56% of abnormal psychology instructors state that fostering critical thinking in students is their greatest challenge.

THINK CRITICALLY

The diagnosis of PTSD has been questioned recently on two fronts. First, some researchers suggest that the criteria for PTSD are too broad and that too many stressful events are accepted as possible triggers (Spitzer, First, & Wakefield, 2007). As noted earlier, the upcoming *DSM-5* is likely to narrow the PTSD diagnostic criteria (Rosen, Spitzer, & McHugh, 2008).

Second, the PTSD field has been criticized for ignoring evidence that most people who experience severe trauma do not develop significant symptoms of PTSD or other mental disorders. A study of New Yorkers 6 months after the attacks on the World Trade Center in 2001 found that 65 percent of the 2,752 adults studied had at most one PTSD symptom (Bonanno, Galea, Bucciarelli, & Vlahov, 2006). This was a randomly selected sample of people with a range of exposures to the attack. But even those most directly affected showed resilience—over half who saw the attack in person or lost a friend or relative did not develop PTSD symptoms. Among the 22 participants who had been in the World Trade Center at the time, 7 developed PTSD, but 5 had two or fewer symptoms, and 10 had only one symptom or none at all (Bonanno et al., 2006).

Have mental health professionals exaggerated the effects of trauma on mental health? Or should PTSD have a broad definition so that individuals who suffer after experiencing a trauma are not overlooked? *(Discussion appears on p. 518 at the back of this book.)*

At the end of each chapter, Nolen-Hoeksema asks students to analyze and apply what they have learned by examining a specific case, designing an intervention, or stating and supporting an opinion on a controversial topic.

TEST YOURSELF

1. What are the positive symptoms of schizophrenia?
2. What are the negative symptoms of schizophrenia?
3. Describe the characteristics of delusions, hallucinations, and catatonic behavior.
4. What are the cognitive deficits of schizophrenia?
5. What are prodromal and residual symptoms?
6. Define the major subtypes of schizophrenia given by the *DSM-IV-TR*.
7. Provide the primary characteristics of schizoaffective disorder, schizophreniform disorder, brief psychotic disorder, delusional disorder, and shared psychotic disorder.

APPLY IT Sonia has schizophrenia. During an acute episode, she might exhibit the positive symptom ______ and the negative symptom ______.

a. hallucination; catatonic behavior
b. disorganized thought; delusion
c. avolition; disorganized speech
d. catatonic behavior; blunted affect

Answers appear online at www.mhhe.com/nolen5e.

Half of abnormal psychology instructors give in-class quizzes to test students' comprehension of the material.

Questions at the end of each major section in Nolen-Hoeksema allow students to check their understanding of the material they have just read by applying it to a real-world scenario.

If you would like to participate in any of the McGraw-Hill research initiatives please contact us **research@mcgraw-hill.com.**

Understanding Abnormal Psychology Along the Continuum

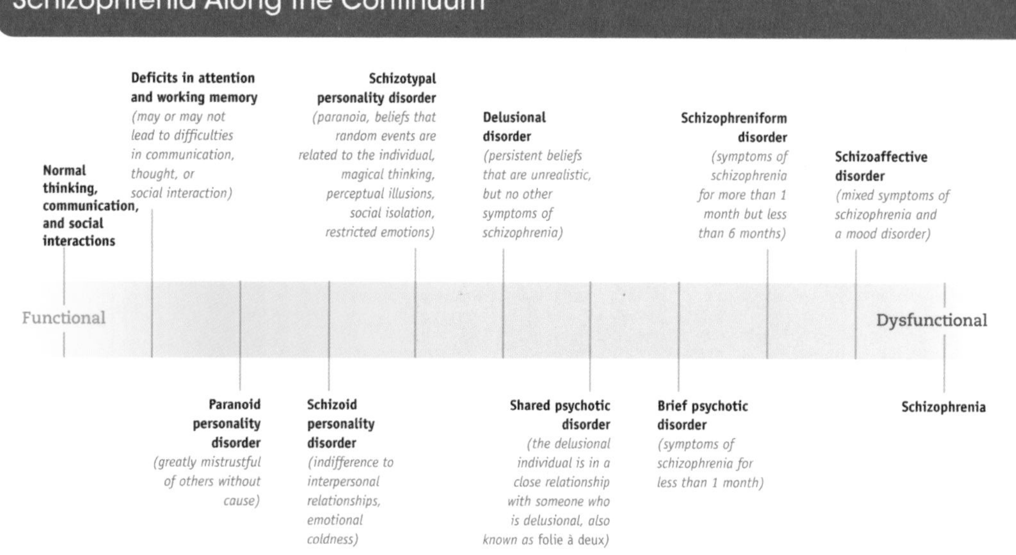

Schizophrenia Along the Continuum
Normal thinking, communication, and social interactions
Deficits in attention and working memory (may or may not lead to difficulties in communication, thought, or social interaction)
Schizotypal personality disorder (paranoia, beliefs that random events are related to the individual, magical thinking, perceptual illusions, social isolation, restricted emotions)
Delusional disorder (persistent beliefs that are unrealistic, but no other symptoms of schizophrenia)
Schizophreniform disorder (symptoms of schizophrenia for more than 1 month but less than 6 months)
Schizoaffective disorder (mixed symptoms of schizophrenia and a mood disorder)
Functional
Dysfunctional
Paranoid personality disorder (greatly mistrustful of others without cause)
Schizoid personality disorder (indifference to interpersonal relationships, emotional coldness)
Shared psychotic disorder (the delusional individual is in a close relationship with someone who is delusional, also known as folie à deux)
Brief psychotic disorder (symptoms of schizophrenia for less than 1 month)
Schizophrenia

After reading John Nash's story, you may think schizophrenia is so different in nature from normal experience that it couldn't possibly be on a continuum. However, the symptoms that make up schizophrenia can appear in mild to moderate form in many people who do not meet the full criteria for any disorder (Linscott & van Os, 2010). For example, in a study of 8,580 people from an unselected community sample, 28 percent reported having had at least one symptom characteristic of schizophrenia, such as hearing voices that no one else heard or believing that their thoughts were being controlled by someone else (Johns et al., 2004). In addition, biological family members of people with schizophrenia often show problems in attention and memory, as well as neurological abnormalities similar to those seen in schizophrenia.

Further along the continuum are personality disorders—such as schizoid personality disorder, paranoid personality disorder, and especially schizotypal personality disorder (see Chapter 9)—that involve moderate symptoms resembling those of schizophrenia but with a retained grasp on reality. People with these personality disorders often speak in odd and eccentric ways, have unusual beliefs or perceptions, and have difficulty relating to other people. Many investigators consider these personality disorders to be along the "schizophrenia spectrum"—that part of the continuum that includes diagnosable disorders that share similarities with schizophrenia but are not as severe.

Still further along the continuum are other disorders, also considered part of the schizophrenia spectrum, in which people lose touch with reality. In delusional disorder, individuals have persistent beliefs that are contrary to reality, but they lack other symptoms of schizophrenia and often are not impaired in their functioning. Their delusions tend to be about things that are possible but untrue. When these delusions are shared by others in close relationship with the delusional person, they warrant a diagnosis of shared psychotic disorder. In brief psychotic disorder, individuals have symptoms of schizophrenia for 1 month or less. In schizophreniform disorder, individuals have symptoms of schizophrenia for 1 to 6 months but usually resume normal lives. Schizoaffective disorder presents a mixed picture of schizophrenia and depression or bipolar disorder.

This chapter focuses primarily on schizophrenia, which has been researched much more than any of the other disorders on the continuum. You will read about schizophrenia's symptoms, subtypes, causes, and prognosis. Most theorists view schizophrenia primarily as a biological disorder, but psychological and social factors can influence its severity and its frequency of relapses. Effective biological treatments for schizophrenia have been developed in the past 50 years. Often, they are supplemented by psychological and social therapies that help the person with schizophrenia cope with the impact of the disorder on his or her life. This chapter considers theoretical perspectives and treatments that integrate knowledge of the biological and psychosocial contributors to schizophrenia.

As reflected in anticipated revisions to the *Diagnostic and Statistical Manual of Mental Disorders (DSM)*, psychologists increasingly believe that "normal" and "abnormal" psychology represent different points along a continuum from functional to dysfunctional thoughts, behaviors, and feelings. Most disorders, such as anxiety and depression, are extreme versions of normal functioning. We choose to draw the line between "normal" and "abnormal" at a point on this continuum.

Nolen-Hoeksema includes new, unique continuum model diagrams in each chapter that show how disorders vary in degree both from one another and from normal functioning. The diagrams also illustrate the point on the continuum where individuals are likely to be diagnosed with a mental disorder under the DSM-IV-TR criteria.

Abnormal Psychology

Abnormal Psychology

Fifth Edition

Susan Nolen-Hoeksema
Yale University

The McGraw-Hill Companies

Published by McGraw-Hill, an imprint of The McGraw-Hill Companies, Inc., 1221 Avenue of the Americas, New York, NY 10020.

This book is printed on acid-free paper.

2 3 4 5 6 7 8 9 0 DOW/DOW 10 9 8 7 6 5 4 3 2 1

ISBN: 978-0-07-338278-4
MHID: 0-07-338278-7

Vice President Editorial: *Michael Ryan*
Publisher: *Mike Sugarman*
Sponsoring Editor: *Krista Bettino*
Executive Marketing Manager: *Julia Larkin*
Director of Development: *Dawn Groundwater*
Developmental Editor: *Anne Kemper*
Supplements Editor: *Sarah Colwell*
Production Editor: *Holly Paulsen*
Manuscript Editor: *Mary Roybal*
Design Manager: *Laurie Entringer*
Text Designer: *Jesi Lazar*
Cover Designer: *Heidi Baughman*
Illustrators: *Joanne Brummett, Kathryn Rathke, Ayelet Arbel, Kristin Mount*
Photo Research Coordinator: *Nora Agbayani*
Photo Research: *Toni Michaels/PhotoFind, LLC*
Media Project Manager: *Jennifer Barrick*
Buyer II: *Louis Swaim*
Composition: *10/12 Palatino by Aptara®, Inc.*
Printing: *RR Donnelley*

Credits: The credits section for this book begins on page 587 and is considered an extension of the copyright page.

Library of Congress Cataloging-in-Publication Data has been applied for.

To Michael and Richard

ABOUT THE AUTHOR

Susan Nolen-Hoeksema, Ph.D., is a professor of psychology at Yale University. She has also been a professor at Stanford University and the University of Michigan. She received her B.A. from Yale University and her Ph.D. from the University of Pennsylvania. Her research focuses on mood regulation and on gender differences in psychopathology. The recipient of three major teaching awards, Professor Nolen-Hoeksema has received research funding from the National Institutes of Health, the National Science Foundation, and the William T. Grant Foundation. She was awarded the Leadership Award from the Committee on Women, as well as the Early Career Award from the American Psychological Association. She lives near New Haven, Connecticut, with her husband, Richard, and her son, Michael.

CONTENTS IN BRIEF

CONTENTS

PREFACE

We are in the midst of a revolutionary change in our understanding of psychological disorders. The distinction between "normal" and "abnormal" has blurred as emerging evidence shows that many disorders, such as depression and anxiety, represent extremes of common experiences. Today, psychological problems are increasingly seen by clinicians as part of a continuum that ranges from healthy, functional behaviors, thoughts, and feelings to unhealthy, dysfunctional behaviors, thoughts, and feelings. This continuum model stands in contrast to older, categorical models—either one has a disorder or one does not—that traditionally have characterized diagnostic classification systems such as the *Diagnostic and Statistical Manual*. While categorical models still dominate both the research and the practice of abnormal psychology, continuum (dimensional) models will play a strong role in the forthcoming *DSM-5* (scheduled for release in 2013 as of this writing).

In a world where distinctions between normal and abnormal are not black-and-white, students must be even more discerning in their study of abnormal psychology. This revision discusses where each disorder falls along a continuum of functioning and builds students' skills in thinking critically about such continuum models. It also provides a strong foundation in the *DSM* system of diagnosis. The *DSM-IV-TR* criteria for diagnosing each disorder are presented in *DSM-IV-TR* tables like the one shown here; the likely changes in these criteria in the *DSM-5* are then described, often with some discussion of why these changes are being considered. Thus, students learn the diagnostic system currently being used and also gain an appreciation of how these criteria evolve as our science progresses.

Along with its new features, this revision retains the previous edition's integrated coverage of biological, psychological, and social perspectives on abnormality and continues to focus on the roles of gender and culture in abnormality. It also highlights personal accounts of people with mental disorders.

TABLE 5.4 *DSM-IV-TR* Criteria for Specific Phobia

A. Marked and persistent fear that is excessive or unreasonable, cued by the presence or anticipation of a specific object or situation (e.g., flying, heights, animals, receiving an injection, seeing blood).

B. Exposure to the phobic stimulus almost invariably provokes an immediate anxiety response, which may take the form of a situationally bound or situationally predisposed panic attack. *Note:* In children, the anxiety may be expressed by crying, tantrums, freezing, or clinging.

C. The person recognizes that the fear is excessive or unreasonable. *Note:* In children, this feature may be absent.

D. The phobic situation(s) is avoided or else is endured with intense anxiety or distress.

E. The avoidance, anxious anticipation, or distress in the feared situation(s) interferes significantly with the person's normal routine, occupational (or academic) functioning, or social activities or relationships, or there is marked distress about having the phobia.

F. In individuals under age 18, the duration is at least 6 months.

G. The anxiety, panic attacks, or phobic avoidance associated with the specific object or situation are not better accounted for by another mental disorder, such as obsessive-compulsive disorder (e.g., fear of dirt in someone with an obsession about contamination), posttraumatic stress disorder (e.g., avoidance of stimuli associated with a severe stressor), separation anxiety disorder (e.g., avoidance of school), social phobia (e.g., avoidance of social situations because of fear of embarrassment), panic disorder with agoraphobia, or agoraphobia without history of panic disorder.

Specify type:
Animal Type
Natural Environment Type (e.g., heights, storms, water)
Blood-Injection-Injury Type
Situational Type (e.g., airplanes, elevators, enclosed places)
Other Type (e.g., phobic avoidance of situations that may lead to choking, vomiting, or contracting an illness; in children, avoidance of loud sounds or costumed characters)

Source: Reprinted with permission from the *Diagnostic and Statistical Manual of Mental Disorders,* Fourth Edition, Text Revision. Copyright © 2000 American Psychiatric Association.

A FOCUS ON THE CONTINUUM OF EXPERIENCE

Because continuum models help students understand and relate to psychopathology, *Abnormal Psychology,* Fifth Edition, places these models front and center in **Along the Continuum** features. The continuum model is introduced in the first chapter and is illustrated with a diagram in each chapter. Each later chapter begins with a discussion of how the continuum model applies to the disorders discussed in that chapter. For example, Chapter 7 on mood disorders presents a range of experiences from feeling blue after a loss to chronic, debilitating depression.

Mood Disorders Along the Continuum

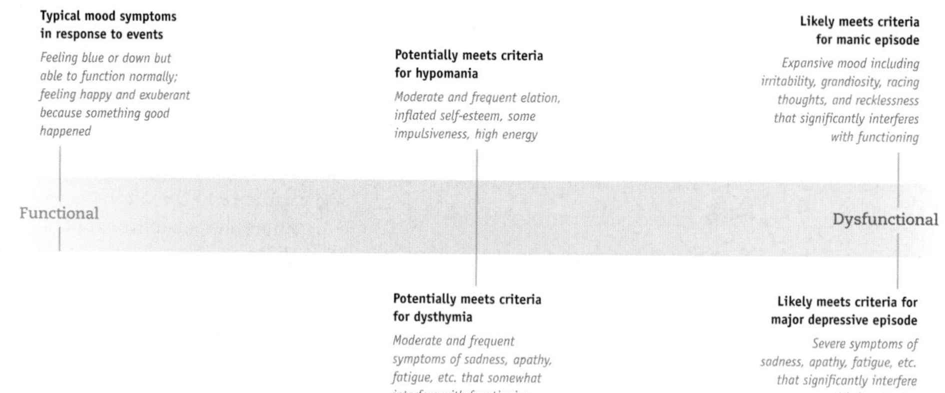

Typical mood symptoms in response to events
Feeling blue or down but able to function normally; feeling happy and exuberant because something good happened
Potentially meets criteria for hypomania
Moderate and frequent elation, inflated self-esteem, some impulsiveness, high energy
Likely meets criteria for manic episode
Expansive mood including irritability, grandiosity, racing thoughts, and recklessness that significantly interferes with functioning
Functional
Dysfunctional
Potentially meets criteria for dysthymia
Moderate and frequent symptoms of sadness, apathy, fatigue, etc. that somewhat interfere with functioning
Likely meets criteria for major depressive episode
Severe symptoms of sadness, apathy, fatigue, etc. that significantly interfere with functioning

"I'm depressed" is a phrase that you may have uttered, perhaps after you didn't do as well as you expected on an exam or when a friend became angry and wouldn't speak to you. Such events often sap our energy and motivation, shake our self-esteem, and make us feel down and blue—all symptoms of depression.

More significant events, such as the death of a loved one, the break-up of a marriage, or the loss of a job, can lead to more serious symptoms of depression. In some people, the symptoms may be mild or moderate and not interfere with daily functioning. Sometimes, however, symptoms of depression following negative events become debilitating and can last for long periods of time. And in some cases, severe symptoms of depression emerge without any obvious cause. A diagnosis of depression depends on both the severity and the duration of symptoms.

Like symptoms of depression, symptoms of mania also vary in severity and duration. Perhaps you've experienced a "fizzing over" feeling of exuberance when something in your life is going particularly well—such as getting an acceptance to college or beginning a relationship with somebody special. As in depression, moderate symptoms of mania usually are tied to specific situations and lessen as those situations pass. Symptoms of a manic episode, however, go beyond feeling happy when something good has happened. People diagnosed with mania are often irritable and impatient with others. Their extreme self-confidence may lead them to carry out grandiose schemes to earn money or influence others, or to engage in extremely risky or impulsive behaviors.

Each chapter also includes a new feature titled **Shades of Gray,** which presents an ambiguous case study illustrating the complexities of judging normal and abnormal. Students are asked whether a diagnosis is warranted in the case; then, near the end of the chapter, the issues involved in making this judgment are discussed so the student understands how the case would be viewed in the *DSM*.

SHADES OF GRAY

Read the following case study.

At the insistence of her parents, Rachel, a 19-year-old freshman at a competitive liberal arts college, received a psychiatric evaluation during spring break. According to her parents, Rachel had lost 16 pounds since her precollege physical the previous August. She now weighed 104 pounds at a height of 5 feet, 5 inches, when a healthy weight for a small-framed woman her height is about 120 pounds. Rachel explained that she had been a successful student and field hockey player in high school. After deciding not to play field hockey in college, she began running several mornings each week during the summer and "cut out junk food" to protect herself from gaining "that freshman 10." Rachel lost a few pounds that summer and received compliments from friends and family for looking so "fit." She reported feeling more confident and ready for college than she had expected. Once she began school, Rachel increased her running to daily, often skipped breakfast in order to get to class on time, and selected from the salad bar for her lunch and dinner. She worked hard in school and made the dean's list the first semester.

When Rachel returned home for Christmas vacation, her family noticed that she looked thin and tired. Despite encouragement to catch up on rest, she awoke early each morning to run. She returned to school in January and thought she might be developing depression. Courses seemed less interesting, and she wondered whether the college she attended was right for her after all. She was sleeping less well and felt cold much of the day. The night Rachel returned home for spring break, her parents asked her to step on the bathroom scale. Rachel was surprised to learn that her weight had fallen to 104 pounds, and she agreed to a visit to her pediatrician, who found no evidence of a medical illness and recommended a psychiatric consultation. (Adapted from Evelyn Attia and B. Timothy Walsh (2007). Anorexia Nervosa, *American Journal of Psychiatry,* 164. Reprinted with permission from the American Journal of Psychiatry, copyright © 2007 American Psychiatric Association.)

Does Rachel have an eating disorder? What criteria does she meet? Are there any criteria that she doesn't meet? (Discussion appears at the end of this chapter.)

THINK CRITICALLY

Imagine yourself a juror in the following murder case (from Loftus, 1993). The defendant is George Franklin, Sr., 51 years old, standing trial for a murder that occurred more than 20 years earlier. The victim was 8-year-old Susan Kay Nason. Franklin's daughter, Eileen, only 8 years old herself at the time of the murder, provided the major evidence against her father. Eileen's memory of the murder, however, had re-emerged only recently, after 20 years of being repressed.

Eileen's memory first began to come back when she was playing with her 2-year-old son and her 5-year-old daughter. At one moment, her daughter looked up and asked a question like "Isn't that right, Mommy?" A memory of Susan Nason suddenly came to Eileen. She recalled the look of betrayal in Susie's eyes just before the murder. Later, more fragments would return, until Eileen had a rich and detailed memory. She remembered her father sexually assaulting Susie in the back of a van. She remembered that Susie was struggling as she said "No, don't!" and "Stop!" She remembered her father saying "Now Susie," and she even mimicked his precise intonation. Next, her memory took the three of them outside the van, where she saw her father raise a rock above his head. She remembered screaming and walking back to where Susie lay, covered with blood, the silver ring on her finger smashed. When questioned by prosecutors, Eileen was highly confident in her memory.

Would you convict George Franklin of the murder of Susan Nason? Why or why not? (*Discussion appears at the back of this book, on p. 518.*)

A FOCUS ON CRITICAL THINKING

Distinguishing between normal and abnormal is only one of many difficult issues in clinical psychology. How can we ever really know the causes of disorders? How can we apply what we know generally about a disorder to treat an individual? In this edition, students hone their ability to think critically about such difficult issues with **Think Critically** questions that appear at the end of the chapter. Some challenge students to apply what they have learned about the causes of or treatments for a disorder to a specific case. Others prompt students to design an experiment or intervention, reflect on their personal experience, or voice their opinion on controversial topics in clinical psychology.

TEST YOURSELF

1. What are the criteria for a diagnosis of major depression?
2. What are the criteria for a diagnosis of dysthymic disorder?
3. How do rates of depression vary by age group and gender?

APPLY IT Over the past 2 months, Brandon has had a severely depressed mood, has lost 30 pounds, and has been chronically exhausted. He believes he has been possessed by the devil and hears voices telling him to kill himself. With which subtype of major depression would Brandon most likely be diagnosed?

a. seasonal pattern
b. melancholic
c. psychotic
d. catatonic

Answers appear online at www.mhhe.com/nolen5e.

Critical-thinking skills are also built with new **Test Yourself** question sets that follow each major section of text. Each set includes an **Apply It** question that asks students to apply key topics from the text to an everyday scenario.

A FOCUS ON CONNECTING WITH STUDENTS

Our knowledge of psychological disorders is rapidly expanding, as are demands on students' and instructors' time. The fifth edition has been revised to address what students really need to know, providing a thorough but focused discussion of the nature, causes, and treatments of each disorder. The Test Yourself question sets after each major section help students review and apply the most important topics in that section. To engage students, many new examples and case studies feature familiar contemporary figures, such as soccer star David Beckham. The Think Critically questions pique students' interest by asking their personal opinion regarding controversial topics, such as lowering the drinking age to 18.

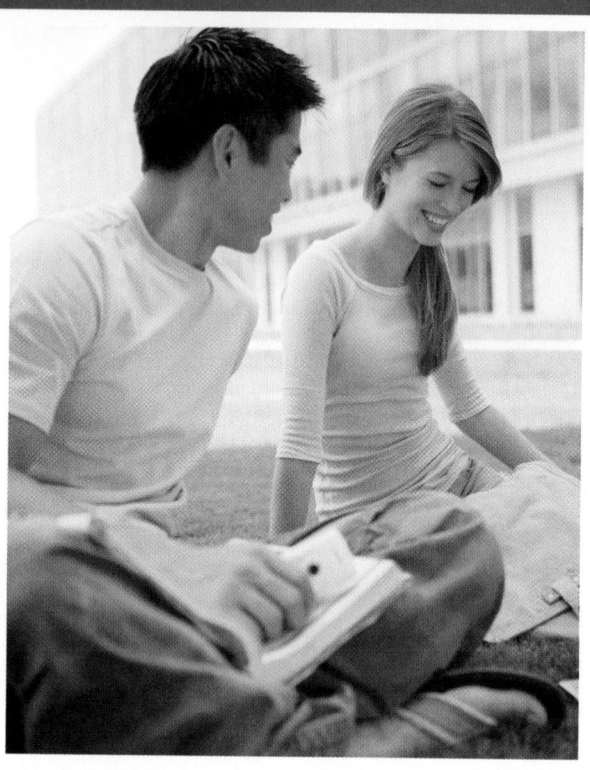

A FOCUS ON EMPIRICISM AND INTEGRATION

The fifth edition reflects recent trends in the field of abnormal psychology, which has become both more empirically based and more interdisciplinary. Empirically supported theories and treatments are the focus of every chapter and are accompanied by fully updated reviews of the research on theories and treatments for each disorder. The text clearly states when particular theories or treatments have not been supported empirically or have not been adequately tested. The reviews of recent research have benefited greatly from the many preprints and in-press manuscripts sent by some of the most respected researchers in the field. As a result, this book presents what the best and brightest researchers believe is the most important new work and where the field is going.

Integrative biopsychosocial models of psychopathology continue to be a feature of the fifth edition. Every chapter ends with a section called **Chapter Integration,** which describes an integrative approach to the disorders discussed in that chapter and illustrates this approach with a figure.

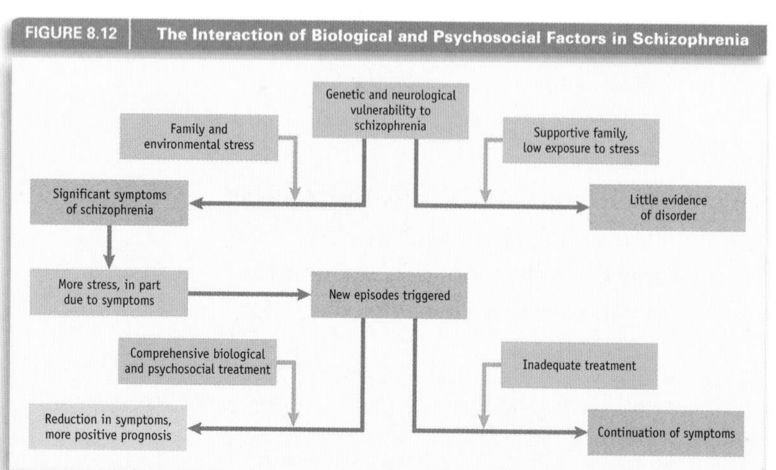

Extraordinary People

David Beckham, *Perfection On and Off the Field*

Soccer star David Beckham's extraordinary ability to curve shots on corner kicks was immortalized in the movie *Bend It Like Beckham*. Beckham's perfectionism on the field is paralleled by his perfectionism about order and symmetry: "I've got this obsessive-compulsive disorder where I have to have everything in a straight line or everything has to be in pairs" (quoted in Dolan, 2006). Beckham spends hours ordering the furniture in his house in a particular way or lining up the clothes in his closet by color. His wife, Victoria (the former Posh Spice), says, "If you open our fridge, it's all coordinated down either side. We've got three fridges—food in one, salad in another and drinks in the third. In the drinks one, everything is symmetrical. If there's three cans he'll throw away one because it has to be an even number" (quoted in Frith, 2006).

Beckham has traveled around the world, playing for top teams including Real Madrid, Manchester United, Los Angeles Galaxy, and AC Milan. Each time he enters a new hotel room, he has to arrange everything in order: "I'll go into a hotel room. Before I can relax I have to move all the leaflets and all the books and put them in a drawer. Everything has to be perfect" (quoted in Frith, 2006). His teammates on Manchester United knew of his obsessions and compulsions and would deliberately rearrange his clothes or move the furniture around in his hotel room to infuriate him.

A FOCUS ON PEOPLE

Abnormal Psychology, Fifth Edition, is not only about theories or research. It is fundamentally about people—people who suffer and struggle and sometimes triumph over their mental health problems. Their voices are heard throughout this book, offering us glimpses of the personal experience of mental disorders.

Every chapter begins with a feature called **Extraordinary People,** which highlights the lives of people with mental disorders. Some of these people have achieved tremendous success, such as Nobel Prize winner John Nash or researcher and professor Kay Redfield Jamison. Some, such as Mary-Kate Olsen or Heath Ledger, will be known to students through the media. Others have led more ordinary lives, which itself is a great accomplishment for people with serious mental disorders. These stories take students far beyond lists of diagnostic criteria and into the subjective experience of a disorder.

Also, throughout the text of each chapter is a feature called **Voices,** which includes quotes from people with mental disorders. These quotes give students a subjective sense of the symptoms of each disorder by allowing people who suffer these symptoms to describe their experience. From this feature students can gain a deeper understanding of the symptoms of mental disorders and their impact on people's lives.

A FOCUS ON CULTURE AND GENDER

Since the first edition, *Abnormal Psychology* has explored the role of culture and gender in mental disorders as they influence people's vulnerability to a disorder, expression of a disorder, or response to treatment. The fifth edition features updated discussions of the empirical research on culture and gender and highlights debates, such as the impact of culture on the diagnosis of personality disorders (Chapter 9).

CHAPTER-BY-CHAPTER CHANGES IN THE FIFTH EDITION

In addition to the major changes across all the chapters, the following changes were made to individual chapters.

Chapter 1: Looking at Abnormality

- Added an introduction and illustration of the concept of the continuum model
- Integrated the four Ds of abnormality (dysfunction, distress, deviance, and danger) with the continuum model of abnormality

Chapter 2: Theories and Treatment of Abnormality

- Integrated formerly separate chapters on theories and treatments of abnormality
- Added a discussion of the biological, sociocultural, and psychological approaches in relation to the continuum model
- Provided more information on the basic structure of the brain
- Added a section on gene-environment interactions, the effects of genes on choice of environment, and epigenetics
- Updated the section on family systems approaches
- Added material on recent emotion-focused approaches to psychopathology and therapy (e.g., acceptance and commitment therapy)
- Expanded the section on sociocultural approaches to discuss the effects of discrimination, stigma, war, and refugee status on mental health, as well as the role of culture in treatment

Chapter 3: Assessing and Diagnosing Abnormality

- Added a discussion of the major changes proposed for the *DSM-5*, including collapsing Axes I, II, and III into one axis and incorporating assessments along a continuum of severity into several diagnoses

Chapter 4: The Research Endeavor

- Added a discussion of the differences between research that assumes a continuum model of psychopathology and research that focuses only on diagnosed disorders
- Added a discussion of the differences between statistical significance and clinical significance of a research result
- Expanded the discussion of ethical issues in research
- Added information on multiple-baseline designs
- Added a section on methods of studying genetic factors

Chapter 5: Anxiety Disorders

- Moved the section on post-traumatic stress disorder from the chapter on stress to this chapter on anxiety disorders to be in line with *DSM* diagnostic categories
- Added information on proposed changes in the *DSM-5* diagnoses for all anxiety disorders, including redefinitions of trauma in PTSD and acute stress disorder, as wells as changing the name of social phobia to social anxiety disorder and of generalized anxiety disorder to generalized anxiety and worry disorder
- Added content on the proposed addition to the *DSM-5* of diagnoses of hoarding and post-traumatic stress disorder in preschool children
- Moved the section on agoraphobia to the section on panic disorder to reflect the close affiliation between these disorders
- Expanded the discussion of conditioned avoidance response

Chapter 6: Somatoform and Dissociative Disorders

- Added information on proposed changes in the *DSM-5* diagnoses for all somatoform and dissociative disorders, including collapsing most somatoform disorders into the diagnosis of complex somatic symptom disorder, moving body dysmorphic disorder to the anxiety and obsessive compulsive disorders, and subsuming dissociative fugue under dissociative amnesia

Chapter 7: Mood Disorders and Suicide

- Added information on proposed changes in the *DSM-5* diagnoses for all mood disorders, including the addition of mixed anxiety depression and chronic depressive disorder
- Incorporated material on suicide that previously had been in a separate chapter
- Added a discussion of nonsuicidal self-injury
- Added a discussion of pediatric bipolar disorder and the proposed *DSM-5* diagnosis in children of temper dysregulation disorder with dysphoria
- Separated the discussions of theories of unipolar mood disorders and theories of bipolar disorder
- Substantially expanded coverage of theories of bipolar disorder, including recent work on the role of reward systems and social rhythms
- Expanded and reorganized the discussion of sociocultural perspectives of unipolar mood disorders to focus on cohort effects, gender differences, ethnicity/race differences, and cross-cultural differences

- Added a section on psychosocial therapies for bipolar disorder, including interpersonal and social rhythm therapy and family-focused therapy

Chapter 8: Schizophrenia and Related Psychotic Disorders

- Added information on proposed changes in the *DSM-5* diagnoses for schizophrenia and other psychotic disorders, including elimination of subtypes for schizophrenia
- Added a discussion of the "schizophrenia spectrum"
- Expanded coverage of cognitive deficits in schizophrenia and their role in producing other symptoms
- Expanded the discussion of psychotic disorders other than schizophrenia

Chapter 9: Personality Disorders

- Added content on the extensive reconceptualization of personality disorders proposed for the *DSM-5* to include dimensional assessments and the reduction of personality disorder diagnoses from ten to five

Chapter 10: Childhood Disorders

- Added information on proposed changes in the *DSM-5* diagnoses for childhood disorders, including eliminating subtypes for attention-deficit/hyperactivity disorder and possibly adding the diagnosis of attention-deficit disorder; moving separation anxiety disorder to the anxiety and obsessive-compulsive disorders; renaming some of the learning disorders (to dyslexia and dyscalculia) and mental retardation (to intellectual disability); changing the criteria for mental retardation (intellectual disability); and eliminating separate diagnoses for different pervasive developmental disorders, with all of them placed in a new category of autism spectrum disorders
- Distinguished between adolescent-limited antisocial behavior and life-course-persistent antisocial behavior
- Expanded discussion of drug therapies for ADHD and conduct disorder
- Expanded coverage of the etiology of learning disabilities

Chapter 11: Cognitive Disorders and Life-Span Issues

- Added information about proposed changes in the *DSM-5* diagnoses of cognitive disorders, including subsuming all forms of dementia and amnesic disorders under one diagnosis of major neurocognitive disorder or minor neurocognitive disorder
- Expanded the discussion of the effects of traumatic brain injury and related these effects to soldiers returning from the Iraq and Afghanistan wars

Chapter 12: Eating Disorders

- Added information about proposed changes in the *DSM-5* diagnoses of eating disorders, including formal recognition of binge-eating disorder, the dropping of the amenorrhea criterion from the diagnosis of anorexia nervosa, and the deletion of subtypes of bulimia nervosa
- Added a major new section on obesity and attempts to treat it

Chapter 13: Sexual Disorders

- Added information about proposed changes in the *DSM-5* diagnoses of sexual disorders, including subsuming hypoactive sexual desire disorder and female sexual arousal disorder under the diagnosis of sexual interest/arousal disorder in women or sexual interest/arousal disorder in men; dropping the diagnosis of sexual aversion disorder; specifying the frequency of problems necessary for male erectile disorder, female orgasmic disorder, premature ejaculation, and male orgasmic disorder (to be renamed delayed ejaculation); subsuming dyspareunia and vaginismus under the diagnosis of genito-pelvic pain/penetration disorder; specifying the frequency of behavior required for each of the paraphilias; adding a diagnosis of paraphillic coercion disorder; adding a diagnosis of hypersexual disorder; changing the criteria for pedophilia to cover sexual interest in pubescent children and changing the name of the disorder to pedohebephilic disorder; renaming gender identity disorder gender incongruence, with some changes in the diagnostic criteria
- Expanded the discussion of controversies in the definitions and diagnoses of sexual dysfunctions, paraphilias, and gender identity disorder
- Expanded coverage of the etiology and treatment of gender identity disorder

Chapter 14: Substance-Related and Impulse-Control Disorders

- Added information about proposed changes in the *DSM-5* diagnoses of substance-related disorders, including changing the name of the category to addiction and related disorders; subsuming substance abuse and substance dependence under one diagnosis of substance use disorder, with some changes in the criteria; moving pathological gambling to the new category addiction and related disorders
- Included coverage of the *DSM-IV-TR* impulse-control disorders
- Added a discussion of the role of reward sensitivity in substance use disorders

- Presented new material on psychological treatment of substance use disorders, including contingency management programs and motivational interviewing
- Added comparisons of different treatments for alcohol abuse and dependence

Chapter 15: Health Psychology

- Reorganized the chapter to emphasize a biopsychosocial approach to health psychology
- Added new material on the effects of culture and gender on the experience of and responses to stress
- Added new sections on the effects of psychological disorders on physical health and, specifically, of depression on coronary heart disease
- Included coverage of the controversy over whether psychosocial interventions can impact the course of cancer
- Added a new section on the use of the Internet to improve people's health-related behaviors
- Expanded material on sleep and health, including new content on assessing sleep and new material on the causes and treatments of sleep disorders
- Added information about proposed changes in the *DSM-5* diagnoses of sleep disorders, including subsuming insomnia and hypersomnia related to a general medical condition under primary insomnia and primary hypersomnia, respectively, and subsuming sleepwalking and sleep terrors under the diagnosis disorders of arousal

Chapter 16: Mental Health and the Law

- Expanded the discussion of individuals who are coerced into receiving mental health care
- Added contemporary cases of social and legal policy dealing with people with mental disorders, including Major Nidal Hasan, who killed 13 people in Texas in 2009, and recent school shooters
- Included discussion of legal issues involved in viewing mental disorders along a continuum rather than as discrete illnesses

SUPPLEMENTS

The text has an outstanding ancillary package to support student learning and classroom teaching.

For the Student

Online Learning Center for Students—www.mhhe.com/nolen5e (updated by Jennifer Boothby, Indiana State University) The official Web site for the text contains chapter outlines, practice quizzes that can be e-mailed to the professor, key term flash cards, Internet activities, and Web links to relevant abnormal psychology sites.

Faces Interactive Available through the Online Learning Center, this resource includes the diagnosis, a case history, an interview, treatment, and assessment tools for 11 disorders. It includes more than 14 hours of video featuring real people and more than 400 interview questions students can use to elicit diagnostic information. Responses inform students' completion of a case report and prepare them for the built-in assessment of each client.

For the Instructor

Online Learning Center for Instructors—www.mhhe.com/nolen5e The password-protected instructor side of the text Web site contains the Instructor's Manual, the Test Bank, a sample chapter from the text, PowerPoint presentations, CPS questions, Image Gallery, and other teaching resources.

Instructor's Manual (revised by Jonathan Weinstein, University of Mississippi) This comprehensive guide includes an overview of each chapter, learning objectives, suggestions and resources for lecture topics, classroom activities, projects, suggestions for video and multimedia lecture enhancements, and a media integration guide to help instructors link the electronic resources to the syllabus.

Test Bank By increasing the rigor of the Test Bank development process, McGraw-Hill aims to raise the bar for student assessment. Over 100 test items for each chapter of the text were prepared by a coordinated team of subject-matter experts. Each question and set of possible answers were methodically vetted by Frederic Desmond, University of Florida, for accuracy, clarity, effectiveness, and accessibility, and each is annotated for level of difficulty, Bloom's Taxonomy, and corresponding coverage in the text. The Test Bank is compatible with McGraw-Hill's computerized testing program EZ Test and with most course management systems.

PowerPoint Lectures (revised by Crystal Park, University of Connecticut, Storrs) Available on the text Web site, these presentations cover the key points of each chapter and include graphics. Helpful lecture guidelines are provided in the "notes" section for each slide. They can be used as is or may be modified to meet your needs.

Classroom Performance System (CPS) With text-specific multiple-choice questions and polling questions created by Elisabeth Sherwin (University of Arkansas, Little Rock) for in-class use, the CPS questions allow instructors to gauge immediately what students are learning during lectures. Instructors can ask questions, take polls, or host classroom demonstrations and get instant feedback. In addition, CPS makes it easy to take attendance, give and grade pop quizzes, or give formal, paper-based class tests with multiple versions of the test, using CPS for immediate grading.

Faces of Abnormal Psychology, Volumes I and II This series of twenty 8- to 10-minute video clips suitable for classroom viewing is available on DVD for instructors who adopt this text. Each video features an interview with an individual who has experienced a mental disorder. Schizophrenia, post-traumatic stress disorder, bulimia nervosa, obsessive-compulsive disorder, and Asperger's disorder are some of the conditions covered.

Taking Sides: Clashing Views on Controversial Issues in Abnormal Psychology This debate-style reader introduces students to controversial viewpoints on important issues in the field. Each topic is carefully framed for students, and the pro and con essays represent the arguments of leading scholars and commentators in their fields. An instructor's guide containing testing materials is also available.

CourseSmart is a new way for faculty to find and review eTextbooks. It's also a great option for students who are interested in accessing their course materials digitally and saving money. CourseSmart offers thousands of the most commonly adopted textbooks across hundreds of courses from a wide variety of higher-education publishers. It is the only place for faculty to review and compare the full text of textbooks online, and it provides immediate access without the environmental impact of requesting a print exam copy. At CourseSmart, students can save up to 50 percent of the cost of a print book, reduce their impact on the environment, and gain access to powerful Web tools for learning, including full-text search, notes and highlighting, and e-mail tools for sharing notes among classmates.

Tegrity Campus is a service that makes class time available all the time by automatically capturing every lecture in a searchable format for students to review when they study and complete assignments. With a simple one-click start-and-stop process, you capture all computer screens and corresponding audio. Students replay any part of any class with easy-to-use browser-based viewing on a PC or Mac. Educators know that the more students can see, hear, and experience class resources, the better they learn. With Tegrity Campus, students can quickly recall key moments by using Tegrity Campus's unique search feature. This search helps students efficiently find what they need when they need it across an entire semester of class recordings. Help turn all your students' study time into learning moments immediately supported by your lectures. To learn more about Tegrity Campus, watch a 2-minute Flash demo at http://tegritycampus.mhhe.com.

ACKNOWLEDGMENTS

I greatly appreciate the hard work and creativity of the McGraw-Hill staff who have contributed to this fifth edition. I especially wish to thank Anne Kemper for her thoughtful editing of the manuscript and for her creativity in helping me develop new features for this edition. I also wish to thank Krista Bettino, Megan Stotts, Dawn Groundwater, Yasuko Okada, Julia Larkin, James Headley, Mike Sugarman, Holly Paulsen, Laurie Entringer, Nora Agbayani, Jennifer Barrick, Marty Moga, and Louis Swaim at McGraw-Hill, and Toni Michaels for her terrific photo research. Sarah Colwell coordinated the development of the supplements.

Many colleagues provided invaluable feedback for the fifth edition. I gratefully acknowledge their contributions.

Manuscript Reviewers

Diana Anson
College of Southern Nevada

Nicole Buchanan
Michigan State University

Mark Deskovitz
Central Michigan University

Frederic Desmond
University of Florida

Mitch Earleywine
University at Albany, State University of New York

Runae Edwards-Wilson
Rutgers University–New Brunswick

Brian Fisak
University of North Florida

Amy Fiske
West Virginia University

Martha Hubertz
Florida Atlantic University

Barbara Kennedy
Brevard Community College

Travis Langley
Henderson State University

Marvin Lee
Tennessee State University

Mary Livingston
Louisiana Technical University

Suzanne Meeks
University of Louisville

Adam Mullins
University at Buffalo, State University of New York

Ken Rice
University of Florida

Alan Roberts
Indiana University Bloomington

Kathryn Roecklein
University of Pittsburgh

Wayne Stein
Brevard Community College

Jonathan Weinstein,
University of Mississippi

Design Reviewers

Dean Cruess
University of Connecticut

Marvin Lee
Tennessee State University

Crystal Park
University of Connecticut

Brady Phelps
South Dakota State University

Judith Rauenzahn
Kutztown University of Pennsylvania

Michael Steger
Colorado State University

Sally Vyain
Ivy Technical Community College of Indiana

Content Consultants

Janine Buxton
Marist College

Holly Chalk
McDaniel College

Koun Eum
University of Florida

Jeffrey B. Henriques
University of Wisconsin

R. Peter Johnson
North Platte Community College

Karen L. Marsh
University of Minnesota–Duluth

Daniel Philip
University of North Florida

Evette Flores Reagan
Orange Coast College

Jean Strand
Campbell University

Franklin V. Thompson
University of Maine at Presque Isle

Robert Weis
Denison University

As always, my family provided tremendous support as I worked on this edition. I thank Richard Nolen-Hoeksema and Michael Hoeksema for their persistent love and patience.

—Susan Nolen-Hoeksema
New Haven, Connecticut

Abnormal Psychology

Chapter 1

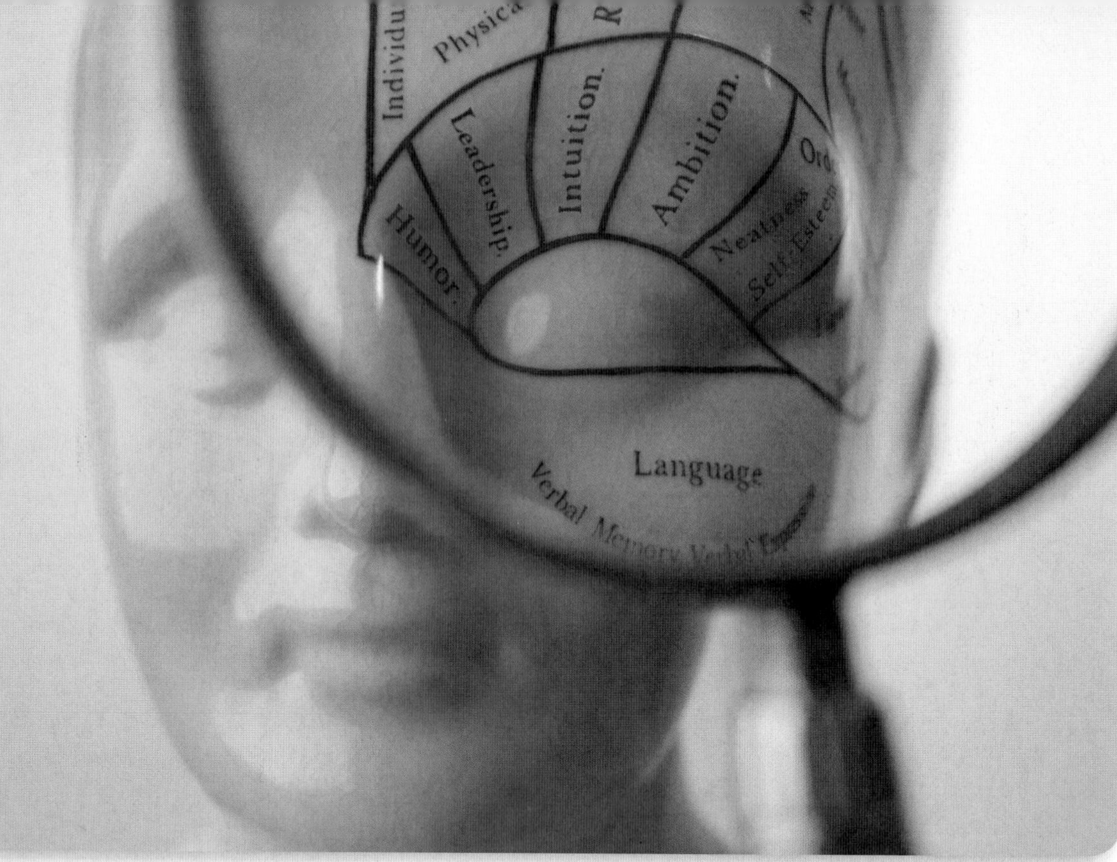

Looking at Abnormality

CHAPTER OUTLINE

Extraordinary People

Clifford Beers, *A Mind That Found Itself*

Clifford Beers was always an energetic child, moody, with little self-control. Still, he was intelligent and ambitious enough to do well in school, and he graduated from college. However, Beers's moodiness increased with time, particularly after his brother Sam began to have severe, convulsive seizures. In March 1890, as his brother lay dying in the family home, Beers's moodiness grew to despair, accompanied by deep paranoia. He began contemplating suicide and eventually jumped out a fourth-floor window, fortunately suffering only broken bones. Beers was hospitalized, first in a private mental hospital but later, when his family ran out of money, in public mental hospitals.

In the early 1900s, there were no effective treatments for symptoms such as those Beers suffered. He was given drugs that physicians thought might help, including strychnine and arsenic tonics. He also was beaten, choked, put in a straitjacket for up to 21 days, and locked away with no clothes for long periods in dark, cold cells. Despite these experiences, Beers's symptoms ultimately subsided, and after spending 3 years in various hospitals, he was declared recovered enough to be released.

These experiences inspired Beers to start a movement for the reform of mental health treatment, which he called the **mental hygiene movement.** After his release from the mental hospital, Beers wrote a personal account of his time there, which was published in 1908 as *A Mind That Found Itself.* This book forever changed how physicians and the public viewed mental patients and hospitals.

The study of abnormal psychology is the study of people, like Clifford Beers, who suffer mental, emotional, and often physical pain, often referred to as **psychopathology.** Sometimes the experiences of people with psychopathology are as unusual as those that this young woman describes:

VOICES

My illness began slowly, gradually, when I was between the ages of 15 and 17. During that time reality became distant and I began to wander around in a sort of haze, foreshadowing the delusional world that was to come later. I also began to have visual hallucinations in which people changed into different characters, the change indicating to me their moral value. For example, the mother of a good friend always changed into a witch, and I believed this to be indicative of her evil nature. Another type of visual hallucination I had at this time is exemplified by an occurrence during a family trip through Utah: The cliffs along the side of the road took on a human appearance, and I perceived them as women, bedraggled and weeping. At the time I didn't know what to make of these changes in my perceptions. On the one hand, I thought they came as a gift from God, but on the other hand, I feared that something was dreadfully wrong. (Anonymous, 1992, pp. 333–334)

Sometimes, however, people with psychopathology have experiences that are familiar to many of us but more extreme, as Kay Redfield Jamison (1995, p. 110) describes in *An Unquiet Mind.*

VOICES

From the time I woke up in the morning until the time I went to bed at night, I was unbearably miserable and seemingly incapable of any kind of joy or enthusiasm. Everything—every thought, word, movement—was an effort. Everything that once was sparkling now was flat. I seemed to myself to be dull, boring, inadequate, thick brained, unlit, unresponsive, chill skinned, bloodless, and sparrow drab. I doubted, completely, my ability to do anything well. It seemed as though my mind had slowed down and burned out to the point of being virtually useless. The wretched, convoluted, and pathetically confused mass of gray worked only well enough to torment me with a dreary litany of my inadequacies and shortcomings in character and to taunt me with the total, the desperate hopelessness of it all.

In this book, we explore the lives of people with troubling psychological symptoms to understand how they think, what they feel, and how they behave. We investigate what is known about the causes of and treatments for various types of symptoms. The purpose of this book is not only to provide you with information, facts and figures, theories, and research. It is also to help you understand the experience of people with psychological symptoms. The good news is that, thanks to an explosion of research in the past few decades, effective biological and psychological treatments are available for many of the mental health problems we discuss in this book.

DEFINING ABNORMALITY

Consider these behaviors:

1. A man kissing another man
2. A man driving a nail through his hand
3. A woman refusing to eat for several days
4. A man barking like a dog and crawling on the floor on his hands and knees
5. A woman building a shrine to her dead husband in her living room and leaving food and gifts for him at the altar

Do you think these behaviors are abnormal? You may reply, "It depends." Several of these behaviors are accepted in certain circumstances. In many European cultures, for example, men commonly greet other men with a kiss. In many religious traditions, refusing to eat for a period, or fasting, is a common ritual of cleansing and penitence. You might expect that some of the other behaviors listed, such as driving a nail through one's hand or barking like a dog, are abnormal in all circumstances, yet even these behaviors are accepted in certain situations. In Mexico, some Christians have themselves nailed to crosses on Good Friday to commemorate the crucifixion of Jesus. Among the Yoruba of Africa, traditional healers act like dogs during healing rituals (Murphy, 1976). Shinto and Buddhist customs include building altars to dead loved ones, offering them food and gifts, and speaking with them as if they were in the room (Stroebe, Gergen, Gergen, & Stroebe, 1992). Thus, the *context*, or circumstances, surrounding a behavior influences whether the behavior is viewed as abnormal.

In Mexico, some Christians have themselves nailed to a cross to commemorate the crucifixion of Jesus.

A number of criteria in addition to context have been used over the years to draw the line between normal and abnormal. We will talk about some of those criteria next.

Cultural Relativism

Cultural relativism is the view that there are no universal standards or rules for labeling a behavior as abnormal; instead, behaviors can only be abnormal relative to cultural norms (Snowden & Yamada, 2005). Proponents of cultural relativism believe that there are different definitions of abnormality across different cultures.

Bereavement practices provide a good example of cultural influences on definitions of abnormality. In Western countries, bereaved people are expected to mourn their dead loved ones for a period of time, perhaps a few weeks or months, then to "let go" of the loved ones and move on in their lives (Stroebe, Hansson, Schut, & Stroebe, 2008). People who continue to think and talk a great deal about their dead loved ones after the specified period of mourning are thought to have "complicated bereavement" and may be encouraged to seek counseling. More often, their family members and friends simply tell them to "get over it." Other cultures have very different bereavement traditions. In Egypt, the bereaved are encouraged to dwell profusely on their grief, and other people support them by recounting their own losses and openly expressing their sorrow in emotional outpourings (Wikan, 1991).

Opponents of cultural relativism argue that dangers arise when cultural norms are allowed to dictate what is normal or abnormal. In particular, psychiatrist Thomas Szasz (1971) noted that, throughout history, societies have labeled individuals and groups as abnormal in order to justify controlling or silencing them. Hitler branded Jews

Abnormality Along the Continuum

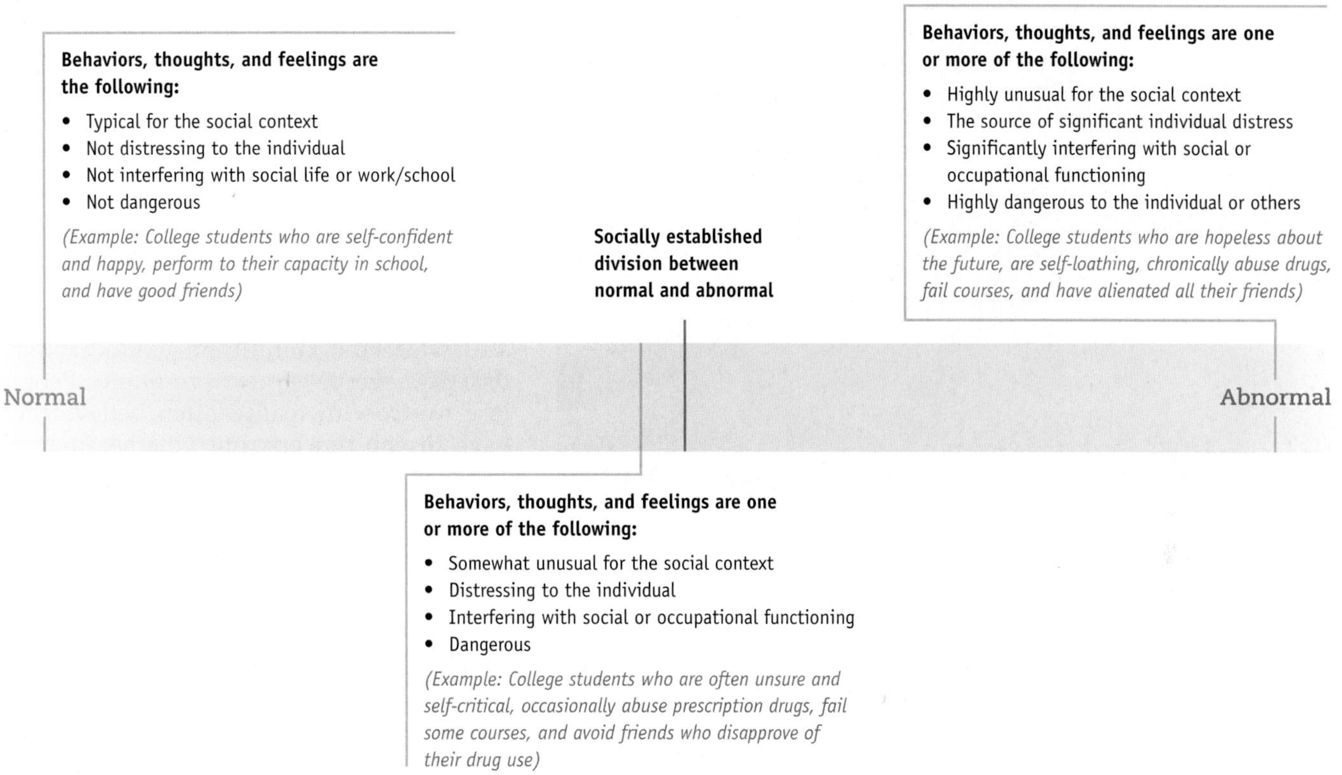

Behaviors, thoughts, and feelings are the following:

- Typical for the social context
- Not distressing to the individual
- Not interfering with social life or work/school
- Not dangerous

(Example: College students who are self-confident and happy, perform to their capacity in school, and have good friends)

Socially established division between normal and abnormal

Behaviors, thoughts, and feelings are one or more of the following:

- Highly unusual for the social context
- The source of significant individual distress
- Significantly interfering with social or occupational functioning
- Highly dangerous to the individual or others

(Example: College students who are hopeless about the future, are self-loathing, chronically abuse drugs, fail courses, and have alienated all their friends)

Normal — Abnormal

Behaviors, thoughts, and feelings are one or more of the following:

- Somewhat unusual for the social context
- Distressing to the individual
- Interfering with social or occupational functioning
- Dangerous

(Example: College students who are often unsure and self-critical, occasionally abuse prescription drugs, fail some courses, and avoid friends who disapprove of their drug use)

"It's not just black and white, there is a gray area in between." You've probably heard this said about a number of issues, such as thorny political issues. When it comes to mental health, we'd like to think there is a clear dividing line—either a person has a mental health problem or he or she doesn't. Unfortunately, however, there are gray areas even in the determination of mental health problems. Many psychologists are coming to believe that there is no clear line between normal and abnormal that, once crossed, labels an individual as having a disorder or not having one. Because no clear line exists, all psychological problems fall along a continuum, and psychologists must make subjective decisions about what warrants a diagnosis or treatment (see the continuum diagram above). This **continuum model of abnormality** applies to all disorders we discuss in this book.

abnormal and used this label as one justification for the Holocaust. The former Soviet Union branded political dissidents mentally ill and confined them in mental hospitals.

When the slave trade was active in the United States, slaves who tried to escape their masters could be diagnosed as having *drapetomania,* a sickness that caused them to desire freedom. This diagnosis provided a justification for capturing them and returning them to their masters (Szasz, 1971). In 1851, Dr. Samuel Cartwright, a prominent physician, published an essay in the prestigious *New Orleans Medical and Surgical Journal* titled "Report on the Diseases and Physical Peculiarities of the Negro Race," in which he argued that

> the cause, in most cases, that induces the Negro to run away from service, is as much a disease of the mind as any other species of mental alienation, and much more curable, as a general rule. With the advantages of proper medical advice, strictly followed, this troublesome practice that many Negroes have of running away can be almost entirely prevented.

Cartwright also described a disease called *dysaesthesia Aethiopis,* or the refusal to work for one's

When the slave trade was active, slaves who tried to escape were sometimes labeled as having mental illness and were beaten to "cure" them.

master. To cure this "disease," Cartwright prescribed the following:

> The liver, skin and kidneys should be stimulated to activity, and be made to assist in decarbonising the blood. The best means to stimulate the skin is, first, to have the patient well washed with warm water and soap; then to anoint it all over with oil, and to slap the oil with a broad leather strap; then to put the patient to some hard kind of work in the open air and sunshine, that will compel him to expand his lungs, as chopping wood, splitting rails, or sawing with the cross-cut or whip saw.

According to Cartwright, whipping slaves who refused to work and then forcing them to do hard labor would "revitalize" their lungs and bring them back to their senses. We might like to believe that Cartwright's essay represented the extreme views of just one person, but he was writing on behalf of a prestigious medical association.

In our modern society, gender-role expectations also influence the labeling of behaviors as normal or abnormal (Addis, 2008). Men who display sadness or anxiety, who choose to stay home to raise their children while their wives work, or who otherwise violate the male gender role are at risk of being labeled as abnormal. Women who are too aggressive, who don't want to have children, or who otherwise violate the female gender role are at risk of being labeled as abnormal. On the other hand, aggression in men and chronic anxiety or sadness in women are often dismissed as normal, because they do not violate gender roles—we expect these behaviors, so we may label them as normal.

The cultural-relativist perspective creates many difficulties in defining abnormality. Most mental health professionals these days do not take an extreme relativist view on abnormality, recognizing the dangers of basing our definitions of abnormality solely on cultural norms. Yet even those who reject an extreme cultural-relativist position recognize that culture and gender have a number of influences on the *expression* of abnormal behaviors and on the way those behaviors are *treated*. First, culture and gender can influence the ways people express symptoms: People who lose touch with reality often believe that they have divine powers, but whether they believe they are Jesus or Mohammed depends on their religious background.

Second, culture and gender can influence people's willingness to admit to certain types of behaviors (Snowden & Yamada, 2005). People in Eskimo and Tahitian cultures may be reluctant to admit to feeling anger because of strong cultural norms against the expression of anger. However, the Kaluli of New Guinea and the Yanomamo of Brazil value the expression of anger and have elaborate and complex rituals for expressing anger (Jenkins, Kleinman, & Good, 1991).

Third, culture and gender can influence the types of treatments deemed acceptable or helpful for maladaptive behaviors. Some cultures may view drug therapies for psychopathology as most appropriate, while others may be more willing to accept psychotherapy (Snowden & Yamada, 2005). Throughout this book, we will explore these influences of culture and gender on maladaptive behaviors.

Unusualness

Another second standard that has been used for designating behaviors as abnormal is **unusualness.** Behaviors that are *deviant*, or unusual, are considered abnormal, whereas behaviors that are typical, or usual, are considered normal. This criterion has some ties to the relativist criterion, because the unusualness of any behavior depends in part on a culture's norms for that behavior. For example, how unusual is it for a bereaved person to wail in public? The answer depends on whether that person is in Minneapolis or Cairo.

The unusualness criterion for abnormality has other problems. For one, how unusual must a behavior be in order for it to be labeled abnormal? Are behaviors that only 10 percent of the population exhibit

"Do people hate us because we dress this way or do we dress this way because people hate us?"
ScienceCartoonsPlus.com

abnormal? Or do we want to set a stricter cutoff and say that only behaviors that 1 percent or less of the population exhibit are abnormal? Choosing a cutoff is as subjective as relying on personal opinions as to what behaviors are abnormal or normal.

Another problem with the unusualness criterion is that many rare behaviors are positive for the individual and for society, and most people would object to labeling such behaviors abnormal. For example, we don't label the playing of a piano virtuoso abnormal; rather, we label it gifted. Other people have hobbies or activities that are rare but are a source of great joy for them and do no harm to others. These people are often referred to as *eccentrics.* For example, consider Gary Holloway, an environmental planner who works for the city of San Francisco and is described in the following case study.

CASE STUDY

He is fascinated by Martin Van Buren, the eighth president of the United States. Eighteen years ago, he discovered that Van Buren was the only president not to have a society dedicated to his memory, so he promptly founded the Martin Van Buren Fan Club. "This man did absolutely nothing to further the course of our national destiny," Holloway told us proudly, "yet hundreds of people now follow me in commemorating him." Holloway has served as the club's president for eighteen consecutive terms, and he has also been the winner for eighteen consecutive years of the Marty, its award for excellence in Van Burenism. Holloway is also a lifelong devotee of St. Francis of Assisi, and frequently dresses in the habit of a Franciscan monk. "It's comfortable, fun to wear, and I like the response I get when I wear it," he explained. "People always offer me a seat on the bus." Holloway has an obsession with the British Commonwealth and has an encyclopedic knowledge of places such as Tristan da Cunha and Fiji. During the Falklands war he passionately espoused the cause of the islanders, to the point of flying the Falklands flag on the flagpole on his front lawn. After the war he celebrated Britain's victory by renaming his home Falklands House, where he continues to fly its flag. His bedroom at Falklands House still has everything in it that it had when he was a boy. He calls it the Peanuts Room because of his huge collection of stuffed Snoopies and other memorabilia pertaining to the comic strip *Peanuts.* He has slept on the same twin bed there for forty years. He has dozens of toy airplanes, relics of his boyhood, and the walls are covered with pennants. "As a monk," he explained, "I'm always doing pennants"—thereby demonstrating the sly sense of humor that many eccentrics possess. (Weeks & James, 1995, pp. 36–37)

Gary Holloway's activities certainly are eccentric, but would we call them abnormal?

Gary Holloway's activities certainly are eccentric, but would we call them abnormal?

Distress

Proponents of a **distress** criterion for abnormality suggest that behaviors should be considered abnormal only if the individual suffers distress and wishes to be rid of the behaviors. This criterion avoids, to some extent, the problems of using societal norms as the criterion for abnormality. If a person's behaviors violate societal norms but do not cause him or her any distress, then the behaviors should not be considered abnormal.

Some clinicians object to the distress criterion, however, because people are not always aware of problems their behaviors create for themselves or for others. For example, some people who have lost touch with reality wander the streets aimlessly, not eating or taking care of themselves, putting themselves in danger of starvation or exposure to the elements. These people may not be fully aware that they have severe problems and therefore do not seek help. If we require that people acknowledge and seek help for their behaviors before we call those behaviors abnormal, some people who could benefit greatly from help might never receive it.

In addition, the behaviors of some people cause great distress to others, if not to themselves. An example is people who engage in highly antisocial behavior, such as lying, cheating, or even being violent toward others. They may suffer no distress, and may even experience pleasure, at causing others great pain. Thus, we might want to call their behaviors abnormal despite their not experiencing distress.

Mental Illness

Some might think that we should not label behaviors abnormal unless they are part of a **mental illness.** This implies that a disease process, much like hypertension or diabetes, is causing the behavior. For example, when many people say that an individual "has schizophrenia," they imply that he or she has a disease that should show up on some sort of biological test, just as hypertension shows up when a person's blood pressure is taken.

To date, however, no biological test is available to diagnose any of the types of abnormality we discuss in this book. This may be simply because we do not yet have the right biological tests. But many theorists believe that most mental health problems are due to a number of complex biological and psychosocial factors, rather than to single abnormal genes or disease processes, and that we will never have simple or definitive tests to show that a person has a mental disorder.

When we give a person's psychological symptoms a diagnosis, it is simply a label for that set of symptoms. For example, when we say someone "has" obsessive-compulsive disorder, we can mean only that he or she is exhibiting a set of symptoms, including obsessive thoughts and compulsive behaviors. The term *obsessive-compulsive disorder* does not refer to an identifiable physical process that is found in all people who exhibit these symptoms.

The Four Ds of Abnormality

Modern judgments of abnormality are not based on any one of the criteria we have discussed but instead are influenced by the interplay of four dimensions, often called *"the four Ds": dysfunction, distress, deviance, and dangerousness*. Behaviors and feelings are *dysfunctional* when they interfere with the person's ability to function in daily life, to hold a job, or to form close relationships. The more dysfunctional behaviors and feelings are, the more likely they are to be considered abnormal by mental health professionals. Behaviors and feelings that cause *distress* to the individual or to others around him or her are also likely to be considered abnormal. Highly *deviant* (unusual) behaviors, such as chronic lying and stealing, or hearing voices when no one is around, lead to judgments of abnormality. Finally, some behaviors and feelings are of potential harm to the individual, such as suicidal gestures, or to others, such as excessive aggression. Such *dangerous* behaviors and feelings are often seen as abnormal. The four Ds together make up mental health professionals' definition of behaviors or feelings as abnormal or *maladaptive*. Julia's experiences and the feelings described by Jamison, presented at the beginning of this chapter, would be labeled abnormal based on these criteria because the symptoms interfere with these people's daily functioning, cause them suffering, are highly unusual, and are potentially dangerous to them.

The four Ds of abnormality capture what most of us mean when we call something abnormal or maladaptive while avoiding some of the problems of using only the cultural relativism, unusualness, distress, and illness criteria. We are still left making subjective judgments, however. How much emotional pain or harm must a person be suffering? How much should the behaviors be interfering with daily functioning? We return to the continuum model to acknowledge that each of the four Ds lies along its own continuum. A person's behaviors and feelings can be more or less dysfunctional, distressing, deviant, or dangerous (see the continuum model on page 5). Thus, there is no sharp line between what is normal and what is abnormal.

SHADES OF GRAY

Consider whether the two students described here show abnormal behavior.

In the year between her eighteenth and nineteenth birthdays, Jennifer, who is 5 feet 6 inches tall, dropped from a weight of 125 pounds to 105 pounds. The weight loss began when she had an extended case of the flu and lost 10 pounds. Friends complimented her on being thinner, and Jennifer decided to lose more weight. She cut her daily intake of food to about 1200 calories, avoiding carbs as much as possible, and began running a few miles every day. Sometimes she is so hungry she has trouble concentrating on her schoolwork, but she values her new, lean look so much that she is terrified of gaining the weight back. She'd even like to lose a few more pounds so she can fit into a size 2.

Mark is what you might call a "heavy drinker." Although he is only 18, he has ready access to alcohol, and most nights he drinks at least five or six beers. He rarely feels drunk after that much alcohol, though, so he might throw back a few shots, especially when he is out partying on Saturday nights. He's gotten caught a few times and has received tickets for underage drinking, but he proudly displays them on his dorm wall as badges of honor. Mark's grades are not what they could be, but he finds his classes boring and has a hard time doing the work.

Are Jennifer's and Mark's behaviors abnormal? How would you rate the level of dysfunction, distress, deviance, and danger for each? (Discussion appears at the end of this chapter.)

TEST YOURSELF

1. What is the continuum model of abnormality?
2. What is cultural relativism? What are the greatest advantage and disadvantage of this perspective on abnormality?
3. What is the unusualness criterion for abnormality? What are its major advantages and disadvantages?
4. What is the distress criterion for abnormality? What about it is useful, and what about it is problematic?
5. What is the mental illness criterion for abnormality? What about it is useful, and what about it is problematic?
6. What are the four Ds of abnormality?

APPLY IT Henry has had multiple arrests for sexual assault and recently was convicted of beating a store clerk unconscious during a holdup. He has been diagnosed with several mental disorders, including attention-deficit/hyperactivity disorder, conduct disorder, and alcohol dependence. The judge at Henry's last trial commented that Henry seemed unconcerned about his own behavior or the prospect of going to prison. Which of the following is the one criterion by which Henry would *not* be considered abnormal?

a. cultural relativism

b. unusualness

c. distress

d. mental illness

Answers appear online at www.mhhe.com/nolen5e.

HISTORICAL PERSPECTIVES ON ABNORMALITY

Three types of theories of the causes of abnormal behaviors have competed for dominance across history. The **biological theories** saw abnormal behavior as similar to physical diseases, caused by the breakdown of systems in the body. The appropriate cure was the restoration of bodily health. The **supernatural theories** saw abnormal behavior as a result of divine intervention, curses, demonic possession, and personal sin. To rid the person of the perceived affliction, religious rituals, exorcisms, confessions, and atonement were prescribed. The **psychological theories** saw abnormal behavior as a result of traumas, such as bereavement, or of chronic stress. According to these theories, rest, relaxation, a change of environment, and certain herbal medicines were sometimes helpful. These three types of theories influenced how people who behaved abnormally were regarded in the society. A person thought to be abnormal because he or she was a sinner, for example, would be regarded differently than would a person thought to be abnormal because of a disease.

Ancient Theories

Our understanding of prehistoric people's conceptions of abnormality is based on inferences from archaeological artifacts—fragments of bones, tools, artwork, and so on. Ever since humans developed written language, they have been writing about abnormal behavior. It seems that humans have always viewed abnormality as something needing special explanation.

Driving Away Evil Spirits

Historians speculate that even prehistoric people had a concept of insanity, probably one rooted in supernatural beliefs (Selling, 1940). A person who acted oddly was suspected of being possessed by evil spirits. The typical treatment for abnormality, according to supernatural beliefs, was exorcism—driving the evil spirits from the body of the suffering person. Shamans, or healers, would recite prayers or incantations, try to talk the spirits out of the body, or make the body an uncomfortable place for the spirits to reside—often through extreme measures such as starving or beating the person. At other times, the person thought to be possessed by evil spirits would simply be killed.

One treatment for abnormality in the Stone Age and well into the Middle Ages may have been to drill holes in the skull of a person displaying abnormal behavior to allow the spirits to depart (Feldman & Goodrich, 2001). Archaeologists have found skulls dating back to a half-million years ago in which sections of the skull have been drilled or cut away. The tool used for this drilling is called a trephine, and the operation is called **trephination.** Some historians believe that people who were seeing or hearing things that were not real and people who were chronically sad were subjected to this form of brain surgery (Feldman & Goodrich, 2001). Presumably, if the person survived this surgery, the evil spirits would have been released and the person's abnormal behavior would have declined. However, we cannot know with certainty that trephination was used to drive away evil spirits. Other historians suggest that it was used primarily for the removal of blood clots caused by stone weapons during warfare and for other medical purposes (Maher & Maher, 1985). It is clear, however, that supernatural theories of abnormality have been around for a very long time.

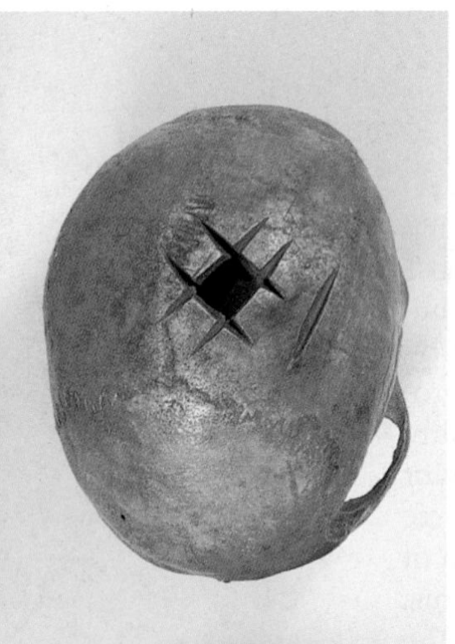

Some scholars believe that holes found in ancient skulls are from trephination, a crude form of brain surgery possibly performed on people acting abnormally.

Ancient China: Balancing Yin and Yang

Some of the earliest written sources on abnormality are ancient Chinese medical texts (Tseng, 1973). *Nei Ching (Classic of Internal Medicine)* was probably written around 2674 BCE by Huang Ti, the legendary third emperor of China.

Ancient Chinese medicine was based on the concept of yin and yang. The human body was said to contain a positive force (yang) and a negative force (yin), which confronted and complemented each other. If the two forces were in balance, the individual was healthy. If not, illness, including insanity, could result. For example, *excited insanity* was considered the result of an excessive positive force:

Some of the earliest medical writings on mental disorders came from ancient Chinese texts. The illustration shows a healer at work.

> The person suffering from excited insanity initially feels sad, eating and sleeping less; he then becomes grandiose, feeling that he is very smart and noble, talking and scolding day and night, singing, behaving strangely, seeing strange things, hearing strange voices, believing that he can see the devil or gods, etc. As treatment for such an excited condition withholding food was suggested, since food was considered to be the source of positive force and the patient was thought to be in need of a decrease in such force. (Tseng, 1973, p. 570)

Another theory in ancient Chinese medical philosophy was that human emotions were controlled by internal organs. When the "vital air" was flowing on one of these organs, an individual experienced a particular emotion. For example, when air flowed on the heart, a person felt joy; when on the lungs, sorrow; when on the liver, anger; when on the spleen, worry; and when on the kidney, fear. This theory encouraged people to live in an orderly and harmonious way so as to maintain the proper movement of vital air.

Although the perspective on psychological symptoms represented by ancient texts such as the *Nei Ching* was largely a biological one, the rise of

Taoism and Buddhism during the Chin and T'ang dynasties (420–618 CE) led to some religious interpretations of abnormal behavior. Evil winds and ghosts were blamed for bewitching people and for inciting people's erratic emotional displays and uncontrolled behavior. Religious theories of abnormality declined in China after this period (Tseng, 1973).

Ancient Egypt, Greece, and Rome: Biological Theories Dominate

Other ancient writings on abnormal behavior are found in the papyri of Egypt and Mesopotamia (Veith, 1965). The oldest of these, a document known as the Kahun Papyrus after the ancient Egyptian city in which it was found, dates from about 1900 BCE. This document lists a number of disorders, each followed by a physician's judgment of the cause of the disorder and the appropriate treatment.

Several of the disorders apparently left people with unexplainable aches and pains, sadness or distress, and apathy about life, such as "a woman who loves bed; she does not rise and she does not shake it" (Veith, 1965, p. 3). These disorders were said to occur only in women and were attributed to a "wandering uterus." The Egyptians believed that the uterus could become dislodged and wander throughout a woman's body, interfering with her other organs. Later, the Greeks, holding to the same theory of the anatomy of women, named this disorder hysteria (from the Greek word *hystera,* which means "uterus"). These days, the term *hysteria* is used to refer to physiological symptoms that probably are the result of psychological processes. In the Egyptian papyri, the prescribed treatment for this disorder involved the use of strong-smelling substances to drive the uterus back to its proper place.

Beginning with Homer, the Greeks wrote frequently of people thought to be mad (Wallace & Gach, 2008). The physician Hippocrates (460–377 BCE) described a case of a common phobia: A man could not walk alongside a cliff, pass over a bridge, or jump over even a shallow ditch without feeling unable to control his limbs and having his vision impaired.

Most Greeks and Romans saw madness as an affliction from the gods. The afflicted retreated to temples honoring the god Aesculapius, where priests held healing ceremonies. Plato (429–347 BCE) and Socrates (384–322 BCE) argued that some forms of madness were divine and could be the source of great literary and prophetic gifts.

For the most part, however, Greek physicians rejected supernatural explanations of abnormal behavior (Wallace & Gach, 2008). Hippocrates, often regarded as the father of medicine, argued that abnormal behavior was like other diseases of the body. According to Hippocrates, the body was composed of four basic humors: blood, phlegm, yellow bile, and black bile. All diseases, including abnormal behavior, were caused by imbalances in the body's essential humors. Based on careful observation of his many patients, which included listening to their dreams, Hippocrates classified abnormal behavior into four categories: epilepsy, mania, melancholia, and brain fever.

The treatments prescribed by the Greek physicians were intended to restore the balance of the four humors. Sometimes these treatments were physiological and intrusive, for example, bleeding a patient to treat disorders thought to result from an excess of blood. Other treatments consisted of rest, relaxation, a change of climate or scenery, a change of diet, or living a temperate life. Some nonmedical treatments prescribed by these physicians sound remarkably like those prescribed by modern psychotherapists. Hippocrates, for example, believed that removing a patient from a difficult family could help restore mental health. Plato argued that madness arose when the rational mind was overcome by impulse, passion, or appetite. Sanity could be regained through a discussion with the individual designed to restore rational control over emotions (Maher & Maher, 1985).

Among the Greeks of Hippocrates' and Plato's time, the relatives of people considered mad were encouraged to confine their afflicted family members to the home. The state claimed no responsibility for insane people; there were no asylums or institutions, other than the religious temples, to house and care for them. The state could, however, take rights away from people declared mad. Relatives could bring suit against those they considered mad, and the state could award the property of insane people to their relatives. People declared mad could not marry or acquire or dispose of their own property. Poor people who were considered mad were simply left to roam the streets if they were not violent. If they were violent, they were locked away. The general public greatly feared madness of any form, and people thought to be mad often were shunned or even stoned (Maher & Maher, 1985).

Medieval Views

The Middle Ages (around 400–1400 CE) are often described as a time of backward thinking dominated by an obsession with supernatural forces, yet even within Europe supernatural theories of abnormal behavior did not dominate until the late

Middle Ages, between the eleventh and fifteenth centuries (Neugebauer, 1979). Prior to the eleventh century, witches and witchcraft were accepted as real but were considered mere nuisances, overrated by superstitious people. Severe emotional shock and physical illness or injury most often were seen as the causes of bizarre behaviors. For example, English court records attributed mental health problems to factors such as a "blow received on the head," explained that symptoms were "induced by fear of his father," and noted that "he has lost his reason owing to a long and incurable infirmity" (Neugebauer, 1979, p. 481). Laypeople probably did believe in demons and curses as causes of abnormal behavior, but there is strong evidence that physicians and government officials attributed abnormal behavior to physical causes or traumas.

Witchcraft

Beginning in the eleventh century, the power of the Catholic Church in Europe was threatened by the breakdown of feudalism and by rebellions. The Church interpreted these threats in terms of heresy and Satanism. The Inquisition was established originally to rid the Earth of religious heretics, but eventually those practicing witchcraft or Satanism also became the focus of hunts. The witch hunts continued long after the Reformation, perhaps reaching their height during the fifteenth to seventeenth centuries—the period known as the Renaissance (Mora, 2008).

Some psychiatric historians have argued that persons accused of witchcraft must have been mentally ill (Veith, 1965; Zilboorg & Henry, 1941). Accused witches sometimes confessed to speaking with the devil, flying on the backs of animals, or engaging in other unusual behaviors. Such people may have been experiencing delusions (false beliefs) or hallucinations (unreal perceptual experiences), which are signs of some psychological disorders. However, such confessions may have been extracted through torture or in exchange for a stay of execution (Spanos, 1978).

Some people burned at the stake as witches may have had mental disorders that caused them to act abnormally.

In 1563, Johann Weyer published *The Deception of Dreams,* in which he argued that those accused of being witches were suffering from melancholy (depression) and senility. The Church banned Weyer's writings. Twenty years later, Reginald Scot, in his *Discovery of Witchcraft* (1584), supported Weyer's beliefs: "These women are but diseased wretches suffering from melancholy, and their words, actions, reasoning, and gestures show that sickness has affected their brains and impaired their powers of judgment" (Castiglioni, 1946, p. 253). Again, the Church—joined this time by the state—refuted the arguments and banned Scot's writings.

As is often the case, change came from within. In the sixteenth century, Teresa of Avila, a Spanish nun who was later canonized, explained that the mass hysteria that had broken out among a group of nuns was not the work of the devil but was the result of infirmities or sickness. She argued that these nuns were *comas enfermas,* or "as if sick." She sought out natural causes for the nuns' strange behaviors and concluded that they were due to melancholy, a weak imagination, or drowsiness and sleepiness (Sarbin & Juhasz, 1967).

The culture so completely accepted the existence of witches and witchcraft that some perfectly sane people may have self-identified as witches. In addition, most writings of medieval and Renaissance times, as well as writings from the witch hunt period in Salem, Massachusetts, clearly distinguish between people who were mad and people who were witches. The distinction between madness and witchcraft continues to this day in cultures that believe in witchcraft.

Psychic Epidemics

Psychic epidemics are defined as a phenomenon in which large numbers of people engage in unusual behaviors that appear to have a psychological origin. During the Middle Ages, reports of dance frenzies or manias were frequent. A monk, Peter of Herental, described a rash of dance frenzies that broke out over a 4-month period in 1374 in Germany:

> Both men and women were abused by the devil to such a degree that they danced in

> their homes, in the churches and in the streets, holding each other's hands and leaping in the air. While they danced they called out the names of demons, such as Friskes and others, but they were unaware of this nor did they pay attention to modesty even though people watched them. At the end of the dance, they felt such pains in the chest, that if their friends did not tie linen clothes tightly around their waists, they cried out like madmen that they were dying. (cited in Rosen, 1968, pp. 196–197)

Other instances of dance frenzy were reported in 1428 during the feast of Saint Vitus, at Schaffhausen, at which a monk danced himself to death. In 1518, a large epidemic of uncontrolled dance frenzy occurred at the chapel of Saint Vitus at Hohlenstein, near Zabern. According to one account, more than 400 people danced during the 4 weeks the frenzy lasted. Some writers of the time began to call the frenzied dancing *Saint Vitus' dance.*

A similar phenomenon, *tarantism,* was noted in Italy as early as the fourteenth century and became prominent in the seventeenth century. People suddenly developed an acute pain, which they attributed to the bite of a tarantula. They jumped around and danced wildly in the streets, tearing at their clothes and beating each other with whips. Some people dug holes in the earth and rolled on the ground; others howled and made obscene gestures. At the time, many people interpreted dance frenzies and tarantism as the results of possession by the devil. The behaviors may have been the remnants of ancient rituals performed by people worshipping the Greek god Dionysus.

We see episodes of psychic epidemics in modern times. On February 8, 1991, a number of students and teachers in a high school in Rhode Island thought they smelled noxious fumes coming from the ventilation system. The first person to detect these fumes, a 14-year-old girl, fell to the floor, crying and saying that her stomach hurt and her eyes stung. Other students and the teacher in that room then began to experience symptoms. They were moved into the hallway with a great deal of commotion. Soon students and teachers from adjacent rooms, who could see clearly into the hallway, began to experience symptoms. Eventually, 21 people (17 students and 4 teachers) were admitted to the local hospital emergency room. All were hyperventilating, and most complained of dizziness, headache, and nausea. Although some initially showed symptoms of mild carbon monoxide intoxication in blood tests, no evidence of toxic gas in the school could be found. The physicians treating the children and teachers concluded that the outbreak was a case of mass hysteria prompted by the fear of chemical warfare during the Persian Gulf War (Rockney & Lemke, 1992).

Psychic epidemics are no longer viewed as the result of spirit possession or the bite of a tarantula. Rather, psychologists attempt to understand them using research from social psychology about the influence of others on individuals' self-perceptions. The social context can affect even our perceptions of our own bodies, as we will see when we discuss people's differing reactions to psychoactive substances such as marijuana (see Chapter 14) and people's interpretations of physical sensations in their bodies (see Chapter 5).

The Spread of Asylums

As early as the twelfth century, many towns in Europe took some responsibility for housing and caring for people considered mentally ill (Kroll, 1973). Remarkable among these towns was Gheel, Belgium, where townspeople regularly took into their homes the mentally ill visiting the shrine of Saint Dymphna for cures.

In about the eleventh or twelfth century, general hospitals began to include special rooms or facilities for people exhibiting abnormal behavior. The mentally ill were little more than inmates in these early hospitals, housed against their will, often in extremely harsh conditions. One of the most famous of these hospitals was the Hospital of Saint Mary of Bethlehem, in London, which officially became a mental hospital in 1547. This hospital, nicknamed *Bedlam*, was famous for its deplorable conditions. At Bedlam and other mental hospitals established in Europe in the sixteenth, seventeenth, and eighteenth centuries, patients were exhibited to the public for a fee. They lived in filth and confinement, often chained to walls or locked inside small boxes. The following description of the treatment of patients in La Bicêtre Hospital, an asylum for male patients in Paris, provides an example of typical care:

> The patients were ordinarily shackled to the walls of their dark, unlighted cells by iron collars which held them flat against the wall and permitted little movement. Ofttimes there were also iron hoops around the waists of the patients and both their hands and feet were chained. Although these chains usually permitted enough movement that the patients could feed

Bedlam—the Hospital of Saint Mary of Bethlehem—was famous for the chaotic and deplorable conditions in which people with mental disorders were kept.

In the medieval and early modern periods, doctors used bleeding to treat people with mental disorders and many other ailments.

> themselves out of bowls, they often kept them from being able to lie down at night. Since little was known about dietetics, and the patients were presumed to be animals anyway, little attention was paid to whether they were adequately fed or whether the food was good or bad. The cells were furnished only with straw and were never swept or cleaned; the patient remained in the midst of all the accumulated ordure. No one visited the cells except at feeding time, no provision was made for warmth, and even the most elementary gestures of humanity were lacking. (adapted from Selling, 1940, pp. 54–55)

The laws regarding the confinement of the mentally ill in Europe and the United States were concerned with the protection of the public and the ill person's relatives (Busfield, 1986; Scull, 1993). For example, Dalton's 1618 edition of *Common Law* states that "it is lawful for the parents, kinsmen or other friends of a man that is mad, or frantic . . . to take him and put him into a house, to bind or chain him, and to beat him with rods, and to do any other forcible act to reclaim him, or to keep him so he shall do no hurt" (Allderidge, 1979).

The first *Act for Regulating Madhouses* in England was not passed until 1774, with the intention of cleaning up the deplorable conditions in hospitals and madhouses and protecting people from being unjustly jailed for insanity. This act provided for the licensing and inspection of madhouses and required that a physician, a surgeon, or an apothecary sign a certificate before a patient could be admitted. These provisions applied only to paying patients in private madhouses, however, and not to the poor people confined to workhouses.

These asylums typically were established and run by people who thought that abnormal behaviors were medical illnesses. For example, Benjamin Rush (1745–1813), one of the founders of American psychiatry, believed that abnormal behavior was caused by excessive blood in the brain and prescribed bleeding the patient, or drawing huge amounts of blood from the body. Thus, although the supernatural theories of the Middle Ages have often been decried as leading to brutal treatment of people with mental illnesses, the medical theories of those times and of the next couple of centuries did not always lead to better treatment.

Moral Treatment in the Eighteenth and Nineteenth Centuries

Fortunately, the eighteenth and nineteenth centuries saw the growth of a more humane treatment of people with mental health problems. This new treatment was based on the psychological view that people developed problems because they had become separated from nature and succumbed to the stresses imposed by the rapid social changes of the period (Rosen, 1968). The treatment was rest and relaxation in a serene and physically appealing place.

A leader of the movement for **moral treatment** of people with abnormality was Philippe Pinel (1745–1826), a French physician who took charge of La Bicêtre in Paris in 1793. Pinel argued, "To detain maniacs in constant seclusion and to load them with chains; to leave them defenceless, to the brutality of underlings . . . in a word, to rule them with a rod of iron . . . is a system of superintendence, more distinguished for its convenience than for its humanity or success" (Grob, 1994, p. 27). Pinel believed that many forms of abnormality could be cured by restoring the dignity and tranquility of patients.

Philippe Pinel, a leader in the moral movement in France, helped free mental patients from the horrible conditions of the hospitals.

Pinel ordered that patients be allowed to walk freely around the asylum. They were provided with clean and sunny rooms, comfortable sleeping quarters, and good food. Nurses and professional therapists were trained to work with the patients to help them restore their sense of tranquility and engage in planned social activities. Although many physicians thought Pinel himself was mad for releasing the patients from confinement, his approach was remarkably successful. Many people who had been locked away in darkness for decades became able to control their behavior and reengage in life. Some improved so much that they could be released from the asylum. Pinel later successfully reformed La Salpetrière, a mental hospital in Paris for female patients (Grob, 1994).

In 1796, the Quaker William Tuke (1732–1819) opened an asylum in England, called The Retreat, in direct response to the brutal treatment he saw being delivered at other facilities to people with abnormal behavior. Tuke's treatment was designed to restore patients' self-restraint by treating them with respect and dignity and encouraging them to exercise self-control (Grob, 1994).

One of the most militant crusaders for moral treatment of the insane was Dorothea Dix (1802–1877). A retired schoolteacher living in Boston, Dix visited a jail on a cold Sunday morning in 1841 to teach a Sunday school class to women inmates. There she discovered the negligence and brutality that characterized the treatment of poor people with abnormal behavior, many of whom were simply warehoused in jails.

That encounter began Dix's tireless quest to improve the treatment of people with mental health problems. Dix's lobbying efforts led to the passage of laws and appropriations to fund the cleanup of mental hospitals and the training of mental health professionals dedicated to the moral treatment of patients. Between 1841 and 1881, Dix personally helped establish more than 30 mental institutions in the United States, Canada, Newfoundland, and Scotland. Hundreds more public hospitals for the insane established during this period by others were run according to humanitarian perspectives.

Unfortunately, the moral treatment movement grew too fast. As more asylums were built and more people went into them, the capacity of the asylums to recruit mental health professionals and to maintain a humane, individual approach to each patient declined (Grob, 1994; Scull, 1993). The physicians, nurses, and other caretakers simply did not have enough time to give each patient the calm and dedicated attention needed. The fantastic successes of the early moral treatment movement gave way to more modest successes, and to many outright failures, as patients remained impaired or got worse. Even some patients who received the best moral treatment could not benefit from it because their problems were not due to a loss of dignity or tranquility. With so many patients receiving moral treatment, the number of patients who failed to benefit from it increased, and questions about its effectiveness grew louder (Grob, 1994).

Dorothea Dix fought for the moral treatment of mental patients in the United States.

At the same time, the rapid pace of immigration into the United States in the late nineteenth century meant that an increasing percentage of its asylum patients were from different cultures and often from lower socioeconomic classes. Prejudice against these "foreigners," combined with increasing attention to the failures of moral treatment, led to declines in public support for funding such institutions. Reduced funding led to even greater declines in the quality of care. At the turn of the twentieth century, many public hospitals were no better than warehouses (Grob, 1994; McGovern, 1985; Scull, 1993).

Effective treatments for most major mental health problems were not developed until well into the twentieth century. Until then, patients who could not afford private care were warehoused in large, overcrowded, physically isolated state institutions that did not offer treatment (Deutsch, 1937). Clifford Beers, highlighted at the beginning of this chapter, was one extraordinary man who suffered the conditions of mental hospitals at the turn of the twentieth century, survived them, and worked to change them.

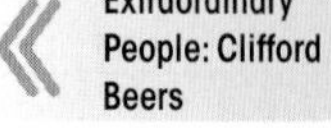

TEST YOURSELF

1. Define the biological, supernatural, and psychological perspectives on abnormality.
2. What is trephination?
3. How did the ancient Chinese medical texts view abnormality?
4. How did Greek and Roman philosophers and physicians view abnormality?
5. How did the witch hunts of the late Middle Ages reflect the views of abnormality in those times?
6. What are psychic epidemics?
7. What is moral treatment? What roles did Philippe Pinel and Dorothea Dix play in reforming the care of people with psychological problems?

APPLY IT Suppose you were being treated for symptoms of depression during ancient Greek times by a physician following Hippocrates' beliefs about the causes of abnormal behavior. To what would this physician likely attribute your symptoms?

a. possession by evil spirits
b. an excess of one of the bodily humors
c. witchcraft
d. vital air flowing over internal organs

Answers appear online at www.mhhe.com/nolen5e.

THE EMERGENCE OF MODERN PERSPECTIVES

Although the treatment of people who exhibited abnormal behavior deteriorated somewhat at the turn of the twentieth century, tremendous advances in the scientific study of disorders took place in the early twentieth century. These advances laid the groundwork for the biological, psychological, and social theories of abnormality that now dominate psychology and psychiatry.

The Beginnings of Modern Biological Perspectives

Basic knowledge of the anatomy, physiology, neurology, and chemistry of the body increased rapidly in the late nineteenth century. With the advancement of this basic knowledge came an increasing focus on biological causes of abnormality. In 1845, German psychiatrist Wilhelm Griesinger (1817–1868) published *The Pathology and Therapy of Psychic Disorders,* presenting a systematic argument that all psychological disorders can be explained in terms of brain pathology. In 1883, one of Griesinger's followers, Emil Kraepelin (1856–1926), also published a textbook emphasizing the importance of brain pathology in psychological disorders. More important, Kraepelin developed a scheme for classifying symptoms into discrete disorders that is the basis for our modern classification systems, as we will discuss in Chapter 3. Having a good classification system gives investigators a common set of labels for disorders, as well as a set of criteria for distinguishing between them, contributing immensely to the advancement of the scientific study of the disorders.

Emil Kraepelin (1856–1926) developed a classification system for mental disorders that remains influential today.

One of the most important discoveries underpinning modern biological theories of abnormality was the discovery of the cause of **general paresis,** a disease that leads to paralysis, insanity, and eventually death (Duffy, 1995). In the mid-1800s, reports that patients with paresis also had a history of syphilis led to the suspicion that syphilis might be a cause of paresis. In 1897, Viennese psychiatrist Richard Krafft-Ebing injected paretic patients with matter from syphilitic sores. None of the patients developed syphilis, and Krafft-Ebing concluded that they must already have been infected with it. The discovery that syphilis is the cause of one form of insanity lent great weight to the idea that biological factors can cause abnormal behaviors (Duffy, 1995).

As we will discuss in more detail in Chapter 2, modern biological theories of the psychological disorders have focused on the role of genetics, structural abnormalities in the brain, and biochemical imbalances. The advances in our understanding of the biological aspects of psychological disorders have contributed to the development of therapeutic medications.

Anton Mesmer (1734–1815) pioneered the use of suggestion to treat psychological problems. His work influenced Charcot and Freud.

The Psychoanalytic Perspective

The development of psychoanalytic theory begins with the odd story of Franz Anton Mesmer (1734–1815), an Austrian physician who believed that people had a magnetic fluid in the body that must be distributed in a particular pattern in order to maintain health. The distribution of magnetic fluid in one person could be influenced by the magnetic forces of other people, as well as by the alignments of the planets. In 1778, Mesmer opened a clinic in Paris to treat all sorts of diseases by applying *animal magnetism.*

The psychological disorders that were the focus of much of Mesmer's treatment were the hysterical disorders, in which people lose functioning or feeling in some part of the body for no apparent physiological reason. His patients sat in darkness around a tub containing various chemicals, and the affected areas of their bodies were prodded by iron rods emerging from the tub. With music playing, Mesmer emerged wearing an elaborate robe, touching each patient as he passed by, supposedly realigning people's magnetic fluids through his own powerful magnetic force. This process, Mesmer said, cured illness, including psychological disorders.

Mesmer eventually was labeled a charlatan by a scientific review committee that included Benjamin Franklin, yet his methods, known as **mesmerism,** continued to fuel debate long after he had faded into obscurity. The "cures" Mesmer effected in his psychiatric patients were attributed to the trance-like state that Mesmer seemed to induce in his patients. Later, this state was labeled *hypnosis*. Under hypnosis, Mesmer's patients appeared very suggestible, and the mere suggestion that their ailments would disappear seemed enough to make them actually disappear.

The connection between hypnosis and hysteria fascinated several leading scientists of the time, although not all scientists accepted this connection. In particular, Jean Charcot (1825–1893), head of La Salpetrière Hospital in Paris and the leading neurologist of his time, argued that hysteria was caused by degeneration in the brain. The work of two physicians practicing in the French town of Nancy, Hippolyte-Marie Bernheim (1840–1919) and Ambroise-Auguste Liebault (1823–1904), eventually won over Charcot, however. Bernheim and Liebault showed that they could induce the symptoms of hysteria, such as paralysis in an arm or the loss of feeling in a leg, by suggesting these symptoms to patients who were hypnotized. Fortunately, they could also remove these symptoms under hypnosis. Charcot was so impressed by the evidence that hysteria has psychological roots that he became a leading researcher of the psychological causes of abnormal behavior. The experiments of Bernheim and Liebault, along with the leadership of Charcot, did a great deal to advance psychological perspectives on abnormality.

One of Charcot's students was Sigmund Freud (1856–1939), a Viennese neurologist who went to study with Charcot in 1885. In this work, Freud became convinced that much of the mental life of an individual remains hidden from consciousness. This view was further supported by Freud's interactions with Pierre Janet (1858–1947) in Paris. Janet was investigating multiple personality disorder, in which people appear to have multiple, distinct personalities, each of which operates independently of the others, often not knowing the others exist (Matarazzo, 1985).

When he returned to Vienna, Freud worked with Josef Breuer (1842–1925), another physician interested in hypnosis and in the unconscious processes behind psychological problems. Breuer had discovered that encouraging patients to talk about their problems while under hypnosis led to a great upswelling and release of emotion, which eventually was called *catharsis.* The patient's discussion of his or her problems under hypnosis was less censored than conscious discussion, allowing the therapist to elicit important psychological material more easily.

Breuer and Freud collaborated on a paper published in 1893 as *On the Psychical Mechanisms of Hysterical Phenomena*, which laid out their discoveries about hypnosis, the unconscious, and the therapeutic value of catharsis. This paper proved to be a foundation stone in the development of **psychoanalysis,** the study of the unconscious. Freud introduced his ideas to America in 1909 in a series of lectures at Clark University in Worcester, Massachusetts, at the invitation of G. Stanley Hall, one of the founders of American psychology.

Freud wrote dozens of papers and books on his theory of psychoanalysis (discussed in detail in Chapter 2), and he became the best-known figure in psychiatry and psychology. The impact of Freud's theories on the development of psychology over the next century cannot be overestimated. Freudian ideas not only influenced the professional literature on psychopathology but also are used heavily in literary theory, anthropology, and other humanities. They pervade popular notions of psychological processes to this day.

The Roots of Behaviorism

In what now seems like a parallel universe, while psychoanalytic theory was being born, the roots of behaviorism were being planted first in Europe and then in the United States. Ivan Pavlov (1849–1936), a Russian physiologist, developed methods and theories for understanding behavior in terms of stimuli and responses rather than in terms of the internal workings of the unconscious mind. He discovered that dogs could be conditioned to salivate when presented with stimuli other than food if the food was paired with these other stimuli—a process later called *classical conditioning.* Pavlov's discoveries inspired American John Watson (1878–1958) to study important human behaviors, such as phobias, in terms of classical conditioning (see Chapter 5). Watson rejected psychoanalytic and biological theories of abnormal behaviors, such as phobias, and explained them entirely on the basis of the individual's history of conditioning. Watson (1930) went so far as to boast that he could train any healthy child to become any kind of adult he wished:

> Give me a dozen healthy infants, well-formed, and my own specified world to bring them up in, and I'll guarantee to take any one at random and train him to be any type of specialist I might select—doctor, lawyer, artist, merchant-chief, and yes, even beggar-man and thief, regardless of his talents, penchants, tendencies, abilities, vocations, and the race of his ancestors. (p. 104)

At the same time, two other psychologists, E. L. Thorndike (1874–1949) and B. F. Skinner (1904–1990), were studying how the consequences of behaviors shape their likelihood of recurrence. They argued that behaviors followed by positive consequences are more likely to be repeated than are behaviors followed by negative consequences. This process came to be known as *operant*, or *instrumental*, *conditioning*. This idea may seem simple to us now (one sign of how much it has influenced thinking over the past century), but at the time it was considered radical to argue that even complex behaviors, such as violence against others, can be explained by the reinforcement or punishment these behaviors have received in the past.

Behaviorism—the study of the impact of reinforcements and punishments on behavior—has had as profound an impact on psychology and on our common knowledge of psychology as has psychoanalytic theory. Behavioral theories have led to many of the effective psychological treatments for disorders that we will discuss in this book.

The Cognitive Revolution

In the 1950s, some psychologists argued that behaviorism was limited in its explanatory power by its refusal to look at internal thought processes that mediate the relationship between stimulus and response. It wasn't until the 1970s that psychology shifted its focus substantially to the study of **cognitions**, thought processes that influence behavior and emotion. An important player in this cognitive revolution was Albert Bandura, a clinical psychologist trained in behaviorism who had contributed a great deal to the application of behaviorism to psychopathology (see Chapters 2 and 5). Bandura argued that people's beliefs about their ability to execute the behaviors necessary to control important events—which he called **self-efficacy beliefs**—are crucial in determining people's well-being. Again, this idea seems obvious to us now, but only because it took hold in both professional psychology and lay notions of psychology.

Another key figure in cognitive perspectives was Albert Ellis, who argued that people prone to psychological disorders are plagued by irrational negative assumptions about themselves and the world. Ellis developed a therapy for emotional problems based on his theory called *rational-emotive therapy*. This therapy was controversial because it required therapists to challenge, sometimes harshly, their patients' irrational belief systems. It became very popular, however, and moved psychology into the study of the thought processes behind serious emotional problems. Another therapy, developed by Aaron Beck, focused on the irrational thoughts of people with psychological problems. Beck's *cognitive therapy* has become one of the most widely used therapies for many disorders (see Chapter 2). Since the 1970s, theorists have continued to emphasize cognitive factors in psychopathology, although behavioral theories have remained strong and interpersonal theories, which we will examine in Chapter 2, have become more prominent.

TEST YOURSELF

1. What role did Kraepelin's classification scheme play in the development of modern biological theories and therapies?
2. What role did the discovery that syphilis causes general paresis play in the emergence of modern theories of abnormality?
3. What is the connection between Anton Mesmer and the development of psychoanalysis?
4. How do behavioral perspectives explain abnormality?
5. How do cognitive perspectives explain abnormality?

APPLY IT Roy went to see a therapist to understand why he had trouble getting motivated in school. The therapist asked Roy to describe situations in which he felt less motivated and those in which he felt more motivated. What approach is Roy's therapist likely taking?

a. behavioral
b. cognitive
c. psychoanalytic
d. biological

Answers appear online at www.mhhe.com/nolen5e.

MODERN MENTAL HEALTH CARE

Halfway through the twentieth century, major breakthroughs were made in drug treatments for some of the major forms of abnormality. In particular, the discovery of a class of drugs that can reduce hallucinations and delusions, known as the phenothiazines (see Chapter 2), made it possible for many people who had been institutionalized for years to be released from asylums and hospitals. Since then, there has been an explosion of new drug therapies for psychopathology. In addition, as we will discuss in Chapter 2, several types of psychotherapy have been developed that have proven effective in treating a wide range of psychological problems. However, there are still significant problems in the delivery of mental health care, some of which began with the deinstitutionalization movement of the mid-twentieth century.

Deinstitutionalization

By 1960, a large and vocal movement known as the **patients' rights movement** had emerged. Patients' rights advocates argued that mental patients can recover more fully or live more satisfying lives if they are integrated into the community, with the support of community-based treatment facilities—a process known as **deinstitutionalization.** Many of these patients would continue to need around-the-clock care, but it could be given in treatment centers based in neighborhoods rather than in large, impersonal institutions. In the United States, the **community mental health movement** was officially launched in 1963 by President John Kennedy as a "bold new approach" to mental health care. This movement attempted to provide coordinated mental health services to people in community-based centers.

FIGURE 1.1 **Trends in the Numbers of Psychiatric Beds in Western Europe, 1978–2002**

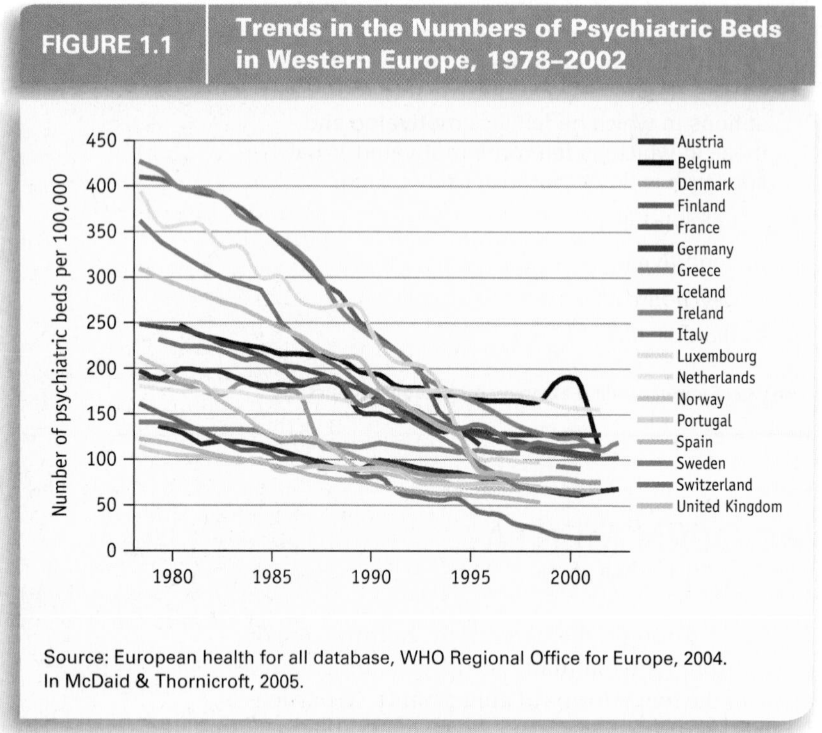

Source: European health for all database, WHO Regional Office for Europe, 2004. In McDaid & Thornicroft, 2005.

The deinstitutionalization movement had a massive effect on the lives of people with serious psychological problems. Between 1955 and 1998, the number of patients in state psychiatric hospitals in the United States went from a high of 559,000 to about 57,000, almost a 90 percent reduction (Lamb & Weinberger, 2001). Parallel trends occurred in Europe (Figure 1.1). Many former mental patients who had lived for years in cold, sterile facilities, receiving little useful care, experienced dramatic increases in their quality of life on their release. Moreover, they suddenly had the freedom to live where they wanted, as they saw fit.

Several types of community-based treatment facilities that were created at this time continue to serve people with mental health problems. **Community mental health centers** often include teams of social workers, therapists, and physicians who coordinate care. **Halfway houses** offer people with long-term mental health problems the opportunity to live in a structured, supportive environment as they try to reestablish a job and ties to family and friends. **Day treatment centers** allow people to obtain treatment during the day, along with occupational and rehabilitative therapies, but to live at home at night.

People who have acute problems that require hospitalization may go to inpatient wards of general hospitals or specialized psychiatric hospitals. Sometimes, their first contact with a mental health professional is in the emergency room of a hospital. Once their acute problems have subsided, however, they often are released back to their community treatment center rather than remaining for the long term in a psychiatric hospital.

Unfortunately, the resources to care for all the mental patients released from institutions have never been adequate. There were not enough halfway houses built or community mental health centers funded to serve the thousands of men and women who formerly were institutionalized or would have been institutionalized if the movement had not taken place. Meanwhile, the state psychiatric hospitals to which they would have retreated were closed down by the hundreds. The community mental health movement spread to Europe, with similar consequences. Currently, 28 percent of European countries have few or no community-based services for people with serious mental health problems (WHO World Mental Health Survey Consortium, 2004).

Men and women released from mental institutions began living in nursing homes and other types of group homes, where they received little mental health treatment, or with their families, many of whom were ill-equipped to handle serious mental illness (Lamb, 2001). Some began living on the streets. Certainly not all homeless people are mentally ill, but some researchers estimate that up to four-fifths of all long-term homeless adults in the United States and Europe have a major mental disorder, a severe substance use disorder (such as alcohol dependence), or both (WHO World Mental Health Survey Consortium, 2004). In emergencies, these people end up in general or private hospitals that are not equipped to treat them appropriately. Many end up in jail. One study of prison inmates found that two-thirds had experienced some form of diagnosable mental disorder in their lifetime (Trestman, Ford, Zhang, & Wiesbrock, 2007).

Thus, although deinstitutionalization began with laudatory goals, many of these goals were never fully reached, leaving many people who formerly would have been institutionalized in mental hospitals no better off. In recent years, the financial strains on local, state, and federal governments have led to the closing of many more community mental health centers.

Managed Care

The entire system of private insurance for health care in the United States underwent a revolution in the second half of the twentieth century, when managed care emerged as the dominant means for organizing health care. **Managed care** is a collection of methods for coordinating care that ranges from simple monitoring to total control over what care can be provided and paid for. The goals are to coordinate services for an existing medical problem and to prevent future medical problems. Often, health care providers are given a set amount of money per member (patient) per month and then must determine how best to serve each patient with that money.

Managed care can solve some of the problems created by deinstitutionalization. For example, instead of leaving it up to people with a serious psychological problem, or their families, to find appropriate care, the primary provider might find this care and ensure that patients have access to it. Suppose an individual patient reported to his physician that he was hearing voices when no one was around. The physician might refer the patient to a psychiatrist for an evaluation to determine if the patient might be suffering from schizophrenia. In some cases, the primary care physician might coordinate care offered by other providers, such as drug treatments, psychotherapy, and rehabilitation services. The primary provider also might ensure continuity of care so that patients do not "fall through the cracks." Thus, theoretically, managed care can have tremendous benefits for people with long-term, serious mental health problems. For people with less severe psychological problems, the availability of mental health care through managed care systems and other private insurance systems has led to a large increase in the number of people seeking psychotherapy and other types of mental health care.

Unfortunately, however, mental health care often is not covered, or not covered fully, by health insurance. Of course, many people do not have any health insurance. Mental health services are expensive, because mental health problems are sometimes chronic and mental health treatment can take a long time.

The Medicaid program, which covers one-fifth of all mental health care spending in the United States, has been a target for reductions in recent years, even as the number of people seeking mental health care has risen. Many states have reduced or restricted eligibility and benefits for mental health care, increased copayments, controlled drug costs, and reduced or frozen payments to providers (Mechanic & Bilder, 2004). At the same time, reductions in state and city welfare programs and other community services targeted at the poor have made daily life more difficult for poor people in general, and in particular for people with serious mental disorders, who often have exhausted their financial resources.

Only 50–60 percent of those in the United States with serious psychological problems receive stable mental health treatment, with much lower percentages receiving care in less-developed and poorer countries (Kessler et al., 2001; Wang et al., 2007). Sometimes, people refuse care that might help them. Other times, they fall through holes in the medical safety net because of bureaucratic rules designed to shift the burden of mental health care costs from one agency to another, as in the case of Rebecca J.

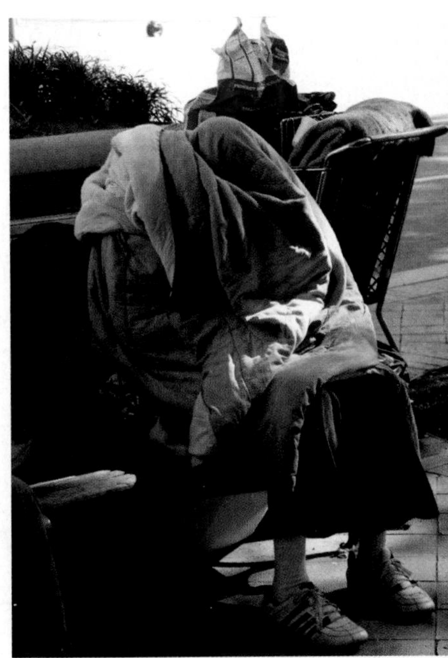

Deinstitutionalization led to a rise in homelessness among people with mental illnesses, which often go untreated.

CASE STUDY

Because of severe schizoaffective disorder, Rebecca J., age 56, had spent 25 years in a New York State psychiatric hospital. She lived in a group home in the community but required rehospitalization for several weeks approximately once a year when she relapsed despite taking medications. As a result of the reduction in state hospital beds (for people with mental disorders) and attempts by the state to shift readmissions for fiscal reasons, these rehospitalizations increasingly took place on the psychiatric wards of general hospitals that varied widely in quality. In 1994, she was admitted to a new hospital because the general hospital where she usually went was full. The new hospital was inadequately staffed to provide care for patients as sick as Rebecca J. In addition, the psychiatrist was poorly trained and had access to only a small fraction of Rebecca J.'s complex and voluminous past history. During her 6-week hospitalization, Rebecca J. lost 10 pounds because the nursing staff did not help her eat, had virtually all her clothing and personal effects lost or stolen, became toxic from her lithium medication, which was not noticed until she was semicomatose, and was prematurely discharged while she was still so psychotic that she had to be rehospitalized in another hospital less than 24 hours later. Meanwhile, less than a mile away in the state psychiatric hospital where she had spent many years, a bed sat empty on a ward with nursing staff and a psychiatrist who knew her case well and with her case records readily available in a file cabinet. (Torrey, 1997, pp. 105–106)

As we discuss the research showing the effectiveness of various treatments for specific disorders throughout the remainder of the book, it is important to keep in mind that those treatments can work only if people have access to them.

Professions Within Abnormal Psychology

In our times, a number of professions are concerned with abnormal or maladaptive behavior. *Psychiatrists* have an MD degree and have received specialized training in the treatment of psychological problems. Psychiatrists can prescribe medications for the treatment of these problems, and some have been trained to conduct psychotherapies as well.

Clinical psychologists typically have a PhD in psychology, with a specialization in psychological problems. Some have a PsyD degree from a graduate program that emphasizes clinical training more than research training. Clinical psychologists can conduct psychotherapy, but in most states they do not currently prescribe medications. (They do have limited prescription privileges in some states, and psychologists are lobbying for prescription privileges in many others.)

Marriage and family therapists specialize in helping families, couples, and children overcome problems that are interfering with their well-being. *Clinical social workers* have a master's degree in social work and often focus on helping people with psychological problems overcome social conditions contributing to their problems, such as joblessness or homelessness. Some states have *licensed mental health counselors*, individuals who have graduate training in counseling beyond the bachelor's degree in counseling but have not obtained a PhD *Psychiatric nurses* have a degree in nursing, with a specialization in the treatment of people with severe psychological problems. They often work on inpatient psychiatric wards in hospitals, delivering medical care and certain forms of psychotherapy, such as group therapy to increase patients' contacts with one another. In some states, they have privileges to write prescriptions for psychotherapeutic drugs.

Each of these professions has its rewards and limitations. Students who are interested in one or more of these professions often find it helpful to volunteer as a research assistant in studies of psychological problems or for work in a psychiatric clinic or hospital. Some students find tremendous gratification working with people with psychological problems, whereas others find it more gratifying to conduct research that might answer important questions about these problems. Many mental health professionals of all types combine clinical practice and research in their careers.

TEST YOURSELF

1. What was the goal of the deinstitutionalization movement? What were some of the consequences of this movement?
2. What are managed care systems? What are some of their benefits and problems?

APPLY IT Sabrina conducts psychotherapy with individuals and can prescribe medications. Which of the following is her profession?

a. clinical psychologist
b. clinical social worker
c. psychiatrist
d. marriage and family therapist

Answers appear online at www.mhhe.com/nolen5e.

CHAPTER INTEGRATION

Although the biological, psychological, and social theories of abnormality have traditionally been viewed as competing with one another to explain psychological disorders, many clinicians and researchers now believe that theories that integrate biological, psychological, and social perspectives on abnormality will prove most useful (Figure 1.2). For example, in Chapter 5 we will discuss

FIGURE 1.2 The Integrationist Approach to Understanding Mental Health. Many mental health theories today strive to integrate biological, psychological, and social factors in understanding mental health issues. This integrationist approach will be emphasized in this book.

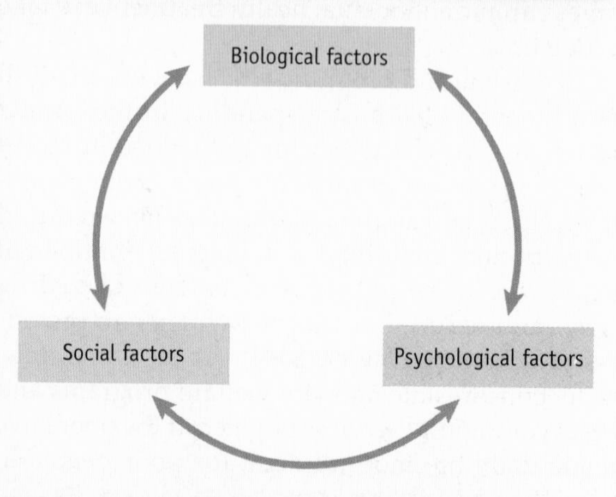

theories of anxiety disorders that take into account individuals' genetic and biochemical vulnerabilities, the impact of stressful events, and the role of cognition in explaining why some people suffer debilitating anxiety. Throughout this book, we will emphasize how biological, psychological, and social factors interact and influence one another to produce and maintain mental health problems. In other words, we will present an *integrationist approach* to psychological problems.

SHADES OF GRAY DISCUSSION (review p. 9)

Given that our society values extreme thinness in women—and that Jennifer has received reinforcement for her weight loss—her behaviors are not very deviant. You may have noted that her dieting causes some dysfunction and distress: She has trouble concentrating in school and is terrified of gaining weight. But her weight loss is also bringing her social benefits. At the same time, you might consider her behaviors to be physically dangerous. Extremely thin women risk medical complications such as reduced bone density and heart arrhythmias (see Chapter 12). So Jennifer's behaviors are somewhat dysfunctional, distressing, and dangerous, but they are so typical for women her age that people will differ in whether they believe her behaviors qualify as *abnormal.*

Mark's behaviors may also seem familiar to you, since many college students view drinking as a "rite of passage." But you probably noticed that he drinks considerably more than most young men (see Chapter 14), making his level of drinking deviant. Mark's legal trouble and low grades are signs of dysfunction resulting from his drinking. When you consider risks such as his increased likelihood of accidents while drunk and the potential alcohol poisoning from the amount he consumes, Mark's behaviors qualify as dangerous. Meanwhile, he doesn't seem distressed about his drinking. For all these reasons, you might consider Mark's behaviors more abnormal than Jennifer's, but again, people will differ as to the degree of abnormality.

Would your judgments of these behaviors change if it were Jennifer who was drinking heavily and Mark who was excessively losing weight? Cultural norms for thinness and for drinking alcohol differ significantly for women and men. This is just one example of how gender influences our views of normality and abnormality.

THINK CRITICALLY

Chances are you have known a family member, friend, or acquaintance whom you suspected might have a psychological problem. Now that you have read about the factors that influence judgments of abnormality, think back to that person. What factors contributed to your concerns about this person? Where would you say his or her behaviors or feelings fall along the four Ds of dysfunction, distress, deviance, and dangerousness? (*Discussion appears on p. 517 at the back of this book.*)

CHAPTER SUMMARY

- Cultural relativists argue that the norms of a society must be used to determine the normality of a behavior. Others have suggested that unusual behaviors, or behaviors that cause subjective distress in a person, should be labeled abnormal. Still others have suggested that only behaviors resulting from mental illness or disease are abnormal. All these criteria have serious limitations, however.
- The current consensus among professionals is that behaviors that cause a person to suffer distress, prevent him or her from functioning in daily life, are unusual, and pose a threat to the person or others are abnormal. These criteria can be remembered as the four Ds: distress, dysfunction, deviance, and dangerousness. Abnormal behaviors fall along a continuum from adaptive to maladaptive, and the location of the line designating behaviors as disordered is based on a subjective decision (review diagram on page 5).
- Historically, theories of abnormality have fallen into one of three categories. Biological theories

saw psychological disorders as similar to physical diseases, caused by the breakdown of a system of the body. Supernatural theories saw abnormal behavior as a result of divine intervention, curses, demonic possession, and personal sin. Psychological theories saw abnormal behavior as being a result of stress.

- In prehistoric times, people probably had largely supernatural theories of abnormal behavior, attributing it to demons or ghosts. A treatment for abnormality in the Stone Age may have been to drill holes in the skull to allow demons to depart, a procedure known as trephination.
- Ancient Chinese, Egyptian, and Greek texts suggest that these cultures took a biological view of abnormal behavior, although references to supernatural and psychological theories also can be found.
- During the Middle Ages, abnormal behavior may have been interpreted as being due to witchcraft.
- In psychic epidemics and mass hysterias, groups of people show similar psychological and behavioral symptoms. Usually, these have been attributed to common stresses or beliefs.
- Even well into the nineteenth and twentieth centuries, many people who acted abnormally were shut away in prisonlike conditions, tortured, starved, or ignored.
- As part of the mental hygiene movement, the moral management of mental hospitals became more widespread. Patients in these hospitals were treated with kindness and given the best biological treatments available. Effective biological treatments for most psychological problems were not available until the mid-twentieth century, however.
- Modern biological perspectives on psychological disorders were advanced by Kraepelin's development of a classification system and the discovery that general paresis is caused by a syphilis infection.
- The psychoanalytic perspective began with the work of Anton Mesmer. It grew as Jean Charcot, and eventually Sigmund Freud, became interested in the role of the unconscious in producing abnormality.
- Behaviorist views on abnormal behavior began with John Watson and B. F. Skinner, who used principles of classical and operant conditioning to explain normal and abnormal behavior.
- Cognitive theorists such as Albert Ellis, Albert Bandura, and Aaron Beck focused on the role of thinking processes in abnormality.
- The deinstitutionalization movement attempted to move mental patients from mental health facilities to community-based mental health centers. Unfortunately, community-based mental health centers have never been fully funded or supported, leaving many former mental patients with few resources in the community.
- Managed care systems are meant to provide coordinated, comprehensive medical care to patients. This can be a great asset to people with long-term, serious psychological disorders.
- The professions within abnormal psychology include psychiatrists, psychologists, marriage and family therapists, clinical social workers, licensed mental health counselors, and psychiatric nurses.

KEY TERMS

mental hygiene movement 3
psychopathology 3
continuum model of abnormality 5
cultural relativism 4
unusualness 6
distress 8
mental illness 8
biological theories 9
supernatural theories 9
psychological theories 9
trephination 10
psychic epidemics 12
moral treatment 15
general paresis 17
mesmerism 17
psychoanalysis 18
behaviorism 18
cognitions 19
self-efficacy beliefs 19
patients' rights movement 19
deinstitutionalization 19
community mental health movement 19
community mental health centers 20
halfway houses 20
day treatment centers 20
managed care 21

Chapter 2

Theories and Treatment of Abnormality

CHAPTER OUTLINE

Chapter 2

Theories and Treatment of Abnormality

CHAPTER OUTLINE

Extraordinary People

Albert Ellis, *The Phobic Psychologist*

Albert Ellis is best known as the psychologist who developed a cognitive theory of emotional problems called rational-emotive theory and a form of therapy based on this theory. According to Ellis's theory, which we will discuss in more detail in this chapter, emotional problems are the result of irrational beliefs. In rational-emotive therapy, therapists confront clients with their irrational beliefs in an attempt to change those beliefs.

What most people don't know about Albert Ellis is that he had a fear of public speaking that was so severe it could have prevented his career. Fortunately, Ellis was a born psychologist. He devised methods for treating himself that hadn't been discovered by psychologists at the time but now are part of many therapists' tool kit:

> At 19, Ellis became active in a political group but was hampered by his terror of public speaking. Confronting his worst demons in the first of many "shame-attacking" exercises he would devise, Ellis repeatedly forced himself to speak up in any political context that would permit it. "Without calling it that, I was doing early desensitization on myself," he says. "Instead of just getting good at this, I found I was very good at it. And now you can't keep me away from a public platform." After mastering his fear of public speaking, Ellis decided to work on the terrors of more private communication. "I was always . . . interested in women," he says. "I would see them and flirt and exchange glances, but I always made excuses not to talk to them and was terrified of being rejected.
>
> "Since I lived near The New York Botanical Garden in the Bronx, I decided to attack my fear and shame with an exercise in the park. I vowed that whenever I saw a reasonably attractive woman up to the age of 35, rather than sitting a bench away as I normally would, I would sit next to her with the specific goal of opening a conversation within one minute. I sat next to 130 consecutive women who fit my criteria. Thirty of the women got up and walked away, but about 100 spoke to me—about their knitting, the birds, a book, whatever. I made only one date out of all these contacts—and she stood me up.
>
> "According to learning theory and strict behavior therapy, my lack of rewards should have extinguished my efforts to meet women. But I realized that throughout this exercise no one vomited, no one called a cop, and I didn't die. The process of trying new behaviors and understanding what happened in the real world instead of in my imagination led me to overcome my fear of speaking to women." (Warga, 1988, p. 56)

Thus was born rational-emotive therapy.

Albert Ellis was able to integrate his personal experiences with contemporary theory and research on anxiety to develop a new theory and therapy of his own. A **theory** is a set of ideas that provides a framework for asking questions about a phenomenon and for gathering and interpreting information about that phenomenon. A *therapy* is a treatment, usually based on a theory of a disorder, that addresses the factors the theory says cause the disorder.

Ellis believed that his fears were due to irrational beliefs, but other theories suggest alternative causes of his fears. If you took a **biological approach** to abnormality, you would suspect that Ellis's symptoms were caused by a biological factor, such as a genetic vulnerability to anxiety, inherited from his parents. Alternately, any one of the several **psychological approaches** looks for the causes of abnormality in people's beliefs, life experiences, and relationships. Finally, if you took a **sociocultural approach,** you would consider the ways Ellis's cultural values or social environment might affect his anxiety.

Traditionally, these different approaches have been seen as incompatible. People frequently ask, "Is the cause of this disorder biological *or* psychological *or* social?" This question is often called the *nature-nurture question*: Is the cause of the disorder something in the *nature* or biology of the person, or in the person's *nurturing* or history of events to which the person was exposed? This question implies that a disorder has to have one cause, rather than multiple causes. Indeed, most theories of psychological disorders over history have searched for the one factor—the one gene, the one traumatic experience, the one personality

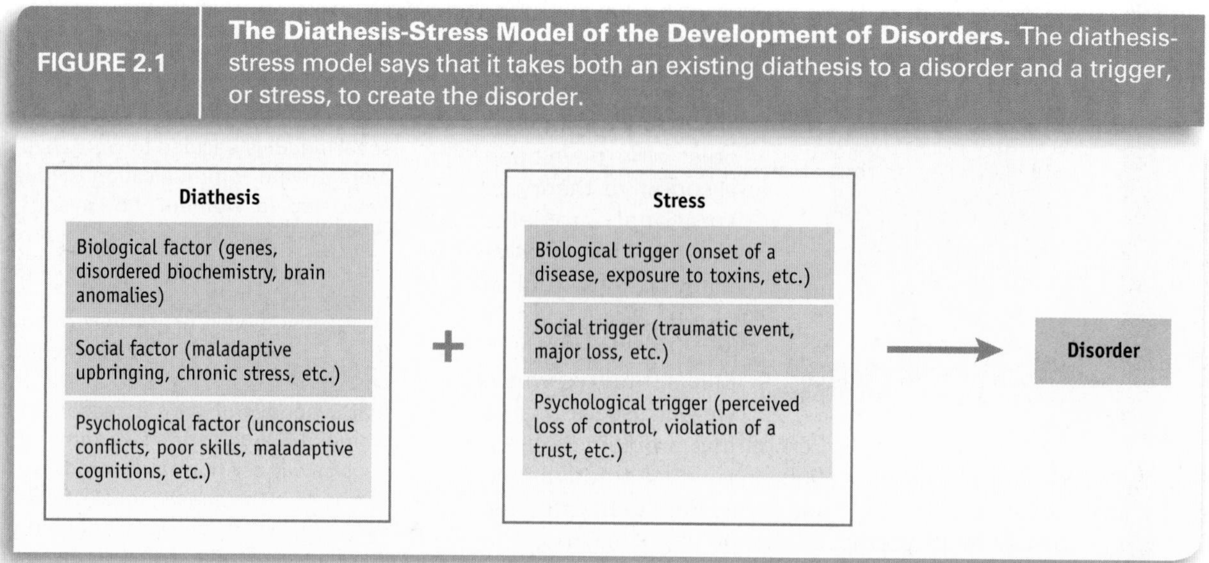

FIGURE 2.1 **The Diathesis-Stress Model of the Development of Disorders.** The diathesis-stress model says that it takes both an existing diathesis to a disorder and a trigger, or stress, to create the disorder.

trait—that causes people to develop a particular disorder.

Many contemporary theorists, however, take a **biopsychosocial approach** to disorders, recognizing that it often takes a combination of biological, psychological, and sociocultural factors to result in the development of a specific disorder. People may carry a *diathesis*, or vulnerability, for a particular disorder. This vulnerability can be a biological one, such as a genetic predisposition to the disorder. It may also be a psychological one, such as a personality trait that increases the person's risk of developing the disorder. Or it may be a sociocultural one, such as growing up with the stress of discrimination based on ethnicity or race.

But in many cases, the vulnerability or diathesis may not be enough to lead to a disorder. For the person to actually develop the disorder, he or she has to experience some type of stress, or trigger. Again, this trigger can be a biological one, such as an illness that changes the person's balance of certain hormones. Or the trigger can be a psychological or social one, such as a traumatic event. Only when the diathesis and the stress come together in the same individual does the full-blown disorder emerge. These are known as **diathesis-stress models** (Figure 2.1). Although Ellis may indeed have a genetic vulnerability to anxiety (his diathesis), it was only when he experienced particular stressors that he developed significant anxiety.

Each of the different approaches to abnormality has led to treatments meant to relieve the symptoms people suffer. Proponents of biological theories of mental disorders most often prescribe medication, although several other types of biological treatments are discussed in this book. Proponents of psychological and some sociocultural approaches to abnormality most often prescribe psychotherapy. There are many forms of psychotherapy, but most involve a therapist (psychiatrist, psychologist, clinical social worker) talking with the person suffering from the disorder (typically called a patient or client) about his or her symptoms and what is contributing to these symptoms. The specific topic of these conversations depends on the therapist's theoretical approach. Both medications and psychotherapy have proven effective in the treatment of many disorders. Medications and psychotherapy are often used together in an integrated approach to disorders (Benjamin, 2005). Proponents of sociocultural approaches also may work to change social policies or the social conditions of vulnerable individuals so as to improve their mental health.

In this chapter, we introduce the major theories of abnormality that have dominated the field in its modern history, along with the treatments that derive from these theories. We present the theories and treatments one at a time to make them easier to understand. Keep in mind, however, that most mental health professionals now take an integrated biopsychosocial approach to understanding mental disorders, viewing them as the result of a combination of biological, psychological, and social vulnerabilities and stresses that come together and feed off one another. We will discuss these integrated biopsychosocial approaches throughout this book.

Approaches Along the Continuum

Sociocultural approaches and, increasingly, biological and psychological approaches, tend to accept a continuum view, represented by the top bar, while traditional biological approaches and some psychological approaches accept a threshold view, represented by the bottom bar.

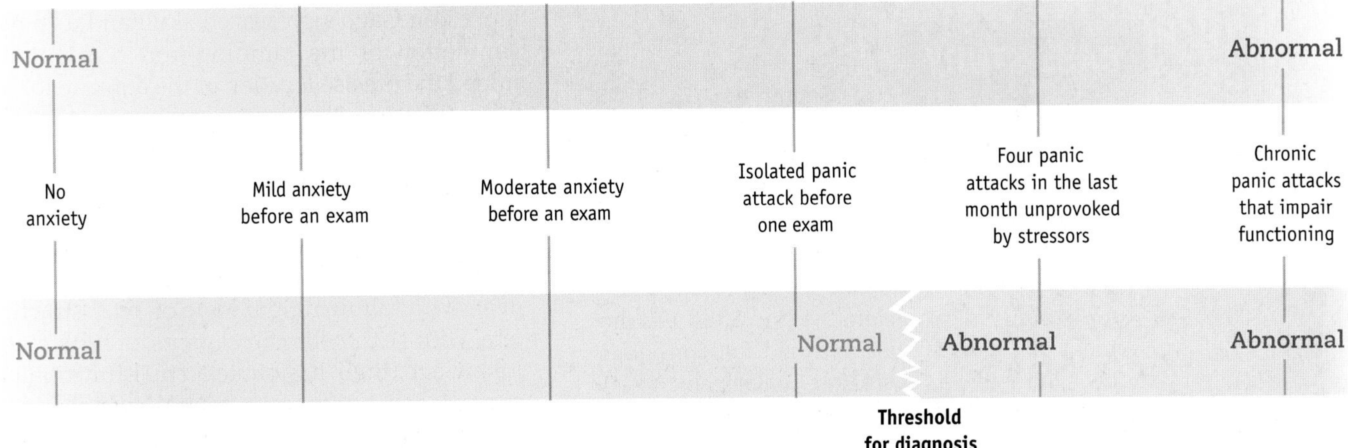

People who favor a sociocultural approach generally embrace the continuum model because they do not view psychological disorders as vastly different from normal functioning. Instead, they think of psychological disorders as labels that society puts on people whose behaviors and feelings differ from social and cultural norms (Castro, Barrera, & Holleran Steiker, 2010). While they agree that these behaviors may be dysfunctional, distressing, deviant, and dangerous, they see them as understandable consequences of social stress in the individuals' lives.

People who take a biological approach traditionally have not accepted a continuum model of abnormality, viewing psychological disorders (such as schizophrenia) as either present or absent—much the way they view medical or physical disorders (such as cancer). More recently, however, those who use biological approaches have begun to view many disorders as part of a spectrum (Cannon & Keller, 2006). Several disorders may have similar symptoms of varying intensity. For example, recent research on autism, a disorder characterized by problems in communication, social skills, and activities and interests, suggests that it may be part of a spectrum of disorders with some of the same symptoms, but which vary in severity. A disorder on the less severe end of that spectrum may be Asperger's syndrome, which is characterized by some of the same problems in social skills and activities as autism but not by severe communication difficulties. Thus, researchers now often speak of the "autism spectrum" of disorders (Sigman, Spence, & Wang, 2006). However, all disorders on the spectrum are qualitatively different from normal functioning.

Similarly, psychological approaches to disorders have been moving toward a continuum model of psychopathology in recent years (Widiger & Mullins-Sweatt, 2009). According to these approaches, psychological processes such as cognition, learning, and emotional control also fall along a continuum. This continuum ranges from very typical processes to those that are highly dysfunctional; minor learning difficulties, for example, would be placed on the more "typical" end of the continuum, and severe mental retardation on the "dysfunctional" end (Sherman, 2008). Likewise, emotional control might range from feeling blue (typical) to feeling severe depression with suicidal intentions (dysfunctional). A continuum perspective would suggest that people on the less severe end of the spectrum (who do not meet the criteria for the disorder) give us insight into the behavior of those on the more severe end (those who do meet the criteria) (Angst et al., 2007).

Not everyone who subscribes to a psychological approach accepts this continuum model, however. Some have argued that individuals with disorders have unique psychological processes that differ from typical functioning. For example, the thinking processes of people diagnosed with mania may be completely different from the thinking processes of people who generally are happy and self-confident. According to this view, psychological studies should focus only on people who meet full criteria for disorders, because studies of people with subclinical symptoms do not inform us about the processes that cause a disorder.

BIOLOGICAL APPROACHES

Let's start by considering the story of Phineas Gage, one of the most dramatic examples of the effect of biological factors on psychological functioning.

CASE STUDY

On September 13, 1848, Phineas P. Gage, a 25-year-old construction foreman for the Rutland and Burlington Railroad in New England, became the victim of a bizarre accident. On the fateful day, a powerful explosion sent a fine-pointed, 3-cm-thick, 109-cm-long tamping iron hurling, rocket-like, through Gage's face, skull, brain, and then into the sky. Gage was momentarily stunned but regained full consciousness immediately thereafter. He was able to talk and even walk with the help of his men. The iron landed many yards away.

Phineas Gage not only survived the momentous injury, in itself enough to earn him a place in the annals of medicine, but he survived as a different man. Gage had been a responsible, intelligent, and socially well-adapted individual, a favorite with peers and elders. He had made progress and showed promise. The signs of a profound change in personality were already evident during the convalescence under the care of his physician, John Harlow. But as the months passed, it became apparent that the transformation was not only radical but difficult to comprehend. In some respects, Gage was fully recovered. He remained as able-bodied and appeared to be as intelligent as before the accident; he had no impairment of movement or speech; new learning was intact, and neither memory nor intelligence in the conventional sense had been affected. On the other hand, he had become irreverent and capricious. His respect for the social conventions by which he once abided had vanished. His abundant profanity offended those around him. Perhaps most troubling, he had taken leave of his sense of responsibility. He could not be trusted to honor his commitments. His employers had deemed him "the most efficient and capable" man in their "employ" but now they had to dismiss him. In the words of his physician, "the equilibrium or balance, so to speak, between his intellectual faculty and animal propensities" had been destroyed. In the words of his friends and acquaintances, "Gage was no longer Gage." (Adapted from Damasio et al., 1994, p. 1102)

As a result of damage to his brain from the accident, Gage's basic personality seemed to change. He was transformed from a responsible, socially appropriate man into an impulsive, emotional, and socially inappropriate man. Almost 150 years later, researchers using modern neuroimaging techniques on Gage's preserved skull and a computer simulation of the tamping-iron accident determined the precise location of the damage to Gage's brain (Figure 2.2).

Studies of people today who suffer damage to this area of the brain reveal that they have trouble making rational decisions in personal and social matters and have trouble processing information about emotions. They do not have trouble, however, with following the logic of an abstract problem, with arithmetic calculations, or with memory. Like Gage, their basic intellectual functioning remains intact, but their emotional control and social judgment are impaired (Damasio et al., 1994).

The damage Gage suffered caused areas of his brain to not function properly. *Brain dysfunction* is one of three causes of abnormality on which biological approaches often focus. The other two are *biochemical imbalances* and *genetic abnormalities*. Brain dysfunction, biochemical imbalances, and genetic abnormalities can all influence one another. For example, brain dysfunction may be the result of genetic factors and may cause biochemical imbalances. We explore these three biological causes of abnormality in this section.

FIGURE 2.2 **Phineas Gage's Brain Injury.** Modern neuroimaging techniques have helped identify the precise location of damage to Phineas Gage's brain.

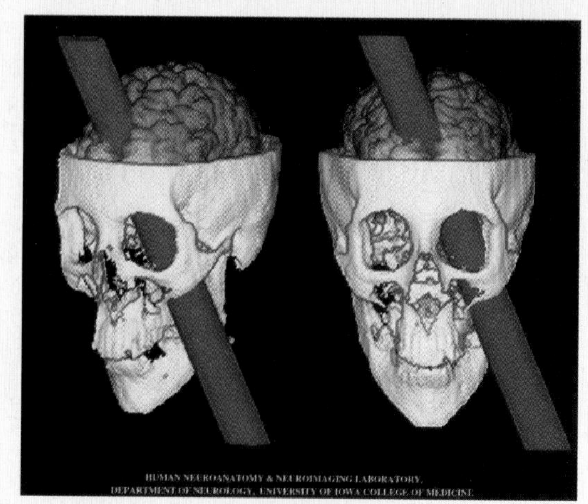

Brain Dysfunction

Like Phineas Gage, people whose brains do not function properly often show problems in psychological functioning. The brain can be divided into three main regions (Kalat, 2007): the *hindbrain,* which includes all the structures located in the hind (posterior) part of the brain, closest to the spinal cord; the *midbrain,* located in the middle of the brain; and the *forebrain,* which includes the structures located in the front (anterior) part of the brain (Figures 2.3 and 2.4). The hindbrain sits on top of the spinal cord and is crucial for basic life functions. It contains the *medulla,* which helps control breathing and reflexes; the *pons,* which is important for attentiveness and the timing of sleep; the *reticular formation,* a network of neurons that control arousal and attention to stimuli; and the *cerebellum,* which is concerned primarily with the coordination of movement (Thompson & Krupa, 1994). The midbrain contains the *superior colliculus* and *inferior colliculus,* which relay sensory information and control movement, and the *substantia nigra,* a crucial part of the pathway that regulates responses to reward.

The human forebrain is relatively large and developed compared to that of other organisms (Kalat, 2007). The outer layer of the cerebrum is called the **cerebral cortex** (or simply *cortex;* Figure 2.5a and b); it is this area of the brain that was damaged in Phineas Gage's accident. The cerebral cortex is involved in many of our most advanced thinking processes. It is composed of two hemispheres on the left and right sides of the brain that are connected by the *corpus collosum.*

FIGURE 2.3 Organization of the Brain.

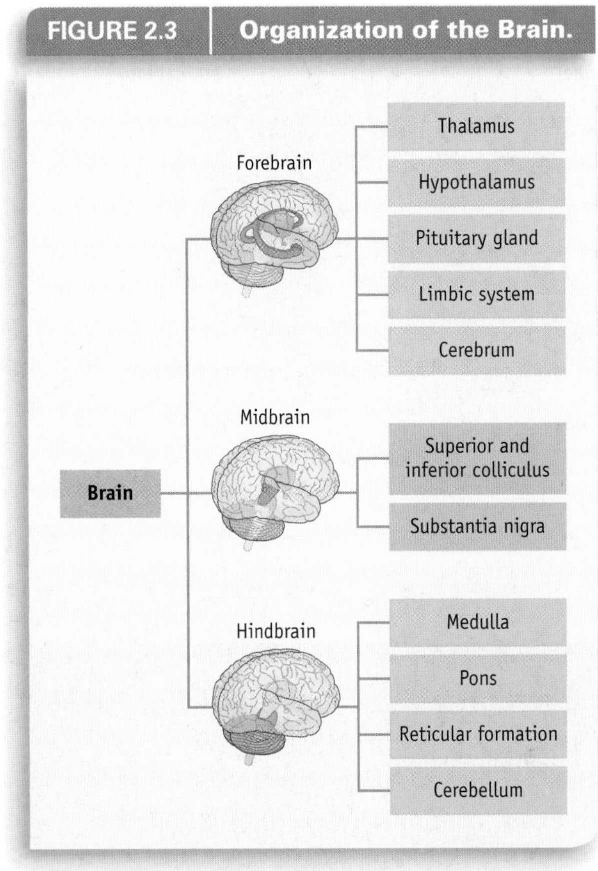

FIGURE 2.4 Some of the Major Structures of the Brain.

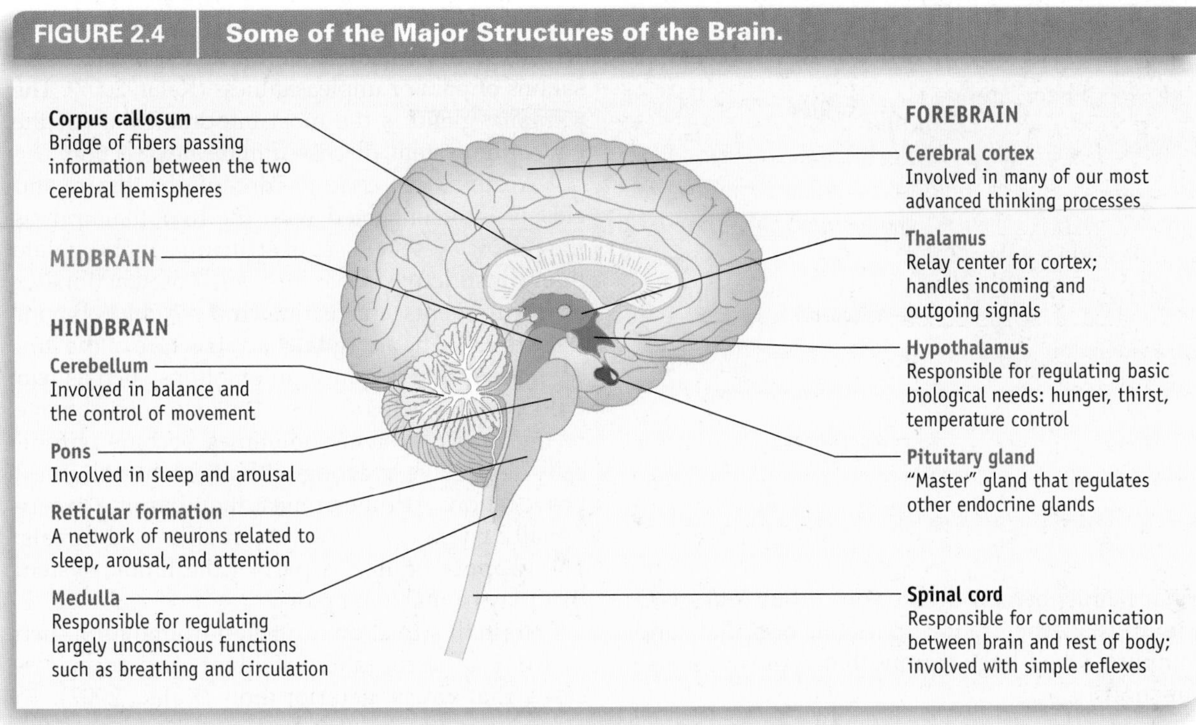

FIGURE 2.5 **Major Sections of the Cerebral Cortex.**

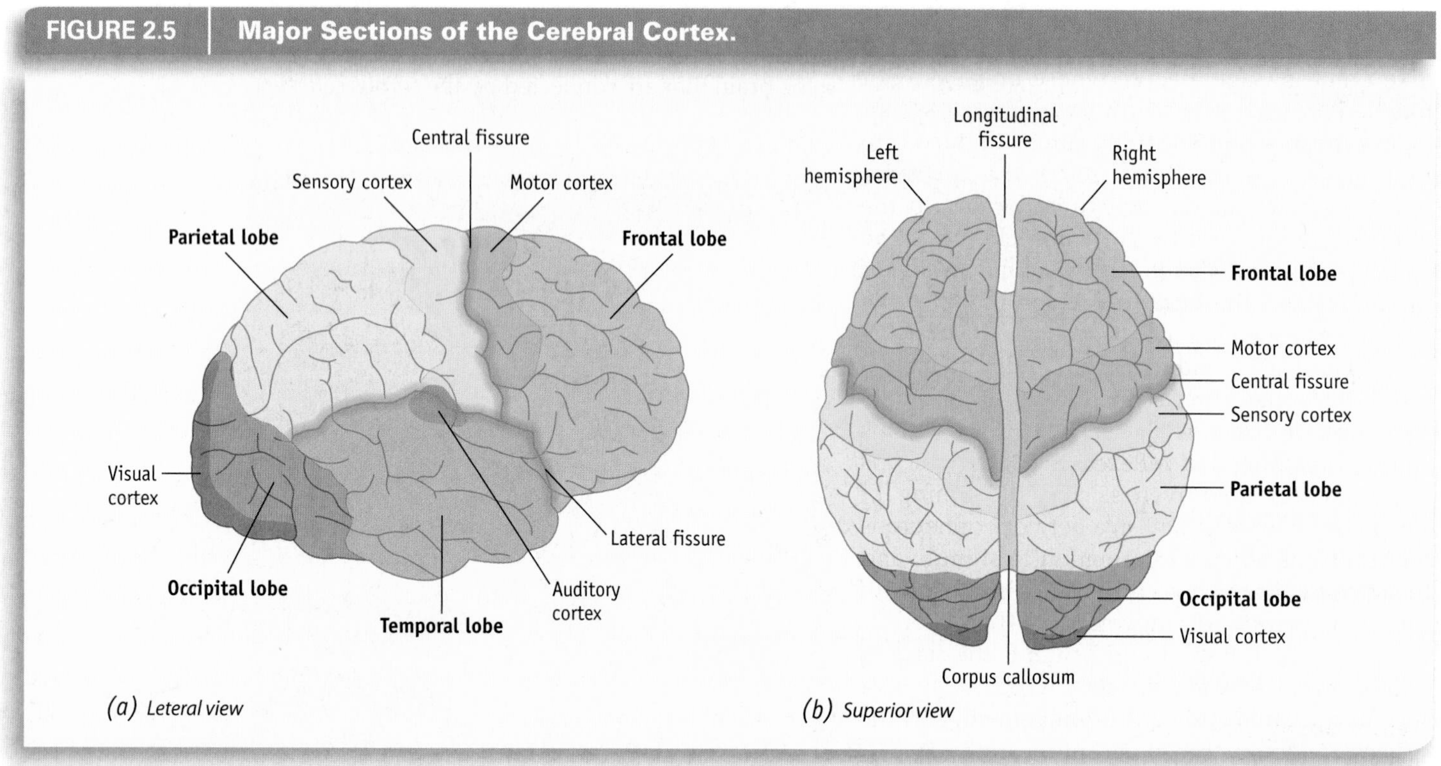

FIGURE 2.6 **Structures of the Limbic System.** The limbic system is a collection of structures that are closely interconnected with the hypothalamus. They appear to exert additional control over some of the instinctive behaviors regulated by the hypothalamus, such as eating, sexual behavior, and reaction to stressful situations.

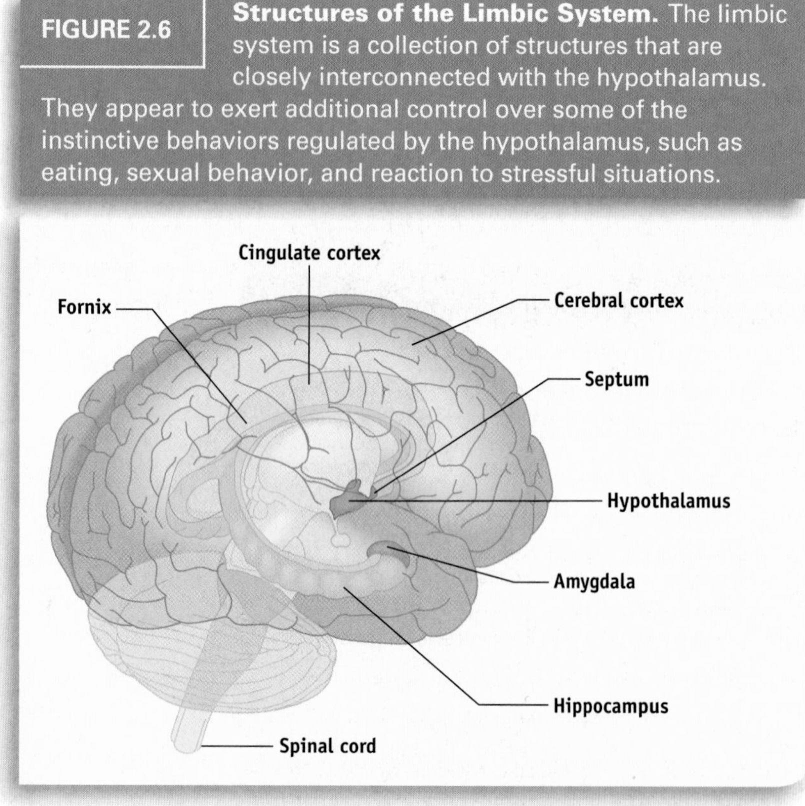

Each hemisphere is divided into four lobes (see Figure 2.5): the frontal, parietal, occipital, and temporal lobes, large regions that perform diverse functions.

The other structures of the forebrain are found just under the cerebrum and therefore are called *subcortical structures.* The **thalamus** directs incoming information from sense receptors (such as vision and hearing) to the cerebrum. The **hypothalamus,** a small structure just below the thalamus, regulates eating, drinking, and sexual behavior. The hypothalamus is also involved in processing basic emotions. For example, the stimulation of certain areas of the hypothalamus produces sensations of pleasure, whereas the stimulation of other areas produces sensations of pain or unpleasantness (Kalat, 2007). The pituitary gland is the most important part of the endocrine system, discussed in the next section.

Around the central core of the brain and closely interconnected with the hypothalamus is the **limbic system,** a set of structures that regulate many instinctive behaviors, such as reactions to stressful events and eating and sexual behavior (Figure 2.6). The **amygdala** is a structure of the limbic system that is critical in emotions such as fear (Le Doux & Phelps, 2000). Monkeys with damage to the limbic system sometimes become chronically aggressive, reacting with rage to the slightest provocation. At other times, they become exceptionally passive, not reacting at all to real threats. The **hippocampus** is a part of the limbic system that plays a role in memory.

Brain dysfunction can result from injury, such as from an automobile accident, and from diseases that cause deterioration (Kalat, 2007). In schizophrenia, a severe disorder in which people have hallucinations (unreal perceptual experiences) and delusions (unreal beliefs), the cerebral cortex does not function effectively or normally (see Chapter 8). We will encounter other examples of psychological disorders that appear to be associated with dysfunction in specific areas of the brain. We will also consider examples of how environmental and psychological factors can change brain functioning. For example, a number of studies have shown that psychotherapy alone, without drug therapy, can change brain activity (Frewen, Dozois, & Lanius, 2008).

Biochemical Imbalances

The brain requires a number of chemicals to work efficiently and effectively. These chemicals include neurotransmitters and hormones, the latter produced by the endocrine system.

Neurotransmitters

Neurotransmitters are biochemicals that act as messengers carrying impulses from one *neuron*, or nerve cell, to another in the brain and in other parts of the nervous system (Figure 2.7). Each neuron has a *cell body* and a number of short branches, called *dendrites*. The dendrites and cell body receive impulses from adjacent neurons. The impulse then travels down the length of a slender, tubelike extension, called an *axon*, to small swellings at the end of the axon, called *synaptic terminals*. Here the impulse stimulates the release of neurotransmitters (Kalat, 2007).

FIGURE 2.7 **Neurotransmitters and the Synapse.** The neurotransmitter is released into the synaptic gap. There it may bind with the receptors on the postsynaptic membrane.

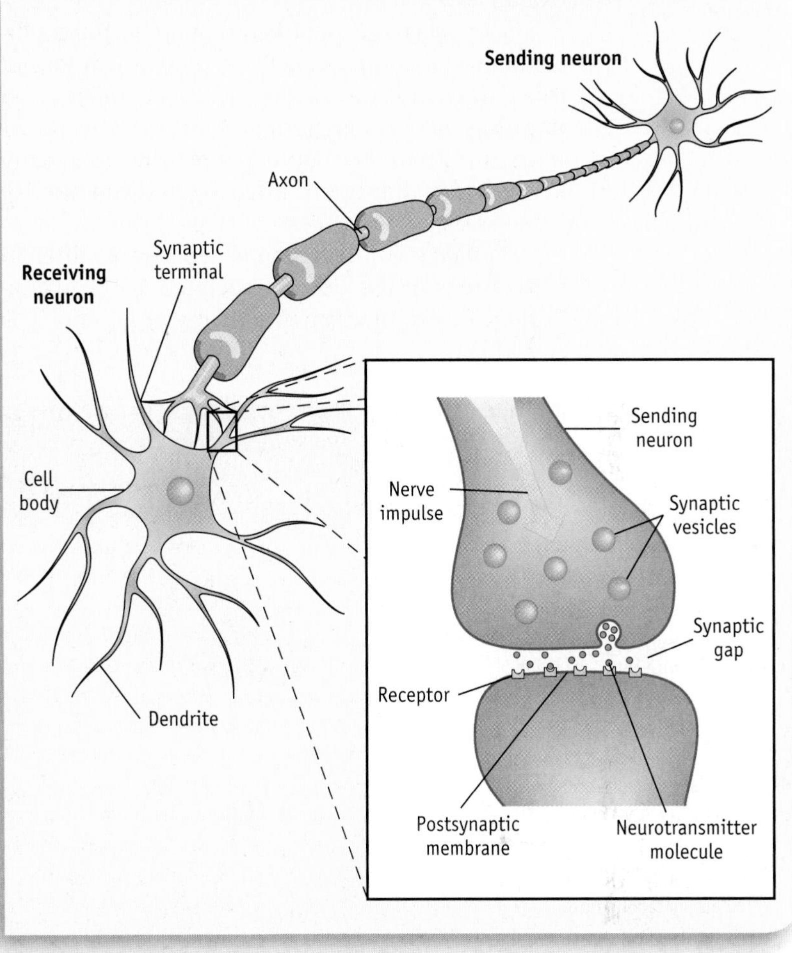

The synaptic terminals do not actually touch the adjacent neurons. There is a slight gap between the synaptic terminals and the adjacent neurons, called the *synaptic gap* or **synapse.** The neurotransmitter is released into the synapse. It then binds to special **receptors,** which are molecules on the membrane of adjacent neurons. This binding works somewhat the way a key fits into a lock. The binding stimulates the adjacent neuron to initiate the impulse, which then runs through its dendrites and cell body and down its axon to cause the release of more neurotransmitters between it and other neurons.

Many biochemical theories of psychopathology suggest that the amount of certain neurotransmitters in the synapses is associated with specific types of psychopathology (Kalat, 2007). The amount of a neurotransmitter available in the synapse can be affected by two processes. The process of **reuptake** occurs when the initial neuron releasing the neurotransmitter into the synapse reabsorbs the neurotransmitter, decreasing the amount left in the synapse. Another process, called **degradation,** occurs when the receiving neuron releases an enzyme into the synapse that breaks down the neurotransmitter into other biochemicals. The reuptake and degradation of neurotransmitters happen naturally. When one or both of these processes malfunction, abnormally high or low levels of neurotransmitter in the synapse result.

Psychological symptoms may also be associated with the number and functioning of the receptors for neurotransmitters on the dendrites (Kalat, 2007). If there are too few receptors or if the receptors are not sensitive enough, the neuron will not be able to make adequate use of the neurotransmitter available in the synapse. If there are too many receptors or if they are too sensitive, the neuron may be overexposed to the neurotransmitter that is in the synapse. Within the neuron, a complex system of biochemical changes takes place as the result of the presence or absence of neurotransmitters. Psychological symptoms may be the consequence of malfunctioning in neurotransmitter systems; psychological experiences also may cause changes in neurotransmitter system functioning (Kalat, 2007).

Scientists have identified more than 100 different neurotransmitters. *Serotonin* plays an important role in mental health, particularly in emotions and impulses, such as aggressive impulses (Belmaker & Agam, 2008). Serotonin travels through many key areas of the brain, affecting the function of those areas.

Dopamine is a prominent neurotransmitter in those areas of the brain associated with our experience of reinforcements or rewards, and it is affected by substances, such as alcohol, that we find rewarding (Ruiz, Strain, & Langrod, 2007). Dopamine also is important to the functioning of muscle systems and plays a role in disorders involving control over muscles, such as Parkinson's disease.

Norepinephrine (also known as noradrenaline) is a neurotransmitter produced mainly by neurons in the brain stem. Two well-known drugs, cocaine and amphetamine, prolong the action of norepinephrine by slowing its reuptake process. Because of the delay in reuptake, the receiving neurons are activated for a longer period of time, causing the stimulating psychological effects of these drugs (Ruiz et al., 2007). On the other hand, when there is too little norepinephrine in the brain, the person's mood is depressed. Another prominent neurotransmitter is *gamma-aminobutyric acid*, or *GABA*, which inhibits the action of other neurotransmitters. Certain drugs have a tranquilizing effect because they increase the inhibitory activity of GABA. GABA is thought to play an important role in anxiety symptoms, so one contributor to Albert Ellis's anxiety could be a dysfunction in his GABA system (Kalivas & Volkow, 2005).

FIGURE 2.8 **The Endocrine System.** The hypothalamus regulates the endocrine system, which produces most of the major hormones of the body.

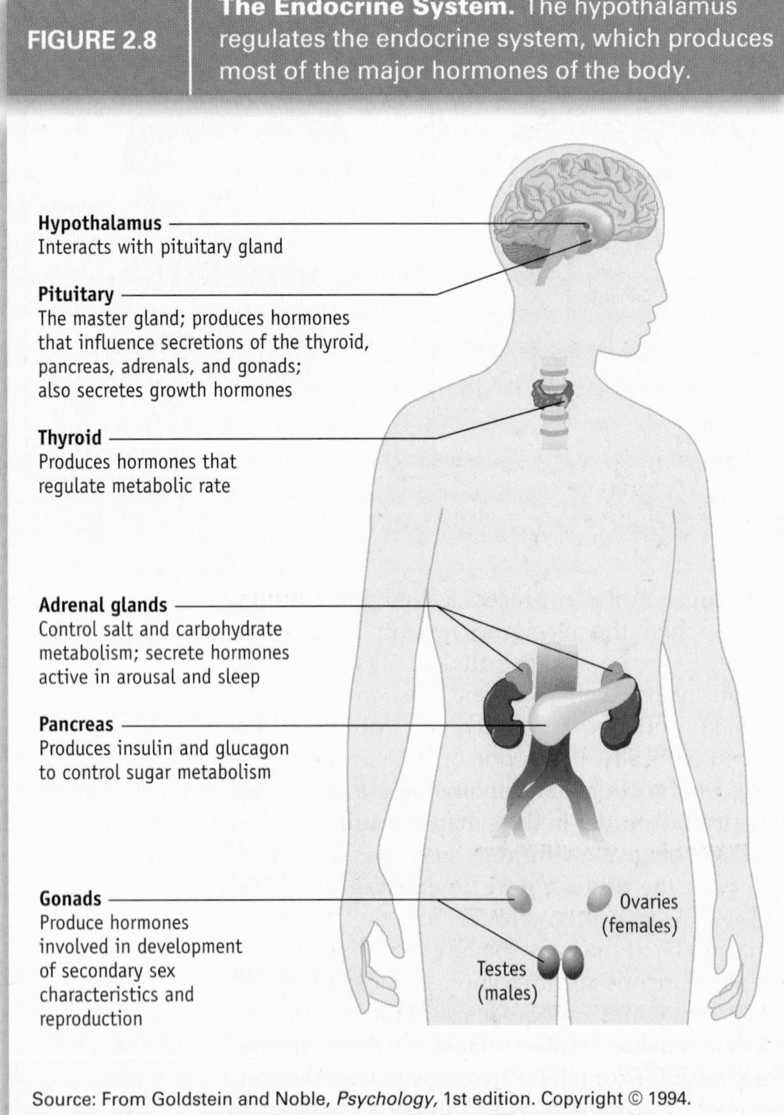
Hypothalamus
Interacts with pituitary gland
Pituitary
The master gland; produces hormones that influence secretions of the thyroid, pancreas, adrenals, and gonads; also secretes growth hormones
Thyroid
Produces hormones that regulate metabolic rate
Adrenal glands
Control salt and carbohydrate metabolism; secrete hormones active in arousal and sleep
Pancreas
Produces insulin and glucagon to control sugar metabolism
Gonads
Produce hormones involved in development of secondary sex characteristics and reproduction
Ovaries (females)
Testes (males)

Source: From Goldstein and Noble, *Psychology,* 1st edition. Copyright © 1994. Reprinted with permission of Wadsworth, a division of Thomson Learning; www.thomsonrights.com. Fax 800-730-2215.

The Endocrine System

Other biochemical theories of psychopathology focus on the body's **endocrine system** (Figure 2.8). This system of glands produces chemicals called *hormones,* which are released directly into the blood. A **hormone** carries messages throughout the body, potentially affecting a person's moods, levels of energy, and reactions to stress (Kalat, 2007).

One of the major endocrine glands, the **pituitary,** has been called the *master gland* because it produces the largest number of different hormones and controls the secretion of other endocrine glands. It is partly an outgrowth of the brain and lies just below the hypothalamus.

The relationship between the pituitary gland and the hypothalamus illustrates the complex interactions between the endocrine and central nervous systems. For example, in response to stress (fear, anxiety, pain, and so forth), neurons on the hypothalamus secrete a substance called corticotropin-release factor (CRF). CRF is carried from the hypothalamus to the pituitary through a channel-like structure. The CRF stimulates the pituitary to release the body's major stress hormone, adrenocorticotrophic hormone (ACTH). ACTH, in turn, is carried by the bloodstream to the adrenal glands and to various other organs of the body, causing the release of about 30 hormones, each of which plays a role in the body's adjustment to emergency situations (Sapolsky, 2007).

As we will discuss in Chapters 5 and 7, some theories of anxiety and depression suggest that these disorders result from dysregulation, or malfunctioning, of a system called the *hypothalamic-pituitary-adrenal axis* (or *HPA axis*). People who have a dysregulated HPA axis may have abnormal physiological reactions to stress that make it more difficult for them to cope with the stress, resulting in symptoms of anxiety and depression.

The proper working of the neurotransmitter and endocrine systems requires a delicate balance, and many forces can upset this balance. For example, a genetic abnormality can affect biochemical systems and brain development, leading to a psychological disturbance.

Genetic Abnormalities

Behavior genetics, the study of the genetics of personality and abnormality, is concerned with two questions: (1) To what extent are behaviors or behavioral tendencies inherited? and (2) What are the processes by which genes affect behavior (Loehlin, 2009)?

Let us begin by reviewing the basics of genetics. At conception, the fertilized embryo has 46 chromosomes, 23 from the female egg and 23 from the male sperm, making up 23 pairs of chromosomes. One of these pairs is referred to as the *sex chromosomes* because it determines the sex of the embryo: The XX combination results in a female embryo, and the XY combination results in a male embryo. The mother of an embryo always contributes an X chromosome, and the father can contribute either an X or a Y.

Alterations in the structure or number of chromosomes can cause major defects. For example, Down syndrome results when chromosome 21 is present in triplicate instead of as the usual pair. Down syndrome is characterized by mental retardation, heart malformations, and facial features such as a flat face, a small nose, protruding lips and tongue, and slanted eyes.

Chromosomes contain individual genes, which are segments of long molecules of deoxyribonucleic acid (DNA; Figure 2.9). Genes give coded instructions to cells to perform certain functions, usually to manufacture certain proteins. Genes, like chromosomes, come in pairs. One half of the pair comes from the mother, and the other half from the father. Abnormalities in genes that make up chromosomes are much more common than are major abnormalities in the structure or number of chromosomes.

FIGURE 2.9 **Chromosome.** Chromosomes consist of individual genes, long molecules of deoxyribonucleic acid (DNA).

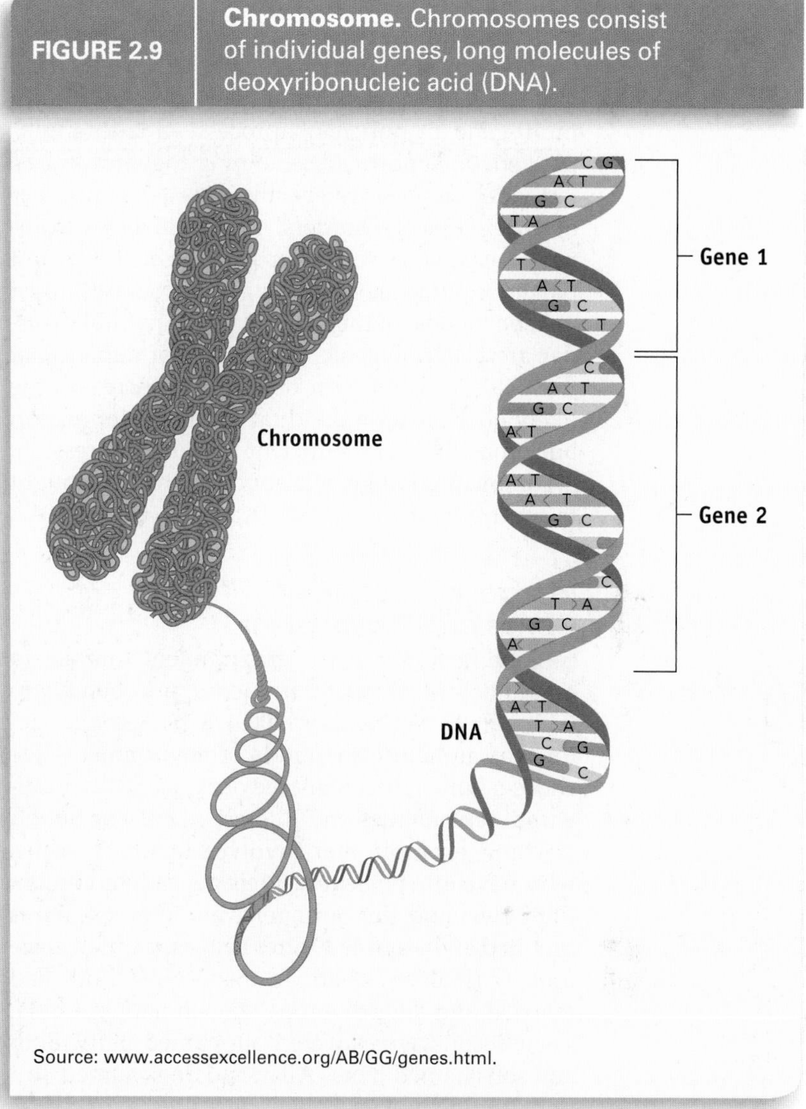

Source: www.accessexcellence.org/AB/GG/genes.html.

For example, as noted earlier, the neurotransmitter serotonin appears to play a role in depression. One gene that influences the functioning of serotonin systems in the brain is the serotonin transporter gene. Every gene has two *alleles,* or coding sequences. Alleles for the serotonin transporter gene can be either short (s) or long (l). Thus, any given individual could have two short alleles (s/s genotype), two long alleles (l/l genotype), or one short and one long allele (s/l genotype). Some studies have suggested that the presence of at least one s allele on the serotonin transporter gene may increase an individual's chance of developing depression (Levinson, 2006).

Although you may often hear of scientists having discovered "the gene" for a major disorder, most disorders are associated not with single abnormal genes but with multiple abnormal genes. Each of these altered genes may make only a partial contribution to vulnerability for the disorder, some more than others. But when a critical number of these altered genes come together, the individual may develop the disorder. This is known as a multi-gene, or **polygenic,** process—it takes multiple genetic abnormalities coming together in one individual to create a specific disorder. A number of physiological disorders, such as diabetes, coronary heart disease, epilepsy, and cleft lip and palate, result from such polygenic processes. Most genetic models of the major types of mental disorder are also polygenic. In the case of depression, the presence of at least one s allele increases the likelihood that an individual will have depression but probably is not sufficient to cause depression. A combination of genetic abnormalities is thought to contribute to depression (Kaufman et al., 2004).

Interactions Between Genes and Environment

Genetic factors and the environment interact in a number of ways to influence our behaviors (Ulbricht & Neiderhiser, 2009). First, genetic factors can influence the kinds of environments we choose, which then reinforce our genetically influenced personalities and interests. Let's consider a startling example that involves identical twins, who have 100 percent of their genes in common. Jim Lewis and Jim Springer were identical twins reunited at the age of 39 after being separated since infancy (Holden, 1980). To their shock, both had married and later divorced women named Linda. Their second wives were both named Betty. Both had sons named James Allan and dogs named Toy. Both chain-smoked Salem cigarettes, worked as sheriffs' deputies, drove Chevrolets, chewed their fingernails, enjoyed stock car racing, had basement workshops, and had built circular white benches around trees in their yards.

Studies of identical twins reared apart have revealed amazing similarities. Jim Lewis and Jim Springer were reared apart but, when reunited, found that they were identical in more than appearance.

Could there possibly be genes for marrying women named Linda or Betty or for having basement workshops that account for the similarities between these twins, who had never before met each other? Genetic researchers think not. Instead, people with identical genes may have similar temperaments and talents that cause them to choose similar environments (Bouchard & Loehlin, 2001; Johnson, McGue, Krueger, & Bouchard, 2004). For example, both of the Jim twins may have woodworking talent that causes them to build workshops in their basements and circular benches in their yards.

Most examples of genes influencing our choices of environment are not as startling as in the case of the Jim twins, but such influences may be important in producing psychological symptoms. For example, children with tendencies toward aggression and impulsive behavior, both of which appear to be influenced by genetic factors, tend to choose friends who encourage their aggressive and impulsive behaviors and provide opportunities to engage in antisocial acts (Dishion & Patterson, 1997).

Second, genes and environment can interact by the environment acting as a catalyst for a genetic tendency. For example, as noted earlier, the presence of at least one s allele on the serotonin transporter gene may increase an individual's chance of developing depression, but it does not determine whether an individual will develop depression. Researchers Avshalom Caspi, Terri Moffitt, and colleagues (2003) found that individuals who carried at least one s allele for the serotonin transporter gene were at increased risk for depression as adults only if they had a history of being maltreated as young children (Figure 2.10). Among individuals with no history of maltreatment, their genotype for the serotonin transporter gene had no relationship to depression. But those with the s/l genotype showed a greater probability of depression if they had been maltreated, and those with the s/s genotype showed an even greater probability of depression if they had been maltreated. Some subsequent studies have failed to replicate the findings of Caspi and colleagues (see Risch et al., 2009), but this intriguing study inspired many other researchers to search for gene-environment interactions

Third, the fascinating new line of research called **epigenetics** indicates that environmental conditions can affect the expression of genes. DNA can be chemically modified by different environ-

FIGURE 2.10 **Gene by Environment Interaction.** In this study, the interaction of certain genes and a history of maltreatment predicted the probability of depression.

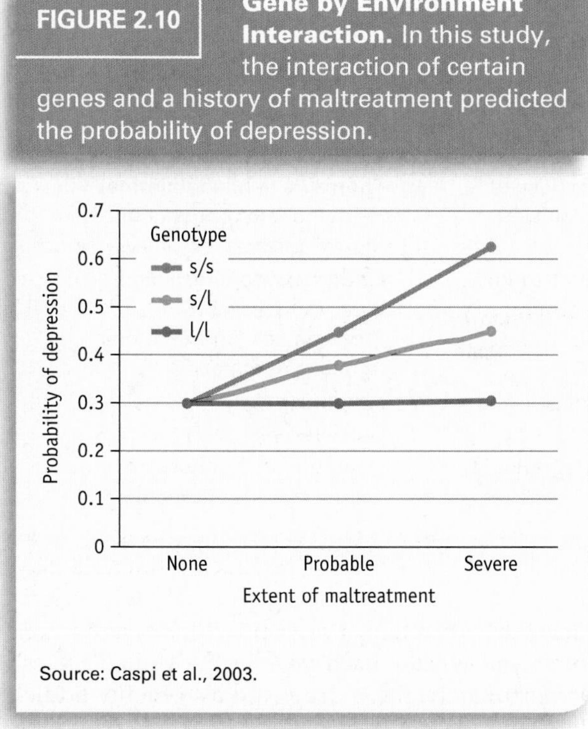

Source: Caspi et al., 2003.

mental conditions, resulting in genes being turned on or off. As a result, cells, tissues, and organs are altered in their development. Epigenetics is the study of heritable changes in the expression of genes without change in the gene sequence.

Researcher Michael Meany studied the effects of epigenetic processes on stress responses in rats (Meaney, 2001; Weaver et al., 2004). Mother rats typically lick and groom their infants (called pups), but the amount of licking and grooming varies from one mother to another. Pups who are licked and groomed more tend to grow into adult rats that are less fearful and show more modest physiological responses to stress, compared to pups who are licked and groomed less. In addition, when the biological offspring of mothers who lick and groom less are raised by mothers who lick and groom more, they are less fearful and physiologically reactive to stress than when they are raised by their own mothers; and when the biological offspring of mothers who lick and groom more are raised by mothers who lick and groom less, they are more fearful and physiologically reactive to stress than when they are raised by their own mothers. This pattern of results suggests that the mother's behavior influences the development of the pups' reactions to stress (Francis, Diorio, Liu, & Meany, 1999). The amount that mother rats lick and groom pups in the first week of life affects the release of certain hormones in the pup. These hormones in turn affect the expression of a gene that influences the development of the hippocampus (refer to Figure 2.6), an area of the brain that influences the stress response. So the mother's behavior toward the pup during the first week of life affects the expression of key genes, which change the development of an area of the brain and, in turn, influence the pups' behavioral and physiological responses to stress.

The role of epigenetics in psychopathology in humans is only beginning to be studied, but it likely is very important. For example, epigenetic processes could help explain how identical twins who share the same DNA sequence could differ in their expression of a disorder. Both twins may carry genes that increase their risk for a disorder, but if the environments of the twins differ during fetal development or in critical stages of development after birth, the expression of these genes may differ, leading one twin but not the other to develop the disorder (see Chapter 8).

Drug Therapies

Most of the biological treatments for abnormality are drug treatments (Table 2.1). These drugs are thought to relieve psychological symptoms by improving the functioning of neurotransmitter systems.

Antipsychotic drugs help reduce the symptoms of psychosis, which include hallucinations (unreal perceptual experiences) and delusions (fantastic, unrealistic beliefs). The first group of antipsychotic drugs were known as the *phenothiazines* (Valenstein, 1998). These drugs have been extremely helpful in reducing psychotic symptoms, but they carry a number of dangerous side effects. These effects include severe sedation, visual disturbances, and *tardive dyskinesia,* a neurological disorder characterized by involuntary movements of the tongue, face, mouth, or jaw (see Chapter 8). Fortunately, newer medications, referred to as the *atypical antipsychotics,* seem to be effective in treating psychosis without inducing some of the same side effects (see Chapter 8).

Antidepressant drugs reduce symptoms of depression (sadness, low motivation, and sleep and appetite disturbance). The most frequently used antidepressants, the *selective serotonin reuptake inhibitors* (SSRIs; see Chapter 7), affect the serotonin neurotransmitter system. Some of the newest antidepressant drugs, *selective serotonin-norepinephrine reuptake inhibitors* (SNRIs; see Chapter 7), are designed to target both serotonin and norepinephrine. Common side effects of SSRIs and SNRIs include nausea, diarrhea, headache, tremor, daytime

TABLE 2.1 Drug Therapies for Mental Disorders

These are the major types of drugs used to treat several kinds of mental disorders.

Type of Drug	Purpose	Examples
Antipsychotic drugs	Reduce symptoms of psychosis (loss of reality testing, hallucinations, delusions)	Thorazine (a phenothiazine) Haldol (a butyrophenone) Clozaril (an atypical antipsychotic)
Antidepressant drugs	Reduce symptoms of depression (sadness, loss of appetite, sleep disturbances)	Parnate (an MAO inhibitor) Elavil (a tricyclic) Prozac (a selective serotonin reuptake inhibitor)
Lithium	Reduce symptoms of mania (agitation, excitement, grandiosity)	Lithobid Cibalith-S
Antianxiety drugs	Reduce symptoms of anxiety (fearfulness, worry, tension)	Nembutal (a barbiturate) Valium (a benzodiazepine)

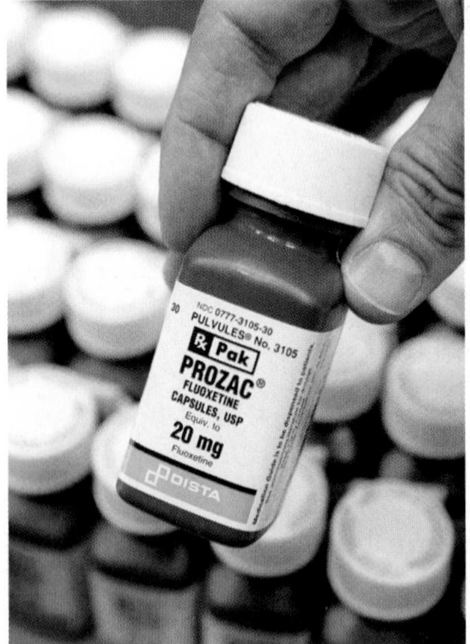

Media stories about so-called wonder drugs, including Prozac, often tout their ability to alleviate a wide range of problems beyond the treatment of serious psychological disorders.

sedation, sexual dysfunction, and agitation. Older classes of antidepressants include the *tricyclic antidepressants* and the *monoamine oxidase inhibitors* (see Chapter 7).

Lithium is a metallic element that is present in the sea, in natural springs, and in animal and plant tissue. It is widely used as a mood stabilizer, particularly in the treatment of bipolar disorder, which involves swings back and forth from depression to mania (highly elevated mood, irritability, grandiosity, and involvement in dangerous activities). Lithium's significant side effects include extreme nausea, blurred vision, diarrhea, tremors, and twitches (see Chapter 7). Other drugs, known as the **anticonvulsants,** are also being used in the treatment of mania (see details in Chapter 7) and have fewer side effects than lithium.

The first group of **antianxiety drugs** were the *barbiturates,* introduced at the beginning of the twentieth century. Although these drugs are effective in inducing relaxation and sleep, they are highly addictive, and withdrawal from them can cause life-threatening symptoms such as increased heart rate, delirium, and convulsions.

The other major class of anxiety-reducing drugs, the *benzodiazepines,* appear to reduce the symptoms of anxiety without interfering substantially with an individual's ability to function in daily life. Their most frequent use is as sleeping pills. As many as 70 million prescription for benzodiazepines are written each year in the United States. Unfortunately, these drugs are also highly addictive, and up to 80 percent of the people who take them for 6 weeks or more show withdrawal symptoms, including heart rate acceleration, irritability, and profuse sweating.

Electroconvulsive Therapy and Newer Brain Stimulation Techniques

An alternative to drug therapies in the treatment of some disorders is **electroconvulsive therapy,** or **ECT.** ECT was introduced in the early twentieth century, originally as a treatment for schizophrenia. Eventually, clinicians found that ECT is effective for depression but not for schizophrenia.

ECT consists of a series of treatments in which a brain seizure is induced by passing electrical current through the patient's brain. Patients are first anesthetized and given muscle relaxants so that they are not conscious when they have the seizure and their muscles do not jerk violently during it. Metal electrodes are taped to the head, and a current of 70 to 150 volts is passed through one side of the brain for about ½ second. Patients typically have a convulsion, which lasts about 1 minute. The full series of treatments consists of 6 to 12 sessions. The side effects of ECT include confusion and memory loss (Sackeim et al., 2007).

More recently, researchers have been developing alternative techniques for stimulating the brain that can be more targeted and have fewer side effects (Dougherty & Rauch, 2007b; George, 2007). One procedure, known as *repetitive transcranial magnetic stimulation (rTMS),* exposes patients to repeated, high-intensity magnetic pulses focused on particular brain structures. In the procedure known as *deep brain stimulation,* electrodes are surgically implanted in specific areas of the brain. These electrodes are then connected to a pulse generator that is placed under the skin and delivers stimulation to the specific brain areas. Similarly, in *vagus nerve stimulation,* electrodes are attached to the vagus nerve, a part of the nervous system that carries information to several areas of the brain, including the hypothalamus and amygdala. These electrodes are connected to a pulse generator that delivers stimulation to the vagus nerve, which in turn travels to targeted areas of the brain.

Some studies have suggested that these newer brain stimulation techniques can be helpful in relieving the symptoms of depression and auditory hallucinations (hearing voices that aren't there) in patients (George, 2007). Electrical stimulation of neurons can result in long-term changes in neurotransmission across synapses (George et al., 2000). Patients who receive these newer brain stimulation treatments report few side effects—usually only minor headaches treatable by aspirin. Thus, there is a great deal of hope that these techniques will be effective and safe alternative therapies, particularly for people who do not respond to drug therapies and may not be able to tolerate ECT.

Psychosurgery

In Chapter 1, we described theories that prehistoric peoples performed crude brain surgery, called trephination, on people with mental disorders in order to release the evil spirits causing the disorders. In modern times, brain surgery did not become a mode of treatment for mental disorders until the early twentieth century. A Portuguese neurologist, Antonio de Egas Moniz, introduced a procedure in 1935 in which the frontal lobes of the brain are severed from the lower centers of the brain in people with psychosis. This procedure eventually developed into the procedure known as *prefrontal lobotomy.* Although Moniz won the Nobel Prize for his work, prefrontal lobotomies eventually were criticized as a cruel and ineffective means of treating psychosis (Valenstein, 1986). Patients often would experience severe and permanent side effects, including either an inability to control impulses or an inability to initiate activity, extreme listlessness and loss of emotions, seizures, and sometimes even death.

By the 1950s, the use of **psychosurgery** had declined dramatically, especially in countries outside the United States. Today, psychosurgery is used rarely, and only with people who have severe disorders that do not respond to other forms of treatment. Modern neurological assessment and surgical techniques make psychosurgery more precise and safer than it was formerly, although it remains highly controversial, even among professionals. Neurosurgeons attempt to lesion, or destroy, minute areas of the brain thought to be involved in a patient's symptoms. One of the greatest remaining problems in psychosurgery, however, is that we do not yet know what areas of the brain are involved in the production of most psychiatric symptoms, and it is likely that many areas of the brain are involved in any given disorder (Valenstein, 1986).

Assessing Biological Approaches

The biological therapies have revolutionized the treatment of people with psychological disorders. We entered the twentieth century able only to house and comfort people with severe psychological disturbances. We entered the twenty-first century able to treat many of these people so successfully that they can lead normal lives, thanks in part to the biological therapies that have been developed in recent decades.

Many people find the biological theories appealing because they seem to erase any blame or responsibility that might be placed on the sufferer of a disorder. Indeed, many organizations that advocate for people with mental disorders argue that mental disorders should be seen as medical diseases, just like diabetes or high blood pressure. They argue that people who suffer these disorders simply must accept that they have a disease and obtain the appropriate medical treatment.

Despite their current popularity, however, the biological therapies are not a panacea. They do not work for everyone. Indeed, some people with psychological disorders do not respond to any of the drugs or other biological treatments currently available. In addition, for some disorders, such as phobias (see Chapter 5), psychotherapy works better than drug therapies in alleviating symptoms.

Most of the biological therapies have significant side effects, as the rest of this book will describe. Often, these side effects are tolerable, and people endure them because they are getting relief from their psychological disorder. For some people, however, the side effects are worse than the disorder itself. For yet others, the side effects can be dangerous and even deadly.

Some critics of biological theories and drug therapies worry that people will turn to the drugs rather than dealing with the issues in their lives that cause or contribute to their psychological problems. Critics also argue that biological theories often ignore the fact that environmental and psychological processes can affect biological functioning.

TEST YOURSELF

1. What three causes of psychopathology do the biological theories focus on?
2. Which neurotransmitter systems have frequently been implicated in specific forms of psychopathology?
3. What are three types of gene-environment interactions?
4. What types of symptoms are antipsychotic and antidepressant drugs, barbiturates, benzodiazepines, and lithium used to treat?
5. What are four methods used to stimulate the brain electrically or magnetically?

APPLY IT Phineas Gage lost his ability to control his impulses and to act in a socially responsible manner. Damage to what major area of the brain was likely responsible for these changes in his behavior?

a. hindbrain

b. midbrain

c. forebrain

Answers appear online at www.mhhe.com/nolen5e.

PSYCHOLOGICAL APPROACHES

We turn now to a discussion of different psychological approaches to understanding and treating abnormality. We begin with behavioral and cognitive approaches, which are the focus of much research in psychopathology. We then discuss psychodynamic and humanistic approaches, family systems approaches, and emotion-focused approaches.

Behavioral Approaches

Behavioral approaches focus on the influences of reinforcements and punishments in producing behavior. The two core principles or processes of learning according to behaviorism are *classical conditioning* and *operant conditioning*. Learning can also occur through *modeling* and *observational learning*.

Classical Conditioning

Around the turn of the twentieth century, Ivan Pavlov, a Russian physiologist, was conducting experiments on the salivary glands of dogs when he made discoveries that would revolutionize psychological theory. Not surprisingly, his dogs would salivate when Pavlov or an assistant put food in their mouths. Pavlov noticed that, after a while, the dogs would salivate when he or his assistant simply walked into the room.

Pavlov had paired a previously neutral stimulus (himself) with a stimulus that naturally leads to a certain response (the dish of food, which leads to salivating), and eventually the neutral stimulus (Pavlov) was able to elicit that response (salivation). This process gained the name **classical conditioning.** The stimulus that naturally produces a response is the **unconditioned stimulus (US),** and the response created by the unconditioned stimulus is the **unconditioned response (UR).** Thus, in Pavlov's experiments, the dish of food was the US, and salivation in response to this food was the UR. The previously neutral stimulus is the **conditioned stimulus (CS),** and the response that it elicits is the **conditioned response (CR).** Thus, Pavlov was the CS, and when the dogs salivated in response to seeing him, this salivation became the CR (Figure 2.11).

Classical conditioning has been used to explain people's seemingly irrational responses to a host of neutral stimuli. For example, a college student who failed a test in a particular classroom may break out in a cold sweat when she enters that room again—this response is the result of classical conditioning. The room has become a conditioned stimulus, eliciting a response of anxiety, because it was paired with an unconditioned stimulus (failing an exam) that elicited anxiety.

Operant Conditioning

E. L. Thorndike observed that behaviors that are followed by a reward are strengthened, whereas behaviors that are followed by a punishment are weakened. This simple but important observation, which Thorndike labeled the *law of effect*, led to the development of the principles of **operant conditioning**—the shaping of behaviors by providing rewards for desired behaviors and providing punishments for undesired behaviors.

In the 1930s, B. F. Skinner showed that a pigeon will learn to press on a bar if pressing it is associated with the delivery of food and will learn to avoid pressing another bar if pressing it is associated with an electric shock. Similarly, a child will learn to make his bed if he receives a hug and a

FIGURE 2.11 **Stimulus and Response in Classical Conditioning.** Classical conditioning is a major way abnormal behaviors are learned, according to behavioral theories.

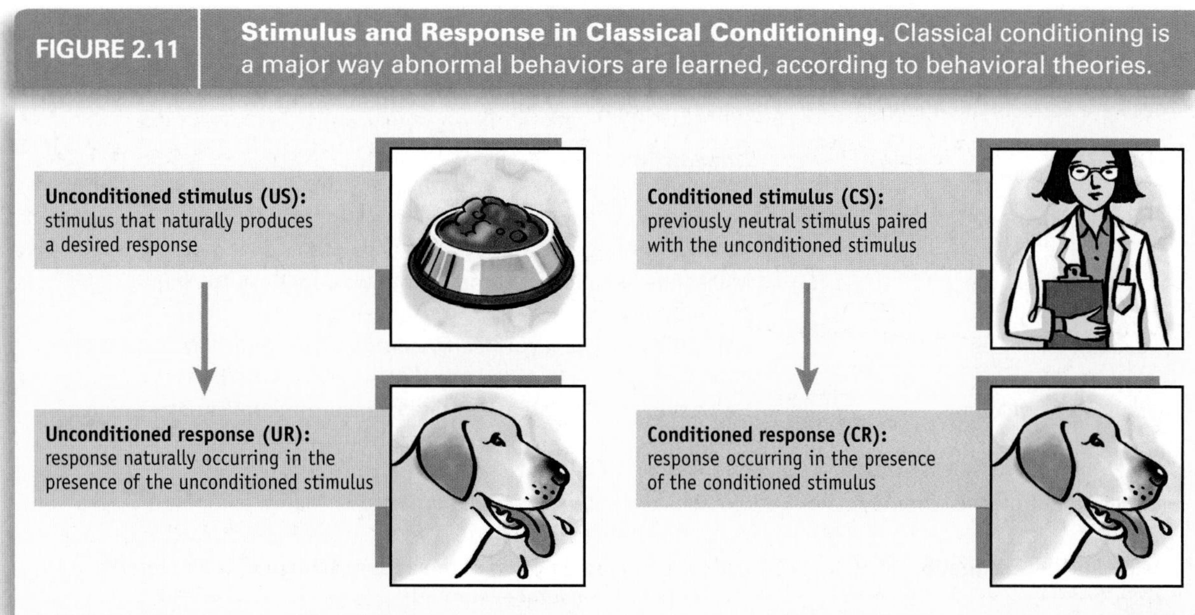

kiss from his mother each time he makes the bed, and he will learn to stop hitting his brother if he doesn't get to watch his favorite television show every time he hits his brother.

Unconditioned stimulus (US):
stimulus that naturally produces a desired response
Conditioned stimulus (CS):
previously neutral stimulus paired with the unconditioned stimulus
Unconditioned response (UR):
response naturally occurring in the presence of the unconditioned stimulus
Conditioned response (CR):
response occurring in the presence of the conditioned stimulus

In operant conditioning, behaviors will be learned most quickly if they are paired with the reward or punishment every time the behavior is emitted. This consistent response is called a *continuous reinforcement schedule.* Behaviors can be learned and maintained, however, on a *partial reinforcement schedule,* in which the reward or punishment occurs only sometimes in response to the behavior. *Extinction*—eliminating a learned behavior—is more difficult when the behavior was learned through a partial reinforcement schedule than when the behavior was learned through a continuous reinforcement schedule. This is because the behavior was learned under conditions of occasional reward, so a constant reward is not needed to maintain the behavior. A good example is gambling behavior. People who frequently gamble are seldom rewarded, but they continue to gamble in anticipation of that occasional, unpredictable win.

Hobart Mowrer's (1939) two-factor model suggests that combinations of classical and operant conditioning can explain the persistence of fears. Initially, people develop fear responses to previously neutral stimuli through classical conditioning. Then, through operant conditioning, they develop behaviors designed to avoid triggers for that fear. For example, a woman may have a fear of bridges developed through classical conditioning: She fell off a bridge into icy waters as a child, and now any time she nears a bridge she feels very anxious. This woman then develops elaborate means of getting around her hometown without having to cross any bridges. Avoiding the bridges reduces her anxiety, and thus her avoidant behavior is reinforced. This woman has developed a *conditioned avoidance response* through operant conditioning. As a result, however, she never exposes herself to a bridge and never has the opportunity to extinguish her initial fear of bridges. As we shall see, many of the therapeutic techniques developed by behavioral theorists are designed to extinguish conditioned avoidance responses, which can interfere greatly with a person's ability to function in everyday life.

Gambling is reinforced by wins only occasionally, but this makes it more difficult to extinguish the behavior.

Modeling and Observational Learning

Skinner and other "pure" behaviorists argued that humans and animals learn behaviors only by directly experiencing rewards or punishments for the behaviors. In the 1950s, however, psychologist Albert Bandura argued that people can also learn behaviors by watching other people, a view that came to be known as *social learning theory.* First, in **modeling,** people learn new behaviors from imitating the behaviors modeled by important people in their lives, such as their parents. Learning through modeling is more likely to occur when the person modeling the behavior is seen as an authority figure or is perceived to be like oneself. For

TABLE 2.2 Behavior Change Techniques

These are some of the methods used in behavior therapy.

Label	Description
Removal of reinforcements	Removes the individual from the reinforcing situation or environment
Aversion therapy	Makes the situation or stimulus that was once reinforcing no longer reinforcing
Relaxation exercises	Helps the individual voluntarily control physiological manifestations of anxiety
Distraction techniques	Helps the individual temporarily distract from anxiety-producing situations; diverts attention from physiological manifestations of anxiety
Flooding, or implosive, therapy	Exposes the individual to the dreaded or feared stimulus while preventing avoidant behavior
Systematic desensitization	Pairs the implementation of relaxation techniques with hierarchical exposure to the aversive stimulus
Response shaping through operant conditioning	Pairs rewards with desired behaviors
Behavioral contracting	Provides rewards for reaching proximal goals
Modeling and observational learning	Models desired behaviors, so that the client can learn through observation

example, Bandura (1969) argued that children are most likely to imitate the behaviors modeled by their same-sex parent, because this parent is an authority figure and because their same-sex parent seems more similar to them than does their opposite-sex parent.

Second, **observational learning** takes place when a person observes the rewards and punishments that another person receives for his or her behavior and then behaves in accord with those rewards and punishments. For example, a child who views her sibling being punished for dropping food on the floor will learn, through observation, the consequences of dropping food on the floor and will be less likely to engage in this behavior herself. Some theorists argue that even extremely negative behaviors, such as teenagers going on a shooting rampage, are also due to observational learning. Teenagers see figures in the media being rewarded for violent behavior with fame and thus learn that behavior. They also are directly rewarded for violent behavior in certain video games.

Behavioral Therapies

Behavioral therapies focus on identifying the reinforcements and punishments contributing to a person's maladaptive behaviors and on changing specific behaviors. The foundation for behavioral therapy is the *behavioral assessment* of the client's problem. The therapist works with the client to identify the specific circumstances that seem to elicit the client's unwanted behavior or emotional responses: What situations seem to trigger anxiety symptoms? When is the client most likely to begin heavy drinking? What types of interactions with other people make the client feel most distressed?

There are many specific techniques for behavior change (Table 2.2). A mainstay of behavior therapy is **systematic desensitization therapy,** a gradual method for extinguishing anxiety responses to stimuli and the maladaptive behavior that often accompanies this anxiety. In systematic desensitization, the client first learns relaxation exercises and then develops a hierarchy of feared stimuli, ranging from stimuli that would cause him or her only mild anxiety to stimuli that would cause severe anxiety or panic. A person with a snake phobia might put at the bottom of his hierarchy "imagining a snake in a closed container across the room." A little further up on the hierarchy might be "watching someone else handle a snake." At the top of his hierarchy might be "touching a snake myself." Then the therapist would help him proceed through this hierarchy,

Behavioral therapy for phobias is very effective.

starting with the least-feared stimulus. He would be instructed to vividly imagine the feared stimulus or even be exposed to the feared stimulus for a short period, while implementing relaxation exercises to control the anxiety. When he gets to the point where he can imagine or experience the least-feared stimulus without feeling anxious, he moves on to the next-most-feared stimulus, imagining or experiencing it while implementing relaxation exercises. This proceeds until he reaches the most-feared stimulus on the list and is able to experience this stimulus without anxiety. Thus, by the end of systematic desensitization therapy, a person with a snake phobia should be able to pick up and handle a large snake without becoming anxious.

Often, systematic desensitization therapy is combined with modeling—the client might watch as the therapist picks up a snake, pets it, and plays with it, observing that the therapist is not afraid, is not bitten or choked, and seems to enjoy playing with the snake. Eventually, the client is encouraged to imitate the therapist's behaviors with and reactions to the snake. In some cases, people undergoing systematic desensitization are asked only to imagine experiencing the feared stimuli. In other cases, they are asked to experience these stimuli directly, actually touching and holding the snake, for example. This latter method, known as *in vivo exposure,* generally has stronger results than exposure only in the client's imagination (Follette & Hayes, 2000).

Assessing Behavioral Approaches

Behavioral theorists set the standard for scientifically testing hypotheses about how normal and abnormal behaviors develop. The hypotheses developed from these theories are precise, and the studies that have been done to test these hypotheses are rigorously controlled and exact. As we will see in subsequent chapters, these studies have provided strong support for behavioral explanations of many types of abnormal behavior, particularly anxiety disorders such as phobias and panic disorder (Craske & Waters, 2005). Similarly, the effectiveness of behavior therapies has been extensively and systematically supported in controlled studies (Follette & Hayes, 2000).

The behavioral theories do have limitations. How behavioral principles could account for some disorders, such as schizophrenia, is unclear. Also, most evidence for behavioral theories is from laboratory studies, but, as we discuss in Chapter 4, lab results do not always apply to the complexity of the real world. Further, the behavioral theories have been criticized for not recognizing free will in people's behaviors—the active choices people make to defy the external forces acting on them.

Cognitive Approaches

Cognitive theories argue that it is not simply rewards and punishments that motivate human behavior. Instead, our **cognitions**—thoughts or beliefs—shape our behaviors and the emotions we experience.

When something happens to us, we ask ourselves why that event happened (Abramson, Metalsky, & Alloy, 1989; Abramson, Seligman, & Teasdale, 1978). The answer to this "why" question is our **causal attribution** for the event. The attributions we make for events can influence our behavior because they impact the meaning we give to events and our expectations for similar events in the future.

The attributions we make for our own behavior can affect our emotions and self-concept. For example, if we act rudely toward another person and attribute this behavior to situational factors (the other person acted rudely first), we

Aaron Beck is one of the founders of cognitive theories of psychopathology.

may feel slightly guilty but we may also feel justified. However, if we attribute this behavior to personality factors (I am a rude person), then we may feel guilty and diminish our self-esteem.

In addition to the attributions we make for specific events, we have broad beliefs about ourselves, our relationships, and the world. These can be either positive and helpful to us or negative and destructive. These broad beliefs are called **global assumptions.** Two prominent proponents of this view are Albert Ellis, whom we met in the Extraordinary People opening segment, and Aaron Beck. They argued that most negative emotions or maladaptive behaviors are the result of one or more of the dysfunctional global assumptions that guide a person's life. Some of the most common dysfunctional assumptions are these:

« Extraordinary People: Albert Ellis

1. I should be loved by everyone for everything I do.
2. It is better to avoid problems than to face them.
3. I should be completely competent, intelligent, and achieving in all I do.
4. I must have perfect self-control.

People who hold such beliefs often will react to situations with irrational thoughts and behaviors and negative emotions. For example, someone who believes that she must be completely competent, intelligent, and achieving in all areas of her life will be extremely upset by even minor failures or bad events. If she were to score poorly on an exam, she may have thoughts such as "I am a total failure. I will never amount to anything. I should have gotten a perfect score on that exam."

Cognitive Therapies

Cognitive therapies help clients identify and challenge these negative thoughts and dysfunctional belief systems. Cognitive therapists also help clients learn more effective problem-solving techniques for dealing with the concrete problems in their lives. Cognitive therapy is designed to be short-term, on the order of 12 to 20 weeks in duration, with one or two sessions per week (Beck, Rush, Shaw, & Emery, 1979). There are three main goals in cognitive therapy (Beck, 1976):

1. Assist clients in identifying their irrational and maladaptive thoughts. A client might be asked to keep a diary of thoughts she has whenever she feels anxious.
2. Teach clients to challenge their irrational or maladaptive thoughts and to consider alternative ways of thinking. A client might be asked to evaluate the evidence for a belief or to consider how other people might think about a difficult situation.
3. Encourage clients to face their worst fears about a situation and recognize ways they could cope.

Cognitive techniques are often combined with behavioral techniques, in what is known as **cognitive-behavioral therapy,** or **CBT.** The therapist may use behavioral assignments to help the client gather evidence concerning his or her beliefs, to test alternative viewpoints about a situation, and to try new methods of coping with different situations. These assignments are presented to the client as ways of testing hypotheses and gathering information that will be useful in therapy regardless of the outcome. The assignments can also involve trying out new skills, such as skill in communicating more effectively, between therapy sessions.

The following case study illustrates how a therapist might use behavioral assignments to provide a depressed student with opportunities to practice new skills and to gather information about thoughts that contribute to negative emotions.

A socially anxious client may be given the behavioral assignment to talk to a clerk in a checkout line as part of cognitive-behavioral therapy.

CASE STUDY A student was unable to complete her degree because she feared meeting with a professor to discuss an incomplete grade she had received in a course. She was quite convinced that the professor would "scream at her" and had been unable to complete a homework assignment to call the professor's secretary to arrange a meeting. An in vivo task was agreed on in which she called the professor from her therapist's office. Her thoughts and feelings before, during, and after the call were carefully examined. As might be expected, the professor was quite glad to hear from his former student and was pleased to accept her final paper. She was able to see that her beliefs were both maladaptive and erroneous. (Adapted from Freeman & Reinecke, 1995, pp. 203–204)

Assessing Cognitive Approaches

Particularly in studies of mood disorders and anxiety disorders, and increasingly in studies of sexual disorders and substance use disorders, evidence demonstrates the effect of maladaptive cognitions (Joormann, 2008). Further, as we will see in subsequent chapters, cognitive therapies have proven useful in the treatment of these disorders (Hollon & Dimidjian, 2008).

The greatest limitation of the cognitive theories has been the difficulty of proving that maladaptive cognitions precede and cause disorders, rather than being the symptoms or consequences of the disorders. For example, it is clear that depressed people think depressing thoughts. But is this a cause of their depression or a symptom of it? It turns out to be harder than you might think to answer this question definitively (Coyne & Gotlib, 1983).

Psychodynamic Approaches

The **psychodynamic theories** of abnormality suggest that all behavior, thoughts, and emotions, whether normal or abnormal, are influenced to a large extent by unconscious processes (McWilliams & Weinberger, 2003). The psychodynamic theories began with Sigmund Freud in the late nineteenth century and have expanded to include several newer theories. These theories accept many of Freud's basic assumptions about the workings of the human mind but emphasize different processes from those that Freud emphasized.

Freud developed **psychoanalysis,** which refers to (1) a theory of personality and psychopathology, (2) a method of investigating the mind, and (3) a form of treatment for psychopathology (McWilliams & Weinberger, 2003). As we noted in Chapter 1, Freud was a Viennese neurologist who became interested in unconscious processes while working with Jean Charcot in Paris in the late nineteenth century. He then returned to Vienna and worked with physician Josef Breuer, most notably on the case of "Anna O."

Sigmund Freud believed that normal and abnormal behaviors are driven by needs and drives, most of which are unconscious.

Anna O. had extensive symptoms of hysteria—physical ailments with no apparent physical cause—including paralysis of the legs and right arm, deafness, and disorganized speech. Breuer attempted to hypnotize Anna O., hoping he could cure her symptoms by suggestion. Anna O. began to talk about painful memories from her past, which apparently were tied to the development of her hysterical symptoms. She expressed a great deal of distress about these memories, but following the recounting of the memories under hypnosis, many of her symptoms went away. Breuer labeled the release of emotions connected to these memories **catharsis,** and Anna O. labeled the entire process her "talking cure."

Breuer and Freud suggested that hysteria is the result of traumatic memories that have been repressed from consciousness because they are too painful. They defined **repression** as the motivated forgetting of a difficult experience, such as being abused as a child, or of an unacceptable wish, such as the desire to hurt someone. Repression does not dissolve the emotion associated with the memory or wish. Instead, argued Breuer and Freud, this emotion is "dammed up" and emerges as symptoms.

The Id, Ego, and Superego

Freud believed that the two basic drives that motivate human behavior are the sexual drive, which he referred to as **libido,** and the aggressive drive (McWilliams & Weinberger, 2003). The energy from these drives continually seeks to be released but can be channeled or harnessed by different psychological systems. Most of Freud's writings focused primarily on libido (or libidinal drive), so our discussion will do so as well.

According to Freud, three systems of the human psyche that help regulate the libido are the id, the ego, and the superego (McWilliams &

ScienceCartoonsPlus.com

Weinberger, 2003). The **id** is the system from which the libido emerges, and its drives and impulses seek immediate release. The id operates by the *pleasure principle*—the drive to maximize pleasure and minimize pain, as quickly as possible.

Freud argued that as children grow older, they become aware that they cannot always quickly satisfy their impulses. A part of the id splits off and becomes the **ego,** the force that seeks to gratify our wishes and needs in ways that remain within the rules of society for their appropriate expression. A preschooler who may wish to suckle at the mother's breast but is aware that this is no longer allowed may satisfy himself with cuddling in his mother's lap.

Freud further argued that the **superego** develops from the ego a little later in childhood. It is the storehouse of rules and regulations for the conduct of behavior that are learned from one's parents and from society. These rules and regulations are in the form of absolute moral standards. We internalize these moral standards because living according to them reduces anxiety (McWilliams & Weinberger, 2003).

Freud believed that most interactions among the id, ego, and superego occur in the **unconscious,** completely out of our awareness. The **preconscious** is intermediate between the unconscious and the **conscious.** Some material (wishes, needs, or memories) from the unconscious can make its way into the preconscious but rarely reaches the conscious level. Because these unconscious desires are often unacceptable to the individual or society, they cause anxiety if they seep into the conscious, prompting the ego to push them back into the unconscious. This pushing of material back into the unconscious is repression (McWilliams & Weinberger, 2003).

Freud—and later his daughter, Anna Freud—described certain strategies, or **defense mechanisms,** that the ego uses to disguise or transform unconscious wishes. The particular defense mechanisms that a person regularly uses shape his or her behavior and personality. Table 2.3 provides a list and examples of the basic defense mechanisms. Everyone uses defense mechanisms to a degree, because everyone must protect against awareness of unacceptable wishes and conform to societal norms. When a person's behavior becomes ruled by defense mechanisms or when the mechanisms themselves are maladaptive, then these mechanisms can result in abnormal, pathological behavior.

Psychosexual Stages

Psychoanalytic theory argues that the nurturance a child receives from his or her early caregivers strongly influences personality development. Freud proposed that as children develop they pass through a series of universal **psychosexual stages.** In each stage, sexual drives are focused on the stimulation of certain body areas, and particular psychological issues can arouse anxiety in the child. The responses of caregivers, usually parents, to the child's attempts to satisfy basic needs and wishes can greatly influence whether a given stage is negotiated successfully. If the parents are not appropriately responsive, helping the child learn acceptable ways of satisfying and controlling his or her drives and impulses, the child can become *fixated* at a stage, trapped in the concerns and issues of that stage and never successfully moving beyond that stage and through the subsequent stages.

According to Freud, the earliest stage of life, the *oral stage,* lasts for the first 18 months following birth. In the oral stage, libidinal impulses are best satisfied through stimulation of the mouth area, usually through feeding or sucking. At this stage, the child is entirely dependent on caregivers for gratification, and the central issues of this stage are issues of one's dependence and the reliability of others. If the child's caregiver, typically the mother, is not adequately available to the child, he or she can develop deep mistrust and fear of abandonment. Children fixated at the oral stage develop an "oral personality," characterized by excessive dependence on others but mistrust of others' love. A number of habits focused on the mouth area—for example, smoking or excessive drinking and eating—are said to reflect an oral character.

The *anal stage* lasts from about 18 months to 3 years of age. During this phase, the focus of gratification is the anus. The child becomes very interested in toilet activities, particularly the passing

TABLE 2.3 Defense Mechanisms

These defense mechanisms were described by Sigmund and Anna Freud.

Defense Mechanism	Definition	Example
Regression	Retreating to a behavior of an earlier developmental period to prevent anxiety and satisfy current needs	A woman abandoned by her lover curls up in a chair, rocking and sucking her fingers.
Denial	Refusing to perceive or accept reality	A husband whose wife recently died denies she is gone and actively searches for her.
Displacement	Discharging unacceptable feelings against someone or something other than the true target of these feelings	A woman who is angry at her children kicks a dog.
Rationalization	Inventing an acceptable motive to explain unacceptably motivated behavior	A soldier who killed innocent civilians rationalizes that he was only following orders.
Intellectualization	Adopting a cold, distanced perspective on a matter that actually creates strong, unpleasant feelings	An emergency room physician who is troubled by seeing young people with severe gunshot wounds every night has discussions with colleagues that focus only on the technical aspects of treatment.
Projection	Attributing one's own unacceptable motives or desires to someone else	A husband who is sexually attracted to a colleague accuses his wife of cheating on him.
Reaction formation	Adopting a set of attitudes and behaviors that are the opposite of one's true dispositions	A man who cannot accept his own homosexuality becomes extremely homophobic.
Identification	Adopting the ideas, values, and tendencies of someone in a superior position in order to elevate self-worth	Prisoners adopt the attitudes of their captors toward other prisoners.
Sublimation	Translating wishes and needs into socially acceptable behavior	An adolescent with strong aggressive impulses trains to be a boxer.

and retaining of feces. Parents can cause a child to become fixated at this stage by being too harsh or critical during toilet training. People with an "anal personality" are said to be stubborn, overcontrolling, stingy, and too focused on orderliness and tidiness.

During the *phallic stage*, lasting from about age 3 to 6, the focus of pleasure is the genitals. During this stage one of the most important conflicts of sexual development occurs, and it occurs differently for boys and girls. Freud believed that boys become sexually attracted to their mother and hate their father as rivals. Freud labeled this the *Oedipus complex*, after the character in Greek mythology who unknowingly kills his father and marries his mother. Boys fear that their father will retaliate against them by castrating them. This fear leads them to put aside their desire for their mother and aspire to become like their father. The successful resolution of the Oedipus complex helps instill a strong superego in boys, because it results in boys identifying with their father and their father's value system.

Freud believed that, during the phallic stage, girls recognize that they do not have a penis and are horrified at this discovery. They also recognize that their mother does not have a penis and disdain their mother and all females for this deficit. Girls develop an attraction for their father, in hopes that he will provide the penis they lack. Freud labeled this the *Electra complex*, after the character in Greek mythology who conspires to murder her mother to avenge her father's death. Girls cannot have castration anxiety, because, according to Freud, they feel they have already been castrated. As a result, girls do not have as strong a motivation as boys to develop a superego. Freud argued that females never develop superegos as strong as those of males and that this leads to a greater reliance on emotion than on reason in the lives of women. Freud also thought that much of women's behavior is driven by *penis envy*—the wish to have the male sex organ.

The unsuccessful resolution of the phallic stage can lead to a number of psychological problems in children. If children do not fully identify with their same-sex parent, they may not develop "appropriate" gender roles or a heterosexual orientation. They also may not develop a healthy superego and may become either too self-aggrandizing or too self-deprecating. If children's sexual attraction to their parents is not met with gentle but firm discouragement, they may become overly seductive or sexualized and have a number of problems in future romantic relationships.

After the turmoil of the phallic stage, children enter the *latency stage*, during which libidinal drives are quelled somewhat. Their attention turns to developing skills and interests and becoming fully socialized into the world in which they live. They play with friends of the same sex and avoid children of the opposite sex.

At about age 12, children's sexual desires emerge again as they enter puberty, and they enter the *genital stage*. If they have successfully resolved the phallic stage, their sexual interests turn to heterosexual relationships. They begin to pursue romantic alliances and learn to negotiate the world of dating and early sexual encounters with members of the opposite sex.

Later Psychodynamic Theories

Many of Freud's followers modified his original psychoanalytic theory, leading to a group of theories collectively referred to as *psychodynamic theories*. Anna Freud extended her work on defense mechanisms to develop the field of **ego psychology,** emphasizing the importance of the individual's ability to regulate defenses in ways that allow healthy functioning within the realities of society.

Other theorists also focused on the role of the ego as an independent force striving for mastery and competence (e.g., Jacobson, 1964; Mahler, 1968). The **object relations** perspective integrated significant aspects of Sigmund Freud's drive theory with the role of early relationships in the development of self-concept and personality. According to proponents of this perspective—such as Melanie Klein, Margaret Mahler, Otto Kernberg, and Heinz Kohut—our early relationships create images, or representations, of ourselves and others. We carry these images throughout adulthood, and they affect all our subsequent relationships.

Carl Jung, who was a student of Freud, rejected many of Freud's ideas about the importance of sexuality in development. He argued that spiritual and religious drives were as important as sexual drives, and he suggested that the wisdom accumulated by a society over hundreds of years of human existence is stored in the memories of individuals. He referred to this wisdom as the **collective unconscious.**

Psychodynamic Therapies

Therapies based on Freud's classical psychoanalytic theory and on later psychodynamic theories focus on uncovering and resolving unconscious processes that are thought to drive psychological symptoms. The goal of **psychodynamic therapies** is to help clients recognize their maladaptive coping strategies and the sources of their unconscious conflicts. These insights are thought to free clients from the grip of the past and give them a sense of agency in making changes in the present (Vakoch & Strupp, 2000).

Freud and others developed the method of **free association,** in which a client is taught to talk about whatever comes to mind, trying not to censor any thoughts. The therapist notices what themes seem to recur in a client's free associations, exactly how one thought seems to lead to another, and the specific memories that a client recalls.

The material the client is reluctant to talk about during psychotherapy—that is, the client's **resistance** to certain material—is an important clue to the client's central unconscious conflicts, because the most threatening conflicts are those the ego tries hardest to repress (Vakoch & Strupp, 2000). The therapist eventually puts together these pieces of the puzzle into a suggestion or an interpretation of a conflict the client might be facing and voices this interpretation to the client. Sometimes, the client accepts the interpretation as a revelation. Other times, the client is resistant to the interpretation. The therapist might interpret resistance as a good indication that the interpretation has identified an important issue in the client's unconscious.

The client's **transference** to the therapist is also a clue to unconscious conflicts and needs. Transference occurs when the client reacts to the therapist as if the therapist were an important person in the client's early development, such as his father or mother. For example, a client may find himself reacting with rage or extreme fear when a therapist is just a few minutes late for an appointment, a reaction that might stem from his feelings of having been emotionally abandoned by a parent during childhood. The therapist might point out the ways the client behaves that represent transference and might then help the client explore the roots of his behavior in his relationships with significant others.

By **working through,** or going over and over, painful memories and difficult issues, clients are able to understand them and weave them into their self-definition in acceptable ways. This allows them to move forward in their lives. Many therapists believe that *catharsis,* or the expression of emotions connected to memories and conflicts, is also central to the healing processes in psychodynamic therapy. Catharsis unleashes the energy bound in unconscious memories and conflicts, allowing this material to be incorporated into a more adaptive self-view.

What is the difference between classical psychoanalysis and modern psychodynamic therapy? Psychoanalysis typically involves three or four sessions per week over a period of many years. The focus of psychoanalysis is primarily on the interpretation of transferences and resistances, as well as on experiences in the client's past (Luborsky & Barrett, 2006). Psychodynamic therapy also may go on for years, but it can be as short as 12 weeks (Crits-Christoph & Barber, 2000). Transferences, resistances, and the client's relationships with early caregivers are also the focus of psychodynamic therapy, but the psychodynamic therapist, compared with the psychoanalyst, may focus more on current situations in the client's life.

Interpersonal therapy, or **IPT,** emerged out of modern psychodynamic theories of psychopathology, which shifted the focus from the unconscious conflicts of the individual to the client's pattern of relationships with important people in his or her life (Klerman, Weissman, Rounsaville, & Chevron, 1984; Weissman & Markowitz, 2002). IPT differs from psychodynamic therapies in that the therapist is much more structuring and directive in the therapy, offering interpretations much earlier and focusing on how to change current relationships. IPT is designed to be a short-term therapy, often lasting only about 12 weeks.

Assessing Psychodynamic Approaches

Psychodynamic theories are among the most comprehensive theories of human behavior established to date. For some people, they are also the most satisfying theories. They explain both normal and abnormal behavior with similar processes. And they have an "Aha!" quality about them that leads us to believe they hold important insights. Psychodynamic theories have played a major role in shaping psychology and psychiatry in the past century.

Psychodynamic theories also have many limitations and weaknesses. Chief among these is that it is difficult or impossible to test their fundamental assumptions scientifically (Erdelyi, 1992; but see Luborsky & Barrett, 2006; Westen, 1998). The processes described by these theories are abstract and difficult to measure. The theories themselves often provide ways to explain away the results of studies that seem to dispute their fundamental assumptions.

As for psychodynamic therapy, its long-term, intensive nature makes it unaffordable for many people. In addition, people suffering from acute problems, such as severe depression or anxiety, often cannot tolerate the lack of structure in traditional psychodynamic therapy and need more immediate relief from their symptoms (Bachrach, Galatzer-Levy, Skolnikoff, & Waldron, 1991).

For these reasons, modern psychodynamic therapists have developed some shorter-term, more structured versions of psychodynamic therapy (Luborsky, 1984). Studies conducted on the effectiveness of these short-term therapies suggest that they can result in significant improvement in symptoms for people with psychological symptoms (Gibbons, Crits-Christoph, & Hearon, 2008).

In this book, we will focus on those theories of specific disorders, and the therapies for these disorders, that have received substantial scientific support. Because psychodynamic theories and therapies have had much less empirical support than many newer psychological theories and therapies, we will not discuss them in detail in reviewing the research on most disorders.

Humanistic Approaches

Humanistic theories are based on the assumption that humans have an innate capacity for goodness and for living a full life (Rogers, 1951). Pressure from society to conform to certain norms rather than to seek one's most-developed self interferes with the fulfillment of this capacity. The humanistic theorists recognized that we often are not aware of the forces shaping our behavior and that the environment can play a strong role in our happiness or unhappiness. But they were optimistic that once people recognized these forces and became freer to direct their own lives, they would naturally make good choices and be happier.

Carl Rogers (1951) developed the most widely known version of humanistic theory. Rogers believed that, without undue pressure from others, individuals naturally move toward personal growth, self-acceptance, and **self-actualization,** the fulfillment of their potential for love, creativity, and meaning. Under the stress of pressure from society and family, however, people can develop rigid and distorted

Carl Rogers (1902–1987) was one of the founders of humanistic theory.

perspectives of the self. People often experience conflict because of differences between their true self—the ideal self they wish to be—and the self they feel they ought to be to please others. This conflict can lead to emotional distress, unhealthy behaviors, and even loss of touch with reality.

Humanistic Therapy

The stated goal of **humanistic therapy** is to help clients discover their greatest potential through self-exploration (Bohart, 1995). The job of the therapist in humanistic therapy is not to act as an authority who provides healing to the client but rather to provide the optimal conditions for the client to heal him- or herself. Humanistic therapists do not push clients to uncover repressed painful memories or unconscious conflicts. Instead, they believe that when clients are supported and empowered to grow, the clients eventually will face the past when necessary for their further development (Bohart, 1995).

The best known of these therapies is Carl Rogers's **client-centered therapy** (**CCT;** Rogers, 1951). In CCT, the therapist communicates a genuineness in his or her role as helper to the client, acting as an authentic person rather than an authority figure. The therapist also shows *unconditional positive regard* for the client and communicates an empathic understanding of the client's underlying feelings and search for self.

The main strategy for accomplishing these goals is the use of reflection. **Reflection** is a method of responding in which the therapist expresses an attempt to understand what the client is experiencing and trying to communicate (Bohart, 1995). The therapist does not attempt to interpret the unconscious aspects of the client's experience. Rather, the therapist tries to communicate an understanding of the client and explicitly asks for feedback from the client about this understanding.

Assessing Humanistic Approaches

The humanistic theories struck a positive chord in the 1960s and still have many proponents, especially among self-help groups and peer-counseling programs. The optimism and attribution of free will of these theories is a refreshing change from the emphasis on pathology and external forces in other theories. Humanistic theories shift our focus from what is wrong with people to questions about how we can help people achieve their greatest potential. These theories have been criticized, however, for being vague and impossible to test scientifically (Bohart, 1990).

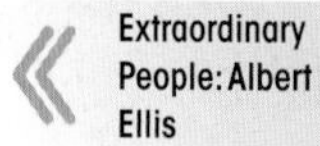

Client-centered therapy has been used to treat people with a wide range of problems, including depression, alcoholism, schizophrenia, anxiety disorders, and personality disorders (Bohart, 1990). Although some studies have shown that CCT results in better outcomes than comparison therapies, other studies have not (Greenberg, Elliot, & Lietaer, 1994). Some therapists believe that CCT may be appropriate for people who are moderately distressed but insufficient for people who are seriously distressed (Bohart, 1995).

Family Systems Approaches

Most of the theories we have discussed thus far have implicated the family in the development of both normal and abnormal behavior. **Family systems theories** and therapies focus on the family in a different way (Mirsalimi, Perleberg, Stovall, & Kaslow, 2003). These theories see the family as a complex interpersonal system, with its own hierarchy and rules that govern family members' behavior. The family system can function well and promote the well-being of its members, supporting their growth and accepting their change. Or the system can be dysfunctional, creating and maintaining psychopathology in one or more members.

When a member of the family has a psychological disorder, family systems theorists see it not as a problem within the individual but as an indication of a dysfunctional family system. The particular form that any individual's psychopathology takes depends on the complex interactions among the family's cohesiveness, adaptability to change, and communication style (Mirsalimi et al., 2003).

For example, an *inflexible family* is resistant and isolated from all forces outside the family and does not adapt well to changes within the family, such as a child moving into adolescence. In an *enmeshed family,* each member is overly involved in the lives of the others, to the point that individuals do not have personal autonomy and can feel controlled. A *disengaged family,* in contrast, is one in which the members pay no attention to each other and operate as independent units isolated from other family members. And in *pathological triangular relationships,* parents avoid dealing with conflicts with each other by always keeping their children involved in their conversations and activities (Mirsalimi et al., 2003). So a family theorist trying to understand Albert Ellis's anxiety would examine how his family functioned as he grew up and how that continues to influence him even now that he is an adult.

Some of the research on family systems theories of psychopathology has focused on disorders in the children in the family, particularly eating disorders (e.g., Minuchin, Rosman, & Baker, 1978; Robin, 2003). This research suggests that many young girls who develop eating disorders are members of enmeshed families. The parents of these girls are overcontrolling and overinvested in their children's success, and in turn the children feel smothered and dependent on their parents. Anorexia nervosa, a disorder in which an individual refuses to eat and becomes emaciated, may be a girl's way of claiming some control over her life. The family system of these girls supports the anorexia rather than helping them overcome it. The anorexia becomes a focal point and excuse for the family's enmeshment. (See also Chapter 12.)

Family systems therapy is based on the belief that an individual's problems are always rooted in interpersonal systems, particularly family systems. According to this viewpoint, you cannot help an individual without treating the entire family system that created and is maintaining the individual's problems. In fact, these theorists argue that the individual may not actually even have a problem but has become the "identified patient" in the family, carrying the responsibility or blame for the dysfunction of the family system (Minuchin, 1981; Satir, 1967).

Behavioral family systems therapy (BFST) targets family communication and problem solving, beliefs of parents and adolescents that impede communication, and systemic barriers to problem solving (Robin, 2003). Behavioral and cognitive methods are used to teach problem-solving and communication skills and to challenge unhelpful beliefs of parents and teens. Therapists also address dysfunctional family system characteristics, such as weak coalitions between parents. Therapists actively provide instructions, feedback, and opportunities for the rehearsal of skills and role playing.

Assessing Family Systems Approaches

The family systems theories have led to therapeutic approaches that have proven useful for some types of disorders (Mirsalimi et al., 2003). Family systems therapies may be particularly appropriate in the treatment of children, because children are so much more entwined in their families than are adults. Although the details of many family systems theories have not been thoroughly tested in research, it is clear that families can contribute to or help diminish psychological symptoms in their members (e.g., Mirsalimi et al., 2003). However, much more research is needed on family systems theories and therapies. This research is difficult to carry out, because it usually involves observing people in the context of their relationships, which is difficult to "capture in the laboratory."

Family therapists work with the entire family rather than only with the "identified patient."

Emotion-Focused Approaches

Some of the most recent developments in theory and therapy for psychopathology focus on people's ability to understand and regulate their emotions. These **emotion-focused approaches,** often referred to as *third-wave approaches,* view poor regulation of emotions as being at the core of many types of psychopathology, including depression, anxiety, substance abuse, and most personality disorders (Campbell-Sills & Barlow, 2007). They combine techniques from behavioral and cognitive therapy with mindfulness practices derived from Zen Buddhism to help individuals accept, understand, and better regulate their emotions.

The most-established emotion-focused approach is *dialectical behavior therapy* (DBT; Linehan, 1999). The term *dialectical* in dialectical behavior therapy refers to the constant tension between conflicting images or emotions in people prone to certain forms of psychopathology. Dialectical behavior therapy focuses on difficulties in managing negative emotions and in controlling impulsive behaviors. The therapy involves a number of behavioral and cognitive techniques, as well as mindfulness exercises, aimed at increasing problem-solving skills, interpersonal skills, and skill at

SHADES OF GRAY

A student comes into a therapist's office to discuss her feelings about her schoolwork and career. She says, "I'm feeling so lost in my career. Every time I seem to be getting close to doing something really good, like acing a class, I somehow manage to screw it up. I never feel like I am really using my potential. There is a block there." (Bohart, 1995, p. 101).

How might a humanistic therapist respond to this student's concerns? How would this response differ from that of a psychodynamic therapist? (Discussion appears at the end of this chapter.)

managing negative emotions. DBT originally was developed to treat people with borderline personality disorder who were suicidal, and studies comparing this therapy to control conditions suggest that it can reduce suicidal thoughts and behaviors as well as improve interpersonal skills (Lynch, Trost, Salsman, & Linehan, 2007). Most recently, DBT has been adapted for the treatment of eating disorders (Safer, Telch, & Chen, 2009) and is being used to treat other individuals with difficulties in emotional regulation and impulse control (Lynch et al., 2007).

A key assumption behind *acceptance and commitment therapy* (ACT; Hayes, et al., 2006) is that *experiential avoidance*—that is, avoidance of painful thoughts, memories, and feelings—is at the heart of many mental health problems. Accepting one's feelings, thoughts, and past and learning to be present in the moment are key to positive change. ACT uses a variety of techniques to help individuals accept their emotions, be present in the moment, relate to their thoughts differently (e.g., watching them as external objects), and commit to changing behaviors in accord with their goals and values. ACT has been used in preliminary trials in the treatment of a wide variety of problems, especially substance abuse and dependence (Hayes et al., 2006).

Assessing Emotion-Focused Approaches

The emotion-focused approaches have their roots in well-established behavioral and cognitive theories and techniques, but they draw innovative ideas and techniques from spiritual and philosophical traditions, such as Buddhism, and theories of adaptive emotion-regulation. Existing studies of the effectiveness of therapies based on emotion-focused approaches suggest that these therapies may be helpful in the treatment of a wide range of mental health problems (Hayes et al., 2006; Lynch et al., 2007). Much more research is needed, however, particularly on claims for how and why these therapies may help individuals change their behaviors and emotional reactions.

TEST YOURSELF

Match each psychological approach below with the factors that approach argues are involved in psychopathology.

Approach	***Factors Leading to Psychopathology***
1. Behavioral	Unconscious conflicts
2. Cognitive	Pressure to conform to societal norms
3. Psychodynamic	Dysfunctional interpersonal dynamics
4. Humanistic	Poor regulation of emotions
5. Family systems	Classical and operant conditioning
6. Emotion-focused	Thoughts and beliefs

APPLY IT Imagine that you sought psychotherapy because you feel you are not good at making new friends. Which of the following is *not* true?

a. A behavioral therapist would inquire about positive and negative social interactions in your past.
b. A cognitive therapist would inquire about the evidence for your belief that you are not good at making friends.
c. A psychodynamic therapist would be interested in your relationships with early caregivers.
d. A humanistic therapist would challenge your motives for wanting more friends.

Answers appear online at www.mhhe.com/nolen5e.

SOCIOCULTURAL APPROACHES

Sociocultural approaches suggest that we need to look beyond the individual or even the family to the larger society to understand people's problems (Ensminger & Hee-Soon, 2001). First, socioeconomic disadvantage is a risk factor for a wide range of mental health problems (Gustafsson, Larsson, Nelson, & Gustafsson, 2009). Individuals who are poor tend to live in neighborhoods in which they are exposed to violence and inadequate schools and where there are few resources for everyday living (such as grocery stores) and little cohesion among neighbors (Gustafsson et al., 2009). In turn, people living in poverty-stricken urban neighborhoods experience more substance abuse, juvenile delinquency, depression, and anxiety (Belle & Doucet, 2003).

Second, the upheaval and disintegration of societies due to war, famine, and natural disaster are potent risk factors for mental health problems. As we will discuss in Chapter 5, individuals whose countries are ravaged by war or who must flee their homelands and live as refugees show high rates of posttraumatic stress disorder and other mental health problems. For example, a study of citizens of Afghanistan found that 42 percent could be diagnosed with posttraumatic stress disorder and 72 percent had some sort of anxiety symptoms (Cardozo et al., 2004).

Third, social norms and policies that stigmatize and marginalize certain groups put individuals in these groups at increased risk for mental health problems even if they do not suffer socioeconomic stress. For example, gay, lesbian, bisexual, and transgender individuals suffer higher rates of depression, anxiety, and substance use compared to heterosexuals (Hatzenbuehler, 2009; Meyer, 2003). These higher rates have been linked to the experience of discrimination based on sexual orientation and to social policies that disadvantage sexual minorities (Hatzenbuehler, Nolen-Hoeksema, & Erickson, 2008; Meyer, 2003). For example, data from a nationally representative study of over 34,000 participants found higher rates of mental health problems in lesbian, gay, and bisexual (LGB) respondents living in states with social policies that do not confer protection for LGB individuals (e.g., states that do not treat anti-LGB violence as a hate crime) compared to LGB respondents who reside in states with protective policies (Hatzenbuehler, Keyes, & Hasin, 2009). Another long-term study found increases in mental health problems among LGB individuals living in states that instituted bans on gay marriage in the 2004–2005 elections (Hatzenbuehler, McLaughlin, Keyes, & Hasin, 2010). Thus, sociocultural discrimination at the level of state policies can affect citizens' mental health.

Fourth, societies may influence the types of psychopathology their members show by having implicit or explicit rules about what types of abnormal behavior are acceptable (Castro et al., 2010). Throughout this book, we will see that the rates of disorders vary from one culture or ethnic group to another and between males and females. For example, people from "traditional" cultures, such as the Old Order Amish in the United States, appear to have less depression than people in modern cultures (Egeland & Hostetter, 1983). In addition, the particular manifestations of disorders seem to vary from one culture to another. For example, the symptoms of anorexia nervosa, the disorder in which people refuse to eat, appear to be different in Asian cultures than in American culture.

Indeed, some disorders appear to be specific to certain cultures (Alarcón et al., 2009). In Japan, there is a disorder called *taijin kyofusho,* in which individuals have intense fears that their body displeases, embarrasses, or is offensive to other people. Throughout Latin American and Mediterranean cultures, *ataque de nervios* is a common reaction to stress. People may feel out of control, with uncontrollable shouting, crying, and trembling and verbal or physical aggression. We discuss the influence of culture on the manifestation of distress further in Chapter 3.

Cross-Cultural Issues in Treatment

For the most part, people from diverse cultures who seek psychotherapy are treated with the types of psychotherapy described in this chapter, with little adaptation of these approaches to specific cultures (Castro et al., 2010). A number of the assumptions inherent in mainstream psychological therapies, however, can clash with the values and norms of people from different cultures. Therefore, therapists must take a culturally sensitive approach to their clients (Snowden & Yamada, 2005; Sue & Lam, 2002). First, most psychotherapies are focused on the individual—the individual's unconscious conflicts, dysfunctional ways of thinking, maladaptive behavior patterns, and so on. In contrast, many cultures focus on the group, or collective, rather than on the individual (Sue &

Sue, 2003). In these cultures, the identity of the individual is not seen apart from the groups to which that individual belongs—his or her family, community, ethnic group, and religion. If therapists fail to recognize this when working with clients from collectivist cultures, they may make useless or perhaps even harmful recommendations, leading to conflicts between their clients and important groups in the clients' lives that the clients cannot handle.

Second, most psychotherapies value the expression of emotions and the disclosure of personal concerns, whereas many cultures value restraint of emotions and personal concerns, for example, Japanese culture (Sue & Sue, 2003). Some counselors may see this restraint as a problem and try to encourage clients to become more expressive. Again, this effort can clash with the self-concepts of clients and with the norms of their culture.

Third, in many psychotherapies, clients are expected to take the initiative in communicating their concerns and desires to the therapist and in generating ideas about what is causing their symptoms and what changes they might want to make. These expectations can clash with cultural norms that require deference to people in authority (Sue & Sue, 2003). A client from a culture in which one speaks only when spoken to and never challenges an elder or authority figure may be extremely uncomfortable with a therapist who does not tell the client what is wrong and how to fix it in a very direct manner.

Fourth, many clients who are in ethnic minority groups may also be in lower socioeconomic groups, while their therapists are likely to be in middle- or upper-class socioeconomic groups. This situation can create tensions due to class differences as well as cultural differences (Miranda et al., 2005).

Some studies suggest that people from Latino, Asian, and Native American cultures are more comfortable with structured and action-oriented therapies, such as behavioral and cognitive-behavioral therapies, than with the less structured therapies (Miranda et al., 2005). The specific form of therapy may not matter as much as the cultural sensitivity the therapist shows toward the client, whatever therapy is being used. Stanley Sue and Nolan Zane (1987, pp. 42–43) give the following example of the importance of cultural sensitivity in the interaction between client and therapist. First, they describe the problems the client faced; then they describe how the therapist (one of the authors of the study) responded to these problems.

CASE STUDY

At the advice of a close friend, Mae C. decided to seek services at a mental health center. She was extremely distraught and tearful as she related her dilemma. An immigrant from Hong Kong several years ago, Mae met and married her husband (also a recent immigrant from Hong Kong). Their marriage was apparently going fairly well until six months ago when her husband succeeded in bringing over his parents from Hong Kong. While not enthusiastic about having her parents-in-law live with her, Mae realized that her husband wanted them and that both she and her husband were obligated to help their parents (her own parents were still in Hong Kong).

After the parents arrived, Mae found that she was expected to serve them. For example, the mother-in-law would expect Mae to cook and serve dinner, to wash all the clothes, and to do other chores. At the same time, she would constantly complain that Mae did not cook the dinner right, that the house was always messy, and that Mae should wash certain clothes separately. The parents-in-law also displaced Mae and her husband from the master bedroom. The guest room was located in the basement, and the parents refused to sleep in the basement because it reminded them of a tomb.

Mae would occasionally complain to her husband about his parents. The husband would excuse his parents' demands by indicating "They are my parents and they're getting old." In general, he avoided any potential conflict; if he took sides, he supported his parents. Although Mae realized that she had an obligation to his parents, the situation was becoming intolerable to her.

I (the therapist) indicated (to Mae) that conflicts with in-laws were very common, especially for Chinese, who are obligated to take care of their parents. I attempted to normalize the problems because she was suffering from a great deal of guilt over her perceived failure to be the perfect daughter-in-law. I also conveyed my belief that in therapy we could try to generate new ideas to resolve the problem—ideas that did not simply involve extreme courses of action such as divorce or total submission to the in-laws (which she believed were the only options).

I discussed Mae during a case conference with other mental health personnel. It is interesting that many suggestions were generated: Teach Mae how to confront her parents-in-law; have her invite the husband for marital counseling so that husband and wife could form a team in negotiation with his parents; conduct extended family therapy so that Mae, her husband, and her in-laws could agree on contractual give-and-take relationships. The staff agreed that working solely with Mae would not change the situation. . . . Confronting her in-laws was discrepant with her role of daughter-in-law, and she felt very uncomfortable in asserting herself in the situation. Trying to involve her husband or in-laws in treatment was ill advised. Her husband did not want to confront his parents. More important, Mae was extremely fearful that her family might find out that she had sought psychotherapy. Her husband as well as her in-laws would be appalled at her disclosure of family problems to a therapist who was an outsider. . . . How could Mae's case be handled? During the case conference, we discussed the ways that Chinese handle interpersonal family conflicts which are not unusual to see. Chinese often use third-party intermediaries to resolve conflicts. The intermediaries obviously have to be credible and influential with the conflicting parties. At the next session with Mae, I asked her to list the persons who might act as intermediaries, so that we could discuss the suitability of having someone else intervene. Almost immediately, Mae mentioned her uncle (the older brother of the mother-in-law) whom she described as being quite understanding and sensitive. We discussed what she should say to the uncle. After calling her uncle, who lived about 50 miles from Mae, she reported that he wanted to visit them. The uncle apparently realized the gravity of the situation and offered to help. He came for dinner, and Mae told me that she overheard a discussion between the uncle and Mae's mother-in-law. Essentially, he told her that Mae looked unhappy, that possibly she was working too hard, and that she needed a little more praise for the work that she was doing in taking care of everyone. The mother-in-law expressed surprise over Mae's unhappiness and agreed that Mae was doing a fine job. Without directly confronting each other, the uncle and his younger sister understood the subtle messages each conveyed. Older brother was saying that something was wrong and younger sister acknowledged it. After this interaction, Mae reported that her mother-in-law's criticisms did noticeably diminish and that she had even begun to help Mae with the chores.

If Mae's therapist had not been sensitive to Mae's cultural beliefs about her role as a daughter-in-law and had suggested some of the solutions put forward by his colleagues in the case conference, Mae might even have dropped out of therapy. People from ethnic minority groups in the United States are much more likely than European Americans to drop out of psychosocial therapy (Snowden & Yamada, 2005). Because Mae's therapist was willing to work within the constraints of her cultural beliefs, he and Mae found a solution to her situation that was acceptable to her.

In treating children, cultural norms about childrearing practices and the proper role of doctors can make it difficult to include the family in a child's treatment. For example, in a study of behavior therapy for children, Hong Kong Chinese parents were very reluctant to be trained to engage in behavioral techniques, such as responding with praise or ignoring certain behaviors. Such techniques violated the parents' views of appropriate childrearing practices and their expectations that the therapist should be the person "curing" the child. However, several clinicians argue that family-based therapies are more appropriate than individual therapy in cultures that are highly family-oriented, including Native American, Hispanic, African American, and Asian American cultures (Miranda et al., 2005).

Jeannette Rosselló and Guillermo Bernal (2005) adapted both cognitive-behavioral therapy and interpersonal therapy to be more culturally sensitive in the treatment of depressed Puerto Rican adolescents. The Puerto Rican value of *familism,* a strong attachment to family, was incorporated into the therapy. Issues of the balance between dependence and independence were explicitly discussed in family groups. The adapted therapies proved effective in treating the adolescents' depression.

Must a therapist come from the same culture as the client to fully understand the client? A review of several studies suggests that ethnic matching is not an important predictor of how long clients remain in therapy or the outcomes of therapy (Maramba & Nagayama Hall, 2002). Cultural sensitivity probably can be acquired through training and experience (Castro et al., 2010). In fact, a therapist's being from the same ethnic or racial group as the client does not mean that therapist and client share the same value system (Teyber & McClure, 2000). For example, a fourth-generation Japanese American who has fully adopted American competitive and individualistic values may clash with a recent immigrant from Japan who subscribes to the self-sacrificing, community-oriented

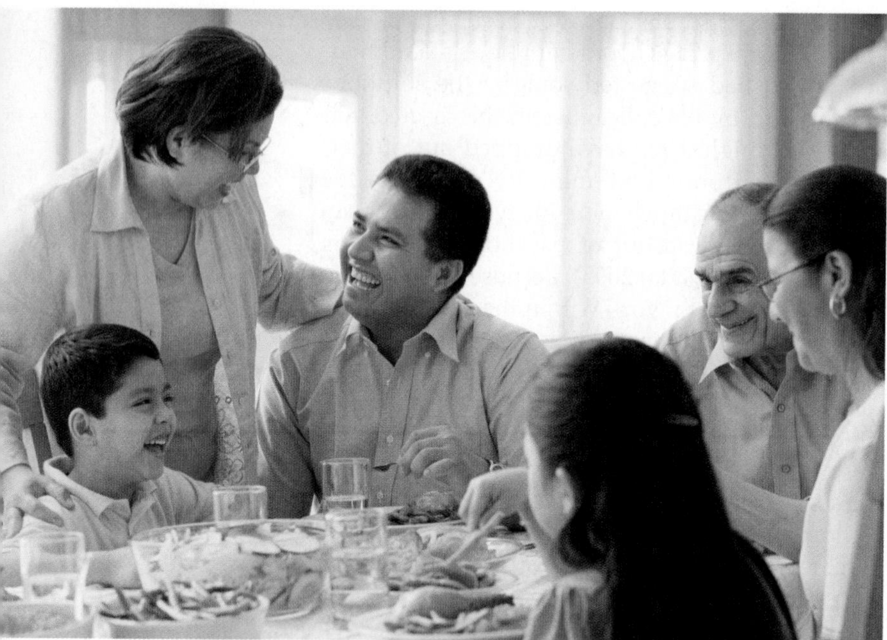

Therapy adapted for Puerto Rican families incorporated the values of familism.

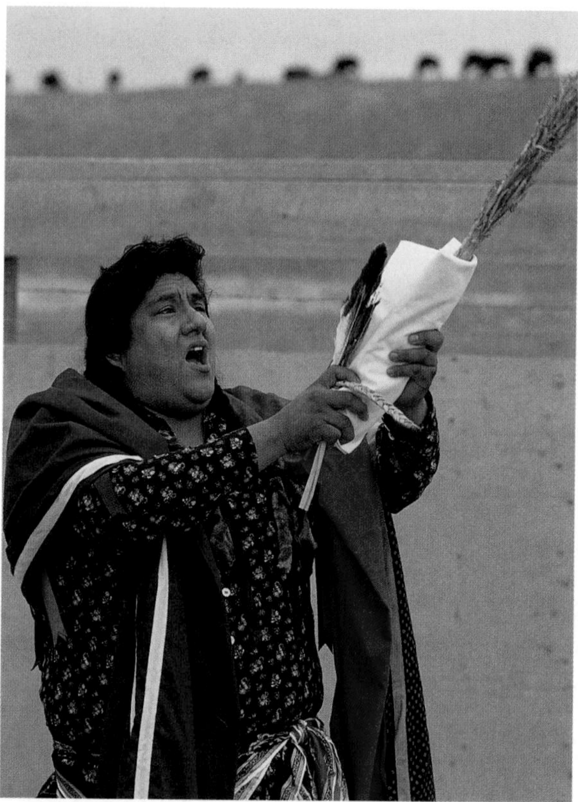

Several cultures have healing rituals that have been part of their cultural traditions for generations.

values of Japanese culture. These value differences among people of the same ethnic/racial group may explain why studies show that matching the ethnicity, race, or gender of the therapist and client does not necessarily lead to a better outcome for the client (Maramba & Nagayama Hall, 2002). On the other hand, the relationship between client and therapist and a client's beliefs about the likely effectiveness of a therapy contribute strongly to a client's full engagement in the therapy and its effectiveness.

However, the treatment outcome literature essentially has ignored the question of whether the effectiveness of treatments varies by cultural group or ethnicity (Miranda et al., 2005). An analysis conducted for the report of the Surgeon General (U.S. Department of Health and Human Services, 2001a) found that of 9,266 participants involved in the efficacy studies forming the major treatment guidelines for bipolar disorder, schizophrenia, depression, and attention-deficit/hyperactivity disorder, only 561 African Americans, 99 Americans of Latin descent, 11 Asian Americans/Pacific Islanders, and no Native Americans were included. Few of these studies could examine the impact of care on specific minorities. The need for more studies specifically examining cultural variation in the efficacy of psychotherapy is obvious.

As for gender, there is little evidence that women or men do better in therapy with a therapist of the same gender (Garfield, 1994; Huppert et al., 2001; Teyber & McClure, 2000). Women and men do tend to report that they prefer a therapist of the same gender, however (Garfield, 1994; Simons & Helms, 1976). Because the client's comfort with a therapist is an important contributor to a client's seeking therapy and continuing it for an entire course, gender matching may be important in therapy.

Culturally Specific Therapies

Our review of the relationships between culture or gender and therapy has focused on those forms of therapy most often practiced in modern, industrialized cultures, such as behavioral, cognitive, and psychodynamic therapies. Cultural groups, even within modern, industrialized countries, often have their own forms of therapy for distressed people, however (Hall, 2001; Koss-Chioino, 2000). Let us examine two of these.

Native American healing processes focus simultaneously on the physiology, psychology, and religious practices of the individual (LaFromboise, Trimble, & Mohatt, 1998). "Clients" are encouraged to transcend the self and experience the self as embedded in the community and as an expression of the community. Family and friends are brought together with the individual in traditional ceremonies involving prayers, songs, and dances emphasizing Native American cultural heritage and the reintegration of the individual into the cultural network. These ceremonies may be supplemented by a variety of herbal medicines used for hundreds of years to treat people with physical and psychological symptoms.

Hispanics in the southwestern United States and Mexico suffering from psychological problems may consult folk healers, known as *curanderos* or *curanderas* (Chevez, 2005; Koss-Chioino, 2000). Curanderos use religion-based rituals to overcome the folk illnesses believed to cause psychological and physical problems. The healing rituals include prayers and incantations. Curanderos also may apply healing ointments or oils and prescribe herbal medicines (Chevez, 2005; Koss-Chioino, 2000).

Native Americans and Hispanics often seek both folk healers and psychiatric care from mental health professionals who practice the therapies described in this chapter. Mental health professionals need to be aware of the practices and beliefs of folk healing when treating clients from these cultural groups, keeping in mind the possibility that clients will combine these different forms of therapy and follow some of the recommendations of both types of healers.

Assessing Sociocultural Approaches

The sociocultural approaches to abnormality argue that we should analyze the larger social and cultural forces that may be influencing people's behavior. It is not enough to look only at what is going on within individuals or their immediate surroundings. Sociocultural approaches are often credited for not "blaming the victim," as other theories seem to do by placing responsibility for psychopathology within the individual. The sociocultural approaches also raise our consciousness about our responsibility as a society to change the social conditions that put some individuals at risk for psychopathology. *Community psychology* and *social work* are two professions focused on empowering individuals to change their social conditions in order to help them improve their psychological well-being and quality of life.

The sociocultural structural theories can be criticized, however, for being vague about the exact ways social and cultural forces lead to psychological disturbance in individuals. Just how does social change or stress lead to depression, schizophrenia, and so on? Why does it lead to depression in some people but to drug abuse in others? Why do most people exposed to social stress and change develop no psychological disturbance at all?

TEST YOURSELF

What aspects of an individual's experience do sociocultural approaches consider key to understanding abnormality?

APPLY IT Which of the following is *true?*

a. Evidence indicates that a therapist's ethnicity and gender should match that of the client in order to provide maximum effectiveness of psychotherapy.
b. There is no evidence that social policies affect citizens' mental health.
c. Some psychological disorders appear to be specific to certain cultures.
d. Sociocultural theories explain why some individuals who encounter poverty or discrimination develop psychological problems while others do not.

Answers appear online at www.mhhe.com/nolen5e.

PREVENTION PROGRAMS

To prevent people from developing psychopathology in the first place would be better than waiting to treat it once it develops. Stopping the development of disorders before they start is called **primary prevention** (Muñoz et al., 2010). Some primary prevention strategies for reducing drug abuse and delinquency might include changing neighborhood characteristics that seem to contribute to drug use or delinquency.

Secondary prevention is focused on detecting a disorder at its earliest stages and thereby preventing the development of the full-blown disorder (Muñoz et al., 2010). Secondary prevention often involves screening for early signs of a disorder, for example, administering a questionnaire to detect mild symptoms of depression. Then an intervention might be administered to individuals with mild symptoms to prevent them from developing depressive disorders. Several studies have shown that administering a cognitive-behavioral intervention to individuals with mild depressive symptoms can significantly reduce their chances of developing depressive disorders (Cuijpers et al., 2008).

Tertiary prevention focuses on people who already have a disorder and on preventing relapse and reducing the impact of the disorder on the person's quality of life. As we will see in Chapter 8, programs that provide job-skills training and social support to people with schizophrenia can help prevent relapses into psychotic episodes (Liberman et al., 2002).

TEST YOURSELF

APPLY IT At many colleges, groups of women give presentations to other students about the dangers of eating disorders. The presenters talk about their personal experiences with eating disorders. Often these presentations are given to all the residents in a dormitory or a sorority. These programs represent efforts at which of the following?

a. primary prevention

b. secondary prevention

c. tertiary prevention

Answers appear online at www.mhhe.com/nolen5e.

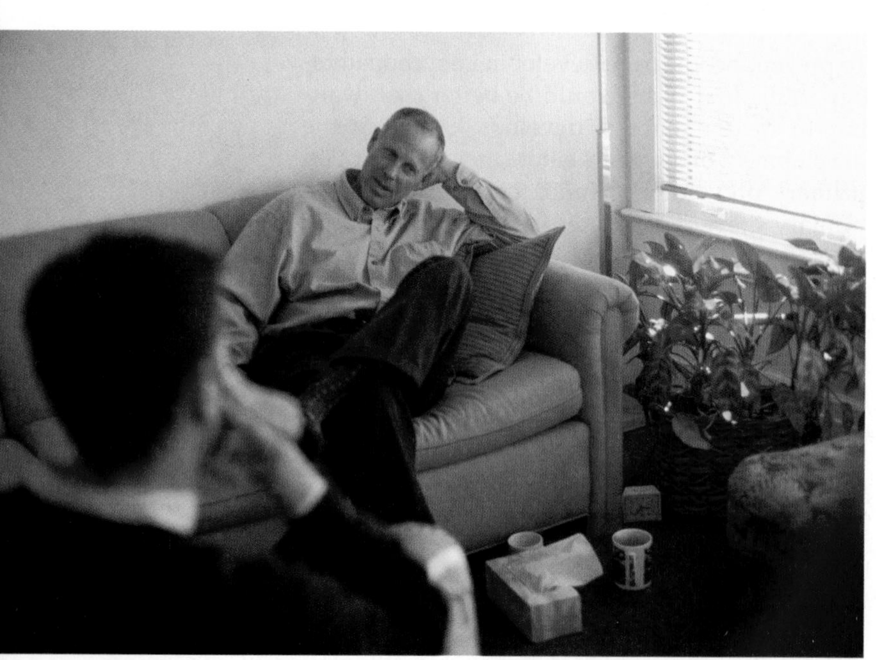

A positive relationship between therapist and client is important to successful treatment.

COMMON ELEMENTS IN EFFECTIVE TREATMENTS

On the surface, the different types of therapy described in this chapter may seem radically different. There is increasing evidence, however, that successful therapies share some common components, even when the specific techniques of the therapies differ greatly.

The first of these components is a *positive relationship* with the therapist (Norcross, 2002). Clients who trust their therapists and believe that the therapists understand them are more willing to reveal important information, engage in homework assignments, and try new skills or coping techniques suggested by the therapists. In addition, simply having a positive relationship with a caring and understanding human being helps people overcome distress and change their behaviors (Teyber & McClure, 2000).

Second, all therapies provide clients with an *explanation* or *interpretation* of why they are suffering (Ingram, Hayes, & Scott, 2000). Simply having a label for painful symptoms and an explanation for those symptoms seems to help many people feel better. In addition, the explanations that therapies provide for symptoms usually are accompanied by a set of recommendations for how to overcome those symptoms and following the recommendations may provide the main relief from the symptoms.

In any case, it seems clear that a client must believe the explanation given for the symptoms for the therapy to help (Frank, 1978). For example, studies of cognitive-behavioral therapy for depression have found that the extent to which clients believe and accept the rationale behind this therapy is a significant predictor of the effectiveness of the therapy (Fennell & Teasdale, 1987). Clients to whom the rationale behind cognitive therapy makes sense engage more actively in therapy and are less depressed after a course of therapy than are clients who don't accept the rationale for the therapy from the outset. A major problem in drug therapies is the high dropout rate. Often, people drop out either because they do not experience quick enough relief from the drugs and therefore believe the drugs will not work or because they feel they need to talk about problems to overcome them.

Third, most therapies encourage clients to *confront painful emotions* and use techniques for helping them become less sensitive to these emotions (Frank, 1978; Prochaska, 1995; Snyder, Ilardi, Michael, & Cheavens, 2000). In behavior therapy, systematic desensitization or flooding might be used. In psychodynamic therapy, clients are encouraged to express painful emotions and thoughts. Whatever technique is used, the goal is to help the client stop denying, avoiding, or repressing the painful emotions and become able to accept, experience, and express the emotions without being debilitated by them.

TEST YOURSELF

APPLY IT If you were designing a new form of psychotherapy, you would want to be sure to include all the following elements *except* which?

a. an explanation for the client's symptoms
b. a positive therapist-client relationship
c. examination of the client's upbringing
d. strategies to help the client confront painful emotions

Answers appear online at www.mhhe.com/nolen5e.

FIGURE 2.12 **How Some Biological, Psychological, and Social Factors Might Interact to Cause Depression.**

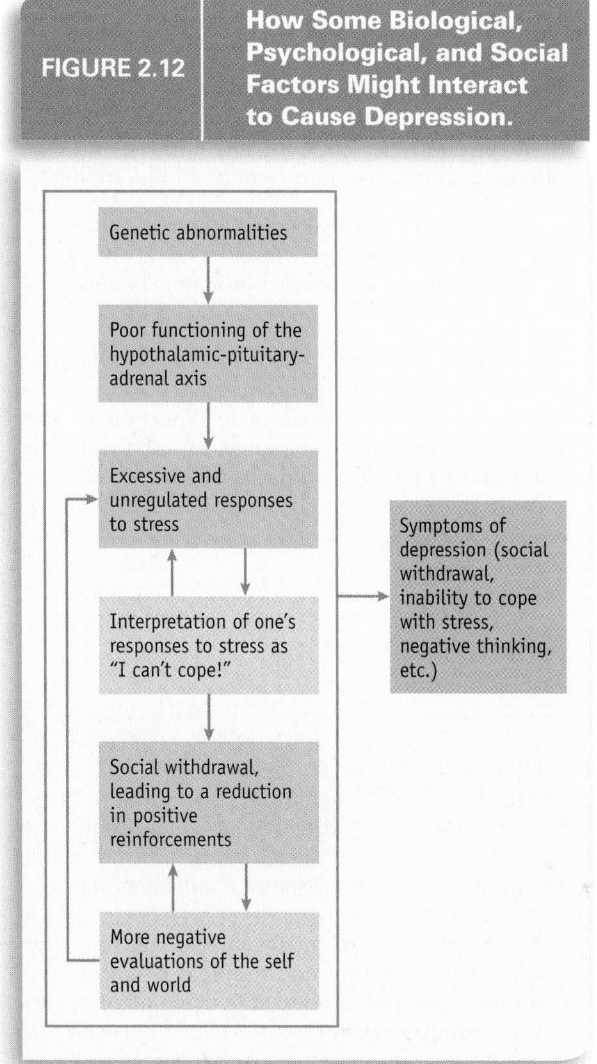

CHAPTER INTEGRATION

As we noted at the beginning of this chapter, many scientists believe that only models that *integrate* biological, psychological, and social factors can provide comprehensive explanations of psychological disorders. Only integrated models can explain why many people with disordered genes or deficiencies in neurotransmitters do *not* develop painful emotional symptoms or bizarre thoughts. Similarly, only integrated models can suggest how traumatic experiences and toxic interpersonal relationships can cause changes in the basic biochemistry of the brain, which then cause changes in a person's emotions, thoughts, and behaviors.

Figure 2.12 illustrates how some of the biological, psychological, and social factors discussed in this chapter might come together to contribute to symptoms of depression, for example. First, some people's genetic characteristics lead to poor functioning of the hypothalamic-pituitary-adrenal axis. Chronic arousal of this axis may lead individuals to be overly responsive to stress. If they tend to interpret their reactions to stress in terms of "I can't cope!" they may develop a negative thinking style. This negative thinking style can then cause them to withdraw socially, leading to a reduction in positive reinforcements. This in turn could feed negative evaluations of themselves and of the world, further contributing to depression. Then, when they are confronted with new stressors, they might not have good strategies for coping with them and might overreact psychologically as well as physiologically. All these processes come together to produce the key symptoms of depression—social withdrawal, an inability to cope with stress, negative thinking, and so on.

SHADES OF GRAY DISCUSSION (review p. 52)

A humanistic therapist would provide a reflection that attempts to accurately restate what the student said and the emotions she expressed, without suggesting any interpretation of her feelings:

> **Reflection:** "It's really frustrating to screw up and kill your chances; and it feels like it's something in you that's making that happen again and again."

A psychodynamic therapist might infer that the student's expressed concerns reflect unconscious conflicts about success. When he or she feels there is enough evidence, an interpretation such as the following might be offered:

> **A psychodynamic interpretation:** "It sounds like every time you get close to success you unconsciously sabotage yourself. Perhaps success means something to you that is troubling or uncomfortable, and you are not aware of what that is."

The psychodynamic interpretation might be true, but the client-centered therapist would view it as inappropriate because it brings to the client's attention something that is not currently in the client's awareness (adapted from Bohart, 1995, p. 101).

THINK CRITICALLY

Read the following case study about Anika. Then explain the causes of her symptoms according to three different approaches: the biological approach, at least one of the psychological approaches, and the sociocultural approach. (*Discussion appears on p. 517 at the back of this book.*)

Anika was born to a 16-year-old mother who was addicted to alcohol and multiple illegal drugs. While Anika's mother tried to stop using alcohol and drugs after Anika was born, the addiction proved too powerful. She lost custody of Anika because of her continued substance abuse and her neglect and abuse of her daughter. While her mother returned to the streets, Anika went from foster home to foster home. Some of the families were loving people who did their best to calm Anika during her frequent temper tantrums, while other families became abusive when she acted out.

Anika did very poorly in school. She was always daydreaming and seldom did any of her homework, finding it impossible to concentrate long enough to read and retain material. On top of that, Anika was constantly in trouble for being aggressive toward other students or skipping classes to smoke cigarettes with some of the other students.

When Anika reached puberty, she became self-destructive, sometimes cutting herself with razors and twice attempting to kill herself. She was forced to see therapists, and she told them that she was "no good" and "defective" and that she wanted to die.

CHAPTER SUMMARY

- Biological theories of psychopathology typically attribute symptoms to structural abnormalities in the brain, disordered biochemistry, or faulty genes.
- Structural abnormalities in the brain can be caused by faulty genes, by disease, or by injury. Which particular area of the brain is damaged influences the symptoms individuals show.
- Many biological theories attribute psychopathology to imbalances in neurotransmitters or to the functioning of receptors for neurotransmitters.
- Genetic theories of abnormality usually suggest that it takes an accumulation of faulty genes to cause a psychopathology.
- Genes can influence the environments people choose, which then influence the expression of genetic tendencies. Epigenetics is the study of how environmental conditions can influence the expression of genes.
- Biological therapies most often involve drugs intended to regulate the functioning of the brain neurotransmitters associated with a

psychological disorder or to compensate for structural brain abnormalities or the effects of genetics.

- Antipsychotic medications help reduce unreal perceptual experiences, unreal beliefs, and other symptoms of psychosis. Antidepressant drugs help reduce symptoms of depression. Lithium and anticonvulsants help reduce mania. Barbiturates and benzodiazepines help reduce anxiety.
- Electroconvulsive therapy is used to treat severe depression. Various new methods are being developed to stimulate the brain without using electricity. Psychosurgery is used in rare circumstances.
- The behavioral theories of abnormality reject notions of unconscious conflicts and focus only on the rewards and punishments in the environment that shape and maintain behavior.
- Classical conditioning takes place when a previously neutral stimulus is paired with a stimulus that naturally creates a certain response; eventually, the neutral stimulus also will elicit the response.
- Operant conditioning involves rewarding desired behaviors and punishing undesired behaviors.
- People also learn by imitating the behaviors modeled by others and by observing the rewards and punishments others receive for their behaviors.
- Behavior therapies focus on changing specific maladaptive behaviors and emotions by changing the reinforcements for them.
- Cognitive theories suggest that people's cognitions (e.g., attributions for events, global assumptions) influence the behaviors and emotions with which they react to situations.
- Cognitive therapies focus on changing the way a client thinks about important situations.
- Psychodynamic theories of psychopathology focus on unconscious conflicts that cause anxiety in the individual and result in maladaptive behavior. Freud argued that these conflicts arise when the libidinal impulses of the id clash with the constraints on behavior imposed by the ego and superego.
- People use various types of defense mechanisms to handle their internal conflicts. How caregivers handle children's transitions through the psychosexual stages determines the concerns or issues the children may become fixated on.
- More recent psychodynamic theorists focus less on the role of unconscious impulses and more on the development of the individual's self-concept in the context of interpersonal relationships. They see a greater role for the environment in shaping personality and have more hope for change during adulthood than Freud had.
- Psychodynamic therapy focuses on unconscious conflicts that lead to maladaptive behaviors and emotions. Interpersonal therapies are based on psychodynamic theories but focus more on current relationships and concerns.
- Humanistic theories suggest that all humans strive to fulfill their potential for good and to self-actualize. The inability to fulfill one's potential arises from the pressures of society to conform to others' expectations and values.
- Humanistic therapies seek to help a client realize his or her potential for self-actualization.
- Sociocultural theories suggest that socioeconomic stress, discrimination, and social upheaval can lead to mental health problems in individuals. Cultures also have implicit and explicit rules regarding the types of abnormal behavior they permit.
- Some clients may wish to work with therapists of the same culture or gender, but it is unclear whether matching therapist and client in terms of culture and gender is necessary for therapy to be effective. It is important that therapists be sensitive to the influences of culture and gender on a client's attitudes toward therapy and toward various solutions to problems.
- Prevention programs focus on preventing disorders before they develop, retarding the development of disorders in their early stages, and reducing the impact of disorders on people's functioning.
- Common components of effective therapy seem to be a good therapist-client relationship, an explanation for symptoms, and the confrontation and expression of negative emotions.

KEY TERMS

theory 27
biological approach 27
psychological approaches 27
sociocultural approach 27
biopsychosocial approach 28
diathesis-stress models 28
cerebral cortex 31
thalamus 32

Chapter 3

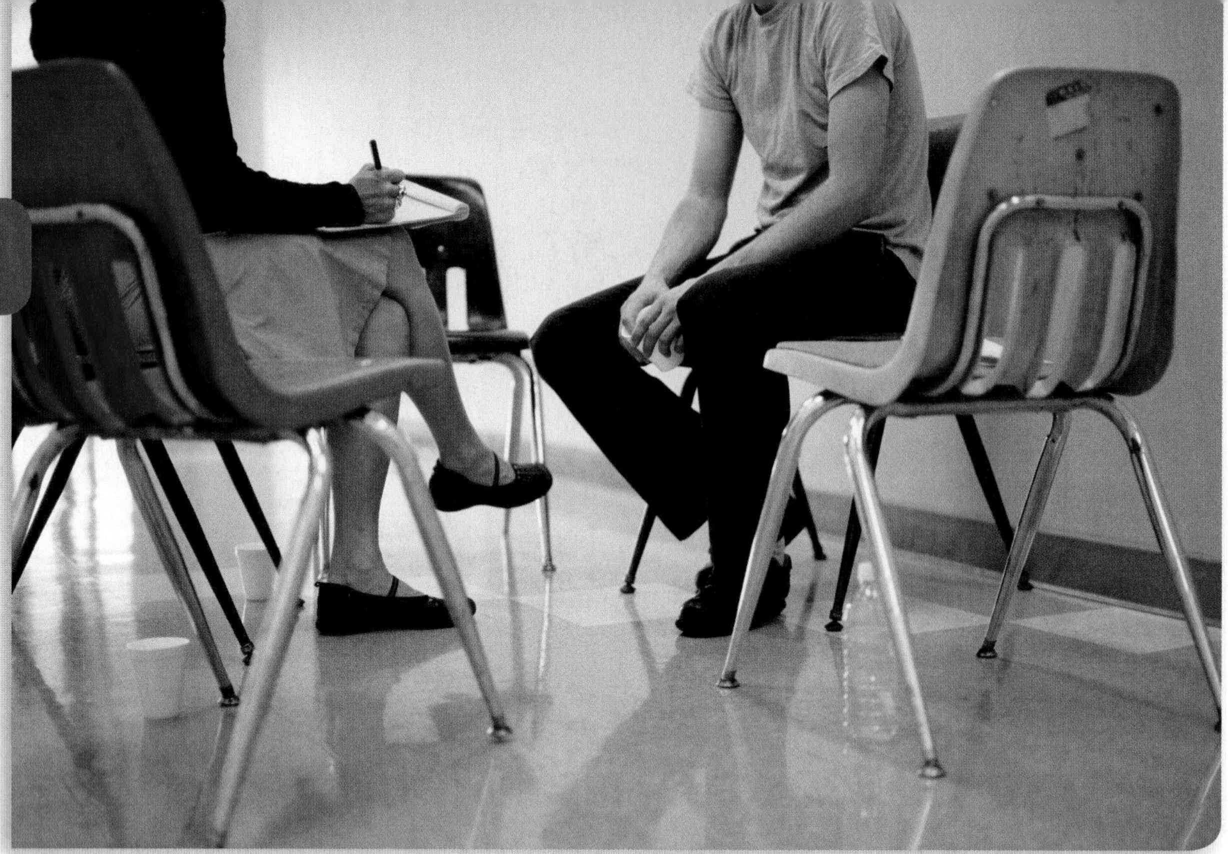

Assessing and Diagnosing Abnormality

CHAPTER OUTLINE

Extraordinary People

Marya Hornbacher, *Madness*

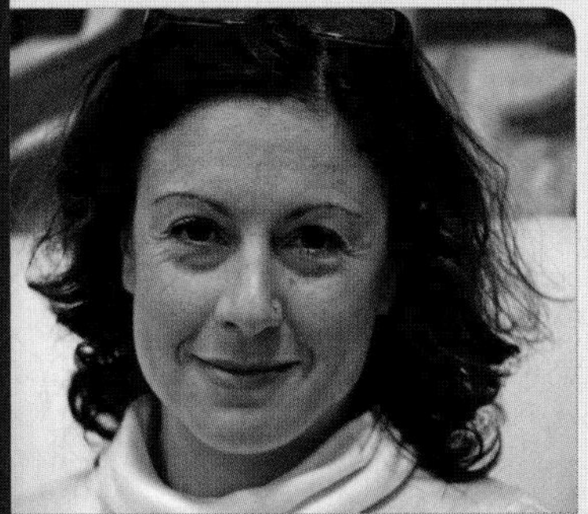

By her late twenties, Marya Hornbacher appeared to be an amazing success story. She had published her first book, *Wasted,* a few years before, to much acclaim. The book was heralded as an eloquent account of her many years with severe eating disorders, and Hornbacher was sought after for speaking engagements and readings across the United States and Europe. Apparently cured of her disorders, she served as a living testament both to the horrors of bulimia and anorexia nervosa and to a young woman's ability to recover from these disorders.

But those who knew her had doubts that she was well, as she recounts in her book *Madness* (2008). She was drinking, which was nothing new for her. But the volume and ferocity of her drinking surprised everyone around her. Even though she is a petite woman, it took a dozen glasses of wine or hard-liquor drinks to even give her a buzz. Marya seemed to have boundless energy and was bouncing off the walls much of the time—that is, except when she went crashing down into depression and retreated to her bed for days on end. Hoping to gain some control over her life, she resorted to controlling her eating again and began to lose weight rapidly.

Marya Hornbacher presents a puzzling picture. She shows signs of alcohol abuse, mood swings, and a lingering eating disorder. Why did these symptoms emerge after she had apparently recovered from her eating disorder and achieved success as a writer? Which of these problems is a cause of the other symptoms, and which is a consequence? How would we go about diagnosing her problems? The assessment and diagnosis of symptoms is the focus of this chapter.

Assessment is the process of gathering information about people's symptoms and the possible causes of these symptoms. The information gathered in an assessment is used to determine the appropriate diagnosis for a person's problems. A **diagnosis** is a label for a set of symptoms that often occur together. Marya Hornbacher's symptoms qualify for several diagnoses we will discuss in later chapters, including eating disorders, substance use disorders, and bipolar disorder.

In this chapter, we discuss the modern tools of assessment and how they are used to diagnose psychological symptoms and to help us understand and treat psychological problems. Some of these tools are very new, while others have been around for many years. These tools provide information on the individual's personality characteristics, cognitive deficits (such as learning disabilities or problems in maintaining attention), emotional well-being, and biological functioning.

We also consider modern systems of diagnosing psychological problems. A standardized system of diagnosis is crucial to communication among mental health professionals and to research into psychological problems. We must agree on what we mean when we use a diagnostic label. A standardized diagnostic system provides agreed-on definitions of disorders.

ASSESSMENT TOOLS

A number of assessment tools have been developed to help clinicians gather information. All assessment tools must be valid, reliable, and standardized. We first discuss these important concepts and then look at specific types of assessment tools.

Validity

If you administer a test to determine a person's behaviors and feelings, you want to be sure that the test is an accurate measure. The *accuracy* of a test in assessing what it is supposed to measure is called its **validity.** The best way to determine the validity of a test is to see if the results of the test yield the same information as an objective and accurate indicator of what the test is supposed to measure. For example, if there were a blood test that definitively proved whether a person had a particular psychological disorder, you would want any other test for that disorder (such as a questionnaire) to yield the same results when administered to the person.

So far there are no definitive blood tests, brain scans, or other objective tests for any of the psychological disorders we discuss in this book. Fortunately, the validity of a test can be estimated

FIGURE 3.1 **Types of Validity for a Questionnaire or Test.** There are a number of types of validity.

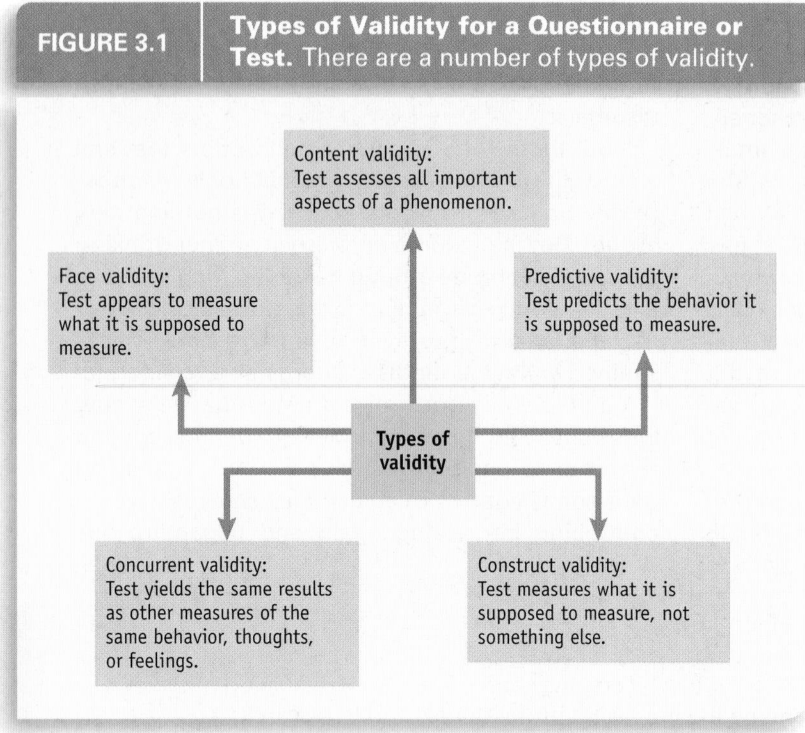
Content validity:
Test assesses all important aspects of a phenomenon.
Face validity:
Test appears to measure what it is supposed to measure.
Predictive validity:
Test predicts the behavior it is supposed to measure.
Types of validity
Concurrent validity:
Test yields the same results as other measures of the same behavior, thoughts, or feelings.
Construct validity:
Test measures what it is supposed to measure, not something else.

FIGURE 3.2 **Types of Reliability for a Questionnaire or Test.** Reliability can be determined in several ways.

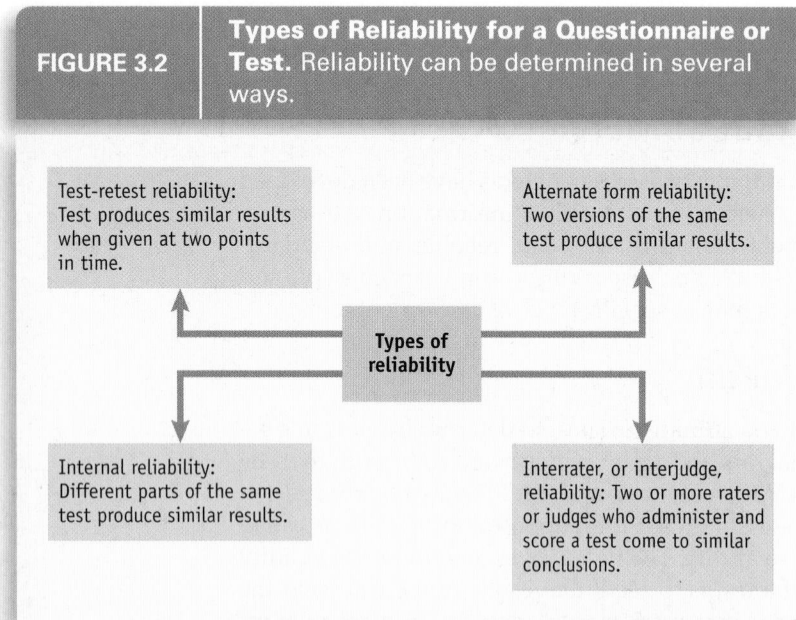
Test-retest reliability:
Test produces similar results when given at two points in time.
Alternate form reliability:
Two versions of the same test produce similar results.
Types of reliability
Internal reliability:
Different parts of the same test produce similar results.
Interrater, or interjudge, reliability: Two or more raters or judges who administer and score a test come to similar conclusions.

in a number of other ways (Figure 3.1). A test is said to have *face validity* when, on face value, the items seem to measure what the test is intended to measure. For example, a questionnaire for anxiety that asks "Do you feel jittery much of the time?" and "Do you worry about many things?" has face validity because it seems to assess symptoms of anxiety. If it also meets other standards of validity, researchers are more likely to trust its results.

Content validity is the extent to which a test assesses all the important aspects of a phenomenon that it purports to measure. For example, if a measure of anxiety asked only about physical symptoms (nervousness, restlessness, stomach distress, rapid heartbeat) and not cognitive symptoms (apprehensions about the future, anticipation of negative events), then we might question whether it is a good measure of anxiety.

Concurrent validity is the extent to which a test yields the same results as other, established measures of the same behavior, thoughts, or feelings. A person's score on a new anxiety questionnaire should bear some relation to information gathered from the person's answers to an established anxiety questionnaire.

A test has *predictive validity* if it is good at predicting how a person will think, act, or feel in the future. An anxiety measure has good predictive validity if it correctly predicts which people will behave in anxious ways when confronted with stressors in the future and which people will not.

Construct validity is the extent to which a test measures what it is supposed to measure and not something else altogether (Cronbach & Meehl, 1955). Consider the construct validity of multiple-choice exams in school. They are supposed to measure a student's knowledge and understanding of content. However, they may also measure the student's ability to take multiple-choice tests—to determine the instructor's intent in asking each question and to recognize any tricks and obviously incorrect answer choices.

Reliability

It is important that a test provide consistent information about a person. The **reliability** of a test indicates its *consistency* in measuring what it is supposed to measure. As with validity, there are several types of reliability (Figure 3.2). *Test-retest reliability* describes how consistent the results of a test are over time. If a test supposedly measures an enduring characteristic of a person, then the person's scores on that test should be similar when he or she takes the test at two different points in time. For example, if an anxiety questionnaire is supposed to measure people's general tendencies to be anxious, then their scores should be similar if they complete the questionnaire once this week and then again next week. On the other hand, if an anxiety questionnaire is a measure of people's current symptoms of anxiety (asking questions such as "Do you feel jittery right now?"), then we might expect low test-retest reliability on

Assessment and Diagnosis Along the Continuum

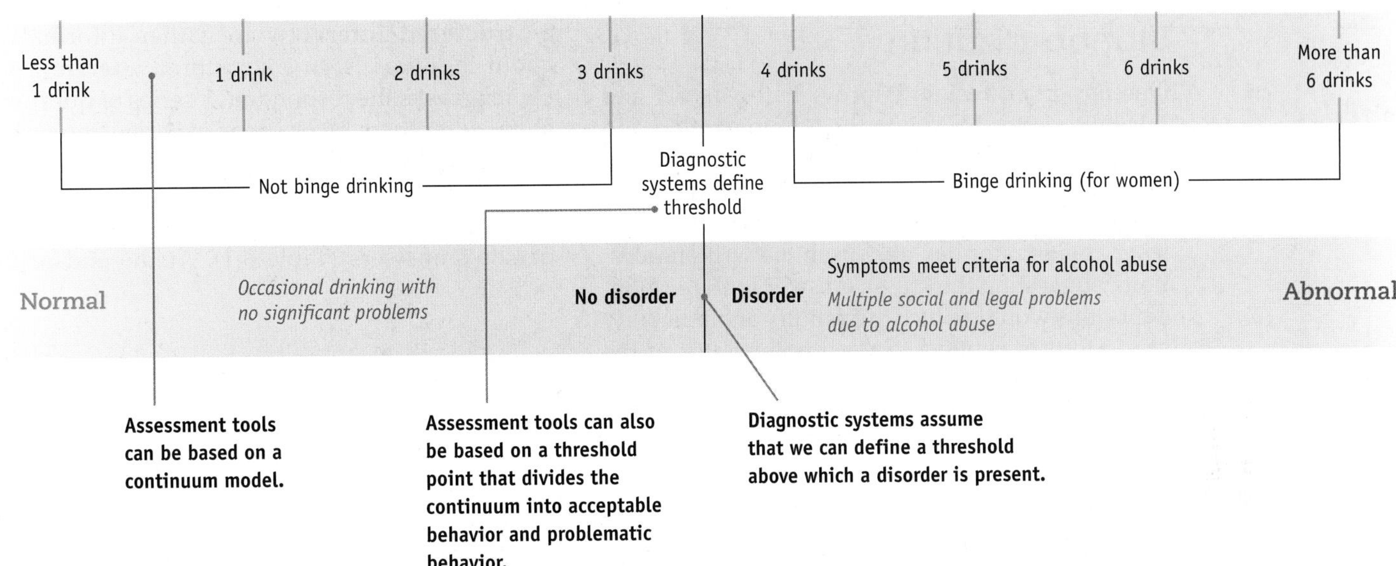

When you drink alcohol, how many drinks do you normally have in one 2-hour period?
Less than 1 drink
1 drink
2 drinks
3 drinks
4 drinks
5 drinks
6 drinks
More than 6 drinks
Not binge drinking
Diagnostic systems define threshold
Binge drinking (for women)
Normal
Occasional drinking with no significant problems
No disorder
Disorder
Symptoms meet criteria for alcohol abuse
Multiple social and legal problems due to alcohol abuse
Abnormal
Assessment tools can be based on a continuum model.
Assessment tools can also be based on a threshold point that divides the continuum into acceptable behavior and problematic behavior.
Diagnostic systems assume that we can define a threshold above which a disorder is present.

As a student, you have taken a variety of tests intended to assess your learning in different subjects. Similarly, mental health professionals use different tests or tools to assess mental health. Some assessment tools described in this chapter are based on the assumption that behaviors or feelings lie along a continuum—the task is to determine where an individual's experiences fall along that continuum. For example, a questionnaire that asked Marya Hornbacher about her drinking behavior might have several options indicating different levels of drinking. Other tools, however, are more like true/false tests: They are based on the assumption that there is a threshold for the behaviors they are assessing, and either people have these behaviors or they do not. For example, some researchers set the threshold for an alcohol "binge" for women at four drinks (Chapter 14); Marya Hornbacher's drinking clearly falls above that threshold, and thus she would be considered a binge drinker, whereas a woman having three drinks would not be considered a binge drinker.

Currently, diagnostic systems use a threshold—a specific cutoff point—to determine whether a person has a disorder; therefore, they seem to oppose a continuum model. Increasingly, researchers and clinicians are building a continuum perspective into the diagnostic process. The forthcoming revision to the manual used to diagnose psychological problems (the *DSM*), which we will discuss in this chapter, is expected to incorporate a continuum approach in several diagnoses, particularly in the personality disorders (Chapter 9). For most disorders, however, diagnostic systems set criteria for when a person's behaviors and feelings cross the line into a disorder, even though there is no purely scientific way to draw that line.

this measure. Typically, measures of general and enduring characteristics should have higher test-retest reliability than measures of transient characteristics.

When people take the same test a second time, they may try to give the same answers so as to seem consistent. For this reason, researchers often will develop two or more forms of a test. When people's answers to different forms of a test are similar, the tests are said to have *alternate form reliability.* Similarly, a researcher may split a test into two or more parts to determine whether people's answers to one part of a test are similar to their answers to another part. When there is similarity in people's answers among different parts of the same test, the test is said to have high *internal reliability.*

Finally, many of the tests we examine in this chapter are interviews or observational measures that require a clinician or researcher to make judgments about the people being assessed. These tests should have high *interrater,* or *interjudge, reliability.*

That is, different raters or judges who administer and score the interview or test should come to similar conclusions when they are evaluating the same people.

Standardization

One important way to improve both validity and reliability is to *standardize* the administration and interpretation of tests. A standard method of administering a test prevents extraneous factors from affecting a person's response. For example, if the test administrator deviated from the written questions, suggesting the "right" answer to the respondents, this would reduce the validity and reliability of the test. In contrast, if the administrator of the test only read aloud the specific questions on the test, this would increase the validity and reliability of the test. Similarly, a standard way of interpreting results (e.g., scores above a certain cutoff are considered severe) makes the interpretation of the test more valid and reliable. Thus, standardization of both the administration and the interpretation of tests is important to their validity and reliability.

With these concepts in mind, let's explore some commonly used assessment tools.

Clinical Interview

Much of the information for an assessment is gathered in an initial interview. This interview may include a mental status exam, which assesses the person's general functioning. In the mental status exam, the clinician probes for five types of information. First is the individual's *appearance and behavior.* Is he or she dressed neatly and well groomed? Or does he or she appear disheveled? The ability to care for one's basic grooming indicates how well one is functioning generally. Also, the clinician will note if the individual seems to be moving particularly slowly, which may indicate depression, or seems agitated.

Second, in a mental status exam a clinician will take note of the individual's *thought processes,* including how coherently and quickly he or she speaks. Third, the clinician will be concerned with the individual's *mood and affect*. Does he or she appear down and depressed, or perhaps elated? Is the affect appropriate to the situation or inappropriate? For example, the individual may seem to laugh excessively at his own jokes, which may indicate nervousness or an inability to relate well to others. Fourth, the clinician will observe the individual's *intellectual functioning,* that is, how well the person speaks and any indications of memory or attention difficulties. Fifth, the clinician will note whether the individual seems appropriately *oriented* to place, time, and person; that is, does the individual understand where he or she is, what day and time it is, and who he or she is, as well as who the clinician is.

Increasingly, clinicians and researchers use a **structured interview** to gather information about individuals. In a structured interview, the clinician asks the respondent a series of questions about symptoms he or she is experiencing or has experienced in the past. The format of the questions and the entire interview is standardized, and the clinician uses concrete criteria to score the person's answers (Table 3.1). At the end of the

TABLE 3.1 Sample Structured Interview

ANXIETY DISORDERS

Panic Disorder Questions

Have you ever had a panic attack, when you *suddenly* felt frightened, anxious, or extremely uncomfortable?

If Yes: Tell me about it. When does that happen? (Have you ever had one that just seemed to come out of the blue?) IF PANIC ATTACKS IN EXPECTED SITUATIONS: Did you ever have one of these attacks when you weren't in (EXPECTED SITUATION)?

Have you ever had four attacks like that in a four-week period?

If No: Did you worry a lot about having another one? (How long did you worry?)

When was the last bad one (EXPECTED OR UNEXPECTED)?

Now I am going to ask you about that attack. What was the first thing you noticed? Then what?

During the attack . . .

. . . were you short of breath? (have trouble catching your breath?)

. . . did you feel dizzy, unsteady, or as if you might faint?

. . . did your heart race, pound, or skip?

. . . did you tremble or shake?

. . . did you sweat?

. . . did you feel as if you were choking?

. . . did you have nausea, upset stomach, or the feeling that you were going to have diarrhea?

. . . did things around you seem unreal or did you feel detached from things around you or detached from part of your body?

Source: Data from First, Spitzer, Gibbon, & Williams, 1997.

interview, the clinician should be able to determine whether the respondent's symptoms qualify for a diagnosis of any major psychological problems.

Symptom Questionnaires

Often, when clinicians or researchers want a quick way to determine a person's symptoms, they will ask the person to complete a **symptom questionnaire.** These questionnaires can cover a wide variety of symptoms representing several different disorders. Other questionnaires focus on the symptoms of specific disorders.

One of the most common questionnaires used to assess symptoms of depression is the *Beck Depression Inventory,* or *BDI* (Beck & Beck, 1972). The most recent form of the BDI has 21 items, each of which describes four levels of a given symptom of depression (Table 3.2). The respondent is asked to indicate which description best fits how he or she has been feeling in the past week. The items are scored to indicate the level of depressive symptoms the person is experiencing. Cutoff scores have been established to indicate moderate and severe levels of depressive symptoms.

Critics of the BDI have argued that it does not clearly differentiate between the clinical syndrome of depression and the general distress that may be related to an anxiety disorder or to several other disorders (see Kendall et al., 1987). The BDI also cannot indicate whether the respondent would qualify for a diagnosis of depression. But because the BDI is extremely quick and easy to administer and has good test-retest reliability, it is widely used, especially in research on depression.

Clinicians treating depressed people also use the BDI to monitor those individuals' symptom levels from week to week. An individual may be asked to complete the BDI at the beginning of each therapy session, and both the individual and the clinician then have a concrete indicator of any changes in symptoms.

TABLE 3.2 Sample Items from the Beck Depression Inventory®—Second Edition (BDI®—II)

UNHAPPINESS	
0	I do not feel unhappy.
1	I feel unhappy.
2	I am unhappy.
3	I am so unhappy that I can't stand it.
CHANGES IN ACTIVITY LEVEL	
0	I have not experienced any change in activity level.
1a	I am somewhat more active than usual.
1b	I am somewhat less active than usual.
2a	I am a lot more active than usual.
2b	I am a lot less active than usual.
3a	I am not active most of the day.
3b	I am active all of the day.

Source: Simulated Items similar to those in the Beck Depression Inventory-II (BDI-II).

Information concerning the BDI®—II is available from:
Pearson
Attn: Customer Service
19500 Bulverde Road
San Antonio, TX 78259
Phone: (800) 627-7271
Fax: (800) 232-1223
Website: www.pearsonassessments.com
E-mail: ClinicalCustomerSupport@Pearson.com

Personality Inventories

Personality inventories usually are questionnaires meant to assess people's typical ways of thinking, feeling, and behaving. These inventories are used as part of an assessment procedure to obtain information on people's well-being, self-concept, attitudes and beliefs, ways of coping, perceptions of their environment and social resources, and vulnerabilities.

The most widely used personality inventory in professional clinical assessments is the *Minnesota Multiphasic Personality Inventory (MMPI),* which has been translated into more than 150 languages and used in more than 50 countries (Groth-Marnat, 2003). The original MMPI was first published in 1945 and contained 550 items. In 1989, an updated version published under the name MMPI-2 contained 567 items. Both versions of the MMPI present respondents with sentences describing moral and social attitudes, behaviors, psychological states, and physical conditions and ask them to respond "true," "false," or "can't say" to each sentence. Here are some examples of items from the MMPI:

> I would rather win than lose in a game.
>
> I am never happier than when alone.
>
> My hardest battles are with myself.
>
> I wish I were not bothered by thoughts about sex.

TABLE 3.3 Clinical and Validity Scales of the Original MMPI

The MMPI is one of the most widely used questionnaires for assessing people's symptoms and personalities. It also includes scales to assess whether respondents are lying or trying to obfuscate their answers.

CLINICAL SCALES		
Scale Number	**Scale Name**	**What It Measures**
Scale 1	Hypochondriasis	Excessive somatic concern and physical complaints
Scale 2	Depression	Symptomatic depression
Scale 3	Hysteria	Hysterical personality features and tendency to develop physical symptoms under stress
Scale 4	Psychopathic deviate	Antisocial tendencies
Scale 5	Masculinity-femininity	Sex-role conflict
Scale 6	Paranoia	Suspicious, paranoid thinking
Scale 7	Psychasthenia	Anxiety and obsessive behavior
Scale 8	Schizophrenia	Bizarre thoughts and disordered affect
Scale 9	Hypomania	Behavior found in mania
Scale 0	Social introversion	Social anxiety, withdrawal, overcontrol
VALIDITY SCALES		
	Scale Name	**What It Measures**
	Cannot say scale	Total number of unanswered items
	Lie scale	Tendency to present favorable image
	Infrequency scale	Tendency to falsely claim psychological problems
	Defensiveness scale	Tendency to see oneself in unrealistically positive manner

Source: *Minnesota Multiphasic Personality Inventory (MMPI).* Copyright © 1942, 1943, 1951, 1967 (renewed 1970), 1983. Reprinted by permission of the University of Minnesota. "MMPI" and "Minnesota Multiphasic Personality Inventory" are trademarks owned by the University of Minnesota.

I am afraid of losing my mind.

When I get bored, I like to stir up some excitement.

People often disappoint me.

The MMPI was developed *empirically,* meaning that a large group of possible items was given to psychologically "healthy" people and to people with various psychological problems. Then the items that reliably differentiated among groups of people were included in the inventory.

The items on the original MMPI are clustered into 10 scales that measure different types of psychological characteristics or problems, such as paranoia, anxiety, and social introversion. Another 4 scales have been added to the MMPI-2 to assess vulnerability to eating disorders, substance abuse, and poor functioning at work. A respondent's scores on each scale are compared with scores from the normal population, and a profile of the respondent's personality and psychological problems is derived. Also, 4 validity scales determine whether the person responds honestly to the items on the scale or distorts his or her answers in a way that might invalidate the test (Table 3.3). For example, the Lie scale measures the respondent's tendency to respond to items in a socially desirable way in order to appear unusually positive or good.

Because the items on the MMPI were chosen for their ability to differentiate people with specific types of psychological problems from people without psychological problems, the concurrent validity of the MMPI scales was "built in" during their development. The MMPI may be especially useful as a general screening device for detecting people who are functioning very poorly psychologically. The test-retest reliability of the MMPI has also proven to be high (Dorfman & Leonard, 2001).

Many criticisms have been raised about the use of the MMPI in culturally diverse samples (Groth-Marnat, 2003). The norms for the original MMPI—the scores that were considered "healthy" scores—were based on samples of people in the United States who were not representative of people from a wide range of ethnic and racial backgrounds, age groups, and social classes. In response to this problem, the publishers of the MMPI established new norms based on more representative samples of eight communities across the United States. Still, there are concerns that the MMPI norms do not reflect variations across cultures in what is considered normal or abnormal. In addition, the linguistic accuracy of the translated versions of the MMPI and the comparability of these versions to the English version have been questioned (Dana, 1998).

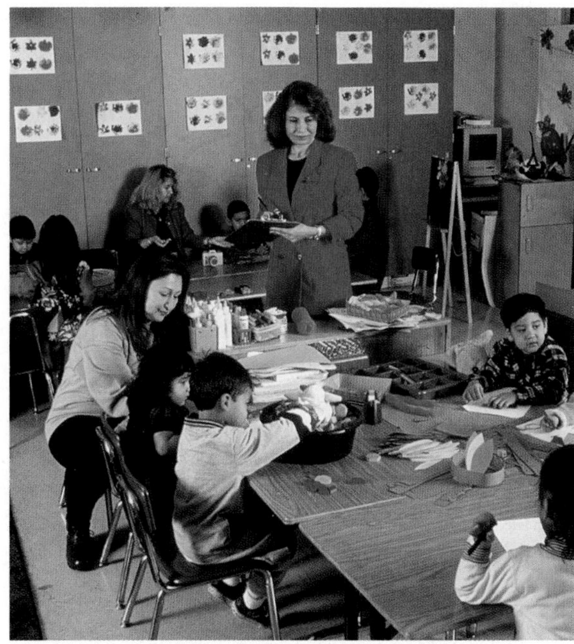

Behavioral observation is a good way to gather data.

Behavioral Observation and Self-Monitoring

Clinicians will often use **behavioral observation** of individuals to assess deficits in their skills or ways of handling situations. The clinician will look for specific behaviors and what precedes and follows these behaviors. For example, a clinician might watch a child interact with other children to determine what situations provoke the child to act aggressively. The clinician can then use information from the behavioral observation to help the individual learn new skills, stop negative habits, and understand and change the way he or she reacts to certain situations. A couple seeking marital therapy might be asked to discuss with each other a topic on which they disagree. The clinician would observe this interaction, noting the specific ways the couple handles conflict. For example, one member of the couple may lapse into statements that blame the other member for problems in their marriage, escalating conflict to the boiling point.

Direct behavioral observation has the advantage of not relying on individuals' reporting and interpretation of their own behaviors. Instead, the clinician sees how the individuals handle important situations. One disadvantage is that individuals may alter their behavior when they are being watched. Another disadvantage is that different observers may draw different conclusions about individuals' skills; that is, direct behavioral observations may have low interrater reliability, especially without a standard means of making the observations. In addition, any individual rater may miss the details of an interpersonal interaction. For example, two raters watching a child play with others on a playground may focus on different aspects of the child's behaviors or be distracted by the chaos of the playground. For these reasons, when behavioral observation is used in research settings, the situations are highly standardized and observers watch for a set list of behaviors. Finally, direct observation may not be possible in some situations. In that case, a clinician may have a client role-play a situation, such as his or her interactions with an employer.

If direct observation or role playing is not possible, clinicians may require **self-monitoring** by individuals—that is, keeping track of the number of times per day they engage in a specific behavior (e.g., smoking a cigarette) and the conditions under which this behavior happens. Following is an example (adapted from Thorpe & Olson, 1997, p. 149):

> Steve, a binge drinker, was asked to self-monitor his drinking behavior for two weeks, noting the situational context of urges to drink and his associated thoughts and feelings. These data revealed that Steve's drinking was completely confined to bar situations, where he drank in the company of friends. Gaining relief from stress was a recurring theme.

Self-monitoring is open to biases in what individuals notice about their behavior and are willing to report. However, individuals can discover the triggers of unwanted behaviors through self-monitoring, which in turn can lead them to change these behaviors.

Intelligence Tests

In clinical practice, **intelligence tests** are used to get a sense of an individual's intellectual strengths and weaknesses, particularly when mental retardation or brain damage is suspected (Ryan & Lopez, 2001). Intelligence tests are also used in schools to identify "gifted" children and children with intellectual difficulties. They are used in occupational settings and the military to evaluate adults' capabilities for certain jobs or types of service. Some examples of these tests are the *Wechsler Adult Intelligence Scale*, the *Stanford-Binet Intelligence Test*, and the *Wechsler Intelligence Scale for Children*.

These tests were designed to measure basic intellectual abilities, such as the ability for abstract reasoning, verbal fluency, and spatial memory. The term *IQ* is used to describe a method of comparing an individual's score on an intelligence test with the performance of individuals of the same age group. An IQ score of 100 means that the person performed similarly to the average performance of other people the same age.

Intelligence tests are controversial in part because there is little consensus as to what is meant by intelligence (Sternberg, 2004). The most widely used intelligence tests assess verbal and analytical abilities but do not assess other talents or skills, such as artistic and musical ability. Some psychologists argue that success in life is as strongly influenced by social skills and other talents not measured by intelligence tests as it is by verbal and analytical skills (Gardner, 2003; Sternberg, 2004).

Another important criticism of intelligence tests is that they are biased in favor of middle- and upper-class, educated European Americans because these people have more familiarity with the kinds of reasoning assessed on the tests (Sternberg, 2004). In addition, educated European Americans may be more comfortable taking intelligence tests because testers often are also European Americans and the testing situation resembles testing situations in their educational experience. In contrast, different cultures within the United States and in other countries may emphasize forms of reasoning other than those assessed on intelligence tests, and members of these cultures may not be comfortable with the testing situations of intelligence tests.

A "culture-fair" test would have to include items that are equally applicable to all groups or that are different for each culture but psychologically equivalent for the groups being tested. Attempts have been made to develop culture-fair tests, but the results have been disappointing. Even if a universal test were created, it would be difficult to make statements about intelligence in different cultures because different nations and cultures vary in the emphasis they place on "intellectual achievement."

FIGURE 3.3 **The Bender-Gestalt Test.** On the left are the figures as presented to the clients. On the right are the figures as copied by a child with a brain tumor that is creating perceptual-motor difficulties.

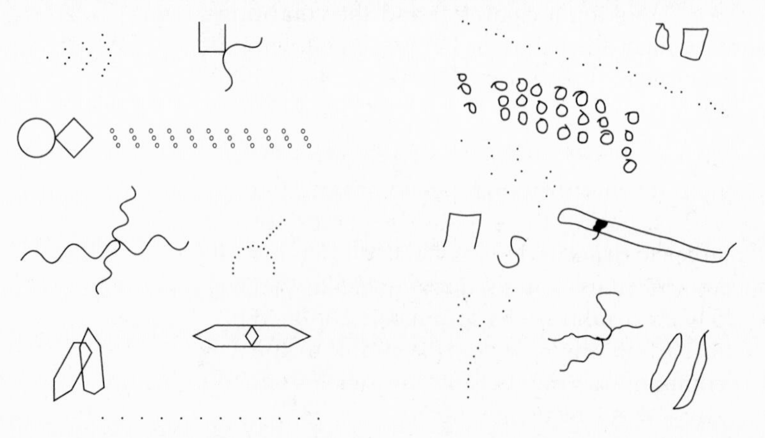

Neuropsychological Tests

If the clinician suspects neurological impairment in a person, paper-and-pencil **neuropsychological tests** may be useful in detecting specific cognitive deficits such as a memory problem, as occurs in dementia (Golden & Freshwater, 2001). One frequently used neuropsychological test is the Bender-Gestalt Test (Bender, 1938). This test assesses individuals' sensorimotor skills by having them reproduce a set of nine drawings (Figure 3.3). People with brain damage may rotate or change parts of the drawings or be unable to reproduce the drawings. When asked to remember the drawings after a delay, they may show significant memory deficits. The Bender-Gestalt Test appears to be good at differentiating people with brain damage from those without brain damage, but it does not reliably identify the specific type of brain damage a person has (Groth-Marnat, 2003).

More extensive batteries of tests have been developed to pinpoint types of brain damage. Two of the most popular batteries are the Halstead-Reitan Test (Reitan & Davidson, 1974) and the Luria-Nebraska Test (Luria, 1973). These batteries contain several tests that provide specific information about an individual's functioning in several skill areas, such as concentration, dexterity, and speed of comprehension.

Brain-Imaging Techniques

Increasingly, neuropsychological tests are being used with brain-imaging techniques to identify specific deficits and possible brain abnormalities. Clinicians use brain imaging to determine if a patient has a brain injury or tumor. Researchers use brain imaging to search for differences in brain activity or structure between people with a psychological disorder and people with no disorder. Ideally, this research will tell us enough about the biology of psychological disorders that we can develop valid and reliable biological tests for these disorders in the future.

Indeed, both technology and our understanding of the biology of disorders are advancing so rapidly that major breakthroughs in biological techniques for assessing and diagnosing psychological disorders are likely in the near future. Let us review existing brain-imaging technologies and what they can tell us now.

Computerized tomography (CT) is an enhancement of X-ray procedures. In CT, narrow X-ray beams are passed through the person's head in a single plane from a variety of angles. The amount of radiation absorbed by each beam is measured, and from these measurements a computer program constructs an image of a slice of the brain. By taking many such images, the computer can construct a three-dimensional image showing the brain's major structures. A CT scan can reveal brain injury, tumors, and structural abnormalities. The two major limitations of CT technology are that it exposes patients to X-rays, which can be harmful, and it provides an image of brain structure rather than brain activity.

Positron-emission tomography (PET) can provide a picture of activity in the brain. PET requires injecting the patient with a harmless radioactive isotope, such as fluorodeoxyglucose (FDG). This substance travels through the blood to the brain. The parts of the brain that are active need the glucose in FDG for nutrition, so FDG accumulates in active parts of the brain. Subatomic particles in FDG called *positrons* are emitted as the isotope decays. These positrons collide with electrons, and both are annihilated and converted to two photons traveling away from each other in opposite directions. The PET scanner detects these photons and the point at which they are annihilated and constructs an image of the brain, showing those areas that are most active. PET scans can be used to show differences in the activity level of specific areas of the brain between people with a psychological disorder and people without a disorder.

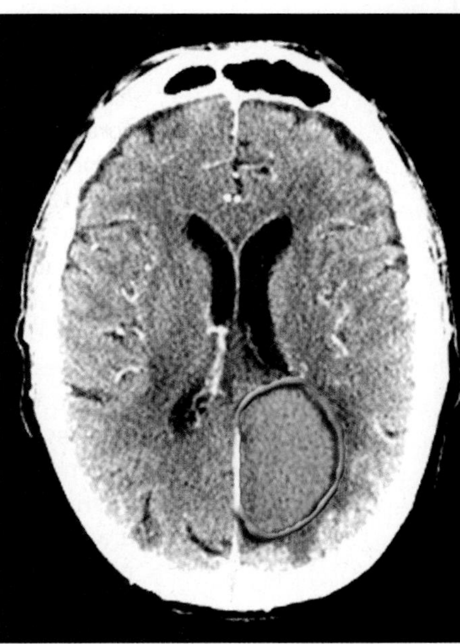

CT scans can detect structural abnormalities such as brain tumors.

Another procedure to assess brain activity is **single photon emission computed tomography,** or **SPECT.** The procedures of SPECT are much like those used in PET except that a different tracer substance is injected. It is less accurate than PET but also less expensive.

Magnetic resonance imaging (MRI) has several advantages over CT, PET, and SPECT technology. It does not require exposing the patient to any radiation or injecting radioisotopes, so it can be used repeatedly for the same individual. It provides much more finely detailed pictures of the anatomy of the brain than do other technologies, and it can image the brain at any angle. Structural MRI provides static images of brain structure. Functional MRI (fMRI) provides images of brain activity.

MRI involves creating a magnetic field around the brain that causes realignment of hydrogen atoms in the brain. When the magnetic field is turned off and on, the hydrogen atoms change position, causing them to emit magnetic signals. These signals are read by a computer, which reconstructs a three-dimensional image of the brain. To assess activity in the brain, many images are taken only milliseconds apart, showing how the brain changes from one moment to the next or in response to some stimulus. Researchers are using MRI to study structural and functional brain abnormalities in almost every psychological disorder.

Psychophysiological Tests

Psychophysiological tests are alternative methods to CT, PET, SPECT, and MRI used to detect changes in the brain and nervous system that reflect emotional and psychological changes. An **electroencephalogram (EEG)** measures electrical activity along the scalp produced by the firing of specific neurons in the brain. EEG is used most often to detect seizure activity in the brain and can also be used to detect tumors and stroke. When EEG patterns over brief periods (such as ½ second) are recorded in response to specific stimuli, such as the individual viewing an emotional picture, the EEG patterns are referred to as *evoked potentials* or *event-related potentials*. Clinicians can compare an individual's response to the standard response of healthy individuals.

Heart rate and respiration are highly responsive to stress and can be easily monitored. Sweat gland activity, known as *electrodermal response* (formerly called *galvanic skin response*), can be assessed with a device that detects electrical conductivity between two points on the skin. This can reflect emotional arousal.

Psychophysiological measures are used to assess people's emotional response to specific types of stimuli, such as response to war scenes in a veteran with post-traumatic stress disorder. Unfortunately, such tests can be difficult to administer, resulting in low validity and reliability. They are less direct measures of brain activity than are the neuroimaging methods.

Projective Tests

A **projective test** is based on the assumption that when people are presented with an ambiguous stimulus, such as an oddly shaped inkblot or a captionless picture, they will interpret the stimulus in line with their current concerns and feelings, their relationships with others, and conflicts or desires. People are thought to project these issues onto their description of the "content" of the stimulus, hence the name *projective tests*. Proponents of these tests argue that they are useful in uncovering the unconscious issues or motives of a person or in cases when the person is resistant or heavily biasing the information he or she presents to the assessor. Two of the most frequently used projective tests are the Rorschach Inkblot Test and the Thematic Apperception Test (TAT).

"Rorschach! What's to become of you?"
ScienceCartoonsPlus.com

The *Rorschach Inkblot Test,* commonly referred to simply as the *Rorschach,* was developed in 1921 by Swiss psychiatrist Hermann Rorschach. The test consists of 10 cards, each containing a symmetrical inkblot in black, gray, and white or in color. The examiner tells the respondent something like "People may see many different things in these inkblot pictures; now tell me what you see, what it makes you think of, what it means to you" (Exner, 1993). Clinicians are interested in both the content and the style of the individual's responses to the inkblot. In the content of responses, they look for particular themes or concerns, such as frequent mention of aggression or fear of abandonment. Important stylistic features may include the person's tendency to focus on small details of the inkblot rather than the inkblot as a whole or hesitation in responding to certain inkblots (Exner, 1993).

The *Thematic Apperception Test (TAT)* consists of a series of pictures. The individual is asked to make up a story about what is happening in the pictures (Murray, 1943). Proponents of the TAT argue that people's stories reflect their concerns and wishes as well as their personality traits and motives. As with the Rorschach, clinicians are interested in both the content and the style of people's responses to the TAT cards. Some cards may stimulate more emotional responses than others or no response at all. These cards are considered to tap the individuals' most important concerns.

Clinicians operating from psychodynamic perspectives value projective tests as tools for assessing the underlying conflicts and concerns that individuals cannot or will not report directly. Clinicians operating from other perspectives question the usefulness of these tests. The validity and reliability of all the projective tests have not proven strong in research (Groth-Marnat, 2003). In addition, because these tests rely so greatly on subjective interpretations by clinicians, they are open to a number of biases. Finally, the criteria for interpreting the tests do not take into account the individual's cultural background (Dana, 2001).

TEST YOURSELF

What do the terms *validity* and *reliability* mean in assessment? List and define the different types of validity and reliability presented in this chapter.

APPLY IT You are a clinical psychologist assessing a client. Which of the following assessment tools might you hesitate to use because they suffer from low reliability and validity?

a. structured clinical interviews
b. symptom questionnaires
c. projective tests
d. personality inventories
e. behavioral observation and self-monitoring

Answers appear online at www.mhhe.com/nolen5e.

CHALLENGES IN ASSESSMENT

Some challenges that arise in assessing people's problems include people's inability to provide information or resistance to providing information. In addition, special challenges arise when evaluating children and people from cultures different from that of the assessor.

Resistance and Inability to Provide Information

One of the greatest challenges to obtaining valid information from an individual can be his or her *resistance* to providing information. Sometimes, the person does not want to be assessed or treated, for example, when a teenager is forced to see a psychologist because of parental concern about his behavior. The teenager may be resistant to providing any information. Because much of the information a clinician needs must come directly from the person being assessed, resistance can be a formidable problem.

Even when a person is not completely resistant to being assessed, he or she may have a strong interest in the outcome of the assessment and thus may be highly selective in the information he or she provides, may bias his or her presentation of the information, or may even lie to the assessor. Such problems often arise when assessments are being done as part of a legal case, for example, when parents are fighting for custody of their children in a divorce. Each parent will want to present him- or herself in the best light and also may negatively bias his or her reports on the other parent when speaking to psychologists who have been appointed to assess each parent's fitness for custody of the children.

Evaluating Children

Consider the following conversation between a mother and her 5-year-old son, Jonathon, who was sent home from preschool for fighting with another child.

Mom: Jonathon, why did you hit that boy?

Jonathon: I dunno. I just did.

Mom: But I want to understand what happened. Did he do something that made you mad?

Jonathon: Yeah, I guess.

Mom: What did he do? Did he hit you?

Jonathon: Yeah.

Mom: Why did he hit you?

Jonathon: I dunno. He just did. Can I go now?

Mom: I need to know more about what happened.

Jonathon: [Silence]

Mom: Can you tell me more about what happened?

Jonathon: No. He just hit me and I just hit him. Can I go now?

Anyone who has tried to have a conversation with a distressed child about why he or she misbehaved has some sense of how difficult it can be to engage a child in a discussion about emotions or behaviors. Even when a child talks readily, his or her understanding of the causes of his or her behaviors or emotions may not be very well developed. Children, particularly preschool-age children, cannot describe their feelings or associated events as easily as adults can. Young children may not differentiate among different types of emotions, often just saying that they feel "bad," for example (Harter, 1983). When distressed, children may talk about physical aches and pains rather than the emotional pain they are feeling. Or a child might show distress only in nonverbal behavior, such as making a sad face, withdrawing, or behaving aggressively.

These problems with children's self-reporting of emotional and behavioral concerns have led clinicians and researchers to rely on other people, usually adults in the children's lives, to provide information about children's functioning. Parents are often the first source of information about a child's functioning. A clinician may interview a child's parents when the child is taken for treatment, asking the parents about changes in the child's behavior and corresponding events in the child's life. A researcher studying children's functioning may ask parents to complete questionnaires assessing the children's behavior in a variety of settings.

Because parents typically spend more time with their child than any other person does, they potentially have the most complete information about the child's functioning and a sense of how the child's behavior has or has not changed over time. Unfortunately, however, parents are not always accurate in their assessments of their children's functioning. One study found that parents and children disagreed as to what problems had brought the child to a psychiatric clinic in 63 percent of cases (Yeh & Weisz, 2001). Parents' perceptions of their children's well-being can be influenced by their own symptoms of psychopathology and their expectations for their children's behavior (Nock & Kazdin, 2001). Indeed, sometimes parents take children for assessment and treatment of psychological problems as a way of seeking treatment for themselves.

Parents also may be the source of a child's psychological problems and, as a result, may be unwilling to acknowledge or seek help for the child's problems. The most extreme example is parents who are physically or sexually abusive. Such parents are unlikely to acknowledge the psychological or physical harm they are causing the child or to seek treatment for the child.

Cultural norms for children's behaviors differ, and parents' expectations for their children and their tolerance of deviant behavior in children are affected by these norms. For example, Jamaican parents appear to be more tolerant than American parents of unusual behaviors in children, including both aggressive behavior and behavior indicating shyness and inhibition. In turn, Jamaican parents have a higher threshold than American parents in terms of the appropriate time to take a child to a clinician (Lambert et al., 1992).

Teachers also provide information about children's functioning. Teachers and other school personnel (such as guidance counselors and coaches) are often the first to recognize that a child has a problem and to initiate an intervention to address the problem. Teachers' assessments of children, however, are often different from the assessments made by other adults, including parents and trained clinicians (Weisz, Donenberg, Han, & Kauneckis, 1995). Such discrepancies may arise because these other adults are providing invalid assessments of the children whereas the teachers are providing valid assessments. The discrepancies may also arise because children function differently in different settings. At home, a child may be well behaved, quiet, and withdrawn, while at school the same child may be impulsive, easily angered, and distractible.

Cultural differences between clients and clinicians can lead to misinterpretations of clients' problems.

Evaluating Individuals Across Cultures

A number of challenges to assessment arise when there are significant cultural differences between the assessor and the person being assessed (Dana, 2000; Tsai, Butcher, Muñoz, & Vitousek, 2001; Tseng, 2001). Imagine having to obtain all the information needed to evaluate someone from a culture very different from your own. The first problem you may run into is that the person may not speak your language or may speak it only partially (and you may not speak his or hers at all). Symptoms can be both underdiagnosed and overdiagnosed when the individual and the assessor do not share a language (Okazaki & Sue, 2003). Overdiagnosis may occur when an individual tries to describe symptoms in the assessor's language but the assessor interprets the individual's slow and confused description of symptoms as indicating more pathology than is really present. Underdiagnosis may occur when the individual cannot articulate complex emotions or strange perceptual experiences in the assessor's language and thus does not even try to do so.

One solution is to find an interpreter to translate between the clinician and the person. While interpreters can be invaluable to good communication, those who are not trained assessors themselves can misunderstand and mistranslate a clinician's questions and the person's answers, as in the following example (Marcos, 1979, p. 173).

Clinician to Spanish-speaking patient: Do you feel sad or blue? Do you feel that life is not worthwhile sometimes?

Interpreter to patient: The doctor wants to know if you feel sad and if you like your life.

Patient's response: No, yes, I know that my children need me, I cannot give up, I prefer not to think about it.

Interpreter to clinician: She says no, she says that she loves her children and that her children need her.

In this case, the interpreter did not accurately reflect the person's answer to the clinician's question, giving the clinician a sense that the person was doing better than the person reported she was. In addition, different people from the same country can speak different dialects of a language or may have different means of expressing feelings and attitudes. Mistranslation can occur when the interpreter does not speak the particular dialect spoken by the individual or comes from a different subculture.

Cultural biases can arise when everyone supposedly is speaking the same language but comes from a unique cultural background. There is evidence that African Americans in the United States are overdiagnosed as having symptoms of schizophrenia (Neighbors, Trierweiler, Ford, & Muroff, 2003). Some investigators believe that cultural differences in the presentation of symptoms play a role (Neighbors, 1984). African Americans may present more intense symptoms than European Americans, and these symptoms then are misunderstood by European American assessors as representing more severe psychopathology. Some European American assessors may be too quick to diagnose psychopathology in African Americans because of negative stereotypes.

Even when clinicians avoid all these biases, they are still left with the fact that people from other cultures often think and talk about their psychological symptoms differently than do members of the clinician's culture. We discuss examples of cultural differences in the presentation of symptoms throughout this book. One of the most pervasive differences is in whether cultures experience and report psychological distress in emotional or somatic (physical) symptoms. European Americans tend to view the body and mind separately, whereas many other cultures do not make sharp distinctions between the experiences of the body and those of the mind (Okazaki & Sue, 2003). Following a psychologically distressing event, European Americans tend to report that they feel anxious or sad, but members of many other cultures tend to report having physical aches and maladies. To conduct an accurate assessment, clinicians must be aware of cultural differences in the manifestation of disorders and in the presentation of symptoms, and they must use this information correctly in interpreting the symptoms individuals report. Cultural differences are further complicated by the fact that not every member of a culture conforms to what is known about that culture's norms. Within every culture, people differ in their acceptance of cultural norms for behavior.

TEST YOURSELF

1. What are some important challenges in assessing adults?
2. What are some challenges specific to assessing children? What role do parents and teachers play in assessing children?

APPLY IT A man who speaks only Laotian comes to a mental health clinic in obvious distress. Which of the following is a common barrier to a clinician's accurately determining what is upsetting this man?

a. language differences
b. translators misinterpreting what the man is saying
c. the man's description of culture-specific symptoms, such as believing that spirits are upsetting him
d. all of the above

Answers appear online at www.mhhe.com/nolen5e.

DIAGNOSIS

Recall that a *diagnosis* is a label we attach to a set of symptoms that tend to occur together. This set of symptoms is called a **syndrome.** In biological models of psychological disorders, a syndrome is thought to be the observable manifestation of an underlying biological disorder. Thus, if you have the symptoms that make up the syndrome *schizophrenia,* you are thought also to have a biological disorder called schizophrenia. As we have noted, however, there are no definitive biological tests for psychological disorders. For this reason, it is impossible to verify whether a given person *has* schizophrenia by conducting a biological test.

We are left to observe humans and identify syndromes based on frequently co-occurring symptoms—no easy task. Typically, several symptoms make up a syndrome, but people differ in which of these symptoms they experience most strongly. The last time you were in a sad or depressed mood, did you also feel tired and have trouble sleeping? Do you feel tired and have trouble sleeping every time you are in a sad or depressed mood, or just sometimes? Does everyone you know also experience fatigue and sleeplessness when in a sad mood? Or do some of them instead lose their appetite and their ability to concentrate?

Syndromes are not lists of symptoms that all people have all the time if they have any of the

FIGURE 3.4 **Syndromes as Clusters of Symptoms.** Syndromes are clusters of symptoms that frequently co-occur. The symptoms of one syndrome, such as major depressive disorder, can overlap the symptoms of another syndrome, such as generalized anxiety disorder.

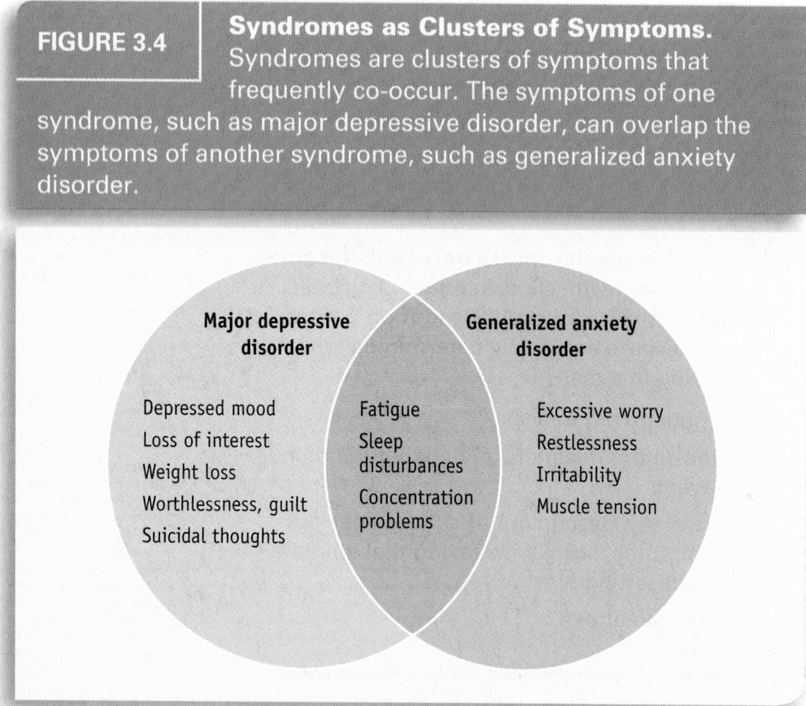

symptoms at all. Rather, they are lists of symptoms that tend to co-occur within individuals. The symptoms of one syndrome may overlap those of another. Figure 3.4 shows the overlap in the symptoms that make up two common psychological disorders: *major depressive disorder* (see Chapter 7) and *generalized anxiety disorder* (see Chapter 5). The two disorders both include symptoms of fatigue, sleep disturbances, and concentration problems. However, each disorder has symptoms that are more specific to it.

For centuries, people have tried to organize the confusing array of psychological symptoms into a limited set of syndromes. This set of syndromes and the rules for determining whether an individual's symptoms are part of one of these syndromes constitute a **classification system.**

One of the first classification systems for psychological symptoms was proposed by Hippocrates in the fourth century BCE. Hippocrates divided all mental disorders into mania (states of abnormal excitement), melancholia (states of abnormal depression), paranoia, and epilepsy. In 1883, Emil Kraepelin published the first modern classification system, which is the basis of our current systems. These systems divide the world of psychological symptoms into a much larger number of syndromes than did Hippocrates. Let us focus on the classification system most widely used in the United States, the ***Diagnostic and Statistical Manual of Mental Disorders,*** or **DSM.** The classification system used in Europe and much of the rest of the world, the *International Classification of Disease,* or ICD-10, shares many similarities with the most recent editions of the *DSM.*

Diagnostic and Statistical Manual of Mental Disorders (*DSM*)

For more than 50 years, the official manual for diagnosing psychological disorders in the United States has been the *Diagnostic and Statistical Manual of Mental Disorders* of the American Psychiatric Association. The first edition of the *DSM,* published in 1952, outlined the diagnostic criteria for all the mental disorders recognized by the psychiatric community at the time. These criteria were somewhat vague descriptions heavily influenced by psychoanalytic theory. For example, the diagnosis of *anxiety neurosis* could have been manifested in a great variety of behaviors and emotions. The key to the diagnosis was whether the clinician inferred that unconscious conflicts were causing the individual to experience anxiety. The second edition of the *DSM* (*DSM-II*), published in 1968, included some new disorders that had been recognized since the publication of the first edition but otherwise was not much different.

Because the descriptions of disorders in the first and second editions of the *DSM* were so abstract and theoretically based, the reliability of the diagnoses was low. For example, one study found that four experienced clinicians using the first edition of the *DSM* to diagnose 153 patients agreed on their diagnoses only 54 percent of the time (Beck et al., 1962). This low reliability eventually led psychiatrists and psychologists to call for a radically new system of diagnosing mental disorders.

DSM-III, DSM-IV, and *DSM-5*

In response to the reliability problems of the first and second editions of the *DSM,* in 1980 the American Psychiatric Association published the third edition of the *DSM,* known as *DSM-III.* This third edition was followed in 1987 by a revised third edition, known as *DSM-IIIR,* and in 1994 by a fourth edition, known as *DSM-IV,* revised as *DSM-IV-TR* in 2000. TR stands for *text revision.* Based on new research, this version of *DSM-IV* included minor changes to the criteria for diagnoses as well as revised descriptions of the behaviors and symptoms associated with disorders. In 2013, the newest edition of the *DSM, DSM-5,* is due to be released. This new edition will remove some diagnoses that are in the *DSM-IV-TR,* add a few new diagnoses, and

TABLE 3.4 *DSM-IV-TR* Diagnostic Criteria for Panic Disorder

These are the *DSM-IV-TR* criteria for a diagnosis of panic disorder. They specify core symptoms that must be present and several other symptoms, a certain number of which must be present, for the diagnosis.

A. At some time during the disturbance, one or more panic attacks have occurred that were (1) unexpected, and (2) not triggered by situations in which the person was the focus of another's attention.

B. Either four attacks, as defined in criterion A, have occurred within a four-week period, or one or more attacks have been followed by a period of at least a month of persistent fear of having another attack.

C. At least four of the following symptoms developed during at least one of the attacks:

1. Shortness of breath or smothering sensations
2. Dizziness, unsteady feelings, or faintness
3. Palpitations or accelerated heart rate
4. Trembling or shaking
5. Sweating
6. Choking
7. Nausea or abdominal distress
8. Depersonalization or derealization
9. Numbness or tingling sensations
10. Flushes or chills
11. Chest pain or discomfort
12. Fear of dying
13. Fear of going crazy or doing something uncontrolled

D. During at least some of the attacks, at least four of the C symptoms developed suddenly and increased in intensity within 10 minutes of the beginning of the first C symptom.

E. It cannot be established that an organic factor initiated the disturbance, such as caffeine intoxication.

Source: Reprinted with permission from the *Diagnostic and Statistical Manual of Mental Disorders,* Fourth Edition, Text Revision.

modify the criteria for others. Throughout this book, we will highlight the changes in the *DSM-IV-TR* criteria likely to appear in the *DSM-5* (for full descriptions of these likely changes, see American Psychiatric Association, 2010).

In these newer editions of the *DSM,* the developers replaced the vague descriptions of disorders with specific and concrete criteria for each disorder. These criteria are in the form of behaviors people must show or experiences or feelings they must report in order to be given a diagnosis. The developers tried to be as atheoretical and descriptive as possible in listing the criteria for each disorder. A good example is the diagnostic criteria for panic disorder in the *DSM-IV-TR,* which are given in Table 3.4. A person must have 4 of 13 possible symptoms as well as meet other criteria in order to be diagnosed with panic disorder. These criteria reflect the fact that not all the symptoms of panic disorder are present in every individual.

Two other elements distinguish the *DSM-III, DSM-IIIR, DSM-IV, DSM-IV-TR,* and *DSM-5* from their predecessors. First, the later editions specify how long a person must show symptoms of the disorder in order to be given the diagnosis (see Table 3.4, item B). Second, the criteria for most disorders require that symptoms interfere with occupational or social functioning. This emphasis on symptoms that are long-lasting and severe reflects the consensus among psychiatrists and psychologists that abnormality should be defined in terms of the impact of behaviors on the individual's ability to function and on his or her sense of well-being (see Chapter 1). While the *DSM* attempts to precisely define the threshold between

SHADES OF GRAY

As you read the following case study, compare Brett's symptoms to the criteria in Table 3.4.

When Brett went to an appointment with his physician, he looked pale and visibly nervous. He told his doctor that twice in the past month he had an episode in which his heart suddenly started racing, he felt short of breath and cold all over, and he trembled uncontrollably. He was sure, when these feelings were happening, that he was dying of a heart attack. The symptoms lasted about 10 minutes and then subsided. His doctor asked Brett where he was when these symptoms began. Brett said the first time he felt this way was when he was about to give a presentation in an important class. The second time was when he was on his way to meet his parents for dinner.

Do Brett's symptoms meet the criteria for panic disorder? (Discussion appears at the end of this chapter.)

normality and abnormality, remember that the setting of the threshold along the continuum is a subjective judgment.

Reliability of the *DSM*

Despite the use of explicit criteria for disorders, the reliability of many of the diagnoses listed in the *DSM-III* and *DSM-IIIR* was disappointing. On average, experienced clinicians agreed on their diagnoses using these manuals only about 70 percent of the time (Kirk & Kutchins, 1992). The reliability of some of the diagnoses, particularly the personality disorder diagnoses, was much lower.

Low reliability of diagnoses can be due to many factors. Although the developers of the *DSM-III* and *DSM-IIIR* attempted to make the criteria for each disorder explicit, many criteria still were vague and required the clinician to make inferences about the individual's symptoms or to rely on the individual's willingness to report symptoms. For example, most of the symptoms of the mood disorders and anxiety disorders are subjective experiences (e.g., sadness, apprehensiveness, hopelessness), and only the individual can report whether he or she has these symptoms and how severe they are. To diagnose any of the personality disorders, the clinician must establish that the person has a lifelong history of specific dysfunctional behaviors or ways of relating to the world. Unless the clinician has known the person his or her entire life, the clinician must rely on the person and his or her family to provide information about the person's history. Different sources of information can provide very different pictures of the person's functioning.

To increase the reliability of diagnoses in the *DSM-IV,* the task force that developed it conducted numerous field trials. The criteria for most of the diagnoses to be included in the *DSM-IV* were tested in clinical and research settings. In a field trial, testing determines whether diagnostic criteria can be applied reliably and whether they fit individuals' experiences. As a result, the reliability of the *DSM-IV* and *DSM-IV-TR* diagnoses are higher than the reliability of their predecessors, although clearly they are not completely reliable (Widiger, 2002). In developing the *DSM-5,* researchers have conducted numerous field trials, and panels of experts have reviewed hundreds of relevant research studies.

Multiaxial System

The *DSM-III, DSM-IV,* and *DSM-IV-TR* specify five *axes,* or dimensions, along which a clinician evaluates a person's behavior (Table 3.5). Only the first two axes list actual disorders and the criteria required for their diagnoses. The other three axes are meant to provide information on physical conditions that might be affecting the person's mental health (Axis III), psychosocial and environmental stressors in the person's life (Axis IV), and the degree of impairment in the person's mental health and functioning (Axis V). Let us take a look at these five axes, one by one, and consider how they would apply to Brett in the Shades of Gray case study.

On Axis I, a clinician lists any major disorders for which the person qualifies, with the exclusion of mental retardation and personality disorders. The clinician also notes whether these disorders are chronic or acute. *Chronic* disorders last for long periods of time. *Acute* disorders have a more recent and abrupt onset of severe symptoms. The Axis I disorder that most closely matches Brett's symptoms is panic disorder.

On Axis II, the clinician lists mental retardation or any personality disorders for which the person qualifies. In general, disorders listed on

TABLE 3.5 *DSM-IV-TR* Axes

The *DSM-IV-TR* has five axes, along which each client should be evaluated.

Axis I	Clinical disorders
Axis II	Personality disorders Mental retardation
Axis III	General medical conditions
Axis IV	Psychosocial and environmental problems
Axis V	Global assessment of functioning

Source: Reprinted with permission from the *Diagnostic and Statistical Manual of Mental Disorders,* Fourth Edition, Text Revision. Copyright © 2000 American Psychiatric Association.

Axis II are lifelong, whereas most Axis I disorders tend to wax and wane across the life span. For example, a person with an antisocial personality disorder has a lifelong pattern of being abusive toward others and violating basic norms of social relationships (see Chapter 9). Brett, in Shades of Gray, does not appear to have any Axis II disorders.

On Axis III, the clinician notes any medical or physical diseases from which the person is suffering. These diseases may or may not be related directly to the psychological disorders from which the person is also suffering. For example, a person may have lung cancer, which has nothing to do with the fact that he or she also has schizophrenia. However, the clinician should know about any physical diseases. For one thing, these diseases could affect the person's mental health. Also, any prescription drugs the person takes may have side effects that could influence diagnosis or potentially interact with any drugs the clinician might prescribe. Brett's panic attacks could be exacerbated by a number of medical conditions, such as a tendency toward heart palpitations, and a clinician would note this on Axis III.

On Axis IV, the clinician rates the severity of the psychosocial stressors the individual is facing. Again, these psychosocial stressors may be related to the individual's mental disorder, as either causes or consequences. Or they may merely be coincidental with the disorder. However, knowing the types of stressors that confront the individual will help the clinician provide successful treatment. A clinician diagnosing Brett would note whether he was under a great deal of stress, which could make him more vulnerable to panic attacks.

On Axis V, the clinician rates the level at which the individual is able to function in daily life. This helps the clinician quantify and communicate the degree to which the disorder is impairing the individual's functioning. Thus, a clinician diagnosing Brett would note how much his panic attacks were interfering with his life.

The authors of the *DSM-5* have recommended that Axes I, II, and III be collapsed into one axis that contains all psychological disorders and general medical conditions. This change would bring the *DSM-5* more in line with the manual used internationally—the *International Classification of Diseases (ICD),* published by the World Health Organization (WHO). Axes IV and V are likely to remain in the *DSM-5* but may be modified so that they are coded more like the way the ICD codes these dimensions. These changes reflect the globalization of research on mental health problems and the desire of researchers to have similar diagnostic systems around the world.

Continuing Concerns About the *DSM*

Although the criteria for diagnosing mental disorders represented in the *DSM-IV-TR* are more standardized and research-based than those of earlier versions of the *DSM,* many researchers see room for improvement (Widiger, 2002). Let us consider some of the ongoing controversies about the *DSM-IV-TR* that have been debated in development of the *DSM-5.*

Considering the Continuum One of the greatest controversies concerns the assumption in the *DSM-IV-TR* that it is possible to define where normality ends and psychopathology begins. Some psychologists advocate a diagnostic system that recognizes many disorders as extremes of ordinary behavior, rather than implying that they are qualitatively different from normal functioning. The *DSM-5* will reflect a continuum model in the diagnosis of at least some disorders, particularly the personality disorders (see Chapter 9) and autism (see Chapter 10).

Differentiating Mental Disorders from Each Other Another ongoing problem with the *DSM-IV-TR* is the difficulty in differentiating the mental disorders from each other (Watson, 2009). Most people who are diagnosed with one *DSM-IV-TR* disorder also meet the criteria for at least one other disorder. This overlap occurs, in part, because certain symptoms show up in the criteria for several different disorders. For example, irritability or agitation can be part of depression, mania, anxiety, schizophrenia, some of the personality disorders, and some of the childhood disorders.

We might want to make the diagnostic criteria for disorders more distinct. But recent research suggests that much of the *comorbidity* (or overlap) among disorders represents the natural co-occurrence of problems in mood, behavior, and thought (Krueger & Markon, 2006). This finding suggests that there are some fundamental dimensions of functioning and that people vary in where they fall along these dimensions, with the extremes being "maladaptive" or "dysfunctional." Diagnostic systems of the future might specify how these dimensions come together to create different types of psychopathology, as well as how and why these psychopathologies are related to each other. This dimensional approach to diagnosis is very different from the approach of the *DSM-IV-TR,* which designates discrete categories of disorders that supposedly represent distinct types of pathology.

The *DSM-5* will go partway toward recognizing the underlying dimensions that make up disorders. The authors are developing a set of instruments to assess variations in fundamental cognitive, emotional, and behavioral processes that cut across many disorders, such as sleep problems, depressed or anxious mood, and substance use. These instruments will not be part of the *DSM-5* but will be available for use by researchers and clinicians to obtain ratings for important dimensions regardless of the specific disorder the individual might be diagnosed with (see Helzer, et al., 2008).

Addressing Cultural Issues Researchers and clinicians also see room for improvement in the *DSM-IV-TR*'s treatment of culture. Different cultures have distinct ways of conceptualizing mental disorders. Some disorders that are defined in one culture do not seem to occur in other cultures. The *DSM-IV-TR* includes an appendix that lists many of these culture-specific disorders and brief guidelines for gathering information during the assessment process regarding a person's culture. Table 3.6 describes some of these culture-bound syndromes.

The *DSM-IV-TR* also includes short descriptions of cultural variation in the presentation of each major mental disorder recognized in the manual. For example, it notes differences among cultures in the content of delusions (beliefs out of touch with reality) in schizophrenia. The manual encourages clinicians to consider cultural issues such as the kinds of symptoms acceptable to the individual's culture. Some critics do not believe the *DSM-IV-TR* goes far enough in recognizing cultural variation in what is considered healthy or unhealthy (Kirmayer, 2001; Tsai et al., 2001). In developing the *DSM-5,* researchers are trying to better understand cultural variations in the expression and characterization of disorders. Throughout the remainder of this book, we will comment on cultural variations in the experience and prevalence of each disorder recognized by the *DSM.*

The Dangers of Diagnosis

One influential critic of psychiatry, Thomas Szasz, has argued that so many biases are inherent in who is labeled as having a mental disorder that the entire system of diagnosis is corrupt and should be abandoned. Szasz (1961) believes that people in power use psychiatric diagnoses to label and dispose of people who do not "fit in." He suggests that mental disorders do not really exist and that people who seem to be suffering from mental disorders are oppressed by a society that does not accept their alternative ways of behaving and looking at the world.

Even psychiatrists and psychologists who do not fully agree with Szasz's perspective on labeling recognize the great danger of labeling behaviors or people as abnormal. The person labeled as abnormal is treated differently by society, and this treatment can continue long after the person stops exhibiting the behaviors labeled abnormal. This point was made in a classic study of the effects of labeling by psychologist David Rosenhan (1973). He and seven colleagues had themselves admitted to 12 different mental hospitals by reporting to hospital staff that they had been hearing voices saying the words *empty, hollow,* and *thud.* When they were questioned by hospital personnel, they told the truth about every other aspect of their lives, including the fact that they had never experienced mental health problems before. All eight were admitted to the hospitals, all but one with a diagnosis of schizophrenia (see Chapter 8).

Once they were admitted to the hospital, the pseudopatients stopped reporting that they were hearing voices and behaved as normally as they usually did. When asked how they were doing by hospital staff, the pseudopatients said they felt fine and no longer heard voices. They cooperated in activities. The only thing they did differently than

TABLE 3.6 Culture-Bound Syndromes

Certain syndromes appear to occur only in some cultures.

Syndrome	Cultures Where Found	Symptoms
Amok	Malaysia, Laos, Philippines, Polynesia, Papua New Guinea, Puerto Rico	Brooding followed by an outburst of violent, aggressive, or homicidal behavior
Ataque de nervios	Latin America and Latin Mediterranean cultures	Uncontrollable shouting, attacks of crying, trembling, heat in the chest rising into the head, verbal or physical aggression, a sense of being out of control
Dhat	India, Sri Lanka, China	Severe anxiety about the discharge of semen, whitish discoloration of the urine, feelings of weakness and exhaustion
Ghost sickness	Native American cultures	Preoccupation with death and the deceased; manifested in dreams and in severe anxiety
Koro	Malaysia, China, Thailand	Episode of sudden and intense anxiety that the penis (or, in women, the vulva and nipples) will recede into the body and possibly cause death
Mal de ojo	Mediterranean cultures	Fitful sleep, crying without apparent cause, diarrhea, vomiting, fever
Shinjing shuairuo	China	Physical and mental fatigue, dizziness, headaches, other pains, concentration difficulties, sleep disturbance, memory loss
Susto	U.S. Latinos, Mexico, Central America, South America	Appetite disturbances, sleep problems, sadness, lack of motivation, low self-worth, aches and pains; follows a frightening experience
Taijin kyofusho	Japan	Intense fear that one's body displeases, embarrasses, or is offensive to other people

other patients was to write down their observations on notepads occasionally during the day.

Not one of the pseudopatients was ever detected as normal by hospital staff, although they remained in the hospitals for an average of 19 days. Several of the other patients in the mental hospitals detected the pseudopatients' normality, however, making comments such as "You're not crazy, you're a journalist, or a professor [referring to the continual note taking]. You're checking up on the hospital" (Rosenhan, 1973). When the pseudopatients were discharged, they were given the diagnosis of schizophrenia in remission, meaning that the physicians still believed the pseudopatients had schizophrenia but the symptoms had subsided for the time being.

Rosenhan (1973) concluded, "It is clear that we cannot distinguish the sane from the insane in psychiatric hospitals. The hospital itself imposes a special environment in which the meanings of behavior can be easily misunderstood." He also noted that, if even mental health professionals cannot distinguish sanity from insanity, the dangers of diagnostic labels are even greater in the hands of nonprofessionals: "Such labels, conferred by mental health professionals, are as influential on the patient as they are on his relatives and friends, and it should not surprise anyone that the diagnosis acts on all of them as a self-fulfilling prophecy. Eventually, the patient himself accepts the diagnosis, with all of its surplus meanings and expectations, and behaves accordingly."

Not surprisingly, Rosenhan's study created a furor in the mental health community. How could seasoned professionals have made such mistakes—admitting mentally healthy people to psychiatric hospitals on the basis of one symptom (hearing voices), not recognizing the pseudopatients' behavior as normal, allowing them to be discharged carrying a diagnosis that suggested they still had schizophrenia? Even today, Rosenhan's study is held up as an example of the abuses of power, specifically, the power to label people as sane or insane, normal or abnormal, good or bad.

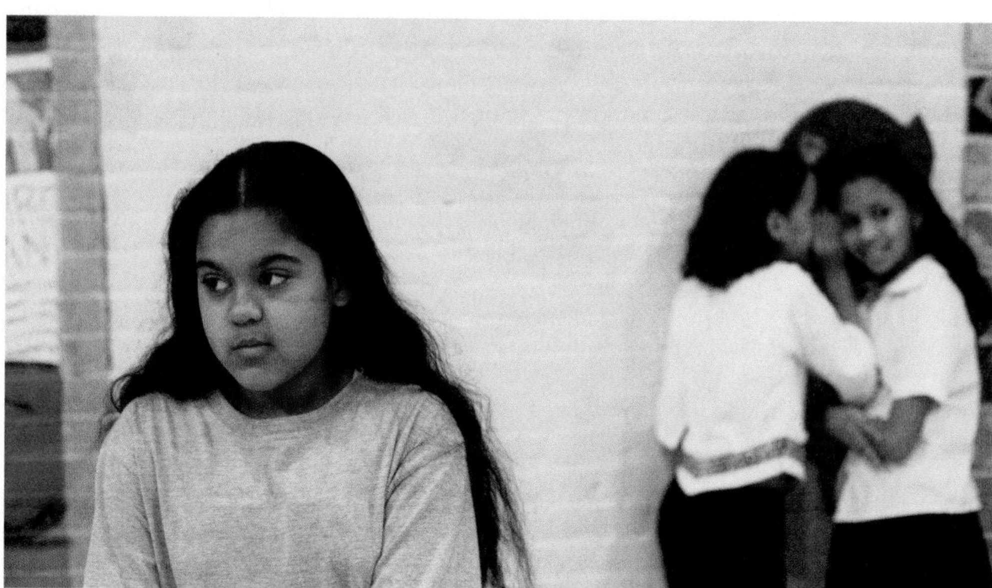

Children who are labeled as *different* can be ostracized by other children.

The label *abnormal* may be even more dangerous when it is applied to children, as illustrated by one study of boys in grades 3 through 6 (Harris, Milich, Corbitt, & Hoover, 1992). Researchers paired boys who were the same age. In half the pairs, one of the boys was told that his partner had a behavior problem that made him disruptive. In reality, only some of the boys labeled as having a behavior problem actually had a behavior problem. In the other half of the pairs, the boys were not told anything about each other, although some of the boys actually did have behavior problems. All the pairs worked together on a task while researchers videotaped their interaction. After the interaction, the boys were asked several questions about each other and about their enjoyment of the interaction.

The boys who had been told that their partners had a behavior problem were less friendly toward their partners during the task, talked with them less often, and were less involved in the interaction with their partners than were the boys who had been told nothing about their partners. In turn, the boys who had been labeled as having a behavior problem enjoyed the interaction less, took less credit for their performance on the task, and said that their partners were less friendly toward them than did the boys who had not been so labeled. Most important, labeling a boy as having a behavior problem influenced his partner's behaviors toward him and his enjoyment of the task regardless of whether he actually had a behavior problem. These results show that labeling a child as abnormal strongly affects other children's behaviors toward him or her, even when there is no reason for the child to be so labeled.

Should we avoid psychiatric diagnoses altogether? Probably not. Despite the potential dangers of diagnostic systems, they serve vital functions. The primary role of diagnostic systems is to organize the confusing array of psychological symptoms in an agreed-on manner. This organization facilitates communication from one clinician to another and across time.

For example, if Dr. Jones reads in a patient's history that he was diagnosed with schizophrenia according to the *DSM-IV-TR,* she knows what criteria were used to make that diagnosis and can compare the patient's diagnosis then with his symptoms now. Such information can assist Dr. Jones in making an accurate assessment of the patient's current symptoms and in determining the proper treatment for his symptoms. For example, if the patient's current symptoms also suggest schizophrenia and the patient responded to Drug X when he had schizophrenia a few years ago, this history indicates that he might respond well to Drug X now.

Having a standard diagnostic system also greatly facilitates research on psychological disorders. For example, if a researcher at State University is using the *DSM-IV-TR* criteria to identify people with obsessive-compulsive disorder and a researcher at Private University is using the same criteria for the same purpose, the two researchers will be better able to compare the results of their research than if they were using different criteria to diagnose obsessive-compulsive disorder. This can lead to faster advances in our understanding of the causes of and effective treatment for disorders.

TEST YOURSELF

1. What is the *Diagnostic and Statistical Manual of Mental Disorders* (*DSM*)?
2. What are the major changes from the first two editions of the *DSM* to more recent editions?
3. What are some remaining criticisms of the DSM?

APPLY IT A clinician using the *DSM-IV-TR* evaluates individuals on each of the following axes except which?

a. clinical disorders
b. personality disorders and mental retardation
c. general medical conditions
d. psychosocial and environmental problems
e. ethnicity/race

Answers appear online at www.mhhe.com/nolen5e.

FIGURE 3.5 **Integration of Biological, Psychological, and Social Factors in Assessment and Diagnosis**

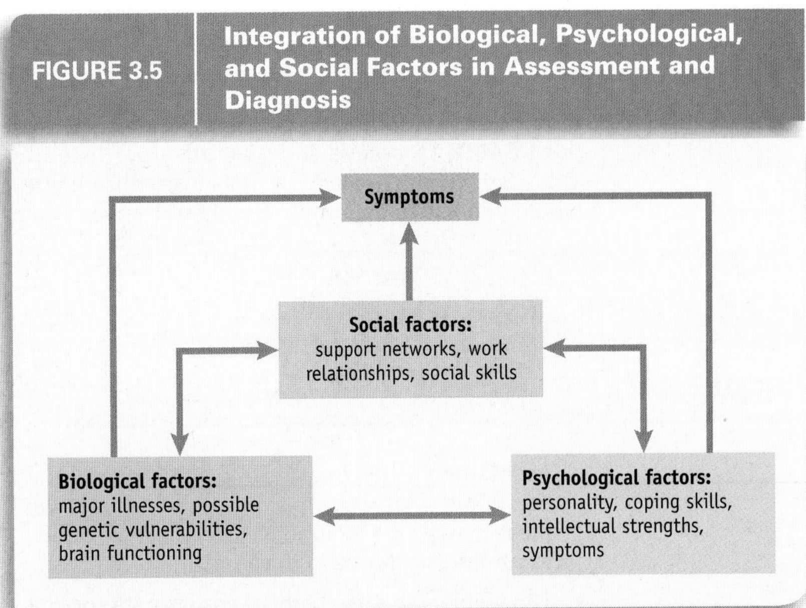

CHAPTER INTEGRATION

Assessment is inherently a process of biopsychosocial integration of pieces of information about an individual. After clinicians administer a battery of assessment tests to a person, they must then integrate the information gathered from these tests to form a coherent picture of the person's strengths and weaknesses. This picture weaves together information on biological functioning (major illnesses, possible genetic vulnerability to psychopathology), psychological functioning (personality, coping skills, intellectual strengths), and social functioning (support networks, work relationships, social skills) (Figure 3.5).

The *DSM-IV-TR* was revised to reflect a more integrated and dynamic view of how biology, psychology, and social factors influence one another. The manual now includes information on cultural differences and similarities for each disorder and the biological symptoms associated with each disorder. In addition, the *DSM-IV* and *DSM-IV-TR* dropped the label *organic disorders,* which had been used previously for a set of disorders including delirium, dementia, and amnesia. The developers of the *DSM-IV* made this change because the label *organic* implied that only these disorders were caused by biological factors. Thus, both the assessment process and the *DSM-IV-TR* itself reflect a biopsychosocial approach to psychopathology. As we will see as we discuss each of the major disorders recognized by the *DSM-IV-TR,* this approach appears warranted.

SHADES OF GRAY DISCUSSION (review p. 80)

If you determined that Brett has experienced panic attacks, you are correct. The *DSM-IV-TR* requires four symptoms from Criterion C to diagnose a panic attack, and Brett reports five: rapid heartbeat, shortness of breath, chills, trembling, and feeling as though he were going to die. Further, these symptoms seem to have developed suddenly and increased in intensity within 10 minutes, meeting Criterion D in Table 3.4.

It is less clear whether Brett's symptoms meet Criterion A or B for panic disorder. Because his panic attacks occurred before giving an important presentation and before meeting with his parents, they may be triggered by being the "focus of another person's attention." If this is the case, his attacks are not "unexplained." In addition, Criterion B requires him to have experienced four panic attacks in 4 weeks or to have been persistently fearful of another panic attack for at least 1 month. Brett has reported only two panic attacks in the past month. He may have had more that he has not mentioned. And we cannot tell if he has been persistently fearful of another attack for at least a month. We also cannot rule out the possibility of an organic factor, such as too much coffee, having caused his panic attacks.

THINK CRITICALLY

Reread the Shades of Gray case study of Brett and the *DSM-IV-TR* criteria for panic disorder listed in Table 3.4. What assessment tools from this chapter would you use to determine whether Brett has panic disorder? How would these assessments help you decide? (*Discussion appears on p. 517 at the back of this book.*)

CHAPTER SUMMARY

- Assessment is the process of gathering information about people's symptoms and the causes of these symptoms. Diagnosis is a label we attach to symptoms that tend to co-occur.
- The validity and reliability of assessment tools indicate their quality. Validity is the accuracy of a test in assessing what it is supposed to assess. Five types of validity are face validity, content validity, concurrent validity, predictive validity, and construct validity. Reliability is the consistency of a test. Types of reliability include test-retest reliability, alternate form reliability, internal reliability, and interrater reliability. Standardization of the implementation and interpretation of an assessment tool can increase both validity and reliability.
- In a mental status exam, the clinician assesses the individual's (a) appearance and behavior, (b) thought processes, (c) mood and affect, (d) intellectual functioning, and (e) orientation.
- To assess emotional and behavioral functioning, clinicians use structured clinical interviews, symptom questionnaires, personality inventories, behavioral observation, and self-monitoring.
- Paper-and-pencil neuropsychological tests can assess specific cognitive deficits that may be related to brain damage in patients. Intelligence tests provide a more general measure of verbal and analytical skills.
- Brain-imaging techniques such as CT, PET, SPECT, and MRI scans currently are being used primarily for research purposes, but in the future they may contribute to the diagnosis and assessment of psychological disorders.
- Psychophysiological tests, including the electroencephalogram (EEG) and electrodermal responses, assess brain and nervous system activity detectable on the periphery of the body (such as on the scalp and skin).
- Projective tests present individuals with ambiguous stimuli. Clinicians interpret individuals' reactions to the stimuli. The validity and reliability of these tests are low.
- During the assessment procedure, many problems and biases can be introduced. Individuals may be resistant to being assessed and thus distort the information they provide. They may be too impaired by cognitive deficits, distress, or lack of development of verbal skills to provide information. Further, many biases can arise when the clinician and the individual are from different cultures.
- A classification system is a set of definitions of syndromes and rules for determining when a person's symptoms are part of each syndrome. In the United States, the predominant classification system for psychological problems is the *Diagnostic and Statistical Manual of Mental Disorders* (*DSM*) of the American Psychiatric Association. Its most recent editions provide specific criteria for diagnosing each of the recognized psychological disorders, as well as information on the course and prevalence of disorders.
- The explicit criteria in the *DSM* have increased the reliability of diagnoses, but there is still room for improvement.
- The *DSM-IV-TR* provides five axes along which clinicians can assess individuals. On Axis I, major clinical syndromes are noted. Axis II contains diagnoses of mental retardation and personality disorders. On Axis III, the clinician notes any medical conditions individuals have. On Axis IV, psychosocial and environmental stressors are noted. On Axis V, individuals' general levels of functioning are assessed. The *DSM-5* will likely collapse Axes I, II, and III into one axis for all psychological disorders and general medical conditions.
- Critics point to many dangers in labeling people as having psychiatric disorders, including the danger of stigmatization. Diagnosis is important, however, to communication between clinicians and researchers. Only when a system of definitions of disorders is agreed on can communication about disorders be improved.

KEY TERMS

assessment 65
diagnosis 65
validity 65
reliability 66
structured interview 68
symptom questionnaire 69
personality inventories 69
behavioral observation 71
self-monitoring 71
intelligence tests 72
neuropsychological tests 72
computerized tomography (CT) 73
positron-emission tomography (PET) 73
single photon emission computed tomography (SPECT) 73
magnetic resonance imaging (MRI) 73
psychophysiological tests 73
electroencephalogram (EEG) 73
projective test 74
syndrome 77
classification system 78
Diagnostic and Statistical Manual of Mental Disorders (*DSM*) 78

Chapter 4

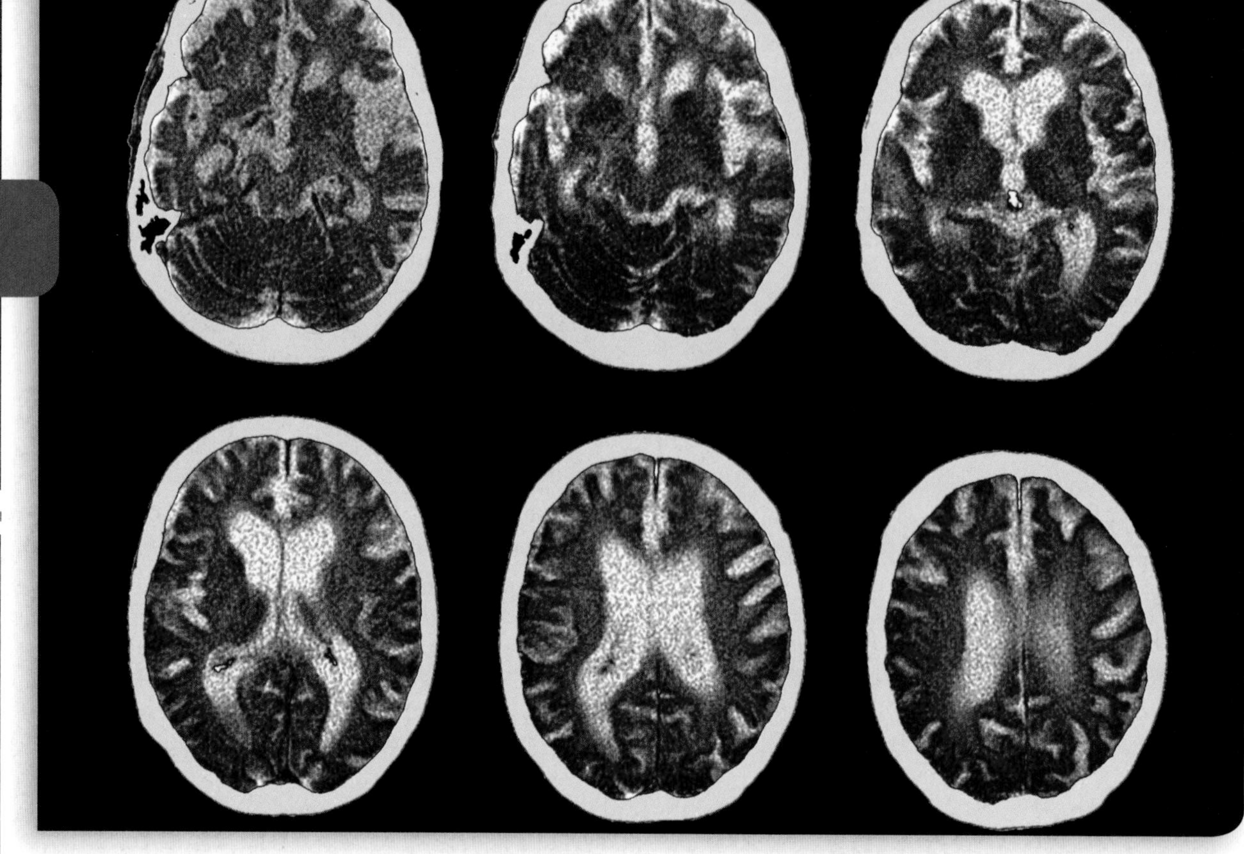

The Research Endeavor

CHAPTER OUTLINE

Extraordinary People

The Old Order Amish of Pennsylvania

The Old Order Amish are a religious sect whose members avoid contact with the modern world and live a simple, agrarian life, much as people lived in the eighteenth century. The Amish use horse and buggy as transportation, most of their homes do not have electricity or telephones, and there is little movement of people into or out of their culture. The rules of social behavior among the Amish are very strict, and roles within the community are clearly set. Members who do not comply with community norms are isolated or shunned.

Despite their self-enforced isolation from mainstream American society, the Amish of southeastern Pennsylvania welcomed researcher Janice Egeland and several of her colleagues to conduct some of the most intensive studies of depression and mania ever done (Egeland, 1986, 1994; Egeland & Hostetter, 1983; Pauls, Morton, & Egeland, 1992). These researchers examined the records of local hospitals looking for Amish people who had been hospitalized for psychological problems. They also interviewed thousands of members of this community to discover people with mood disorders who had not been hospitalized. The closed society of the Amish and their meticulous record-keeping of family histories proved a perfect setting in which to study the transmission of psychological disorders within families. The result was groundbreaking research on genetic factors that contribute to mood disorders.

While research in abnormal psychology in many ways resembles research in other fields, the study of psychopathology brings some special challenges. One challenge is accurately measuring abnormal behaviors and feelings. We cannot see, hear, or feel other people's emotions and thoughts. Researchers often must rely on people's own accounts, or *self-reports,* of their internal states and experiences. Self-reports can be distorted in a number of ways, intentionally or unintentionally. Similarly, relying on an observer's assessments of a person has its own pitfalls. The observer's assessments can be biased by stereotypes involving gender and culture, idiosyncratic biases, and lack of information. A second challenge is the difficulty of obtaining the participation of populations of interest, such as people who are paranoid and hearing voices.

A third challenge is that most forms of abnormality probably have multiple causes. Unless a single study can capture all the biological, psychological, and social causes of the psychopathology of interest, it cannot fully explain the causes of that abnormality. Rarely can a single study accomplish so much. Instead, we usually are left with partial answers to the question of what causes a certain disorder or symptom, and we must piece together the partial answers from several studies to get a full picture.

Despite these challenges, researchers have made tremendous strides in understanding many forms of abnormality in the past 50 years or so. They have overcome many of the challenges of researching psychopathology by using a *multimethod approach,* that is, using different methods to study the same issue. Each of the different research methods may have some limitations, but taken together they can provide convincing evidence concerning an abnormality.

In this chapter we discuss the most common methods of mental health research. In our discussion, we will use various research methods to test the idea that stress contributes to depression. Of course, these research methods also can be used to test many other ideas.

THE SCIENTIFIC METHOD

Any research project involves a basic series of steps designed to obtain and evaluate information relevant to a problem in a systematic way. This process is often called the **scientific method.**

First, researchers must select and define a problem. In our case, the problem is to determine the relationship between stress and depression. Then a **hypothesis,** or testable statement of what we predict will happen in our study, must be formulated. Next, the method for testing the hypothesis must be chosen and implemented. Once the data are collected and analyzed, the researcher draws the appropriate conclusions and documents the results in a research report.

Defining the Problem and Stating a Hypothesis

Throughout this chapter, we will examine the idea that stress causes depression. This simple idea is too broad and abstract to test directly. Thus, we must state a hypothesis, or a testable prediction of what relationship between stress and depression we expect to find in our study.

To generate a hypothesis, we might ask, "What kind of evidence would support the idea that stress causes depression?" If we find that people who had recently experienced stress are more likely to be depressed than people who had not recently experienced stress, this evidence would support our idea. One hypothesis, then, is that people who have recently been under stress are more likely to be depressed than people who have not. This hypothesis can be tested by a number of research methods.

The alternative to our hypothesis is that people who experience stress are *not* more likely to develop depression than people who do not experience stress. This prediction that there is *no relationship* between the phenomena we are studying—in this case, stress and depression—is called the **null hypothesis.** Results often support the null hypothesis instead of the researcher's primary hypothesis.

Does support for the null hypothesis mean that the underlying idea has been disproved? No. The null hypothesis can be supported for many reasons, including flaws in the study design. Researchers often will continue to test their primary hypothesis, using a variety of methodologies. If the null hypothesis continues to get much more support than the primary hypothesis, the researchers eventually either modify or drop the primary hypothesis.

Choosing and Implementing a Method

Once we have stated a hypothesis, the next step in testing our idea that stress leads to depression is to choose how we are going to define the phenomena we are studying.

A **variable** is a factor or characteristic that can vary within an individual or between individuals. Weight, mood, and attitudes toward one's mother are all factors that can vary over time, so they are considered variables. Characteristics such as sex and ethnicity do not vary for an individual over time, but because they vary from one individual to another, they too can be considered variables. A **dependent variable** is the factor we are trying to predict in our study. In our studies of stress and depression, we will be trying to predict depression, so depression is our dependent variable. An **independent variable** is the factor we believe will affect the dependent variable. In our studies, the independent variable will be the amount of stress an individual has experienced.

In order to research depression and stress, we must first define what we mean by these terms. As we will discuss in Chapter 7, *depression* is a syndrome or a collection of the following symptoms: sadness, loss of interest in one's usual activities, weight loss or gain, changes in sleep, physical agitation or slowing down, fatigue and loss of energy, feelings of worthlessness or excessive guilt, problems in concentration or indecisiveness, and suicidal thoughts (American Psychiatric Association, 2000). Researchers who adopt a continuum model of depression focus on the full range of depressive symptoms, from no symptoms to moderate symptoms to the most severe symptoms. To researchers who do not accept a continuum model, anyone who has some of these symptoms of depression but does not meet the criteria for one of the depressive disorders would be considered not depressed.

Stress is more difficult to define, because the term has been used in so many ways in research and in the popular press. Many researchers consider stressful events to be events that are uncontrollable, unpredictable, and challenging to the limits of people's abilities to cope (see Chapter 15).

Operationalization is the way we measure or manipulate the variables in a study. Our definitions of depression and stress will influence how we measure these variables. For example, if we define depression as a diagnosable depressive disorder, then we will measure depression in terms of whether people's symptoms meet the criteria for a depressive disorder. If we define depression as symptoms along the entire range of severity, then we might measure depression as scores on a depression questionnaire.

In measuring stress, we might assess how often a person has encountered events that most people would consider stressful. Or we might devise a way of manipulating or creating stress so that we can then examine people's depression in response to this stress. In the remaining sections of this chapter, we will discuss different methods for testing hypotheses, as well as the conclusions that can and cannot be drawn from these methods.

Research Along the Continuum

Research with Continuum Approach

Studies focus on people with symptoms that range in severity from the everyday *(occasional sad mood)* to the highly impairing and likely to meet criteria for a disorder *(paralyzing depression)*

Research with Threshold Approach

Studies focus on people with diagnosed disorders of various severities *(adjustment disorder with depressed mood, major depressive disorder)* or on comparisons of people with diagnosed disorders and people without disorders

Depressive symptoms:

No symptoms	*Low symptoms*	*Moderate symptoms*	*Severe symptoms meeting diagnostic criteria*

This text helps you understand psychopathology using a continuum model. This model actually is a hot topic for debate in the field of abnormal psychology. Researchers disagree on whether studies should reflect a continuum model of psychopathology or focus only on disorders as diagnosed in the *DSM-IV-TR* and related diagnostic schemes. The difference lies mainly in how the researchers view people who have some symptoms of a disorder but do not meet the criteria for diagnosis. Researchers who favor continuum models believe that such individuals provide valuable insights into people who have diagnosable disorders. For example, they argue that the results of studies of people with moderate depression can be generalized to individuals with diagnosed depressive disorders (Angst et al., 2007). Researchers who do not support continuum models argue that people who fall short of a diagnosable disorder are inherently different from those who have a disorder and therefore studies of these people cannot be applied to those who have a disorder. To continue our example, these researchers believe that the results of studies of people with moderate depression cannot be generalized to people with diagnosed depressive disorders (Gotlib, Lewinsohn, & Seeley, 1995).

The debate continues, with evidence supporting both points of view. Some research methods use a continuum model, such as a study of the relationship between how many stressors individuals have experienced and how many depressive symptoms they report. In contrast, investigators who are interested only in differences between people with diagnosed disorders and people who do not meet diagnostic criteria would be more likely to compare these two groups on the number of stressors they have experienced. We will explore several research methods.

Ethical Issues in Research

Any type of research, whether experimental or some other type, must be evaluated for whether it is ethical. All colleges and universities have *human participants committees* (sometimes referred to as human subjects committees, institutional review boards, or ethics committees). These committees review the procedures of studies done with humans to ensure that the benefits of the study substantially outweigh any risks to the participants and that the risks to the participants have been minimized. The committees ensure that each research study includes certain basic rights for all participants:

1. *Understanding the study.* Participants have the right to understand the nature of the research they are participating in, particularly any factors that might influence their willingness to participate. For example, if they are likely to experience discomfort (psychological or physical) as a result of participating in the study or if the study entails any risk to their well-being, the researcher should explain this in plain language to the participants. Individuals not capable of understanding the risks of a study, such as young children or adults with mental impairments, must have a parent, guardian, or other responsible adult make the judgment about the individual's participation in the study.
2. *Confidentiality.* Participants should expect their identity and any information gathered from them in the study to be held in strict

confidence. Researchers usually report data aggregated across participants, rather than reporting data gathered from individual participants. Researchers who intend to report data gathered from individuals should obtain their explicit permission.

3. *Right to refuse or withdraw participation.* Participants should be allowed to refuse to participate in the study or to withdraw from participation once the study has begun without suffering adverse consequences. If students are participating in a study as a course requirement or as an opportunity for extra credit for a class, they should be given the choice of equitable alternative activities if they wish not to participate. Payment or other inducements for being in a study should not be so great that individuals essentially cannot afford to refuse to participate.
4. *Informed consent.* Usually, participants' consent to participate in the study should be documented in writing. In some cases, a written informed consent document is not used, as when participants are filling out an anonymous survey (in this case, their willingness to complete the survey is taken as their consent to participate). Also, if obtaining written documentation of participants' consent could put them at risk, the researcher sometimes is allowed to obtain only verbal consent. Examples of when this would be permitted include research being done in countries where a civil war is ongoing or an oppressive regime is in power, in which case participants may be at risk if it is discovered they have talked with researchers.
5. *Deception.* Researchers should use deception in studies only when such techniques are absolutely essential and justified by the study's potential contributions. Participants should not be deceived about those aspects of the research that might affect their willingness to participate, such as physical risks, discomfort, or unpleasant emotional experiences. If deception is necessary, researchers should explain the deception to the participants after the research is completed.
6. *Debriefing.* At the end of the study, researchers should explain the purpose of the research and answer participants' questions.

Although these rights may seem straightforward, human participants committees must make judgment calls as to whether a given study adequately protects participants' rights and whether the potential benefits of the study outweigh any risks to the participants.

TEST YOURSELF

1. What is the scientific method?
2. What are a hypothesis and a null hypothesis?
3. What is a variable?
4. What are the basic rights that research participants have?

APPLY IT If you did a study that looked at the relationship between the density of the population in different cities and the proportion of citizens who had mental disorders, the independent variable would be ________ and the dependent variable would be ______.

a. density of cities; proportion of citizens with mental disorders
b. proportion of citizens with mental disorders; density of cities
c. Both the density of cities and the proportion of citizens with mental disorders are independent variables.
d. Both the density of cities and the proportion of citizens with mental disorders are dependent variables.

Answers appear online at www.mhhe.com/nolen5e.

CASE STUDIES

Throughout this book, you will see **case studies**—detailed histories of individuals who have some form of psychological disorder. Case studies have been used for centuries as a way to understand the experiences of individuals and to make more general inferences about the sources of psychopathology.

If we wanted to use a case study to test our idea that stress causes depression, we would focus on an individual, interviewing him or her at length to discover the links between periods of depression and stressful events in his or her life. We might also interview close friends and family to obtain additional information. Based on the information we gathered, we would create a detailed description of the causes of his or her depressive episodes, with emphasis on the role of stressful events in these episodes. For example, this brief case study describes singer Kurt Cobain of the hit 1990s rock band Nirvana, who committed suicide.

CASE STUDY

Cobain always had a fragile constitution (he was subject to bronchitis, as well as the recurrent stomach pains he claimed drove him to a heroin addiction). The image one gets is that of a frail kid batted between warring parents. "[The divorce] just destroyed his life," Wendy O'Connor tells Michael Azerrad in the Nirvana biography *Come As You Are*. "He changed completely. I think he was ashamed. And he became very inward—he just held everything [in]. . . . I think he's *still* suffering." As a teen, Cobain dabbled in drugs and punk rock and dropped out of school. His father persuaded him to pawn his guitar and take an entrance exam for the navy. But Cobain soon returned for the guitar. "To them, I was wasting my life," he told the *Los Angeles Times*. "To me, I was fighting for it." Cobain didn't speak to his father for 8 years. When Nirvana went to the top of the charts, Don Cobain began keeping a scrapbook. "Everything I know about Kurt," he told Azerrad, "I've read in newspapers and magazines."

The more famous Nirvana became, the more Cobain wanted none of it. . . . Nirvana—with their stringy hair, plaid work shirts, and torn jeans—appealed to a mass of young fans who were tired of false idols like Madonna and Michael Jackson and who'd never had a dangerous rock-and-roll hero to call their own. Unfortunately, the band also appealed to the sort of people Cobain had always hated: poseurs and band wagoneers, not to mention record company execs and fashion designers who fell over themselves cashing in on the new sights and sounds. Cobain, who'd grown up as an angry outsider, tried to shake his celebrity. . . .

By 1992, it became clear that Cobain's personal life was as tangled and troubling as his music. The singer married [Courtney] Love in Waikiki—the bride wore a moth-eaten dress once owned by actress Frances Farmer—and the couple embarked on a self-destructive pas de deux widely referred to as a 90s version of *Sid and Nancy*. As Cobain put it, "I was going off with Courtney and we were scoring drugs and we were f—king up against a wall and stuff . . . and causing scenes just to do it. It was fun to be with someone who would stand up all of a sudden and smash a glass on the table." In September 1992, *Vanity Fair* reported that Love had used heroin while she was pregnant with [their daughter] Frances Bean. She and Cobain denied the story (the baby is healthy). But authorities were reportedly concerned enough to force them to surrender custody of Frances to Love's sister, Jamie, for a month, during which time the couple was, in Cobain's words, "totally suicidal." . . .

[T]hose who knew the singer say there was a real fragility buried beneath the noise of his music and his life. . . . If only someone had heard the alarms ringing at that rambling, gray-shingled home near the lake. Long before there was a void in our hearts, there was a void in Kurt Cobain's. (From J. Giles, "The poet of Alienation." *Newsweek*, April 18, 1994 (c) 1994 Newsweek, Inc. All rights reserved. Used by permission and protected by the Copyright Laws of the United States. The printing, copying, redistribution, or retransmission of the Material without express written permission is prohibited.)

Case studies are a time-honored method of research, for several reasons. No other method captures the uniqueness of the individual as much as a case study. The nuances of an individual's life and experiences can be detailed, and the individual's own words can be used to describe these experiences. Exploring the unique experiences of individuals and honoring their perspectives on these experiences are important goals for many researchers, and in-depth case studies of individual lives have become even more popular in recent years.

In-depth histories of troubled people, such as Kurt Cobain, may be rich in detail but not generalizable.

Case studies can be the only way to study rare problems, because there simply are not enough people with such problems to study through some other method. For example, much of the research on people with multiple personalities has come from case studies, because this form of psychopathology historically has been quite rare.

Case studies can be invaluable in helping generate new ideas and providing tentative support for those ideas. Today one of the most common uses of case studies is in drug treatment research to report unusual reactions patients have had to certain drugs. These reports can alert other clinicians to watch for similar reactions in their patients. If enough case reports of these unusual reactions emerge in the literature, larger-scale research to study the sources of the reactions may be warranted.

Case studies have drawbacks, however. The first involves **generalizability**—the ability to apply what we have learned to other individuals or groups. The conclusions drawn from the study of an individual may not apply to many other individuals. This limitation is especially obvious when case studies focus on people whose experiences may have been dramatic but unusual. For example, the circumstances leading to Kurt Cobain's death may be interesting, but they may not tell us anything about why other people commit suicide.

Case studies also suffer from a lack of *objectivity* on the part of both the individuals telling their stories and the therapists or researchers listening to the stories. People might have biased recollections of their pasts and may selectively report events that happen in the present. The therapists or researchers might selectively remember parts of the stories that support their beliefs and assumptions about the causes of human behavior and forget parts that do not. Thus, two case studies of the same person conducted by two different researchers may arrive at different conclusions about the motivations and key events in that person's life.

TEST YOURSELF

1. Define case studies.
2. What advantages do case studies provide researchers compared to other types of research?

APPLY IT If you chose to conduct research by case study, which disadvantage would you *not* face?

a. Case studies lack generalizability.
b. Case studies lack objectivity.
c. Case studies are difficult to replicate.
d. Case studies are uninteresting.

Answers appear online at www.mhhe.com/nolen5e.

CORRELATIONAL STUDIES

Correlational studies examine the relationship between an independent variable and a dependent variable without manipulating either variable. Correlational studies are the most common type of study in psychology and medicine. For example, you will often read about studies of the link between television watching and violence, smoking and heart disease, and Internet use and depression in which researchers have examined the naturally occurring relationships between variables.

There are many kinds of correlational studies. The most common type of correlational study in abnormal psychology is a study of two or more continuous variables. A **continuous variable** is measured along a continuum. For example, on a scale measuring severity of depression, scores might fall along a continuum from 0 (no depression) to 100 (extreme depression). On a scale measuring number of recent stressors, scores might fall along a continuum from 0 (no stressors) to 20 (20 or more recent stressors). If we measured severity of depression and number of recent stressors in the same group of people and then looked at the relationship between these two continuous variables, we would be doing a continuous variable correlational study.

Another type of correlational study is a **group comparison study.** In this type of study, researchers are interested in the relationship between people's membership in a particular group and their scores on some other variable. For example, we might be interested in the relationship between depression and whether people have experienced a specific type of stress, such as failing a test. In this case, the groups of interest are students who failed a test and students who did not. We would find people who represented these two groups, then measure depression in both groups. This is still a correlational study because we are only observing the relationship between two variables—test failure and depression—and are not manipulating any variable. In this type of study, however, at least one of the variables—group membership—is not a continuous variable.

Both continuous variable studies and group comparison studies can be either **cross-sectional**—observing people at only one point in time—or **longitudinal**—observing people on two or more occasions over time. Longitudinal studies have a major advantage over cross-sectional studies, because they can show that the independent variable precedes and predicts changes in the dependent variable over time. For example, a longitudinal study of stress and depression can show that people who are not depressed at the beginning of the study are much more likely to be depressed later in the study if they have experienced a stressful event in the interim than if they have not.

FIGURE 4.1 **Correlations.** Correlations can be positive (a) or negative (b). A zero correlation (c) indicates that there is no relationship between the independent and dependent variables. Most correlations are moderate (d), indicating that the value of the dependent variable is not perfectly predicted by that of the independent variable.

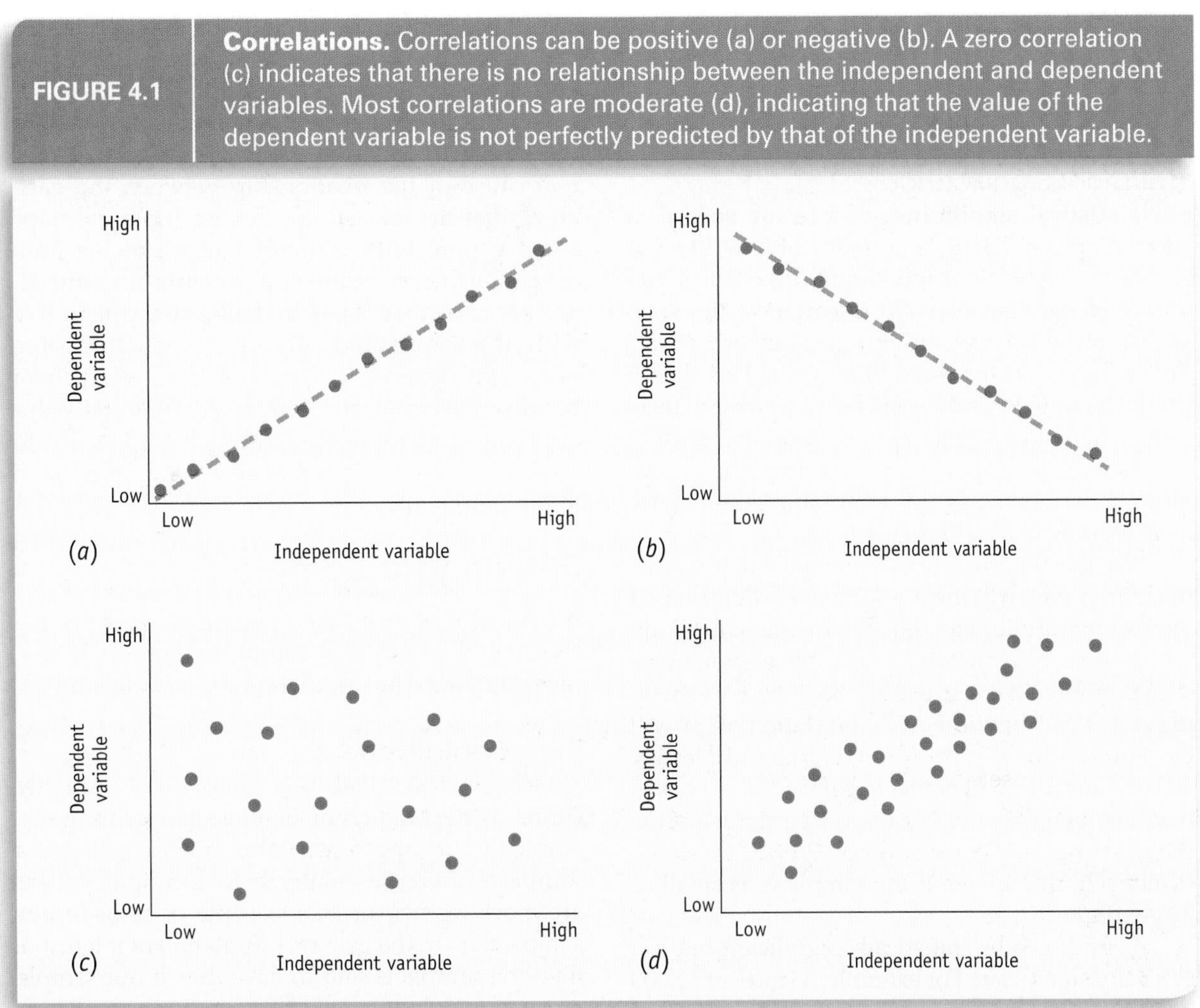

Measuring the Relationship Between Variables

In most correlational studies, the relationship between the variables is indicated by a correlation coefficient. Let us review what this statistic is and how to interpret it.

Correlation Coefficient

A **correlation coefficient** is a statistic used to represent the relationship between variables, usually denoted by the symbol *r*. A correlation coefficient can fall between −1.00 and +1.00. A positive correlation coefficient indicates that as values of the independent variable increase, values of the dependent variable also increase (Figure 4.1a). For example, a *positive correlation* between stress and depression would mean that people who report more stressors have higher levels of depression.

A negative correlation coefficient indicates that as values of the independent variable increase, values of the dependent variable decrease (Figure 4.1b). If we were measuring stressors and depression, a *negative correlation* would mean that people who report more stressors actually have lower levels of depression. This is an unlikely scenario, but there are many instances of negative correlations between variables. For example, people who have more positive social support from others typically have lower levels of depression.

The magnitude (size) of a correlation is the degree to which the variables move in tandem with each other. It is indicated by how close the correlation coefficient is to either +1.00 or −1.00. A correlation (*r*) of 0 indicates no relationship between the variables (Figure 4.1c). A value of *r* of +1.00 or −1.00 indicates a perfect relationship between the two variables (as illustrated in Figure 4.1a and b)—the value of one variable is perfectly predicted by the value of the other variable; for example, every time people experience stress they become depressed.

Seldom do we see perfect correlations in psychological research. Instead, correlations often are in the low to moderate range (for example, .2 to .5), indicating some relationship between the two variables but a far from perfect relationship (Figure 4.1d). Many relationships between variables happen by chance and are not meaningful. Scientists evaluate the importance of a correlation coefficient by examining its statistical significance.

Statistical Significance

The **statistical significance** of a result, such as a correlation coefficient, is an index of how likely it is that the result occurred simply by chance. You will often see statements in research studies such as "The result was statistically significant at $p < .05$." This means that the probability (p) is less than 5 in 100 that the result occurred only by chance. Researchers typically accept results at this level of significance as support of their hypotheses, although the choice of an acceptable significance level is somewhat arbitrary.

Whether a correlation coefficient will be statistically significant at the $p < .05$ level is determined by its magnitude and the size of the sample on which it is based. Both larger correlations and larger sample sizes increase the likelihood of achieving statistical significance. A correlation of .30 will be significant if it is based on a large sample, say 200 or more, but will not be significant if it is based on a small sample, say 10 or fewer participants. On the other hand, a correlation of .90 will be statistically significant even if the sample is as small as 30 people.

A result can be statistically significant but not clinically significant. For example, a study of 10,000 people might find a correlation of .15 between the number of stressors people experienced and their scores on a depression questionnaire. This correlation would likely be statistically significant because of the very large sample, but it is so small as to suggest that stress is not a very good predictor of depression. Similarly, two groups may differ in their mean levels of depression to a statistically significant degree because the sample sizes of both groups are very large. But if the two groups actually differ only by 1 or 2 points on a depression questionnaire in which scores can range from 0 to 60, the clinical significance of the difference in the two groups would be questionable. Increasingly, research is being examined for whether an effect is not only statistically significant but also clinically significant.

Correlation Versus Causation

A high correlation between an independent and a dependent variable does not tell us that the independent variable caused the dependent variable. If we found a strong positive correlation between stress and depression, we still could not conclude that stress causes depression. All a positive correlation tells us is that there is a relationship between stress and depression. It could be that depression causes stress, or some other variable may cause both stress and depression. This latter situation is called the **third variable problem**—the possibility that variables not measured in a study are the real cause of the relationship between the variables that are measured. For example, perhaps some people with difficult temperaments both are prone to depression and generate stressful experiences in their lives by being difficult to live with. If we measured only stress and depression, we might observe a relationship between them because they co-occur within the same individuals. But this relationship actually would be due to the common relationship of stress and depression to temperament.

Selecting a Sample

A critical choice in a correlational study is the choice of the sample. A **sample** is a group of people taken from the population we want to study.

Representativeness

A *representative sample* is a sample that is highly similar to the population of interest in terms of sex, ethnicity, age, and other important variables. If a sample is not representative—for example, if there are more women or more people of color in our sample than in the general population of interest—then the sample is said to have *bias*. If our sample represents only a small or unusual group of people, then we cannot generalize the results of our study to the larger population. For example, if all the people in our study are White, middle-class females, we cannot know whether our results generalize to males, people of color, or people in other socioeconomic classes.

An effective way to obtain a representative sample of a population is to generate a random sample of that population. For example, some studies have obtained random samples of the entire U.S. population by randomly dialing phone numbers throughout the country and then recruiting into the study the people who answer the phone. Often, researchers can settle for random samples of smaller populations, such as particular cities. When a sample is truly random, the chances are high that it will be similar to the population of interest in terms of ethnicity, sex, age, and all the other important variables in the study.

Selection of a Comparison Group

A group comparison study compares the experiences of one group with those of another group. For example, we may be interested in the depression levels of students who are athletes and students who are not athletes. We might begin by recruiting our sample of student athletes, attempting to make this sample as representative as possible of student athletes at our university.

Our comparison group of non-athletes should match our group of athletes on any variable (other than stress) that might influence levels of depression. If the two groups are not as similar as possible, then any differences in their levels of depression could be attributable to other variables. For example, women generally are more likely to be depressed than men. If we had more women in our athlete group than in our non-athlete group, then higher levels of depression in the athlete group might be attributable to a third variable—the fact that there are more women in that group—rather than to the effects of participation in athletics. For this reason, our athlete and non-athlete groups should be alike on all third variables that might influence our dependent variable, depression.

If we decide to match our two groups on sex, age, race or ethnicity, and socioeconomic status, we can then generate the comparison group by consulting student demographic records. For every student in our athlete group, we would recruit a student of the same sex, age, race, and socioeconomic status into our comparison group. Although not a simple task, this is a good way to generate a matched comparison group.

Some group comparison studies focus on different age groups or *cohorts*, for example, young adults age 20 to 30 and older adults age 70 to 80. Some studies have found that older adults are less likely to report depression than are younger adults (Fiske, Wetherell, & Gatz, 2009). Are the differences in levels of depression between these two cohorts due to the greater maturity of the older adults? Are they due to the different historical periods the two groups have experienced? Determining whether differences between age groups are due to age itself or to the different experiences of each cohort can be extremely difficult. When differences are due to the experiences one group had because all the individuals were born in a particular era or lived through certain historical events, this is known as a **cohort effect.**

A study of depression in student athletes might need to include a comparison group of students who are not athletes.

Evaluating Correlational Studies

Correlational studies have provided much important information for abnormal psychology. One major advantage of correlational studies is that they focus on situations occurring in the real world, rather than those manipulated in a laboratory. This gives them relatively good **external validity,** the extent to which a study's results can be generalized to real-life phenomena. The results of these studies may be generalizable to wider populations and to people's actual life experiences.

Longitudinal correlational studies have several advantages over cross-sectional correlational studies. In longitudinal correlational studies, researchers can determine whether there are differences between the groups before the crucial event occurs. If there are no differences before the event but significant differences after the event, then researchers can have more confidence that it was the event that actually led to the differences between the groups. Longitudinal designs also allow researchers to follow groups long enough to assess both short-term and long-term reactions to the event.

Longitudinal studies can be time-consuming and expensive to run. Chapter 8 reports studies in which children at high risk for schizophrenia were studied from their preschool years to their early adult years to determine what characteristics could predict who would develop schizophrenia and who would not (Erlenmeyer-Kimling, Rock, Squires-Wheeler, & Roberts, 1991). Some of these studies have been going on for more than 25 years and have cost millions of dollars. They are producing extremely valuable data, but at a high cost in both researchers' time and research dollars.

The greatest disadvantage of all correlational studies is that they cannot indicate what is a cause and what is a consequence. For example, many stressful events that depressed people report may be the consequences of their depression, rather than the causes (Hammen, 2005). The symptoms of depression can cause stress by impairing interpersonal skills, interfering with concentration on the job, and causing insomnia. The same problem exists for studies of many types of psychopathology. For example, the symptoms of schizophrenia can disrupt social relationships, alcoholism can lead to unemployment, and so on.

Finally, all correlational studies suffer from the third variable problem. Researchers seldom can measure all possible influences on their participants' levels of depression or other psychopathologies. Third variable problems are one of the major reasons why researchers turn to experimental studies.

TEST YOURSELF

1. What is a correlational study?
2. What is statistical significance?
3. What is the difference between a cross-sectional study and a longitudinal study?
4. What is a group comparison study?
5. What are the limitations of correlational studies?

APPLY IT A study found that cities with a greater population density had a greater proportion of citizens with mental disorders. This is a ________ correlation and indicates ________.

a. positive; that population density is related to the proportion of citizens with mental disorders
b. positive; that a greater population density causes a greater proportion of citizens to have mental disorders
c. negative; that population density is related to the proportion of citizens with mental disorders
d. negative; that a greater population density causes a greater proportion of citizens to have mental disorders

Answers appear online at www.mhhe.com/nolen5e.

EPIDEMIOLOGICAL STUDIES

Epidemiology is the study of the frequency and distribution of a disorder, or a group of disorders, in a population. An epidemiological study asks how many people in a population have the disorder and how this number varies across important groups within the population, such as men and women or people with high and low incomes.

TABLE 4.1 Lifetime and 12-Month Prevalence of Major Depressive Disorder

	Lifetime Prevalence (%)	12-Month Prevalence (%)
Males	12.7	7.7
Females	21.3	12.9
Total	17.1	10.3

Source: Kessler et al., 1994.

Epidemiological research focuses on three types of data. First, the **prevalence** of a disorder, or the proportion of the population that has the disorder at a given point or period in time, may be the focus of research. For example, a study might report the *lifetime prevalence* of a disorder, or the number of people who will have the disorder at some time in their life. The *12-month prevalence* of a disorder would be the proportion of the population who will be diagnosed with the disorder in any 12-month period.

Table 4.1 shows the lifetime and 12-month prevalences of one of the more severe forms of depression—major depressive disorder—from a nationwide epidemiological study conducted in the United States (Kessler et al., 1994). Not surprisingly, the proportion of the population who will be diagnosed with major depressive disorder at some time in their life is larger than the proportion who will be diagnosed with the disorder in any 12-month period. Table 4.1 illustrates the fact, mentioned earlier, that the prevalence of major depression is greater for women than for men. As we will discuss in Chapter 7, this fact, revealed by many epidemiological studies, has been an important focus of research into depression.

Second, epidemiological research seeks to determine the **incidence** of a disorder, or the number of new cases of the disorder that develop during a specified period of time. The 1-year incidence of a disorder is the number of people who develop the disorder during a 1-year period.

Third, epidemiological research is concerned with the **risk factors** for a disorder—those conditions or variables that are associated with a higher risk of having the disorder. If women are more likely than men to have a disorder, then being a woman is a risk factor for the disorder. In terms of our interest in the relationship between stress and depression, an epidemiological study might show that people who live in high-stress areas of a city are more likely to have depression than people who live in low-stress areas of the city.

How do researchers determine the prevalence, incidence, and risk factors for a disorder? Epidemiological researchers first identify the population of interest and next identify a random sample of that population, for example, by randomly phoning residential telephone numbers. They then use *structured clinical interviews* that ask specific questions of participants to assess whether they have the symptoms that make up the disorder and risk factors, such as gender or socioeconomic status, being studied. Recall our discussion of structured clinical interviews in Chapter 3. From these data, epidemiologists estimate how many people in different categories of risk factors have the disorder.

Evaluating Epidemiological Studies

Epidemiological studies have provided valuable information on the prevalence, incidence, and risk factors for disorders, and we will discuss evidence from some major nationwide and international epidemiological studies throughout this book. This research can give us important clues as to who is at highest risk for a disorder. This information can be used in turn to test hypotheses about why those people are at higher risk.

Epidemiological studies are affected by many of the same limitations as correlational studies. First and foremost, they cannot establish that any risk factor causes a disorder. While a study may show that people living in higher-stress neighborhoods are more likely to have a disorder, this does not mean that the high-stress environment caused the disorder. Similarly, as in correlational studies, third variables may explain the relationship between any risk factor and the rates of a disorder.

TEST YOURSELF

1. What is epidemiology?
2. What is the prevalence of a disorder?
3. What is the incidence of a disorder?

APPLY IT Several epidemiological studies have found higher rates of depression in women than in men. This means that female gender is which of the following?

a. a cause of depression
b. a risk factor for depression
c. irrelevant, because women are more likely than men to admit to depression

Answers appear online at www.mhhe.com/nolen5e.

EXPERIMENTAL STUDIES

The hallmark of **experimental studies** is control. Researchers attempt to control the independent variable and any potentially problematic third variables rather than simply observing them as they occur naturally. There are various types of experimental studies we could do to investigate whether stress leads to depression. We will examine four types in particular.

Human Laboratory Studies

To test our hypothesis that stress leads to depression, we could expose participants to a stressor in the laboratory and then determine whether it causes an increase in depressed mood. This method is known as a **human laboratory study.**

Several studies of this type have been done (see Peterson & Seligman, 1984). The stressor that is often used in this study is an unsolvable task or puzzle, such as an unsolvable anagram. In this case, our index of stress is participants' exposure to unsolvable anagrams. In this study, we are manipulating stress, not simply measuring it. This gives us the advantage of knowing precisely what type of stress participants are exposed to and when. We cannot create in the laboratory many of the types of stress that may cause depression in the real world, such as the destruction of a person's home in a hurricane or continual physical abuse. Instead, we can create analogues—situations that capture some of the key characteristics of these real-world events, such as their uncontrollability and unpredictability.

Internal Validity

We want to ensure that our experiment has **internal validity,** meaning that changes in the dependent variable can confidently be attributed to our manipulation of the independent variable and not to other factors. For example, people who participate in our experiment using anagrams might become more depressed over the course of the experiment simply because participating in an experiment is a difficult experience, not because the anagrams are unsolvable. This threat to internal validity is basically the same type of third variable problem we encountered previously.

Researchers may give participants an unsolvable puzzle to observe the effects of stress on mental health.

To control third variables, researchers create a **control group** or *control condition,* in which participants have all the same experiences as the group of main interest in the study except that they do not receive the key manipulation—in our case, the stressor of the unsolvable puzzles. The control group for our study could be given similar but solvable anagrams. Thus, the control group's experience would be identical to that of the other group—the **experimental group** or *experimental condition*—with the exception of receiving the unsolvable puzzles.

Another threat to internal validity can arise if the participants in our experimental group (the group given the unsolvable anagrams) and in our control group (the group given the solvable anagrams) differ in important ways before beginning the experiment. If such differences exist, we could not be sure that our manipulation is the cause of any changes in our dependent variable. Internal validity requires **random assignment;** that is, each participant must have an equal chance of being in the experimental group or the control group. Often, a researcher will use a table of random numbers to assign participants to groups.

Yet another threat to internal validity is the presence of **demand characteristics**—situations that cause participants to guess the purpose of the study and change their behavior as a result. For example, if our measure of depression is too obvious, participants could guess what hypothesis we are testing. To avoid demand characteristics, we could use subtler measures of depression, embedded in other tests to obscure the real purpose of our study. These other tests are often called *filler measures.* Researchers also often use *cover stories,* telling participants a false story to prevent them from guessing the true purpose of the experiment and changing their behavior accordingly. After the study, participants should be debriefed about the deception they were exposed to in the study, as well as its purpose.

If participants know what group they are in ahead of time, their behavior in the study can be affected. Similarly, if experimenters know what condition a participant is in, they might inadvertently behave in ways that affect how the participant responds to the manipulations. In order to reduce these demand characteristics, both the participants and the experimenters who interact with them should be *unaware* of whether the participants are in the experimental condition or the control condition. This situation is referred to as a **double-blind experiment.**

We have instituted a number of safeguards for internal validity in our study: Participants have been randomly selected and assigned, and our participants and experimenters are unaware of which condition participants are in. Now the study can be conducted. When our data are collected and analyzed, we find that, as we predicted, participants given the unsolvable anagrams showed greater increases in depressed mood than did participants given the solvable anagrams.

What can we conclude about our idea of depression, based on this study? Our experimental controls have helped us rule out third variable explanations, so we can be relatively confident that it was the experience of the uncontrollable stressor that led to the increases in depression in the experimental group. Thus, we can say that we have supported our hypothesis that people exposed to uncontrollable stress will show more depressed mood than will people not exposed to such stress.

Evaluating Human Laboratory Studies

The primary advantage of human laboratory studies is control. Researchers have more control over third variables, the independent variable, and the dependent variable in these studies than they do in any other type of study they can do with humans.

Yet human laboratory studies also have their limitations. Because we cannot know if our results generalize to what happens outside the laboratory, their external validity can be low. Is being exposed to unsolvable anagrams anything like being exposed to major, real-world uncontrollable stressors, such as the death of a loved one? Clearly, the severity of the two types of experiences differs, but is this the only important difference? Similarly, do the increases in depressed mood in the participants in our study, which probably were small, tell us anything about why some people develop extremely severe, debilitating episodes of depression? Experimental studies such as this have been criticized for the lack of generalizability of their results to the major psychopathology that occurs in real life.

Apart from posing problems of generalizability, human laboratory studies sometimes pose serious ethical issues. Is it ethical to deliberately induce distress, even mild distress, in people? Different people will have different answers to this question.

Therapy Outcome Studies

Therapy outcome studies are experimental studies designed to test whether a specific therapy—whether a psychological therapy or a biological therapy—reduces psychopathology in individuals who receive it. Because therapies target supposed causes of psychopathology, therapy outcome studies can produce evidence that reducing these causes reduces psychopathology, which in turn supports the hypothesis that these factors played a role in creating the psychopathology in the first place.

Control Groups

Sometimes, people simply get better with time. Thus, we need to compare the experiences of people who receive our experimental therapy with those of a control group made up of people who do not receive the therapy to see whether our participants' improvement has anything to do with our therapy. Sometimes, researchers use a *simple control group* consisting of participants who do not receive the experimental therapy but are tracked for the same period of time as the participants who do receive the therapy.

A variation on this simple control group is the **wait list control group.** The participants in this type of group do not receive the therapy when the experimental group does but instead go onto a wait list to receive the intervention at a later date when the study is completed. Both groups of participants are assessed at the beginning and end of the study, but only the experimental group receives the therapy as part of the study.

Another type of control group, the **placebo control group,** is used most often in studies of the effectiveness of drugs. The participants in this group have the same interactions with experimenters as the participants in the experimental group, but they take pills that are *placebos* (inactive substances) rather than the drug being studied. Usually, to prevent demand effects, both the participants and the experimenters in these studies are unaware of which group the participants are in; thus, this type of experiment is double-blind.

Evaluating Therapy Outcome Research

Although therapy outcome studies might seem the most ethical way of conducting research on people in distress, they carry their own methodological challenges and ethical issues. Most psychological therapies involve a package of techniques for responding to people's problems. For example, depressed people in an experimental therapy group might be taught assertiveness skills, social problem-solving skills, and skills in changing self-defeating thinking. Which of these skills was most responsible for alleviating their depression? Even when a therapy works, researchers often cannot know exactly what it is about the therapy that works.

Ethical problems arise in using simple control groups, wait list control groups, and placebo control groups in therapy outcome research. Some researchers believe it is unethical to withhold treatment or to provide a treatment believed to be ineffective for people in distress. For example, many depressed participants assigned to a control group may be in severe distress or in danger of harming themselves and therefore would require immediate treatment.

In response to this concern, many therapy outcome studies now compare the effectiveness of two or more therapies expected to have positive effects. These studies basically are a competition between rival therapies and the theories behind these therapies. In theory, all the participants in such a study will benefit, but the study will also yield useful information about the most effective type of therapy for the participants. Regardless of which type of control or comparison group experimenters use in a therapy outcome study, participants must be informed of the types of groups the study involves and of the fact that they will be randomly assigned to one group or another (and thus run the risk of not receiving useful treatment as part of the study).

Another ethical issue concerns the obligation of the therapist to respond to the needs of the patient. How much can a therapy be modified to respond to a specific participant's needs without compromising the scientific integrity of the study? Therapists may feel the need to vary the dosage of a drug or to deviate from a study's procedure for psychological intervention. Departing too far from the standard therapy, however, will lead to great variation in the therapy that participants in the intervention group receive, which could compromise the results of the study.

A related methodological issue has to do with generalizing results from therapy outcome studies to the real world. In these studies, the therapeutic intervention usually is delivered to patients in a controlled, high-quality atmosphere by the most

Therapy outcome studies focus on the experiences of people receiving therapy.

competent therapists. Patients usually are screened so that they fit a narrow set of criteria for being included in the study, and often only patients who stick with the therapy to its end are included in the final analyses.

In the real world, mental health services are not always delivered in controlled, high-quality atmospheres by the most competent therapists. Patients are who they are, with their complicated symptom pictures and lives that may not fit neatly into the criteria for an "optimal patient." Also, patients often leave and return to therapy and may not receive "full trials" of the therapy before they drop out for financial or personal reasons.

Therapy outcome research that tests how well a therapy works in highly controlled settings with a narrowly defined group of people is said to test the **efficacy** of a therapy. In contrast, therapy outcome research that tests how well a therapy works in real-world settings, with all the complications we have mentioned, is said to test the **effectiveness** of a therapy.

Single-Case Experimental Designs

Another type of experimental study is the **single-case experimental design,** in which a single individual or a small number of individuals are studied intensively. Unlike the case studies we discussed earlier, a single-case experimental design exposes the individual to some manipulation or intervention, and his or her behavior is examined before and after to determine the effects. In addition, in a single-case experimental design, the participant's behaviors are measured repeatedly over time through some standard method, whereas a case study often is based on the researcher's impressions of the participant and the factors affecting him or her.

FIGURE 4.2 **Effects Over Time of Drug Treatment for Depression in an Individual.** This graph shows an individual's level of depression during a 4-week baseline assessment (A), during 4 weeks of drug treatment (B), when the drug treatment is withdrawn for 4 weeks (A), and when the drug treatment is reinstated for 4 weeks (B).

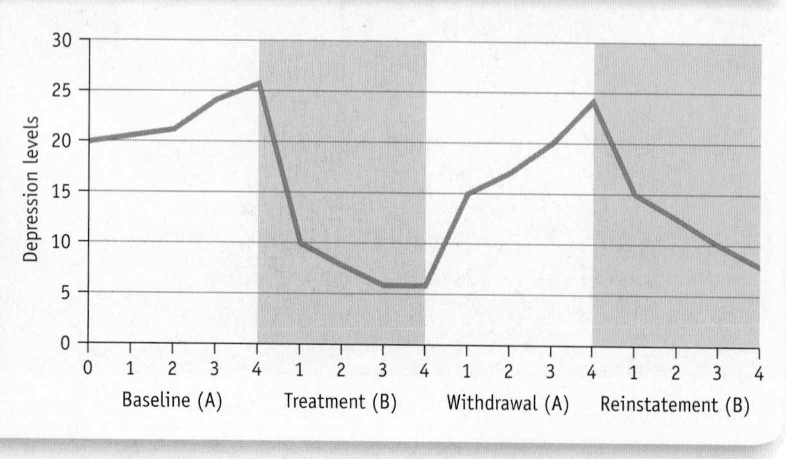

ABAB Design

A specific type of single-case experimental design is the **ABAB,** or **reversal, design,** in which an intervention is introduced, withdrawn, and then reinstated and the behavior of a participant is examined both on and off the treatment. For example, in the study of the effects of a drug for depression, an individual depressed participant might be assessed for her level of depression each day for 4 weeks. This is the baseline assessment (A; Figure 4.2). Then the participant would be given the drug for 4 weeks (B), and her level of depression would be assessed each day during that period. The drug then would be withdrawn for 4 weeks (A), and, again, her level of depression would be assessed each day. Finally, the drug would be reinstated for 4 weeks (B), and her level of depression assessed each day during that period. If the participant's levels of depression followed the pattern seen in Figure 4.2, this result would suggest that her depression level was much lower when she was taking the drug (B) than when she was not taking the drug (A).

Multiple Baseline Designs

In a **multiple baseline design,** an intervention might be given to the same individual but in different settings or to different individuals at different points in time. To test whether a meditation exercise reduces depression, a researcher might teach a depressed person how to use the exercise while at work when she feels depressed. If the participant's depression decreased at work but not at home, where she did not use the meditation exercise, the researcher has some evidence that the exercise was responsible for the reduction in depression. If the participant were then told to use the meditation exercise at home and her depression decreased in this setting also, this would be further evidence of the exercise's utility.

Similarly, the researcher might teach the meditation exercise to multiple individuals, but at different points in time when their experiences are likely to be different. For example, the researcher might teach the meditation exercise to one depressed college student during the first week of classes, to another student during spring break, and to still another during exam week. If all the students experienced relief of their depression symptoms after learning the meditation exercise, despite their different levels of stress, this would be evidence that the effects of the meditation exercise were generalizable across individuals and settings.

Evaluating Single-Case Experimental Designs

A major advantage of single-case experimental designs is that they allow much more intensive assessment of participants than might be possible if there were more participants. For example, an individual child could be observed for hours each day as he was put on and then taken off a treatment. This intensity of assessment can allow researchers to pinpoint the types of behaviors that are and are not affected by the treatments.

The major disadvantage of single-case experimental designs is that their results may not be generalizable to the wider population. One individual's experience on or off a treatment may not be the same as other individuals' experiences. In addition, not all hypotheses can be tested with single-case experimental designs. Some treatments have lingering effects after they end. For example, if a person is taught new skills at coping with stress during the treatment, these skills will continue to be present even after the treatment is withdrawn.

FIGURE 4.3 **Shuttle Box for Learned Helplessness Experiments.** Researchers used an apparatus like this to deliver controllable or uncontrollable shocks to dogs in order to investigate the phenomenon of learned helplessness.

Animal Studies

Researchers sometimes try to avoid the ethical issues involved in experimental studies with humans by conducting the studies with animals. Animal research has its own set of ethical issues, but many researchers feel it is acceptable to expose animals to situations in the laboratory that it would not be ethical to impose on humans. **Animal studies** thus provide researchers with even more control over laboratory conditions and third variables than is possible in human laboratory studies.

In a well-known series of animal studies designed to investigate depression (discussed in Chapter 7), Martin Seligman, Bruce Overmier, Steven Maier, and their colleagues subjected dogs to an uncontrollable stressor in the laboratory (Overmier & Seligman, 1967; Seligman & Maier, 1967). The experimental group of dogs received a series of uncontrollable electric shocks. Let us call this *Group E,* for *experimental.*

In addition, there were two control groups. One control group of dogs received shocks but could control them by jumping over a barrier (Figure 4.3). Let us call this *Group J,* for *jump.* The dogs in Groups E and J received the same number and duration of shocks. The only difference between the groups was that the dogs in Group E could not control the shocks, whereas the dogs in Group J could. The second control group of dogs received no shock. Let us call this *Group N,* for *none.*

Dogs in Group E initially responded to the shocks by jumping around their cages. Soon, however, the majority became passive. Later, when the researchers provided the dogs with an opportunity to escape the shock by jumping over a barrier, these dogs did not learn to do so. It seemed that they had learned they could not control the shock, so they did not recognize opportunities for control when offered. The researchers labeled this set of behaviors *learned helplessness deficits.*

The dogs in the controllable shock group, Group J, learned to control the shock and did not develop learned helplessness deficits. The fact that the two groups of dogs experienced the same number and

SHADES OF GRAY

Imagine that you were the student member of the human participants committee that considered the ethics of research at your school. A researcher proposed a study in which participants would believe they were taking a test that indicated their intellectual ability. In truth, half the participants would be randomly assigned to receive feedback that they had done poorly on the test, and half would be randomly assigned to receive feedback that they had done well on the test. The researcher would measure participants' moods before and after taking the test and receiving the feedback.

At a minimum, what would you require of the researcher in order to consider this study ethical? (Discussion appears at the end of this chapter.)

duration of shocks suggests that lack of control, not the shocks alone, led to the learned helplessness deficits in the experimental group. The dogs in Group N, which received no shocks, also did not develop learned helplessness deficits.

Seligman and colleagues likened the learned helplessness deficits shown by their dogs to the symptoms of depression in humans: apathy, low initiation of behavior, and the inability to see opportunities to improve one's environment (see Seligman, 1975). They argued that many human depressions result from people learning they have no control over important outcomes in their lives. This learned helplessness theory of depression seems helpful in explaining the depression and passivity seen in chronically oppressed groups, such as battered spouses and some people who grow up in poverty.

Another type of animal study is similar to therapy outcome studies. In studies of the effectiveness of drugs, animals often are given the drugs to determine their effects on different bodily systems and behaviors. Sometimes, the animals are killed after receiving the drugs, to enable detailed physiological analyses of their effects. Obviously, such studies could not be done with humans. Animal studies of drugs are particularly useful in the early stages of research, when the possible side effects of the drugs are unknown.

Evaluating Animal Studies

There clearly are problems with animal studies. First, some people believe it is no more ethical to conduct painful, dangerous, or fatal experiments with animals than it is to do so with humans. Second, from a scientific vantage point, we must ask whether we can generalize the results of experiments with animals to humans. Are learned helplessness deficits in dogs really analogous to human depression? The debate over the ethical and scientific issues of animal research continues. Particularly in research on drug effectiveness, however, animal research may very well be crucial to the advancement of our knowledge of how to help people overcome psychopathology.

TEST YOURSELF

1. What is the critical difference between the independent variables in human laboratory studies and those in nonexperimental studies?
2. What are control groups?
3. What are demand characteristics and the concern about generalizability?
4. What is a therapy outcome study? What are some types of control groups in therapy outcome studies? What are some limitations of therapy outcome studies?
5. What are single-case experimental designs? What are ABAB, or reversal, designs? What are multiple baseline designs? What are some advantages and disadvantages of these types of studies?
6. What are animal studies? What are some of the pros and cons of animal studies?

APPLY IT A researcher wants to understand the effects of being bullied on the playground on children's well-being. He hires a child actor to go onto a playground and begin bullying targeted children. He videotapes the emotional reactions of the targeted children. To avoid biasing the results, the researcher does not tell the targeted children or their parents that he is conducting the study until the study is completed. Which of the following ethical principles does this study violate?

a. the right of participants never to be deceived
b. the requirement that research studies never inflict psychological distress on participants
c. the right of participants to give informed consent before participating.
d. the right of participants to be debriefed about the purposes of the study once it is completed

Answers appear online at www.mhhe.com/nolen5e.

GENETIC STUDIES

Identifying genetic factors associated with psychopathology involves a variety of research methods. Researchers investigate the degree to which genes play a role in a particular disorder, or its heritability, through *family history studies, twin studies,* and *adoption studies*. To investigate specific genes that may be involved in a disorder, they may use *molecular genetic studies* (also called *association studies*) or *linkage analyses*.

Family History Studies

Disorders that are genetically transmitted should, on average, show up more often in the families of people who have the disorder than they do in families of people who do not have the disorder. This is true whether the disorder is associated with one or with many genes. To conduct a **family history study,** scientists first identify people who clearly have the disorder in question. This group is called the *probands*. The researchers also identify a *control group* of people who clearly do not have the disorder. They then trace the *family pedigrees,* or family trees, of individuals in these two groups and determine how many of their relatives have the disorder. Researchers are most interested in *first-degree* relatives, such as full siblings, parents, or children, because these relatives are most genetically similar to the subjects (unless they have an identical twin, who will be genetically identical to them).

Figure 4.4 illustrates the degree of genetic relationship between an individual and various categories of relatives. This figure gives you an idea of why the risk of inheriting the genes for a disorder quickly decreases as the relationship between an individual and the relative with the disorder becomes more distant: The percentage of genes the individual and the relative with the disorder have in common decreases greatly with distance.

Although family history studies provide very useful information about the possible genetic transmission of a disorder, they have their problems. The most obvious is that families share not only genes but also environment. Several members of a family might have a disorder because they share the same environmental stresses. Family history studies cannot tease apart the genetic and environmental contributions to a disorder. Researchers often turn to twin studies to do this.

Twin Studies

Notice in Figure 4.4 that identical twins or **monozygotic (MZ) twins,** share 100 percent of their genes. This is because they come from a single fertilized egg, which splits into two identical parts. In contrast, nonidentical twins, or **dizygotic (DZ) twins,** share, on average, 50 percent of their genes because they come from two separate eggs fertilized by separate sperm, just as non-twin siblings do.

FIGURE 4.4 **Degrees of Genetic Relationship.** People with whom you share 50 percent of your genes are your first-degree relatives. People with whom you share 25 percent of your genes are your second-degree relatives. People with whom you share 12.5 percent of your genes are your third-degree relatives.

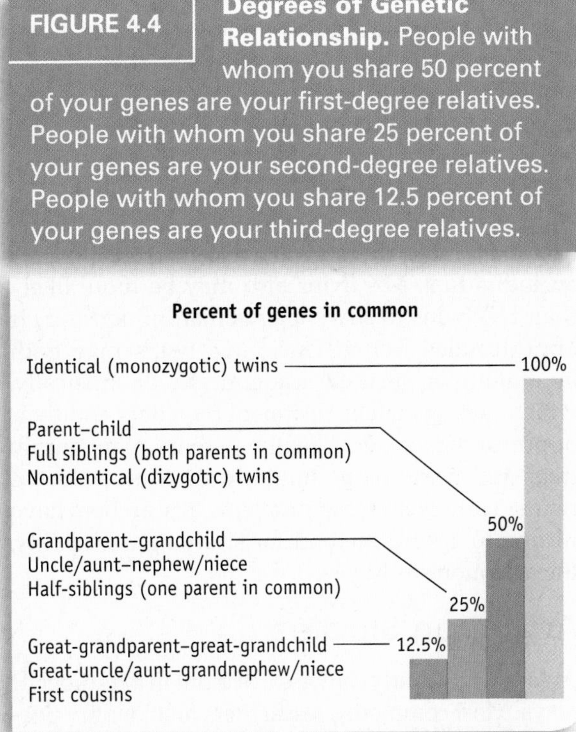

Researchers have capitalized on this difference between MZ and DZ twins to conduct **twin studies** on the contribution of genetics to many disorders. If a disorder is determined *entirely* by genetics, then when one member of a monozygotic (MZ) twin pair has a disorder, the other member of the pair should always have the disorder. This probability that both twins will have the disorder if one twin has it is called the **concordance rate** for the disorder. Thus, if a disorder is entirely determined by genes, the concordance rate among MZ twins should be close to 100 percent. The concordance rate for the disorder among dizygotic (DZ) twins will be much lower than 100 percent. Even when a disorder is transmitted only partially by genes, the concordance rate for MZ twins should be considerably higher than the concordance rate for DZ twins, because MZ twins are genetically identical but DZ twins share only about half their genes.

For example, suppose the concordance rate for Disorder X for MZ twins is 48 percent, whereas the concordance rate for DZ twins is 17 percent. These concordance rates tell us two things. First, because the concordance rate for MZ twins is considerably higher than that for DZ twins, we have evidence that Disorder X is genetically transmitted. Second, because the concordance rate for MZ twins is well under 100 percent, we have evidence that a combination of a genetic predisposition and other factors (biological or environmental) causes an individual to develop Disorder X.

Extraordinary People: Amish

Twin studies do not fully separate genetic and environmental factors, because MZ twins may have more similar environments and experiences than do DZ twins. For example, MZ twins typically look alike, whereas DZ twins often do not, and physical appearance can affect other people's reactions to an individual. MZ twins also may be more likely than DZ twins to share talents that influence their opportunities. For instance, MZ twins may both be athletic or talented academically or musically, which can affect their treatment by others and their opportunities in life. Finally, parents may simply treat MZ twins more similarly than they do DZ twins. To address these problems, researchers have turned to a third method for studying heritability, the adoption study.

Adoption Studies

An **adoption study** can be carried out in a number of ways. Most commonly, researchers first identify people who have the disorder of interest who were adopted shortly after birth. They then determine the rates of the disorder in the biological relatives of these adoptees and in the adoptive relatives of the adoptees. If a disorder is strongly influenced by genetics, then researchers should see higher rates of the disorder among the biological relatives of the adoptee than among the adoptive relatives. If the disorder is strongly influenced by environment, then they should see higher rates of the disorder among the adoptive relatives than among the biological relatives.

Molecular Genetic Studies and Linkage Analyses

The technology for examining human genes has advanced rapidly in recent decades, allowing researchers to search for associations between specific genetic abnormalities (also referred to as *genetic markers*) and psychopathology in what are called **molecular genetic studies** or **association studies.** A typical study might compare a group of people who have been diagnosed with a particular disorder, such as depression, with people who have no form of psychopathology. DNA from individuals in both groups is obtained either through blood samples or by swabbing the inside of the individuals' cheeks to obtain a small amount of tissue. This DNA is then analyzed (genotyped) to determine whether each individual has a genetic characteristic or marker of interest.

Because the human genome is so vast, researchers may try to narrow down the location of the gene marker associated with a psychological disorder by looking for other characteristics that co-occur with the disorder and have known genetic markers, a process called **linkage analysis.** For example, in the study of mood disorders among the Amish described in the Extraordinary People segment at the beginning of this chapter, researchers found that two markers on chromosome 11, one for insulin and one for a known cancer gene, were linked to the presence of mood disorder in one large family (Biron et al., 1987). This suggests that a gene that plays a role in vulnerability to mood disorders may be on chromosome 11. Unfortunately, this linkage has not been replicated in other studies. In Chapter 8, we will discuss genetic linkage studies that have identified possible genetic markers for schizophrenia.

TEST YOURSELF

APPLY IT A researcher contacts all known relatives of patients who have schizophrenia and determines whether these relatives have schizophrenia. This is an example of which of the following?

a. a twin study
b. an adoption study
c. a family history study
d. an association study
e. a linkage analysis

Answers appear online at www.mhhe.com/nolen5e.

CROSS-CULTURAL RESEARCH

Not long ago, most psychological research was conducted with college students, most of whom were White and middle- or upper-class. Researchers believed that any results they obtained from these samples could be generalized to any other relevant sample. Only anthropologists and a handful of psychologists and psychiatrists argued that what is true of one ethnic group, culture, or gender is not necessarily true of others.

In the past three decades, however, there has been an explosion of cross-cultural research in abnormal psychology. Researchers are investigating the similarities and differences across culture in the nature, causes, and treatment of psychopathology. These cross-cultural researchers face several special challenges.

First, researchers must be careful in applying theories or concepts that were developed in one culture to another culture (Rogler, 1999). Because the manifestations of disorders can differ across cultures, researchers who insist on narrow definitions of disorders may fail to identify many people manifesting disorders in culturally defined ways. Similarly, theoretical variables can have different meanings or manifestations across cultures.

A good example is the variable known as *expressed emotion*. Families high in expressed emotion are highly critical of and hostile toward other family members and emotionally overinvolved with each other. Several studies of the majority cultures in America and Europe have shown that people with schizophrenia whose families are high in expressed emotion have higher rates of relapse than those whose families are low in expressed emotion (Hooley, 2007). The meaning and manifestation of expressed emotion can differ greatly across cultures, however:

> Criticism within Anglo-American family settings, for example, may focus on allegations of faulty personality traits (e.g., laziness) or psychotic symptom behaviors (e.g., strange ideas). However, in other societies, such as those of Latin America, the same behaviors may not be met with criticism. Among Mexican-descent families, for example, criticism tends to focus on disrespectful or disruptive behaviors that affect the family but not on psychotic symptom behavior and individual personality characteristics. Thus, culture plays a role in creating the content or targets of criticism. Perhaps most importantly, culture is influential in determining *whether* criticism is a prominent part of the familial emotional atmosphere. (Jenkins & Karno, 1992, p. 10)

Today's researchers are more careful to search for culturally specific manifestations of the characteristics of interest in their studies and for the possibility that the characteristics or variables that predict psychopathology in one culture may be irrelevant in other cultures.

Second, even if researchers believe they can apply their theories across cultures, they may have difficulty translating their questionnaires or other assessment tools into different languages. A key concept in English, for example, may not be precisely translated into another language. Many languages contain variations on pronouns and verbs whose usage is determined by the social relationship between the speaker and the person being addressed. For example, in Spanish, the second-person pronoun *usted* ("you") connotes respect, establishes an appropriate distance in a social relationship, and is the correct way for a young interviewer to address an older respondent (Rogler, 1989). In contrast, when a young interviewer addresses a young respondent, the relationship is more informal, and the appropriate form of address is *tú* (also "you"). An interviewer who violates the social norms implicit in a language can alienate a respondent and impair the research.

Third, there may be cultural or gender differences in people's responses to the social demands of interacting with researchers. For example, people of Mexican origin, older people, and people of a lower socioeconomic class are more likely to answer yes to researchers' questions, regardless of the content, and also to attempt to answer questions in socially desirable ways than are Anglo-Americans, younger people, and people of higher socioeconomic class. These differences appear to result from differences among groups in their deference to authority figures and concern over presenting a proper appearance (Ross & Mirowsky, 1984). Similarly, it is often said that men are less likely than women to admit to "weaknesses," such as symptoms of distress or problems coping. If researchers do not take biases into account when they design assessment tools and analyze data, erroneous conclusions can result.

TEST YOURSELF

APPLY IT Which of the following is *not* one of the challenges of conducting cross-cultural research discussed in this chapter?

a. difficulty in applying theories appropriate in one culture to other cultures
b. difficulty in translating concepts and measures across cultures
c. differences in how people from different cultures react to being in studies and interacting with researchers
d. difficulty in getting funding for cross-cultural research

Answers appear online at www.mhhe.com/nolen5e.

META-ANALYSIS

Often the research literature contains many studies that have investigated a particular idea (e.g., that stress leads to depression). An investigator may want to know what the overall trend across all studies is and what factors might account for some studies supporting their hypothesis and others not. A researcher could read over all the studies and draw conclusions about whether most of them support or do not support the hypothesis. These conclusions can be biased, however, by the reader's interpretations of the studies.

A more objective way to draw conclusions about a body of research is to conduct a **meta-analysis,** a statistical technique for summarizing results across several studies. The first step in a meta-analysis is to do a thorough literature search, usually with the help of computer search engines that will identify all studies with certain keywords. Often, studies use different methods and measures for testing a hypothesis, so the second step of a meta-analysis is to transform the results of each study into a statistic common across all the studies. This statistic, called the *effect size,* gives an indication of how big the differences are between two groups (such as a group that received a specific form of therapy and one that did not) or how large the relationship is between two continuous variables (such as the correlation between levels of stress and levels of depression). Researchers can then examine the average effect size across studies and relate the effect size to characteristics of the study, such as the year it was published, the type of measure used, or the age or gender of the participants. For example, a meta-analysis of studies of children's depression levels found that studies done in more recent years tend to find lower levels of depression than studies done previously (Twenge and Nolen-Hoeksema, 2002). This finding suggests that levels of depression may be decreasing in more recent groups of children.

Evaluating Meta-Analysis

Meta-analysis can overcome some of the problems of small numbers of participants in an individual study by pooling the data from thousands of study participants, providing more power to find significant effects. The studies examined by Twenge and Nolen-Hoeksema (2002) generally had small numbers of ethnic minority children, making it difficult to compare their depression scores with those of nonminority children. By pooling studies, however, the overall sample sizes of Hispanic and African American children were large enough to allow comparisons by race/ethnicity. The meta-analysis found that Hispanic children generally had higher depression scores than African American or White children.

Meta-analyses have their problems, however. First, some published studies have methodological flaws. These flawed studies may be included in a meta-analysis along with methodologically stronger studies, influencing the overall results. Second, there is the *file drawer effect*—studies that do not support the hypothesis they are designed to test are less likely to get published than studies that do. For example, a study that finds that a psychotherapy is not any more effective than a wait list control is less likely to get published than a study that finds that the same psychotherapy is more effective than the wait list control. The bias toward publishing studies with positive results means that many perfectly good studies that fail to find the expected effects do not get published and therefore do not end up in meta-analyses. This file drawer effect biases the results of meta-analyses toward finding an overall positive effect of a treatment or some other type of difference between groups.

TEST YOURSELF

What is meta-analysis? What is an effect size?

APPLY IT What is the file drawer effect?

a. the fact that so many studies are published in a given year that it is difficult to tabulate all of them in a meta-analysis
b. the fact that studies that result in support for their hypothesis are more likely to get published than those that do not
c. the fact that researchers who do meta-analyses tend to exclude studies that do not show significant relationships between the independent and dependent variables

Answers appear online at www.mhhe.com/nolen5e.

CHAPTER INTEGRATION

We noted in Chapter 2 that theories or models of psychopathology are increasingly based on the integration of concepts from biological, psychological, and social approaches. These concepts often are viewed from a vulnerability-stress perspective. The characteristics that make a person more vulnerable to abnormality might include biological characteristics, such as a genetic predisposition, or psychological characteristics, such as maladaptive styles of thinking about the world. These personal characteristics must interact with characteristics of the situation or environment to create the abnormality. For example, a woman with a genetic predisposition to depression may never develop the disorder in its full form if she has a supportive family and never faces major stressors.

Conducting research that reflects this integrationist perspective on abnormality is not easy. Researchers must gather information about people's biological, psychological, and social vulnerabilities and strengths. This work may require specialized equipment or expertise. It also may require following participants longitudinally to observe what happens when people with vulnerabilities face stressors that may trigger episodes of their disorder.

Increasingly, researchers work together in teams to share both their expertise in specialized research methods and resources, making multidisciplinary longitudinal research possible. Researchers also train in multiple disciplines and methods. For example, psychologists are learning to use magnetic resonance imaging (MRI), positron-emission tomography (PET) scans, and other advanced biological methods in investigating abnormality.

If you pursue a career in researching abnormality, you might integrate methods from psychology (which have been the focus of this chapter), sociology, and biology to create the most comprehensive picture of the disorder you are investigating. This task may seem daunting, but the interactionist approach holds out the possibility of producing breakthroughs that can greatly improve the lives of people vulnerable to psychopathology.

SHADES OF GRAY DISCUSSION (review p. 104)

Your greatest challenge in deciding the ethics of this particular study is that the study involves deception. Some ethics committees would never accept a study in which students were deceived about their results on an intelligence test. Other committees might approve this study if it ensured all or most of the basic rights discussed on pages 91–92. Participants must be aware that they may experience psychological distress as a result of participating. They must know that they may decline participation or withdraw at any point. Usually, these statements must appear in an informed consent document that individuals should read before deciding to participate. This document should also tell participants how confidential their responses in the study will be. In this case, there is no reason why participants' responses should not be confidential.

If the researcher told participants before the study began that the feedback they will receive is bogus, this clearly would affect participants' responses to the feedback. The researcher would argue that participants cannot be told in the informed consent document that the study involves deception. Your ethics committee then must decide whether the potential benefits of the information obtained in this study warrant this deception.

Following the study, the researcher should reveal the nature of the deception and the justification for using it. Many participants, especially college students, continue to believe negative feedback they receive in an experiment even after being told that they were deceived. The researchers who discovered this phenomenon recommended conducting a *process debriefing* (Ross, Lepper, & Hubbard, 1975). In such a debriefing, experimenters discuss at length the purposes and procedures of the experiment, explaining that the feedback was not a reflection of participants' abilities.

THINK CRITICALLY

Imagine that you want to test the hypothesis that pressures to be thin lead women to develop eating disorders.

1. What are your dependent variable and independent variable?
2. What type of sample would you recruit for your study?
3. How are you going to define pressures to be thin and eating disorders?
4. What would be the advantages and disadvantages of using a case study to test your hypothesis?
5. Outline a correlational study that you could do to test your hypothesis.
6. Outline an experimental study that you could do to test your hypothesis.
7. Outline a therapy outcome study that you could do to test your hypothesis.
8. How could a meta-analysis be useful in testing your hypothesis?

(Discussion appears on pp. 517–518 at the back of this book.)

CHAPTER SUMMARY

- A hypothesis is a testable statement of what we predict will happen in a study.
- The dependent variable is the factor the study aims to predict. The independent variable is the factor used or manipulated to predict the dependent variable.
- A sample is a group taken from the population of interest to participate in the study. The samples for the study must be representative of the population of interest, and the research must be generalizable to the population of interest.

- A control group consists of people who are similar in most ways to the primary group of interest but who do not experience the variable the theory hypothesizes causes changes in the dependent variable. Matching the control group to the group of primary interest can help control third variables, which are variables unrelated to the theory that still may have some effect on the dependent variable.
- The basic rights of participants in studies include being told the risks of participation, having their information kept confidential, having the right to refuse participation or withdraw from the study, giving informed consent, not being exposed to deception unless well justified, and being debriefed following the study.
- Case studies of individuals provide detailed information about their subjects. They are helpful in generating new ideas and in studying rare problems. They suffer from problems in generalizability and in the subjectivity of both the person being studied and the person conducting the study.
- Correlational studies examine the relationship between two variables without manipulating the variables. A correlation coefficient is an index of the relationship between two variables. It can range from −1.00 to +1.00. The magnitude of the correlation indicates how strong the relationship between the variables is.
- A positive correlation indicates that as values of one variable increase, values of the other variable increase. A negative correlation indicates that as values of one variable increase, values of the other variable decrease.
- A result is said to be statistically significant if it is unlikely to have happened by chance. The convention in psychological research is to accept results for which there is probability of less than 5 in 100 that they happened by chance.
- A correlational study can show that two variables are related, but it cannot show that one variable causes the other. All correlational studies have the third variable problem—the possibility that variables not measured in the study actually account for the relationship between the variables measured in the study.
- Continuous variable studies evaluate the relationship between two variables that vary along a continuum.
- A representative sample resembles the population of interest on all important variables. One way to generate a representative sample is to obtain a random sample.
- Whereas cross-sectional studies assess a sample at one point in time, longitudinal studies assess a sample at multiple points in time. A longitudinal study often assesses a sample that is expected to experience some key event in the future both before and after the event, then examines changes that occurred in the sample. Group comparison studies evaluate differences between key groups, such as a group that experienced a certain stressor and a matched comparison group that did not.
- Epidemiology is the study of the frequency and distribution of a disorder in a population. The prevalence of a disorder is the proportion of the population that has the disorder at a given point or period in time. The incidence of a disorder is the number of new cases of the disorder that develop during a specific period of time. Risk factors for a disorder are conditions or variables associated with a higher risk of having the disorder.
- Experimental studies can provide evidence that a given variable causes psychopathology. A human laboratory study has the goal of inducing the conditions that we hypothesize will lead to our outcome of interest (e.g., increasing stress to cause depression) in people in a controlled setting. Participants are randomly assigned to either the experimental group, which receives a manipulation, or a control group, which does not.
- Generalizing experimental studies to real-world phenomena sometimes is not possible. In addition, manipulating people who are in distress in an experimental study can create ethical problems.
- A therapy outcome study allows researchers to test a hypothesis about the causes of a psychopathology while providing a service to participants.
- In therapy outcome studies, researchers sometimes use wait list control groups, in which control participants wait to receive the interventions until after the studies are completed. Alternatively, researchers may try to construct placebo control groups, in which participants receive the general support of therapists but none of the elements of the therapy thought to be active. Both types of control groups have practical and ethical limitations.
- Difficult issues associated with therapy outcome studies include problems in knowing what elements of therapy were effective, questions about the appropriate control groups to use, questions about whether to allow modifications of the therapy to fit individual participants' needs, and the lack of generalizability of the results of these studies to the real world.
- Single-case experimental designs involve the intensive investigation of single individuals or small groups of individuals, before and after a manipulation or intervention. In an ABAB, or reversal, design, an intervention is introduced, withdrawn, and then reinstated, and the behavior of a participant on and off the treatment is examined.
- In multiple baseline designs, an individual is given a treatment in different settings or multiple individuals are given a treatment at different

times across different settings, and the effects of the treatment are systematically observed.

- Animal studies allow researchers to manipulate their subjects in ways that are not ethically permissible with human participants, although many people feel that such animal studies are equally unethical. Animal studies raise questions about their generalizability to humans.
- Family history studies determine whether biological relatives of someone with a disorder are more likely to have it than are people not related to someone with the disorder. Adoption studies determine whether the biological family members of adoptees with a disorder are more likely to have the disorder than are the adoptive family members. Twin studies determine whether monozygotic twins are more alike in the presence or absence of a disorder than are dizygotic twins. Molecular genetic (or association) studies look for specific genes associated with a disorder. Linkage analyses investigate the relationship between a biological characteristic for which the genes are known and a psychological disorder for which they are not.
- Cross-cultural research poses challenges. Theories and concepts that make sense in one culture may not be applicable to other cultures. Questionnaires and other assessment tools must be translated accurately. Also, culture can affect how people respond to the social demands of research. Finally, researchers must be careful not to build into their research any assumptions that one culture is normal and another is deviant.
- Meta-analysis is a statistical technique for summarizing the results across several studies. In a meta-analysis, the results of individual studies are standardized by a statistic called the effect size. Then the magnitude of the effect size and its relationship to characteristics of the study are examined.
- Meta-analyses reduce bias that can occur when investigators draw conclusions across studies in a more subjective manner, but they can include studies that have poor methods or exclude good studies that did not get published because they did not find significant effects.

KEY TERMS

scientific method 89
hypothesis 89
null hypothesis 90
variable 90
dependent variable 90
independent variable 90
operationalization 90
case studies 92
generalizability 94
correlational studies 94
continuous variable 94
group comparison study 94
cross-sectional 94
longitudinal 94
correlation coefficient 95
statistical significance 96
third variable problem 96
sample 96
cohort effect 97
external validity 97
epidemiology 98
prevalence 98
incidence 98
risk factors 98
experimental studies 99
human laboratory study 99
internal validity 99
control group 100
experimental group 100
random assignment 100
demand characteristics 100
double-blind experiment 100
therapy outcome studies 100
wait list control group 101
placebo control group 101
efficacy 102
effectiveness 102
single-case experimental design 102
ABAB (reversal) design 102
multiple baseline design 102
animal studies 103
family history study 105
monozygotic (MZ) twins 105
dizygotic (DZ) twins 105
twin studies 105
concordance rate 105
adoption study 106
molecular genetic studies 106
association studies 106
linkage analysis 106
meta-analysis 108

Chapter 5

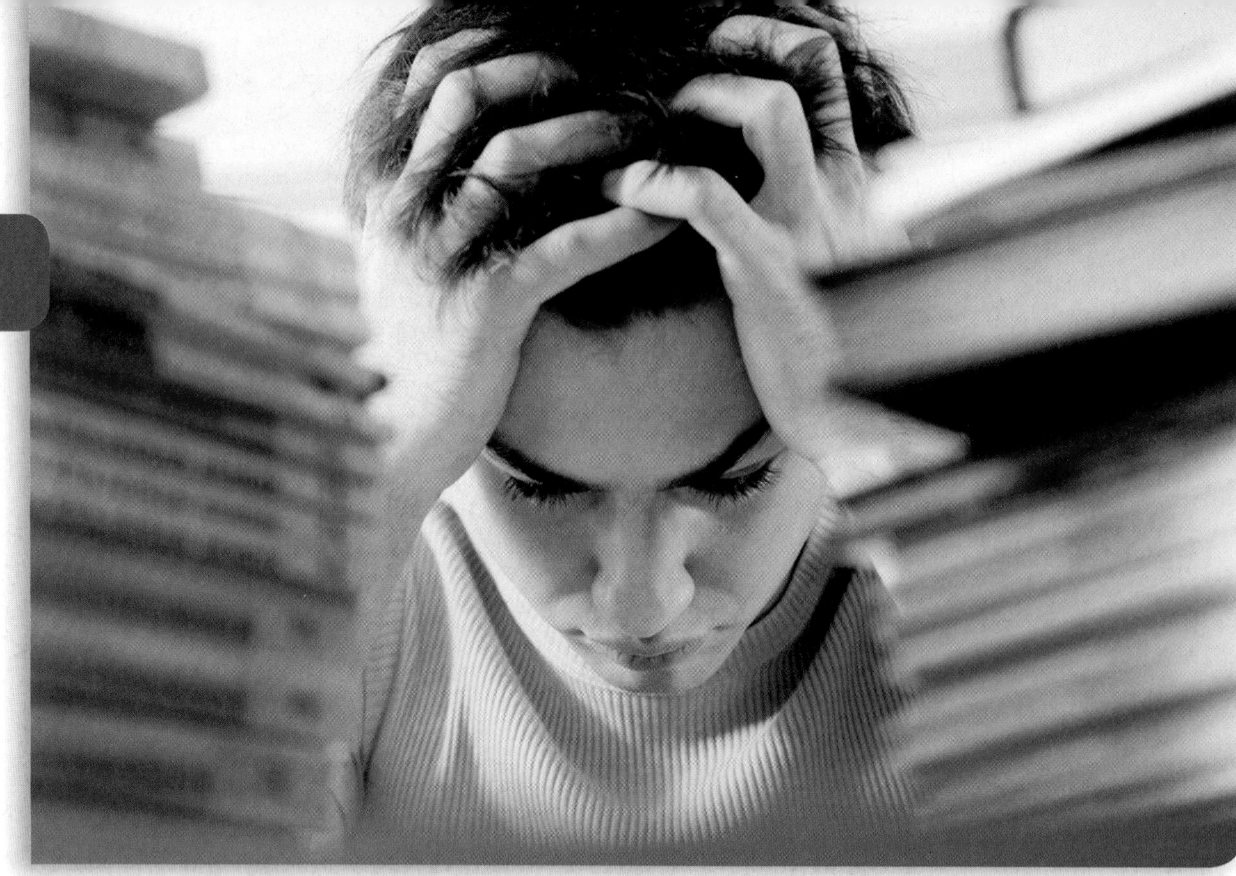

Anxiety Disorders

CHAPTER OUTLINE

Extraordinary People

David Beckham, *Perfection On and Off the Field*

Soccer star David Beckham's extraordinary ability to curve shots on corner kicks was immortalized in the movie *Bend It Like Beckham*. Beckham's perfectionism on the field is paralleled by his perfectionism about order and symmetry: "I've got this obsessive-compulsive disorder where I have to have everything in a straight line or everything has to be in pairs" (quoted in Dolan, 2006). Beckham spends hours ordering the furniture in his house in a particular way or lining up the clothes in his closet by color. His wife, Victoria (the former Posh Spice), says, "If you open our fridge, it's all coordinated down either side. We've got three fridges—food in one, salad in another and drinks in the third. In the drinks one, everything is symmetrical. If there's three cans he'll throw away one because it has to be an even number" (quoted in Frith, 2006).

Beckham has traveled around the world, playing for top teams including Real Madrid, Manchester United, Los Angeles Galaxy, and AC Milan. Each time he enters a new hotel room, he has to arrange everything in order: "I'll go into a hotel room. Before I can relax I have to move all the leaflets and all the books and put them in a drawer. Everything has to be perfect" (quoted in Frith, 2006). His teammates on Manchester United knew of his obsessions and compulsions and would deliberately rearrange his clothes or move the furniture around in his hotel room to infuriate him.

When we face any type of threat or stressor, our bodies mobilize to handle it. Over evolutionary history, humans have developed a characteristic **fight-or-flight response**, a set of physical and psychological responses that help us fight a threat or flee from it.

The physiological changes of the fight-or-flight response result from the activation of two systems controlled by the hypothalamus, as seen in Figure 5.1: the *autonomic nervous system* (in particular, the sympathetic division of this system) and the *adrenal-cortical system* (a hormone-releasing system; see Chapter 2). The hypothalamus first activates the sympathetic division of the autonomic nervous system. The sympathetic system acts directly on the smooth muscles and internal organs to produce key bodily changes: The liver releases extra sugar (glucose) to fuel the muscles, and the body's metabolism increases in preparation for expending energy on physical action. Heart rate, blood pressure, and breathing rate increase, and the muscles tense. Less essential activities, such as digestion, are curtailed. Saliva and mucus dry up, increasing the size of the air passages to the lungs. The body secretes endorphins, natural painkillers, and the surface blood vessels constrict to reduce bleeding in case of injury. The spleen releases more red blood cells to help carry oxygen.

The hypothalamus activates the adrenal-cortical system by releasing corticotropin-release factor (CRF), which signals the pituitary gland to secrete adrenocorticotropic hormone (ACTH), the body's major stress hormone. ACTH stimulates the outer layer of the adrenal glands (the adrenal cortex), releasing a group of hormones, the major one being **cortisol.** The amount of cortisol in blood or urine samples is often used as a measure of stress. ACTH also signals the adrenal glands to release about 30 other hormones, each of which plays a role in the body's adjustment to emergency situations. Eventually, when the threatening stimulus has passed, the hormones signal the hippocampus, a part of the brain that helps regulate emotions, to turn off this physiological cascade. The fight-or-flight system thus has its own feedback loop that normally regulates the level of physiological arousal we experience in response to a stressor. In many of the anxiety disorders we discuss in this chapter, the normal response becomes abnormal, and the fight-or-flight system becomes dysregulated.

In addition to these physiological responses to a threat, characteristic emotional, cognitive, and

FIGURE 5.1 **The Fight-or-Flight Response.** The body's fight-or-flight response is initiated by the part of the brain known as the hypothalamus. The hypothalamus stimulates the sympathetic division of the autonomic nervous system, which acts on smooth muscles and internal organs to produce the bodily changes shown in the figure. The hypothalamus also releases corticotropin-release factor (CRF), which triggers the pituitary gland to release adrenocorticotropic hormone (ACTH). In turn, ACTH stimulates the adrenal glands to release about 30 other hormones. These hormones act on organs and muscles to prepare the body to fight or flee.

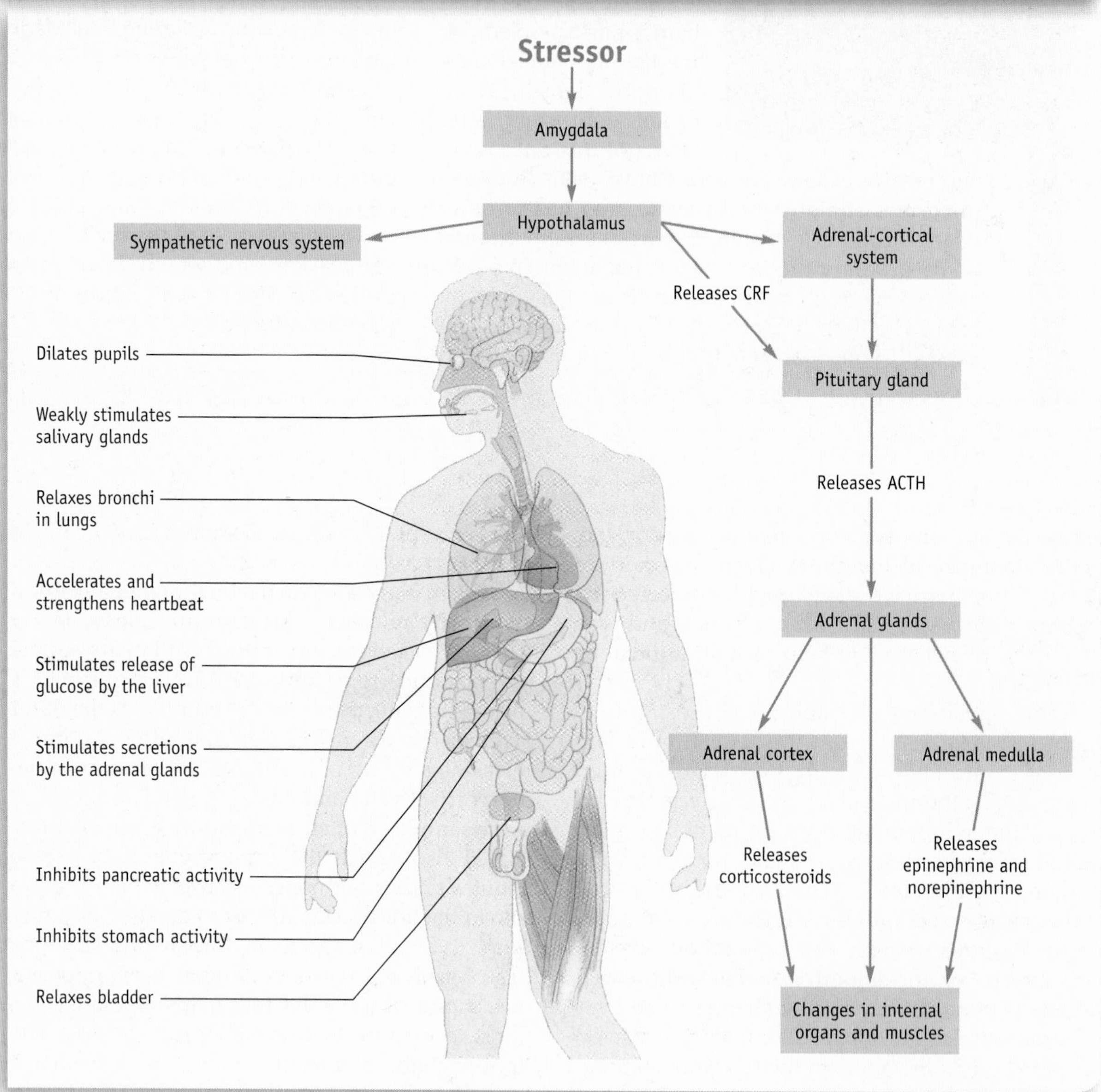

behavioral responses occur (Table 5.1 on page 116). Emotionally, we experience terror and dread, and we often are irritable or restless. Cognitively, we are on the lookout for danger. Behaviorally, we seek to confront the threat or escape from it. In a realistic fear response, these emotional, cognitive, and behavioral responses subside when the threat subsides. In anxiety disorders, these responses may persist in the absence of any objective threat.

Anxiety is a large part of many psychological disorders. Most people with serious depression report bouts of anxiety (Kessler et al., 1994; Lewinsohn et al., 1997). People with schizophrenia often feel anxious when they believe they are slipping into a

Fear and Anxiety Along the Continuum

Functional — Dysfunctional

- Fear is in response to **objectively threatening** events *(fearing you will fail a class after failing the midterm)*
- Fear is of **appropriate severity** given the threat *(being concerned because you need this class to graduate)*
- Fear **subsides when threat has passed** *(relaxing when you learn there was a grading error and you actually did well)*
- Fear leads to **adaptive behaviors** to confront or avoid threat *(asking your instructor if you can improve your grade with extra work)*

- Fear may be **somewhat unrealistic** *(fear of appearing foolish when giving a presentation in class)*
- Fear may be **somewhat more than is warranted** given the severity of the threat *(being unable to sleep the night before a presentation)*
- Fear **persists after the threat has passed** *(after you give the presentation, analyzing it and worrying about what people thought)*
- Fear **leads to behaviors that may be somewhat inappropriate** *(taking a tranquilizer before the presentation to relax)*

Potentially meets diagnostic criteria for an anxiety disorder:

- Fear is **moderately unrealistic** *(fearing a car accident if you drive on Friday the 13th)*
- Fear is **definitely more than is warranted** given the severity of the threat *(being very nervous when forced to drive on Friday the 13th)*
- Fear **persists for quite a while after the threat has passed** *(worrying about the next Friday the 13th)*
- Fear leads to **behaviors that are potentially dangerous or impairing** *(skipping class to avoid driving on Friday the 13th)*

Likely meets diagnostic criteria for an anxiety disorder:

- Fears are **completely unrealistic** *(fearing that every ache or pain is a sign of terminal illness)*
- Fears are **excessive** given the objective threat *(thinking one is dying when one feels pain)*
- Fears **persist long after the threat has passed,** and chronic anticipatory anxiety exists *(believing one has a terminal illness despite physician reassurance)*
- Fear **leads to dangerous behavior or impairment** *(seeking out surgery to cure the terminal illness your physician says you do not have)*

Think of a time you felt fearful or anxious—perhaps on the first day of college. Chances are you responded in an adaptive way—that is, you had an appropriate response that helped you handle the threat (e.g., you went to school and made an effort to meet new people). But other people might have had *unrealistic* fears that they responded to in a way that was *out of proportion* to the threat—they were so afraid of saying something embarrassing to a new classmate that they avoided going to class completely.

Adaptive fear responses subside when the threat ends, while maladaptive **anxiety** *persists* after the threat passes and can even lead to *anticipatory anxiety* about the future. In adaptive fear, people behave appropriately to confront or avoid the threat. In maladaptive anxiety, people behave in ways that are dangerous or lead to impairment. Someone whose wallet was stolen may keep alert when going out (adaptive), while a person with agoraphobia may become housebound due to fear of venturing out (maladaptive).

new episode of psychosis. Many people who abuse alcohol and other drugs do so to dampen anxious symptoms (Schuckit, 1991). In addition, people with one anxiety disorder are likely to have another (Craske & Waters, 2005).

This chapter focuses on disorders that the *DSM* classifies as anxiety disorders. We begin with two disorders in which an initial, potentially adaptive fear response develops into a maladaptive anxiety disorder.

TABLE 5.1 Responses to Threat

These characteristic responses to threat can also be symptoms of an anxiety disorder.

Somatic	Emotional	Cognitive	Behavioral
Goosebumps	Sense of dread	Anticipation of harm	Escape
Tense muscles	Terror	Exaggeration of danger	Avoidance
Increased heart rate	Restlessness	Problems in concentrating	Aggression
Accelerated respiration	Irritability	Hypervigilance	Freezing
Deepened respiration		Worried, ruminative thinking	Decreased appetitive responding
Spleen contraction		Fear of losing control	Increased aversive responding
Dilated peripheral blood vessels		Fear of dying	
Widened bronchioles		Sense of unreality	
Dilated pupils			
Increased perspiration			
Adrenaline secretion			
Inhibited stomach acid			
Decreased salivation			
Bladder relaxation			

POST-TRAUMATIC STRESS DISORDER AND ACUTE STRESS DISORDER

Two psychological disorders, **post-traumatic stress disorder (PTSD)** and **acute stress disorder,** are by definition the consequences of experiencing extreme stressors. Blair, a survivor of the terrorist attacks on the World Trade Center on September 11, 2001, describes many core symptoms of both.

VOICES

I just can't let go of it. I was working at my desk on the 10th floor of the World Trade Center when the first plane hit. We heard it but couldn't imagine what it was. Pretty soon someone started yelling, "Get out—it's a bomb!" and we all ran for the stairs.

The dust and smoke were pouring down the staircase as we made our way down. It seemed to take an eternity to get to the ground. When I got outside, I looked up and saw that the top of the tower was on fire. I just froze; I couldn't move. Then the second plane hit. Someone grabbed my arm and we started running. Concrete and glass began to fly everywhere. People were falling down, stumbling. Everyone was covered in *(continued)* dust. When I got far enough away, I just stood and stared as the towers fell. I couldn't believe what I was seeing. Other people were crying and screaming, but I just stared. I couldn't believe it.

Now, I don't sleep very well. I try, but just as I'm falling asleep, the images come flooding into my mind. I see the towers falling. I see people with cuts on their faces. I see the ones who didn't make it out, crushed and dead. I smell the dust and smoke. Sometimes, I cry to the point that my pillow is soaked. Sometimes, I just stare at the ceiling, as I stared at the towers as they fell. During the day, I go to work, but often it's as if my head is in another place. Someone will say something to me, and I won't hear them. I often feel as if I'm floating around, not touching or really seeing anything around me. But if I do hear a siren, which you do a lot in the city, I jump out of my skin.

Immediately after the World Trade Center attacks, about 20 percent of people living nearby had symptoms meeting the diagnosis of PTSD, including reexperiencing the event (e.g., flashbacks or nightmares), feeling numb and detached, and being hypervigilant and chronically aroused (Galea et al., 2002). Even those not physically present were traumatized by the event. Nationwide studies showed that just after September 11, 2001, 44 percent

Traumatic events such as the attacks on the World Trade Center can lead to post-traumatic stress.

of adults reported symptoms of PTSD (Schuster et al., 2001). Two months later, 21 percent of adults nationwide reported still being "quite a bit" or "extremely" bothered by distress symptoms (Stein et al., 2004). Those in this study with persistent distress reported accomplishing less at work (65 percent), avoiding public gathering places (24 percent), and using alcohol or other drugs to quell worries about terrorism (38 percent).

A wide range of traumas can induce post-traumatic stress disorder or acute stress disorder, ranging from extraordinary events, such as a terrorist attack, to common events, such as a traffic accident. About 7 percent of adults will be exposed to a traumatic event and develop post-traumatic stress disorder at some time in their lives, with women at greater risk than men (Kessler et al., 2005). The symptoms can be mild to moderate, permitting normal functioning. For other people, however, the symptoms can be immobilizing, causing deterioration in their work, family, and social lives.

A diagnosis of PTSD requires the presence of three types of symptoms (Table 5.2). The first is repeated *reexperiencing of the traumatic event.* PTSD sufferers may experience intrusive images or thoughts, recurring nightmares, or flashbacks in which they relive the event. Memories of the World Trade Center attack intrude into Blair's consciousness against her will, particularly when she encounters something that reminds her of the event. She also relives her emotional reaction to the event, and she chronically experiences negative emotions that have not diminished with time.

The second type of symptoms in PTSD involves persistent avoidance of stimuli associated with the trauma and *emotional numbing.* People will shun activities, places, or other people that remind them of the event. They become withdrawn, reporting that they feel numb and detached from others. Especially immediately after the trauma, they may also feel detached from themselves and their ongoing experiences, as does Blair. They may have a sense of a foreshortened future, not expecting to reach typical milestones such as having a career, a marriage, or a normal life span.

The third type of symptoms includes *hypervigilance* and *chronic arousal.* People with PTSD are always on guard for the traumatic event to recur. Sounds or images that remind them of their trauma can instantly create panic and flight. A war veteran, hearing a car backfire, may jump into a ditch and begin to have flashbacks of the war, reexperiencing the terror he or she felt on the front lines. Those with PTSD may report "survivor guilt" about having lived through the traumatic event or about things they had to do to survive.

The *DSM* recognizes another disorder associated with traumas: *acute stress disorder.* Acute stress disorder occurs in response to traumas similar to those involved in PTSD but is diagnosed when symptoms arise within 1 month of exposure to the stressor and last no longer than 4 weeks. As in PTSD, the individual with acute stress disorder persistently reexperiences the trauma through flashbacks, nightmares, and intrusive thoughts; avoids reminders of the trauma; and is constantly aroused. In acute stress disorder, *dissociative symptoms* are common, including numbing or detachment, reduced awareness of surroundings, derealization (experiencing the world as unreal or dreamlike), depersonalization (feeling detached from one's body or mental processes), and an inability to recall important aspects of the trauma. Although acute stress disorder is defined as a short-term response to trauma, people who experience acute stress disorder are at high risk of continuing to experience post-traumatic stress symptoms for many additional months.

Another trauma- and stress-related diagnosis is **adjustment disorder,** which consists of emotional and behavioral symptoms (depressive symptoms, anxiety symptoms, and/or antisocial behaviors) that arise within 3 months of the experience of a stressor. The stressors that lead to adjustment disorder can be of any severity, while those that lead to PTSD and acute stress disorder are, by definition, extreme. Adjustment disorder is a diagnosis for people experiencing emotional and behavioral symptoms following a stressor who do not meet the criteria for a diagnosis of PTSD, acute stress disorder, or an anxiety or mood disorder resulting from stressful experience.

In the *DSM-IV-TR,* "traumatic event" was not clearly defined in the criteria for PTSD or acute

TABLE 5.2 *DSM-IV-TR* Criteria for Post-traumatic Stress Disorder

A. The person has been exposed to a traumatic event in which both of the following have been present:
   1. The person experienced, witnessed, or was confronted with an event or events that involved actual or threatened death or serious injury, or a threat to the physical integrity of self or others.
   2. The person's response involved intense fear, helplessness, or horror. *Note:* In children, may be expressed by disorganized or agitated behavior.

B. The traumatic event is persistently reexperienced in one (or more) of the following ways:
   1. Recurrent and intrusive distressing recollections of the event, including images, thoughts, or perceptions. *Note:* In young children, repetitive play with themes of the trauma may occur.
   2. Recurrent distressing dreams of the event. *Note:* In children, there may be frightening dreams without recognizable content.
   3. Acting or feeling as if the traumatic event were recurring (includes a sense of reliving the experience, illusions, hallucinations, and dissociative flashback episodes, including those that occur upon awakening or when intoxicated). *Note:* In young children, trauma-specific reenactment may occur.
   4. Intense psychological distress at exposure to internal or external cues that symbolize or resemble an aspect of the traumatic event.
   5. Physiological reactivity on exposure to internal or external cues that symbolize or resemble an aspect of the traumatic event.

C. Persistent avoidance of stimuli associated with the trauma and numbing of general responsiveness (not present before the trauma), as indicated by three (or more) of the following:
   1. Efforts to avoid thoughts, feelings, or conversations associated with the trauma
   2. Efforts to avoid activities, places, or people that arouse recollections of the trauma
   3. Inability to recall an important aspect of the trauma
   4. Markedly diminished interest or participation in significant activities
   5. Feeling of detachment or estrangement from others
   6. Restricted range of affect (e.g., unable to have loving feelings)
   7. Sense of a foreshortened future (e.g., does not expect to have a career, marriage, children, or a normal life span)

D. Persistent symptoms of increased arousal (not present before the trauma), as indicated by two (or more) of the following:
   1. Difficulty falling or staying asleep
   2. Irritability or outbursts of anger
   3. Difficulty concentrating
   4. Hypervigilance
   5. Exaggerated startle response

E. Duration of the disturbance (symptoms in Criteria B, C, and D) is more than 1 month.

F. The disturbance causes clinically significant distress or impairment in social, occupational, or other important areas of functioning.

Source: Reprinted with permission from the *Diagnostic and Statistical Manual of Mental Disorders,* Fourth Edition, Text Revision.

stress disorder, leading to questions about whether any type of event could be considered traumatic if the person responded to the event with intense fear, helplessness, or horror (Criterion A2 in Table 5.2). The *DSM-5* will more explicitly define "traumatic event" as death, serious injury, or sexual assault (or a serious threat of experiencing these events) (American Psychiatric Association, 2010). To get a diagnosis of PTSD, the *DSM-5* will require that an individual personally experience the event or witness it happen to others, have a close relative or friend who experienced it, or be repeatedly exposed to aversive details of the event (American Psychiatric Association, 2010). The *DSM-5* will drop the requirement that individuals experience "intense fear, helplessness or horror" because this subjective criterion was judged not to be useful.

Another change that may occur in the *DSM-5* relates to the diagnosis of PTSD in young children. Young children can manifest somewhat different symptoms of PTSD (see Scheeringa, Zeanah, Myers, & Putnam, 2003). Rather than reporting distressing memories of the event, children may express their recollections in their play. For example, a child who witnessed a parent being shot and killed may repeatedly have one doll kill another. Children also may reenact the traumatic event in their interactions with other children, such as by assaulting another child just as they were assaulted by an adult. The dreams of traumatized children may be frightening but lack clear content. The *DSM-IV-TR* notes these differences (see Table 5.2). The *DSM-5*, however, may introduce a separate diagnosis called *post-traumatic stress disorder in preschool children*. In addition to the different symptoms of PTSD described, this new diagnosis will detail how young children manifest other core symptoms (e.g., their irritable or aggressive behavior may be expressed as tantrums) and will require children to show fewer symptoms than adults to meet the criteria for the diagnosis.

Survivors of natural disasters, such as Hurricane Katrina in 2005, the tsunami in Asia in 2004, or the 2010 earthquake in Haiti, often experience post-traumatic stress disorder.

Traumas Leading to PTSD

The traumas that can lead to PTSD unfortunately are common. Among these are natural disasters such as floods, tsunamis, earthquakes, fires, hurricanes, and tornadoes. One of the largest natural disasters in recent history was the tsunami that struck south and southeast Asia on December 26, 2004. It is estimated that over 280,000 people were killed, while 27,000 remain missing and are assumed dead and 1.2 million were displaced. In the state of Tamil Nadu, India, 7,983 people were killed, and 44,207 had to be relocated to camps due to damage to their homes. Two months after the tsunami, researchers found that 13 percent of adults in this area were experiencing PTSD (Kumar et al., 2007).

Hurricane Katrina, one of the greatest U.S. natural disasters, hit the Gulf of Mexico coastline in August 2005. Nearly 90,000 square miles of land, an area the size of Great Britain, was declared a disaster area. More than 500,000 people were evacuated, over 1,600 were confirmed dead, and hundreds are still missing. Five months later, 30 percent of people from the New Orleans metropolitan area and 12 percent from the remainder of the hurricane area were diagnosed with PTSD (Galea et al., 2007). The 2010 earthquake in Haiti, with a death toll over 230,000 and widespread devastation, may have produced thousands of new cases of PTSD.

Human-made disasters such as wars, terrorist attacks, and torture may be even more likely to lead to PTSD than natural disasters. PTSD symptoms went by different names in the two world wars and the Korean War: "combat fatigue syndrome," "war zone stress," and "shell shock." In follow-up studies of soldiers experiencing these syndromes, the soldiers showed chronic post-traumatic stress symptoms for decades after the war (Elder & Clipp, 1989; Sutker, Allain, & Winstead, 1993). PTSD became widely recognized after the Vietnam War. Large numbers of Vietnam veterans had the disorder, and as many as half a million still had it 15 years after their service ended (Schlenger, Kulkan, Fairbank, & Hough, 1992).

Recent and ongoing wars and conflicts have left thousands of PTSD sufferers in their wake. Studies of U.S. Army soldiers and Marines have found that approximately 15 to 19 percent of those deployed in Iraq and about 11 percent of those deployed in Afghanistan could be diagnosed with PTSD (Erbes, Westermeyer, Engdahl, & Johnsen, 2007; Hoge et al., 2004; Hoge, Auchterlonie, & Milliken, 2006). Follow-up studies of soldiers returning from Iraq have found that as many as 42 percent report some mental health problems, most often PTSD symptoms (Milliken, Auchterlonie, & Hoge, 2007). Army sergeant Kristofer Goldsmith, who served 4 years in active duty, is one of those soldiers.

CASE STUDY

Kristopher Goldsmith was a 19-year-old, fresh out of high school, when he joined the Army. He was soon deployed to Sadr City, one of the most violent places in Iraq. Goldsmith's duty was to photograph and document the incidents his platoon encountered, including mutilated men, women, and children.

When his unit was back home for a while, family and friends noticed that Goldsmith was a

(continued)

different man. His drinking escalated to binges every day. He also seemed to get into fights or be violent in some way every day. He was constantly hypervigilant for any threats. Simply walking through a crowded shopping mall was enough to spark paranoia as he scanned every person and scene for enemies who might spring out and hurt him. Innocent remarks by clerks or being touched by someone as he was walking by could spark violent outbursts. There were times when he seemed not to know what he was doing and was totally out of control. At one party, he suddenly grabbed another guy and choked him until he stopped breathing.

Soon Goldsmith's unit was ordered to re-deploy to Iraq. Believing he couldn't face the scenes of devastation and death that now haunted him, he attempted suicide, swallowing massive numbers of painkillers and gulping a liter and a half of vodka. Goldsmith survived, and was eventually diagnosed with PTSD (see Gajilan, 2008).

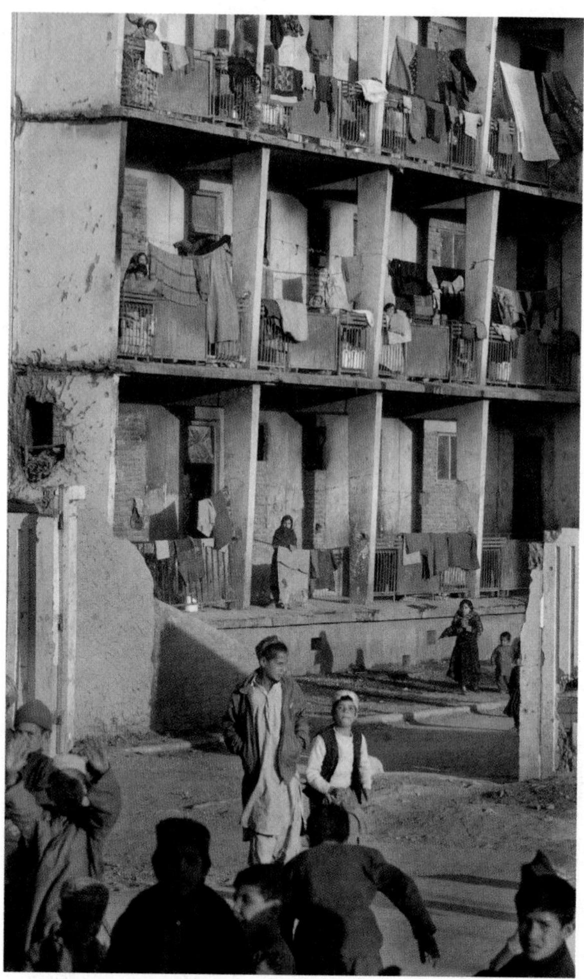

The people of Afghanistan have lived in desperate conditions for many years, and many suffer from PTSD.

The citizens of countries besieged by war are also at high risk for PTSD. The Afghan people have endured decades of war and occupation, the repressive regime of the Taliban, the U.S. bombing of their country after the September 11 attacks, and since 2001 protracted violence. Thousands of Afghanis have been killed, injured, or displaced from their homes. Many of the displaced now live in makeshift tents without adequate food or water. Post-traumatic stress disorder was found in 42 percent of Afghan citizens, and other anxiety symptoms were found in 72 percent (Cardozo et al., 2004). Afghan women may be especially likely to experience PTSD, because the Taliban deprived them of their basic human rights, killed their husbands and male relatives, and then made it impossible for them to survive without those men. In a study of women living in Kabul under the Taliban regime, 84 percent reported having lost at least one family member to war, 69 percent reported that they or a family member had been detained and abused by Taliban militia, and 68 percent reported extremely restricted social activities (Rasekh, Bauer, Manos, & Iacopino, 1998). Over 90 percent of these women reported some symptoms, and 42 percent were diagnosed with PTSD (see also Scholte et al., 2004).

A common precipitator of PTSD is abuse, physical (domestic violence) or sexual (rape and incest). About 95 percent of rape survivors experience post-traumatic stress symptoms severe enough to qualify for a diagnosis of the disorder in the first 2 weeks following the rape (Figure 5.2). About 50 percent still qualify for the diagnosis 3 months after the rape, and as many as 25 percent still experience PTSD 4 to 5 years later (Faravelli, Giugni, Salvatori, & Ricca, 2004; Foa & Riggs, 1995; Resnick, Kilpatrick, Dansky, & Saunders, 1993; Rothbaum, Foa, Riggs, & Murdock, 1992).

In the United States alone, an estimated 794,000 cases of verified child abuse and neglect are reported each year (U.S. Department of Health and Human Services, 2009). Studies of children who have been sexually and/or physically assaulted show that they remain at increased risk for PTSD—as well as other anxiety disorders, depression, substance abuse, and sexual dysfunction—well into adulthood (Cicchetti & Toth, 2005; Kessler, Davis, & Kendler, 1997). Indeed, over 60 percent of childhood rape survivors develop PTSD at some time in their life (Saunders et al., 1992).

Explanations of PTSD Vulnerability

What kind of trauma is most likely to cause long-term, severe psychological impairment? And why do some people develop PTSD in the wake of trauma, whereas others do not? Researchers have identified a number of factors that seem to increase the risk for developing PTSD.

Environmental and Social Factors

Strong predictors of people's reactions to trauma include its *severity* and *duration* and the individual's *proximity* to it (Cardozo, Vergara, Agani, & Gotway, 2000; Ehlers et al., 1998; Hoge et al., 2004; Kessler et al., 1995). People who experience more severe and longer-lasting traumas and are directly affected by a traumatic event are more prone to developing PTSD. For example, veterans are more likely to experience PTSD if they were on the front lines for an extended period (Iverson et al., 2008). People at Ground Zero during the World Trade Center attacks were more likely to develop PTSD than were those who were not at the site (Galea et al., 2002). Rape survivors who were violently and repeatedly raped over an extended period are particularly likely to experience PTSD (Epstein, Saunders, & Kilpatrick, 1997; Merrill et al., 2001; Resick, 1993). Victims of natural disasters who are injured or who lose their homes or loved ones are more likely to experience PTSD than are those whose lives are less severely affected (Galea, Tracy, Norris, & Coffey, 2008).

Another predictor of vulnerability to PTSD is the available *social support*. People who have the emotional support of others after a trauma recover more quickly than do people who do not (Kendall-Tackett, Williams, & Finkelhor, 1993; King et al., 1999; LaGreca, Silverman, Vernberg, & Prinstein, 1996; Sutker, Davis, Uddo, & Ditta, 1995). Survivors of Hurricane Katrina who could talk with others about their experiences and who received emotional and practical support were less likely to develop PTSD than were those who did not receive such support (Galea et al., 2008).

Psychological Factors

People already experiencing increased symptoms of anxiety or depression before a trauma occurs are more likely to develop PTSD following the trauma (Cardozo, Kaiser, Gotway, & Agani, 2003; Hoge et al., 2004; Mayou, Bryant, & Ehlers, 2001). Children who were anxious prior to Hurricane Katrina were more likely to develop symptoms of PTSD than were those who were not (Weems et al., 2007).

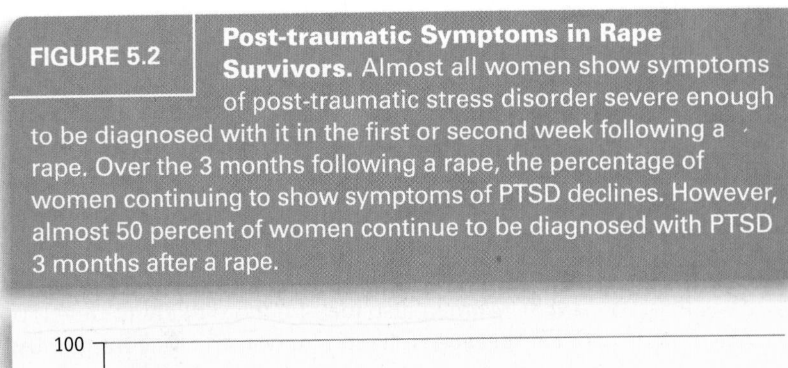
FIGURE 5.2 **Post-traumatic Symptoms in Rape Survivors.** Almost all women show symptoms of post-traumatic stress disorder severe enough to be diagnosed with it in the first or second week following a rape. Over the 3 months following a rape, the percentage of women continuing to show symptoms of PTSD declines. However, almost 50 percent of women continue to be diagnosed with PTSD 3 months after a rape.

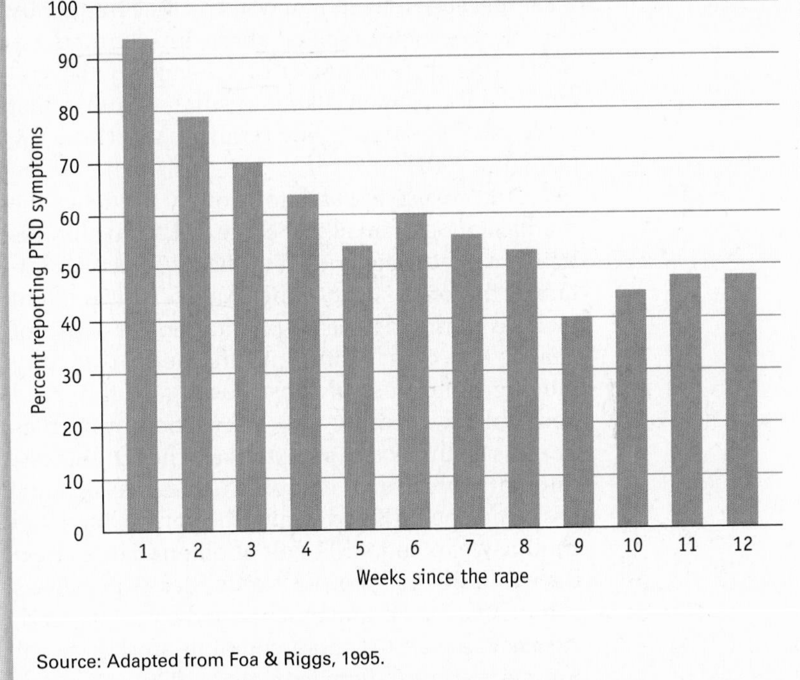

Source: Adapted from Foa & Riggs, 1995.

War veterans who have psychological distress or poor interpersonal relationships before they enter combat are more likely to develop symptoms of PTSD (Koenen et al., 2002).

Once a trauma occurs, people's styles of *coping* may also influence their vulnerability. Several studies have shown that people who use self-destructive or avoidant coping strategies, such as drinking and self-isolation, are more likely to experience PTSD (Fairbank, Hansen, & Fitterling, 1991; Merrill et al., 2001; Sutker et al., 1995). Another form of coping that may increase the likelihood of PTSD is dissociation, or psychological detachment from the trauma and ongoing events. People who dissociate may feel they are in another place, or in someone else's body watching the trauma and its aftermath unfold. Those who dissociate shortly after a trauma are at increased risk of developing PTSD (Fauerbach et al., 2000; Koopman, Classen, & Spiegel, 1994; Mayou et al., 2001; Shalev, Peri, Canetti, & Schreiber, 1996).

Gender and Cross-Cultural Differences

Women are more likely than men to be diagnosed with PTSD, as well as most other anxiety disorders including panic disorder, social phobias, and generalized anxiety disorder (Hanson et al., 2008). Women may experience some of the triggers for anxiety disorders more often than men, particularly sexual abuse, a potent risk factor for most anxiety disorders (Burnam, Stein, Golding, & Siegel, 1988). Women also may be more likely to develop PTSD because the types of traumas they frequently experience, such as sexual abuse, are stigmatized, decreasing the amount of social support they receive. Men are more likely to suffer traumas that carry less stigma, such as exposure to war (Resick & Calhoun, 2001).

Culture also appears to strongly influence the manifestation of anxiety. People in Latino cultures report a syndrome known as *ataque de nervios* (attack of the nerves). A typical *ataque de nervios* might include trembling, heart palpitations, a sense of heat in the chest rising into the head, difficulty moving limbs, loss of consciousness or the mind going blank, memory loss, a sensation of needles in parts of the body (paresthesia), chest tightness, difficulty breathing (dyspnea), dizziness, faintness, and spells. Behaviorally, the person begins to shout, swear, and strike out at others. The person then falls to the ground and either experiences convulsive body movements or lies as if dead. *Ataque de nervios* is more common among recent trauma victims (Guarnaccia et al., 1996).

More chronic anxiety-like symptoms, known as *nervios*, are common in Latino communities, particularly among the poor and uneducated (Guarnaccia et al., 1996). The term *nervios* encompasses a broad array of symptoms, including physical ailments (headaches, stomach problems, dizziness) and emotional symptoms (sadness, irritability, anger, absent-mindedness), as well as the presence of intrusive worries or negative thoughts. One study of 942 adults in rural Mexico found that 21 percent of the women and 10 percent of the men had chronic *nervios* (de Snyder, Diaz-Perez, & Ojeda, 2000). The authors suggest that among the underprivileged, particularly women, *nervios* expresses the anger and frustration of "being at the bottom" and provides temporary release from the grinding everyday burdens of life (see also Lopez & Guarnaccia, 2000).

Culture and gender may interact to influence vulnerability to PTSD. One study compared random community samples of survivors of Hurricane Andrew, which hit Florida in 1992, with survivors of Hurricane Paulina, which hit Acapulco, Mexico, in 1997 (Norris et al., 2001). The hurricanes were similar in many ways, rated as Category 4 storms and causing widespread property damage, physical injury, and death as well as high rates of PTSD symptoms. Women had more symptoms than men in both countries (Figure 5.3), yet the difference between Mexican women and men was much greater than that between U.S. women and men. Differences were also significantly greater between U.S. White women and men than between African American women and men.

FIGURE 5.3 Cultural and Sex Differences in PTSD. In a study of reactions to a hurricane, sex differences in rates of PTSD were greatest among Mexicans, followed by non-Hispanic White Americans and last by African Americans.

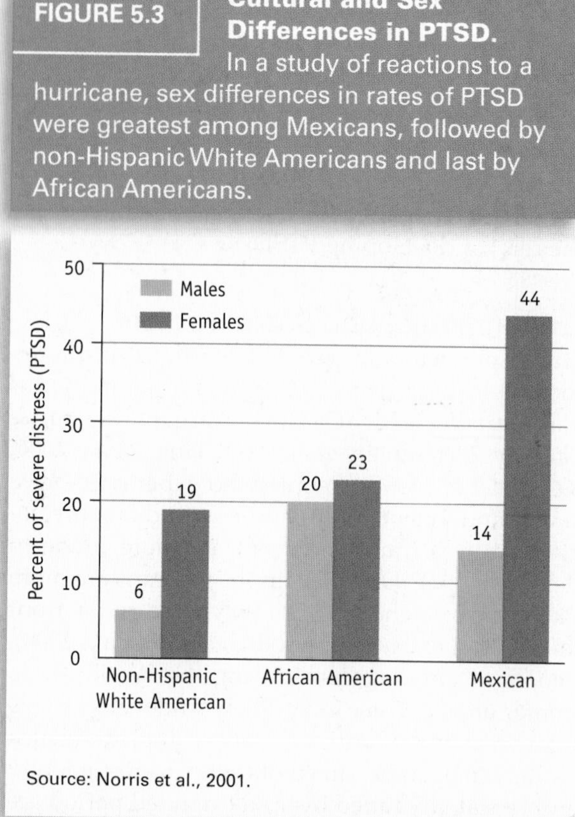

Source: Norris et al., 2001.

The researchers suggest that the relative strength of traditional sex roles across the Mexican, Caucasian American, and African American cultures influenced sex differences in PTSD symptoms. There is more social pressure in Mexican than U.S. culture for women to be passive, self-sacrificing, and compliant and for men to be dominant, fearless, and strong (Vazquez-Nuttall, Romero-Garcia, & DeLeon, 1987). This may lead Mexican women to feel more helpless than Mexican men following a trauma and to be less able to get the material support they need. The tendency to dissociate in response to severe stress also appears greater among Latinos, which may increase the risk of PTSD in Latino cultures generally (Hough, Canino, Abueg, & Gusman, 1996; Marshall & Orlando, 2002). Within U.S. culture, there is some evidence that sex roles are more egalitarian among African Americans than among Caucasians (Davenport & Yurick, 1991). This may explain why African American women did not experience much more PTSD than African American men in the aftermath of Hurricane Andrew.

Biological Factors

The search for biological factors in PTSD has focused on differences between those with the disorder and those without in the functioning of the brain and biochemical systems that act in the stress response. Some research also suggests that genetics plays a role.

Neuroimaging Findings Positron-emission tomography (PET) and magnetic resonance imaging (MRI; see Chapter 3) have shown differences between people with PTSD and those without. These differences occur in brain areas that regulate emotion, the fight-or-flight response, and memory, including the amygdala, hippocampus, and prefrontal cortex (Francati, Vermetten, & Bremner, 2007). The *amygdala* appears to respond more actively to emotional stimuli in those with PTSD. Further, the medial prefrontal cortex, which modulates the reactivity of the amygdala to emotional stimuli, is less active in people with more severe symptoms of PTSD than in people with less severe symptoms. Thus, the brains of people with severe PTSD may be both more reactive to emotional stimuli and less able to dampen that reactivity when it occurs (Shin et al., 2005).

Some studies also show shrinkage in the *hippocampus* among PTSD patients, possibly due to overexposure to neurotransmitters and hormones released in the stress response (Bremner et al., 2000; Villarreal et al., 2002). The hippocampus functions in memory, and damage to it may result in some of the memory problems reported by PTSD patients. It also helps regulate the body's fear response, as discussed earlier. Thus, damage to the hippocampus may interfere with returning the fear response to a normal level after the threat has passed (Bremner et al., 2000).

Biochemical Findings Recall that one of the major hormones released as part of the fight-or-flight response is *cortisol* and that high levels usually indicate an elevated stress response. Interestingly, resting levels of cortisol among people with PTSD (when not exposed to trauma reminders) tend to be *lower* than among people without PTSD (Ballenger et al., 2004; Yehuda, 2004). One longitudinal study assessed cortisol levels in people injured in a traffic accident 1 to 2 hours previously (Yehuda, McFarlane, & Shalev, 1998). Six months later, these people were evaluated for the presence of PTSD. Those who developed the disorder had significantly lower cortisol levels immediately after the trauma than did people who did not develop the disorder. Cortisol down-regulates sympathetic nervous system activity after stress, so lower levels may result in prolonged activity of the sympathetic nervous system following stress. As a result, some people may more easily develop a conditioned fear of stimuli associated with the trauma and subsequently develop PTSD (Ballenger et al., 2004).

Some other physiological responses to stress are exaggerated in PTSD sufferers, including elevated heart rate and increased secretion of the neurotransmitters epinephrine and norepinephrine (Ballenger et al., 2004; Pole et al., 2007). In people vulnerable to PTSD, different components of the stress response may not be working in sync with one another. The hypothalamic-pituitary-adrenal (HPA) axis may be unable to shut down the response of the sympathetic nervous system by secreting necessary levels of cortisol, resulting in overexposure of the brain to epinephrine, norepinephrine, and other neurochemicals. This overexposure may cause memories of the traumatic event to be "overconsolidated" or planted more firmly in memory (Ballenger et al., 2004).

Increasing evidence suggests that exposure to trauma during childhood may permanently alter children's biological stress response, making them more vulnerable to PTSD, as well as to other anxiety disorders and depression, throughout their lives (Cicchetti & Toth, 2005; Nemeroff, 2004). Studies of maltreated (severely neglected or physically, emotionally, or sexually abused) children show abnormal cortisol responses to stressors (Cicchetti & Rogosch, 2001) and a diminished startle response (Klorman, Cicchetti, Thatcher, & Ison, 2003). Adults abused as children continue to have abnormal cortisol responses and elevated startle and anxiety responses to laboratory stressors, even when they no longer show symptoms of PTSD or depression (Heim, Meinlschmidt, & Nemeroff, 2003; Pole et al., 2007). Depressed women abused as children show lower volume of the hippocampus than depressed women who were not abused as children (Vythilingam et al., 2002). Thus, early childhood trauma may leave permanent physical and emotional scars that predispose individuals to later psychological problems, including PTSD.

Genetics Vulnerability to PTSD may be inherited (Koenen, Nugent, & Amstadter, 2008). One study of about 4,000 twins who served in the Vietnam War found that if one developed PTSD, the other was much more likely to also if the twins were identical rather than fraternal (True et al., 1993;

see also Stein et al., 2002). The adult children of Holocaust survivors with PTSD are over three times more likely also to develop it than are matched comparison groups. They also have abnormally low levels of cortisol, whether or not they have ever been exposed to traumatic events or developed PTSD (Yehuda, Blair, Labinsky & Bierer, 2007). These findings suggest that abnormally low cortisol levels may be one heritable risk factor for PTSD.

Treatments for PTSD

Psychotherapies for PTSD generally have three goals: exposing clients to what they fear in order to extinguish that fear, challenging distorted cognitions that contribute to symptoms, and helping clients reduce stress in their lives. These goals are addressed in cognitive-behavioral therapy for PTSD and in stress-management therapies. Some clients also benefit from antianxiety and antidepressant medications.

Cognitive-Behavioral Therapy and Stress Management

Cognitive-behavioral therapy has proven effective in the treatment of PTSD in both adults (Davidson, 2004; Resick & Calhoun, 2001) and children (Cohen, Deblinger, Mannarino, & Steer, 2004). A major element is *systematic desensitization* (see Chapter 2). The client identifies thoughts and situations that create anxiety, ranking them from most anxiety-provoking to least. The therapist takes the client through this hierarchy, using relaxation techniques to quell the anxiety (Resick & Calhoun, 2001). It usually is impossible to return to the actual traumatic event, so imagining it vividly must replace actual exposure. A combat veteran being treated for PTSD imagines the bloody battles and scenes of killing and death that haunt him; a rape survivor imagines the minute details of the assault. The therapist also watches for unhelpful thinking patterns, such as survivor guilt, and helps the client challenge these thoughts (Resick & Calhoun, 2001).

Repeatedly and vividly imagining and describing the feared events in the safety of the therapist's office allows the client to habituate to his or her anxiety and distinguish memory from present reality (Foa & Jaycox, 1999; Resick & Calhoun, 2001). It may also allow the client to integrate the events into his or her concepts of self and of the world (Foa & Jaycox, 1999; Horowitz, 1976). Studies of rape survivors, combat veterans, survivors of traffic collisions, and refugees have found that this kind of repeated exposure therapy significantly decreases PTSD symptoms and helps prevent relapse (Foa et al., 1999; Keane, Gerardi, Quinn, & Litz, 1992; Paunovic & Öst, 2001; Resick & Schnicke, 1992; Taylor et al., 2001).

Another approach to treating clients with PTSD, particularly those who cannot tolerate exposure to their traumatic memories, is **stress-management interventions.** Therapists teach clients skills for overcoming problems in their lives that increase their stress and may result from PTSD, such as marital problems or social isolation (Keane et al., 1992; Wolfsdorf & Zlotnick, 2001).

Biological Therapies

The **selective serotonin reuptake inhibitors (SSRIs)** and, to a lesser extent, the benzodiazepines can be useful in treating symptoms of PTSD, particularly sleep problems, nightmares, and irritability (Ballenger et al., 2004). One study showed that PTSD patients treated with an SSRI were more likely to be symptom-free for 5 months than were other patients (Martenyi et al., 2002). Patients who continue to take an SSRI after acute symptoms have subsided are even more likely to remain symptom-free (Davidson, et al., 2001).

TEST YOURSELF

1. What are the three categories of symptoms of PTSD?
2. How does acute stress disorder differ from PTSD?
3. What are the social and psychological risk factors for PTSD?
4. What biological differences have been found between people with PTSD and people without?
5. What medications have been useful in treating people with PTSD?

APPLY IT Henry is undergoing treatment for combat-related PTSD. He is asked to rank, in order of least to most upsetting, his thoughts and experiences from the battle in which he was seriously injured. He is later asked to recall these thoughts and experiences in rank order while relaxing. Which answer below *best* describes Henry's therapy?

a. systematic desensitization
b. behavioral therapy
c. cognitive restructuring
d. thought stopping

Answers appear online at www.mhhe.com/nolen5e.

SHADES OF GRAY

Read the following case study.

Last week, Ramon was turning left at a light when another driver sped through the intersection and ran into his car, smashing the entire passenger side. Fortunately, Ramon was uninjured, thanks in part to his air bag. He got out of his car screaming at the driver who hit him but then saw that he was unconscious and bleeding. Ramon immediately called 911, and the ambulance came within a few minutes.

Since the accident, Ramon has been having nightmares in which he is in the accident again, only this time his 3-year-old daughter is in the backseat and is seriously injured. He wakes up sweating and sometimes screaming. He has to go into his daughter's bedroom and touch her to convince himself she is okay. His concentration at work is diminished because he is tired from loss of sleep and because he keeps going over the accident, thinking about how he could have prevented it. Today he was at his desk, replaying the accident again in his mind, when his boss came by to ask him a question. Ramon jumped so badly at the sound of his name that he spilled his coffee all over his desk.

Would you diagnose Ramon with a disorder that we have discussed in this chapter? (Discussion appears at the end of this chapter.)

PANIC DISORDER AND AGORAPHOBIA

CASE STUDY

The first time Celia had a panic attack, two days before her twentieth birthday, she was working at McDonald's. As she was handing a customer a Big Mac, the earth seemed to open up beneath her. Her heart began to pound, she felt she was smothering, she broke into a sweat, and she was sure she was going to have a heart attack and die. After about 20 minutes of terror, the panic subsided. Trembling, she got in her car, raced home, and barely left the house for the next 3 months.

Since that time, Celia has had about three attacks a month. She does not know when they are coming. During them she feels dread, searing chest pain, smothering and choking, dizziness, and shakiness. She sometimes thinks this is all not real and she is going crazy. She also thinks she is going to die. (Adapted from Seligman, 1993, p. 61)

Celia is suffering from **panic attacks,** short but intense periods in which she experiences many symptoms of anxiety: heart palpitations, trembling, a feeling of choking, dizziness, intense dread, and so on (Table 5.3). Celia's panic attacks appear to come "out of the blue," in the absence of any environmental triggers. Simply handing a customer a hamburger should not cause such terror. This is one of the baffling characteristics of some panic attacks.

Other people have panic attacks triggered by specific situations or events. Someone with a social phobia, for instance, may have a panic attack

TABLE 5.3 *DSM-IV-TR* Criteria for Panic Disorder

A. Recurrent unexpected panic attacks, defined as a discrete period of intense fear or discomfort in which four (or more) of the following symptoms develop abruptly and reach a peak within 10 minutes:
   1. Palpitations, pounding heart
   2. Sweating
   3. Trembling or shaking
   4. Shortness of breath or choking
   5. Feeling of choking
   6. Chest pain or discomfort
   7. Nausea or abdominal distress
   8. Feeling dizzy, light-headed, or faint
   9. Derealization or depersonalization
   10. Fear of losing control or going crazy
   11. Fear of dying
   12. Chills or hot flushes
   13. Paresthesia (tingling, pricking, or burning sensation on the skin)

B. At least one of the attacks followed by one month (or more) of one (or more) of the following:
   1. Persistent concern about having additional attacks
   2. Worry about the implications of the attack or its consequences
   3. A clinically significant change in behavior related to the attacks

Source: Reprinted with permission from the *Diagnostic and Statistical Manual of Mental Disorders,* Fourth Edition, Text Revision.

when forced into a social situation. Most commonly, panic attacks arise in certain situations but not every time. In all cases, however, they are terrifying experiences, causing a person intense fear or discomfort, the physiological symptoms of anxiety, and the feeling of losing control, going crazy, or dying.

Panic Disorder

As many as 28 percent of adults have occasional panic attacks, especially during times of stress (Kessler, Chiu, et al., 2006). For most, the attacks are annoying but isolated events that do not change how they live their lives. However, when they become a common occurrence, when they are not usually provoked by any particular situation, and when a person begins to worry about having them and changes behaviors as a result of this worry, a diagnosis of **panic disorder** may be made.

Some people with panic disorder have many episodes in a short period of time, such as every day for a week, and then go weeks or months without any episodes, followed by another period of frequent attacks. Other people have attacks less frequently but more regularly, such as once every week for months. Between full-blown attacks, they might experience minor bouts of panic.

People with panic disorder often fear that they have a life-threatening illness, and they are more likely to have a personal or family history of serious chronic illness. Even after such an illness is ruled out, they may continue to believe they are about to die of a heart attack, seizure, or other physical crisis. Another common but erroneous belief is that they are "going crazy" or "losing control." Many people with panic disorder feel ashamed and try to hide it from others. If left untreated, people with panic disorder may become demoralized and depressed (Craske & Waters, 2005).

About 3 to 5 percent of people will develop panic disorder at some time (Craske & Waters, 2005; Kessler et al., 2005), usually between late adolescence and the mid-thirties. It is more common in women and tends to be chronic (Craske & Waters, 2005).

Panic disorder can be debilitating. Many sufferers also show chronic generalized anxiety, depression, and alcohol abuse (Wilson & Hayward, 2005). Those with panic disorder who are depressed or who abuse alcohol may be at increased risk for suicide attempts (Goodwin & Roy-Byrne, 2006).

Agoraphobia

About one-third to one-half of people diagnosed with panic disorder develop **agoraphobia** (Kessler et al., 2005). The term *agoraphobia* comes from the Greek for "fear of the marketplace." People with agoraphobia fear places where they might have trouble escaping or getting help if they become anxious or have a panic attack. People with agoraphobia also often fear that they will embarrass themselves if others notice their symptoms or their efforts to escape during an attack. Actually, other people can rarely tell when a person is having a panic attack (Craske & Barlow, 2001).

People with agoraphobia may become housebound.

Agoraphobia can occur in people who do not have panic attacks, but most people who seek treatment for agoraphobia do experience either full-blown panic attacks, more moderate panic attacks, or severe social phobia, in which they experience panic-like symptoms in social situations (Craske & Barlow, 2001). In most cases, agoraphobia begins within 1 year after a person begins experiencing frequent anxiety symptoms.

People with agoraphobia often reach the point where they will not leave their homes. Sometimes, they are able to venture out with a close family member who makes them feel safe. However, family and friends may not be willing to chaperone them everywhere they go. When people with agoraphobia force themselves to enter situations that frighten them, they experience persistent and intense anxiety, causing many to retreat to their homes. Some turn to alcohol and other substances to dampen their anxiety symptoms (Craske & Barlow, 2001).

Theories of Panic Disorder

The biological and psychological theories of panic disorder have been integrated into a model (Figure 5.4) that helps us understand how different factors work together to create panic disorder and agoraphobia (Bouton, Mineka, & Barlow, 2001; Craske & Waters, 2005). We next review the model's components.

The Role of Genetics

About 10 percent of the first-degree relatives of people with panic disorder also have it, compared to only about 2 percent of the first-degree relatives of people without it (Hettema, Neale, & Kendler, 2001). In particular, those whose parents have panic disorder are at increased risk for developing it (Biederman, Faraone et al., 2001). Twin studies of panic disorder find that 30 to 40 percent of the variation is due to genetics (Roy-Byrne, Craske, & Stein, 2006). These studies suggest a genetically transmitted vulnerability to panic disorder. Family history studies of agoraphobia find that about 10 to 11 percent of first-degree relatives of people with this disorder also have it, compared to 3 to 4 percent of relatives of people who do not (Fyer et al., 1995), suggesting that agoraphobia also may be attributable in part to genetic factors.

FIGURE 5.4 **An Integrated Model of Panic Disorder.** Biological and psychological factors come together to create panic disorder and agoraphobia.

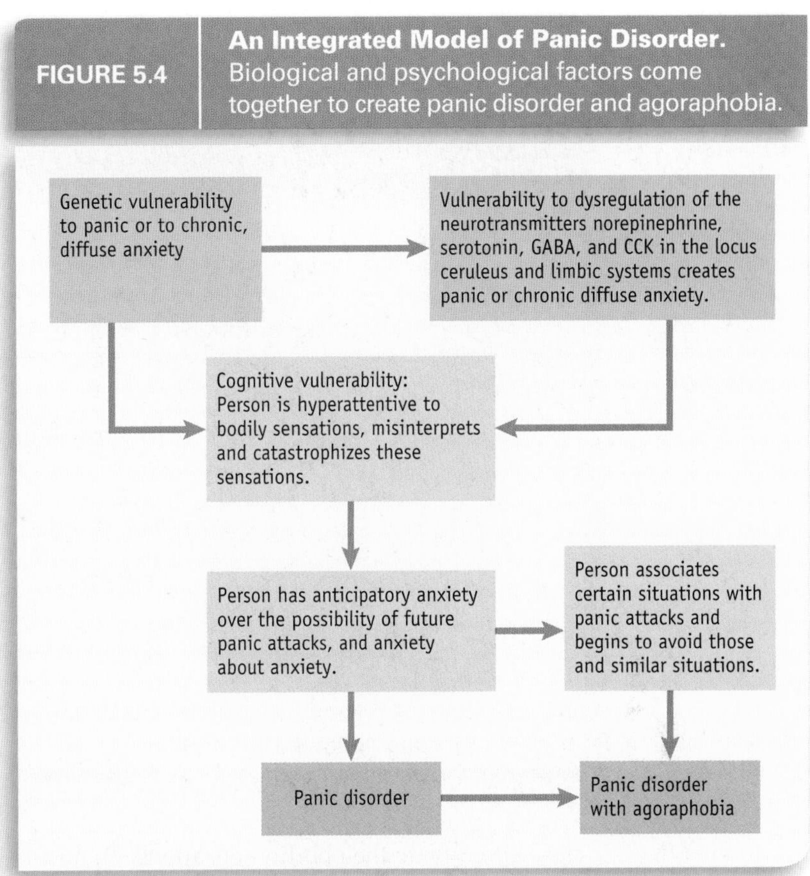

Neurobiological Contributors

Panic attacks can easily be triggered in sufferers of panic disorder if they hyperventilate, inhale a small amount of carbon dioxide, ingest caffeine, breathe into a paper bag, or take infusions of sodium lactate, a substance that resembles the lactate produced during exercise (Craske & Barlow, 2001). These activities initiate the physiological changes of the fight-or-flight response. People without a history of panic attacks may experience some physical discomfort during these activities, but rarely a full-blown attack.

The fight-or-flight response appears to be poorly regulated in people who develop panic disorder, perhaps due to poor regulation of several neurotransmitters, including norepinephrine, serotonin, gamma-aminobutyric acid (GABA), and cholecystokinin (CCK; Charney et al., 2000).

Neuroimaging studies show differences between people with panic disorder and those without panic disorder in several areas of the **limbic system** involved in the stress response, including the amygdala, hypothalamus, and hippocampus (Figure 5.5; Roy-Byrne et al., 2006). People with the disorder also show dysregulation of norepinephrine systems in an area of the brain stem called the **locus ceruleus** (see Figure 5.5). The locus ceruleus has well-defined pathways to the limbic system. Poor regulation in the locus ceruleus may cause panic attacks, which then stimulate the limbic system, lowering the threshold for the activation of diffuse and chronic anxiety (Gorman et al., 1995). This anticipatory anxiety may, in turn, increase the likelihood of dysregulation of the locus ceruleus and thus of another panic attack.

Some women with panic disorder report increased anxiety symptoms during premenstrual periods and postpartum (Brawman-Mintzer & Yonkers, 2001). The hormone progesterone can affect the activity of both serotonin and GABA neurotransmitter systems. Fluctuations in progesterone levels with the menstrual cycle or postpartum might lead to an imbalance or dysfunction of the serotonin or GABA systems, thereby influencing susceptibility. Increases in progesterone also can induce mild chronic hyperventilation. In women prone to panic attacks, this may be enough to induce full-blown attacks.

The Cognitive Model

Although many people with panic disorder may have a biological vulnerability to it, psychological factors also appear to help determine who develops the disorder. Cognitive theorists argue that people prone to panic attacks tend to (1) pay very

FIGURE 5.5 **Areas of the Brain Involved in Panic Disorder.** Several areas of the limbic system shown here, along with the locus ceruleus, may be involved in panic attacks.

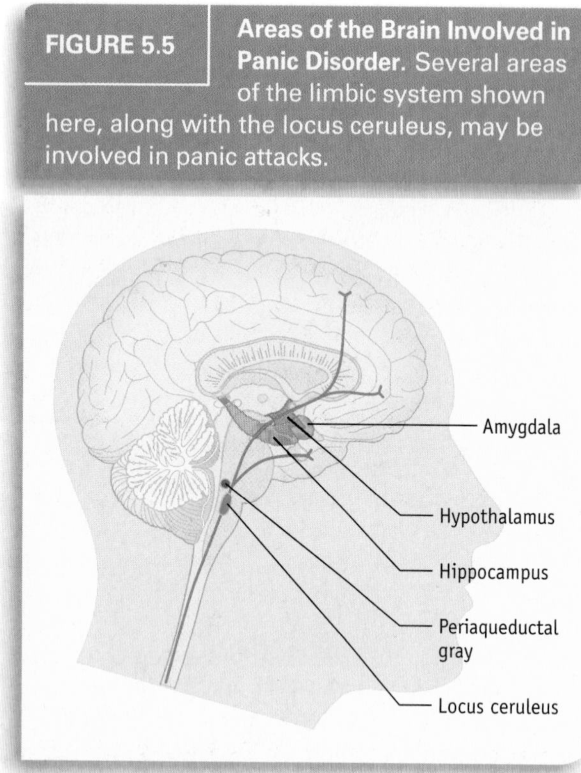

close attention to their bodily sensations, (2) misinterpret these sensations in a negative way, and (3) engage in snowballing catastrophic thinking, exaggerating symptoms and their consequences (Clark, 1988; Craske & Barlow, 2001). A person prone to panic disorder who feels a bit dizzy after standing up too quickly might think, "I'm really dizzy. I think I'm going to faint. Maybe I'm having a seizure. Oh God, what's happening?" This kind of thinking increases the subjective sense of anxiety as well as physiological changes such as increased heart rate. The person interprets these feelings catastrophically and is on the way to a full panic attack. Between attacks, the person is hypervigilant for any bodily sensations, worrying about his or her health generally and about having more panic attacks specifically. This constant arousal makes further attacks more likely (Clark, 1988; Craske & Barlow, 2001).

The belief that bodily symptoms have harmful consequences is labeled **anxiety sensitivity** (McNally, 1999a). People high in anxiety sensitivity are more likely than people low in it to already have panic disorder, to have more frequent panic attacks, or to develop panic attacks over time (Hayward, Killen, Kraemer, & Taylor, 2000).

Those prone to panic attacks also appear to have increased *interoceptive awareness*—a heightened awareness of bodily cues (such as slight sensations of arousal or anxiety) that may signal a coming panic attack (Razran, 1961). These bodily cues have occurred at the beginning of previous panic attacks and have become conditioned stimuli signaling new attacks, a process called **interoceptive conditioning** (Bouton et al., 2001). Thus, slight increases in anxiety, even if not consciously recognized, can elicit conditioned fear that grows into a full panic attack. If the individual doesn't recognize this process, the attack seems to come from nowhere.

Beliefs about the controllability of symptoms appear to be important to the development of panic attacks. In one study, two groups of people with panic disorder were asked to wear breathing masks, which delivered air slightly enriched with carbon dioxide. Participants were warned that inhaling carbon dioxide could induce an attack. One group was told they could not control the amount of carbon dioxide that came through their masks. The other group was told they could control it by turning a knob. Actually, neither group had any control over the amount of carbon dioxide, and both groups inhaled the same amount. However, 80 percent of the people who believed they had no control experienced a panic attack, compared to 20 percent of those who believed they had control (Sanderson, Rapee, & Barlow, 1989).

The Integrated Model

We can now summarize the integrated model of panic disorder illustrated in Figure 5.4. Many people who develop panic disorder seem to have a biological vulnerability to a hypersensitive fight-or-flight response. With only a mild stimulus, their heart begins to race, their breathing becomes rapid, and their palms begin to sweat.

They typically will not develop frequent panic attacks or a panic disorder, however, unless they engage in catastrophizing thinking about their physiological symptoms. Such cognitions increase the intensity of initially mild physiological systems to the point of a panic attack. They also make the individuals hypervigilant for signs of another panic attack, putting them at a constant mild to moderate level of anxiety. This anxiety increases the probability that they will become panicked again, and the cycle continues.

Some people then begin to associate certain situations with symptoms of panic and may begin to feel them again if they return to the situations. By avoiding these places, they reduce their symptoms, thereby reinforcing their avoidance behavior. This process is known as a **conditioned avoidance response** (Mowrer, 1939). Thus, a man who has a panic attack while sitting in a theater may later associate the theater with his symptoms and begin to feel anxious whenever he is near it. By avoiding it, he can reduce his anxiety. He may associate other places, such as his home or a specific room, with lowered anxiety levels, so being in these places is reinforcing. Eventually, he confines himself only to his safe places and avoids a wide range of places he feels are unsafe. Thus develops agoraphobia.

Treatments for Panic Disorder

Both biological and psychological treatments for panic disorder have been developed. Certain antidepressant drugs effectively treat panic and agoraphobia, and the benzodiazepines can help some people. Cognitive-behavioral therapies appear to be as successful as medications in reducing symptoms, and better than medications at preventing relapse.

Biological Treatments

The tricyclic antidepressants, such as imipramine, can reduce panic attacks in the majority of patients (Katon, 2006). Recall that one of the neurotransmitters potentially involved in panic disorder is norepinephrine. The tricyclic antidepressants are thought to improve the functioning of the norepinephrine system, possibly explaining why they are effective in treating panic. These drugs also may influence the levels of a number of other neurotransmitters, including serotonin, thereby affecting levels of anxiety.

The tricyclic antidepressants have two disadvantages. First, possible side effects include blurred vision, dry mouth, difficulty urinating, constipation, weight gain, and sexual dysfunction. Second, most patients relapse when they discontinue the drugs (Katon, 2006).

Other antidepressants useful in treating panic disorder are the selective serotonin reuptake inhibitors (SSRIs such as Paxil, Prozac, Zoloft) and the serotonin-norepinephrine reuptake inhibitors (SNRIs such as Effexor). Studies suggest that the SSRIs and SNRIs are more effective than a placebo; about half of patients with panic disorder experience significant reductions in symptoms. Possible side effects include gastrointestinal upset and irritability, initial feelings of agitation, insomnia, drowsiness, tremor, and sexual dysfunction. Patients frequently tolerate these side effects better than those of the tricyclic antidepressants (Katon, 2006).

The third type of drug used to treat panic disorder is the benzodiazepines, which suppress the central nervous system and influence functioning in the GABA, norepinephrine, and serotonin neurotransmitter systems. The benzodiazepines approved to treat panic are alprazolam and clonazepam. These drugs work quickly to reduce panic attacks and general symptoms of anxiety in most patients (Culpepper, 2004). Unfortunately, they are physically (and psychologically) addictive. When patients stop using the drug, they experience difficult withdrawal symptoms, including irritability, tremors, insomnia, anxiety, tingling sensations, and, more rarely, seizures and paranoia. Benzodiazepines can also interfere with cognitive and motor functioning. The ability to drive or to avoid accidents is impaired, and performance on the job, at school, and in the home suffers. These impairments can be especially severe if the benzodiazepines are combined with alcohol (Culpepper, 2004).

Cognitive-Behavioral Therapy

As in treatment for PTSD, cognitive-behavioral therapy for panic disorder has clients confront the situations or thoughts that arouse anxiety. Confrontation seems to help in two ways: It allows irrational thoughts about these situations to be challenged and changed, and it helps anxious behaviors be extinguished.

Cognitive-behavioral interventions have multiple components (Barlow, Gorman, Shear, & Woods, 2000). First, clients are taught relaxation and breathing exercises, which impart some control over symptoms and permit clients to engage in the other components of the therapy. Second, the clinician guides clients in identifying the catastrophizing cognitions they have about changes in bodily sensations. Clients may keep diaries of their thoughts about their bodies on days between sessions, particularly at times when they begin to feel they are going to panic. Figure 5.6 shows one man's panic thoughts diary. He noted mild symptoms of panic at work but more severe symptoms while riding the subway home. In both situations, he had thoughts about feeling trapped, suffocating, and fainting.

Many clients, too overwhelmed while having symptoms to pay attention to their thoughts, need to experience panic symptoms in the presence of their therapist in order to identify their catastrophizing cognitions (Barlow, 2002). The therapist may try to induce symptoms during sessions by having clients exercise to elevate their heart rate, spin to get dizzy, or put their head between their knees and then stand up quickly to get lightheaded (due to sudden changes in blood pressure). None of these activities is dangerous, but all are likely to produce the kind of symptoms clients catastrophize. As clients experience these symptoms

FIGURE 5.6 **A Panic Thoughts Diary.** This man recorded the thoughts he had had during panic attacks and then worked on these thoughts in cognitive therapy.

SITUATION	SYMPTOMS AND SEVERITY	THOUGHTS
Office at work	Choking (mild) Dizziness (mild) Heart racing (mild)	Oh, I can't have an attack here. People will see me and I might get fired. I'm suffocating! I'm going to faint.
Riding subway home	Sweating (severe) Choking (severe) Shaking (severe) Heart racing (severe) Dizziness (severe)	I can't stand this! I've got to get out of here. I'm going to choke to death. I'm trapped. I'm going to faint!
At home	Sweating (mild) Heart still racing (moderate) A little faintness	I can't believe I made it home.

and their catastrophizing cognitions, the therapist helps them collect their thoughts.

Third, clients practice relaxation and breathing exercises while experiencing panic symptoms in the session. If attacks occur during sessions, the therapist talks clients through them, coaching them in the use of relaxation and breathing skills, suggesting ways of improving their skills, and noting clients' success in using the skills to stop the attacks.

Fourth, the therapist challenges clients' catastrophizing thoughts about their bodily sensations and teaches them to challenge these thoughts themselves, using the cognitive techniques described in Chapter 2. The therapist might help clients reinterpret the sensations accurately. For example, the client whose thoughts are listed in Figure 5.6 frequently felt as if he were choking. His therapist might explore whether his choking sensation might be due to the stuffiness of a small office or a subway on a warm summer day. If he interprets the increase in his heart rate as a heart attack, the therapist might have him collect evidence from his physician that he is in perfect cardiac health. The therapist might also explore the client's expectations that he will die of a heart attack because a relative did. If relaxation techniques allow a client to reduce panic symptoms during a therapy session, the therapist will challenge the client's belief that the symptoms are uncontrollable (Barlow, 2002).

Fifth, the therapist uses systematic desensitization therapy to expose clients gradually to the situations they fear most while helping them maintain control over their symptoms (Barlow, 2002). The client and therapist will compose a list of panic-inducing situations, from most to least threatening. Then, after learning relaxation and breathing skills and perhaps gaining some control over panic symptoms induced during therapy sessions, clients begin to expose themselves to their panic-inducing situations, beginning with the least threatening. The therapist might accompany clients in this exercise, coaching them in their relaxation and breathing skills and in how to challenge catastrophic cognitions that arise.

A large-scale, multisite study compared tricyclic antidepressants to cognitive-behavioral therapy (CBT) in the treatment of 312 people with panic disorder and found them equally effective in eliminating symptoms (Barlow et al., 2000). Several other studies have found that 85 to 90 percent of panic disorder patients treated with CBT experience complete relief from their panic attacks within 12 weeks (Addis et al., 2004; Mitte, 2005; Schmidt & Keough, 2010). In follow-up studies of patients receiving CBT, nearly 90 percent were panic-free 2 years after treatment (Mitte, 2005; Westen & Morrison, 2001). Cognitive-behavioral therapy appears to be considerably better than antidepressants at preventing relapse after treatment ends (Barlow et al., 2000), probably because this therapy teaches people strategies to prevent the recurrence of panic symptoms.

TEST YOURSELF

1. What are the key features of panic disorder and agoraphobia?
2. What biological factors play a role in panic disorder?
3. What role do cognitive factors and conditioning play in panic disorder?
4. What medications are useful in treating panic disorder?
5. What are the components of cognitive-behavioral therapy treatment for panic disorder and agoraphobia?

APPLY IT According to the conditioning model for the development of agoraphobia, which of the following is true?

a. Individuals avoid places associated with panic attacks, which *increases* short-term anxiety but reinforces avoidance, leading to agoraphobia in the long term.
b. Individuals avoid places associated with panic attacks, which *reduces* short-term anxiety but reinforces avoidance, leading to agoraphobia in the long term.
c. Individuals avoid places associated with panic attacks, which *increases* short-term anxiety but punishes avoidance, leading to agoraphobia in the long term.
d. Individuals avoid places associated with panic attacks, which *reduces* short-term anxiety and punishes avoidance, leading to agoraphobia in the long term.

Answers appear online at www.mhhe.com/nolen5e.

TABLE 5.4 *DSM-IV-TR* Criteria for Specific Phobia

A. Marked and persistent fear that is excessive or unreasonable, cued by the presence or anticipation of a specific object or situation (e.g., flying, heights, animals, receiving an injection, seeing blood).

B. Exposure to the phobic stimulus almost invariably provokes an immediate anxiety response, which may take the form of a situationally bound or situationally predisposed panic attack. *Note:* In children, the anxiety may be expressed by crying, tantrums, freezing, or clinging.

C. The person recognizes that the fear is excessive or unreasonable. *Note:* In children, this feature may be absent.

D. The phobic situation(s) is avoided or else is endured with intense anxiety or distress.

E. The avoidance, anxious anticipation, or distress in the feared situation(s) interferes significantly with the person's normal routine, occupational (or academic) functioning, or social activities or relationships, or there is marked distress about having the phobia.

F. In individuals under age 18, the duration is at least 6 months.

G. The anxiety, panic attacks, or phobic avoidance associated with the specific object or situation are not better accounted for by another mental disorder, such as obsessive-compulsive disorder (e.g., fear of dirt in someone with an obsession about contamination), post-traumatic stress disorder (e.g., avoidance of stimuli associated with a severe stressor), separation anxiety disorder (e.g., avoidance of school), social phobia (e.g., avoidance of social situations because of fear of embarrassment), panic disorder with agoraphobia, or agoraphobia without history of panic disorder.

Specify type:
Animal Type
Natural Environment Type (e.g., heights, storms, water)
Blood-Injection-Injury Type
Situational Type (e.g., airplanes, elevators, enclosed places)
Other Type (e.g., phobic avoidance of situations that may lead to choking, vomiting, or contracting an illness; in children, avoidance of loud sounds or costumed characters)

SPECIFIC PHOBIAS AND SOCIAL PHOBIA/SOCIAL ANXIETY DISORDER

People can develop phobias related to many objects and situations. Here we consider phobias of specific items or situations, as well as the more general social phobias.

Specific Phobias

Most **specific phobias** fall into one of four categories (American Psychiatric Association, 2000): animal type, natural environment type, situational type, and blood-injection-injury type. When people with these phobias encounter their feared objects or situations, their anxiety is immediate and intense, sometimes producing panic attacks. They also become anxious over the possibility of encountering the objects or situations and will go to great lengths to avoid them. The *DSM-IV-TR* criteria for specific phobia are given in Table 5.4.

Most phobias develop during childhood. Adults with phobias recognize that their anxieties are unreasonable, although children may not. As many as 13 percent of people will have a specific phobia at some time in their lives, making phobias one of the most common disorders (Kessler et al., 2005). Almost 90 percent of those with a specific phobia never seek treatment (Regier et al., 1993).

Animal type phobias focus on specific animals or insects, such as dogs, cats, snakes, or spiders. Snakes and spiders are the most common objects of animal phobias (Jacobi et al., 2004). While most people who come across a feared animal or insect will startle and move away quickly, they would not be diagnosed with a phobia because they do not live in terror of encountering a snake or spider or organize their lives around avoiding them.

Natural environment type phobias focus on events or situations in the natural environment, such as storms, heights, or water. Mild to moderate fears of these natural events or situations are extremely common and are adaptive in that they help us avoid dangerous situations. A diagnosis of

John Madden's phobia of flying leads him to travel to sports events by bus.

phobia is warranted only when people reorganize their lives to avoid the feared situations or have severe anxiety attacks when confronted with them.

Situational type phobias usually involve fear of public transportation, tunnels, bridges, elevators, flying, or driving. *Claustrophobia*, or fear of enclosed spaces, is a common situational phobia. People with situational phobias fear having a panic attack in their phobic situations. Indeed, they often have had panic attacks when forced into those situations, but, unlike people with agoraphobia, *only* then. One prominent person with a situational phobia is John Madden, the former coach and sports announcer. Madden is so afraid of flying that he travels over 60,000 miles a year on his personal bus to get to sports events around the United States.

Blood-injection-injury type phobias are diagnosed in people who fear seeing blood or an injury. Whereas people with another type of specific phobia typically experience increases in heart rate, blood pressure, and other fight-or-flight responses when confronted with their feared object or situation, people with blood-injection-injury type phobia experience significant *drops* in heart rate and blood pressure and are likely to faint. This type of phobia runs more strongly in families than do the other types (Öst, 1992).

Social Phobia/Social Anxiety Disorder

People with **social phobia**—to be called *social anxiety disorder* in the *DSM-5*—fear being judged or embarrassing themselves in front of others (see the *DSM-IV-TR* criteria in Table 5.5). Social phobia is more likely than a specific phobia to create severe

TABLE 5.5 *DSM-IV-TR* Criteria for Social Phobia

A. A marked and persistent fear of one or more social or performance situations in which the person is exposed to unfamiliar people or to possible scrutiny by others. The individual fears that he or she will act in a way (or show anxiety symptoms) that will be humiliating or embarrassing. *Note:* In children, there must be evidence of the capacity for age-appropriate social relationships with familiar people, and the anxiety must occur in peer settings, not just in interactions with adults.

B. Exposure to the feared social situation almost invariably provokes anxiety, which may take the form of a situationally bound or situationally predisposed panic attack. *Note:* In children, the anxiety may be expressed by crying, tantrums, freezing, or shrinking from social situations with unfamiliar people.

C. The person recognizes that the fear is excessive or unreasonable. *Note:* In children, this feature may be absent.

D. The feared social or performance situations are avoided or else are endured with intense anxiety or distress.

E. The avoidance, anxious anticipation, or distress in the feared social or performance situation(s) interferes significantly with the person's normal routine, occupational (academic) functioning, or social activities or relationships, or there is marked distress about having the phobia.

F. In individuals under age 18, the duration is at least 6 months.

G. The fear or avoidance is not due to the direct physiological effects of a substance (e.g., a drug of abuse, a medication) or a general medical condition and is not better accounted for by another mental disorder.

H. If a general medical condition or another mental disorder is present, the fear in Criterion A is unrelated to it.

Specify if: Generalized: If the fears include most social situations (also consider the additional diagnosis of avoidant personality disorder)

Source: Reprinted with permission from the *Diagnostic and Statistical Manual of Mental Disorders,* Fourth Edition, Text Revision.

disruption in a person's daily life (Kessler, 2003). It is easier in most cultures to avoid snakes or spiders than it is to avoid social situations. Consider the inner pain this person with social phobia experiences and the way he has organized his life to avoid social situations.

CASE STUDY

Malcolm was a computer expert who worked for a large software firm. One of the things he hated most was to ride the elevator at his office when there were other people on it. He felt that everyone was watching him, commenting silently on his rumpled clothes, and noticing every time he moved. He held his breath for almost the entire elevator ride, afraid that he might say something or make an embarassing sound. Often, he walked up the eight flights of stairs to his office, rather than take the risk that someone might get on the elevator with him.

Malcolm rarely went anywhere except to work and home. He hated even to go to the grocery store for fear he would run his cart into someone or say something stupid to a clerk. He found a grocery store and several restaurants that took orders online for food to be delivered to customers' homes. He liked this service because he could avoid even talking to someone over the phone to place an order.

In the past, Malcolm's job had allowed him to remain quietly in his office all day, without interacting with other people. Recently, however, his company was reorganized and took on a number of new projects. Malcolm's supervisor said that everyone in Malcolm's group needed to begin working together more closely to develop new products. Malcolm was supposed to make a presentation to his group about some software he was developing, but he called in sick the day of the presentation because he could not face it. Malcolm was thinking that he had to change jobs and perhaps go into private consulting, so he could work from his home rather than having to work with anyone else.

Many people get nervous when speaking in front of an audience or joining a group already engaged in conversation (Table 5.6). One study of college students found that 48 percent could be classified as "shy" (Heiser, Turner, & Beidel, 2003). However, only 18 percent of these shy students qualified for a diagnosis of social phobia.

TABLE 5.6 Lifetime Prevalence of Social Fears in a National Survey

Social Fear	Percentage of People Saying They Experienced the Fear in Their Lifetimes
Public speaking	30.2%
Talking in front of a small group	15.2
Talking with others	13.7
Using a toilet away from home	6.6
Writing while someone watches	6.4
Eating or drinking in public	2.7
Any social fear	38.6

Source: Kessler, Stein, & Berglund, 1998, p. 614.

In social situations, people with social phobia may tremble and perspire, feel confused and dizzy, have heart palpitations, and eventually have a full panic attack. Like Malcolm, they think others see their nervousness and judge them as inarticulate, weak, stupid, or crazy. Malcolm avoided speaking in public and having conversations with others for fear of being judged. People with social phobia may avoid eating or drinking in public, for fear that they will make noises when they eat, drop food, or otherwise embarrass themselves. They may avoid writing in public, afraid that others will see their hands tremble. Men with social phobia often avoid urinating in public bathrooms.

People with social phobia tend to fall into one of three groups (Eng et al., 2000). Some fear only public speaking. Others have moderate anxiety about a variety of social situations. Finally, people who have severe fear of many social situations, like Malcolm, are said to have a generalized type of social phobia.

Social phobia is relatively common, with a lifetime prevalence of about 12 percent in the United States (Kessler et al., 2005) and 3 to 7 percent internationally (Alonso et al., 2004; Wittchen & Fehm, 2003). Women are somewhat more likely than men to develop this disorder (Lang & Stein, 2001). One study found that women with social phobia have more severe social fears than men, particularly with regard to performance situations (such as giving a presentation) (Turk, Heimberg, & Hope, 2001).

Social phobia tends to develop in either the early preschool years or adolescence , when many people become self-conscious and concerned about others' opinions of them (Deardorff et al., 2007; Turk et al., 2001). Over 90 percent of adults with social phobia report humiliating experiences that contributed to their symptoms, such as extreme teasing as a child (McCabe et al., 2003). Others report feeling uncomfortable in social situations all their lives. Social phobia often co-occurs with mood disorders, other anxiety disorders, and avoidant personality disorder (Neal & Edelmann, 2003; Wittchen & Fehm, 2003). Once it develops, social phobia tends to be chronic if left untreated. Most people do not seek treatment (Kessler, 2003).

In Japan, the term *taijin kyofu-sho* describes an intense fear of interpersonal relations. *Taijin kyofu-sho* is characterized by shame about and persistent fear of causing others offense, embarrassment, or even harm through one's personal inadequacies. It is most frequently encountered, at least in treatment settings, among young men. People with this disorder may fear blushing, emitting body odor, displaying unsightly body parts, speaking their thoughts aloud, or irritating others (Chapman, Manuzza, & Fyer, 1995). Although *taijin kyofu-sho* may share some features with social phobia, it reflects concerns about offending others rather than about embarrassing oneself. This concern is in line with the emphasis in Japan on deference to others (Kirmayer, 2001).

Theories of Phobias

The phobias have been a battleground among various psychological approaches to abnormality. Freud (1909) argued that phobias result when unconscious anxiety is displaced onto a neutral or symbolic object. That is, people become phobic of objects not because they have any real fear of the objects but because they have displaced their anxiety over other issues onto them.

This theory is detailed in a 150-page case history of a little boy named Hans, who had a phobia of horses after seeing a horse fall on the ground and writhe violently. How did Hans's phobia develop? According to Freud, young boys have a sexual desire for their mothers and jealously hate their fathers, but they fear that their fathers will castrate them in retaliation for this desire. As we discussed in Chapter 2, this phenomenon is known as the Oedipus complex. In Freud's interpretation, little Hans unconsciously displaced this anxiety onto horses, which symbolized his father for him. Freud's evidence came from Hans' answers to a series of leading questions. After long conversations about what Hans was "really" afraid of, Hans reportedly became less fearful of horses because, according to Freud, he had gained insight into the true source of his anxiety.

There is little reason to accept Freud's theory of phobias. Hans never provided any spontaneous or direct evidence that his real problem was Oedipal concerns rather than fear of horses. In addition, Hans's phobia of horses decreased slowly over time, rather than suddenly in response to an insight. Many children have specific fears that simply fade over time. In general, psychodynamic therapy is not highly effective for treating phobias, suggesting that insight into unconscious anxieties is not what is needed in their treatment.

Behavioral Theories

In contrast to the psychodynamic theories, the behavioral theories have been very successful in explaining phobias. According to Mowrer's (1939) two-factor theory, classical conditioning leads to the fear of the phobic object, and operant conditioning helps maintain it. As discussed in Chapter 2, in classical conditioning a previously neutral object (the conditioned stimulus) is paired with an object that naturally elicits a reaction (an unconditioned stimulus that elicits an unconditioned response) until the previously neutral object elicits the same reaction (now called the conditioned response). When a tone is paired with an electric shock, the conditioned stimulus is the tone, the unconditioned stimulus is the electric shock, the unconditioned response is anxiety in response to the shock, and the conditioned response is anxiety in response to the tone.

The first application of these theories to phobias came in a series of studies done 90 years ago by John Watson and Rosalie Raynor (1920). Watson and Raynor placed a white rat in front of an 11-month-old boy named Little Albert. As Little Albert reached for the white rat, they banged a

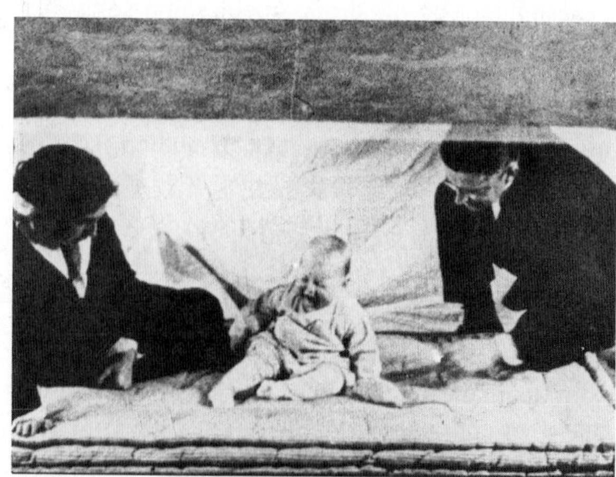

Little Albert, shown in this photo, developed a fear of white rats through classical conditioning.

FIGURE 5.7 **The Behavioral Account of Little Albert's Phobia.** The pairing of the banged bar (the US), which naturally leads to a startle response (the UR), and the white rat (the CS) eventually leads to the white rat producing the same startle response (now referred to as the CR).

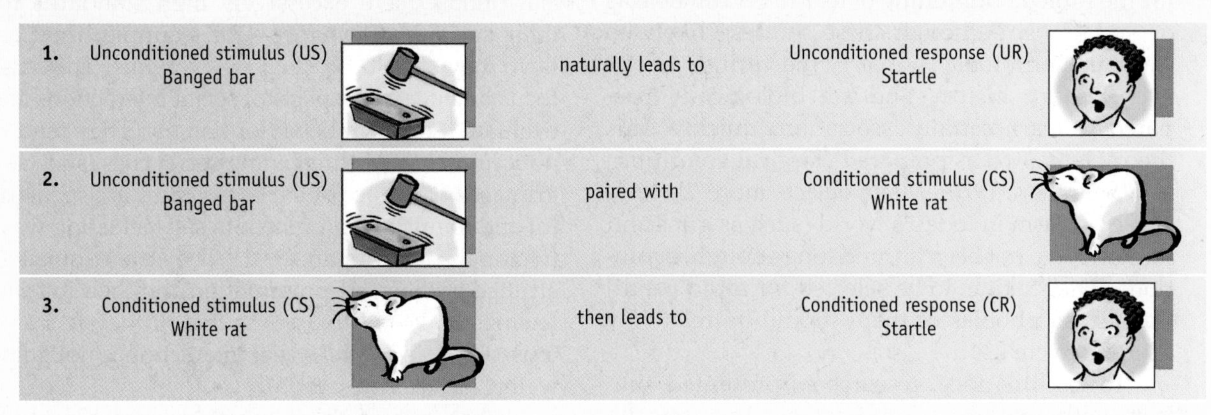

metal bar loudly just above his head. Naturally, Little Albert was startled and began to cry. After several more pairings of the white rat with the loud noise from the metal bar, Little Albert would have nothing to do with the rat. When presented with it, he retreated and showed distress. Little Albert's fear also generalized to other white furry animals—he would not approach white rabbits either.

Although by today's standards this experiment would raise serious ethical questions, it showed the creation of a phobia through classical conditioning. The unconditioned stimulus (US) was the loud noise from the banged bar, and the unconditioned response (UR) was Little Albert's startle response to the noise. The conditioned stimulus (CS) was the white rat, and the conditioned response (CR) was the startle-and-fear response to the white rat (Figure 5.7). If Little Albert had later been presented with the white rat several times without the noise, his fear of white rats should have been extinguished.

Most people who develop a phobia, however, try to avoid being exposed to their feared object, thus avoiding what could extinguish the phobia. If they are suddenly confronted with their feared object, they experience extreme anxiety and run away as quickly as possible. Running away reduces their anxiety; thus, their avoidance of the feared object is reinforced by the reduction of their anxiety—an operant conditioning process known as **negative reinforcement** (Mowrer, 1939). Thereafter, they avoid the feared object. This is the same type of *conditioned avoidance response* found in agoraphobia.

Malcolm, the person with social phobia described earlier, had developed an array of avoidant behaviors to prevent his exposure to what he feared most: the possibility of scrutiny by others. He walked up several flights of stairs rather than be trapped in an elevator for a few minutes with another person. He paid to have his groceries delivered rather than risk going to a crowded grocery store. He was even prepared to quit his job to avoid having to make presentations or work closely with others. These avoidant behaviors created hardship for Malcolm, but they reduced his anxiety and therefore were reinforced. As a result of this avoidance, Malcolm never had the chance to extinguish his anxiety about social situations.

Some theorists argue that phobias can develop through observational learning as well as through direct classical conditioning (see Mineka & Zinbarg, 2006). For example, small children may learn to fear snakes if their parents show severe fright when seeing snakes (Bandura, 1969; Mineka, Davidson, Cook, & Keir, 1984).

An extension of the behavioral theory of phobias may answer the question of why humans develop phobias of some objects or situations and not others (deSilva, Rachman, & Seligman, 1977; Mineka, 1985; Seligman, 1970). Phobias of spiders, snakes, and heights are common, but phobias of flowers are not. Many phobic objects appear to be things whose avoidance, over evolutionary history, has been advantageous for humans. Our distant ancestors had many nasty encounters with insects, snakes, heights, loud noises, and strangers. Those who quickly learned to fear and avoid these objects or events were more likely to survive and bear offspring. Thus, evolution may have selected for the rapid conditioning of fear to certain objects or situations. Although these are less likely to cause us harm today, we carry the vestiges of our evolutionary history and are biologically prepared to learn certain associations quickly. This theory is known as **prepared classical conditioning** (Seligman, 1970). Many objects more likely to cause us harm in today's world (such as guns and knives) have not been around long enough, evolutionarily speaking, to be selected for rapid conditioning, so phobias of them should be relatively difficult to create.

To test this idea, researchers presented subjects with pictures of objects that theoretically should be evolutionarily selected for conditioning (snakes and spiders) and objects that should not be selected (houses, faces, and flowers). They paired the presentation of these pictures with short but painful electric shocks. The subjects developed anxiety reactions to the pictures of snakes and spiders within one or two pairings with shock, but it took four or five pairings of the pictures of houses, faces, or flowers with shock to create a fear reaction. Extinguishing the subjects' anxiety reactions to houses or faces was relatively easy once the pictures were no longer paired with shock, but the anxiety reactions to spiders and snakes were difficult to extinguish (Hugdahl & Ohman, 1977; Ohman, Fredrikson, Hugdahl, & Rimmo, 1976).

The behavioral theory seems to provide a compelling explanation for phobias, particularly when we add the principles of observational learning and prepared classical conditioning. It has also led to effective therapies. Its most significant problem is that many people with phobias can identify no traumatic event in their own lives or the lives of people they are close to that triggered their phobias. Without conditioned stimuli, it is hard to argue that they developed their phobias through classical conditioning or observational learning. Michelle Craske and Allison Waters (2005) argue that many individuals who develop phobias have a chronic low-level anxiety or reactivity, which makes them more susceptible to the development of phobias given even mildly aversive experiences.

Evolution may have prepared us to fear dangerous creatures, such as snakes, more readily than creatures that have not been dangerous to us over human history.

Cognitive Theories

The cognitive theories of phobias have focused primarily on the development of social phobia (Clark & Wells, 1995; Rapee & Heimberg, 1997; Turk et al., 2001). According to these theories, people with social phobia have excessively high standards for their social performance—for example, they believe they should be liked by everyone. They also focus on negative aspects of social interactions and evaluate their own behavior harshly. They tend to notice potentially threatening social cues (such as a grimace on the face of the person they are speaking to) and to misinterpret them in self-defeating ways (Heinrichs & Hofman, 2001). They are exquisitely attuned to their self-presentation and their internal feelings and tend to assume that, if they feel anxious, it is because the social interaction is not going well (Clark & Wells, 1995).

What creates these cognitive biases? Adults with social phobia often describe their parents as having been overprotective and controlling but also critical and negative (Craske & Waters, 2005; Neal & Edelmann, 2003). Such retrospective accounts could be incorrect. To date, we lack prospective studies of the family environments of people who develop social phobia. Nor have studies established whether the biases described by cognitive theories are causes of social phobia or symptoms. Cognitive-behavioral therapies based on these theories can, however, help people overcome the avoidant and anxious symptoms of social phobia.

Biological Theories

The first-degree relatives of people with phobias are three to four times more likely to have a phobia than the first-degree relatives of people without phobias. Twin studies suggest that this is due, at least in part, to genetics (Hettema et al., 2001; Merikangas, Lieb, Wittchen, & Avenevoli, 2003).

Several researchers suggest that a particular phobia in itself is not strongly heritable but that the general tendency toward anxiety is, leading to a temperament that makes it easier for phobias to be conditioned (Eysenck, 1967; Gray, 1987). Children who are behaviorally inhibited as toddlers—excessively timid and shy—are at higher risk for the development of specific phobias and social phobia than are others (Biederman, Hirshfeld-Becker et al., 2001; Craske & Waters, 2005). One study found that socially inhibited children were four times more likely to develop social phobia in high school than were others (Hayward, Killen, Kraemer, & Taylor, 1998). Again, however, children who have a genetic predisposition toward anxiety or are behaviorally inhibited may not develop social phobia, or a specific phobia, unless the parenting they receive exacerbates their anxiety (Craske & Waters, 2005; Neal & Edelmann, 2003).

Treatments for Phobias

A number of behavioral techniques can treat phobias. Some therapists include cognitive techniques and medications.

Behavioral Treatments

Behavioral therapies for phobias use exposure to extinguish the person's fear of the object or situation. These therapies cure the majority of phobias (Christophersen & Mortweet, 2001; Emmelkamp, 1994; Wolpe, 1997). Some studies suggest that just one session of behavior therapy can lead to major reductions in phobic behaviors and anxiety (Öst, Svensson, Hellström, & Lindwall, 2001). Three basic components of behavior therapy for phobias are *systematic desensitization, modeling,* and *flooding.*

As we have already discussed, in systematic desensitization clients formulate lists of situations or objects they fear, ranked from most to least feared (Emmelkamp, 1994). They learn relaxation techniques and begin to expose themselves to the items on their "hierarchy of fears," beginning with the least feared. A person with a severe dog phobia who has "seeing a picture of a dog in a magazine" first on her list might look at a picture of a dog. The therapist will coach her to use relaxation techniques to replace her anxiety with a calm reaction. When she can look at a picture of a dog without experiencing anxiety, she might move on to looking at a dog in a pet store window, again using relaxation techniques to lower her anxiety reaction and replace it with calm. Gradually, the client and therapist will move through the entire list, until the client is able to pet a big dog without feeling overwhelming anxiety.

Blood-injection-injury phobia requires a different approach, because people with this phobia experience severe *decreases* in heart rate and blood pressure (Öst & Sterner, 1987). Thus, therapists teach them to tense the muscles in their arms, legs, and chest until they feel the warmth of their blood rising in their faces. This **applied tension technique** increases blood pressure and heart rate and can keep people with this type of phobia from fainting when confronted with the feared object. Then systematic desensitization can help extinguish fear of blood, injury, or injections.

Modeling techniques are often adopted in conjunction with systematic desensitization. A therapist treating a person with a snake phobia may perform (model) each behavior on the client's hierarchy of fears before asking the client to perform them. The therapist will stand in the room with the snake before asking the client to do so, touch the snake before asking the client to do so, and hold the snake before the client does. Through observational

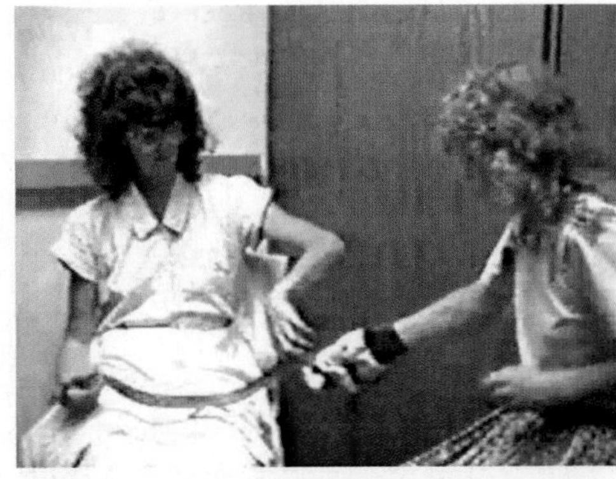
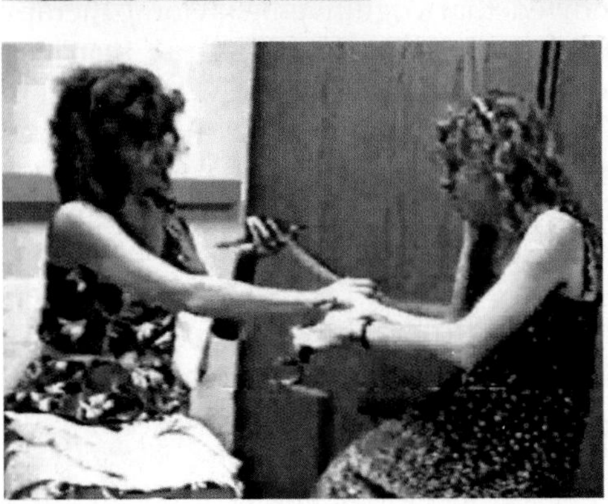
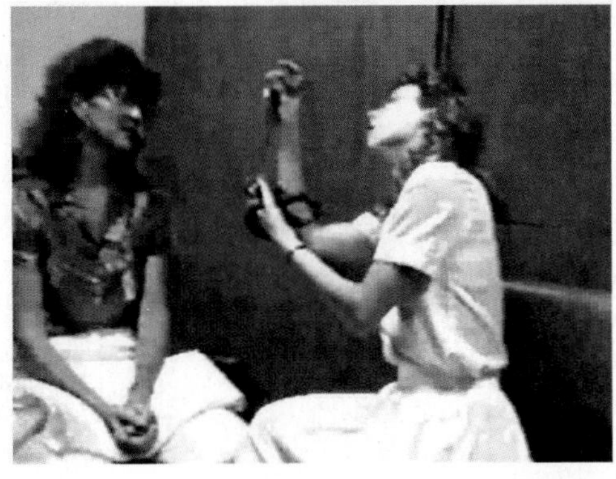

The therapist first models handling a snake for this woman with a snake phobia. Then gradually the woman is able to handle it herself.

learning, the client associates these behaviors with a calm response in the therapist, which reduces anxiety about engaging in the behaviors. Modeling is as effective as systematic desensitization in reducing phobias (Bandura, 1969; Thorpe & Olson, 1997).

Flooding intensively exposes a client to his or her feared object until anxiety is extinguished. In a flooding treatment, a person with claustrophobia might lock himself in a closet for several hours, a person with a dog phobia might spend the night in a dog kennel, and a person with social phobia might volunteer to teach a class that meets every day for a semester. The therapist typically will prepare clients with relaxation techniques they can use to reduce their fear. Flooding is as effective as systematic desensitization or modeling and often works more quickly. However, it is more difficult to get clients to agree to this type of therapy, because it is frightening to contemplate (Thorpe & Olson, 1997).

Cognitive-Behavioral Treatments

Many therapists combine behavioral techniques with cognitive techniques that help phobic clients identify and challenge negative, catastrophizing thoughts they have when anxious (Beck & Emery, 1985; Turk et al., 2001). Cognitive-behavioral therapy (CBT) seems particularly useful for social phobia and can be implemented in a group setting in which everyone except the therapist is phobic (Coles, Hart, & Heimberg, 2005; Heimberg, 2001; Turk et al., 2001). Group members are an audience for one another, providing exposure to the very situation each member fears. An individual can practice her feared behaviors in front of the others while the therapist coaches her in the use of relaxation techniques to calm her anxiety. The group can also help the individual challenge her negative, catastrophizing thoughts about her behavior, as in the following excerpt from a group cognitive therapy session with Gina.

VOICES

Therapist: So your automatic thought is, "I don't know how to have a conversation," is that right?

Gina: Yeah, I always screw it up.

Therapist: All right, let's ask the rest of the group what they think about that. Who has had a conversation with Gina or noticed her talking with someone else?

Ed: We walked out to our cars together last week and talked in the parking lot for a while. [Several other group members list similar conversations.]

Therapist: So it sounds like you have had a number of conversations with the rest of the group.

Gina: I guess so.

Therapist: Group, how did she do? How did the conversations go?

Sally: It was fine. She was asking me about my car, because she has been looking for a new one, so we talked mostly about that. [Other group members provide similar answers.]

Therapist: Well, Gina, the rest of the group doesn't seem to agree that you don't know how to have conversations.

Gina: I guess I've always been so nervous that I never stopped to think that sometimes the conversations go OK.

(Adapted from Turk et al., 2001, pp. 124–125)

Group-administered cognitive-behavioral therapy has proven effective even for people with generalized social phobia (Heimberg, 2001; Turk et al., 2001). In one study, 133 people with social phobia were randomly assigned to receive group cognitive-behavioral therapy (CBT), to take an antidepressant, to receive a pill placebo, or simply to meet in a group to receive support and education about social phobia (Heimberg et al., 1998). After 12 weeks, 75 percent of the group cognitive-behavioral therapy patients showed significant improvement, compared to 77 percent of the people who had received the antidepressant. Both of these groups had significantly better recovery than the pill placebo or the education/support group. A follow-up study showed that cognitive-behavioral therapy was much better at preventing relapse than was the antidepressant treatment—only 17 percent of the CBT group had relapsed 1 year later, compared to 50 percent of the antidepressant treatment group. Other studies have found similar results (Clark et al., 2003; Hofmann, 2004).

Biological Treatments

Some people use the benzodiazepines to reduce their anxiety when forced to confront their phobic objects; for example, they use Valium before flying or giving a presentation. These drugs produce temporary relief, but the phobia remains (Jefferson, 2001).

Antidepressants, particularly the monoamine oxidase inhibitors and the selective serotonin reuptake inhibitors, are more effective than placebos in treating social anxiety (Davidson, 2003). However, follow-up studies suggest that people relapse soon after discontinuing the drug (Davidson, 2003).

In contrast, behavioral techniques can cure most phobias in a few hours (Öst et al., 2001), and cognitive-behavioral therapy effectively treats social phobia (Zaider & Heimberg, 2003). For now, it appears that the age-old advice to "confront your fears" through behavior therapy is the best strategy.

APPLY IT Katie enjoys shooting guns at a firing range but has a severe fear of snakes. She has never been bitten or attacked by a snake, but she panics if she encounters one. Which theory helps explain why Katie is afraid of snakes but not guns?

a. negative reinforcement
b. classical conditioning
c. operant conditioning
d. prepared classical conditioning

Answers appear online at www.mhhe.com/nolen5e.

TEST YOURSELF

1. What are the four types of specific phobias?
2. What is the main feature of social phobia?
3. What are the behavioral and cognitive theories of the development of phobias?
4. What biological factors may play a role in the development of phobias?
5. What are the most effective treatments for phobias?

GENERALIZED ANXIETY DISORDER

The phobias, panic disorder, and agoraphobia involve periods of anxiety that are acute, usually short-lived, and more or less specific to certain object or situations. Some people are anxious all the time, however, in almost all situations. These people may be diagnosed with **generalized anxiety disorder (GAD;** Table 5.7). People with GAD worry about many things in their lives, as Claire describes in the following excerpt.

TABLE 5.7 *DSM-IV-TR* Criteria for Generalized Anxiety Disorder

A. Excessive anxiety and worry (apprehensive expectation), occurring more days than not for at least 6 months, about a number of events or activities (such as work or school performance).

B. The person finds it difficult to control the worry.

C. The anxiety and worry are associated with three (or more) of the following six symptoms (with at least some symptoms present for more days than not for the past 6 months). *Note:* Only one item is required in children.

1. Restlessness or feeling keyed up or on edge
2. Being easily fatigued
3. Difficulty concentrating or mind going blank
4. Irritability
5. Muscle tension
6. Sleep disturbance (difficulty falling or staying asleep, or restless unsatisfying sleep)

D. The focus of the anxiety and worry is not attributable to another disorder.

E. The anxiety, worry, or physical symptoms cause clinically significant distress or impairment in social, occupational, or other important areas of functioning.

F. The disturbance is not due to the direct physiological effects of a substance (e.g., a drug of abuse, a medication) or a general medical condition (e.g., hyperthyroidism).

Source: Reprinted with permission from the *Diagnostic and Statistical Manual of Mental Disorders,* Fourth Edition, Text Revision.

VOICES

I just feel anxious and tense all the time. It started in high school. I was a straight-A student, and I worried constantly about my grades, whether the other kids and the teachers liked me, being prompt for classes—things like that. . . . Now I vacuum four times a week and clean the bathrooms every day. There have even been times when I've backed out of going out to dinner with my husband because the house needed to be cleaned.

I get so upset and irritated over minor things. . . . I still worry about being on time to church and to appointments. Now I find I worry a lot about my husband. He's been doing a tremendous amount of traveling for his job, some of it by car, but most of it by plane. Because he works on the northeastern seaboard, and because he frequently has to travel in the winter, I worry that he'll be stuck in bad weather and get into an accident or, God forbid, a plane crash.

Oh, and I worry about my son. He just started playing on the varsity football team, so he's bound to get an injury some time. It's so nerve-wracking to watch him play that I've stopped going to his games. I'm sure my son must be disappointed . . . , but it's simply too much for me to take. (Adapted from Brown, O'Leary, & Barlow, 2001, p. 187)

People with GAD may worry about their performance on the job, their relationships, and their health. Like Claire, they also may worry about minor issues such as being late. The focus of their worries may shift frequently, and they tend to worry about many things instead of focusing on only issue of concern (Borkovec, 1994).

Their worry is accompanied by physiological symptoms, including muscle tension, sleep disturbances, and chronic restlessness. People with GAD feel tired much of the time, probably due to chronic muscle tension and sleep loss (Craske & Waters, 2005).

GAD is relatively common, with cross-national studies showing a lifetime prevalence of about 5 percent of women and 3 percent of men. It tends to be chronic (Kessler et al., 2002). Many people with this disorder report that they have been anxious all their lives; the disorder most commonly begins in childhood or adolescence. Over 50 percent of people with GAD also develop another anxiety disorder. Over 70 percent experience a mood disorder, and 33 percent have a substance use disorder (Craske & Waters, 2005; Kessler et al., 2002).

In the *DSM-5*, the name for this disorder is proposed to be changed to generalized anxiety and worry disorder to reflect the fact that worry is a central feature. The criteria for the new disorder are likely to undergo a number of other changes as well. The criterion that the excessive anxiety and worry must be persistently present will be reduced from 6 months to 3 months. The individual must show both restlessness and muscle tension. The other symptoms listed in Criterion C of Table 5.7 will be dropped, because research has shown these to be less common symptoms (Andrews et al., 2010). The proposed new criteria will require that because of anxiety and worry about situations, individuals frequently spend inordinate amounts of time and energy preparing for feared situations or avoiding those situations, are immobilized by procrastination and indecision, and seek reassurance from others (American Psychiatric Association, 2010). These behavioral symptoms of anxiety have been added to the proposed criteria in response to evidence that they are very common and lead to significant impairment (Andrews et al., 2010).

Theories of Generalized Anxiety Disorder

Cognitive theories have dominated recent psychological theories of GAD. Biological factors also may play a role.

Cognitive Theories

Cognitive theories suggest that the cognitions of people with GAD are focused on threat, at both the conscious and unconscious levels (Beck, 1997; Borkovec, 1994; Mathews & MacLeod, 2005). At the conscious level, people with GAD make a number of maladaptive assumptions, such as "It's always best to expect the worst" and "I must anticipate and prepare myself at all times for any possible danger" (Beck & Emery, 1985; Ellis, 1997). Many of these assumptions reflect concerns about losing control.

People with GAD believe that worrying can help them avoid bad events by motivating them to engage in problem solving. Yet they seldom get to the problem solving. Although they are always anticipating a negative event, they tend not to think it through (Borkovec, 2002). Indeed, they actively avoid visual images of what they worry about, perhaps as a way of avoiding the associated negative emotion. This avoidance prevents them from habituating to the negative emotions associated with the event or considering ways they might cope.

Their maladaptive assumptions lead people with GAD to respond to situations with automatic thoughts that stir up anxiety, cause them to be hypervigilant, and lead them to overreact (Beck & Emery, 1985). When facing an exam, a person with GAD might reactively think, "I don't think I can do this," "I'll fall apart if I fail this test," and "My parents will be furious if I don't get good grades."

The unconscious cognitions of people with GAD also appear to focus on detecting possible threats in the environment (Mathews & MacLeod, 2005). In the Stroop color-naming task, participants are presented with words printed in color on a computer screen (Figure 5.8). Their role is to say what color the word is printed in. In general, people are slower in naming the color of words that have special significance to them (such as *disease* or *failure* for people with chronic anxiety) than in naming the color of nonsignificant words. Presumably they are paying more attention to the content of those words than to the colors (Mathews & MacLeod, 2005).

Why do some people become vigilant for signs of threat? One theory is that they have experienced stressors or traumas that were uncontrollable and came without warning (Mineka & Zinbarg, 2006). Animals given unpredictable and uncontrollable shocks often exhibit symptoms of chronic fear or anxiety. Studies have shown that the level of control and predictability in an infant monkey's life is related to its symptoms of anxiety as an adolescent or adult (Mineka, Gunnar, & Champoux, 1986; Suomi, 1999). People who have had unpredictable and uncontrollable life experiences—such as an abusive parent—also may develop chronic anxiety.

Biological Theories

The discovery in the 1950s that the benzodiazepines provide relief from generalized anxiety has led to theories about the neurotransmitters active in generalized anxiety. The benzodiazepines increase the activity of GABA, a neurotransmitter that carries inhibitory messages from one neuron to another. When GABA binds to a neuronal receptor, it prevents the neuron from firing. One theory is that people with generalized anxiety disorder have a deficiency of GABA or GABA receptors, which results in excessive firing of neurons through many areas of the brain, particularly the limbic system, which is involved in emotional, physiological, and behavioral responses to threat (Charney, 2004; Le Doux, 1996). As a result of excessive and chronic neuronal activity, the person experiences chronic, diffuse symptoms of anxiety.

Genetic studies suggest that GAD, as a specific disorder, has a modest heritability (Kendler, Neale, Kessler, & Heath, 1992; Rapee & Barlow, 1993). The more general trait of anxiety is much more clearly heritable and puts individuals at risk for GAD (Craske & Waters, 2005).

FIGURE 5.8 **The Stroop Color-Naming Task.** In this task, words are flashed on a computer screen for a brief period of time, and the person is asked to name the color the word is printed in. People with generalized anxiety disorder are slower to name the color of words with threatening content than that of neutral words, presumably because they are attending to the content of the threatening words.

DISEASE

CHAIR

Treatments for Generalized Anxiety Disorder

The effective treatments for GAD are cognitive-behavioral or biological.

Cognitive-Behavioral Treatments

Cognitive-behavioral treatments focus on helping people with GAD confront the issues they worry about most; challenge their negative, catastrophizing thoughts; and develop coping strategies. In the following excerpt, a cognitive-behavioral therapist helps Claire challenge her tendency to overestimate the probability that her son will be injured while playing football.

VOICES

Therapist: Claire, you wrote that you were afraid about your son playing in his football game. What specifically were you worried about?

Claire: That he'd get seriously hurt. His team was playing last year's state champions, so you know that those boys are big and strong.

Therapist: How specifically do you imagine your son getting hurt?

Claire: Getting a broken back or neck. Something that will result in paralysis or death. It happened to two NFL players this past year, remember?

Therapist: What happened to your son when he played in the game?

Claire: Nothing, really. He came home that afternoon with a sore thumb, but that went away after a while. He said he scored a touchdown and had an interception. I guess he played really well.

Therapist: So you had predicted that he would be injured during the game, but that didn't happen. When we're anxious, we tend to commit a common cognitive error, called "probability overestimation." In other words, we overestimate the likelihood of an unlikely event. While you were feeling anxious and worried, what was the probability in your mind that your son would be hurt, from 0 to 100 percent?

Claire: About 75 percent.

Therapist: And now what would you rate the probability of your son getting hurt in a future game?

Claire: Well, if you put it that way, I suppose around a 50 percent chance of him getting injured.

Therapist: So that means for every two times that your son plays football, he gets hurt once. Is that correct?

Claire: Umm, no. I don't think it's that high. Maybe about 30 percent.

Therapist: That would be one out of every three times that your son gets hurt. What evidence can you provide from your son's playing history to account for your belief that he'll get hurt one out of every three games?

Claire: Well, none. He had a sprained ankle during summer training, but that's it.

Therapist: So what you're saying is that you don't have very much evidence at all to prove that your son has a 30 percent chance of getting hurt in a game.

Claire: Gee, I never thought of it that way.

(Adapted from Brown, O'Leary, & Barlow, 2001, pp. 193–194)

Cognitive-behavioral therapy is more effective than benzodiazepine therapy, placebos, or nondirective supportive therapy in the treatment of GAD (Borkovec, Newman, & Castonguay, 2003; Siev & Chambless 2007). In one follow-up study, its positive effects remained after 2 years (Borkovec, Newman, Pincus, & Lytle, 2002).

Biological Treatments

The benzodiazepine drugs (such as Xanax, Librium, Valium, and Serax) provide short-term relief from anxiety symptoms (Gorman, 2003). However, their side effects and addictiveness preclude long-term use. Once people discontinue the drugs, their anxiety symptoms return (Davidson, 2001).

Both the tricyclic antidepressant imipramine (trade name Tofranil) and the selective serotonin reuptake inhibitor paroxetine (trade name Paxil) have been shown to be better than a placebo in reducing anxiety symptoms in GAD, and paroxetine improves anxiety more than a benzodiazepine. Venlafaxine (trade name Effexor), a serotonin-norepinephrine reuptake inhibitor, also reduces symptoms of anxiety in GAD better than a placebo (Davidson et al., 2008).

TEST YOURSELF

1. What is the key feature of generalized anxiety disorder?
2. What cognitive processes appear to play a role in GAD?
3. What biological factors appear to play a role in GAD?
4. What is the focus of cognitive-behavioral treatments for GAD?
5. What medications are used to treat GAD?

APPLY IT A biological theorist would attribute GAD to excessive firing of neurons in which area of the brain?

a. prefrontal cortex
b. hippocampus
c. limbic system
d. brain stem

Answers appear online at www.mhhe.com/nolen5e.

OBSESSIVE-COMPULSIVE DISORDER

Obsessions are thoughts, images, ideas, or impulses that are persistent, that uncontrollably intrude on consciousness, and that cause significant anxiety or distress. **Compulsions** are repetitive behaviors or mental acts that an individual feels he or she must perform.

Obsessive-compulsive disorder (OCD) is classified as an anxiety disorder because people experience anxiety as a result of their obsessional thoughts and when they cannot carry out their compulsive behaviors (Table 5.8). OCD differs enough from the other anxiety disorders, however, that the *DSM-5* authors have proposed renaming the category anxiety disorder as *anxiety and obsessive-compulsive spectrum disorders*.

Like adults. children can suffer from OCD. Zach's account in the following excerpt illustrates how overwhelming the disorder can be.

VOICES

When I was 6 I started doing all these strange things when I swallowed saliva. When I swallowed saliva I had to crouch down and touch the ground. I didn't want to lose any saliva—for a bit I had to sweep the ground with my hand—and later I had to blink my eyes if I swallowed. I was frustrated because I couldn't stop the compulsions. Each time I swallowed I had to do something. For a while I had to touch my shoulders to my chin. I don't know why. I had no reason. I was afraid. It was just so unpleasant if I didn't. If I tried not to do these things, all I got was failure. I had to do it, and no matter how hard I tried, I just *still* had to.

It wrecked my life. It took away all the time. I couldn't do anything. If you put it all together I did it maybe an hour and a half or sometimes three hours a day. (Rapoport, 1990, pp. 43–44)

TABLE 5.8 *DSM-IV-TR* Criteria for Obsessive-Compulsive Disorder

A. Either obsessions or compulsions.

Obsessions as defined by 1, 2, 3, and 4:

1. Recurrent and persistent thoughts, impulses, or images that are experienced, at some time during the disturbance, as intrusive and inappropriate and that cause marked anxiety or distress.
2. The thoughts, impulses, or images are not simply excessive worries about real-life problems.
3. The person attempts to ignore or suppress such thoughts, impulses, or images, or to neutralize them with some other thought or action.
4. The person recognizes that the obsessional thoughts, impulses, or images are a product of his or her own mind (not imposed from without as in thought insertion).

Compulsions as defined by 1 and 2:

1. Repetitive behaviors (e.g., hand washing, ordering, checking) or mental acts (e.g., praying, counting, repeating words silently) that the person feels driven to perform in response to an obsession, or according to rules that must be applied rigidly.
2. The behaviors or mental acts are aimed at preventing or reducing distress or preventing some dreaded event or situation; however, these behaviors or mental acts either are not connected in a realistic way with what they are designed to neutralize or prevent or are clearly excessive.

B. At some point during the course of the disorder, the person has recognized that the obsessions or compulsions are excessive or unreasonable. *Note:* This does not apply to children.

C. The obsessions or compulsions cause marked distress, are time consuming (take more than 1 hour a day), or significantly interfere with the person's normal routine, occupational (or academic) functioning, or usual social activities or relationships.

D. If another Axis I disorder is present, the content of the obsessions or compulsions is not restricted to it (e.g., preoccupation with food in the presence of an eating disorder).

E. The disturbance is not due to the direct physiological effects of a substance (e.g., a drug of abuse, a medication) or a general medical condition.

Source: Reprinted with permission from the *Diagnostic and Statistical Manual of Mental Disorders,* Fourth Edition, Text Revision.

Hand-washing is one of the most common compulsions in OCD.

Zach's thoughts and behaviors might seem "crazy"—out of touch with reality. However, people with OCD know that their thoughts and behaviors are irrational yet cannot control them.

OCD often begins at a young age. The peak age of onset for males is between 6 and 15, and for females between 20 and 29 (Angst et al., 2004; Foa & Franklin, 2001). Children often hide their symptoms, even from their parents; as a result, the symptoms can go undetected for years (Rapoport et al., 2000).

OCD tends to be chronic if left untreated (Foa & Franklin, 2001). Obsessional thoughts are distressing to people with OCD, and engaging in compulsive behaviors can be time-consuming or harmful (e.g., hand-washing to the point of bleeding). As many as 66 percent of people with OCD are also significantly depressed (Foa & Franklin, 2001). Panic attacks, phobias, and substance abuse are common.

Between 1 and 3 percent of people will develop OCD at some time (Angst et al., 2004; Kessler et al., 2005). In the United States, European Americans show higher rates of OCD than African Americans or Hispanic Americans (Hewlett, 2000). The prevalence of OCD does not seem to differ greatly across countries that have been studied, including the United States, Canada, Mexico, England, Norway, Hong Kong, India, Egypt, Japan, and Korea (Escobar, 1993; Insel, 1984; Kim, 1993). Although some studies have found slightly higher rates in women (Angst et al., 2004), other studies have not (Edelmann, 1992; Karno & Golding, 1991).

Symptoms of OCD

The focus of obsessive thoughts seems to be similar across cultures, most commonly consisting of dirt and contamination (Akhtar et al., 1975; Hewlett, 2000; Rachman & Hodgson, 1980). Howie Mandel, comedian and host of *Deal or No Deal,* has obsessions about germs and contamination that keep him from shaking hands with anyone (Mandel, 2005). When contestants win big money on the show, he will do a fist bump with them but will not shake their hand. He keeps his head shaved because it helps him feel cleaner.

Other common obsessions include aggressive impulses (such as to hurt one's child), sexual thoughts (such as recurrent pornographic images), impulses to do something against one's moral code (such as to shout obscenities in church), and repeated doubts (such as worrying that you have not turned off the stove) (Rachman & Hodgson, 1980). Although thoughts of this kind occur to most people occasionally, most of us can dismiss or ignore them. People with OCD cannot.

Sometimes, an individual's compulsion is tied logically to his or her obsession. If Howie Mandel does touch someone's hand or an object he feels is dirty, he will wash his hands over and over until he feels clean (Mandel, 2005). The compulsive behavior becomes so extreme and repetitive that it is irrational. "Checking" compulsions, which are extremely common, are tied to obsessional doubts, as illustrated in the following story.

Howie Mandel, host of *Deal or No Deal,* has a severe germ phobia and cannot shake hands with other people, but he can tolerate fist bumps.

VOICES

I'm driving down the highway doing 55 MPH. Out of nowhere an obsessive-compulsive disorder (OCD) attack strikes. While in reality no one is on the road, I'm intruded by the heinous thought that I *might* have hit someone . . . a human being!

I think about this for a second and then say to myself, "That's ridiculous. I didn't hit anybody." Nonetheless, a gnawing anxiety is born.

I reason, "Well, if I hit someone while driving, I would have *felt* it." This brief trip into reality helps the pain dissipate . . . but only for a second. Why? Because the gnawing anxiety that I really did commit the illusionary accident is growing larger—so is the pain.

The pain is a terrible guilt that I have committed an unthinkable, negligent act. At one level, I know this is ridiculous, but there's a terrible pain in my stomach telling me something quite different.

I start ruminating, "Maybe I did hit someone and didn't realize it. . . . Oh, my God! I might have killed somebody! I have to go back and check." Checking is the only way to calm the anxiety. It brings me closer to truth somehow. I can't live with the thought that I actually may have killed someone—I have to check it out. (Rapoport, 1990, pp. 21–22)

This man's compulsive checking makes some sense, given what he is thinking. However, what he is thinking—that he hit someone on the road without knowing it—is highly improbable. The compulsive checking briefly quells his obsessional thoughts, but they recur with even more force.

Often, the link between the obsession and the compulsion is the result of "magical thinking" (Rapoport, 1991). Many people with OCD believe that repeating a behavior a certain number of times will ward off danger to themselves or others. Their rituals often become stereotyped and rigid, and they develop obsessions and compulsions about not performing them correctly. An individual might feel compelled to read a passage in a book 25 times perfectly, fearing that something bad will happen to his family if he does not.

At times, there is no discernible link between a specific obsession and the compulsions an individual develops. Recall that Zach engaged in several behaviors, such as touching the floor, when he had an obsession about losing his saliva. He could not even say how these behaviors were related to his obsession; he just knew he had to engage in them. Thus, although compulsions often may seem purposeful, they are not functional.

One compulsive behavior that has been featured in a reality television show, and may be included as a new diagnosis in the *DSM-5*, is *hoarding*. People who hoard cannot throw away their possessions, even those that most of us regard as trash, such as newspapers or take-out food containers. They stockpile these items in their homes and cars to the point of creating hazards, making these spaces unusable (American Psychiatric Association, 2010). Epidemiological studies suggest that 2 to 5 percent of the population engage in hoarding (Iervolino et al., 2009). People who hoard usually do not meet the criteria for obsessive-compulsive disorder, however, so the *DSM-5* authors have proposed a separate diagnosis for hoarding.

FIGURE 5.9 **OCD in the Brain.** A three-dimensional view of the human brain (with parts shown as they would look if the overlying cerebral cortex were transparent) clarifies the locations of the orbital frontal cortex and the basal ganglia—areas implicated in obsessive-compulsive disorder. Among the basal ganglia's structures are the caudate nucleus, which filters powerful impulses that arise in the orbital frontal cortex so that only the most powerful ones reach the thalamus. Perhaps the orbital frontal cortex, the caudate nucleus, or both are so active in people with obsessive-compulsive disorder that numerous impulses reach the thalamus, generating obsessive thoughts or compulsive actions.

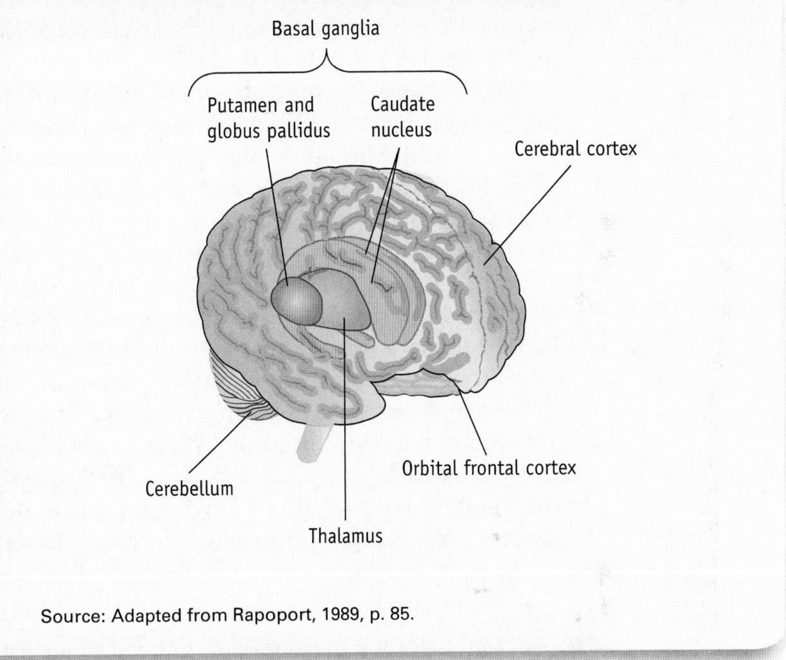

Source: Adapted from Rapoport, 1989, p. 85.

Theories of OCD

The biological theories of OCD have dominated research in recent years. Cognitive-behavioral theories have also been proposed.

Biological Theories

Biological theories of obsessive-compulsive disorder have focused on a circuit in the brain involved in executing primitive patterns of behavior, such as aggression, sexuality, and bodily excretion (Rauch et al., 2003). This circuit begins in the orbital region of the frontal cortex (Figure 5.9). Impulses are then carried to a part of the basal ganglia called the *caudate nucleus*, which allows the strongest of the impulses to flow through to the thalamus. If these impulses reach the thalamus, the person is motivated to think further about and possibly act on them. The action might be a set of stereotyped behaviors appropriate to the impulse. Once these behaviors are executed, the impulse diminishes.

For people with OCD, dysfunction in this circuit may result in the system's inability to turn off the primitive impulses or the execution of the stereotyped behaviors. When most of us think our hands are dirty, we engage in a fairly stereotyped form of cleansing: We wash them. People with OCD, however, continue to have the impulse to wash their hands because their brains do not shut off their thoughts about dirt or their hand-washing behavior when the behavior is no longer necessary. Proponents of this biological theory point out that many of the obsessions and compulsions of people with OCD have to do with contamination, sex, aggression, and repeated patterns of behavior—all issues with which this primitive brain circuit deals (Rapoport, 1991; Rauch et al., 2003).

PET scans show more activity in this primitive circuit in people with OCD than in people without it (Figure 5.10; Micallef & Blin, 2001; Saxena et al., 2003). In addition, people with OCD often get some relief from their symptoms when they take drugs that regulate the neurotransmitter serotonin, which plays an important role in the circuit's proper functioning (Micallef & Blin, 2001; Saxena et al., 2003). Those patients who respond to serotonin-enhancing drugs tend to show more reduction in the rate of activity in these brain areas than patients who do not respond well to the drugs (Baxter, Schwartz, Bergman, & Szuba, 1992; Saxena et al., 1999, 2003). Interestingly, people with OCD who respond to behavior therapy also tend to show decreases in the rate of activity in the caudate nucleus and thalamus (Schwartz et al., 1996).

FIGURE 5.10 **PET Scans of OCD.** PET scans of people with OCD show more activity in the frontal cortex, basal ganglia, and thalamus than do PET scans of people without OCD.

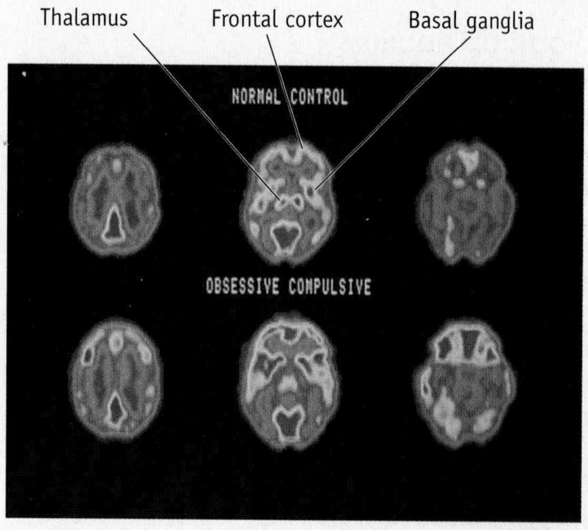

Piecing together these studies, researchers have argued that people with OCD have a fundamental dysfunction in those areas of the brain that regulate primitive impulses, perhaps due to a depletion of serotonin in these systems. As a result, primitive impulses about sex, aggression, and cleanliness break through to their consciousness and motivate the execution of stereotyped behaviors much more often than in people without OCD (Baxter, Clark, Iqbal, & Ackermann, 2001; Rapoport, 1989, 1991; Hurley et al., 2008).

Finally, genes may help determine who is vulnerable to OCD (Mundo, Zanoni, & Altamura, 2006). Family history studies clearly show that OCD runs in families, and twin studies support a substantial genetic component in obsessive and compulsive behaviors (Eley et al., 2003; Hudziak et al., 2004).

Cognitive-Behavioral Theories

Most people, including those without OCD, occasionally have negative, intrusive thoughts (Angst et al., 2004; Rachman & deSilva, 1978). People are more prone to having such thoughts and to engaging in rigid, ritualistic behaviors when they are distressed (Clark & Purdon, 1993; Rachman, 1997). Many new mothers, exhausted from sleep deprivation and the stress of caring for a newborn, think of harming their baby even though they are horrified by such thoughts and would never carry them out.

According to cognitive-behavioral theories of OCD, what differentiates people with OCD from people without the disorder is the inability to turn off these negative, intrusive thoughts (Clark, 1988; Rachman & Hodgson, 1980; Salkovskis, 1998). Most people can ignore or dismiss the thoughts, attributing them to their distress. With the passage of time, the thoughts subside.

Why do people who develop OCD have trouble turning off their thoughts, according to cognitive-behavioral theories? First, they may be depressed or generally anxious much of the time so that even minor negative events are likely to invoke intrusive, negative thoughts (Clark & Purdon, 1993). Second, people with OCD may have a tendency toward rigid, moralistic thinking (Rachman, 1993; Salkovskis, 1998). They judge their negative, intrusive thoughts as more unacceptable than most people would and become more anxious and guilty about having them. This anxiety then makes it harder for them to dismiss the thoughts (Salkovskis, 1998). People who feel more responsible for events that happen in their lives and the lives of others will also have more trouble dismissing thoughts such as "Did I hit someone on the road?" and thus might be more likely to develop OCD.

Third, people with OCD appear to believe that they *should* be able to control all thoughts and have trouble accepting that everyone has horrific notions from time to time (Clark & Purdon, 1993; Freeston, Ladouceur, Thibodeau, & Gagnon, 1992). They tend to believe that having these thoughts means they are going crazy, or they equate having the thoughts with actually engaging in the behaviors ("If I'm thinking about hurting my child, I'm as guilty as if I actually did"). Of course, this just makes them more anxious when they have the thoughts, making the thoughts harder to dismiss.

According to these theories, compulsions develop largely through operant conditioning. People with anxiety-provoking obsessions discover that if they engage in certain behaviors, their anxiety is reduced. Each time the obsessions return and the person uses the behaviors to reduce them, the behaviors are negatively reinforced. Thus, compulsions are born.

Research has supported pieces of the cognitive-behavioral view of OCD (Julien, O'Connor, & Aardema, 2007), but more work is needed. In particular, whether the dysfunctions the cognitive-behavioral theories point to are causes or consequences is not clear.

Treatment of OCD

Both biological and cognitive-behavioral treatments are helpful for people with OCD.

Biological Treatments

Until the 1980s, few effective biological treatments for OCD were available. The antianxiety drugs, the benzodiazepines, were not useful in most cases. Then, fortuitously, it was discovered that antidepressant drugs affecting levels of serotonin helped relieve symptoms of OCD in many patients (Marazziti, Catena, & Pallanti, 2006). Clomipramine (trade name Anafranil) was the first (Rapoport, 1989). Then the SSRIs, including fluoxetine (trade name Prozac), paroxetine (trade name Paxil), sertraline (trade name Zoloft), and fluvoxamine (trade name Luvox) proved effective. Controlled studies suggest that 50 to 80 percent of OCD patients experience decreases in their obsessions and compulsions while on these drugs, compared to only 5 percent of patients on placebos (Marazziti et al., 2006; Hurley et al., 2008).

These drugs are not the complete answer for people with OCD, however. A substantial number of OCD sufferers do not respond to SSRIs. Among those who do, obsessions and compulsions are reduced only 40 to 50 percent, and patients tend to relapse if they discontinue the drugs (Hewlett, 2000). Significant side effects, which include drowsiness, constipation, and loss of sexual interest, prevent many people from taking them. Studies suggest that adding an atypical antipsychotic (see Chapter 8) can further help people who do not respond fully to SSRIs (Bystritsky et al., 2004).

Behavioral Treatments

Many clinicians believe that drugs must be combined with behavioral therapies using **exposure and response prevention** to help people recover completely from OCD. Exposure and response prevention therapy repeatedly exposes the client to the focus of the obsession and prevents compulsive responses to the resulting anxiety (Foa & Franklin, 2001; Marks & Swinson, 1992; Rachman & Hodgson, 1980). The repeated exposure to the content of the obsession extinguishes the client's anxiety about the obsession. Preventing the person from engaging in compulsive behavior allows this extinction to take place. The client learns that not engaging in the compulsive behavior does not lead to a terrible result.

Clients may be given homework that helps them confront their obsessions and compulsions. Early in therapy, a client might be assigned simply to refrain from cleaning the house every day and instead to clean it only every 3 days. Later he might be asked to drop a cookie on a dirty kitchen floor and then pick it up and eat it, or to drop the kitchen knives on the floor and then use them to prepare food.

These behavior therapies lead to significant improvement in obsessions and compulsive behavior in 60 to 90 percent of OCD clients (Abramowitz, 1997; Fals-Stewart, Marks, & Schafer, 1993; Foa & Franklin, 2001; Marks & Swinson, 1992; McLean et al., 2001; Steketee & Frost, 2003). In most clients, the improvements remain for up to 6 years (Foa & Franklin, 2001; Foa & Kozak, 1993).

TEST YOURSELF

1. What are obsessions and compulsions?
2. What biological factors have been implicated in OCD?
3. What is the cognitive model of OCD?
4. What biological therapies have proven useful in treating OCD?
5. What is exposure and response prevention therapy for OCD?

APPLY IT A therapist explaining OCD to a client might say which of the following?

a. Obsessions are only mental phenomena, whereas compulsions are behaviors.

(continued)

b. Obsessions are rigid rituals, such as making sure the stove is turned off, whereas compulsions are disturbing thoughts.
c. Obsessions are intrusive thoughts that increase anxiety, whereas compulsions are physical or mental acts that decrease it.
d. Some individuals experience only compulsions, but all who have obsessions also engage in compulsions.

Answers appear online at www.mhhe.com/nolen5e.

FIGURE 5.11 **Vulnerability-Stress Models.** Vulnerability-stress models of anxiety disorders describe how biological, psychological, and social factors work together to create these disorders.

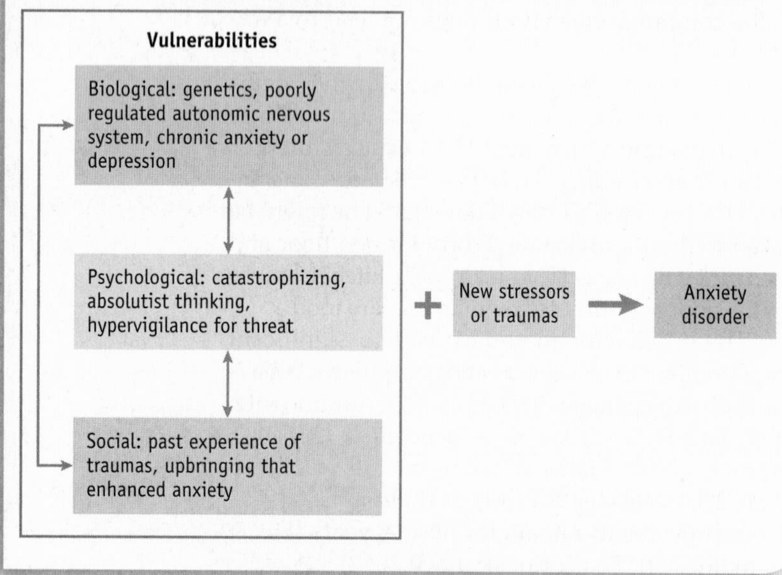

CHAPTER INTEGRATION

Biology clearly influences the experience of anxiety. Evolution has prepared our bodies to respond to threatening situations with physiological changes that make it easier for us to flee from or confront a threat. For some people, this natural physiological response may be impaired, leading to overreactivity, chronic arousal, or poorly regulated arousal. These people may be more prone to severe anxiety reactions to threatening stimuli and to anxiety disorders.

Psychological and social factors also clearly play a role in anxiety and the anxiety disorders. Frightening experiences lead to the development of some anxiety disorders, particularly PTSD. People differ in what they perceive as threatening, leading to differences in the level of anxiety they feel in potentially threatening situations. These differences may be due to specific traumas that some people have experienced or to upbringing. A child may develop a phobia of dogs because her mother modeled a fearful response to dogs. Another child may be chronically anxious and believe he must be perfect because his parents punish him severely if he makes any type of mistake.

Vulnerability (diathesis)-stress models (Figure 5.11) stipulate that people who develop an anxiety disorder have pre-existing biological or psychological vulnerabilities due in part to trauma or severe stress and that these vulnerabilities interact with new stressors to create anxiety disorders. Such models help explain why some people, but not others, experience anxiety so severe and chronic that it develops into a disorder.

SHADES OF GRAY DISCUSSION (review p. 125)

Neither posttraumatic stress disorder nor acute stress disorder applies to Ramon. His response at the time of the accident was characterized more by anger at the other driver than by the fear, helplessness, or horror necessary for either diagnosis in the *DSM-IV-TR.* Although his recurrent nightmares meet the "re-experiencing" criterion for PTSD and acute stress disorder, he actively thinks about the accident rather than avoiding thoughts of it. We have no evidence that he displays a lack of interest in activities, feels detached or estranged from others, has restricted affect, or has a sense of a foreshortened future. We also lack evidence that Ramon has significant arousal symptoms; the exaggerated startle response he had in the interchange with his boss seems to be an isolated incident, and his sleep difficulties are caused primarily by his nightmares.

For now, Ramon appears to be having an understandable, but not diagnosable, reaction to a very frightening event. If you were his psychologist, you would want to check up in a week or two. If his nightmares and thoughts about the accident persist, and if they begin to more significantly impair his functioning, you might then diagnose him with an adjustment disorder.

THINK CRITICALLY

The diagnosis of PTSD has been questioned recently on two fronts. First, some researchers suggest that the criteria for PTSD are too broad and that too many stressful events are accepted as possible triggers (Spitzer, First, & Wakefield, 2007). As noted earlier, the upcoming *DSM-5* is likely to narrow the PTSD diagnostic criteria (Rosen, Spitzer, & McHugh, 2008).

Second, the PTSD field has been criticized for ignoring evidence that most people who experience severe trauma do not develop significant symptoms of PTSD or other mental disorders. A study of New Yorkers 6 months after the attacks on the World Trade Center in 2001 found that 65 percent of the 2,752 adults studied had at most one PTSD symptom (Bonanno, Galea, Bucciarelli, & Vlahov, 2006). This was a randomly selected sample of people with a range of exposures to the attack. But even those most directly affected showed resilience—over half who saw the attack in person or lost a friend or relative did not develop PTSD symptoms. Among the 22 participants who had been in the World Trade Center at the time, 7 developed PTSD, but 5 had two or fewer symptoms, and 10 had only one symptom or none at all (Bonanno et al., 2006).

Have mental health professionals exaggerated the effects of trauma on mental health? Or should PTSD have a broad definition so that individuals who suffer after experiencing a trauma are not overlooked? *(Discussion appears on p. 518 at the back of this book.)*

CHAPTER SUMMARY

- Anxiety has physiological, emotional, cognitive, and behavioral symptoms.
- Post-traumatic stress disorder (PTSD) occurs after a severe trauma. It manifests three types of symptoms: (1) repeatedly reexperiencing the traumatic event through intrusive images or thoughts, recurring nightmares, flashbacks, and psychological and physiological reactivity to stimuli that remind the person of the traumatic event; (2) withdrawal, emotional numbing, and avoidance of anything that might arouse memories of the event; and (3) hypervigilance and chronic arousal. PTSD sufferers also report survivor guilt.
- Acute stress disorder has symptoms similar to those of PTSD but occurs within 1 month of a stressor and usually lasts less than 1 month.
- Social factors appear to influence the risk for PTSD. The more severe and longer-lasting a trauma and the more deeply involved a person is in it, the more likely he or she is to show PTSD. People with less social support are at increased risk.
- Psychological factors also play a role in PTSD. People who are already depressed or anxious before a trauma or who cope through avoidance or dissociation may be at increased risk.
- The biological factors that increase vulnerability to PTSD may include abnormally low cortisol levels and a genetic risk. People with PTSD show hyperarousal of the amygdala, atrophy in the hippocampus, and exaggerated heart rate responses to stressors.
- An effective treatment for PTSD exposes a person to memories of a trauma through systematic desensitization and flooding to extinguish the anxiety these memories elicit. Some people cannot tolerate such exposure, however, and may do better with supportive therapy to reduce and prevent stress.
- The benzodiazepines and antidepressant drugs can quell some of the symptoms of PTSD.
- A panic attack is a short, intense experience of several physiological symptoms of anxiety, plus thoughts that one is going crazy, losing control, or dying. Panic disorder is diagnosed when a person has spontaneous panic attacks frequently, worries about having them, and changes his or her lifestyle as a result. About one-third to one-half of people diagnosed with panic disorder also develop agoraphobia; they avoid a wide range of places in which they fear they will have a panic attack.
- One biological theory of panic disorder holds that sufferers have overreactive autonomic nervous systems, putting them into a full fight-or-flight response with little provocation. This reaction may be the result of imbalances in norepinephrine or serotonin in areas of the brain stem and limbic system. Evidence also exists for genetic contributions to panic disorder.
- Psychological theories of panic disorder suggest that people who have it pay close attention to bodily sensations, misinterpret these in a negative way, and engage in snowballing, catastrophic thinking. This thinking

increases physiological activation, and a full panic attack ensues.

- Antidepressants and benzodiazepines are effective in reducing panic attacks and agoraphobic behavior, but people tend to relapse when they discontinue the drugs.
- An effective cognitive-behavioral therapy for panic attacks and agoraphobia teaches clients to use relaxation exercises and to identify and challenge their catastrophic styles of thinking, often during panic attacks induced in therapy sessions. Systematic desensitization techniques reduce agoraphobic behavior.
- The specific phobias are fears of certain objects or situations. Common categories are animal type, natural environment type, situational type, and blood-injection-injury type. Social phobia is fear of being judged or embarrassed.
- Behavioral theories suggest that phobias develop through classical and operant conditioning. The person has learned that avoiding the phobic object reduces fear, so avoidance is reinforced. Phobias also develop through observational learning. It appears that, through prepared classical conditioning, humans more readily develop phobias to objects our distant ancestors had reason to fear, such as snakes.
- Cognitive theories suggest that social phobia develops in people who have overly high standards for their social performance, assume others will judge them harshly, and give biased attention to signs of social rejection.
- Behavioral treatments focus on extinguishing fear responses to phobic objects and have proven effective. People with blood-injection-injury phobias must learn to tense their muscles when they confront their phobic objects to prevent decreases in blood pressure and heart rate. Drug therapies have not proven useful for phobias.
- Group cognitive-behavioral therapy effectively treats social phobia.
- People with generalized anxiety disorder (GAD) are chronically anxious in most situations. Cognitive theories argue that people with GAD appear more vigilant for threatening information, even on an unconscious level.
- Benzodiazepines can produce short-term relief for some people with GAD but are not suitable in long-term treatment. Antidepressants appear helpful in treating GAD.
- Cognitive-behavioral therapies focus on changing the catastrophic thinking styles of people with GAD and have been shown to reduce acute symptoms and prevent relapse in most patients.
- Obsessions are thoughts, images, ideas, or impulses that are persistent, intrusive, and distressing. They commonly focus on contamination, sex, violence, and repeated doubts. Compulsions are repetitive behaviors or mental acts the individual feels he or she must perform to dispel obsessions.
- One biological theory of obsessive-compulsive disorder (OCD) speculates that areas of the brain responsible for the execution of primitive patterns of behavior, such as washing rituals, may be impaired in people with OCD. These brain areas are rich in the neurotransmitter serotonin. Drugs that regulate serotonin have proven helpful in treatment.
- Cognitive-behavioral theories suggest that people with OCD are unable to turn off the negative, intrusive thoughts most people occasionally have. Compulsive behaviors develop through operant conditioning when people are reinforced for behaviors that reduce anxiety.
- The most effective drug therapies for OCD are the SSRIs.
- Exposure and response prevention therapies have also proven helpful for OCD sufferers. These therapies expose OCD clients to the content of their obsessions while preventing compulsive behavior, so anxiety over the obsessions and the compulsions to perform the behaviors is extinguished.

KEY TERMS

fight-or-flight response 113
cortisol 113
anxiety 115
post-traumatic stress disorder (PTSD) 116
acute stress disorder 116
adjustment disorder 117
stress-management interventions 124
selective serotonin reuptake inhibitors (SSRIs) 124
panic attacks 125
panic disorder 126
agoraphobia 126
limbic system 127
locus ceruleus 127
anxiety sensitivity 128

interoceptive conditioning 128
conditioned avoidance response 128
specific phobias 131
animal type phobias 131
natural environment type phobias 131
situational type phobias 132
blood-injection-injury type phobias 132
social phobia 132
negative reinforcement 135
prepared classical conditioning 136
applied tension technique 137
modeling 137
flooding 138
generalized anxiety disorder (GAD) 139
obsessions 143
compulsions 143
obsessive-compulsive disorder (OCD) 143
exposure and response prevention 147

Chapter 6

Somatoform and Dissociative Disorders

CHAPTER OUTLINE

Extraordinary People

Anna O., *The Talking Cure*

One of the most famous cases in the annals of psychology and psychiatry was that of Anna O., a young Viennese woman whose real name was Bertha Pappenheim. She was born in Vienna in 1859, into a wealthy Orthodox Jewish family. Highly intelligent, she craved intellectual stimulation but rarely received it after leaving school. She was strong-willed and slightly temperamental. In 1880, at age 21, Pappenheim became ill around the time of her father's serious illness and eventual death. Josef Breuer, a colleague of Freud who treated Pappenheim, noted, "Up to the onset of the disease, the patient showed no sign of nervousness, not even during pubescence. . . . Upon her father's illness, in rapid succession there seemingly developed a series of new and severe disturbances" (quoted in Edinger, 1963).

These new disturbances were a variety of physical ailments that didn't appear to have any physical causes. She experienced head pain, dizziness and profound visual disturbances, an inability to move her head and neck, and numbness and contractions in her lower-right limbs. Breuer treated Pappenheim by asking her to talk about her symptoms under hypnosis, and after 18 months her symptoms seemed to subside. Pappenheim dubbed this the "talking cure." After Breuer told her that he thought she was well and he would not be seeing her again, he was called to her house later that evening, where she was thrashing around in her bed, going through imaginary childbirth. She claimed that the baby was Breuer's. He calmed her down by hypnotizing her, but he soon fled the house and never saw her again.

Breuer collaborated with Sigmund Freud in writing about Anna O., and their descriptions of the talking cure launched psychoanalysis as a form of psychotherapy. Pappenheim, however, did not credit psychoanalysis with the eventual decline in her symptoms. She spent the remainder of her life as an advocate for the poor and for the Jewish minority in Europe.

Bertha Pappenheim, or Anna O., appeared to suffer from what we now call a *somatoform disorder*—she experienced physiological symptoms that Breuer argued were the result of painful emotions or memories she was not able to confront. In this chapter, we discuss the somatoform disorders as well as the *dissociative disorders*, in which people develop multiple separate personalities or completely lose their memory of significant portions of their lives.

The somatoform and dissociative disorders have a long history in psychology. As the story of Bertha Pappenheim illustrates, these phenomena provided the material for much of the early theorizing by Breuer, Freud, and other psychoanalysts. In recent years, these disorders and the idea that people can completely lose conscious access to painful memories and emotions through dissociation have become controversial. We will discuss this controversy at the end of the chapter.

SOMATOFORM DISORDERS

The **somatoform disorders** are a group of disorders in which people experience significant physical symptoms for which there is no apparent organic cause. This group of disorders may be renamed *somatic symptom disorders* in the *DSM-5.* Often, the symptoms are inconsistent with possible physiological processes, and there is strong reason to believe that psychological factors are involved. People with somatoform disorders do not consciously produce or control their symptoms. Instead, they truly experience the symptoms, and the symptoms pass only when the psychological factors that led to them are resolved.

One difficulty in diagnosing somatoform disorders is the possibility that an individual has a real physical disorder that is difficult to detect or diagnose. Many of us have friends or relatives who have complained to their physicians for years about physical symptoms that the physicians attributed to "nervousness" or "attention seeking" but that later were determined to be early symptoms of serious disease. The diagnosis of somatoform disorder is easier when psychological factors leading to the development of the symptoms can be identified clearly or when physical examination proves that the symptoms cannot be physiologically possible. For example, when a child is perfectly healthy on weekends but has stomachaches in the morning just before going to school, it is possible that the stomachaches are due to distress over going to school. A more extreme example of a clear somatoform disorder is *pseudocyesis,* or false pregnancy, in which a woman believes she is pregnant but physical examination and laboratory tests confirm that she is not. Bertha Pappenheim apparently displayed pseudocyesis.

Distinguishing Somatoform Disorders from Related Disorders

The somatoform disorders are not the same as **psychosomatic disorders,** in which people have an actual, documented physical illness or defect, such as high blood pressure, that is being worsened by psychological factors. Instead, a person with a somatoform disorder does not have any illness or defect that can be documented with tests (Table 6.1).

Somatoform disorders are also different from **malingering,** in which people fake a symptom or disorder in order to avoid an unwanted situation, such as military service, or in order to gain something, such as insurance payments. Again, the individual with a somatoform disorder subjectively experiences the symptoms, but the symptoms have no organic basis.

TABLE 6.1 Distinctions Between Somatoform Disorders and Related Syndromes

Somatoform Disorders	Psychosomatic Disorders	Malingering	Factitious Disorders
Subjective experience of many physical symptoms, with no organic cause	Actual physical illness present with psychological factors seemingly contributing to the illness	Deliberate faking of physical symptoms to avoid an unpleasant situation, such as military duty	Deliberate faking of physical illness to gain medical attention

TABLE 6.2 Dissociative Experiences in the General Population

These are the percentages of people in a random sample of 1,055 adults in Winnipeg, Canada, who acknowledged ever having experienced each item and who fell into the pathological range for frequency of experiences of the item.

Experience	Percentage Acknowledging	Percent in Pathological Range
Missing part of a conversation	83%	29%
Not sure whether one has done something or only thought about it	73	25
Remembering the past so vividly one seems to be reliving it	60	19
Talking out loud to oneself when alone	56	18
Not sure if remembered event happened or was a dream	55	13
Feeling as though one were two different people	47	12
So involved in fantasy that it seems real	45	11
Driving a car and realizing that one doesn't remember part of the trip	48	8
Finding notes or drawings that one must have done but doesn't remember doing	34	6
Seeing oneself as if looking at another person	29	4
Hearing voices inside one's head	26	7
Other people and objects do not seem real	26	4
Finding unfamiliar things among one's belongings	22	4
Feeling as though one's body is not one's own	23	4
Finding oneself in a place but unaware of how one got there	19	2
Finding oneself dressed in clothes one doesn't remember putting on	15	1
Not recognizing one's reflection in a mirror	14	1

Source: From C. A. Ross, *Dissociative Identity Disorder.* Copyright © 1997 John Wiley & Sons, Inc. Reprinted with permission of John Wiley & Sons, Inc.

Somatoform and Dissociative Disorders Along the Continuum

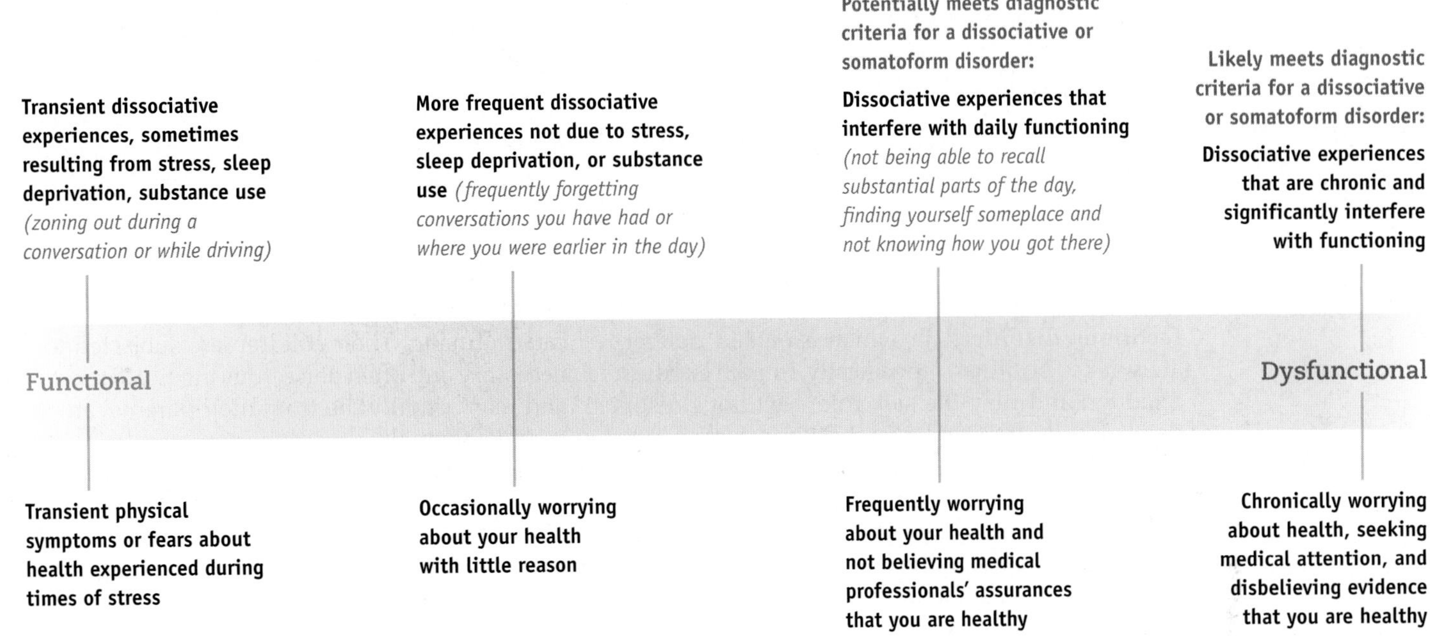
Potentially meets diagnostic criteria for a dissociative or somatoform disorder:
Likely meets diagnostic criteria for a dissociative or somatoform disorder:
Transient dissociative experiences, sometimes resulting from stress, sleep deprivation, substance use (zoning out during a conversation or while driving)
More frequent dissociative experiences not due to stress, sleep deprivation, or substance use (frequently forgetting conversations you have had or where you were earlier in the day)
Dissociative experiences that interfere with daily functioning (not being able to recall substantial parts of the day, finding yourself someplace and not knowing how you got there)
Dissociative experiences that are chronic and significantly interfere with functioning
Functional
Dysfunctional
Transient physical symptoms or fears about health experienced during times of stress
Occasionally worrying about your health with little reason
Frequently worrying about your health and not believing medical professionals' assurances that you are healthy
Chronically worrying about health, seeking medical attention, and disbelieving evidence that you are healthy

Both somatoform and dissociative disorders are considered by some theorists to be the result of a psychological process known as **dissociation,** in which different parts of an individual's identity, memories, or consciousness split off from one another. You may not realize it, but you likely have had dissociative experiences (Aderibigbe, Bloch, & Walker, 2001; Seedat, Stein, & Forde, 2003): You are driving down a familiar road, thinking about a recent conversation with a friend, and suddenly you realize that you've driven several miles and don't remember traveling that section of the road. That's a dissociative experience, as is daydreaming. When we daydream, we can lose consciousness of where we are and of what is going on around us. Becoming absorbed in a movie or book is also a dissociative experience.

Researcher Colin Ross (1997) asked more than a thousand adults from the general community about a number of different dissociative experiences. His findings are listed in Table 6.2. Missing part of a conversation appears to be the most common dissociative experience, followed by being unsure of whether you have actually carried through with something (such as brushing your teeth) or have only thought about it. These experiences are not harmful. Farther down the list are somewhat more bizarre experiences, such as hearing voices in your head, feeling as though your body is not your own, and not recognizing objects or other people as real. As the table shows, even these bizarre experiences happen, at least occasionally, to a substantial percentage of the general population.

Fatigue and stress are probably the most common causes of dissociation. A study of mentally healthy soldiers undergoing survival training in the U.S. Army found that over 90 percent reported dissociative symptoms in response to the stress of the training; the symptoms included feeling separated from what was happening, as if they were watching themselves in a movie (Morgan et al., 2001).

Binge-drinking alcohol or taking other psychoactive drugs can cause many of the memory lapses described in Table 6.2. Older adults whose short-term memories are fading often forget having done things, and, as we will discuss in Chapter 11, several cognitive disorders can lead to memory lapses and even to the inability to recognize faces. Most of the time, however, dissociative experiences pass quickly and do not signal any long-term problem.

Some people do have dissociative experiences frequently enough that dissociation interferes with their functioning. Ross (1997) placed these people in the "pathological range" of dissociative experiences. The percentage of people in his sample falling in this range for each experience he studied is given in the right-hand column of Table 6.2. As you can see, most of the more bizarre dissociative experiences occur infrequently enough that only a small percentage of people are categorized in the pathological range. In

(continued)

fact, only a very small percentage of the population is ever diagnosed with a dissociative disorder.

Just as we all experience mild dissociative symptoms, so too do many of us "carry our stress in our body," experiencing tension and unexplained aches, pains, and illnesses when we feel stressed. This may be the result of dissociation, a case when our consciousness of our psychological pain is diminished and instead we are aware only of physical pain. Usually, these aches and pains subside when our stress subsides. For a small number of people, however, their attention to their perceived aches and pains is chronic and persists even when they have strong evidence that nothing is wrong. Their lives focus on fears about their physical health, and they may be diagnosed with a somatoform disorder.

Also, somatoform disorders are different from **factitious disorders,** in which a person deliberately fakes an illness specifically to gain medical attention and play the sick role. Factitious disorders are also referred to as *Munchhausen's syndrome*. Note that the major difference between malingering and factitious disorders is the motivation for faking symptoms—in malingering the symptoms help an individual avoid an unwanted situation, while in factitious disorders the symptoms are intentionally created to gain medical attention.

Factitious disorder by proxy is diagnosed when parents fake or even create illnesses in their children in order to gain attention for themselves. They act as devoted and long-suffering protectors of their children, drawing praise for their dedicated nursing. Their children are subjected to unnecessary and often dangerous medical procedures and may actually die from their parents' attempts to make them ill.

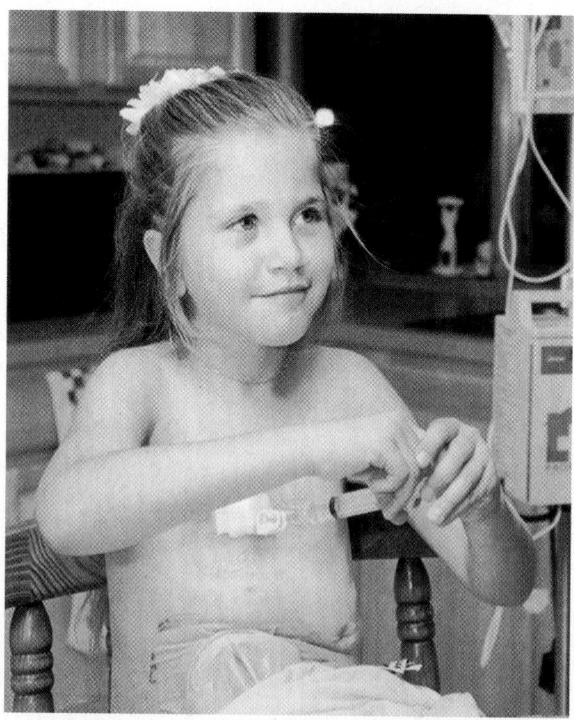

Jennifer Bush endured hundreds of medical treatments and surgeries. Her mother was accused of causing Jennifer's illness to gain the attention of physicians and the media.

Seven-year-old Jennifer Bush appeared to be one victim of factitious disorder by proxy. Jennifer underwent almost 200 hospitalizations and 40 operations in efforts to cure the puzzling array of ailments she seemed to have. Her mother, Kathleen Bush, was with her through it all, dealing with medical professionals and standing by as the family's finances were ruined by Jennifer's medical bills. All the while, however, it seems Kathleen Bush was actually causing her daughter's illnesses by giving her unprescribed drugs, altering her medications, and even putting fecal bacteria in her feeding tube. Bush was eventually arrested and convicted of child abuse and fraud and served 3 years in prison (Toufexis, Blackman, & Drummond, 1996).

There are five distinct types of somatoform disorders: *conversion disorder, somatization disorder, pain disorder, hypochondriasis,* and *body dysmorphic disorder.* Except for body dysmorphic disorder, each of these is characterized by the experience of one or more physical symptoms. Body dysmorphic disorder involves a preoccupation with an imagined defect in one's appearance that is so severe that it interferes with one's functioning in life.

One study of 294 patients admitted to a hospital for medical symptoms found somatoform disorders (excluding body dysmorphic disorder) to be quite common. About 20 percent of patients were diagnosed with one or more somatoform disorders (Fink, Hansen, & Oxhøj, 2004). About one-third of these patients also had another psychiatric diagnosis, most often depression or anxiety. They were four times more likely than patients without somatoform disorders to have been admitted frequently to the hospital in the past, and six times more likely to be heavy users of outpatient primary care facilities.

TABLE 6.3 *DSM-IV-TR* Criteria for Conversion Disorder

A. One or more symptoms or deficits affecting voluntary motor or sensory function that suggest a neurological or other general medical condition.

B. Psychological factors are judged to be associated with the symptom or deficit because the initiation or exacerbation of the symptom or deficit is preceded by conflicts or other stressors.

C. The symptom or deficit is not intentionally produced or feigned (as in factitious disorder or malingering).

D. The symptom or deficit cannot, after appropriate investigation, be fully explained by a general medical condition, or by the direct effects of a substance, or as a culturally sanctioned behavior or experience.

E. The symptom or deficit causes clinically significant distress or impairment in social, occupational, or other important areas of functioning or warrants medical evaluation.

F. The symptom or deficit is not limited to pain or sexual dysfunction, does not occur exclusively during the course of somatization disorder, and is not better accounted for by another mental disorder.

Specify type of symptom or deficit:
With motor symptom or deficit
With sensory symptom or deficit
With seizures or convulsions
With mixed presentation

Source: Reprinted with permission from the *Diagnostic and Statistical Manual of Mental Disorders,* Fourth Edition, Text Revision.

Conversion Disorder

The most dramatic type of somatoform disorder is **conversion disorder** (Table 6.3). People with this disorder lose functioning in a part of their bodies, apparently due to neurological or other general medical causes. Some of the most common conversion symptoms are paralysis, blindness, mutism, seizures, loss of hearing, severe loss of coordination, and anesthesia in a limb. Conversion disorder typically involves one specific symptom, such as blindness or paralysis, but a person can have repeated episodes of conversion involving different parts of the body. Usually, the symptom develops suddenly following exposure to an extreme psychological stressor. Conversion disorder is relatively rare. One study of nearly 300 hospital patients estimated that 2.7 percent of the men and none of the women were suffering from a conversion disorder (Fink, Hansen, & Oxhøj, 2004).

Theories of Conversion Disorder

Sigmund Freud became fascinated with conversion symptoms early in his career. One particularly dramatic conversion symptom is **glove anesthesia,** in which people lose all feeling in one hand, as if they were wearing a glove that wiped out physical sensation. This pattern of feeling loss cannot be caused physiologically, however, because the nerves in the hand do not provide feeling in a glovelike pattern. Freud found that these people tended to regain feeling in their hands when, usually under hypnosis, they recalled painful memories or emotions that had been blocked from their consciousness. Freud and his contemporaries viewed conversion symptoms as the result of the transfer of the psychic energy attached to repressed emotions or memories to physical symptoms. The symptoms often symbolized the specific concerns or memories being repressed.

It is difficult to prove the psychoanalytic theory, but some studies have provided evidence that could be interpreted as supporting it. Conversion symptoms apparently were quite common during the two world wars, when soldiers inexplicably would become paralyzed or blind and therefore unable to return to the front (Ironside & Batchelor, 1945). Many of the soldiers seemed unconcerned about their paralysis or blindness, a phenomenon called *la belle indifference.* Sometimes, the physical symptoms represented traumas the soldiers had witnessed. For example, a soldier who had shot a civilian in the chest might have chest pains.

Children can have conversion symptoms as well. Most often, their symptoms mimic those of someone they are close to who has a real illness (Grattan-Smith, Fairly, & Procopis, 1988; Spierings et al., 1990). For example, a child whose cherished grandfather has had a stroke and has lost functioning on his right side may become unable to use his right arm.

Conversion symptoms may occur among some victims of sexual abuse (Anderson, Yasenik, & Ross, 1993). Consider the following case study of a woman who was raped and later developed both post-traumatic stress disorder (see Chapter 5) and conversion mutism.

CASE STUDY At the time she sought treatment, Jane was a 32-year-old woman living with her 15-year-old son and employed as a lower-level executive. When she was 24, two men entered her home after midnight, held a knife to her throat, and threatened to kill her if she made a sound or struggled. They raped her orally and vaginally in front of her son, who was 7 at the time, and then locked them in the basement before leaving. Several weeks after the rape, Jane's mother, to whom she was very close, died of cancer. Jane felt she had to be "the strong one" in the family and prided herself because she "never broke down."

At age 31, during an abusive relationship with a live-in boyfriend, Jane developed conversion mutism. In the midst of attempting to ask her boyfriend to leave her house, she was unable to produce any sound. After several months of treatment with a speech therapist, Jane became able to whisper quietly but did not regain her normal speech. The speech therapist referred Jane to a clinic for the treatment of rape-related PTSD.

The pretreatment interview confirmed that Jane suffered from chronic PTSD as a result of the rape. She presented with fears, panicky reactions, nightmares, flashbacks, and intrusive thoughts about the assault. She reported attempts to avoid thinking about the assault and situations that reminded her of it and feelings of detachment from others. She also complained of sleep problems, exaggerated startle, and hyperalertness. Jane was moderately depressed and quite anxious. During the intake interview, Jane indicated that she had never verbally expressed her feelings about the assault and believed that this constriction underlied her inability to speak. (From Rothbaum & Foa, 1991)

Research suggests that people with conversion symptoms are highly hypnotizable (Roelofs et al., 2002). This supports the idea that conversion symptoms result from spontaneous self-hypnosis, in which sensory or motor functions are dissociated, or split off, from consciousness in reaction to extreme stress.

FIGURE 6.1 **Glove Anesthesia.** In the conversion symptom called glove anesthesia, the entire hand from fingertips to wrist becomes numb. Actual physical damage to the ulnar nerve, in contrast, causes anesthesia in the ring finger and little finger and beyond the wrist partway up the arm; damage to the radial nerve causes anesthesia only in parts of the ring, middle, and index fingers and the thumb and partway up the arm.

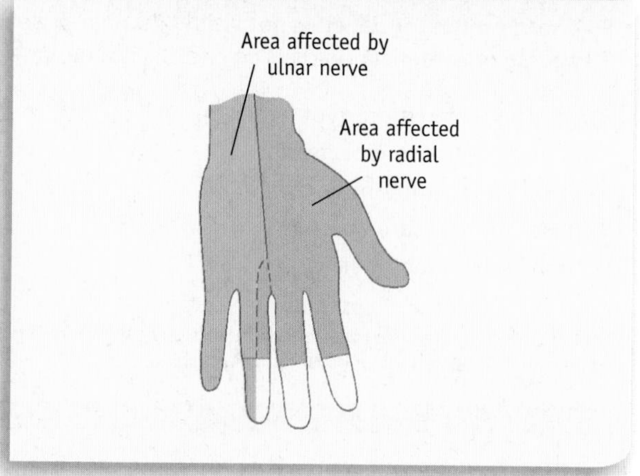

Distinguishing Conversion Disorder from Physical Disorders

Over the years, a number of studies have suggested that many people diagnosed with conversion disorder actually were suffering from a physical disorder that the diagnostic tests of the time could not identify. For example, one study found that 62.5 percent of people diagnosed with conversion symptoms later were found to have a medical disease, compared to only 5.3 percent of people not diagnosed with conversion symptoms (Watson & Buranen, 1979). The most common medical problem found in the conversion group was head injury, which usually occurred about 6 months before the conversion symptoms began. Other common problems were stroke, encephalitis, and brain tumors (see also Fishbain & Goldberg, 1991).

If diagnostic tests cannot establish a physical cause for puzzling symptoms, then clinicians will try to determine whether the conversion symptoms are consistent with the way the body works. For example, recall that glove anesthesia violates what we know about the innervation of the hand, because the anesthesia usually begins abruptly at the wrist and extends throughout the hand. As Figure 6.1 shows, however, the nerves in the hand are distributed in a way that makes this pattern of anesthesia highly unlikely. Similarly, a person with a conversion paralysis from the waist down may not show the deterioration of the muscles in the legs that a person with a physical paralysis typically shows over time. Still, distinguishing conversion disorder from a physical disorder that simply is difficult to diagnose can be tricky.

With increases in the sophistication of tests to diagnose physical disorders, such as the use of neuroimaging techniques to identify pathologies not detectable by other methods, physicians have become better able to differentiate physical disorders from conversion symptoms. Some investigators are using neuroimaging techniques to try to understand how an individual's conversion symptoms might occur (Ron, 2001). For example, researchers used single photon emission computerized tomography (SPECT) to examine seven patients for whom no organic cause could be found for their loss of functioning (Vuilleumier et al., 2001). They applied a vibration to both hands, a stimulus that typically causes widespread activity in the sensory and motor areas of the brain. The SPECT recorded activity in sensory and motor areas on both sides of the brain but reduced activity in the thalamus and basal ganglia on the side of the brain opposite the side of the body in which the patient had loss of functioning. The authors suggested that emotional stressors can inhibit the circuits between sensorimotor areas of the brain and areas more involved in emotions (e.g., the thalamus and basal ganglia), resulting in loss of sensation or motor control.

Treatment of Conversion Disorder

People with conversion disorder can be difficult to treat because they do not believe there is anything wrong with them psychologically. Psychoanalytic treatment for conversion disorder focuses on the expression of painful emotions and memories and on insight into the relationship between these and the conversion symptoms (Temple, 2001). Chronic conversion disorder is more difficult to treat. When symptoms are present for more than a month, the person's history often resembles somatization disorder (discussed in the next section), and the symptoms are treated as such.

Behavioral treatments focus on relieving the person's anxiety around the initial trauma that caused the conversion symptoms and on reducing any benefits the person is receiving from the conversion symptoms (Rothbaum & Foa, 1991). For example, the treatment of Jane, the woman in the case study, involved both systematic desensitization therapy and exposure therapy (see Chapters 2 and 5). A hierarchy of situations that Jane avoided—mostly situations that reminded her of her rape—was constructed. For the exposure therapy, Jane was aided in approaching the situations that made her feel anxious and in progressing up her hierarchy to increasingly more feared situations while practicing relaxation techniques. During the imagery sessions, Jane recounted the details of the assault first in general terms and later in great detail, including the details of the situation and the details of her physiological and cognitive reactions to the assault. At first, Jane was able to describe the assault only in a whisper, but she cried in full volume. After crying, Jane's speech became increasingly louder, with occasional words uttered in full volume. Eventually, she regained a full-volume voice. Following treatment, Jane's PTSD symptoms also decreased, and they diminished further over the following year (Rothbaum & Foa, 1991).

Somatization and Pain Disorders

A person with **somatization disorder** has a long history of complaints about physical symptoms, affecting many different areas of the body, for which medical attention has been sought but that appear to have no physical cause (Table 6.4). To receive a diagnosis of somatization disorder, a person has to complain of pain symptoms in at least four areas of the body, two non-pain-related gastrointestinal symptoms (e.g., nausea and diarrhea), a non-pain-related sexual symptom (e.g., erectile dysfunction or low libido), and an apparent neurological symptom not limited to pain (e.g., double vision or paralysis) (American Psychological Association, 2000). People with somatization disorder often go from physician to physician looking for attention, sympathy, and proof of illness.

People with somatization disorder may also report loss of functioning in a part of the body, as do people with conversion disorder. In somatization disorder, this loss of functioning is only one of a multitude of physical complaints; in conversion disorder, the loss of functioning may be the person's only complaint.

The complaints of people with somatization disorder are usually presented in vague, dramatic, or exaggerated ways, and the individual may have insisted on medical procedures—even surgeries—that clearly were not necessary. One study of 191 persons in a general medicine outpatient clinic found that about 40 percent who had physical symptoms for which no organic causes could be found met the diagnostic criteria for a somatization disorder, meaning that they had long histories of vague and multiple physical complaints with no

TABLE 6.4 *DSM-IV-TR* Criteria for Somatization Disorder

A. A history of many physical complaints beginning before age 30 that occur over several years and result in treatment being sought or significant impairment in social, occupational, or other important areas of functioning.

B. Each of the following criteria must have been met, with individual symptoms occurring at any time during the course of the disturbance:

1. Four pain symptoms: a history of pain related to at least four different sites or functions (e.g., head, abdomen, back, joints, extremities, chest, rectum, during menstruation, during sexual intercourse, or during urination)
2. Two gastrointestinal symptoms: a history of at least two gastrointestinal symptoms other than pain (e.g., nausea, bloating, vomiting other than during pregnancy, diarrhea, or intolerance of several foods)
3. One sexual symptom: a history of at least one sexual or reproductive symptom other than pain (e.g., sexual indifference, erectile or ejaculatory dysfunction, irregular menses, excessive menstrual bleeding, vomiting throughout pregnancy)
4. One pseudo-neurological symptom: a history of at least one symptom or deficit suggesting a neurological condition not limited to pain (conversion symptoms such as impaired coordination or balance, paralysis or localized weakness, difficulty swallowing or breathing, aphonia, urinary retention, hallucinations, loss of touch or pain sensation, double vision, blindness, deafness, seizures; dissociative symptoms such as amnesia; or loss of consciousness other than fainting)

C. Either 1 or 2:

1. After appropriate investigation, each of the symptoms in Criterion B cannot be fully explained by a known general medical condition or the direct effects of a substance (e.g., a drug of abuse, a medication).
2. When there is a related general medical condition, the physical complaints or resulting social or occupational impairment are in excess of what would be expected from the history, physical examination, or laboratory findings.

D. The symptoms are not intentionally feigned or produced (as in factitious disorder or malingering).

Source: Reprinted with permission from the *Diagnostic and Statistical Manual of Mental Disorders,* Fourth Edition, Text Revision.

apparent organic causes (Van Hemert, Hengeveld, Bolk, & Rooijmans, 1993).

People who complain only of chronic pain due to or maintained by psychological factors may be given the diagnosis of **pain disorder** (Table 6.5), in contrast to people with somatization disorder, who report a variety of symptoms. Because most of what we know about pain disorder is encompassed in what we know about somatization disorder, we discuss these two disorders together in this section.

As with conversion disorder, people with somatization or pain disorder may be prone to periods of anxiety and depression that they cannot express or cope with adaptively. They either express their distress as physical symptoms or mask the distress in alcohol abuse or antisocial behavior. Studies of people with somatization disorder find that the majority have a lifetime history of episodes of major depression (Rief, Hiller, & Margraf, 1998; see also Feder et al., 2001; Katon, Sullivan, & Walker, 2001) and that many have a history of anxiety disorders, drug abuse, and personality disorders (Noyes et al., 2001). Their symptoms become their identity.

Moderate degrees of somatization are common, but very few people meet the diagnostic criteria for somatization disorder (Katon et al., 2001). For example, one study found that 4.4 percent of a randomly selected sample of adults had a history of significant somatization but only 0.03 percent met the criteria for somatization disorder (Escobar, Burnam, Karno, & Forsythe, 1987). A study of hospital patients found that 3.3 percent of the women and none of the men qualified for a diagnosis of somatization disorder (Fink et al., 2004).

In the United States, somatization disorder appears to be more common in older adults than in middle-aged adults (Feder et al., 2001). The cultural norms with which older adults were raised often prohibited admitting to depression or anxiety. For this reason, older adults who are depressed or anxious may be more likely to express their negative emotions in somatic complaints, which are

TABLE 6.5 *DSM-IV-TR* Criteria for Pain Disorder

A. Pain in one or more anatomical sites is the predominant focus of the clinical presentation and is of sufficient severity to warrant clinical attention.

B. The pain causes clinically significant distress or impairment in social, occupational, or other important areas of functioning.

C. Psychological factors are judged to have an important role in the onset, severity, exacerbation, or maintenance of the pain.

D. The symptom or deficit is not intentionally produced or feigned (as in factitious disorder or malingering).

E. The pain is not better accounted for by a mood, anxiety, or psychotic disorder and does not meet criteria for dyspareunia.

Specify if:

Acute: duration of less than 6 months

Chronic: duration of 6 months or longer

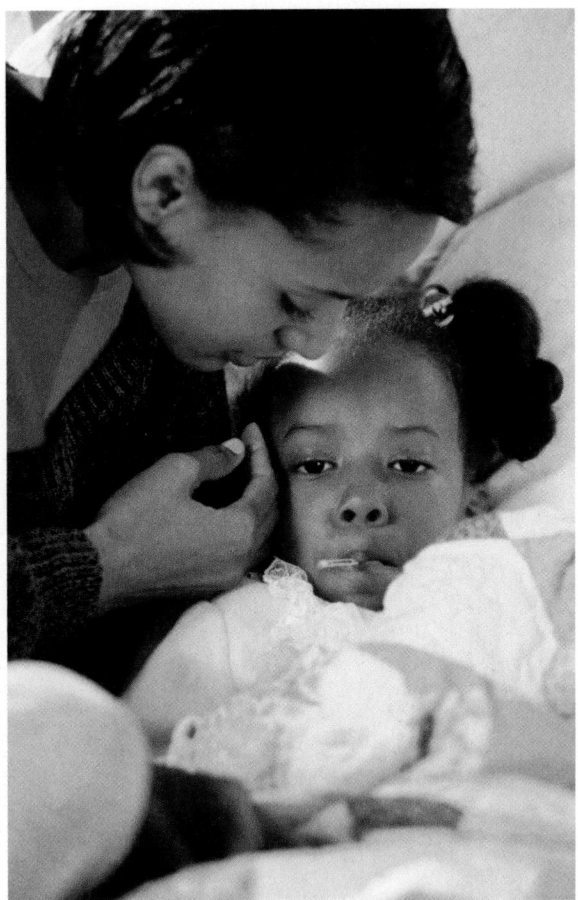

Children sometimes express distress through somatic symptoms.

acceptable and expected in old age. Young children also often express their distress in somatic complaints (Garber, Walker, & Zeman, 1991). They may not have the language to express difficult emotions but can say that they feel "bad" or that they have a stomachache or headache. From 10 to 30 percent of children and adolescents report having headaches or abdominal pain on a weekly basis (Fritz, Fritsch, & Hagino, 1997).

Somatization disorder tends to be a long-term problem. The symptoms of people with somatization disorder tend to last longer than the symptoms of people with similar physical complaints for which an organic cause can be found (Craig, Boardman, Mills, & Daly-Jones, 1993). Moreover, changes in the symptoms of people with somatization disorder mirrored their emotional well-being: When they were anxious or depressed, they reported more physical complaints than when they were not anxious or depressed.

Theories of Somatization and Pain Disorders

Family history studies of somatization and pain disorders find that the disorders run in families, primarily among female relatives (Phillips, 2001). Anxiety and depression are also common in the female relatives of people with somatization disorder (Garber et al., 1991). The male relatives of persons with somatization disorder also have higher than usual rates of alcoholism and antisocial personality disorder. Similarly, patients with pain disorder tend to have family histories of psychological problems, most often pain disorder among the female relatives and alcoholism among the male relatives (Phillips, 2001).

It is not clear that the transmission of somatization or pain disorder in families is related to genetics. A study of more than 3,400 twins could not determine whether genetics or shared environments were responsible for the fact that somatization disorder clusters in families (Gillespie et al., 2000). The children of parents with somatization or pain disorder may model their parents' tendencies to somatize distress (Marshall et al., 2007). Parents who somatize also are more likely to neglect their children, and the children may learn that the only way to receive care and attention is to be ill. This finding is in accord with a behavioral account of somatization and

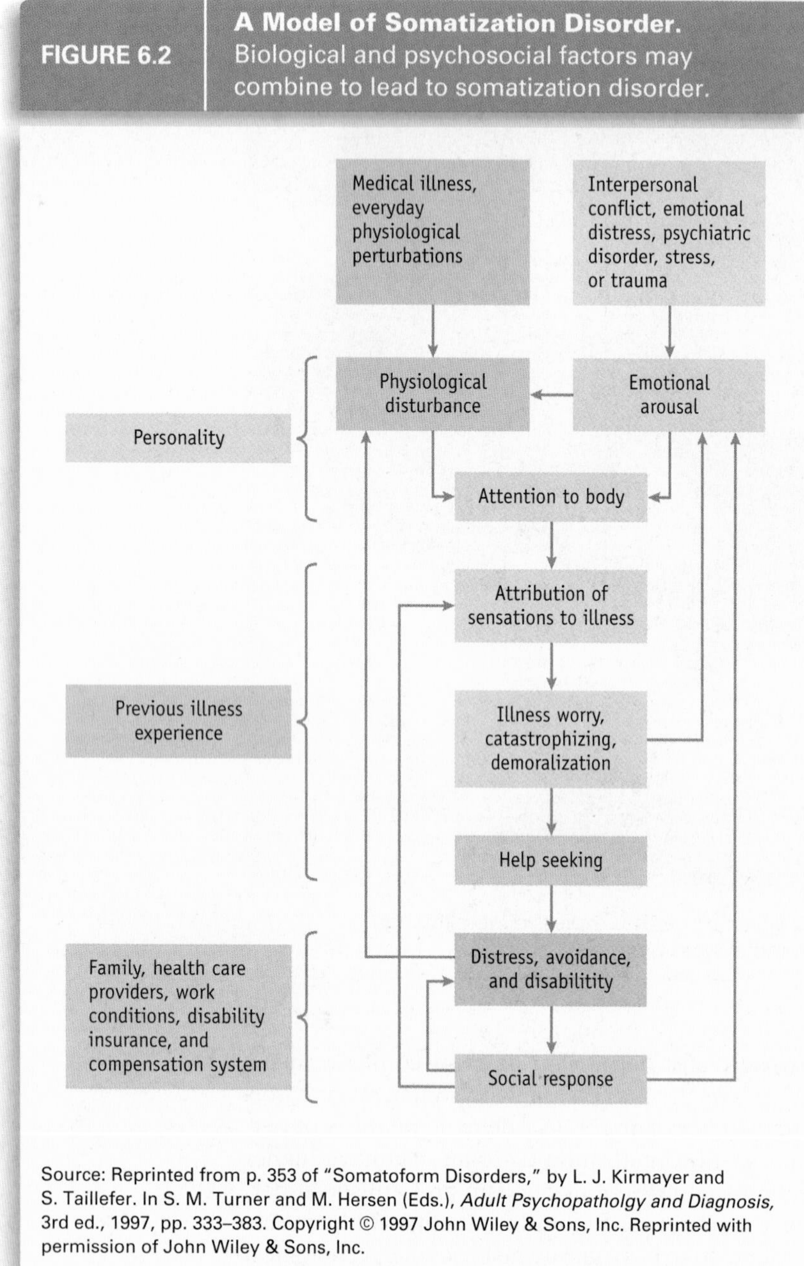

FIGURE 6.2 **A Model of Somatization Disorder.** Biological and psychosocial factors may combine to lead to somatization disorder.

Source: Reprinted from p. 353 of "Somatoform Disorders," by L. J. Kirmayer and S. Taillefer. In S. M. Turner and M. Hersen (Eds.), *Adult Psychopatholgy and Diagnosis*, 3rd ed., 1997, pp. 333–383. Copyright © 1997 John Wiley & Sons, Inc. Reprinted with permission of John Wiley & Sons, Inc.

pain disorders, which views them as the result of reinforcements for "sickness behavior" that the individual has received over much of his or her lifetime (Ullman & Krasner, 1975).

A cognitive theory of somatization and pain disorders suggests that people with these disorders tend to experience bodily sensations more intensely than do other people, to pay more attention than others to physical symptoms, and to catastrophize these symptoms (Figure 6.2; Kirmayer & Taillefer, 1997). For example, such a person might have a slight case of indigestion but experience it as severe chest pain and interpret the pain as a sure sign of a heart attack. The person's interpretation of his experience may have a direct influence on his physiological processes by increasing his heart rate or blood pressure, thereby maintaining and exacerbating the pain. Further, his cognitions will influence the way he presents symptoms to his physician and his family. As a result, physicians may prescribe more potent medication or order more diagnostic tests, and family members may express more sympathy, excuse the person from responsibilities, and otherwise encourage passive behavior (Turk & Ruby, 1992). In this way, the person's misinterpretation and catastrophizing of his symptoms are reinforced by his physician and his family, increasing the likelihood that he will interpret future symptoms similarly.

As with conversion disorders, somatization disorder may be part of post-traumatic stress disorder experienced by a person who has survived a severe stressor. Many people with somatization disorder have a history of physical or sexual abuse or other severe childhood adversity (Katon et al., 2001; Pribor, Yutzy, Dean, & Wetzel, 1993).

Refugees and recent immigrants also have an increased risk of somatization disorder. For example, a study found that immigrants to the United States from Central America and Mexico had higher rates of post-traumatic stress disorder and somatization disorder than either U.S.-born Mexican Americans or European Americans: Fifty-two percent of Central Americans who fled to the United States to escape war or political unrest had post-traumatic stress disorder and somatization disorder (Cervantes, Salgado de Snyder, & Padilla, 1989). Similarly, a study of Hmong immigrants to the United States, who had fled Cambodia during the Khmer Rouge regime, found that 17 percent had post-traumatic stress disorder characterized by moderate to severe somatizing symptoms (Westermeyer, Bouafuely, Neider, & Callies, 1989).

Treatment of Somatization and Pain Disorders

Convincing people with somatization or pain disorder that they need psychological treatment is not easy. They strongly believe that they are physically ill despite dozens of physicians telling them they are not and hundreds of medical tests establishing no physical illness. If they do agree to psychological treatment, people with these disorders appear to respond well to interventions that teach them to express negative feelings or memories and to understand the relationship between their emotions and their physical symptoms (Beutler, Daldrup, Engle, & Guest, 1988).

Psychodynamic therapies focus on providing insight about the connections between emotions and physical symptoms by helping people recall events and memories that may have triggered their symptoms. Behavioral therapies attempt to determine the reinforcements individuals receive for their symptoms and to eliminate these reinforcements while increasing positive rewards for healthy behavior. Cognitive therapies for these disorders help people learn to interpret their physical symptoms appropriately and to avoid catastrophizing physical symptoms, much as in the cognitive treatment of panic symptoms (see Chapter 5; Campo & Fritz, 2001). One study found that antidepressant medications (selective serotonin reuptake inhibitors) led to significant improvement in somatization symptoms in a sample of 15 people with somatization disorder (Menza et al., 2001).

Some clinicians use the belief systems and cultural traditions of the clients they are treating to motivate the clients to engage in therapy and help them overcome their physical complaints. Following is an example of the use of cultural beliefs in treating a Hispanic woman with somatization disorder.

CASE STUDY

Ellen was a 45-year-old woman who consulted many doctors for "high fever, vomiting, diarrhea, inability to eat, and rapid weight loss." After numerous negative lab tests, her doctor told her, "I can't go on with you; go to one of the *espiritistas* or a *curandera* (traditional healers)." A cousin then took her to a Spiritist center "for medicine." She was given herbal remedies: some baths and a tea of *molinillo* to take in the morning before eating. But the treatment focused mainly on the appearance of the spirit of a close friend who had died a month earlier from cancer. The spirit was looking for help from Ellen, who had not gone to help during her friend's illness because of her own family problems. The main thrust of the healers' treatment plan was to help Ellen understand how she had to deal with the feelings of distress related to the stress of a paralyzed husband and caring for two small daughters alone. The spirit's influence on Ellen's body was an object lesson that was aimed at increasing her awareness of how her lifestyle was causing her to neglect the care of her own body and feelings much as she had neglected her dying friend. (Adapted from Koss, 1990, p. 22)

The spiritual healer in this case recognized the cause of Ellen's somatic complaints as stress, anger, and guilt; helped her link her physical symptoms to these emotions; and helped her find ways to cope more adaptively with the emotions. The context for this intervention was not cognitive therapy or another type of psychotherapy used by the dominant, non-Hispanic culture but rather the cultural belief system concerning the role of spirits in producing physical symptoms.

Hypochondriasis

Somatization disorder and **hypochondriasis** are quite similar. The primary distinction in the *DSM-IV-TR* between the two disorders is that people with somatization disorder actually experience physical symptoms and seek help for them, whereas people with hypochondriasis worry that they have a serious disease but do not always experience severe physical symptoms (Table 6.6). However, when they

TABLE 6.6 *DSM-IV-TR* Criteria for Hypochondriasis

A. Preoccupation with fears of having, or the idea that one has, a serious disease based on the person's misinterpretation of bodily symptoms.

B. The preoccupation persists despite appropriate medical evaluation and reassurance.

C. The belief in Criterion A is not of delusional intensity (as in delusional disorder, somatic type) and is not restricted to a circumscribed concern about appearance (as in body dysmorphic disorder).

D. The preoccupation causes clinically significant distress or impairment in social, occupational, or other important areas of functioning.

E. The duration of the disturbance is at least 6 months.

F. The preoccupation is not better accounted for by generalized anxiety disorder, obsessive-compulsive disorder, panic disorder, a major depressive episode, separation anxiety, or another somatoform disorder.

Specify if:

With Poor Insight: If, for most of the time during the current episode, the person does not recognize that the concern about having a serious illness is excessive or unreasonable do have any physical complaints, people with hypochondriasis are more alarmed and more likely to seek out medical attention immediately. People with somatization disorder tend to wait and see how the bodily sensations develop (Rief, Hiller, & Margraf, 1998). People with hypochondriasis may go through many medical procedures and float from physician to physician, sure that they have a dread disease. Often, their fears focus on a particular organ system. Carlos, in this case study, was convinced something was wrong with his bowels.

CASE STUDY

Carlos, a married man of 39, came to the clinic complaining, "I have trouble in my bowels and then it gets me in my head. My bowels just spasm on me, I get constipated." The patient's complaints dated back 12 years to an attack of "acute indigestion" in which he seemed to bloat up and pains developed in his abdomen and spread in several directions. He traced some of these pathways with his finger as he spoke. Carlos spent a month in bed at this time and then, based on an interpretation of something the doctor said, rested for another 2 months before working again. Words of reassurance from his doctor failed to take effect. He felt "sick, worried, and scared," feeling that he would never really get well again.

Carlos became very dependent on the woman he married when he was 22 years old. He left most of the decisions to her and showed little interest in sexual relations. His wife was several years older than he and did not seem to mind his totally passive approach to life. His attack of "acute indigestion" followed her death, 5 years after marriage, by 3 months during which he felt lost and hopeless. In time, he moved to a rural area and remarried. His second wife proved less willing to assume major responsibilities for him than the first, and she made sexual demands on him that he felt unable to meet. He became more and more preoccupied with his gastrointestinal welfare. (Adapted from Cameron & Rychlak, 1985)

Diagnosable hypochondriasis is not very common. A study of 1,456 patients in a general medical practice found that only 3 percent met the diagnostic criteria for hypochondriasis (Escobar et al., 1998). Another study of hospital patients found that 2.1 percent of the men and 7.8 percent of the women were diagnosed with hypochondriasis (Fink et al., 2004).

Most studies of hypochondriasis have grouped people who have this disorder with people who have somatization disorder, in part because people often will qualify for the diagnosis of both disorders. Thus, most of what is known about the causes of somatization disorder also applies to the causes of hypochondriasis. In particular, people with hypochondriasis appear to be prone to chronic depression and anxiety and to have family histories of these disorders (Barsky, Wyshak, & Klerman, 1992; Escobar et al., 1998). Their fears about their health often stem from general distress and an inability to cope with that distress in adaptive ways. People with hypochondriasis also tend to have dysfunctional beliefs about illness, assuming that serious illnesses are common, and they tend to misinterpret any physical change in themselves as a sign for concern (Marcus & Church, 2003).

As is the case with people who have somatization disorder, people who have hypochondriasis do not appreciate suggestions that their problems are caused by psychological factors and thus tend not to seek psychological treatment. Cognitive-behavioral treatments for hypochondriasis that focus on identifying and challenging illness beliefs and misinterpretations of physical sensations have shown some positive effects (Barsky & Ahern, 2005; Clark et al., 1998).

If the distinctions between somatization disorder, pain disorder, and hypochondriasis seem small to you, you are not alone. The authors of the *DSM-5* have proposed that these disorders be collapsed into one new diagnosis named *complex somatic symptom disorder.* To receive this diagnosis, individuals must have multiple bodily symptoms that are upsetting, or one severe symptom, for at least 6 months. They must also worry intensely about their health, tend to catastrophize their health, and organize their lives around their health concerns. This new diagnosis may include specifiers to indicate whether the individual's symptoms are most like the *DSM-IV-TR* diagnoses of somatization disorder, pain disorder, or hypochondriasis (American Psychiatric Association, 2010).

Body Dysmorphic Disorder

People with **body dysmorphic disorder** are excessively preoccupied with a part of their body that they believe is defective (Table 6.7). Although it is not clear whether there are gender differences in the prevalence of this disorder, men and women with body dysmorphic disorder tend to obsess about different

TABLE 6.7 *DSM-IV-TR* Criteria for Body Dysmorphic Disorder

A. Preoccupation with an imagined defect in appearance. If a slight physical anomaly is present, the person's concern is markedly excessive.

B. The preoccupation causes clinically significant distress or impairment in social, occupational, or other important areas of functioning.

C. The preoccupation is not better accounted for by another mental disorder (e.g., dissatisfaction with body shape and size in anorexia nervosa).

People with body dysmorphic disorder become obsessed with the imagined defects of a body part.

parts of their bodies (Perugi et al., 1997; Phillips & Diaz, 1997). Women seem to be more concerned with their breasts, legs, hips, and weight, whereas men tend to be preoccupied with a small body build, their genitals, excessive body hair, and thinning hair. These gender differences likely represent extreme versions of societal norms concerning attractiveness in women and men. People with this disorder will spend hours looking at their "deformed" body parts and will perform elaborate rituals to try to improve or hide the parts. For example, they may spend hours styling their hair to hide the defects in their ears or wear heavy makeup to hide their defects. People with this disorder also often seek out plastic surgery to change the offensive body parts (Phillips, 2001).

Case studies of people with this disorder indicate that their perceptions of deformation can be so severe and bizarre as to be considered out of touch with reality (Phillips, Didie, Feusner, & Wilhelm, 2008). Even if they do not lose touch with reality, some people with body dysmorphic disorder have severe impairment in their functioning. Most people with this disorder avoid social activities because of their "deformity," and many become housebound (Phillips & Diaz, 1997). About 30 percent attempt suicide (Phillips et al., 2008).

Body dysmorphic disorder tends to begin in the teenage years and to become chronic if left untreated. The average age of onset of this disorder is 16 years, and the average number of bodily preoccupations is about four. Those who seek treatment wait an average of 6 years from the onset of their concerns before doing so (Cororve & Gleaves, 2001).

CASE STUDY

"Mr. H," a 33-year-old single white male, presented with preoccupations focused on his "thinning" hair, facial "acne," and "short" fingers. He began to worry excessively about his appearance at age 15, focusing at that time on his "pale" skin and "uneven" cheekbones. Mr. H described his appearance preoccupations as "severely upsetting," but he was too embarrassed to reveal them to family or friends. Even though he looked normal to others, Mr. H was "100% convinced" that these body areas appeared "abnormal and deformed," although in the past he had sometimes thought that "maybe I don't look so bad." He believed that other people took special notice of him and "laugh at me behind my back because I look so ugly." Mr. H spent 5 to 6 hours a day thinking about his perceived appearance flaws. He also performed compulsive behaviors for 4 to 5 hours a day, which included excessive mirror checking, comparing his appearance with that of other people, wearing and frequently adjusting a baseball cap to cover his hair, picking his skin to remove tiny blemishes, and searching the Internet for acne and hair loss treatments. Mr. H's appearance preoccupations and compulsive behaviors made it difficult to concentrate on his job as a store clerk and often made him late for work. In the past few weeks, he had missed work several times because he thought his skin looked particularly bad on those days. Mr. H avoided many social events with family and friends as well as sexual intimacy with his

(continued)

girlfriend because of shame over how he looked. In addition, he reported depressed mood, *anhedonia* [inability to experience pleasure], feelings of worthlessness, and passive suicidal ideation, and he had attempted suicide 5 years ago. He attributed his depressive symptoms and suicidal thinking to his appearance concerns, stating, "If I didn't look like such a freak, I wouldn't feel so hopeless and depressed." Mr. H had received treatment from a dermatologist for his acne concerns, which did not diminish his preoccupations. He had never received psychiatric treatment and was ambivalent about trying it because, as he stated, "my appearance problems are real." (Phillips et al., 2008, p. 1111)

Body dysmorphic disorder is highly comorbid with several disorders, including anxiety and depressive disorders, personality disorders, and substance use disorders (Cororve & Gleaves, 2001). Obsessive-compulsive disorder is relatively common among people with body dysmorphic disorder (Stewart, Stack, & Wilhelm, 2008). Some theorists believe that body dysmorphic disorder may be a form of obsessive-compulsive disorder, in which the person obsesses about a part of the body and engages in compulsive behaviors to change that part (Cororve & Gleaves, 2001; Phillips, 2001). An MRI study of the brains of eight women with body dysmorphic disorder found that they showed some of the same abnormalities in the caudate nucleus as are seen in obsessive-compulsive disorder (Rauch et al., 2003). The authors of the *DSM-5* are proposing that body dysmorphic disorder be moved out of the category of somatoform disorders into the category of anxiety and obsessive-compulsive disorders.

Cognitive-behavioral therapies focus on challenging clients' maladaptive cognitions about their body, exposing them to feared situations concerning their body, extinguishing anxiety about their body parts, and preventing compulsive responses to those body parts (Cororve & Gleaves, 2001). For example, a client may identify her ears as her deformed body part. The client could develop her hierarchy of things she would fear doing related to her ears, ranging from looking at herself in the mirror with her hair fully covering her ears to going out in public with her hair pulled back and her ears fully exposed. After learning relaxation techniques, the client would begin to work through the hierarchy and engage in the feared behaviors, beginning with the least feared and using the relaxation techniques to quell her anxiety. Eventually, the client would work up to the greatly feared situation of exposing her ears in public. At first, the therapist might contract with the client that she could not engage in behaviors intended to hide the body part (such as putting her hair over her ears) for at least 5 minutes after going out in public. The eventual goal in therapy would be for the client's concerns about her ears to diminish totally and no longer affect her behavior or functioning. Empirical studies have supported the efficacy of cognitive-behavioral therapies in treating body dysmorphic disorder (Cororve & Gleaves, 2001). Some studies suggest that selective serotonin reuptake inhibitors can be effective in reducing obsessional thoughts and compulsive behaviors in some persons with this disorder (Phillips & Najjar, 2003; Phillips, Pagano, & Menard, 2006).

TEST YOURSELF

1. What are the primary characteristics of somatoform disorders?
2. What is conversion disorder? What are possible causes of conversion disorder? How is conversion disorder treated?
3. What is somatization disorder? What is pain disorder? What is hypochondriasis? What are some possible causes of these disorders? How are they treated?
4. What is body dysmorphic disorder? How is it treated?

APPLY IT As a clinician formulating a diagnosis, what difference between hypochondriasis and somatization disorder would you want to keep in mind?

a. Somatization disorder primarily affects women; the incidence of hypochondriasis is roughly equal across genders.
b. Hypochondriasis rarely follows traumatic episodes; somatization disorder usually is caused by such events.
c. Somatization disorder usually affects the hands; hypochondriasis focuses on the gastrointestinal system.
d. People with hypochondriasis usually seek out medical attention immediately; people with somatization disorder wait to see how their symptoms develop.

Answers appear online at www.mhhe.com/nolen5e.

SHADES OF GRAY

Consider this description of a young boy with health worries.

Ben is a 9-year-old whose teachers refer to him as "the worrier." At least once a week, he ends up in the school nurse's office with complaints of a headache or a stomachache, insisting he needs to rest or go home. The school nurse always dutifully takes Ben's temperature, which is always normal. Still, Ben will not go back to class. His frequent absences are causing his grades to decline. Ben's mother has taken him to his pediatrician a number of times, and multiple tests have revealed no medical problems that could be causing his frequent headaches and stomachaches.

Ben's health worries seem to have started about 8 months ago, after he had a serious case of the flu that kept him home in bed for over a week. Shortly after that, his parents separated because of marital conflict that had been escalating for years. When his mother has tried to talk with Ben about the possibility that his aches and pains are connected to his parents' separation, he has acknowledged that this could be true. But within a few days, he has experienced another headache or stomachache, saying "this time it's real, and it really hurts!"

Does Ben appear to have a somatoform disorder? If so, which one? (Discussion appears at the end of this chapter.)

DISSOCIATIVE DISORDERS

Scientific interest in dissociative disorders has waxed and waned over the past century (Kihlstrom, 2005). There was a great deal of interest in dissociation in nineteenth-century France and in the United States among neurologists and psychologists such as Charcot, Freud, Carl Jung, and William James. French neurologist Pierre Janet viewed dissociation as a process in which systems of ideas are split off from consciousness but remain accessible through dreams and hypnosis. One case he investigated was that of a woman named Irene, who had no memory of the fact that her mother had died. However, during her sleep, Irene physically dramatized the events surrounding her mother's death.

After about 1910, interest in dissociative phenomena waned, partly because of the rise within psychology of behaviorism and biological approaches, which rejected the concept of repression and the use of techniques such as hypnosis in therapy. Ernest Hilgard (1977/1986) revitalized interest in dissociation in his experiments on the *hidden observer* phenomenon. He argued that there is an *active mode* to consciousness, which includes our conscious plans and desires and voluntary actions. In its passive *receptive mode,* the conscious registers and stores information in memory without being aware that the information has been processed, as if hidden observers were watching and recording events in people's lives without their awareness.

Hilgard and his associates (Hilgard, 1977/1986) conducted experimental studies in which participants were hypnotized and given a suggestion that they would feel no pain during a painful procedure but would remember the pain when the hypnotist gave them a specific cue. These subjects indeed showed no awareness of pain during the procedure. When cued, they reported memories of the pain in a matter-of-fact fashion, as if a lucid, rational observer of the event had registered the event for the subject. Other research showed that some anesthetized surgical patients could later recall, under hypnosis, specific pieces of music played during the surgery. Again, it was as if a hidden observer was registering the events of the operations even while the patients were completely unconscious under anesthesia (see Kihlstrom, 2001; Kihlstrom & Couture, 1992; Kirsch & Lynn, 1998).

For most people, the active and receptive modes of consciousness weave our experiences together so seamlessly that we do not notice any division between them. People who develop dissociative disorders, however, may have chronic problems integrating their active and their receptive consciousness (Hilgard, 1992; Kihlstrom, 2001). That is, different aspects of consciousness in these people do not integrate with each other in normal ways but instead remain split and operate independently of each other.

We begin our discussion of specific dissociative disorders with *dissociative identity disorder (DID),* formerly known as *multiple personality disorder.*

We then move to *dissociative fugue, dissociative amnesia,* and *depersonalization disorder.* All these disorders involve frequent experiences in which various aspects of a person's "self" are split off from each other and felt as separate.

Dissociative Identity Disorder

CASE STUDY

Eve White was a quiet, proper, and unassuming woman, a full-time homemaker and devoted mother to a young daughter. She sought help from a psychiatrist for painful headaches that were occurring with increasing frequency. The psychiatrist decided that her headaches were related to arguments she was having with her husband over whether to raise their young daughter in the husband's church (which was Catholic) or in her church (which was Baptist). After undergoing some marital therapy, Mrs. White's marriage improved and her headaches subsided for a year or so.

Then, her husband recontacted her therapist, alarmed over changes in his wife's behavior. She had gone to visit a favorite cousin in a town 50 miles away and during the visit had behaved in a much more carefree and reckless manner than she usually did. Mrs. White told her husband over the phone that she was not going to return home, and the two had a terrible fight that ended in an agreement to divorce. When Mrs. White did return home a few days later, however, she said she had no memory of the fight with her husband or, for that matter, of the visit with her cousin.

Shortly thereafter, Mrs. White apparently went shopping and bought hundreds of dollars worth of elaborate clothing, which the couple could not afford. When confronted by her husband about her expenditures, Mrs. White claimed to have no memory of buying the clothing.

At the urging of her husband, Mrs. White made an appointment with the therapist whom she had originally consulted about her headaches. In the session, she admitted that her headaches had returned and were much more severe now than before. Eventually, she also tearfully admitted that she had begun to hear a voice other than her own speaking inside her head and that she feared she was going insane. The therapist asked her more questions about the clothes-buying spree, and Mrs. White became more tense and had difficulty getting words out to discuss the incident. Then, as her therapist reported,

> The brooding look in her eyes became almost a stare. Eve seemed momentarily dazed. Suddenly her posture began to change. Her body slowly stiffened until she sat rigidly erect. An alien, inexplicable expression then came over her face. This was suddenly erased into utter blankness. The lines of her countenance seemed to shift in a barely visible, slow, rippling transformation. For a moment there was the impression of something arcane. Closing her eyes, she winced as she put her hands to her temples, pressed hard, and twisted them as if to combat sudden pain. A slight shudder passed over her entire body.
>
> Then the hands lightly dropped. She relaxed easily into an attitude of comfort the physician had never before seen in this patient. A pair of blue eyes popped open. There was a quick reckless smile. In a bright, unfamiliar voice that sparked, the woman said, "Hi, there, Doc!"
>
> Still busy with his own unassimilated surprise, the doctor heard himself say, "How do you feel now?"
>
> "Why just fine—never better! How you doing yourself, Doc? . . . She's been having a real rough time. There's no doubt about that," the girl said carelessly. "I feel right sorry for her sometimes. She's such a damn dope though. . . . What she puts up with from that sorry Ralph White—and all her mooning over that little brat . . . ! To hell with it, I say!" . . .
>
> The doctor asked, "Who is 'she'?"
>
> "Why, Eve White, of course. Your long-suffering, saintly, little patient."
>
> "But aren't you Eve White?" he asked.
>
> "That's for laughs," she exclaimed, a ripple of mirth in her tone. . . . "Why, I'm Eve Black," she said. . . . "I'm me and she's herself," the girl added. "I like to live and she don't. . . . Those dresses—well, I can tell you about them. I got out the other day, and I needed some dresses. I like good clothes. So I just went into town and bought what I wanted. I charged 'em to her husband, too!" She began to laugh softly. "You ought've seen the look on her silly face when he showed her what was in the cupboard!" (Reprinted with permission from C. H. Thigpen and H. M. Cleckley, *The Three Faces of Eve.* Copyright © 1957 McGraw-Hill)

The movie *The Three Faces of Eve* depicted the story of a woman with dissociative identity disorder. Here, she discovered extravagant articles of clothing in her closet that she didn't remember buying.

In later sessions, Eve Black told the psychiatrist of escapades in which she had stayed out all night drinking and then had gone "back in" in the morning to let Eve White deal with the hangover. At the beginning of therapy, Eve White had no consciousness of Eve Black or of more than 20 personalities eventually identified during therapy.

This story, depicted in the movie *The Three Faces of Eve,* is one of the most detailed and gripping accounts of a person diagnosed with dissociative identity disorder. Eve White eventually recovered from her disorder, integrating the aspects of her personality represented by Eve Black and her other personalities into one entity and living a healthy, normal life.

Dissociative identity disorder (DID) is one of the most controversial and fascinating disorders recognized in clinical psychology and psychiatry. People with this disorder appear to have more than one distinct identity or personality, and many have more than a dozen (Table 6.8). Each personality has different ways of perceiving and relating to the world, and each takes control over the individual's behavior on a regular basis. As was true of Eve White/Black, the alternate personalities can be extremely different from one another, with distinct facial expressions, speech characteristics, physiological responses, gestures, interpersonal styles, and attitudes (Putnam, 1991; Vermetten et al., 2006). Often they are different ages and different genders and perform specific functions.

TABLE 6.8 *DSM-IV-TR* Criteria for Dissociative Identity Disorder

A. The presence of two or more distinct identities or personality states (each with its own relatively enduring pattern of perceiving, relating to, and thinking about the environment and self).

B. At least two of these identities or personality states recurrently take control of the person's behavior.

C. Inability to recall important personal information that is too extensive to be explained by ordinary forgetfulness.

D. The disturbance is not due to the direct physiological effects of a substance (e.g., blackouts or chaotic behavior during alcohol intoxication) or a general medical condition (e.g., complex partial seizures). *Note:* In children, the symptoms are not attributable to imaginary playmates or other fantasy play.

Source: Reprinted with permission from the *Diagnostic and Statistical Manual of Mental Disorders,* Fourth Edition, Text Revision. Copyright © 2000 American Psychiatric Association.

Reliable estimates of the prevalence of dissociative identity disorder are hard to come by. One study of psychiatric inpatients found that 1 percent could be diagnosed with DID (Rifkin et al., 1998). The vast majority of people diagnosed with this disorder are adult women. Males with dissociative identity disorder appear to be more aggressive than females with the disorder. In one study, 29 percent of male dissociative identity patients had been convicted of crimes, compared to 10 percent of female dissociative identity patients (Ross & Norton, 1989). Case reports suggest that females with dissociative identity disorder tend to have more somatic complaints than do males with the disorder and may engage in more suicidal behavior (Kluft, 1987).

Symptoms

The cardinal symptom in dissociative identity disorder is the apparent presence of multiple personalities with distinct qualities, referred to as *alters.* These alters can take many forms and perform many functions. *Child alters*—alters that are young children, who do not age as the individual ages—appear to be the most common type of alter (Ross, Norton, & Wozney, 1989). Childhood trauma is often associated with the development of dissociative identity disorder. A child alter may be created during a traumatic experience to take on the role of victim in the trauma, while the *host* personality escapes into the protection of psychological oblivion. Or, an alter may be created as a type of big brother or sister to protect the host personality from trauma. When a child alter is "out," or in control of the individual's behavior, the adult may speak and act in a childlike way.

Another type of alter is the *persecutor personality.* These alters inflict pain or punishment on the other personalities by engaging in self-mutilative behaviors, such as self-cutting or -burning and suicide attempts (Coons & Milstein, 1990; Ross et al., 1989). A persecutor alter may engage in a dangerous behavior, such as taking an overdose of pills or jumping in front of a truck, and then "go back inside," leaving the host personality to experience the pain. Persecutors may believe that they can harm other personalities without harming themselves.

Yet another type of alter is the *protector,* or *helper, personality.* The function of this personality is to offer advice to other personalities or perform functions the host personality is unable to perform, such as engaging in sexual relations or hiding from abusive parents. Helpers sometimes control the switching from one personality to another or act as passive observers who can report on the thoughts and intentions of all the other personalities (Ross, 1989).

People with dissociative identity disorder typically claim to have significant periods of amnesia, or blank spells. They describe being completely amnesic for the periods when other personalities are in control or having one-way amnesia between certain personalities. In these instances, one personality is aware of what the other is doing, but the second personality is completely amnesic for periods when the first personality is in control. As with Eve White, people with dissociative identity disorder may suddenly discover unknown objects in their home or may lose objects. People they do not recognize might approach them on the street, claiming to know them. They may consistently receive mail or phone calls addressed to someone with a different first or last name. Verifying claims of amnesia is difficult, but some studies suggest that information and memories tend to transfer between identities, even in individuals who believe that certain personalities experience amnesia (Allen & Iacono, 2001; Kong, Allen, & Glisky, 2008).

Self-destructive behavior is common among people with dissociative identity disorder and often is the reason they seek or are taken for treatment (Ross, 1999). This behavior includes self-inflicted burns or other injuries, wrist slashing, and overdoses. About three-quarters of patients with dissociative identity disorder have a history of suicide attempts, and over 90 percent report recurrent suicidal thoughts (Ross, 1997).

Like adults, children diagnosed with dissociative identity disorder exhibit a host of behavioral and emotional problems (Putnam, 1991). Their performance in school may be erratic, sometimes very good and sometimes very poor. They are prone to

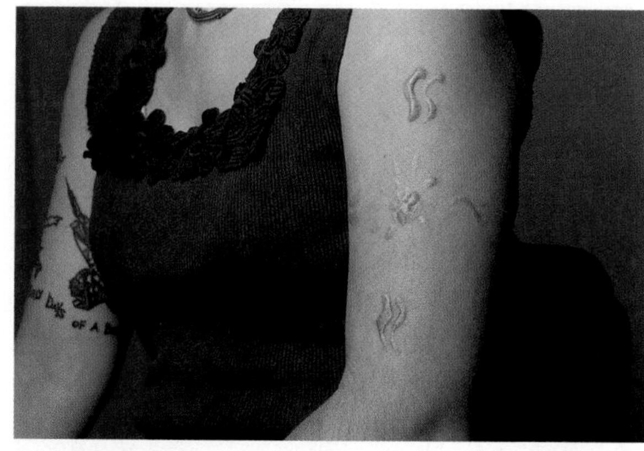

People with dissociative identity disorder may engage in self-mutilative behavior.

antisocial behavior, such as stealing, fire-setting, and aggression. They may engage in sexual relations and abuse alcohol or illicit drugs at an early age. They tend to show many symptoms of post-traumatic stress disorder (PTSD; see Chapter 5), including hypervigilance, flashbacks to traumas they have endured, traumatic nightmares, and an exaggerated startle response. Their emotions are unstable, alternating among explosive outbursts of anger, deep depression, and severe anxiety.

Most children and many adults with dissociative identity disorder report hearing voices inside their heads. Some report awareness that their actions or words are being controlled by other personalities. For example, Joe, an 8-year-old boy with dissociative identity disorder, described how "a guy inside of me," called B. J. (for Bad Joey), would make him do "bad things."

VOICES

Well, say B. J. hears someone call me names, then he would strike me to do something, like I'd be running at the other kid, but it wouldn't be my legs, I'd be saying to my legs, "no . . . , stop . . . , " but they'd keep going on their own because that's B. J. doing that. Then my arm would be going at the other kid, hitting him, and I could see my arm doing that, but I couldn't stop it, and it wouldn't hurt when my hand hit him, not until later when B. J. goes back in and then my arm is my own arm. Then it starts hurting. (Hornstein & Putnam, 1992, p. 1081)

Issues in Diagnosis

Dissociative identity disorder was rarely diagnosed before about 1980, but there was a great increase in the number of reported cases after this time (Braun, 1986; Coons, 1986). This is due in part to the fact that dissociative identity disorder was first included as a diagnostic category in the *DSM* in its third edition, published in 1980. The availability of specific diagnostic criteria for this disorder made it more likely that it would be diagnosed. At the same time, the diagnostic criteria for schizophrenia were made more specific in the 1980 version of the *DSM*, possibly leading to some cases that would have been diagnosed as schizophrenia being diagnosed as dissociative identity disorder. One final, and important, influence on diagnostic trends was the publication of a series of influential papers by psychiatrists describing persons with dissociative identity disorder whom they had treated (Bliss, 1980; Coons, 1980; Greaves, 1980; Rosenbaum, 1980). These cases aroused interest in the disorder within the psychiatric community.

Still, most mental health professionals are reluctant to give this diagnosis. Most people diagnosed with dissociative identity disorder have previously been diagnosed with at least three other disorders (Kluft, 1987). Some of the other disorders diagnosed may be secondary to or the result of the dissociative identity disorder. For example, one study of 135 patients with dissociative identity disorder found that 97 percent could also be diagnosed with major depression; 90 percent had an anxiety disorder, most often post-traumatic stress disorder; 65 percent were abusing substances; and 38 percent had an eating disorder (Ellason, Ross, & Fuchs, 1996). In addition, most people with dissociative identity disorder also are diagnosed with a personality disorder (Dell, 1998). Some of the earlier diagnoses may be misdiagnoses of the dissociative symptoms. For example, when people with dissociative identity disorder report hearing voices talking inside their heads, they may be misdiagnosed as having schizophrenia (Kluft, 1987).

Dissociative identity disorder is diagnosed more frequently in the United States than in Great Britain, Europe, India, or Japan (Ross, 1989; Saxena & Prasad, 1989; Takahashi, 1990). Some studies suggest that Latinos, both within and outside the United States, may be more likely than other ethnic groups to experience dissociative symptoms in response to traumas. For example, a study of Vietnam veterans found that Latino veterans were more likely than non-Latino veterans to show dissociative symptoms (Koopman et al., 2001). Another study conducted with Latino survivors of community violence in the United States found that those who were less acculturated to mainstream U.S. culture were more likely to show dissociative symptoms than were those who were more acculturated (Marshall & Orlando, 2002). Dissociative symptoms may be part of the syndrome *ataque de nervios*, a culturally accepted reaction to stress among Latinos that involves transient periods of loss of consciousness, convulsive movements, hyperactivity, assaultive behaviors, and impulsive acts (see Chapter 5). Some researchers have argued that psychiatrists in the United States are too quick to diagnose dissociative identity disorder; others argue that psychiatrists in other countries misdiagnose it as another disorder (Coons, Cole, Pellow, & Milstein, 1990; Fahy, 1988).

Explanations of Dissociative Identity Disorder

Some theorists who study dissociative identity disorder view it as the result of coping strategies used by persons faced with intolerable trauma, most often childhood sexual and/or physical abuse, that they are powerless to escape (Bliss, 1986; Kluft, 1987; Putnam, Zahn, & Post, 1990). As Ross (1997, p. 64) describes:

> The little girl being sexually abused by her father at night imagines that the abuse is happening to someone else, as a way to distance herself from the overwhelming emotions she is experiencing. She may float up to the ceiling and watch the abuse in a detached fashion. Now not only is the abuse not happening to her, but she blocks it out of her mind—that other little girl remembers it, not the original self. In this model, DID is an internal divide-and-conquer strategy in which intolerable knowledge and feeling is split up into manageable compartments. These compartments are personified and take on a life of their own.

Most studies find that the majority of people diagnosed with dissociative identity disorder self-report having been the victims of sexual or physical abuse during childhood (Coons, 1994; Dell & Eisenhower, 1990; Hornstein & Putnam, 1992) and, in turn, that dissociative experiences are commonly reported by survivors of child sexual abuse (Butzel et al., 2000; Kisiel & Lyons, 2001). For example, in a study of 135 persons with dissociative identity disorder, 92 percent reported having been sexually abused and 90 percent reported having been repeatedly physically abused (Ellason et al., 1996; see also Putnam, Guroff, Silberman, & Barban, 1986). Researchers have found similar results in studies in which patients' reports of abuse were corroborated by at least one family member or by emergency room reports (Coons, 1994; Coons & Milstein, 1986). The abuse most often was carried out by parents or other family members and was chronic over an extended period of childhood. Other types of trauma that have been associated with the development of dissociative identity disorder include kidnapping, natural disasters, war, famine, and religious persecution (Ross, 1999).

People who develop dissociative identity disorder tend to be highly suggestible and hypnotizable and may use self-hypnosis to dissociate and escape their traumas (Kihlstrom, Glisky, & Angiulo, 1994). They may create the alternate personalities to help them cope with their traumas, much as a child might create imaginary playmates to ease pangs of loneliness. These alternate personalities can provide the safety, security, and nurturing that they are not receiving from their caregivers. Retreating into their alternate personalities or using these personalities to perform frightening functions becomes a chronic way of coping with life.

A contrasting view is that the alternate identities are created by patients who adopt the idea or narrative of dissociative identity disorder as an explanation that fits their lives (Merckelbach, Devilly, & Rassin, 2002; Spanos, 1994). The identities are not true personalities with clear-cut demarcations but rather a metaphor used by the patients to understand their subjective experiences.

A few family history studies suggest that dissociative identity disorder may run in some families (Coons, 1984; Dell & Eisenhower, 1990). In addition, studies of twins and of adopted children have found evidence that the tendency to dissociate is substantially affected by genetics (Becker-Blease et al., 2004; Jang, Paris, Zweig-Frank, & Livesley, 1998). Perhaps the ability and tendency to dissociate as a coping response is to some extent biologically determined.

Treatment of Dissociative Identity Disorder

Treating dissociative identity disorder can be extremely challenging. The goal of treatment is the integration of all the alter personalities into one coherent personality (Lemke, 2007). This integration is achieved by identifying the functions or roles of each personality, helping each personality confront and work through the traumas that led to the disorder and the concerns each one has or represents, and negotiating with the personalities for fusion into one personality who has learned adaptive styles of coping with stress. Hypnosis is used heavily in the treatment of dissociative identity disorder to contact alters (Putnam & Lowenstein, 1993).

One of the few studies to empirically evaluate the treatment of DID found that patients who were able to integrate their personalities through treatment remained relatively free of symptoms over the subsequent 2 years (Ellason & Ross, 1997). These patients also reported few symptoms of substance abuse or depression and were able to reduce their use of antidepressants and antipsychotic medications. In contrast, patients who had not achieved integration during treatment continued to show symptoms of DID and a number of other disorders. This study did not compare the outcome of the patients who received therapy with that of patients who did not, nor did it compare different types of therapy.

Dissociative Fugue

A person in the midst of a **dissociative fugue** may suddenly pick up and move to a new place, assume a new identity, and have no memory of his previous identity. He will behave quite normally in his new environment, and it will not seem odd to him that he cannot remember anything from his past. Just as suddenly, he may return to his previous identity and home, resuming his life as if nothing had happened, with no memory of what he did during the fugue. A fugue may last for days or years, and a person may experience repeated fugue states or a single episode.

An extreme and classic case of fugue was that of Reverend Ansel Bourne, reported by American philosopher and psychologist William James (1890, pp. 391–393).

CASE STUDY

The Rev. Ansel Bourne, of Greene, R.I., was brought up to the trade of a carpenter; but, in consequence of a sudden temporary loss of sight and hearing under very peculiar circumstances, he became converted from Atheism to Christianity just before his thirtieth year, and has since that time for the most part lived the life of an itinerant preacher. He has been subject to headaches and temporary fits of depression of spirits during most of his life, and has had a few fits of unconsciousness lasting an hour or less. . . . He is of a firm and self-reliant disposition, a man whose yea is yea and his nay, nay; and his character for uprightness is such in the community that no person who knows him will for a moment admit the possibility of his case not being perfectly genuine.

On January 17, 1887, he drew 551 dollars from a bank in Providence with which to pay for a certain lot of land in Greene, paid certain bills, and got into a Pawtucket horse-car. This is the last incident which he remembers. He did not return home that day, and nothing was heard of him for two months. He was published in the papers as missing, and foul play being suspected, the police sought in vain his whereabouts. On the morning of March 14th, however, at Norristown, Pennsylvania, a man calling himself A. J. Brown, who had rented a small shop six weeks previously, stocked it with stationery, confectionery, fruit, and small articles, and carried on his quiet trade without seeming to anyone unnatural or eccentric, woke up in a fright and called the people of the house to tell him where he was. He said that his name was Ansel Bourne, that he was entirely ignorant of Norristown, and that he knew nothing of shop-keeping, and that the last thing he remembered—it seemed only yesterday—was drawing the money from the bank, etc. in Providence. He would not believe that two months had elapsed. . . .

This was all that was known of the case up to June 1890, when I induced Mr. Bourne to submit to hypnotism, so as to see whether, in the hypnotic trance, his "Brown" memory would not come back. It did so with surprising readiness; so much so indeed that it proved quite impossible to make him whilst in the hypnosis remember any of the facts of his normal life. He had heard of Ansel Bourne, but "didn't know as he had ever met the man." When confronted with Mrs. Bourne he said that he had "never seen the woman before," etc. . . . He gives no motive for the wandering except that there was "trouble back there" and "he wanted rest."

Some, but not all, persons who experience fugue episodes do so after traumatic events. Many others, such as the Reverend Bourne, seem to escape into a fugue state in response to chronic stress in their lives that is within the realm of most people's experience. People typically are depressed before the onset of fugues (Kopelman, 1987). As with dissociative identity disorder, fugue states may be more common in people who are highly hypnotizable. Unlike a person with dissociative identity disorder, however, a person in a fugue state actually leaves the scene of the trauma or stress and leaves his or her former identity behind.

Fugue states appear to be more common among people with a history of amnesia, including amnesias due to head injuries (Kopelman, 1987). No accurate estimate of the prevalence of fugue states is available, although they appear to be quite rare, and in part because of their rarity we do not know much about their causes. Clinicians who treat people with this disorder tend to use many of the same techniques used to treat dissociative identity disorder, but again, little is known about the outcomes of treatment. Because this disorder involves amnesia about one's identity, and because it is so rare, in the *DSM-5* it is likely to be subsumed under dissociative amnesia.

Dissociative Amnesia

In both dissociative identity disorder and dissociative fugue states, individuals claim to have amnesia for those periods of time when their alternate personalities are in control or when they are in a fugue state. Yet some people have significant periods of amnesia without assuming new personalities or identities. They cannot remember important facts about their lives and their personal identities and typically are aware of large gaps in their memory or knowledge of themselves. These people are said to have **dissociative amnesia.**

Amnesia is considered to be either organic or psychogenic (Table 6.9). **Organic amnesia** is caused by brain injury resulting from disease, drugs, accidents (such as blows to the head), or surgery. Organic amnesia often involves the inability to remember new information; this is known as **anterograde amnesia.**

Psychogenic amnesia arises in the absence of any brain injury or disease and is thought to have psychological causes. Psychogenic amnesia rarely involves anterograde amnesia. **Retrograde amnesia,** the inability to remember information from the past, can have both organic and psychogenic causes. For example, people who have been in a serious car accident can have retrograde amnesia for the few minutes just before the accident. This retrograde amnesia can be due to brain injury resulting from blows to the head during the accident, or it can be a motivated forgetting of the events leading up to the trauma. Retrograde amnesia can also occur for longer periods of time.

When such amnesias are due to organic causes, people usually forget everything about the past, including both personal information, such as where they lived and people they knew, and general information, such as the identity of the president and major historical events of the period. They typically retain memory of their personal identities, however; while they may not remember their children, they know their own names. When long-term retrograde amnesias are due to psychological causes, people typically lose their identity and forget personal information but retain their memory for general information.

Following is a case study of a man with a psychogenic retrograde amnesia.

TABLE 6.9 Differences Between Psychogenic and Organic Amnesia

There are several important differences between psychogenic amnesia and organic amnesia.

Psychogenic Amnesia	Organic Amnesia
Caused by psychological factors	Caused by biological factors (such as disease, drugs, and blows to the head)
Seldom involves anterograde amnesia (inability to learn new information acquired since onset of amnesia)	Often involves anterograde amnesia
Can involve retrograde amnesia (inability to remember events from the past)	Can involve retrograde amnesia
Retrograde amnesia often only for personal information, not for general information	Retrograde amnesia usually for both personal and general information

CASE STUDY

Some years ago a man was found wandering the streets of Eugene, Oregon, not knowing his name or where he had come from. The police, who were baffled by his inability to identify himself, called in Lester Beck . . . , a psychologist they knew to be familiar with hypnosis, to see if he could be of assistance. He found the man eager to cooperate and by means of hypnosis and other methods was able to reconstruct the man's history. . . .

Following domestic difficulties, the man had gone on a drunken spree completely out of keeping with his earlier social behavior, and he had subsequently suffered deep remorse. His amnesia was motivated in the first place by the desire to exclude from memory the mortifying experiences that had gone on during the guilt-producing episode. He succeeded in forgetting all the events before and after this behavior that reminded him of it. Hence the amnesia spread from the critical incident to events before and after it, and he completely lost his sense of personal identity. (Hilgard 1977/1986, p. 68)

Loss of memory due to alcohol intoxication is common, but usually the person forgets only the events occurring during the period of intoxication. People who have severely abused alcohol much of their lives can develop a more global retrograde amnesia, known as *Korsakoff's syndrome* (see Chapter 14), in which they cannot remember much personal or general information for a period of several years or decades. However, the type of retrograde amnesia in the previous case study, which apparently involved only one episode of heavy drinking and the loss of only personal information, typically has psychological causes.

Some theorists argue that psychogenic amnesias may be the result of using dissociation as a defense against intolerable memories or stressors (Freyd, 1996; Gleaves, Smith, Butler, & Spiegel, 2004). Psychogenic amnesias most frequently occur following traumatic events, such as wars or sexual assaults. Alternatively, amnesia for specific events may occur because individuals were in such a high state of arousal during the events that they did not encode and store information during them and thus were unable to retrieve information about them later.

Amnesias for specific periods of time around traumas appear to be fairly common, but generalized retrograde amnesias for people's entire pasts and identities appear to be very rare. Studies of people in countries that have been the site of attempted genocides, ethnic cleansings, and wars have suggested that the rate of dissociative amnesias in these countries may be elevated. For example, a study of 810 Bhutanese refugees in Nepal found that almost 20 percent of those who had been tortured during conflicts in their countries could be diagnosed with dissociative amnesia (van Ommeren et al., 2001).

One complication that arises in diagnosing amnesias is the possibility that the amnesias are being faked by people trying to escape punishment for crimes they committed during the periods for which they claim to be amnesic. True amnesias also can occur in conjunction with the commission of crimes. Many crimes are committed by persons under the influence of alcohol or other drugs, and the drugs can cause blackouts for the periods of intoxication (Kopelman, 1987). Similarly, people who

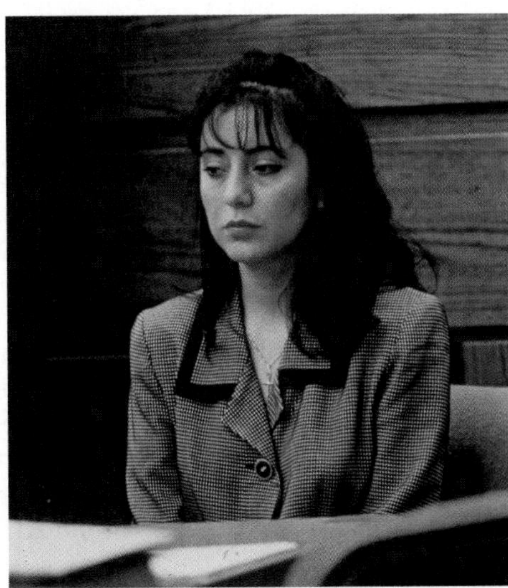

Lorena Bobbit cut off her husband's penis, after years of experiencing his abuse. She claimed to have amnesia for the act of cutting it off.

incur head injuries during the commission of a crime—for example, by falling while trying to escape the scene of a crime—can have amnesia for the commission of the crime.

Amnesia is seen most often in homicide cases, with between 25 and 45 percent of persons arrested for homicide claiming to have amnesia for the killings (Kopelman, 1987). In most of these cases, the victims are closely related to the killers (as lovers, spouses, close friends, or family members), the killings appear to be unpremeditated, and the killers are in a state of extreme emotional arousal at the time of the killings. More rarely, the killers appear to have been in a psychotic state at the time of the killings.

There is no clear-cut way to differentiate true amnesias from feigned ones. Head injuries leading to amnesia may be detectable through neuroimaging of the brain. Some clinicians advocate the use of hypnosis to assist people in remembering events around crimes if it is suspected that the amnesia is due to psychological causes. However, the possibility that hypnosis will "create" memories through the power of suggestion has led many courts to deny the use of hypnosis in such cases (Kopelman, 1987). In most cases, it is impossible to determine whether the amnesia is real.

Depersonalization Disorder

People with **depersonalization disorder** have frequent episodes in which they feel detached from their own mental processes or body, as if they are outside observers of themselves. Occasional experiences of depersonalization are common, particularly when people are sleep-deprived or under the influence of drugs (Baker et al., 2003). Approximately half of all adults report having had at least one brief episode of depersonalization, usually following a severe stressor (American Psychiatric Association, 2000).

Depersonalization disorder is diagnosed when episodes of depersonalization are so frequent and distressing that they interfere with individuals' ability to function. One study of people diagnosed with depersonalization disorder found that the average age of onset was about 23 years and two-thirds reported having had chronic experiences of depersonalization since the onset (Baker et al., 2003). Seventy-nine percent reported impaired social or work functioning, and the majority also had another psychiatric diagnosis, most often depression. People diagnosed with depersonalization disorder often report a history of childhood emotional, physical, or sexual abuse (Simeon et al., 2001).

Controversies Around the Dissociative Disorders

Surveys of psychiatrists in the United States and Canada find that less than one-quarter of them believe there is strong empirical evidence that the dissociative disorders are valid diagnoses (Lalonde, Hudson, Gigante, & Pope, 2001; Pope et al., 1999). Skeptics argue that the disorders are artificially created in suggestible clients by clinicians who reinforce clients for creating symptoms of dissociative disorders and may even induce symptoms of the disorder through hypnotic suggestion (see Kihlstrom, 2005; Lilienfeld et al., 1999; Spanos, 1994).

Controversy over the diagnosis of dissociative amnesia increased in response to claims that some survivors of childhood sexual abuse repressed their memories of the abuse for years and then eventually recalled these memories, often in the context of psychotherapy. These *repressed memories* represent a form of dissociative amnesia. Believers in repressed memories argue that the clinical evidence for dissociative or psychogenic amnesia is ample and that the empirical evidence is growing (Freyd, DePrince, & Gleaves, 2007). Nonbelievers argue that the empirical evidence against the validity of dissociative amnesia is ample and that the supportive evidence is biased (Kihlstrom, 2005; Loftus, Garry, & Hayne, 2008).

Most of the evidence for the phenomenon of repressed memories comes from studies of people who either are known to have been abused or self-report abuse and who claim to have forgotten or repressed their abuse at some time in the past. For example, Linda Williams (1995) surveyed 129 women who had documented histories of having been sexually abused sometime between 1973 and 1975. These women, who were between 10 months and 12 years old at the time of their abuse, were interviewed about 17 years after their abuse. Williams found that 49 of these 129 women had no memory of the abuse events that were documented or had forgotten about them.

John Briere and Jon Conte (1993) located 450 therapy patients who self-identified as abuse victims. Briere and Conte asked these people if there had ever been a time before their eighteenth birthdays when they "could not remember" their abuse. Fifty-nine percent answered yes to this question. As another example, Judith Herman and Mary Harvey (1997) examined interviews of 77 women who had reported memories of childhood trauma. They found that 17 percent spontaneously reported having had some delayed recall of the trauma and that 16 percent reported a period of complete amnesia following the trauma.

Nonbelievers in repressed memories have raised questions about the methods and conclusions of these studies (Kihlstrom, 2005; Loftus, 2003; McNally, 2003). For example, regarding the Williams study, it turns out that 33 of the 49 women who said they could not remember the specific abuse incidents they were asked about could remember other abuse incidents during their childhoods. Thus, they had not completely forgotten or repressed all memories of abuse. Instead, they simply could not remember the specific incident about which they were being asked. Williams did not give any additional information about the 16 women who could remember no incidents of molestation in their childhoods. They may have been too young to remember the incidents, because memory for anything that happens before about age 3 tends to be very sketchy.

Nonbelievers in repressed memories also cite numerous studies from the literature on eyewitness identification and testimony indicating that people can be made to believe that events occurred that in fact never happened (Ceci & Bruck, 1995; Loftus, 1993; Read & Lindsay, 1997). For example, Elizabeth Loftus and her colleagues developed a method for instilling a childhood memory of being lost on a specific occasion at age 5 (Loftus, 2003). This method involved a trusted family member engaging the subject in a conversation about the time he or she was lost (Loftus, 1993, p. 532):

> Chris (14 years old) was convinced by his older brother Jim that he had been lost in a shopping mall when he was 5 years old. Jim told Chris this story as if it were the truth: "It was 1981 or 1982. I remember that Chris was 5. We had gone shopping in the University City shopping mall in Spokane. After some panic, we found Chris being led down the mall by a tall, oldish man (I think he was wearing a flannel shirt). Chris was crying and holding the man's hand. The man explained that he had found Chris walking around crying his eyes out just a few moments before and was trying to help him find his parents." Just two days later, Chris recalled his feelings about being lost: "That day I was so scared that I would never see my family again. I knew that I was in trouble." On the third day, he recalled a conversation with his mother: "I remember Mom telling me never to do that again." On the fourth day: "I also remember that old man's flannel shirt." On the fifth day, he started remembering the mall itself: "I sort of remember the stores." In his last recollection, he could even remember a conversation with the man who found him: "I remember the man asking me if I was lost." . . . A couple of weeks later, Chris described his false memory and he greatly expanded on it. "I was with you guys for a second and I think I went over to look at the toy store, the Kay-Bee Toy and uh, we got lost and I was looking around and I thought, 'Uh-oh, I'm in trouble now.' You know. And then I . . . I thought I was never going to see my family again. I was really scared you know. And then this old man, I think he was wearing a blue flannel, came up to me. . . . He was kind of old. He was kind of bald on top. . . . He had like a ring of gray hair . . . and he had glasses."

Other studies have found that repeatedly asking adults about childhood events that never actually happened leads a percentage (perhaps 20 to 40 percent) eventually to "remember" these events and even explain them in detail (Hyman & Billings, 1998; Schacter, 1999). In addition, if a psychologist suggests that an individual's dreams reflect repressed memories of childhood events, a majority of subjects subsequently report that the events depicted in their dreams actually happened (Mazzoni & Loftus, 1998).

Critics of this line of work question the application of these studies to claims of repressed memories of sexual abuse (Gleaves & Freyd, 1997; Gleaves, Hernandez, & Warner, 2003). They argue that people might be willing to go along with experimenters who try to convince them that they were lost in a shopping mall as a child but are unlikely to be willing to go along with a therapist who tries to convince them that they were sexually abused if such abuse did not in fact happen. Abuse is such a terrible thing to remember, and the social consequences of admitting the abuse and confronting the abuser are so negative, that people simply would not claim it was true if it was not.

Researchers have used paradigms from cognitive psychology to test hypotheses about the reality of repressed memories. In a series of studies, Richard McNally and colleagues (McNally, 2003; McNally, Clancy, & Schacter, 2001; McNally, Clancy, Schacter, & Pitman, 2000a, 2000b) have found that individuals reporting recovered memories of either childhood sexual abuse or abduction by space aliens have a greater tendency to form false memories during certain laboratory tasks. For example, one task required participants to say whether they recognized words similar to other words they previously had learned, but not exactly the same. People who claimed to have recovered memories of alien abductions were more prone than comparison groups to falsely recognize words they had not seen previously (Clancy, Schacter, McNally, & Pitman, 2000; Clancy et al., 2002). The researchers argue that these people are characterized by an information-processing style that may render them more likely to believe they experienced specific events, such as childhood sexual abuse, when in fact they experienced other broadly similar events, such as physical abuse or emotional neglect.

Jennifer Freyd and colleagues (2007) have argued that the kinds of cognitive tasks McNally and colleagues have used do not tap into the specific cognitive phenomena associated with repressed memories. Specifically, they suggest that individuals who dissociate from, and forget, their abusive experiences are most likely to perform differently than other individuals on cognitive tasks that require divided attention—that is, paying attention to more than one thing at a time—because a division of attention is critical to dissociation (DePrince & Freyd, 1999, 2001; Freyd et al., 1998). One divided-attention task requires participants to press a key on a keyboard in response to a secondary task while attending to words on a computer screen and committing them to memory. Under these divided-attention conditions, people who score high on measures of dissociation recall fewer trauma-related words but more neutral words they previously had been instructed to remember, compared to low-dissociation participants, who show the opposite pattern. This suggests that people high in dissociation are better able to keep threatening information from their explicit awareness, particularly if they can turn their attention to other tasks or to other events in their environment at the time.

The repressed memory (or, as some researchers call it, false memory) debate continues and is likely to do so for some time. Researchers are trying to apply scientific techniques to support their views, and psychologists are being called on to testify in court cases involving claims of recovered or false memories. People who are trying to understand their distressing symptoms are at the center of this scientific maelstrom.

TEST YOURSELF

1. What are the four dissociative disorders, and what are the characteristics of this class of disorders?
2. What are proposed causes of and treatments for the dissociative disorders?
3. What are the characteristics of dissociative identity disorder?
4. What are the characteristics of dissociative fugue disorder? What are the characteristics of dissociative amnesia?
5. What is depersonalization disorder?

APPLY IT To determine whether Jaime's retrograde amnesia is organic or psychogenic, what criterion could his clinician use?

a. Psychogenic retrograde amnesia prevents short-term memory formation; organic retrograde amnesia prevents long-term memory recall.
b. Organic retrograde amnesia preserves memories for general information, while psychogenic retrograde amnesia does not.
c. Psychogenic retrograde amnesia preserves memories for general information, while organic retrograde amnesia does not.
d. Psychogenic retrograde amnesia impairs spontaneous speech, while organic retrograde amnesia does not.

Answers appear online at www.mhhe.com/nolen5e.

CHAPTER INTEGRATION

Philosophers and scientists have long debated the *mind-body problem:* Does the mind influence bodily processes? Do changes in the body affect a person's sense of "self"? Exactly how do the body and the mind influence each other?

The dissociative and somatoform disorders provide excellent evidence that the mind and body are complexly interwoven (Figure 6.3). In conversion disorder, psychological stress causes the person to lose eyesight, hearing, or functioning in another important physiological system. In somatization and pain disorders, a person under psychological stress experiences physiological symptoms, such as severe headaches. An underlying theme of these disorders is that for some people it is easier or

FIGURE 6.3 **Mind and Body in the Somatoform Dissociative Disorders**

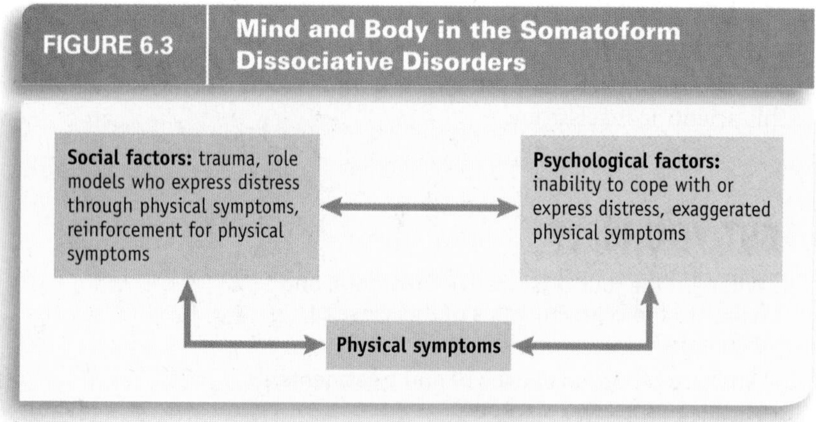

more acceptable to experience psychological distress through changes in their bodies than to express it more directly as sadness, fear, or anger, perhaps because of cultural or social norms.

We all somatize our distress to some degree—we feel more aches and pains when we are upset about something than when we are happy. People who develop somatoform and perhaps dissociative disorders may somatize their distress to an extreme degree. Their tendency to differentiate between what is going on in their mind and what is going on in their body may be low, and they may favor an extreme bodily expression of what is going on in their mind.

SHADES OF GRAY DISCUSSION (review p. 167)

Ben's health concerns do seem to be linked to his parents' separation and not to a medical condition. His insistence of real pain and his refusal to return to class signal that he experiences significant physical and emotional distress over his perceived headaches and stomachaches. Therefore, his symptoms are more in line with a somatization or pain disorder than with hypochondriasis. The diagnosis of somatization disorder requires multiple types of symptoms, and Ben has only headaches and stomachaches. You would give a diagnosis of pain disorder.

THINK CRITICALLY

Imagine yourself a juror in the following murder case (from Loftus, 1993). The defendant is George Franklin, Sr., 51 years old, standing trial for a murder that occurred more than 20 years earlier. The victim was 8-year-old Susan Kay Nason. Franklin's daughter, Eileen, only 8 years old herself at the time of the murder, provided the major evidence against her father. Eileen's memory of the murder, however, had re-emerged only recently, after 20 years of being repressed.

Eileen's memory first began to come back when she was playing with her 2-year-old son and her 5-year-old daughter. At one moment, her daughter looked up and asked a question like "Isn't that right, Mommy?" A memory of Susan Nason suddenly came to Eileen. She recalled the look of betrayal in Susie's eyes just before the murder. Later, more fragments would return, until Eileen had a rich and detailed memory. She remembered her father sexually assaulting Susie in the back of a van. She remembered that Susie was struggling as she said "No, don't!" and "Stop!" She remembered her father saying "Now Susie," and she even mimicked his precise intonation. Next, her memory took the three of them outside the van, where she saw her father raise a rock above his head. She remembered screaming and walking back to where Susie lay, covered with blood, the silver ring on her finger smashed. When questioned by prosecutors, Eileen was highly confident in her memory.

Would you convict George Franklin of the murder of Susan Nason? Why or why not? (*Discussion appears at the back of this book, on p. 518.*)

CHAPTER SUMMARY

- The somatoform disorders are a group of disorders in which the individual experiences or fears physical symptoms for which no organic cause can be found. These disorders may result from the dissociation of painful emotions or memories and the re-emergence of these emotions or memories in the form of symptoms as cries for help or as sources of gain people may receive for exhibiting these symptoms.
- One of the most dramatic somatoform disorders is conversion disorder, in which individuals lose all functioning in a part of their body, such as the eyes or the legs. Conversion symptoms often occur after trauma or stress. People with conversion disorder tend to have high rates of depression, anxiety, alcohol abuse, and antisocial personality disorder. Treatment for the disorder focuses on the expression of associated emotions or memories.

- Somatization disorder involves a long history of multiple physical complaints for which people have sought treatment but for which there is no apparent organic cause. Pain disorder involves only the experience of chronic, unexplainable pain. People with these disorders show high rates of anxiety and depression.
- Somatization and pain disorders run in families. The cognitive theory of these disorders is that affected people focus excessively on physical symptoms and catastrophize these symptoms. People with these disorders often have experienced recent traumas. Treatment involves understanding the traumas and helping the patient find adaptive ways to cope with distress.
- Hypochondriasis is a disorder in which individuals fear they have a disease despite medical proof to the contrary. Hypochondriasis shares many of the features and causes of somatization disorder and typically is comorbid with this disorder.
- A disorder questionably categorized as a somatoform disorder is body dysmorphic disorder, in which individuals have an obsessional preoccupation with parts of their body and engage in elaborate behaviors to mask or improve these body parts. They frequently are depressed, anxious, and suicidal. This disorder may be a feature of an underlying depression or anxiety disorder, or it may be a form of obsessive-compulsive disorder. Treatment includes psychodynamic therapy to uncover the emotions driving the obsession about the body, systematic desensitization therapy to decrease obsessions and compulsive behaviors focused on the body part, and the use of selective serotonin reuptake inhibitors to reduce obsessional thoughts.
- In the dissociative disorders, the individual's identity, memories, and consciousness become separated, or dissociated, from one another. In dissociative identity disorder (DID), the individual develops two or more distinct personalities, which alternate their control over the individual's behavior. Persons with dissociative identity disorder often engage in self-destructive and mutilative behaviors.
- The vast majority of diagnosed cases of dissociative identity disorder are women, and they tend to have a history of childhood sexual and/or physical abuse. The alternate personalities may have been formed during the traumatic experiences as a way of defending against these experiences, particularly among people who are highly hypnotizable. The treatment of dissociative identity disorder typically has involved helping the various personalities integrate into one functional personality.
- Dissociative fugue is a disorder in which the person suddenly moves away from home and assumes an entirely new identity, with complete amnesia for the previous identity. Fugue states usually occur in response to a stressor and can disappear suddenly, with the person returning to his or her previous identity. Little is known about the prevalence or causes of fugue states.
- Dissociative, or psychogenic, amnesia involves the loss of memory due to psychological causes. It differs from organic amnesia, which is caused by brain injury and in which a person may have difficulty remembering new information (anterograde amnesia), rare in psychogenic amnesia. In addition, with organic amnesia loss of memory for the past (retrograde amnesia) usually is complete, whereas with psychogenic amnesia it is limited to personal information.
- Psychogenic amnesia typically occurs following traumatic events. It may be due to motivated forgetting of events, to poor storage of information during events due to hyperarousal, or to avoidance of the emotions experienced during traumatic events and of the associated memories of these events.
- Depersonalization disorder involves frequent episodes in which individuals feel detached from their mental processes or body. Transient depersonalization experiences are common, especially under the influence of drugs or sleep deprivation. The causes of depersonalization disorder are unknown.

KEY TERMS

Chapter 7

Mood Disorders and Suicide

CHAPTER OUTLINE

Extraordinary People

Kay Redfield Jamison, *An Unquiet Mind*

"I was a senior in high school when I had my first attack. At first, everything seemed so easy. I raced about like a crazed weasel, bubbling with plans and enthusiasms, immersed in sports, and staying up all night, night after night, out with friends, reading everything that wasn't nailed down, filling manuscript books with poems and fragments of plays, and making expansive, completely unrealistic plans for my future. The world was filled with pleasure and promise; I felt great. Not just great, I felt *really* great. I felt I could do anything, that no task was too difficult. My mind seemed clear, fabulously focused, and able to make intuitive mathematical leaps that had up to that point entirely eluded me. Indeed, they elude me still. At the time, however, not only did everything make perfect sense, but it all began to fit into a marvelous kind of cosmic relatedness. My sense of enchantment with the laws of the natural world caused me to fizz over, and I found myself buttonholing my friends to tell them how beautiful it all was. They were less than transfixed by my insights into the webbings and beauties of the universe although considerably impressed at how exhausting it was to be around my enthusiastic ramblings: You're talking too fast, Kay. Slow down, Kay. You're wearing me out, Kay. Slow down, Kay. And those times when they didn't actually come out and say it, I still could see it in their eyes: For God's sake, Kay, slow down.

I did, finally, slow down. In fact, I came to a grinding halt. The bottom began to fall out of my life and my mind. My thinking, far from being clearer than a crystal, was tortuous. I would read the same passage over and over again only to realize that I had no memory at all for what I had just read. My mind had turned on me: It mocked me for my vapid enthusiasms; it laughed at all my foolish plans; it no longer found anything interesting or enjoyable or worthwhile. It was incapable of concentrated thought and turned time and again to the subject of death: I was going to die, what difference did anything make? Life's run was only a short and meaningless one; why live? I was totally exhausted and could scarcely pull myself out of bed in the mornings. It took me twice as long to walk anywhere as it ordinarily did, and I wore the same clothes over and over again, as it was otherwise too much of an effort to make a decision about what to put on. I dreaded having to talk with people, avoided my friends whenever possible, and sat in the school library in the early mornings and late afternoons, virtually inert, with a dead heart and a brain as cold as clay." (Jamison, 1995, pp. 35–38)

The emotional roller-coaster ride Kay Jamison describes is known as **bipolar disorder,** or *manic-depression.* First, Jamison had **mania,** with great energy and enthusiasm for everything, talking and thinking so fast that her friends could not keep up with her. Eventually, though, she crashed into a **depression.** Her energy and enthusiasm were gone, and she was slow to think, to talk, and to move. The joy had been drained from her life. Bipolar disorder is one of the two major types of mood disorders. The other type is **unipolar depression.** People with unipolar depression experience only depression, and not mania.

CHARACTERISTICS OF UNIPOLAR DEPRESSION

We will consider unipolar depression first. In unipolar depression, the symptoms of depression take over the whole person—emotions, bodily functions, behaviors, and thoughts.

Symptoms of Depression

A cardinal symptom of depression is depressed mood out of proportion to any cause. Many people diagnosed with depression report that they have lost interest in everything in life, a symptom referred to as *anhedonia*. Even when they try to do something enjoyable, they may feel no emotion. As Kay Jamison (1995, p. 110) writes, she was "unbearably miserable and seemingly incapable of any kind of joy or enthusiasm."

In depression, changes in appetite, sleep, and activity levels can take many forms. Some people with depression lose their appetite, while others find themselves eating more, perhaps even binge eating. Some people with depression want to sleep all day, while others find it difficult to sleep and may experience early morning wakening, in which they awaken at 3 or 4 A.M. every morning and cannot go back to sleep.

Behaviorally, many people with depression are slowed down, a condition known as *psychomotor*

TABLE 7.1 ***DSM-IV-TR* Diagnostic Criteria for Major Depression**

A. Five or more of the following symptoms present nearly every day for at least 2 weeks; at least one of the symptoms is either depressed mood or loss of interest or pleasure:
   1. Depressed mood
   2. Markedly diminished interest or pleasure in all, or almost all, activities
   3. Significant weight loss, or change in appetite
   4. Insomnia or hypersomnia
   5. Psychomotor retardation or agitation
   6. Fatigue or loss of energy
   7. Feelings of worthlessness or excessive or inappropriate guilt
   8. Diminished ability to think or concentrate, or indecisiveness
   9. Recurrent thoughts of death, or a suicide attempt or specific plan

B. The symptoms do not meet criteria for a mixed episode.

C. The symptoms cause clinically significant distress or impairment in social, occupational, or other important areas of functioning.

D. The symptoms are not due to the direct physiological effects of a substance (e.g., a drug of abuse or medication) or a general medical condition (e.g., hypothyroidism).

E. The symptoms are not better accounted for by bereavement; major depression can still be diagnosed if symptoms following a loss of a loved one persist for longer than 2 months or are characterized by marked functional impairment, morbid preoccupation with worthlessness, suicidal ideation, psychotic symptoms, or psychomotor retardation.

Source: Reprinted with permission from the *Diagnostic and Statistical Manual of Mental Disorders,* Fourth Edition, Text Revision.

retardation. They walk more slowly, gesture more slowly, and talk more slowly and quietly. They have more accidents because they cannot react quickly enough to avoid them. Many people with depression lack energy and report feeling chronically fatigued. A subset of people with depression exhibit *psychomotor agitation* instead of retardation—they feel physically agitated, cannot sit still, and may move around or fidget aimlessly.

The thoughts of people with depression may be filled with themes of worthlessness, guilt, hopelessness, and even suicide. They often have trouble concentrating and making decisions. As Jamison (1995, p. 100) describes, "It seemed as though my mind had slowed down and burned out to the point of being virtually useless."

In some severe cases, people with depression lose touch with reality, experiencing delusions (beliefs with no basis in reality) and hallucinations (seeing, hearing, or feeling things that are not real). These delusions and hallucinations usually are negative. People with depression may have delusions that they have committed a terrible sin, that they are being punished, or that they have killed or hurt someone. They may hear voices accusing them of having committed an atrocity or instructing them to kill themselves.

Diagnosing Depressive Disorders

Depression takes several forms. The *DSM-IV-TR* recognizes two categories of unipolar depression: **major depression** and **dysthymic disorder.** The diagnosis of major depression requires that a person experience either depressed mood or loss of interest in usual activities, plus at least four other symptoms of depression, chronically for at least 2 weeks (Table 7.1). In addition, these symptoms must be severe enough to interfere with the person's ability to function in everyday life. People who experience only one depressive episode receive a diagnosis of *major depression, single episode.* Two or more episodes separated by at least 2 months without symptoms merit the diagnosis of *major depression, recurrent*.

Mood Disorders Along the Continuum

Typical mood symptoms in response to events
Feeling blue or down but able to function normally; feeling happy and exuberant because something good happened
Potentially meets criteria for hypomania
Moderate and frequent elation, inflated self-esteem, some impulsiveness, high energy
Likely meets criteria for manic episode
Expansive mood including irritability, grandiosity, racing thoughts, and recklessness that significantly interferes with functioning
Functional
Dysfunctional
Potentially meets criteria for dysthymia
Moderate and frequent symptoms of sadness, apathy, fatigue, etc. that somewhat interfere with functioning
Likely meets criteria for major depressive episode
Severe symptoms of sadness, apathy, fatigue, etc. that significantly interfere with functioning

"I'm depressed" is a phrase that you may have uttered, perhaps after you didn't do as well as you expected on an exam or when a friend became angry and wouldn't speak to you. Such events often sap our energy and motivation, shake our self-esteem, and make us feel down and blue—all symptoms of depression.

More significant events, such as the death of a loved one, the break-up of a marriage, or the loss of a job, can lead to more serious symptoms of depression. In some people, the symptoms may be mild or moderate and not interfere with daily functioning. Sometimes, however, symptoms of depression following negative events become debilitating and can last for long periods of time. And in some cases, severe symptoms of depression emerge without any obvious cause. A diagnosis of depression depends on both the severity and the duration of symptoms.

Like symptoms of depression, symptoms of mania also vary in severity and duration. Perhaps you've experienced a "fizzing over" feeling of exuberance when something in your life is going particularly well—such as getting an acceptance to college or beginning a relationship with somebody special. As in depression, moderate symptoms of mania usually are tied to specific situations and lessen as those situations pass. Symptoms of a manic episode, however, go beyond feeling happy when something good has happened. People diagnosed with mania are often irritable and impatient with others. Their extreme self-confidence may lead them to carry out grandiose schemes to earn money or influence others, or to engage in extremely risky or impulsive behaviors.

Dysthymic disorder is less severe than major depression but more chronic. A person diagnosed with dysthymic disorder must experience depressed mood plus two of the following symptoms for at least 2 years: (a) poor appetite or overeating, (b) insomnia or hypersomnia, (c) low energy or fatigue, (d) low self-esteem, (e) poor concentration or difficulty making decisions, (f) feelings of hopelessness. During these 2 years, the person must never have been without the symptoms of depression for longer than a 2-month period. Some individuals with dysthymic disorder also experience episodes of major depression intermittently, a condition referred to as *double depression*.

In the *DSM-5*, both dysthymic disorder and major depressive episodes lasting longer than 2 years may fall under the proposed diagnosis *chronic depressive disorder* (American Psychological Association, 2010), reflecting evidence that these two disorders have similar symptom patterns, treatment response, and family history (McCullough et al., 2008).

Over 70 percent of the people diagnosed with *DSM-IV-TR* major depression or dysthymia also have another psychological disorder at some time

TABLE 7.2 *DSM-IV-TR* Subtypes of Major Depression (and the Depressive Phase of Bipolar Disorder)

The *DSM-IV-TR* specifies a number of subtypes of major depression and the depressive phase of bipolar disorder.

Subtype	Characteristic Symptoms
With melancholic features	Inability to experience pleasure, distinct depressed mood, depression regularly worse in morning, early morning awakening, marked psychomotor retardation or agitation, significant anorexia or weight loss, excessive guilt
With psychotic features	Presence of depressing delusions or hallucinations
With catatonic features	Catatonic behaviors: catalepsy, excessive motor activity, severe disturbances in speech
With atypical features	Positive mood reactions to some events, significant weight gain or increase in appetite, hypersomnia, heavy or laden feelings in arms or legs, long-standing pattern of sensitivity to interpersonal rejection
With postpartum onset	Onset of major depressive episode within four weeks of delivery of child
With seasonal pattern	History of at least two years in which major depressive episodes occur during one season of the year (usually the winter) and remit when the season is over

in their lives. The most common disorders that are comorbid with (occur with) depression are substance abuse (e.g., alcohol abuse); anxiety disorders, such as panic disorder; and eating disorders (Kessler et al., 2003). Sometimes, the depression precedes and may cause the other disorder. In other cases, the depression follows and may be the consequence of the other disorder.

The combination of major depression and anxiety is so common that the authors of the *DSM-5* have proposed the diagnosis *mixed anxiety depression.* This diagnosis would require three or four symptoms of major depression, including depressed mood and/or anhedonia, and two or more symptoms of anxiety (American Psychological Association, 2010).

The *DSM-IV-TR* recognizes several subtypes of depression—different forms the disorder can take (Table 7.2). These subtypes apply both to major depression and to the depressive phase of bipolar disorder. The first subtype of depression is *depression with melancholic features,* in which the physiological symptoms of depression are particularly prominent (see Table 7.2). Second is *depression with psychotic features,* in which people experience delusions and hallucinations during a major depressive episode. Third, people with *depression with catatonic features* show the strange behaviors collectively known as *catatonia,* which can range from a complete lack of movement to excited agitation. Fourth is *depression with atypical features.* The criteria for this subtype are an odd assortment of symptoms (see Table 7.2).

Fifth is *depression with postpartum onset.* This diagnosis is given to women when the onset of a major depressive episode occurs within 4 weeks of delivery of a child. More rarely, some women develop mania postpartum and are given the diagnosis of *bipolar disorder with postpartum onset.* In the first few weeks after giving birth, as many as 30 percent of women experience the *postpartum blues*—emotional lability (unstable and quickly shifting moods), frequent crying, irritability, and fatigue. For most women, these symptoms cease completely within 2 weeks of the birth. About 1 in 10 women experience postpartum depression serious enough to warrant a diagnosis of a depressive disorder (Steiner, Dunn, & Born, 2003).

The sixth subtype of major depressive disorder is *depression with seasonal pattern,* also referred to as **seasonal affective disorder,** or **SAD.** People with SAD have a history of at least 2 years of experiencing and fully recovering from major depressive episodes. They become depressed when the daylight hours are short and recover when the daylight hours are long. In the northern hemisphere, this means that people are depressed from November through February and not depressed from June through August. Some people with this disorder actually develop mild forms of mania or have full manic episodes during the summer months and are diagnosed with *bipolar disorder with seasonal pattern.* In order to be diagnosed with seasonal affective disorder, a person's mood changes cannot be the result of psychosocial events, such as regularly being unemployed during the winter.

Rather, the mood changes must seem to come on without reason or cause.

Although many of us may experience mood changes with the seasons, only about 1 percent of the U.S. population have a diagnosable seasonal affective disorder, and only 1 to 5 percent internationally (Blazer, Kessler, & Swartz, 1998; Westrin & Lam, 2007). SAD is more common in latitudes with fewer hours of daylight in the winter months (Michalak & Lam, 2002; Rosen et al., 1990). For example, a study in Greenland found a relatively high rate of SAD, 9 percent, and found that individuals living in northern latitudes were more likely to meet the criteria for SAD than individuals living in southern latitudes (Kegel, Dam, Ali, & Bjerregaard, 2009).

Another subtype that may be added to the *DSM-5* is *premenstrual dysphoric disorder.* It would describe women who frequently have significant increase in distress symptoms prior to menstruation (American Psychiatric Association, 2010).

Prevalence and Course of Unipolar Depressive Disorders

At some time in their lives, 16 percent of Americans experience an episode of major depression (Kessler, Merikangas, & Wang, 2007). International studies in North America, Latin America, Europe, and Japan show that the lifetime prevalence of major depression ranges from 3 percent in Japan to the 16 percent rate in the United States (Andrade et al., 2003).

In the United States, 18- to 29-year-olds are most likely to have had a major depressive episode in the past year (Kessler et al., 2003). Rates of depression in the past year go down steadily and are lowest in people over age 60. The rates of depression do go up among those over age 85. When they do occur, depressions in older people tend to be severe, chronic, and debilitating (Fiske, Wetherell, & Gatz, 2009).

It may be surprising that the rate of depression is so low among adults over age 60. The diagnosis of depression in older adults is complicated (Fiske et al., 2009). First, older adults may be less willing than younger adults to report the symptoms of depression, because they grew up in a society less accepting of depression. Second, depressive symptoms in older adults often occur in the context of a serious medical illness, which can interfere with making an appropriate diagnosis. Third, older people are more likely than younger people to have mild to severe cognitive impairment, and it is often difficult to distinguish between a depressive disorder and the early stages of a cognitive disorder (see Chapter 11).

Although these factors are important, other researchers suggest that the low rate is valid, and they have offered several explanations (Lyness, 2004). The first is quite grim: Depression appears to interfere with physical health, and as a result people with a history of depression may be more likely to die before they reach old age. The second explanation is more hopeful: As people age, they may develop more adaptive coping skills and a psychologically healthier outlook on life (Fiske et al., 2009). We consider a third explanation, that there have been historical changes in people's vulnerability to depression, later in this chapter.

Depression is less common among children than among adults. Still, at any point in time, as many as 2.5 percent of children and 8.3 percent of adolescents can be diagnosed with major depression, and as many as 1.7 percent of children and 8.0 percent of adolescents can be diagnosed with dysthymic disorder (for reviews, see Garber & Horowitz, 2002; Merikangas & Knight, 2009). As many as 24 percent of youth will experience an episode of major depression at some time before age 20.

Women are about twice as likely as men to experience both mild depressive symptoms and severe depressive disorders (Nolen-Hoeksema & Hilt, 2009). This gender difference in depression has been found in many countries, in most ethnic groups, and in all adult age groups. We discuss possible reasons for these differences later in the chapter.

Depression appears to be a long-lasting, recurrent problem for some people. One nationwide study found that people with major depression had spent an average of 16 weeks during the previous year with significant symptoms of depression (Kessler et al., 2003). The picture that emerges is of a depressed person spending much of his or her time at least moderately depressed. After recovery from one episode of depression, people with depression remain at high risk for a relapse. As many as 75 percent of people who experience a first episode of depression will experience subsequent episodes (Kessing, Hansen, & Andersen, 2004). People with a history of multiple episodes of depression are even more likely to remain depressed for long periods of time.

Depression is a costly disorder, both to the individual and to society. People who have a diagnosis of major depression lose an average of 27 days of work per year because of their symptoms. Depression in workers costs employers an estimated $37 billion per year in lost productivity alone (not including the cost of treatment) (Kessler et al., 2007).

SHADES OF GRAY

Consider the following case study of a college student, who may resemble someone you know.

Carmen's friends were shocked to find her passed out in her dorm room with an empty bottle of sleeping pills on the floor next to her. Carmen had experienced years of unhappiness, a sense of low self-worth, pessimism, and chronic fatigue. She often told her friends she couldn't remember a time when she was happy for more than a few days at a time. Since the beginning of the winter term, however, Carmen's depressed mood had deepened, and she had spent days on end locked in her bedroom, apparently sleeping. She had said it was no use going to class because she couldn't concentrate. She had been skipping meals and had lost 12 pounds.

Based on the time frame and symptoms described, what diagnosis would Carmen most likely receive? (Discussion including answer appears at the end of the chapter.)

The good news is that once people undergo treatment for their depression, they tend to recover much more quickly than they would without treatment and reduce their risk of relapse. The bad news is that many people with depression never seek care or wait years after their symptoms have begun before they seek care (Kessler et al., 2003). Why don't people experiencing the terrible symptoms of depression seek treatment? They may lack insurance or the money to pay for care. But often they expect to get over their symptoms on their own. They believe that the symptoms are simply a phase that will pass with time and won't affect their lives over the long term.

TEST YOURSELF

1. What are the criteria for a diagnosis of major depression?
2. What are the criteria for a diagnosis of dysthymic disorder?
3. How do rates of depression vary by age group and gender?

APPLY IT Over the past 2 months, Brandon has had a severely depressed mood, has lost 30 pounds, and has been chronically exhausted. He believes he has been possessed by the devil and hears voices telling him to kill himself. With which subtype of major depression would Brandon most likely be diagnosed?

a. seasonal pattern

b. melancholic

c. psychotic

d. catatonic

Answers appear online at www.mhhe.com/nolen5e.

CHARACTERISTICS OF BIPOLAR DISORDER

VOICES

There is a particular kind of pain, elation, loneliness, and terror involved in this kind of madness. When you're high it's tremendous. The ideas and feelings are fast and frequent like shooting stars and you follow them until you find better and brighter ones. Shyness goes, the right words and gestures are suddenly there, the power to seduce and captivate others a felt certainty. There are interests found in uninteresting people. Sensuality is pervasive and the desire to seduce and be seduced irresistible. Feelings of ease, intensity, power, well-being, financial omnipotence, and euphoria now pervade one's marrow.

But, somewhere, this changes. The fast ideas are far too fast and there are far too many; overwhelming confusion replaces clarity. Memory goes. Humor and absorption on friends' faces are replaced by fear and concern. Everything previously moving with the grain is now against—you are irritable, angry, frightened, uncontrollable, and enmeshed totally in the blackest caves of the mind. You never knew those caves were there. It will never end. (Goodwin & Jamison, 1990, pp. 17–18)

This person is describing an episode of bipolar disorder. When she is manic, she has tremendous energy and vibrancy, her self-esteem is soaring, and she is filled with ideas and confidence. Then, when she becomes depressed, she is despairing and fearful, she doubts herself and everyone around her, and she wishes to die. This alternation

TABLE 7.3 *DSM-IV-TR* Criteria for Manic Episode

A. A distinct period of abnormally and persistently elevated, expansive, or irritable mood, lasting at least 1 week.

B. During the period of mood disturbance, three (or more) of the following symptoms (four if the mood is only irritable):
   1. Inflated self-esteem or grandiosity
   2. Decreased need for sleep
   3. More talkative than usual or pressure to keep talking
   4. Flight of ideas or subjective experience that thoughts are racing
   5. Distractibility
   6. Increase in goal-directed activity or psychomotor agitation
   7. Excessive involvement in pleasurable activities with a high potential for painful consequences (e.g., engaging in unrestrained buying sprees, sexual indiscretions, or foolish business investments)

C. The symptoms do not meet criteria for a mixed episode.

D. The mood disturbance is sufficiently severe to cause marked impairment in occupational functioning or in usual social activities or relationships with others, or to necessitate hospitalization to prevent harm to self or others, or there are psychotic features.

E. The symptoms are not due to the direct physiological effects of a substance (e.g., a drug of abuse, a medication, or other treatment) or a general medical condition (e.g., hyperthyroidism).

Source: Reprinted with permission from the *Diagnostic and Statistical Manual of Mental Disorders,* Fourth Edition, Text Revision.

between periods of mania and periods of depression is the classic manifestation of bipolar disorder.

Symptoms of Mania

We have already discussed the symptoms of depression in detail, so here we focus on the symptoms of mania (Table 7.3). The moods of people who are manic can be elated, but that elation is often mixed with irritation and agitation.

People with mania have unrealistically positive and grandiose (inflated) self-esteem. They experience racing thoughts and impulses. At times, these grandiose thoughts are delusional and may be accompanied by grandiose hallucinations. People experiencing a manic episode may speak rapidly and forcefully, trying to convey a rapid stream of fantastic thoughts. Some people may become agitated and irritable, particularly with people they perceive as "getting in the way." They may engage in a variety of impulsive behaviors, such as sexual indiscretions or spending sprees. Often, they will frenetically pursue grand plans and goals.

In order to be diagnosed with mania, an individual must show an elevated, expansive, or irritable mood for at least 1 week, as well as at least three of the other symptoms listed in Table 7.3. These symptoms must impair the individual's functioning.

People who experience manic episodes meeting these criteria are said to have **bipolar I disorder.** Almost all these people eventually will fall into a depressive episode; mania without any depression is rare (Goodwin & Jamison, 2007). For some people with bipolar I disorder, the depressions are as severe as major depressive episodes, whereas for others the episodes of depression are relatively mild and infrequent. Some people diagnosed with bipolar I disorder have mixed episodes in which they experience the full criteria for manic episodes and major depressive episodes in the same day, every day for at least 1 week.

People with **bipolar II disorder** experience severe episodes of depression that meet the criteria for major depression, but their episodes of mania are milder and are known as **hypomania** (Table 7.4). Hypomania involves the same symptoms as mania. The major difference is that in hypomania these symptoms are not severe enough to interfere with daily functioning and do not involve hallucinations or delusions.

Just as dysthymic disorder is the less severe but more chronic form of depressive disorder,

TABLE 7.4 *DSM-IV-TR* Criteria for Bipolar I and Bipolar II Disorders

Bipolar I and II disorders differ in the presence of major depressive episodes, episodes meeting the full criteria for mania, and hypomanic episodes.

Criteria	Bipolar I	Bipolar II
Major depressive episodes	Can occur but are not necessary for diagnosis	Are necessary for diagnosis
Episodes meeting full criteria for mania	Are necessary for diagnosis	Cannot be present for diagnosis
Hypomanic episodes	Can occur between episodes of severe mania or major depression but are not necessary for diagnosis	Are necessary for diagnosis

there is a less severe but more chronic form of bipolar disorder, known as **cyclothymic disorder.** A person with cyclothymic disorder alternates between episodes of hypomania and moderate depression chronically over at least a 2-year period. During the periods of hypomania, the person may be able to function reasonably well. Often, however, the periods of depression significantly interfere with daily functioning, although the episodes are less severe than major depressive episodes. People with cyclothymic disorder are at increased risk of developing bipolar disorder (Goodwin & Jamison, 2007).

Children with bipolar disorder may be highly agitated and irritable.

About 90 percent of people with bipolar disorder have multiple episodes or cycles during their lifetimes (Merikangas et al., 2007). The length of an individual episode of bipolar disorder varies greatly from one person to the next. Some people are in a manic state for several weeks or months before moving into a depressed state. More rarely, people switch from mania to depression and back within a matter of days or, as noted above, even in the same day. The number of lifetime episodes also varies tremendously from one person to the next, but a relatively common pattern is for episodes to become more frequent and closer together over time. Four or more cycles of mania and depression within 1 year lead to a diagnosis of **rapid cycling bipolar disorder.**

One area of great interest and controversy is bipolar disorder in youth. Until the past decade, it was assumed that bipolar disorder could not be diagnosed reliably until individuals were in their late teens or early adulthood. Increasingly, researchers and clinicians have been interested in identifying early signs of bipolar disorder in children and young teenagers so that interventions could be initiated and researchers could investigate the causes and course of the disorder in youth (Leibenluft & Rich, 2008; Taylor & Miklowitz, 2009).

Although some children show bipolar disorder with alternating episodes of mania and depression interspersed with periods of normal mood (Birmaher et al., 2006), others show chronic symptoms and rapid mood switches. Individuals in the latter group tend toward severe irritability characterized by frequent temper tantrums or rages (Leibenluft & Rich, 2008). These irritable children are at increased risk of developing anxiety and unipolar depressive disorders later in life but do not tend to develop classic bipolar disorder (Stringaris, Cohen, Pine, & Leibenluft, 2009). In addition, the agitation and risky behavior accompanying mania in youth are difficult to distinguish from the symptoms of attention-deficit/hyperactivity disorder (ADHD; see Chapter 10), which include hyperactivity, poor judgment, and impulsivity, or from the symptoms of oppositional defiant disorder (see Chapter 10), which include chronic irritability and refusal to follow rules. There has been considerable debate as to whether these agitated, irritable children have bipolar disorder, ADHD, or oppositional defiant disorder, none of which seems to fit their symptoms perfectly.

The *DSM-5* may include a new diagnosis for youth age 6 and older called *temper dysregulation disorder with dysphoria* (American Psychiatric Association, 2010). To qualify for this diagnosis, a young person would have to show immature and inappropriate temper outbursts three or more times per week on average. In between these outbursts, the youth must be consistently and obviously irritable, angry, or sad. For the diagnosis, the symptoms must first occur before age 10 and be present for at least 1 year (without more than 3 symptom-free months) (American Psychological Association, 2010).

Prevalence and Course of Bipolar Disorder

Bipolar disorder is less common than unipolar depression. About 1 or 2 in 100 people will experience at least one episode of bipolar disorder at some time in their lives (Merikangas et al., 2007). Men and women seem equally likely to develop the disorder, and there are no consistent differences in the prevalence of the disorder among ethnic groups. These facts suggest that biological factors may be more responsible for bipolar disorder than for unipolar disorder, which shows more variability across sociodemographic groups. Most people who develop bipolar disorder do so in late adolescence or early adulthood (Merikangas et al., 2007).

Like people with unipolar depression, people with bipolar disorder often face chronic problems on the job and in their relationships (Marangell, 2004). One study followed people who had been hospitalized for an episode of bipolar disorder and found that over the year following hospitalization, only about one in four recovered fully from the symptoms and was able to lead a relatively normal life (Keck et al., 1998). The best predictors of recovery were full compliance with medication taking and higher social class, which may have afforded people better health care and social support. In addition, people with bipolar disorder often abuse substances such as alcohol and hard drugs, impairing their control over their disorder, their willingness to take medications, and their functioning (Merikangas et al., 2007).

Creativity and the Mood Disorders

Some theorists have argued that the symptoms of mania—increased self-esteem, a rush of ideas and the courage to pursue these ideas, high energy, little need for sleep, hypervigilance, and decisiveness—can actually have benefits. In turn, the melancholy of depression is often seen as inspirational for artists. Indeed, some of the most influential people in history have suffered, and perhaps benefited, from bipolar disorder or depression (Jamison, 1993).

Political leaders including Abraham Lincoln, Alexander Hamilton, Winston Churchill, Napoleon Bonaparte, and Benito Mussolini and religious leaders including Martin Luther and George Fox (founder of the Society of Friends, or Quakers) have been posthumously diagnosed by psychiatric biographers as having had periods of mania, hypomania, or depression (Jamison, 1993). Although during periods of depression these leaders often were incapacitated, during periods of mania and hypomania they accomplished extraordinary feats. While manic, they devised brilliant and daring strategies for winning wars and solving national problems and had the energy, self-esteem, and persistence to carry out these strategies.

Winston Churchill had periods of manic symptoms that may have been both an asset and a liability.

Writers, artists, and composers have a higher-than-normal prevalence of mania and depression. For example, a study of 1,005 famous twentieth-century artists, writers, and other professionals found that the artists and writers experienced two to three times the rate of mood disorders, psychosis, and suicide attempts than comparably successful people in business, science, and public life. The poets in this group were most likely to have been manic (Ludwig, 1992). More recently, actor Zach Braff, actress Kirsten Dunst, game-show host Drew Carey, rapper DMX, and singers Amy Winehouse and Janet Jackson are among the celebrities who have publicized their mood disorder.

Abraham Lincoln suffered periods of severe depression.

Although many creative people with bipolar disorder may have been able to learn from their periods of depression and to exploit their periods

Game-show host Drew Carey has struggled with depression.

of mania, many also have found the highs and lows of the disorder unbearable and have attempted or completed suicide. In general, the mood disorders substantially impair thinking and productivity. As Elizabeth Wurtzel (1995, p. 295) notes:

> While it may be true that a great deal of art finds its inspirational wellspring in sorrow, let's not kid ourselves in how much time each of those people wasted and lost by being mired in misery. So many productive hours slipped by as paralyzing despair took over. This is not to say that we should deny sadness its rightful place among the muses of poetry and of all art forms, but let's stop calling it madness, let's stop pretending that the feeling itself is interesting. Let's call it depression and admit that it is very bleak.

TEST YOURSELF

1. What are the symptoms of mania?
2. What is cyclothymic disorder?
3. How do the prevalence and course of bipolar disorder differ from those of unipolar disorder?

APPLY IT Steve had a great idea—he would take the money his parents had put aside for him to attend college and use it to start a new company. He and some friends were building a new type of computer. Steve often stayed up all night working on the prototype, feeling exhilarated, with too many ideas to be able to sleep. He would call friends and relatives in the middle of the night asking them for money to fund his new company, talking excitedly until they hung up on him. Would Steve meet the criteria for a manic episode?

A. clearly yes

B. clearly no

C. maybe

Answers appear online at www.mhhe.com/nolen5e.

THEORIES OF UNIPOLAR DEPRESSION

Unipolar depression is one of the most researched of all the psychological disorders. We will discuss biological, behavioral, cognitive, interpersonal, and sociocultural theories.

Biological Theories of Depression

A number of different biological processes appear to be involved in depression, including genetics, neurotransmitter systems, structural and functional abnormalities of the brain, and neuroendocrine systems.

Genetic Factors

Family history studies find that the first-degree relatives of people with unipolar depression are two to three times more likely to also have depression than are the first-degree relatives of people without the disorder (Klein, Lewinsohn, Seeley, & Rohde, 2001). Twin studies of major depression find higher concordance rates for monozygotic twins than for dizygotic twins, implicating genetic processes in the disorder (Kendler, Myers, Prescott, & Neale, 2001). Depression that begins early in life appears to have a stronger genetic base than depression that begins in adulthood (Holmans et al., 2007).

Some twin studies of major depression suggest that genetics plays a greater role in this disorder for women than for men (Kendler et al., 2001), while other twin studies have found no gender difference in the heritability of depression (Eaves et al., 1997; Kendler & Prescott, 1999; Rutter, Silberg, O'Connor, & Simonoff, 1999). Still other studies suggest that the types of genes responsible for depression may differ in women and men (Zubenko et al., 2002).

It is probable that multiple genetic abnormalities contribute to depression. Several studies suggest that the serotonin transporter gene may play a role (Belmaker & Agam, 2008). As we will discuss below, serotonin is one of the neurotransmitters implicated in depression. Abnormalities on the serotonin transporter gene could lead to dysfunction in the regulation of serotonin, which in turn could affect the stability of individuals' moods. In a longitudinal study, Avshalom Caspi and colleagues (2003) found that people with abnormalities on the serotonin transporter gene were at increased risk for depression when they faced negative life events (see also Kaufman et al., 2004, 2006). Not all studies have replicated these findings, however (Risch et al., 2009).

Neurotransmitter Theories

The neurotransmitters that have been implicated most often in depression are the **monoamines,** specifically, **norepinephrine, serotonin,** and, to a lesser extent, **dopamine.** These neurotransmitters are found in large concentrations in the *limbic system,* a part of the brain associated with the regulation of sleep, appetite, and emotional processes. The early theory of the role of these neurotransmitters in mood disorders was that depression is caused by a reduction in the amount of norepinephrine or serotonin in the synapses between neurons (Glassman, 1969; Schildkraut, 1965).

Our understanding of the functioning of neurotransmitters in the brain has increased tremendously, and, consequently, theories of their role in depression have become much more complex (Belmaker & Agam, 2008). A number of processes within brain cells that affect the functioning of neurotransmitters may go awry in depression (Figure 7.1). For example, serotonin and norepinephrine are synthesized in neurons from tryptophan and tyrosine, respectively, and some studies suggest that abnormalities in this synthesis process may contribute to depression (Zhang et al., 2004). Both serotonin and norepinephrine are released by one neuron (referred to as the presynaptic neuron) into the synapse and then bind to receptors on other neurons (referred to as the postsynaptic neurons; see Figure 7.1). The release process, which is regulated by the serotonin transporter gene, may be abnormal in depression. In addition, the receptors for serotonin and norepinephrine on the postsynaptic neurons may be less sensitive than normal in people with depression, or they may sometimes malfunction (Svenningsson et al., 2006).

FIGURE 7.1 **Neurotransmitter Abnormalities Implicated in Depression.** Several problems in the production and regulation of serotonin and norepinephrine may contribute to depression.

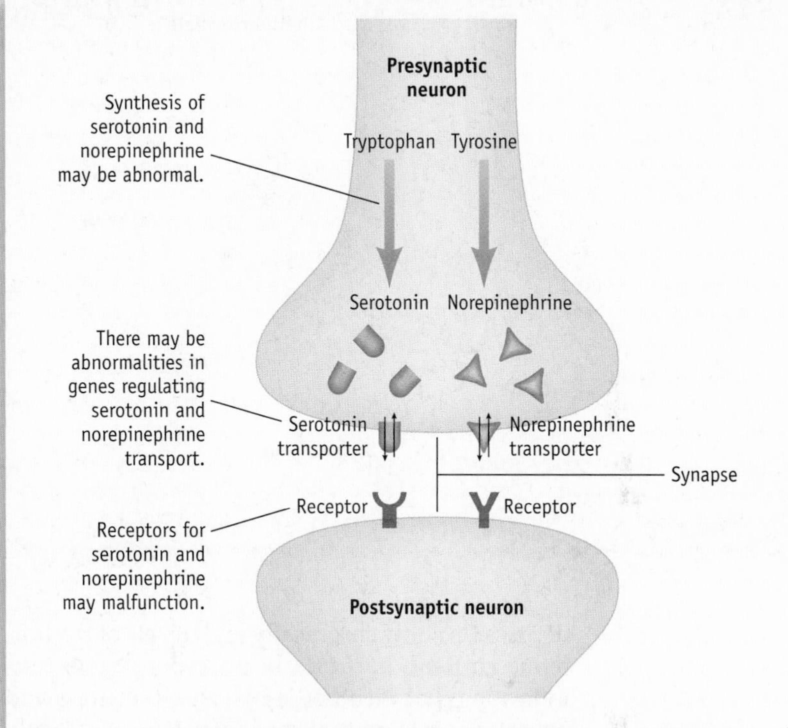

Brain Abnormalities

Neuroimaging studies have found consistent abnormalities in at least four areas of the brain in people with depression: the prefrontal cortex, anterior cingulate, hippocampus, and amygdala (Figure 7.2).

Critical functions of the prefrontal cortex include attention, short-term memory, planning, and problem solving. Many studies have shown reduced metabolic activity and a reduction in the volume of gray matter in the prefrontal cortex, particularly on the left side, in people with serious depression (Dougherty & Rauch, 2007a). In addition, electroencephalographic (EEG) studies show lower brain-wave activity on the left side of the prefrontal cortex in depressed people compared to nondepressed people (Davidson, Pizzagalli, & Nitschke, 2009). The left prefrontal cortex is particularly involved in motivation and goal-orientation, and inactivity in this region may be associated with motivational difficulties as seen in depression. The successful treatment of depression with antidepressant medications is associated with increases in metabolic and brain-wave activity in the left prefrontal cortex (Kennedy et al., 2001).

The anterior cingulate, a subregion of the prefrontal cortex, plays an important role in the body's response to stress, in emotional expression, and in social behavior (Davidson et al., 2009). People with depression show different levels of activity in the anterior cingulate relative to controls (Dougherty & Rauch, 2007a). This altered activity may be associated with problems in attention, in the planning of appropriate responses, and in coping, as well as with anhedonia found in depression. Again, activity normalizes in this region of the brain when people are successfully treated for their depression (Dougherty & Rauch, 2007a).

The hippocampus is critical in memory and in fear-related learning. Neuroimaging studies show smaller volume and lower metabolic activity in the hippocampus of people with major depression (Konarski et al., 2008). Damage to the hippocampus could be the result of chronic arousal of the body's stress response. As we will discuss, people with

FIGURE 7.2 **Areas of the Brain Implicated in Major Depression.** Neuroimaging studies have found abnormalities in the prefrontal cortex, anterior cingulate, amygdala, and hippocampus.

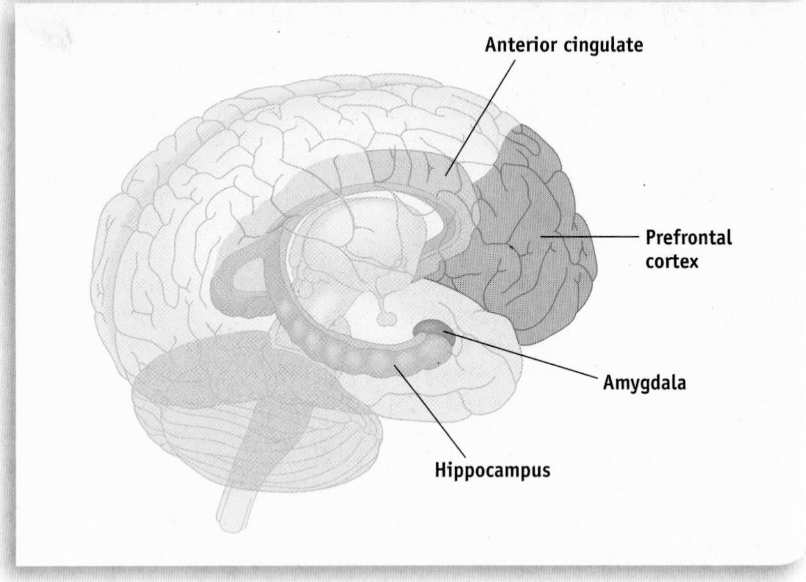

depression show chronically high levels of the hormone **cortisol,** particularly in response to stress, indicating that their bodies overreact to stress and do not return to normal levels of cortisol as quickly as the bodies of nondepressed people. The hippocampus contains many receptors for cortisol, and chronically elevated levels of this hormone may kill or inhibit the development of new neurons in the hippocampus (Pittenger & Duman, 2008). Treatment with antidepressants or electroconvulsive therapy results in the growth of new cells in the hippocampus in rats (Pittenger & Duman, 2008).

Abnormalities in the structure and functioning of the amygdala also are found in depression (Konarski et al., 2008). The amygdala helps direct attention to stimuli that are emotionally salient and have major significance for the individual. Studies of people with mood disorders show an enlargement and increased activity in this part of the brain, and activity in the amygdala has been observed to decrease to normal values in people successfully treated for depression (Drevets, 2001). The effects of overactivity in the amygdala are not yet entirely clear, but the overactivity may bias people toward aversive or emotionally arousing information and lead to rumination over negative memories and negative aspects of the environment (Davidson et al., 2009).

Neuroendocrine Factors

Hormones have long been thought to play a role in mood disorders, especially depression. The *neuroendocrine system* regulates a number of important hormones, which, in turn, affect basic functions such as sleep, appetite, sexual drive, and the ability to experience pleasure (to review the neuroendocrine system, see Chapter 2). These hormones also help the body respond to environmental stressors.

FIGURE 7.3 **The Hypothalamic-Pituitary-Adrenal Axis.** The hypothalamus synthesizes corticotropin-releasing hormone (CRH). CRH is transported to the pituitary gland, where it stimulates the synthesis and release of adrenocorticotropic hormone (ACTH), which then circulates to the adrenal glands, producing cortisol. Cortisol then inhibits the production of further ACTH and CRH. Normally, this process prevents too much or too prolonged physiological arousal following a stressor. In major depression, however, people often show abnormal cortisol functioning, suggesting that there is dysregulation in the hypothalamic-pituitary-adrenal (HPA) axis.

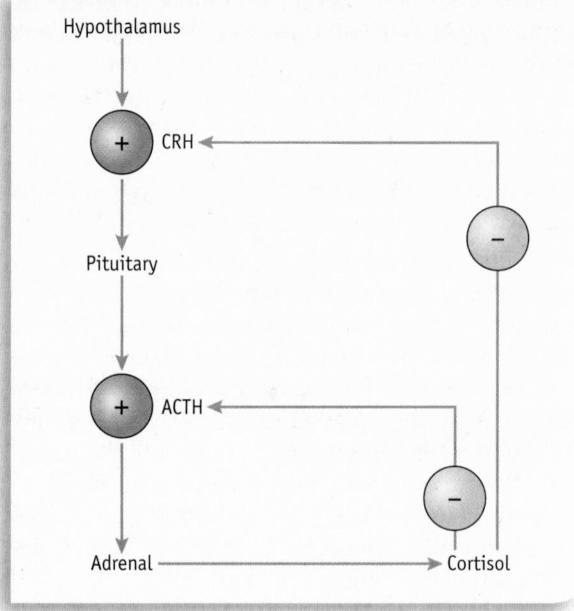

Three key components of the neuroendocrine system—the hypothalamus, pituitary, and adrenal cortex—work together in a biological feedback system richly interconnected with the amygdala, hippocampus, and cerebral cortex. This system, often referred to as the **hypothalamic-pituitary-adrenal axis** or **HPA axis,** is involved in the fight-or-flight response (see Chapter 5).

Normally, when we are confronted with a stressor, the hypothalamus releases corticotropin-releasing hormone (CRH) onto receptors on the anterior pituitary (Figure 7.3). This results in secretion of corticotropin into the plasma in the bloodstream, stimulating the adrenal cortex to release cortisol into the blood. This process helps the body fight the stressor or flee from it. The hypothalamus has cortisol receptors that detect when cortisol levels have increased and normally responds by decreasing CRH to regulate the stress response. Thus, this biological feedback loop both helps activate the HPA system during stress and calms the system when the stress is over.

People with depression tend to show elevated levels of cortisol and CRH, indicating chronic hyperactivity in the HPA axis and difficulty in the HPA axis returning to normal functioning following a stressor (Belmaker & Agam, 2008; Young & Korszun, 1998). In turn, the excess hormones produced by heightened HPA activity seem to have an inhibiting effect on receptors for the monoamine neurotransmitters. One model for the development of depression proposes that people exposed to chronic stress may develop poorly regulated neuroendocrine systems. Then, when they are exposed even to minor stressors later in life, the HPA axis overreacts and does not easily return to baseline. This overreaction creates a change in the functioning of the monoamine neurotransmitters in the brain, and an episode of depression is likely to follow (Southwick, Vythilingam, & Charney, 2005). In addition, chronic excessive exposure to cortisol may account for the reductions in volume in several areas of the brain seen in depressed people, including the hippocampus, the prefrontal cortex, and the amygdala.

Early traumatic stress, such as being the victim of incest, severe neglect, or other serious chronic stress, may lead to some of the neuroendocrine abnormalities that perhaps predispose people to depression (Southwick et al., 2005). Studies of children who have been abused or neglected show that their biological responses to stress—particularly the response of their HPA axis—often are either exaggerated or blunted (Cicchetti & Toth, 2005). Christine Heim and colleagues (Heim & Nemeroff, 2001; Heim, Plotsky, & Nemeroff, 2004) have found that women who were sexually abused as children show altered HPA responses to stress as adults, even when they are not depressed. Similarly, animal studies show that early stress (such as separation from mothers) promotes exaggerated neurobiological stress reactivity and vulnerability to depression-like responses to future stressors (Belmaker & Agam, 2008). Notably, these neurobiological vulnerabilities can be reduced in animals by providing them with subsequent supportive maternal care and/or pharmacological interventions.

Hormonal factors have often been implicated in women's greater vulnerability to depression (Nolen-Hoeksema & Hilt, 2009). Changes in the ovarian hormones, estrogen and progesterone, affect the serotonin and norepinephrine neurotransmitter systems and thus theoretically could affect mood. Some women show increases in depressed mood when their levels of estrogen and progesterone are in flux, such as during pregnancy and the postpartum period and premenstrually (DeRose, Wright, & Brooks-Gunn, 2006; Somerset, Newport, Ragan, & Stow, 2006). Further, girls show increases in their rate of depression around ages 13 to 15 (Twenge & Nolen-Hoeksema, 2002), possibly because of the hormonal changes of puberty (Angold, Castello, & Worthman, 1998). Direct links between changes in estrogen and progesterone levels and vulnerability to depression have not been found consistently, however. The hormonal changes of puberty, the menstrual cycle, the postpartum period, and menopause may trigger depression only in women with a genetic or other biological vulnerability to the disorder (Steiner, Dunn, & Born, 2003; Young & Korszun, 1999).

Psychological Theories of Depression

Behavioral theorists have focused on the role of uncontrollable stressors in producing depression. Cognitive theorists have argued that the ways people think can contribute to, and maintain, depression. Interpersonal theorists have considered the role of relationships in causing and maintaining depression. Sociocultural theorists have focused on explanations for the differences in rates of depression among sociodemographic groups.

Behavioral Theories

Depression often arises as a reaction to stressful negative events, such as the breakup of a relationship, the death of a loved one, a job loss, or a serious medical illness (Hammen, 2005). Up to 80 percent of people with depression report a negative life event prior to the onset of their depression (Mazure, 1998). People with depression are more likely than people without depression to have chronic life stressors, such as financial strain or a bad marriage. They also tend to have a history of traumatic life events, particularly events involving loss (Hammen, 2005).

Behavioral theories of depression suggest that life stress leads to depression because it reduces the positive reinforcers in a person's life (Lewinsohn & Gotlib, 1995). The person begins to withdraw, which results in a further reduction in reinforcers, which leads to more withdrawal, creating a self-perpetuating chain.

For example, a man having difficulty in his marriage may initiate interactions with his wife less often because these interactions are no longer

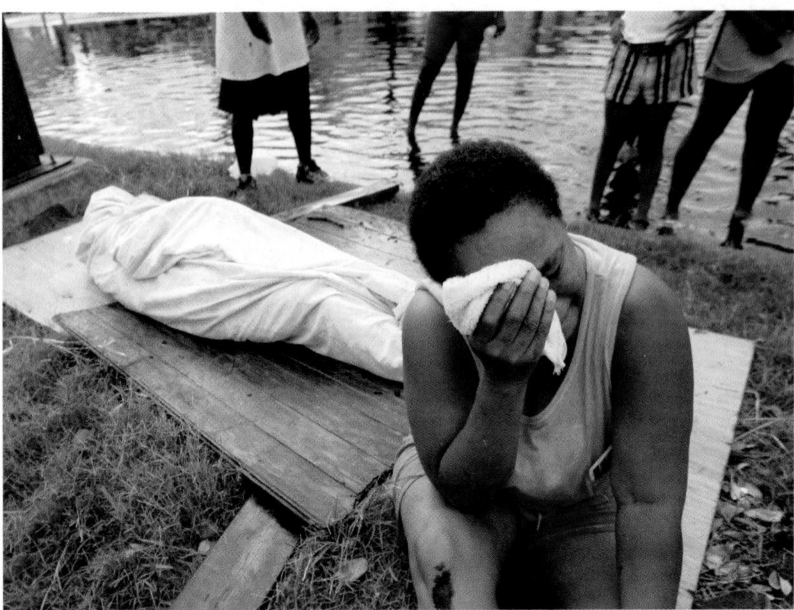

Loss of a loved one can increase the risk of depression.

as positively reinforcing as they were formerly. This only worsens the communication between him and his wife, so the relationship deteriorates. He then withdraws further and becomes depressed about this area of his life. Behavioral theorists suggest that such a pattern is especially likely in people with poor social skills, because they are more likely to experience rejection by others and to withdraw in response to this rejection than to find ways to overcome it (Lewinsohn, 1974). In addition, once a person begins engaging in depressive behaviors, these behaviors are reinforced by the sympathy and attention they engender in others.

Another behavioral theory—the **learned helplessness theory**—suggests that the type of stressful event most likely to lead to depression is an uncontrollable negative event (Seligman, 1975). Such events, especially if they are frequent or chronic, can lead people to believe they are helpless to control important outcomes in their environment. In turn, this belief in helplessness leads people to lose their motivation and to reduce actions on their part that might control the environment and leaves them unable to learn how to control situations that are controllable. These *learned helplessness deficits* are similar to the symptoms of depression: low motivation, passivity, and indecisiveness (Seligman, 1975). For example, battered women may develop the belief that they cannot control their beatings or other parts of their lives. This belief may explain their high rates of depression and their tendency to remain in abusive relationships (Koss & Kilpatrick, 2001).

Cognitive Theories

Aaron Beck (1967) argued that people with depression look at the world through a **negative cognitive triad:** They have negative views of themselves, the world, and the future. They then commit errors in thinking that support their negative cognitive triad, such as ignoring good events and exaggerating negative events. Their negative thinking both causes and perpetuates their depression. Many studies have demonstrated that people with depression show these negative ways of thinking, and some longitudinal studies have shown that these thinking styles predict depression over time (Abramson et al., 2002). Beck's theory led to one of the most widely used and successful therapies for depression—cognitive behavioral therapy.

Another cognitive theory of depression, the **reformulated learned helplessness theory,** explains how cognitive factors might influence whether a person becomes helpless and depressed following a negative event (Abramson et al., 1978; Peterson & Seligman, 1984). This theory focuses on people's causal attributions for events. A **causal attribution** is an explanation of why an event happened. According to this theory, people who habitually explain negative events by causes that are internal, stable, and global tend to blame themselves for these negative events, expect negative events to recur in the future, and expect to experience negative events in many areas of their lives. In turn, these expectations lead them to experience long-term learned helplessness deficits as well as loss of self-esteem in many areas of their lives.

For example, consider a student who becomes depressed after failing a psychology exam. The reformulated learned helplessness theory would suggest that she has blamed her failure on internal causes—she didn't study hard enough—rather than external causes—the exam was too hard. Further, she has assumed that the failure was due to stable causes, such as a lack of aptitude in psychology, rather than to unstable causes, such as the instructor not allowing enough time. Therefore, she expects to fail again. Finally, she has attributed her failure to a global cause, such as her difficulty learning the material. This global attribution would lead her to expect failure in other academic areas.

Hopelessness depression develops when people make pessimistic attributions for the most important events in their lives and perceive that they have no way to cope with the consequences of these events (Abramson, Metalsky, & Alloy, 1989). Both the reformulated learned helplessness theory and the hopelessness theory have led to much additional research (Abramson et al., 2002).

People who attribute negative events, such as failing an exam, to internal ("*I* failed"), stable ("I *always* fail"), and global causes ("I *always* fail at *everything*") may be at greater risk for depression.

One of the most definitive studies of the hopelessness theory of depression was a long-term study of college students (Alloy, Abramson, & Francis, 1999). The researchers interviewed first-year students at two universities and identified those with hopeless attributional styles and those with optimistic attributional styles. They then tracked these students for the next 2½ years, interviewing them every 6 weeks. Among the students with no history of depression, those with a hopeless attributional style were much more likely to develop a first onset of major depression than were those with an optimistic attributional style (17 percent versus 1 percent). In addition, among those who had a history of depression, students with a hopeless style were more likely to have a relapse of depression than were those with an optimistic style (27 percent versus 6 percent). Thus, a pessimistic attributional style predicted both first onset and relapse of depression.

Another cognitive theory, the *ruminative response styles theory*, focuses more on the process of thinking than on the content of thinking as a contributor to depression (Nolen-Hoeksema, Wisco, & Lyubomirsky, 2008). Some people, when they are sad, blue, and upset, focus intently on how they feel—their symptoms of fatigue and poor concentration and their sadness and hopelessness—and can identify many possible causes. They do not attempt to do anything about these causes, however, and instead continue to engage in **rumination** about their depression. Several studies have shown that people with this more ruminative coping style are more likely to develop major depression (Nolen-Hoeksema et al., 2008).

Finally, people who are depressed show a bias toward negative thinking in basic attention and memory processes (Harvey, Watkins, Mansell, & Shafran, 2004; Joormann, 2009). Depressed people are more likely than nondepressed people to dwell on negative stimuli, such as sad faces (Gotlib, Krasnoperova, Yue, & Joormann, 2004) and to have trouble disengaging their attention from negative stimuli (Joormann, 2004). After learning a list of words and then being surprised with the task of recalling those words, depressed people tend to recall more negative words than positive words, while nondepressed people show the opposite memory bias (Blaney, 1986; Matt, Vasquez, & Campbell, 1992). These biases in attention to and memory for negative information could form the basis of, and help maintain, depressed people's tendency to see the world in a negative light.

In addition, depressed people tend to show *overgeneral memory* (Williams et al., 2007). When given a simple word cue such as "angry" and asked to describe a memory that is prompted by that cue, depressed people are more likely than nondepressed people to offer memories that are highly general (e.g., "People who are mean") instead of concrete (e.g., "Jane being rude to me last Friday"). Mark Williams and colleagues (2007) suggest that depressed people develop the tendency to store and recall memories in a general fashion as a way of coping with a traumatic past. Vague, general memories are less emotionally charged and painful than memories that are rich in concrete detail, and thus they help reduce the emotional pain depressed people feel over their past. Interestingly, the one other disorder characterized by overgeneral memory is post-traumatic stress disorder (see Chapter 5), which develops specifically in response to traumatic events (Williams et al., 2007).

Interpersonal Theories

The interpersonal relationships of people with depression often are fraught with difficulty. The **interpersonal theories of depression** focus on these relationships (Coyne, 1976; Joiner & Timmons, 2009; Rudolph, 2008). Interpersonal difficulties and losses frequently precede depression and are the stressors most commonly reported as triggering depression (Hammen, 2005). Depressed people are more likely than nondepressed people to have chronic conflict in their relationships with family, friends, and co-workers (Hammen, 2005).

Depressed people may act in ways that engender interpersonal conflict (Hammen, 2005). Some depressed people have a heightened need for approval and expressions of support from others (Leadbeater, Kuperminc, Blatt, & Herzog, 1999; Rudolph & Conley, 2005) but at the same time easily perceive rejection by others, a characteristic called **rejection sensitivity** (Downey & Feldman, 1996). They engage in **excessive reassurance seeking,** constantly looking for assurances from others that they are accepted and loved (Joiner & Timmons, 2009). They never quite believe the affirmations other people give, however, and anxiously keep going back for more. After a while, their family and friends can become weary of this behavior and may become frustrated or hostile. The insecure person picks up on these cues of annoyance and panics over them. The person then feels even more insecure and engages in even more excessive reassurance seeking. Eventually, the person's social support may be withdrawn altogether, leading to even more depression.

Sociocultural Theories

Sociocultural theorists have focused on how differences in the social conditions of demographic groups lead to differences in vulnerability to depression.

Cohort Effects Historical changes may have put more recent generations at higher risk for depression than previous generations (Kessler et al., 2003; Klerman & Weissman, 1989). This age-based variation in risk is called a **cohort effect.** For example, fewer than 20 percent of people born before 1915 appear to have experienced major depression, whereas over 40 percent of people born after 1955 appear to be at risk for major depression at some time in their life. Some theorists suggest that more recent generations are at higher risk for depression because of the rapid changes in social values beginning in the 1960s and the disintegration of the family unit (Klerman & Weissman, 1989). Another possible explanation is that younger generations have unrealistically high expectations for themselves that older generations did not have.

Gender Differences We noted earlier that women are about twice as likely as men to suffer from depression (Kessler et al., 2003). Several explanations have been offered for this gender difference (Nolen-Hoeksema & Hilt, 2009).

When faced with distress, men are more likely than women to turn to alcohol to cope and to deny that they are stressed, while women are more likely than men to ruminate about their feelings and problems (Nolen-Hoeksema & Hilt, 2009). Men therefore may be more likely to develop disorders such as alcohol abuse, while women's tendency to ruminate appears to make them more likely to become depressed. These different responses to stress may be due to social norms—it is more acceptable for men to turn to alcohol and for women to ruminate (Addis, 2008; Nolen-Hoeksema & Hilt, 2009).

Perhaps also due to gender socialization, women tend to be more interpersonally oriented than men (Feingold, 1994). On one hand, women's strong interpersonal networks may give tham support in times of need. However, when bad things happen to others or when there is conflict in their relationships, women are more likely than men to report depressive symptoms (Hammen, 2003; Rudolph, 2009). Women also appear more likely than men to base their self-worth on the health of their relationships (Jack, 1991). In addition, women in most societies have less status and power than do men, and as a result they experience more prejudice, discrimination, and violence (Nolen-Hoeksema & Hilt, 2009). Sexual abuse, particularly in childhood, contributes to depression in women throughout their lifetime (Widom, DuMont, & Czaja, 2007).

Earlier in this chapter, we noted biological explanations for women's greater vulnerability to depression compared to men. Biological and sociocultural factors likely interact to lead to the large gender difference in the incidence of depression (Nolen-Hoeksema & Hilt, 2009).

Ethnicity/Race Differences In one large study done in the United States, Hispanics had a higher prevalence of depression in the previous year than European Americans (Blazer, Kessler, McGonagle, & Swartz, 1994). This may reflect the higher rates of poverty, unemployment, and discrimination among Hispanics compared to European Americans. A study of adolescents also found higher rates of depression in Hispanic youth, especially in Hispanic girls (McLaughlin, Hilt, & Nolen-Hoeksema, 2007).

Adult studies indicate that African Americans have lower rates of depression than European Americans (e.g., Blazer et al., 1994). This may seem puzzling given the disadvantaged status of African Americans in U.S. society. However,

African Americans have high rates of anxiety disorders, suggesting that the stress of their social status may make them especially prone to anxiety disorders rather than to depression. Other studies have found extremely high rates of depression among Native Americans, especially the young (Saluja et al., 2004). Depression among Native American youth is tied to poverty, hopelessness, and alcoholism.

Cross-Cultural Differences Cross-national studies have suggested that the prevalence of major depression is lower in less industrialized and less modern countries than in more industrialized and more modern countries (Cross-National Collaborative Group, 1992; Lepine, 2001). The fast-paced lifestyles of people in modern industrialized societies, with their lack of stable social support and community values, may be toxic to mental health. In contrast, the community- and family-oriented lifestyles of less modern societies may be beneficial to mental health, despite the physical hardships faced by many people in these societies.

Alternately, some researchers have suggested that people in less modern cultures may tend to manifest depression through physical complaints rather than psychological symptoms of depression such as sadness, loss of motivation, and hopelessness about the future (Tsai & Chentsova-Dutton, 2002). For example, a study of refugees in Somalia found that they had a concept similar to the concept of sadness, which they called *murug* (Carroll, 2004). *Murug* presents itself when an individual has lost a loved one or when some other major negative life event has occurred. The symptoms of *murug,* however, are headaches and social withdrawal. Similarly, people in China facing severe stress often complain of *neurasthenia,* a collection of physical symptoms that include chronic headaches, pain in the joints, nausea, lack of energy, and palpitations, as described in this case study.

CASE STUDY

Lin Hung is a 24-year-old worker in a machine factory in China who complains of headaches, dizziness, weakness, lack of energy, insomnia, bad dreams, poor memory, and a stiff neck. Pain, weakness, and dizziness, along with bouts of palpitations, are his chief symptoms. His symptoms began 6 months ago, and they are gradually worsening. His factory doctors believe he has a heart problem, but repeated electrocardiograms have been normal. He believes he has a serious bodily disorder that is worsened by his work and that interferes with his ability to carry out his job responsibilities. Until his father retired from the job Lin now holds, Lin was a soldier living not far from home. He didn't want to leave the army, but his father was anxious to retire so he could move to a new apartment owned by his factory in another city. Fearing that his son would not be able to stay in the army and thereafter would not find work, Lin's father pressured him to take over his job, a job the younger Lin never liked or wanted for himself. Lin Hung reluctantly agreed but now finds he cannot adjust to the work. He did not want to be a machinist and cries when he recounts that this is what he must be for the rest of his life. Moreover, he is despondent and lonely living so far away from his parents. He has no friends at work and feels lonely living in the dormitory. He has a girlfriend, but he cannot see her regularly anymore, owing to the change in work sites. They wish to marry, but his parents, who have a serious financial problem because of a very low pension, cannot provide the expected furniture, room, or any financial help.The leaders of his work unit are against the marriage because he is too young. They also criticize him for his poor work performance and frequent days missed from work owing to sickness. (Adapted from Kleinman & Kleinman, 1985, pp. 454–455)

When questioning Lin Hung, psychiatrists trained in Western medicine diagnosed major depressive disorder. Like many Chinese, Lin rejected the psychological diagnosis, believing firmly that he was suffering solely from a physical disorder. A psychological diagnosis would not have garnered any sympathy from Lin's co-workers or family; a physical diagnosis, on the other hand, could provide him with an acceptable reason to leave his job and return to his family.

Indeed, the very concept of depression may be unique to Western cultures (Tsai & Chentsova-Dutton, 2002). Symptoms such as a decrease in self-esteem and lack of interest in pleasurable activities are abnormal only in cultures that expect people to have high self-esteem and to seek out sources of positive emotions. These are expectations in Western culture but not in many other cultures around the world.

TEST YOURSELF

1. What neurotransmitters and brain abnormalities are implicated in depression?
2. What abnormalities of the hypothalamic-pituitary-adrenal (HPA) axis do depressed people tend to show?
3. What do the behavioral theories say about the causes of depression?
4. How do cognitive theorists explain depression?
5. How do interpersonal theorists explain depression?
6. What factors do sociocultural theories of depression focus on?

APPLY IT Suppose a new study found that depressed people show less activity than nondepressed people in an area of the brain called the caudate nucleus. What could you conclude?

a. Low activity of the caudate causes depression.
b. Depression causes low activity of the caudate.
c. Low activity of the caudate and depression are related to each other.
d. Some other biological factor causes both low activity of the caudate and depression.

Answers appear online at www.mhhe.com/nolen5e.

THEORIES OF BIPOLAR DISORDER

Most existing theories of bipolar disorder focus on biological causes. In recent years, however, there has been increasing interest in psychological and social contributors to new episodes in bipolar disorder.

Biological Theories of Bipolar Disorder

Genetic Factors

Bipolar disorder is strongly and consistently linked to genetic factors, although the specific genetic abnormalities that contribute to bipolar disorder are not yet known. First-degree relatives (parents, children, and siblings) of people with bipolar disorder have 5 to 10 times higher rates of both bipolar disorder and depressive disorders than relatives of people without bipolar disorder (Farmer, Elkin, & McGuffin, 2007). Also, the identical twins of individuals with bipolar disorder are 45 to 75 times more likely to develop the disorder than are people in the general population (McGuffin et al., 2003).

Brain Abnormalities

Like unipolar depression, bipolar disorder is associated with abnormalities in the structure and functioning of the amygdala, which is involved in the processing of emotions (Figure 7.4; Rich et al., 2007), and the prefrontal cortex, which is involved in cognitive control of emotion, planning, and judgment (Konarski et al., 2008). In contrast to unipolar depression, bipolar disorder has not consistently been associated with alterations in the size or functioning of the hippocampus.

An area of the brain called the *striatum,* part of a structure called the basal ganglia, is involved in the processing of environmental cues of reward. For example, this brain structure becomes active when rewarding stimuli, such as tasty food or opportunities to earn money, are perceived by the individual. This area of the brain is activated abnormally in people with bipolar disorder, but not consistently so in people with major depression, suggesting that people with bipolar disorder may be hypersensitive to rewarding cues in the environment (Caligiuri et al., 2003; Saxena et al., 2002). A circuit from the prefrontal cortex through the striatum to the amygdala is involved in adaptation to changing contingencies of reward (i.e., knowing when you should drop one strategy in favor of another in order to get a reward). Some researchers suggest that individuals with bipolar disorder have abnormalities in the functioning of this circuit that lead them to have inflexible responses to reward (Leibenluft & Rich, 2008). When they are in a manic phase, they inflexibly and excessively seek reward; when they are in a depressive phase, they are highly insensitive to reward (Depue & Iacono, 1989).

Some studies suggest that youth with bipolar disorder have abnormalities in the white matter of the brain, particularly in the prefrontal cortex (Frazier et al., 2007; Pillai et al., 2002). White matter is tissue that connects various structures in the brain and transmits messages between them. White matter abnormalities are found in children at their first episodes of bipolar disorder, before they have been medicated (Adler et al., 2006), and in children at risk for bipolar disorder because of family history (Frazier et al., 2007). White matter abnormalities could result in the prefrontal area of the brain having difficulty communicating with and exerting control over other areas, such as the amygdala, and thus in the disorganized emotions and extreme behavior characteristic of bipolar disorder.

Neurotransmitter Factors

The monoamine neurotransmitters have been implicated in bipolar disorder as well as in unipolar depression. In particular, several studies have suggested that dysregulation in the dopamine system contributes to bipolar disorder (Leibenluft & Rich, 2008). High levels of dopamine are thought to be associated with high reward seeking, while low levels are associated with insensitivity to reward. Thus, dysregulation in the dopamine system may lead to excessive reward seeking during the manic phase and a lack of reward seeking in the depressed phase (Berk et al., 2007; Depue & Iacono, 1989).

FIGURE 7.4 **Amygdala Activation in Youth with Bipolar Disorder.** Youth with bipolar disorder showed significantly greater amygdala activation (yellow area) than did healthy youth when rating their fear of neutral faces.

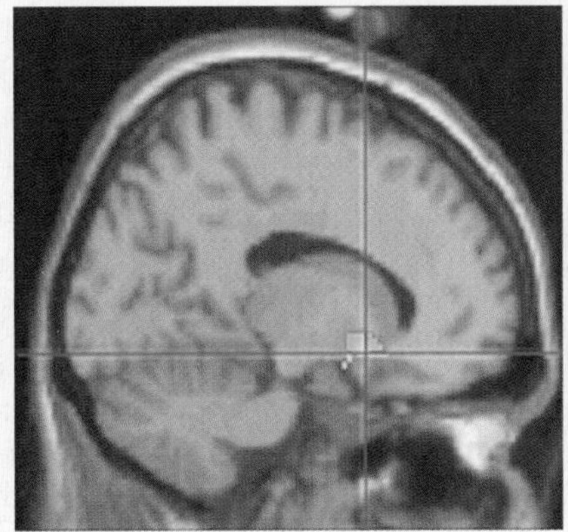
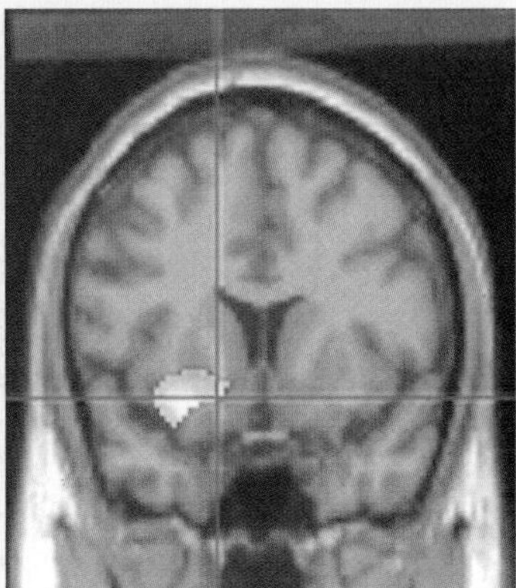

Source: Leibenluft & Rich, 2008.

Psychosocial Contributors to Bipolar Disorder

In line with biological evidence that dysregulation of reward systems plays a role in bipolar disorder, psychologists have been examining relationships between bipolar disorder and behavioral indicators of sensitivity to reward. In some of these studies, individuals play games on the computer, such as gambling games, that assess their willingness to take risks in order to pursue possible rewards and their ability to detect what kinds of behaviors will be rewarded. These studies confirm that people with bipolar disorder, even when they are asymptomatic, show greater sensitivity to reward than do people without the disorder (Alloy et al., 2008; Johnson, Cuellar, & Miller, 2009). In addition, a study that followed people with bipolar disorder for nearly 3 years found that those with greater sensitivity to reward relapsed into manic or hypomanic symptoms sooner than did those with lower sensitivity to reward (Alloy et al., 2008). In contrast, individuals with high sensitivity to punishment relapsed into depressive episodes sooner than did those with lower sensitivity.

Another psychological factor that has been studied in people with bipolar disorder is stress. Experiencing stressful events and living in an unsupportive family may trigger new episodes of bipolar disorder (Altman et al., 2006; Frank, Swartz, & Kupfer, 2000; Hlastsala et al., 2000). Even positive events can trigger new episodes of mania or hypomania, particularly if they involve striving for goals seen as highly rewarding. A study of college students found that among those with bipolar disorder, preparing for and completing exams tended to trigger hypomanic symptoms, particularly among students who were highly sensitive to rewards (Nusslock et al., 2007). Thus, goal-striving situations may trigger high reward sensitivity, which in turn triggers manic or hypomanic symptoms in people with bipolar disorder.

Changes in bodily rhythms or usual routines also can trigger episodes in people with bipolar disorder (Frank et al., 2000). For example, changes in sleep and eating patterns can lead to relapse. Significant changes in daily routine can do the same, particularly if they are due to changes in the social climate, such as starting a new job. A psychosocial therapy we discuss later in this chapter, interpersonal and social rhythm therapy, helps people with bipolar disorder keep their bodily and social rhythms regular.

TEST YOURSELF

1. How strong a role do genetic factors play in bipolar disorder?
2. What areas of the brain are implicated in bipolar disorder?
3. What neurotransmitters are implicated in bipolar disorder?
4. What psychosocial factors play a role in bipolar disorder?

APPLY IT The reward sensitivity theories suggest that people with bipolar disorder would do which of the following:

a. gamble more during manic episodes
b. gamble more during depressed episodes
c. dislike gambling because they don't like to lose

Answers appear online at www.mhhe.com/nolen5e.

TREATMENT OF MOOD DISORDERS

Many forms of treatment are now available for sufferers of mood disorders. In any given year, however, only about half the people who have bipolar disorder and about 60 percent of the people having an episode of major depression seek treatment (Kessler et al., 2003; Merikangas et al., 2007). Most often, those who eventually do seek treatment do so a number of years after the onset of their symptoms.

Biological Treatments for Mood Disorders

Most of the biological treatments for depression and bipolar disorder are drug treatments. In addition to being treated with drugs, some people with mood disorders are treated with electroconvulsive therapy (ECT). Three new treatments for mood disorders—repetitive transcranial magnetic stimulation (rTMS), vagus nerve stimulation, and deep brain stimulation—hold out hope for many people. People with seasonal affective disorder (SAD) can benefit from a simple therapy: exposure to bright lights.

Drug Treatments for Depression

The late twentieth century saw rapid growth in the number of drugs available for depression and in their use by large numbers of people. Table 7.5 summarizes the classes of drugs commonly used in the treatment of unipolar depressive disorders and the depressive symptoms of bipolar disorder. Initially, they were thought to work by altering levels of the neurotransmitters serotonin, norepinephrine, or dopamine in synapses or by affecting the receptors for these neurotransmitters. However, these changes occur within hours or days of taking the drugs, whereas reductions in depressive symptoms typically don't appear for weeks. More recent theories suggest that these drugs have slow-emerging effects on intracellular processes in the neurotransmitter systems discussed earlier (see Figure 7.1) and on the action of genes that regulate neurotransmission, the limbic system, and the stress response (Thase & Denko, 2008).

All the different antidepressant drugs currently available reduce depression in about 50 to 60 percent of people who take them (Thase & Denko, 2008). These medications appear to work better for treating severe and chronic depression than for treating mild-to-moderate depression. A meta-analysis of 718 patients from six studies found that antidepressants were substantially better than a placebo in reducing symptoms only in very severely depressed patients; in patients with mild-to-moderate depression, the effects of the antidepressants were small to nonexistent (Fournier et al., 2010; see also Khan et al., 2002; Kirsch et al., 2008).

The choice of which drug to begin with tends to be based on the experience of the physician and concerns about the patient's ability to tolerate side effects. It typically takes a few weeks to know whether a person will respond to a drug. Most people try more than one medication before they find the one that works for them. These days, antidepressant drugs are used to relieve the acute symptoms of depression. Then individuals usually are maintained on antidepressant drugs for at least 6 months after their symptoms have subsided, to prevent relapse. Discontinuing antidepressant use during the first 6 to 9 months after symptoms subside seems to double the risk of relapse in severe unipolar depression (Geddes et al., 2004). People with bipolar disorder take antidepressants continually to prevent a relapse of depression.

Selective Serotonin Reuptake Inhibitors

The **selective serotonin reuptake inhibitors,** or **SSRIs,** are widely used to treat depressive symptoms. SSRIs are not more effective in the treatment of depression than the other available antidepressants, but they have fewer difficult-to-tolerate side effects (Thase & Denko, 2008). In addition, they are much safer if taken in overdose than many of the older antidepressants, such as the tricyclic antidepressants and the monoamine oxidase inhibitors, described below. Finally, they have positive effects on a wide range of symptoms that co-occur with depression, including anxiety, eating disorders, and impulsiveness.

The SSRIs do have side effects, however, and 5 to 10 percent of people have to discontinue their use because of these side effects (Thase & Denko, 2008). The most common side effects are gastrointestinal symptoms (e.g., nausea and diarrhea), tremor, nervousness, insomnia, daytime sleepiness, diminished sex drive, and difficulty achieving orgasm. When people first begin taking an SSRI, they sometimes report feeling "jittery" or having a feeling of "crawling out of one's skin." Some people who have bipolar disorder may develop manic symptoms when they take an SSRI. The agitation some people experience while taking an SSRI may contribute to an increase in suicidal thought and behavior. This risk may be greatest for children and adolescents; reviews of controlled studies show that approximately 4 percent of youth treated with an SSRI show suicidal thought and behavior, about double the percentage of youth on a placebo (Thase & Denko, 2008). SSRIs

TABLE 7.5 Antidepressant Medications

A number of different types of medication are available for the treatment of depression.

Class	Generic Name	Brand Name	Prominent Side Effects
Selective serotonin reuptake inhibitors	Citalopram Escitalopram Fluoxetine Flovoxamine Paroxetine Sertraline	Celexa Lexapro Prozac Luvox Paxil Zoloft	Nausea, diarrhea, insomnia, tremor, sexual dysfunction, daytime sedation, agitation/restlessness, possible increases in suicidal thought and behavior.
Selective serotonin-norepinephrine reuptake inhibitors	Venlafaxine Duloxetine	Effexor Cymbalta	Nausea, diarrhea, insomnia, tremor, sexual dysfunction, daytime sedation, agitation/restlessness, possible increases in suicidal thought and behavior, increased sweating, dry mouth, rapid heartbeat, headaches.
Norepinephrine-dopamine reuptake inhibitor	Bupropion	Wellbutrin Zyban	Nausea, vomiting, insomnia, headaches, seizures.
Tricyclic antidepressants	Amitriptyline Clomipramine Doxepin Imipramine Trimipramine Desipramine Nortriptyline Protriptyline Amoxapine Maprotiline	Elavil Anafranil Sinequan Tofranil Surmontil Norpramin Aventyl Vivactil Ascendin Ludiomil	Anticholinergic effects (dry mouth, constipation, difficulty urinating, blurred vision, memory impairment, confusion). Less commonly: difficulty sleeping, headaches, tremor, appetite change. Especially problematic: drop in blood pressure, cardiac arrhythmias for people with heart problems, can be lethal in overdose.
Monoamine oxidase inhibitors	Isocarboxazid Phenelzine Tranylcypromine	Marplan Nardil Parnate	Dry mouth, constipation, difficulty urinating, blurred vision, memory impairment, confusion. Less commonly: difficulty sleeping, headaches, tremor, appetite change. Especially problematic: drop in blood pressure, cardiac arrhythmias for people with heart problems, potentially life-threatening increase in blood pressure following ingestion of certain foods or medications.

are associated with a smaller increase in suicidal thought and behavior among adults than among children, and among the elderly SSRIs are associated with a reduction in suicidal thought and behavior.

Selective Serotonin-Norepinephrine Reuptake Inhibitors The **selective serotonin-norepinephrine reuptake inhibitors (SNRIs)** were designed to affect levels of norepinephrine as well as serotonin. Perhaps because these drugs influence both neurotransmitters, they show a slight advantage over the selective serotonin reuptake inhibitors in preventing a relapse of depression (Nemeroff et al., 2007). The dual action of these drugs also may account for their slightly broader array of side effects compared to the SSRIs (see Table 7.5).

Bupropion: A Norepinephrine-Dopamine Reuptake Inhibitor Bupropion affects the norepinephrine and dopamine systems and thus is known as a **norepinephrine-dopamine reuptake inhibitor.** It may be especially useful in treating people suffering from psychomotor retardation, anhedonia, hypersomnia, cognitive slowing, inattention,

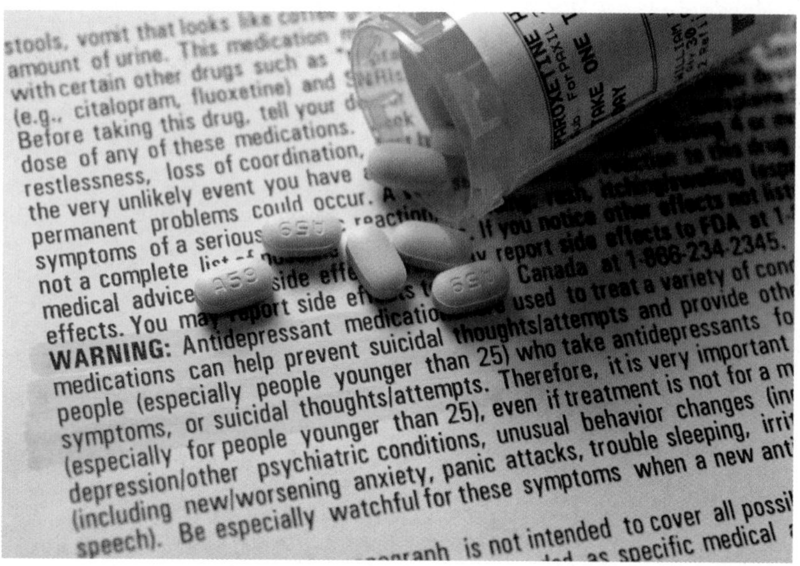

The Federal Drug Administration (FDA) requires warnings for SSRIs saying that they may increase the risk of suicide.

and craving (e.g., bupropion can help people stop craving cigarettes). In addition, bupropion appears to overcome the sexual dysfunction side effects of the SSRIs and thus sometimes is used in conjunction with them (Thase & Denko, 2008).

Tricyclic Antidepressants Although the **tricyclic antidepressant drugs** were some of the first drugs shown to consistently relieve depression, they are used less frequently these days than the other drugs reviewed in this section (Thase & Denko, 2008). This is due in large part to their numerous side effects, many of which are called *anticholinergic effects* because they are related to levels of the neurotransmitter acetylcholine. The tricyclic antidepressants also can cause a drop in blood pressure and cardiac arrhythmia in people with heart problems. Further, the tricyclics can be fatal in overdose, which is only three to four times the average daily prescription for the drug; for this reason, physicians are wary of prescribing these drugs, particularly for people with depression who might be suicidal.

Monoamine Oxidase Inhibitors Another older class of drugs that is no longer used frequently to treat depression is the **monoamine oxidase inhibitors (MAOIs).** MAO is an enzyme that causes the breakdown of the monoamine neurotransmitters in the synapse. MAOIs decrease the action of MAO and thereby increase the levels of the neurotransmitters in the synapses.

The MAOIs are as effective as the tricyclic antidepressants, but their side effects are potentially quite dangerous (Thase & Denko, 2008). When people taking MAOIs ingest aged cheese, red wine, or beer, they can experience a potentially fatal rise in blood pressure. The MAOIs also can interact with several drugs, including antihypertension medications and over-the-counter drugs such as antihistamines. The MAOIs also can cause liver damage, weight gain, severe lowering of blood pressure, and several of the same side effects caused by the tricyclic antidepressants.

Mood Stabilizers

People with bipolar disorder may take antidepressants to relieve their depressive symptoms, but they also must take a mood stabilizer (lithium or an anticonvulsant medication) to relieve or prevent symptoms of mania. Lithium can also have positive effects on depressive symptoms in people with unipolar depression. In addition, many people are prescribed atypical antipsychotic medications.

Lithium **Lithium** may work by improving the functioning of the intracellular processes that appear to be abnormal in the mood disorders (Belmaker, 2004). Most people with bipolar disorder take lithium even when they have no symptoms of mania or depression in order to prevent relapses. People maintained on adequate doses of lithium have significantly fewer relapses of mania and depression than people with bipolar disorder not maintained on lithium (Geddes et al., 2004; Ghaemi, Pardo, & Hsu, 2004). Lithium is also quite effective in reducing suicide risk, as we discuss later in this chapter.

Although lithium has literally been a lifesaver for many people with mood disorders, it poses some problems. The difference between an effective dose of lithium and a toxic dose is small, leaving a narrow window of therapeutic effectiveness. People who take lithium must be monitored carefully by physicians, who can determine whether the dosage of lithium is adequate to relieve their symptoms but not so large as to induce toxic side effects. The side effects of lithium range from annoying to life threatening. Many patients experience abdominal pain, nausea, vomiting, diarrhea, tremors, and twitches. People on lithium complain of blurred vision and problems in concentration and attention that interfere with their ability to work. Lithium can cause diabetes, hypothyroidism, and kidney dysfunction and can contribute to birth defects if taken during the first trimester of pregnancy. Up to 55 percent of patients develop resistance to lithium within 3 years, and only about 33 percent of patients remain symptom-free on lithium (Nemeroff, 2000).

Anticonvulsant and Atypical Antipsychotic Medications In the mid-1990s, it was discovered that a medication that helps reduce convulsions, valproate (trade name Depakote), also helped stabilize mood in people with bipolar disorder. Another **anticonvulsant** medication, carbamazepine (trade names Tegretol, Equetro) has been approved for use in treating bipolar disorder. The side effects of carbamazepine include blurred vision, fatigue, vertigo, dizziness, rash, nausea, drowsiness, and liver disease. Valproate seems to induce many fewer side effects and is used more often than carbamazepine (Thase & Denko, 2008). But the anticonvulsants can cause birth defects if women take them while pregnant, and they do not prevent suicide as effectively as lithium does. The anticonvulsants may work by restoring the balance between the neurotransmitter systems in the amygdala (Thase & Denko, 2008).

The **atypical antipsychotic** medications, which are described in more detail in Chapter 8, are also used to quell the symptoms of severe mania (Thase & Denko, 2008). These drugs, which include olanzapine (Zyprexa), ariprizole (Abilify), quetiapine (Seroquel), and risperidone (Risperdal), reduce functional levels of dopamine and seem to be especially useful in the treatment of psychotic manic symptoms. The side effects of these drugs can include weight gain and metabolic changes.

Electroconvulsive Therapy

Perhaps the most controversial of the biological treatments for mood disorders is **electroconvulsive therapy (ECT).** ECT was introduced in the early twentieth century, originally as a treatment for schizophrenia (see Chapter 2). It consists of a series of treatments in which a brain seizure is induced by passing electrical current through the patient's brain. Patients are first anesthetized and given muscle relaxants so they are not conscious when they have the seizure and so their muscles do not jerk violently during the seizure. Metal electrodes are taped to the head, and a current of 70 to 130 volts is passed through one side of the brain for about ½ second. Patients typically have a convulsion that lasts about 1 minute. The full ECT treatment consists of 6 to 12 sessions. Neuroimaging studies show that ECT results in decreases in metabolic activity in several regions of the brain, including the frontal cortex and the anterior cingulate, although the mechanisms by which ECT relieves depressive symptoms are not clear (Henry et al., 2001; Oquendo et al., 2001).

ECT can lead to memory loss and difficulty learning new information (Sackeim et al., 2007). When ECT was first developed, it was administered to both sides of the brain, and the effects on memory and learning sometimes were severe and permanent. These days, ECT usually is delivered to only one side of the brain—usually the right side, because this side is less involved in learning and memory. As a result, patients undergoing modern ECT are less likely to experience significant or long-term memory loss or learning difficulties, but people who have undergone ECT still experience a significant increase in memory problems (Sackeim et al., 2007). In addition, because this unilateral administration sometimes is not as effective as bilateral administration, some people are still given bilateral ECT. Although ECT can be extremely effective in eliminating the symptoms of depression, the relapse rate among people who have undergone ECT can be as high as 85 percent (Fink, 2001).

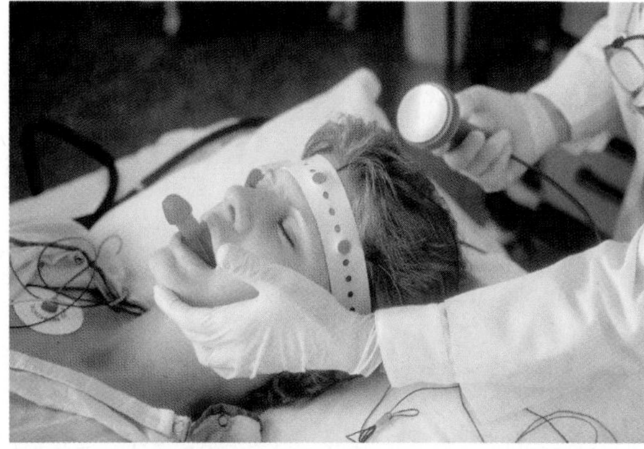

Electroconvulsive therapy is a controversial but effective treatment for depression.

Newer Methods of Brain Stimulation

In recent years, researchers have been investigating new methods of stimulating the brain without applying electric current. Each of these methods has been shown in randomized clinical trials to result in more improvement in depressive symptoms than a placebo in patients with unipolar depression or bipolar disorder whose depressive symptoms have not responded to other forms of treatment (see reviews by Dougherty & Rauch, 2007b; George, 2007). However, more research on these methods is needed.

In the procedure known as **repetitive transcranial magnetic stimulation (rTMS),** scientists expose patients to repeated, high-intensity magnetic pulses that are focused on particular brain structures (Figure 7.5a). In treating people with depression, researchers have targeted the left prefrontal cortex, which tends to show abnormally low metabolic activity in some people with

FIGURE 7.5 Newer Methods of Brain Stimulation. (a) Transcranial magnetic stimulation exposes patients to repeated, high-intensity magnetic pulses focused on particular brain structures. (b) In vagus nerve stimulation, electrodes are attached to the vagus nerve, a part of the autonomic nervous system that carries information to several areas of the brain. (c) In deep brain stimulation, electrodes are implanted deep in the brain and connected to a pulse generator placed under the skin. The generator then delivers stimulation to targeted brain areas.

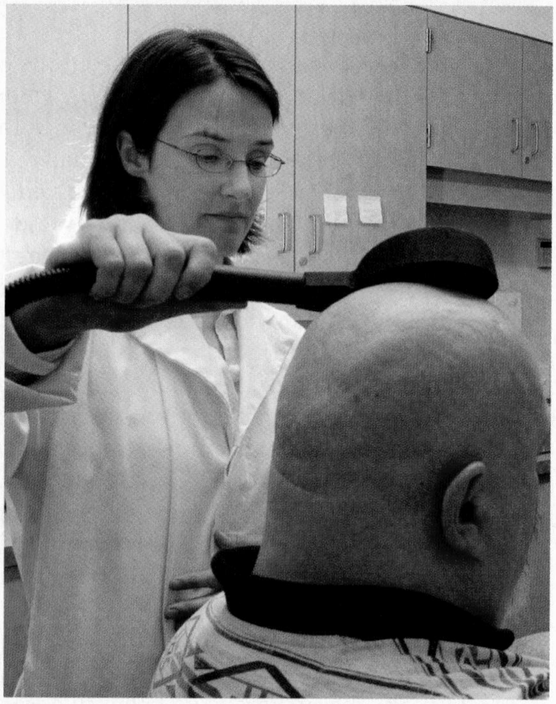

(a)

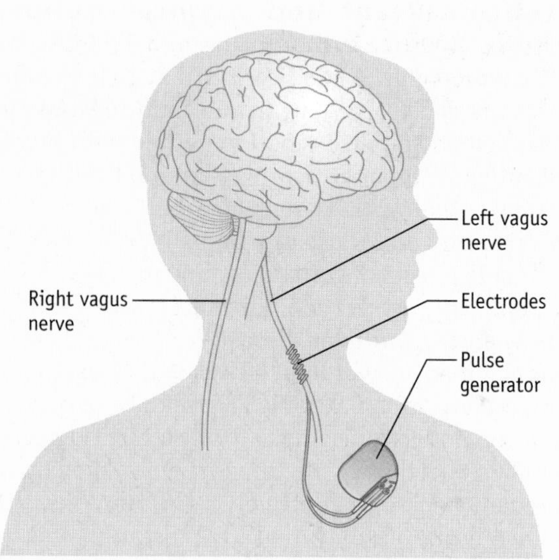

(b)

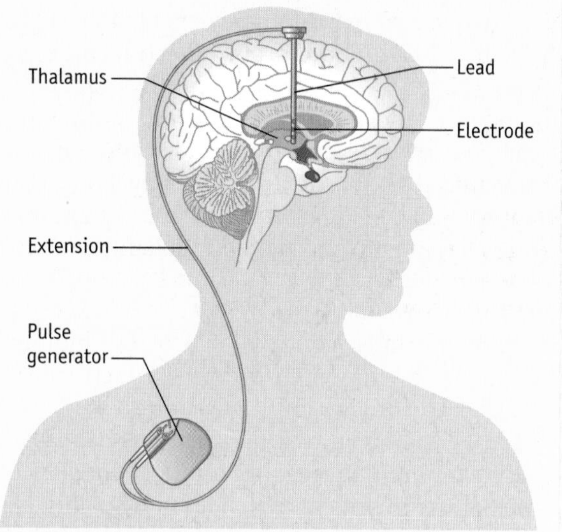

(c)

depression. Patients who receive rTMS report few side effects—usually only minor headaches treatable by aspirin. Patients can remain awake, rather than having to be anesthetized as in electroconvulsive therapy (ECT), thereby avoiding possible complications of anesthesia.

Another new method that holds considerable promise in the treatment of serious depression is **vagus nerve stimulation (VNS;** Figure 7.5b). The vagus nerve, part of the autonomic nervous system, carries information from the head, neck, thorax, and abdomen to several areas of the brain, including the hypothalamus and amygdala, which are involved in depression. In vagus nerve stimulation, the vagus nerve is stimulated by a small electronic device, much like a cardiac pacemaker, that is surgically implanted under the patient's skin in the left chest wall. How VNS relieves depression is not entirely clear, but positron-emission studies show that VNS results in increased activity in the hypothalamus and amygdala, which may have antidepressant effects (George et al., 2000).

The newest and least studied procedure to date is **deep brain stimulation,** in which electrodes are surgically implanted in specific areas of the brain (Figure 7.5c). The electrodes are connected to a pulse generator that is placed under the skin

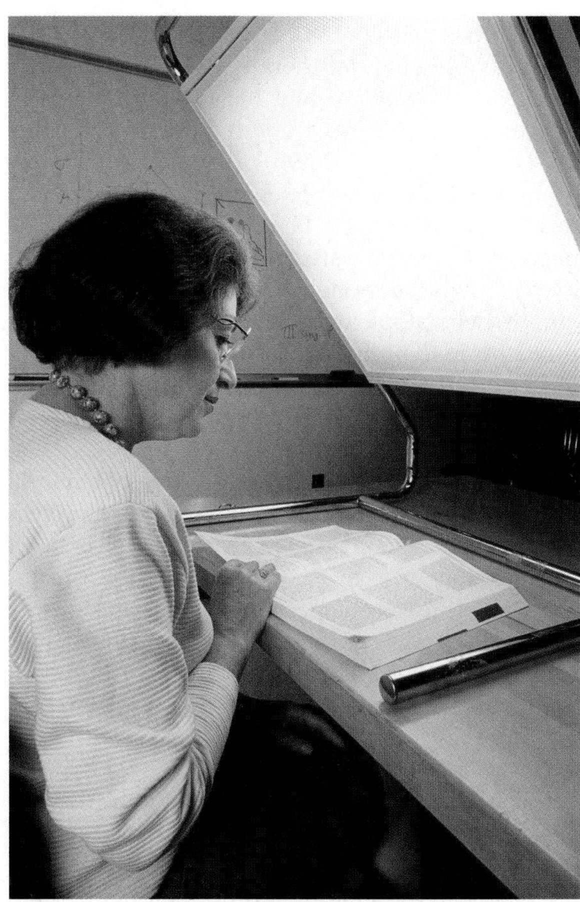

Use of light boxes can reduce depression in some people with seasonal affective disorder.

and stimulates these brain areas. Very small trials of deep brain stimulation have shown promise in relieving intractable depression (Mayberg et al., 2005).

Light Therapy

Recall that seasonal affective disorder (SAD) is a form of mood disorder in which people become depressed during the winter months, when there are the fewest hours of daylight. Their moods improve in the summer months, when there are more hours of daylight each day. It turns out that exposing people with SAD to bright lights for a few hours each day during the winter months can significantly reduce some people's symptoms. One study found that 53 percent of people with SAD responded to light therapy (Rohan et al., 2007).

Light therapy may help reduce seasonal affective disorder by resetting circadian rhythms, natural cycles of biological activity that occur every 24 hours. The production of several hormones and neurotransmitters varies over the course of the day according to circadian rhythms. These rhythms are regulated by internal clocks but can be affected by environmental stimuli, including light. People with depression sometimes show dysregulation of their circadian rhythms. Light therapy may work by resetting circadian rhythms, thereby normalizing the production of hormones and neurotransmitters (Westrin & Lam, 2007).

Another theory is that light therapy works by decreasing levels of the hormone melatonin, which is secreted by the pineal gland (Westrin & Lam, 2007). Decreasing melatonin levels can increase the levels of norepinephrine and serotonin, reducing the symptoms of depression. Also, studies suggest that exposure to bright lights may directly increase serotonin levels, also decreasing depression.

Psychological Treatments for Mood Disorders

Each of the psychological theories has led to a treatment designed to overcome those factors that the theory asserts cause mood disorders.

Behavior Therapy

Behavior therapy focuses on increasing positive reinforcers and decreasing aversive experiences in an individual's life by helping the depressed person change his or her patterns of interaction with the environment and with other people (Hollon, Haman, & Brown, 2002). Behavior therapy is designed to be short-term, lasting about 12 weeks.

The first phase of behavior therapy involves a *functional analysis* of the connections between specific circumstances and the depressed person's symptoms. When does the depressed person feel worst? Are there any situations in which he or she feels better? This analysis helps the therapist pinpoint the behaviors and interaction patterns that need to be the focus of therapy. It also helps the client understand the intimate connections between his or her symptoms and his or her daily activities or interactions.

Once the circumstances that precipitate the client's depressive symptoms are identified, therapists help the client change aspects of the environment that are contributing to the depression, such as isolation. They will teach depressed clients skills for changing their negative circumstances, particularly negative social interactions. They also will help clients learn new skills, such as relaxation techniques, for managing their moods in unpleasant situations. For example, consider the following case study.

Inactivity may contribute to depression. Behavioral therapy encourages people to become more active.

CASE STUDY

Mark worked constantly. When he was not actually at work, he was working at home. He had a position of considerable responsibility and was convinced that if he didn't stay focused on his job, he'd miss something that would result in his being fired or kicked off the career ladder. Mark had not taken a vacation in several years. Although he wanted to continue to get pay raises and promotions, as he has each year, he was also painfully aware that life was passing him by. He felt stressed, depressed, and hopeless about ever having a "normal" life.

Mark clearly felt rewarded for his one-dimensional life with praise, pay raises, promotions, and the absence of mistakes for which he might get punished. Mark's behavior was governed by his work focus. He engaged in no social activities, lived alone, and did not organize his time to include anything but his work. The behavior therapist suggested that if he wanted to improve his quality of life, and his outlook on life, he must learn some very specific new behaviors. Mark was encouraged to schedule time for social and recreational opportunities. He learned he needed to actively and deliberately do things that are fun and pleasurable. He and the therapist practiced new ways to meet people and form social relationships (friendships, dating). The therapist also taught him relaxation skills to reduce his stress. Eventually, Mark felt a new sense of control over his life and his depression lifted. (Adapted from Yapko, 1997)

Cognitive-Behavioral Therapy

Cognitive-behavioral therapy (CBT) represents a blending of cognitive and behavioral theories of depression (Beck, Weissman, Lester, & Trexler, 1974; Ellis & Harper, 1961; Lewinsohn, Muñoz, Youngren, & Zeiss, 1986; Rehm, 1977). This therapy has two general goals. First, it aims to change the negative, hopeless patterns of thinking described by the cognitive models of depression. Second, it aims to help people with depression solve concrete problems in their lives and develop skills for being more effective in their world so they no longer have the deficits in reinforcers described by behavioral theories of depression.

Like behavior therapy, cognitive-behavioral therapy is designed to be brief and time-limited. The therapist and client usually will agree on a set of goals they wish to accomplish in 6 to 12 weeks. These goals focus on specific problems that clients believe are connected to their depression, such as problems in their marriage or dissatisfaction with their job. From the beginning of therapy, the therapist urges clients to set their own goals and make their own decisions.

The first step in cognitive behavioral therapy is to help clients discover the negative automatic thoughts they habitually have and understand the link between those thoughts and their depression. Often, the therapist will assign clients the homework of keeping track of times when they feel sad or depressed and writing down on record sheets, such as the one in Figure 7.6, what is going through their mind at such times.

The second step in cognitive-behavioral therapy is to help clients challenge their negative thoughts. People with depression often believe that there is only one way to interpret a situation—their negative way. Therapists use a series of questions to help clients consider alternative ways of thinking about a situation and the pros and cons of these alternatives, such as "What is the evidence that you are right in the way you are interpreting this situation?" "Are there other ways of looking at this situation?" and "What can you do if the worst-case scenario comes true?"

The third step in cognitive-behavioral therapy is to help clients recognize the deeper, basic beliefs or assumptions they might hold that are feeding their depression. These might be beliefs such as "If I'm not loved by everyone, I'm a failure" or "If I'm not a complete success at everything, my life is worthless." The therapist will help clients question such beliefs and decide if they truly want to base their lives on them. The case of Susan illustrates some of the cognitive components of cognitive-behavioral therapy.

FIGURE 7.6 **An Automatic Thoughts Record Used in Cognitive-Behavioral Therapy.** In cognitive-behavioral therapy, patients keep a record of the negative thoughts that arise when they feel negative emotions. This record is then used in therapy to challenge the patients' depressive thinking.

Date	Event	Emotion	Automatic thoughts
April 4	Boss seemed annoyed.	Sad, anxious, worried	Oh, what have I done now? If I keep making him mad, I'm going to get fired.
April 5	Husband didn't want to make love.	Sad	I'm so fat and ugly.
April 7	Boss yelled at another employee.	Anxious	I'm next.
April 9	Husband said he's taking a long business trip next month.	Sad, defeated	He's probably got a mistress somewhere. My marriage is falling apart.
April 10	Neighbor brought over some cookies.	A little happy, mostly sad	She probably thinks I can't cook. I look like such a mess all the time. And my house was a disaster when she came in!

CASE STUDY

Susan was a young, single, 24-year-old woman. Her goals for therapy were to learn how to overcome chronic feelings of depression and temptations to overeat. Susan was unemployed and living with her aunt and uncle in a rural area. She had no means of personal transportation. Hypersensitivity to the reactions of significant others and the belief that they could control her feelings seemed to be central to her low self-concept and feelings of helplessness. Susan described her mother as knowing which "buttons to push." This metaphor was examined and challenged. She was questioned as to how her mother controlled her emotions: Where were these buttons? Once again, the principle was asserted that it is not the actions of others that cause emotions, but one's cognitions about them.

Then the cognitions she had concerning certain looks or critical statements were examined. When her aunt was looking "sickly and silent," Susan believed that it was because she was displeased with her for not helping enough. The evidence for this belief was examined, and there was none. Alternative explanations were explored, such as that the aunt might be truly ill, having a bad day, or upset with her spouse. Susan admitted that all explanations were equally plausible. Furthermore, it was noted that in ambiguous social situations, she tended to draw the most negative and personalized conclusions.

(continued)

TABLE 7.6 Interpersonal Therapy

Interpersonal therapists focus on four types of interpersonal problems as sources of depression.

Type of Problem	Therapeutic Approach
Grief, loss	Help the client accept feelings and evaluate a relationship with a lost person; help the client invest in new relationships
Interpersonal role disputes	Help the client make decisions about concessions willing to be made and learn better ways of communicating
Role transitions	Help the client develop more realistic perspectives toward roles that are lost and regard new roles in a more positive manner
Interpersonal skills deficits	Review the client's past relationships, helping the client understand these relationships and how they might be affecting current relationships; directly teach the client social skills, such as assertiveness

During the last stage of therapy, Susan's mother visited. This provided a real test of the gains Susan had made, as it was her mother's criticism that she feared the most. At first, she reported feeling easily wounded by her mother's criticism. These examples were used as opportunities to identify and challenge self-defeating thoughts. Soon, Susan was able to see her mother's critical statements as her mother's problem, not her own. She also discovered that, as she became better at ignoring her mother's critical remarks and not taking them to heart, her mother began to be more relaxed and open around her and criticized her less. (Adapted from Thorpe & Olson, 1997, pp. 225–227)

Cognitive-behavioral therapists also use behavioral techniques to train clients in new skills they might need to cope better. Often people with depression are unassertive in making requests of other people or in standing up for their rights and needs. This lack of assertiveness can be the result of their negative automatic thoughts. For example, a person who often thinks "I can't ask for what I need because the other person might get mad and that would be horrible" is not likely to make even reasonable requests of other people. The therapist first will help clients recognize the thoughts behind their actions (or lack of action). The therapist then may work with the clients to devise exercises or homework assignments in which they practice new skills, such as assertiveness, between therapy sessions.

Interpersonal Therapy

In **interpersonal therapy (IPT),** therapists look for four types of problems in depressed individuals (Table 7.6, Weissman & Markowitz, 2002). First, many depressed people are *grieving* the loss of a loved one, perhaps not from death but instead from the breakup of an important relationship. Interpersonal therapists help clients face such losses and explore their feelings about them. Therapists also help clients begin to invest in new relationships.

Another type of problem on which interpersonal therapy focuses is *interpersonal role disputes,* which arise when people do not agree on their roles in a relationship. For example, a college student and a parent may disagree on the extent to which the student should follow the parent's wishes in choosing a career. Interpersonal therapists first help the client recognize the dispute and then guide him or her in making choices about what concessions might be made to the other person in the relationship. Therapists also may need to help clients modify and improve their patterns of communicating with others in relationships. For example, a student who resents his parents' intrusions into his private life may tend to withdraw and sulk rather than directly confront his parents about their intrusions. He would be helped to develop more effective ways of communicating his distress over his parents' intrusions.

The problems of *role transitions* are also addressed in interpersonal therapy, problems such as the transition from college to work or from work to full-time motherhood. People sometimes become depressed over the role they must leave behind. Therapists help clients develop more realistic perspectives toward roles that are lost and learn to regard new roles in a more positive manner. If clients feel unsure about their ability to perform new roles, therapists help them develop a sense of mastery in their new roles. Sometimes, clients need help in developing new networks of social support to replace the support systems they have left behind in their old roles.

People with depression also turn to interpersonal therapy for help with problems caused by *deficits in interpersonal skills*. Such skill deficits can be the reason people with depression have inadequate social support networks. Therapists review with clients past relationships, especially important childhood relationships, helping them understand these relationships and how they might be affecting their current relationships. Therapists also might directly teach clients social skills such as assertiveness.

Interpersonal and Social Rhythm Therapy and Family-Focused Therapy

Interpersonal and social rhythm therapy (ISRT) is an enhancement of interpersonal therapy designed specifically for people with bipolar disorder (Frank et al., 2005). When people with bipolar disorder experience disruptions in either their daily routines or their social environment, they sometimes experience an upsurge in symptoms. ISRT combines interpersonal therapy techniques with behavioral techniques to help patients maintain regular routines of eating, sleeping, and activity, as well as stability in their personal relationships. By having patients self-monitor their patterns over time, therapists help patients understand how changes in sleep patterns, circadian rhythms, and eating habits can provoke symptoms. Then therapists and patients work together to develop a plan to stabilize the patients' routines and activities. Similarly, patients learn how stressors in their family and work relationships affect their moods, and they develop better strategies for coping with these stressors. Studies show that patients who receive ISRT in conjunction with medication show fewer symptoms and relapses over time than patients who do not receive ISRT (Frank et al., 2005).

Family-focused therapy (FFT) also focuses on reducing interpersonal stress in people with bipolar disorder, particularly within the context of families. Patients and their families are educated about bipolar disorder and trained in communication and problem-solving skills. Studies comparing family-focused therapy with standard therapy (medication with periodic individual check-ups with a psychiatrist) have found that adults receiving family-focused therapy show lower relapse rates over time (Miklowitz et al., 2003). In addition, applications of FFT to adolescents with bipolar disorder show promise in helping these youths and their families manage symptoms and reduce the impact of the disorder on the adolescents' functioning and development (Taylor & Miklowitz, 2009).

Comparison of Treatments

Which of the many treatments for mood disorders is best? In the past few decades, several studies have compared behavioral, cognitive-behavioral, interpersonal, and drug therapies in the treatment of unipolar depression. Perhaps surprisingly, these therapies, despite their vast differences, appear to be about equally effective in treating most people with depression (Cuijpers et al., 2008; DeRubeis, Gelfand, Tang, & Simons, 1999; Dimidjian et al., 2006; Hollon et al., 2002; Weissman & Markowitz, 2002). For example, in one study, 240 people with major depression were randomly assigned to receive either the SSRI paroxetine (Paxil) or cognitive-behavioral therapy for 16 weeks (DeRubeis et al., 2005). At the end of treatment, equal percentages of patients (about 60 percent) in each group no longer experienced major depression. Another study compared the results of behavioral therapy, cognitive therapy (without behavioral interventions), and drug therapy (paroxetine) in 240 patients with major depression (Dimidjian et al., 2006). In this study, behavioral therapy led to improvement in the greatest number of patients, followed by cognitive therapy and then drug therapy.

We might expect the combination of psychotherapy and drug therapy to be more effective in treating people with chronic depression than either type of therapy alone, and some studies support this idea (Cuijpers, Dekker, Hollon & Andersson, 2009; Cuijpers, van Straten, Warmerdam, & Andersson, 2009). For example, in one study, 681 patients with chronic major depression were randomly assigned to receive a serotonin modulator (nefazadone, a drug that is no longer sold because of adverse side effects), cognitive-behavioral therapy, or both for 12 weeks (Keller, 2000). About 50 percent of the people receiving medication or cognitive behavioral therapy alone experienced relief from their depression, while 85 percent of the patients receiving both medication and cognitive-behavioral therapy experienced relief.

FIGURE 7.7 Relapse Rates After Drug Versus Cognitive-Behavioral Therapy for Major Depression. Patients with major depression who had received CBT showed lower relapse rates in the next year than those who continued to take only an SSRI. Both groups showed lower rates of re-lapse than patients who received a placebo pill.

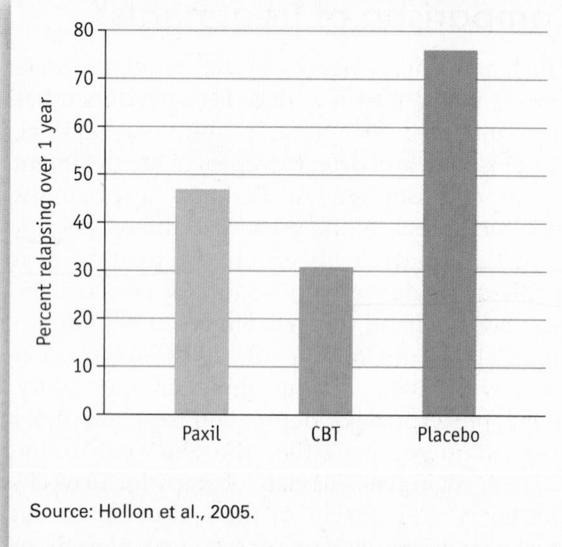

Source: Hollon et al., 2005.

Relapse rates in depression are quite high, even among people whose depressions completely disappear with treatment. For this reason, many psychiatrists and psychologists argue that people with a history of recurrent depression should be kept on a maintenance level of therapy even after their depression is relieved (Thase & Denko, 2008). Usually, the maintenance therapy is a drug therapy, and many people remain on antidepressant drugs for years after their initial episodes of depression have passed. Studies of behavioral therapy, interpersonal therapy, and cognitive-behavioral therapy show that maintenance levels of these therapies—usually consisting of once-a-month meetings with therapists—also can substantially reduce relapse (Hollon et al., 2002; Weissman & Markowitz, 2002).

Even when maintenance doses of psychotherapy are not available, people who have had any of the empirically supported psychotherapies appear to be less likely to relapse than those who have had only drug therapy. For example, researchers followed the 240 patients in one of the studies described earlier for a year after they had recovered from acute depression. They found that those who had had cognitive-behavioral therapy showed a lower rate of relapse than those who continued with the drug therapy (paroxetine) only and that both groups had much lower rates of relapse than those who were taking a placebo pill over that 12 months (Figure 7.7; Hollon et al., 2005).

In the case of bipolar disorder, combining drug treatment with the psychological therapies may reduce the rate at which patients stop taking their medication and may lead more patients to achieve full remission of their symptoms, compared to lithium treatment alone (Miklowitz et al., 2000; Swartz & Frank, 2001). Psychotherapy can help people with bipolar disorder understand and accept their need for lithium treatment as well as help them cope with the impact of the disorder on their lives.

TEST YOURSELF

1. What categories of drugs are used to treat depression?
2. How is lithium used in the treatment of mood disorders?
3. What are anticonvulsants and atypical anti-psychotic medications?
4. What is electroconvulsive therapy (ECT)? What are some newer methods used to stimulate the brain?
5. What are the goals of behavior therapy?
6. What are the goals of cognitive-behavioral therapy?
7. What does interpersonal therapy focus on?

APPLY IT Sam is seeking treatment for major depression. According to recent studies, the most effective therapy for him is likely to be which of the following?

a. cognitive-behavioral therapy
b. interpersonal therapy
c. serotonin reuptake inhibitors
d. combined psychotherapy and drug therapy

Answers appear online at www.mhhe.com/nolen5e.

SUICIDE

Suicide is among the three leading causes of death worldwide among people ages 15 to 44 (World Health Organization [WHO], 2008). Around the world, more people die from suicide than from homicide. Suicide is associated with mood disorders, and thus we address it in the final section of this chapter. Note, however, that the risk of suicide is increased in people with any mental disorder.

Defining and Measuring Suicide

The Centers for Disease Control and Prevention (CDC), one of the federal agencies in the United States that tracks suicide rates, defines **suicide** as "death from injury, poisoning, or suffocation where there is evidence (either explicit or implicit) that the injury was self-inflicted and that the decedent intended to kill himself/herself." As clear as this definition seems, there is great variability in the form that suicide takes, and whether to call particular types of death suicide is open to debate. We may easily agree that a young man who is despondent and shoots himself in the head has committed suicide. It is harder to agree on whether an unhappy young man who goes on a drinking binge and crashes his car into a tree has committed suicide. Is an elderly person who refuses life support when dying from a painful disease committing suicide? Is a middle-aged person with severe heart disease who continues to smoke cigarettes, eat fatty foods, and drink excessive amounts of alcohol committing suicide? Clearly, suicide-like behaviors fall along the type of continuum we discuss throughout this book.

We can distinguish among *completed suicides,* which end in death; **suicide attempts,** which may or may not end in death; and **suicidal ideation** or thought. Many people with mental disorders think about committing suicide but never attempt to kill themselves. Also, actual suicide attempts are much more common than completed suicides, with some studies estimating that suicide attempts are 20 times as common as completed suicides (WHO, 2008).

Given the difficulty of defining suicide, it is not surprising that accurate suicide rates are difficult to obtain. Many deaths are ambiguous, particularly when no notes are left behind and no clues exist as to the victim's mental state before the death. Recorded rates probably are low, because the stigma against suicide is a great incentive for labeling a death as anything but a suicide. Accurate data on nonlethal suicide attempts are even harder to obtain.

Even so, the statistics indicate that suicide is more common than we would like to believe. More than 33,000 people kill themselves each year in the United States, an average of 90 people per day. In addition, as many as 3 percent of the population make a suicide attempt (with intent to die) sometime in their lives (Nock & Kessler, 2006), and more than 13 percent report having had suicidal thoughts at some time (Borges et al., 2008). Suicide is not just an American phenomenon, however. Internationally, an estimated 1 million people die by suicide each year, or 1 person about every 40 seconds (WHO, 2008).

FIGURE 7.8 **Gender and Suicide.** In many nations of the world, males are more likely to commit suicide than females across almost all age groups.

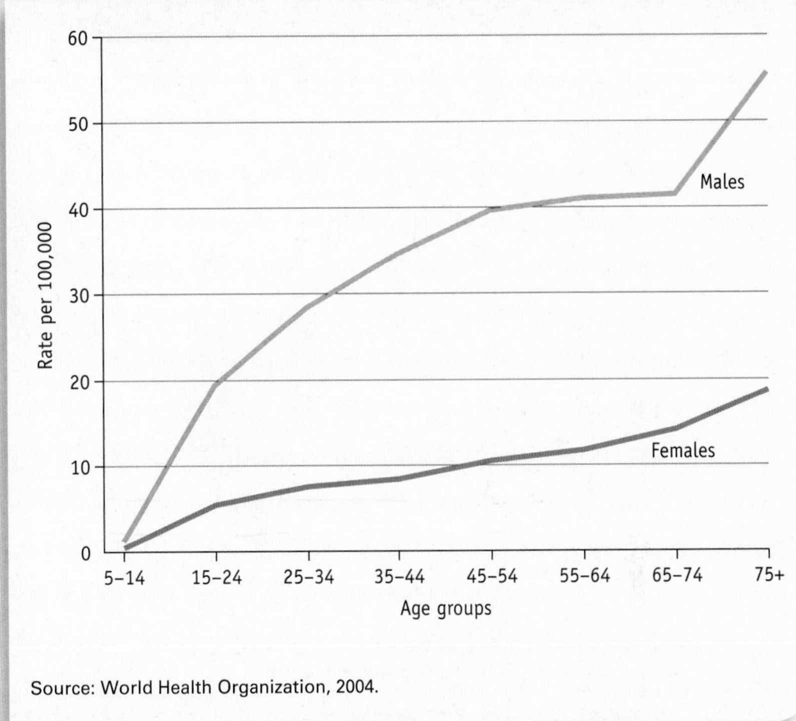

Source: World Health Organization, 2004.

Gender Differences

While two to three times more women than men *attempt* suicide (Nock & Kessler, 2006), men are four times more likely than women to complete suicide (CDC, 2007). This gender difference is true across all age groups, as seen in Figure 7.8.

The gender difference in rates of completed suicide may be due in part to gender differences in the means of attempting suicide. Men tend to choose more lethal methods of suicide than do women, with more than half of men who kill themselves using a firearm (CDC, 2007). For women the most common method of suicide is poisoning.

FIGURE 7.9 **Map of Suicide Rates.** There are significant differences across countries in suicide rates. This map shows the rate per 100,000 people in different regions.

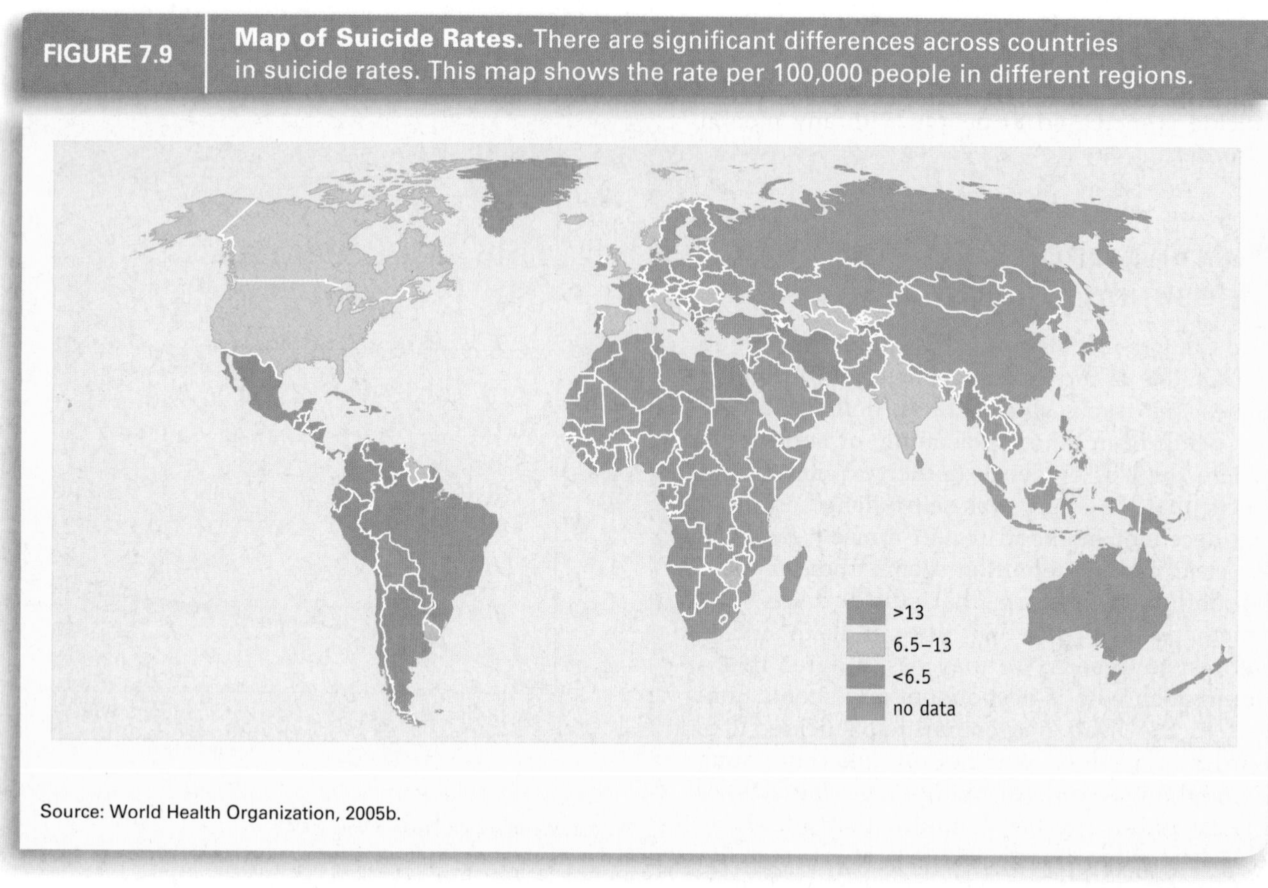

Source: World Health Organization, 2005b.

In addition, men who attempt suicide tend to be more sure in their intent to die than are women (Jack, 1992; Linehan, 1973).

Ethnic and Cross-Cultural Differences

Within the United States, there are substantial differences in suicide rates among ethnic/racial groups (CDC, 2005; Oquendo et al., 2001). European Americans have higher suicide rates than all other groups, approximately 12 people per 100,000 population, and Native Americans are close behind at approximately 11 per 100,000. Suicide among Native Americans is tied to poverty, lack of education and hope, discrimination, substance abuse, and the easy availability of firearms (Berman & Jobes, 1995). Suicide rates among African American males have increased greatly in recent decades (Joe & Kaplan, 2001).

There are cross-national differences in suicide rates, with higher rates in much of Europe, the former Soviet Union, and Australia and lower rates in Latin America and South America (Figure 7.9; WHO, 2004). The suicide rates in the United States, Canada, and England fall between these two extremes. The differences may be due in part to cultural and religious norms. People who belong to religions that expressly forbid suicide are less likely to attempt it (O'Donnell, O'Donnell, Wardlaw, & Stueve, 2004; Statham et al., 1998).

Suicide in Children and Adolescents

Although suicide is relatively rare in young children, it is not unheard of. The rate of suicide increases substantially in early adolescence. Each year, 17 percent of teenagers in the United States seriously consider suicide, 15 percent make a specific plan to attempt suicide, more than 8 percent attempt suicide, and about 2 percent make a serious suicide attempt that requires medical attention (Jacobson & Gould, 2009). Suicide may become more common in adolescence than in childhood because the rates of several types of psychopathology that are tied to suicide, including depression, anxiety disorders, and substance abuse, increase in adolescence. Suicide rates also may rise during the teen years because adolescents are more sophisticated than children in their thinking and can contemplate suicide more clearly. Finally, adolescents simply may have readier access to the means to commit suicide (e.g., drugs and guns) than do children.

As with adults, girls are much more likely to attempt suicide than boys, but boys are more likely to succeed (Jacobson & Gould, 2009). Males are six times more likely than females in this age range to commit suicide (CDC, 2004). Homosexual and bisexual adolescents have rates of suicide attempts 2 to 6 times higher than those of heterosexual adolescents (Jacobson & Gould, 2009).

Hispanic females have especially high rates of suicidal thoughts and plans and attempted suicides compared to Hispanic males and adolescents from other racial/ethnic groups (Jacobson & Gould, 2009). Luis Zayas and colleagues (2005) suggest that these high rates are linked to clashes between Hispanic girls, who are highly acculturated to American values, and their parents, who may hold traditional cultural values of *familism* (centrality of family to one's life) and may reject the girls' bids for independence.

Rates of suicide among children and teenagers more than doubled between the 1950s and the early 1990s, but they have steadily declined since 1994 (Jacobson & Gould, 2009). The initial increase may have been linked to the increase in substance use by teenagers during that same period, coupled with an increased availability of firearms. The decrease in suicide rates since the mid-1990s is thought to be related to an increase in the use of antidepressants, particularly SSRIs, to treat depression in adolescents (Zalsman, Shoval, & Rotstein, 2009). Unfortunately, there has been a spike in adolescent suicide rates since 2004—the same year the FDA mandated a warning regarding the use of SSRIs by youth. Since that warning was required, prescriptions for SSRIs for teenagers have declined (Nemeroff et al., 2007). Some experts are concerned that the FDA warning has had the unintended consequence of leaving many depressed teenagers untreated and vulnerable to suicidal thoughts and behaviors (Zalsman et al., 2009).

College Students

The college years are full of academic and social pressures and challenges. In a survey of students in college, 9 percent said they had thought about committing suicide since entering college, and 1 percent said they had attempted suicide while at college (Furr, Westefeld, McConnell, & Jenkins, 2001). Students who had contemplated or attempted suicide were more likely than those who had not to have experienced depression and hopelessness, loneliness, and problems with their parents. Unfortunately, only 20 percent of the students who had contemplated suicide had sought any type of counseling.

Illness is often a precursor to suicide among older adults.

Suicide in Older Adults

Although there has been a 50 percent decline in suicide rates among adults over age 65 in the past few decades, older people, particularly older men, still remain at relatively high risk for suicide. The highest risk is among European American men over age 85 (CDC, 2004). When they attempt suicide, older people are much more likely than younger people to be successful. It seems that most older people who attempt suicide fully intend to die (McIntosh, 1995).

Some older people commit suicide because they cannot tolerate the loss of their spouse or other loved ones. Suicide rates are highest in the first year after a loss but remain relatively high for several years (McIntosh, 1995). Other older people who commit suicide wish to escape the pain and suffering of debilitating illness. Escape from illness and disabilities may be a particularly strong motive for suicide among men, who are reluctant to become a burden to others (Conwell & Thompson, 2008). In one study of older people who committed suicide, 44 percent had said they could not bear being placed in a nursing home and would rather be dead (Loebel et al., 1991).

Most older people who lose a spouse or become ill do not commit suicide. Those with a history of depression or other psychological problems are at greatest risk for responding to the challenges of old age with suicide (Harwood, Hawton, Hope, & Jacoby, 2000).

Nonsuicidal Self-Injury

Some people—often adolescents—repeatedly cut, burn, puncture, or otherwise significantly injure their skin with no intent to die, a behavior known as **nonsuicidal self-injury** or **NSSI** (Nock, 2010). NSSI seems to be relatively common, with estimates of adolescents reporting having engaged in NSSI at some time in their lives ranging from 13 to 45 percent (Lloyd-Richardson, Perrine, Dierker, & Kelley, 2007; Plener et al., 2009; Ross & Heath, 2002). Clinicians, teachers, and other health professionals report a dramatic increase in NSSI in recent years, but longitudinal data are lacking (Nock, 2010).

Individuals who engage in NSSI are at increased risk for suicide attempts (Nock, 2010). Theories of NSSI suggest that it functions as a way of regulating emotion and/or influencing the social environment (Nock & Prinstein, 2004). People who engage in NSSI often report that feeling the pain and seeing the blood actually calms them and releases tension (Lloyd-Richardson et al., 2007). Self-injury also draws support and sympathy from others or may punish others (Nock & Prinstein, 2004). Much more research on the triggers for self-injury is needed, however.

The *DSM-5* may add diagnostic criteria for NSSI, in part to motivate and organize research into it (Shaffer & Jacobson, 2010). To receive this diagnosis, individuals must have engaged in NSSI behaviors on 5 or more days in the past year, without suicidal intent. The diagnostic criteria are also likely to require that the NSSI behaviors be accompanied by negative thoughts or feelings that the individual intends to alleviate with the NSSI behaviors and frequent preoccupations with, and urges to engage in, NSSI acts (American Psychological Association, 2010).

Understanding Suicide

Our ability to understand the causes of suicide is hampered by many factors. First, although suicide is more common than we would hope, it is still rare enough to make it difficult to study scientifically. Second, in the wake of a suicide, family members and friends may selectively remember certain information about the victim (e.g., evidence that he or she was depressed) and forget other information. Third, most people who kill themselves do not leave notes. The notes that are left often do not provide much understanding of what led the people to take their lives (Jamison, 1993). In this section, we briefly discuss historical perspectives on suicide and then discuss research findings on the factors contributing to suicide.

Historical Perspectives on Suicide

Freud argued that depressed people express anger at themselves instead of at the people they feel have betrayed or abandoned them. When that anger becomes so great in depressed people that they wish to annihilate the image of the lost person, they destroy themselves. For example, teenagers who cannot express anger at their parents may attempt suicide to punish them. Like many of Freud's theories, this idea is difficult to test because it involves emotions that people are unable of unwilling to express or acknowledge.

In his classic work on suicide, sociologist Émile Durkheim (1897) focused on the mind-sets certain societal conditions can create that increase the risk for suicide. He proposed that there are three types of suicide. **Egoistic suicide** is committed by people who feel alienated from others, empty of social contacts, and alone in an unsupportive world. The patient with schizophrenia who kills herself because she is completely isolated from society may be committing egoistic suicide. **Anomic suicide** is committed by people who experience severe disorientation because of a major change in their relationship to society. A man who loses his job after 20 years of service may feel *anomie,* a complete confusion of his role and his worth in society, and may commit anomic suicide. Finally, **altruistic suicide** is committed by people who believe that taking their life will benefit society. For instance, during the Vietnam War, Buddhist monks publicly burned themselves to death to protest the war.

Durkheim's theory suggests that social ties and integration into a society will help prevent suicide if the society discourages suicide and supports individuals in overcoming negative situations in ways other than suicide. However, if a society supports suicide as a beneficial act in some situations, then ties with such a society may promote suicide. For example, some terrorist groups promote suicide as an honorable, even glorious, act in the service of striking at enemies.

Modern empirical research has identified a number of psychological, biological, and environmental factors that increase the risk for suicide. We turn now to this research.

Psychological Disorders and Suicide

More than 90 percent of people who commit suicide probably have been suffering from a diagnosable mental disorder (Jacobson & Gould, 2009; Joiner, Brown, & Wingate, 2005). Depression increases the odds of a suicide attempt by approximately 6 times, and bipolar disorder increases the odds of a suicide attempt by 7 times (Nock et al., 2008).

By far the best predictor of future suicidal thought and behavior is past suicidal thought and behavior (Borges et al., 2008). Among adolescents, a history of a previous suicide attempt increases the odds of suicide by 30 times among boys and by 3 times among girls (Shaffer et al., 1996). Thus, it is critically important that suicidal thought and behavior be assessed and intervention made, regardless of what other psychological problems it is related to.

Stressful Life Events and Suicide

Stressful life events increase the risk of suicide, perhaps because they cause or worsen mood disorders. One stressful event consistently linked to increased vulnerability to suicide is economic hardship (Borges et al., 2008; Fanous, Prescott, & Kendler, 2004). Loss of a job, for example, can precipitate suicidal thoughts and attempts (Crosby, Cheltenham, & Sacks, 1999; Platt & Hawton, 2000). The high suicide rate among African American males in recent years may be tied to perceptions that their economic futures are uncertain at best, as well as to comparisons of their economic status with that of the majority culture. One study found that rates of suicide among African American males in the United States were highest in communities where the occupational and income inequalities between African Americans and European Americans were greatest (Burr, Hartman, & Matteson, 1999).

Loss of a loved one through death, divorce, or separation often immediately precedes suicide attempts or completions (Jacobson & Gould, 2009). People feel they cannot go on without the lost relationship and wish to end their pain. In addition, people who have experienced certain traumas in childhood, especially sexual abuse or the loss of a parent, also appear to be at increased risk for suicide (Fanous et al., 2004). For example, a nationwide study in the United States found that a history of child sexual abuse increased the odds of a suicide attempt by 2 to 4 times for women and by 4 to 11 times for men (Molnar, Berkman, & Buka, 2001; see also Brent et al., 2002). Studies focusing on women have found that physical abuse by a partner is a potent predictor of suicide attempts (Kaslow et al., 2000; Ragin et al., 2002).

Suicide Contagion

Can suicide be contagious? When a well-known member of society commits suicide, people who closely identify with that person may see suicide as more acceptable (Jacobson & Gould, 2009). When two or more suicides or attempted suicides are nonrandomly bunched in space or time, such as a series of suicide attempts in the same high school or a series of completed suicides in response to the suicide of a celebrity, scientists refer to it as a **suicide cluster** (Joiner, 1999). Suicide clusters seem to occur primarily among adolescents (Jacobson & Gould, 2009).

Suicide clusters appear to be most likely among people who knew the person who committed suicide. One well-documented example occurred in a high school of about 1,500 students in which 2 students committed suicide within 4 days. Over an 18-day span, 7 other students attempted suicide, and an additional 23 students reported having suicidal thoughts (Brent et al., 1989). Many of those who attempted suicide or had active suicidal thoughts were friends of one another and of the students who had completed suicide.

Other suicide clusters occur not among close friends but among people who are linked by media exposure to the suicide of a stranger, often a celebrity. Some studies have suggested that suicide rates, at least among adolescents, increase after a publicized suicide (Gould, Jamieson, & Romer, 2003). For example, after the suicide of Kurt Cobain, the popular lead singer of the band Nirvana, there were concerns that young people who identified with Cobain and the message in his music would view suicide as an appropriate way of dealing with the social anomie expressed in that music. One fan, a 28-year-old man, went home after a candlelight vigil honoring Cobain and killed himself with a shotgun, just as Cobain had.

What is the reason for suicide clustering? Some theorists have labeled it **suicide contagion** (Stack, 1991). Survivors who become suicidal may be modeling the behavior of the friend or admired celebrity who committed suicide. That suicide also may make the idea of suicide more acceptable and thus lower inhibitions for suicidal behavior in survivors. In addition, the local and media attention given to a suicide can be attractive to some people who are feeling alienated and abandoned. After the murder-suicide rampage of two teenagers at Columbine High School in Littleton, Colorado, some teenagers said that receiving the media attention that was given to the shooters would be an attractive way to "go out."

Personality and Cognitive Factors in Suicide

The personality characteristic that seems to predict suicide best is **impulsivity,** the general tendency to act on one's impulses rather than to inhibit them when it is appropriate to do so (Joiner

Could media coverage of school shootings and suicides inspire other students to commit similar acts?

et al., 2005). When impulsivity is overlaid on other psychological problems—such as depression, substance abuse, or living in a chronically stressful environment—it can be a potent contributor to suicide. One family history study showed that the children of parents with a mood disorder who also scored high on measures of impulsivity were at much greater risk of attempting suicide (Brent et al., 2002).

The cognitive variable that has most consistently predicted suicide is **hopelessness**—the feeling that the future is bleak and there is no way to make it more positive (Beck, Steer, Kovacs, & Garrison, 1985). Thomas Joiner and colleagues (2005) suggest that hopeless feelings about being a burden on others and about never belonging with others are especially linked to suicide. Hopelessness also may be one reason why people who are suicidal often do not seek treatment.

Biological Factors in Suicide

Suicide runs in families. For example, one study found that the children of parents who had attempted suicide were 6 times more likely to also attempt suicide than were the children of parents who had a mood disorder but had not attempted suicide (Brent et al., 2002, 2003).

Although some of this clustering of suicide within families may be due to environmental factors, such as family members modeling each other or sharing common stressors, twin and adoption studies suggest that genetics is involved as well (Joiner et al., 2005). Twin studies estimate that the risk of suicide attempts increases by 5.6 times if a person's monozygotic twin has attempted suicide, and by 4.0 times if a person's dizygotic twin has attempted suicide (Glowinski et al., 2001; Joiner et al., 2005). Strong evidence of a genetic component to suicide remained when researchers controlled for histories of psychiatric problems in the twins and their families, for recent and past negative life events, for how close the twins were to each other socially, and for personality factors.

Many studies have found a link between suicide and low levels of the neurotransmitter serotonin (Asberg & Forslund, 2000; Mann, Brent, & Arango, 2001). For example, postmortem studies of the brains of people who committed suicide find low levels of serotonin (Gross-Isseroff, Biegon, Voet, & Weizman, 1998). Also, people with a family history of suicide or who have attempted suicide are more likely to have abnormalities on genes that regulate serotonin (Courtet et al., 2004; Joiner et al., 2005; Joiner, Johnson, & Soderstrom, 2002). People with low serotonin levels who attempt suicide are 10 times more likely to make another suicide attempt than are those with higher serotonin levels (Roy, 1992). Low serotonin levels are linked to suicidal tendencies even in people who are not depressed, suggesting that the connection between serotonin and suicide is not due entirely to a common connection to depression.

Treatment and Prevention

Some intervention and prevention programs appear to reduce the risk of suicide.

Treatment of Suicidal Persons

A person who is gravely suicidal needs immediate care. Sometimes people require hospitalization to prevent an imminent suicide attempt. They may voluntarily agree to be hospitalized. If they do not agree, they can be hospitalized involuntarily for a short period of time (usually about 3 days). We will discuss the pros and cons of involuntary hospitalization in Chapter 16.

Community-based *crisis intervention* programs are available to help highly suicidal people deal in the short term with their feelings and then refer them to mental health specialists for longer-term care. Some crisis intervention is done over the phone, on *suicide hotlines*. Some communities have walk-in clinics or suicide prevention centers, which may be part of a more comprehensive mental health system.

Crisis intervention aims to reduce the risk of an imminent suicide attempt by providing suicidal persons someone to talk with who understands their feelings and problems. The counselor can help them mobilize support from family members and friends and can make a plan to deal with specific problem situations in the short term. The crisis intervention counselor may contract with the suicidal person that he or she will not attempt suicide, or at least will recontact the counselor as soon as suicidal feelings return. The counselor will help the person identify other people he or she can turn to when feeling panicked or overwhelmed and make follow-up appointments with the suicidal person or refer him or her to another counselor for long-term treatment.

The medication most consistently shown to reduce the risk of suicide is lithium. A review of 33 published treatment studies of people with major depression or bipolar disorder found that those not treated with lithium were 13 times more likely to commit or attempt suicide than those who had been treated with lithium (Baldessarini, Tondo, & Hennen, 2001).

The selective serotonin reuptake inhibitors also may reduce the risk of suicide, because they reduce depressive symptoms and possibly because they regulate levels of serotonin, which may have independent effects on suicidal intentions (Thase & Denko, 2008). As we discussed earlier, however, there is some evidence that the serotonin reuptake inhibitors increase the risk of suicide in children and adolescents. Clinicians must weigh the potential benefits and risks and carefully monitor individuals for signs of increased suicidal thoughts when they begin taking an SSRI (Zalsman et al., 2008).

Psychological therapies designed to treat depression can be effective in treating suicidality. *Dialectical behavior therapy (DBT)* was developed to treat people with borderline personality disorder, who frequently attempt suicide (Linehan, 1999). This therapy focuses on managing negative emotions and controlling impulsive behaviors. It aims to increase problem-solving skills, interpersonal skills, and skill at managing negative emotions. Studies suggest that dialectical behavior therapy can reduce suicidal thoughts and behaviors, as well as improve interpersonal skills (Lynch et al., 2007).

What is clearest from the literature on the treatment of suicidal people is that they are woefully undertreated. Most people who are suicidal never seek treatment (Crosby et al., 1999). Even when their families know they are suicidal, they may not be taken for treatment because of denial and a fear of being stigmatized.

Suicide Prevention

Suicide hotlines and crisis intervention centers provide help to suicidal people in times of their greatest need, hoping to prevent a suicidal act until the suicidal feelings have passed. In addition, many prevention programs aim to educate entire communities about suicide. These programs often are based in schools or colleges. Students are given information about the rate of suicide in their age group, the risk factors for suicide, and actions to take if they or a friend is suicidal.

Unfortunately, broad-based prevention or education programs do not tend to be very helpful and might even do harm (Gould, Greenberg, et al., 2003). One major problem with these programs is that they often simultaneously target both the general population of students and those students at high risk for suicide. The programs may attempt to destigmatize suicide by making it appear quite common and by not mentioning that most suicidal people are suffering from a psychological disorder, in hopes that suicidal students will feel freer to seek help. But such messages can backfire among students who are not suicidal, making suicide seem like an understandable response to stress. In addition, studies of school-based suicide prevention programs have found that adolescents who had made prior suicide attempts generally reacted negatively to the programs, saying that they were less inclined to seek help after attending the program than before (Gould, Greenberg, et al., 2003).

Researchers have tailored suicide prevention messages to specific populations—particularly high-risk populations—in hopes of getting the right kind of help to the neediest people. David Shaffer and his colleagues at Columbia University have designed a program that involves screening adolescents for risk of suicide, doing a diagnostic interview with high-risk adolescents, and then interviewing them to determine the most appropriate referral to a mental health specialist (Shaffer & Gould, 2000). This program has had some success in identifying high-risk youth and getting them into effective treatment. Similar programs have been developed for college students (Haas, Hendin, & Mann, 2003).

Parents and school officials often worry that asking teenagers about thoughts of suicide might "put the idea in their head." One study addressed this concern directly (Gould et al., 2005). The researchers randomly assigned more than 2,000 teenagers to complete questionnaires that either included or did not include questions about suicidal thoughts and behaviors. Two days later the researchers had all the teenagers fill out a measure of suicidal thought. Teenagers who had completed the suicide questionnaire did not report any more (or less) suicidal thought or distress than the teenagers who had not been asked about suicide. Thus, there was no evidence that answering questions about suicide induced teenagers to consider suicide or made them highly distressed.

Guns and Suicide

In the United States, 57 percent of suicides involve guns (National Institute of Mental Health [NIMH], 2002). A longitudinal study of people who had purchased handguns in California found that their risk of suicide increased 57 times in the first week after the purchase (Wintemute et al., 1999). The majority of people who commit suicide by gun, however, use a gun that has been in their household for some time; the presence of a gun in the home increases the risk of suicide by 4 to 5 times (Brent & Bridge, 2003).

Indeed, the most frequent use of a gun in the home is for suicide. Researchers examined 398 consecutive deaths by gun in the homes of families who owned guns (usually handguns). Of these deaths, only 0.5 percent involved intruders shot by families protecting themselves. In contrast, 83 percent were suicides of adolescent or adult family members. Another 12 percent were homicides of one adult in the home by another family member, usually in the midst of a quarrel. The final 3 percent of deaths were due to accidental shootings of a family member (Kellermann, Rivara, Somes, & Reay, 1992).

The mere presence of a firearm in the home appears to be a risk factor for suicide when other risk factors are taken into account, especially when handguns are improperly secured or are kept loaded (Brent et al., 1991). These suicides do not occur only in people with mental disorders. One study found that while the presence of a gun in the home increased the risk of suicide by 3 times for people with a mental disorder, it increased the risk of suicide by 33 times for people without a mental disorder (Kellerman, Rivara, Somes, & Reay, 1992; see also Brent et al., 1993). This apparently counterintuitive finding is the result of the dramatic increase in impulsive suicides conveyed by having a loaded gun in the home, even among people without a known risk factor such as psychopathology (Brent & Bridges, 2003).

Restricting access to guns appears to lower suicide rates.

Can the number of such suicides be reduced by laws that restrict access to guns? Although not all studies find this to be the case (Ludwig & Cook, 2000), several studies have found that suicide rates are lower in cities, states, or countries with strict antigun legislation that limits people's access to guns (Brent & Bridges, 2003; Leenaars, 2007). For example, one international study showed that the proportion of suicides by gun decreased proportionately with the number of households owning guns; in addition, after countries enacted stricter gun control laws, the proportion of suicides involving guns decreased (Ajdacic-Gross et al., 2006; see also Bridges, 2004). Similarly, in the United States, states with unrestrictive firearm laws (e.g., Alaska, Kentucky, Montana) or modest firearm laws (e.g., Colorado, North Carolina, Pennsylvania) were shown to have 50 to 65 percent higher rates of suicide by firearms than states with restrictive firearm laws (e.g., California, Illinois, New York), even after controlling for differences in socioeconomic status, race/ethnicity, and urbanization (Conner & Zhong, 2003).

Although people who are intent on committing suicide can find other means to do so when guns are not available, restricting ready access to them appears to reduce impulsive suicides with guns. In addition, some studies suggest that suicides by means other than guns (e.g., by jumping off buildings or inhaling carbon monoxide) show no increase when access to guns is restricted, suggesting that people do not consistently substitute different means of committing suicide when guns are not available (Connor & Zhong, 2003; but see Brent & Bridges, 2003). Instead, the unavailability of guns seems to give people a cooling off period, during which their suicidal impulses can wane (Brent & Bridges, 2003; Lambert & Silva, 1998).

What to Do If a Friend Is Suicidal

What should you do if you suspect that a friend or family member is suicidal? The Depression and Bipolar Support Alliance (2008), a patient-run advocacy group, makes the following suggestions in *Suicide and Depressive Illness:*

1. *Take the person seriously.* Although most people who express suicidal thoughts do not go on to attempt suicide, most people who do commit suicide have communicated their suicidal intentions to friends or family members beforehand.
2. *Get help.* Call the person's therapist, a suicide hotline, 911, or any other source of professional mental health care.
3. *Express concern.* Tell the person concretely why you think he or she is suicidal.
4. *Pay attention.* Listen closely, maintain eye contact, and use body language to indicate that you are attending to everything the person says.
5. *Ask direct questions about whether the person has a plan for suicide, and if so, what that plan is.*
6. *Acknowledge the person's feelings in a nonjudgmental way.* For example, you might say something like "I know you are feeling really horrible right now, but I want to help you get through this" or "I can't begin to completely understand how you feel, but I want to help you."
7. *Reassure the person that things can be better.* Emphasize that suicide is a permanent solution to a temporary problem.
8. *Don't promise confidentiality.* You need the freedom to contact mental health professionals and tell them precisely what is going on.
9. *Make sure guns, old medications, and other means of self-harm are not available.*
10. *If possible, don't leave the person alone until he or she is in the hands of professionals.* Go with him or her to the emergency room if need be. Then, once he or she has been hospitalized or has received other treatment, follow up to show you care.
11. *Take care of yourself.* Interacting with a person who is suicidal can be extremely stressful and disturbing. Talk with someone you trust about it—perhaps a friend, family member, or counselor—particularly if you worry about how you handled the situation or that you will find yourself in that situation again.

TEST YOURSELF

1. How is suicide defined?
2. What groups show the highest rates of suicide?
3. What are some risk factors for suicide?
4. What are some effective treatments for suicidal persons?
5. What are some effective prevention methods for suicide?

APPLY IT If you were concerned that a friend was suicidal, which of the following would *not* be an appropriate response?

a. avoiding saying anything to your friend about your concern for fear of putting ideas in his or her head
b. calling for professional help
c. refusing to promise to keep your friend's suicidal thought and behavior a secret
d. seeking support for yourself by discussing the matter rather than trying to handle it alone

Answers appear online at www.mhhe.com/nolen5e.

CHAPTER INTEGRATION

The mood disorders affect the whole person. Depression and mania involve changes in every aspect of functioning, including biology, cognitions, personality, social skills, and relationships. Some of these changes may be causes of the depression or mania, while some may be consequences.

The fact that the mood disorders are phenomena affecting the whole person illustrates the intricate connections among biology, cognitions, personality, and social interactions. These areas of functioning are so intertwined that major changes in any one area almost necessarily will provoke changes in other areas. Many recent models of the mood disorders suggest that most people who become depressed carry a vulnerability to depression for much of their lives. This may be a biological vulnerability, such as dysfunction in the neurotransmitter systems, or a psychological vulnerability, such as overdependence on others. Not until these vulnerabilities interact with certain stressors is a full-blown depression triggered, however (Figure 7.10).

Fortunately, the interconnections among these areas of functioning may mean that improving functioning in one area can improve functioning in other areas: Improving people's biological functioning can improve their cognitive and social functioning and their personalities, improving people's cognitive and social functioning can improve their biological functioning, and so on. Thus, although there may be many pathways into mood disorders (biological, psychological, and social), there also may be many pathways out.

FIGURE 7.10 An Integrative Model of Depression Proposed by Kendler and Colleagues

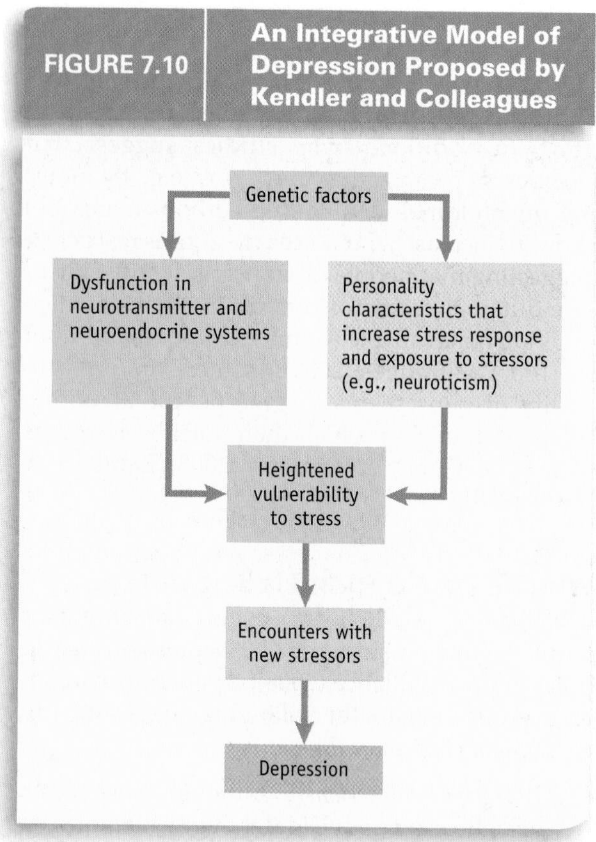

SHADES OF GRAY DISCUSSION (review p. 186)

Carmen's symptoms—severe depressed mood, chronic sleeping, trouble concentrating, weight loss, and a suicide attempt—are characteristic of a major depressive episode. She has a long history of moderate depression with pessimism, unhappiness, and chronic fatigue. These symptoms are probably too mild to meet the criteria for major depression but warrant a diagnosis of dysthymic disorder. Episodes of major depression often are superimposed on dysthymic disorder, a condition called double depression.

Because Carmen's more severe symptoms began in the winter term, you may wonder if she is experiencing the subtype of major depression called seasonal affective disorder, or SAD. A diagnosis of SAD is not warranted because (a) this diagnosis requires evidence that the individual has experienced seasonal changes in mood for at least 2 years, and we only have evidence that Carmen's depression has worsened in this year, and (b) the diagnosis of SAD requires that the individual's depressive symptoms lift during the spring or summer, and Carmen's low-level depressive symptoms appear to persist throughout the year.

THINK CRITICALLY

Depression can have devastating effects on people's lives, from marring their quality of life to leading to a tragic end, as it did for singer Kurt Cobain. How might you design a program to prevent depression in vulnerable people based on techniques from cognitive-behavioral and interpersonal therapies for depression? *(Discussion appears on pp. 518–519 at the back of this book.)*

CHAPTER SUMMARY

- There are two general categories of mood disorder: unipolar depression and bipolar disorder. People with unipolar depression experience only the symptoms of depression (sad mood, loss of interest, disruption in sleep and appetite, motor retardation or agitation, loss of energy, feelings of worthlessness and guilt, suicidality). People with bipolar disorder experience both depression and mania (elated or agitated mood, grandiosity, little need for sleep, racing thoughts and speech, increase in goals and dangerous behavior).
- Within unipolar depression the two major diagnostic categories are major depression and dysthymic disorder. Major depression is a more severe, acute form of depression, and dysthymic disorder is a less severe but more chronic form. In addition, there are several subtypes of major depression: with melancholic features, with psychotic features, with catatonic features, with atypical features, with postpartum onset, and with seasonal onset. Cyclothymic disorder is a less severe but more chronic form of bipolar disorder.
- Depression is one of the most common disorders, but there are substantial age, gender, and cross-cultural differences in depression. Bipolar disorder is much less common than the depressive disorders and tends to be a lifelong problem. The length of individual episodes of bipolar disorder, as in depression, varies dramatically from one person to the next and over the life course.
- The neurotransmitters norepinephrine, serotonin, and dopamine have been implicated in the mood disorders. Disordered genes may lead to dysfunction in these neurotransmitter systems. In addition, neuroimaging studies show abnormal structure or activity in several areas of the brain, including the prefrontal cortex, hippocampus, anterior cingulate cortex, and amygdala. There is evidence that people with depression have chronic hyperactivity in the hypothalamic-pituitary-adrenal axis, which may make them more susceptible to stress.
- Behavioral theories of depression suggest that people with much stress in their lives may have too low a rate of reinforcement and too high a rate of punishment, leading to depression. Stressful events also can lead to learned helplessness—the belief that nothing you do can control your environment—which is linked to depression.
- The cognitive theories argue that depressed people have negative views of themselves, the world, and the future and engage in biased thinking that promotes this negativity. People who ruminate in response to distress are more prone to depression.
- Interpersonal theories suggest that people prone to depression are highly sensitive to rejection and engage in excessive reassurance seeking. Levels or interpersonal stress and conflict are high in the lives of depressed people.
- Sociocultural theorists have tried to explain the differences in rates of depression among different demographic groups. The decreased risk of depression in older adults may be due to historical cohort effects. Women's greater risk of depression may be due to differences in the ways women and men respond to distress and to women's greater interpersonal orientation, lesser power and status, and higher rates of victimization. High rates of depression in Hispanic Americans may be due to low socioeconomic status. Cross-cultural differences in depression have been attributed to industrialization; also, different cultures may experience distress differently.
- Bipolar disorder has an even greater connection to genetic factors than does unipolar depression. The areas of the brain most implicated in bipolar disorder are the amygdala, prefrontal cortex, and striatum. Adolescents with bipolar disorder show abnormalities in white-matter tissue. Dopamine is the neurotransmitter most implicated in bipolar disorder.
- People with bipolar disorder may have dysfunctional reward systems: They are hypersensitive to reward when in a manic state and insensitive when in a depressed state.
- Most of the biological therapies for the mood disorders are drug therapies, including antidepressants and mood stabilizers. Electroconvulsive therapy is used to treat severe depressions that do not respond to drugs. Newer methods of stimulating the brain, including transcranial magnetic stimulation, vagus nerve stimulation, and deep brain stimulation, hold promise for the treatment of mood disorders. Light therapy is helpful in treating seasonal affective disorder.
- Behavior therapies focus on increasing positive reinforcers and decreasing negative events by building social skills and teaching clients how to engage in pleasant activities and cope with their moods. Cognitive-behavioral therapies help people with depression develop more adaptive ways of thinking. Interpersonal therapy helps people with depression identify and change the patterns in their relationships.

- Interpersonal social rhythm therapy helps people with bipolar disorder manage their social relationships and daily rhythms to try to prevent relapse. Family-focused therapy may help people with bipolar disorder manage their disorder.
- Direct comparisons of various psychotherapies and drug therapies show that they tend to be equally effective in treating depression. Psychotherapies may be more effective than drug therapies in reducing relapse.
- Suicide is defined as death from injury, poisoning, or suffocation when there is evidence (either explicit or implicit) that the injury was self-inflicted and that the decedent intended to kill him- or herself.
- Women are more likely than men to attempt suicide, but men are more likely than women to complete suicide. Cross-cultural differences in suicide rates may have to do with religious prescriptions, stressors, or cultural norms about suicide. Young people are less likely than adults to commit suicide, but suicide rates among youth have been fluctuating dramatically in recent decades. The elderly, particularly elderly men, are at high risk for suicide.
- Several mental disorders increase the risk for suicide, including depression, bipolar disorder, substance abuse, schizophrenia, and anxiety disorders.
- Several negative life events or circumstances increase the risk for suicide, including economic hardship, serious illness, loss, and abuse.
- Suicide clusters (also called suicide contagion) occur when two or more suicides or attempted suicides are nonrandomly bunched in space or time.
- Impulsivity and hopelessness predict suicidal tendencies.
- Family history, twin, and adoption studies all suggest a genetic vulnerability to suicide. Many studies have found a link between low serotonin levels and suicide.
- Drug treatments for suicidal patients most often involve lithium or antidepressant medications. Psychotherapies for suicide are similar to those for depression. Dialectical behavior therapy addresses skill deficits and thinking patterns in people who are suicidal.
- Suicide hotlines and crisis intervention programs provide immediate help to people who are highly suicidal. Community prevention programs aim to educate the public about suicide and to encourage suicidal people to enter treatment.
- Guns are involved in the majority of suicides, and some research suggests that restricting access to guns can reduce the number of suicide attempts.

KEY TERMS

repetitive transcranial magnetic stimulation (rTMS) 203
vagus nerve stimulation (VNS) 204
deep brain stimulation 204
light therapy 204
behavior therapy 205
cognitive-behavioral therapy (CBT) 206
interpersonal therapy (IPT) 208
interpersonal and social rhythm therapy (ISRT) 209
family-focused therapy (FFT) 209
suicide 211
suicide attempts 211
suicide ideation 211
nonsuicidal self-injury (NSSI) 214
egoistic suicide 214
anomic suicide 214
altruistic suicide 214
suicide cluster 215
suicide contagion 215
impulsivity 215
hopelessness 216

Chapter 8

Schizophrenia and Related Psychotic Disorders

CHAPTER OUTLINE

Extraordinary People

John Nash, *A Beautiful Mind*

In 1959, at age 30, John Nash was a widely recognized mathematician and professor at the Massachusetts Institute of Technology. While still a graduate student at Princeton, he had introduced the notion of equilibrium to game theory, which eventually would revolutionize the field of economics and win him the Nobel Prize.

As writer Sylvia Nasar details in her biography of John Nash, *A Beautiful Mind*—the basis for the Academy Award–winning film—Nash had always been eccentric and had few social skills. But in 1959 Nash began writing letters to the United Nations, the FBI, and other government agencies complaining of conspiracies to take over the world. He also began talking openly about his belief that powers from outer space, or perhaps from foreign governments, were communicating with him through the front page of the *New York Times.* He gave a series of incoherent lectures at Columbia and Yale universities. Nash later described one of his delusions:

> I got the impression that other people at MIT were wearing red neckties so I would notice them. As I became more and more delusional, not only persons at MIT but people in Boston wearing red neckties [would seem significant to me] . . . [there was some relation to] a crypto-communist plot." (Nasar, 1998, p. 242)

Nash's wife, Alicia, saw him become increasingly distant and cold toward her. His behavior grew more and more bizarre:

> Several times, Nash had cornered her with odd questions when they were alone, either at home or driving in the car. "Why don't you tell me about it?" he asked in an angry, agitated tone, apropos of nothing. "Tell me what you know," he demanded. (Nasar, 1998, p. 248)

Alicia had him committed to McLean Hospital in April 1959 after his threats to harm her became more severe and his behavior became increasingly unpredictable. There Nash was diagnosed with paranoid schizophrenia and was given medication and daily psychoanalytic therapy. Nash learned to hide his delusions and hallucinations and to behave rationally, although his inner world remained unchanged. On his release, Nash resigned from MIT, furious that the institution had "conspired" in his commitment to McLean Hospital.

After traveling around Europe for 2 years, Nash walked the streets of Princeton with a fixed expression and a dead gaze, wearing Russian peasant garments and going into restaurants in his bare feet. He wrote endless letters and made many phone calls to friends and eminences around the world, talking of numerology and world affairs.

Alicia was forced to have him committed again, this time in Trenton State Hospital. After 6 weeks, Nash was considered much improved and was moved to another ward of the hospital. There he began to work on a paper on fluid dynamics. After 6 months of hospitalization, a month after his thirty-third birthday, he was discharged. Nash appeared to be well for some time, but then his thinking, speech, and behavior began to slip again. Eventually, he ended up living with his mother in Roanoke, Virginia.

His daily rounds extended no farther than the library or the shops at the end of Grandin Road, but in his mind he traveled to the remotest reaches of the globe and lived in refugee camps, foreign embassies, prisons, and bomb shelters. At other times, he felt that he was inhabiting an inferno, a purgatory, or a polluted heaven. His many identities included a Palestinian refugee, a Japanese shogun, and even, at times, a mouse (Nasar, 1998).

After his mother died, Nash returned to Princeton and lived with Alicia, who had divorced him. During the 1970s and 1980s, his illness gradually subsided without treatment. Nash was awarded the Nobel Prize in economics for his contributions to game theory. He and Alicia remarried and now live in Princeton, where Nash works on his mathematical theories. He helps care for their son, Johnny, who obtained his Ph.D. in mathematics several years ago and who also has developed paranoid schizophrenia. Although Johnny is receiving the newest treatments for schizophrenia, they help only a little, and he is hospitalized frequently.

What must it be like to walk around with perceptions that do not map onto reality, as John Nash did during the acute phases of his illness? You might see things that do not really exist. You might hear voices that are not coming from other people but are only in your head. You might believe that the ideas you are having are being broadcast over television, so that others already know what you are thinking. If you are unable to tell the difference between what is real and what is unreal, you have a **psychosis.**

Psychosis can take many forms. One of the most common and puzzling psychotic disorders is **schizophrenia.** At times, people with schizophrenia think and communicate clearly, have an accurate view of reality, and function well in daily life. At other times, their thinking and speech are garbled, they lose touch with reality, and they are unable to care for themselves.

Schizophrenia exacts a heavy toll, including medical costs. More than 90 percent of people with schizophrenia seek treatment in a mental health or general medicine facility in any given year (Narrow et al., 1993). International studies show that nations spend up to 3 percent of their health care budget treating people with schizophrenia, and tens of billions of dollars more are lost in declines in productivity (Knapp, Mangalore, & Simon, 2004). Most people who develop schizophrenia do so in the late teenage or early adult years. By then, they have been educated and are ready to contribute to society. Then the disorder strikes, often preventing them from contributing. They may instead need continual services, including residential care, rehabilitative therapy, subsidized income, and the help of social workers to obtain needed resources—and they need these services for the rest of their lives, because schizophrenia tends to be chronic.

Within the United States, 1 to 2 percent of the population will develop schizophrenia at some time in their lives (Walker, Kestler, Bollini, & Hochman, 2004). Similarly, studies around the globe find that between 0.5 and 2 percent of the general population will develop from schizophrenia (Gottesman, 1991; Linscott & van Os, 2010). Because schizophrenia is one of the most stigmatized psychological disorders, people often hide away their loved ones who have it.

E. Fuller Torrey (2006) compiled data from several sources to estimate where people with schizophrenia are living; his estimates are given in Figure 8.1. Note that the majority of people with schizophrenia live independently or with their family. Note also in Figure 8.1 that almost as many people with schizophrenia are in jails, prisons, homeless shelters, and on the street as are in hospitals and nursing homes. The criminal justice system and shelters often are repositories for people with schizophrenia who do not have families to support them or the resources to get psychiatric help.

FIGURE 8.1 **Distribution of People with Schizophrenia.** Most people with schizophrenia live with family members or independently, but a number are in hospitals, in nursing homes, in group homes, in jail, or on the street.

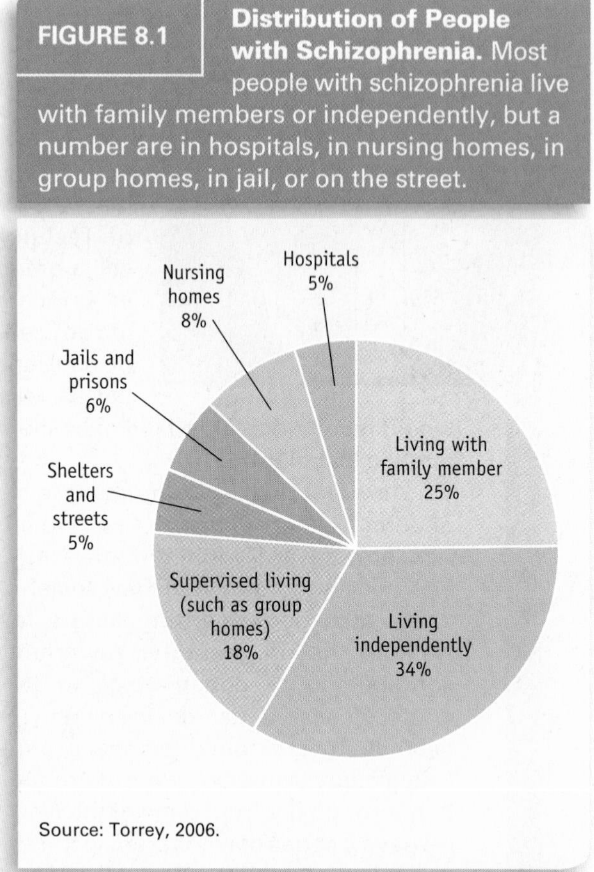

Source: Torrey, 2006.

SYMPTOMS, DIAGNOSIS, AND COURSE

Schizophrenia is a complex disorder that can take many forms. Indeed, many researchers and clinicians talk about "the schizophrenias," reflecting their belief that several disorders currently are captured by the diagnostic criteria for schizophrenia (Mueser & McGurk, 2004). In the *DSM-IV-TR*, delusions, hallucinations, and disorganized speech are not necessary for the diagnosis of schizophrenia (Criterion A in Table 8.1), but in the *DSM-5* the presence of at least one of these symptoms will likely be required for the diagnosis. There are three categories of symptoms: positive symptoms, negative symptoms, and cognitive deficits (Mueser & McGurk, 2004).

Positive Symptoms

The **positive symptoms** of schizophrenia include delusions, hallucinations, disorganized thought and speech, and disorganized or catatonic behavior.

Schizophrenia Along the Continuum

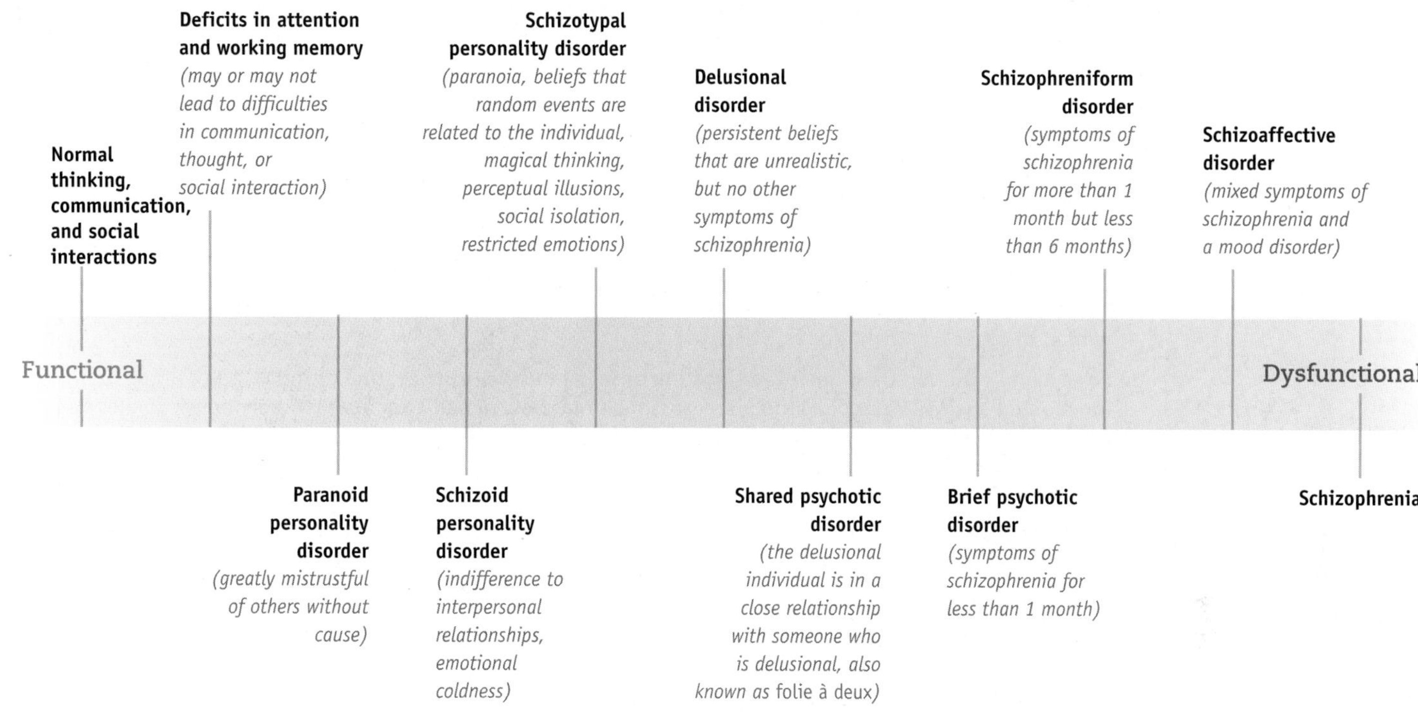

Deficits in attention and working memory
(may or may not lead to difficulties in communication, thought, or social interaction)
Schizotypal personality disorder
(paranoia, beliefs that random events are related to the individual, magical thinking, perceptual illusions, social isolation, restricted emotions)
Delusional disorder
(persistent beliefs that are unrealistic, but no other symptoms of schizophrenia)
Schizophreniform disorder
(symptoms of schizophrenia for more than 1 month but less than 6 months)
Schizoaffective disorder
(mixed symptoms of schizophrenia and a mood disorder)
Normal thinking, communication, and social interactions
Functional
Dysfunctional
Paranoid personality disorder
(greatly mistrustful of others without cause)
Schizoid personality disorder
(indifference to interpersonal relationships, emotional coldness)
Shared psychotic disorder
(the delusional individual is in a close relationship with someone who is delusional, also known as folie à deux)
Brief psychotic disorder
(symptoms of schizophrenia for less than 1 month)
Schizophrenia

After reading John Nash's story, you may think schizophrenia is so different in nature from normal experience that it couldn't possibly be on a continuum. However, the symptoms that make up schizophrenia can appear in mild to moderate form in many people who do not meet the full criteria for any disorder (Linscott & van Os, 2010). For example, in a study of 8,580 people from an unselected community sample, 28 percent reported having had at least one symptom characteristic of schizophrenia, such as hearing voices that no one else heard or believing that their thoughts were being controlled by someone else (Johns et al., 2004). In addition, biological family members of people with schizophrenia often show problems in attention and memory, as well as neurological abnormalities similar to those seen in schizophrenia.

Further along the continuum are personality disorders—such as schizoid personality disorder, paranoid personality disorder, and especially schizotypal personality disorder (see Chapter 9)—that involve moderate symptoms resembling those of schizophrenia but with a retained grasp on reality. People with these personality disorders often speak in odd and eccentric ways, have unusual beliefs or perceptions, and have difficulty relating to other people. Many investigators consider these personality disorders to be along the "schizophrenia spectrum"—that part of the continuum that includes diagnosable disorders that share similarities with schizophrenia but are not as severe.

Still further along the continuum are other disorders, also considered part of the schizophrenia spectrum, in which people lose touch with reality. In delusional disorder, individuals have persistent beliefs that are contrary to reality, but they lack other symptoms of schizophrenia and often are not impaired in their functioning. Their delusions tend to be about things that are possible but untrue. When these delusions are shared by others in close relationship with the delusional person, they warrant a diagnosis of shared psychotic disorder. In brief psychotic disorder, individuals have symptoms of schizophrenia for 1 month or less. In schizophreniform disorder, individuals have symptoms of schizophrenia for 1 to 6 months but usually resume normal lives. Schizoaffective disorder presents a mixed picture of schizophrenia and depression or bipolar disorder.

This chapter focuses primarily on schizophrenia, which has been researched much more than any of the other disorders on the continuum. You will read about schizophrenia's symptoms, subtypes, causes, and prognosis. Most theorists view schizophrenia primarily as a biological disorder, but psychological and social factors can influence its severity and its frequency of relapses. Effective biological treatments for schizophrenia have been developed in the past 50 years. Often, they are supplemented by psychological and social therapies that help the person with schizophrenia cope with the impact of the disorder on his or her life. This chapter considers theoretical perspectives and treatments that integrate knowledge of the biological and psychosocial contributors to schizophrenia.

TABLE 8.1 *DSM-IV-TR* Criteria for Schizophrenia

A. Two (or more) of the following, each present for a significant portion of time during a 1-month period (or less if successfully treated):

1. Delusions
2. Hallucinations
3. Disorganized speech (e.g., frequent derailment or incoherence)
4. Grossly disorganized or catatonic behavior
5. Negative symptoms, i.e., affective flattening, alogia, or avolition

Note: Only one Criterion A symptom is required if delusions are bizarre or hallucinations consist of a voice keeping up a running commentary on the person's behavior or thoughts, or two or more voices conversing with each other.

B. For a significant portion of the time since the onset of the disturbance, one or more major areas of functioning such as work or school, interpersonal relations, or self-care are markedly below the level expected for the individual or achieved prior to the onset.

C. Continuous signs of the disturbance persist for at least 6 months. This 6-month period must include at least 1 month of symptoms (or less if successfully treated) that meet Criterion A and may include periods of prodromal or residual symptoms. During these prodromal or residual periods, the signs of the disturbance may be manifested by only negative symptoms or two or more symptoms listed in Criterion A present in an attenuated form (e.g., odd beliefs, unusual perceptual experiences).

D. Schizoaffective disorder and mood disorder with psychotic features have been ruled out.

E. The disturbance is not due to the direct physiological effects of a substance (e.g., a drug of abuse, a medication) or a general medical condition.

F. If there is a history of autistic disorder or another pervasive developmental disorder, the additional diagnosis of schizophrenia is made only if prominent delusions or hallucinations are also present for at least a month (or less if successfully treated).

Source: Reprinted with permission from the *Diagnostic and Statistical Manual of Mental Disorders,* Fourth Edition, Text Revision.

Delusions

Delusions are ideas that an individual believes are true but are highly unlikely and often simply impossible. Of course, most people occasionally hold beliefs that are likely to be wrong, such as the belief that they will win the lottery. These kinds of *self-deceptions* differ from delusions in at least three ways (Strauss, 1969). First, self-deceptions are at least possible, whereas delusions often are not. It is possible, if highly unlikely, that you are going to win the lottery, but it is not possible that your body is dissolving and floating into space. Second, people harboring self-deceptions may think about these beliefs occasionally, but people harboring delusions tend to be preoccupied with them. Delusional people look for evidence in support of their beliefs, attempt to convince others of these beliefs, and take actions based on them, such as filing lawsuits against the people they believe are trying to control their mind. Third, people holding self-deceptions typically acknowledge that their beliefs may be wrong, but people holding delusions often are highly resistant to arguments or compelling facts that contradict their delusions. They may view the arguments others make against their beliefs as a conspiracy to silence them and as evidence of the truth of their beliefs.

Common Types of Delusions Table 8.2 lists some of the more common types of delusions. Most common are **persecutory delusions** (Bentall et al., 2008). People with persecutory delusions may believe they are being watched or tormented by people they know, such as their professors, or by agencies or persons in authority with whom they have never had direct contact, such as the FBI or a particular member of Congress. Pamela Spiro Wagner, a person with schizophrenia, writes about delusions she had after having a tooth filled at the dentist's office.

TABLE 8.2 Types of Delusions

These are some types of delusions that are often woven together in a complex and frightening system of beliefs.

Delusion	Definition	Example
Persecutory delusion	False belief that oneself or one's loved ones are being persecuted, watched, or conspired against by others	Belief that the CIA, FBI, and local police are conspiring to catch you in a sting operation
Delusion of reference	Belief that random events are directed at oneself	Belief that a newscaster is reporting on your movements
Grandiose delusion	False belief that one has great power, knowledge, or talent or that one is a famous and powerful person	Belief that you are Martin Luther King Jr. reincarnated
Delusions of being controlled	Beliefs that one's thoughts, feelings, or behaviors are being imposed or controlled by an external force	Belief that an alien has taken over your body and is controlling your behavior
Thought broadcasting	Belief that one's thoughts are being broadcast from one's mind for others to hear	Belief that your thoughts are being transmitted via the Internet against your will
Thought insertion	Belief that another person or object is inserting thoughts into one's head	Belief that your spouse is inserting blasphemous thoughts into your mind through the microwave
Thought withdrawal	Belief that thoughts are being removed from one's head by another person or an object	Belief that your roommate is stealing all your thoughts while you sleep
Delusion of guilt or sin	False belief that one has committed a terrible act or is responsible for a terrible event	Belief that you have killed someone
Somatic delusion	False belief that one's appearance or part of one's body is diseased or altered	Belief that your intestines have been replaced by snakes

VOICES

A few days later, I come to understand that amalgam is not all the dentist filled the tooth with. I realize from various signs and evidence around me that he implanted a computer microchip for reasons I can't yet determine. The computers at the drugstore across the street, programmed by the Five People, have tapped into my TV set and monitor my activities with radar. If I go out, special agents keep every one of my movements under surveillance. (Wagner & Spiro, 2001, p. 205)

Another common type of delusion is the **delusion of reference,** in which people believe that random events or comments by others are directed at them. People with delusions of reference may believe that the comments of a local politician at a rally are directed at them. John Nash believed that people in Boston were wearing red neckties so he would notice them as part of some crypto-communist plot.

Grandiose delusions are beliefs that one is a special being or possesses special powers (Mueser & McGurk, 2004). A person may believe herself a deity incarnated. Or she may believe that she is the most intelligent person on earth or has discovered the cure for a disease.

Another common type of delusion is **delusions of thought insertion,** or beliefs that one's thoughts are being controlled by outside forces, as this person with schizophrenia describes.

VOICES

"Suggestions" or "commands" are being transmitted (by a parapsychologist) straight into an unknowing victim's hearing-center, becoming strong impressions on his mind. Those "voices" (which are sometimes accompanied by melodious tones and sounds that either please or irritate the mind) will subliminally change his personality by controlling what kinds of suggestions go into his "subconscious memory" to govern how he feels, or mind-boggle him (trick his mind

(continued)

into believing that they are its own thoughts) during these brainwash and thought-control techniques. Psychotropic medications are given to the victims who can "discern the voices" over other sounds in order to keep them ignorant to the real truth about their dilemma, and to enhance the chemical-reaction in the brain to the stimulation as their souls: (minds): are enslaved by computers programmed to "think" for them.

Delusional beliefs can be simple and transient, such as when a person with schizophrenia believes the pain he has just experienced in his stomach is the result of someone across the room shooting a laser beam at him. However, delusional beliefs often are complex and elaborate with the person clinging to these beliefs for long periods. The following account illustrates how several types of delusions—grandiose delusions, persecutory delusions, delusions of reference, and delusions of thought control—may work together in one person's belief system. Although the passage is written by a person with schizophrenia about his own experience, he speaks of himself in the third person.

VOICES

A drama that profoundly transformed David Zelt began at a conference on human psychology. David respected the speakers as scholars and wanted their approval of a paper he had written about telepathy. A week before the conference, David had sent his paper "On the Origins of Telepathy" to one speaker, and the other speakers had all read it. He proposed the novel scientific idea that telepathy could only be optimally studied during the process of birth. . . .

David's paper was viewed as a monumental contribution to the conference and potentially to psychology in general. If scientifically verified, his concept of telepathy, universally present at birth and measurable, might have as much influence as the basic ideas of Darwin and Freud. Each speaker focused on David. By using allusions and nonverbal communications that included pointing and glancing, each illuminated different aspects of David's contribution. Although his name was never mentioned, the speakers enticed David into feeling that he had accomplished something supernatural in writing the paper. . . . David was described as having a halo around his head, and the Second Coming was announced as forthcoming. Messianic feelings took hold of him. His mission would be to aid the poor and needy, especially in underdeveloped countries. . . .

David's sensitivity to nonverbal communication was extreme; he was adept at reading people's minds. His perceptual powers were so developed that he could not discriminate between telepathic reception and spoken language by others. He was distracted by others in a way that he had never been before. It was as if the nonverbal behavior of people interacting with him was a kind of code. Facial expressions, gestures, and postures of others often determined what he felt and thought.

Several hundred people at the conference were talking about David. He was the subject of enormous mystery, profound in his silence. Criticism, though, was often expressed by skeptics of the anticipated Second Coming. David felt the intense communication about him as torturous. He wished the talking, nonverbal behavior, and pervasive train of thoughts about him would stop. (Zelt, 1981, pp. 527–531)

David's *grandiose delusions* were that he had discovered the source of telepathy, that all the scientists thought highly of him, and that he might be the Messiah. These grandiose delusions were accompanied by *persecutory delusions*—that the scientists were criticizing him because they were jealous. David's delusions of reference were that all the scientists were talking about him, both directly and indirectly. David believed that he could read others' minds. Finally, he had *delusions of thought control*—that the scientists were determining his feelings with their facial expressions, gestures, and postures.

Delusions also occur in other disorders. In particular, individuals with severe forms of depression or bipolar disorder (Chapter 7) often have delusions that are consistent with their moods: When they are depressed they may believe they have committed some unforgivable sin, and when they are manic they may believe they are a deity (Bentall et al., 2008).

Delusions Across Cultures Although the types of delusions we have discussed probably occur in all cultures, the specific content of delusions can differ across cultures (Suhail & Cochrane, 2002; Tateyama et al., 1998). For example, persecutory delusions often focus on intelligence agencies or persons of authority in the person's culture. European Americans with schizophrenia often fear that the Central Intelligence Agency is after them; Afro-Caribbeans with schizophrenia sometimes believe that people are killing them with curses (Westermeyer, 1993; for similar results comparing British and Pakistani patients, see Suhail & Cochrane, 2002). Studies comparing Japanese and Western Europeans who have schizophrenia have found that, among the Japanese, delusions of being slandered by others and delusions that others know something terrible about them are relatively common, perhaps due to the emphasis in Japanese culture on how one is thought of by others. In contrast, among Germans and Austrians with schizophrenia, religious delusions of having committed a sin (e.g., "Satan orders me to pray to him; I will be punished") are relatively common, perhaps due to the influence of Christianity in Western Europe (Tateyama et al., 1993).

Some theorists argue that odd or impossible beliefs that are part of a culture's shared belief system cannot be considered delusions (Fabrega, 1993). If the people of a culture believe that the spirits of dead relatives watch over the living, then individuals in that culture who hold that belief are not considered delusional. However, people who hold extreme manifestations of their culture's shared belief systems are considered delusional. For example, a person in the culture described who believed that her dead relatives were causing her heart to rot would be considered delusional.

Hallucinations

Have you ever had a strange perceptual experience, such as thinking you saw someone when no one was near, thinking you heard a voice talking to you, or feeling as though your body was floating through the air? In one study, 15 percent of mentally healthy college students reported sometimes hearing voices, such as their "conscience" giving them advice, or two voices (usually both their own) debating a topic (Chapman, Edell, & Chapman, 1980). Most of these students probably would not be diagnosed with schizophrenia because their auditory "hallucinations" are occasional and brief—often occurring when they are tired, stressed, or under the influence of alcohol or other drugs—and do not impair their daily functioning in any way. In addition, the hallucinations that occur due to alcohol or drug use usually are arbitrary perceptual phenomena, such as flashes of light or blasts of noise (Aleman & Laroi, 2008).

The **hallucinations**—unreal perceptual experiences—of people with schizophrenia tend to be much more bizarre and complex than these college students' hallucinations and are precipitated not only by sleep deprivation, stress, or drugs, as this person describes.

VOICES

At one point, I would look at my coworkers and their faces would become distorted. Their teeth looked like fangs ready to devour me. Most of the time I couldn't trust myself to look at anyone for fear of being swallowed. I had no respite from the illness. Even when I tried to sleep, the demons would keep me awake, and at times I would roam the house searching for them. I was being consumed on all sides whether I was awake or asleep. I felt I was being consumed by demons. (Long, 1996)

An **auditory hallucination** (hearing voices, music, and so on) is the most common hallucination, and it is more common in women than in men (American Psychiatric Association, 2000). These hallucinations may consist of a voice speaking the individual's thoughts aloud or carrying on a running commentary on the person's behavior, a collection of voices speaking about the individual in the third person, or voices issuing commands and instructions (Aleman & Laroi, 2008). The voices may seem to come either from inside the person's head or from somewhere outside. They often have a negative quality, criticizing or threatening the individuals or telling them to hurt themselves or others (Aleman & Laroi, 2008). People with schizophrenia may talk back to the voices even as they are trying to talk to people who are actually in the room with them. The second most common hallucination is the **visual hallucination,** often accompanied by auditory hallucinations. For example, a woman may see a figure of a man standing at her bedside, telling her she is damned and must die. An individual's hallucinations may be consistent with her delusions—the person seeing Satan telling her she must die may think that she is Satan.

Hallucinations can involve any of the senses (Aleman & Laroi, 2008). **Tactile hallucinations** involve the perception that something is happening to the outside of the person's body—for example, that bugs are crawling up her back. **Somatic hallucinations** involve the perception that something is happening inside the person's body—for example, that worms are eating his intestines. These hallucinations often are frightening (NIMH, 2008; Torrey, 2006).

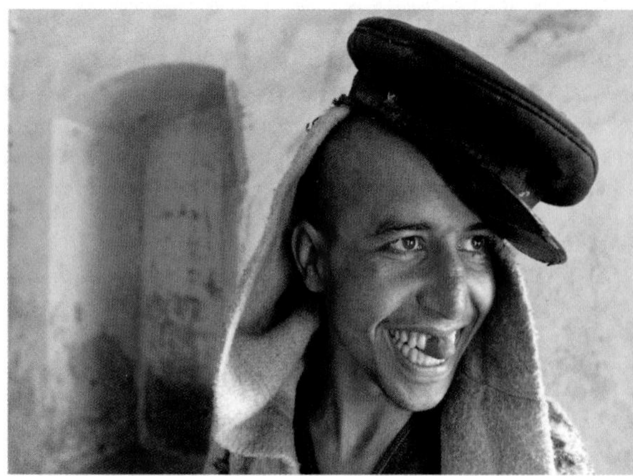

The specific content of hallucinations and delusions may be influenced by culture.

Hallucinations do not occur only in schizophrenia and other psychotic disorders (Aleman & Laroi, 2008). One study of individuals with visual hallucinations (Gauntlett-Gilbert & Kuipers, 2003) found that 60 percent were diagnosed with schizophrenia or schizoaffective disorders (described below) but that 25 percent were diagnosed with depression and 15 percent with bipolar disorder (see Chapter 7),

As with delusions, the types of hallucinations people have in different cultures appear similar, but the specific content of hallucinations can be culturally specific. For example, a person from Asia may see the ghosts of ancestors haunting him or her, but this is not a common experience for Europeans (Browne, 2001; Westermeyer, 1993). As with delusions, clinicians must interpret hallucinations in a cultural context (Aleman & Laroi, 2008). For example, a Puerto Rican woman might be diagnosed with schizophrenia by a European American interviewer because she believes she has special powers to anticipate events and because she describes what sound like hallucinations, such as "I see images of saints and virgins in the house. I also see the image of Jesus Christ, with the crown of thorns and bleeding." Interviewers who know Puerto Rican culture, however, might recognize this woman's beliefs and experiences as consistent with a spiritual group common in Latin America that believes in clairvoyance and religious visions (Guarnaccia et al., 1992).

Disorganized Thought and Speech

The disorganized thinking of people with schizophrenia is often referred to as a **formal thought disorder.** One of the most common forms of disorganization in schizophrenia is a tendency to slip from one topic to a seemingly unrelated topic with little coherent transition, often referred to as the *loosening of associations,* or *derailment.* For example, one person with schizophrenia posted this "announcement."

VOICES

Things that relate, the town of Antelope, Oregon, Jonestown, Charlie Manson, the Hillside Strangler, the Zodiac Killer, Watergate, King's trial in L.A., and many more. In the last 7 years alone, over 23 Starwars scientists committed suicide for no apparent reason. The AIDS coverup, the conference in South America in 87 had over 1,000 doctors claim that insects can transmit it. To be able to read one's thoughts and place thoughts in one's mind without the person knowing it's being done. Realization is a reality of bioelectromagnetic control, which is thought transfer and emotional control, recording individual brain-wave frequencies of thought, sensation, and emotions.

The person who wrote this announcement saw clear connections among the events he listed in the first half of the paragraph and between these events and his concerns about mind reading and bioelectromagnetic control. However, it is hard for us to see these connections.

A person with schizophrenia may answer questions with barely related or unrelated comments. For example, when asked why he is in the hospital, a man with schizophrenia might answer, "Spaghetti looks like worms. I really think it's worms. Gophers dig tunnels but rats build nests." At times, the person's speech is so disorganized as to be totally incoherent to the listener, known as *word salad.* For example, "Much of abstraction has been left unsaid and undone in these products milk syrup, and others, due to economics, differentials, subsidies, bankruptcy, tools, buildings, bonds, national stocks, foundation craps, weather, trades, government in levels of breakages and fuses in electronics too all formerly states not necessarily factuated" (Maher, 1966, p. 395). The person may make up words that mean something only to him or her, known as *neologisms.* Or, the person may make associations between words that are based on the sounds of the words rather than on the content, known as *clangs.* Or the person may repeat the same word or statement over and over again (NIMH, 2008).

Men with schizophrenia tend to show more severe deficits in language than do women with schizophrenia, possibly because language is controlled more bilaterally—that is, by both sides of the brain—in women than in men (Goldstein et al., 2002). Thus, the brain abnormalities associated with schizophrenia may not affect women's language and thought as much as they do men's because women can use both sides of their brain to compensate for problems. In contrast, language is more localized in men, so when these areas of the brain are affected by schizophrenia, men may not be as able to compensate for the deficits.

Disorganized or Catatonic Behavior

The disorganized behavior of people with schizophrenia often frightens others. People with schizophrenia may display unpredictable and apparently untriggered agitation—suddenly shouting, swearing, or pacing rapidly. These behaviors may occur in response to hallucinations or delusions. For example, a man who believes he is being persecuted may hallucinate a frightening figure chasing him; in response, he screams and runs. Another man who believes a computer chip has been implanted under his skin to control him may pace agitatedly because no one will believe him and offer him help.

People with schizophrenia often have trouble organizing their daily routines of bathing, dressing properly, and eating regularly. Because their attention and memory are impaired, it takes all their concentration to accomplish even one simple task, such as brushing their teeth (NIMH, 2008; Torrey, 2006). They may engage in socially unacceptable behavior, such as public masturbation. Many are disheveled and dirty, sometimes wearing few clothes on a cold day or heavy clothes on a very hot day.

Catatonia is disorganized behavior that reflects unresponsiveness to the world. In *catatonic excitement,* the person becomes wildly agitated for no apparent reason. The individual may articulate a number of delusions or hallucinations or may be incoherent (Mueser & Jeste, 2008; NIMH, 2008).

Negative Symptoms

The **negative symptoms** of schizophrenia involve losses, or deficits, in certain domains. Three types of negative symptoms are recognized as core symptoms of schizophrenia: affective flattening, alogia, and avolition.

Affective Flattening

Affective flattening or *blunted affect* is a severe reduction or absence of affective (emotional) responses to the environment. The person's face may

A significant percentage of people with schizophrenia end up homeless and on the streets.

remain immobile most of the time, and his or her body language may be unresponsive (Kring & Moran, 2008). One man set fire to his house and then sat down to watch TV. When it was called to his attention that his house was on fire, he calmly got up and walked outside (Torrey, 1995). People with blunted affect may speak in a monotone and avoid eye contact with others.

This affective flattening may reflect the severe *anhedonia* (a loss of interest in everything in life) that some people with schizophrenia experience. They lose the ability to experience emotion, no matter what happens. This emotional void itself can be highly aversive (Torrey, 2006).

We cannot assume, however, that people with affective flattening are not experiencing emotion. In one study, people with schizophrenia and people without it were shown emotionally charged films while their facial expressions were observed and their physiological arousal was recorded (Kring & Neale, 1996). The people with schizophrenia showed less facial responsiveness to the films than did the normal group, but they reported experiencing just as much emotion and showed even more physiological arousal. Thus, people with schizophrenia who show no emotion may be experiencing intense emotion that they cannot express.

Alogia

Alogia, or poverty of speech, is a reduction in speaking. The person may not initiate speech with others and, when asked direct questions, may give brief, empty replies. The person's lack of speech presumably reflects a lack of thinking, although it may be caused in part by a lack of motivation to speak (Torrey, 2006).

Avolition

Avolition is an inability to persist at common, goal-directed activities, including those at work, school, and home. The person has great trouble completing tasks, is disorganized and careless, and apparently is completely unmotivated. He or she may sit around all day doing almost nothing and may withdraw and become socially isolated.

Cognitive Deficits

People with schizophrenia show deficits in basic cognitive processes, including attention and memory (Savla, Moore, & Palmer, 2008). Compared to people without schizophrenia, they have greater difficulty focusing and maintaining their attention at will, for example, in tracking a moving object with their eyes. In addition, people with schizophrenia show deficits in *working memory,* the ability to hold information in memory and manipulate it (Barch, 2005). These deficits in attention and working memory make it difficult for people with schizophrenia to pay attention to relevant information and to suppress unwanted or irrelevant information. As a result, they find it difficult to distinguish the thoughts in their mind that are relevant to the situation at hand and to ignore stimuli in their environment that are not relevant to what they are doing. These deficits taken together may contribute to the hallucinations, delusions, and disorganized thought and behavior of people with schizophrenia (Barch, 2005). Information and stimulation constantly flood their consciousness, and they are unable to filter out what is irrelevant or to determine the source of the information. This makes it difficult for them to concentrate, maintain a coherent stream of thought or conversation, perform a basic task, or distinguish real from unreal. Social relationships and work performance are severely affected, and daily functioning is impaired. Delusions and hallucinations may develop as individuals try to make sense of the thoughts and perceptions bombarding their consciousness (Beck & Rector, 2005).

The relatives of people with schizophrenia also show many of these cognitive deficits, even if they do not show the symptoms of schizophrenia (Snitz, MacDonald, & Carter, 2003). In addition, longitudinal studies of people who develop schizophrenia suggest that many show these cognitive deficits before they develop acute symptoms of the disorder (Cannon et al., 2003). Thus, cognitive deficits may be an early marker of risk for schizophrenia and may contribute to the development of other symptoms (Gur et al., 2007).

Diagnosis

Schizophrenia has been recognized as a psychological disorder since the early 1800s (Gottesman, 1991). In 1883, German psychiatrist Emil Kraepelin labeled the disorder *dementia praecox* (precocious dementia), because he believed that the disorder results from premature deterioration of the brain. He viewed the disorder as progressive, irreversible, and chronic (Lavretsky, 2008).

Eugen Bleuler disagreed with Kraepelin's view that this disorder develops at an early age and always leads to severe deterioration of the brain (Lavretsky, 2008). Bleuler introduced the label *schizophrenia* for this disorder, from the Greek words *schizein*, meaning "to split," and *phren*, meaning "mind." Bleuler believed that this disorder involves the splitting of usually integrated psychic functions of mental associations, thoughts, and emotions. (Bleuler did not view schizophrenia as the splitting of distinct personalities, as in dissociative identity disorder, nor do modern psychiatrists and psychologists.)

Bleuler argued that the primary problem underlying the symptoms of schizophrenia is the "breaking of associative threads," that is, a breaking of associations among thought, language, memory, and problem solving. He argued that the attentional problems seen in schizophrenia are due to a lack of the necessary links between aspects of the mind and that the behavioral symptoms (such as alogia) are similarly due to an inability to maintain a train of thought (Lavretsky, 2008).

The *DSM-IV-TR* states that, in order to be diagnosed with schizophrenia, an individual must show some symptoms of the disorder for at least 6 months. During this 6-month period, there must be at least 1 month of acute symptoms during which two or more of the broad groups of symptoms (e.g., delusions, hallucinations, disorganized speech, disorganized or catatonic behavior, negative symptoms) are present and severe enough to impair the individual's social or occupational functioning (see Table 8.1). Some people seek treatment shortly after the onset of symptoms, but most do not and may experience significant symptoms for months or years before seeking treatment (Castle & Morgan, 2008).

Prodromal symptoms are symptoms that are present before people go into the acute phase of schizophrenia, and **residual symptoms** are symptoms that are present after they emerge from it. During the prodromal and residual phases, people with schizophrenia may express beliefs that are unusual but not delusional (Nelson & Yung, 2008). They may have strange perceptual experiences, such as sensing another person in the room, without reporting full-blown hallucinations. They may speak in a somewhat disorganized and tangential way but remain coherent. Their behavior may be peculiar—for example, collecting scraps of paper—but not grossly disorganized. The negative symptoms are especially prominent in the prodromal and residual phases of the disorder. The person may be withdrawn and uninterested in others or in work or school. During the prodromal phase, family members and friends may perceive the person with schizophrenia as "gradually slipping away" (Torrey, 2006). Left untreated, schizophrenia is both chronic and episodic; after the first onset of an acute episode, individuals may have chronic residual symptoms punctuated by relapses into acute episodes.

The impact of schizophrenia symptoms on peoples' lives is enormous. One review of 37 longitudinal studies that had followed individuals for an average of 3 years after their first episode of acute schizophrenia symptoms found that only about 40 percent were employed or in school and only about 37 percent had recovered a good level of functioning (Menezes, Arenovich, & Zipursky, 2006). Difficulties in functioning are tied to the negative symptoms of schizophrenia—the lack of motivation and appropriate emotional responding—as well as to the positive symptoms. People with schizophrenia who show many negative symptoms have lower levels of educational attainment and less success in holding jobs, poorer performance on cognitive tasks, and a poorer prognosis than do those with predominantly positive symptoms (Andreasen et al., 1990; Eaton, Thara, Federman, & Tien, 1998). In addition, the negative symptoms are less responsive to medication than are the positive symptoms: With medication, a person with schizophrenia may be able to overcome the hallucinations, delusions, and thought disturbances but may not be able to overcome the affective flattening, alogia, and avolition. Thus, the person may remain chronically unresponsive, unmotivated, and socially isolated even when not acutely psychotic (Fenton & McGlashan, 1994).

The *DSM-IV-TR* officially divides schizophrenia into five subtypes (Table 8.3). Three of these types—*paranoid, disorganized*, and *catatonic schizophrenia*—have specific symptoms that differentiate them from one another. The other two types—*undifferentiated* and *residual schizophrenia*—are characterized not by specific differentiating symptoms but rather by a mix of symptoms that are either acute (in the undifferentiated type) or attenuated (in the residual type). In the *DSM-5,* these subtypes are likely to be dropped, because, except perhaps for the paranoid subtype, the evidence for their validity and usefulness has not been strong (Linscott, Allardyee, & van Os, 2009).

TABLE 8.3 Types of Schizophrenia in the *DSM-IV-TR*

The *DSM-IV-TR* recognizes five subtypes of schizophrenia.

Type	Major Features
Paranoid schizophrenia	Delusions and hallucinations with themes of persecution and grandiosity
Disorganized schizophrenia	Incoherence in cognition, speech, and behavior and flat or inappropriate affect
Catatonic schizophrenia	Nearly total unresponsiveness to the environment, as well as motor and verbal abnormalities
Undifferentiated schizophrenia	Diagnosed when a person experiences schizophrenic symptoms but does not meet the criteria for paranoid, disorganized, or catatonic schizophrenia
Residual schizophrenia	History of at least one episode of acute positive symptoms but currently no prominent positive symptoms

Source: Reprinted with permission from the *Diagnostic and Statistical Manual of Mental Disorders,* Fourth Edition, Text Revision. Copyright © 2000 American Psychiatric Association.

Paranoid Schizophrenia

The best-known, and most researched, type of schizophrenia is the paranoid type. This is the type John Nash appeared to suffer from. People with **paranoid schizophrenia** have prominent delusions and hallucinations that involve themes of persecution and grandiosity. They often do not show grossly disorganized speech or behavior. They may be lucid and articulate, relating elaborate stories of plots against them.

People with paranoid schizophrenia are highly resistant to any arguments against their delusions and may become angry if someone argues with them. They may act arrogantly, as if they are superior to others, or may remain aloof and suspicious. The combination of persecutory and grandiose delusions can lead people with this type of schizophrenia to be suicidal or violent toward others.

The prognosis for people with paranoid schizophrenia is better than the prognosis for people with other types of schizophrenia (Hwu et al., 2002).

They are more likely to be able to live independently and to hold down a job and show better cognitive and social functioning (Kendler, McGuire, Gruenberg, & Walsh, 1994). The onset of paranoid schizophrenia tends to occur later in life than does the onset of other forms of schizophrenia, and episodes of psychosis are often triggered by stress. In general, paranoid schizophrenia is considered a milder, less insidious form of schizophrenia (Hafner & van der Heiden, 2008).

Disorganized Schizophrenia

Unlike people with paranoid schizophrenia, people with **disorganized schizophrenia** do not have well-formed delusions or hallucinations. Instead, their thoughts and behaviors are severely disorganized. People with this type of schizophrenia may speak in word salads and be completely incoherent to others. They are prone to odd, stereotyped behaviors, such as frequent grimacing or mannerisms such as flapping their hands. They may be so disorganized that they do not bathe, dress, or eat if left on their own.

The emotional experiences and expressions of people with disorganized schizophrenia are also disturbed. They may not show any emotional reactions, or they may have inappropriate emotional reactions to events, such as laughing uncontrollably at a funeral. When they talk, they may display emotions that appear unrelated to what they are saying or to what is going on in the environment. For example, a young woman with disorganized schizophrenia might respond as follows when asked about her mother: "Mama's sick. [Giggle.] Sicky, sicky, sicky. [Giggle.] I flipped off a doctor once, did you know that? Flip. I wanta wear my blue dress tomorrow. Dress mess. [Giggle.]"

This type of schizophrenia tends to have an early onset and a continuous course, which often is unresponsive to treatment. People with disorganized schizophrenia are among the most disabled by the disorder (Hafner & van der Heiden, 2008).

Catatonic Schizophrenia

People with **catatonic schizophrenia** show a variety of motor behaviors and ways of speaking that suggest almost complete unresponsiveness to their environment (Ungvari et al., 2005). The diagnostic criteria for catatonic schizophrenia require two of the following symptoms: (1) catatonic stupor (remaining motionless for long periods of time); (2) catatonic excitement (excessive and purposeless motor activity); (3) the maintenance of rigid postures or being completely mute for long periods of time; (4) odd mannerisms, such as grimacing or hand flapping; and (5) *echolalia* (the senseless repetition of words just spoken by others) or *echopraxia* (repetitive imitation of the movements of others).

Undifferentiated Schizophrenia and Residual Schizophrenia

People with **undifferentiated schizophrenia** have symptoms that meet the criteria for schizophrenia (delusions, hallucinations, disorganized speech, disorganized behavior, negative symptoms) but do not meet the criteria for paranoid, disorganized, or catatonic schizophrenia. This type of schizophrenia tends to have an early onset and to be chronic and difficult to treat (Hwu et al., 2002).

People with **residual schizophrenia** have had at least one acute episode of acute positive symptoms of schizophrenia but do not currently show any prominent positive symptoms. They continue to have signs of the disorder, however, including the negative symptoms and mild versions of the positive symptoms. These residual symptoms may be chronic over several years (Hwu et al., 2002).

Prognosis

Between 50 and 80 percent of people hospitalized for one schizophrenic episode will be rehospitalized sometime in their lives (Eaton, Moortonsenk, Herrman, & Freeman, 1992). The life expectancy of people with schizophrenia is as much as 10 years shorter than that of people without schizophrenia (McGlashan, 1988; Mortensen, 2003). People with schizophrenia suffer from infectious and circulatory diseases at a higher rate than do people without the disorder, for unclear reasons. As many as 10 to 15 percent of people with schizophrenia commit suicide (Joiner, 2005). The following account of a woman about her suicidal thoughts gives a sense of the pain that many people with schizophrenia live with and wish to end through suicide.

VOICES

I had major fantasies of suicide by decapitation and was reading up on the construction of guillotines. I had written several essays on the problem of the complete destruction of myself; I thought my inner being to be a deeply poisonous substance. The problem, as I saw it, was to kill myself, but then to get rid of my essence in such a way that it did not harm creation. (Anonymous, 1992, p. 334)

Despite the dire statistics, most people with schizophrenia do not show a progressive deterioration in functioning across the life span. Instead, most stabilize within 5 to 10 years of their first episode, showing few or no relapses and regaining a moderately good level of functioning (Eaton et al., 1992, 1998; Menezes et al., 2006). Studies suggest that between 20 and 30 percent of treated people with schizophrenia recover substantially or completely within 10 to 20 years of onset (Breier, Schreiber, Dyer, & Pickar, 1991; Jablensky, 2000).

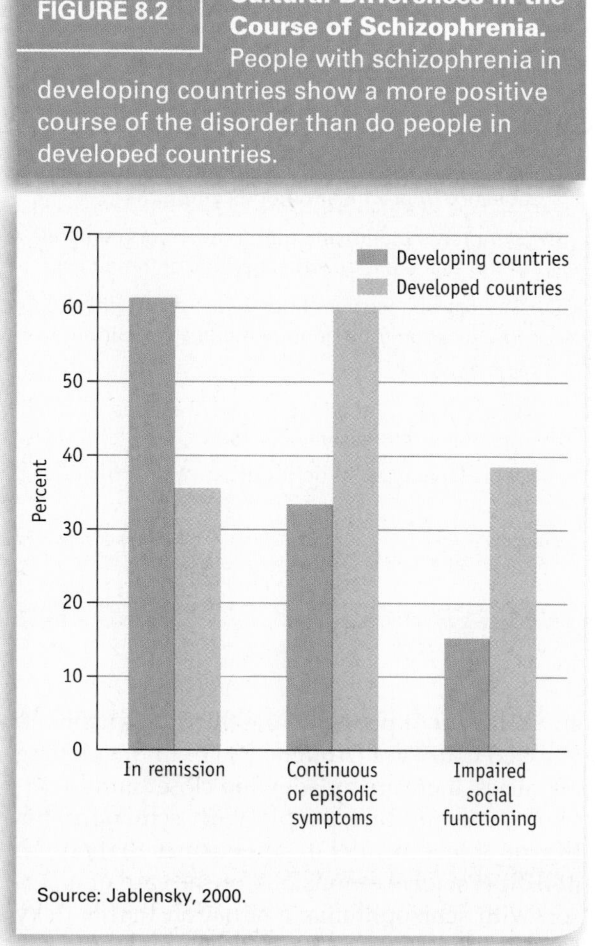

FIGURE 8.2 Cultural Differences in the Course of Schizophrenia. People with schizophrenia in developing countries show a more positive course of the disorder than do people in developed countries.

Source: Jablensky, 2000.

Gender and Age Factors

Women with schizophrenia tend to have better predisorder histories than men (Seeman, 2008). They are more likely to have graduated from high school or college, to have married and had children, and to have developed good social skills. This may be, in part, because the onset of schizophrenia in women tends to be in the late twenties or early thirties, whereas men more often develop schizophrenia in their late teens or early twenties (Goldstein & Lewine, 2000). Women are hospitalized less often and for briefer periods of time than are men, show milder negative symptoms between periods of acute positive symptoms, and have better social adjustment when they are not psychotic. Women also show fewer cognitive deficits than men (Goldstein et al., 2002).

The reasons for these gender differences in the age of onset, course, and cognitive deficits in schizophrenia are not yet well understood. Estrogen may affect the regulation of dopamine, a neurotransmitter implicated in schizophrenia, in ways that are protective for women (Seeman, 2008). Some of the sex differences, particularly in cognitive deficits, may also be due to normal sex differences in the brain (Goldstein et al., 2002). The pace of prenatal brain development, which is hormonally regulated, is slower in males than in females and may place males at higher risk than females for poor brain development. Exposure to toxins and illnesses in utero increases the risk for abnormal brain development and the development of schizophrenia. Several studies suggest that males with schizophrenia show greater abnormalities in brain structure and functioning than do females with schizophrenia (Goldstein & Lewine, 2000).

In both men and women with schizophrenia, functioning seems to improve with age (Jablensky, 2000). Why? Perhaps they find treatments that help them stabilize, or maybe they and their families learn to recognize the early symptoms of a relapse and seek aggressive treatment before the symptoms become acute (Torrey, 2006). Alternatively, the aging of the brain might somehow reduce the likelihood of new episodes of schizophrenia. Some think this might be related to a reduction in dopamine levels in the brain with age; as we will discuss, high dopamine levels have been implicated in schizophrenia (Downar & Kapur, 2008).

Sociocultural Factors

Culture appears to play a strong role in the course of schizophrenia. Schizophrenia tends to have a more benign course in developing countries than in developed countries (Anders, 2003; Jablensky, 2000). Cross-national studies find that persons who develop schizophrenia in countries such as India, Nigeria, and Colombia are less likely to remain incapacitated by the disorder in the long term than are persons who develop schizophrenia in countries such as Great Britain, Denmark, and the United States (Figure 8.2; Jablensky, 2000).

The social environment of people with schizophrenia in developing countries may facilitate adaptation and recovery better than the social

TABLE 8.4 *DSM-IV-TR* Criteria for Schizoaffective Disorder

A. An uninterrupted period of illness during which, at some time, there is either a major depressive episode, a manic episode, or a mixed episode concurrent with symptoms that meet Criterion A for schizophrenia.

Note: The major depressive episode must include Criterion A1: depressed mood.

B. During the same period of illness, there have been delusions or hallucinations for at least 2 weeks in the absence of prominent mood symptoms.

C. Symptoms that meet criteria for a mood episode are present for a substantial portion of the total duration of the active and residual periods of the illness.

D. The disturbance is not due to the direct physiological effects of a substance (e.g., a drug of abuse, a medication) or a general medical condition.

Specify type:

Bipolar Type: if the disturbance includes a manic or a mixed episode (or a manic or a mixed episode and major depressive episodes)

Depressive Type: if the disturbance only includes major depressive episodes

Source: Reprinted with permission from the *Diagnostic and Statistical Manual of Mental Disorders,* Fourth Edition, Text Revision.

environment of people with schizophrenia in developed countries (Anders, 2003). In developing countries, there are broader and closer family networks surrounding people with schizophrenia (Karno & Jenkins, 1993). This ensures that no one person is solely responsible for the care of a person with schizophrenia, a situation that is risky for both the person with schizophrenia and the caregiver. Families in some developing countries also score lower on measures of hostility, criticism, and over-involvement than do families in some developed countries (Hooley, 2007). This may help lower relapse rates for their family members with schizophrenia.

Social factors likely contribute to the gender differences in the course of schizophrenia. Deviant behavior may be more socially acceptable in women than in men, so women who develop schizophrenia may lose less social support than men (Mueser, Bellack, Morrison, & Wade, 1990). Also, women with schizophrenia may have better social skills than men with the disorder. These social skills may help women maintain and use their social support networks and reduce the level of stress in their lives, thereby lowering their risk of relapse (Mueser et al., 1990).

Whatever the reasons for variations in the course of schizophrenia among cultures and between men and women, the conventional wisdom that schizophrenia is inevitably a progressive disorder, marked by more deterioration with time, has been replaced by new evidence that many people with schizophrenia achieve a good level of functioning over time.

Other Psychotic Disorders

The *DSM-IV-TR* recognizes other psychotic disorders that share features with schizophrenia. **Schizoaffective disorder** is a mix of schizophrenia and a mood disorder (Table 8.4). People with schizoaffective disorder simultaneously experience schizophrenic symptoms (delusions, hallucinations, disorganized speech and behavior, and/or negative symptoms) and mood symptoms meeting the criteria for a major depressive episode, a manic episode, or an episode of mixed mania/depression (see Chapter 7). Mood symptoms must be present for much of the period of schizophrenic symptoms. Unlike mood disorders with psychotic features, schizoaffective disorder requires at least 2 weeks of hallucinations or delusions without mood symptoms.

The diagnosis of schizoaffective disorder is controversial; many clinicians believe that it is used when clinicians can't decide between a diagnosis of schizophrenia and one of a mood disorder. Clinicians often disagree on whether an individual warrants this diagnosis (Rudnick & Roe, 2008).

The diagnosis of **schizophreniform disorder** requires that individuals meet Criteria A, D, and E for schizophrenia but show symptoms that last only 1 to 6 months (Table 8.5). This is a relatively rare disorder, with only approximately 0.2 percent of the population meeting the diagnosis (American Psychiatric Association, 2000). Individuals with this disorder who have a good prognosis have a quick onset of symptoms, functioned well previously, and experience confusion but not blunted or flat affect. Individuals who do not show two or more

TABLE 8.5 *DSM-IV-TR* Criteria for Schizophreniform Disorder

A. Criteria A, D, and E for schizophrenia are met.

B. An episode of the disorder (including prodromal, active, and residual phases) lasts at least 1 month but less than 6 months. (When the diagnosis must be made without waiting for recovery, it should be qualified as "provisional.")

C. *Specify if:*

With good prognostic features, as evidenced by two or more of the following:

1. Onset of prominent psychotic symptoms within 4 weeks of the first noticeable change in usual behavior or functioning
2. Confusion or perplexity at the height of the psychotic episode
3. Good premorbid social and occupational functioning
4. Absence of blunted or flat affect

Without good prognostic features

Source: Reprinted with permission from the *Diagnostic and Statistical Manual of Mental Disorders,* Fourth Edition, Text Revision.

TABLE 8.6 *DSM-IV-TR* Criteria for Brief Psychotic Disorder

A. Presence of one (or more) of the following symptoms:

1. Delusions
2. Hallucinations
3. Disorganized speech (e.g., frequent derailment or incoherence)
4. Grossly disorganized or catatonic behavior

Note: Do not include a symptom if it is a culturally sanctioned response pattern.

B. Duration of an episode of the disturbance is at least 1 day but less than 1 month, with eventual full return to premorbid level of functioning.

C. The disturbance is not better accounted for by a mood disorder with psychotic features, schizoaffective disorder, or schizophrenia and is not due to the direct physiological effects of a substance (e.g., a drug of abuse, a medication) or a general medical condition.

Specify if:

With marked stressor(s) (brief reactive psychosis): if symptoms occur shortly after and apparently in response to events that, singly or together, would be markedly stressful to almost anyone in similar circumstances in the person's culture

Without marked stressor(s): if psychotic symptoms do not occur shortly after, or are not apparently in response to, events that, singly or together, would be markedly stressful to almost anyone in similar circumstances in the person's culture

With postpartum onset: if onset within 4 weeks postpartum

Source: Reprinted with permission from the *Diagnostic and Statistical Manual of Mental Disorders,* Fourth Edition, Text Revision.

of these features are said to be without good prognostic features.

Individuals with **brief psychotic disorder** show a sudden onset of delusions, hallucinations, disorganized speech, and/or disorganized behavior. However, the episode lasts only between 1 day and 1 month, after which the symptoms vanish completely (Table 8.6). Symptoms sometimes emerge after a major stressor, such as being in an accident. At other times, no stressor is apparent.

TABLE 8.7 *DSM-IV-TR* Criteria for Delusional Disorder

A. Nonbizarre delusions (i.e., involving situations that occur in real life, such as being followed, poisoned, infected, loved at a distance, or deceived by spouse or lover, or having a disease) of at least 1 month's duration.

B. Criterion A for schizophrenia has never been met. *Note:* Tactile and olfactory hallucinations may be present in delusional disorder if they are related to the delusional theme.

C. Apart from the impact of the delusion(s) or its ramifications, functioning is not markedly impaired and behavior is not obviously odd or bizarre.

D. If mood episodes have occurred concurrently with delusions, their total duration has been brief relative to the duration of the delusional periods.

E. The disturbance is not due to the direct physiological effects of a substance (e.g., a drug of abuse, a medication) or a general medical condition.

Specify type (the following types are assigned based on the predominant delusional theme):

Erotomanic Type: delusions that another person, usually of higher status, is in love with the individual

Grandiose Type: delusions of inflated worth, power, knowledge, identity, or special relationship to a deity or famous person

Jealous Type: delusions that the individual's sexual partner is unfaithful

Persecutory Type: delusions that the person (or someone to whom the person is close) is being malevolently treated in some way

Somatic Type: delusions that the person has some physical defect or general medical condition

Mixed Type: delusions characteristic of more than one of the above types but no one theme predominates

Unspecified Type

Source: Reprinted with permission from the *Diagnostic and Statistical Manual of Mental Disorders,* Fourth Edition, Text Revision.

TABLE 8.8 *DSM-IV-TR* Criteria for Shared Psychotic Disorder

A. A delusion develops in an individual in the context of a close relationship with another person(s), who has an already-established delusion.

B. The delusion is similar in content to that of the person who already has the established delusion.

C. The disturbance is not better accounted for by another psychotic disorder (e.g., schizophrenia) or a mood disorder with psychotic features and is not due to the direct physiological effects of a substance (e.g., a drug of abuse, a medication) or a general medical condition.

Source: Reprinted with permission from the *Diagnostic and Statistical Manual of Mental Disorders,* Fourth Edition, Text Revision.

Approximately 1 in 10,000 women experience brief psychotic episodes shortly after giving birth (Steiner et al., 2003).

Individuals with **delusional disorder** (Table 8.7) have delusions lasting at least 1 month regarding situations that occur in real life, such as being followed, being poisoned, being deceived by a spouse, or having a disease. They do not show any other symptoms. Other than the behaviors that may follow from their delusions, they do not act oddly or have difficulty functioning. In the general population, delusional disorder may be rare, affecting 24 to 30 of every 100,000 people. It appears to affect females more than males. Onset tends to be later in life than most disorders, with an average age of first admission to a psychiatric facility of 40 to 49 (Munro, 1999).

Individuals with **shared psychotic disorder** (also referred to as *folie à deux*) have a delusion that develops from a relationship with another person who already has delusions (Table 8.8). For example, a woman may have the delusion that she is pregnant and convince her husband of this. Shared psychotic disorder usually occurs in relationships of only two people, but it can occur in

SHADES OF GRAY

Read the following case study (adapted from Andreasen, 1998).

Jeff, age 19, had been a normal but somewhat shy kid until about 2 years ago. On a high school trip to France, he had become acutely anxious and returned home early. After that, Jeff began to withdraw. He no longer wanted to be with friends and dropped off the football team. His grades plummeted from his usual As and Bs, but he was able to graduate. His parents commented that a gradual but dramatic personality change had taken place over the past 2 years, and he just seemed "empty." All their efforts to encourage him, to help him find new directions, or to reassess his goals seem to have led nowhere.

Jeff had begun coursework in college but was unable to study and dropped out. He got a job delivering pizzas but couldn't even find his way around the town he had grown up in to deliver the pizzas to the right addresses. His parents reported that he seemed suspicious much of the time and that he had no desire to be around friends or peers. Jeff didn't seem to care about anything. His grooming and hygiene had deteriorated. The apartment he rented was filthy and full of decaying food and dirty laundry. There was no history of drug abuse of any type.

When interviewed by a psychiatrist, Jeff said he did not feel sad or blue, just "empty." Jeff reported no experiences of hearing voices when no one was around, seeing things that other people can't see, or feeling like he'd lost control of his mind or body.

Does Jeff have schizophrenia or one of the disorders along the schizophrenia spectrum? (Discussion appears at the end of the chapter.)

larger groups, as when a family adopts a parent's delusion. Apart from the delusional belief, the individual with shared psychotic disorder may not otherwise act oddly or be impaired.

TEST YOURSELF

1. What are the positive symptoms of schizophrenia?
2. What are the negative symptoms of schizophrenia?
3. Describe the characteristics of delusions, hallucinations, and catatonic behavior.
4. What are the cognitive deficits of schizophrenia?
5. What are prodromal and residual symptoms?
6. Define the major subtypes of schizophrenia given by the *DSM-IV-TR*.
7. Provide the primary characteristics of schizoaffective disorder, schizophreniform disorder, brief psychotic disorder, delusional disorder, and shared psychotic disorder.

APPLY IT Sonia has schizophrenia. During an acute episode, she might exhibit the positive symptom ______ and the negative symptom ______.

a. hallucination; catatonic behavior
b. disorganized thought; delusion
c. avolition; disorganized speech
d. catatonic behavior; blunted affect

Answers appear online at www.mhhe.com/nolen5e.

BIOLOGICAL THEORIES

Given the similarity in the symptoms and prevalence of schizophrenia across cultures and time, biological factors have long been thought key to its development. There are several biological theories of schizophrenia. First, evidence indicates genetic transmission, although genetics does not fully explain who develops this disorder. Second, some people with schizophrenia show structural and functional abnormalities in specific areas of the brain, which may contribute to the disorder. Third, many people with schizophrenia have a history of birth complications or prenatal exposure to viruses, which may affect brain development. Fourth, neurotransmitter theories hold that excess levels of dopamine contribute to schizophrenia; new research also is focusing on the neurotransmitters serotonin, GABA, and glutamate.

Genetic Contributors to Schizophrenia

Family, twin, and adoption studies all indicate a genetic component to the transmission of schizophrenia (Gottesman & Reilly, 2003; Lichtermann, Karbe, & Maier, 2000). Many scientists believe that no single genetic abnormality accounts for this complex disorder (or set of disorders). Indeed, it may be that different genes are responsible for different symptoms of the disorder; for example, one set of genes may contribute to the positive symptoms, and a different set of genes may contribute to the negative symptoms (Gur et al., 2007).

FIGURE 8.3 **Risk for Schizophrenia and Genetic Relatedness.** One's risk of developing schizophrenia decreases substantially as one's genetic relationship to a person with schizophrenia becomes more distant.

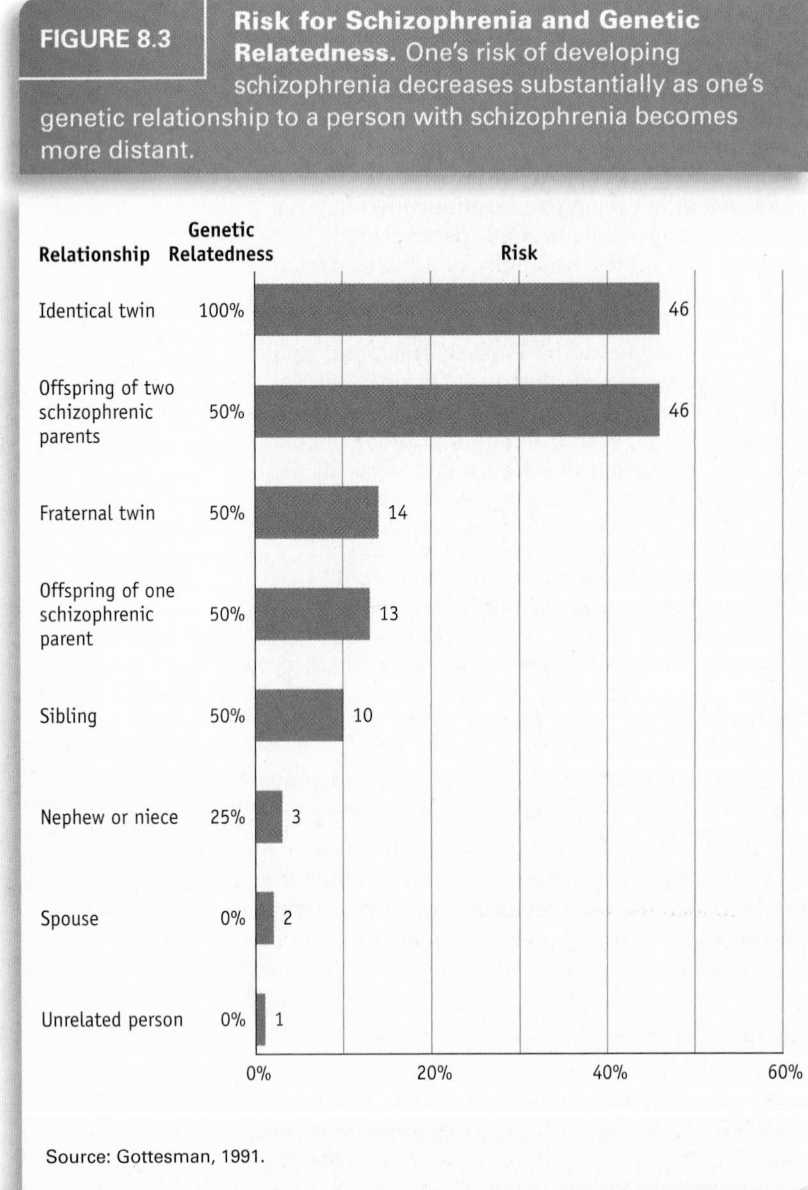

Source: Gottesman, 1991.

The Genain quadruplets all have schizophrenia, but the specific forms of schizophrenia differ among the sisters.

Family Studies

Psychologist Irving Gottesman compiled more than 40 studies to determine the lifetime risk of developing schizophrenia for people with various familial relationships to a person with schizophrenia. His conclusions are summarized in Figure 8.3. Children of two parents with schizophrenia and monozygotic (identical) twins of people with schizophrenia share the greatest number of genes with people with schizophrenia. As the top bars of the graph in Figure 8.3 show, these individuals also have the greatest risk of developing schizophrenia at some time in their lives.

As the genetic similarity to a person with schizophrenia decreases, an individual's risk of developing schizophrenia also decreases. Thus, a first-degree relative of a person with schizophrenia, such as a non-twin sibling, who shares about 50 percent of genes with the person with schizophrenia, has about a 10 percent chance of developing the disorder. In contrast, a niece or nephew of a person with schizophrenia, who shares about 25 percent of genes with the person with schizophrenia, has only a 3 percent chance of developing the disorder. The general population has a risk of about 1 to 2 percent. The relationship between an individual's degree of genetic similarity to a schizophrenic relative and the individual's own risk of developing schizophrenia strongly suggests that genes play a role in the development of the disorder.

Having a biological relative with schizophrenia increases an individual's risk for the disorder but does not mean that the individual will develop it. For example, of all children who have one parent with schizophrenia, 87 percent will *not* develop the disorder. Also, 63 percent of people with schizophrenia have *no* first- or second-degree relative with the disorder (Gottesman & Erlenmeyer-Kimling, 2001).

Adoption Studies

Even when the child of a person with schizophrenia develops the disorder, it may not be due to genetics. A home with a parent with schizophrenia is likely to be a stressful environment. When a parent is psychotic, the child may be exposed to illogical thought, mood swings, and chaotic behavior. Even when the parent is not acutely psychotic, the residual negative symptoms of schizophrenia—flattening of affect, lack of motivation, and disorganization—may impair the parent's child-care skills.

Several adoption studies addressing the question of genes versus environment indicate that genetics plays an important role in schizophrenia. For example, Seymour Kety and colleagues (1994) found that the biological relatives of adoptees with schizophrenia were 10 times more likely to have a diagnosis of schizophrenia than were the biological relatives of adoptees who did not have schizophrenia. In contrast, the adoptive relatives of adoptees with schizophrenia showed no increased risk for the disorder.

In one of the largest adoption studies, Pekka Tienari (1991) tracked 155 offspring of mothers with schizophrenia and 185 children of mothers without schizophrenia; all the children had been given up for adoption early in life. Approximately 10 percent of the children whose biological mothers had schizophrenia developed schizophrenia or another psychotic disorder, compared to about 1 percent of the children whose biological mothers did not have schizophrenia.

Twin Studies

Figure 8.3 also shows the compiled results of several twin studies of schizophrenia. These suggest that the concordance rate for monozygotic (identical) twins is 46 percent, while the concordance rate for dizygotic (fraternal) twins is 14 percent. A study that assessed all twins born in Finland between 1940 and 1957 using statistical modeling estimated that 83 percent of the variation in schizophrenia is due to genetic factors (Cannon et al., 1998).

Even when a person carries a genetic risk for schizophrenia, however, many other biological and environmental factors may influence whether and how he or she manifests the disorder. The classic illustration of this point is found in the Genain quadruplets, who shared the same genes and family environment. While all developed schizophrenia, their specific symptoms, onset, course, and outcomes varied substantially (Mirsky et al., 2000).

Recently, researchers have been investigating *epigenetic* factors that influence the expression of genes. Recall from Chapter 2 that DNA can be chemically modified by different environmental conditions, resulting in genes being turned on or off, thereby altering the development of cells, tissues, and organs. When MZ twins who were discordant for schizophrenia (i.e., one twin had schizophrenia but the other twin did not) were compared with MZ twins who both had schizophrenia, researchers found that the MZ twins discordant for schizophrenia showed numerous differences in the molecular structure of their DNA, particularly on genes regulating dopamine systems. In contrast, the MZ twins concordant for schizophrenia showed many fewer molecular differences in their DNA (Petronis et al., 2003). The reasons for these epigenetic differences are unclear. However, a number of environmental events that could affect development in utero appear to increase the risk for schizophrenia. Some of these events might alter genes that guide brain development.

FIGURE 8.4 **Enlarged Ventricles in People with Schizophrenia.** The left panel shows the brain of a healthy male. The right panel shows the brain of his identical twin, who has schizophrenia. Notice the larger ventricles (blue spaces midbrain) in the brain of the twin with schizophrenia.

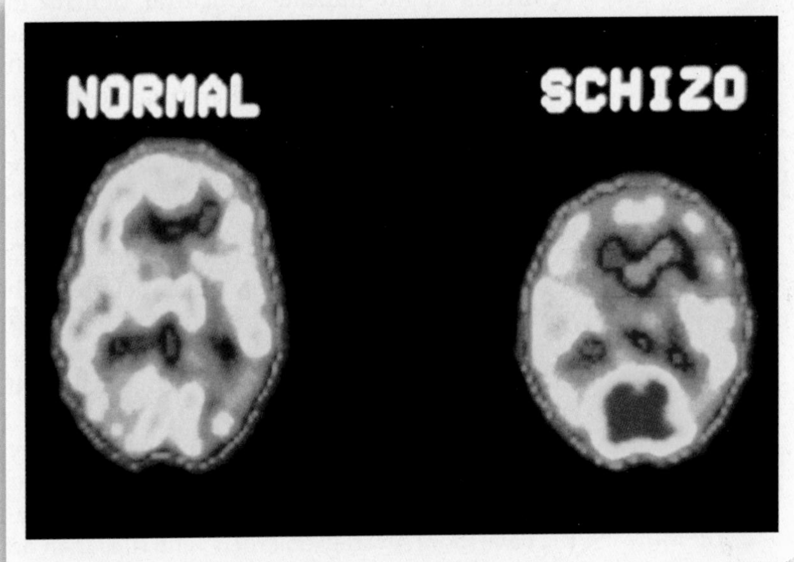

Structural and Functional Brain Abnormalities

Clinicians and researchers have long believed that the brains of people with schizophrenia differ fundamentally from those of people without schizophrenia. Only in the past 20 years, with the development of technologies such as positron-emission tomography (PET scans), computerized axial tomography (CAT scans), and magnetic resonance imaging (MRI), have scientists been able to examine in detail the structure and functioning of the brain. These new technologies have shown major structural and functional deficits in the brains of some people with schizophrenia (Andreasen, 2001; Barch, 2005). Most theorists think of it as a *neurodevelopmental disorder,* in which a variety of factors lead to abnormal development of the brain in the uterus and early in life.

Enlarged Ventricles

The most consistent structural brain abnormality found in schizophrenia is *enlarged ventricles* (Figure 8.4; Lawrie et al., 2008). The *ventricles* are fluid-filled spaces in the brain. Enlarged ventricles suggest atrophy, or deterioration, in other brain tissue. People with schizophrenia with enlarged ventricles also show reductions in the prefrontal areas of the brain and an abnormal connection between the prefrontal cortex and the amygdala and hippocampus. However, enlarged ventricles might indicate structural deficits in other areas of the brain. Indeed, the different areas of the brain that can deteriorate to create enlarged ventricles might lead to different manifestations of schizophrenia.

People with schizophrenia with enlarged ventricles tend to show social, emotional, and behavioral deficits long before they develop the core symptoms of schizophrenia. They also tend to have more severe symptoms than other people with schizophrenia and are less responsive to medication. These characteristics suggest gross alterations in the functioning of the brain, which are difficult to alleviate with treatment.

The gender differences in schizophrenia may be tied, in part, to gender differences in ventricular size. Some studies find that men with schizophrenia have more severely enlarged ventricles than do women with schizophrenia (Nopoulos, Flaum, & Andreasen, 1997). This difference may be due to the fact that men generally show greater loss of tissue volume and increase in ventricle size with age than do women. The normal effects of aging on men's brains may exacerbate the neuroanatomical abnormalities of schizophrenia, causing more severe symptoms and thus a worse course (Nopoulos et al., 1997).

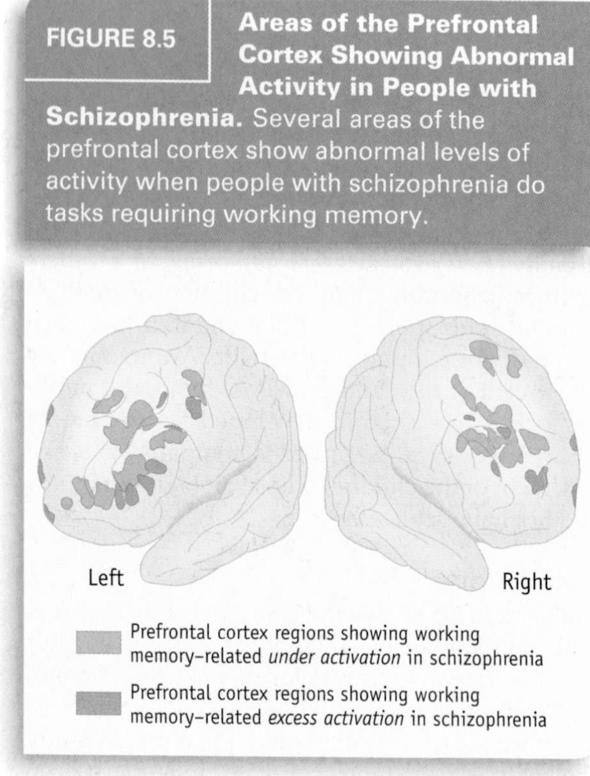

FIGURE 8.5 **Areas of the Prefrontal Cortex Showing Abnormal Activity in People with Schizophrenia.** Several areas of the prefrontal cortex show abnormal levels of activity when people with schizophrenia do tasks requiring working memory.

Prefrontal Cortex and Other Key Areas

Studies have shown abnormalities in the volume, density of neurons, and metabolic rate in several brain areas in people with schizophrenia, including the frontal cortex, temporal lobe, basal ganglia, and limbic area (including the hippocampus, thalamus, and amygdala) (Andreasen, 2001; Barch, 2005; Suhara et al., 2002). The *prefrontal cortex* of the brain consistently is smaller and shows less activity in people with schizophrenia than in other people (Figure 8.5). In addition, people who are at risk for schizophrenia because of a family history but have not yet developed the disorder show abnormal prefrontal activity (Lawrie et al., 2008).

The prefrontal cortex connects to all other cortical regions, as well as to the *limbic system,* which is involved in emotion and cognition, and *the basal ganglia,* which is involved in motor movement. The prefrontal cortex is important in language, emotional expression, planning, and carrying out plans (Barch, 2005). Thus, it seems logical that a person with an unusually small or inactive prefrontal cortex would show the deficits in cognition, emotion, and social interactions seen with schizophrenia, such as difficulty holding conversations, appropriately responding to social situations, and carrying out tasks.

The prefrontal cortex undergoes major development in the adolescent-to-young-adult years (Steinberg et al., 2006). Aberrations in the normal development of the prefrontal cortex during mid- to late adolescence may help explain the emergence of the disorder during this period (Cannon et al., 2003). Neuroimaging studies of individuals who developed schizophrenia in adolescence show significant structural changes across the cortex from ages 13 to 18, particularly in the prefrontal cortex (Figure 8.6; Thompson et al., 2001).

The *hippocampus* is another brain area that consistently differs from the norm in people with schizophrenia (Barch, 2005). The hippocampus plays a critical role in the formation of long-term memories. In some studies, people with schizophrenia show abnormal hippocampal activation when they are doing tasks that require them to encode information for storage in their memory or to retrieve information from memory (Barch,

Csernansky, Conturo, & Snyder, 2002; Schacter, Chiao, & Mitchell, 2003). Other studies show that people with schizophrenia have abnormalities in the volume and shape of their hippocampus and at the cellular level (Knable et al., 2004; Shenton et al., 2001). Similar abnormalities in the hippocampus are found in first-degree relatives of people with schizophrenia (Seidman et al., 2002).

Damage to the Developing Brain

What causes the neuroanatomical abnormalities in schizophrenia? There might be a number of causes, including specific genetic abnormalities, brain injury due to birth complications, head injury, viral infections, nutritional deficiencies, and deficiencies in cognitive stimulation (Barch, 2005; Conklin & Iacono, 2002). In some studies of MZ twins in which one twin has schizophrenia, only the twin with schizophrenia tends to show neuroanatomical abnormalities, even though both twins have identical genetic makeups (Gur et al., 2007; Suddath, Christison, Torrey, & Casanova, 1990; Thermenos et al., 2004). As noted earlier, epigenetic factors could contribute to these twin differences. In addition, damage to the developing brain could be due to other causes.

Birth Complications Serious prenatal and birth difficulties are more frequent in the histories of people with schizophrenia than in those of people without schizophrenia and may play a role in the development of neurological difficulties (Cannon et al., 2003). Individuals with schizophrenia who had delivery complications and who also have a familial risk for schizophrenia show greater enlargement of the ventricles and abnormalities in the hippocampus.

One type of birth complication that may be especially important in neurological development is *perinatal hypoxia* (oxygen deprivation at birth or in the few weeks before or after birth) (Goldstein et al., 2000). As many as 30 percent of people with schizophrenia have a history of perinatal hypoxia. A prospective study of 9,236 people born in Philadelphia between 1959 and 1966 found that the odds of an adult diagnosis of schizophrenia increased in direct proportion to the degree of perinatal hypoxia (Cannon et al., 1999). The authors of this study suggest that the effects of oxygen deprivation interact with a genetic vulnerability to schizophrenia, resulting in a person's developing the disorder. Most people experiencing oxygen deprivation prenatally or at birth do not develop schizophrenia, however.

FIGURE 8.6 Mapping Early and Late Deficits in Schizophrenia. Deficits occurring during development of schizophrenia are detected by comparing average profiles of gray matter between patients and controls at their first scan (age 13; top row) and their last scan 5 years later (age 18; bottom row). Although severe parietal, motor, and diffuse frontal loss has already occurred (top row) and subsequently continues, the temporal and dorsolateral prefrontal loss characteristic of adult schizophrenia is not found until later in adolescence (bottom row), where a process of fast attrition occurs over the next 5 years. The color code shows the significance of these effects.

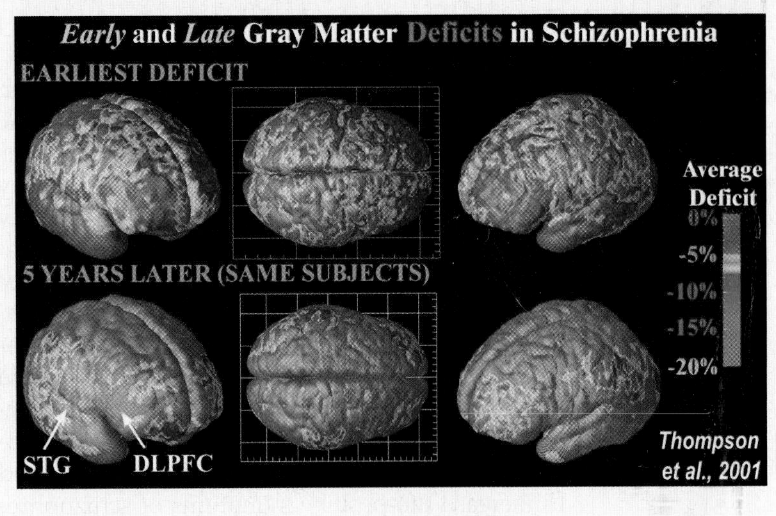

Note: DLPFC = dorsolateral prefrontal cortex
Source: Reprinted from Thompson et al. (2001) with permission from the National Academy of Sciences of the United States of America.

Prenatal Viral Exposure Epidemiological studies have shown high rates of schizophrenia among persons whose mothers were exposed to viral infections while pregnant (Cannon et al., 2003). For example, people whose mothers were exposed to the influenza epidemic that swept Helsinki, Finland, in 1957 were significantly more likely to develop schizophrenia than people whose mothers were not exposed. The link was particularly strong among people whose mothers were exposed during the second trimester of pregnancy (Mednick et al., 1988, 1998). The second trimester is a crucial period for the development of the central nervous system of the fetus. Disruption in this phase of brain development could cause the major structural deficits found in the brains of some people with schizophrenia. Interestingly, people with schizophrenia are somewhat more likely to be born in the spring months than at other times of the year

(Ellman & Cannon, 2008). Pregnant women may be more likely to contract influenza and other viruses at critical phases of fetal development if they are pregnant during the fall and winter.

Another study found that individuals whose mothers had been exposed to the herpes simplex virus while pregnant were more likely to have a psychotic disorder, most often schizophrenia (Buka et al., 2008). The authors of this study suggest that viral infections prompt a mother's immune system to be more active, which can negatively impact the development of brain cells and dopamine systems in the fetus.

Neurotransmitters

The neurotransmitter **dopamine** has long been thought to play a role in schizophrenia (Conklin & Iacono, 2002). The original dopamine theory was that the symptoms of schizophrenia are caused by excess levels of dopamine in the brain, particularly in the prefrontal cortex and limbic system.

This theory was supported by several lines of evidence. First, a group of drugs that tend to reduce the symptoms of schizophrenia, the **phenothiazines** or **neuroleptics,** reduces the functional level of dopamine in the brain (Dolder, 2008). Second, drugs that increase the functional level of dopamine in the brain, such as amphetamines, tend to increase the positive symptoms of schizophrenia (Davis, Kahn, Ko, & Davidson, 1991). Third, neuroimaging studies suggest the presence of more receptors for dopamine and higher levels of dopamine in some areas of the brain in people with schizophrenia than in people without the disorder (Conklin & Iacono, 2002).

More recent research, however, suggests that the original dopamine theory of schizophrenia was too simple (Conklin & Iacono, 2002; Downar & Kapur, 2008). Many people with schizophrenia do not respond to the phenothiazines. In addition, even people with schizophrenia who respond to the phenothiazines tend to experience more relief from positive symptoms (hallucinations and delusions) than from negative symptoms (Kutscher, 2008). This suggests that simple dopamine depletion does not fully explain the negative symptoms. Further, levels of dopamine change relatively soon after drug therapy begins, while changes in symptoms often take longer. This suggests that the level of dopamine in the brain is not the only determinant of symptoms.

Although the original dopamine theory of schizophrenia (that the brains of people with schizophrenia generally have higher functional levels of dopamine) does not entirely explain the disorder, it is clear that dopamine systems are involved in schizophrenia. A more complex version of the dopamine theory can explain both the positive symptoms and the negative symptoms (Conklin & Iacono, 2002; Davis et al., 1991; Talkowski, Bamne, Mansour, & Nimgaonkar, 2007).

FIGURE 8.7 **Areas of Abnormal Dopamine Activity in the Brain in Schizophrenia.** There may be *excess* dopamine activity in the mesolimbic pathway, which begins in the ventral tegmental area and projects to the hypothalamus, amygdala, and hippocampus. But there may be unusually *low* dopamine activity in the prefrontal cortex.

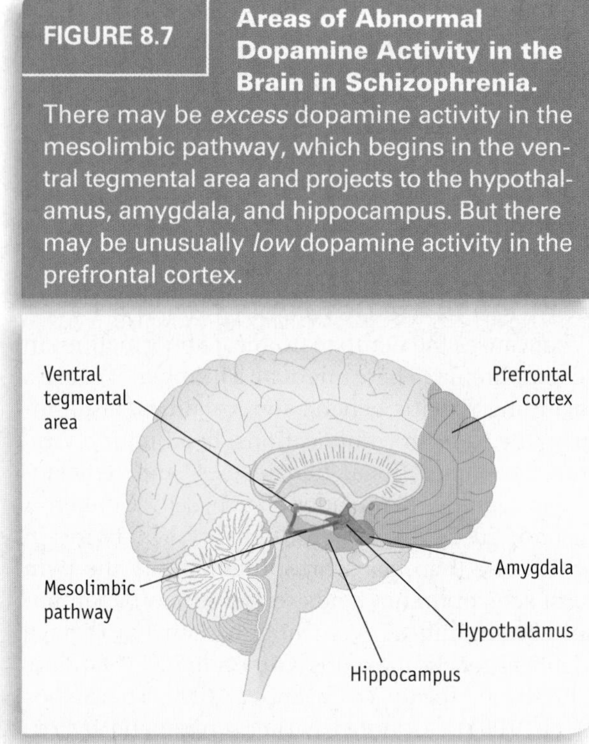

First, there may be *excess* dopamine activity in the **mesolimbic pathway,** a subcortical part of the brain involved in cognition and emotion (Figure 8.7). Newer drugs in the treatment of schizophrenia, the *atypical antipsychotics,* may work to reduce the symptoms of schizophrenia by binding to a specific type of dopamine receptor common in the mesolimbic system, blocking the action of dopamine (Sajatovic, Madhusoodanan, & Fuller, 2008).

Second, there may be *unusually low* dopamine activity in the prefrontal area of the brain, which is involved in attention, motivation, and the organization of behavior (Barch, 2005). Low dopamine activity here may lead to the negative symptoms of schizophrenia: lack of motivation, inability to care for oneself in daily activities, and the blunting of affect. This idea fits the evidence associating structural and functional abnormalities in this part of the brain with the negative symptoms of schizophrenia. It also helps explain why the phenothiazines, which reduce dopamine activity, do not effectively alleviate the negative symptoms.

Third, research suggests that other neurotransmitters also play an important role in schizophrenia.

Serotonin neurons regulate dopamine neurons in the mesolimbic system, and some of the newest drugs for treating schizophrenia bind to serotonin receptors (Bondolfi et al., 1998). The interaction between serotonin and dopamine may be critical in schizophrenia (Breier, 1995). Still other research has found abnormal levels of the neurotransmitters glutamate and gamma-aminobutyric acid (GABA) in people with schizophrenia (Tiihonen & Wahlbeck, 2006). Glutamate and GABA are widespread in the brain, and deficiencies could contribute to cognitive and emotional symptoms. Glutamate neurons are the major excitatory pathways linking the cortex, limbic system, and thalamus, regions of the brain shown to behave abnormally in people with schizophrenia. Drugs, such as PCP and ketamine, that block glutamate receptors cause hallucinations and delusions in otherwise healthy individuals (Tiihonen & Wahlbeck, 2006).

An Integrative Model

Deanna Barch (2003, 2005) and others (Docherty, Grosh, & Wexler, 1996; Fitzgerald et al., 2004) have argued that the functional and structural brain abnormalities seen in the brains of people with schizophrenia lead to basic cognitive deficits that create many of the symptoms of schizophrenia. These core symptoms include disorganized speech and difficulties in communication, logical reasoning, and performing the tasks of daily living (such as getting oneself out of bed, dressed, fed, and to work).

According to this integrative model, abnormalities in the dopamine system, particularly in the prefrontal cortex, lead to deficits in working memory (Figure 8.8; Barch, 2005). These deficits make it difficult to keep irrelevant information from intruding into one's attention. They also interfere with communication with others, as a woman with schizophrenia describes.

VOICES

Everything seems to grip my attention although I am not particularly interested in anything. I am speaking to you just now, but I can hear noises going on next door and in the corridor. I find it difficult to shut these out, and it makes it more difficult for me to concentrate on what I am saying to you. (McGhie & Chapman, 1961, p. 104)

Working memory deficits also impair the ability both to learn new information and to retrieve it.

FIGURE 8.8 An Integrated Model of the Links Between Cognitive Deficits and the Symptoms of Schizophrenia. Theorists have argued that abnormalities in the function of the dopamine system, particularly in the prefrontal cortex, lead to deficits in working memory, which then make it difficult for people with schizophrenia to attend only to relevant information. This difficulty impairs their ability to reason, communicate, and solve problems.

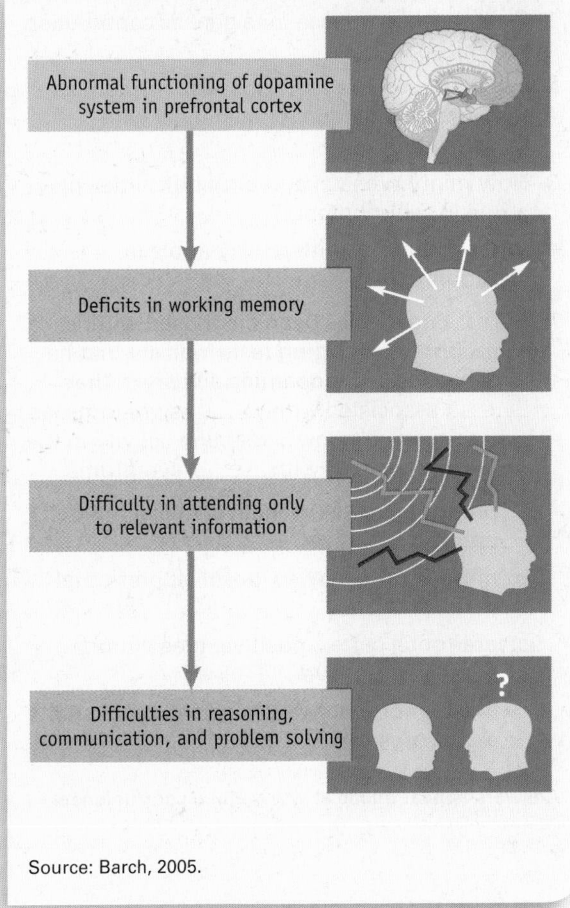

Source: Barch, 2005.

Together, these deficits may contribute to the difficulties in reasoning, communication, and problem solving experienced by people with schizophrenia (Barch, 2005).

This model has been supported by a wide range of studies showing deficits in working memory and related cognitive functions in people with schizophrenia and in their first-degree relatives (Barch, 2005). In addition, these cognitive deficits are linked to abnormalities in the functioning of the prefrontal cortex and in the dopamine system

(Gur et al., 2007). The model explains how basic cognitive deficits, tied to abnormalities in brain functioning that may be genetically based, can lead to the problems in communication, reasoning, and functioning in daily life that are some of the most damaging symptoms of schizophrenia. As noted above, hallucinations and delusions may be an individual's attempt to make sense of strange perceptual experiences (Beck & Rector, 2005).

TEST YOURSELF

1. Describe the evidence for a genetic contribution to schizophrenia.
2. What areas of the brain show abnormalities in structure and function in people with schizophrenia?
3. How might prenatal and birth difficulties play a role in schizophrenia?
4. What neurotransmitters play a role in schizophrenia?

APPLY IT Eugene has been diagnosed with schizophrenia. Imaging tests indicate that he may have excess dopamine activity in the ______, associated with ______ symptoms, as well as unusually low dopamine activity in the ______, associated with ______ symptoms.

a. prefrontal cortex, negative, mesolimbic pathway, positive
b. mesolimbic pathway, positive, prefrontal cortex, negative
c. prefrontal cortex, positive, mesolimbic pathway, negative
d. mesolimbic pathway, negative, prefrontal cortex, positive

Answers appear online at www.mhhe.com/nolen5e.

PSYCHOSOCIAL PERSPECTIVES

Although schizophrenia is strongly linked to biological factors, social factors can influence its course.

Social Drift and Urban Birth

People with schizophrenia are more likely than people without schizophrenia to experience chronically stressful circumstances, such as impoverished inner-city neighborhoods and low-status occupations or unemployment (Dohrenwend, 2000). Most research supports a **social drift** explanation of this link: Because schizophrenia symptoms interfere with a person's ability to complete an education and hold a job, people with schizophrenia tend to drift downward in social class compared to the class of their family of origin.

A classic study showing social drift tracked the socioeconomic status of men with schizophrenia and compared it to the status of their brothers and fathers (Goldberg & Morrison, 1963). The men with schizophrenia tended to end up in socioeconomic classes well below those of their fathers. In contrast, the healthy brothers of the men with schizophrenia tended to end up in socioeconomic classes equal to or higher than those of their fathers. More recent data also support the social drift theory (Dohrenwend, 2000).

Several studies have shown that people with schizophrenia and other forms of psychosis are more likely to have been born in a large city than in a small town (Kendler, Gallagher, Abelson, & Kessler, 1996; Lewis, David, Andreasson, & Allebeck, 1992; Takei et al., 1992, 1995; Torrey, Bowler, & Clark, 1997; van Os, Hanssen, Bijl, & Vollebergh, 2001). For example, studies in the United States find that people with psychotic disorders are as much as five times more likely to have been born and raised in a large metropolitan area than in a rural area. Does the stress of the city lead to psychosis? E. Fuller Torrey and Robert Yolken (1998) argue that the link between urban living and psychosis is due not to stress but to overcrowding, which increases the risk that a pregnant woman or newborn will be exposed to infectious agents. Many studies have shown that the rates of many infectious diseases—including influenza, tuberculosis, respiratory infections, herpes, and measles—are higher in crowded urban areas than in less crowded areas. As noted earlier, there is a link between prenatal or perinatal exposure to infectious disease and schizophrenia.

Stress and Relapse

Stressful circumstances may not cause someone to develop schizophrenia, but they may trigger new episodes in people with the disorder. Researchers found higher levels of stress occurring shortly before the onset of a new episode compared to other times in the lives of people with schizophrenia (Norman & Malla, 1993). For example, in one study, researchers followed a group of people with schizophrenia for 1 year, interviewing them every 2 weeks to determine if they had experienced any stressful events and/or any increase in their symptoms. People who experienced relapses of psychosis were more likely than people who did not to have experienced negative life events in the month before their relapse (Ventura, Neuchterlein, Lukoff, & Hardesty, 1989).

One major stressor linked to an increased risk for episodes in schizophrenia is immigration. Recent immigrants often have left behind extended networks of family and friends to move to a new country where they may know few people. They may face financial stress, particularly if the education they received in their native country isn't recognized in their new country. They may not know the language of their new country and may not be comfortable in the new culture. Studies in the United States and Britain find that first- and second-generation immigrants have a higher incidence of acute schizophrenia symptoms than individuals from their ethnic group who have been in the country longer or individuals native to the country (Cantor-Graae & Selten, 2005; Coid et al., 2008; Kirkbride et al., 2006).

It is important not to overstate the link between stressful life events and new episodes of schizophrenia. In the study that followed people with schizophrenia for a year, more than half the participants who had a relapse of acute symptoms in the year they were followed had *not* experienced negative life events just before their relapse (Ventura et al., 1989). In addition, other studies suggest that many of the life events that people with schizophrenia experience prior to relapse actually may be caused by the prodromal symptoms that occur just before a relapse into psychosis (Dohrenwend et al., 1987). For example, one of the prodromal symptoms of a schizophrenic relapse is social withdrawal. The negative life events most often preceding a relapse, such as the breakup of a relationship or the loss of a job, might be caused partially by this social withdrawal.

Schizophrenia and the Family

Historically, theorists blamed schizophrenia on mothers. Early psychodynamic theorists suggested that schizophrenia results when mothers are at the same time overprotective and rejecting of their children (Fromm-Reichmann, 1948). These *schizophrenogenic (schizophrenia-causing) mothers* dominated their children, not letting them develop an autonomous sense of self and simultaneously making the children feel worthless and unlovable. Similarly, Gregory Bateson and his colleagues (1956) argued that parents (particularly mothers) of children who develop schizophrenia put their children in *double binds* by constantly communicating conflicting messages to their children. Such a mother might physically comfort her child when he falls down and is hurt but, at the same time, be verbally hostile to and critical of the child. Children chronically exposed to such mixed messages supposedly cannot trust their feelings or their perceptions of the world and thus develop distorted views of themselves, of others, and of their environment that contribute to schizophrenia. These theories did not hold up to scientific scrutiny, but they did heap guilt on the families of people with schizophrenia.

One family interaction factor that research shows is associated with schizophrenia is **expressed emotion.** Families high in expressed emotion are overinvolved with one another, are overprotective of the ill family member, and voice self-sacrificing attitudes toward the family member while at the same time being critical, hostile, and resentful toward him or her (Hooley, 2007). Although high-expressed-emotion family members do not doubt their loved one's illness, they talk as if the ill family member can control his or her symptoms (Hooley & Campbell, 2002). They often have ideas about how the family member can improve the symptoms.

Expressed emotion has been assessed through lengthy interviews with people with schizophrenia and their families, through projective tests, and through direct observation of family interactions. A number of studies have shown that people with schizophrenia whose families are high in expressed emotion are more likely to suffer relapses of psychosis than those whose families are low in expressed emotion (e.g., Hooley, 2007). An analysis of 27 studies of expressed emotion and schizophrenia showed that 70 percent of patients in high-expressed-emotion families relapsed within a follow-up year, compared to 31 percent of patients in low-expressed-emotion families (Butzlaff & Hooley, 1998). Being in a high-expressed-emotion family may create stresses for persons with schizophrenia that overwhelm their ability to cope and thus trigger new episodes of psychosis.

The link between high levels of family expressed emotion and higher relapse rates has been replicated in studies of several cultures, including Europe, the United States, Mexico, and India. In Mexico and India, however, families of people with schizophrenia tend to score lower on measures of expressed emotion than do their counterparts in Europe or the United States (Figure 8.9; Karno & Jenkins, 1993; Karno et al., 1987). The lower levels of expressed emotion in families in developing countries may help explain the lower relapse rates of people with schizophrenia in these countries.

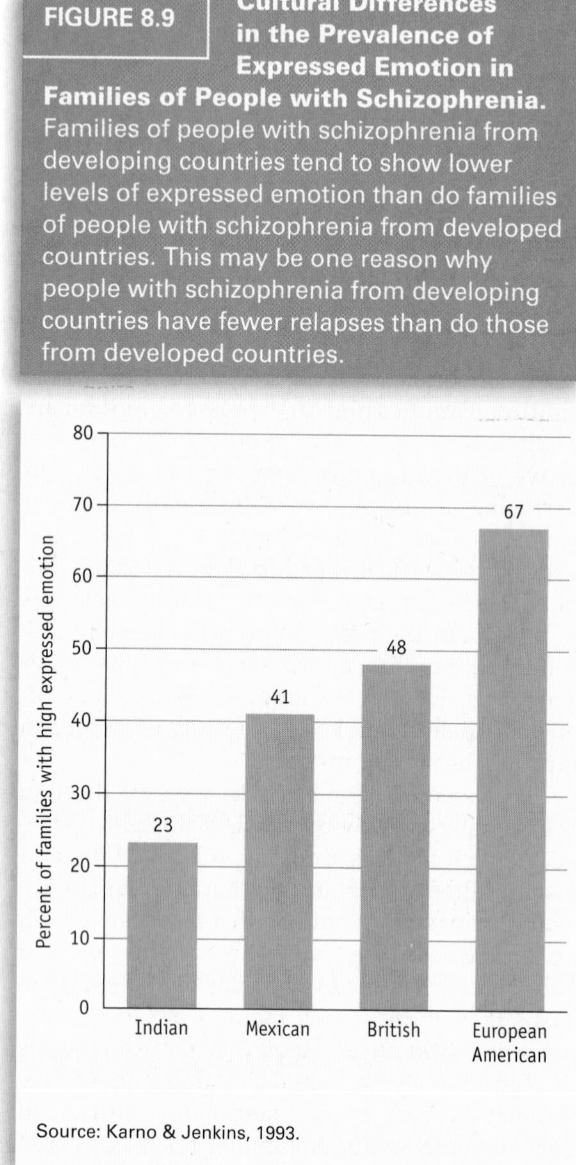

FIGURE 8.9 **Cultural Differences in the Prevalence of Expressed Emotion in Families of People with Schizophrenia.** Families of people with schizophrenia from developing countries tend to show lower levels of expressed emotion than do families of people with schizophrenia from developed countries. This may be one reason why people with schizophrenia from developing countries have fewer relapses than do those from developed countries.

Source: Karno & Jenkins, 1993.

Critics of the literature on expressed emotion argue that the hostility and intrusiveness observed in some families of people with schizophrenia might be the result of the symptoms exhibited by the person with schizophrenia rather than contributors to relapse (Parker, Johnston, & Hayward, 1988). Although families often are forgiving of the positive symptoms of schizophrenia (e.g., hallucinations, delusions) because they view them as uncontrollable, they can be unforgiving of the negative symptoms (e.g., lack of motivation, blunted affect), viewing them as controllable by the person with schizophrenia (Hooley & Campbell, 2002). People with more of the negative symptoms may elicit more expressed emotion from their families. They also may be especially prone to relapse, but for reasons other than exposure to expressed emotion.

Family members who rate particularly high on expressed emotion are themselves more likely to have some form of psychopathology (Goldstein, Talovic, Nuechterlein, & Fogelson, 1992). Thus, people with schizophrenia in these families may have high rates of relapse because they have a greater genetic loading for psychopathology, rather than because their family members show high levels of expressed emotion. Perhaps the best evidence that family expressed emotion does in fact influence relapse in schizophrenic patients is that interventions to reduce family expressed emotion tend to reduce the relapse rate in family members with schizophrenia (Hooley, 2007).

Cognitive Perspectives

Aaron Beck and Neil Rector (Beck & Rector, 2005) suggest that fundamental difficulties in attention, inhibition, and adherence to rules of communication lead people with schizophrenia to try to conserve their limited cognitive resources. One way they do this is to use certain biases or schemas for understanding the overwhelming information streaming through their brain. Delusions arise as the person with schizophrenia tries to explain strange perceptual experiences. Hallucinations result from a hypersensitivity to perceptual input, coupled with a tendency to attribute experiences to external sources. Rather than thinking "I'm hearing things," the person with schizophrenia will think "Someone is trying to talk to me." The negative symptoms of schizophrenia arise from expectations that social interactions will be aversive and from the need to withdraw and conserve scarce cognitive resources.

This cognitive conceptualization has led to cognitive strategies for treating people with schizophrenia. These strategies help patients identify and cope with stressful circumstances associated with the development and worsening of symptoms. They also teach patients to dispute their delusional beliefs or hallucinatory experiences. Negative symptoms are treated by helping patients develop the expectation that being more active and interacting more with other people will have positive benefits. This cognitive intervention has shown greater success in reducing symptoms than does simply providing patients with support (Beck & Rector, 2005).

Cross-Cultural Perspectives

Different cultures vary greatly in how they explain schizophrenia (Anders, 2003; Karno & Jenkins, 1993). Most have a biological explanation for the disorder, including the general idea that it runs in families. Intermingled with biological explanations are theories that attribute the disorder to stress, lack of spiritual piety, and family dynamics. Kevin Browne (2001) offers a case study of a woman from Java, whose understanding of her schizophrenia symptoms included all these factors.

CASE STUDY

Anik is a 29-year-old Javanese woman who was born in a rural area but has lived in the city of Yogyakarta for the past four years. She has been married 1½ years, but is very unhappy in her marriage, feeling her husband is lacking in openness and compassion. Anik has been unable to care for her 8-month-old daughter for the past several months, so the daughter was living with Anik's aunt in Jakarta. When her illness began, Anik first became withdrawn and didn't sleep or eat. She developed hallucinations of accusatory voices criticizing her husband, his family, and their landlady. Anik also suffered from jealous delusions that her husband was having an affair. She was taken to the hospital by her brother, where her symptoms included *mondar-mandir* ("wandering without purpose"), *ngamuk* ("being irritable"), being easily offended and suspicious, talking to herself, crying, insomnia, *malmun* ("daydreaming"), and quickly changing emotions. Her sister-in-law reported that she had been chronically fearful and irritable for some time and would frequently slam doors and yell. In Javanese culture, the control of emotions in social situations is of great importance, so Anik's outbursts were seen as clear signs of some sort of pathology.

Anik had several explanations for her behavior. First and foremost, she believed that she was in a bad marriage, and this stress was a contributing factor. Shortly before her symptoms began, her landlady said something harsh to her, and Anik believed that her startle reaction to this (*goncangan*) led to *sajit hati,* literally "liver sickness." In addition, Anik's mother had a brief period during Anik's childhood when she "went crazy," becoming loud and violent, and Anik believes she may have inherited this tendency from her mother. Anik initially sought to overcome her symptoms by increasing the frequency with which she repeated Muslim prayers and asking to be taken to a Muslim boarding house. Once she was taken to the hospital, she agreed to take antipsychotic medications, which helped her symptoms somewhat. She was discharged from the hospital after a short time, but was rehospitalized multiple times over the next year.

Anik's experience illustrates the interweaving in people with schizophrenia symptoms of traditional beliefs and practices and modern biological treatments. Although she agreed to take antipsychotic medications, the understanding she and her family had of her symptoms was not primarily a biological one but rather one rooted in concerns about stress and, to some extent, religion.

TEST YOURSELF

1. What is social drift? What is the connection between urban living and schizophrenia? What role does stress play in schizophrenia?
2. What types of family interaction patterns might play a role in schizophrenia?
3. How do cognitive theorists explain schizophrenia?

APPLY IT If you lived in a developing country such as Java and had a family member with schizophrenia, which of the following probably would be true?

a. You would believe that your family member's schizophrenia was caused entirely by biological factors.
b. You would be less likely than someone from a developed nation to show high levels of expressed emotion toward your family member with schizophrenia.
c. You would be likely to institutionalize your family member with schizophrenia.
d. You would be unlikely to observe hallucinations or delusions in your family member with schizophrenia.

Answers appear online at www.mhhe.com/nolen5e.

TREATMENTS

Comprehensive treatment for people with schizophrenia includes medications to help quell symptoms, therapy to help people cope with the consequences of the disorder, and social services to aid their reintegration into society and to ensure their access to the resources they need for daily life.

Biological Treatments

History of Biological Treatments

Over the centuries, many treatments for schizophrenia have been developed, based on the scientific theories of the time (Valenstein, 1998).

Physicians have performed brain surgery on people with schizophrenia in an attempt to "fix" or eliminate the part of the brain causing hallucinations or delusions. These patients sometimes were calmer after their surgeries, but they often also experienced significant cognitive and emotional deficits as a result of the surgery. *Insulin coma therapy* was used in the 1930s to treat schizophrenia. People with schizophrenia would be given massive doses of insulin—the drug used to treat diabetes—until they went into a coma. When they emerged from the coma, however, patients rarely were much better, and the procedure was highly dangerous (Valenstein, 1998). *Electroconvulsive therapy*, or *ECT*, was also used to treat schizophrenia until it became clear that it had little effect (although it is effective in treating serious depression, as discussed in Chapter 7).

Mostly, however, people with schizophrenia were simply warehoused. In 1955, one out of every two people housed in psychiatric hospitals had been diagnosed with schizophrenia, although by today's standards of diagnosis they may have actually had different disorders (Rosenstein, Milazzo-Sayre, & Manderscheid, 1989). These patients received custodial care—they were bathed, fed, and prevented from hurting themselves, often with the use of physical restraints—but few received any treatment that actually reduced their symptoms. Not until the 1950s was an effective drug treatment for schizophrenia—chlorpromazine—introduced. Since then, several other antipsychotic drugs have been added to the arsenal of treatments for schizophrenia. Most recently, the atypical antipsychotics hold out the promise of relieving positive symptoms while inducing fewer side effects than the traditional antipsychotics.

Antipsychotic Drugs

In the early 1950s, French researchers Jean Delay and Pierre Deniker found that **chlorpromazine** (Thorazine), one of a class of drugs called the *phenothiazines*, calms agitation and reduces hallucinations and delusions in patients with schizophrenia (Valenstein, 1998). Other phenothiazines that became widely used include trifluoperazine (Stelazine), thioridazine (Mellaril), and fluphenazine (Prolixin). These drugs appear to block receptors for dopamine, thereby reducing its action in the brain. For the first time, many people with schizophrenia could control the positive symptoms of the disorder (hallucinations, delusions, thought disturbances) by taking these drugs even when they were asymptomatic.

Thanks to these drugs, by 1971 the number of people with schizophrenia who required hospitalization had decreased to half of what would have been expected without the use of the drugs (Lavretsky, 2008). Other classes of antipsychotic drugs were introduced after the phenothiazines, including the *butyrophenones* (such as Haldol) and the *thioxanthenes* (such as Navane). Collectively, these drugs are known as the *neuroleptics*.

Effectiveness and Side Effects of Neuroleptics Although the neuroleptic drugs revolutionized the treatment of schizophrenia, about 25 percent of people with schizophrenia do not respond to them (Adams, Awad, Rathbone, & Thornley, 2007). Among people who do respond, the neuroleptics are more effective in treating the positive symptoms of schizophrenia than in treating the negative symptoms (lack of motivation and interpersonal deficits). Many people with schizophrenia who take these drugs are not actively psychotic but still are unable to hold a job or build positive social relationships. People with schizophrenia typically must take neuroleptic drugs all the time in order to prevent new episodes of acute symptoms. If the drug is discontinued, about 78 percent of people with schizophrenia relapse within 1 year, and 98 percent within 2 years, compared to about 30 percent of people who continue on their medications (Gitlin et al., 2001).

Unfortunately, however, these drugs have significant side effects that cause many people to want to discontinue their use (Adams et al., 2007). The side effects include grogginess, dry mouth, blurred vision, drooling, sexual dysfunction, visual disturbances, weight gain or loss, constipation, menstrual disturbances in women, and depression. Another common side effect is *akinesia*, which includes slowed motor activity, monotonous speech, and an expressionless face. Patients taking the phenothiazines often show symptoms similar to those seen in Parkinson's disease, including muscle stiffness, freezing of the facial muscles, tremors and spasms in the extremities, and *akathesis*, an agitation that causes people to pace and be unable to sit still (Adams et al., 2007). The fact that Parkinson's disease is caused by a lack of dopamine in the brain suggests that these side effects occur because the drugs reduce the functional levels of dopamine.

One serious side effect is **tardive dyskinesia**, a neurological disorder that involves involuntary movements of the tongue, face, mouth, or jaw. People with this disorder may involuntarily smack their lips, make sucking sounds, stick out their tongue, puff their cheeks, or make other bizarre movements over and over again. Tardive dyskinesia often is irreversible and may occur in over 20 percent of persons with long-term use of the phenothiazines (Kutscher, 2008).

The side effects of the neuroleptics can be reduced by reducing dosages. For this reason, many clinicians prescribe for people with schizophrenia the lowest dosage possible that still keeps acute symptoms at bay, known as a *maintenance dose.* Unfortunately, maintenance doses often do not restore an individual to full functioning (Kutscher, 2008). The negative symptoms of schizophrenia may still be strongly present, along with mild versions of the positive symptoms, making it hard for the individual to function in daily life. Some people with schizophrenia live a revolving-door existence marked by frequent hospitalizations and a marginal life outside the hospital.

Some modern treatment facilities provide people with schizophrenia with comprehensive services in a positive, pleasant setting.

Atypical Antipsychotics Fortunately, newer drugs, the **atypical antipsychotics**, seem to be more effective in treating schizophrenia than the neuroleptics, without the neurological side effects of the latter (Dossenbach et al., 2004). One of the most common of these drugs, *clozapine* (sold in the United States as Clozaril), binds to the D4 dopamine receptor, but it also influences several other neurotransmitters, including serotonin (Sajotovic et al., 2008). Clozapine has helped many people with schizophrenia who never responded to the phenothiazines, and it appears to reduce the negative as well as the positive symptoms in many patients (Dossenbach et al., 2004).

While clozapine does not induce tardive dyskinesia, it does have some side effects, including dizziness, nausea, sedation, seizures, hypersalivation, weight gain, and tachycardia. In addition, in 1 to 2 percent of the people who take clozapine, a condition called *agranulocytosis* develops (Spaulding et al., 2001). This is a deficiency of granulocytes, substances produced by bone marrow that fight infection. This condition can be fatal, so patients taking clozapine must be carefully monitored.

Physicians now often begin treatment with another atypical antipsychotic, such as risperidone. This drug affects serotonin receptors and is a weak blocker of dopamine receptors (Ananth, Burgoyne, Gadasalli, & Aquino, 2001). Risperidone (Risperdal) is as effective as clozapine and may work more quickly (Bondolfi et al., 1998). It also has been shown to be more effective at preventing relapse than the typical antipsychotic medications, such as haloperidol (Csernansky, Mahmoud, & Brenner, 2002). Risperidone does not induce tardive dyskinesia, but it can cause sexual dysfunction, sedation, low blood pressure, weight gain, seizures, and problems with concentration.

Other atypical antipsychotic drugs stabilize dopamine levels across the brain, increasing the level of dopamine where it is deficient and decreasing it where it is in excess (Stahl, 2001). Some of these drugs, including olanzapine (Zyprexa), decrease symptoms of schizophrenia while inducing significantly fewer neurological side effects than either the typical antipsychotics or clozapine (Dossenbach et al., 2004; Lieberman et al., 2003). Aripiprazole (Abilify) is an atypical antipsychotic that affects both dopamine and serotonin systems; it has been effective in treating both schizophrenia and mood disorders (Stahl, 2006). Side effects include akathesis, headache, tiredness or weakness, vomiting, stomach upset, light-headedness, sleep disturbances, and blurred vision.

Despite the potentially serious side effects of the drugs used to treat schizophrenia, many people with schizophrenia and their families regard these drugs as lifesavers. The drugs have released many people with schizophrenia from lives of psychosis and isolation, enabling them to pursue the everyday activities and goals that most of us take for granted.

Psychological and Social Treatments

If drugs control the symptoms of schizophrenia, why would anyone need psychological or social interventions? As the following excerpt illustrates, drugs cannot completely restore the life of a person with schizophrenia.

VOICES

Medicine did not cause sanity; it only made it possible. Sanity came through a minute-by-minute choice of outer reality, which was often without meaning, over inside reality, which was full of meaning. Sanity meant choosing reality that was not real and having faith that someday the choice would be worth the fear involved and that it would someday hold meaning. (Anonymous, 1992, p. 335)

Many individuals who are able to control the acute positive symptoms of schizophrenia with drugs still experience many of the negative symptoms, particularly problems in motivation and in social interactions. Psychological interventions can help them increase their social skills and reduce their isolation and immobility (Bustillo, Lauriello, Horan, & Keith, 2001). Such interventions also can help people with schizophrenia and their families reduce the stress and conflict in their lives, thereby reducing the risk of relapse into psychosis (Pharoah, Mari, Rathbone, & Wong, 2006). Psychological interventions can help people with schizophrenia understand their disorder, appreciate the need to remain on their medications, and cope more effectively with the side effects of the medications. Because of the severity of their disorder, many people with schizophrenia have trouble finding or holding a job, feeding and sheltering themselves, and obtaining necessary medical or psychiatric care. Psychologists, social workers, and other mental health professionals can assist people with schizophrenia in meeting these basic needs.

Behavioral, Cognitive, and Social Interventions

Most experts in the treatment of schizophrenia argue for a comprehensive approach that addresses the wide array of behavioral, cognitive, and social deficits in schizophrenia and is tailored to the specific deficits of each individual with the disorder (Liberman et al., 2002). These treatments are given in addition to medication and can increase the level of everyday functioning and significantly reduce the risk for relapse (Gumley et al., 2003).

Cognitive interventions include helping people with schizophrenia recognize and change demoralizing attitudes they may have toward their illness so that they will seek help when needed and participate in society to the extent that they can (Beck & Rector, 2005). Behavioral interventions, based on social learning theory (see Chapter 2), include the use of operant conditioning and modeling to teach persons with schizophrenia skills such as initiating and maintaining conversations with others, asking for help or information from physicians, and persisting in an activity, such as cooking or cleaning (Liberman et al., 2002). These interventions may be administered by the family. In that case, a therapist would teach a client's family members to ignore schizophrenia symptoms, such as bizarre comments, but to reinforce socially appropriate behavior by giving it attention and positive emotional responses. In psychiatric hospitals and residential treatment centers, *token economies* sometimes are established, based on the principles of operant conditioning. Patients earn tokens that they can exchange for privileges (such as time watching television) by completing assigned duties (such as making their bed) or even by simply engaging in appropriate conversations with others.

Social interventions include increasing contact between people with schizophrenia and supportive others, often through self-help support groups (Liberman et al., 2002). These groups discuss the impact of the disorder on their lives, the frustration of trying to make people understand their disorder, their fear of relapse, their experiences with various medications, and other day-to-day concerns. Group members also can help one another learn social and problem-solving skills by giving feedback and providing a forum in which individual members can role-play new skills. People with schizophrenia also are often directly taught problem-solving skills applicable to common social situations (Liberman, Eckman, & Marder, 2001). For example, they may practice generating and role-playing solutions for when a receptionist tells them no one is available at a company to interview them for a potential job.

Family Therapy

Recall that high levels of expressed emotion within the family of a person with schizophrenia can substantially increase the risk for and frequency of relapse. Many researchers have examined the effectiveness of family-oriented therapies for people with schizophrenia. Successful therapies combine basic education on schizophrenia with training of family members in coping with their loved one's inappropriate behaviors and the disorder's impact on their lives (Bustillo et al., 2001; Falloon, Brooker, & Graham-Hole, 1992; Hogarty et al., 1991; Pharoah et al., 2006).

In the educational portion of these therapies, families are taught about the disorder's biological causes, its symptoms, and the medications and their side effects. The hope is that this information will reduce self-blame in family members, increase their tolerance for the uncontrollable symptoms of the disorder, and allow them to monitor their family member's use of medication and possible side effects. Family members also learn communication skills to reduce harsh, conflictual interactions, as well as problem-solving skills to manage issues in the family, such as lack of money, so as to reduce the overall level of stress in the family. They also learn specific behavioral techniques for encouraging appropriate behavior and discouraging inappropriate behavior by their family member with schizophrenia.

These family-oriented interventions, when combined with drug therapy, appear to be more effective at reducing relapse rates than drug therapy alone. On average, approximately 24 percent of people who receive family-oriented therapy in addition to drug therapy relapse into schizophrenia, compared to 64 percent of people who receive routine drug therapy alone (Bustillo et al., 2001; Pitschel-Walz et al., 2001).

For example, Gerard Hogarty and colleagues (1986, 1991; see also Hogarty, Greenwald, et al., 1997; Hogarty, Kornblith, et al., 1997) compared the effectiveness of four types of intervention for persons with schizophrenia. The first group received medication only. The other three groups received medication plus one of the following types of psychosocial intervention: social skills training for the person with schizophrenia only, family-oriented treatment for his or her family members, or a combination of social skills training for the person and family-oriented treatment. In the first year following these treatments, 40 percent of the people in the medication-only group relapsed, compared to only 20 percent in the first two psychosocial intervention groups and no one in the group that received medication as well as both individual social skills training and family-oriented therapy (Figure 8.10). In the second year of follow-up, the groups that received family-oriented therapy continued to fare better than those who received medication alone. In this study and others, however, the effects of psychosocial intervention diminished with time if the intervention was not continued. Thus, like the medications for schizophrenia, psychosocial interventions must be ongoing if they are to continue to reduce the risk of relapse.

In some cultures, people with schizophrenia are more likely to be cared for and be deeply embedded in their family than in other cultures. Family-oriented interventions may be even more critical for people in these cultures (Lopez, Kopelowicz, & Canive, 2002). The interventions must be culturally sensitive. One study found that behavior therapies to increase communication actually backfired in some Hispanic families, perhaps because these families already had low levels of expressed emotion and found the techniques suggested by the therapists to violate their cultural norms for how family members should interact (Telles et al., 1995). For example, some of the most traditional family members in this study expressed great discomfort during exercises that encouraged them to establish eye contact or express negative feelings to authority figures, because these actions were considered disrespectful. This is another example of how therapists must take into account the culture of their clients in designing interventions.

FIGURE 8.10 **Effects of Psychosocial Intervention (with Medication) on Relapse Rates.** In one study, patients with schizophrenia who received social skills training, family therapy, or both in addition to medication had much lower relapse rates in the first year after treatment than did patients who received only medication.

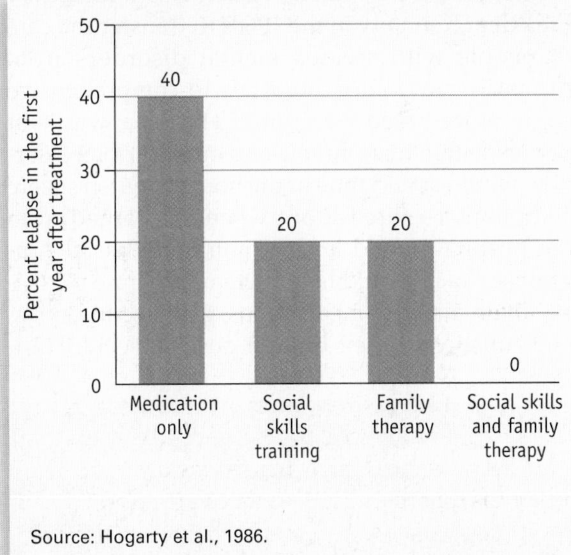

Source: Hogarty et al., 1986.

Assertive Community Treatment Programs

Many people with schizophrenia lack families to care for them. Even those with families have such a wide array of needs—for the monitoring and adjustment of their medications, occupational training, assistance in receiving financial resources (such as Social Security and Medicaid), social skills training, emotional support, and sometimes basic housing—that comprehensive community-based treatment programs are necessary. **Assertive community treatment programs** provide comprehensive services for people with schizophrenia, relying on the expertise of medical professionals, social workers, and psychologists to meet the variety of patients' needs 24 hours a day (Test & Stein, 1980).

In Chapter 1, we discussed the community mental health movement, which was initiated by President Kennedy in the 1960s to transfer the care of people with serious mental disorders from primarily psychiatric hospitals to comprehensive community-based programs. The idea was that people with schizophrenia and other serious disorders would spend time in the hospital when severe symptoms required it but when discharged from the hospital would go to community-based programs, which would help them reintegrate to society, maintain their medications, gain needed skills, and function at their highest possible level. Hundreds of halfway houses, group homes, and therapeutic communities were established for people with serious mental disorders who needed a supportive place to live.

FIGURE 8.11 **Effects of Home-Based Treatment on Need for Institutional Care.** In one study, patients with schizophrenia who received intensive home-based skills training and care were much less likely to be hospitalized for psychotic symptoms or to need other types of institutional care.

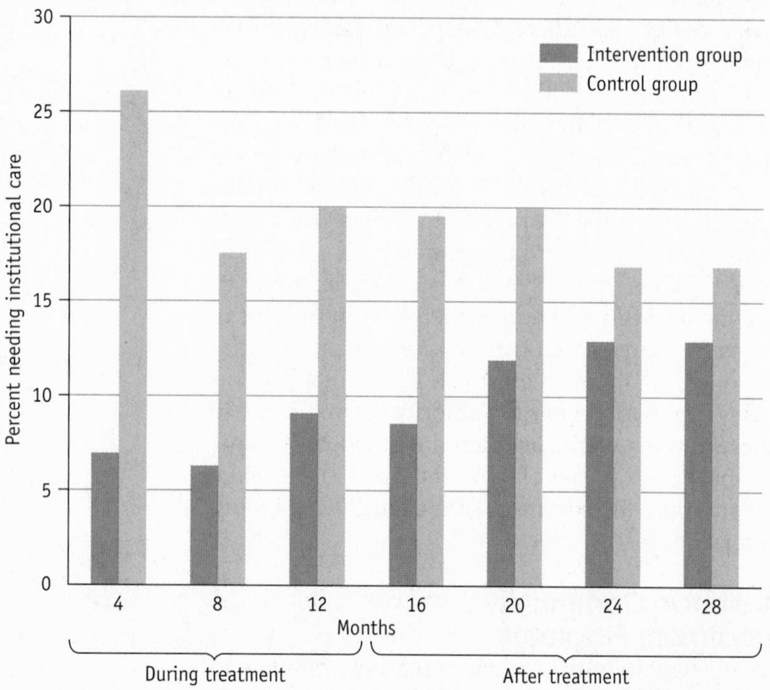

Source: Test & Stein, 1980.

One classic example of this was The Lodge, a residential treatment center for people with schizophrenia established by George Fairweather and his colleagues (1969). At The Lodge, mental health professionals were available for support and assistance, but residents ran the household and worked with other residents to establish healthy behaviors and discourage inappropriate behaviors. The residents also established their own employment agency to assist with finding jobs. Follow-up studies showed that Lodge residents fared much better than people with schizophrenia who were simply discharged from the hospital into the care of their families or into less intensive treatment programs (Fairweather et al., 1969). For example, Lodge residents were less likely to be rehospitalized and much more likely to hold jobs than were those in a comparison group, even after The Lodge closed.

Other comprehensive treatment programs provide skills training, vocational rehabilitation, and social support to people with schizophrenia who live at home. Studies of these programs find that they reduce the amount of time spent in the hospital and, as a result, can be cost-effective (Bustillo et al., 2001).

In a model program established in Madison, Wisconsin, by founders of the *assertive community program movement* (Test & Stein, 1980), mental health professionals worked with chronically disabled people with schizophrenia. Interventions were provided in the homes or communities of the patients for 14 months, and then the patients were followed for another 28 months. Their progress was compared with that of another group of patients, who received standard hospital treatment for their positive symptoms. Both groups were treated with antipsychotic medications. The patients who received the home-based intensive skills interventions were less likely than the control-group patients to be hospitalized and more likely to be employed both during the treatment and in the 28 months of follow-up (Figure 8.11). The home-based intervention group also showed lower levels of emotional distress and of positive symptoms during the intervention than did the control group.

The difference in levels of symptoms between the two groups diminished after the intervention period ended. In general, the gains that people in skills-based interventions make tend to decline once the interventions end, suggesting that these interventions need to be ongoing (Liberman, 1994). However, their benefits can be great.

Despite the proven effectiveness of intensive treatment programs such as these, they have been few and far between. About 800 community mental health centers now operate in the United States, only one-third the number needed (Torrey, 2006). Those that do exist tend to be understaffed and underfunded and thus unable to provide adequate care to the people they serve.

The *community mental health movement* was never funded to a level that could support its lofty goals. With the changes in medical insurance in recent years, funding for mental health care for the seriously mentally ill has been even tighter. Although billions of dollars are spent on mental health care per year in the United States, much of that money goes not to direct services to people with schizophrenia but rather to subsistence programs such as Social Security disability income and to community services for people with less serious mental disorders (Torrey, 2006). Much of the financial burden of caring for people with schizophrenia falls to state and local governments, which lack the necessary resources, or to families, who too often are bankrupted by the cost of care.

As a result, 40 to 60 percent of people with schizophrenia receive little or no care in a given year (Torrey, 2006). Those who do receive care often are hospitalized only when their symptoms are acute, and they remain in the hospital for an inadequate period of time for their symptoms to stabilize. They may be discharged with little or no follow-up. Some return to their families, but many end up in nursing homes, where they receive only custodial care, or in single-room-occupancy hotels or rooming houses, often in run-down inner-city neighborhoods. Many end up homeless or in prison (Torrey, 2006).

Cross-Cultural Treatments: Traditional Healers

In developing countries and in parts of industrialized countries, the symptoms of schizophrenia sometimes are treated by folk or religious healers, according to cultural beliefs about the meaning and causes of the symptoms. Anthropologists and cultural psychiatrists have described four models that traditional healers tend to follow in treating schizophrenic symptoms (Karno & Jenkins, 1993). According to the *structural model,* there are interrelated levels of experience—such as the body, emotion, and cognition or the person, society, and culture—and symptoms arise when the integration of these levels is lost. Healing thus involves reintegrating these levels through a change of diet or environment, the prescription of herbal medicines, or rituals.

The *social support model* holds that symptoms arise from conflictual social relationships and healing involves mobilizing a patient's kin to support him or her through the crisis and reintegrating the patient into a positive social support network. The *persuasive model* suggests that rituals can transform the meaning of symptoms for the patient, diminishing their pain. And, in the *clinical model,* the faith the patient puts in the traditional healer to provide a cure for the symptoms is sufficient. In developing countries, care for people with schizophrenia is more likely to be carried out by the extended family than by a mental health institution (Karno & Jenkins, 1993). Thus, it may be especially important in these countries that interventions for a person with schizophrenia also include his or her family.

TEST YOURSELF

1. What are the phenothiazines? Describe the symptoms they treat and their side effects.
2. What are the atypical antipsychotics? What advantages do they have over the traditional antipsychotics? What are their side effects?
3. How can psychosocial therapies help people with schizophrenia?

APPLY IT Will's assertive community treatment program likely provides him with all of the following *except* which?

a. analysis of the childhood events that contributed to his illness
b. occupational rehabilitation
c. education of his family about schizophrenia
d. support for maintaining his medications

Answers appear online at www.mhhe.com/nolen5e.

CHAPTER INTEGRATION

There is probably more consensus among mental health professionals about the biological roots of schizophrenia than of any other psychopathology discussed in this book. The evidence that the fundamental vulnerability to schizophrenia is biological is compelling, yet there is growing consensus that psychosocial factors also contribute to the risk for schizophrenia among people who have the biological vulnerability. Theorists are increasingly developing models that integrate the biological and psychosocial contributors to schizophrenia in order to provide comprehensive explanations of the development of this disorder (Figure 8.12).

FIGURE 8.12 The Interaction of Biological and Psychosocial Factors in Schizophrenia

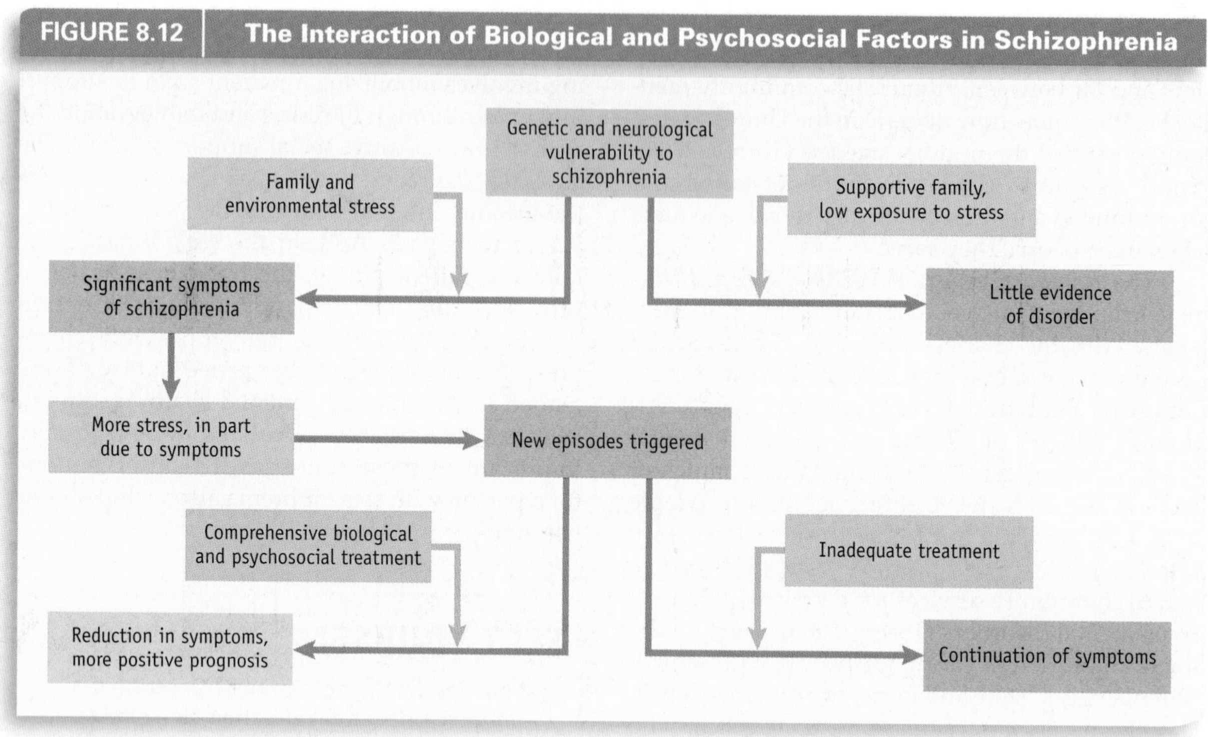

A person with a biological vulnerability to schizophrenia who is raised in a supportive, low-expressed-emotion family and who escapes exposure to major stressors may never develop the full syndrome of schizophrenia. He or she still may have mild symptoms, however, because the biological underpinnings of this disorder play such an important role. Alternatively, a person who has a biological vulnerability and grows up in a stressful atmosphere is more likely to develop the full syndrome of schizophrenia. Psychosocial stress also clearly contributes to new episodes of psychosis in people with this disorder.

There is widespread consensus among mental health professionals that the most effective therapies for schizophrenia are those that address both the biological and the psychosocial contributors to the disorder.

SHADES OF GRAY DISCUSSION (review p. 241)

As you may have noticed, Jeff's symptoms do not fit neatly into any of the categories in the *DSM-IV-TR*. You might wonder if he is depressed, because he reports feelings of emptiness. But because he does not show most of the other symptoms of depression (see Chapter 7), this is not an appropriate diagnosis. His emptiness, social isolation, lack of motivation, and general deterioration in functioning all look like negative symptoms of schizophrenia. However, he does not appear to have the positive symptoms—delusions, hallucinations, incoherence in speech or thought.

The psychiatrist treating Jeff believed that he was showing prodromal or early symptoms of schizophrenia, which often are predominantly negative. He was given antipsychotic medications and allowed to go home with his parents. Remaining isolated and apathetic, he stopped taking the medications. Two months later, he said he was experiencing severe electrical sensations in his head that he believed were being transmitted through his father's mind. He also began to have "horrible thoughts" that were put there by his father. He became agitated and one night grabbed a knife, went into his parents' bedroom, and threatened to kill his father if he would not stop tormenting him. Fortunately, his father was able to talk him into dropping the knife and going to the emergency room.

Jeff was admitted to the hospital, given a diagnosis of schizophrenia, and placed on a higher dose of antipsychotic medications. His positive symptoms diminished, but his negative symptoms remained. (Adapted from Andreasen, 1998)

THINK CRITICALLY

In their book *Divided Minds,* identical twins Carolyn Spiro and Pamela Spiro Wagner describe a close childhood relationship, apart from typical sibling rivalries. Carolyn often felt she had to prove that she was as intelligent and creative as Pamela. As they entered their teenage years, however, the twins grew apart. Pamela's increasingly bizarre behaviors became an embarrassment to Carolyn. By the time the twins were college students at Brown University, Pamela was becoming more and more reclusive. Eventually, Pamela had a psychotic episode, although it was years before she was diagnosed with paranoid schizophrenia. Carolyn went on to graduate from first Brown and then Harvard Medical School. She is now a practicing psychiatrist. Pamela lives nearby, doing her artwork when she can but constantly battling to keep her schizophrenia under control with medications and therapy. The twins once again are very close emotionally.

Given what you have learned about the causes of schizophrenia, how might you explain why Pamela developed schizophrenia but Carolyn did not? (*Discussion appears on p. 519 at the back of this book.*)

CHAPTER SUMMARY

- The positive symptoms of schizophrenia include delusions (ideas the individual believes are true but are certainly false), hallucinations (unreal perceptual experiences), thought disturbances (incoherent thought and speech), and grossly disorganized or catatonic behavior.
- The negative symptoms of schizophrenia include affective flattening, alogia (poverty of speech), and avolition (the inability to initiate and persist in goal-directed activities). In addition, people with schizophrenia often show inappropriate affect, anhedonia, and impaired social skills. Prodromal and residual symptoms are mild versions of the psychotic and negative symptoms that occur before and after episodes of acute symptoms.
- Cognitive deficits in schizophrenia include problems in attention, working memory, problem solving, and abstract thinking.
- There are five subtypes of schizophrenia. People with the paranoid subtype have delusions and hallucinations with themes of persecution and grandiosity. This type of schizophrenia tends to begin later in life, and its episodes often are triggered by stress. People with this type of schizophrenia have a better prognosis than do people with other types.
- The disorganized subtype of schizophrenia shows especially marked disorganization in thought and behavior and either a flattening of affect or frequent inappropriate affect. People with this subtype of schizophrenia are prone to odd, stereotyped behaviors, and their speech often is incoherent. This type of schizophrenia tends to have an early onset and a continuous course, which often is unresponsive to treatment.
- The catatonic subtype of schizophrenia is characterized by motor behaviors and ways of speaking that suggest the person is completely unresponsive to the environment. The symptoms include motor immobility, excessive and purposeless motor activity, extreme negativism, peculiar movements, and echolalia or echopraxia.
- People with the undifferentiated subtype of schizophrenia have symptoms that meet the criteria for schizophrenia but do not meet the criteria for paranoid, disorganized, or catatonic schizophrenia.
- People with the residual subtype of schizophrenia have had at least one episode of active symptoms but do not currently have prominent positive symptoms of schizophrenia. They continue to have mild positive symptoms and significant negative symptoms.
- Estimates of the prevalence of schizophrenia in various countries range from about 0.1 to 2.0 percent, but most estimates are between 0.5 and 1.0 percent. There are some slight ethnic differences in rates of schizophrenia, but these may be due to differences in socioeconomic status.
- The content of delusions and hallucinations changes somewhat across cultures, but the form of these symptoms remains similar, and many clinicians and researchers believe that schizophrenia can be diagnosed reliably across cultures.

- Men may be more prone to schizophrenia than women, and there are some differences in symptoms between genders.
- A number of other psychotic disorders are recognized by the *DSM-IV-TR.* Schizoaffective disorder is diagnosed when symptoms of schizophrenia occur with significant mood symptoms. Individuals with schizophreniform disorder meet the criteria for schizophrenia but for a period of only 1 to 6 months. Those with brief psychotic disorder meet the criteria for schizophrenia but for a period of less than 1 month and sometimes in response to a major stressor. Delusional disorder is characterized primarily by the presence of nonbizarre delusions. Shared psychotic disorder is diagnosed when one individual comes to share the delusion of another individual with whom she or he has a close relationship.
- Biological theories of schizophrenia focus on genetics, structural and functional abnormalities in the brain, and neurotransmitters. There is clear evidence of a genetic transmission of schizophrenia. People with schizophrenia show abnormal functioning in the prefrontal areas of the brain and the hippocampus, as well as enlarged ventricles, suggesting atrophy in parts of the brain. Many people with schizophrenia have a history of prenatal difficulties, such as exposure to the influenza virus during the second trimester of gestation, or birth complications, including perinatal hypoxia. Brain abnormalities and dysfunction in dopamine systems may contribute to the fundamental cognitive deficits in attention and memory seen in people with schizophrenia.
- Stressful events probably cannot cause schizophrenia in people who lack a vulnerability to the disorder, but they may trigger new episodes of psychosis in people with the disorder.
- Expressed emotion theorists argue that some families of people with schizophrenia are simultaneously overprotective and hostile and that this increases the risk for relapse.
- Cognitive theories suggest that some schizophrenic symptoms are attempts by the individual to understand and manage cognitive deficits.
- Drugs known as the phenothiazines, introduced in the 1950s, brought relief to many people with schizophrenia. The phenothiazines reduce the positive symptoms of schizophrenia but often are not effective in reducing the negative symptoms. Major side effects include tardive dyskinesia, an irreversible neurological disorder characterized by involuntary movements of the tongue, face, mouth, or jaw.
- Newer drugs, called atypical antipsychotics, seem to induce fewer side effects and are effective in treating both the positive symptoms and the negative symptoms of schizophrenia for many people.
- Psychological and social therapies focus on helping people with schizophrenia reduce stress, improve family interactions, learn social skills, and cope with the impact of the disorder on their lives. Comprehensive treatment programs combining drug therapy with an array of psychological and social therapies have been shown to reduce relapse significantly. These programs tend to be few and underfunded, however.

KEY TERMS

undifferentiated schizophrenia 236
residual schizophrenia 236
schizoaffective disorder 238
schizophreniform disorder 238
brief psychotic disorder 239
delusional disorder 240
shared psychotic disorder 240
dopamine 246
phenothiazines 246
neuroleptics 246
mesolimbic pathway 246
social drift 248
expressed emotion 249
chlorpromazine 252
tardive dyskinesia 252
atypical antipsychotics 253
assertive community treatment programs 256

Chapter 9

Personality Disorders

CHAPTER OUTLINE

Extraordinary People

Susanna Kaysen, *Girl, Interrupted*

Susanna Kaysen was 18, depressed, drifting through life and endlessly oppositional toward her parents and teachers. She tried to commit suicide and eventually was hospitalized, remaining there for nearly 2 years. Later, Kaysen discovered that her diagnosis had been borderline personality disorder. In her autobiography, *Girl, Interrupted,* she raises many questions about this diagnosis.

> . . . I had to locate a copy of the *Diagnostic and Statistical Manual of Mental Disorders* and look up Borderline Personality to see what they really thought about me.
>
> It's a fairly accurate picture of me at eighteen, minus a few quirks like reckless driving and eating binges. . . . I'm tempted to try refuting it, but then I would be open to the further charges of "defensiveness" and "resistance."
>
> All I can do is give the particulars: an annotated diagnosis.
>
> . . . "Instability of self-image, interpersonal relationships, and mood . . . uncertainty about . . . long-term goals or career choice . . . ." Isn't this a good description of adolescence? Moody, fickle, faddish, insecure: in short, impossible.
>
> "Self-multilating behavior (e.g., wrist-scratching) . . . ." I've skipped forward a bit. This is the one that caught me by surprise as I sat on the floor of the bookstore reading my diagnosis. Wrist-scratching! I thought I'd invented it. Wrist-banging, to be precise. . . .
>
> "The person often experiences this instability of self-image as chronic feelings of emptiness or boredom." My chronic feelings of emptiness and boredom came from the fact that I was living a life based on my incapacities, which were numerous. A partial list follows. I could not and did not want to: ski, play tennis, or go to gym class; attend to any subject in school other than English and biology; write papers on any assigned topics (I wrote poems instead of papers for English; I got Fs); plan to go or apply to college; give any reasonable explanation for these refusals.
>
> My self-image was not unstable. I saw myself, quite correctly, as unfit for the educational and social systems. But my parents and teachers did not share my self-image. Their image of me was unstable, since it was out of kilter with reality and based on their needs and wishes. They did not put much value on my capacities, which were admittedly few, but genuine. I read everything, I wrote constantly, and I had boyfriends by the barrelful. . . .
>
> I often ask myself if I'm crazy. I ask other people too. "Is this a crazy thing to say?" I'll ask before saying something that probably isn't crazy.
>
> I start a lot of sentences with "Maybe I'm totally nuts," or "Maybe I've gone 'round the bend." If I do something out of the ordinary—take two baths in one day, for example—I say to myself: Are you crazy? (Kaysen, 1993, pp. 150–159)

Was Susanna Kaysen just a mixed-up teenager whose parents expected too much of her and locked her away when she didn't comply? Or was she a deeply troubled young woman whose stay in the hospital prevented her complete psychological deterioration? Is the diagnosis of borderline personality disorder valid, or is it a label we give to people who don't conform? Kaysen's *Girl, Interrupted* (which was made into a 1999 film starring Winona Ryder) brings life to the enduring debate about the validity and ethics of the diagnosis of borderline personality disorder.

Personality is all the ways we have of acting, thinking, believing, and feeling that make each of us unique. A *personality trait* is a complex pattern of behavior, thought, and feeling that is stable across time and across many situations. People vary greatly in their personalities. Some people have personalities that are very appealing to others and lead them to have many strong, positive social relationships. They may be gregarious and outgoing, caring and compassionate, or humorous and witty. Others have personalities that interfere with their social functioning. They may be shy and withdrawn, exploitative or critical, hostile or dull. Some people have personalities that make them high-achieving. They may be disciplined and goal-oriented, have good leadership skills, and be able to handle stress. Others have personalities that interfere with their achievement. They may be impulsive, unstable, or unreliable or so perfectionistic that they never get anything done.

One of the leading theories of personality is the **five-factor model,** which posits that everyone's personality is organized along five broad dimensions or factors of personality. These factors are often referred to as the Big 5: *negative emotionality, extraversion, openness to experience, agreeableness,* and *conscientiousness* (McCrae & Costa, 1999). Each factor has a number of *facets,* or dimensions, as shown in Table 9.1. Considerable research supports

TABLE 9.1 The Big 5 Personality Factors

Each of the Big 5 personality factors is composed of different facets or components, as described here.

FACTOR 1: NEGATIVE EMOTIONALITY VERSUS EMOTIONAL STABILITY

Facet	Individuals high on this facet are	Individuals low on this facet are
Anxiousness	fearful, apprehensive	relaxed, unconcerned, cool
Angry hostility	angry, bitter	even-tempered
Depressiveness	pessimistic, glum	optimistic
Self-consciousness	timid, embarrassed	self-assured, glib, shameless
Impulsivity	tempted, urgent	controlled, restrained
Vulnerability	helpless, fragile	clear-thinking, fearless, unflappable

FACTOR 2: EXTRAVERSION VERSUS INTROVERSION

Facet	Individuals high on this facet are	Individuals low on this facet are
Warmth	cordial, affectionate, attached	cold, aloof, indifferent
Gregariousness	sociable, outgoing	withdrawn, isolated
Assertiveness	dominant, forceful	unassuming, quiet, resigned
Activity	unassuming, quiet, resigned	passive, lethargic
Excitement seeking	reckless, daring	cautious, monotonous, dull
Positive emotions	high-spirited	placid, anhedonic

FACTOR 3: OPENNESS VERSUS CLOSEDNESS TO ONE'S OWN EXPERIENCE

Facet	Individuals high on this facet are	Individuals low on this facet are
Fantasy	dreamers, unrealistic, imaginative	practical, concrete
Aesthetics	aberrant interests, aesthetic	uninvolved, no aesthetic interests
Feelings	self-aware	constricted, unaware
Actions	unconventional, eccentric	routine, predictable, habitual, stubborn
Ideas	unusual, creative	pragmatic, rigid
Values	permissive, broad-minded	traditional, inflexible, dogmatic

FACTOR 4: AGREEABLENESS VERSUS ANTAGONISM

Facet	Individuals high on this facet are	Individuals low on this facet are
Trust	gullible, naïve, trusting	skeptical, cynical, suspicious, paranoid
Straightforwardness	confiding, honest	cunning, manipulative, deceptive
Altruism	sacrificial, giving	stingy, selfish, greedy, exploitative
Compliance	docile, cooperative	oppositional, combative, aggressive
Modesty	meek, self-effacing, humble	confident, boastful, arrogant
Tender-mindedness	soft, empathetic	tough, callous, ruthless

FACTOR 5: CONSCIENTIOUSNESS VERSUS UNDEPENDABILITY

Facet	Individuals high on this facet are	Individuals low on this facet are
Competence	perfectionistic, efficient	lax, negligent
Order	ordered, methodical, organized	haphazard, disorganized, sloppy
Dutifulness	rigid, reliable, dependable	casual, undependable, unethical
Achievement	workaholic, ambitious	aimless, desultory
Self-discipline	dogged, devoted	hedonistic, negligent
Deliberation	cautious, ruminative, reflective	hasty, careless, rash

Source: T. A. Widiger, personal communication, 2009.

Personality Disorders Along the Continuum

Long-standing patterns of behavior, thought, and feelings that lead to positive social and occupational functioning

A student who is interested in classes, has good friends, and generally enjoys life

Long-standing patterns of behavior, thought, and feeling that are unusual but do not interfere with social or occupational functioning

A student who is awkward or sometimes inappropriate with others, struggles in school or at work, and/or sometimes overreacts emotionally

Potentially meets diagnostic criteria for a personality disorder:

Long-standing patterns of behavior, thought, and feeling that somewhat interfere with social and/or occupational functioning

A student who is often inappropriate with others or socially withdrawn, is having significant difficulties at school or work, and/or frequently overreacts emotionally

Likely meets diagnostic criteria for a personality disorder:

Long-standing patterns of behavior, thought, and feeling that substantially interfere with social and/or occupational functioning

A student who is chronically inappropriate with others or socially withdrawn, has chronic and severe difficulties at school or work, and/or becomes out of control emotionally in distressing situations

Functional — Dysfunctional

Your personality affects your daily life constantly. It determines how you perceive the events of your day, how you feel, and how you interact with others. A core aspect of your personality is your sense of self (Cloninger, 2000; Livesley, 1998). On the functional end of the continuum are people who have a sense of themselves that is coherent and relatively stable and is distinct from their views of others. They have a sense of meaning and purpose in their life and the ability to pursue personally important goals. Another core aspect of personality is the way we relate to others (Livesley, 1998; Rutter, 1987). People with adaptive personalities can empathize and cooperate with others, can be intimate with others appropriately, and appreciate the uniqueness of the different people in their life.

Some people have difficulty in their sense of self and their relationships to others. Their identity may be too susceptible to social pressure, as when a teenager succumbs to peer pressure and engages in illegal behavior. They may wander through life without goals or purpose. They may find it difficult to care about others or to maintain healthy relationships. When an individual fails to develop a sense of self-identity and a capacity for interpersonal functioning that are adaptive in the individual's relationships, he or she may be diagnosed with a **personality disorder**.

the five-factor model of personality. These dimensions seem to capture a great deal of the variation in people's personalities, and they have been replicated in cultures very different from that of the United States, where they have been studied most (Benet-Martinez & John, 1998; Yang et al., 2002). The personality traits in the five-factor model appear to be strongly influenced by genetics (Jang et al., 1998). You can probably find yourself among the dimensions and facets of the Big 5.

As we discuss later in this chapter, the *DSM-5* is likely to incorporate a continuum model of personality disorders such as that represented in the Big 5 model. The *DSM-IV-TR,* in contrast, treats personality disorders as if they were entirely different from "normal" personality traits. It groups

TABLE 9.2 ***DSM-IV-TR* Personality Disorders**
The *DSM-IV-TR* groups personality disorders into three clusters.
CLUSTER A: ODD-ECCENTRIC PERSONALITY DISORDERS
People with these disorders have symptoms similar to those of people with schizophrenia, including inappropriate or flat affect, odd thought and speech patterns, and paranoia. People with these disorders maintain their grasp on reality, however.
CLUSTER B: DRAMATIC-EMOTIONAL PERSONALITY DISORDERS
People with these disorders tend to be manipulative, volatile, and uncaring in social relationships. They are prone to impulsive, sometimes violent behaviors that show little regard for their own safety or the safety or needs of others.
CLUSTER C: ANXIOUS-FEARFUL PERSONALITY DISORDERS
People with these disorders are extremely concerned about being criticized or abandoned by others and thus have dysfunctional relationships with others.
Source: Reprinted with permission from the *Diagnostic and Statistical Manual of Mental Disorders,* Fourth Edition, Text Revision. Copyright © 2000 American Psychiatric Association.

personality disorders into three clusters (Table 9.2). *Cluster A* includes three disorders characterized by *odd or eccentric behaviors and thinking:* paranoid personality disorder, schizoid personality disorder, and schizotypal personality disorder. Each of these has some of the features of schizophrenia, but people diagnosed with these personality disorders are not out of touch with reality. Their behaviors simply are odd and often inappropriate. For example, they may be chronically suspicious of others or speak in odd ways that are difficult to understand.

Cluster B includes four disorders characterized by *dramatic, erratic, and emotional behavior and interpersonal relationships:* antisocial personality disorder, histrionic personality disorder, borderline personality disorder, and narcissistic personality disorder. People diagnosed with these disorders tend to be manipulative, volatile, and uncaring in social relationships and prone to impulsive behaviors. They may behave in exaggerated ways or even attempt suicide to try to gain attention.

Cluster C includes three disorders characterized by *anxious and fearful emotions and chronic self-doubt:* dependent personality disorder, avoidant personality disorder, and obsessive-compulsive personality disorder. People diagnosed with these disorders have little self-confidence and difficulty in relationships.

The *DSM-IV-TR* treats personality disorders as different from the acute disorders, such as major depression and schizophrenia, by placing the personality disorders on Axis II of the diagnostic system instead of on Axis I with the acute disorders (see Chapter 3). The *DSM-IV-TR* uses Axis II to signal that personality disorders are especially chronic and pervasive, rather than occurring in distinct episodes. People diagnosed with a personality disorder often experience one of the acute Axis I disorders as well at some time in their life (Grant, Stinson, et al., 2004). In fact, the acute disorders are often what bring these people to the attention of clinicians.

In this chapter, we first describe how the *DSM-IV-TR* defines and diagnoses personality disorders. Then we explain how the proposed changes for the *DSM-5* reconceptualize personality disorders along a continuum model.

ODD-ECCENTRIC PERSONALITY DISORDERS

The behavior of people diagnosed with the **odd-eccentric personality disorders** (Table 9.3) is similar to that of people with schizophrenia, but these people retain their grasp on reality to a greater degree than do people who are psychotic. They may be paranoid, speak in odd and eccentric ways that make them difficult to understand, have difficulty relating to other people, and have unusual beliefs or perceptual experiences that fall short of delusions and hallucinations. Some researchers consider this group of personality disorders to be part of the *schizophrenia spectrum* (Nigg & Goldsmith, 1994). That is, these disorders may be precursors to

TABLE 9.3 Odd-Eccentric Personality Disorders

People with an odd-eccentric personality disorder may exhibit mild signs of schizophrenia.

Label	Key Features	Relationship to Schizophrenia
Paranoid personality disorder	Chronic and pervasive mistrust and suspicion of other people that is unwarranted and maladaptive	Weak relationship
Schizoid personality disorder	Chronic lack of interest in and avoidance of interpersonal relationships, emotional coldness toward others	Unclear relationship
Schizotypal personality disorder	Chronic pattern of inhibited or inappropriate emotion and social behavior, aberrant cognitions, disorganized speech	Strong relationship—considered a mild version of schizophrenia

Source: Reprinted with permission from the *Diagnostic and Statistical Manual of Mental Disorders,* Fourth Edition, Text Revision.

schizophrenia in some people or may even be milder versions of schizophrenia. These disorders often occur in people with first-degree relatives who have schizophrenia.

Paranoid Personality Disorder

The defining feature of **paranoid personality disorder** is a pervasive and unwarranted mistrust of others. People diagnosed with this disorder believe that other people are chronically trying to deceive or exploit them, and they are preoccupied with concerns about the loyalty and trustworthiness of others. They are hypervigilant for evidence confirming their suspicions. Often they are penetrating observers of situations, noting details most other people miss. For example, they notice a slight grimace on the face of their boss or an apparently trivial slip of the tongue by their spouse that would go unnoticed by everyone else. Moreover, people diagnosed with paranoid personality disorder consider these events to be highly meaningful and spend a great deal of time trying to decipher such clues to other people's true intentions. They are also sensitive to criticism.

People with paranoid personality disorder tend to misinterpret situations in line with their suspicions. For example, a husband might interpret his wife's cheerfulness one evening as evidence that she is having an affair with someone at work. These people are resistant to rational arguments against their suspicions and may consider the fact that another person is arguing with them as evidence that the person is part of the conspiracy against them. Some withdraw from other people in an attempt to protect themselves, but others become aggressive and arrogant, sure that their way of looking at the world is right and superior and that the best defense against the conspiring of others is a good offense. Felix, in the following case study, was diagnosed with paranoid personality disorder.

CASE STUDY

Felix is a 59-year-old construction worker who worries that his co-workers might hurt him. Last week, while he was using a table saw, Felix's hand slipped and his fingers came very close to being cut badly. Felix wonders if someone sabotaged the saw, so that somehow the piece of wood he was working with slipped and drew his hand into the saw blade. Since this incident, Felix has observed his co-workers looking at him and whispering to each other. He mentioned his suspicion that the saw had been tampered with to his boss, but the boss told him that was a crazy idea and that Felix obviously had just been careless.

Felix does not have any close friends. Even his brothers and sisters avoid him, because he frequently misinterprets things they say to be criticisms of him. Felix was married for a few years, but his wife left him when he began to demand that she not see any of her friends or go out without him, because he suspected she was having affairs with other men. Felix lives in a middle-class neighborhood in a small town that has very little crime. Still, he owns three handguns and a shotgun, which are always loaded, in expectation of someone breaking into his house.

Epidemiological studies suggest that between 0.7 and 5.1 percent of people in the general population can be diagnosed with paranoid personality disorder (Lenzenweger, 2008). People diagnosed with this disorder appear to be at increased risk for a number of acute psychological problems, including major depression, anxiety disorders, substance abuse, and psychotic episodes (Bernstein, Useda, & Siever, 1995; Grant, Stinson, et al., 2004). Not surprisingly, their interpersonal relationships, including intimate relationships, tend to be unstable. Retrospective studies suggest that their prognosis generally is poor, with their symptoms intensifying under stress.

Theories of Paranoid Personality Disorder

Some family history studies have shown that paranoid personality disorder is more common in the families of people with schizophrenia than in the families of healthy control subjects. This finding suggests that paranoid personality disorder may be part of the schizophrenia spectrum of disorders (Chang et al., 2002; Nigg & Goldsmith, 1994). One twin study found the heritability of paranoid personality disorder to be .50 (Coolidge, Thede, & Jang, 2004).

Cognitive theorists view paranoid personality disorder as the result of an underlying belief that other people are malevolent and deceptive, combined with a lack of self-confidence about being able to defend oneself against others (Beck & Freeman, 1990). Thus, the person must always be vigilant for signs of others' deceit or criticism and must be quick to act against others. A study of 17 patients diagnosed with paranoid personality disorder found that they endorsed beliefs as predicted by this cognitive theory more than did patients diagnosed with other personality disorders (Beck et al., 2001).

Treatment of Paranoid Personality Disorder

People diagnosed with paranoid personality disorder usually come into contact with clinicians only when they are in crisis. They may seek treatment for severe symptoms of depression or anxiety but often do not feel a need for treatment of their paranoia. In addition, therapists' attempts to challenge their paranoid thinking are likely to be misinterpreted in line with their paranoid belief system. For this reason, treating paranoid personality disorder can be quite difficult (Millon et al., 2000).

In order to gain the trust of a person diagnosed with a paranoid personality disorder, the therapist must be calm, respectful, and extremely straightforward (Siever & Kendler, 1985). The therapist cannot directly confront the client's paranoid thinking but instead must rely on indirect means of raising questions in the client's mind about his or her typical way of interpreting situations. Although many therapists do not expect paranoid clients to achieve full insight into their problems, they hope that, by developing at least some degree of trust in the therapist, the client can learn to trust others a bit more and thus develop somewhat improved interpersonal relationships.

Cognitive therapy for people diagnosed with this disorder focuses on increasing their sense of self-efficacy in dealing with difficult situations, thus decreasing their fear and hostility toward others. As an example, consider the following interchange between a cognitive therapist and a woman, Ann, who believed that her co-workers were intentionally trying to annoy her and to turn her supervisor against her.

VOICES

Therapist: You're reacting as though this is a very dangerous situation. What are the risks you see?

Ann: They'll keep dropping things and making noise to annoy me.

Therapist: Are you sure nothing worse is at risk?

Ann: Yeah.

Therapist: So you don't think there's much chance of them attacking you or anything?

Ann: Nah, they wouldn't do that.

Therapist: If they do keep dropping things and making noises, how bad will that be?

Ann: Like I told you, it's real aggravating. It really bugs me.

Therapist: So it would continue pretty much as it's been going for years now.

Ann: Yeah. It bugs me, but I can take it.

Therapist: And you know that if it keeps happening, at the very least you can keep handling it the way you have been—holding the aggravation in, then taking it out on your husband when you get home. Suppose we could come up with some ways to handle the aggravation even better or to have them get to you less. Is that something you'd be interested in?

Ann: Yeah, that sounds good.

Therapist: Another risk you mentioned earlier is that they might talk to your supervisor and turn her against you. As you see it, how long have they been trying to do this?

Ann: Ever since I've been there.

Therapist: How much luck have they had so far in doing that?

Ann: Not much.

Therapist: Do you see any indications that they're going to have any more success now than they have so far?

Ann: No, I don't guess so.

Therapist: So your gut reaction is as though the situation at work is really dangerous. But when you stop and think it through, you conclude that the worst they're going to do is to be really aggravating, and that even if we don't come up with anything new, you can handle it well enough to get by. Does that sound right?

Ann: [Smiling] Yeah, I guess so.

Therapist: And if we can come up with some ways to handle the stress better or handle them better, there will be even less they can do to you.

(Beck & Freeman, 1990, pp. 111–112)

In this interchange, the therapist did not directly challenge Ann's beliefs about her co-workers' intentions but did try to reduce the sense of danger Ann felt about her workplace by helping her redefine the situation as aggravating rather than threatening. The therapist also enlisted Ann in an effort to develop new coping skills that might further reduce her aggravation.

Schizoid Personality Disorder

People diagnosed with **schizoid personality disorder** lack the desire to form interpersonal relationships and are emotionally cold in their interactions with others. Other people describe them as aloof, reclusive, and detached or as dull, uninteresting, and humorless. People diagnosed with this disorder show little emotion in interpersonal interactions. They view relationships with others as unrewarding, messy, and intrusive. The man described next shows several of these symptoms.

CASE STUDY

Roy was a successful sanitation engineer involved in the planning and maintenance of water resources for a large city; his job called for considerable foresight and independent judgment but little supervisory responsibility. In general, he was appraised as an undistinguished but competent and reliable employee. There were few demands of an interpersonal nature made of him, and he was viewed by most of his colleagues as reticent and shy and by others as cold and aloof.

Difficulties centered around his relationship with his wife. At her urging they sought marital counseling, for, as she put it, "he is unwilling to join in family activities, he fails to take interest in the children, he lacks affection and is disinterested in sex."

The pattern of social indifference, flatness of affect and personal isolation which characterized much of Roy's behavior was of little consequence to those with whom a deeper or more intimate relationship was not called for; with his immediate family, however, these traits took their toll. (Millon, 1969, p. 224)

Roy would be diagnosed with schizoid personality disorder because of his long-standing avoidance of relationships with other people and his lack of intimate relationships with family members.

Schizoid personality disorder is quite rare, with about 0.8 to 1.7 percent of adults manifesting the disorder at some time in their life (Lenzenweger, 2008). Among people seeking treatment for this disorder, males outnumber females (Zimmerman, Rothschild, & Chelminski, 2005). People with schizoid personality disorder can function in society, particularly in occupations that do not require interpersonal interactions.

Theories of Schizoid Personality Disorder

There is a slightly increased rate of schizoid personality disorder in the relatives of persons with schizophrenia, but the link between the two disorders is not clear (Kendler, Neale, Kessler, Heath, & Eaves, 1993; Nigg & Goldsmith, 1994). Twin studies of the personality traits associated with schizoid personality disorder, such as low sociability and low warmth, strongly suggest that these personality traits may be partially inherited (Costa & Widiger, 2002). The evidence for the heritability of schizoid personality disorder is only indirect, however.

Treatment of Schizoid Personality Disorder

Psychosocial treatments for schizoid personality disorder focus on increasing the person's awareness of his or her own feelings, as well as increasing his or her social skills and social contacts (Beck & Freeman, 1990; Quality Assurance Project, 1990). The therapist may model the expression of feelings for the client and help the client identify and express his or her own feelings. Social skills training, done through role-playing with the therapist and homework assignments in which the client tries out new social skills with other people, is an important component of cognitive therapies. Some therapists recommend group therapy for people with schizoid personality disorder. In the context of group sessions, the group members can model interpersonal relationships, and each person with schizoid personality disorder can practice new social skills directly with other group members.

Schizotypal Personality Disorder

Like people diagnosed with schizoid personality disorder, people diagnosed with **schizotypal personality disorder** tend to be socially isolated, to have a restricted range of emotions, and to be uncomfortable in interpersonal interactions. As children, people who develop schizotypal personality disorder are passive, socially unengaged, and hypersensitive to criticism (Olin et al., 1999). The distinguishing characteristics of schizotypal personality disorder are the oddities in cognition, which generally fall into four categories (Beck & Freeman, 1990).

Group therapy can help people with schizoid personality disorder increase their social skills.

The first category of odd cognition is *paranoia or suspiciousness.* As in paranoid personality disorder, people diagnosed with schizotypal personality disorder perceive other people as deceitful and hostile, and much of their social anxiety emerges from this paranoia. The second category is *ideas of reference.* People diagnosed with schizotypal personality disorder tend to believe that random events or circumstances are related to them. For example, they may think it highly significant that a fire occurred in a store in which they had shopped only yesterday. The third category is *odd beliefs and magical thinking.* For example, they may believe that others know what they are thinking. The fourth category is *illusions* that are just short of hallucinations. For example, they may think they see people in the patterns of wallpaper.

In addition to possessing these oddities of thought, people diagnosed with schizotypal personality disorder tend to have speech that is tangential, circumstantial, vague, or overelaborate. In interactions with others, they may have inappropriate emotional responses or no emotional response to what other people say or do. Their behaviors also are odd, sometimes reflecting their odd thoughts. They may be easily distracted or fixate on an object for long periods of time, lost in thought or fantasy. On neuropsychological tests (see Chapter 3), people with schizotypal personality disorder show deficits in working memory, learning, and recall similar to those shown by people with schizophrenia (Barch, 2005).

Although the quality of these oddities of thought, speech, and behavior is similar to that in schizophrenia, their severity is not as great as in schizophrenia, and people diagnosed with schizotypal personality disorder retain basic contact with reality. The man in the following case study shows many of the oddities of schizotypal personality disorder.

CASE STUDY

A 41-year-old man was referred to a community mental health center's activities program for help in improving his social skills. He had a lifelong pattern of social isolation, with no real friends, and spent long hours worrying that his angry thoughts about his older brother would cause his brother harm. He had previously worked as a clerk in civil service, but had lost his job because of poor attendance and low productivity.

On interview the patient was distant and somewhat distrustful. He described in elaborate and often irrelevant detail his rather uneventful and routine daily life. For two days he had studied the washing instructions on a new pair of jeans: Did "Wash before wearing" mean that the jeans were to be washed before wearing the first time, or did they need, for some reason, to be washed each time before they were worn? He did not regard concerns such as these as senseless, though he acknowledged that the amount of time spent thinking about them might be excessive. He could recite from memory his most recent monthly bank statement, including the amount of every check and the running balance as each check was written. He knew his balance on any particular day, but sometimes got anxious if he considered whether a certain check or deposit had actually cleared. (Adapted from Spitzer et al., 2002, pp. 289-290)

Between 0.6 and 1.1 percent of people will be diagnosed with schizotypal personality disorder at some time in their life (Lenzenweger, 2008). Among people seeking treatment, it is more commonly diagnosed in males than in females (Zimmerman et al., 2005). As with the other odd-eccentric personality disorders, people diagnosed with schizotypal personality disorder are at increased risk for depression and for schizophrenia or isolated psychotic episodes (Siever, Bernstein, & Silverman, 1995).

For a person to be given a diagnosis of schizotypal personality disorder, his or her odd or eccentric thoughts cannot be part of cultural beliefs, such as a cultural belief in magic or specific superstitions. Still, some psychologists have argued that people of color are diagnosed more often with schizophrenia-like disorders, such as schizotypal personality disorder, than are Whites because White clinicians often misinterpret culturally bound beliefs as evidence of schizotypal thinking (Snowden & Cheung, 1990).

One large study of people in treatment found that African American patients were more likely than White or Hispanic patients to be diagnosed with schizotypal personality disorder on both self-report and standardized diagnostic interviews (Chavira et al., 2003). This finding suggests that African Americans may be diagnosed with this disorder relatively frequently even when steps are taken to avoid clinician bias. It is possible that African Americans are more likely to be exposed to conditions that enhance a biological vulnerability to schizophrenia-like disorders. These conditions include perinatal brain damage, urban living, and low socioeconomic status (see Chapter 8 for a discussion of these conditions in schizophrenia).

Theories of Schizotypal Personality Disorder

Many more studies of the genetics of schizotypal personality disorder have been conducted than studies of the other odd-eccentric personality disorders. Family history, adoption, and twin studies all suggest that schizotypal personality disorder is transmitted genetically (Siever & Davis, 2004). Indeed, a twin study found the heritability of schizotypal personality disorder to be .81 (Coolidge et al., 2004). In addition, schizotypal personality disorder is much more common in the first-degree relatives of people with schizophrenia than in the relatives of either psychiatric patients or healthy control groups (Gilvarry, Russell, Hemsley, & Murray, 2001; Kendler, Neale, Kessler, Heath, & Eaves, 1993). This supports the view that schizotypal personality disorder is a mild form of schizophrenia that is transmitted through genes in ways similar to those in schizophrenia.

Similarly, some of the nongenetic biological factors implicated in schizophrenia also are present in people with schizotypal personality disorder (Barch, 2005). In particular, people diagnosed with this disorder show problems in their ability to sustain their attention on cognitive tasks, as well as deficits in memory similar to those seen in people with schizophrenia (Mitropoulou et al., 2003). People with schizotypal personality disorder, like people with schizophrenia, tend to show dysregulation of the neurotransmitter dopamine in the brain (Abi-Dargham et al., 2004). Thus, like people with schizophrenia, people with schizotypal personality disorder may have abnormally high levels of dopamine in some areas of the brain. People with schizotypal personality disorder also show abnormalities in the structure of the brain similar to those seen in people with schizophrenia (Barch, 2005).

Treatment of Schizotypal Personality Disorder

Schizotypal personality disorder is most often treated with the same drugs used to treat schizophrenia, including traditional neuroleptics such as haloperidol and thiothixene and atypical antipsychotics such as olanzapine (Keshavan, Shad, Soloff, & Schooler, 2004; Siever et al., 1998). As in schizophrenia, these drugs appear to relieve psychotic-like symptoms, which include ideas of reference, magical thinking, and illusions. Antidepressants sometimes are used to help people with schizotypal personality disorder who are experiencing significant distress.

Although there are few psychological theories of schizotypal personality disorder, psychological therapies have been developed to help people with this disorder overcome some of their symptoms. In psychotherapy for schizotypal personality disorder, it is especially important for therapists to first establish good relationships with their clients, because these clients typically have few close relationships and tend to be paranoid (Beck & Freeman, 1990). The next step in therapy is to help clients increase social contacts and learn socially appropriate behaviors through social skills training. Group therapy may be especially helpful in increasing clients' social skills. The crucial component of cognitive therapy with clients diagnosed with schizotypal personality disorder is teaching them to look for objective evidence for their thoughts in the environment and to disregard bizarre thoughts. For example, a client who often thinks he or she is not real can be taught to identify that thought as bizarre and to discount the thought when it occurs, rather than taking it seriously and acting on it.

TEST YOURSELF

1. What are the odd-eccentric personality disorders, and what characteristics do they share?
2. What are the defining characteristics of paranoid personality disorder?
3. What are the defining characteristics of schizoid personality disorder?
4. What are the defining characteristics of schizotypal personality disorder?
5. What treatments exist for people with paranoid, schizoid, or schizotypal personality disorders?

APPLY IT Joe has been diagnosed with schizotypal personality disorder. The Axis I disorder that is most likely to run in his family is which of the following?

a. major depression

b. panic disorder

c. depersonalization disorder

d. schizophrenia

Answers appear online at www.mhhe.com/nolen5e.

DRAMATIC-EMOTIONAL PERSONALITY DISORDERS

People diagnosed with the **dramatic-emotional personality disorders** engage in behaviors that are dramatic and impulsive, and they often show little regard for their own safety or the safety of others (Table 9.4). For example, they may engage in suicidal behaviors or self-damaging acts such as self-cutting. They also may act in hostile, and even violent, ways against others. One core feature of this group of disorders is a lack of concern for others. Two of the disorders in this cluster, antisocial personality disorder and borderline personality disorder, have been the focus of a great deal of research, whereas the other two, histrionic personality disorder and narcissistic personality disorder, have not.

Antisocial Personality Disorder

People with severe antisocial tendencies were labeled *psychopaths* in the late nineteenth and early twentieth centuries (Sher & Trull, 1994). Today, the label *psychopath* is not part of the official *DSM-IV-TR* nomenclature. Instead, the *DSM-IV-TR* diagnoses people who exhibit chronic antisocial behaviors as having **antisocial personality disorder** (**ASPD**; Table 9.5).

The key features of antisocial personality disorder, as defined by the *DSM-IV-TR*, are an impairment in the ability to form positive relationships with others and a tendency to engage in behaviors that violate basic social norms and values. People with this disorder are deceitful, repeatedly lying or conning others for personal profit or pleasure. They commit violent criminal offenses against others—including assault, murder, and rape—much more frequently than do people without the disorder (Hart & Hare, 1997). When caught, they tend to have little remorse and seem indifferent to the pain and suffering they have caused others.

A prominent characteristic of antisocial personality disorder is poor control of impulses. People with this disorder have a low tolerance for frustration and often act impetuously, with no apparent concern for the consequences of their behavior. They often take chances and seek thrills with no concern for danger. They are easily bored and restless, unable to endure the tedium of routine or to persist at the day-to-day responsibilities of marriage or a job (Millon et al., 2000). As a result, they tend to drift from one relationship to another and often are in lower-status jobs. They may engage in criminal activity impulsively—50 to 80 percent of men and about 20 percent of women

TABLE 9.4 Dramatic-Emotional Personality Disorders

People with dramatic-emotional personality disorders tend to have unstable emotions and to engage in dramatic and impulsive behavior.

Label	Key Features	Similar Disorders on Axis I
Antisocial personality disorder	Pervasive pattern of criminal, impulsive, callous, or ruthless behavior; disregard for the rights of others; no respect for social norms	Conduct disorder (diagnosed in children)
Borderline personality disorder	Rapidly shifting and unstable mood, self-concept, and interpersonal relationships; impulsive behavior; transient dissociative states; self-effacement	Mood disorders
Histrionic personality disorder	Rapidly shifting moods, unstable relationships, and intense need for attention and approval; dramatic, seductive behavior	Somatoform disorders, mood disorders
Narcissistic personality disorder	Grandiose thoughts and feelings of one's own worth; obliviousness to others' needs; exploitative, arrogant demeanor	Manic symptoms

Source: Reprinted with permission from the *Diagnostic and Statistical Manual of Mental Disorders,* Fourth Edition, Text Revision.

TABLE 9.5 *DSM-IV-TR* Criteria for Antisocial Personality Disorder

A. There is a pervasive pattern of disregard for and violation of the rights of others occurring since age 15 years, as indicated by three (or more) of the following:
   1. Failure to conform to social norms with respect to lawful behaviors as indicated by repeatedly performing acts that are grounds for arrest
   2. Deceitfulness, as indicated by repeated lying, use of aliases, or conning others for personal profit or pleasure
   3. Impulsivity or failure to plan ahead
   4. Irritability and aggressiveness, as indicated by repeated physical fights or assaults
   5. Reckless disregard for safety of self or others
   6. Consistent irresponsibility, as indicated by repeated failure to sustain consistent work behavior or honor financial obligations
   7. Lack of remorse, as indicated by being indifferent to or rationalizing having hurt, mistreated, or stolen from another

B. The individual is at least age 18 years.

C. There is evidence of conduct disorder with onset before age 15 years.

D. The occurrence of antisocial behavior is not exclusively during the course of schizophrenia or a manic episode.

Source: Reprinted with permission from the *Diagnostic and Statistical Manual of Mental Disorders,* Fourth Edition, Text Revision.

in prison may be diagnosable with antisocial personality disorder (Cale & Lilienfeld, 2002; Fazel & Danesh, 2002; Warren et al., 2002).

Although **psychopathy** is not an official diagnosis in the *DSM-IV-TR*, it is still the focus of considerable research. Antisocial personality disorder, as defined by the *DSM-IV-TR* (see Table 9.5), differs in some important ways from the characterization of psychopathy. While the *DSM-IV-TR* emphasizes observable antisocial behaviors in the diagnosis of ASPD, Hervey Cleckley (1941/1982), a pioneer in the study of psychopathy, emphasized certain broad personality traits in psychopathy. More recently, Robert Hare and colleagues (Hare & Neumann, 2008) have built on Cleckley's work to develop criteria for the diagnosis of psychopathy that have been supported in research. These criteria include a superficial charm, a grandiose sense of self-worth, a tendency toward boredom and a need for stimulation, pathological lying, being cunning and manipulative, and a lack of remorse. People with psychopathy are cold and callous, gaining pleasure by competing with and humiliating everyone and anyone. They can be cruel and malicious. They often insist on being seen as faultless and are dogmatic in their opinions. However, when they need to, people with psychopathy can be gracious and cheerful—until they get what they want. Then they may revert to being brash and arrogant. Cleckley (1941/1982) noted that, although psychopaths often end up in prison or dead, many become successful businesspeople and professionals. He suggested that the difference between successful psychopaths and those who end up in prison is that the successful ones are better able to maintain an outward appearance of normality. They may be able to do this because they have superior intelligence and can put on a "mask of sanity" and superficial social charm in order to achieve their goals.

Anthony Hopkins played a terrifying antisocial personality in the film *Silence of the Lambs.*

Epidemiological studies assessing antisocial personality disorder, as defined by the *DSM-IV-TR,* suggest that it is one of the most common personality disorders, with as many as 4.1 percent of the general population being diagnosed with the disorder at some time in their life (Lenzenweger, 2008). Men are substantially more likely than women to be diagnosed with this disorder (Lenzenweger, Lane, Lorangor, & Kessler, 2007). Although some theorists have argued that clinicians are more likely to see antisociality in African Americans than in Caucasians (Iwamasa, Larrabee, & Merritt, 2000), epidemiological studies have not found ethnic/racial differences in rates of diagnosis (Lenzenweger et al., 2007).

As many as 80 percent of people with antisocial personality disorder abuse substances such as alcohol and illicit drugs (Kraus & Reynolds, 2001; Trull, Waudby, & Sher, 2004). Substance use, such as binge drinking, may be just one form of impulsive behavior that is part of antisocial personality disorder. Substance use probably feeds impulsive and antisocial behavior in people with this personality disorder. Alcohol and other substances may reduce any inhibitions they do have, making them more likely to lash out violently at others. People with this disorder also are at somewhat increased risk for suicide attempts (particularly females) and for violent death (Cale & Lilienfeld, 2002).

The tendency to engage in antisocial behaviors is one of the stablest personality characteristics of people with this disorder (Loeber & Farrington, 1997; Moffitt, 1993; Perry, 1993). Adults with antisocial personality disorder typically have shown a disregard for societal norms and a tendency for antisocial behavior since childhood, and most would have been diagnosed with conduct disorder as children. For some people with this disorder, however, there is a tendency for antisocial behavior to diminish as they age. This is particularly true of people who were not antisocial as children but became antisocial as adolescents or young adults (Moffitt, 1993). This tendency may be due to psychological or biological maturation or to the possibility that many people with this disorder have been jailed or otherwise constrained by society from acting out their antisocial tendencies.

Theories of Antisocial Personality Disorder

A variety of biological and psychosocial theories of antisocial personality disorder have received some empirical support. There is substantial evidence of a genetic influence on antisocial behaviors, particularly criminal behaviors (Baker et al., 2007; Eley, Lichenstein, & Stevenson, 1999; Taylor, Iacono, & McGue, 2000). Twin studies find that the concordance rate for such behaviors is nearly

50 percent in MZ twins, compared to 20 percent or lower in DZ twins (Larsson et al., 2007; Rutter et al., 1990). Adoption studies find that the criminal records of adopted sons are more similar to the criminal records of their biological fathers than to those of their adoptive fathers (Cloninger & Gottesman, 1987; Mednick, Reznick, Hocevar, & Baker, 1987).

Most theorists suggest that antisocial behavior is not the result of one gene or even a small number of genes. Instead, some people appear to be born with a number of genetically influenced deficits that make them ill-equipped to manage ordinary life, putting them at risk for antisocial behavior (Dodge & Pettit, 2003). Some researchers argue that poor impulse control is at the heart of antisocial personality disorder (Rutter, 1997). What might be the biological causes of poor impulse control? Many animal studies have shown that impulsive and aggressive behaviors are linked to low levels of the neurotransmitter serotonin, leading to the suggestion that people with antisocial personality disorder also may have low levels of serotonin (Krakowski, 2003). Several studies of humans suggest that impulsiveness and aggressiveness are correlated with low levels of serotonin (Mann, Brent, & Arango, 2001). Young adults who have a genotype that influences serotonin functioning and who grow up in socioeconomically deprived circumstances are at particularly increased risk for symptoms of antisocial personality disorder (Lyons-Ruth et al., 2007).

People with antisocial personalities also show deficits in verbal skills and in the executive functions of the brain: the ability to sustain concentration, abstract reasoning, concept and goal formation, the ability to anticipate and plan, the capacity to program and initiate purposive sequences of behavior, self-monitoring and self-awareness, and the ability to shift from maladaptive patterns of behavior to more adaptive ones (Henry & Moffitt, 1997). In turn, some, but not all, studies have found differences between antisocial adults (usually prison inmates) and the general population in the structure or functioning of the temporal and frontal lobes of the brain (Morgan & Lilienfeld, 2000). These deficits in structure and brain functioning could be tied to medical illnesses or exposure to toxins during infancy and childhood, both of which are more common among people who develop criminal records than among those who do not. On the other hand, these deficits might be tied to genetic abnormalities. Whatever their causes, low verbal intelligence and deficits in the executive functions of the brain might contribute to poor impulse control and difficulty in anticipating the consequences of one's actions.

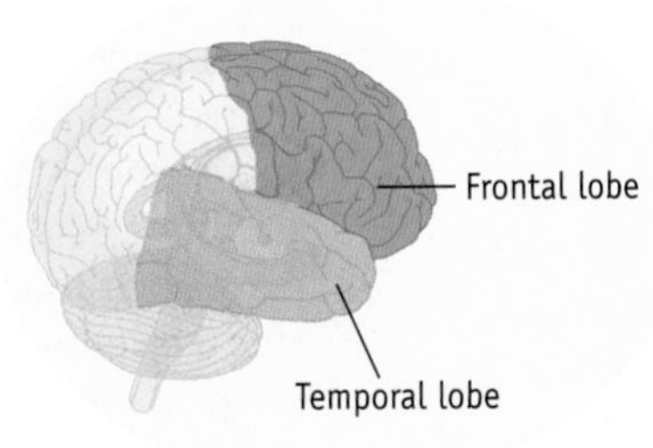

The temporal and frontal lobes of the brain may be implicated in deficits in executive functions in antisocial personality disorder.

People with antisocial personality disorder show low levels of arousability as measured by relatively low resting heart rates, low skin conductance activity, or excessive slow-wave electroencephalogram readings (Sylvers et al., 2008). One interpretation of these data is that low levels of arousal indicate low levels of fear in response to threatening situations (Raine, 1997). Fearlessness can be put to good use—bomb disposal experts and British paratroopers also show low levels of arousal (McMillan & Rachman, 1987; O'Connor, Hallam, & Rachman, 1985). However, fearlessness also may predispose some people to antisocial and violent behaviors that require fearlessness to execute, such as fighting and robbery. In addition, low-arousal children may not fear punishment and may not be deterred from antisocial behavior by the threat of punishment.

Another theory of how low arousability might contribute to antisocial personality is that chronically low arousal is an uncomfortable state and leads to stimulation seeking (Eysenck, 1994). If an individual seeks stimulation through prosocial or neutral acts, such as skydiving, stimulation seeking may not lead to antisocial behavior. But some individuals may seek stimulation through antisocial acts that are dangerous or impulsive, such as fighting. The direction stimulation seeking takes—toward antisocial activities or toward more neutral activities—may depend on the reinforcement individuals receive for their behaviors. Those who are rewarded for antisocial behaviors by family and peers may develop antisocial personalities, whereas those who are consistently punished for such behaviors and are given alternative, more neutral, options for behavior may not (Dishion & Patterson, 1997).

Intelligence also may influence the direction stimulation seeking takes (Henry & Moffitt, 1997). Children who are intelligent experience more rewards from school and thus may be more influenced by the norms held to by adults and positive peer groups in the choices they make for seeking stimulation. In contrast, children who are less intelligent may find school punishing and thus may turn to deviant peer groups for gratification and stimulating activities.

One long-standing theory is that aggressiveness, such as that shown by people with antisocial personality disorder, is linked to the hormone testosterone. Although some studies have found that highly aggressive males have higher levels of testosterone than nonaggressive males, the evidence for a role for testosterone in most forms of aggression is weak (Brain & Susman, 1997). Hormones such as testosterone may play a more important role during prenatal development in organizing the fetal brain in ways that promote or inhibit aggressiveness, rather than having a direct influence on behavior in adolescence or adulthood.

Much of the empirical research on the social and cognitive factors that contribute to antisocial behavior has been conducted with children. Many children with antisocial tendencies have experienced harsh and inconsistent parenting and physical abuse (Dishion & Patterson, 1997; Dodge & Pettit, 2003). Their parents alternately neglect them and show hostility and violence toward them. These children learn ways of thinking about the world that promote antisocial behavior (Crick & Dodge, 1994). They enter social interactions with the assumption that other children will be aggressive toward them, and they interpret the actions of their peers in line with this assumption. As a result, they are quick to engage in aggressive behaviors toward others. These social and cognitive factors alone may be enough to lead to antisocial personalities in some children and adults.

Kenneth Dodge and Gregory Pettit (2003) integrated the myriad biological, social, and cognitive factors associated with antisociality into a comprehensive model (Figure 9.1). According to this model, some people are born with neural, endocrine, and psychophysiological dispositions or into sociocultural contexts that put them at risk for antisocial behavior throughout their lifetime. Early symptoms of aggression and oppositional behavior in a child lead to, and interact with, harsh discipline and a lack of warmth from parents and conflicts with aggressive peers. These children are at risk for academic and social problems in school, which can motivate them to turn to deviant peer groups that encourage antisocial behavior. All along, such children learn that the world is hostile and that they must defend themselves rapidly and aggressively. They are prone to impulsive behaviors or reactions to others. These children enter adulthood with a long history of negative interactions with others, violent and impulsive outbursts, and alienation from mainstream society. All these factors feed on each other, perpetuating the cycle of antisocial behavior into adulthood.

FIGURE 9.1 **An Integrative Model of the Development of Antisociality.** Biological, social, and psychological factors interact across a child's development to lead to a lifetime of antisociality in some children.

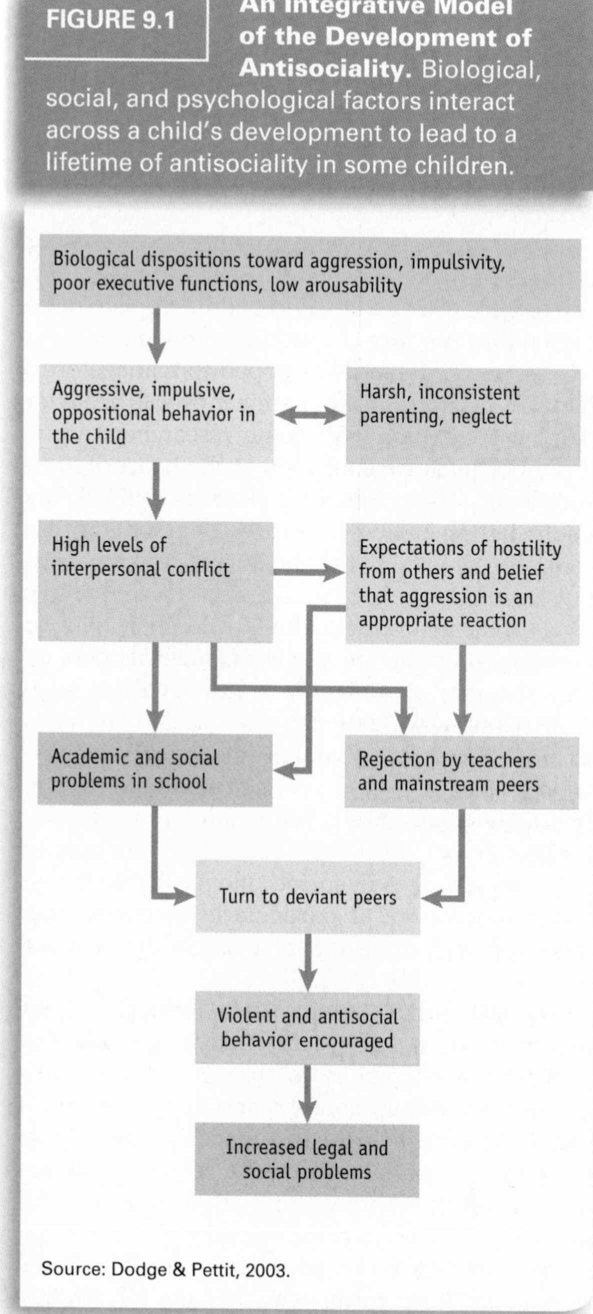

Source: Dodge & Pettit, 2003.

Treatments for Antisocial Personality Disorder

People with antisocial personality disorder tend to believe they do not need treatment. They may submit to therapy when forced to because of marital discord, work conflicts, or incarceration, but they are prone to blaming others for their current situation rather than accepting responsibility for their actions. As a result, many clinicians do not hold much hope for effectively treating persons with this disorder through psychotherapy (Kraus & Reynolds, 2001; Millon et al., 2000).

When clinicians attempt psychotherapy, they tend to focus on helping the person with antisocial personality disorder gain control over his or her anger and impulsive behaviors by recognizing triggers and developing alternative coping strategies (Kraus & Reynolds, 2001). Some clinicians also try to increase the individual's empathy for the effects of his or her behaviors on others (Hare & Hart, 1993).

Lithium and the atypical antipsychotics have been used successfully to control impulsive and aggressive behaviors in people with antisocial personality disorder (Karper & Krystal, 1997; Markovitz, 2004). Based on the evidence of low levels of serotonin in some animals prone to impulsive and aggressive behavior, researchers have recommended the use of drugs that inhibit the reuptake of serotonin into the synapses, such as the selective serotonin reuptake inhibitors (Karper & Krystal, 1997; Kraus & Reynolds, 2001). The efficacy of these drugs in treating antisocial personality disorder is not yet clear.

Borderline Personality Disorder

Recall that Susanna Kaysen, whom we met in the opener to this chapter, suffered a variety of symptoms and received a diagnosis of borderline personality disorder, which she later questioned. In the following passage, a clinician describes her introduction to another woman who later was diagnosed with **borderline personality disorder.**

CASE STUDY

At the initial meeting, Cindy was a 30-year-old, white, married woman with no children who was living in a middle-class suburban area with her husband. She had a college education and had successfully completed almost 2 years of medical school. Cindy was referred by her psychiatrist of 1½ years, who was no longer willing to provide more than pharmacotherapy following a recent hospitalization for a near-lethal suicide attempt. In the 2 years prior to referral, Cindy had been hospitalized at least 10 times (one lasting 6 months) for psychiatric treatment of suicidal ideation; had engaged in numerous instances of parasuicidal behavior, including at least 10 instances of drinking Clorox bleach, multiple deep cuts, and burns; and had had three medically severe or nearly lethal suicide attempts, including cutting an artery in her neck.

Until age 27 Cindy was able to function well in work and school settings, and her marriage was reasonably satisfactory to both partners, although the husband complained of Cindy's excessive anger. When Cindy was in the second year of medical school, a classmate she knew only slightly committed suicide. Cindy stated that when she heard about the suicide, she immediately decided to kill herself also, but had very little insight into what about the situation actually elicited the inclination to kill herself. Within weeks she left medical school and became severely depressed and actively suicidal. Although Cindy presented herself as a person with few psychological problems before the classmate's suicide, further questioning revealed a history of severe anorexia nervosa, bulimia nervosa, and alcohol and prescription medication abuse, originating at age 14.

Over the course of therapy, a consistent pattern associated with self-harm became apparent. The chain of events would often begin with an interpersonal encounter (almost always with her husband), which culminated in her feeling threatened, criticized, or unloved. These feelings would often be followed by urges either to self-mutilate or to kill herself, depending somewhat on her levels of hopelessness, anger, and sadness. Decisions to self-mutilate and/or to attempt suicide were often accompanied by the thought "I'll show you." At other times, hopelessness and a desire to end the pain permanently seemed predominant. Following the conscious decision to self-mutilate or attempt suicide, Cindy would then immediately dissociate and at some later point cut or burn herself, usually while in a state of "automatic pilot." Consequently, Cindy often had difficulty remembering specifics of the actual acts. At one point, Cindy burned her leg so badly (and then injected it with dirt to convince the doctor that he should give her more attention) that reconstructive surgery was required. (Adapted from Linehan, Cochran, & Kehrer, 2001, pp. 502–504)

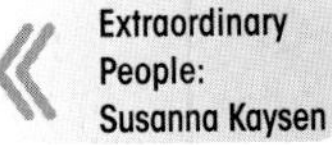
Extraordinary People: Susanna Kaysen

TABLE 9.6 *DSM-IV-TR* Criteria for Borderline Personality Disorder

A pervasive pattern of instability of interpersonal relationships, self-image, and affects, and marked impulsivity beginning by early adulthood and present in a variety of contexts, as indicated by five (or more) of the following:

1. Frantic efforts to avoid real or imagined abandonment. *Note:* Do not include suicidal or self-mutilating behavior covered in Criterion 5.
2. A pattern of unstable and intense interpersonal relationships characterized by alternating between extremes of idealization and devaluation
3. Identity disturbance: markedly and persistently unstable self-image or sense of self
4. Impulsivity in at least two areas that are potentially self-damaging (e.g., spending, sex, substance abuse, reckless driving, binge eating). *Note:* Do not include suicidal or self-mutilating behavior covered in Criterion 5.
5. Recurrent suicidal behavior, gestures, or threats, or self-mutilating behavior
6. Affective instability due to a marked reactivity of mood (e.g., intense episodic dysphoria, irritability, or anxiety usually lasting a few hours and only rarely more than a few days)
7. Chronic feelings of emptiness
8. Inappropriate, intense anger or difficulty controlling anger (e.g., frequent displays of temper, constant anger, recurrent physical fights)
9. Transient, stress-related paranoid ideation or severe dissociative symptoms

Cindy's symptoms represent some of the benchmarks of borderline personality disorder: out-of-control emotions that cannot be smoothed, a hypersensitivity to abandonment, a tendency to cling too tightly to other people, and a history of hurting oneself (see the *DSM-IV-TR* criteria in Table 9.6).

Instability is a key feature of borderline personality disorder. The *mood* of people with borderline personality disorder is unstable, with bouts of severe depression, anxiety, or anger seeming to arise frequently, often without good reason. Their *self-concept* is unstable, with periods of extreme self-doubt alternating with periods of grandiose self-importance. Their *interpersonal relationships* are extremely unstable—they can switch from idealizing others to despising them without provocation. People with borderline personality disorder often describe an emptiness, which leads them to cling to new acquaintances or therapists in an attempt to fill their internal void. They worry about abandonment and misinterpret other people's innocent actions as desertion or rejection. For example, if a therapist has to cancel an appointment because she is ill, a client with borderline personality disorder might interpret this as a rejection by the therapist and become extremely depressed or angry.

With the instability of mood, self-concept, and interpersonal relationships comes a tendency toward impulsive, self-damaging behaviors, including self-mutilating behavior and suicidal behavior. Cindy's self-mutilating behavior was to cut and burn herself. Further, like Cindy, people with borderline personality disorder are prone to transient dissociative states, in which they feel unreal, lose track of time, and may even forget who they are.

The variety of symptoms that make up the criteria for a diagnosis of borderline personality disorder reflects, to some extent, the complexity of this disorder. The manifestation of this disorder varies from one person to the next and from one day to the next in any one person. The varied list of symptoms also reflects the difficulty clinicians have had in agreeing on a conceptualization of this disorder (Gunderson, Zanarini, & Kisiel, 1995). One result of the variety of symptoms listed in the diagnostic criteria for the disorder is a great deal of overlap between the borderline diagnosis and several other personality disorders, including paranoid, antisocial, narcissistic, histrionic, and schizotypal personality disorders (Grilo, Sanislow, & McGlashan, 2002). Indeed, the majority of persons diagnosed with borderline personality disorder also meet the diagnostic criteria for at least one other personality disorder.

People with borderline personality disorder also tend to receive diagnoses of one of the acute disorders, including substance abuse, depression, generalized anxiety disorder, simple phobias, agoraphobia, post-traumatic stress disorder, panic disorder, or somatization disorder (Kraus & Reynolds, 2001; Lenzenweger et al., 2007). About 75 percent of people with this disorder attempt suicide, and about 10 percent die by suicide (Kraus & Reynolds, 2001; Linehan et al., 2001). The greatest risk for suicide appears to be in the first year or two after diagnosis with borderline personality disorder, possibly because people often are not diagnosed until a crisis brings them to the attention of the mental health system.

The symptoms of borderline personality disorder create a number of severe and debilitating problems for people with this disorder and for the people in their environment. A longitudinal study that followed 351 young adults diagnosed with the disorder found that their impulsivity and emotional instability led to difficulties in relating to other people, in meeting their social role obligations (e.g., as a parent), and in achieving their academic and work goals (Bagge et al., 2004).

Epidemiological studies suggest that between 1.4 and 3.9 percent of the population develop borderline personality disorder at some time in their life (Lenzenweger, 2008; Lenzenweger et al., 2007). In clinical settings, borderline personality disorder is much more often diagnosed in women than in men. It is somewhat more commonly diagnosed in people of color than in Whites, and in people in lower socioeconomic classes than in people in other classes (Chavira et al., 2003; Grilo et al., 2002). A large study of people in treatment for personality disorders found that Hispanics were more likely than Whites or African Americans to be diagnosed with borderline personality disorder (Chavira et al., 2003). This difference could occur because factors that contribute to the disorder, such as extreme stress, are more common among Hispanics. Or clinicians may overdiagnose this disorder in Hispanic people because they do not take into account Hispanic cultural norms that permit greater expression of strong emotions such as anger, aggressiveness, and sexual attraction (Chavira et al., 2003).

People with borderline personality disorder are high users of outpatient mental health services (Bender et al., 2001). One community study found that 50 percent had used some form of mental health service in the past 6 months (Swartz, Blazer, George, & Winfield, 1990). Follow-up studies of people treated for borderline personality disorder as inpatients suggest that about 50 percent continue to meet the diagnostic criteria for the disorder 7 years later (Links, Heslegrave, & van Reekum, 1998). The more severe the symptoms at the time of treatment, the more likely the disorder is to be chronic.

Theories of Borderline Personality Disorder

Given the emotional instability characteristic of borderline personality disorder, it is not surprising that several theorists have argued that people with this disorder have fundamental deficits in emotion regulation (Gunderson, 2001). Marsha Linehan (Linehan et al., 2001) suggests that these deficits in emotion regulation are physiologically based. Extreme emotional reactions to situations lead to impulsive actions. In addition, Linehan argues that people with borderline personality disorder have a history of significant others discounting and criticizing their emotional experiences. Such a history makes it even harder for them to learn appropriate emotion-regulation skills and to understand and accept their emotional reactions to events. People with this disorder come to rely on others to help them cope with difficult situations but do not have enough self-confidence to ask for help from others in mature ways. They become manipulative and indirect in their attempt to gain support from others.

People with borderline personality disorder score higher on measures of difficulty in regulating emotions and in laboratory tasks assessing unwillingness to tolerate emotional distress in order to reach a goal (Gratz et al., 2006; Rosenthal et al., 2008). In one study, participants carried beepers that randomly cued them to provide ratings of their moods. People with borderline personality disorder showed greater variability in their moods, particularly with regard to hostility, fear, and sadness, than people with no personality disorder (Trull et al., 2008).

Psychoanalytic theorists, particularly those in the object relations school (Kernberg, 1979; Klein, 1952), suggest that people with this disorder have poorly developed views of themselves and others. Their caregivers may have encouraged dependence on them early in life. They may have punished the children's attempts at individuation and separation with the result that the children never learned to fully differentiate their view of themselves from their view of others, making them extremely reactive to others' opinions of them and to the possibility of abandonment. When they perceive others as rejecting them, they reject themselves and may engage in self-punishment or self-mutilation.

They also have never been able to integrate the positive and negative qualities of either their self-concept or their concept of others, because their early caregivers were rewarding when they remained dependent and compliant but hostile when they tried to separate from the caregivers. They tend to see themselves and other people as either all good or all bad and to vacillate between these two views, a process known as *splitting*. The instability in emotions and interpersonal relationships is due to such splitting: Their emotions and their perspectives on their interpersonal relationships reflect their vacillation between the all-good and the all-bad self and the all-good and the all-bad other.

Empirical studies have found that people with borderline personality disorder are more likely than people without the disorder to report childhoods marked by instability, abuse, neglect, and parental psychopathology (Helgeland & Torgersen, 2004). Of course, this is true of the childhoods of people with many different types of psychopathology and does not directly address the object relations theory of the development of this disorder.

People with borderline personality disorder often have histories of physical and sexual abuse during childhood (Horesh, Ratner, Laor, & Toren, 2008; Zanarini, 1997). Some theorists believe that the severe problems in self-concept and emotion regulation seen in people with borderline personality disorder frequently are the result of childhood abuse (Kraus & Reynolds, 2001).

Emotional instability and impulsivity also could be due to biological factors. Twin studies provide evidence that the symptoms of borderline personality disorder are heritable (Distel et al., 2007). Functional magnetic resonance imaging (fMRI) studies show that people with borderline personality disorder, like people with mood and anxiety disorders, have greater activation of the amygdala in response to pictures of emotional faces, which may contribute to the difficulty they have in regulating their moods (Figure 9.2; Donegan et al., 2003). Recall that the amygdala is a part of the brain that is important in the processing of emotion. Similarly, positron emission tomography studies have found decreased metabolism in the prefrontal cortex of patients with borderline personality disorder, as is also found in patients with mood disorders (Soloff et al., 2000). Most researchers do not suggest that borderline personality disorder is simply a type of affective disorder, but there are clear links between the two.

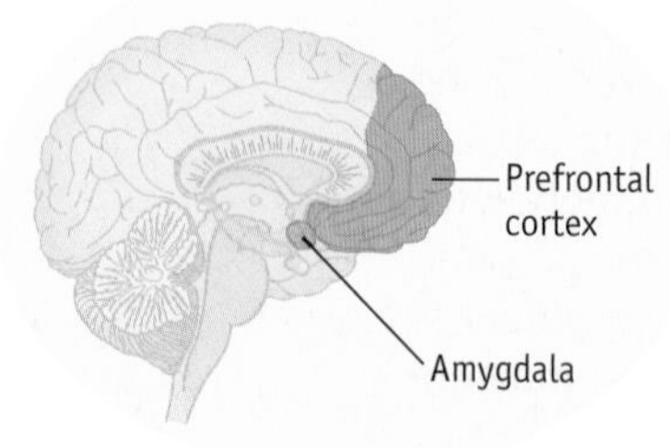

The amygdala and the prefrontal cortex have been implicated in borderline personality disorder.

Impulsive behaviors in people with borderline personality disorder are correlated with low levels of serotonin (Weston & Siever, 1993). Recall that impulsive behaviors in people with antisocial personality disorder also have been linked to low serotonin levels. This link suggests that a low level of serotonin is associated not just with one diagnostic category but rather with impulsive behaviors in general.

FIGURE 9.2 **Map Showing Activated Regions in the Amygdala for Normal Control and Borderline Personality Disorder Groups for Four Facial Expressions.** People with borderline personality disorder showed more activity in the amygdala in response to all emotional faces.

Treatments for Borderline Personality Disorder

One of the first psychotherapies shown to have positive effects in patients with borderline personality disorder was **dialectical behavior therapy** (Linehan et al., 2001). This therapy focuses on helping clients with borderline personality disorder gain a more realistic and positive sense of self, learn adaptive skills for solving problems and regulating emotions, and correct dichotomous thinking. Therapists teach clients to monitor self-disparaging thoughts and black-or-white evaluations of people and situations and to challenge these thoughts and evaluations. Therapists also help clients learn appropriate assertiveness skills for close relationships so that they can express their needs and feelings in a mature manner. Clients may learn how to control their impulsive behaviors by monitoring situations most likely to lead to such behaviors and learning alternative ways to handle those situations. Controlled clinical trials comparing dialectical behavior therapy to wait list controls have found that the therapy reduces depression, anxiety, and self-mutilating behavior while increasing interpersonal functioning (Bohus et al., 2004; Linehan, Heard, & Armstrong, 1993).

Cognitive therapy treatments for borderline personality disorder have also proven helpful. *Systems training for emotional predictability and problem solving* (STEPPS) is a group intervention for people with borderline personality disorder that combines cognitive techniques challenging irrational and maladaptive cognitions and behavioral techniques addressing self-management and problem solving. A clinical trial of STEPPS compared to usual therapy (support plus medication) showed that clients receiving STEPPS showed greater improvement in negative affect, impulsivity, and functioning than clients receiving the usual therapy (Blum et al., 2008). Similarly, trials of cognitive-behavioral therapy focusing on challenging patients' maladaptive core beliefs and teaching them more adaptive ways to function in daily life resulted in significant reductions in hospitalizations and suicide attempts, as well as improvements in mood, compared to treatment as usual (Davidson et al., 2006; Giesen-Bloo et al., 2006).

Psychodynamically oriented therapies also show promise in the treatment of borderline personality disorder. *Transference-focused therapy* uses the relationship between patient and therapist to help patients develop a more realistic and healthy understanding of themselves and their interpersonal relationships. Patients with borderline personality disorder receiving this therapy showed reductions in suicidality, impulsivity, aggression, and anger (Clarkin, Levy, Lenzenweger, & Kernberg, 2007). *Mentalization-based treatment* is based on the argument that people with borderline personality disorder have fundamental difficulty understanding the mental states of themselves and others because of traumatic experiences in childhood and poor attachment to their caregivers (Fonagy & Bateman, 2008). This psychodynamically oriented therapy provides patients with validation and support. Further, it attempts to help patients appreciate alternative points of view to their own subjective sense of self and others by using the relationship between the patient and the therapist, and the patient and others, to illustrate those alternatives. One long-term study found significant improvement in mood and functioning in patients receiving mentalization-based therapy compared to patients receiving typical community care; further, over a 5-year follow-up, patients receiving mentalization-based therapy needed less medication, had fewer suicide attempts, and continued to function better on several dimensions than patients receiving the usual care (Bateman & Fonagy, 2008).

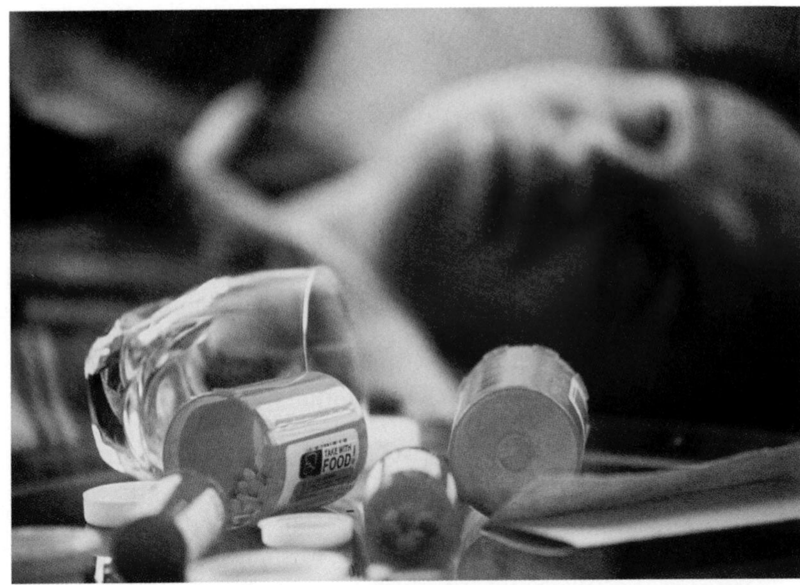

Suicidal behavior is common among people with borderline personality disorder.

Antianxiety and antidepressant drugs are used to treat anxiety and depressive symptoms in people with borderline personality disorder. Serotonin reuptake inhibitors can reduce aggressiveness and impulsivity (Hollander et al., 2001; Markovitz, 2004). Antipsychotic drugs are sometimes used with people who have severe borderline personality disorder, particularly when they exhibit signs of psychosis. The neurological side effects of the phenothiazines (see Chapter 8) lead many people to discontinue taking these drugs (Soloff et al., 1993). Studies of the atypical antipsychotics clozapine and olanzapine have suggested that these drugs may relieve psychotic-like symptoms and other symptoms of borderline personality disorder in many people with the diagnosis (Benedetti et al., 1998; Hough, 2001; Markovitz, 2004). Anticonvulsant drugs, such as lamotrigine, have been useful in reducing aggression in people with borderline personality disorder. Overall, however, the results of drug treatment studies have been mixed, and adding a drug treatment to an effective psychotherapy such as dialectical behavior therapy does not appear to improve recovery rates (Linehan et al., 2001; Paris, 2008; Simpson et al., 2004).

Histrionic Personality Disorder

Histrionic personality disorder shares features with borderline personality disorder, including rapidly shifting emotions and intense, unstable relationships. However, whereas people with borderline personality disorder often are self-effacing in an attempt to win favor from others, people with

Flamboyance is one symptom of histrionic personality disorder.

histrionic personality disorder usually want to be the center of attention. The person with borderline personality disorder may desperately cling to others as an expression of self-doubt and need, but the person with histrionic personality disorder simply wants the attention of others. Individuals with histrionic personality disorder pursue others' attention by being highly dramatic and overtly seductive and by emphasizing the positive qualities of their physical appearance. Others see them as self-centered and shallow, unable to delay gratification, demanding, and overly dependent. Debbie, in the following case study, was diagnosed with histrionic personality disorder.

CASE STUDY

Debbie was a 26-year-old woman who worked as a salesclerk in a trendy clothing store and who sought therapy for panic disorder with agoraphobia. She dressed flamboyantly, with an elaborate and dramatic hairdo. Her appearance was especially striking, since she was quite short (under 5 feet tall) and at least 75 pounds overweight. She wore sunglasses indoors throughout the evaluation and constantly fiddled with them, taking them on and off nervously and waving them to emphasize a point. She cried loudly and dramatically at various points in the interview, going through large numbers of tissue. She continually asked for reassurance. ("Will I be OK?" "Can I get over this?") She talked nonstop throughout the evaluation. When gently interrupted by the evaluator, she was very apologetic, laughing and saying, "I know I talk too much"; yet she continued to do so throughout the session. (Beck & Freeman, 1990, pp. 211–212)

Between 0.2 and 0.9 percent of the population will develop histrionic personality disorder at some time in their life, and the vast majority of persons diagnosed with this disorder are women (Lenzenweger, 2008). People with this disorder are more likely to be separated or divorced than married. Like people with the somatoform disorders, they tend to exaggerate medical problems and make more medical visits than the average person, and this group has an increased rate of suicidal behavior and threats (Kraus & Reynolds, 2001; Nestadt, Romanowski, Chahal, & Merchant, 1990). People with this disorder most often seek treatment for depression or anxiety (Fabrega, Ulrich, Pilkonis, & Mezzich, 1991).

Theories of Histrionic Personality Disorder

Although discussions of histrionic personalities date back to the ancient Greek philosophers, little is known about causes or effective treatments. Family history studies indicate that histrionic personality disorder clusters in families, along with borderline personality disorder, antisocial personality disorder, and somatization disorder (Dahl, 1993). Whether this disorder is genetically caused or results from processes within the family or the environment is unclear.

Treatment of Histrionic Personality Disorder

Psychodynamic treatments focus on uncovering repressed emotions and needs and helping people with histrionic personality disorder express these emotions and needs in more socially appropriate ways. Cognitive therapy focuses on identifying these patients' assumptions that they cannot function on their own and helping them formulate goals and plans for their life that do not rely on the approval of others (Beck & Freeman, 1990). Therapists attempt to help clients tone down their dramatic evaluations of situations by challenging these evaluations and suggesting more reasonable ones. None of the therapies for this disorder have been tested empirically.

Narcissistic Personality Disorder

The characteristics of **narcissistic personality disorder** are similar to those of histrionic personality disorder. In both disorders, individuals act in a dramatic and grandiose manner, seek admiration from others, and are shallow in their emotional expressions and relationships with others. Whereas people with histrionic personality disorder look to others for approval, however, people with narcissistic personality disorder rely on their self-evaluations and see dependency on others as weak and dangerous. They are preoccupied with thoughts of their self-importance and with fantasies of power and success, and they view themselves as superior to most other people. In interpersonal relationships, they make unreasonable demands on others to follow their wishes, ignore the needs and wants of others, exploit others to gain power, and are arrogant and demeaning. David, in the following case study, has been diagnosed with narcissistic personality disorder.

CASE STUDY

David was an attorney in his early 40s when he sought treatment for depressed mood. He cited business and marital problems as the source of his distress and wondered if he was having a midlife crisis. David had grown up in a comfortable suburb of a large city, the oldest of three children and the only son of a successful businessman and a former secretary. David spoke of being an "ace" student and a "super" athlete but could not provide any details that would validate a superior performance in these areas. He also recollected that he had his pick of girlfriends, as most women were "thrilled" to have a date with him.

David went to college, fantasizing about being famous in a high-profile career. He majored in communications, planning to go on to law school and eventually into politics. He met his first wife during college, the year she was the university homecoming queen. They married shortly after their joint graduation. He then went on to law school, and she went to work to support the couple.

During law school, David became a workaholic, fueled by fantasies of brilliant work and international recognition. He spent minimal time with his wife and, after their son was born, even less time with either of them. At the same time, he continued a string of extramarital affairs, mostly brief sexual encounters. He spoke of his wife in an annoyed, devaluing way, complaining about how she just did not live up to his expectations. He waited until he felt reasonably secure in his first job so that he could let go of her financial support and then he sought a divorce. He continued to see his son occasionally, but he rarely paid his child support.

After his divorce, David decided that he was totally free to just please himself. He loved spending all his money on himself, and he lavishly decorated his condominium and bought an attention-getting wardrobe. He constantly sought the companionship of attractive women. He was very successful at making initial contacts and getting dates, but he rarely found anyone good enough to date more than once or twice.

At work, David believed that because he was "different" from other people, they had no right to criticize him. But he had every right to criticize others. He also believed that other people were weak and needed contact with someone like him in order to bring direction or pleasure into their lives. He saw no problem in taking advantage of other people if they were "stupid" enough to allow him to do so. (Adapted from Beck & Freeman, 1990, pp. 245–247)

People with narcissistic personality disorder can be extremely successful in societies that reward self-confidence and assertiveness, such as the United States (Millon et al., 2000). When they grossly overestimate their abilities, however, they can make poor choices in their careers and may experience many failures. In addition, they annoy other people and can alienate the important people in their lives. People with this disorder seek treatment most often for depression and for trouble adjusting to life stressors (Fabrega et al., 1991).

Some epidemiological studies suggest that narcissistic personality disorder is rare, with a lifetime prevalence of less than 1 percent (Lenzenweger, 2008), although one community study found a prevalence of 2.2 percent (Crawford et al., 2005). In clinical populations, it is more frequently diagnosed in men (Zimmerman et al., 2005).

Theories of Narcissistic Personality Disorder

Cognitive theorists have argued that some people with narcissistic personality disorder develop unrealistically positive assumptions about their self-worth as the result of indulgence and overvaluation by significant others during childhood (Beck and Freeman, 1990). Other people with this disorder develop the belief that they are unique or exceptional as a defense against rejection by important people in their lives. One study found that people diagnosed with narcissistic personality disorder were significantly more likely to endorse beliefs such as "I don't have to be bound by rules that apply to other people" than were people diagnosed with other disorders (Beck et al., 2001).

Treatment of Narcissistic Personality Disorder

People with narcissistic personality disorder tend not to seek treatment except when they develop depression or are confronted with severe interpersonal problems (Beck & Freeman, 1990). In general, they see any problems they encounter as due to the weaknesses of others. Cognitive techniques can help these clients develop more realistic expectations of their abilities and more sensitivity to the needs of others by teaching them to challenge their initially self-aggrandizing ways of interpreting situations (Millon et al., 2000). Such self-challenging doesn't come easily for people with narcissistic personality disorder, however, and often they do not remain in therapy once their acute symptoms or interpersonal problems lessen.

TEST YOURSELF

1. What are the dramatic-emotional personality disorders, and what are the general characteristics of this group of disorders?
2. What are the characteristics of antisocial personality disorder? What factors may be involved in its development?
3. What are the characteristics of borderline personality disorder? What factors may be involved in its development? What treatments have been helpful for people with borderline personality disorder?
4. What are the characteristics of histrionic and narcissistic personality disorders?

APPLY IT Some star athletes, successful politicians, and business leaders have been caught having extramarital affairs or enriching themselves at the expense of others. Often they seem surprised at the public's outrage, acting as though they were merely exercising the privileges due them. Which personality disorder does this pattern fit best?

a. antisocial personality disorder
b. borderline personality disorder
c. histrionic personality disorder
d. narcissistic personality disorder

Answers appear online at www.mhhe.com/nolen5e.

ANXIOUS-FEARFUL PERSONALITY DISORDERS

The **anxious-fearful personality disorders**—avoidant personality disorder, dependent personality disorder, and obsessive-compulsive personality disorder—are characterized by a chronic sense of anxiety or fearfulness and behaviors intended to ward off feared situations (Table 9.7). People with each of the three disorders fear something different, but they are all nervous and unhappy.

Avoidant Personality Disorder

People with **avoidant personality disorder** are extremely anxious about being criticized by others and thus avoid interactions in which there is any possibility of being criticized. They might choose occupations that are socially isolated, such as wilderness park rangers. When they must interact with others, people with avoidant personality disorder are restrained, nervous, and hypersensitive to signs of being evaluated or criticized. They are terrified of saying something silly or doing something that will embarrass themselves. They tend to be depressed and lonely. While they may crave relationships with others, they feel unworthy of these relationships and isolate themselves, as the following case study illustrates.

CASE STUDY

Ruthann is a 32-year-old postal employee who petitioned her supervisors to assign her to a rural route where she wouldn't have to talk with anyone most of the day. Ruthann has always been terrified of interacting with others, believing that they would judge her. When she was forced to interact, she was sure other people found her stupid and ugly and caught the many "social mistakes" she felt she committed in these interactions. Ruthann lived alone and did not date because she was sure men would find her unattractive and silly and would reject her.

Studies suggest that from 0.8 to 6.4 percent of people can be diagnosed with avoidant personality disorder (Lenzenweger, 2008). There are no strong gender differences in its prevalence (Ekselius, Tilfors, Furmark, & Fredrikson, 2001). People with this disorder are prone to chronic dysthymic disorder and to bouts of major depression and severe anxiety (Grant, Stinson, et al., 2004).

There is overlap between the characteristics of avoidant personality disorder and those of social phobia/social anxiety disorder (see Chapter 5); in general, people with avoidant personality disorder tend to have more severe and generalized anxiety

TABLE 9.7 Anxious-Fearful Personality Disorders

People with the anxious-fearful personality disorders are chronically anxious.

Label	Key Features	Similar Disorders on Axis I
Avoidant personality disorder	Pervasive anxiety, a sense of inadequacy, and a fear of being criticized, which lead to the avoidance of social interactions and nervousness	Social phobia
Dependent personality disorder	Pervasive selflessness, a need to be cared for, and a fear of rejection, leading to total dependence on and submission to others	Separation anxiety disorder, dysthymic disorder
Obsessive-compulsive personality disorder	Pervasive rigidity in one's activities and interpersonal relationships, including emotional constriction, extreme perfectionism, and anxiety about even minor disruptions in one's routine	Obsessive-compulsive disorder

about social situations than people with social phobia and are more impaired by their anxiety (Huppert et al., 2008). People with social phobia tend to want to connect with others, while people with avoidant personality disorder do not. People with schizoid personality disorder also withdraw from social situations, but unlike people with avoidant personality disorder, they do not view themselves as inadequate and incompetent.

Theories of Avoidant Personality Disorder

Twin studies show that genetics plays a role in avoidant personality disorder and that the same genes likely are involved in avoidant personality disorder and social phobia (Reichborn-Kuennerud et al., 2007).

Cognitive theorists suggest that people with avoidant personality disorder develop dysfunctional beliefs about being worthless as a result of rejection by important others early in life (Beck & Freeman, 1990). They contend that children whose parents reject them conclude, "If my parents don't like me, how could anyone?" Thus, they avoid interactions with others. Their thoughts are of this sort: "Once people get to know me, they see I'm really inferior." When they must interact with others, they are unassertive and nervous, thinking, "I must please this person in every way or she will criticize me." They also tend to discount any positive feedback they receive from others, believing that other people are simply being nice or do not see how incompetent they really are. A study of 130 patients with avoidant personality disorder found that they endorsed such beliefs more often than patients with other personality disorders (Beck et al., 2001).

Treatment of Avoidant Personality Disorder

Cognitive and behavior therapies have proven helpful for people with avoidant personality disorder (Shea, 1993). These therapies have included graduated exposure to social settings, social skills training, and challenges to negative automatic thoughts about social situations. People receiving these therapies show increases in the frequency and

People with avoidant personality disorder may choose professions that allow them to avoid other people.

range of social contacts, decreases in avoidance behaviors, and increases in comfort and satisfaction when engaging in social activities (Emmelkamp et al., 2006; Pretzer, 2004).

Dependent Personality Disorder

People with **dependent personality disorder** are anxious about interpersonal interactions, but their anxiety stems from a deep need to be cared for by others, rather than from a concern that they will be criticized. Their desire to be loved and taken care of by others leads persons with dependent personality disorder to deny any of their own thoughts and feelings that might displease others, to submit to even the most unreasonable demands, and to cling frantically to others. People with this personality disorder cannot make decisions for themselves and do not initiate new activities except in an effort to please others. In contrast to people with avoidant personality disorder, who avoid relationships, people with dependent personality disorder can function only within a relationship. They deeply fear rejection and abandonment and may allow themselves to be exploited and abused rather than lose relationships, as in the following case of Francesca.

CASE STUDY

Francesca was in a panic because her husband seemed to be getting increasingly annoyed with her. Last night, he became very angry when Francesca asked him to cancel an upcoming business trip because she was terrified of being left at home alone. In a rage, her husband shouted, "You can't ever be alone! You can't do anything by yourself! You can't even decide what to have for dinner by yourself! I'm sick of it. Grow up and act like an adult!"

It was true that Francesca had a very difficult time making decisions for herself. While she was in high school, she couldn't decide which courses to take and talked with her parents and friends for hours about what she should do, finally doing whatever her best friend or her mother told her to do. When she graduated from high school, she didn't feel smart enough to go to college, even though she had gotten good grades in high school. She drifted into a job because her best friend had a job with the same company, and she wanted to remain close to that friend. The friend eventually dumped Francesca, however, because she was tired of Francesca's incessant demands for reassurance. Francesca frequently bought gifts for the friend and offered to do the friend's laundry or cooking, in obvious attempts to win the friend's favor. But Francesca also kept the friend for hours in the evening, asking her whether she thought Francesca had made the right decision about some trivial issue, such as what to buy her mother for Christmas and how she thought Francesca was performing on the job.

Soon after her friend dumped her, Francesca met her future husband, and when he showed some interest in her, she quickly tried to form a close relationship with him. She liked the fact that he seemed strong and confident, and when he asked her to marry him, Francesca thought that perhaps finally she would feel safe and secure. But especially since he has begun to get angry with her frequently, Francesca has been worrying constantly that he is going to leave her.

Between 0.1 percent and 0.8 percent of people will develop dependent personality disorder at some time in their life (Lenzenweger, 2008). Higher rates of the disorder are found with self-report methods than with structured clinical interviews, suggesting that many people feel they have this disorder when clinicians would not diagnose it in them. More women than men are diagnosed with this disorder in clinical settings (Fabrega et al., 1991). Periods of dysthymia, major depression, and chronic anxiety over being separated from important others are common in people with dependent personality disorder (Grant, Stinson, et al., 2004).

Theories of Dependent Personality Disorder

Dependent personality disorder runs in families, and one twin study estimated the heritability of this disorder to be .81 (Coolidge et al., 2004). Children with a history of anxiety about separation from their parents or of chronic physical illness appear to be more prone to developing dependent personality disorder.

Cognitive theories argue that people with dependent personality disorder have beliefs, such as "I am needy and weak," that drive their dependent behaviors. A study of 38 patients with dependent personality disorder found that they endorsed such beliefs more often than patients with other personality disorders (Beck et al., 2001).

Treatment of Dependent Personality Disorder

Unlike people with many of the other personality disorders, persons with dependent personality disorder frequently seek treatment (Millon et al., 2000). Although many psychosocial therapies are used in the treatment of this disorder, none have been systematically tested for their effectiveness. Psychodynamic treatment focuses on helping clients gain insight into the early experiences with caregivers that led to their dependent behaviors by using free association, dream interpretation, and interpretation of the transference process. Nondirective and humanistic therapies may be helpful in fostering autonomy and self-confidence in persons with dependent personality disorder (Millon et al., 2000).

Cognitive-behavioral therapy for dependent personality disorder includes behavioral techniques designed to increase assertive behaviors and decrease anxiety, as well as cognitive techniques designed to challenge clients' assumptions about the need to rely on others (Beck & Freeman, 1990). Clients might be given graded exposure to anxiety-provoking situations, such as requesting help from a salesperson. They also may be taught relaxation skills to enable them to overcome their anxiety enough to engage in homework assignments. They and their therapists might develop a hierarchy of increasingly difficult independent actions that the clients gradually attempt on their own, beginning with deciding what to have for lunch and ending with deciding what job to take. After making each decision, clients are encouraged to recognize their competence and to challenge any negative thoughts they had about making the decision.

Obsessive-Compulsive Personality Disorder

Self-control, attention to detail, perseverance, and reliability are highly valued in many societies, including U.S. society. Some people, however, carry these traits to an extreme and become rigid, perfectionistic, dogmatic, ruminative, and emotionally blocked. These people are said to have **obsessive-compulsive personality disorder.** This disorder shares features with obsessive-compulsive disorder (see Chapter 5), but it represents a more generalized way of interacting with the world than does obsessive-compulsive disorder, which often involves only specific and constrained obsessional thoughts and compulsive behaviors.

People with obsessive-compulsive personality disorder often seem grim and austere, tensely in control of their emotions, and lacking in spontaneity (Millon et al., 2000). They are workaholics who see little need for leisure activities or friendships. Other people experience them as stubborn, stingy, possessive, moralistic, and officious. They tend to relate to others in terms of rank or status and are ingratiating and deferential to "superiors" but dismissive, demeaning, or authoritarian toward "inferiors." Although they are extremely concerned with efficiency, their perfectionism and obsession about following rules often interfere with their completion of tasks, as in the following case study.

People with obsessive-compulsive personality disorder are very concerned with orderliness.

CASE STUDY

Ronald Lewis is a 32-year-old accountant who is "having trouble holding on to a woman." He does not understand why, but the reasons become very clear as he tells his story. Mr. Lewis is a remarkably neat and well-organized man who tends to regard others as an interference to the otherwise mechanically perfect progression of his life. For many years he has maintained an almost inviolate schedule. On weekdays he arises at 6:47, has two eggs soft-boiled for 2 minutes, 45 seconds, and is at his desk at 8:15. Lunch is at 12:00, dinner at 6:00, bedtime at 11:00. He has separate Saturday and Sunday schedules, the latter characterized by a methodical and thorough trip through the *New York Times.* Any change in schedule causes him to feel varying degrees of anxiety, annoyance, and a sense that he is doing something wrong and wasting time.

Orderliness pervades Mr. Lewis's life. His apartment is immaculately clean and meticulously arranged. His extensive collections of books, records, and stamps are all carefully catalogued, and each item is reassuringly always in the right and familiar place. Mr. Lewis is highly valued at his work because his attention to detail has, at times, saved the company considerable embarrassment. . . . His perfectionism also presents something of a problem, however. He is

(continued)

SHADES OF GRAY

Ellen Farber, a single 35-year-old insurance company executive, came to a psychiatric emergency room of a university hospital with complaints of depression and the thought of driving her car off a cliff. . . . She reported a 6-month period of increasingly persistent dysphoria and lack of energy and pleasure. Feeling as if she were "made of lead," Ms. Farber had recently been spending 15–20 hours a day in her bed. She also reported daily episodes of binge-eating, when she would consume "anything I can find," including entire chocolate cakes or boxes of cookies. She reported problems with intermittent binge-eating since adolescence, but these episodes had recently increased in frequency, resulting in a 20-pound weight gain over the past few months. . . .

She attributed her increasing symptoms to financial difficulties. Ms. Farber had been fired from her job 2 weeks before coming to the emergency room. She claimed it was because she "owed a small amount of money." When asked to be more specific, she reported owing $150,000 to her former employers and another $100,000 to various local banks due to spending sprees.

In addition to lifelong feelings of emptiness, Ms. Farber described chronic uncertainty about what she wanted to do in life and with whom she wanted to be friends. She had many brief, intense relationships with both men and women, but her quick temper led to frequent arguments and even physical fights. Although she had always thought of her childhood as happy and carefree, when she became depressed, she began to recall episodes of abuse by her mother. Initially, she said she had dreamt that her mother had pushed her down the stairs when she was only 6, but then she began to report previously unrecognized memories of beatings or verbal assaults by her mother. (Adapted from Spitzer et al., 2002, pp. 395–397)

What diagnosis would you give Ms. Farber? (Discussion appears at the end of this chapter.)

the slowest worker in the office and probably the least productive. He gets the details right but may fail to put them in perspective. His relationships to coworkers are cordial but formal. He is on a "Mr. and Ms." basis with people he has known for years in an office that generally favors first names. Mr. Lewis's major problems are with women and follow the same repetitive pattern.

At first, things go well. Soon, however, he begins to resent the intrusion upon his schedule a woman inevitably causes. This is most strongly illustrated in the bedtime arrangements. Mr. Lewis is a light and nervous sleeper with a rather elaborate routine preceding his going to bed. He must spray his sinuses, take two aspirin, straighten up the apartment, do 35 sit-ups and read two pages of the dictionary. The sheets must be of just the right crispness and temperature and the room must be noiseless. Obviously, a woman sleeping over interferes with his inner sanctum and, after sex, Mr. Lewis tries either to have the woman go home or sleep in the living room. No woman has put up with this for very long. (From Spitzer, R. L., Skodol, A. E., Gibbon, M., & Williams, J. B. W., 1983, *Psychopathology: A Case Book,* pp. 63–64. Copyright © 1983 The McGraw-Hill Companies, Inc. Reprinted with Permission.

Between 1.9 and 4.7 percent of the population can be diagnosed with obsessive-compulsive personality disorder, and it is more common in men than in women (Lenzenweger, 2008). People with this disorder are prone to depression and anxiety, but not to the same extent as people with avoidant or dependent personality disorder (Grant, Stinson, et al., 2004).

Theories of Obsessive-Compulsive Personality Disorder

Cognitive theories suggest that people with this disorder harbor beliefs such as "Flaws, defects, or mistakes are intolerable." One study found that people diagnosed with obsessive-compulsive personality disorder endorsed such beliefs significantly more often than people diagnosed with other personality disorders (Beck et al., 2001).

Treatment of Obsessive-Compulsive Personality Disorder

Supportive therapies may assist people with this disorder in overcoming the crises that bring them in for treatment, and behavioral therapies can decrease their compulsive behaviors (Beck & Freeman, 1990; Millon et al., 2000). For example, a client may be given the assignment to alter his usual rigid schedule for the day, first by simply getting up 15 minutes later than usual and then by gradually changing additional elements of his schedule. The client may be taught to use relaxation techniques to overcome the anxiety created by alterations in the schedule. He might also write down the automatic negative thoughts he has about changes in the schedule ("Getting up 15 minutes later is going to put my entire day off"). In the next therapy session, he and the therapist might discuss the evidence for and against these automatic thoughts.

TEST YOURSELF

1. What are the anxious-fearful personality disorders, and what are their general characteristics?
2. What are the characteristics of avoidant personality disorder?
3. What are the characteristics of dependent personality disorder?
4. What are the characteristics of obsessive-compulsive personality disorder?

APPLY IT Rose frequently asks her husband "Do you really love me?" despite his repeated reassurances that he does. Which anxious-fearful personality disorder might Rose have?

a. avoidant personality disorder
b. dependent personality disorder
c. obsessive-compulsive personality disorder

Answers appear online at www.mhhe.com/nolen5e.

PROBLEMS WITH THE *DSM-IV-TR* PERSONALITY DISORDERS

As you may have noticed, there are many problems with the way the *DSM-IV-TR* defines the personality disorders. Let's discuss several of these problems.

Diagnostic Overlap and Reliability

First, there is a great deal of overlap in the diagnostic criteria for the various personality disorders. The majority of people who are diagnosed with one disorder meet the diagnostic criteria for at least one other personality disorder (Lenzenweger et al., 2007). This overlap suggests that there actually may be fewer personality disorders that adequately account for the variation in personality disorder symptoms. The overlap also makes it very difficult to obtain reliable diagnoses of the personality disorders. Thus, one goal of the developers of the *DSM-5* has been to collapse the 10 *DSM-IV-TR* personality disorders into a smaller number of personality disorders that are more distinct from one another.

Second, diagnosing a personality disorder often requires information that is hard for a clinician to obtain. For example, the clinician may need accurate information about how an individual treats other people, how an individual behaves in a wide variety of situations, or how stable an individual's behaviors have been since childhood or adolescence. Again, this difficulty makes it hard to obtain reliable diagnoses of the personality disorders.

Third, the personality disorders are conceptualized as stable characteristics of an individual. Longitudinal studies have found, however, that people diagnosed with these disorders vary over time in how many symptoms they exhibit and the severity of these symptoms, going in and out of the diagnosis (Shea et al., 2002). In particular, people often look as if they have a personality disorder when they are suffering from an acute Axis I disorder, such as major depression, but then their personality disorder symptoms seem to diminish when their Axis I disorder symptoms subside.

All these problems make it difficult for clinicians to be confident of diagnoses of personality disorders. Indeed, the diagnostic reliability of the personality disorders is only fair (Trull & Durrett, 2005; Zanarini et al., 2000). These problems also make it difficult to do research on personality disorders, which explains why much less research is available on the epidemiology, causes, and treatment of the personality disorders than on most of the other disorders described in this book.

Gender and Ethnic/Racial Biases in Construction and Application

We have seen throughout this chapter that there are differences in the frequency with which men and women are diagnosed with certain personality disorders, as well as some differences in the frequency with which different ethnic or racial groups are diagnosed. One of the troubling controversies in the literature on personality disorders concerns claims that these apparent differences actually result from biases in the construction of these disorders in the *DSM-IV-TR* or in clinicians' applications of the diagnostic criteria (Cale & Lilienfeld, 2002; Hartung & Widiger, 1998; Widiger, 1998).

Some theorists have argued that the diagnoses of histrionic, dependent, and borderline personality disorders, which are characterized by flamboyant behavior, emotionality, and dependence on others,

Women and men may exhibit flamboyant and self-aggrandizing behavior in different ways.

are simply extreme versions of negative stereotypes of women's personalities (Kaplan, 1983; Sprock, 2000; Walker, 1994). For this reason, clinicians sometimes may be too quick to see these characteristics in women clients and to apply these diagnoses. It has also been argued that the diagnostic criteria for antisocial, paranoid, and obsessive-compulsive personality disorders, which are characterized by violent, hostile, and controlling behaviors, represent extremes of negative stereotypes of men's personalities. Clinicians may overapply these diagnoses to men but not to women (Sprock, Blashfield, & Smith, 1990). Similarly, clinicians may overapply diagnoses of antisocial and paranoid personality disorders to African Americans because they selectively perceive violence and hostility in their African American clients (Iwamasa et al., 2000). Hispanics are more likely to receive diagnoses of borderline personality disorder, perhaps because the symptoms of this disorder parallel cultural stereotypes of Hispanics (Chavira et al., 2003).

Another way the *DSM-IV-TR* constructions of personality disorders may be biased is in not recognizing that the expressions of the symptoms of a disorder may vary naturally between groups. For example, the diagnostic criteria for antisocial personality disorder emphasize overt signs of callous and cruel antisocial behavior, including committing crimes against property and people. However, women with antisocial personality disorder may be less likely than men with the disorder to engage in such overt antisocial behaviors because of the greater social sanctions against women for doing so. Instead, women with antisocial personality disorder may find subtler ways of being antisocial, such as acting cruelly toward their children or covertly sabotaging people at work (Cale & Lilienfeld, 2002). As we will see when we discuss childhood disorders in Chapter 10, the same argument has been made about possible gender differences in the expression of a childhood precursor to antisocial personality disorder: conduct disorder. It also may be that certain ethnic or racial groups, such as Whites, are better able to hide their symptoms of callous and cruel behavior because they hold more social power and can exercise these tendencies in ways deemed acceptable in the majority culture (e.g., being ruthless in business deals).

Similarly, some theorists have argued that the *DSM-IV-TR* ignores or downplays possible masculine ways of expressing dependent, histrionic, and borderline personality disorders and that this bias contributes to an underdiagnosis of these disorders in men (see Widiger et al., 1995). For example, one criterion for histrionic personality disorder is "consistently uses physical appearance to draw attention to the self" (American Psychiatric Association, 2000). Although the *DSM-IV-TR* notes that men may express this characteristic by acting "macho" and bragging about their athletic skills, the wording of the criterion brings to mind everyday behaviors more common among women, such as wearing seductive clothing.

Even if the *DSM-IV-TR* criteria for personality disorders are not biased in their construction, they may be biased in their application. Clinicians may be too quick to see histrionic, dependent, and borderline personality disorders in women or antisocial personality disorder in men. Several studies have shown that when clinicians are presented with the description of a person who exhibits many of the symptoms of one of these disorders—say, a histrionic personality disorder—they are more likely to make that diagnosis if the person is described as a female than if the person is described as a male (Widiger, 1998).

Among people with personality disorders who have been reliably diagnosed through a structured clinical interview, African Americans and Hispanics are less likely to receive good mental health care for their disorder (Bender et al., 2007). This disparity in care is not due simply to lower socioeconomic resources among minority patients. The researchers in this study found that minority patients perceived less positive support from their clinicians and thus were more likely to become alienated from mental health treatment providers.

TEST YOURSELF

1. What major problems exist in the *DSM-IV-TR* conceptualizations of the personality disorders?

APPLY IT Dr. Smith is a psychologist who tends to believe in traditional gender stereotypes. You might suspect that Dr. Smith tends to overdiagnose ______ personality disorders in female clients and ______ personality disorders in male clients.

a. borderline; antisocial
b. borderline; histrionic
c. narcissistic; dependent
d. obsessive-compulsive; antisocial

Answers appear online at www.mhhe.com/nolen5e.

DSM-5 RECONCEPTUALIZATION OF PERSONALITY DISORDERS

A major proposed change in the *DSM-5* is the incorporation of a continuum model into the diagnosis of the personality disorders. This change is in response to ample evidence that personality disorders, for the most part, represent extreme versions of typical personality traits (Krueger et al., 2008; Trull & Durrett, 2005; Widiger & Mullins-Sweatt, 2009). Specifically, four of the five dimensions in the Big 5—negative emotionality, extraversion, agreeableness, and conscientiousness—capture most of the characteristics of the *DSM-IV-TR* personality disorders (see O'Connor, 2005; Saulsman & Page, 2004; Widiger & Simonsen, 2005). The fifth factor, openness, is not strongly related to the personality disorders (O'Connor, 2005). Thus, the *DSM-5* authors propose that all individuals being assessed for a personality disorder be rated on the four dimensions characteristic of personality disorders. They further propose that two other dimensions, schizotypy (odd or unusual patterns of thinking and behaving) and compulsivity, be added in order to capture features of the *DSM-IV-TR* disorders not reflected in negative emotionality, extraversion, agreeableness, and conscientiousness.

The *DSM-5* is likely to retain five specific personality disorder types that have received the most empirical support over the years (Skodol, 2010). These are the antisocial (psychopathic) type, the avoidant type, the borderline type, the obsessive-compulsive type, and the schizotypal type. Unlike in the *DSM-IV-TR*, however, the criteria for the diagnosis of each of these types will not be in the form of specific behaviors, thoughts, or feelings individuals must show. Instead, individuals will be rated on the extent to which their sense of self and their interpersonal functioning are a good match with the core traits of that type. So, for example, for antisocial/psychopathic type, individuals will be rated on the dimensions of antagonism toward others (e.g., callousness, hostility, narcissism) and disinhibition (e.g., irresponsibility, recklessness, impulsivity). For the obsessive-compulsive type, individuals will be rated on the dimensions of compulsivity (e.g., perfectionism, rigidity, orderliness, perseveration), negative emotionality (e.g., anxiousness, pessimism, guilt/shame), introversion (i.e., restricted affect), and antagonism (i.e., oppositionality) (American Psychiatric Association, 2010). Individuals will be diagnosed when their traits are a good match to the core dimensions of a disorder and when the level of personal, social, and occupational impairment stemming from these traits is severe or extreme, as suggested in the continuum model on page 265 (Livesley, 2010).

What about those *DSM-IV-TR* diagnoses not explicitly included in the *DSM-5*, including the paranoid, schizoid, histrionic, narcissistic, and dependent personality disorders? These will be captured by ratings on the six personality traits the *DSM-5* authors recommend all individuals be assessed for: negative emotionality, introversion, antagonism, disinhibition, compulsivity, and schizotypy (American Psychiatric Association, 2010).

The major advantages of the *DSM-5* dimensional reconceptualization of personality disorders are that it is based on solid research and that it should reduce the amount of overlap among individual personality disorders. It remains to be seen whether these changes will overcome the problem of needing information that is difficult to obtain and the possibility of gender bias in diagnosis.

TEST YOURSELF

1. What dimensions are likely to be used in the *DSM-5* for rating people's personalities?
2. What five personality disorder types are likely to be included in the *DSM-5*?

APPLY IT If you were a proponent of the *DSM-5* dimensional approach to personality disorders, which of the following arguments could you *not* currently make in its favor?

a. This approach should reduce overlap between diagnoses of specific personality disorders.
b. There is strong empirical evidence that personality disorders can be conceptualized on the basis of dimensions of normal personality.
c. The dimensional approach eliminates diagnostic bias against women and against persons of some races.
d. The *DSM-5* approach retains personality type diagnoses that have had the most empirical support.

Answers appear online at www.mhhe.com/nolen5e.

FIGURE 9.3 An Integrated Model of the Personality Disorders. A difficult temperament may combine with ineffective parenting to lead to personality disorders.

Biological predisposition to a difficult temperament
↓
Parenting that is harsh, critical, or unsupportive or is alternately overprotective and indulgent
↓
Behavioral and emotional dysregulation; maladaptive beliefs about the self
↓
Negative reactions from peers and adults
↓
Worsening of temperamental difficulties in controlling emotions and behaviors

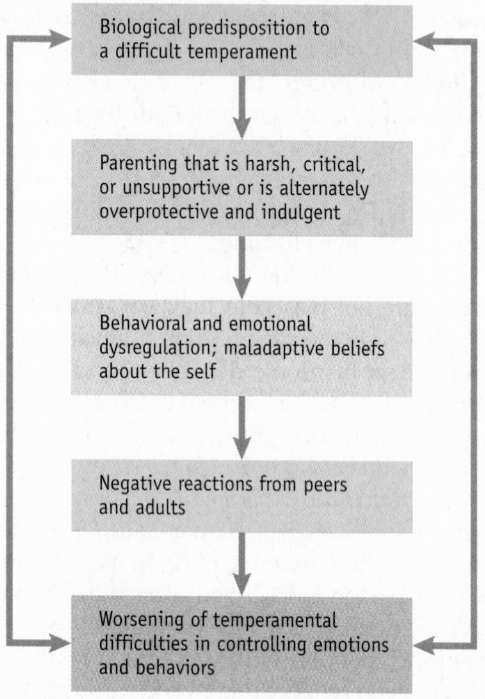

CHAPTER INTEGRATION

Although empirical research on the personality disorders is insufficient to allow a clear integration of biological, psychological, and social factors impinging on these disorders, some theoretical models have attempted such an integration. These serve as a basis for current research (Millon et al., 2000; Siever & Davis, 1991; Trull & Durrett, 2005). According to these models, at the root of many of the personality disorders may lie a biological predisposition to a certain kind of difficult temperament (Figure 9.3).

For example, in the case of avoidant, dependent, and obsessive-compulsive personality disorders, an anxious and fearful temperament may be involved. An impulsive and aggressive temperament may contribute to narcissistic and antisocial personality disorders. In borderline and histrionic personality disorders, an unstable, overly emotional temperament may play a role.

Children born with any of these temperaments are difficult to parent effectively. If parents can be supportive of these children and still set appropriate limits on their behavior, the children may never develop severe enough behavioral or emotional problems to be diagnosed with a personality disorder. If parents are unable to counteract their children's temperamental vulnerabilities or if they exacerbate these vulnerabilities with harsh, critical, unsupportive parenting or overprotective, indulgent parenting, then the children's temperamental vulnerabilities may grow into severe behavior and emotional problems and maladaptive beliefs about the self. These problems will influence how others—teachers, peers, and eventually employers and mates—interact with the individuals, perhaps further exacerbating their temperamental vulnerabilities.

In this way, a lifelong pattern of dysfunction, called a personality disorder, may emerge out of the interaction between a child's biologically based temperament and others' reactions to that temperament.

SHADES OF GRAY **DISCUSSION** (review p. 288)

Ms. Farber shows signs of a mood disorder, with dysphoria, lack of energy or pleasure, and suicidal thoughts. Her sleeping and eating patterns have changed dramatically as well. But other details of her story point to the possibility of a personality disorder. Ms. Farber's spending sprees, intense and even violent relationships with others, feelings of emptiness, and unstable sense of herself and her relationships suggest borderline personality disorder. This case illustrates a common problem clinicians face in making diagnoses of personality disorder: People with personality disorders often come to the attention of mental health professionals when they are in a crisis, making it difficult to diagnose whether they only have an acute disorder, such as depression, or a personality disorder as well.

THINK CRITICALLY

Read the following true case history of "Ted." Then determine whether he meets the criteria for any of the *DSM-IV-TR* personality disorders. Next, rate Ted on each facet of each of the Big 5 personality factors described in Table 9.1, using a scale from 1 (extremely low on this facet) to 5 (extremely high on this facet). Do you think the *DSM-IV-TR* diagnoses or the Big 5 personality factor facets are more useful in describing Ted? (Discussion appears on p. 519 at the back of this book.)

Ted was born in Burlington, Vermont. He did well in school and typically earned As in most of his classes, although he was sometimes in trouble for fighting with other children. He later attributed much of his scholastic success to the diligent efforts of his mother to encourage him. Despite his fondness for his mother, they never discussed personal matters, and he stated that their relationship was not an open one.

Ted reported that he found it difficult to socialize and often chose to be alone or engage in solitary hobbies when in high school. Although he was described as charming, intelligent, and attractive, he had limited social contacts because he did not enjoy drinking and preferred the role of a scholar. He also had relatively few experiences with girls in high school and only went on one date. After graduation, Ted became involved with politics and worked on several successful campaigns, where he was described as being responsible, dedicated, and hard-working. Through this experience he was able to establish a wide social network. Ted used his charm and quick wit to establish himself as an up- and-coming politician and even was referred to as a "young JFK" for his political savvy.

At age 27, Ted began abducting, raping, and murdering young women. He often lured these women into his car by deception, such as by impersonating a police detective. The brutal murders included bludgeoning, mutilation, and rape.

Ted's murders attracted media and police attention, yet he continued to abduct women and evade detection. He planned and executed the kidnappings with great care, in order to avoid discovery. His colleagues found him charming and endearing, and they could not imagine him capable of such acts. Ted was finally arrested approximately 15 months after his first murder. After his arrest, he was linked to several murders and was scheduled to stand trial. While in custody, his charm, good looks, and cooperation soon won over his captors. They gave him special treatment, including the least restrictive restraints. He insisted on defending himself in court and was allowed access to the local library, where he diligently studied legal documents. He proved to be a quick study in the field of law and was able to delay his hearings and trial for quite some time. During this delay he lost enough weight to fit his body through a 12-inch aperture and escape by crawling through openings above the jail cells and offices.

After escaping custody he settled near Florida State University. Not long after, he was once again raping, beating, and killing women. During this time, he lived under a false name and supported himself by using stolen credit cards. He was eventually arrested after bludgeoning to death many members of a sorority house as they slept. He was subsequently found guilty and twice sentenced to death. However, his legal acumen was so high during the trial that, after sentencing him, the judge stated that Ted "should have been a lawyer." These legal skills continued to serve him while in prison as he delayed his execution for 10 years. Others, however, suggested that his arrogant self-confidence contributed to a failure to obtain competent legal counsel and that his effort to serve as his own lawyer ultimately was harmful to his defense. While in prison, Ted granted numerous interview requests and revealed that he committed the murders as a means of gaining full possession of the women. He claimed that the rapes were not brutal and that he had attempted to make the murders as painless as possible for the victims. Ted never expressed any explicit or compelling feelings of remorse for the murders. He in fact withheld the identities of many of his victims as a means of delaying his execution. (Adapted from T. A. Widiger, personal communication, 2009)

CHAPTER SUMMARY

- The *DSM-IV-TR* divides the personality disorders into three clusters: the odd-eccentric disorders, the dramatic-emotional disorders, and the anxious-fearful disorders. This organization is based on symptom clusters. It assumes that there is a dividing line between normal personality and pathological personality.
- The odd-eccentric disorders include paranoid personality disorder (extreme mistrust of others), schizoid personality disorder (extreme social withdrawal and detachment), and schizotypal personality disorder (inappropriate social interactions and magical thinking). These disorders, particularly schizotypal personality disorder, may be genetically linked to schizophrenia and may represent mild versions of schizophrenia. People with these disorders tend to have poor social relationships and to be at increased risk for depression and schizophrenia.
- Psychotherapies for the odd-eccentric disorders have not been empirically tested for their efficacy. Neuroleptic and atypical antipsychotic drugs appear to reduce the odd thinking of people with schizotypal personality disorder.
- The dramatic-emotional personality disorders include four disorders characterized by dramatic, erratic, and emotional behavior and interpersonal relationships: antisocial personality disorder, borderline personality disorder, histrionic personality disorder, and narcissistic personality disorder. People with antisocial personality disorder show impulsive behavior that disregards the rights of others. People with borderline personality disorder show instability in mood, self-concept, and interpersonal relationships, along with impulsive behavior. People with histrionic personality disorder show rapidly shifting moods, unstable relationships, a need for attention and approval, and dramatic, seductive behavior. People with narcissistic personality disorder show grandiosity and are oblivious to others' needs.
- Antisocial personality disorder (ASPD) is one of the most common personality disorders and is more common in men than in women. Potential contributors include a genetic predisposition; the effects of testosterone on fetal brain development; low levels of serotonin; low levels of arousability; harsh, inconsistent parenting; and assumptions about the world that promote aggressive responses.
- Psychotherapy is not considered to be extremely effective for people with antisocial personality disorder. Lithium, the selective serotonin reuptake inhibitors, and antipsychotic drugs may help control their impulsive behaviors.
- Borderline personality disorder is more common in women than in men. People with the disorder may have low levels of serotonin, which may lead to impulsive behaviors. There is little evidence that borderline personality disorder is transmitted genetically, but the family members of people with this disorder show high rates of mood disorders.
- Several theorists argue that fundamental deficits in emotion regulation are at the core of borderline personality disorder. Psychoanalytic theorists argue that borderline personality disorder is the result of poorly developed and integrated views of the self, which in turn are due to poor early relationships with caregivers. Many people with this disorder were the victims of physical and sexual abuse in childhood.
- Dialectical behavior therapy, psychodynamic therapies, and cognitive therapies have shown greater success than drug treatments for borderline personality disorder. Transference-focused

psychodynamic therapy and mentalization therapy also appear promising as treatments for this disorder.

- The anxious-fearful personality disorders include three disorders characterized by anxious and fearful emotions and chronic self-doubt, leading to maladaptive behaviors: dependent personality disorder (extreme need to be cared for and fear of rejection), avoidant personality disorder (social anxiety and sense of inadequacy leading to social avoidance), and obsessive-compulsive personality disorder (rigidity in activities and interpersonal relationships).
- Dependent personality disorder is more common in women, obsessive-compulsive personality disorder is more common in men, and avoidant personality disorder is equally common in men and women. Dependent and avoidant personality disorders tend to run in families, but whether this is due to genetics or to family environments is not clear.
- The *DSM-5* likely will reconceptualize personality disorders along the trait dimensions of negative emotionality, introversion, antagonism, disinhibition, compulsivity, and schizotypy. The personality disorder types—antisocial/psychopathic type, avoidant type, borderline type, obsessive-compulsive type, and schizotypal type—are likely to be retained.

KEY TERMS

five-factor model 263
personality disorder 265
odd-eccentric personality disorders 266
paranoid personality disorder 267
schizoid personality disorder 269
schizotypal personality disorder 270
dramatic-emotional personality disorders 272
antisocial personality disorder (ASPD) 272
psychopathy 274
borderline personality disorder 277
dialectical behavior therapy 280
histrionic personality disorder 281
narcissistic personality disorder 282
anxious-fearful personality disorders 284
avoidant personality disorder 284
dependent personality disorder 286
obsessive-compulsive personality disorder 287

Chapter 10

Childhood Disorders

CHAPTER OVERVIEW

Extraordinary People

Temple Grandin, *Thinking in Pictures*

Dr. Temple Grandin, professor of animal sciences at Colorado State University, has designed one-third of livestock-handling facilities in the United States. She has published dozens of scientific papers and gives lectures throughout the world. Some of her lectures describe her new equipment and procedures for safer and more humane animal handling. Others describe her life with autism.

Grandin showed the classic symptoms of autism during childhood. As a baby, she had no desire to be held by her mother, though she was calm if left alone. As a young child, she seldom made eye contact with others and seemed to lack interest in people. She frequently threw wild tantrums. If left alone, she rocked back and forth or spun around indefinitely. She could sit for hours on the beach, watching sand dribble through her fingers, in a trancelike state. At 2½ she still had not begun talking and was labeled "brain-damaged" because doctors at the time did not know about autism.

Fortunately, Grandin's mother was determined to find good teachers, learn ways to calm her daughter, and encourage her to speak and engage with others. Grandin did learn to speak by the time she entered elementary school, although most of her deficits in social interactions remained. When she was 12, Grandin scored 137 on an IQ test but still was thrown out of a regular school because she didn't fit in. She persisted, however, and eventually went to college, where she earned a degree in psychology, and then to graduate school for a PhD in animal sciences.

Grandin has been able to thrive in her career and personal life. Still, she finds it very difficult to understand emotions and social relationships. She does not "read" other people well and often finds herself offending others or being stared at for her social awkwardness:

> I have always felt like someone who watches from the outside. I could not participate in the social interactions of high school life. . . . My peers spent hours standing around talking about jewelry or some other topic with no real substance. What did they get out of this? I just did not fit in. I never fit in with the crowd, but I had a few friends who were interested in the same things, such as skiing and riding horses. Friendship always revolved around what I did rather than who I was. (Grandin, 1995, p. 132)

Still, Grandin does not regret that she has autism. She says,

> If I could snap my fingers and be a nonautistic person, I would not. Autism is part of what I am. (p. 60)

We like to think of childhood as a time relatively free of stress and psychological problems. Yet it was not so for Temple Grandin, nor is it for many children. Many of the disorders discussed in other chapters of this book, including mood disorders (Chapter 7), anxiety disorders (Chapter 5), and eating disorders (Chapter 12), can occur in children or adolescents. In this chapter we consider disorders that, by definition, emerge during childhood or adolescence. The study of childhood disorders is known as *developmental psychopathology*.

Developmental psychopathologists try to understand when children's behaviors cross the line from the normal difficulties of childhood into abnormal problems that warrant concern (Cicchetti & Toth, 2005). Developmental psychopathologists also try to understand how children's levels of cognitive, social, and emotional development can affect the symptoms they show. These developmental considerations make the assessment, diagnosis, and treatment of childhood disorders challenging, but helping children overcome their problems can be highly rewarding.

BEHAVIOR DISORDERS

The *behavior disorders* have been the focus of much research, probably because children with these disorders can be disruptive and their behaviors can exact a heavy toll on society. The three behavior disorders we discuss are *attention-deficit/hyperactivity disorder, conduct disorder,* and *oppositional defiant disorder*.

TABLE 10.1 ***DSM-IV-TR*** **Criteria for Attention-Deficit/Hyperactivity Disorder**

I. Either A or B:

A. Six or more of the following symptoms of *inattention* for at least 6 months to a point that is disruptive and developmentally inappropriate:

1. Often does not give close attention to details or makes careless mistakes in schoolwork, work, or other activities
2. Often has trouble keeping attention on tasks or play activities
3. Often does not seem to listen when spoken to directly
4. Often does not follow instructions and fails to finish schoolwork, chores, or duties in the workplace (not due to oppositional behavior or failure to understand instructions)
5. Often has trouble organizing activities
6. Often avoids, dislikes, or doesn't want to do tasks involving prolonged mental effort (such as schoolwork or homework)
7. Often loses things needed for tasks and activities (e.g., toys, school assignments)
8. Is often easily distracted
9. Is often forgetful in daily activities

B. Six or more of the following symptoms of *hyperactivity-impulsivity* for at least 6 months to a point that is disruptive and developmentally inappropriate:

Hyperactivity

1. Often fidgets with hands or feet or squirms in seat
2. Often gets up from seat when remaining in seat is expected
3. Often runs about or climbs when and where it is not appropriate (adolescents or adults may feel very restless)
4. Often has trouble playing or enjoying leisure activities quietly
5. Is often "on the go" or often acts as if "driven by a motor"
6. Often talks excessively

Impulsivity

1. Often blurts out answers before questions have been finished
2. Often has trouble waiting one's turn
3. Often interrupts or intrudes on others (e.g., butts into conversations or games)

C. Some symptoms that cause impairment were present before age 7 years.

D. Some impairment from the symptoms is present in two or more settings (e.g., at school/work and at home).

E. Clear evidence of significant impairment in social, school, or work functioning.

Source: Reprinted with permission from the *Diagnostic and Statistical Manual of Mental Disorders,* Fourth Edition, Text Revision.

Attention-Deficit/Hyperactivity Disorder

"Pay attention! Slow down! You're so hyper today!" Most parents say this at least occasionally. A major focus of socialization is helping children learn to pay attention, control their impulses, and organize their behaviors so that they can accomplish long-term goals. Some children have tremendous trouble learning these skills, however, and may be diagnosed with **attention-deficit/hyperactivity disorder,** or **ADHD** (see *DSM-IV-TR* criteria in Table 10.1). Eddie is a young boy with ADHD.

Childhood Disorders Along the Continuum

Resilience even in stressful situations

Passing emotional or behavioral problems caused by a specific situation

(fearfulness after a car accident, being aggressive in response to teasing)

Potentially meets diagnostic criteria for a childhood disorder:

Moderately persistent emotional or behavioral problems

(persistent fear of being separated from parents, aggressive behavior combined with stealing and lying)

Likely meets diagnostic criteria for a childhood disorder:

Persistent emotional or behavioral problems that significantly interfere with the child's schoolwork, development of friends, and interactions with family

(refusal to go to school so as not to separate from parents, physical aggression toward peers combined with acts of vandalism)

Functional — Dysfunctional

Walking through the grocery store, you suddenly hear a child screaming. You look around and see that it is a toddler throwing a temper tantrum because her mother won't give her candy. Temper tantrums and periods of fearfulness or shyness are common in children. It is not unusual for children to struggle with emotions and to misbehave in ways that can be as serious as lying or stealing. But how can we tell when a child's behavior or emotional difficulty crosses the line into abnormality?

Some statistics can help us put the continuum of childhood disorders into perspective. Large-scale epidemiological studies suggest that more than one-third of children suffer from a significant emotional or behavior disorder by age 16 (Costello, Mustillo, et al., 2003). As Table 10.2 on page 300 shows, prior to age 16, boys have more mental health problems than girls—particularly behavioral disorders and attention-deficit/hyperactivity disorder. Still, only a minority of all children have any disorder.

Even when children experience significant stressors such as poverty or a parent's death, many remain psychologically healthy. We call such children *resilient* (Garmezy, 1991; Luthar, 2003) because they keep a positive sense of themselves and develop their talents. We do not know what makes children resilient, but having at least one competent adult to rely on helps. Studies of homeless children suggest that those who receive support from a parent are no more likely to develop psychological problems than are children with homes (Masten & Powell, 2003).

However, most children who develop psychological problems do not receive the care they need. One study of children living in a rural area in the southeastern United States found that two-thirds of those who met the criteria for a *DSM-IV-TR* diagnosis had not received mental health services (Costello, Copeland, Cowell, & Keeler, 2007). Of those who did receive help, only 7 percent received it from mental health professionals. In most cases, schools or juvenile justice facilities provided counseling and other services. The study estimated the annual national cost of providing mental health services to adolescents at $10.2 billion to $12.3 billion.

Table 10.3 on page 301 lists several disorders that commonly are diagnosed in childhood or infancy. Because all children experience some emotional and behavioral problems, the continuum of childhood disorders is especially challenging to discern. This chapter will help you meet the challenge by presenting biological and psychosocial factors in the development and treatment of childhood disorders.

This chapter includes changes in the diagnosis of childhood disorders likely to appear in the *DSM-5.* Other chapters cover three additional childhood disorders proposed for the *DSM-5:* post-traumatic stress disorder in preschool children (Chapter 5), temper dysregulation disorder with dysphoria (Chapter 7), and nonsuicidal self-injury (Chapter 7).

TABLE 10.2 Prevalence of Mental Disorders in Children

Estimated percentages of children who suffer psychological disorders by age 16 years (note that children can be diagnosed with more than one disorder).

Diagnosis	Total	Girls	Boys
Any disorder	36.7%	31.0%	42.3%
Any anxiety disorder	9.9	12.1	7.7
Any depressive disorder	9.5	11.7	7.3
Any behavior disorder	23.0	16.1	29.9
Conduct disorder	9.0	3.8	14.1
Oppositional defiant disorder	11.3	9.1	13.4
ADHD*	4.1	1.1	7.0
Substance use disorder (e.g., alcohol abuse)	12.2	10.1	14.3

Source: Costello, Mustillo, et al., 2003.
*ADHD = attention-deficit/hyperactivity disorder

CASE STUDY

Eddie, age 9, was referred to a child psychiatrist at the request of his school because of the difficulties he creates in class. His teacher complains that he is so restless that his classmates are unable to concentrate. He is hardly ever in his seat and mostly roams around talking to other children while they are working. In his seat, he fidgets with his hands and feet and drops things on the floor. His most recent suspension from school was for swinging from the fluorescent light fixture over the blackboard. Because he was unable to climb down again, the class was in an uproar.

His mother says that Eddie's behavior has been difficult since he was a toddler and that, as a 3-year-old, he was extremely restless and demanding. He has always required little sleep and awoken before anyone else. When he was small, "he got into everything," particularly in the early morning, when he would get up at 4:30 or 5:00 and go downstairs by himself. His parents would awaken to find the living room or kitchen "demolished." When he was 4, he unlocked the door of the apartment and wandered off into a busy street; fortunately, he was rescued by a passerby.

Eddie has no interest in TV and dislikes games or toys that require any concentration or patience. He is not popular with other children and at home prefers to be outdoors, playing with his dog or riding his bike. If he plays with toys, his games are messy and destructive. His mother cannot get him to keep his things in any order. (Reprinted from the *DSM-IV-TR Casebook: A Learning Companion to the Diagnostic and Statistical Manual of Mental Disorders,* Fourth Edition, Text Revision. Copyright © 2000 American Psychiatric Association.)

Most elementary-school-age children can sit still for some period of time and engage in games that require patience and concentration. They can inhibit their impulses to jump up in class or walk into traffic. Eddie cannot. His behavior is driven and disorganized, as is common in children with ADHD.

There are three subtypes of ADHD in the *DSM-IV-TR*. The *predominantly inattentive type* is diagnosed if six or more symptoms of inattention but fewer than six symptoms of hyperactivity-impulsivity are present. Some researchers argue that symptoms indicating a *sluggish cognitive tempo* are also important parts of the inattentive type. These symptoms include slow retrieval of information from memory and slow processing of information, low levels of alertness, drowsiness, and daydreaming (McBurnett, Pfiffner, & Frick, 2001). The *predominantly hyperactive-impulsive type* is diagnosed if six or more symptoms of hyperactivity-impulsivity but fewer than six symptoms of inattention are present. Eddie appears to have this latter type. The *combined type* includes six or more symptoms of inattention and six or more symptoms of hyperactivity-impulsivity.

The *DSM-5* may eliminate these subtypes based on criticisms that the criteria for them have not been well validated in research (American Psychiatric Association, 2010). It is also possible that a diagnosis of attention-deficit disorder will

TABLE 10.3 Disorders of Childhood

These disorders have their first onset in childhood.

Category	Specific Disorders
Behavior disorders	Attention-deficit/hyperactivity disorder Conduct disorder Oppositional defiant disorder
Separation/anxiety disorder	
Elimination disorders	Enuresis Encopresis

Disorders in cognitive, motor, and communication skills	Learning disorders
	  Reading disorder (dyslexia)
	  Mathematics disorder
	  Disorder of written expression
	Motor skills disorder
	  Developmental coordination disorder
	Communication disorders
	  Expressive language disorder
	  Mixed receptive-expressive language disorder
	  Phonological disorder
	  Stuttering

Mental retardation	Mild, moderate, severe, and profound mental retardation
Pervasive developmental disorders	Autism Rett's disorder Childhood disintegrative disorder Asperger's disorder
Tic disorders	Tourette's disorder Chronic motor or focal tic disorder Transient tic disorder
Feeding and eating disorders	Pica Rumination disorder Feeding disorder of infancy or early childhood
Other disorders	Selective mutism Reactive attachment disorder Stereotypic movement disorder

be added for children who have attentional problems but no hyperactivity. Also, the current onset age, before age 7 may be raised to before age 12.

Children with ADHD often do poorly in school. Because they cannot pay attention or calm their hyperactivity, they do not learn the material and perform below their intellectual capabilities. In addition, 20 to 25 percent of children with ADHD may have a serious learning disability that makes it doubly hard for them to concentrate in school and to learn (Wilens, Biederman, & Spencer, 2002).

Children with ADHD may have poor relationships with other children and, like Eddie, often are rejected outright (Hoza et al., 2005). When interacting with their peers, children with ADHD may be intrusive, irritable, and demanding. They want to play by their own rules and have an explosive temper, so when things do not go their way they may become physically violent.

The behavior problems of some children with ADHD are severe enough to be diagnosed as a *conduct disorder.* Children with conduct disorders

Children normally have high energy levels, but only a minority of children can be labeled hyperactive.

grossly violate the norms for appropriate behavior toward others by acting in uncaring and even violent ways. Between 45 and 60 percent of children with ADHD develop a conduct disorder, abuse drugs, or violate the law (Waschbusch, 2002; Wilens et al., 2002). For some individuals, conduct problems persist into adulthood (Abramowitz, Kosson, & Seidenberg, 2004).

Epidemiological studies indicate that 5 percent of children develop ADHD (Polanczyk & Jensen, 2008). Boys are about three times more likely than girls to develop ADHD in childhood and early adolescence (Angold et al., 2002). Girls with ADHD tend to have less disruptive behavior than boys with ADHD, which may lead to an under-identification of ADHD in girls (Biederman et al., 2002). ADHD is found across most cultures and ethnic groups. Contrary to some media accounts, the percentage of children diagnosed with ADHD is not much greater in the United States than in other countries (Polanczyk & Jensen, 2008).

The long-term outcomes for children with ADHD vary considerably. Symptoms persist into young adulthood in about 75 percent of cases (Wilens et al., 2002). Adults diagnosed with ADHD as children are at increased risk for antisocial personality disorder, substance abuse, mood and anxiety disorders, marital problems, traffic accidents, legal infractions, and frequent job changes (Fischer & Barkley, 2006; Wilens et al., 2002).

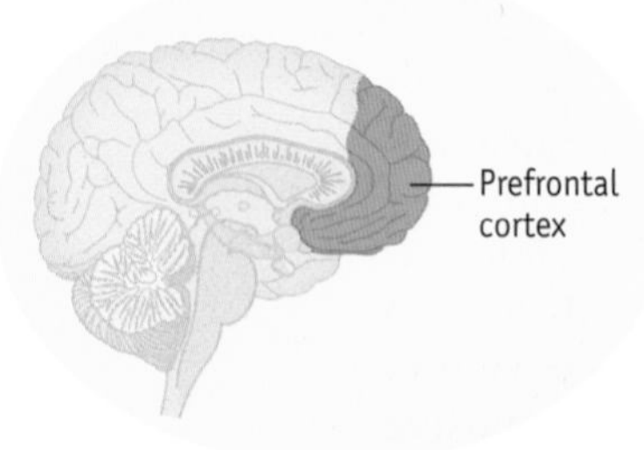

The prefrontal cortex is smaller and shows abnormal activity in children with ADHD.

Some adults who have had lifelong problems achieving success in school and at work as well as difficulties in social relationships might have had undiagnosed ADHD as children. An epidemiological study of the United States found that 4.4 percent of adults could be diagnosed with ADHD (Kessler, Adler, et al., 2006). They were more likely to be male, and they showed a wide range of difficulties at work and in their social lives. Most had not received treatment for ADHD specifically, although many had been treated for other disorders. Adults with ADHD are at high risk for depression, anxiety disorders, substance abuse, and antisocial personality disorder (Biederman et al., 2004).

Biological Factors

Modern studies have shown that children with ADHD differ from children with no psychological disorder on a variety of measures of neurological functioning and cerebral blood flow (Valera, Faraone, Murray, & Seidman, 2007; Wilens et al., 2002). The prefrontal cortex, which regulates attention, organization, and planning, is smaller in volume in children with ADHD and shows abnormal activation when these children attempt to inhibit their responses (Sheridan, Hinshaw, & D'Esposito, 2007). Because the prefrontal cortex continues to develop well into adolescence, one hypothesis is that children with ADHD are neurologically immature—their brains are slower to develop than the brains of other children—leaving them unable to maintain attention and control their behavior at a level appropriate for their age. This *immaturity hypothesis* helps explain why in some children the symptoms of ADHD decline with age.

The catecholamine neurotransmitters, which include dopamine, serotonin, and norepinephrine, appear to function abnormally in individuals with ADHD (Prince, 2008). Dopamine is implicated most frequently; serotonin, which influences impulsivity, may also play a role (Winstanley, Theobald, Dalley, & Robbins, 2005). As we will see, drugs that affect levels of norepinephrine are useful in treating ADHD, suggesting that norepinephrine systems also are dysfunctional in the disorder.

ADHD runs in families. Siblings of children with ADHD are three to four times more likely to develop it than siblings of children without the disorder (Todd, Lobos, Sun, & Neuman, 2003). Several other disorders also tend to run in the families of children with ADHD, including antisocial personality disorder, alcoholism, and depression (Barkley, 1991; Faraone, Biederman, Keenan, & Tsuang, 1991). Twin studies and adoption studies suggest that genetic factors play a role in vulnerability to ADHD (Mick & Faraone, 2008). It is not clear what aspects of the ADHD syndrome are inherited, such as problems with attention, hyperactivity, impulsivity, or aggression. Molecular genetics studies suggest that the dopamine transporter genes may be abnormal in ADHD (Brookes et al., 2006).

Children with ADHD often have a history of prenatal and birth complications. ADHD is associated with low birth weight, premature delivery, and difficult delivery leading to oxygen deprivation (Bradley & Golden, 2001). Some investigators suspect that moderate to severe drinking or heavy use of nicotine or barbiturates by mothers during pregnancy can lead to the kinds of problems in inhibiting behaviors seen in children with ADHD. Some children with ADHD were exposed to high concentrations of lead as preschoolers when they ingested lead-based paint (Fergusson, Horwood, & Lynskey, 1993).

The popular notion that hyperactivity in children is caused by dietary factors, such as the consumption of large amounts of sugar, has not been supported in controlled studies (Whalen & Henker, 1998). A few studies suggest that some children with ADHD have severe allergies to food additives and that removing these additives from their diet can reduce hyperactivity (Bradley & Golden, 2001).

Psychological and Social Factors

Children with ADHD are more likely than children without a psychological disturbance to belong to families that experience frequent disruptions, such as moving or divorce (Barkley, Fischer, Smallish, & Fletcher, 1990). Their fathers are more prone to antisocial and criminal behavior, and the children's interactions with their mothers often are marked by hostility and conflict (Barkley et al., 1990). Some investigators argue that there is a nongenetic form of ADHD that is caused by environmental adversity (Bauermeister et al., 1992). Others argue, however, that both ADHD and difficult family environments are the result of a genetic predisposition to problems with lack of control (Barkley, 1996).

Treatments for ADHD

Most children with ADHD are treated with stimulant drugs, such as Ritalin, Dexedrine, and Adderall. It may seem odd to give a stimulant to a hyperactive child, but between 70 and 85 percent of ADHD children respond to these drugs with *decreases* in demanding, disruptive, and noncompliant behavior (Joshi, 2004; Swanson et al., 2008). They also show increases in positive mood, in the ability to be goal-directed, and in the quality of their interactions with others. The stimulants may work by increasing levels of dopamine in the synapses of the brain, enhancing release and inhibiting reuptake of this neurotransmitter (Joshi, 2004).

The side effects of stimulants include reduced appetite, insomnia, edginess, and gastrointestinal upset. Stimulants also can increase the frequency of tics in children with ADHD. There has been concern that stimulants may stunt growth, and some evidence exists that children with ADHD who begin taking stimulants show decreases in their growth rate (Swanson et al., 2007). Stimulants also carry a risk of abuse by people looking for a high or hoping to gain an edge in college or the workplace (Joshi, 2004; Wilens et al., 2002).

Nationwide, the number of children prescribed stimulant medications increased by 200 to 300 percent in the past two decades (Joshi, 2004). Some researchers have argued that this increase reflects greater recognition and treatment seeking for children with ADHD. Others say that it represents an inappropriate overuse of the drugs, particularly for children who are difficult to control (Angold, Erkanli, Egger, & Costello, 2000). There is scant empirical evidence on which to judge these competing claims.

In a longitudinal study of children in the southeastern United States, 72 percent of those with ADHD received stimulants at some point during the 4 years they were followed, suggesting that most children with ADHD are being treated (Angold et al., 2000). In this study, however, the majority of the children taking stimulants did *not* have symptoms meeting the diagnostic criteria for ADHD, suggesting that stimulants were misprescribed, especially for the boys and younger children in the study. More research is needed to determine how appropriately stimulants are being used in treating children.

Other drugs that treat ADHD include atomoxetine, clonidine, and guanfacine, which are not stimulants but affect norepinephrine levels. These drugs can help reduce tics, common in children with ADHD, and increase cognitive performance (Joshi, 2004; Kratochvil et al., 2007). Side effects of these drugs include dry mouth, fatigue, dizziness, constipation, and sedation.

Antidepressant medications sometimes are prescribed to children and adolescents with ADHD, particularly if they also have depression. These drugs have some positive effects on cognitive performance but are not as effective as the stimulants against ADHD (Wilens et al., 2002). Bupropion, an antidepressant with particularly strong effects on dopamine levels, appears to be more effective against ADHD than some other antidepressants. Unfortunately, the gains made by ADHD children treated with medications alone are short-term (Joshi, 2004). As soon as medication is stopped, symptoms often return.

Behavioral therapies for ADHD focus on reinforcing attentive, goal-directed, and prosocial behaviors and extinguishing impulsive and hyperactive behaviors (DuPaul & Barkley, 1993). These therapies typically engage parents and teachers in changing rewards and punishments in every aspect of the child's life. A child and his parents might agree that he will earn a chip every time he obeys a request to wash his hands or put away his toys. At the end of each week, he can exchange his chips for fun activities. Each time the child refuses to comply, he loses a chip. Such techniques can help parents break the cycle of arguments with their children that escalate behaviors, which in turn lead to more arguments and perhaps physical violence. The children learn to anticipate the consequences of their behaviors and to make less impulsive choices. They are taught to interact more appropriately with others, including waiting their turn in games, finding nonaggressive ways to express frustration, and listening when others speak. A meta-analysis of 174 studies evaluating the effectiveness of behavioral therapy found strong and consistent evidence that behavioral therapy is highly effective in reducing symptoms of ADHD in children (Fabiano et al., 2009).

Some studies suggest that the combination of stimulant therapy and psychosocial therapy is more likely to produce short-term improvements than either therapy alone. In one multisite study, 579 children with ADHD were randomly assigned to receive the combination of Ritalin and behavior therapy, one therapy alone, or routine community care (Jensen et al., 2001). After 14 months, 68 percent of the combined-treatment group had reduced or discontinued their ADHD behaviors, such as aggression and lack of concentration. In the medication-alone group, 56 percent showed reduced or discontinued symptoms. Behavior therapy alone reduced symptoms in only 34 percent of group members, and only 25 percent of those given routine community care showed reductions in their symptoms. In a follow-up 3 years later, all three treatment groups were doing equally well (Jensen et al., 2007).

Conduct Disorder and Oppositional Defiant Disorder

Have you ever lied, stolen something, or hit someone? Most of us would have to answer yes to at least one of these. However, few would answer yes to the following questions:

- Have you ever pulled a knife or a gun on another person?
- Have you ever forced someone into sexual activity?
- Have you ever deliberately set a fire with the hope of damaging someone's property?
- Have you ever broken into someone else's car or house with the intention of stealing?

Many young people who have **conduct disorder** answer yes to these questions and engage in other serious transgressions of societal norms for behavior (see the *DSM-IV-TR* criteria in Table 10.4). These children have a chronic pattern of unconcern for the basic rights of others. Consider Phillip, in the following case study.

CASE STUDY

Phillip, age 12, was suspended from a small-town Iowa school and referred for psychiatric treatment by his principal, who sent the following note:

"This child has been a continual problem since coming to our school. He does not get along on the playground because he is mean to other children. He disobeys school rules, teases the patrol children, steals from the other children, and defies all authority. Phillip keeps getting into fights with other children on the bus.

"The truth is not in Phillip. When caught in actual misdeeds, he denies everything and takes upon himself an air of injured innocence. He believes we are picking on him. His attitude is sullen when he is refused anything. He pouts, and when asked why he does these things, he points to his head and says, Because I'm not right up here. This boy needs help badly. He does not seem to have any friends. His aggressive behavior prevents the children from liking him. Our school psychologist tested Phillip, and the results indicated average intelligence, but his school achievement is only at the third- and low fourth-grade level." (From Jenkins, 1973, pp. 60–64)

We all have known bullies and "troublemakers." While only 3 to 7 percent of children and adolescents exhibit behaviors serious enough for a diagnosis of conduct disorder (Costello et al., 2003; Maughan et al., 2004), those with the disorder exact a high cost from society. The cost to schools of vandalism by juveniles in the United States is estimated to be over $600 million per year. About 50 percent of adolescent boys and 25 percent of adolescent girls report being attacked by someone at school (Offord, 1997).

The conduct problems of some youth diminish with age, a pattern called *adolescent-limited* antisocial behavior (Moffitt, 2006). Unfortunately, many children with conduct disorder continue to violate social norms in adolescence and adulthood, a pattern called *life-course-persistent* antisocial behavior (Moffitt, 2006). As adolescents, about 50 percent engage in criminal behavior and drug abuse. As adults, about 75 to 85 percent are chronically unemployed, have a history of unstable personal relationships, frequently engage in impulsive physical aggression, or abuse their spouse (Moffitt et al.,

TABLE 10.4 *DSM-IV-TR* Diagnostic Criteria for Conduct Disorder

A. A repetitive and persistent pattern of behavior in which the basic rights of others or major age-appropriate societal norms or rules are violated, with the presence of three (or more) of the following in the past 12 months, with at least one in the past 6 months:

Aggression to people and/or animals

1. Often bullies, threatens or intimidates others
2. Often initiates physical fights
3. Has used a weapon that can cause serious physical harm to others
4. Has been physically cruel to people
5. Has been physically cruel to animals
6. Has stolen while confronting a victim
7. Has forced someone into sexual activity

Destruction of property

1. Has deliberately engaged in fire setting with the intention of causing serious damage
2. Has deliberately destroyed others' property (other than by fire setting)

Deceitfulness or theft

1. Has broken into someone else's house, building, or car
2. Often lies to obtain goods or favors or to avoid obligations (i.e., cons others)
3. Has stolen items of nontrivial value without confronting the victim (e.g., shoplifting, but without breaking and entering; forgery)

Serious violations of rules

1. Often stays out at night despite parental prohibitions, beginning before age 13 years
2. Has run away from home overnight at least twice while living in a parental or parental surrogate home (or once without returning for a lengthy period)
3. Is often truant from school, beginning before age 13 years

B. The disturbance in behavior causes clinically significant impairment in social, academic, or occupational functioning.

C. If the individual is age 18 years or older, criteria are not met for antisocial personality disorder.

Source: Reprinted with permission from the *Diagnostic and Statistical Manual of Mental Disorders,* Fourth Edition, Text Revision.

2008). Between 35 and 40 percent are diagnosed with antisocial personality disorder as adults. Children who develop conduct disorder are more likely than those whose conduct problems begin in adolescence to show a wide range of psychological problems and violent behavior as adults. One study of children in three countries found that boys who exhibited physical aggression early in life were most likely to show chronic conduct problems in adulthood (Broidy et al., 2003).

The *DSM-5* will likely retain the *DSM-IV-TR* criteria for this disorder. A specifier may be added for *callous and unemotional traits* to represent children who meet the full criteria for conduct disorder and also seem to be unemotional and unable to care about their performance in school or about others (American Psychiatric Association, 2010). These traits characterize *psychopathy,* an adult personality pattern related to antisocial personality disorder (see Chapter 9).

The *DSM-IV-TR* also recognizes a less severe pattern of chronic misbehavior known as **oppositional defiant disorder.** The criteria for oppositional defiant disorder are that children show at least four of the following symptoms for at least 6 months: (a) frequently lose their temper, (b) quarrel with grownups, (c) actively disobey requests or rules, (d) intentionally irritate others, (e) blame others for their errors or misconduct, (f) are easily annoyed by other people, (g) are angry and resentful, and (h) are spiteful or vindictive. Unlike children with conduct disorder, children with oppositional defiant disorder are not aggressive toward people or animals, do not destroy property, and do not show a pattern of theft and deceit. The *DSM-IV-TR* criteria for oppositional defiant disorder will largely be retained in the *DSM-5.*

We see several symptoms of oppositional defiant disorder in 9-year-old Jeremy.

CASE STUDY

Jeremy has been increasingly difficult to manage since nursery school. At school, he teases and kicks other children, trips them, and calls them names. He is described as bad-tempered and irritable, though at times he seems to enjoy school. Often he appears to be deliberately trying to annoy other children, though he always claims that others have started the arguments. He does not get in serious fights but does occasionally exchange a few blows with another child.

Jeremy sometimes refuses to do what his two teachers tell him to do, and this year he has been particularly difficult during arithmetic, art, and science lessons. He gives many reasons why he should not have to do his work and argues when told to do it. At home, Jeremy's behavior varies. Some days he is defiant and rude to his mother, needing to be told to do everything several times, though he usually complies eventually. Other days he is charming and volunteers to help, but his unhelpful days predominate. His mother says, "The least little thing upsets him, and then he shouts and screams." Jeremy is described as spiteful and mean with his younger brother, Rickie. His mother also says that he tells many minor lies, though when pressed he is truthful about important things. (Reprinted from the *DSM-IV-TR Casebook: A Learning Companion to the Diagnostic and Statistical Manual of Mental Disorders,* Fourth Edition, Text Revision. Copyright © 2000 American Psychiatric Association.)

Symptoms of oppositional defiant disorder often begin during the toddler and preschool years. Some affected children seem to outgrow these behaviors by late childhood or early adolescence. Others, however, particularly those who tend to be aggressive, go on to develop conduct disorder in childhood and adolescence. Indeed, almost all children who develop conduct disorder during elementary school seem to have had symptoms of oppositional defiant disorder at a younger age.

Across cultures, boys are about three times more likely than girls to be diagnosed with conduct disorder or oppositional defiant disorder (Moffitt, Caspi, Rutter, & Silva, 2001). Males are 10 to 15 times more likely than females to have life-course-persistent antisocial behavior (Moffitt, 2006). The biological and psychosocial causes of these disorders may be present more frequently in boys than in girls. Also, boys with conduct disorder tend to be more physically aggressive than girls with conduct disorder and thus more likely to draw attention (Maughan et al., 2000; Tiet et al., 2001).

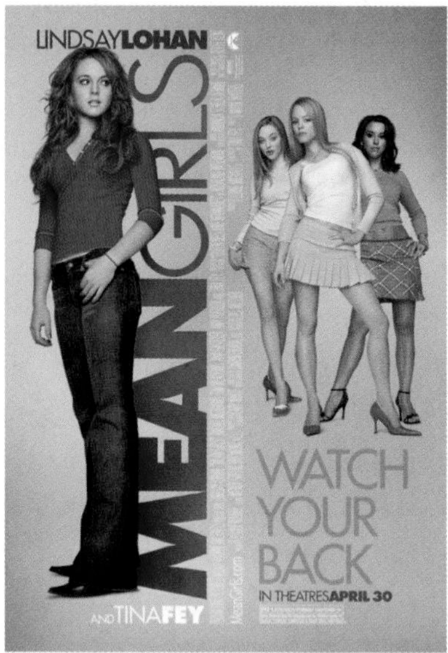

Girls may be aggressive toward others in different ways than boys.

Some researchers have suggested that antisocial behavior is not rarer in girls than in boys—it just looks different (Crick & Grotpeter, 1995; Zoccolillo, 1993). Girls' aggression is more likely to be indirect and verbal rather than physical. Girls appear to engage in *relational aggression,* such as excluding their peers, gossiping about them, and colluding with others to damage the social status of their targets (Crick & Grotpeter, 1995).

However, girls and boys with conduct disorder are equally likely to engage in stealing, lying, and substance abuse (Tiet et al., 2001). Long-term studies of girls diagnosed with conduct disorder find that, as adolescents and adults, they also show high rates of depression and anxiety disorders, severe marital problems, criminal activity, and early, unplanned pregnancies (Moffitt et al., 2001).

Biological Factors

Children with conduct disorder are more likely than children without the disorder to have parents with antisocial personalities (Odgers et al., 2007). Their fathers tend to have a history of criminal arrest and alcohol abuse, and their mothers tend to have a history of depression.

Twin and adoption studies indicate that both conduct disorder and oppositional defiant disorder are heritable. For example, one study of 1,116 pairs of 5-year-old twins found that 82 percent of the variability in conduct disorder was due to genetic factors (Arsenault et al., 2003). Genetics appears to play a particularly strong role in conduct disorder that begins in early childhood.

Several specific genes have been associated with an increased risk of conduct disorder and oppositional defiant disorder, primarily genes involved in the regulation of the neurotransmitters dopamine, serotonin, and norepinephrine (Moffitt et al., 2008). One study found an interaction between childhood maltreatment (including physical and sexual abuse as well as neglect) and the MAOA gene, which encodes an enzyme that metabolizes dopamine, serotonin, and norepinephrine. Children who both were maltreated and had the abnormal variant of the MAOA gene were especially likely to develop conduct disorder (Caspi et al., 2002). This is another example of gene-and-environment interactions contributing to psychopathology.

Children with conduct disorder may have fundamental neurological deficits in those brain systems responsible for planning and controlling behavior. Neuroimaging studies show abnormalities in the functioning of the anterior cingulate, an area of the prefrontal cortex involved in responding to emotional stimuli (Stadler et al., 2006; Sterzer et al., 2005). They also show less amygdala activity in response to emotional stimuli (Sterzer et al., 2005), possibly suggesting that children with conduct disorder do not process emotional cues the way healthy children do. Indeed, children with conduct disorder have deficits, not seen in healthy children, on tasks that measure planning and organizing ability and the processing of emotional cues, (Blair et al., 2006; Nigg & Huang-Pollock, 2003).

One source of the neurological deficits these children have may be exposure to neurotoxins and drugs while in the womb or during the preschool years. Boys whose mothers smoke during pregnancy are 2.6 times more likely to develop oppositional behavior in early childhood, followed by increasingly more aggressive and severe antisocial behavior as they grow older (Wakschlag, Pickett, Kasza, & Loeber, 2006).

Another clue that biological factors are involved in conduct disorder is that signs of trouble often appear in infancy. Children who develop conduct disorder tend to have been difficult babies and toddlers, at least as reported by their parents (Shaw, Keenan, & Vondra, 1994; Shaw & Winslow, 1997). They are described as having been irritable, demanding, disobedient, and impulsive. They seemed to lack self-control and responded to frustration with aggression. Some theorists argue that such children are born with a biologically based difficult temperament that interacts with parenting and environmental factors to produce behavioral problems (Caspi, Harrington, et al., 2003).

Children with conduct disorder have a slower heart rate than children without the disorder, both while resting and especially when confronted with a stressor (Ortiz & Raine, 2004). They also show abnormal cortisol levels both at rest and in response to a stressor (van Goozen, Fairchild, Snoek, & Harold, 2007). Because they become less physiologically aroused than other children when confronted by stressors, children with conduct disorder may be more willing to take risks and may have more difficulty learning from being punished for their behavior.

The role of serotonin in violent behavior has been the focus of many studies. One study of a large community-based sample found that young men with high blood serotonin levels relative to those of other men their age were much more likely to have committed a violent crime (Moffitt et al., 1998). Several other studies, but not all, have found an association between measures of serotonin activity and antisocial behavior in children (van Goozen, et al., 2007).

Also, a popular theory links aggressive behavior to the hormone testosterone. A meta-analysis of studies of testosterone and aggression in humans found a small but statistically significant correlation of 0.14 (Book, Starzyk, & Quinsey, 2001). The association between testosterone and aggression depends on the social context of the participants. In a study of 9- to 15-year-old-boys, higher testosterone levels were associated with more conduct disorder symptoms in boys whose peers engaged in socially deviant behaviors (Rowe et al., 2004). In boys whose peers did not engage in these behaviors, testosterone was associated with leadership rather than with conduct disorder symptoms.

Social Factors

Conduct disorder and oppositional defiant disorder are found more frequently in children in lower socioeconomic classes and in urban areas than in children in higher socioeconomic classes and in rural areas (Costello, Keeler, & Angold, 2001). A tendency toward antisocial behavior may run in families, and families whose members engage in antisocial behavior may experience *downward social drift:* The adults in these families cannot maintain good jobs, and the families' socioeconomic status tends to decline. This tendency also may be due to differences in some environmental causes of antisocial behavior, such as exposure to toxins.

An "experiment of nature" provided more evidence of a causal role for poverty in antisocial behavior than of support for a downward-drift hypothesis. For several years, researchers had been following 1,420 children in rural North Carolina,

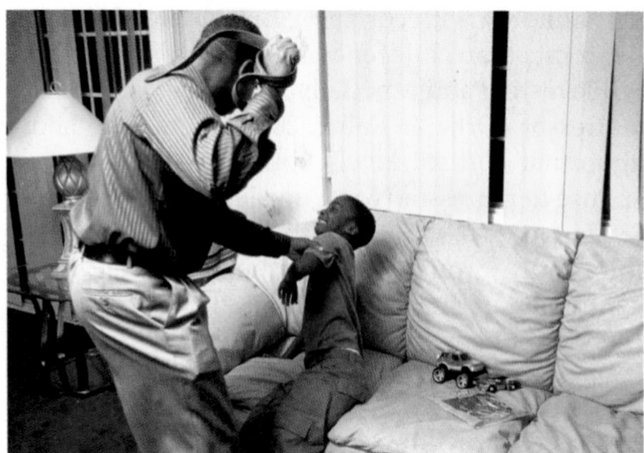

Children are more likely to exhibit disruptive and delinquent behavior if they are physically abused.

about one-quarter of whom were Native American (Costello, 2003). During the study, a casino operated by Native Americans opened, providing a sudden and substantial increase in income for the families of some of these children. The rates of conduct and oppositional defiant disorder decreased in those Native American children whose families benefited from the casino money.

The quality of parenting that children receive, particularly children with vulnerability to hyperactivity and conduct disturbances, is strongly related to whether they develop the full syndrome of conduct disorder (Kim-Cohen et al., 2006; Smith & Farrington, 2004). Children who are physically abused or severely neglected by their parents are more likely to develop disruptive and delinquent behavior (Stouthamer-Loeber, Loeber, Homish, & Wei, 2001). Children whose parents are not involved in their everyday life—for example, whose parents do not know who their friends are or what they are doing in school—are more likely to develop conduct disturbances. When parents do interact with their children with conduct disturbances, the interactions often are characterized by hostility, physical violence, and ridicule (Dishion & Patterson, 1997). Such parents frequently ignore their children or are absent from home, but when the children transgress the parents lash out violently (Kim-Cohen et al., 2006; Smith & Farrington, 2004). These parents are more likely to physically punish boys severely than girls, which may account partially for the higher rate of conduct disturbances in boys than in girls (Lytton & Romney, 1991).

Young people living in such families may turn to their peers to receive validation and escape their parents. Unfortunately, these peer groups may consist of others with similar conduct disturbances who tend to encourage delinquent acts and even provide opportunities for them (Dishion & Patterson, 1997). They may dare a new group member to commit a robbery to "show he is a man" and provide him with a weapon and a getaway car. Children who become part of deviant peer groups are especially likely to begin abusing alcohol and illicit drugs, abuse that in turn leads to increased deviant acts (McBride, Joe, & Simpson, 1991).

Individuals with antisocial tendencies also tend to choose mates with similar tendencies (Smith & Farrington, 2004). Conversely, those who form close relationships with others who do not have a conduct disturbance are much more likely to grow out of their behaviors. Delinquent young men who marry young women with no history of conduct problems tend to cease their delinquent acts permanently (Sampson & Laub, 1992).

Biological and family factors contributing to conduct disorder often may coincide, sending a child on a trajectory toward antisocial behaviors that is difficult to stop (Figure 10.1; Loeber, 1990; Reid & Eddy, 1997). The neuropsychological problems associated with antisocial behaviors are linked to maternal drug use, poor prenatal nutrition, pre- and postnatal exposure to toxic agents, child abuse, birth complications, and low birth weight (Moffitt, 1993; Silberg et al., 2003). Infants and toddlers with these neuropsychological problems are more irritable, impulsive, awkward, overreactive, inattentive, and slow to learn than their peers. This makes them difficult to care for and puts them at increased risk for maltreatment and neglect. Their parents are likely to be teenagers with their own psychological problems that contribute to ineffective, harsh, or inconsistent parenting. Thus, children who carry a biological predisposition to antisocial behaviors may experience parenting that contributes to these behaviors and grow up in a disadvantaged or dangerous setting.

In a longitudinal study following children from age 3 into adulthood, Terri Moffit, Avshalom Caspi, and colleagues (Moffit & Caspi, 2001; Moffit et al., 2001) found that the combination of a biological disposition toward cognitive deficits and a difficult temperament plus growing up in a risky environment characterized by inadequate parenting and disrupted family bonds tended to lead to pernicious conduct disorder that developed in childhood and persisted into adulthood. In contrast, youth who were antisocial only in adolescence were much less likely to have this combination of biological and environmental risk factors. Another study found impulsivity in boys to be linked to a greater risk for late-adolescent delinquency only among those who grew up in poor, violent neighborhoods (Lynam et al., 2000).

Cognitive Factors

Children with conduct disorder tend to process information about social interactions in ways that promote aggressive reactions (Crick & Dodge, 1994).

FIGURE 10.1 **Developmental Model of Behavior Disorders.** Several biological and environmental factors come together to create behavior disorders.

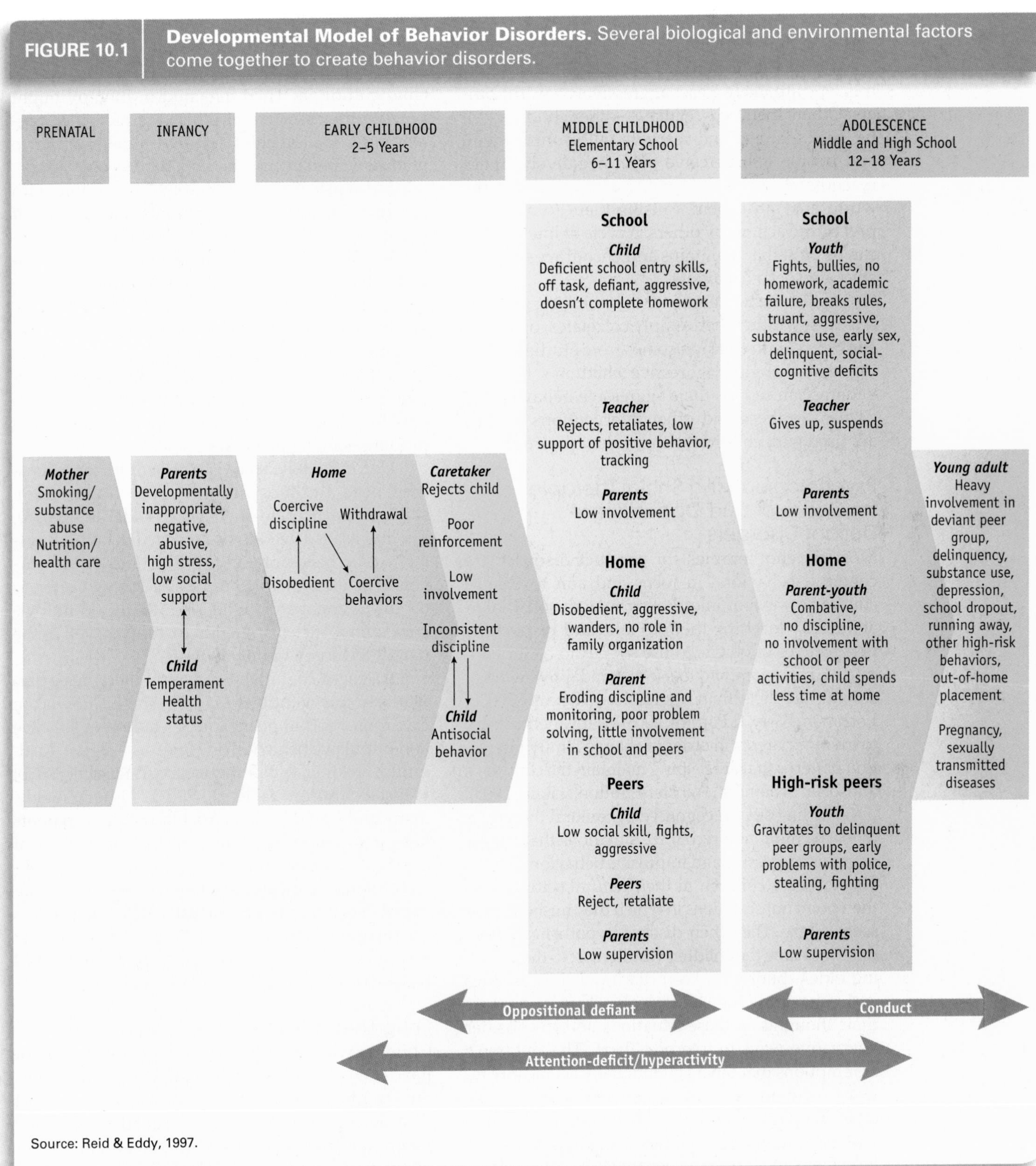

Source: Reid & Eddy, 1997.

They assume that others will be aggressive toward them, and they use these assumptions—rather than cues from specific situations—to interpret the actions of their peers (Dodge & Schwartz, 1997). For example, when accidentally bumped into by another child, a child with conduct disorder will assume that the bump was intentional and meant to provoke a fight. Children with conduct disorder tend to consider a narrow range of responses to perceived provocation by a peer, usually including aggression (Pettit, Dodge, & Brown, 1988). When pressed to consider other responses, they generate ineffective or vague ideas and often judge anything besides aggression as useless or unattractive (Crick & Ladd, 1990).

Children who think about social interactions this way are likely to act aggressively toward others. Others then may retaliate—other children will hit back, parents and teachers will punish them, and people will perceive them negatively. These reactions feed the children's assumption that the world is against them, causing them to misinterpret future actions by others. A cycle of interactions can be built that maintains and encourages aggressive, antisocial behaviors.

Again, the best evidence that thinking patterns are causes, rather than simply correlates, of antisocial behavior in children comes from studies showing that changing aggressive children's thinking patterns can reduce their aggressive behavior. Let us turn to these and other interventions as they are used with children with conduct disorder.

Psychological and Social Therapies for Conduct and Oppositional Defiant Disorders

Most psychotherapies for conduct disorder are cognitive-behavioral in focus and aim to change children's ways of interpreting interpersonal interactions by teaching them to take and respect the perspectives of others, to use *self-talk* to control impulsive behaviors, and to use more adaptive ways of solving conflicts than aggression (Kazdin, 2003b; Lochman, Barry, & Pardini, 2003). Many therapies try to involve parents in order to change family interaction patterns that are helping maintain the children's antisocial behaviors (Webster-Stratton & Reid, 2003).

The first step in cognitive-behavioral therapy is to teach children to recognize situations that trigger anger or aggressive and impulsive behaviors. Therapists observe children in their natural settings and then point out situations in which they misbehave or seem angry. They then discuss hypothetical situations and how the children would react to them, asking older children to keep diaries of their feelings and behaviors. The children also learn to analyze their thoughts in these situations and to consider alternative ways to interpret them. The children's assumptions that others intentionally act meanly toward them are challenged, and they learn to take other people's perspectives on situations. Children may be taught to use self-talk, repeating phrases to help them avoid reacting negatively to situations.

Therapists teach adaptive problem-solving skills by discussing real and hypothetical problem situations with children and helping them generate positive solutions. For example, if a therapist and a child are discussing how to respond to another child who has cut in line in the lunchroom, the therapist initially might model an assertive (rather than aggressive) response, such as saying "I would like you to move to the back of the line" to the child cutting in. Then the child in therapy might practice the assertive response, perhaps also pretending to be the child cutting in line in order to gain some perspective on the other's behavior.

Some psychosocial therapies for children with conduct disorder include parents, particularly if the family dynamics support the children's behavior (Kazdin, 2003a). Parents learn to reinforce positive behaviors in their children and to discourage aggressive or antisocial behaviors. They also are given nonviolent discipline techniques and strategies for controlling their own angry outbursts. These behavioral techniques are especially important in treating younger children, who may not be able to analyze and challenge their thinking and problem-solving processes.

Unfortunately, it can be difficult to get parents who need the most improvement in parenting skills to participate in therapy (Kazdin, 2003a). Therapists also need to be sensitive to cultural differences in behavioral norms for children and parents. For example, in families of color it often is useful to engage the extended family (grandparents, aunts, uncles) in family therapy as well as the parents (Dudley-Grant, 2001).

All these cognitive-behavioral therapies—particularly interventions made in the home, in the classroom, and in peer groups—reduce aggressive and impulsive behaviors in children (August, Realmutto, Hektner, & Bloomquist, 2001; Kazdin, 2003b; Webster-Stratton & Reid, 2003). Unfortunately, many children relapse, particularly if their parents have poor parenting skills, a history of alcoholism or drug abuse, or some other psychopathology. Interventions are most likely to have long-term positive effects if they begin early in a disturbed child's life (Estrada & Pinsof, 1995). Booster sessions after a course of initial therapy can help a child avoid relapse (Lochman, White, & Wayland, 1991).

Drug Therapies for Conduct Disorder

Children who exhibit severely aggressive behavior have been prescribed a variety of drugs. Stimulants are the most widely prescribed drugs for conduct disorder in the United States, Canada, and many other countries, in part because conduct disorder often is comorbid with ADHD (Michelson, 2004). A meta-analysis of clinical trials found that stimulants are highly effective in relieving ADHD symptoms in children with conduct disorder, and moderately effective in reducing aggression in these children (Pappadopulos et al., 2006). Antidepressants, particularly the selective serotonin reuptake inhibitors and serotonin-norepinephrine reuptake inhibitors, may help reduce irritable and agitated behavior in children (Emslie, Portteus, Kumar, & Hume, 2004). Children with conduct disorder sometimes are prescribed atypical antipsychotics (see Chapter 8), which seem to suppress aggressive behavior (Pappadopulos et al., 2006). Whether they affect other symptoms of conduct disorder, such as lying and stealing, is unclear. Traditional antipsychotic medications, such as Haldol and Mellaril (see Chapter 8), also have been used to treat children with conduct disorder, with some success (Pappadopulos et al., 2006). The neurological side effects of these drugs (see Chapter 8) have discouraged many physicians from prescribing them, however. Some controlled studies suggest that mood stabilizers, including lithium and anticonvulsants (see Chapter 7), may effectively treat children with aggressive conduct disorder (Chang & Simeonova, 2004).

TEST YOURSELF

1. What are the diagnostic criteria for attention-deficit/hyperactivity disorder (ADHD)?
2. What biological and social factors play a role in ADHD?
3. What biological and psychosocial treatments are most effective for ADHD?
4. What are the diagnostic criteria for conduct disorder and oppositional defiant disorder?
5. What biological and social factors play a role in conduct disorder?
6. What biological and psychosocial treatments are effective for conduct disorder?

APPLY IT A therapist is working with a boy with conduct disorder, using cognitive-behavioral therapy. The boy is asked to imagine being pushed off a swing by another boy at school. Which of the following would the therapist encourage the boy to do in response?

a. Think of possible actions he could take.
b. Quickly run to a teacher to report the incident.
c. Cry to show his feelings about the situation.
d. Turn around and walk away.

Answers appear online at www.mhhe.com/nolen5e.

TABLE 10.5 *DSM-IV-TR* Criteria for Separation Anxiety Disorder

A. Developmentally inappropriate and excessive anxiety concerning separation from home or from those to whom the individual is attached, as evidenced by three (or more) of the following:
   1. Recurrent excessive distress when separation from home or major attachment figures occurs or is anticipated
   2. Persistent and excessive worry about losing, or about possible harm befalling, major attachment figures
   3. Persistent and excessive worry that an untoward event will lead to separation from a major attachment figure (e.g., getting lost or being kidnapped)
   4. Persistent reluctance or refusal to go to school or elsewhere because of fear of separation
   5. Persistently and excessively fearful or reluctant to be alone or without major attachment figures at home or without significant adults in other settings
   6. Persistent reluctance or refusal to go to sleep without being near a major attachment figure or to sleep away from home
   7. Repeated nightmares involving the theme of separation
   8. Repeated complaints of physical symptoms (such as headaches, stomachaches, nausea, or vomiting) when separation from major attachment figures occurs or is anticipated

B. The duration of the disturbance is at least 4 weeks.

C. The onset is before age 18 years.

D. The disturbance causes clinically significant distress or impairment in social, academic (occupational), or other important areas of functioning.

SEPARATION ANXIETY DISORDER

Children, like adults, can suffer from depression, panic attacks, obsessive-compulsive disorder, generalized anxiety disorder, posttraumatic stress disorder, and phobias (see Chapters 5 and 7). One emotional disorder whose onset is specific to childhood is **separation anxiety disorder** (see the *DSM-IV-TR* criteria in Table 10.5). In the *DSM-5,* the criteria for separation anxiety disorder are unlikely to change, but the disorder probably will be categorized with the anxiety disorders to allow diagnosis in adults.

Many infants become anxious and upset if they are separated from their primary caregivers. With development, however, most come to understand that their caregivers will return, and they find ways to comfort themselves while their caregivers are away.

Some children continue to be extremely anxious when they are separated from their caregivers, even into childhood and adolescence. They may be very shy, sensitive, and demanding of adults. They may refuse to go to school because they fear separation, and they may experience stomachaches, headaches,

Children with separation anxiety disorder often cling desperately to their parents.

nausea, and vomiting if forced to leave their caregivers. They may follow their caregivers around the house, have nightmares with themes of separation, and be unable to sleep at night unless they are with their caregivers. When separated from their caregivers, they worry that something bad will happen to the caregivers and harbor exaggerated fears of natural disasters. kidnappings, and accidents. Younger children may cry inconsolably. Older children may avoid activities, such as being on a baseball team, that might take them away from their caregivers.

Many children go through a few days of these symptoms after a traumatic event, such as getting lost in a shopping mall or seeing a parent hospitalized for a sudden illness. Separation anxiety disorder is not diagnosed unless symptoms persist for at least 4 weeks and significantly impair the child's functioning.

About 3 percent of children under age 11 years, more commonly girls, experience separation anxiety disorder (Angold et al., 2002; Bowen, Offord, & Boyle, 1990). Left untreated, the disorder can recur throughout childhood and adolescence, significantly interfering with the child's academic progress and peer relationships. One study examined the adult outcomes of children with separation anxiety who had refused to go to school. They had more psychiatric problems as adults than did the comparison group, were more likely to continue to live with their parents, and were less likely to have married and had children (Flakierska-Praquin, Lindstrom, & Gilberg, 1997).

Biological Factors

Children with separation anxiety disorder tend to have family histories of anxiety and depressive disorders (Biederman, Faraone, et al., 2001; Manicavasagar et al., 2001). Twin studies suggest that separation anxiety disorder is heritable, more so in girls than in boys (Eaves et al., 1997; Feigon, Waldman, Levy, & Hay, 2001).

Some children are born high in **behavioral inhibition**—they are shy, fearful, and irritable as toddlers and cautious, quiet, and introverted as school-age children (Kagan, Reznick, and Snidman, 1987). These children tend to avoid or withdraw from novel situations, are clingy with their parents, and become excessively aroused in unfamiliar situations.

Some studies suggest that individuals high in behavioral inhibition as infants are at increased risk for developing anxiety disorders in childhood (Biederman et al., 1990, 1993; Caspi et al., 2003). These children's parents also are prone to anxiety disorders—particularly panic disorder—that a sometimes date to their own childhood. One study found that children who were behaviorally inhibited had abnormalities on the gene that regulates corticotropin-releasing hormone (CRH), a hormone that plays an important role in stress responses (Smoller et al., 2003). This association was particularly strong in children whose parents also had an anxiety disorder.

Psychological and Sociocultural Factors

Children may learn to be anxious from their parents or as an understandable response to their environment. In some cases, such as the following,

CASE STUDY

In the early morning hours, 7-year-old Maria was abruptly awakened by a loud rumbling and violent shaking. She sat upright in bed and called out to her 10-year-old sister, Rosemary, who was leaping out of her own bed 3 feet away. The two girls ran for their mother's bedroom as their toys and books plummeted from shelves and dresser tops. The china hutch in the hallway teetered in front of them and then fell forward with a crash, blocking their path to their mother's room. Mrs. Marshall called out to them to go back and stay in their doorway. They huddled there together until the shaking finally stopped. Mrs. Marshall climbed over the hutch and broken china to her daughters. Although they were all very scared, they were unhurt.

Two weeks later, Maria began to complain every morning of stomachaches, headaches, and dizziness, asking to stay home with her mother. After 4 days, when a medical examination revealed no physical problems, Maria was told she must return to school. She protested tearfully, but her mother insisted, and Rosemary promised to hold her hand all the way to school. In the classroom, Maria could not concentrate on her schoolwork and was often out of her seat, looking out the window in the direction of home. She told her teacher she needed to go home to see whether her mother was okay. When told she couldn't go home, she began to cry and tremble so violently that the school nurse called Mrs. Marshall, who picked Maria up and took her home.

The next morning, Maria's protests grew stronger and she refused to go to school until her mother promised to go with her and sit in her classroom for the first hour. When Mrs. Marshall began to leave, Maria clung to her, crying, pleading for her not to leave, and following her into the hallway. The next day, Maria refused to leave the house for her Brownie meeting and her dancing lessons or even to play in the front yard. She followed her mother around the house and insisted on sleeping with her at night. "I need to be with you, Mommy, in case something happens," she declared.

separation anxiety disorder develops following a traumatic event.

Observational studies of interactions between anxious children and their parents show that the parents tend to be more controlling and intrusive both behaviorally and emotionally, and also more critical and negative in their communications with their children (Hughes, Hedtke, & Kendall, 2008). Some of this behavior may be in response to the children's anxious behaviors, but many parents of anxious children are themselves anxious or depressed.

Some of the best evidence that environmental and parenting factors can influence the development of anxiety disorders in youngsters comes from studies of primates (Mineka, Gunnar, & Champoux, 1986; Suomi, 1999). Susan Mineka and colleagues found that rhesus monkeys who, from ages 2 to 6 months, were given adequate food and water but could not control their access to them became fearful and inhibited. Other monkeys given the same amount of food and water but under conditions that allowed them to exert some control did not become fearful. This result suggests that some human children raised in conditions over which they have little control may develop anxiety symptoms.

Moreover, Stephen Suomi (1999) found that although some rhesus monkeys seem to be born behaviorally inhibited, the extent to which they develop serious signs of fearfulness and anxiety later in life depends on the parenting they receive. Those raised by anxious mothers, who are inhibited and inappropriately responsive to the infants, are prone to develop monkey versions of anxiety disorders. Those raised by calm, responsive mothers who model appropriate reactions to stressful situations typically are no more likely to develop anxiety problems as adolescents or adults than those not born behaviorally inhibited.

Treatments for Separation Anxiety

Cognitive-behavioral therapies (CBT) most often are used to treat separation anxiety disorder (Kendall, Aschenbrand, & Hudson, 2003). Children are taught new skills for coping and for challenging cognitions that feed their anxiety. They might learn relaxation exercises to practice when they are separated from their parents. Their fears about separation are challenged, and they are taught to use self-talk to calm themselves when they become anxious.

As therapy progresses, periods of separation from parents are increased in number and duration. Parents must be willing to participate in therapy and to cope with their children's (and their own) reactions to increased periods of separation. Parents may need to be taught to model nonanxious reactions to separations from their children and to reinforce nonanxious behavior in their children.

Controlled clinical trials of this type of therapy show that it can be effective in the short term and maintain its effects over the long term (Shortt, Barrett, & Fox, 2001; Velting, Setzer, & Albano, 2004). Philip Kendall and his colleagues (2008) provided three treatments: individualized CBT to anxious children, family-based CBT to anxious children and their parents, or simply education and support. At the end of therapy, the children in both the individualized and the family-based CBT showed substantial declines in anxiety symptoms, while the children who received only education and support showed less improvement. These declines were sustained over a 1-year follow-up period.

Here is how Maria was treated for her separation anxiety.

CASE STUDY

Mrs. Marshall was instructed to take Maria to school and leave four times during the period she was there. Initially, Mrs. Marshall left for 30 seconds each time. Over time, she gradually increased the amount of time and distance she was away while Maria remained in the classroom. Maria was given a sticker at the end of the school day for each time she remained in her seat while her mother was out of the room. In addition, she was praised by her teacher and her mother, and positive self-statements ("My mommy will be okay; I'm a big girl and I can stay at school") were encouraged. No response was made when Maria failed to stay in her chair. Maria could exchange her stickers for prizes at the end of each week.

At home, Mrs. Marshall was instructed to give minimal attention to Maria's inquiries about her well-being and to ignore excessive, inappropriate crying. Eventually, Maria was given a sticker and praise each morning for sleeping in her own bed.

The first few times Mrs. Marshall left the classroom, Maria followed her out. Soon, however, she began to stay in her chair and receive stickers. At home, she remained in her own bed the first night, even though she was told she had to stay only 2 hours to earn her sticker. At her own request, she returned to Brownie meetings and attended summer camp.

Drugs used to treat childhood anxiety disorders include antidepressants; antianxiety drugs, such as the benzodiazepines; stimulants; and antihistamines. The selective serotonin reuptake inhibitors, such as fluoxetine, are used most frequently and have been shown to be most consistent in effectively reducing anxiety symptoms in children (Birmaher et al., 2003; Thienemann, 2004).

TEST YOURSELF

1. What are the diagnostic criteria for separation anxiety disorder?
2. What biological factors may play a role in separation anxiety disorder?
3. What psychosocial factors may play a role in separation anxiety disorder?
4. What are effective psychosocial and biological treatments for separation anxiety disorder?

APPLY IT Kirsten has been diagnosed with separation anxiety disorder. Which of the following is most likely to be true of her?

a. She also shows symptoms of conduct disorder.
b. She refuses to go to school.
c. She is thrill seeking and impulsive.
d. She has neglectful parents.

Answers appear online at www.mhhe.com/nolen5e.

ELIMINATION DISORDERS

Most children gain sufficient control over their bladder and bowel movements by about age 4 as to no longer need to wear diapers. They may view the ability to control their bladder and bowel movements as a sign of being "a big boy or girl." Understandably, children who lose this control, particularly past the preschool years and into middle childhood, can experience shame and distress. These children might be diagnosed with one of the two **elimination disorders:** enuresis or encopresis.

Enuresis

Occasional wetting of the bed at night is common among elementary school children, particularly during times of stress. Children over age 5 are diagnosed with **enuresis** when they have wet the bed or their clothes at least twice a week for 3 months. Most children with enuresis wet only at night. A subset of children with enuresis wet only during the daytime, most often at school. These children may be socially anxious about using the public toilets at school or prone to preoccupation with other activities. They do not use the toilet when they need to and have wetting accidents.

Bed-wetting is relatively common among young children, but the prevalence decreases with age. About 15 to 20 percent of 5-year-olds wet the bed at least once per month. By adolescence, the prevalence of bed-wetting decreases to 1 to 2 percent (Angold et al., 2002; Houts, 2003).

Enuresis runs in families, and approximately 75 percent of children with enuresis have biological relatives who had the disorder. Some of these children may have inherited an unusually small bladder or a lower bladder threshold for involuntary voiding. About 5 to 10 percent of children with enuresis have a urinary tract infection (Mellon & McGrath, 2000).

Enuresis can arise when a child experiences distress caused by disruptions or dysfunction in the family (Olmos de Paz, 1990). For example, some children develop enuresis when a new baby is born into the family, perhaps because they feel threatened by the attention their parents are giving to the new baby. Behaviorists suggest that enuresis may be due to lax or inappropriate toilet training—enuretic children never learned appropriate bladder control and thus have recurrent problems during childhood (Erickson, 1992).

Children with enuresis usually are taken to their pediatrician rather than a mental health specialist, and physicians overwhelmingly prescribe antidepressants to treat enuresis (Glazener, Evans, & Peto, 2003). Tricyclic antidepressants, particularly imipramine, are commonly used. About half of children treated with imipramine show reductions in wetting, but up to 95 percent relapse when the medication is discontinued (Glazener et al., 2003). In addition, the tricyclic antidepressants have dangerous side effects in children, including sleep disturbances, tiredness, gastrointestinal distress, and cardiac irregularities. Overdoses can be fatal.

The synthetic antidiuretic hormone desmopressin also is frequently prescribed for nighttime enuresis (Glazener et al., 2003). This drug concentrates urine, thus reducing urine output from the kidney to the bladder. It reliably reduces nighttime wetting, but, again, children typically relapse into wetting when the medication is discontinued.

A behavioral method referred to as the **bell and pad method** is a reliable, long-term solution (Glazener, Evans, & Peto, 2005). The child sleeps on a pad that has a sensory device to detect urine. If the child wets during her sleep, a bell rings and wakes her. Through classical conditioning, the child learns to wake up when she has a full bladder and needs to urinate. Reviews of dozens of studies of the bell and pad method and related methods conclude that they are highly effective, with over 70 percent of children completely cured of bed-wetting, often within 4 weeks (Glazener et al., 2005; Houts, 2003).

Encopresis

Encopresis involves repeated defecation into clothing or onto the floor and is rarer than enuresis. To be diagnosed, children must have at least one such event a month for at least 3 months and must be at least age 4 years. Fewer than 1 percent of children are diagnosed with encopresis, and it is more common in boys than in girls (Angold et al., 2002).

Encopresis usually begins after one or more episodes of severe constipation. Constipation may result from environmental factors, such as the withholding of bowel movements during toilet training or when at school, a genetic predisposition, food intolerance, or certain medications (Stark et al., 1997). Constipation can cause distention of the colon (decreasing the child's ability to detect the urge to have a bowel movement), fecal hardening and buildup in the colon, and subsequent leakage of fecal material. The child may make the problem worse by avoiding use of the toilet because of large or painful bowel movements, in turn becoming more insensitive to fecal matter in the colon and thus less able to know when it is time to use the toilet.

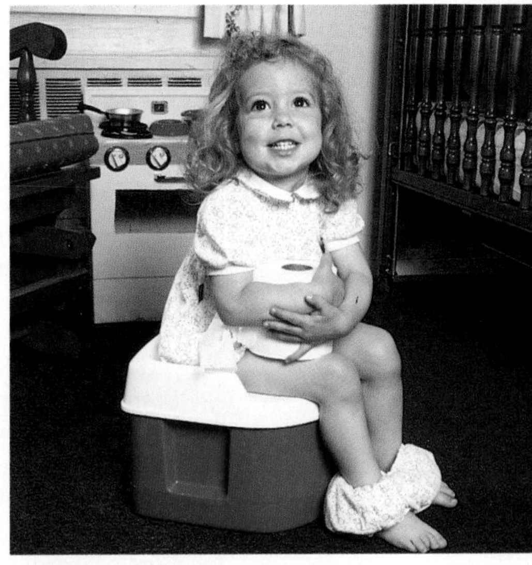

Children are very proud of themselves when they learn to control their bowel and bladder movements; thus, loss of control can be very distressing.

Encopresis typically is treated by a combination of medications to clear out the colon, laxatives or mineral oil to soften stools, recommendations to increase dietary fiber, and encouragement to the child to sit on the toilet a certain amount of time each day. This medical management strategy works for 60 to 80 percent of children with encopresis.

Kevin Stark and colleagues (1997) used a behavioral treatment program with a group of encopretic children who did not respond to medical management alone. In addition to medical management, the program included relaxation techniques and rewards for appropriate toilet use. Eighty-six percent of the children stopped soiling by the end of the intervention and did not require further treatment.

TEST YOURSELF

1. What is enuresis? What are some causes? What are the effective treatments for enuresis?
2. What is encopresis? What are some causes? How is it treated?

APPLY IT Billy has been diagnosed with enuresis. The most effective treatment for him would be which of the following?

a. antidepressants

b. antipsychotics

c. cognitive therapy

d. the bell and pad method

Answers appear online at www.mhhe.com/nolen5e.

DISORDERS OF COGNITIVE, MOTOR, AND COMMUNICATION SKILLS

From their first day home from the hospital with a new baby, parents eagerly track their child's development, watching for the emergence of cognitive, motor, and communication skills. Although most parents worry when it seems their children are not developing a skill "on time," their fears usually are allayed as their children's skills eventually emerge.

Sometimes important skills do not emerge or fully develop in a child. A child might not learn to crawl or walk until many months after most children do. Or a child might have severe trouble with reading or arithmetic despite having good teachers. Approximately 20 percent of children, more commonly boys, have significant impairment in important learning, motor, or communication skills (American Psychiatric Association, 2000). Such impairments can greatly affect a child's achievement in school and lower self-esteem and well-being. When deficits in fundamental skills are severe enough to interfere with a child's progress, the child may be diagnosed with a learning disorder, a motor skills disorder, or a communication disorder.

Learning Disorders

The *DSM-IV-TR* describes three specific *learning disorders*. They are diagnosed only when an individual's performance on standardized tests of these skills is significantly below that expected for his or her age, schooling, and overall level of intelligence as indicated by intelligence tests. **Reading disorder** involves deficits in the ability to read and usually is apparent by the fourth grade. It affects about 4 percent of children, more commonly boys (Katusic et al., 2001, 2005; Rutter et al., 2004). In the *DSM-5,* reading disorder is likely to be renamed *dyslexia*.

Mathematics disorder includes problems in understanding mathematical terms, recognizing numerical symbols, clustering objects into groups, counting, and understanding mathematical principles. Although many people feel that they are not great at math, deficits in math skills severe enough to warrant this diagnosis occur in only about 1 percent of children (Tannock, 2005). The disorder usually is apparent by about second or third grade. It probably will be renamed *dyscalculia* in the *DSM-5.*

Disorder of written expression involves deficits in the ability to write. Children with this rare disorder have severe trouble spelling, constructing a sentence or paragraph, or writing legibly. This diagnosis may be omitted from the *DSM-5* or be made part of the new diagnosis *learning disability*.

Children with learning disorders can become demoralized and be disruptive in class. If left untreated, they are at high risk for dropping out of school, with as many as 40 percent never finishing high school. As adults, they may have problems getting and keeping a good job. The emotional side effects of a learning disorder may also affect their social relationships (Fletcher, Lyon, Fuchs, & Barnes, 2007).

Motor Skills Disorder

The one *motor skills disorder,* **developmental coordination disorder,** involves deficits in fundamental motor skills, such as walking, running, or holding on to objects.

Communication Disorders

The *communication disorders* involve deficits in the ability to communicate verbally because of a limited vocabulary, stuttering, or an inability to articulate words correctly. Children with **expressive language disorder** have a limited vocabulary, difficulty in learning new words, difficulty in retrieving words, and poor grammar. They may use a limited variety of sentence types (e.g., only questions or declarations), omit critical parts of sentences, or use words in an unusual order. Some children with this disorder show signs of it from a very early age, whereas others develop language normally for a while before showing signs of the disorder. Between 3 and 7 percent of children may be affected by this disorder (Kartheiser, Ursano, & Barnhill, 2007). Some also have problems understanding the language produced by others. These children are said to have a **mixed receptive-expressive language disorder.**

Children with **phonological disorder** do not use speech sounds appropriate for their age or dialect. They may substitute one sound for another (e.g., use a *t* for a *k* sound) or omit certain sounds (such as final consonants on words). Their words come out sounding like baby talk. They may say *wabbit* for *rabbit,* or *bu* for *blue*. Approximately 2 to 3 percent of 6- to 7-year-olds have moderate to severe phonological disorder. The prevalence falls to 0.5 percent by age 17 (Kartheiser et al., 2007).

Children who suffer from **stuttering** have significant problems with speaking evenly and fluently, often voicing frequent repetitions of sounds or syllables (such as "I-I-I-I see him"). Some children also repeat whole words or short phrases, as in "Kids tease me about my, about my s-s-s-stutter."

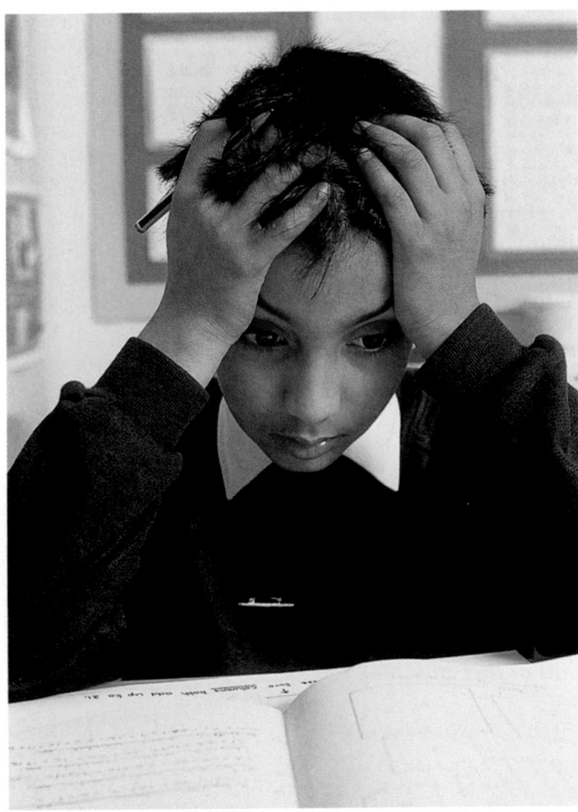

Learning disorders can lead to frustration and low self-esteem.

The severity of their speech problems varies situationally but usually is worse when they are under pressure to speak well, as when giving an oral report. Stuttering often begins gradually and almost always before age 10. Estimates of the prevalence of stuttering range from 0.3 percent to 5 percent, with roughly twice as many boys as girls diagnosed (Howell, 2007; McKinnon, McLeod, & Reilly, 2008; Proctor, Yairi, Duff, & Zhang, 2008). As many as 80 percent of children who stutter recover on their own by age 16 (Howell, 2007). Others, however, go on to stutter as adults. Stuttering can reduce a child's self-esteem and cause him or her to limit goals and activities.

Causes and Treatment of Disorders of Cognitive, Motor, and Communication Skills

Genetic factors are implicated in several of the learning disorders (Davis, Haworth, & Plomin, 2009; Wittke-Thompson et al., 2007). While there may not be specific genes responsible for specific disorders in most cases, certain genetic abnormalities may account for a number of different learning disorders (Davis et al., 2009).

Abnormalities in brain structure and functioning have long been thought to cause learning disorders. Studies of people with reading disorder have identified three areas of the brain involved in three separate but interrelated skills (Shaywitz & Shaywitz, 2008). An area of the inferior frontal gyrus called *Broca's area* is involved in the ability to articulate and analyze words. An area in the parietotemporal region is involved in the ability to map the visual perception of the printed word onto the basic structures of language. Another area, in the occipitotemporal region, is involved in the rapid, automatic, fluent identification of words (Shaywitz & Shaywitz, 2008). In individuals with *dyslexia,* a form of reading disorder in which the individual has difficulty with accurate and fluent word recognition, neuroimaging studies show unusually low activity in the parietotemporal and occipitotemporal regions (Shaywitz, 2003).

Environmental factors linked to the learning disorders include lead poisoning, birth defects, sensory deprivation, and low socioeconomic status (Fletcher et al., 2007). These conditions may create the risk of damage to critical brain areas. Children whose environments offer fewer opportunities to develop language skills are less likely to overcome biological contributors to learning problems (Shaywitz & Shaywitz, 2008).

The treatment of these disorders usually involves therapies designed to build missing skills (Fletcher et al., 2007). According to the Individuals with Disabilities Education Act, reauthorized by the U.S. Congress in 2004, these interventions are bundled in a child's comprehensive Individualized Education Plan (IEP). The IEP describes the child's specific skills deficits, based on formal tests and observations by parents and teachers. The plan also involves parents and teachers in strategies to help the child overcome these deficits. A child with dyslexia might receive systematic instruction in word recognition while in school, supplemented with practice at home, possibly using computerized exercises. Children with developmental coordination disorder might receive physical therapy, and children with communication disorders might receive speech therapy. Such programs appear to significantly improve skills in children with learning disorders (Gajria, Jitendra, Sood, & Sacks, 2007).

Studies suggest that specialized instruction to overcome skills deficits actually can change brain functioning. In one study, children with dyslexia received daily individual tutoring. Before, immediately after, and 1 year after the intervention, the children underwent neuroimaging. Children who received this intervention not only improved their

SHADES OF GRAY

Read the following description of Jake, a college student.

Jake had just earned a 2.4 GPA in his freshman year at the University of Washington when his parents took him to see a psychologist about his academic performance. At the meeting with the psychologist, his parents described their middle son as lazy, unmotivated, stubborn, and disorganized. His brothers were successful at school, as his parents had been. Growing up, Jake had seemed smart, but he often sabotaged his grades by forgetting to do his homework, quitting in the middle of assignments, and not finishing tests. When he completed a project, he would often leave it behind or lose it. He could be engrossed in TV or a video game, but when it came to his homework, he lacked focus. His parents also noted that he was constantly late and didn't seem to care about making everyone else wait for him.

When the psychologist spoke with Jake alone, Jake seemed like a nice, polite teenager. He felt discouraged and confused about school. He agreed that he didn't get the good grades his brothers did and knew his parents expected more of him. When he was younger he did well in school, and in elementary school he thought of himself as smart. But his grades had slipped when he transitioned into middle school, then again when he entered high school, and now again in college. He thought he understood what was going on in class but was always forgetting or losing things, or his mind would wander. Outside of the classroom, he had a small but supportive group of friends, and he was involved in a wide variety of sports and activities. He denied any involvement with drugs or illegal activity. (Adapted from Vitkus, 2004, pp. 193–199)

What might be causing Jake's problems? What additional information would you want before making a diagnosis? (Discussion appears at the end of this chapter.)

reading but also demonstrated increased activation in the parietotemporal and occipitotemporal systems (Shaywitz et al., 2004). Other researchers also have seen neural effects of specialized training overcome learning problems (Richards et al., 2000; Temple et al., 2003).

TEST YOURSELF

1. What are the individual learning disorders, and what skills deficits characterize each?
2. What is developmental coordination disorder?
3. What are the individual communication disorders, and what skills deficits characterize each?
4. What are some causes of the disorders in questions 1 to 3? What treatments are used for them?

APPLY IT Jeremy is receiving specialized training to overcome dyslexia. According to research, this training is likely to do which of the following?

a. have little long-term effect
b. result in changes in brain activity
c. improve emotional functioning but not cognitive functioning
d. stigmatize Jeremy

Answers appear online at www.mhhe.com/nolen5e.

MENTAL RETARDATION

Mental retardation involves deficits in a wide range of skills and is defined as significantly subaverage intellectual functioning. A child's level of intellectual functioning can be assessed by standardized tests, usually referred to as *IQ tests* (see Chapter 3). In addition to low test scores, a diagnosis of mental retardation requires that a child show deficits relative to his or her age group in at least two of the following skill areas: communication, self-care, home living, social or interpersonal skills, use of community resources (such as riding a bus), self-direction, academic skills, work, leisure, health, and personal safety (see the *DSM-IV-TR* criteria in Table 10.6). Mental retardation is listed on Axis II of the *DSM-IV-TR* because it is assumed to be lifelong.

The *DSM-IV-TR* divides mental retardation into four levels: mild, moderate, severe, and profound. Children with *mild mental retardation* can feed and dress themselves with minimal help, may or may not have average motor skills, and can learn to talk and write in simple terms. They can navigate their own neighborhoods well, although they may not be able to venture farther without help. If they receive training that addresses their specific deficits, they can achieve a high school education and become self-sufficient. As adults, they can shop for specific items and cook simple meals for themselves. They may be employed in

TABLE 10.6 *DSM-IV-TR* Criteria for Mental Retardation

The diagnosis of mental retardation requires that a child show both poor intellectual functioning and significant deficits in everyday skills.

A. Significantly subaverage intellectual functioning, indicated by an IQ of approximately 70 or below.

B. Significant deficits relative to others of the same age in at least two of the following areas:
   1. Communication
   2. Self-care
   3. Home living
   4. Social or interpersonal skills
   5. Use of community resources
   6. Self-direction
   7. Academic skills
   8. Work
   9. Leisure
   10. Health
   11. Personal safety

C. Onset before age 18.

Source: Reprinted with permission from the *Diagnostic and Statistical Manual of Mental Disorders,* Fourth Edition, Text Revision. Copyright © 2000 American Psychiatric Association.

unskilled or semiskilled jobs. Their scores on IQ tests tend to be between about 50 and 70.

Children with *moderate mental retardation* typically have significant delays in language development, such as using only 4 to 10 words by age 3. They may be physically clumsy and have some trouble dressing and feeding themselves. They typically do not achieve beyond the second-grade level in academic skills but, with special education, can acquire simple vocational skills. As adults, they may not be able to travel alone or to shop or cook for themselves. Their scores on IQ tests tend to be between about 35 and 50.

Children with *severe mental retardation* have very limited vocabularies and speak in two- or three-word sentences. They may have significant deficits in motor development and may play with toys inappropriately (e.g., banging two dolls together). As adults, they can feed themselves with a spoon and dress themselves if the clothing is not complicated, with many buttons or zippers. They cannot travel alone for any distance and cannot shop or cook for themselves. Some may be able to learn some unskilled manual labor, but many are not. Their IQ scores tend to be between 20 and 35.

Children and adults with *profound mental retardation* require full-time custodial care. They cannot dress themselves completely. They may be able to use a spoon. Although they may respond to simple commands, they tend to not interact with others socially. They may achieve vocabularies of 300 to 400 words as adults. Many persons with profound mental retardation suffer from frequent illnesses, and their life expectancy is shorter than normal. Their IQ scores tend to be under 20.

In the *DSM-5,* mental retardation will be renamed *intellectual disability*, in line with international usage. The new criteria will move the diagnosis away from a reference to IQ scores and instead describe intellectual deficits in terms of what is expected for the person's age and cultural group. The criteria will also highlight the importance of adaptive functioning, such as social, practical, and thinking skills, specifying that the person must show deficits in at least two of these areas beginning in childhood or adolescence (American Psychiatric Association, 2010).

Biological Causes of Mental Retardation

Many biological factors can cause mental retardation, including chromosomal and gestational disorders, exposure to toxins prenatally and in early childhood, infections, physical trauma, metabolism and nutrition problems, and gross brain disease. We examine these factors first and then turn to sociocultural factors.

Genetic Factors

Intellectual skills are at least partially inherited. The IQs of adopted children correlate much more strongly with those of their biological parents than with those of their adoptive parents. Similarly, the IQs of monozygotic twins are much more strongly correlated than are the IQs of dizygotic twins, even when the twins are reared apart (Davis et al., 2009; Scarr, Weinberg, & Waldman, 1993). Families of children with mental retardation tend to have high incidences of a variety of intellectual problems, including the different levels of mental retardation and autism (Camp, Broman, Nichols, & Leff, 1998).

Two metabolic disorders that are genetically transmitted and cause mental retardation are *phenylketonuria (PKU)* and *Tay-Sachs disease.* PKU is carried by a recessive gene and occurs in about 1 in 20,000 births. Children with PKU are unable to metabolize phenylalanine, an amino acid. As a result, phenylalanine and its derivative, phenyl pyruvic acid, build up in the body and cause brain damage. Fortunately, children who receive a special diet free from phenylalanine from an early age can develop an average level of intelligence. Most states mandate testing for PKU in newborns. If left untreated, children with PKU typically have IQs below 50.

Tay-Sachs disease also is carried by a recessive gene and occurs primarily in Jewish populations. When an affected child is between 3 and 6 months old, a progressive degeneration of the nervous system begins, leading to mental and physical deterioration. These children usually die before age 6, and there is no effective treatment.

Several types of chromosomal disorders can lead to mental retardation (Williams, 2010). Children are born with 23 pairs of chromosomes. Twenty-two of these pairs are known as *autosomes,* and the twenty-third pair contains the *sex chromosomes*. One of the best-known causes of mental retardation is *Down syndrome,* which occurs when chromosome 21 is present in triplicate rather than in duplicate. (For this reason, Down syndrome is also referred to as *trisomy 21.*) Down syndrome occurs in about 1 in every 800 children born in the United States.

Advocates of mainstreaming argue that individuals with intellectual disabilities should be integrated into everyday life.

From childhood, almost all people with Down syndrome have mental retardation, although the level varies from mild to profound. Their ability to care for themselves, live somewhat independently, and hold a job depends on their level of retardation and the training and support they receive. Children with Down syndrome have a round, flat face and almond-shaped eyes; a small nose; slightly protruding lip and tongue; and short, square hands. They tend to be short in stature and somewhat obese. Many have congenital heart defects and gastrointestinal difficulties. As adults, they seem to age more rapidly than normal, and their life expectancy is shorter than average. People with Down syndrome have abnormalities in the neurons in their brains that resemble those found in Alzheimer's disease. Nearly all individuals with Down syndrome past age 40 develop the thinking and memory deficits of Alzheimer's dementia (see Chapter 11) and lose the ability to care for themselves (Visser et al., 1997).

Fragile X syndrome, another common cause of mental retardation, is caused when a tip of the X chromosome breaks off (Bear, Dolen, Osterweil, & Nagarajan, 2008). This syndrome affects primarily males because they do not have a second, normal X chromosome to balance the mutation. The syndrome is characterized by severe to profound mental retardation, speech defects, and severe deficits in interpersonal interaction. Males with fragile X syndrome have large ears, a long face, and enlarged testes. Females with the syndrome tend to have less severe mental retardation (Koukoui & Chaudhuri, 2007). Two other chromosomal abnormalities that cause severe mental retardation and shortened life expectancy are *trisomy 13* (chromosome 13 is present in triplicate) and *trisomy 18* (chromosome 18 is present in triplicate).

The risk of having a child with Down syndrome or any other chromosomal abnormality increases with the age of the parents. This may be because the older a parent is, the more likely chromosomes are to have degenerated or to have been damaged by toxins.

Brain Damage During Gestation and Early Life

The intellectual development of a fetus can be profoundly affected by its prenatal environment (King, Hodapp, & Dykens, 2005). When a pregnant woman contracts the rubella (German measles) virus, herpesvirus, or syphilis, there is a risk of damage to the fetus that can cause mental retardation. Chronic maternal disorders, such as high blood pressure and diabetes, can interfere with fetal nutrition and brain development and therefore can affect the intellectual capacities of the fetus. If these disorders are treated effectively throughout the pregnancy, the risk of damage to the fetus is low.

Children whose mothers abuse alcohol during pregnancy are at increased risk for **fetal alcohol syndrome (FAS).** Children with fetal alcohol syndrome have an average IQ of 68, along with poor judgment, distractibility, and difficulty perceiving social cues. As adolescents, their academic functioning is at only the second- to fourth-grade level, and they have trouble following directions. It is estimated that from 2 to 15 children per 10,000 in the United States have fetal alcohol syndrome, and three times that number are born with lesser alcohol-related neurological and birth defects (CDC, 2008b). Abel Dorris, in the following case study, was born with fetal alcohol syndrome.

CASE STUDY Abel Dorris was adopted when he was 3 years old by Michael Dorris. Abel's mother had been a heavy drinker throughout the pregnancy and after Abel was born. She had subsequently died at age 35 of alcohol poisoning. Abel had been born almost 7 weeks premature, with low birth weight. He had been abused and malnourished before being removed to a foster home. At age 3, Abel was small for his age, was not yet toilet-trained, and could only speak about 20 words. He had been diagnosed as mildly retarded. His adoptive father hoped that, in a positive environment, Abel could catch up.

Yet, at age 4, Abel was still in diapers and weighed only 27 pounds. He had trouble remembering the names of other children and his activity level was unusually high. When alone, he would rock back and forth rhythmically. At age 4, he suffered the first of several severe seizures, which caused him to lose consciousness for days. No drug treatments seemed to help.

When he entered school, Abel had trouble learning to count, to identify colors, and to tie his shoes. He had a short attention span and difficulty following simple instructions. Despite devoted teachers, when he finished elementary school, Abel still could not add, subtract, or identify his place of residence. His IQ was measured in the mid-60s.

Eventually, at age 20, Abel entered a vocational training program and moved into a supervised home. His main preoccupations were his collections of stuffed animals, paper dolls, newspaper cartoons, family photographs, and old birthday cards. At age 23, he was hit by a car and killed. (Adapted from Dorris, 1989; Lyman, 1997)

Studies of the effects of moderate maternal drinking on reproductive outcomes such as birth weight, gestational age, rate of miscarriage or stillbirth, congenital abnormalities, and social and cognitive development suggest that even low to moderate levels of drinking during pregnancy are associated with subtle birth defects (Jacobson & Jacobson, 2000; Kelly, Day, & Streissguth, 2000; Olson et al., 1998). For example, longitudinal studies of children exposed prenatally to alcohol show negative effects on growth at age 6 and on learning and memory skills at age 10, even if the children do not evidence the full syndrome of FAS (Cornelius, Goldschmidt, Day, & Larkby, 2002).

Severe head traumas that damage children's brains also can lead to mental retardation. *Shaken baby syndrome* is caused when a baby is shaken, leading to intracranial injury and retinal hemorrhage (Caffey, 1972). Babies' heads are relatively large and heavy compared to the rest of their body, and their neck muscles are too weak to control their head when they are shaken. The rapid movement of their head when shaken can lead to their brain's being banged against the skull wall and bruised. Bleeding in and around the brain or behind the eyes can lead to seizures, partial or total blindness, paralysis, mental retardation, or death. Although the shaking of a baby may be part of a pattern of chronic abuse, shaken baby syndrome can occur when an otherwise nonabusive parent becomes frustrated and shakes the baby only once.

Young children face a number of other hazards that can cause brain damage. Exposure to toxic substances—such as lead, arsenic, and mercury—during early childhood can lead to mental retardation by damaging areas of the brain. Children also can incur brain damage leading to mental retardation through accidents, including traffic accidents in cars in which they are not properly buckled.

Sociocultural Factors

Children with mental retardation are more likely to come from low socioeconomic backgrounds (Brooks-Gunn, Klebanov, & Duncan, 1996; Camp et al., 1998). This may be because their parents also have mental retardation and have not been able to acquire well-paying jobs. The social disadvantages of being poor also may contribute to lower than average intellectual development. Poor mothers are less likely to receive good prenatal care, increasing the risk of premature birth. Children living in lower socioeconomic areas are at increased risk for exposure to lead, because many older buildings have lead paint, which chips off and can be ingested. Poor children are concentrated in poorly funded schools, where those with lower IQs receive less favorable attention from teachers and fewer learning opportunities, especially if they are also members of minorities (Alexander, Entwisle, & Thompson, 1987). Poor children also are less likely to have parents who read to them and are involved in their schooling. These factors may directly affect a child's intellectual development and exacerbate the biological conditions that impede a child's cognitive development (Camp et al., 1998; Zigler, Gilliam, & Jones, 2006).

Treatments for Mental Retardation

Interventions for mentally retarded children must be comprehensive, intensive, and long-term to show benefits (Zigler et al., 2006; Zigler & Styfco, 2004, 2008).

Behavioral Strategies

A child's parents or caregivers and teachers work together to enhance the child's positive behaviors and reduce negative behaviors. Behavioral strategies help children and adults learn new skills, from identifying colors correctly to using vocational skills. Social and communication skills also may be taught. Individuals may learn to initiate conversations by asking questions and to articulate what they want to say more clearly. The desired behavior may be modeled in incremental steps and rewards given to the individual as he or she comes closer to mastering the skill. Behavioral strategies also can help reduce self-injurious and other maladaptive behaviors. Typically, behavioral methods do not simply focus on isolated skills but rather are integrated into a comprehensive program designed to maximize the individual's ability to function in the community (Feldman, 2004).

Drug Therapy

Medications are used to reduce seizures, which are common among people with mental retardation; to control aggressive or self-injurious behavior; and to improve mood (Singh, Oswald, & Ellis, 1998). Neuroleptic medications (see Chapter 8) can reduce aggressive, destructive, and antisocial behavior; however, the potential for neurological side effects has made these medications controversial. The atypical antipsychotics, such as risperidone, have been shown to reduce aggression and self-injurious behavior in adults with mental retardation without having serious neurological side effects (Cohen, Ohrig, Lott, & Kerrick, 1998). Antidepressant medications can reduce depressive symptoms, improve sleep patterns, and help control self-injurious behavior in individuals with mental retardation (Singh et al., 1998).

Social Programs

Social programs have focused on integration of the child into the mainstream of other children where possible, on group homes that provide comprehensive care, and on institutionalization when necessary. The earlier these interventions begin, the greater the chance that the child will develop to his or her full potential.

Early Intervention Programs Many experts recommend beginning comprehensive interventions with children at risk for mental retardation from the first days of life. These measures include intensive one-on-one interventions to enhance their development of basic skills; efforts to reduce the social conditions that might interfere with the children's development, such as child abuse, malnutrition, or exposure to toxins; and adequate medical care (Zigler & Styfco, 2004).

One such program was the Infant Health and Development Program (Gross, Brooks-Gunn, & Spiker, 1992), which focused on children with a birth weight of 2,500 grams (5½ pounds) or less and a gestational age of 37 completed weeks or less. This program had three components. First, specially trained counselors visited each child's home during the first 3 years of the child's life, providing support to the mother and fostering parent-child activities that would enhance the child's development. The mothers were given training in good parenting practices and in ways to facilitate their children's cognitive development. For example, they were taught ways to calm their babies (who tended to be irritable), provide appropriate levels of stimulation as well as opportunities for exploration, and reduce stress in the family's environment. Second, the children went daily to a child development center with specially trained teachers, who worked to overcome the children's intellectual and physical deficits. Third, parent support groups were started to help the parents cope with the stresses of parenting.

At 36 months of age, the children in the intervention group were significantly less likely to have IQ scores in the low range than were those in the control group, who received only medical care (Infant Health and Development Program, 1990). The children who received the program intervention also showed fewer behavioral and emotional problems at age 36 months than did the children in the control group.

What accounted for the positive effects of the intervention? Several factors were noted. The home environments of the children in the intervention group improved significantly (Berlin, Brooks-Gunn, McCartoon, & McCormick, 1998; McCormick et al., 1998). More learning materials were available, and their mothers more actively stimulated the children's learning. The mothers of the children in the intervention program were better at assisting their children in problem solving, remaining more responsive and persistent with their children. In turn, these children showed more enthusiasm and involvement in learning tasks. In addition, the mothers in the intervention program reported better mental health than the mothers in the control group and also were less likely to use harsh disciplinary strategies with their children. All these factors were associated with better outcomes for the children in the intervention group.

Mainstreaming Controversy exists over whether children with mental retardation should be placed in special education classes or instead be *mainstreamed*—that is, put into regular classrooms. On one hand, special education classes can provide children with extra training in skills they lack. On the other hand, some critics argue that these classes stigmatize children and provide them with an education that asks less of them than they are capable of achieving.

Placing children with mental retardation in a classroom with children of average intelligence can put them at certain disadvantages. One study found that children with mental retardation were viewed negatively by the other children in their classrooms (Zigler & Hodapp, 1991). Also, children with mental retardation who are mainstreamed may not receive the special training they need. Studies of the academic progress of children with mental retardation in special education programs and in regular classrooms, however, tend to find little difference in the performance of these two groups. Many children today spend some time in special education, where they receive intensive training to overcome skills deficits, and some time in regular classrooms over the course of the week.

Group Homes Many adults with mental retardation live in group homes, where they receive assistance in the tasks of daily living (e.g., cooking, cleaning) and training in vocational and social skills. They may work in sheltered workshops during the day, performing unskilled or semiskilled labor. Increasingly, they are being mainstreamed into the general workforce, often in service-related jobs (e.g., in fast-food restaurants or as baggers in grocery stores). Some community-based programs for adults with mental retardation have been shown to be effective in enhancing their social and vocational skills (Chilvers, Macdonald, & Hayes, 2006).

Institutionalization In the past, most children with mental retardation were institutionalized for life. Institutionalization is less common these days, even for children with severe mental retardation. African American and Latino families are less likely than European American families to institutionalize their children with mental retardation (Blacher, Hanneman, & Rousey, 1992). This may be because African American and Latino families are less likely than European American families to have the financial resources to place their children in high-quality institutions, or it may be because African American and Latino cultures place a stronger emphasis on caring for ill or disabled family members within the family.

TEST YOURSELF

1. How is mental retardation defined?
2. What biological factors are implicated in mental retardation?
3. What types of intervention can improve the functioning of people with mental retardation?

APPLY IT Matthew's mother drank alcohol while she was pregnant with Matthew. What are Matthew's chances of showing effects from this exposure?

a. Matthew will show cognitive deficits only if he was exposed to a great deal of alcohol.
b. Matthew will show severe cognitive deficits if he was exposed to low to moderate amounts of alcohol.
c. Matthew may show subtle cognitive deficits if he was exposed to low to moderate amounts of alcohol.
d. Matthew will show no cognitive deficits regardless of how much alcohol he was exposed to.

Answers appear online at www.mhhe.com/nolen5e.

PERVASIVE DEVELOPMENTAL DISORDERS

The **pervasive developmental disorders** involve severe and lasting impairment in several areas of development, including social interactions, communication with others, and everyday behaviors, interests, and activities. The most thoroughly researched pervasive developmental disorder is **autism,** a disorder in which children show deficits in all these areas (see the *DSM-IV-TR* criteria in Table 10.7). Many children with autism also show at least a mild level of mental retardation, although this was not true of Temple Grandin, whose life with autism is described in the chapter opener. Richard, a child with autism, shows a range of deficits characteristic of this disorder.

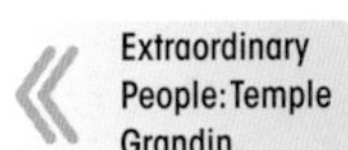
Extraordinary People: Temple Grandin

CASE STUDY

Richard, age 3½, appeared to be self-sufficient and aloof from others. He did not greet his mother in the mornings or his father when he returned from work, though if left with a baby-sitter, he tended to scream much of the time. He had no interest in other children and ignored his younger brother. His babbling had no con-

(continued)

versational intonation. At age 3 he could understand simple practical instructions. His speech consisted of echoing some words and phrases he had heard in the past, with the original speaker's accent and intonation; he could use one or two such phrases to indicate his simple needs. For example, if he said, "Do you want a drink?" he meant he was thirsty. He did not communicate by facial expression or use gesture or mime, except for pulling someone along with him and placing his or her hand on an object he wanted. He was fascinated by bright lights and spinning objects and would stare at them while laughing, flapping his hands, and dancing on tiptoe. He was intensely attached to a miniature car, which he held in his hand, day and night, but he never played imaginatively with this or any other toy. From age 2 he had collected kitchen utensils and arranged them in repetitive patterns all over the floors of the house. These pursuits, together with occasional periods of aimless running around, constituted his whole repertoire of spontaneous activities.

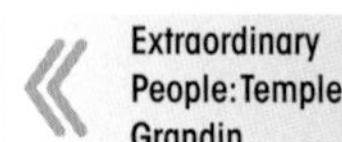
Extraordinary People: Temple Grandin

The major management problem was Richard's intense resistance to any attempt to change or extend his interests. Removing his toy car, even retrieving, for example, an egg whisk or a spoon for its legitimate use in cooking, or trying to make him look at a picture book precipitated temper tantrums that could last an hour or more, with screaming, kicking, and the biting of himself or others. These tantrums could be cut short by restoring the status quo.

His parents had wondered if Richard might be deaf, but his love of music, his accurate echoing, and his sensitivity to some very soft sounds, such as those made by unwrapping chocolate in the next room, convinced them that this was not the cause of his abnormal behavior. Psychological testing gave Richard a mental age of 3 years in non-language-dependent skills (such as assembling objects) but only 18 months in language comprehension. (Reprinted from the *DSM-IV-TR Casebook: A Learning Companion to the Diagnostic and Statistical Manual of Mental Disorders*, Fourth Edition, Text Revision. Copyright © 2000 American Psychiatric Association.)

Diagnosis of Autism

Autism involves three types of deficits. The first type is deficits in *social interaction*, such as a lack of interaction with family members. As infants, children with autism may not smile and coo in response to their caregivers or initiate play with their caregivers, the way most young infants do. They may not want to cuddle with their parents, even when they are frightened. Whereas most infants love to gaze on their caregivers as the caregivers gaze adoringly at them, infants with autism may hardly ever make eye contact. When they are a bit older, children with autism may not be interested in playing with other children, preferring to remain in solitary play. They also do not seem to react to other people's emotions. In the chapter opener, Temple Grandin describes how she had to work hard to overcome her lack of understanding of social interactions.

Formerly, it was thought that children with autism were preoccupied with internal thoughts and fantasies, much as people with schizophrenia might be preoccupied with hallucinations and delusions. Indeed, childhood autism once was considered a precursor to adult schizophrenia (Volkmar, State, & Klin, 2009). However, these children do not develop the classic symptoms of schizophrenia (e.g., hallucinations and delusions) as adults, and adults with schizophrenia do not have a history of autism. In addition, autism and schizophrenia do not co-occur at a high rate in families, suggesting that the disorders have different genetic causes.

The second type of deficits in autism involves *communication*. Approximately 50 percent of children with autism do not develop useful speech. Those who do develop language may not use it as other children do. In the previous case study, Richard showed several of the communication problems of children with autism. Rather than generating his own words, he simply echoed what he had just heard, a phenomenon called *echolalia*. He reversed pronouns, using *you* when he meant *I*. When he did try to generate his own words or sentences, he did not modulate his voice for expressiveness, instead sounding almost like a voice-generating machine.

The third type of deficits concerns the *activities and interests* of children with autism. Rather than engaging in symbolic play with toys, they are preoccupied with one part of a toy or an object, as Richard was preoccupied with his miniature car or as Temple Grandin was interested only in watching sand dribble through her fingers. They may engage in bizarre, repetitive behaviors with toys. Rather than using two dolls to play "dollies have tea," a child with autism might take the arm off one doll and simply pass it back and forth between her two hands. Routines and rituals often are extremely important to children with autism. When any aspect of the daily routine is changed—for example, if their mother stops at the bank on the way

TABLE 10.7 *DSM-IV-TR* Criteria for Autism

I. A total of six (or more) items from A, B, and C, with at least two from A and one each from B and C.

A. Qualitative impairment in social interaction, as manifested by at least two of the following:

1. Marked impairment in the use of multiple nonverbal behaviors such as eye-to-eye gaze, facial expression, body posture, and gestures to regulate social interaction
2. Failure to develop peer relationships appropriate to developmental level
3. A lack of spontaneous seeking to share enjoyment, interests, or achievements with other people
4. Lack of social or emotional reciprocity

B. Qualitative impairments in communication as manifested by at least one of the following:

1. Delay in, or total lack of, the development of spoken language (not accompanied by an attempt to compensate through alternative modes of communication such as gesture or mime)
2. In individuals with adequate speech, marked impairment in the ability to initiate or sustain a conversation with others
3. Stereotyped and repetitive use of language or idiosyncratic language
4. Lack of varied, spontaneous make-believe play or social imitative play appropriate to developmental level

C. Restricted repetitive and stereotyped patterns of behavior, interests, and activities, as manifested by at least two of the following:

1. Encompassing preoccupation with one or more stereotyped and restricted patterns of interest that is abnormal either in intensity or focus
2. Apparently inflexible adherence to specific, nonfunctional routines or rituals
3. Stereotyped and repetitive motor mannerisms (e.g., hand or finger flapping or twisting, or complex whole-body movements)
4. Persistent preoccupation with parts of objects

II. Delays or abnormal functioning in at least one of the following areas, with onset prior to age 3 years: (A) social interaction, (B) language as used in social communication, (C) symbolic or imaginative play.

Source: Reprinted with permission from the *Diagnostic and Statistical Manual of Mental Disorders,* Fourth Edition, Text Revision.

to school—they may fly into a rage. Some children perform stereotyped and repetitive behaviors using some parts of their body, such as incessantly flapping their hands or banging their head against a wall. These behaviors sometimes are referred to as *self-stimulatory behaviors,* under the assumption that these children engage in such behaviors for self-stimulation. It is not clear, however, that this is their true purpose.

Children with autism often do poorly on measures of intellectual ability, such as IQ tests, with 50 to 70 percent of children showing moderate to severe intellectual impairments (Sigman, Spence, & Wang, 2006). The deficits of some children with autism, however, are confined to skills that require language and understanding others' points of view, and they may score in the average range on subtests that do not require language skills. Temple Grandin is clearly of above-average intelligence despite her autism. Much has been made in the popular press about the special talents of some children with autism, such as the ability to play music without having been taught or to draw extremely well, or exceptional memory and mathematical calculation abilities as depicted in the movie *Rain Man*. These persons sometimes are referred to as *savants*. Such cases are quite rare, however (Bölte & Poustka, 2004).

By definition, the symptoms of autism have their onset before age 3. However, children with autism are not simply delayed in their development of important skills. When they do develop language or social interaction patterns, there is a striking deviance in the nature of these. It is important to note that there is a wide variation in the severity and outcome of this disorder. One study

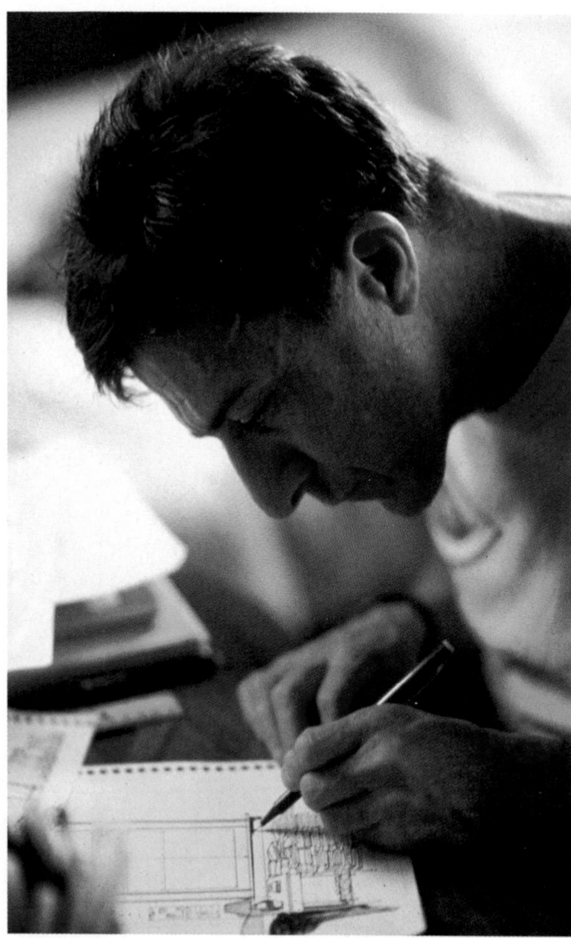

In *Rain Man,* Dustin Hoffman played a man with autism who had some extraordinary abilities.

followed 68 individuals who had been diagnosed with autism as children and who had a performance IQ of at least 50 (Howlin, Goode, Hutton, and Rutter, 2004). As adults, 13 of them had been able to obtain some sort of academic degree, 5 had gone on to college, and 2 had obtained a postgraduate degree. Of the 68, 23 were employed, and 18 had close friendships. The majority, however, remained very dependent on their parents or required some form of residential care. Fifty-eight percent, 39 individuals, had overall outcomes that were rated "poor" or "very poor." They were unable to live alone or hold a job, and had persistent problems in communication and social interactions.

By far the best predictor of the outcome of autism is a child's IQ and the amount of language development before age 6 (Howlin et al., 2004; Nordin & Gillberg, 1998). Children who have IQs above 50 and communicative speech before age 6 have a much better prognosis than do others. In the study by Howlin and colleagues (2004), people with an IQ of 70 or above were especially likely to achieve a "good" or "very good" outcome.

The prevalence of autism has been rising in recent years, probably because of increased attention to and recognition of the disorder (Tager-Flusberg, Joseph, & Folstein, 2001). A review of epidemiological studies estimated the prevalence of autism to be about 1 in 500 children, and the prevalence of all forms of pervasive developmental disorder to be 1 in 160 children (Fombonne, 2009). Boys outnumber girls about four to one. The prevalence of autism does not appear to vary by national origin, race/ethnicity, socioeconomic status, or parental education.

Asperger's Disorder and Other Pervasive Developmental Disorders

Other pervasive developmental disorders recognized in the *DSM-IV-TR* include Asperger's disorder, Rett's disorder, and childhood disintegrative disorder (Tables 10.8 and 10.9).

Asperger's disorder is characterized by deficits in social interactions and in activities and interests that are similar to those in autism (see Table 10.8). It differs from autism in that there are no significant delays or deviance in language and, in the first 3 years of life, children show normal levels of curiosity about the environment and acquire most normal cognitive skills. The children usually have average IQ scores.

Children with Asperger's disorder tend to have difficulty in social relationships. They can be obsessed with arcane facts and issues (such as memorizing zip codes), or they can be formal in their speech—the disorder has been referred to as the *little professor syndrome.*

The prevalence of Asperger's disorder is not clear, and many individuals with the disorder are able to function well enough in life that they go undiagnosed. Current estimates suggest that the prevalence is between 1 and 36 people per 10,000 (Volkmar et al., 2004).

In both **Rett's disorder** and **childhood disintegrative disorder,** children seem to develop normally and then show apparently permanent loss of basic skills in social interactions, language, and/or movement.

The distinctions between the pervasive developmental disorders, particularly between autism and Asperger's disorder, have been controversial (Volkmar et al., 2009). These disorders co-occur in families, and there is no clear evidence that they have different causes. Rett's childhood disintegrative disorder and disorder are very rare, and the validity of these diagnoses has been questioned (Fombonne, 2009).

TABLE 10.8 *DSM-IV-TR* Criteria for Asperger's Disorder

A. Qualitative impairment in social interaction, as manifested by at least two of the following:
   1. Marked impairment in the use of multiple nonverbal behaviors such as eye-to-eye gaze, facial expression, body postures, and gestures to regulate social interaction
   2. Failure to develop peer relationships appropriate to developmental level
   3. A lack of spontaneous seeking to share enjoyment, interests, or achievements with other people (e.g., by a lack of showing, bringing, or pointing out objects of interest to other people)
   4. Lack of social or emotional reciprocity

B. Restricted repetitive and stereotyped patterns of behavior, interests, and activities, as manifested by at least one of the following:
   1. Encompassing preoccupation with one or more stereotyped and restricted patterns of interest that is abnormal either in intensity or focus
   2. Apparently inflexible adherence to specific, nonfunctional routines or rituals
   3. Stereotyped and repetitive motor mannerisms (e.g., hand or finger flapping or twisting, or complex whole-body movements)
   4. Persistent preoccupation with parts of objects

C. The disturbance causes clinically significant impairment in social, occupational, or other important areas of functioning.

D. There is no clinically significant general delay in language (e.g., single words used by age 2 years, communicative phrases used by age 3 years).

E. There is no clinically significant delay in cognitive development or in the development of age-appropriate self-help skills, adaptive behavior (other than in social interaction), and curiosity about the environment in childhood.

F. Criteria are not met for another specific pervasive developmental disorder or schizophrenia.

Source: Reprinted with permission from the *Diagnostic and Statistical Manual of Mental Disorders,* Fourth Edition, Text Revision.

TABLE 10.9 Other Pervasive Developmental Disorders

The *DSM-IV-TR* recognizes two pervasive developmental disorders in addition to autism and Asperger's disorder.

Disorder	Description
Rett's disorder	Apparently normal development through the first 5 months of life and normal head circumference at birth, but then deceleration of head growth between 5 and 48 months, loss of motor and social skills already learned, and poor development of motor skills and language
Childhood disintegrative disorder	Apparently normal development for the first 2 years, followed by significant loss by age 10 in at least two of the following: expressive or receptive language, social skills or adaptive behavior, bowel or bladder control, play, motor skills; also, abnormalities of functioning in at least two of the following areas: social interaction, communication, or restricted, repetitive, and stereotyped patterns of behavior, interests, and activities

Source: Reprinted with permission from the *Diagnostic and Statistical Manual of Mental Disorders,* Fourth Edition, Text Revision.

In the *DSM-5,* all the pervasive developmental disorders are likely to be subsumed under the new category *autism spectrum disorder,* in light of evidence that they fall along a continuum of severity but are not clearly distinct from one another (Volkmar et al., 2009). The diagnosis of autism spectrum disorder will require that children show evidence of shortfalls in social communication and interactions, and restricted and recurring behaviors, such as those in the *DSM-IV-TR* criteria for autism and Asperger's disorder (American Psychiatric Association, 2010). The symptoms must be present in early childhood, but no age by which they must be present is specified. The old distinctions between autism and other pervasive developmental disorders likely will be indicated by a rating scale for severity.

Contributors to Autism

Over the years, a wide variety of theories of autism have been proposed. The psychiatrist who first described autism, Leo Kanner (1943), thought that autism was caused by a combination of biological factors and poor parenting. He and later psychoanalytic theorists (Bettelheim, 1967) described the parents of children with autism as cold, distant, and uncaring. The child's symptoms were seen as a retreat inward to a secret world of fantasies in response to unavailable parents. However, research over the decades has shown clearly that unresponsive parenting plays little or no role in the development of autism.

Several biological factors have been implicated in the development of autism. Family and twin studies strongly suggest that genetics plays a role in the development of the disorder. The siblings of children with autism are 50 times more likely to have the disorder than are the siblings of children without autism (Sigman et al., 2006). Twin studies show concordance rates for autism to be about 60 percent for monozygotic twins and 0 to 10 percent for dizygotic twins (Folstein & Rosen-Sheidley, 2001). In addition, about 90 percent of the MZ twins of children with autism have a significant cognitive impairment, compared to 10 percent of DZ twins. Also, children with autism have a higher than average rate of other genetic disorders associated with cognitive impairment, including fragile X syndrome and PKU (Volkmar et al., 2009). These data suggest that a general vulnerability to several types of cognitive impairment, only one of which is manifested as autism, runs in families. No single gene seems to cause autism; rather, abnormalities in several genes have been associated with autism and with the pervasive developmental disorders as a group (Liu, Paterson, Szatmari, and the Autism Genome Project Consortium, 2008; Sigman et al., 2006).

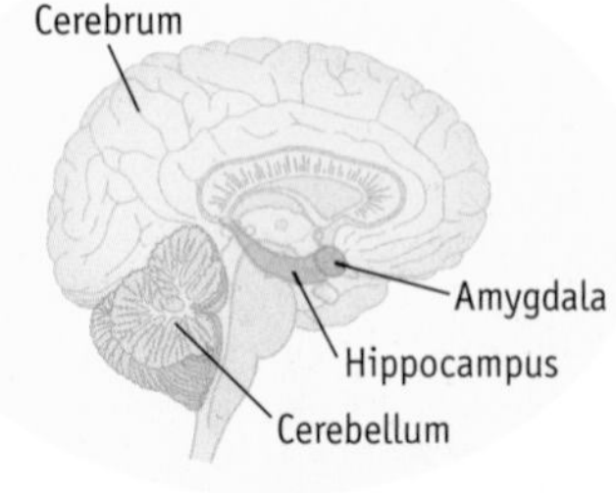

These areas of the brain have been implicated in autism.

Neurological factors probably play a role in autism. The array of deficits seen in autism suggests disruption in the normal development and organization of the brain (Sigman et al., 2006). In addition, approximately 30 percent of children with autism develop seizure disorders by adolescence, suggesting a severe neurological dysfunction (Fombonne, 1999).

Neuroimaging studies have suggested a variety of structural and functional deficits in the brains of individuals with autism, including in the cerebellum, the cerebrum, the amygdala, and possibly the hippocampus (Sigman et al., 2006). A consistent finding is greater head and brain size in children with the disorder than in children without it (Lotspeich et al., 2004).

When children with autism and other pervasive developmental disorders are doing tasks that require perception of facial expressions, joint attention with another person, empathy, or thinking about social situations, they show abnormal functioning in areas of the brain that are recruited for such tasks. For example, when shown photos of faces, children with a pervasive developmental disorder show less activation than do typical children in an area of the brain involved in facial perception called the fusiform gyrus (Figure 10.2; Schultz, 2005). Difficulty in perceiving and understanding facial expressions could contribute to these children's deficits in social interactions.

Children with pervasive developmental disorders perform more poorly than other children on tasks requiring *theory of mind*—the ability to understand that people, including oneself, have mental states and to use this understanding to interact and communicate with others (Baron-Cohen & Swettenham, 1997). Having a theory of mind is essential to comprehending, explaining, predicting, and manipulating the behavior of others. Children with autism often fail at tasks assessing theory of mind, even when they perform appropriately for their age group on other cognitive tasks (Yirmiya, Erel, Shaked, & Solomonica-Levi, 1998). A deficient theory of mind may make it difficult for these children to understand and operate in the social world and to communicate appropriately with others. Their strange play behavior—specifically, the absence of symbolic play—also may represent an inability to understand anything but the concrete realities before them. Positron emission tomography studies show that children with autism show deficits in the medial prefrontal cortex and amygdala when performing theory of mind tasks (Castelli et al., 2002).

Neurological dysfunctions could be the result of genetic factors. Alternately, children with autism have a higher than average rate of prenatal and birth complications, and these complications might create the neurological damage (Sigman et al., 2006). Further, studies have found differences between children with and without autism in levels of the neurotransmitters serotonin and dopamine, although the meaning of these differences is not entirely clear (Anderson & Hoshino, 1997).

FIGURE 10.2 **Brain Activity in Response to Faces.** When shown images of faces, children with autism (image on right) show less activation of the fusiform gyrus than do children without autism (image on left).

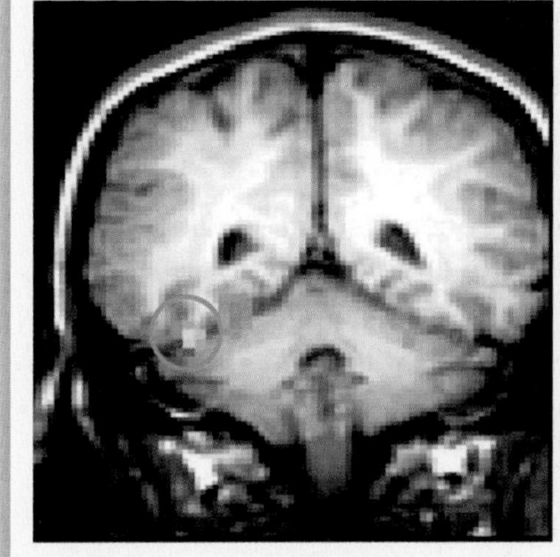

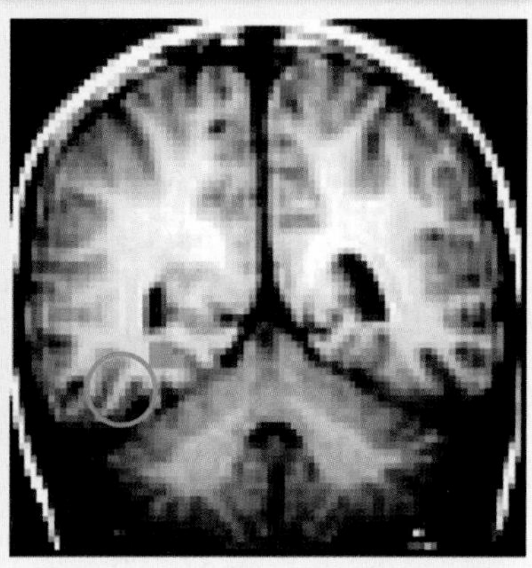

Treatments for Autism

A number of drugs have been shown to improve some of the symptoms of autism, including overactivity, stereotyped behaviors (e.g., head-banging and hand-flapping), sleep disturbances, and tension (Kerbeshian, Burd, & Avery, 2001; Volkmar, 2001). The selective serotonin reuptake inhibitors appear to reduce repetitive behaviors and aggression, and they improve social interactions in some people with autism. The atypical antipsychotic medications are used to reduce obsessive and repetitive behaviors and to improve self-control. Naltrexone, a drug that blocks receptors for opiates, has been shown to be useful in reducing hyperactivity in some children with autism. Finally, stimulants are used to improve attention (Jesner, Aref-Adib, & Coren, 2007). These drugs do not alter the basic autistic disorder, but they may make it easier for people with autism to participate in school and in treatment interventions.

Psychosocial therapies for autism combine behavioral techniques and structured educational services (Koegel, Koegel, & Brookman, 2003; Lovaas & Smith, 2003; Vismara & Rogers, 2010). Operant conditioning strategies are used to reduce excessive behaviors, such as repetitive or ritualistic behaviors, tantrums, and aggression, and to alleviate deficits or delays, such as deficits in communication and in interactions with others. These techniques may be implemented in highly structured schools designed especially for children with autism or in regular classrooms if children are mainstreamed. The specific deficits a child has in cognitive, motor, or communication skills are targeted, and materials that reduce possible distractions (such as books that do not have words printed in bright colors) are used. Parents may be taught to implement the techniques consistently when the children are at home.

Intensive behavior therapy can help children with autism learn communication and social skills.

One pioneering study showed that 47 percent of children with autism given this intensive behavioral treatment for at least 40 hours a week for at least 2 years achieved normal intellectual and educational functioning by age 7, compared to only 2 percent of children who received institutional care alone (Lovaas, 1987). Several other studies have shown remarkable improvements in cognitive skills and behavioral control in children with autism who were treated with a comprehensive behavior therapy administered both by their parents and in their school setting (Bregman & Gerdtz, 1997; Koegel et al., 2003; Lovaas & Smith, 2003; Ozonoff & Cathcart, 1998; Schreibman & Charlop-Christy, 1998; Vismara & Rogers, 2010).

TEST YOURSELF

1. What are the pervasive developmental disorders? What types of impairment are seen in each of these disorders?
2. What biological factors have been implicated in autism?
3. What medications are used to treat autism?
4. How is behavior therapy used to treat autism?

APPLY IT Harry has been diagnosed with autism. Which of the following deficits is he *least* likely to show?

a. deficits in social interaction
b. deficits in intelligence
c. deficits in language and communication
d. deficits in activities and interests

Answers appear online at www.mhhe.com/nolen5e.

FIGURE 10.3 **An Integrated Model of Antisocial Behavior.** The interaction of biological and psychosocial factors may lead to the development of antisocial and hostile behavior in children.

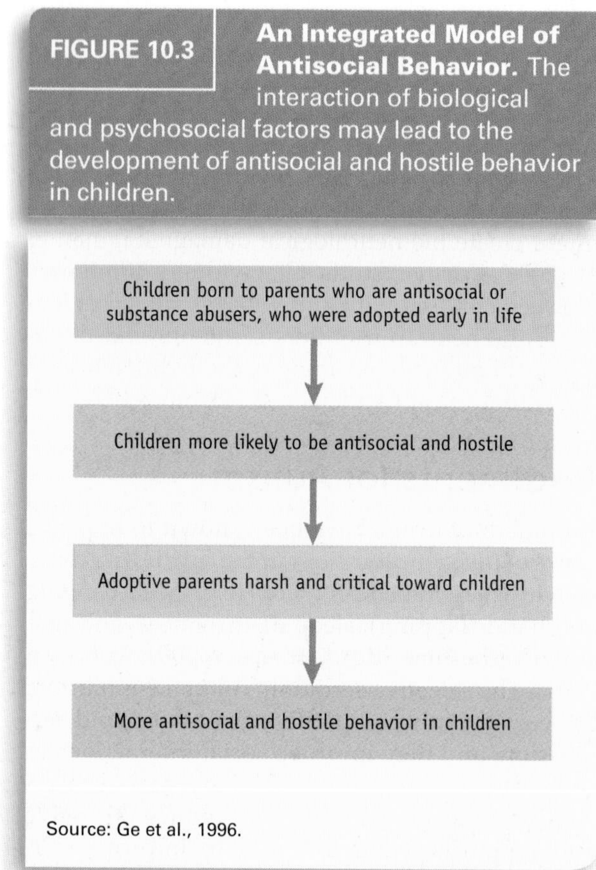

Source: Ge et al., 1996.

CHAPTER INTEGRATION

The field of *developmental psychopathology* begins with the assumption that in order to understand psychopathology in children, researchers must understand normal biological, psychological, and social development. Moreover, developmental psychopathologists are concerned with the interdependence of biological, psychological, and social development in children, recognizing that disruptions in any one of these three systems send perturbations through the other systems. The interdependence of these systems probably is greater in children than in adults, because children are not mature enough to compartmentalize their troubles and are highly dependent on their caregivers and their environment for even their most basic needs.

An example of the interplay among biology, psychology, and the social environment comes from a study of adopted children (Figure 10.3; Ge, Conger, Cadoret, & Neiderhiser, 1996). Some of the adopted children in this study had biological parents with antisocial personalities or a history of substance abuse. The other adopted children had biological parents with no history of psychological problems. The children whose biological parents had a history of psychopathology were more likely than the other children to be hostile and antisocial themselves. Most researchers who do not adopt a biopsychosocial approach to childhood disorders would stop with these results and declare them clear evidence of the genetic inheritance of antisocial and hostile tendencies.

The researchers in this study, however, went further and looked at the parenting behaviors of the children's adoptive parents. They found that the adoptive parents of the antisocial and hostile children were harsher and more critical in their parenting than were the adoptive parents of the children who were not antisocial and hostile. It appeared that the antisocial and hostile children drew out harsh and critical behaviors from their adoptive parents. Harsh and critical parenting then exacerbated the children's antisocial behaviors. Thus, the children with biological parents who were antisocial or were substance abusers appeared to have a genetic predisposition to being antisocial and hostile. Their genes in effect created an environment of parenting practices by their adoptive parents that contributed to more antisocial behavior by the children.

These children were on a developmental trajectory in which their biology and their social environment were acting in synergy to lead them toward serious conduct disturbances. This kind of synergy among biology, psychology, and the social environment is the rule, rather than the exception, in the development of psychopathology, particularly in children.

SHADES OF GRAY DISCUSSION (review p. 318)

Before giving Jake a diagnosis, there are several possibilities worth considering. First, you might consider whether Jake has a learning disability that is hurting his academic performance. You might administer testing to see if this is the case. Second, you may note that people with the inattentive type of ADHD are not hyperactive and often may seem dazed. Jake's tendencies to forget things, to leave projects incomplete, to have his mind wander, and to be late all fit the symptoms of an inattentive type of ADHD. However, they also could be caused by depression. Jake's parents often were critical of him and felt that he wasn't living up to their expectations. Also, the fact that Jake's grades tended to drop at times of transition could suggest trouble coping with change. You would need to thoroughly investigate these possibilities before making a diagnosis.

THINK CRITICALLY

In recent years, increasing concerns have been raised about prescribing psychotropic medications to children when the medications have been tested primarily on adults. For example, the atypical antipsychotic medications, which were developed and tested for adult schizophrenia (see Chapter 8), are now being widely used to treat disruptive and self-injurious behaviors in children with conduct disorder, pervasive developmental disorders, and a variety of other diagnoses (Jensen et al., 2007). The few studies that have compared these medications with a placebo in double-blind, controlled trials generally have found that they are effective in reducing aggressive and disruptive behavior and self-injury in children (see Jensen et al., 2007, for a meta-analysis). Thus, it seems that the atypical antipsychotics are a valuable tool in the treatment of symptoms that can be dangerous for children and severely impair their functioning.

The atypical antipsychotics, however, do raise concerns about safety. The meta-analysis by Peter Jensen and colleagues (2007) showed that the most common side effects of these medications in children are sleepiness and weight gain. Significant weight gain may increase risk for the development of diabetes. Some children who take atypical antipsychotics show increases in levels of the hormone prolactin, and the long-term effects of these elevations are not known. Some rare adverse events have been reported, including heart arrhythmias.

If your child had significant problems with aggressive and disruptive behavior or self-injury, would you agree to having him or her take atypical antipsychotics if they were prescribed by a child psychiatrist? What do you think should be the policy on the prescription of drugs for children when the drugs have been tested primarily on adults? *(Discussion appears on p. 519 at the back of this book.)*

CHAPTER SUMMARY

- The behavior disorders include attention-deficit/hyperactivity disorder (ADHD), conduct disorder, and oppositional defiant disorder.
- ADHD is characterized by inattentiveness, impulsivity, and hyperactivity. Children with ADHD do poorly in school and in peer relationships and are at increased risk for developing conduct disorder. ADHD is more common in boys than in girls.
- Biological factors that have been implicated in the development of ADHD include genetics, exposure to toxins prenatally and early in childhood, and abnormalities in neurological functioning. In addition, many children with ADHD come from families marked by many disruptions, although it is not clear whether this is a cause or simply a correlate of ADHD.
- Treatments for ADHD usually involve stimulant drugs and behavior therapy designed to decrease children's impulsivity and hyperactivity and help them control aggression.
- Conduct disorder is characterized by extreme antisocial behavior and the violation of other people's rights and of social norms. Conduct disorder is more common in boys than in girls and is highly stable across childhood and

adolescence. Adults who had conduct disorder as children are at increased risk for criminal behavior and a host of problems in fitting into society.

- Children with oppositional defiant disorder are easily angered and tend to violate rules and requests. Unlike children with conduct disorder, they do not tend to be aggressive toward other people or animals, to steal, or to destroy property.
- Genetics and neurological problems are implicated in the development of conduct disorder. In addition, children with conduct disorder tend to have parents who are harsh and inconsistent in their discipline practices and who model aggressive, antisocial behavior. Psychologically, children with conduct disorder tend to process information in ways likely to lead to aggressive reactions to the behaviors of others.
- The treatment for conduct disorder is most often cognitive-behavioral, focusing on changing children's ways of interpreting interpersonal situations and helping them control their angry impulses. Antipsychotic drugs, antidepressants, and stimulant drugs also are sometimes used to treat conduct disorder.
- Children can develop all the major emotional disorders (such as mood disorders, anxiety disorders), but separation anxiety is a disorder that, by definition, begins in childhood. Its symptoms include chronic worry about separation from parents or about parents' well-being, dreams and fantasies about separation from parents, refusal to go to school, and somatic complaints. Separation anxiety is more common in girls.
- Separation anxiety runs in families, which may suggest either that genetics plays a role in its development or that interactions between parents and children can arouse anxiety in children. Separation anxiety often arises following a major trauma, particularly if parents are anxious and overprotective of their children.
- The therapy for separation anxiety follows cognitive-behavioral principles and involves relaxation training and increasing periods of separation from parents.
- The elimination disorders are enuresis, the repeated wetting of clothes or bed linens in children over age 5, and encopresis, repeated defecation in the clothes or on the floor in children over age 4. Enuresis is more common and has been studied more extensively than encopresis and has been linked to psychological stress, inappropriate or lax toilet training, and genetics.
- Enuresis often is treated with the bell and pad method, which helps children learn to wake when their bladder is full so that they can go to the bathroom. Antidepressants also are used to treat enuresis, but their effects disappear when the children stop taking them.
- Encopresis most often begins after episodes of constipation. It is treated with medical management and regular toilet sitting.
- Disorders of cognitive, motor, and communication skills involve deficits and delays in the development of fundamental skills.
- Learning disorders include reading disorder (inability to read), mathematics disorder (inability to learn math), and disorder of written expression (inability to write).
- Developmental coordination disorder involves deficits in fundamental motor skills.
- Communication disorders include expressive language disorder (inability to express oneself through language), mixed receptive-expressive language disorder (inability to use or understand language), phonological disorder (the use of speech sounds inappropriate for age and dialect), and stuttering (deficits in word fluency).
- Some of the disorders of cognitive, motor, and communication skills may have genetic roots. Abnormalities in brain structure and functioning have been implicated in these disorders. Environmental factors, including lead poisoning, birth defects, sensory deprivation, and low socioeconomic status, may contribute to brain dysfunction.
- Treatment usually focuses on building skills in problem areas through specialized training, as well as the use of computerized exercises.
- Mental retardation is defined as subaverage intellectual functioning, as measured by an IQ score below 70 and deficits in adaptive behavioral functioning. There are four levels of mental retardation, ranging from mild to profound.
- A number of biological factors are implicated in mental retardation, including metabolic disorders (PKU, Tay-Sachs disease); chromosomal disorders (Down syndrome, fragile X, trisomy 13, and trisomy 18); prenatal exposure to rubella, herpes, syphilis, or drugs (especially alcohol, as in fetal alcohol syndrome); premature delivery; and head trauma (such as that arising from being shaken as an infant).
- There is some evidence that intensive and comprehensive educational interventions, administered very early in a child's life, can help decrease the level of mental retardation.
- The pervasive developmental disorders are characterized by severe and lasting impairment in several areas of development, including social interaction, communication with others, and everyday behaviors, interests, and activities. They include Asperger's disorder, Rett's

disorder, childhood disintegrative disorder, and autism.

- Autism is characterized by significant interpersonal, communication, and behavioral deficits. Many children with autism score in the mental retardation range on IQ tests. Outcomes of autism vary widely, although the majority of people with autism must receive continual care, even as adults. The best predictors of a good outcome in autism are an IQ above 50 and language development before age 6.
- Possible biological causes of autism include a genetic predisposition to cognitive impairment, central nervous system damage, prenatal complications, and neurotransmitter imbalances.
- Drugs reduce some symptoms in autism but do not eliminate the core of the disorder. Behavior therapy is used to reduce inappropriate and self-injurious behaviors and encourage prosocial behaviors.

KEY TERMS

attention-deficit/hyperactivity disorder (ADHD) 297
conduct disorder 304
oppositional defiant disorder 305
separation anxiety disorder 311
behavioral inhibition 312
elimination disorders 314
enuresis 314
bell and pad method 315
encopresis 315
reading disorder 316
mathematics disorder 316
disorder of written expression 316
developmental coordination disorder 316
expressive language disorder 316
mixed receptive-expressive language disorder 316
phonological disorder 316
stuttering 316
mental retardation 318
fetal alcohol syndrome (FAS) 320
pervasive developmental disorders 323
autism 323
Rett's disorder 326
childhood disintegrative disorder 326
Asperger's disorder 326

Chapter 11

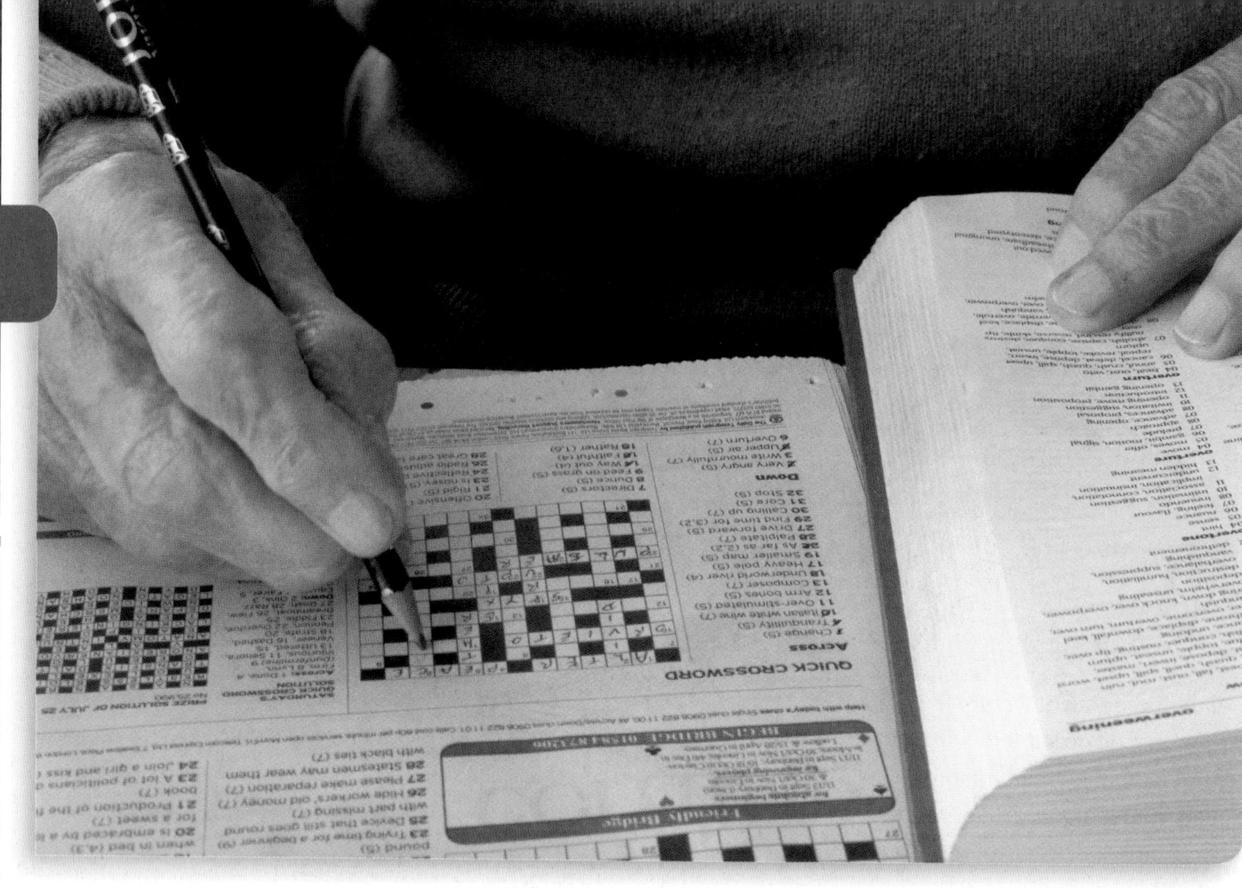

Cognitive Disorders and Life-Span Issues

CHAPTER OVERVIEW

Extraordinary People

John Bayley and Iris Murdoch, *Elegy for Iris*

As a young woman teaching philosophy at Oxford University, Iris Murdoch met John Bayley, a recent graduate in English. They fell in love, married 2 years later, and settled in Oxford, where Bayley eventually taught and became an eminent literary critic. Murdoch wrote 26 novels and several textbooks on philosophy and is now considered one of the greatest writers of the twentieth century. She received honorary doctorates from many major universities and was named a Dame of the British Empire. These two intellectual giants shared a life and love that was extraordinary for its passion, its intimacy, and its fun.

In 1994, after the couple had been married nearly 40 years, Murdoch developed Alzheimer's disease. The brilliant novelist and philosopher was reduced to grunts, squeaks, and murmurs, asking the same questions over and over and becoming unable to care for herself. "Alzheimer's is, in fact, like an insidious fog, barely noticeable until everything around has disappeared. After that, it is no longer possible to believe that a world outside the fog exists," Bayley writes in *Elegy for Iris* (1999, p. 281), his account of his life with Murdoch after she developed Alzheimer's disease.

Rather than give up Murdoch to her disease, Bayley cared for her and even communicated with her through the "insidious fog":

> Our mode of communication seems like underwater sonar, each bouncing pulsations off the other, then listening for an echo. The baffling moments at which I cannot understand what Iris is saying, or about whom or what—moments which can produce tears and anxieties, though never, thank goodness, the raging frustration typical of many Alzheimer's sufferers—can sometimes be dispelled by embarking on a jokey parody of helplessness, and trying to make it mutual, both of us at a loss of words. (pp. 51–52)

His accounts reflect other aspects of Alzheimer's disease:

> The face of an Alzheimer's patient has been clinically described as the "lion face." An apparently odd comparison, but in fact a very apt one. The features settle into a leonine impassivity which does remind one of the king of beasts, and the way his broad expressionless mask is represented in painting and sculpture. . . .
>
> The face of the Alzheimer's sufferer indicates only an absence: It is a mask in the most literal sense. That is why the sudden appearance of a smile is so extraordinary. The lion face becomes the face of the Virgin Mary, tranquil in sculpture and painting, with a gravity that gives such a smile its deepest meaning. (pp. 53–54)

Despite the stresses of caring for someone with severe dementia, Bayley came to see Murdoch's debilitating disease as a natural extension of their life together:

> Life is no longer bringing the pair of us "closer and closer apart," in the poet's tenderly ambiguous words. Every day we move closer and closer together. We could not do otherwise. There is a certain comic irony—happily, not darkly comic—that after more than forty years of taking marriage for granted, marriage has decided it is tired of this, and is taking a hand in the game. Purposefully, persistently, involuntarily, our marriage is now getting somewhere. It is giving us no choice—and I am glad of that.
>
> Every day, we are physically closer; and Iris's little "mouse cry," as I think of it, signifying loneliness in the next room, the wish to be back beside me, seems less and less forlorn, more simple, more natural. She is not sailing into the dark: The voyage is over, and under the dark escort of Alzheimer's she has arrived somewhere. So have I. (pp. 265–266)

Iris Murdoch died in February 1999, just a few months after *Elegy for Iris* was published.

All the disorders we have discussed so far in this book can be found among older people. Near the end of this chapter, we will discuss the prevalence, characteristics, and treatment of depression, anxiety, and substance use disorders in older people. But first we discuss disorders that most often arise for the first time in old age, the **cognitive disorders:** dementia, delirium, and amnesia. These disorders result from medical conditions that cause impairments in cognition (such as the Alzheimer's disease that Iris Murdoch suffered) or from substance intoxication or withdrawal. Cognitive problems include memory deficits, language disturbances, perceptual disturbances, impairment in the capacity to plan and organize, and failure to recognize or identify objects.

DEMENTIA

CASE STUDY

A 61-year-old high school science department head who was an experienced and enthusiastic camper and hiker became extremely fearful while on a trek in the mountains. Gradually, over the next few months, he lost interest in his usual hobbies. Formerly a voracious reader, he stopped reading. He had difficulty doing computations and made gross errors in home financial management. On several occasions he became lost while driving in areas that were formerly familiar to him. He began to write notes to himself so that he would not forget to do errands. Very abruptly, and in uncharacteristic fashion, he decided to retire from work, without discussing his plans with his wife. Intellectual deterioration gradually progressed. He spent most of the day piling miscellaneous objects in one place and then transporting them to another spot in the house. He became stubborn and querulous. Eventually he required assistance in shaving and dressing.

When examined 6 years after the first symptoms had developed, the patient was alert and cooperative. He was disoriented with respect to place and time. He could not recall the names of four or five objects after a 5-minute interval of distraction. He could not remember the names of his college and graduate school or the subject in which he had majored. He could describe his job by title only. In 1978 he thought that Kennedy was president of the United States. He did not know Stalin's nationality. His speech was fluent and well articulated, but he had considerable difficulty finding words and used many long, essentially meaningless phrases. He called a cup a vase and identified the rims of glasses as "the holders." He did simple calculations poorly. He could not copy a cube or draw a house. (Spitzer et al., 2002, p. 302)

This man was slowly losing his ability to remember the most fundamental facts of his life, to express himself through language, and to carry out basic everyday tasks. This is the picture of **dementia,** the most common cognitive disorder.

Dementia typically occurs in late life. The estimated prevalence of the most common type of dementia—that due to Alzheimer's disease—is 5 to 10 percent of people over age 65 (Aguero-Torres, Fratiglioni, & Winblad, 1998; Epple, 2002). The prevalence of most types of dementia increases with age, and experts estimate that 30 percent of individuals age 85 and older are living with dementia (Ferri et al., 2005).

Symptoms of Dementia

Dementia is characterized by a number of cognitive deficits (see the *DSM-IV-TR* criteria for dementia of the Alzheimer's type in Table 11.1). The most prominent is a *memory deficit,* which is required for the diagnosis of dementia. In the early stages of dementia, the memory lapses may be similar to those that we all experience from time to time—forgetting the name of someone we know casually, our phone number, or what we went into the next room to get. Most of us eventually remember what we temporarily forgot, either spontaneously or by using tricks that jog our memory. The difference in dementia is that memory does not return spontaneously and may not respond to reminders or other cues.

People in the early stages of dementia may repeat questions because they do not remember asking them moments ago or do not remember getting an answer. They frequently misplace items, such as keys or wallets. They may try to compensate for their memory loss. For example, they may carefully write down their appointments or things they need to do. Eventually, however, they forget to look at their calendars or lists. As the memory problems become more apparent, they may become angry when asked questions or may make up answers in an attempt to hide their memory loss. Later, as dementia progresses, they may become lost in familiar surroundings and be

Cognitive Disorders and Life-Span Mental Health Along the Continuum

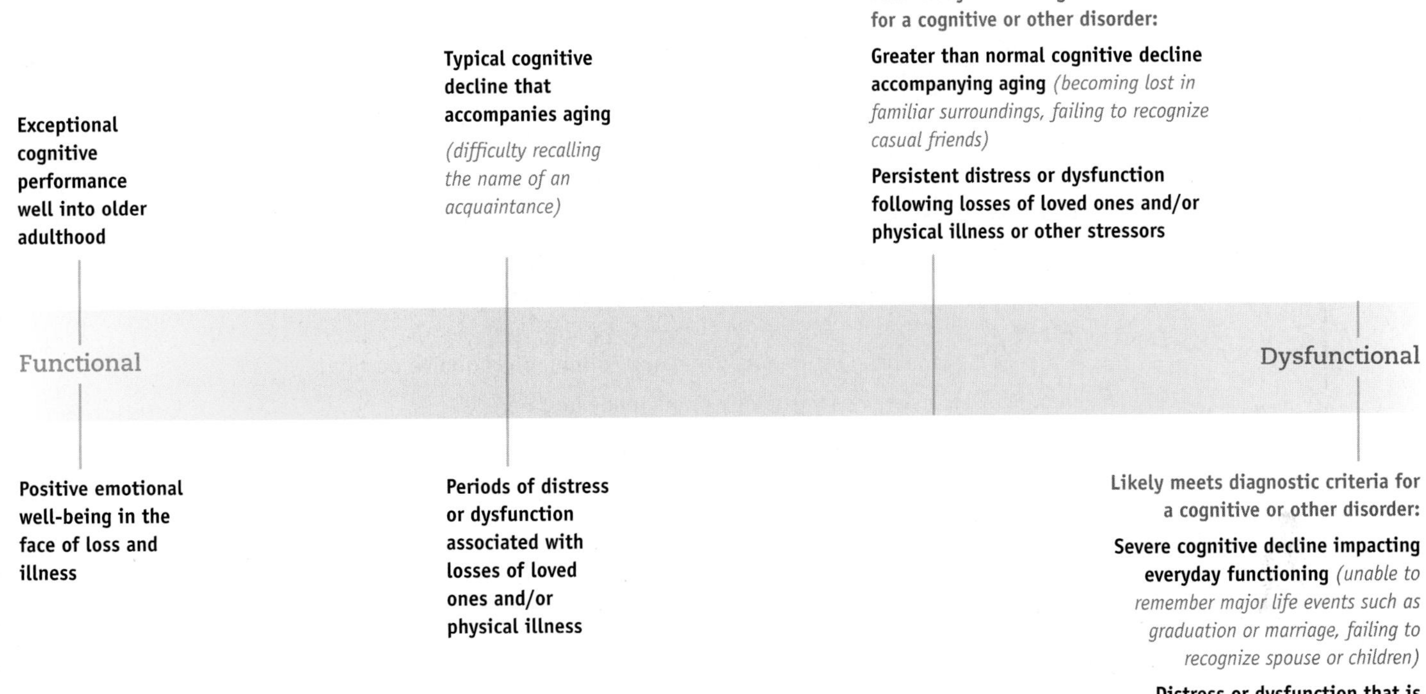
Exceptional cognitive performance well into older adulthood
Typical cognitive decline that accompanies aging
(difficulty recalling the name of an acquaintance)
Potentially meets diagnostic criteria for a cognitive or other disorder:
Greater than normal cognitive decline accompanying aging (becoming lost in familiar surroundings, failing to recognize casual friends)
Persistent distress or dysfunction following losses of loved ones and/or physical illness or other stressors
Functional
Dysfunctional
Positive emotional well-being in the face of loss and illness
Periods of distress or dysfunction associated with losses of loved ones and/or physical illness
Likely meets diagnostic criteria for a cognitive or other disorder:
Severe cognitive decline impacting everyday functioning (unable to remember major life events such as graduation or marriage, failing to recognize spouse or children)
Distress or dysfunction that is chronic and significantly impairing

Reading Iris Murdoch's story, you may have felt that her deterioration was a familiar portrait of older age. Our culture, after all, tends to equate aging with disease and decline. But, while it's true that aging involves some decline in cognitive abilities, most adults remain highly functional well into older adulthood. Figure 11.1 presents data from several cognitive tests given to a large sample of adults ranging from age 20 to 89 (Park & Reuter-Lorenz, 2009). There are gradual age-related declines in how quickly people perceive and process information, in the ability to hold and manipulate information in working memory, and in long-term memory. Verbal ability, which is more a measure of accumulated knowledge than of cognitive processing, generally is protected from the effects of aging. The greater knowledge and expertise people gain as they age compensates in part for their declines in cognitive processing ability. Further, the brain changes the way it processes information as people age, enlisting more help from the prefrontal cortex to enhance the processing capacities of other parts of the brain (Park & Reuter-Lorenz, 2009).

FIGURE 11.1 Changes in Cognitive Processes with Age. Some cognitive processes show declines with age, while world knowledge increases with age.
Source: Park & Reuter-Lorenz, 2009.

As we age, we tend to experience more losses of family and friends and a greater likelihood of physical illness in ourselves. Nevertheless, most older people are mentally healthy and are living happy, productive lives. The rate of most psychological disorders is lower among older people than among younger people, suggesting that older people are highly resilient (Whitbourne, 2000). Only 10 to 20 percent of people over age 65 have diagnosable psychological problems that warrant treatment (Gatz, Kasl-Godley, & Karel, 1996).

Recall from Chapter 10 that developmental psychopathologists try to understand children's psychological problems in the context of normal development during childhood and adolescence. In the same way, specialists in *geropsychology*—the field of later-life psychology—try to understand psychological problems in older people in the context of the many biological, psychological, and social changes people undergo in later life.

TABLE 11.1 *DSM-IV-TR* Criteria for Dementia of the Alzheimer's Type

A. The development of multiple cognitive deficits manifested by both
   1. Memory impairment (impaired ability to learn new information or to recall previously learned information)
   2. One (or more) of the following cognitive disturbances:
      a. aphasia (language disturbance)
      b. apraxia (impaired ability to carry out motor activities despite intact motor function)
      c. agnosia (failure to recognize or identify objects despite intact sensory function)
      d. disturbance in executive functioning (i.e., planning, organizing, sequencing, abstracting)

B. The cognitive deficits each cause significant impairment in social or occupational functioning and represent a significant decline from a previous level of functioning.

C. The course is characterized by gradual onset and continuing cognitive decline.

D. The cognitive deficits are not due to any of the following:
   1. Other central nervous system conditions that cause progressive deficits in memory and cognition
   2. Systemic conditions that are known to cause dementia
   3. Substance-induced conditions

E. The deficits do not occur exclusively during the course of a delirium.

F. The disturbance is not better accounted for by another Axis I disorder (e.g., major depressive episode, schizophrenia).

Without Behavioral Disturbance: if the cognitive disturbance is not accompanied by any clinically significant behavioral disturbance

With Behavioral Disturbance: if the cognitive disturbance is accompanied by a clinically significant behavioral disturbance (e.g., wandering, agitation)

With Early Onset: if onset is at age 65 years or below

With Late Onset: if onset is after age 65 years

Source: Reprinted with permission from the *Diagnostic and Statistical Manual of Mental Disorders,* Fourth Edition, Text Revision.

unable to find their way when not accompanied by others.

Eventually, long-term memory also becomes impaired. People with dementia will forget the order of major events in their life, such as graduation from college, marriage, and the birth of their children. After a time, they will be unable to recall the events at all and may not even know their own name.

The *DSM-IV-TR* requires that for a diagnosis of dementia memory loss plus at least one of four other cognitive deficits must be present. **Aphasia** is a *deterioration of language*. People with dementia will have tremendous difficulty producing the names of objects or people and often may use terms such as *thing* or vague references to *them* to hide their inability to produce concrete names. If asked to identify a cup, for example, they may say that it is a *thing for drinking* but be unable to name it as a cup. They also may be unable to understand what another person is saying or to follow simple requests such as "Turn on the lights and shut the door." In advanced stages of dementia, people may exhibit **echolalia**, simply repeating what they hear, or **palilalia**, repeating sounds or words over and over.

Another common cognitive deficit is **apraxia,** impairment of the ability to execute common actions such as waving good-bye or putting on a shirt. This deficit is not caused by problems in motor functioning (e.g., moving the arm), in sensory functioning, or in comprehending what action is required. People with dementia simply are unable to carry out actions that are requested of them or that they wish to carry out.

Agnosia is the failure to recognize objects or people. People with dementia may not be able to identify common objects, such as chairs or tables. At first, they fail to recognize casual friends or distant family members. With time, they may not recognize their spouse or children or even their own reflection in a mirror.

Most people with dementia eventually lose **executive functions,** those functions of the brain that involve the ability to plan, initiate, monitor, and stop complex behaviors. Cooking Thanksgiving dinner, for example, requires executive functioning. Each menu item (the turkey, the stuffing, the pumpkin pie) requires different ingredients and preparation. The cooking of various menu items must be coordinated so that all the items are ready at the same time. People in the early stages of dementia may attempt to cook Thanksgiving dinner but forget important components (such as the turkey) or fail to coordinate the dinner, burning certain items and undercooking others. People in later stages of dementia are unable even to initiate a complex task such as this.

Deficits in executive functioning also involve difficulty in the kind of abstract thinking required to evaluate new situations and respond appropriately to these situations. For example, if a man with dementia was presented with the proverb "People who live in glass houses shouldn't throw stones," he may be unable to interpret the abstract meaning of the proverb. Instead, he might interpret it concretely to mean "People don't want their windows broken."

In addition to these cognitive deficits, people with dementia often show changes in emotional functioning and personality. Shoplifting and exhibitionism are common manifestations caused by a decline in judgment and an inability to control impulses. People with dementia may become depressed when they recognize their cognitive deterioration. Often, however, they do not recognize or admit to their cognitive deficits. This can lead them to perform unrealistic or dangerous actions, such as driving a car when they are too impaired to do so safely. People with dementia may become paranoid and angry with family members and friends, whom they see as thwarting their desires and freedom. They may accuse others of stealing belongings they have misplaced. They may believe that others are conspiring against them—the only conclusion left for them when they simply do not remember conversations in which they agreed to some action (e.g., starting a new medication or moving into a treatment facility for people with dementia). Violent outbursts are not unusual.

In the *DSM-5,* various forms of dementia are likely to be subsumed under one overarching category, *major neurocognitive disorder*, characterized by significant decline in cognitive functioning that makes it difficult for the person to be independent. A diagnosis of *minor neurocognitive disorder* would apply to individuals with less severe cognitive decline, who might be in the early stages of what eventually will develop into a major neurocognitive disorder (American Psychiatric Association, 2010).

Types of Dementia

Dementia has several causes. The most common is Alzheimer's disease, which accounts for up to two-thirds of all cases of dementia (Gatz, 2007). Dementia also can be caused by vascular disease (blockage of blood to the brain, commonly referred to as a stroke); by head injury; by progressive diseases, such as Parkinson's disease and HIV disease; and by chronic drug abuse.

Former President Ronald Reagan, who died in 2004 at the age of 93, was diagnosed with Alzheimer's disease.

Dementia of the Alzheimer's Type

Dementia due to **Alzheimer's disease** typically begins with mild memory loss, but as the disease progresses the memory loss and disorientation quickly become profound, as they did for Iris Murdoch. About two-thirds of Alzheimer's patients show psychiatric symptoms, including agitation, irritability, apathy, and dysphoria. John Bayley writes in *Elegy for Iris* that these emotional symptoms were as difficult for him to deal with as the cognitive symptoms. As the disease worsens, sufferers may become violent and experience hallucinations and delusions. The disease usually begins after age 65, but there is an early-onset type of Alzheimer's disease that tends to progress more quickly than the late-onset type (Gatz, 2007). On average, people with this disease die within 8 to 10 years of its diagnosis, usually as a result of physical decline or independent diseases common in old age, such as heart disease. Iris Murdoch was diagnosed with Alzheimer's disease in 1994 and died in 1999.

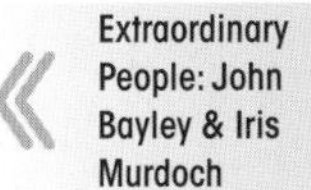

Extraordinary People: John Bayley & Iris Murdoch

Brain Abnormalities in Alzheimer's Disease

What we now call Alzheimer's disease was first

FIGURE 11.2 **Neurofibrillary Tangles and Beta-Amyloid Plaques in Alzheimer's Disease.** Protein deposits build up and cause neurofibrillary tangles and beta-amyloid plaques in neurons in the brains of people with Alzheimer's disease.

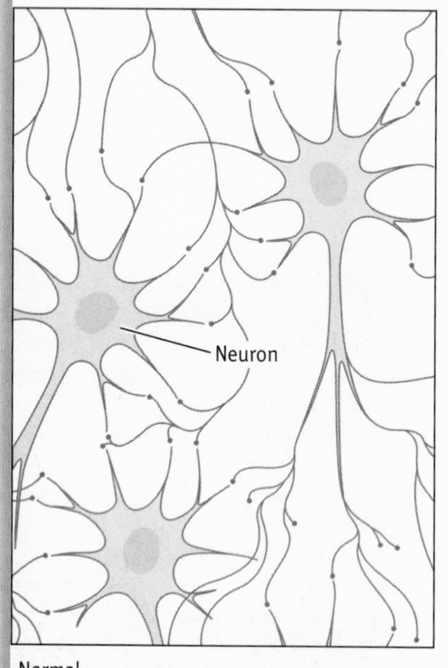

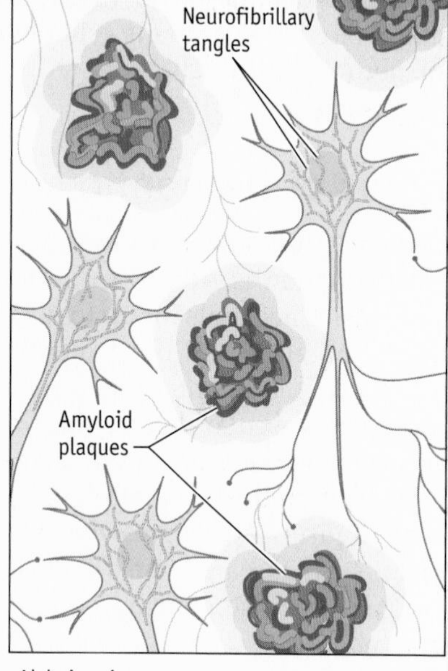

FIGURE 11.3 **Cortical Regions in Alzheimer's Disease.** Cell death causes shrinkage of cortical regions in the brains of people with Alzheimer's disease (left; compare to healthy brain on right).

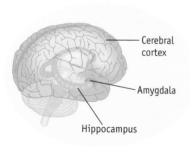

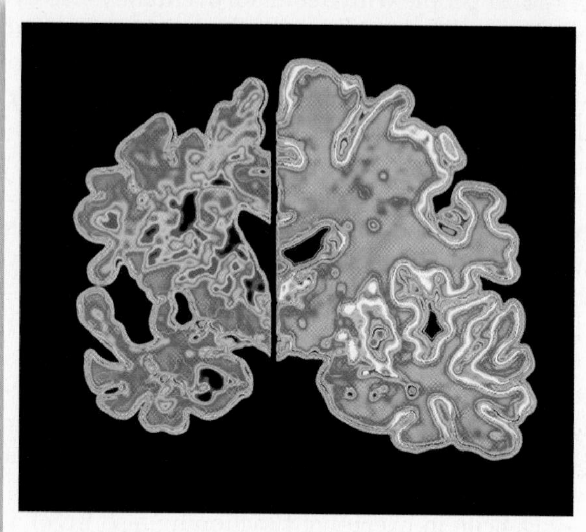

described in 1906 by Alois Alzheimer. He observed severe memory loss and disorientation in a 51-year-old female patient. Following her death at age 55, an autopsy revealed that filaments within nerve cells in her brain were twisted and tangled. These **neurofibrillary tangles** are common in the brains of Alzheimer's patients but rare in people without a cognitive disorder (Figure 11.2). The tangles, which are made up of a protein called tau, impede nutrients and other essential supplies from moving through cells so that cells eventually die. Another brain abnormality seen in Alzheimer's disease is **plaques** (see Figure 11.2). Plaques are deposits of a class of protein, called **beta-amyloid,** that accumulate in the spaces between the cells of the cerebral cortex, hippocampus, amygdala, and other brain structures critical to memory and cognitive functioning (Atiya, Hyman, Albert, & Killiany, 2003; Du et al., 2001).

Cerebral cortex

Amygdala

Hippocampus

Plaques accumulate between cells in these and other areas of the brain in Alzheimer's disease.

There is extensive cell death in the cortex of Alzheimer's patients, resulting in shrinking of the cortex and enlargement of the ventricles of the brain (Figure 11.3). The remaining cells lose many of their dendrites—the branches that link one cell to other cells (Figure 11.4). The result of all these brain abnormalities is profound memory loss and an inability to coordinate activities.

Causes of Alzheimer's Disease What causes the brain deterioration seen with Alzheimer's disease? This is an area of tremendous research activity, and new answers to this question emerge each day. Alzheimer's disease has been attributed to viral infections, immune system dysfunction, exposure to toxic levels of aluminum, deficiencies of the vitamin folate, and head traumas.

Much of the current research, however, has focused on genes that might transmit a vulnerability to this disorder and on the beta-amyloid proteins that form the plaques found in the brains of almost all Alzheimer's patients. Family history studies suggest that 24 to 49 percent of first-degree relatives of patients with Alzheimer's disease eventually develop the disease (Gatz, 2007). The lifetime risk of developing Alzheimer's disease is 1.8 to 4.0 times higher for people with a family history of the disorder than for those without a family history.

Twin studies confirm an important role of genetics in the risk for Alzheimer's disease, as well as for other forms of dementia. Concordance rates for all forms of dementia in monozygotic twins are 44 percent for men and 58 percent for women; concordance rates for dizygotic twins are 25 percent for men and 45 percent for women (Gatz et al., 2006).

Several genes have been linked to Alzheimer's disease. The gene most consistently associated with the disease is the apolipoprotein E gene (APOE), which is on chromosome 19. This gene regulates the ApoE protein, which is involved in the transport of cholesterol through the blood. ApoE also binds to beta-amyloid protein and may play a role in its regulation. The APOE gene has three alleles, or versions: e2, e3, and e4. People who inherit an e4 allele from one parent have a 2 to 4 times greater risk of developing Alzheimer's than people who do not inherit an e4 allele, and people who inherit e4 alleles from both parents have an 8 to 12 times greater risk of developing the disorder (Farrer et al., 1997).

Neuroimaging studies show that people with the e4 version of the APOE gene have reduced cortex and hippocampus volume compared to people without the e4 version of the APOE gene, even as children or adolescents (Jack et al., 2007; Shaw et al., 2007; Thompson et al., 2004). Studies find increased activity in the cortex during cognitive tasks in people with the e4 version of the APOE gene compared to people without this allele (Bookheimer et al., 2000). This increased activity may represent the brain's having to work harder to do cognitive tasks in people at risk for Alzheimer's disease. The greater the activation during the tasks, the more decline in memory functioning people showed after 2 years.

Other genes are implicated in the development of less common forms of Alzheimer's disease, which begin in middle age and are more strongly familial. One of these genes is on chromosome 21 (Bird, Lampe, Wijsman, & Schollenberg, 1998). The first clue that a defective gene on chromosome 21 might be linked with Alzheimer's disease came from the fact that people with Down syndrome are more likely than people in the general population to develop Alzheimer's disease in late life. Researchers hypothesized that the gene responsible for some forms of Alzheimer's disease may be on chromosome 21 and that people with Down syndrome are more prone to Alzheimer's disease because they have an extra chromosome 21.

This hypothesis has been supported by studies of families with high rates of Alzheimer's disease. These studies have found links between the presence of the disease and the presence of an abnormal gene on chromosome 21 (Goate et al., 1991; St. George-Hyslop et al., 1987). Also, this abnormal gene on chromosome 21 is near the gene responsible for producing a precursor of the amyloid protein known as the amyloid precursor protein gene, or APP gene. It may be that defects along this section of chromosome 21 cause an abnormal production and buildup of amyloid proteins in the brain, resulting in Alzheimer's disease. A number of other genes have been implicated in Alzheimer's disease, though somewhat inconsistently (Gatz, 2007). Even taken altogether, however, the genes shown to be associated with Alzheimer's disease account for only about 50 percent of cases.

People with Alzheimer's disease also show deficits in a number of neurotransmitters, including acetylcholine, norepinephrine, serotonin, somatostatin (a corticotropin-releasing factor), and peptide Y (Small, 1998). The deficits in acetylcholine are particularly noteworthy because this neurotransmitter is thought to be critical in memory function. The degree of cognitive decline seen in patients with Alzheimer's is significantly correlated with the degree of deficit in acetylcholine (Knopman, 2003). Drugs that enhance levels of acetylcholine can slow the rate of cognitive decline in some Alzheimer's sufferers.

We will likely know much more about the causes of Alzheimer's disease in the next few years. The technologies for studying the genetic and neurological processes of the disease are

FIGURE 11.4 **Cell Damage in Alzheimer's Disease.** Cells lose their dendrites, which connect cells to one another, in the brains of people with Alzheimer's disease.

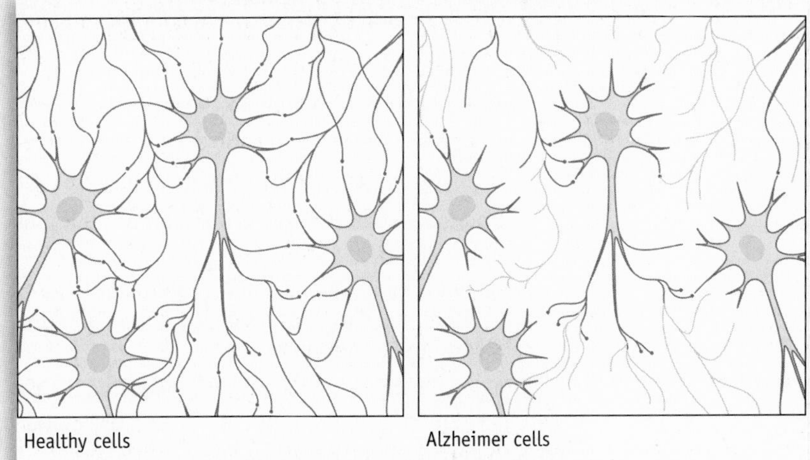

TABLE 11.2 *DSM-IV-TR* Criteria for Vascular Dementia

A. The development of multiple cognitive deficits manifested by both
   1. Memory impairment (impaired ability to learn new information or to recall previously learned information)
   2. One (or more) of the following cognitive disturbances:
      a. aphasia (language disturbance)
      b. apraxia (impaired ability to carry out motor activities despite intact motor function)
      c. agnosia (failure to recognize or identify objects despite intact sensory function)
      d. disturbance in executive functioning (i.e., planning, organizing, sequencing, abstracting)

B. The cognitive deficits each cause significant impairment in social or occupational functioning and represent a significant decline from a previous level of functioning.

C. Focal neurological signs and symptoms or laboratory evidence indicative of cerebrovascular disease (e.g., multiple infarctions involving cortex and underlying white matter) that are judged to be etiologically related to the disturbance.

D. The deficits do not occur exclusively during the course of a delirium.

With Delirium: if delirium is superimposed on the dementia

With Delusions: if delusions are the predominant feature

With Depressed Mood: if depressed mood (including presentations that meet full symptom criteria for a major depressive episode) is the predominant feature

Uncomplicated: if none of the above predominates in the current clinical presentation

Specify if:

With Behavioral Disturbance

Source: Reprinted with permission from the *Diagnostic and Statistical Manual of Mental Disorders,* Fourth Edition, Text Revision.

advancing rapidly, and many researchers are investigating this disorder. Four and a half million people in the United States and 18 million people worldwide have been diagnosed with Alzheimer's disease, and this number is expected to increase by at least 300 percent by 2050 (Hebert et al., 2003; Tariot, 2003). We can hope that, by then, we will understand the disorder well enough to treat it effectively.

Vascular Dementia

Another common type of dementia is **vascular dementia** (formerly called *multi-infarct dementia*). As can be seen in Table 11.2, the symptoms of vascular dementia are the same as those of dementia due to Alzheimer's disease. In addition, to be diagnosed with vascular dementia, a person must have symptoms or laboratory evidence of **cerebrovascular disease.** Cerebrovascular disease occurs when the blood supply to areas of the brain is blocked, causing tissue damage in the brain. Neuroimaging techniques, such as PET and MRI, can detect areas of tissue damage and reduced blood flow in the brain, confirming cerebrovascular disease.

Sudden damage to an area of the brain due to the blockage of blood flow or to hemorrhaging (bleeding) is called a **stroke.** Vascular dementia can occur after one large stroke or after an accumulation of small strokes. Cerebrovascular disease can be caused by high blood pressure and the accumulation of fatty deposits in the arteries, which block blood flow to the brain. It also can be a complication of diseases that inflame the brain and of head injuries.

About 25 percent of stroke patients develop cognitive deficits severe enough to qualify for a diagnosis of dementia (Stephens et al., 2004). A greater risk of developing dementia is seen in stroke patients who are older (over age 80), who have less education, who have a history of strokes, or who have diabetes.

Even stroke patients who do not immediately develop dementia are at increased risk of devel-

TABLE 11.3 *DSM-IV-TR* Criteria for Dementia Due to Other General Medical Conditions

A. The development of multiple cognitive deficits manifested by both
   1. Memory impairment (impaired ability to learn new information or to recall previously learned information)
   2. One (or more) of the following cognitive disturbances:
      a. aphasia (language disturbance)
      b. apraxia (impaired ability to carry out motor activities despite intact motor function)
      c. agnosia (failure to recognize or identify objects despite intact sensory function)
      d. disturbance in executive functioning (i.e., planning, organizing, sequencing, abstracting)

B. The cognitive deficits each cause significant impairment in social or occupational functioning and represent a significant decline from a previous level of functioning.

C. Focal neurological signs and symptoms or laboratory evidence indicative of cerebrovascular disease (e.g., multiple infarctions involving cortex and underlying white matter) that are judged to be etiologically related to the disturbance.

D. The deficits do not occur exclusively during the course of a delirium.

Dementia due to Parkinson's disease
Dementia due to HIV disease
Dementia due to Huntington's disease
Dementia due to Pick's disease
Dementia due to Creutzfeldt-Jakob disease
Dementia due to head trauma
Dementia due to (other medical condition not listed above)

oping dementia compared to people the same age who do not suffer a stroke. Follow-ups of stroke victims who remained free of dementia in the 3 months after their stroke found that about 30 percent developed dementia within the next 52 months, compared to 10 percent of a control group (Desmond & Tatemichi, 1998). The patients most likely to eventually develop dementia tended to have additional strokes over this time, some of which were obvious and others which were silent and detected only later. In addition, patients who had medical events or conditions that caused widespread oxygen or blood deficiency—such as seizures, cardiac arrhythmias, congestive heart failure, and pneumonia—were more likely to develop dementia.

Dementia Associated with Other Medical Conditions

A variety of other serious medical conditions can produce dementia, including Parkinson's disease, the human immunodeficiency virus (HIV), and Huntington's disease (Table 11.3). *Parkinson's disease* is a degenerative brain disorder that affects about 0.3 percent of people in the general population and 1 percent of people over age 60 (Samii, Nutt, & Ransom, 2004). Muhammed Ali and Michael J. Fox are two well-known people with Parkinson's disease. Its primary symptoms are tremors, muscle rigidity, and the inability to initiate movement. The symptoms result from the death of brain cells that produce the neurotransmitter dopamine. Approximately 75 percent of people with Parkinson's disease develop dementia (Aarsland & Kurz, 2009).

The *human immunodeficiency virus (HIV),* the virus that causes AIDS, can cause dementia. People's memory and concentration become impaired. Their mental processes slow—they may have difficulty following conversations or may take much longer to organize their thoughts and to complete simple, familiar tasks. They may withdraw socially and lose their spontaneity. Weakness in the legs or hands, clumsiness, loss of balance, and lack of coordination are also common. If the dementia progresses, the deficits increase. Speech becomes increasingly impaired, as does the understanding of language. People are confined to bed, often with indifference to their surroundings.

HIV-associated dementia is diagnosed when the deficits and symptoms become severe and global, with significant disruption of daily activities and functioning. New onsets of HIV-related dementia have decreased, as has its severity, as antiretroviral therapies have become widely used in treating people with HIV. On the other hand, as more patients with HIV survive into older age due to these drugs, the number of people with HIV-related dementia is increasing, particularly among people who abused drugs or also had hepatitis C infections (Nath et al., 2008).

Huntington's disease is a rare genetic disorder that afflicts people early in life, usually between the ages of 25 and 55. People with this disorder develop severe dementia and chorea—irregular jerks, grimaces, and twitches. Huntington's disease is transmitted by a single dominant gene on chromosome 4 (Gusella, MacDonald, Ambrose, & Duyao, 1993). If one parent has the gene, his or her children have a 50 percent chance of inheriting the gene and developing the disorder. Huntington's disease affects many neurotransmitters in the brain. Which of these changes causes chorea and dementia is unclear.

Dementia can also be caused by two rare diseases, Pick's disease and Creutzfeldt-Jakob disease; by brain tumors; by endocrine conditions, such as hypothyroidism; by nutritional conditions, such as deficiencies of thiamine, niacin, and vitamin B_{12}; by infections, such as syphilis; and by other neurological diseases, such as multiple sclerosis. In addition, the chronic heavy use of alcohol, inhalants, and sedatives, especially in combination with nutritional deficiencies, can cause brain damage and dementia. As many as 10 percent of chronic alcohol abusers may develop dementia (Winger, Hofmann, & Woods, 1992). Alcohol-related dementia usually has a slow, insidious onset. While it can be slowed with nutritional supplements, it often is irreversible.

Traumatic brain injury, another potential cause of dementia, can result from penetrating injuries, such as those caused by gunshots, or closed head injuries, typically caused by blows to the head. In the United States, falls account for 28 percent of traumatic brain injuries, motor vehicle accidents for 20 percent, being struck by an object for 19 percent, violence for 11 percent, and bicycle accidents for 3 percent (Langlois, Rutland-Brown, & Wald, 2006). Leland, in the following case study, developed dementia after a motor vehicle accident.

CASE STUDY

A 41-year-old factory worker named Leland was returning home along a rural road one night after work. A drunk driver ran a stop sign and collided at a high rate of speed with the driver's side of Leland's car. Leland was not wearing a seat belt. The collision sent Leland through the windshield and onto the pavement. He lived but sustained substantial head injuries, as well as many broken bones and cuts. Leland was unconscious for more than 2 weeks and then spent another 2 months in the hospital, recovering from his injuries.

When he returned home to his family, Leland was not himself. Before the accident, he was a quiet man who doted on his family and frequently displayed a wry sense of humor. After the accident, Leland was sullen and chronically irritable. He screamed at his wife or children for the slightest annoyance. He even slapped his wife once when she confronted him about his verbal abuse of the children.

Leland did not fare much better at work. He found he now had great trouble concentrating on his job, and he could not follow his boss's instructions. When his boss approached Leland about his inability to perform his job, Leland could not express much about the trouble he was having. He became angry at his boss and accused him of wanting to fire him. Leland had always been much liked by his co-workers, and they welcomed him back after the accident with sincere joy, but soon he began to lash out at them, as he was lashing out at his wife and children. He accused a close friend of stealing from him.

These symptoms continued acutely for about 3 months. Gradually, they declined. Finally, about 18 months after the accident, Leland's emotional and personality functioning appeared to be back to normal. His cognitive functioning has also improved greatly, but he still finds it more difficult to pay attention and to complete tasks than he did before the accident.

Leland's symptoms are characteristic of people with traumatic brain injury. He showed changes both in his cognitive abilities and in his usual emotional and personality functioning. Fortunately, Leland's symptoms subsided after several months. Many victims of brain injury never fully recover (Beatty, 1995).

Dementias that follow single closed head injuries are more likely to dissipate with time than are dementias that follow repeated closed head injuries, such as those experienced by boxers. Between 1.6 and 3.8 million traumatic brain injuries in the United States each year are the result of sports and recreation activities; young men are most likely to suffer dementia due to head injury because they take more risks associated with head injuries than do other groups (CDC, 2007).

Soldiers serving in Iraq and Afghanistan are suffering high rates of traumatic brain injury due to blasts from roadside bombs and other explosive devices. It is estimated that 22 percent of all injuries in these wars are traumatic brain injuries (Committee on Gulf War and Health, 2008). Soldiers with traumatic brain injuries show declines in neurocognitive function similar to those in dementia, as well as depression, aggressive behavior, long-term unemployment, and problems with social relationships.

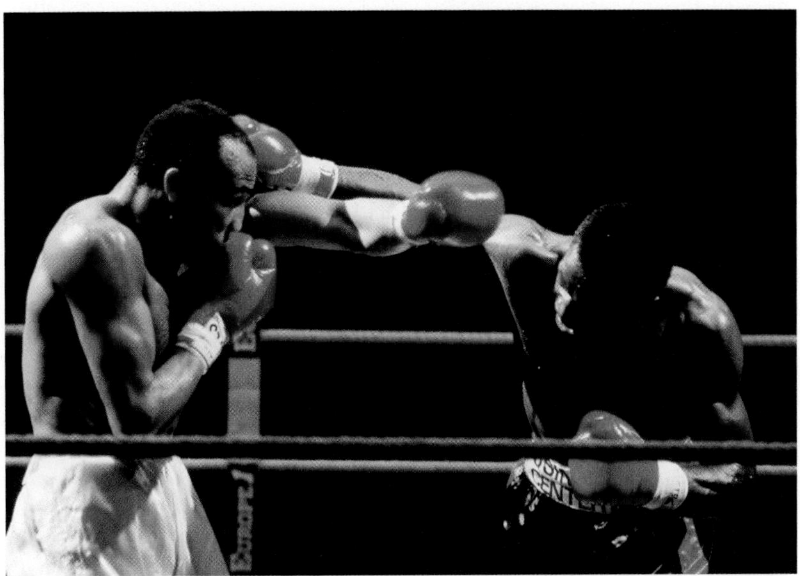

People engaged in sports such as boxing are at risk for brain injuries that can lead to severe cognitive deficits.

The Impact of Gender, Culture, and Education on Dementia

There are more elderly women than elderly men with dementia, particularly Alzheimer's dementia (Gatz, 2007). This may be simply because women tend to live longer than men and thus live long enough to develop age-related dementias. Among people with dementia, women tend to show greater decline in language skills than men, even though among people without dementia women tend to score better than men on tests of language skills (Buckwalter, Sobel, Dunn, & Diz, 1993). The reason for the greater impact of dementia on language in women is unknown. Some researchers have speculated that language skills are distributed across both sides of the brain in women but are more localized in the left side of the brain in men and that this somehow makes women's language skills more vulnerable to the effects of dementia.

In general, African Americans are diagnosed with dementia more frequently than European Americans (Chui & Gatz, 2005). African Americans have higher rates of hypertension and cardiovascular disease, both of which contribute to vascular dementia. However, the genetic factors leading to dementia may be more prevalent in European Americans than in African Americans.

Differences between groups in level of education also may contribute to differences in rates of dementia. Studies in the United States, Europe, Israel, and China show that people with lower levels of education are more likely to be diagnosed with dementia than are people with higher levels of education (Katzman, 1993; Stern, Gurland, Tatemichi, & Tang, 1994). Neuroimaging studies of people with dementia find that those with less education show more of the brain deterioration associated with dementia than do those with more education. It may be that people with more education have a higher socioeconomic status, which in turn provides them with better nutrition and health care that protect them against the conditions contributing to Alzheimer's disease. Education and, more generally, cognitive activity throughout one's life actually may increase brain resources in ways that forestall the development of dementia in people prone to the disorder (Gatz, Prescott, & Pedersen, 2006).

The likelihood that a person with dementia will be institutionalized rather than cared for in the family is greater among European Americans than among Asians or Hispanics and Latinos (Mausbach et al., 2004; Torti et al., 2004). The reason may be that Asian and Latino cultures have a more positive view of caring for sick and elderly family members than does European American culture. Asian and Latino cultures also exert greater societal pressure to care for ill family members in the home.

Treatments for and Prevention of Dementia

Two classes of drugs are approved for treatment of the cognitive symptoms of dementia. The first class is cholinesterase inhibitors, such as donepezil (Aricept), rivastigmine (Exelon), and galantamine (Reminyl). These drugs help prevent the breakdown of the neurotransmitter acetylcholine, and randomized trials show that they have a modest positive effect on dementia symptoms (Rockwood et al., 2007). The side effects of these drugs include

The Sisters of Notre Dame have participated in a fascinating study of the effects of early experiences on mental and physical health in old age.

Many people are interested in behavioral means of reducing their risk for dementia. Aerobic exercise and mental activity may have some protective value (Deeny et al., 2008; Valenzuela, 2008). Reducing the risk factors for stroke—for example, avoiding smoking, obesity, and hypertension—may reduce the risk for vascular dementia (Gatz, 2007).

One of the most fascinating studies to show a link between intellectual activity beginning early in life and a reduced risk of Alzheimer's disease is the Nun Study, a longitudinal study of several hundred elderly nuns in the School Sisters of Notre Dame. Nuns who entered old age with greater intellectual strengths were less likely to develop severe dementia, even when their brain showed evidence of significant neurofibrillary tangles and senile plaques (Snowdon, 1997). For example, the level of linguistic skill the nuns showed in journal writings when they were in their twenties significantly predicted their risk of developing dementia in later life (Snowdon et al., 1996). The best example was Sister Mary, who had high cognitive test scores right up until her death at age 101. An evaluation of Sister Mary's brain revealed that Alzheimer's disease had spread widely through her brain, even though her cognitive test scores slipped only from the "superior" range to the "very good" range as she aged. Other results from this study showed that tiny strokes may lead a mildly deteriorating brain to develop full-fledged dementia (Snowdon et al., 1997).

nausea, diarrhea, and anorexia. The second class is drugs that regulate the activity of the neurotransmitter glutamate, which plays an essential role in learning and memory; memantine (Namenda) is one such drug.

Many other drugs used to treat people with dementia affect the secondary symptoms of the disorder rather than the primary cognitive symptoms. Antidepressants and antianxiety drugs may be used to help control emotional symptoms. Antipsychotic drugs may help control hallucinations, delusions, and agitation (Sultzer et al., 2008).

Behavior therapies can be helpful in controlling patients' angry outbursts and emotional instability (Fitzsimmons & Buettner, 2002; Teri et al., 2003). Often, family members are given training in behavioral techniques to help them manage patients at home. These techniques not only reduce stress and emotional distress among family caregivers but also may result in fewer behavior problems in the family member with dementia (Teri et al., 2003).

TEST YOURSELF

1. What five types of cognitive impairment are seen in dementia?
2. What changes in the brain are seen in people with Alzheimer's disease?
3. What specific genes have been implicated in Alzheimer's disease? What other biological factors may play a role?
4. What are other causes of dementia besides Alzheimer's disease?

APPLY IT Helen is being treated for Alzheimer's disease. Which of the following treatments is *not* one that studies indicate would be useful for her?

a. cholinesterase inhibitors
b. drugs affecting glutamate
c. antianxiety and antidepressant drugs
d. stimulants

Answers appear online at www.mhhe.com/nolen5e.

TABLE 11.4 *DSM-IV-TR* Diagnostic Criteria for Delirium

A. Disturbance of consciousness (i.e., reduced clarity of awareness of the environment) with reduced ability to focus, sustain, or shift attention.

B. A change in cognition (such as memory deficit, disorientation, language disturbance) or the development of a perceptual disturbance that is not better accounted for by a preexisting, established, or evolving dementia.

C. The disturbance develops over a short period of time (usually hours to days) and tends to fluctutate during the course of the day.

D. There is evidence from the history, physical examination, or laboratory findings that the disturbance is caused by the direct physiological consequences of a general medical condition.

Source: Reprinted with permission from the *Diagnostic and Statistical Manual of Mental Disorders,* Fourth Edition, Text Revision.

DELIRIUM

Delirium is characterized by disorientation, recent memory loss, and a clouding of consciousness (Table 11.4). A delirious person has difficulty focusing, sustaining, or shifting attention. These signs arise suddenly, within several hours or days. They fluctuate over the course of a day and often become worse at night, a condition known as *sundowning*. The duration of these signs is short—rarely longer than a month. Delirious patients often are agitated or frightened. They also may experience disrupted sleep-wake cycles, incoherent speech, delusions, and hallucinations.

The symptoms of delirium usually follow a common progression (Cole, 2004). In the early phase, patients report mild symptoms such as fatigue, decreased concentration, irritability, restlessness, or depression. They may experience mild cognitive impairments or perceptual disturbances, or even visual hallucinations. As the delirium worsens, the person's orientation becomes disrupted. A patient may think she is in her childhood home instead of in the hospital. If undetected, the delirium progresses, and the person's orientation to familiar people becomes distorted. For example, a delirious person may misidentify his wife or fail to recognize his child. Immediate memory is the first to be affected, followed by intermediate memory (memories of events occurring in the past 10 minutes) and finally by remote, or distant, memory. When intervals of these symptoms alternate with intervals of lucid functioning and the symptoms become worse at night, a diagnosis of delirium is likely. If the person is not disoriented (to time, place, or person) or if recent memory loss is absent, then a diagnosis of delirium is unlikely.

The onset of delirium may be dramatic, as when a normally quiet person suddenly becomes loud, verbally abusive, and combative or when a compliant hospital patient tries to pull out his IV. Sometimes, though, the onset of delirium manifests as an exaggerated form of an individual's normal personality traits. For example, a generally cranky person recovering from surgery may complain loudly and harshly about the "inadequate" care she is receiving from the attending nurses. It would be easy for attending staff to regard her irritability as consistent with her personality style "She must be feeling better; she's beginning to complain." In this type of case, the delirium may go unrecognized until severe symptoms emerge.

Sometimes, delirious individuals simply appear confused. People who know the person well might say, "He just doesn't seem like himself." These delirious individuals may call acquaintances by the wrong names or forget how to get to familiar locations, such as their room. In such cases, the first indication of delirium often comes from the observations of family or medical staff. They notice that the person seems calm during the day but becomes agitated at night. It is important to monitor such a person around the clock. Detecting delirium also may require the frequent testing of the person's orientation. Close monitoring is also important because, with delirium, accidents such as falling out of bed or stepping into traffic are common.

Delirium typically signals a serious medical condition. When it is detected and the underlying medical condition is treated, delirium is temporary and reversible. The longer delirium continues, however, the more likely the person is to suffer permanent brain damage, because the causes of delirium, if left untreated, can induce permanent changes in the functioning of the brain.

Causes of Delirium

Dementia is the strongest predictor of delirium, increasing the risk fivefold (Cole, 2004). A wide range of medical disorders, including stroke, congestive heart failure, infectious diseases, a high fever, and

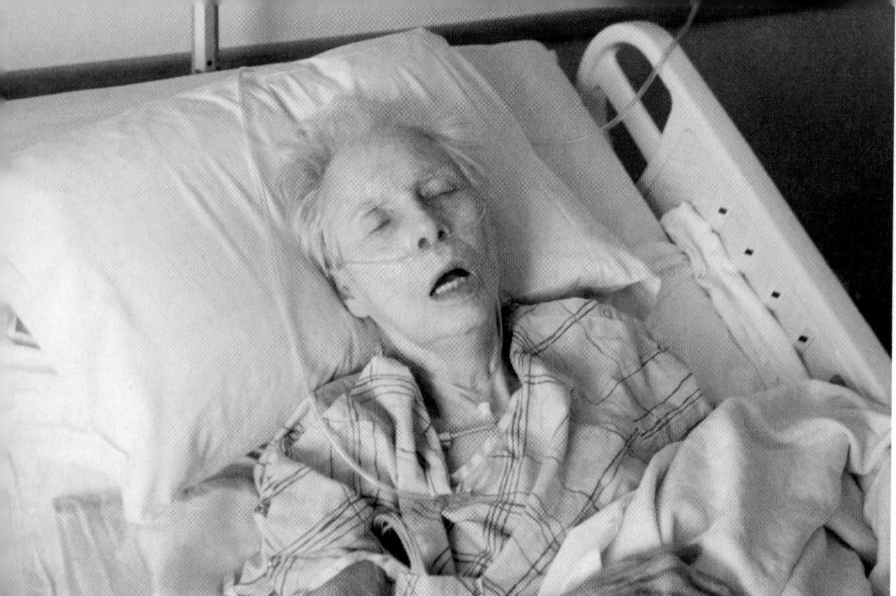

Delirium is a common problem in hospitals.

HIV infection, is associated with a risk for delirium. Intoxication with illicit drugs and withdrawal from these drugs or from prescription medications also can lead to delirium. Other possible causes include fluid and electrolyte imbalances, medications, and toxic substances.

Delirium may be caused when a medical condition, a drug, or a toxic substance affects the level of acetylcholine in the brain (White, 2002). Abnormalities in a number of other neurotransmitters, including dopamine, serotonin, and GABA, are seen in people who are delirious.

Delirium is probably the most common psychiatric syndrome found in general hospitals, particularly in older people. About 15 to 20 percent of older people are delirious on admission to the hospital for a serious illness, and another 10 to 15 percent develop delirium while in the hospital. Older people often experience delirium following surgery (Brown & Boyle, 2002; Cole, 2004). The delirium may be the result of the person's medical disorder or the effect of medications. It also may result from sensory isolation. A syndrome known as *ICU/CCU psychosis* occurs in intensive care and cardiac care units (Maxmen & Ward, 1995). Patients who are kept in unfamiliar surroundings that are monotonous may hear noises from machines as human voices, see the walls quiver, or hallucinate that someone is tapping them on the shoulder.

Among the elderly, a high mortality rate is associated with delirium (Byrne, 1994; Cole, 2004). The typical reason is that the underlying condition or the cause of the delirium is very serious. Between 15 and 40 percent of delirious hospital patients die within 1 month, compared to half that rate for nondelirious patients.

Some people are at increased risk for delirium. Risk factors include age (the older the person, the higher the risk), gender (males are at greater risk than females), and pre-existing brain damage or dementia (Brown & Boyle, 2002). African Americans have higher rates of delirium than European Americans, possibly because African Americans are less likely to have health insurance and thus do not receive early intervention for serious illnesses. As a result, their illnesses may be more likely to become severe enough to cause delirium.

Treatments for Delirium

It is extremely important that delirium be recognized and treated quickly. If a delirious person is not already hospitalized, immediate referral to a physician should be made. If another medical condition is associated with the delirium (e.g., stroke or congestive heart failure), the first priority is to treat that condition (Cole, 2004). Drugs that may contribute to the delirium must be discontinued. Antipsychotic medications sometimes are used to treat the person's confusion. It also may be necessary to prevent people with delirium from harming themselves (Maxmen & Ward, 1995). Often, nursing care is required to monitor people's state and prevent them from wandering off, tripping, or ripping out intravenous tubes and to manage their behavior if they should become noncompliant or violent. In some instances, restraints are necessary. Providing a reassuring atmosphere filled with familiar personal belongings, such as family photographs and the person's own clothing, can help patients prone to delirium be less agitated and feel more in control.

TEST YOURSELF

1. What are the characteristics of delirium?
2. What are some causes of delirium?

APPLY IT Stan, who is in the hospital for heart surgery, is showing symptoms of delirium. Which of the following medications do studies indicate might be useful in treating his symptoms?

a. antipsychotic medications
b. anticoagulant medications
c. stimulants
d. antihistamines

Answers appear online at www.mhhe.com/nolen5e.

SHADES OF GRAY

Consider the following description of a woman named Mariel.

Mariel, age 29, is a single Puerto Rican woman who currently lives with her mother and aunt in the Bronx. She was found to be HIV-positive 8 years ago, when she was donating blood. She contracted the virus when she was raped at age 17 by a family friend, who later died of AIDS. For the past 2 years, Mariel had been living and working as a store clerk in Puerto Rico. When she developed *Pneumocystis carinii* pneumonia, her mother insisted that she return to New York City to obtain better medical care.

In the hospital, Mariel was referred for a psychiatric consultation because she was found wandering in a corridor distant from her room. When the psychiatrist arrived in her room, he found her lying on her bed, with half her body outside the covers, rocking back and forth while clutching a pink teddy bear and staring at the television expressionlessly. When asked a series of questions about where she was, what day it was, and so on, she answered correctly, indicating that she was oriented to the time and place, but her responses were greatly delayed, and it was almost impossible to engage her in conversation. She said she wanted to leave the hospital to find a place to think. Her mother reported that Mariel had told her she wanted to die.

Over the next few days in the hospital, Mariel became increasingly withdrawn. She sat motionless for hours, did not eat voluntarily, and did not recognize her mother when she visited. At times, Mariel became agitated and appeared to be responding to visual hallucinations. When asked to state where she was and her birth date, she did not answer and either turned away or became angry and agitated.

As the pneumonia subsided, these acute psychological symptoms dissipated, but Mariel continued to be inattentive, apathetic, and withdrawn and to take a long time to answer simple questions. Suspecting depression, the psychiatrist prescribed an antidepressant, but the medication had little effect on Mariel's symptoms. After being discharged from the hospital, Mariel showed increasing trouble in expressing herself to her mother and in remembering things her mother had told her. She spent all day in her room, staring out the window, and showing little interest in the activities her mother suggested to her.

What diagnosis would you give Mariel? (Discussion appears at the end of this chapter.)

AMNESIA

CASE STUDY

A 46-year-old divorced housepainter is admitted to the hospital with a history of 30 years of heavy drinking. He has had two previous admissions for detoxification, but his family states that he has not had a drink in several weeks, and he shows no signs of alcohol withdrawal. He looks malnourished, however, and appears confused and mistakes one of his physicians for a dead uncle.

Within a week, the patient seems less confused and can find his way to the bathroom without direction. He remembers the names and birthdays of his siblings but has difficulty naming the past five presidents. More strikingly, he has great difficulty retaining information for longer than a few minutes. He can repeat a list of numbers immediately after he has heard them, but a few minutes later he does not recall being asked to perform the task. Shown three objects (keys, comb, ring), he cannot recall them 3 minutes later. He does not seem worried about this. Asked if he can recall the name of his doctor, he replies, "Certainly," and proceeds to call the doctor "Dr. Masters" (not his name), and he claims to have met him in the Korean War. He tells a long untrue story about how he and Dr. Masters served as fellow soldiers. (Reprinted from the *DSM-IV-TR Casebook: A Learning Companion to the Diagnostic and Statistical Manual of Mental Disorders,* Fourth Edition, Text Revision. Copyright © 2000 American Psychiatric Association.)

In dementia and delirium, people show multiple cognitive deficits, including memory deficits, language deficits, disorientation, an inability to recognize objects or people, and an inability to think abstractly or to plan and carry out an activity. In *amnesic disorders,* only memory is affected. A person with **amnesia** may be impaired either by **anterograde amnesia,** the inability to learn new information, or by **retrograde amnesia,** the inability to recall previously learned information or past events. Amnesic disorders often follow periods of confusion, disorientation, and delirium. Unlike the dissociative amnesia discussed in Chapter 6, the amnesic disorders in this chapter have known organic or biological causes. In the *DSM-5,* the diagnosis of amnesia is likely to be subsumed under the categories *major neurocognitive disorder* and *minor neurocognitive disorder* (American Psychological Association, 2010).

The pattern of amnesia represented in movies and television shows—people suddenly forgetting everything they previously knew—is unrealistic. Commonly, people with amnesia can remember events from the distant but not the recent past. For example, a 60-year-old patient may be able to tell where he went to high school and college but be unable to remember that he was admitted to the hospital yesterday. He also will forget meeting his doctor from one day to the next. In profound amnesia, a person may be completely disoriented about place or time, but rarely does an amnesic person forget his or her identity.

Often, people with amnesia do not realize that they have profound memory deficits and deny evidence of these deficits. They may seem unconcerned with obvious lapses in memory or may make up stories to cover these lapses. They may become agitated with others who point out their memory lapses and may even accuse others of conspiring against them.

Amnesia can be caused by brain damage due to stroke, head injury, chronic nutritional deficiencies, exposure to toxins (e.g., through carbon monoxide poisoning), herpes encephalitis, or chronic substance abuse (Kopelman, 2002). *Korsakoff's syndrome* is an amnesic disorder caused by damage to the thalamus, a part of the brain that acts as a relay station for other parts of the brain (Kopelman, 2002). Chronic and heavy alcohol use is associated with Korsakoff's syndrome, probably because many alcohol abusers neglect their nutrition and develop a thiamin deficiency (see Chapter 14).

The course of amnesic disorders depends on their cause (Kopelman, 2002). If, for example, a stroke occurs in the hippocampus, the memory loss that results will include events after the date of the stroke. Memories prior to the stroke will remain intact. If the memory loss is caused by alcohol or other toxins, it is often broader and the onset can be insidious. For some people, remote memory also may become impaired.

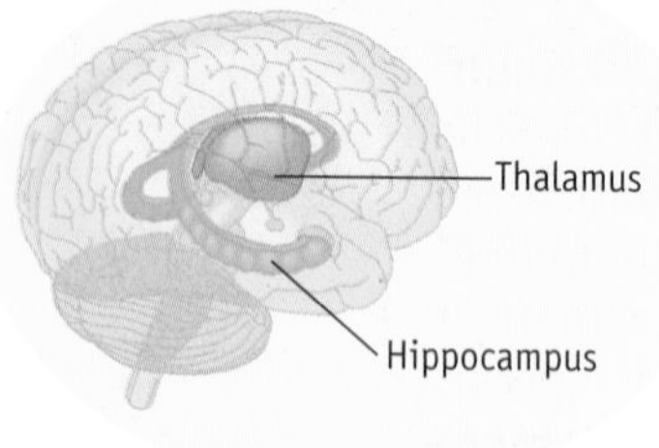

Damage to the thalamus causes Korsakoff's syndrome, and stroke damage to the hippocampus causes memory loss for events that take place after the stroke.

The first step in the treatment of amnesic disorders is to remove, if possible, any conditions contributing to the amnesia, such as alcohol use or exposure to toxins (Grossman, 2008). In addition, attention to nutrition and the treatment of any accompanying health condition (such as hypertension) can prevent further deterioration. Because new surroundings and routines may prove too difficult or impossible for the amnesic person to learn, the environment should be kept as familiar as possible. Often, as with dementia, it can be helpful to prominently display clocks, calendars, photographs, labels, and other reminders.

TEST YOURSELF

1. What are some causes of amnesia?
2. How is amnesia treated?

APPLY IT Rebecca has lost her memory of past events. Jose cannot remember new information. The appropriate diagnosis for Rebecca would be ______, while the appropriate diagnosis for Jose would be ______.

a. anterograde amnesia; retrograde amnesia
b. retrograde amnesia; anterograde amnesia
c. organic amnesia; psychogenic amnesia
d. psychogenic amnesia; organic amnesia

Answers appear online at www.mhhe.com/nolen5e.

MENTAL DISORDERS IN LATER LIFE

All the disorders in other chapters of this book also can occur in later life, sometimes as the continuation of lifelong problems and sometimes arising for the first time in old age. For the remainder of this chapter, we focus on three of the most common mental disorders among older adults—the anxiety disorders, depression, and substance use disorders. Assessing psychopathology in older people can be difficult, in part because psychological problems frequently co-occur with medical problems (Zarit & Haynie, 2000). Sometimes, the symptoms of depression, anxiety, or confusion, for example, can be the result of medical problems. Other times, they are independent of medical problems but contribute to them, as when a depressed person is not motivated to take the medications needed to overcome a medical problem. Still other times, emotional symptoms arise in response to the disability, pain, or loss that occurs because of a medical problem. Further, some psychological symptoms are side effects of medications an older person is taking for a medical problem. Teasing apart psychological symptoms from medical issues is critical to making an accurate assessment, but it can be very difficult.

Assessment is also complicated by the fact that older people may not present the same symptoms of a disorder that younger people do (Fiske et al., 2009). In the mood and anxiety disorders, for example, older people often complain of physical problems rather than the psychological concerns we associate with these disorders. This can lead to misdiagnosis or to the elderly person's somatic complaints being dismissed as "normal for old age." Also, older people may be more reluctant to admit to psychological problems because they grew up in a period when these problems were heavily stigmatized.

Anxiety Disorders

Anxiety is one of the most common problems among older adults, with up to 15 percent of people over age 65 experiencing an anxiety disorder (Bryant, Jackson, & Ames, 2008). Some older people have had anxiety disorders all their lives. For other people, anxiety first arises in old age. It often takes the form of worry about loved ones or about the older person's own health or safety, and it frequently exists along with medical illnesses and with depression, as with Mrs. Johnson in the following case study.

CASE STUDY

Mrs. Johnson is a 71-year-old female who was referred by a family practice physician who works in a nearby town. Mrs. Johnson had become extremely anxious and moderately depressed following a major orthopedic surgery, a total hip replacement. She was a retired office worker.

I was immediately struck by her general level of anxiety. For example, she expressed fears about her ability to get her husband to take her to an appointment and was concerned that she might not be the right type of person for psychological treatment. Her anxiety seemed to interfere with her ability to adequately attend to and process information. For example, she seemed to have difficulty getting down the directions to my office. She stated that she was concerned about being able to find the building and that she would leave her house early in case she got lost. Mrs. Johnson was early to her appointment. She looked distraught throughout the session. She wrung her hands, cried on a couple of occasions, and repeatedly stated, "I don't want to be a burden." Her main concern was that due to her recent surgery, she might not be able to continue living in the home she and her husband had lived in most of her adult life. She was extremely afraid of having a fall and not being found for hours.

Mrs. Johnson stated that when she was raising her children, she worried about their education and about money. Her children were living various distances away from her, so that their involvement, at least physically, was not an option. Mrs. Johnson indicated that she loved all her children but that she worried about two of them. Both had been divorced and she was concerned about their well-being and that of her three grandchildren. She reported not having the desire to eat because her stomach was "fluttery." I asked, "Do you find yourself worrying about things?" to which she responded, "Yes, a lot. I worry that I've begun to be a burden for my husband. I worry about my hip and I worry about not being able to get around. I guess I'm crazy because I worry about being worried so much." I assured her that she was not crazy, just anxious, which can oftentimes make you feel like you are crazy. (Adapted from Scogin, Floyd, & Forde, 2000, pp. 117–118)

Mrs. Johnson was diagnosed with generalized anxiety disorder (GAD; see Chapter 5). One study estimated that 7.3 percent of older adults suffer from GAD (Beekman et al., 1998). This rate is lower than the rate among young adults, but, as in young adults, older women are about twice as likely as older men to suffer from the disorder. Older adults may worry more about health and about family issues than do younger adults (Scogin et al., 2000). Too often, their worries about health are dismissed as understandable when in fact they are part of GAD.

Panic disorder is relatively rare in later life (Bryant et al., 2008). One epidemiological study estimated that only 0.1 percent of people over age 65 can be diagnosed with this disorder (Regier et al., 1988). Obsessive-compulsive disorder also is quite rare, diagnosed in only 0.8 percent of the older people in this study. The symptoms of posttraumatic stress disorder (PTSD) and acute stress disorder, however, are relatively common among older people, often occurring in response to the loss of a loved one (Bryant et al., 2008).

Very few older adults seek treatment for anxiety disorders, and those who do tend to consult their family physicians rather than mental health professionals (Scogin et al., 2000). For those older people who do seek help, cognitive-behavioral therapy has been shown to be effective in treating the anxiety symptoms (Wetherell, Lenze, & Stanley, 2005).

Physicians frequently prescribe an antianxiety drug, such as a benzodiazepine, when an older patient complains of anxiety. With age come changes in drug absorption and distribution, metabolism, and sensitivity to side effects. Side effects such as unsteadiness can lead to falls and bone fractures (Scogin et al., 2000). Also, tolerance can develop with prolonged use of the benzodiazepines, leading to severe withdrawal effects and the rebound of anxiety symptoms when the person discontinues their use. Antidepressant drugs, including buspirone and the selective serotonin reuptake inhibitors, are increasingly used to treat anxiety symptoms and have fewer side effects and withdrawal effects than the benzodiazepines. Older adults often are taking several prescription and over-the-counter medications that can interact with psychotropic drugs. All these factors make the management of drug therapy in older adults more complex than in younger adults (Scogin et al., 2000).

Depression

CASE STUDY

Mrs. Scott was a 76-year-old widowed mother of three children who came to the Clinic for Older Adults, an ambulatory psychiatric clinic for seniors, at the behest of her oldest son, Roger. When first greeted in the waiting room, Mrs. Scott was sitting on the edge of her seat wringing her hands, looking anxiously from one corner of the room to another. Roger was sitting next to his mother, slumped in his chair and visibly irritated. Once she was alone with the interviewer, Mrs. Scott explained that she was terribly upset because her bowel was no longer working. She had been constipated for 5 days and took this as evidence that her bowel had "died" and that she would likely be dead within a matter of days. She further stated that she had been to see her primary care physician repeatedly for the problem and got only false reassurances that she was basically healthy but needed to adjust her diet and take a daily fiber supplement. She then tearfully related how "fed up" her children were with her and her bowel problems, and fervently asked the interviewer not to tell Roger that she had been talking about her problems again. She hinted that her children would be better off without her because "they just don't understand what I'm going through and are too busy with their own lives to worry about me." When asked if she had other difficulties, Mrs. Scott stated only that she was quite lonely and wished her children would visit her more often. In response to specific questions about depressive symptoms, Mrs. Scott stated that her sleep had been quite interrupted for the past several months and that she woke typically around 5 A.M. with abdominal cramping and fears about dying. She estimated that in the past 6 months she had lost about 20 pounds, in part because she had lost her appetite and in part because she was afraid to eat and "clog up" her body. Although she had been an avid reader in the past, she now found it difficult to focus or concentrate on anything other than her bowel. When asked if her problems had gotten so bad that she thought about dying or hurting herself, her eyes welled with tears and she admitted that she asked the Lord each night to take her and put her out of her misery.

Later when asked about her sister, who had died unexpectedly from a stroke 6 months previously, Mrs. Scott initially turned away and then wept bitterly. She began to describe how her sister had been her close companion throughout life and especially since Mrs. Scott's husband died 10 years earlier. After this brief release of sorrow, she then abruptly asked that the interview be terminated because she could not imagine how any of this could help her with her "real" problem. (Adapted from King & Markus, 2000, pp. 141–142)

Among older people living in the community, only about 1 to 5 percent can be diagnosed with major depression (Fiske et al., 2009). Depression is much more common among those living in acute care or chronic care settings, where the prevalence is as high as 12 to 20 percent. Symptoms not quite meeting the criteria for major depression occur in approximately 15 percent of the community-dwelling elderly and in up to 30 percent of the institutionalized elderly (King & Marcus, 2000). As we discussed in Chapter 7, women outnumber men among people with depression, but this gender gap narrows—and in some studies disappears—among people over 65 (Fiske et al., 2009). Bipolar disorder is quite rare among the elderly and even more rarely is diagnosed for the first time in old age (King & Markus, 2000). Thus, we focus our discussion here on unipolar depression.

Depression greatly reduces the quality of life for older people. One study estimated that depression ranks with arthritis and heart disease as the diseases inflicting the greatest burden on quality of life in the elderly (Unützer et al., 2000). Depression can even be lethal for older people. The suicide rate among older White males is the highest of any group in the United States, and 85 percent of older suicide victims are suffering from depression (Conwell et al., 1998; see the discussion of the prevalence of suicide among the elderly in Chapter 7). In addition, depression may hasten the progression of several medical diseases. Among people who have had a heart attack, depression increases the risk of death by five times (Frasure-Smith, Lesperance, & Talajic, 1995). In nursing home patients, major depression is estimated to increase the mortality rate by 59 percent, regardless of what physical ailment patients have (Rovner, 1993).

About half of older people who are depressed were depressed as younger adults, and about half have symptoms that arose initially in older age (Fiske et al., 2009). Older people are less likely than younger people to report the psychological symptoms of depression, such as depressed mood, guilt, low self-esteem, and suicidal ideation. They are more likely to complain of somatic problems (such as Mrs. Scott's constipation), psychomotor abnormalities (such as agitation or extreme slowing), and cognitive impairments (King & Markus, 2000). Many depressed elders show a *depletion syndrome,* consisting of loss of interest, loss of energy, hopelessness, helplessness, and psychomotor retardation (Newmann, Engal, & Jensen, 1991). Depression is less likely to lead to impairment in functioning in older people, perhaps because they are less likely to be in the workforce or in the process of raising children. As a result, depression often is misdiagnosed, or missed altogether, by family members and physicians.

Differentiating a primary depression from one caused by medical illness or medication can be difficult. Several medical illnesses can cause depression-like symptoms, including multiple sclerosis, Cushing's disease, Parkinson's disease, Huntington's disease, Addison's disease, cerebrovascular disease, hypothyroidism, chronic obstructive pulmonary disease, and vitamin deficiency (Fiske et al., 2009). An older adult who appears to be depressed needs a thorough medical examination in order to discern whether a medical disorder might be causing the symptoms.

One of the most difficult differential diagnoses to make is between depression and dementia, particularly because the two disorders often co-occur. Dementia can cause depression, and depression can cause changes in brain functioning that increase the risk for future irreversible dementia (King & Markus, 2000). Some rules of thumb can help differentiate depression from dementia, although they are not foolproof.

First, although depressed people often complain about memory problems, they tend to have cognitive deficits that are less severe than those found in people with dementia and also tend to be more aware of their cognitive problems than people with dementia. Second, the noncognitive symptoms of depression (e.g., hopelessness, fatigue, loss of motivation) tend to be more severe in people with primary depression than in people with dementia. Third, depressed people often have trouble with free recall memory tasks but can recognize things they know when they are shown them, whereas people with dementia have difficulty with both free recall and recognition memory tasks. Fourth, depressed people are likely to have a rapid onset of symptoms, whereas the onset of dementia is much more gradual.

Depression can be a life-threatening disorder in elderly people.

Depression that occurs first in old age is very often associated with the disability and pain of medical illness (Fiske et al., 2009). In addition, older people often are caring for a spouse or other loved ones who are seriously ill, and caregiving is a risk factor for depression. The loss of a spouse or another loved one to death leads to depressive symptoms in the majority of people. These grief-related symptoms are normal and are not diagnosed as depression unless they persist for several months beyond the loss. *Complicated grief,* or grief that eventually is diagnosed as major depression, also tends to be characterized by profound guilt, thoughts that one would be better off dead, profound inactivity, persistent impairment in functioning, and hallucinations that go beyond the common experience of hearing or seeing a dead loved one (American Psychiatric Association, 2000).

A substantial amount of research has been done on the treatment of depression in the elderly, and it is clear that several treatments can be successful (Fiske et al., 2009). Antidepressants are effective in 50 to 70 percent of older depressed people. The tricyclic antidepressants and the monoamine oxidase inhibitors can have dangerous cardiac side effects, however, so the selective serotonin and serotonin-norepinephrine reuptake inhibitors are used more often. Physicians must monitor older patients to ensure that dosage levels are not too high and that serious side effects do not emerge. Electroconvulsive therapy is disproportionately used with older depressed people, particularly among those who have not responded to medication therapy or whose medical conditions (e.g., cardiac problems) preclude the use of antidepressants. ECT is effective in reducing depression in the majority of depressed older people, although it carries the risk of memory loss (see Chapter 7).

Many psychological treatments for depression have been shown to help older adults, including behavioral therapy, cognitive-behavioral therapy, interpersonal therapy, problem-solving therapy, brief psychodynamic therapy, and life review therapy (Scogin et al., 2005). Most of these treatments include a behavioral activation component designed to increase the experience of pleasant activities in the lives of older adults.

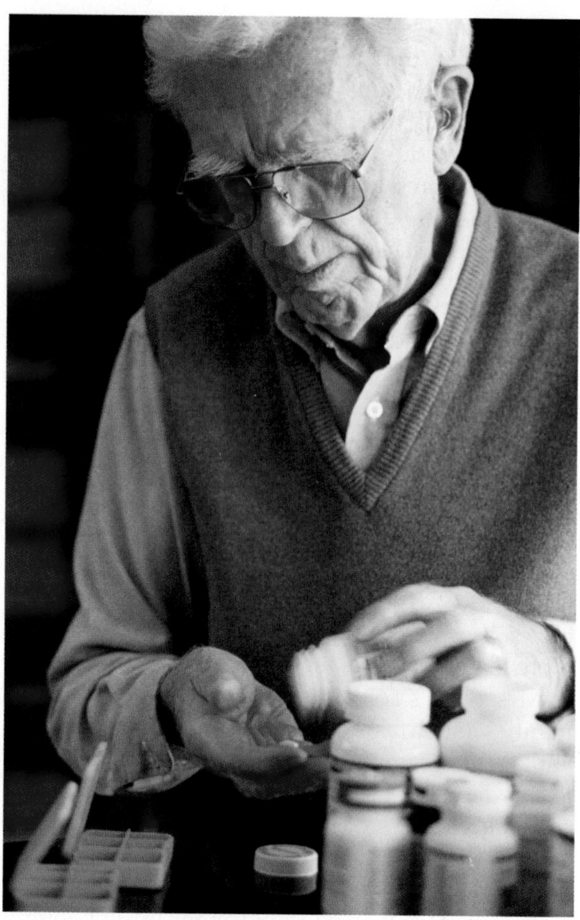

Some elderly people abuse prescription drugs.

Substance Use Disorders

We tend to think of substance use disorders as problems of the young. Indeed, the use of hard drugs, such as cocaine or heroin, is quite rare among the elderly. Many chronic users of illicit substances die before they reach old age, and others grow out of their use. Certain types of substance abuse and dependence are a frequent problem among older people, however, including alcohol-related problems and the misuse of prescription drugs (Lisansky-Gomberg, 2000).

Approximately 2 percent of people over 65 can be diagnosed with alcohol abuse or dependence, and about 10 percent can be considered heavy drinkers (Helzer, Burnam, & McEvoy, 1991; Merrick et al., 2008). One-third to one-half of abusers of alcohol first develop problems after age 65 (Liberto, Oslin, & Ruskin, 1996). Tolerance for alcohol decreases with age, so it takes fewer drinks for an older person to have a high blood-alcohol concentration. Older people also metabolize alcohol (and other drugs and medications) more slowly than younger people, so it can more readily cause toxic effects in the body, including changes in brain chemistry and cognitive deficits. In addition, women tend to metabolize alcohol and some drugs less efficiently than men, so the same dose can lead to greater toxic effects, especially with usage spanning many years.

The abuse of and dependence on prescription drugs is a much greater problem among the elderly than among younger individuals. Although only 13 percent of the U.S. population is over age 65, this group accounts for one-third of all prescription drug expenditures (National Institute on Drug Abuse, 2008b). The most commonly prescribed drugs are diuretics, cardiovascular drugs, and sedatives. Older people also are more likely than younger people to purchase over-the-counter drugs, including analgesics, vitamins, and laxatives.

The abuse of drugs such as the benzodiazepines may begin innocently. Physicians frequently prescribe them for older patients, and as many as one-third of older people take these drugs at least occasionally—for insomnia or after experiencing a loss, for example. As tolerance develops and the withdrawal effects of discontinuing the drug become clear, an individual may try to get more of it by copying prescriptions or seeing multiple physicians. Slurred speech and memory problems caused by drugs may be overlooked in the elderly as normal symptoms of old age. Older adults often can hide their drug abuse for a long period of time.

Eventually, the side effects of the drugs, the withdrawal symptoms people experience when they try to go off the drug cold turkey, or effects of interaction with other medications may land them in a hospital emergency room, as happened with Eleanor in the following case study.

CASE STUDY Eleanor is a widow of 72; she keeps reasonably busy by volunteering in a few community organizations. Since her husband died 10 years ago, she has had difficulty sleeping. Her physician, who perceived the sleep difficulties as based on depression and grieving, prescribed antidepressants. Because her insomnia continued, he also prescribed sedatives. She is now a regular user of sedatives and has appeared in the emergency department of the local hospital recently complaining of loginess and fatigue. (Lisansky-Gomberg, 2000, p. 277)

Treatment for older substance abusers is similar to that for younger abusers (see Chapter 14), although withdrawal symptoms may be more dangerous for older abusers and must be monitored more carefully (Lisansky-Gomberg, 2000). Psychotherapies that have been shown to be useful tend to have the following characteristics (Schonfeld & Dupree, 2002):

- Elders are treated along with people their same age in a supportive, nonconfrontational approach.
- Negative emotional states (such as depression and loneliness) and their relationship to the substance abuse are a focus of the intervention.
- Social skills and social networks are rebuilt.
- Staff members are respectful and interested in working with older adults.
- Linkages are made with medical facilities and community resources (such as housing services).

Due to increasing longevity and the size of the baby-boomer generation, the proportion of the population that is above age 65 will increase dramatically over the next few decades (King & Marcus, 2000). In addition, older adults will become much more ethnically diverse in the future. Although 85 percent of Americans over age 65 in 1995 were non-Hispanic Whites, this proportion is expected to decrease to 66 percent by 2030 (Whitbourne, 2000). In turn, the proportion of older people who are of Hispanic and Asian descent will increase. Much more research is needed on the psychological health needs of older people, particularly older people in ethnic and racial minority groups.

TEST YOURSELF

1. What anxiety disorders are most common in older adults?
2. How are anxiety disorders treated in older adults?
3. How can depression differ in presentation in older adults compared to its presentation in younger adults?
4. What are common substance abuse problems in older adults?

APPLY IT George is a 72-year-old man in good physical health who has been diagnosed with major depression. Which of the following treatments do studies suggest could reduce George's depressive symptoms?

a. cognitive-behavioral therapy and behavioral therapy
b. interpersonal therapy and brief psychodynamic therapy
c. ECT and antidepressant medications
d. all of the above

Answers appear online at www.mhhe.com/nolen5e.

CHAPTER INTEGRATION

Geropsychologists have emphasized the importance of understanding the cognitive disorders and psychological problems experienced by older people in the context of normal aging. Aging is not simply a biological process but rather the interaction of biological, psychological, and social processes, as depicted in Figure 11.5.

Changes that take place in the brain and the rest of the body with aging are influenced by our genetic and other biological vulnerabilities. The impact of these changes on the everyday behavior of older people varies tremendously, however, in part due to differences in personality and in the social environment. Some people become sedentary when they lose some of the strength and endurance they had as younger adults, whereas others institute exercise programs that help them maintain much of their youthful fitness. Similarly, the likelihood of developing many diseases in old age is substantially influenced by a person's

FIGURE 11.5 **Integrating Biological and Psychosocial Factors in Aging.**

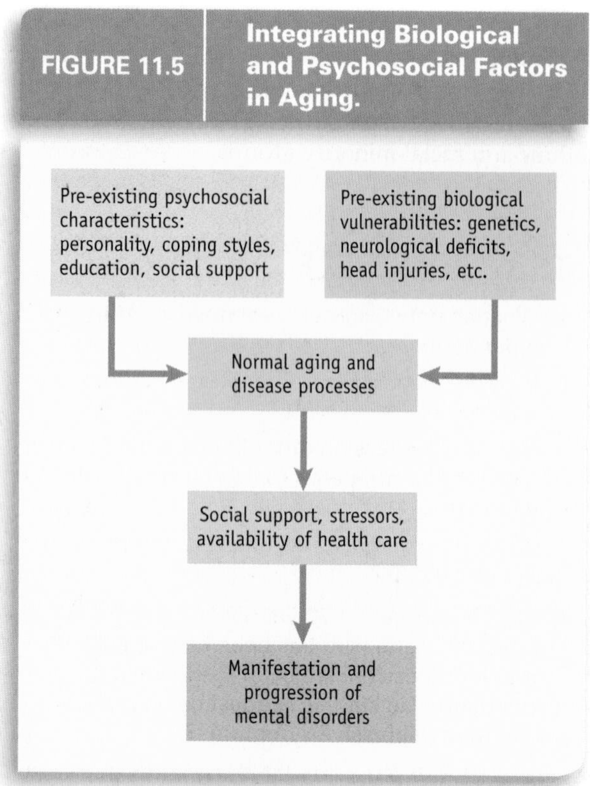

behaviors as a younger adult. For example, people who keep mentally active into middle and old age may be less likely to develop Alzheimer's disease.

Much of what we attribute to biological aging—for example, memory loss—is not the result of aging itself but rather is the effect of diseases such as those discussed in this chapter. But even the progression of these biological diseases is greatly affected by psychological and social variables. For example, many people in the early stages of dementia become paranoid, irritable, and impulsive. These symptoms may be especially pronounced in people who were somewhat paranoid, irritable, and impulsive before they developed dementia.

The social environment can affect the severity of cognitive deficits. If a person who is easily confused or forgetful is further stressed by family members who frequently become annoyed with the person or expect too much of him or her, then the cognitive deficits can become even more severe. Thus, even though the cognitive disorders are rooted in medical disease or in chronic intoxication with substances such as alcohol, psychosocial factors can influence the severity and manifestation of these disorders.

SHADES OF GRAY DISCUSSION (review p. 349)

Mariel shows some signs of delirium. Hospitalized for pneumonia, she is found wandering the halls, disoriented. She is inattentive and agitated, and apparently is hallucinating. Her symptoms persist after the pneumonia subsides, leading the psychiatrist to suspect that she is depressed. Antidepressants have little effect on her symptoms, however. She becomes more withdrawn and has more difficulty expressing herself after she leaves the hospital.

Mariel eventually was given the diagnosis of HIV-associated dementia. This form of dementia is characterized by a slowing of mental processes. As Mariel's case shows, people with this type of dementia experience changes in their behavior—they may withdraw socially, become indifferent to familiar people and responsibilities, and lose their spontaneity. They may complain of fatigue, depression, irritability, and agitation, just as Mariel did.

THINK CRITICALLY

The 2001 movie *Iris*, the Academy Award–winning film version of John Bayley's *Elegy for Iris*, shows Bayley (played by Jim Broadbent) explaining tenderly to his once-brilliant novelist wife (played by Judi Dench) that she had written many beautiful books in her lifetime. Another scene shows him completely frustrated, screaming that there is no reason for her Alzheimer's and that he hates Iris—words he doesn't really mean.

Dementia exacts a heavy toll not only on its sufferers, but also on their family members, as John Bayley's plight shows. The emotional and behavioral symptoms of dementia—paranoia, agitation, anxiety, and depression—can be very stressful for family members to handle in their loved ones. If the person with dementia is cared for in the home, the caregivers may have to deal with the patient losing important items, wandering away from the house and into dangerous situations, or engaging in dangerous behaviors such as putting clothes in the oven and turning it on. Caring for a patient also has a financial cost: From the first onset of symptoms, people with dementia live an average of 8 years and as long as 20 years, with the lifetime cost of treatment reaching hundreds of thousands of dollars per person in the United States.

If you became the primary caregiver of a person with dementia, what could you do to deal effectively with the challenges and stresses this role entails? (*Discussion appears on pp. 519–520 at the back of this book.*)

CHAPTER SUMMARY

- Dementia typically is a permanent deterioration in cognitive functioning, often accompanied by emotional changes. The five types of cognitive impairment in dementia are memory impairment, aphasia, apraxia, agnosia, and loss of executive functioning.
- The most common type of dementia is that due to Alzheimer's disease. The brain of an Alzheimer's patient shows neurofibrillary tangles, plaques made up of beta-amyloid protein, and cortical atrophy. Recent theories of Alzheimer's disease focus on genes that might contribute to the buildup of beta-amyloid protein in the brain of Alzheimer's patients, particularly the APOE gene.
- Dementia also can be caused by cerebrovascular disorder, head injury, and progressive disorders such as Parkinson's disease, HIV infection, Huntington's disease, Pick's disease, and Creutzfeldt-Jakob disease. Chronic drug abuse and the nutritional deficiencies that often accompany it also can lead to dementia.
- Drugs help reduce the cognitive symptoms of dementia and the accompanying depression, anxiety, and psychotic symptoms in some patients.
- Delirium is characterized by disorientation, recent memory loss, and a clouding of consciousness. Delirium typically is a signal of a serious medical condition, such as a stroke, congestive heart failure, an infectious disease, a high fever, or drug intoxication or withdrawal. It is a common syndrome in hospitals, particularly among elderly surgical patients.
- Treating delirium involves treating the underlying condition leading to the delirium and keeping the patient safe until the symptoms subside.
- In amnesic disorders, only patients' memories are affected. Anterograde amnesia, the most common form of amnesia, is characterized by the inability to learn or retain new information. Retrograde amnesia is the inability to recall previously learned information or past events.
- Amnesic disorders can be caused by stroke, head injury, chronic nutritional deficiencies, exposure to toxins, herpes encephalitis, and chronic substance abuse. The course and treatment of amnesic disorders depend on their cause.
- Anxiety disorders, particularly generalized anxiety disorder and post-traumatic stress disorder; are fairly common among older people. Anxiety disorders can be treated with antianxiety drugs, antidepressants, or psychotherapy.
- Depression is a common problem among the elderly, and suicide rates are extremely high among elderly White males. Some older people show a depletion syndrome, consisting of loss of interest, loss of energy, hopelessness, helplessness, and psychomotor retardation. Differentiating depression from dementia can be particularly difficult, but certain patterns of memory loss can help in making the differentiation.
- Antidepressant medications and ECT are commonly used to treat severe depression in older people. Several psychotherapies have been shown to work very well.
- Alcohol use problems can begin in older age, particularly since the metabolism of alcohol and tolerance for it change with age. Abuse of and dependence on prescription drugs are significant problems among older people. The treatment of substance use disorders for older people is similar to that for younger people.

KEY TERMS

Chapter 12

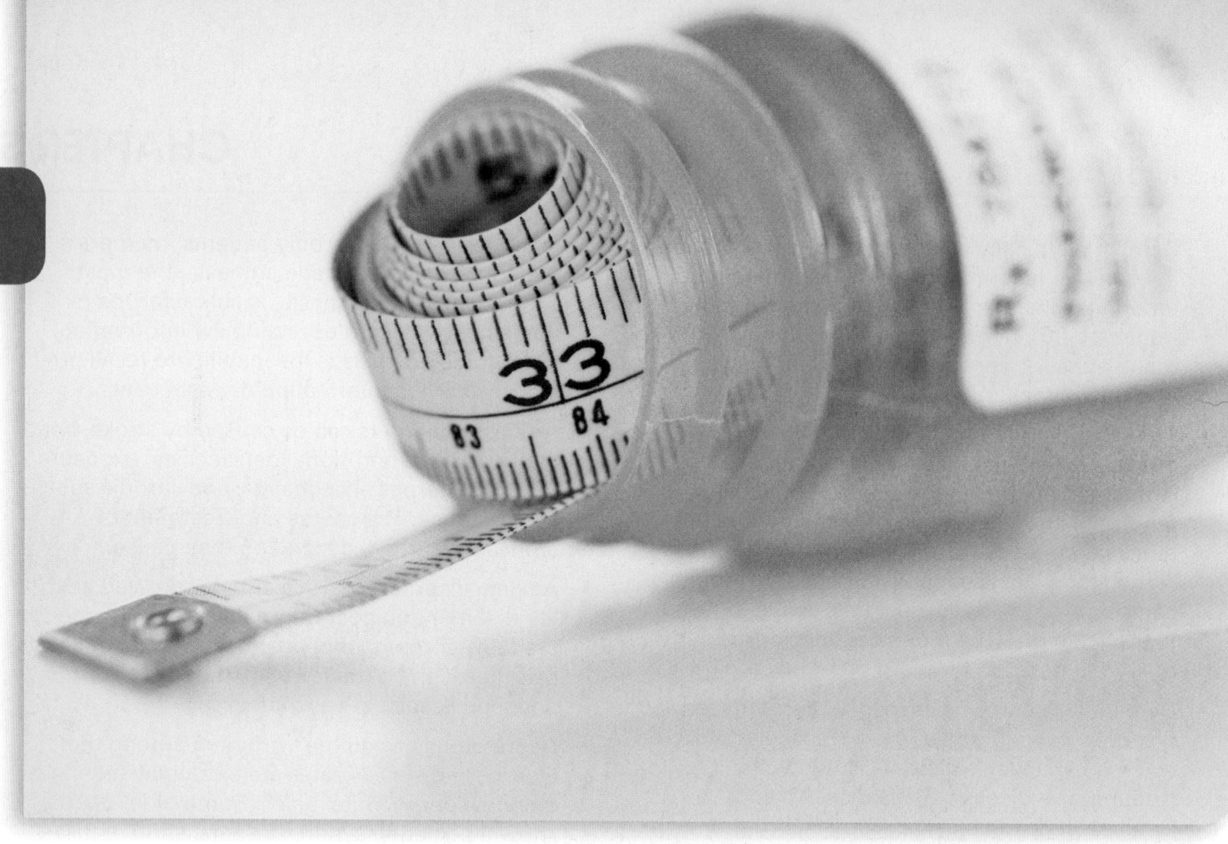

Eating Disorders

CHAPTER OUTLINE

Extraordinary People

Mary-Kate Olsen, *Standards of Beauty*

For years, the Olsen twins, Mary-Kate and Ashley, were the cutest kids on television. Beginning when they were 9 months old, they starred in the long-running hit *Full House.* As teens, they had their own line of straight-to-video films, video games, books, dolls, fragrances, and Wal-Mart clothing. In 2004, on their eighteenth birthday, they took control of an empire worth an estimated $300 million.

Days after that eighteenth birthday, Mary-Kate checked into a treatment facility for anorexia nervosa. Fans had noticed for months that Mary-Kate was becoming rail-thin. Reporters and bloggers speculated that she had an eating disorder. Some Web sites that promote and teach anorexic behaviors even held up Mary-Kate as a standard for other girls to aspire to. When asked whether she had an eating disorder, Mary-Kate and family members denied it. But in a TV interview on *48 Hours,* Mary-Kate showed body image concerns typical of a person with an eating disorder when she compared her looks with those of her twin sister, saying, "Are you kidding me? I look in the mirror and I'm like, why do you look pretty and I look ugly?"

Mary-Kate Olsen has led an unusual life with unusual stresses. Still, the pressure to be thin is familiar to many, as this excerpt from a college student's diary shows.

VOICES

This morning I had a half of a grapefruit for breakfast, and some coffee—no sugar or cream. For lunch, I had an apple and a diet soda. For dinner, I had some plain white rice and a salad with just some lemon squeezed over it. So I was feeling really good about myself, really virtuous. That is, until Jackie came over, and completely messed up my day. She brought over a movie to watch, which was fine. But then she insisted on ordering a pizza. I told her I didn't want any, that I wasn't hungry (which was a lie, because I was starving). But she ordered it anyway. The pizza arrived, and I thought I could be good and not have any. But it was just sitting there on the table, and I couldn't think of anything except having some. I couldn't concentrate on the movie. I kept smelling the pizza and feeling the emptiness in my stomach. Like a weakling, I reached out and got one piece, a small piece. It was ice cold by then, and kind of greasy, but I didn't care. I ate that piece in about 5 seconds flat. Then I had another piece. And another. I stopped after four pieces. But I still couldn't pay attention to the movie. All I could think about was what a pig I was for eating that pizza, and how I'll never lose the 10 pounds I need to lose to fit into size 2 jeans. Jackie's gone now, and I still keep thinking about how ugly and fat I am, and how I have no willpower. I didn't deserve to have that pizza tonight, because I haven't lost enough weight this month. I'm going to have to skip breakfast and lunch tomorrow, and exercise for a couple of hours, to make up for being a complete pig tonight.

CHARACTERISTICS OF EATING DISORDERS

Although we will discuss anorexia nervosa, bulimia nervosa, and binge-eating disorder separately, most individuals who initially meet the criteria for one of these disorders "migrate" between them, meeting criteria for two or more of the disorders at different times (Milos, Spindler, Schnyder, & Fairburn, 2005). Moreover, many individuals show behaviors and concerns characteristic of one or more of the eating disorders without meeting the criteria for one of these diagnoses. Such individuals may be given the diagnosis *eating disorder not otherwise specified.* Subclinical symptoms of eating disorders are extremely common and are risk factors for the development of a full-blown eating disorder and other problems.

Anorexia Nervosa

Diagnosis

People with **anorexia nervosa** starve themselves, subsisting on little or no food for very long periods of time, yet they remain sure that they need to lose

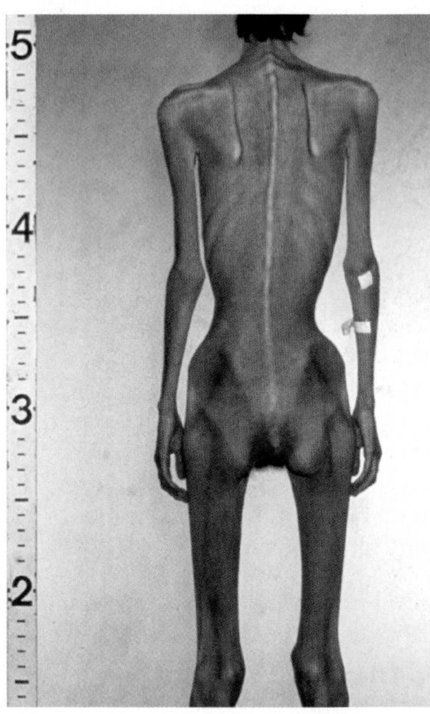
People with anorexia nervosa weigh significantly less than what they should for their age and height.

more weight. The diagnosis of anorexia nervosa requires that a person refuse to maintain a body weight that is normal for his or her age and height (see the *DSM-IV-TR* criteria in Table 12.1). The *DSM-IV-TR* criteria for anorexia nervosa require that a person's weight be at least 15 percent below the minimum healthy weight for the person's age and height (American Psychiatric Association, 2000). Often, the person's weight is much lower. For example, a 5-foot 6-inch young woman with anorexia may weigh 95 pounds, when the healthy weight for a woman this height is between 120 and 159 pounds. The extreme weight loss causes women and girls who have begun menstruating to stop having menstrual periods, a condition known as **amenorrhea.** The requirement of amenorrhea likely will be dropped from the diagnostic criteria for anorexia nervosa in the *DSM-5* because some individuals meet all the other criteria but still report some menstrual activity (Attia & Roberto, 2009). Also, eliminating this requirement allows the diagnosis to be applied to premenarcheal girls, post-menopausal women, and men.

Despite being emaciated, people with anorexia nervosa have an intense fear of becoming fat. Like Mary-Kate Olsen, they have a distorted image of their body, often believing that they are fat and need to lose more weight. They feel good and worthwhile only when they have complete control over their eating and when they are losing weight. Their weight loss causes people with anorexia to be chronically fatigued, yet they drive themselves to exercise excessively and to keep up a grueling schedule at work or school.

People with anorexia often develop elaborate rituals around food, as writer Marya Hornbacher describes in her autobiography, *Wasted.*

TABLE 12.1 *DSM-IV-TR* Diagnostic Criteria for Anorexia Nervosa

The *DSM-IV-TR* specifies that both intentional extreme weight loss and distorted thoughts about one's body are key features of anorexia nervosa.

A. Refusal to maintain body weight at or above a minimally normal weight for age and height (e.g., weight loss leading to a weight at least 15 percent below minimum healthy body weight, or failure to make expected weight gain during a period of growth, resulting in a weight at least 15 percent below minimum healthy body weight).

B. Intense fear of gaining weight or becoming fat, despite being underweight.

C. Distortions in the perception of one's body weight or shape, undue influence of body weight or shape on self-evaluation, or denial of the seriousness of the current low body weight.

D. In females who have reached menarche, amenorrhea (absence of at least three consecutive menstrual cycles).

Source: Reprinted with permission from the *Diagnostic and Statistical Manual of Mental Disorders,* Fourth Edition, Text Revision. Copyright © 2000 American Psychiatric Association.

VOICES

I would spread my paper out in front of me, set the yogurt aside, check my watch. I'd read the same sentence over and over, to prove that I could sit in front of food without snarfing it up, to prove it was no big deal. When five minutes had passed, I would start to skim my yogurt. . . . You take the edge of your spoon and run it over the top of the yogurt, being careful to get only the melted part. Then let the yogurt drip off until there's only a sheen of it on the spoon. Lick it—wait, be careful, you have to only lick a teeny bit at a time, the sheen should last at least four or five licks, and you have to lick the back of the spoon first, then turn the spoon over and lick the front, with the tip of your tongue. Then set the yogurt aside again. Read a full page, but don't look at the yogurt to check the melt progression. Repeat. Repeat. Do not take a mouthful, do not eat any of the yogurt unless it's melted. Do not fantasize about toppings, crumbled Oreos, or chocolate sauce. Do not fantasize about a sandwich. A sandwich would be so *complicated.* (Hornbacher, 1998, pp. 254–255)

Eating Disorders Along the Continuum

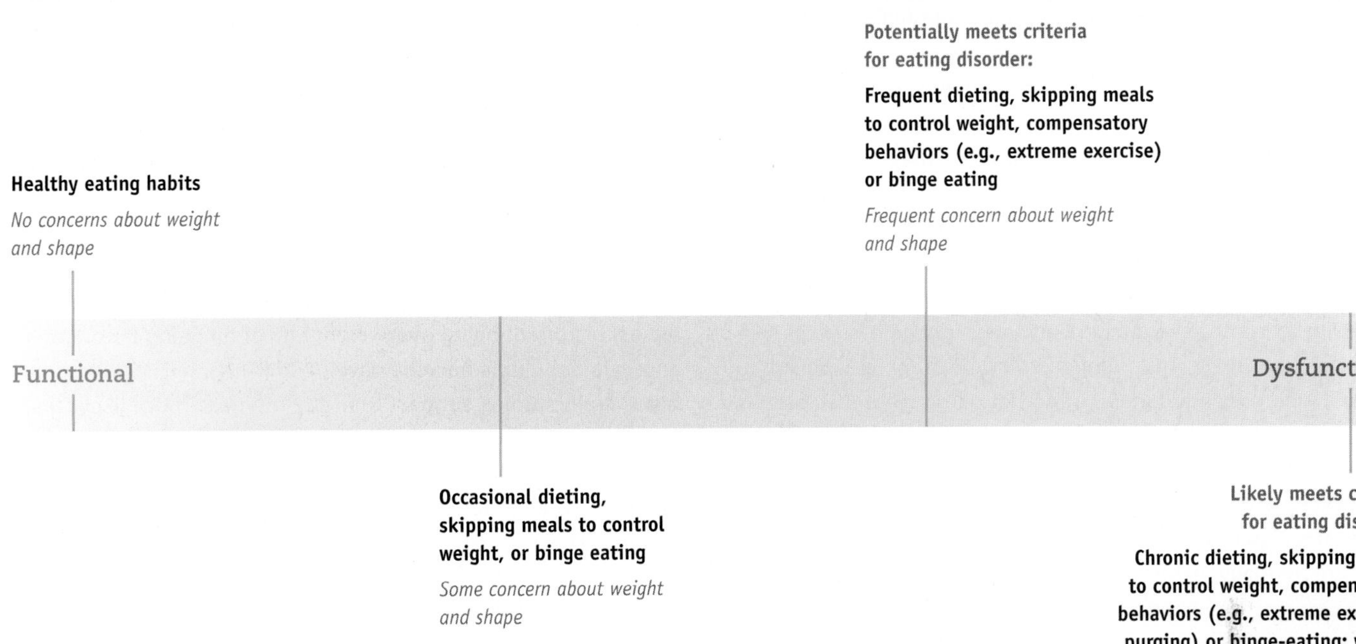
Potentially meets criteria for eating disorder:
Frequent dieting, skipping meals to control weight, compensatory behaviors (e.g., extreme exercise) or binge eating
Frequent concern about weight and shape
Healthy eating habits
No concerns about weight and shape
Functional
Dysfunctional
Occasional dieting, skipping meals to control weight, or binge eating
Some concern about weight and shape
Likely meets criteria for eating disorder:
Chronic dieting, skipping meals to control weight, compensatory behaviors (e.g., extreme exercise, purging) or binge-eating; weight loss of more than 15 percent of normal weight; loss of menses in women
Chronic dissatisfaction about weight and shape

As you go about your daily life, you certainly have seen in movies, ads, TV programs, and magazines that our culture is obsessed with body image and with how much food we eat. If you are a woman, you likely have been dissatisfied with your weight at some time. A nationwide study in the United States found that 38 percent of normal-weight women thought they were overweight (Chang & Christakis, 2003). Weight concerns are even greater among college women: A study of 2,200 college students in six universities across the United States found that two-thirds of the women were unhappy with their weight (Rozin, Bauer, & Catanese, 2003). If you are a man, you are less likely to have battled weight, but in recent years men have become increasingly concerned with attaining the lean lower body and strong, toned upper body celebrated in pop culture and the media. Studies show that toy action figures have grown more muscular over time, with many contemporary action figures appearing even more muscular than the most musclebound human bodybuilders (Baghurst, 2006). The number of magazine articles on achieving such a look has risen dramatically, and television stars tend to have this body type (Nemeroff, Stein, Diehl, & Smilack, 1994). On average, men want to be much more muscular and thinner than they actually are (Pope et al., 2000; Tiggemann, Martins, & Kirkbride, 2007).

Why do people care so much about their weight? Some people care because being overweight can contribute to serious diseases, such as high blood pressure, heart disease, and diabetes. Overweight people have shorter life spans than people who are not overweight. But most people attempt to lose weight because they want to be more attractive and have higher self-esteem. Eating has become more than a source of nourishment, and exercise more than a means of improving health. What we eat and how much we exercise have become linked to feelings of worth, merit, guilt, sin, rebelliousness, and defiance, in turn affecting our self-esteem.

The measures people take to lose weight fall along a continuum. Dieting is the most common way people try to overcome their body dissatisfaction. Only 33 percent of college women say they "never" diet, compared to 58 percent of college men (Rozin et al., 2003). However, successful dieting is hard, and almost all dieters who lose weight regain it—and often gain more (Byrne, Cooper, & Fairburn, 2003). Many people spend their lives in this cycle of yo-yo dieting.

Some people turn to more extreme means to make themselves look better. Each year, almost half a million people have the surgical procedure known as liposuction to remove unwanted body fat. Annually, Americans spend over $20 billion

(continued)

on cosmetic procedures and $30 billion on weight-loss products, including $8 billion on spas and exercise clubs, $382 million on diet books, $10 billion on diet soft drinks, and billions of dollars on low-calorie foods and artificial sweeteners.

At the far end of the continuum are people whose concerns about weight become so overwhelming and whose behaviors surrounding eating get so out of control that they have an eating disorder. There are three specific types of eating disorders: anorexia nervosa, bulimia nervosa, and binge-eating disorder. *Anorexia nervosa* is a pursuit of thinness that leads people to starve themselves. *Bulimia nervosa* is a cycle of bingeing followed by extreme behaviors to prevent weight gain, such as self-induced vomiting. And, *binge-eating disorder* is applied to people who regularly binge but do not purge what they eat. As you will see in this chapter, relatively few people meet the full criteria for these eating disorders, but many more people have some symptoms, which researchers call *partial-syndrome eating disorders* (Lewinsohn, Striegel-Moore, & Seeley, 2000).

Traditionally, eating disorders have been much more common among women than among men because women have felt more pressure to be thin (Figure 12.1). But men who develop eating disorders generally display the same symptoms as women, including body dissatisfaction and the use of purging and excessive exercise to control their weight (McCabe & Ricciardelli, 2004). Both men and women with eating disorders have high rates of depression, anxiety, and substance abuse (Olivardia, Pope, Mangweth, & Hudson, 1995; Striegel-Moore et al., 1998). For both genders, concern with weight can start young. About 12 percent of adolescent girls and 5 percent of adolescent boys report using extreme weight-loss strategies, such as laxative abuse, vomiting, and fasting (Neumark-Sztainer, Story, Hannan, & Croll, 2002).

There are some differences between men and women with regard to eating disorders. Men are more likely than women to have a history of being overweight and of bingeing before their anorexia or bulimia nervosa developed (Andersen, 1990). Some, but not all, studies suggest that gay men are more likely than heterosexual men to have an eating disorder while lesbians and heterosexual women are equally likely to have an eating disorder (Schneider, O'Leary, & Jenkins, 1995; Tiggemann et al., 2007).

In this chapter, we discuss the diagnosis and epidemiology of eating disorders; the causes of eating disorders, including the psychological and biological factors that may lead some people to develop these disorders; and effective treatments for eating disorders.

Types of Anorexia

In the previous Voices excerpt, Hornbacher describes one of the two types of anorexia, the restricting type (Table 12.2). People with the **restricting type of anorexia nervosa** simply refuse to eat as a way of preventing weight gain. Some people attempt to go for days without eating anything; most eat very small amounts of food each day, in part simply to stay alive and in part because of pressure from others to eat. Hornbacher survived for months on one cup of yogurt and one fat-free muffin per day. Daphne, in the following case study, also has the restricting type of anorexia nervosa.

CASE STUDY

Daphne is 5 feet 11 inches tall and weighs 102 pounds. She has felt "large" since her height soared above her schoolmates in the fifth grade. She has been on a diet ever since. During her junior year in high school, Daphne decided that she had to take drastic measures to lose more weight. She began by cutting her calorie intake to about 1,000 calories per day. She lost several pounds, but not fast enough for her liking, so she cut her intake to 500 calories per day. She also began a vigorous exercise program of cross-country running. Each day, Daphne would not let herself eat until she had run at least 10 miles. Then she would have just a few vegetables and a handful of cereal. Later in the day, she might have some more vegetables and some fruit, but she would wait until she was so hungry that she was faint. Daphne dropped to 110 pounds and she stopped menstruating. Her mother expressed some concern about how little Daphne was eating, but as her mother tended to be overweight, she did not discourage Daphne from dieting.

When it came time to go to college, Daphne was excited but also frightened, because she had always been a star student in high school and wasn't sure she could maintain her straight *A*'s in college. In the first examination period in college, Daphne got mostly *A*'s but one *B*. She felt very vulnerable, like a failure, and as if she were losing control. She also was unhappy with her social life, which, by the middle of the first semester, was going nowhere. Daphne decided that things might be better if she lost more weight, so she cut her food intake to two apples

FIGURE 12.1 **Women's and Men's Body Images.** Female and male undergraduates were shown figures of their own sex and asked to indicate figures that looked most like their current shape, their ideal figure, and the figure they felt would be most attractive to the opposite sex. Men selected very similar figures for all three choices, but women selected very different figures for their current figure and either their ideal figure or the figure they thought would be most attractive.

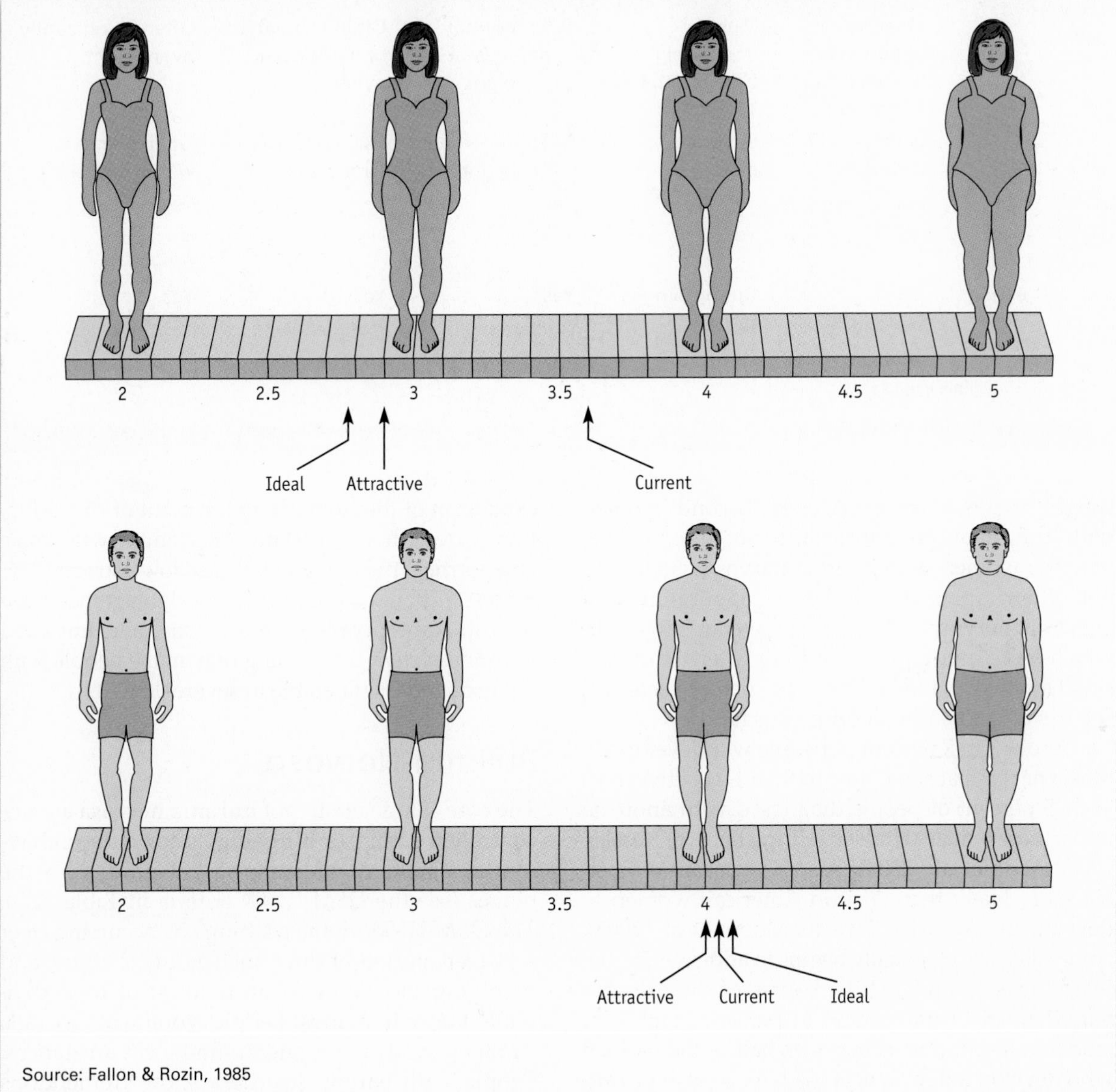

Source: Fallon & Rozin, 1985

and a handful of cereal each day. She also ran at least 15 miles each day. By the end of fall semester, she was down to 102 pounds. She was also chronically tired, had trouble concentrating, and occasionally fainted. Still, when Daphne looked in the mirror, she saw a fat, homely young woman who needed to lose more weight.

The other type of anorexia is the **binge/purge type of anorexia nervosa,** in which people periodically engage in bingeing or purging behaviors (e.g., self-induced vomiting or the misuse of laxatives or diuretics). This disorder is different from bulimia nervosa in at least two ways. First, people with the binge/purge type of anorexia continue to be at least 15 percent below healthy body weight, whereas people with bulimia nervosa typically are at normal

TABLE 12.2 Comparisons of Eating Disorders

The eating disorders vary on these characteristics.

Symptom	AN* Restricting Type	AN* Binge/Purge Type	BN* Purging Type	BN* Nonpurging Type	Binge-Eating Disorder
Body weight	Must be underweight by more than 15 percent	Must be underweight by more than 15 percent	Often normal or somewhat overweight	Often normal or somewhat overweight	Often significantly overweight
Body image	Severely disturbed	Severely disturbed	Overconcerned with weight	Overconcerned with weight	Often disgusted with overweight
Binges	No	Yes	Yes	Yes	Yes
Purges or other compensatory behaviors	No	Yes	Yes	No	No
Sense of lack of control over eating	No	During binges	Yes	Yes	Yes
Amenorrhea in females	Yes	Yes	Not usually	Not usually	No

*AN refers to anorexia nervosa, BN to bulimia nervosa.

weight or somewhat overweight. Second, women with binge/purge anorexia have amenorrhea, whereas women with bulimia nervosa usually do not. Often, a person with the binge/purge type of anorexia nervosa does not engage in binges in which large amounts of food are eaten. If even a small amount of food is eaten, the person feels as if she has binged and will purge this food.

About 1 to 2 percent of people will develop anorexia nervosa at some time in their life; between 90 and 95 percent of people diagnosed with anorexia nervosa are female (Hudson, Hiripi, Pope, & Kessler, 2007; Wade et al., 2006). Also, Caucasian women are more likely than African American women to develop the disorder (Striegel-Moore et al., 2003). Anorexia nervosa usually begins in adolescence, between ages 15 and 19. The course of the disorder varies greatly from person to person. Long-term studies suggest that as many as half of the women who develop anorexia nervosa have a positive outcome 10 to 15 years after treatment, but the remainder continue to have eating-related problems or other psychopathology, particularly depression (Herpertz-Dahlmann, Muller, Herpertz, & Heussen, 2001; Lowe et al., 2001; Wade et al., 2006; Wentz, Gillberg, Gillberg, & Ratsam, 2001).

Anorexia nervosa is a very dangerous disorder, with a death rate of 5 to 8 percent (Polivy & Herman, 2002). Some of the most serious consequences of anorexia are cardiovascular complications, including *bradycardia* (extreme slowing of heart rate), *arrhythmia* (irregular heart beat), and heart failure. Another potentially serious complication of anorexia is acute expansion of the stomach, to the point of rupturing. Bone strength is an issue for women who have amenorrhea, presumably because low estrogen levels lessen bone strength. Kidney damage has been seen in some people with anorexia, and impaired immune system functioning may make people with anorexia more vulnerable to severe illnesses.

Bulimia Nervosa

The core characteristics of **bulimia nervosa** are uncontrolled eating, or **bingeing,** followed by behaviors designed to prevent weight gain from the binges (see the *DSM-IV-TR* criteria in Table 12.3). The *DSM-IV-TR* defines a binge as occurring over a discrete period of time, such as 1 or 2 hours, and involving the eating of an amount of food definitely larger than most people would eat during a similar period of time and in similar circumstances. People with eating disorders show tremendous variation in the size of their binges, however. In laboratory feeding studies, the average binge of people with bulimia nervosa ranges from about 3,000 to 4,500 calories (Mitchell et al., 1998). But many individuals with bulimia nervosa also report binges of under 1,000 calories (Rossiter & Agras, 1990). What makes this lesser amount a binge for people with an eating disorder is the sense that they have no control over their eating and feel compelled to eat even though they are not hungry (Fairburn & Cooper, 2007). Recognizing this aspect of binges, the *DSM-IV-TR* criteria for a binge include a sense of lack of control over eating.

TABLE 12.3 *DSM-IV-TR* Diagnostic Criteria for Bulimia Nervosa

People with bulimia nervosa regularly binge eat and then attempt to avoid gaining weight from their binge.

A. Recurrent episodes of binge eating, characterized by both of the following:
   1. Eating, in a discrete period of time (such as within a 2-hour period), an amount of food that is definitely larger than most people would eat during a similar period of time and under similar circumstances
   2. A sense of lack of control over eating during the episode

B. Recurrent inappropriate behaviors to prevent weight gain, such as self-induced vomiting; misuse of laxatives, diuretics, enemas, or other medications; fasting; or excessive exercise.

C. The binge eating and inappropriate purging behaviors both occur, on average, at least twice a week for 3 months.

D. Self-evaluation is unduly influenced by body shape and weight.

Source: Reprinted with permission from the *Diagnostic and Statistical Manual of Mental Disorders,* Fourth Edition, Text Revision. Copyright © 2000 American Psychiatric Association.

The behaviors people with bulimia use to control their weight include self-induced vomiting; the abuse of laxatives, diuretics, or other purging medications; fasting; and excessive exercise. As with people with anorexia nervosa, the self-evaluations of people with bulimia nervosa are heavily influenced by their body shape and weight. When they are thin, they feel like a "good person." However, people with bulimia nervosa, unlike people with anorexia nervosa, do not tend to show gross distortions in their body images. Whereas a woman with anorexia nervosa who is absolutely emaciated looks in the mirror and sees herself as obese, a woman with bulimia nervosa has a more realistic perception of her actual body shape. Still, people with bulimia nervosa are constantly dissatisfied with their shape and weight and concerned about losing weight.

People with bulimia nervosa are distinguished from people with the binge/purge type of anorexia nervosa primarily by their body weight: The criteria for binge/purge anorexia require that a person be at least 15 percent below normal body weight, whereas there are no weight criteria for bulimia nervosa. People with the restricting type of anorexia nervosa also differ from people with bulimia nervosa in that they do not engage in binges—restrictors severely limit their food intake all the time (see Table 12.2).

Princess Diana struggled with bulimia nervosa.

Self-induced vomiting is the behavior people most often associate with bulimia. Bulimia is often discovered by family members, roommates, and friends when people with the disorder are caught vomiting or leave messes after they vomit.

Dentists also recognize people with bulimia because frequent vomiting can rot teeth due to exposure to stomach acid. People who use self-induced vomiting or purging medications are said in the *DSM-IV-TR* to have a **purging type of bulimia nervosa.** The cycle of bingeing and then purging or using other compensatory behaviors to control weight becomes a way of life, as in the case of Gregory.

CASE STUDY

Gregory, a 43-year-old theatrical manager, was evaluated at an eating disorders clinic in San Francisco. Although he had lost 58 pounds in the last 5 months, dropping from 250 to 192 pounds on a 6-foot, 1-inch frame, he was still terrified of getting fat.

Gregory first began to diet 5 months earlier when his wife told him he was "a fat slob" and implied that she might be considering a divorce. This terrified him and started him on a strict dietary regimen: an omelet and bran for breakfast, coffee for lunch, and salad and shrimp or chicken for dinner. His original goal was to lose about 50 pounds. When dieting did not result in sufficiently rapid loss of weight, he started sticking his finger down his throat to induce vomiting after meals.

Gregory is now "obsessed" with food. Before he goes to a restaurant, he worries about what he will order. He has done a study of what he eats in

(continued)

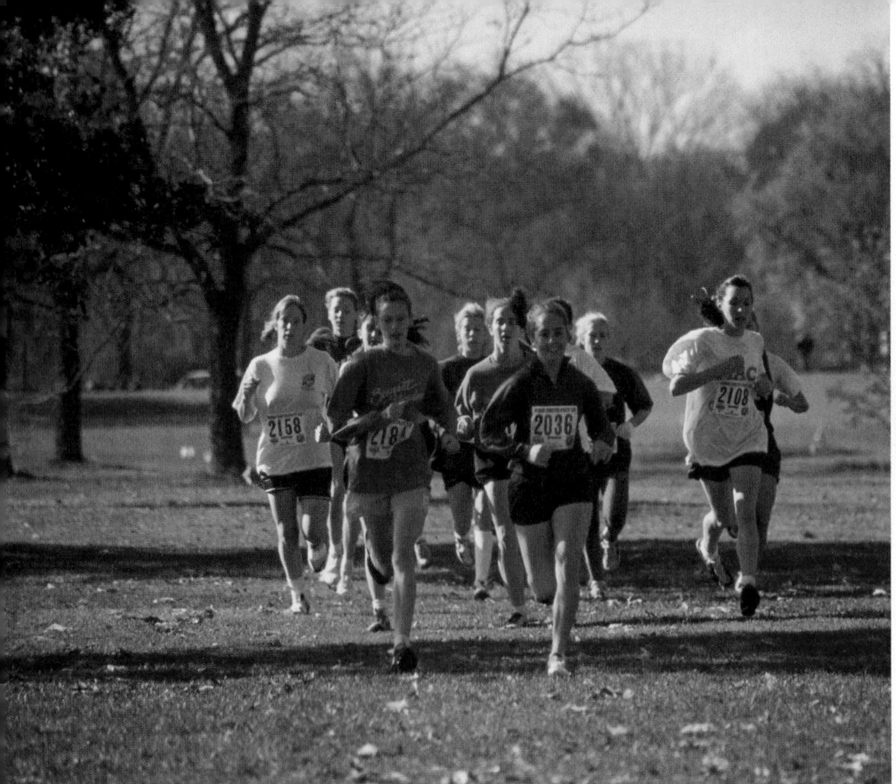

Some people with eating disorders may use excessive exercise to control their weight.

terms of what is easiest to purge, and he knows all the bathrooms in the areas he frequents. Three or four times a week he is unable to resist the urge to binge. At those times he feels that his eating is out of control, and he may gobble down as much as three hamburgers, two orders of French fries, a pint of ice cream, and two packages of Oreo cookies. He always induces vomiting after a binge. (Reprinted from the *DSM-IV-TR Casebook: A Learning Companion to the Diagnostic and Statistical Manual of Mental Disorders,* Fourth Edition, Text Revision. Copyright © 2000 American Psychiatric Association.)

People who use excessive exercise or fasting to control their weight but do not engage in purging are said to have a **nonpurging type of bulimia nervosa.** Using excessive exercise to control weight can easily hide people's bulimia if they are part of a group that values exercise, such as students on a college campus. Because individuals with this subtype resemble individuals with binge-eating disorder (see below), the *DSM-5* authors are recommending that subtypes in the diagnosis of bulimia nervosa be deleted (American Psychiatric Association, 2010).

The following passage was written by a male psychologist who developed the nonpurging type of bulimia nervosa over a period of years. This man grew up viewing food as a source of comfort and bingeing as a way of escaping from overbearing and disapproving parents. To control his weight, he fasted for a day or longer after a binge. As the pressures of his job and a failed marriage increased, his bulimic pattern of bingeing and then fasting grew more serious.

VOICES

I would sigh with relief when Sunday evening came, since I had no work responsibilities until the next morning, and I would have just returned my son to his mother's custody. I would then carefully shop at convenience stores for "just right" combinations of cheese, lunch meats, snack chips, and sweets such as chocolate bars. I would also make a stop at a neighborhood newsstand to buy escapist paperback novels (an essential part of the binge) and then settle down for a three-hour session of reading and slow eating until I could barely keep my eyes open. My binges took the place of Sunday dinner, averaging approximately 6,000 calories in size. Following the binge, my stomach aching with distension, I would carefully clean my teeth, wash all the dishes, and fall into a drugged slumber. I would typically schedule the following day as a heavy working day with evening meetings in order to distract myself from increasing hunger as I fasted. I began running. . . . I would typically run for one hour, four to five days per week, and walked to work as a further weight control measure. . . . As time went on, I increased the frequency of these binges, probably because of the decreasing structured demands for my time. They went from weekly to twice per week, then I was either bingeing or fasting with no normal days in my week at all. My sleep patterns were either near-comatose or restless, with either sweating after a binge or shivering after a fast. I became increasingly irritable and withdrawn . . . prompting increased guilt on my part that I resented the intrusion of my friends, my patients, and even my son into my cycle. . . . The nadir of my life as a bulimic occurred when I found myself calling patients whom I had scheduled for evening appointments, explaining to them that I was ill, then using the freed evening for bingeing. . . . I was physically exhausted most of the time, and my hands, feet, and abdomen were frequently puffy and edematous, which I, of course, interpreted as gain in body fat and which contributed to my obsession with weight and food. I weighed myself several times per day in various locations, attending to half pound variations as though my life depended on them.

("Male Bulimia Nervosa: An Autobiographical Case Study" by Wilps, R. F. Jr. from *Males with Eating Disorder* by A. E. Andersen (ed.), copyright 1990 Taylor & Francis Group LLC—Books. Reproduced with permission of Taylor & Francis Group LLC—Books in the Format Textbook via Copyright Clearance Center.)

The prevalence of bulimia nervosa in the general population is estimated to be between 0.5 and 3 percent (Hudson et al., 2007; Wade et al., 2006). It is much more common in women than in men, and in Caucasians than in African Americans (Striegel-Moore et al., 2003). The onset of bulimia nervosa most often occurs between ages 15 and 29 (Striegel-Moore, 1995). Although the death rate among people with bulimia is not as high as among people with anorexia, bulimia also has serious medical complications (Anderson, Shaw, & McCargar, 1997). One of the most serious is an imbalance in the body's electrolytes, which results from fluid loss following excessive and chronic vomiting, laxative abuse, and diuretic abuse. Imbalances in electrolytes can lead to heart failure.

Bulimia nervosa tends to be a chronic condition. People seeking treatment for this disorder typically report years of unremitting symptoms. A study of the natural course of bulimia nervosa in 102 women, most of whom did not receive treatment, found that over a 5-year period one-half to two-thirds had some form of eating disorder of clinical severity at each of several assessment points within that period (Fairburn et al., 2000, 2003). One-third still had a diagnosable eating disorder at the end of 5 years. Those with a more persistent course tended to have been obese as children, excessively valued shape and low weight, frequently dieted, and had high levels of social maladjustment.

Binge-Eating Disorder

Binge-eating disorder resembles bulimia nervosa, except that a person with binge-eating disorder does not regularly engage in purging, fasting, or excessive exercise to compensate for binges (Table 12.4). Binge-eating disorder was not one of the officially recognized forms of eating disorders in the *DSM-IV-TR,* largely because the authors of the *DSM-IV-TR* felt that too little research had been done on this disorder to sanction the diagnosis at the time the manual was published. Rather, the criteria for binge-eating disorder were placed in an appendix in the *DSM-IV-TR,* for further study. The *DSM-5* probably will include binge-eating disorder as a diagnosis, because additional research clearly supports its validity (Striegel-Moore & Franko, 2008).

TABLE 12.4 *DSM-IV-TR* Criteria for Binge-Eating Disorder

A. Recurrent episodes of binge eating that occur in a discrete period of time (within 2 hours) and a sense of loss of control during the eating.

B. The binge episodes are associated with three or more of the following:
   1. Eating more rapidly than normal
   2. Eating until feeling uncomfortably full
   3. Eating large amounts of food when not hungry
   4. Eating alone due to embarrassment or guilt
   5. Eating amounts that lead to feeling disgusted, depressed, and very guilty

C. Marked distress regarding binge eating is present.

D. Binge eating occurs at least 2 days a week for a 6-month period

E. The binge eating is not associated with the regular use of inappropriate compensatory behaviors, such as purging, fasting, or excessive exercise, and does not occur exclusively during the course of anorexia or bulimia nervosa.

Source: Reprinted with permission from the *Diagnostic and Statistical Manual of Mental Disorders,* Fourth Edition, Text Revision. Copyright © 2000 American Psychiatric Association.

People with binge-eating disorder may eat continuously throughout the day, with no planned mealtimes. Others engage in discrete binges of large amounts of food, often in response to stress and to feelings of anxiety or depression. They may eat very rapidly and appear almost in a daze as they eat, as the man in the following case study describes.

CASE STUDY

"The day after New Year's Day I got my check cashed. I usually eat to celebrate the occasion, so I knew it might happen. On the way to the bank I steeled myself against it. I kept reminding myself of the treatment and about my New Year's resolution about dieting. . . .

"Then I got the check cashed. And I kept out a hundred. And everything just seemed to go blank. I don't know what it was. All of my good intentions just seemed to fade away. They just didn't seem to mean anything anymore. I just said, 'What the hell,' and started eating, and what I did then was an absolute sin."

He described starting in a grocery store where he bought a cake, several pieces of pie, and boxes of cookies. Then he drove through heavy midtown traffic with one hand, pulling food out of the bag

(continued)

with the other hand and eating as fast as he could. After consuming all of his groceries, he set out on a furtive round of restaurants, staying only a short time in each and eating only small amounts. Although in constant dread of discovery, he had no idea what "sin" he felt he was committing. He knew only that it was not pleasurable. "I didn't enjoy it at all. It just happened. It's like a part of me just blacked out. And when that happened there was nothing there except the food and me, all alone." Finally he went into a delicatessen, bought another $20 worth of food and drove home, eating all the way, "until my gut ached." (Stunkard, 1993, pp. 20–21)

People with binge-eating disorder often are significantly overweight and say they are disgusted with their body and ashamed of their bingeing (Striegel-Moore & Franko, 2008). They typically have a history of frequent dieting, membership in weight-control programs, and family obesity (Fairburn et al., 1997). As many as 30 percent of people currently in weight-loss programs may have binge-eating disorder. In contrast, approximately 2 to 3.5 percent of the general population have the disorder (Hudson et al., 2007).

Like anorexia nervosa and bulimia nervosa, binge-eating disorder is more common in women than in men, both in the general community and among people in weight-loss programs—although the gender difference is less than in anorexia or bulimia (Hudson et al., 2007). In the United States, there do not appear to be racial or ethnic differences in rates of binge-eating disorder (Striegel-Moore & Franko, 2008). People with this disorder also have high rates of depression and anxiety and possibly a higher incidence of alcohol abuse and personality disorders (Striegel-Moore & Franko, 2008). Binge-eating disorder tends to be chronic; one retrospective study found the mean duration of the disorder to be 8 years (Hudson et al., 2007), and another study found a mean duration of 14.4 years (Pope et al., 2006).

FIGURE 12.2 **Check Your Attitudes Toward Eating.** Psychologist David Garner and his colleagues developed the Eating Disorder Inventory to assess people's attitudes and behaviors toward eating and their bodies. People who score higher on this questionnaire are more prone to eating disorders. As you read through these items, think about whether you would say each one is true of you always, usually, often, sometimes, rarely, or never. If you find you have answered "usually" or "always" to many of these items, you might want to reconsider your attitudes toward food and your body and perhaps talk to someone you trust about them (Garner, Olmstead, & Polivy, 1984).

Eating Disorder Inventory
I think my stomach is too big.
I eat when I am upset.
I stuff myself with food.
I think about dieting.
I think that my thighs are too large.
I feel ineffective as a person.
I feel extremely guilty after overeating.
I am terrified of gaining weight.
I get confused as to whether or not I am hungry.
If I gain a pound, I worry that I will keep gaining.
I have the thought of trying to vomit in order to lose weight.
I eat or drink in secrecy.

Source: Garner, Cooke, & Marano, 1997.

Variations on Eating Disorders

As noted at the beginning of the chapter, subclinical symptoms of bulimia nervosa are quite common, particularly among adolescent and young adult women. Figure 12.2 lists questions from one survey commonly used to measure maladaptive eating attitudes. A study of 2,200 students in six colleges around the United States found that 15 percent of the women surveyed admitted to having engaged in some purging behavior, and 28 percent classified themselves as obsessed with their weight (Rozin et al., 2003; rates for men on these questions were 4 percent and 11 percent, respectively).

Researchers in Oregon followed a large group of adolescents for several years, examining the ebb and flow of what they called *partial-syndrome eating disorders*—syndromes on the less severe end of the continuum of eating disorders that don't meet the full criteria for anorexia or bulimia nervosa (Lewinsohn et al., 2000; Striegel-Moore, Seeley, & Lewinsohn, 2003). Adolescents with partial-syndrome eating disorders may binge at least once every week but not multiple times every week. They may be underweight but not 15 percent underweight. They tend to be highly concerned with their weight and judge themselves on the basis of their weight. But their symptoms don't add up to a full-blown eating disorder.

The researchers found that adolescents with partial-syndrome eating disorders, the vast majority of whom were girls, were just as likely as those with full-blown eating disorders to have several psychological problems, both as adolescents and in their 20s. These problems included anxiety disorders, substance abuse, depression, and attempted suicide. Almost 90 percent had a diagnosable psychiatric disorder when they were in their early 20s. Those with partial-syndrome eating disorders also had lower self-esteem, poorer social relationships, poorer physical health, and lower levels of life satisfaction than those with no signs of an eating disorder. They were less likely to have earned a bachelor's degree and more likely to be unemployed.

The *DSM-IV-TR* allows the diagnosis **eating disorder not otherwise specified (EDNOS)** for individuals who have some severe symptoms of anorexia nervosa or bulimia nervosa but do not meet all criteria for either disorder. Table 12.5 gives examples of patterns that might be diagnosed as EDNOS. Epidemiological studies show that this is the most common eating disorder, with the majority of individuals seeking treatment receiving this diagnosis and a prevalence of approximately 5 percent of the general population (Fairburn et al., 2007; Wade et al., 2006). EDNOS tends to be as severe and persistent as bulimia nervosa or anorexia nervosa (Fairburn et al., 2007). Proposed changes to the *DSM-5* would lessen the need for this diagnosis, allowing individuals to be more precisely classified in terms of their eating behaviors and concerns (American Psychiatric Association, 2010).

TABLE 12.5 Examples of Eating Disorders Not Otherwise Specified (EDNOS)

In these examples, the behaviors do not meet the full criteria for anorexia nervosa or bulimia nervosa but may be given a diagnosis of eating disorders not otherwise specified (EDNOS).

1. For females, all of the criteria for anorexia nervosa are met except that the individual has regular menses.
2. All of the criteria for anorexia nervosa are met except that, despite significant weight loss, the individual's current weight is in the normal range.
3. All of the criteria for bulimia nervosa are met except that the binge eating and inappropriate compensatory mechanisms occur at a frequency of less than twice a week or for a duration of less than 3 months.
4. The regular use of inappropriate compensatory behavior by an individual of normal body weight after eating small amounts of food (e.g., self-induced vomiting after the consumption of two cookies).
5. Repeatedly chewing and spitting out, but not swallowing, large amounts of food.

Source: Reprinted with permission from the *Diagnostic and Statistical Manual of Mental Disorders*, Fourth Edition, Text Revision. Copyright © 2000 American Psychiatric Association.

Cultural and Historical Trends

Several theorists have argued that the eating disorders are culture-bound syndromes, occurring primarily in wealthy, developed countries where food is abundant and in cultures that highly value thinness (Garner & Garfinkel, 1980; McCarthy, 1990; Sobal & Stunkard, 1989). In addition, the prevalence of eating disorders may have increased in recent decades as the availability of food has increased while cultural norms (at least in the United States and Europe) increasingly prize thinness for women (Striegel-Moore, 1995; Stunkard, 1997).

There is clear evidence of cultural, racial/ethnic, and historical differences in the prevalence of bulimia nervosa. A meta-analysis found that bulimia nervosa is considerably more common in "Westernized" cultures than in "non-Westernized" cultures (Keel and Klump, 2003). In addition, the prevalence of bulimia nervosa increased significantly in the second half of the twentieth century. Since 1990, the prevalence of bulimia nervosa has remained stable in the United States, Europe, and Australia despite the increased availability of effective treatments for the disorder (Crowther et al., 2008; Keel et al., 2006).

There is also evidence of historical trends in rates of anorexia nervosa. The incidence of anorexia nervosa increased substantially from 1930 through 1970, but has since remained unchanged (Hoek & Van Hoeken, 2003). A study of over 30,000 Swedish

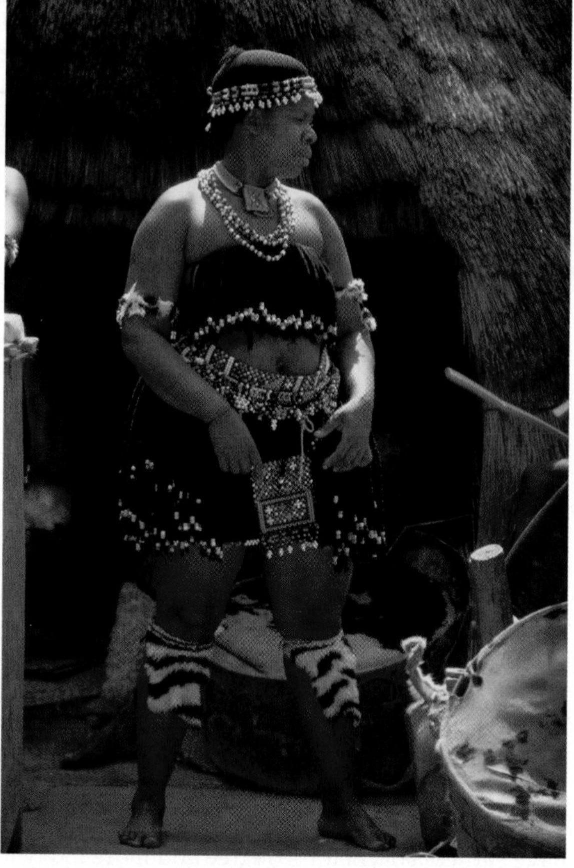

Standards of beauty vary greatly across cultures.

twins found significantly higher rates of anorexia nervosa among those born after 1945 than among those born before 1945 (Bulik et al., 2006).

Few methodologically strong cross-cultural studies of anorexia nervosa have been made. In one excellent study, H. W. Hoek and colleagues (2005) found that the incidence of anorexia nervosa was much higher in the Netherlands and the United States than in Curaçao, an island on which the majority population is Black and values large female bodies. Indeed, the only cases of anorexia nervosa in Curaçao were among White and mixed-race women, most of whom had been abroad to "Westernized" countries and were more affluent than the average Black woman in Curaçao.

The motivations for self-starvation also seem to vary across culture and time. In "non-Westernized" countries and in centuries past, the stated motivations for excessive fasting have had less to do with weight concerns than with stomach discomfort or religious reasons (Keel & Klump, 2003). Patients with anorexia in Asian countries do not have the distorted body image characteristic of anorexia in the United States and Europe and readily admit to being very thin. Nonetheless, they stubbornly refuse to eat, as illustrated by the case of one Chinese woman.

CASE STUDY

Miss Y, age 31, was 5 foot 3 inches. She had formerly weighed 110 pounds but now weighed 48 pounds. Her anorexia began 4 years previously, when she was suddenly deserted by her boyfriend, who came from a neighboring village. Greatly saddened by his departure for England, Miss Y started to complain of abdominal discomfort and reduced her food intake. She became socially withdrawn and unemployed. At her psychiatric examination, she wore long hair and was shockingly emaciated—virtually a skeleton. She had sunken eyes, hollow cheeks, and pale, cold skin. She recognized her striking wasting readily but claimed a complete lack of hunger and blamed the weight loss on an unidentifiable abdominal problem. Her concern over the seriousness of her physical condition was perfunc-

tory. When asked whether she consciously tried to restrict the amount she ate, she said, "No." When questioned why she had gone for periods of 8 or more waking hours without eating anything, she said it was because she had no hunger and felt distended, pointing to the lower left side of her abdomen. All physical examinations revealed no biological source for her feelings of distension, however. Miss Y was often in a low mood and became transiently tearful when her grief over the broken relationship was acknowledged. However, she resisted all attempts to discuss this loss in detail and all other psychological and medical treatments. Miss Y later died of cardiac arrest. Postmortem examination revealed no specific pathology other than multiple organ atrophy due to starvation. (Adapted from Sing, 1995, pp. 27–29)

FIGURE 12.3 **Obesity in the United States.** The percent of adults meeting the criteria for obesity (BMI ≥ 30) in the United States is shown based on age, gender, and ethnic/racial makeup.

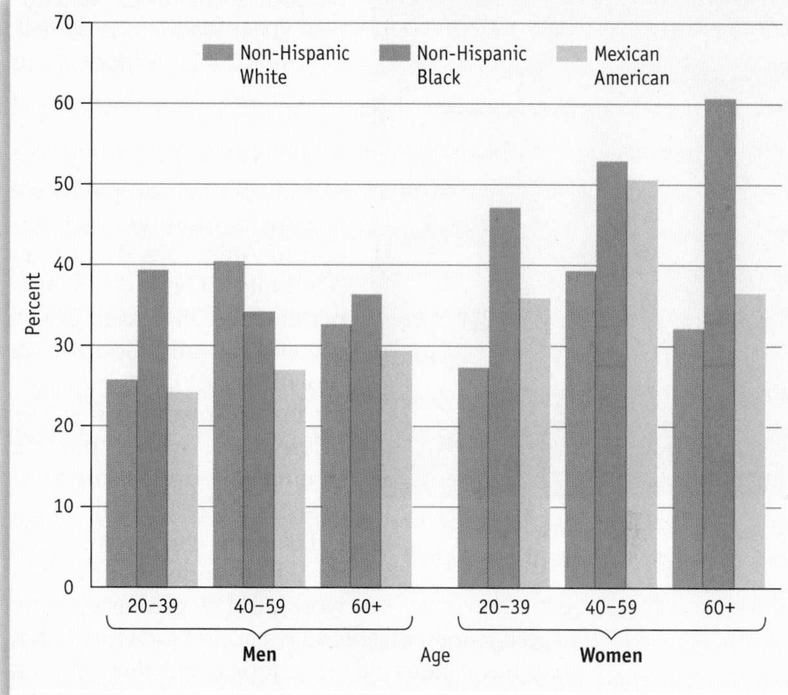

Source: CDC/NCHS, National Health and Nutrition Examination Survey, 1999–2000.

One question that can be raised is whether self-starvation in the absence of weight concerns can be called anorexia nervosa, given that weight concerns are a defining feature of the disorder in the *DSM-IV-TR*. However, the *DSM-IV-TR* itself is a culture-bound document, representing Western views of mental disorders.

In the United States, the overall rates of anorexia and bulimia are lower among African Americans and Hispanics than among Caucasians (Striegel-Moore et al., 2003), perhaps because African Americans and Hispanics are less likely to accept the thin ideal promoted in Caucasian culture (Smolak & Striegel-Moore, 2001). Caucasian women show greater body dissatisfaction than African American women, although the difference is not great (Grabe & Hyde, 2006).

Obesity

One of the greatest public health concerns in the United States and many developed countries is skyrocketing rates of obesity (U.S. Department of Health and Human Services [USDHHS], 2001b). **Obesity** is defined as a body mass index (BMI) of 30 or over, where BMI is calculated as your weight in pounds multiplied by 703, then divided by the square of your height in inches (Centers for Disease Control [CDC], 2010). Between 1980 and 2002, the prevalence of obesity doubled in adults and tripled in children and adolescents (Flegal, Carroll, Ogden, & Johnson, 2002; Hedley et al., 2004; Ogden, Flegal, Carroll, & Johnson, 2002). Rates have continued to climb (Ogden et al., 2006), and in 2010 the Centers for Disease Control estimated that over one-third of Americans were obese (CDC, 2010). African Americans have the highest rate of obesity, followed by Hispanic and non-Hispanic Whites (Figure 12.3). Rates of obesity also are climbing around the world, particularly in countries where the standard of living is increasing (USDHHS, 2001b).

Obesity is not designated as an eating disorder by the *DSM-IV-TR*, but it clearly is a major health hazard. Obesity is associated with an increased risk of coronary heart disease, hypertension and stroke, type 2 diabetes, and some kinds of cancer (USDHHS, 2001b). A BMI of 30 or more increases the risk of death by approximately 30 percent, and a BMI of 40 or more increases the risk of death by 100 percent (Manson et al., 1995). The quality of life for obese people can deteriorate, both because of health effects and because obesity is highly stigmatized. Adults and children who are obese face teasing and ridicule, as well as biases against them in the workplace and at school (Puhl & Heuer, 2009).

The dramatic historical increases in obesity point to environmental causes. Researcher Kelly

The toxic environment includes large portions of high-fat foods at low prices.

Brownell argues that we live in a *toxic environment* of high-fat, high-calorie, inexpensive food and of advertisers who promote the consumption of large quantities (Brownell & Horgen, 2004; Wadden, Brownell, & Foster, 2002). Added to our "Super-Size Me" culture is a significant reduction over the past several decades in the amount of physical activity we engage in. More than 60 percent of Americans do not get 30 minutes of physical exercise per day, and 25 percent get no exercise at all (Godfrey & Brownell, 2008). A typical day for many Americans involves driving to work, passing through the drive-through at a fast-food restaurant to get a fat- and cholesterol-laden breakfast sandwich, sitting at work all day, getting up only to go to another fast-food restaurant for a lunch that may have thousands of calories, and then driving home to spend the evening sitting in front of the television. It is a prescription for obesity.

Evidence that such an environment contributes to obesity comes from studies of immigrants. One study compared Pima Indian women who migrated to Arizona to their female relatives who remained in Mexico. The women in Arizona had an average dietary fat intake of 41 percent of all calories, a body weight of 198 kilograms, and a BMI of 37. In comparison, the women in Mexico had an average dietary fat intake of only 23 percent of all calories, a body weight of 154 kilograms, and a BMI of 25 (Ravussin et al., 1994).

Not everyone living in a toxic environment becomes overweight or obese. Genes appear to account for about 30 percent of the variability in obesity (Bouchard, 1994). Genes affect the number of fat cells and the likelihood of fat storage, the tendency to overeat, and activity level (Cope, Fernandez, & Allison, 2004). These genetic factors interact with the toxic environment to contribute to obesity.

Millions of people try to lose weight on their own, with the aid of self-help books; millions of others participate in commercial weight-loss programs such as Weight Watchers. Evaluations of popular weight-loss programs suggest that they can result in modest weight loss (Dansinger et al., 2005; Sarwer, Magee, & Crerand, 2004). For example, Christopher Gardner and colleagues (2007) randomly assigned women with a BMI of 27 to 40 to follow the Atkins (carbohydrate-restricted), Ornish (fat-restricted), Zone (macronutrients balance), or LEARN (exercise and changes in eating patterns) programs. At the end of 1 year, the women on the Atkins program had lost an average of about 10 pounds, significantly more weight loss than for women on the Zone program (3.5 pounds) but not significantly different from that for women on the Ornish program (4.8 pounds) or the LEARN program (5.7 pounds). Another study that included men and women found that the Atkins, Ornish, Zone, and Weight Watchers programs all resulted in similar weight loss (Dansiger et al., 2005). Weight Watchers led to an average loss of 4 to 7 pounds, but only 50 to 65 percent of people stuck to the diet for 1 year. Even for those who do stick to these programs, the modest weight loss is discouraging, especially given the advertisements suggesting that these programs can result in much greater loss for obese people. Yet even a modest weight loss of 5 to 10 percent of body weight can result in significant health improvements for obese people (Wadden, Brownell, & Foster, 2002).

Two drugs currently approved in the United States for weight loss are sibutramine (Meridia) and orlistat (Xenical). Rimonabant (Acomplia) is approved in Europe but not the United States. A meta-analysis of controlled trials of these drugs showed that they led to more weight loss than a placebo—an average of 11 pounds or less, depending on the drug, over 1 to 4 years (Rucker et al., 2007). All these medications have side effects, including gastrointestinal upset (orlistat), increased blood pressure and heart rate (sibutramine), and negative mood changes (rimonabant).

For obese people with a BMI between 30 and 39, low-calorie diets (900 to 1,200 calories per day), often using prepackaged, portion-controlled servings (such as SlimFast shakes), are recommended (Wadden et al., 2002). Individuals also are encouraged to increase their physical activity. Such a program results in significantly more weight loss than when individuals consume a self-selected diet of conventional food (Fletchner-Mors et al., 2000). For extremely obese people with a BMI of 40 or over who have at least one severe health problem (e.g., diabetes), bariatric surgery is an option. A small pouch is created at the base of the esophagus, severely limiting food intake, and the stomach may be stapled, banded, or bypassed. Such surgery can result in very substantial weight loss of 25 to 30 percent (Wadden et al., 2002). One person who underwent bariatric surgery is TV weatherman Al Roker.

TV weatherman Al Roker underwent bariatric surgery to lose weight.

It is difficult for overweight and obese people to lose weight, and even more difficult to keep it off. To combat the discouragement many people feel about losing weight, researchers are encouraging obese people to adopt reasonably modest goals for weight loss and to focus on increasing their physical activity, both of which can lead to substantial improvements in cardiac functioning and diabetes risk (Wadden et al., 2002). In general, the proven methods for preventing weight gain and reducing weight are these:

- Eat more nutrient-dense foods and fewer foods with empty calories.
- Aim for a minimum of 30 minutes of physical activity daily.
- Structure your environment so that healthy choices are easier to make; for example, keep low-fat foods readily available in your house and purge your cabinets of junk food.
- Be more active throughout the day: Use the stairs rather than the elevator, park in the farthest spot from the building rather than the closest, and seek other opportunities that encourage movement over standing or sitting (Godfrey & Brownell, 2008).

TEST YOURSELF

1. What are the diagnostic criteria and subtypes for anorexia nervosa?
2. What are the criteria and subtypes for bulimia nervosa?
3. What are the criteria for binge-eating disorder?
4. What is eating disorder not otherwise specified?
5. How is obesity defined?

APPLY IT Amelia is obese and is seeking treatment to lose at least 50 pounds. Based on the studies reviewed in this section, what advice should she be given about the effectiveness of various treatments?

a. Medications lead to an average weight loss of 50 to 60 pounds, so they would likely help her reach her goal.
b. Commercial weight-loss programs are not effective in helping people lose weight, so she should avoid them.
c. Dieting does not work, so she should avoid dieting.
d. Increased exercise and a more modest weight-loss goal would help her most.

Answers appear online at www.mhhe.com/nolen5e.

SHADES OF GRAY

Read the following case study.

At the insistence of her parents, Rachel, a 19-year-old freshman at a competitive liberal arts college, received a psychiatric evaluation during spring break. According to her parents, Rachel had lost 16 pounds since her precollege physical the previous August. She now weighed 104 pounds at a height of 5 feet, 5 inches, when a healthy weight for a small-framed woman her height is about 120 pounds. Rachel explained that she had been a successful student and field hockey player in high school. After deciding not to play field hockey in college, she began running several mornings each week during the summer and "cut out junk food" to protect herself from gaining "that freshman 10." Rachel lost a few pounds that summer and received compliments from friends and family for looking so "fit." She reported feeling more confident and ready for college than she had expected. Once she began school, Rachel increased her running to daily, often skipped breakfast in order to get to class on time, and selected from the salad bar for her lunch and dinner. She worked hard in school and made the dean's list the first semester.

When Rachel returned home for Christmas vacation, her family noticed that she looked thin and tired. Despite encouragement to catch up on rest, she awoke early each morning to run. She returned to school in January and thought she might be developing depression. Courses seemed less interesting, and she wondered whether the college she attended was right for her after all. She was sleeping less well and felt cold much of the day. The night Rachel returned home for spring break, her parents asked her to step on the bathroom scale. Rachel was surprised to learn that her weight had fallen to 104 pounds, and she agreed to a visit to her pediatrician, who found no evidence of a medical illness and recommended a psychiatric consultation. (Adapted from Evelyn Attia and B. Timothy Walsh (2007). Anorexia Nervosa, *American Journal of Psychiatry,* 164. Reprinted with permission from the American Journal of Psychiatry, copyright © 2007 American Psychiatric Association.)

Does Rachel have an eating disorder? What criteria does she meet? Are there any criteria that she doesn't meet? (Discussion appears at the end of this chapter.)

UNDERSTANDING EATING DISORDERS

A number of biological, sociocultural, and psychological factors have been implicated in the development of the eating disorders. As we discuss at the end of this chapter, it is likely that it takes an accumulation of several of these factors for any individual to develop an eating disorder. In this section, however, we consider each of these factors separately.

Biological Factors

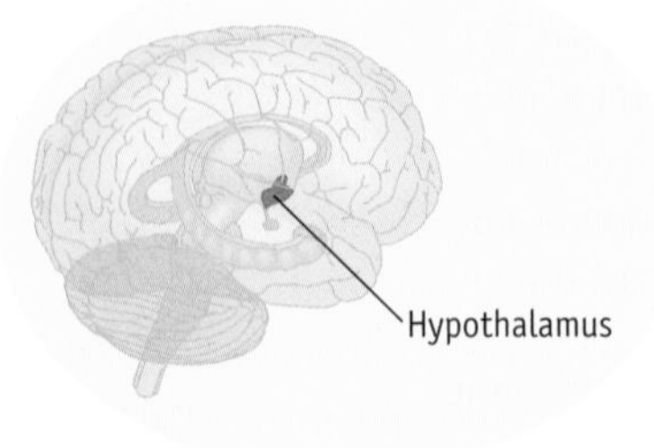

The hypothalamus plays a central role in regulating eating and is implicated in disordered eating behavior in bulimia and anorexia.

As with most psychological disorders, anorexia nervosa, bulimia nervosa, and binge-eating disorder tend to run in families (Striegel-Moore & Bulik, 2007). Twin studies of anorexia nervosa have found that 33 to 84 percent of the variability in the disorder is due to genetic factors (Striegel-Moore & Bulik, 2007). A particularly large study of more than 30,000 twins found a heritability of 56 percent for anorexia nervosa (Bulik et al., 2006). Twin studies of bulimia nervosa found a heritability of 50 to 83 percent (Striegel-Moore & Bulik, 2007). A large twin study of binge-eating disorder found a heritability of 41 percent (Bulik, Sullivan, & Kendler, 2003). The specific genes involved in any of the eating disorders are yet to be identified definitively.

Much of the current research on the biological causes of the eating disorders focuses on those bodily systems that regulate appetite, hunger, satiety, initiation of eating, and cessation of eating. The *hypothalamus* plays a central role in regulating eating (Berthoud & Morrison, 2008). It receives messages about the body's recent food consumption and nutrient level and sends messages to cease eating when the body's nutritional needs are met. These messages are carried by a variety of neurotransmitters, including norepinephrine, serotonin, and dopamine, and by a number of hormones, including cortisol and insulin. Disordered eating behavior might be caused by imbalances in or dysregulation of any of the neurochemicals involved in this system or by structural or functional problems in the hypothalamus. For example, disruptions of this system could cause the individual to have trouble detecting hunger accurately or to stop eating when full, both of which are characteristics of people with eating disorders.

People with anorexia nervosa show lowered functioning of the hypothalamus and abnormalities in the levels of several hormones important to the functioning of the hypothalamus, including serotonin and dopamine (Attia & Walsh, 2007; Brambilla et al., 2001; Frank et al., 2001). Whether these disruptions are causes or consequences of the self-starvation of anorexia is unclear. Some studies find that people with anorexia continue to show abnormalities in hypothalamic and hormonal functioning and neurotransmitter levels after they gain some weight, whereas other studies find that these abnormalities disappear with weight gain (Polivy & Herman, 2002).

Many people with bulimia show abnormalities in the neurotransmitter serotonin (Franko, Wonderlich, Little, & Herzog, 2004). Deficiencies in serotonin might lead the body to crave carbohydrates, and people with bulimia often binge on high-carbohydrate foods. These people may then engage in self-induced vomiting or some other type of purge in order to avoid gaining weight from carbohydrates.

Thus, a number of biological abnormalities have been found to be associated with anorexia nervosa and bulimia nervosa. These abnormalities could contribute to disordered eating behavior by causing the body to crave certain foods or by making it difficult for a person to read the body's signals of hunger and fullness. Exactly why people with eating disorders also develop a distorted body image and the other cognitive and emotional problems seen in the eating disorders is not clear. In addition, many of the biological abnormalities seen in the eating disorders could be the consequences, rather than the causes, of the disorders.

Sociocultural and Psychological Factors

Societal pressures to be thin and attractive probably play a role in the eating disorders, although many people who are exposed to these pressures do not develop an eating disorder. Certain psychological factors may also need to come into play for an eating disorder to develop.

Social Pressures and Cultural Norms

Psychologists have linked the historical and cross-cultural differences in the prevalence of eating disorders to differences in the standards of beauty for women at different historical times and in different cultures (Garner & Garfinkel, 1980; McCarthy, 1990; Sobal & Stunkard, 1989). In addition, certain groups within a culture, such as athletes, may have standards for appearance that put them at greater risk for developing eating disorders.

Standards of Beauty The ideal shape for women in the United States and Europe has become thinner and thinner since the mid-twentieth century. Models in fashion magazines, winners of the Miss America and Miss Universe pageants, and Barbie dolls—icons of beauty for women—all have been getting thinner (Figure 12.4; Garner & Garfinkel, 1980; Keel & Klump, 2003; Wiseman, Gray, Mosimann, & Ahrens, 1992). Indeed, the average model in a fashion magazine these days is pencil thin, with a figure that is physically unattainable by most adult women.

Both anorexia nervosa and bulimia nervosa are much more common in females than in males, perhaps because thinness is more valued and more strongly encouraged in females than in males. For example, studies of popular women's and men's magazines find 10 times more diet articles in women's magazines than in men's magazines (Andersen & DiDomenico, 1992; Nemeroff et al., 1994).

The thin ideal promoted in women's magazines seems to affect women's attitudes toward

Research shows that girls who read fashion magazines may develop unhealthy attitudes toward their own weight and shape.

FIGURE 12.4 **Our Changing Beauty Standards.** In the period from 1959 to 1978, the average weight of women who were *Playboy* centerfolds or who won the Miss America pageant became lower and lower, relative to what would be expected for women of their height.

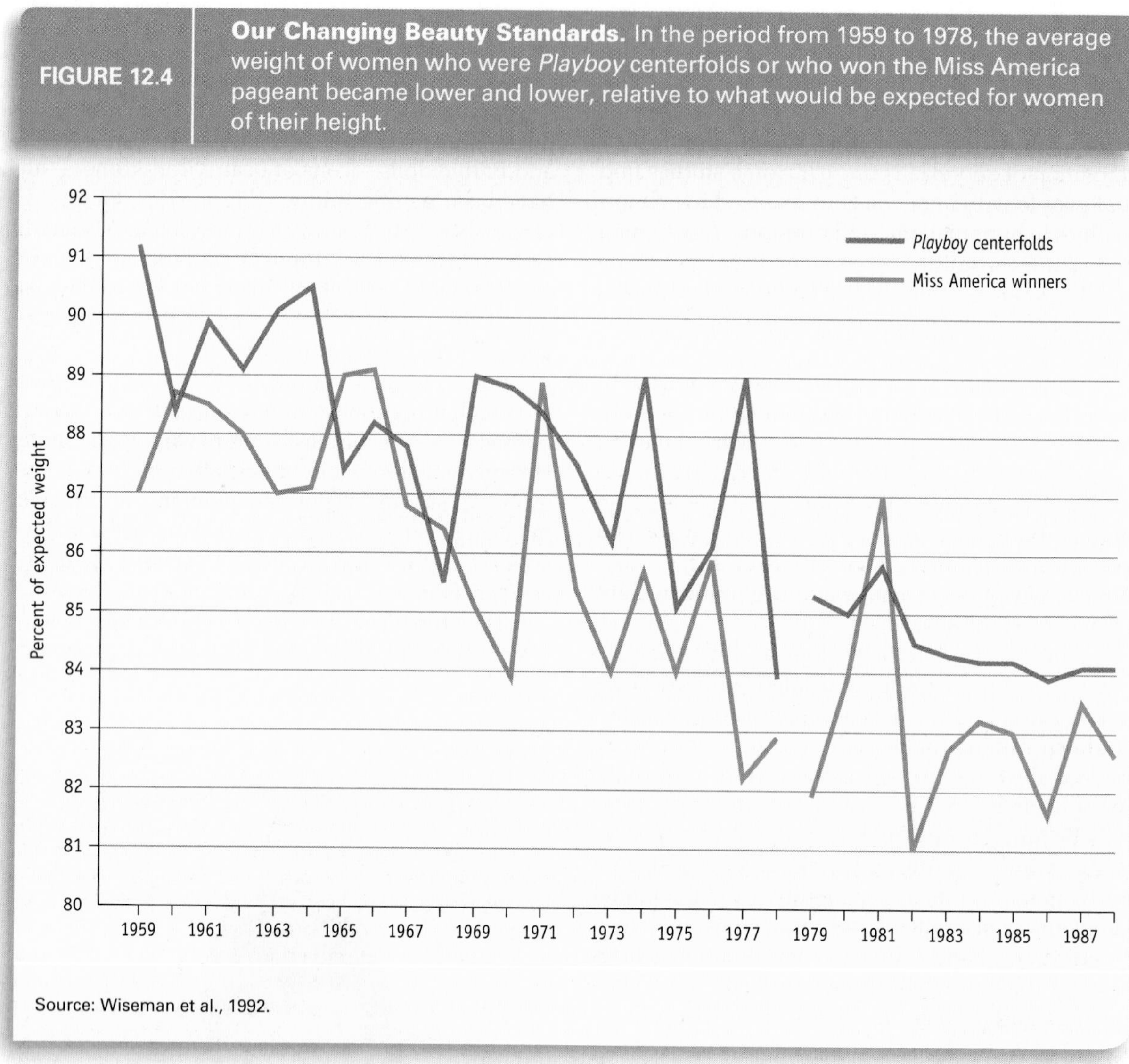

Source: Wiseman et al., 1992.

themselves (see review by Groesz, Levine, & Murnen, 2002). For example, Eric Stice and Heather Shaw (1994) showed young women either images of models from fashion magazines or images that didn't portray thin models, for a 3-minute period. Those women who saw the fashion magazine images experienced increases in depression, shame, guilt, stress, insecurity, and body dissatisfaction compared to those women who were exposed to the other images. In turn, those women who showed the greatest increases in negative mood and body dissatisfaction and who most strongly subscribed to the thin ideal for women also showed increases in the symptoms of bulimia. If only 3 minutes of exposure to these fashion models can have such effects, think what the constant exposure young women experience does to their self-image and well-being.

Stice and colleagues looked at what chronic exposure to the thin ideal in fashion magazines actually does to adolescent girls' mental health (Stice, Spangler, & Agras, 2001). They randomly gave 219 girls ages 13 to 17 a 15-month subscription to a leading fashion magazine or no subscription, then followed them over time. They found that girls who already felt pressured to be thin and were dissatisfied with their bodies became more depressed over time if they had been given the subscription to the fashion magazine than if they had not. In addition, girls who started the study with little social support from family members and friends became more dissatisfied with their bodies, dieted more, and showed more bulimic symptoms if they were given the fashion magazine subscription than if they were not. Similar results have been found in studies that expose adolescent or adult males to media depictions of idealized male bodies (Blond, 2008).

Social pressure to be thin and beautiful has been taken to new extremes with reality TV shows in which individuals undergo cosmetic surgery "makeovers." These shows have been very popular with adults under age 50. One study found that Caucasian college-age women who viewed episodes of one of these shows, *The Swan,* reported greater perceptions of pressures to be thin and greater beliefs that they could control their body's appearance than Caucasian women who viewed a reality TV show about home improvement (Mazzeo, Trace, Mitchell, & Gow, 2007). The NBC show *The Biggest Loser* has been criticized for encouraging contestants and viewers to use extreme measures, including starvation and excessive exercise, to lose weight at an unhealthy pace (Wyatt, 2009).

The TV show *The Biggest Loser* may encourage people to take extreme, dangerous measures to lose weight.

People can avoid some pressures to conform to the ideal of thinness by avoiding fashion magazines and other media depictions. People can't completely avoid their friends, however, and sometimes they are the most effective carriers of appearance-related messages. Stice and colleagues had women college students talk to another college woman they thought was simply another student but actually was an accomplice in the study (Stice, Maxfield, & Wells, 2003). This accomplice was a thin, attractive 19-year-old woman. In the *pressure condition,* the accomplice complained about how dissatisfied she was with her weight and discussed her extreme exercise routine and restrictive diet. In the *neutral condition,* the accomplice talked about classes she was currently taking and her plans for the weekend. The target women in the pressure condition became significantly more dissatisfied with their bodies after talking with the thin accomplice about her weight concerns. In contrast, the women in the neutral condition did not become more dissatisfied with their bodies after talking with the same woman about matters unrelated to weight or dieting.

Of course, not all women accept the thin ideal for themselves. Table 12.6 gives some items from questionnaires designed to assess the internalization of the thin ideal. Longitudinal studies have shown that women who internalize the thin ideal are more likely to develop bulimic symptoms as well as to show increases in dieting and body dissatisfaction over time (Stice, 2003; Thompson & Stice, 2001). Experimental studies have shown that interventions designed to get women to argue against the thin ideal and to recognize pressures from the media to subscribe to this ideal result in reductions in women's acceptance of the ideal and decreases in body dissatisfaction, dieting, and bulimic symptoms (Stice, Mazotti, Weibel, & Agras, 2000; Stice, Chase, Stormer, & Appel, 2001; Stormer & Thompson, 1998).

TABLE 12.6 Items from Questionnaires Measuring Internalization of the Thin Ideal

These are some items assessing women's internalization of the thin ideal promoted in today's media.

I would like my body to look like the women that appear in TV shows and movies.

I wish I looked like the women pictured in magazines that model underwear.

Music videos that show women who are in good physical shape make me wish that I were in better physical shape.

Slender women are more attractive.

Women with toned bodies are more attractive.

Women with long legs are more attractive.

Sources: Stice & Agras, 1998; Thompson et al., 1999.

TABLE 12.7 Rates of Eating Disorders in Elite Women Athletes

Sports that emphasize weight are especially likely to encourage eating disorders.

Sport	Percentage with an Eating Disorder
Aesthetic sports (e.g., figure skating, gymnastics)	35%
Weight-dependent sports (e.g., judo, wrestling)	29
Endurance sports (e.g., cycling, running, swimming)	20
Technical sports (e.g., golf, high jumping)	14
Ball game sports (e.g., volleyball, soccer)	12

Source: Data from Sundgot-Borgen, 1994.

Athletes and Eating Disorders One group at increased risk for unhealthy and disordered eating habits is athletes, especially those participating in sports in which weight is considered an important factor in competitiveness, such as gymnastics, ice skating, dancing, horse racing, wrestling, and bodybuilding (Smolak, Murnen, & Ruble, 2000). Researchers in Norway assessed all 522 elite female athletes between ages 12 and 35 for the presence of eating disorders. They found that those participating in sports classified as "aesthetic" or "weight-dependent," including diving, figure skating, gymnastics, dance, judo, karate, and wrestling, were most likely to have anorexia or bulimia nervosa (Table 12.7; Sundgot-Borgen, 1994). Many of the women athletes with eating disorders reported feeling that the physical changes of puberty had decreased their competitive edge. They had started dieting severely to try to maintain their prepubescent figure. The case of Heidi, described by her therapist, illustrates several of these triggers.

Sports that require certain body shapes or weights, such as bodybuilding, seem to breed eating disorders among participants.

CASE STUDY

Heidi arrived in my office after gymnastics practice. Blond and pretty, she was dressed in a shiny red-and-white warm-up suit. We talked about gymnastics, which Heidi had been involved in since she was six. At that time, she was selected to train with the university coaches. Now she trained four hours a day, six days a week. She didn't expect to make an Olympic team, but she anticipated a scholarship to a Big-8 school.

Heidi glowed when she talked about gymnastics, but I noticed her eyes were red and she had a small scar on the index finger of her right hand. (When a hand is repeatedly stuck down the throat, it can be scarred by the acids in the mouth.) I wasn't surprised when she said she was coming in for help with bulimia.

Heidi said, "I've had this problem for two years, but lately it's affecting my gymnastics. I am too weak, particularly on the vault, which requires strength. It's hard to concentrate.

"I blame my training for my eating disorder," Heidi continued. "Our coach has weekly weigh-ins where we count each other's ribs. If they are hard to count we're in trouble."

I clucked in disapproval. Heidi explained that since puberty she had had trouble keeping her weight down. After meals, she was nervous that she'd eaten too much. She counted calories; she was hungry but afraid to eat. In class she pinched the fat on her side and freaked out. The first time she vomited was after a gymnastics meet. Coach took her and the other gymnasts to a steak house. Heidi ordered a double cheeseburger and onion rings. After she ate, she obsessed about the weigh-in the next day, so she decided, just this once, to get rid of her meal. She slipped into the restaurant bathroom and threw up.

She blushed. "It was harder than you would think. My body resisted, but I was able to do it. It was so gross that I thought, 'I'll never do that again,' but a week later I did. At first it was weekly, then twice a week. Now it's almost every day. My dentist said that acid is eating away the enamel of my teeth." (Adapted from Pipher, 1994, pp. 165–168)

Among men, bodybuilding is an increasingly popular sport, but bodybuilders routinely have substantial weight fluctuations as they shape their bodies for competition and then binge in the off-season. For example, a study that compared male bodybuilders with men with diagnosed eating disorders found that the bodybuilders had a pattern of eating and exercising as obsessive as that of the men with eating disorders, but with a focus on gaining muscle rather than on losing fat (Mangweth et al., 2001). In another study of male bodybuilders, 46 percent reported bingeing after most competitions, and 85 percent reported gaining significant weight (an average of 15 pounds) in the off-season. Then they dieted to prepare for competition, losing an average of 14 pounds. In a parallel study of female bodybuilders and weight lifters, 42 percent reported having been anorexic at some time in their life, 67 percent were terrified of being fat, and 58 percent were obsessed with food (Anderson, Bartlett, Morgan, & Brownell, 1995). A study of female weight lifters found that they often abused ephedrine, a stimulant that helps reduce body fat, particularly if they had symptoms of an eating disorder (Gruber & Pope, 1998).

There is mixed evidence as to whether amateur athletics contributes to eating-disorder behaviors. One study of women college students found that varsity athletes showed the highest rates of eating-disordered behaviors, but club athletes and independent exercisers still had higher rates of some eating-disorder behaviors than did women who did not exercise (Holm-Denoma et al., 2009). However, a meta-analysis of studies (Smolak et al., 2000) concluded that, although elite athletes do show increased rates of eating disorders, nonelite athletes—particularly those participating in sports in which thinness is not emphasized—showed lower rates of eating problems than nonathletes.

Emotion Regulation Difficulties

Eating-disorder behaviors may sometimes serve as maladaptive strategies for dealing with painful emotions (Fairburn et al., 1995; McCarthy, 1990). Depressive symptoms and a history of negative affect predict future onset or exacerbation of anorexic and bulimic symptoms (Bulik, 2005; Cooley & Toray, 2001; Stice, Burton, & Shaw, 2004; Stice, Presnell, & Spangler, 2002) and relapse into binge eating among obese people (Byrne et al., 2003). Stice and colleagues (2002) followed a group of adolescent girls over a period of 2 years. They found that girls who engaged in emotional eating—eating when they felt distressed in an attempt to feel better—were significantly more likely to develop chronic binge eating over the 2 years.

In addition, Stice and colleagues have identified two subtypes of disordered eating patterns involving binge eating (Stice et al., 2002; Stice, Bohon, Marti, & Fischer, 2008). One subtype is connected to excessive attempts to lose weight. Women with this *dieting subtype* are greatly concerned about their body shape and size and try their best to maintain a strict low-calorie diet, but they frequently fall off the wagon and engage in binge eating. They then often use vomiting or exercise to try to purge themselves of the food or the weight it puts on their bodies. The other subtype is the *depressive subtype*. These women also are concerned about their weight and body size, but they are plagued by feelings of depression and low self-esteem and often eat to quell these feelings.

Women with the depressive subtype of disordered eating patterns suffer greater social and psychological consequences over time than do women with the dieting subtype (Stice et al., 2002; Stice, Bohon, et al., 2008). They face more difficulties in their relationships with family and friends; are more likely to suffer significant psychiatric disorders, such as anxiety disorders; and are less likely to respond well to treatment. Longitudinal studies find that women with the depressive subtype are more likely to be diagnosed with major depression or an anxiety disorder over time and also are more likely to continue to engage in severe binge eating, compared to women with the dieting subtype (Stice & Fairburn, 2003; Stice, Bohon, et al., 2008). Indeed, 80 percent of the women with the depressive subtype developed major depression over a 5-year follow-up.

Cognitive Models of Eating Disorders

Christopher Fairburn (1997) suggests that the overvaluation of appearance is of primary importance in the development of the eating disorders. According to Fairburn, people who consider their body shape to be one of the most important aspects of their self-evaluation and who believe that achieving thinness will bring social and psychological benefits will engage in excessive dieting and purging behaviors to reduce their weight. In line with Fairburn's model, a meta-analysis of relevant studies found that women who internalize the thin ideal for women and are dissatisfied with their bodies show greater eating pathology (Stice, 2002).

Kathleen Vohs and colleagues (1999, 2001) suggested that disordered eating is especially likely to result when body dissatisfaction is combined with perfectionism and low self-esteem. Women who feel they need a perfect body, are dissatisfied with their body, and have low self-esteem will engage in maladaptive strategies to control their weight, including excessive dieting and purging. Vohs and colleagues found that young women with all three of these cognitive characteristics were more likely to develop bulimic symptoms than were women with just one or two of the characteristics.

Other research confirms that people with eating disorders are more concerned with the opinions of others, are more conforming to others' wishes, and are more perfectionistic and rigid in their evaluations of themselves and others than are other people (Polivy & Herman, 2002; Striegel-Moore, Silberstein, & Rodin, 1993; Wade et al., 2008). People with eating disorders tend to have a dichotomous thinking style, in which things are either all good or all bad. For example, if they eat one cookie, they may think that they have blown their diet and might as well eat the whole box of cookies.

Individuals who develop eating disorders are overly attentive to their weight and shape.

They will say that they cannot break their rigid eating routines or they will completely lose control over their eating. They obsess over their eating routines and plan their days down to the smallest detail around these routines (Polivy & Herman, 2002).

Women with eating disorders may be concerned with body size at an unconscious level. Women with and without symptoms of bulimia were shown photos of women who varied in terms of both their body size and the emotions shown on their faces. The participants were not told that these were the critical dimensions along which the photos varied. Women with bulimic symptoms were more likely than the other women in the study to attend to information about body size than to information about facial emotion and to classify the photos on the basis of body size rather than facial emotion (Viken et al., 2002). Thus, women who show bulimic symptoms unconsciously organize their perceptions of the world around body size more so than do women who do not show significant bulimic symptoms.

Family Dynamics

Hilde Bruch (1973, 1982), a pioneer in the study of eating disorders, argued that anorexia nervosa often occurs in girls who have been unusually "good girls"—high achievers, dutiful and compliant daughters who are always trying to please their parents and others by being "perfect." These girls tend to have parents who are overinvested in their daughters' compliance and achievements, who are overcontrolling, and who will not allow the expression of feelings, especially negative feelings (see also Minuchin et al., 1978). As a result, the daughters do not learn to identify and accept their own feelings and desires. Instead, they learn to monitor closely the needs and desires of others and to comply with others' demands, as can be seen in the case of Renee and her family.

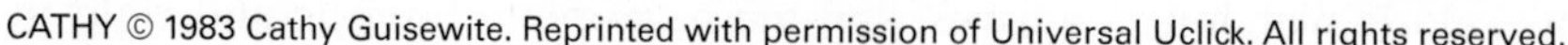

CASE STUDY

Renee is a 16-year-old with anorexia nervosa. Her parents are highly educated and very successful, having spent most of their careers in the diplomatic corps. Renee, her two brothers, and her parents are "very close, as are many families in the diplomatic corps, because we move so much," although the daily care of the children has always been left to nannies. The children had to follow strict rules for appropriate conduct, both in the home and outside. These rules were partly driven by the requirements of the families of diplomats to "be on their best behavior" in their host country and partly driven by Renee's parents' very conservative religious beliefs. Renee, as the only daughter in the family, always had to behave as "a proper lady" to counteract the stereotype of American girls as brash and sexually promiscuous. All the children were required to act mature beyond their years, controlling any emotional outbursts, taking defeats and disappointments without complaint, and happily picking up and moving every couple of years when their parents were reassigned to another country.

Renee's anorexic behaviors began when her parents announced they were leaving the diplomatic corps to return to the United States. Renee had grown very fond of their last post in Europe, because she had finally found a group of friends that she liked *and* whom her parents approved of, and she liked her school. She had always done well in school but often had hated the harshly strict schoolteachers. In her present school, she felt accepted by her teachers as well as challenged by the work. When Renee told her parents she would like to finish her last year of high school in this school rather than go to the United States with them, they flatly refused to even consider it. Renee tried to talk with her parents, suggesting she stay with the family of one of her friends, who was willing to have her, but her parents cut her off and told her they would not discuss the idea further. Renee became sullen and withdrawn and stopped eating shortly after the family arrived in the United States.

One important task of adolescence is separation and individuation from one's family. Bruch argues that girls from overcontrolling families deeply fear separation because they have not developed the ability to act and think independently of their family. They also fear involvement with peers, especially sexual involvement, because they neither understand their feelings nor trust their judgment. Yet at some level they recognize their need to separate from their family. They harbor rage against their parents for their overcontrol and become angry, defiant, and distrustful. They also discover that controlling their food intake both gives them a sense of control over their life and elicits concern from their parents. Their rigid control of their body provides a sense of power over the self and the family that they have never had before. It also provides a way of avoiding peer relationships—the girl dons the persona of an anorexic, presenting herself as sickly, distant, untouchable, and superior in her self-control.

Research has confirmed that the families of girls with eating disorders have high levels of conflict, discourage the expression of negative emotions, and emphasize control and perfectionism (Polivy & Herman, 2002). Several of these negative characteristics are also prevalent in the families of children with depression, anxiety disorders, and several other forms of psychopathology. What may distinguish families in which anorexia nervosa or bulimia nervosa develops is that the mothers in these families believe their daughters should lose more weight, criticize their daughters' weight, and are themselves more likely to show disordered eating patterns (Hill & Franklin, 1998). One longitudinal study showed that eating and weight-related concerns in 10-year-old children were predicted by the amount of conflict over eating habits and issues of control during mealtimes when the children were 5 years old (Stein et al., 2006). In addition, a lack of awareness of their bodily sensations may allow some girls in these families to ignore even the most severe hunger pangs (Leon, Fulkerson, Perry, & Early-Zald, 1995). Girls from these troubled families who cannot completely ignore their hunger may fall into a binge/purge form of anorexia nervosa or into bulimia nervosa.

Studies of adult women with binge-eating disorder suggest that the combination of low parental warmth and high parental demands or control seems to distinguish girls and women who develop binge-eating disorder from those with other forms of psychopathology (Striegel-Moore et al., 2005; Wilfley, Pike, & Striegel-Moore, 1997). Another family characteristic that distinguishes people with binge-eating disorder from individuals with other mental disorders is a history of binge eating among other family members (Striegel-Moore et al., 2005). Thus, individuals who develop the tendency to binge may come from families that modeled and reinforced bingeing behavior.

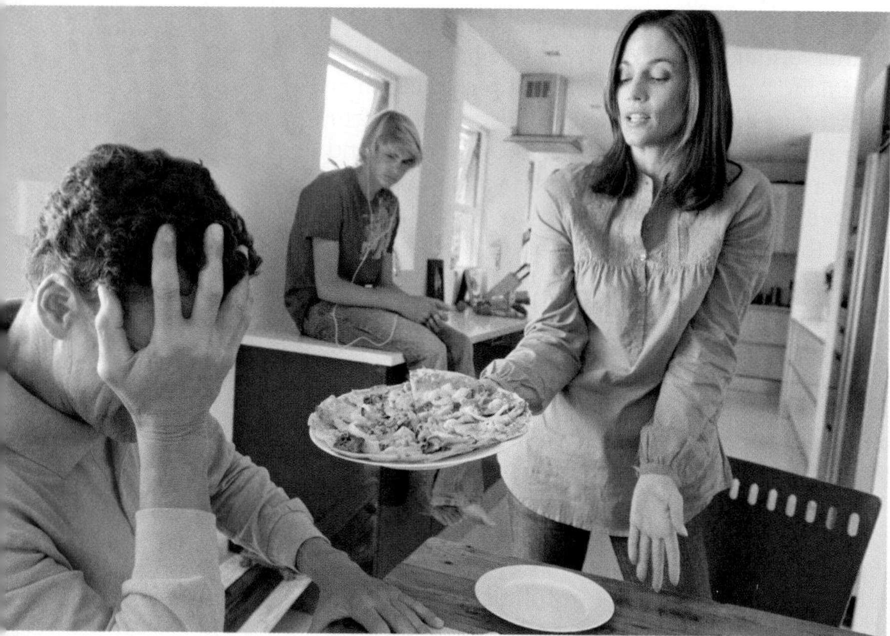

Family conflict around issues of eating may contribute to eating disorders.

Unfortunately, the majority of studies of the families and personality characteristics associated with eating disorders have compared people who already have eating disorders with those who do not (Polivy & Herman, 2002). As a result, we do not know to what extent these family and personality characteristics actually are causes of eating disorders. The controlling nature of parents' behaviors toward their children may be a consequence as well as a cause of the disorder, with parents exerting control in order to try to save their children's lives.

TEST YOURSELF

1. What biological factors seem to be involved in the eating disorders?
2. How are personality characteristics, difficulty in regulating emotions, and patterns of thinking related to eating disorders?
3. What family characteristics may be involved in the eating disorders?

APPLY IT According to the evidence on the role of cultural and societal norms in the eating disorders, which of the following groups should tend to have the lowest rate of eating disorders?

a. gymnasts in the United States
b. traditional dancers in Fiji
c. bodybuilders in Europe
d. casual joggers in the United States

Answers appear online at www.mhhe.com/nolen5e.

TREATMENTS FOR EATING DISORDERS

In this section, we discuss psychotherapies and biological treatments used for people with eating disorders. There are several empirical studies of the effectiveness of treatments for bulimia nervosa, and an increasing number for binge-eating disorder. The number of studies for anorexia nervosa is low, and many of these studies are plagued by small sample sizes and other methodological problems (Fairburn, 2005; Wilson, Grilo, & Vitousek, 2007).

Psychotherapy for Anorexia Nervosa

It can be difficult to engage people with anorexia nervosa in psychotherapy. Because they so highly value the thinness they have achieved and believe they must maintain absolute control over their behaviors, people with anorexia nervosa can be resistant to therapists' attempts to change their behaviors or attitudes. Regardless of the type of psychotherapy a therapist uses with a client with anorexia, he or she must do much work to win the client's trust and participation in the therapy and to maintain this trust and participation as the client begins to regain that dreaded weight (Attia & Walsh, 2007).

Winning the trust of someone with anorexia can be especially difficult if the therapist is forced to hospitalize the client because she has lost so much weight that her life is in danger. However, hospitalization and forced refeeding sometimes are necessary (Attia & Walsh, 2007). Because people with anorexia nervosa typically do not seek treatment themselves, often they do not come to the attention of a therapist until they are so malnourished that they have a medical crisis, such as a cardiac problem, or until their families fear for their lives. During hospitalization, the therapist will try to engage the client in facing and solving the psychological issues causing her to starve herself.

Psychotherapy can help many people with anorexia, particularly adolescents, but it typically is a long process, often marked by many setbacks (Wilson et al., 2007). Along the way, many people with anorexia who have an initial period of recovery, with restoration of their weight to normal levels and of their eating to healthy patterns, relapse into bulimic or anorexic behaviors (Stice & Spoor, 2007). They often continue to have self-esteem deficits, family problems, and periods of depression and anxiety.

Individual Therapy

Cognitive-behavioral therapies are the most researched treatment for anorexia nervosa (Wilson et al., 2007). The client's overvaluation of thinness is confronted, and rewards are made contingent on the person's gaining weight. If the client is hospitalized, certain privileges in the hospital are used as rewards, such as watching television, going outside the hospital, or receiving visitors. The client also may be taught relaxation techniques to use as she becomes extremely anxious about ingesting food. Some studies suggest that this type of therapy can be useful for anorexia nervosa (Halmi et al., 2005; Pike et al., 2003; Serfaty et al., 1999), but all the studies have had methodological problems.

Family Therapy

In family therapy, the person with anorexia and her family are treated as a unit. The best-studied family therapy is known as the Maudsley model (Lock, le Grange, Agras, & Dare, 2001). The intervention involves 10 to 20 sessions over 6 to 12 months. Parents are coached to take control over their child's eating and weight. As the therapy progresses, the child's autonomy is linked explicitly to the resolution of the eating disorder. There is evidence that family therapy can be successful in treating girls with anorexia nervosa (Eisler et al., 2000; le Grange, Eisler, Dare, & Russell, 1992; Lock, Agras, Bryson, & Kraemer, 2005).

Psychotherapy for Bulimia Nervosa and Binge-Eating Disorder

Cognitive-behavioral therapy (CBT) has received the most empirical support for use in treating bulimia nervosa (Fairburn, 2005; Whittal, Agras, & Gould, 1999). CBT is based on the view that the extreme concerns about shape and weight are the central features of the disorder (Fairburn, 1997). The therapist teaches the client to monitor the cognitions that accompany her eating, particularly the binge episodes and purging episodes (Wilson, Fairburn, & Agras, 1997). Then the therapist helps the client confront these cognitions and develop more adaptive attitudes toward weight and body shape. An interchange between a therapist and a client might go like this.

VOICES

Therapist: What were you thinking just before you began to binge?

Client: I was thinking that I felt really upset and sad about having no social life. I wanted to eat just to feel better.

Therapist: And as you were eating, what were you thinking?

Client: I was thinking that the ice cream tasted really good, that it was making me feel good. But I was also thinking that I shouldn't be eating this, that I'm bingeing again. But then I thought that my life is such a wreck that I deserve to eat what I want to make me feel better.

Therapist: And what were you thinking after you finished the binge?

Client: That I was a failure, a blimp, that I have no control, that this therapy isn't working.

Therapist: Okay, let's go back to the beginning. You said you wanted to eat because you thought it would make you feel better. Did it?

Client: Well, as I said, the ice cream tasted good and it felt good to indulge myself.

Therapist: But in the long run, did bingeing make you feel better?

Client: Of course not. I felt terrible afterward.

Therapist: Can you think of anything you might say to yourself the next time you get into such a state, when you want to eat in order to make yourself feel better?

Client: I could remind myself that I'll feel better only for a little while, but then I'll feel terrible.

Therapist: How likely do you think it is that you'll remember to say this to yourself?

Client: Not very likely.

Therapist: Is there any way to increase the likelihood?

Client: Well, I guess I could write it on a card or something and put the card near my refrigerator.

Therapist: That's a pretty good idea. What else could you do to prevent yourself from eating when you feel upset? What other things could you do to relieve your upset, other than eat?

Client: I could call my friend Keisha and talk about how I feel. Or I could go for a walk—someplace away from food—like up in the hills, where it's so pretty. Walking up there always makes me feel better.

Therapist: Those are really good ideas. It's important to have a variety of things you can do, other than eat, to relieve bad moods.

The behavioral components of this therapy involve introducing forbidden foods (such as bread) back into the client's diet and helping the client confront her irrational thoughts about these foods, such as "If I have just one doughnut, I'm inevitably going to binge." Similarly, the client is taught to eat three healthy meals a day and to challenge the thoughts she has about these meals and about the possibility of gaining weight. Cognitive-behavioral therapy for bulimia usually lasts about 3 to 6 months and involves 10 to 20 sessions.

Controlled studies of the efficacy of cognitive-behavioral therapy for bulimia find that about half the clients completely stop the binge/purge cycle (Fairburn, 2005; Wilson et al., 2007). Clients undergoing this therapy also show a decrease in depression and anxiety, an increase in social functioning, and a lessening of concern about dieting and weight. Cognitive-behavioral therapy is more effective than drug therapies in producing complete cessation of binge eating and purging and in preventing relapse over the long term (Fairburn, 2005). Consistent with theories that bulimia nervosa is due to deficits in regulating negative affect, cognitive-behavioral interventions targeting depressive symptoms also reduce bulimic symptoms (Burton, Stice, Bearman, & Rohde, 2007).

Other studies of the treatment of bulimia have compared cognitive-behavioral therapy (CBT) with three other types of psychotherapy: interpersonal therapy (IPT), supportive-expressive psychodynamic therapy, and behavior therapy without a focus on cognitions (Agras et al., 2000; Fairburn et al., 1991, 1995; Garner, Rockert, Davis, & Garner, 1993; Wilson et al., 1999, 2002). In interpersonal therapy, the client and the therapist discuss interpersonal problems related to the client's eating disorder, and the therapist works actively with the client to develop strategies to solve these problems. In supportive-expressive psychodynamic therapy, the therapist also encourages the client to talk about problems related to the eating disorder—especially interpersonal problems—but in a highly nondirective manner. In behavior therapy, the client is taught how to monitor her food intake, is reinforced for introducing avoided foods into her diet, and is taught coping techniques for avoiding bingeing. In the studies, all the therapies resulted in significant improvement in the clients' eating behaviors and emotional well-being, but the cognitive-behavioral and interpersonal therapy clients showed the greatest and most enduring improvements. Comparisons of CBT and IPT suggest that CBT is significantly more effective than IPT in treating bulimia and works more quickly, with substantial improvement being shown by 3 to 6 weeks into treatment with CBT (Agras et al., 2000; Fairburn, 2005; Wilson et al., 1999, 2002). CBT and IPT appear to be equally effective in preventing relapse over 1- and 6-year follow-ups (Agras et al., 2000).

For binge-eating disorder, cognitive-behavioral therapy has been shown to be more effective than both wait-list controls and antidepressant medications (Grilo, Masheb, & Wilson, 2005; Ricca et al., 2001). Intepersonal therapy has proven as effective as CBT for binge-eating disorder (Wilfley et al., 1993, 2002).

Biological Therapies

The *selective serotonin reuptake inhibitors (SSRIs)*, such as fluoxetine (trade name Prozac), have been the focus of much research on biological treatments for bulimia nervosa. These drugs appear to reduce binge-eating and purging behaviors, but often they fail to restore the individual to normal eating habits (de Zwaan, Roerig, & Mitchell, 2004; Reas & Grilo, 2008). Adding cognitive-behavioral therapy to antidepressant treatment increases the rate of recovery from the disorder (Fairburn, 2005). Drug treatments, including antidepressants, are often used to treat anorexia nervosa, but there is no consistent evidence that they are better than a placebo (Attia & Walsh, 2007). A meta-analysis of medications for binge eating found that a number of drugs, including the SSRIs, antiepileptic medications (such as topiramate), and obesity medications (such as orlistat), all are better than a placebo in reducing binge eating (Reas & Grilo, 2008).

TEST YOURSELF

1. Describe cognitive-behavioral therapy for anorexia nervosa.
2. Describe family therapy for anorexia nervosa.
3. What are the goals of cognitive-behavioral therapy for bulimia nervosa and binge-eating disorder?
4. What medications are used to treat eating disorders?

APPLY IT A therapist has a new client with bulimia nervosa. Based on the outcome studies described in this section, what type of treatment should the therapist use for this client?

a. cognitive-behavioral therapy
b. interpersonal therapy
c. family therapy
d. serotonin reuptake inhibitors

Answers appear online at www.mhhe.com/nolen5e.

FIGURE 12.5 Multiple Pathways into the Eating Disorders

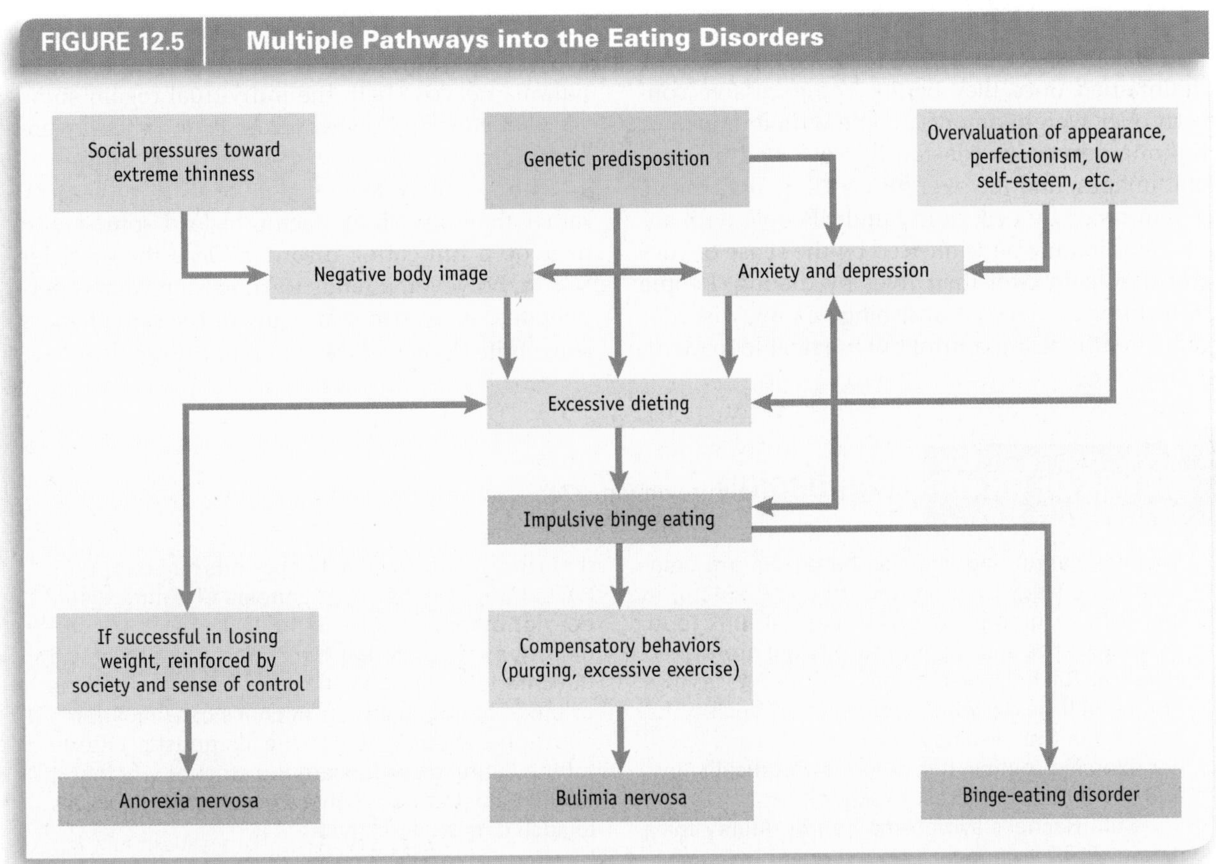

CHAPTER INTEGRATION

Several experts have suggested that a group of biological, psychological, and social factors interact to create the eating disorders (Agras & Kirkley, 1986; Garner & Garfinkel, 1985; Polivy & Herman, 2002; Striegel-Moore, 1993). Any one of these factors alone may not be enough to push someone to develop anorexia or bulimia nervosa, but combined they may do so (Figure 12.5).

First, societal pressures for thinness clearly provide a potent impetus for the development of unhealthy attitudes toward eating, especially for women. If these pressures were simply toward achieving a healthy weight and maintaining fitness, they would not be so dangerous. However, the ideal weight for women promoted by beauty symbols in developed countries is much lower than that considered healthy and normal for the average woman, and thus women may develop a negative body image. This leads them to engage in excessive dieting. Unfortunately, excessive dieting sets up conditions for impulsive binge eating, which leads to negative emotions and even lower self-esteem.

Second, biological factors may interact with these societal pressures to make some people more likely than others to develop eating disorders. People who develop eating disorders may have a genetic predisposition to these disorders or to dysregulation of their hormones or neurotransmitters. Exactly how the genetic vulnerabilities lead to the symptoms of eating disorders is unclear, but they may contribute to an ability to diet excessively. Another biological factor that may predispose some people to acquiesce to the pressures to diet and to be thin is a tendency toward anxiety or mild depression. Many people with eating disorders, especially people with bulimia, are often depressed and eat impulsively in response to their moods. Although problems in mood in people with an eating disorder may be the result of environmental circumstances or of the stresses of the disorder, they also may have a biological origin in some people.

Third, personality factors also may interact with societal pressures to be thin and/or with the biological predispositions described to lead some people to develop eating disorders. Perfectionism, all-or-nothing thinking, and low self-esteem may make people more likely to engage in extreme measures to control their weight in pursuit of an ideal of attractiveness. These personality characteristics are more likely to develop in children whose parents are lacking in affection and nurturance and who at the same time are controlling and demanding of perfection.

Whatever pathway an individual takes into the eating disorders, these behaviors tend to be maintained once they begin. The excessive concern over weight among people with anorexia or bulimia nervosa is constantly reinforced by societal images, and any weight loss they do achieve is reinforced by peers and family. People with anorexia also may be reinforced by the sense of control they gain over their lives by dieting. People with bulimia nervosa and binge-eating disorder may greatly desire control but are unable to maintain it, so they fall into binge eating to escape negative emotions. The compensatory behaviors of bulimia nervosa help the individual regain some sense of control, however fragile, and thereby are reinforced.

Thus, it may take a mixture of these factors, rather than any single factor, to lead someone to develop a full eating disorder. Once the disorder sets in, however, it tends to be reinforced and perpetuated. Note also that many of the same factors contribute to each of the different eating disorders.

SHADES OF GRAY DISCUSSION (review p. 374)

Rachel's eating and exercise behaviors are common for college women and, to some extent, in line with recommendations to cut out junk food, eat more fruits and vegetables, and get more exercise. Yet Rachel's weight has dropped to a level that is well below what is considered healthy for her height. She also has become obsessive about her exercise routine, her mood is chronically low, and she is losing interest in school.

Still, Rachel's symptoms do not qualify for a diagnosis of anorexia nervosa, primarily because there is no evidence that her periods have stopped. Rachel might receive a diagnosis of eating disorder not otherwise specified because she has significant symptoms that nonetheless do not reach the criteria for anorexia nervosa, bulimia nervosa, or binge-eating disorder. Rachel's case illustrates questions about whether the diagnostic criteria for the eating disorders are too strict or whether it would be better not to give a psychiatric diagnosis to such common behavior.

THINK CRITICALLY

Given what you know about the contributors to eating disorders, what kind of prevention program might you design for your school to try to reduce the prevalence of these disorders among students? *(Discussion appears on p. 520 at the back of this book.)*

CHAPTER SUMMARY

- The eating disorders include anorexia nervosa, bulimia nervosa, and binge-eating disorder.
- Anorexia nervosa is characterized by self-starvation, a distorted body image, intense fears of becoming fat, and amenorrhea. People with the restricting type of anorexia nervosa refuse to eat in order to prevent weight gain. People with the binge/purge type periodically engage in bingeing and then purge to prevent weight gain.
- The lifetime prevalence of anorexia is about 1 percent, with 90 to 95 percent of cases being females. Anorexia nervosa usually begins in adolescence, and the course is variable from one person to another. It is a very dangerous disorder; the death rate among people with anorexia is between 5 and 8 percent.
- Bulimia nervosa is characterized by uncontrolled bingeing followed by behaviors designed to prevent weight gain from the binges. People with the purging type of bulimia use self-induced vomiting, diuretics, or laxatives to prevent weight gain. People with the nonpurging type use fasting and exercise to prevent weight gain.
- The prevalence of bulimia nervosa is between 0.5 and 3 percent. The onset of bulimia nervosa

most often is in adolescence. Although people with bulimia do not tend to be underweight, bulimia nervosa has several dangerous medical complications.

- People with binge-eating disorder engage in bingeing, but not in purging or in behaviors designed to compensate for the binges. It is more common in women than in men, and people with the disorder tend to be significantly overweight. Binge-eating disorder is not officially recognized by the *DSM-IV-TR,* but the diagnostic criteria were placed in an appendix for further study.
- People with subclinical eating-disorder symptoms experience significant impairment and are at risk of developing a full-blown eating disorder.
- The diagnosis *eating disorder not otherwise specified* may be given to individuals who show severe symptoms of an eating disorder but do not meet the full criteria for one of the eating disorders.
- Obesity is defined as a body mass index of 30 or more. Obesity rates have skyrocketed in recent years, largely due to increases in the intake of high-fat, low-nutrient food and decreases in physical activity. Genes also play a role in obesity. Treatments for obesity include commercial weight-loss programs, medications, low-calorie diets, and bariatric surgery.
- The biological factors implicated in the development of the eating disorders include genetics, the dysregulation of hormone and neurotransmitter systems, and generally lower functioning in the hypothalamus.
- Sociocultural theorists have attributed the eating disorders to pressures to be thin in Western cultures and in the media.
- Eating disorders may develop in some people as maladaptive strategies for coping with negative emotions. Also, certain cognitive factors, including overvaluation of appearance, perfectionism, low self-esteem, excessive concern about others' opinions, and a rigid, dichotomous thinking style, may contribute to the development of the eating disorders.
- The families of girls with eating disorders may be overcontrolling, overprotective, and hostile and may not allow the expression of feelings. In adolescence, these girls may develop eating disorders as a way of exerting control.
- Cognitive-behavioral therapy and family therapy have been shown in some studies to be effective in the treatment of anorexia nervosa, but more research is needed.
- Cognitive-behavioral therapy has proven to be the most effective therapy for reducing the symptoms of bulimia and preventing relapse. Interpersonal therapy, supportive-expressive psychodynamic therapy, and behavior therapy also appear to be effective in treating bulimia nervosa.
- Antidepressants are effective in treating bulimia, but the relapse rate is high. Antidepressants have not proven to be reliably effective in the treatment of anorexia nervosa.

KEY TERMS

anorexia nervosa 359
amenorrhea 360
restricting type of anorexia nervosa 362
binge/purge type of anorexia nervosa 363
bulimia nervosa 364
bingeing 364
purging type of bulimia nervosa 365
nonpurging type of bulimia nervosa 366
binge-eating disorder 367
eating disorder not otherwise specified (EDNOS) 369
obesity 371

Chapter 13

Sexual Disorders

CHAPTER OUTLINE

Extraordinary People

David Reimer, *The Boy Who Was Raised as a Girl*

In April 1966, 8-month-old Bruce Reimer underwent a routine circumcision to alleviate a painful medical condition on his penis. The operation went terribly wrong, however, and Bruce's penis was accidentally severed. None of the doctors whom Bruce's anguished parents consulted could offer any hope of restoring the penis and suggested that he would never be able to function as a normal male. But Dr. John Money offered them a solution: Raise Bruce as a girl and have him undergo sex reassignment therapy. Money firmly believed that male or female identity depends on the environment in which a child is raised, not on the genes or genitals with which he or she is born. Bruce's condition presented him with the perfect opportunity to prove his theory. Not only had Bruce been born male, but he had an identical twin brother as well. If surgically reassigning Bruce's sex and raising him as a girl resulted in Bruce fully accepting himself as a girl, when his twin brother identified himself as a boy, Money's theories of gender identity would be soundly supported.

Bruce's parents renamed him Brenda Lee and began dressing him in feminine clothes. The child underwent a bilateral orchidectomy—removal of both testicles—at the age of 22 months. Brenda's parents then furnished her with dolls and tried to reinforce her identity as a girl. Brenda, however, resisted. As brother, Brian, recalled, "When I say there was nothing feminine about Brenda . . . I mean there was *nothing* feminine. She walked like a guy. Sat with her legs apart. We both wanted to play with guys, build forts and have snowball fights and play army. She'd get a skipping rope for a gift, and the only thing we'd use that for was to tie people up, whip people with it" (Colapinto, 2000, p. 57).

As Brenda grew up, she refused surgery to create a vagina for her and insisted on urinating standing up. Beginning at the age of 12, Brenda was given estrogen, and as a result she began to develop breasts. However, her voice began to crack just like her brother's. Finally, when Brenda was 14, her father told her the truth about the botched circumcision and her parents' decision to raise her as a girl. Brenda said, "I was *relieved*. . . . Suddenly it all made sense why I felt the way I did. I wasn't some sort of weirdo. I wasn't crazy" (Colapinto, 2000, p. 180).

Brenda immediately decided to revert to her biological sex. She renamed herself David, after the biblical king and giant-slayer. David began to take injections of testosterone and in 1980 underwent a double mastectomy to remove the breasts he had grown. Then, a month before his sixteenth birthday, he had surgery to create a rudimentary penis. Still, David's reentry into life as a boy was difficult. He still looked and talked differently from other boys and, as a result, was teased and shunned. The artificial genitals that had been fashioned for him frequently became blocked, and he went through several additional surgeries and treatments. Over the next few years, David attempted suicide and secluded himself in a mountain cabin for months at a time.

Finally, after his twenty-second birthday, David had a new kind of surgery to create a more acceptable and functional penis. In 1990, David married a young woman named Jane, and things went well for a while. But after losing his job, experiencing financial difficulties, and separating from his wife, David committed suicide in 2004. According to his mother, he had also been grieving the death of his brother, which had occurred 2 years before the suicide.

In a newspaper story after David's death, John Colapinto, his biographer, noted, "David's blighted childhood was never far from his mind. Just before he died, he talked to his wife about his sexual 'inadequacy,' his inability to be a true husband. Jane tried to reassure him. But David was already heading for the door" (*Slate,* 3 June 2004).

David Reimer's story raises many questions about the biological and social contributors to our self-concept as male or female, our sexual preferences, and the role of sexuality and gender in our psychological well-being. In this chapter, we consider how biology interacts with social norms and psychological factors in producing both sexual health and sexual disorders.

SEXUAL DYSFUNCTIONS

The sexual dysfunctions are a set of disorders in which people have trouble engaging in and enjoying sexual relationships (see Table 13.2). To qualify for a diagnosis of a sexual dysfunction, the difficulty must be more than occasional and must cause significant distress or interpersonal difficulty. The

FIGURE 13.1 **The Sexual Response Cycle.** Masters and Johnson divided the sexual response cycle into five phases (see discussion in Sexual Functioning Along the Continuum).

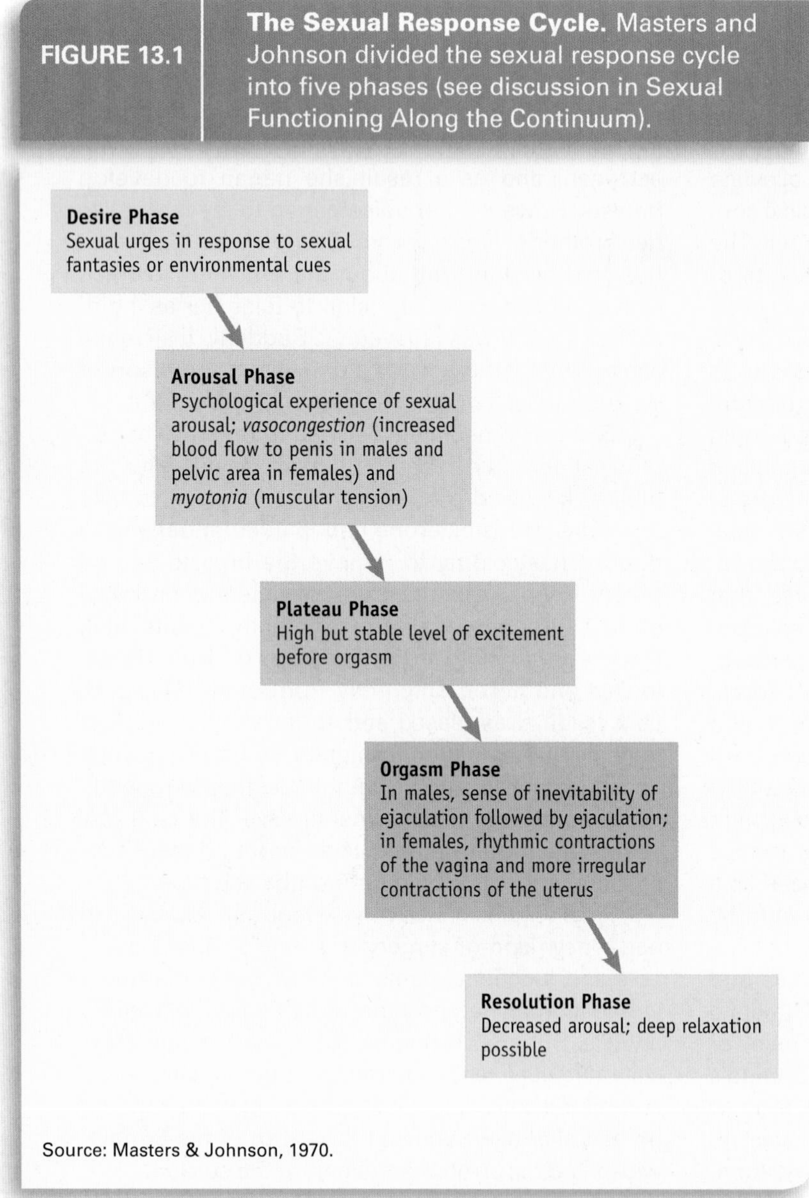
Desire Phase
Sexual urges in response to sexual fantasies or environmental cues
Arousal Phase
Psychological experience of sexual arousal; vasocongestion (increased blood flow to penis in males and pelvic area in females) and myotonia (muscular tension)
Plateau Phase
High but stable level of excitement before orgasm
Orgasm Phase
In males, sense of inevitability of ejaculation followed by ejaculation; in females, rhythmic contractions of the vagina and more irregular contractions of the uterus
Resolution Phase
Decreased arousal; deep relaxation possible

Source: Masters & Johnson, 1970.

DSM-IV-TR divides sexual dysfunctions into four categories: *sexual desire disorders, sexual arousal disorders, orgasmic disorders,* and *sexual pain disorders.* In reality, these dysfunctions overlap significantly, and many people who seek treatment for a sexual problem have more than one of these dysfunctions.

Sexual Desire Disorders

Sexual desire can be manifested in a person's sexual thoughts and fantasies, a person's interest in initiating or participating in sexual activities, and a person's awareness of sexual cues from others (Schiavi & Segraves, 1995). People vary tremendously in their levels of sexual desire, and an individual's level of sexual desire can vary greatly across time (Michael, Gagnon, Laumann, & Kolata, 1994).

Hypoactive Sexual Desire Disorder

People with **hypoactive sexual desire disorder** have little desire for sex—they do not fantasize about sex or initiate sexual activity and may be unresponsive when a partner initiates sex (American Psychiatric Association, 2000). This lack of sexual desire causes them marked distress or interpersonal difficulty. In some rare cases, people report never having had much interest in sex, either with other people or privately, as in the viewing of erotic films, masturbation, or fantasy. These individuals are diagnosed with *lifelong hypoactive sexual desire disorder.* In most cases, the individual used to enjoy sex but has lost interest in it, a condition diagnosed as *acquired hypoactive sexual desire disorder*. A diagnosis of hypoactive sexual desire is not given if the individual's lack of desire is the result of transient circumstances, such as being too fatigued from overwork to care about sex. If the lack of desire is caused by one of the other problems in sexual functioning, such as pain during intercourse or the inability to achieve orgasm, the person would receive a diagnosis focused on that dysfunction instead of a diagnosis of hypoactive sexual desire. Inhibited desire can be either generalized to all partners and situations or specific to certain partners or types of stimulation. A person who has had little desire for sexual activity for most of his or her life has a *generalized sexual desire disorder.* A person who does not desire sex with his or her partner but has sexual fantasies about other people may be diagnosed with a *situational sexual desire disorder.* Obviously, the judgment about when a person's sexual desire has been too low for too long is subjective. The *DSM-IV-TR* specifies that the clinician should make this determination with consideration of other aspects of the person's life, including age. Low sexual desire is one of the most common problems for which people seek treatment (Bach, Wincze, & Barlow, 2001; Hackett, 2008).

In a study of over 31,000 women, hypoactive sexual desire was diagnosed in 9.5 percent (Clayton, 2007). Rates of hypoactive sexual desire increase to 26 percent in postmenopausal women (Leiblum et al., 2006). Between 5 and 13 percent of men report frequent problems with hypoactive sexual desire, with higher rates among older men than among younger men (Laumann et al., 1999; Laumann, Das, & Waite, 2008). Women with hypoactive sexual desire are more likely than men to report anxiety, depression, and life stress. Hypoactive

Sexual Functioning Along the Continuum

Sexual functioning, sexual practices, and gender identity that bring the individual positive well-being and relationships

- **Occasional difficulties in sexual functioning that do not cause distress or difficulties in relationships** *(occasional difficulty reaching orgasm)*
- **Atypical sexual practices that do not cause distress or difficulties in social functioning** *(use of objects as part of sex play with a consenting partner)*
- **Questions about gender identity that eventually are resolved**

Potentially meets diagnostic criteria for a sexual disorder:

- **Difficulties in sexual functioning that cause moderate distress or difficulties in relationships** *(frequent difficulty reaching orgasm)*
- **Atypical sexual practices that cause distress or difficulties in social functioning** *(one's partner disapproves of the objects used in sexual practice)*
- **Uncertainty about gender identity**

Likely meets diagnostic criteria for a sexual disorder:

- **Chronic difficulties in sexual functioning that cause significant distress or difficulties in relationships** *(complete lack of sexual desire)*
- **Atypical sexual practices that cause significant distress or difficulties in social functioning** *(inappropriate objects become the sole focus of sexual activities, arrests for illegal sexual behavior)*
- **Significant distress regarding gender identity, desire to change genders**

Functional — Dysfunctional

Pick up an issue of *Cosmopolitan, Maxim,* or similar magazines targeting young adults and you will quickly discover that much of the content is devoted to sex—from readers' questions about sexual health to tips for giving your partner a more pleasurable experience. Sexual encounters and talk about sex permeate the most popular TV shows, from *How I Met Your Mother* to *Gossip Girl.*

But as sex-oriented as our culture is, we often don't stop to think about sexual behavior in the larger context of a continuum. This section gives you the opportunity to do just that. It focuses on three elements of sexuality: sexual functioning, sexual practices, and gender identity.

Before the work of researchers William Masters and Virginia Johnson in the 1950s and 1960s, we knew little about what happened in the human body during sexual arousal and activity. Masters and Johnson (1970) observed people engaging in a variety of sexual practices in a laboratory setting and recorded the physiological changes that occurred. They found that the sexual response cycle can be divided into five phases: desire, arousal or excitement, plateau, orgasm, and resolution (Figure 13.1).

Sexual desire is the urge to engage in any type of sexual activity. The **arousal phase,** or *excitement phase,* combines a psychological experience of pleasure and the physiological changes known as *vasocongestion* and *myotonia*. Vasocongestion, or *engorgement,* occurs when blood vessels and tissues fill with blood. In males, erection of the penis is caused by an increase in the flow of blood into the arteries of the penis, accompanied by a decrease in the outflow of blood from the penis through the veins. In females, vasocongestion causes the clitoris to enlarge, the labia to swell, and the vagina to become moist. Myotonia is muscular tension. During the arousal phase, many muscles in the body become tenser, culminating in the muscular contractions known as orgasm.

After arousal is the **plateau phase,** when excitement remains at a high but stable level. This period is pleasurable in itself, and some people try to extend the plateau phase as long as possible before reaching **orgasm,** the discharge of the neuromuscular tension built up during the excitement and plateau phases. In males, orgasm involves rhythmic contractions of the prostate and the entire length of the penis and urethra, accompanied by

(continued)

the ejaculation of semen. After ejaculation, a *refractory* period, lasting from a few minutes to a few hours, occurs in which the male cannot achieve full erection and another orgasm, regardless of the type or intensity of sexual stimulation. In females, orgasm generally involves rhythmic contractions of the vagina and more irregular contractions of the uterus, which are not always felt. Because females do not have a refractory period, they are capable of experiencing additional orgasms immediately following one. However, not all women find multiple orgasms easy to achieve or desirable. Following orgasm, the entire musculature of the body relaxes, and men and women tend to experience a state of deep relaxation, the stage known as **resolution.**

If you are sexually active, you may or may not have recognized all these phases in your sexual response cycle. People vary greatly in the length and distinctiveness of each phase. Masters and Johnson's depiction of the sexual response cycle may be more characteristic of men than of women, as women's responses tend to vary (Basson et al., 2001). Sometimes, the excitement and plateau phases are short for a female, and she reaches a discernible orgasm quickly. At other times, the excitement and plateau phases are longer, and she may or may not experience a full orgasm.

Occasional problems with sexual functioning are extremely common. A study of a representative sample of more than 3,000 adults in the United States found that 43 percent of the women and 31 percent of the men reported occasional problems (Laumann, Paik, & Rosen, 1999; Figure 13.2). When people have difficulties in sexual functioning that are persistent and that cause significant distress or interpersonal difficulty, they may be diagnosed with a **sexual dysfunction.**

What one person finds arousing, another may not (Table 13.1). And when people focus their sexual activity on something considered inappropriate—nonliving objects, prepubescent children, nonconsenting adults, or suffering or humiliation—they may be diagnosed with a **paraphilia.** Many people have occasional paraphilic fantasies. One study found that 62 percent of men fantasized about having sex with a young girl, 33 percent fantasized about raping a woman, 12 percent fantasized about being humiliated during sex, 5 percent fantasized about having sexual activity with an animal, and 3 percent fantasized about having sexual activity with a young boy (Crepault & Couture, 1980). Because these men reported making no attempt to carry out the fantasies, and because the fantasies did not make up the primary focus of their sexual arousal or cause them distress, most of them would not be diagnosed with a paraphilia.

For persons diagnosed with a paraphilia, atypical sexual acts are their primary form of sexual arousal. They often feel compelled to engage in their paraphilias, even though their behaviors cause them distress or create social or occupational problems. Their partners in sexual acts are merely vehicles for acting out their paraphilic fantasies, not individuals with needs, and rights.

Just as people vary in sexual functioning and sexual practices, so too do individuals vary in their **gender identity**—their perception of themselves as male or female. Gender identity differs from *gender role,* which is a person's belief about how he or she should behave as a male or female in society. Many females engage in behaviors considered part of the masculine gender role, such as playing aggressive sports or pursuing competitive careers, but still have a fundamental sense of themselves as female. Similarly, many males engage in behaviors considered part of the feminine gender role, such as caring for children, cooking, or sewing, but still have a fundamental sense of themselves as male. David Reimer was forced to dress and behave like a girl in his early childhood, but he still saw himself as male.

Gender identity and gender roles differ from *sexual orientation,* which is a person's preference for sexual partners of the opposite sex and/or of the same sex. Most men who have sex with men have a fundamental sense of themselves as male and therefore have male gender identities. The same is true of women who have sex with women and retain female gender identities.

When an individual believes he or she was born with the body of the wrong gender, the *DSM-IV-TR* defines this as **gender identity disorder (GID).** People with gender identity disorder feel trapped in the wrong body, wish to be rid of their genitals, and want to live as a member of the other gender.

The *DSM-IV-TR* definitions of sexual disorders are controversial because they single out some sexual behaviors as abnormal and disordered but not others. For example, adults whose sexual fantasies, urges, and behaviors focus on children can be diagnosed with a sexual disorder, but adults who rape other adults may not be diagnosed under the *DSM-IV-TR* criteria. The authors of the *DSM-5* have suggested changes to the diagnoses of the sexual and gender identity disorders, some of which are intended to make the lines between what constitutes a disorder and what is simply a variation in people's chosen sexual behavior more rational and clearer. We describe these proposed changes throughout this chapter.

sexual desire is more often connected to problems in relationships for women than for men (Meston & Bradford, 2007).

In the *DSM-5,* hypoactive sexual desire disorder may be subsumed under the new categories *sexual interest/arousal disorder in women* and *sexual interest/arousal disorder in men*. This combined diagnosis reflects the fact that lack of sexual desire or interest very often is tied to difficulties in sexual arousal (Meston & Bradford, 2007).

Thanks in part to endorsements by celebrities such as Rafael Palmeiro, sales of medications to treat male erectile disorder have skyrocketed.

Sexual Aversion Disorder

The other type of sexual desire disorder in the *DSM-IV-TR* is **sexual aversion disorder.** People with this disorder actively avoid sexual activities. When they do engage in sex, they may feel sickened by it or experience acute anxiety. Some people experience a generalized aversion to all sexual activities, including kissing and touching. The *DSM-5* authors are suggesting that this diagnosis be dropped because the disorder resembles a specific phobia (see Chapter 5) and because there is little research on it (American Psychiatric Association, 2010).

Sexual Arousal Disorders

People with *sexual arousal disorders* do not experience the physiological changes that make up the excitement or arousal phase of the sexual response cycle. **Female sexual arousal disorder** involves a recurrent inability to attain or maintain the swelling-lubrication response of sexual excitement. **Male erectile disorder** (previously referred to as *impotence*) involves the recurrent inability to attain or maintain an erection until the completion of sexual activity.

Female sexual arousal disorder is common. About 20 percent of women report difficulties with lubrication or arousal during sexual activity (Laumann et al., 1999; Lewis et al., 2004). The study of

FIGURE 13.2 **Percentage of People Who Have Had a Sexual Difficulty in the Past Year.** A national survey found that many people report having had one or more sexual difficulties in the past year.

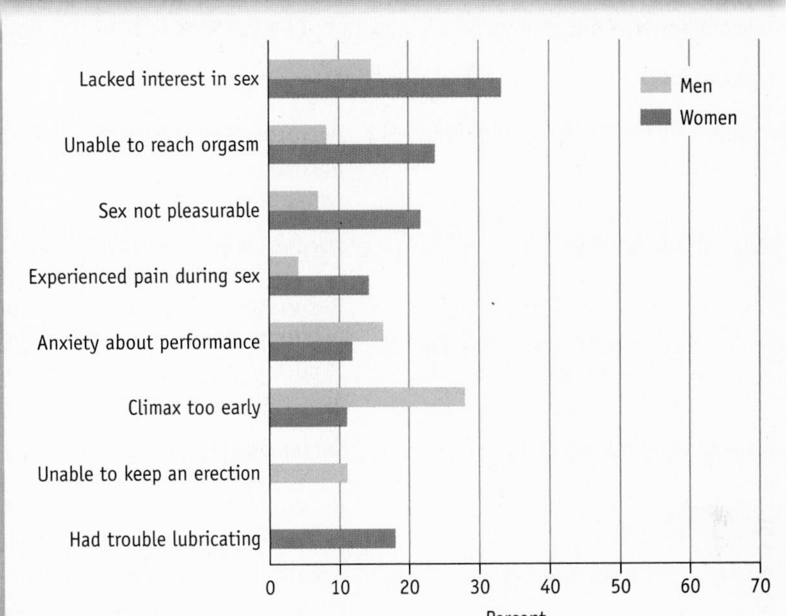

Source: Michael et al., 1994, p. 126.

TABLE 13.1 What Kinds of Sexual Practices Do People Find Appealing?

A national survey of 18- to 44-year-olds found that many different sexual practices appeal to people, with men finding more activities appealing than women do.

	Percent Saying "Very Appealing"	
Practice	**Men**	**Women**
Vaginal intercourse	83%	78%
Watching partner undress	50	30
Receiving oral sex	50	33
Giving oral sex	37	19
Group sex	14	1
Anus stimulated by partner's fingers	6	4
Using dildos/vibrators	5	3
Watching others do sexual things	6	2
Having a same-gender sex partner	4	3
Having sex with a stranger	5	1

Source: Michael et al., 1994.

TABLE 13.2 *DSM-IV-TR* Sexual Dysfunction Disorders

To meet the criteria for a *DSM-IV-TR* sexual dysfunction disorder, a disturbance must cause distress or interpersonal difficulty. It cannot be due to another Axis I Disorder (e.g., mood or anxiety disorders), the physiological effects of a substance (e.g., medication, psychoactive drugs), or a general medical condition. Each disorder can be subtyped as lifelong or acquired, generalized (occurring in all situations) or situational, and due to psychological factors or due to both biological and psychological factors.

Sexual Desire Disorders	Description
Hypoactive sexual desire disorder	Recurrent lack of sexual fantasies and desire for sexual activity
Sexual aversion disorder	Recurrent extreme aversion to, and avoidance of, all (or almost all) genital sexual contact with a sexual partner
Sexual Arousal Disorders	**Description**
Female sexual arousal disorder	Recurrent inability to attain, or to maintain until completion of the sexual activity, an adequate lubrication-swelling response of sexual excitement
Male erectile disorder	Recurrent inability to attain, or to maintain until completion of the sexual activity, an adequate lubrication-swelling response of sexual excitement
Orgasmic Disorders	**Description**
Female orgasmic disorder	Recurrent delay in, or absence of, orgasm following normal sexual excitement phase
Male orgasmic disorder	Recurrent delay in, or absence of, orgasm following normal sexual excitement phase
Premature ejaculation	Recurrent ejaculation with minimal sexual stimulation before, on, or shortly after penetration and before the person wishes it
Sexual Pain Disorders	**Description**
Dyspareunia	Recurrent genital pain associated with sexual intercourse in either a male or a female
Vaginismus	In women, involuntary contractions of the muscles surrounding the vagina, which interfere with sexual functioning

Source: Reprinted with permission from the *Diagnostic and Statistical Manual of Mental Disorders,* Fourth Edition, Text Revision.

over 31,000 women mentioned earlier found that 5.4 percent could be diagnosed with sexual arousal disorder (Clayton, 2007). In the *DSM-5,* female sexual arousal disorder may be subsumed under the category *sexual interest/arousal disorder in women.*

Men with the *lifelong* form of male erectile disorder have never been able to sustain an erection for a desired period of time. Men with the *acquired* form of the disorder were able to sustain an erection in the past but no longer can. Occasional problems in achieving or sustaining an erection are very common, with as many as 30 million men in the United States having erectile problems at some time in their life. Such problems do not constitute a disorder until they become persistent and significantly interfere with a man's interpersonal relationships or cause him distress. In the *DSM-5,* the criteria for male erectile disorder likely will specify that a man must fail to achieve or maintain an erection until completion of sexual activity on 75 percent of occasions over a period of at least 6 months.

One nationwide study (Saigal et al., 2006) found that one in five men over age 20 could be diagnosed with erectile dysfunction. The prevalence of erectile dysfunction increased dramatically with age, with over 77 percent of men over age 75 affected by it (Saigal et al., 2006). Problems with sexual arousal can be both the result and the cause of other difficulties in a couple's relationship, as in the following case study.

CASE STUDY

Paul and Geraldine had been living together for the past 6 months and were contemplating marriage. Geraldine described the problem that brought them to the sex therapy clinic: "For the past 2 months he hasn't been able to keep his erection after he enters me."

The psychiatrist learned that Paul, age 26, was a recently graduated lawyer, and that Geraldine, age 24, was a successful buyer for a large department store. They had both grown up in educated, middle-class, suburban families. They had met through mutual friends and had started to have sexual intercourse a few months after they met, with no problems at that time.

Two months later, Paul had moved from his family home into Geraldine's apartment. This was her idea, and Paul was unsure that he was ready for such an important step. Within a few weeks, Paul noticed that although he continued to be sexually aroused and wanted intercourse, as soon as he entered his partner, he began to lose his erection and could not stay inside. They would try again, but by then his desire had waned and he was unable to achieve another erection.

The psychiatrist learned that sex was not the only area of contention in the relationship. Geraldine complained that Paul did not spend enough time with her and preferred to go to baseball games with his male friends. Even when he was home, he would watch all the sports events that were available on TV and was not interested in going to foreign movies, museums, or the theater with her. Despite these differences, the couple was planning to marry and had set a date. (Reprinted from the *DSM-IV-TR Casebook: A Learning Companion to the Diagnostic and Statistical Manual of Mental Disorders,* Fourth Edition, Text Revision. Copyright © 2000 American Psychiatric Association.)

Orgasmic Disorders

Women with **female orgasmic disorder,** or *anorgasmia,* experience a recurrent delay in or the complete absence of orgasm after having reached the excitement phase of the sexual response cycle. The *DSM-IV-TR* specifies that this diagnosis should be based on the clinician's judgment that the woman's ability to have an orgasm is less than would be reasonable for her age, sexual experience, and the adequacy of sexual stimulation she receives (American Psychiatric Association, 2000). The *DSM-5* likely will make the criteria clearer by specifying that a woman must have difficulty reaching orgasm on 75 percent or more of occasions over a period of at least 6 months (American Psychiatric Association, 2010).

About one in four women reports occasional difficulty reaching orgasm (Laumann et al., 1999), and 4.7 percent can be diagnosed with orgasmic disorder (Clayton, 2007). The problem is greater among postmenopausal women, with about one in three reporting some problem reaching orgasm during sexual stimulation (Clayton, 2007).

The most common form of orgasmic disorder in males is **premature ejaculation.** Men with this disorder persistently ejaculate with minimal sexual stimulation before they wish to ejaculate. Laumann and colleagues (1999) found that 21 percent of men reported problems with premature ejaculation. Again, it is a judgment call as to when premature ejaculation becomes a sexual dysfunction. Premature ejaculation must cause significant distress or interpersonal problems before it is considered a disorder. Some men seeking treatment for this problem simply cannot prevent ejaculation before their partner reaches orgasm. Others ejaculate after very little stimulation, long before their partner is fully aroused. The *DSM-IV-TR* specifies that the clinician considering this diagnosis must take into account factors that affect duration of the excitement phase, such as age, novelty of the sexual partner or situation, and recent frequency of sexual activity (American Psychiatric Association, 2000). A community-based study found that 13 percent of men could be diagnosed with premature ejaculation by the *DSM-IV-TR* criteria (Patrick et al., 2005). The *DSM-5* is likely to make the criteria for this diagnosis clearer by specifying that a man must ejaculate within 1 minute of beginning sexual activity and before the man wishes it on 75 percent of occasions over a period of at least 6 months (American Psychiatric Association, 2010).

Men with premature ejaculation resort to applying desensitizing cream to the penis before sex, wearing multiple condoms, distracting themselves with other thoughts while making love, not allowing their partner to touch them, and masturbating multiple times shortly before having sex (Althof, 1995). These tactics generally are unsuccessful and can make the man's partner feel shut out of the sexual encounter, as in the following account.

CASE STUDY

Bill and Margaret were a couple in their late 20s who had been married for 2 years. They had had a tumultuous dating relationship before marriage. A therapist helped Bill and Margaret deal with issues in their relationship. However, the therapist made an incorrect assumption that with increased intimacy and the commitment of marriage, Bill's ejaculatory control problem would disappear. . . .

Margaret saw the early ejaculation as a symbol of lack of love and caring on Bill's part. As

(continued)

the problem continued over the next 2 years, Margaret became increasingly frustrated and withdrawn. She demonstrated her displeasure by resisting his sexual advances, and their intercourse frequency decreased from three or four times per week to once every 10 days. A sexual and marital crisis was precipitated by Margaret's belief that Bill was acting more isolated and distant when they did have intercourse. When they talked about their sexual relationship, it was usually in bed after intercourse, and the communication quickly broke down into tears, anger, and accusations. Bill was on the defensive and handled the sexual issue by avoiding talking to Margaret, which frustrated her even more.

Unbeknownst to Margaret, Bill had attempted a do-it-yourself technique to gain better control. He had bought a desensitizing cream he'd read about in a men's magazine and applied it to the glans of his penis (the caplike structure at the end of the penis) 20 minutes before initiating sex. During intercourse he tried to keep his leg muscles tense and think about sports as a way of keeping his arousal in check. Bill was unaware that Margaret felt emotionally shut out during sex. Bill was becoming more sensitized to his arousal cycle and was worrying about erection. He was not achieving better ejaculatory control, and he was enjoying sex less. The sexual relationship was heading downhill, and miscommunication and frustration were growing. (McCarthy, 1989, pp. 151–152)

Men with **male orgasmic disorder** experience a recurrent delay in or the absence of orgasm following the excitement phase of the sexual response cycle. In most cases of this disorder, a man cannot ejaculate during intercourse but can ejaculate with manual or oral stimulation. Eight percent of men report problems in reaching orgasm (Laumann et al., 1999); it is estimated that less than 3 percent of men could be diagnosed with male orgasmic disorder (Perelman & Rowland, 2008). In the *DSM-5,* this disorder is likely to be renamed *delayed ejaculation,* and the criteria will specify that delayed or absent ejaculation must occur in 75 percent of sexual encounters over a period of at least 6 months.

Sexual Pain Disorders

The sexual pain disorders are *dyspareunia* and *vaginismus.* **Dyspareunia** is genital pain associated with intercourse. It is rare in men, but in community surveys 12 to 39 percent of women report frequent pain during intercourse (Farmer, Kukkonen, & Binik, 2008). In women, the pain may be shallow during intromission (insertion of the penis into the vagina) or deep during penile thrusting. Some women also experience pain when inserting tampons, having a gynecological exam, riding a bike, or even walking (Farmer, Kao, & Binik, 2009). Dyspareunia in women can be the result of dryness of the vagina caused by antihistamines or other drugs, infection of the clitoris or vulval area, injury or irritation to the vagina, or tumors of the internal reproductive organs. In men, dyspareunia involves painful erections or pain during thrusting (Farmer et al., 2009).

Vaginismus involves the involuntary contraction of the muscles surrounding the outer third of the vagina when penetration with a penis, finger, tampon, or speculum is attempted. Women with vaginismus may experience sexual arousal and have an orgasm when their clitoris is stimulated. In other women with this disorder, even the anticipation of vaginal insertion may result in this muscle spasm. It is estimated that 5 to 17 percent of women experience vaginismus (Reissing, Binik, & Khalife, 1999).

In the *DSM-5*, dyspareunia and vaginismus likely will be subsumed under the general diagnosis *genito-pelvic pain/penetration disorder*. This change reflects difficulty in distinguishing between the two disorders clinically.

Causes of Sexual Dysfunctions

Most sexual dysfunctions probably have multiple causes, including biological and psychosocial causes.

Biological Causes

The *DSM-IV-TR* sets apart sexual dysfunctions caused by medical conditions by giving them the separate diagnosis *sexual dysfunction due to a general medical condition*. Many medical illnesses can cause problems in sexual functioning in both men and women. One of the most common contributors to sexual dysfunction is diabetes, which can lower sexual drive, arousal, enjoyment, and satisfaction, especially in men (Incrocci & Gianotten, 2008). Diabetes often goes undiagnosed, leading people to believe that psychological factors are causing their sexual dysfunctions when the cause actually is undiagnosed diabetes. Other diseases that are common causes of sexual dysfunction, particularly in men, are cardiovascular disease, multiple sclerosis, kidney failure, vascular disease, spinal cord injury, and injury to the autonomic nervous system by surgery or radiation (Lewis, Yuan, & Wang, 2008; Saigal et al., 2006).

As many as 40 percent of cases of male erectile disorder are caused by one of these medical conditions (Lewis et al., 2008). In men with cardiovascular disease, sexual dysfunction can be caused directly by the disease, which can reduce blood flow to the penis, or it may be a psychological response to the presence of the disease. For example, a man who recently has had a heart attack may fear he will have another one if he has sex.

In men, abnormally low levels of the androgen hormones, especially testosterone, or high levels of the hormones estrogen and prolactin can cause sexual dysfunction (Hackett, 2008). In women, levels of both androgens and estrogens may play a role in sexual dysfunction, although less consistently so than in men (Meston & Bradford, 2007). Estrogen problems in women may result in low arousal due to reduced vaginal lubrication. Levels of estrogen drop greatly at menopause; thus, postmenopausal women often complain of lowered sexual desire and arousal. Similarly, women who have had a radical hysterectomy, which removes the main source of estrogen—the ovaries—can experience reductions in both sexual desire and arousal. Androgens seem to play a role in the maintenance of sexual desire and mood and also may enhance the function of vaginal tissue.

Vaginal dryness or irritation, which causes pain during sex and therefore lowers sexual desire and arousal, can be caused by antihistamines, douches, tampons, vaginal contraceptives, radiation therapy, endometriosis, and infections such as vaginitis or pelvic inflammatory disease (Meston & Bradford, 2007). Injuries during childbirth that have healed poorly, such as a poorly repaired episiotomy, can cause sexual pain in women (Masters, Johnson, & Kolodny, 1993). Women who have had gynecological cancers sometimes report pain, changes in the vaginal anatomy, and problems with their body image or sexual self-concept (Lagana, McGarrey, Classen, & Koopman, 2001).

Several prescription drugs can diminish sexual drive and arousal and interfere with orgasm (Clayton, 2007). These include antihypertensive drugs taken by people with high blood pressure, antipsychotic drugs, antidepressants, lithium, and tranquilizers. Indeed, sexual dysfunction is one of the most common side effects of the widely used selective serotonin reuptake inhibitors (Meston & Bradford, 2007).

Many recreational drugs, including marijuana, cocaine, amphetamines, and nicotine, can impair sexual functioning (Schiavi & Segraves, 1995). Although people often drink alcohol to make them feel sexier and less inhibited, even small amounts of alcohol can significantly impair sexual functioning. Chronic alcohol abusers and alcohol dependents often have diagnosable sexual dysfunctions (Lewis et al., 2008). When a sexual dysfunction is caused by substance use, it is given the diagnosis **substance-induced sexual dysfunction.**

Although many people drink alcohol to decrease their sexual inhibitions, alcohol also can impair sexual performance.

To determine whether a man is capable of attaining an erection, clinicians can do a psychophysiological assessment with devices that directly measure men's erections. In a laboratory, strain gauges can be attached to the base and glans (end structure) of a man's penis to record the magnitude, duration, and pattern of arousal while he watches erotic films or listens to erotic audio recordings (Lewis et al., 2008). For women, the physical ability to become aroused can be measured with a vaginal photoplethysmograph, a tampon-shaped device inserted into a woman's vagina that records the changes accompanying vasocongestion, the rush of blood to the vagina during arousal (Geer, Morokoff, & Greenwood, 1974).

Psychological Causes

Our emotional well-being and our beliefs and attitudes about sex greatly influence our sexuality.

Psychological Disorders A number of psychological disorders can cause sexual dysfunction (Meston & Bradford, 2007; van Lankveld, 2008). A person with depression may have no desire for sex or may experience any of the problems in sexual arousal and functioning we have discussed. Unfortunately, the medications used to treat depression often lead to problems in sexual functioning. Similarly, people with an anxiety disorder, such as generalized anxiety disorder, panic disorder, or obsessive-compulsive disorder, may find their sexual desire and functioning waning. Loss of sexual desire and functioning also is common among people with schizophrenia (van Lankveld, 2008).

Attitudes and Cognitions People who have been taught that sex is dirty, disgusting, or sinful or is a "necessary evil" understandably may lack the desire to have sex (van Lankveld, 2008). They also may know so little about their own body and sexual responses that they do not know how to make sex pleasurable. Such is the case with Mrs. Booth in the following case study.

CASE STUDY

Mr. and Mrs. Booth have been married for 14 years and have three children, ages 8 through 12. They are both bright and well educated. Both are from Scotland, from which they moved 10 years ago because of Mr. Booth's work as an industrial consultant. They present with the complaint that Mrs. Booth has been able to participate passively in sex "as a duty" but has never enjoyed it since they have been married.

Before their marriage, although they had had intercourse only twice, Mrs. Booth had been highly aroused by kissing and petting and felt she used her attractiveness to "seduce" her husband into marriage. She did, however, feel intense guilt about their two episodes of premarital intercourse; during their honeymoon, she began to think of sex as a chore that could not be pleasing. Although she periodically passively complied with intercourse, she had almost no spontaneous desire for sex. She never masturbated, had never reached orgasm, thought of all variations such as oral sex as completely repulsive, and was preoccupied with a fantasy of how disapproving her family would be if she ever engaged in any of these activities.

Mrs. Booth is almost totally certain that no woman she respects in any older generation has enjoyed sex and that despite the "new vogue" of sexuality, only sleazy, crude women let themselves act like "animals." These beliefs have led to a pattern of regular but infrequent sex that at best is accommodating and gives little or no pleasure to her or her husband. Whenever Mrs. Booth comes close to having a feeling of sexual arousal, numerous negative thoughts come into her mind such as, "What am I, a tramp?"; "If I like this, he'll just want it more often"; and "How could I look at myself in the mirror after something like this?" These thoughts almost inevitably are accompanied by a cold feeling and an insensitivity to sensual pleasure. As a result, sex is invariably an unhappy experience. Almost any excuse, such as fatigue or being busy, is sufficient for her to rationalize avoiding intercourse. (Adapted from Spitzer et al., 2002, pp. 251–252)

Although the attitudes Mrs. Booth has toward sex may be uncommon among younger people these days, many younger and older women still report a fear of "letting go," which interferes with orgasm (Nobre & Pinto-Gouveia, 2006; Tugrul & Kabakci, 1997). They say they fear losing control or acting in some way that will embarrass them. This fear of loss of control may result from a distrust of one's partner, a sense of shame about sex, a poor body image, or a host of other factors.

Another set of attitudes that interfere with sexual functioning is often referred to as *performance concerns* or **performance anxiety** (LoPiccolo, 1992; Masters & Johnson, 1970). People worry so much about whether they are going to be aroused and have an orgasm that this worry interferes with their sexual functioning: "What if I can't get an erection? I'll die of embarrassment!" "I've got to have an orgasm, or he'll think I don't love him!" These worried thoughts are so distracting that people experiencing them cannot focus on the pleasure that sexual stimulation is giving them and thus do not become as aroused as they want to or need to in order to reach orgasm (Figure 13.3; Barlow, Sakheim, & Beck, 1983; Cranston-Cuebas & Barlow, 1990).

In addition, many people engage in *spectatoring:* They anxiously attend to reactions and performance during sex as if they were spectators rather than participants (Masters & Johnson, 1970). Spectatoring distracts from sexual pleasure and interferes with sexual functioning. Unfortunately, people who have had some problems in sexual functioning only develop more performance concerns, which then further interfere with their functioning. By the time they seek treatment for sexual dysfunction, they may be so anxious about "performing" sexually that they avoid all sexual activity.

Trauma Reductions in sexual desire and functioning often follow personal trauma, such as the loss of a loved one, the loss of a job, or the diagnosis of severe illness in one's child. Unemployment

FIGURE 13.3 A Model Showing How Anxiety and Cognitive Interference Can Produce Erectile Dysfunction and Other Sexual Disorders.

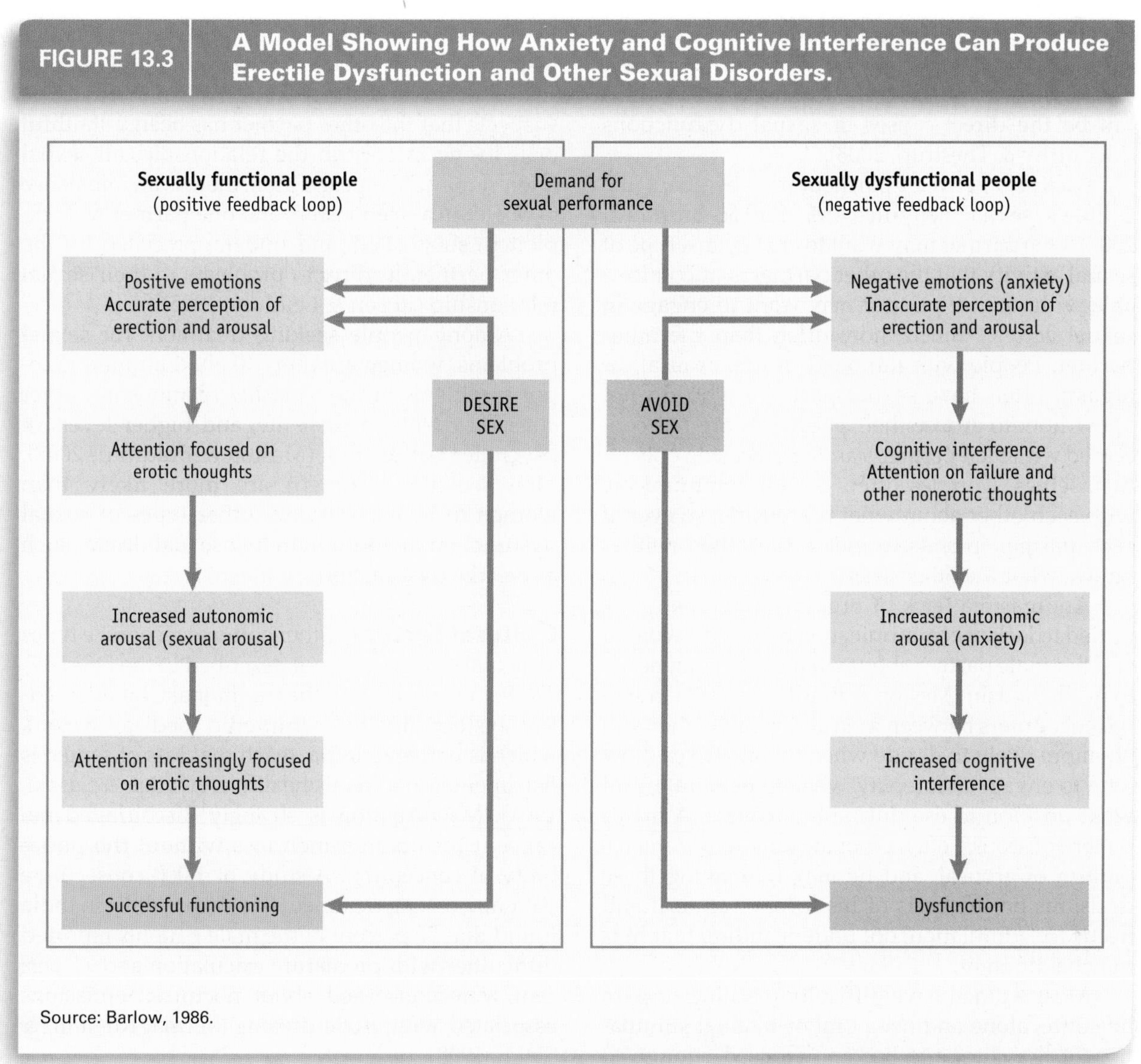

Source: Barlow, 1986.

in men may contribute to declines in sexual desire and functioning (Morokoff & Gillilland, 1993). Traumas such as unemployment can challenge a person's self-esteem, interfering with his or her sexual self-concept. Traumas can also cause a person to experience a depression that includes a loss of interest in most pleasurable activities, including sex. In such cases, clinicians typically focus on treating the depression, with the expectation that sexual desire will resume once the depression has lifted.

One type of personal trauma often associated with sexual desire disorders in women is sexual assault (van Lankveld, 2008). A woman who has been sexually assaulted may lose all interest in sex and become disgusted or extremely anxious when anyone, particularly a man, touches her. Her sexual aversion may become tied to a sense of vulnerability and loss of control or to a conditioned aversion to all forms of sexual contact. In addition, male partners of women who have been sexually assaulted sometimes cannot cope with the trauma and withdraw from sexual encounters with sexual assault survivors. Survivors then may feel victimized yet again, and their interest in sex may decline even further.

Interpersonal and Sociocultural Factors

Although our internal psychological states and beliefs play important roles in our sexuality, sex is largely an interpersonal activity—one that societies attempt to control. For this reason, interpersonal and sociocultural factors also play important roles in people's sexual interests and activities.

Interpersonal Factors Problems in intimate relationships are extremely common among people with sexual dysfunctions. Sometimes, these problems are the consequences of sexual dysfunctions, as when a couple cannot communicate about the sexual dysfunction of one partner and they grow distant from each other. Relationship problems also can be the direct causes of sexual dysfunctions (McCarthy & Thestrup, 2008).

Conflicts between partners may be about the couple's sexual activities (Meston & Bradford, 2007). One partner may want to engage in a type of sexual activity that the other partner is uncomfortable with, or one partner may want to engage in sexual activity much more often than the other partner. People with inhibited desire, arousal, or orgasm often have sexual partners who do not know how to arouse their partner or are not concerned with their partner's arousal, focusing only on themselves. Couples often do not communicate with each other about what is arousing, so even if each partner intends to please the other, neither knows what the other desires.

Anorgasmia (lack of orgasm) in women may be tied to lack of communication between a woman and her male partner about what the woman needs to reach orgasm (Meston & Bradford, 2007). In sexual encounters between men and women, men still are more likely to decide when to initiate sex, how long to engage in foreplay, when to penetrate, and what position to use during intercourse. A man's pattern of arousal often is not the same as a woman's pattern of arousal, and he may be making these decisions on the basis of his level of arousal and needs for stimulation, not understanding that hers may be different.

Most women have difficulty reaching orgasm by coitus alone and need oral or manual stimulation of the clitoris to become aroused enough to reach orgasm (Hite, 1976; Kaplan, 1974). Because many men and women believe that men should be able to bring women to orgasm by penile insertion and thrusting alone, many women never receive the stimulation they need to be sufficiently aroused to orgasm. They may feel inhibited from telling their partner that they would like him to stimulate their clitoris more, because they are afraid of hurting their partner's feelings or angering him or because they believe they do not have the right to ask for the kind of stimulation they want. Some women fake an orgasm to protect their partner's ego. Often, their partner knows that they are not fully satisfied, however. Communication between partners may break down further, and sex may become a forum for hostility rather than pleasure (McCarthy & Thestrup, 2007).

Conflicts between partners that are not directly related to their sexual activity can affect their sexual relationship as well, as we saw in the case of Paul and Geraldine (McCarthy & Thestrup, 2007; Rosen & Leiblum, 1995). Anger, distrust, and lack of respect for one's partner can greatly interfere with sexual desire and functioning. When one partner suspects that the other partner has been unfaithful or is losing interest in the relationship, all sexual interest may disappear. Often, there is an imbalance of power in a relationship, and one partner feels exploited, subjugated, and underappreciated by the other partner, leading to problems in their sexual relationship (Rosen & Leiblum, 1995).

Among people seeking treatment for sexual problems, women are more likely than men to report problems in their marital relationship, other stressful events in their life, and higher levels of psychological distress (Meston & Bradford, 2007). Men seeking treatment are more likely than women to be experiencing other types of sexual dysfunction in addition to low sexual desire, such as erectile dysfunction.

Cultural Factors Other cultures recognize types of sexual dysfunction not described in the *DSM-IV-TR*. For example, both the traditional Chinese medical system and the Ayurvedic medical system, which is native to India, teach that loss of semen is detrimental to a man's health (Dewaraja & Sasaki, 1991). Masturbation is strongly discouraged because it results in semen loss without the possibility of conception. A study of 1,000 consecutive patients seeking treatment in a sexual clinic in India found that 77 percent of the male patients reported difficulties with premature ejaculation and 71 percent were concerned about nocturnal emissions associated with erotic dreams (Verma, Khaitan, & Singh, 1998).

A depersonalization syndrome known as *Koro,* thought to result from semen loss, has been reported among Malaysians, Southeast Asians, and southern Chinese. This syndrome involves an acute anxiety state, characterized by a feeling of panic and impending death, and a delusion that the penis is shrinking into the body and disappearing (American Psychiatric Association, 2000). To stop the penis from disappearing into the body, the patient or his relatives may grab and hold the penis until the attack of Koro is ended.

In Polynesian culture, there is no word for erection problems in men (Mannino, 1999). If a man does not have an erection, it is assumed that he does not want sex. In some African cultures, the preference is for a woman's vagina to be dry and tight for sexual intercourse (Brown, Ayowa, & Brown, 1993). Several herbal treatments are used to achieve this dryness.

In surveys in the United States, less educated and poorer men and women tend to experience more sexual dysfunctions. Problems include having pain during sex, not finding sex pleasurable, being unable to reach orgasm, lacking interest in sex, climaxing too early, and, for men, having trouble maintaining an erection (Laumann, Gagnon, Michael, & Michaels, 1994). People in lower educational and income groups may have more sexual dysfunctions because they are under more psychological stress, because their physical health is worse, or because they have not had the benefit of educational programs that teach people about their bodies and about healthy social relationships. In addition, people from cultural backgrounds that teach negative attitudes toward sex are more likely to develop sexual dysfunctions resulting from these attitudes (Gagnon, 1990).

Trends Across the Life Span

Our culture conveys the message that young adults, particularly men, can't get enough sex but that sexual activity declines steadily with age. Supposedly, older adults (i.e., over about age 65) hardly ever have sex. While sexual activity is greater among younger adults than among older adults, many adults remain sexually active well into old age (Bartlik & Goldstein, 2001a, 2001b; Laumann et al., 2008).

Age-related biological changes can affect sexual functioning (Brotto & Luria, 2008). Both men and women need adequate levels of testosterone to maintain sexual desire. Testosterone levels begin to decline in a person's 50s and continue to decrease steadily throughout life. Lower testosterone levels are associated with increased difficulty in achieving and maintaining an erection (Agronin, 2009). Diminished estrogen levels in postmenopausal women can lead to vaginal dryness and lack of lubrication and thus to a reduction in sexual responsivity (Brotto & Luria, 2008). In many cases of sexual dysfunction in older adults, the cause is not age itself but rather medical conditions, which are more common in older age.

For both older men and older women, the loss of a lifelong spouse, losses of other family members and friends, health concerns, and discomfort with one's own aging can contribute to sexual problems (Brotto & Luria, 2008). Conflicts and dissatisfactions in a couple's relationship can worsen as the couple spends more time together following retirement and/or their children's moving out of the house. Older couples may need to learn to be more flexible and patient with each other as their bodies change and to try new techniques for stimulating each other. A number of biological and psychosocial treatments are available for sexual dysfunctions in both older and younger people.

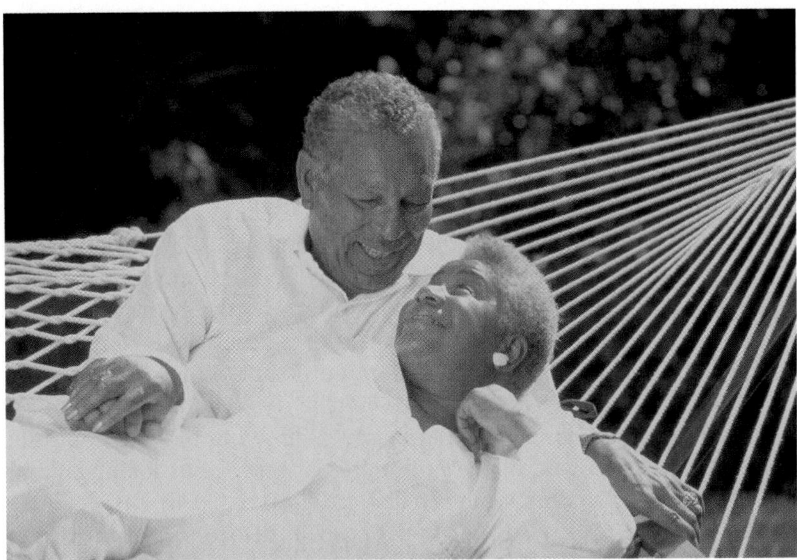

Many older adults remain sexually active and experience little decline in sexual functioning.

Treatments for Sexual Dysfunctions

Because most sexual dysfunctions have multiple causes, treatments may involve a combination of approaches, often including biological interventions, psychosocial therapy focusing on problems in a relationship or on the concerns of an individual client, and sex therapies to help clients learn new skills for increasing their sexual arousal and pleasure.

Biological Therapies

If a sexual dysfunction is the direct result of another medical condition, such as diabetes, treating the medical condition often will reduce the sexual dysfunction (Incrocci & Gianotten, 2008). Similarly, if medications are contributing to a sexual dysfunction, adjusting the dosage or switching to a different type of medication can relieve sexual difficulties. Also, getting a person to stop using recreational drugs such as marijuana can often cure sexual dysfunction.

A number of biological treatments are available for men with male erectile disorder (Lewis et al., 2008). The drug that has received the most media attention in recent years is sildenafil (trade name Viagra). This drug has proven effective both in men whose erectile dysfunction has no known organic cause and in men whose erectile dysfunction is caused by a medical condition, such as hypertension, diabetes, or spinal cord injury (Lewis et al., 2008). Two other drugs, Cialis and Levitra, have similar positive effects. These drugs do have side effects, though, including headaches, flushing, and stomach irritation, and do not work in up to 44 percent of men (Bach et al., 2001).

Some antidepressants, particularly the selective serotonin reuptake inhibitors (SSRIs), can cause sexual dysfunctions. Other drugs can be used in conjunction with these antidepressants to reduce their sexual side effects (Balon & Segraves, 2008). One drug that has proven helpful in this regard is bupropion, which goes by the trade names Wellbutrin and Zyban. Bupropion appears to reduce the sexual side effects of the SSRIs and can itself be effective as an antidepressant. Sildenafil also may help men whose erectile dysfunction is caused by taking antidepressants, allowing them to continue taking the antidepressants without losing sexual functioning (Balon & Segraves, 2008).

In men with erectile disorder, certain drugs can be injected directly into the penis to induce an erection. Although this method is effective, it has the obvious drawback of requiring injections (Lewis et al., 2008).

Mechanical interventions are available for men with erectile dysfunction (Lewis et al., 2008). One device includes a cylinder that fits over the penis and connects to a manual or battery-powered vacuum pump, which induces engorgement of the penis with blood. Alternately, prosthetic devices can be surgically implanted into the penis to make it erect. One prosthetic consists of a pair of rods inserted into the penis. The rods create a permanent erection, which can be bent either up or down against the body. Another type is a hydraulic inflatable device, which allows a man to create an erection by pumping saline into rods inserted in the penis and then to relieve the erection by pumping out the saline. Erections achieved with these devices technically are full erections but frequently do not evoke bodily or mental feelings of sexual arousal (Delizonna et al., 2001).

For men suffering from premature ejaculation, some antidepressants can be helpful, including fluoxetine (Prozac), clomipramine (Anafranil), and sertraline (Zoloft). Several studies suggest that these drugs significantly reduce the frequency of premature ejaculation (Rowland & McMahon, 2008).

Several studies have examined the effects of hormone therapy, specifically the use of testosterone, to increase sexual desire in men and women with hypoactive sexual desire disorder. Hormone replacement therapy can be very effective for men whose low levels of sexual desire or arousal are linked to low levels of testosterone; they are not effective for men whose low sexual desire or arousal is not linked to low levels of testosterone (Segraves, 2003). For women, the effects of testosterone therapy are mixed (see review by Meston & Bradford, 2007). Some studies find that high levels of testosterone increase sexual desire and arousal in women but also run the risk of significant side effects, including masculinization (e.g., chest hair, voice changes; Shifren et al., 2000). More moderate levels of testosterone do not have consistent effects on libido for women. Bupropion has proven helpful in treating some women with hypoactive sexual desire (Segraves et al., 2004).

Large controlled studies investigating the effects of sildenafil for women with sexual dysfunctions report mixed results (Basson et al., 2002 Meston & Bradford, 2007; Nurnberg et al., 2008). The drug does increase vasocongestion and lubrication in women, but these physiological changes do not consistently lead to greater subjective arousal. It seems that, particularly for women, achieving sexual arousal and pleasure takes more than physiological arousal.

Psychotherapy and Sex Therapy

The introduction of drugs, such as sildenafil, that can overcome sexual dysfunctions, at least in men, has dramatically changed the nature of treatments for these disorders. Given the financial and time constraints imposed by managed care, many people seeking treatment for a sexual dysfunction are offered only a medication and not psychotherapy (McCarthy & Thestrup, 2008). Also, many people want only a medication and do not want to engage in psychotherapy to address possible psychological and interpersonal contributors to their sexual problems.

A variety of psychotherapeutic techniques have been developed, however, and have been shown to help people with sexual dysfunctions (Leiblum & Rosen, 2000). One technique is individual psychotherapy, in which individuals explore the thoughts and previous experiences that impede them from enjoying a positive sexual life. Couples therapy often helps couples develop more satisfying sexual relationships. As part of both individual and couples therapy, behavioral techniques are used to teach people skills to enhance their sexual experiences and to improve communication and interactions with their sexual partners.

Individual and Couples Therapy A therapist begins treatment by assessing the attitudes, beliefs, and personal history of an individual client or of both members of a couple in order to discover experiences, thoughts, and feelings that might be contributing to sexual problems. Cognitive-behavioral interventions often are used to address attitudes and beliefs that interfere with sexual functioning (McCarthy & Thestrup, 2008; Pridal & LoPiccolo, 2000; Rosen & Leiblum, 1995). For example, a man who fears that he will embarrass himself by not sustaining an erection in a sexual encounter may be challenged to examine the evidence of this having happened to him in the past. If this has been a common occurrence for the man, his therapist would explore the thought patterns surrounding the experience and then help the man challenge these cognitions and practice more positive ones. Similarly, a woman who has low sexual desire because she was taught by her parents that sex is dirty would learn to challenge this belief and to adopt a more accepting attitude toward sex.

When one member of a couple has a sexual dysfunction, it may be the result of problems in the couple's relationship, or it may be contributing to problems in the relationship. For this reason, many therapists prefer to treat sexual dysfunctions in the context of the couple's relationship, if possible, rather than focusing only on the individual with the sexual dysfunction. The therapist may use role playing during therapy sessions to observe how the couple discusses sex and how the partners perceive each other's role in their sexual encounters (Pridal & LoPiccolo, 2000).

Some couples in long-term relationships have abandoned the *seduction rituals*—those activities that arouse sexual interest in both partners—they followed when they were first together (McCarthy, 2001; Verhulst & Heiman, 1988). Couples in which both partners work may be particularly prone to try squeezing in sexual encounters late at night, when both partners are tired and not really interested in sex. These encounters may be rushed or not fully satisfying and can lead to a gradual decline in interest in any sexual intimacy. A therapist may encourage a couple to set aside enough time to engage in seduction rituals and satisfying sexual encounters (McCarthy, 1997). For example, partners may decide to hire a babysitter for their children, have a romantic dinner out, and then go to a hotel, where they can have sex without rushing or being interrupted by their children.

Partners often differ in their *scripts* for sexual encounters—their expectations about what will take place during a sexual encounter and about what each partner's responsibilities are (Pridal & LoPiccolo, 2000). Resolving these differences in scripts may be a useful goal in therapy. For example, if a woman lacks desire for sex because she feels her partner is too rough during sex, a therapist may encourage the partner to slow down and show the woman the kind of gentle intimacy she needs to enjoy sex. In general, therapists help partners understand what each wants and needs from sexual interactions and helps them negotiate mutually acceptable and satisfying repertoires of sexual exchange.

When the conflicts between partners involve matters other than their sexual practices, the therapist will focus primarily on these conflicts and only secondarily on the sexual dysfunction. Such conflicts may involve an imbalance of power in the relationship, distrust or hostility, or disagreement over important values or decisions. Cognitive-behavioral therapies are used most commonly, although some therapists use psychodynamic interventions and some use interventions based on family systems therapy. Cognitive-behavioral therapies have been researched more than other types of therapy and have been shown to be effective for several types of sexual dysfunction (see Leiblum & Rosen, 2000; Meston, Seal, & Hamilton, 2008).

Sex Therapy Whether a therapist uses a cognitive-behavioral or some other therapeutic approach to address the psychological issues involved in a sexual dysfunction, direct sex therapy using behavioral techniques may be a part of the therapy. When a sexual dysfunction seems to be due, at least in part, to inadequate sexual skill on the part of the client and his or her partner, sex therapy focusing on practicing skills can be useful. Some people have never learned what does give them or their partners pleasure or have fallen out of the habit of engaging in some practices. Sex therapy both teaches skills and helps partners develop a regular pattern of engaging in satisfying sexual encounters.

Sex therapy often includes teaching or encouraging clients to masturbate (Heiman, 2000; Meston et al., 2008). The goals of masturbation are for people to explore their bodies to discover what is arousing and to become less inhibited about their sexuality. Then individuals are taught to communicate their newly discovered desires to their partners. This technique can be especially helpful for anorgasmic women, many of whom have never masturbated and have little knowledge of what they need in order to become aroused (Meston & Bradford, 2007). Studies show that more than 80 percent of anorgasmic women are able to have an orgasm when they learn to masturbate and that 20 to 60 percent are able to have an orgasm with their partner after learning to masturbate (Heiman, 2000). These women also report increased enjoyment and satisfaction from sex, a more relaxed attitude toward sex and life, and increased acceptance of their bodies.

The client's cognitions while engaging in new sexual skills can be evaluated and used as a focus of therapy sessions (McCarthy & Thestrup, 2008). For example, a woman who is learning how to masturbate for the first time may realize that she has thoughts such as "I'm going to get caught, and I'll be so embarrassed"; "I shouldn't be doing this—this is sinful"; and "Only pathetic people do this" while masturbating. A cognitive-behavioral therapist can then help the woman address the accuracy of these thoughts and decide whether she wants to maintain this attitude toward masturbation. If the woman is in psychodynamic therapy, the therapist might explore the origins of the woman's attitudes about masturbation in her early relationships. Thus, the behavioral techniques of sex therapy not only directly teach the client new sexual skills but also provide material for discussion in therapy sessions.

In sensate focus therapy, couples are encouraged to spend time exploring what sexually arouses each of them without feeling pressured to reach orgasm.

Sensate Focus Therapy One of the mainstays of sex therapy is **sensate focus therapy** (Althof, 2000; Masters & Johnson, 1970). In the early phases of this therapy, partners are instructed *not* to be concerned about or even to attempt intercourse. Rather, they are told to focus intently on the pleasure created by the exercises. These instructions are meant to reduce performance anxiety and any concern about achieving orgasm.

In the first phase of sensate focus therapy, partners spend time gently touching each other, but not around the genitals. They are instructed to focus on the sensations and to communicate with each other about what does and does not feel good. The goal is to have the partners spend intimate time together communicating, without pressure for intercourse. This first phase may continue for several weeks, until the partners feel comfortable with the exercises and have learned what gives each of them pleasure.

In the second phase of sensate focus therapy, the partners spend time directly stimulating each other's breasts and genitals, but still without attempting intercourse. If the problem is a female arousal disorder, the woman guides her partner to stimulate her in arousing ways. It is acceptable for a woman to be aroused to orgasm during these exercises, but the partners are instructed not to attempt intercourse until she regularly becomes fully aroused by her partner during the sensate focus exercises. If the problem is a male erectile disorder, the man guides his partner in touching him in ways that feel arousing. If he has an erection, he is to let it come and go naturally. Intercourse is forbidden until he is able to have erections easily and frequently during the sensate focus exercises.

Throughout these exercises, the partner with the problem is instructed to be selfish and to focus only on the arousing sensations and on communicating with his or her partner about what feels good. The touching should proceed in a relaxed and nondemanding atmosphere. Once the partner with the problem regularly experiences arousal with genital stimulation, the partners may begin having intercourse, but the focus remains on enhancing and sustaining pleasure rather than on orgasm or performance.

The following case study indicates how the behavioral techniques of sensate focus therapy can help couples recognize and confront the complex personal and interpersonal issues that may be interfering with their enjoyment of sex.

CASE STUDY

Murray, a 53-year-old successful insurance agent, and his wife, a 50-year-old nutritional counselor, had been married for 28 years. With the exception of time spent on vacation, Murray had a 7-year history of erectile dysfunction. The frequency of their lovemaking had gradually declined to its current level of once every 4 months. Murray reported considerable performance anxiety, enhanced by his competitive personality style. He summed up his dilemma: "When you have a life full of successes, you don't get much practice at how to deal with inadequacy."

During the first hour of therapy, sensate focus exercises were suggested, and instructions given to engage in sensual nongenital touching. They returned in a week, noting how difficult it had been to find time to pleasure one another. Their mutual avoidance was discussed and understood as a means of warding off feelings of inadequacy. Working through the resistance allowed the couple to engage in the exercises three times over the course of the next week. With the pleasuring, Murray began to achieve good, long-lasting erections.

Therapy then progressed to include genital touching. After the first week, they talked about their problem of "silliness." They realized that humor had been used to cope with the dysfunction. Now, however, joking in bed seemed to inhibit sexual closeness. Murray's good erections were maintained, although he was having trouble concentrating on his sensations. Further exploration revealed that he was focusing his attention in a driven, intense manner. To counter this, the therapist redirected him to maintain a relaxed awareness akin to meditation. Murray found this analogy helpful, and the couple felt ready to proceed with vaginal containment. During the following week, they "disobeyed" and moved on to have mutually satisfying intercourse. They feared the recurrence of the old problem, but it did not return, and the remaining two sessions were spent talking about their sexual life. Despite otherwise good communication, they had never been able before to broach this topic with one another. (From Althof, 2000, p. 270)

Techniques for Treating Premature Ejaculation Two techniques are useful in helping a man with premature ejaculation gain control over his ejaculations: the stop-start technique (Semans, 1956) and the squeeze technique (Masters & Johnson, 1970). The **stop-start technique** can be carried out either through masturbation or with a partner. In the first phase, the man is told to stop stimulating himself or to tell his partner to stop stimulating him just before he is about to ejaculate. He then relaxes and concentrates on the sensations in his body until his level of arousal declines. At that point, he or his partner can resume stimulation, again stopping before the point of ejaculatory inevitability. If stimulation stops too late and the man ejaculates, he is encouraged not to feel angry or disappointed but to enjoy the ejaculation and reflect on what he has learned about his body and then resume the exercise. If a man is engaging in this exercise with a female partner, they are instructed not to engage in intercourse until he has sufficient control over his ejaculations during her manual stimulation of him.

In the second phase of this process, when a female partner is involved, the man lies on his back with his female partner on top of him, and she inserts his penis into her vagina but then remains quiet. Most men with premature ejaculation have intercourse only in the man-on-top position, with quick and short thrusting during intercourse, which makes it very difficult for them to exert control over their ejaculations. The goal is for the man to enjoy the sensation of being in the woman's vagina without ejaculating. During the exercise, he is encouraged to touch or massage his partner and to communicate with her about what each is experiencing. If he feels he is reaching ejaculatory inevitability, he can request that she dismount and lie next to him until his arousal subsides. Partners are encouraged to engage in this exercise for at least 10 to 15 minutes, even if they must interrupt it several times to prevent the man from ejaculating.

In the third phase of the stop-start technique, the woman creates some thrusting motion while still on top of her partner but uses slow, long strokes. The partners typically reach orgasm and experience the entire encounter as highly intimate and pleasurable. Female partners of men with premature ejaculation often have trouble reaching orgasm themselves, because the men lose their erection after ejaculating, long before the women are highly aroused, and tension is high between the partners during sex. The stop-start technique can create encounters in which the female partner receives the stimulation she needs to reach orgasm as well.

The **squeeze technique** is used somewhat less often because it is harder to teach to partners (McCarthy, 2001). The man's partner stimulates him to an erection, and then, when he signals that ejaculation is imminent, his partner applies a firm but gentle squeeze to his penis, either at the head or at the base, for 3 or 4 seconds. This results in a partial loss of erection. The partner then can stimulate him again to the point of ejaculation and use the squeeze technique to stop the ejaculation. The goal of this technique, as with the stop-start technique, is for the man with a premature ejaculation disorder to learn to identify the point of ejaculatory inevitability and control his arousal level at that point.

Techniques for Treating Vaginismus Vaginismus is often treated by deconditioning the woman's automatic tightening of her vaginal muscles (Leiblum, 2000). She is taught about the muscular tension at the opening of her vagina and the need to learn to relax those muscles. In a safe setting, she is instructed to insert her fingers into her vagina. She examines her vagina in a mirror and practices relaxation exercises. She may also use silicon or metal vaginal dilators made for this exercise. Gradually, she inserts larger and larger dilators as she practices relaxation exercises and becomes accustomed to the feel of the dilator in her vagina. If she has a partner, his or her fingers may be used instead of the dilator. If the woman has a male partner, eventually she guides his penis into her vagina while remaining in control.

Sexual dysfunctions can also arise in the context of gay, lesbian, and bisexual relationships.

Gay, Lesbian, and Bisexual People

Often, gay, lesbian, and bisexual people experience sexual dysfunctions for the same reasons as heterosexual people, such as medical disorders, medications, aging, or conflicts with partners. However, many problems in sexual functioning experienced by gay, lesbian, and bisexual people may have to do with society's attitudes toward them and the particular stressors they face (Gilman et al., 2001). They may have lost partners and friends to AIDS, and grief and depression can impair sexual functioning. The fear of contracting the human immunodeficiency virus (HIV) or other sexually transmitted diseases also can heighten sexual anxiety and dampen sexual desire. Anxiety over discrimination, harassment, and violence can do the same. Constant challenges to their partnerships and their ability to be parents also can interfere with normal sexual functioning.

Therapists treating gay, lesbian, or bisexual clients must be sensitive to the psychological conflicts and stresses these clients face as a result of society's rejection of their sexual orientation, as well as to the contributions of these stresses to their sexual functioning (American Psychological Association, 2000). Most of the sex therapy treatments can readily be adapted for gay, lesbian, or bisexual couples.

The attitude of clinical psychology as a profession toward homosexuality has changed over the past several decades. Early versions of the *DSM* listed homosexuality, particularly *ego-dystonic homosexuality* (which meant that the person did not want to be homosexual), as a mental disorder. Gay men, lesbians, and bisexual people argue that their sexual orientation is a natural part of themselves. Apart from society's homophobia, their orientation causes them no discomfort. In addition, there was little evidence that psychotherapy could lead a homosexual person to become heterosexual. In 1973, the American Psychiatric Association removed homosexuality from its list of recognized psychological disorders (Spitzer, 1981).

TEST YOURSELF

1. What is the common characteristic of the sexual desire disorders? List these disorders.
2. What is the common characteristic of the sexual arousal disorders? List these disorders.
3. What are the orgasmic disorders, and what are their characteristics?
4. What are the sexual pain disorders, and what are their characteristics?
5. What are common causes of sexual dysfunctions?
6. What treatments are effective for sexual dysfunctions?

TABLE 13.3 *DSM-IV-TR* Paraphilias

The paraphilias involve recurrent, intense sexually arousing fantasies, sexual urges, or behaviors involving (1) nonliving objects, (2) nonconsenting adults, (3) suffering or the humiliation of the person or the person's partner, or (4) children. The fantasies, urges, or behaviors must be present for at least 6 months and must cause clinically significant distress or impairment in social, occupational, or other important areas of functioning. A diagnosis of sexual sadism, pedophilia, exhibitionism, voyeurism, or frotteurism is made if the individual has acted on the urges or fantasies, even if the action does not cause distress or impairment.

Diagnosis	Object of Fantasies, Urges, or Behaviors
Fetishism	Nonliving objects (e.g., female undergarments)
Transvestic fetishism	Cross-dressing
Sexual sadism	Acts (real, not simulated) in which the psychological or physical suffering (including humiliation) of the victim is sexually exciting to the person
Sexual masochism	Acts (real, not simulated) of being humiliated, beaten, bound, or otherwise made to suffer
Voyeurism	The act of observing an unsuspecting person who is naked, in the process of undressing, or engaged in sexual activity
Exhibitionism	Exposure of one's genitals to an unsuspecting stranger
Frotteurism	Touching and rubbing against a nonconsenting person
Pedophilia	Sexual activity with a prepubescent child or children (generally age 13 years or younger) **Note:** The person must be at least age 16 years and at least 5 years older than the target child or children.

Source: Reprinted with permission from the *Diagnostic and Statistical Manual of Mental Disorders,* Fourth Edition, Text Revision.

APPLY IT James had a great deal of performance anxiety during his sexual encounters. This means he tended to do which of the following?

a. perform so well his partners became anxious about keeping up
b. overvalue sexual intercourse
c. focus on his partners more than on his own pleasure
d. focus on how he was performing rather than on the pleasurable sensations

Answers appear online at www.mhhe.com/nolen5e.

PARAPHILIAS

We noted earlier that people vary greatly in the sexual activities they find arousing. Atypical sexual preferences that the *DSM-IV-TR* considers to be disorders are the *paraphilias* (Greek for *besides* and *love*), listed in Table 13.3. Paraphilias are diagnosed when people have sexual fantasies, urges, or behaviors that involve (1) nonliving objects, (2) nonconsenting adults, (3) suffering or the humiliation of the person or the person's partner, or (4) prepubescent children. Paraphilias are sometimes divided into those that involve the consent of others (e.g., some sadomasochistic practices) and those that involve nonconsenting others (e.g., pedophilia). They also can be divided into those that involve contact with others (e.g., frotteurism) and those that do not necessarily involve contact with others (e.g., some fetishes). In order to be diagnosed with a paraphilia, an individual's unusual sexual behavior has to cause clinically significant distress or impairment in social, occupational, or other important areas of functioning. Exceptions are made in this criterion, however, for paraphilias that involve victims—namely, sexual sadism, pedophilia, exhibitionism, voyeurism, and frotteurism. In these cases, a diagnosis is made if the individual has acted on the urges or fantasies, even if the action does not cause that individual distress or impairment (American Psychiatric Association, 2000).

The *DSM-IV-TR* definitions of the paraphilias are highly controversial. Questions exist as to why some variations in sexual behavior are considered mental disorders while others are not (Gijs, 2008). For example, many in the transvestite community argue that cross-dressing for sexual pleasure should not be considered a disorder because their sexual behavior causes neither them nor others harm (Hucker, 2008). A more general argument can be made that we should not medicalize or pathologize variations in sexual preference or behavior by labeling some as mental disorders. Further, labeling sexual behaviors that involve victims, such as pedophilia, as mental disorders runs the risk of providing an "excuse" for behaviors that society wishes to forbid and punish (Gijs, 2008). These controversies are difficult to resolve because they involve moral judgments and strong social norms. In addition, the research literature on most paraphilias is limited and inconsistent, providing little information on which to make judgments about how pathological these behaviors are (Laws & O'Donohue, 2008).

The authors of the *DSM-5* have proposed some changes in an attempt to address these issues. First, they have recommended that the *DSM-5* distinguish between paraphilias and *paraphilic disorders*. A paraphilia would be defined as a specific pattern of urges, fantasies, or behaviors, while diagnosis of a paraphilic disorder would be given only when a paraphilia causes distress or impairment to the individual or harm to others (American Psychiatric Association, 2010). This distinction would avoid automatically labeling a nonnormative sexual behavior as pathological. Second, the proposed revisions are more specific about the necessary frequency of the paraphilic behavior for some diagnoses, in order to set clearer thresholds for the diagnosis. Still, much controversy remains regarding diagnoses of paraphilic disorders.

Fetishism and Transvestic Fetishism

Fetishism involves the use of nonliving objects for sexual arousal or gratification. Soft fetishes are objects that are soft, furry, or lacy, such as frilly lingerie, stockings, and garters. Hard fetishes are objects that are smooth, harsh, or black, such as spike-heeled shoes, black gloves, and garments made of leather or rubber (Darcangelo, Hollings, & Paladino, 2008). These soft and hard objects are somewhat arousing to many people and, indeed, are promoted as such by their manufacturers. For most people, however, the objects simply add to the sexiness of the people wearing them, and their desire is for sex with those people. For the person with a fetish, the desire is for the object itself (Darcangelo et al., 2008), as in the following case study.

CASE STUDY

A 32-year-old, single, male freelance photographer presented with the chief complaint of "abnormal sex drive." The patient related that although he was somewhat sexually attracted by women, he was far more attracted by "their panties."

To the best of the patient's memory, sexual excitement began at about age 7, when he came upon a pornographic magazine and felt stimulated by pictures of partially nude women wearing panties. His first ejaculation occurred at 13 via masturbation to fantasies of women wearing panties. He masturbated into his older sister's panties, which he had stolen without her knowledge. Subsequently, he stole panties from her friends and from other women he met socially. He found pretexts to "wander" into the bedrooms of women during social occasions and would quickly rummage through their possessions until he found a pair of panties to his satisfaction. He later used these to masturbate into and then "saved them" in a "private cache." The pattern of masturbating into women's underwear had been his preferred method of achieving sexual excitement and orgasm from adolescence until the present consultation.

The patient first had sexual intercourse at 18. Since then he had had intercourse on many occasions, and his preferred partner was a prostitute paid to wear panties, with the crotch area cut away, during the act. On less common occasions when sexual activity was attempted with a partner who did not wear panties, his sexual excitement was sometimes weak.

The patient felt uncomfortable dating "nice women" as he felt that friendliness might lead to sexual intimacy and that they would not understand his sexual needs. He avoided socializing with friends who might introduce him to such women. He recognized that his appearance, social style, and profession all resulted in his being perceived as a highly desirable bachelor. He felt anxious and depressed because his social life was limited by his sexual preference. (Reprinted from the *DSM-IV-TR Casebook: A Learning Companion to the Diagnostic and Statistical Manual of Mental Disorders,* Fourth Edition, Text Revision. Copyright © 2000 American Psychiatric Association.)

Fetishism is more common in men than in women. Although many men may engage in fetishistic behavior, perhaps less than 1 percent would be diagnosed with a disorder, because their behavior does not cause significant distress or impairment (Darcangelo, 2008).

One variation on fetishism is **transvestic fetishism,** or dressing in the clothes of the opposite sex as a means of becoming sexually aroused (this disorder likely will be renamed *transvestic disorder* in the *DSM-5*). In the *DSM-IV-TR* and *DSM-5,* the diagnosis requires that the cross-dressing behavior cause the individual significant distress or impairment. Transvestic fetishism can be distinguished from *transvestism,* which is cross-dressing behavior that may or may not be for the purposes of sexual arousal or gratification (Wheeler, Newring, & Draper, 2008). One community-based study found that 2.8 percent of men and 0.4 percent of women reported engaging in cross-dressing for sexual arousal (Langstrom & Zucker, 2005). Controversially, the *DSM-IV-TR* and *DSM-5* limit the diagnosis of transvestic fetishism to men (Newring, Wheeler, & Draper, 2008).

For many men with transvestic fetishism, it is not the women's clothes themselves that are sexually arousing but dressing in women's clothes. They may surreptitiously wear only one women's garment, such as a pair of women's panties. Or they may dress fully in women's garments, complete with makeup and a wig. Some men engage in cross-dressing alone. Others participate in transvestite subcultures, in which groups of men gather for drinks, meals, and dancing while dressed as women (Wheeler et al., 2008). About half of men who engage in cross-dressing for sexual gratification find the behavior acceptable and thus might not meet the *DSM-IV-TR* or *DSM-5* criteria for the disorder (Langstrom & Zucker, 2005).

Most adults who engage in cross-dressing report that the behavior began secretly prior to or during puberty (Wheeler et al., 2008). The function of the cross-dressing at young ages may not be explicitly sexual but instead may be more generally pleasurable or exciting or may alleviate negative psychological states associated with male gender roles. With puberty, cross-dressing activities increasingly are paired with sexual behavior. Most men who engage in cross-dressing are married and have children (Langstrom & Zucker, 2005). With age, the sexual function of cross-dressing may diminish even as men continue to cross-dress as a self-soothing behavior (Newring et al., 2008).

Sexual Sadism and Sexual Masochism

Sexual sadism and **sexual masochism** are two separate diagnoses, although sadistic and masochistic sexual practices often are considered together as a pattern referred to as **sadomasochism.** In sexual sadism, a person's sexual fantasies, urges, or behaviors involve inflicting pain and humiliation on his or her sex partner. Further, for the diagnosis to be given, the urges must cause him or her significant distress or impairment in functioning or the person must have acted on these urges with a nonconsenting person (the *DSM-5* likely will specify that this must occur on two or more occasions for the diagnosis to be given). In sexual masochism, a person's sexual fantasies, urges, or behaviors involve suffering pain or humiliation during sex, and they must cause the person significant distress or impairment in functioning. Some people occasionally engage in moderately sadistic or masochistic behaviors during sex or simulate such behaviors without actually carrying through with the infliction of pain or suffering (Hucker, 2008). These people probably would not be given a diagnosis, especially if their behaviors occur in the context of a trusting relationship in which boundaries have been set and safety measures are in place (e.g., having a "safe word" that, when uttered by either partner, stops the behavior). People diagnosed with sexual sadism or sexual masochism typically engage in sadistic and masochistic behaviors as their preferred or exclusive form of sexual gratification.

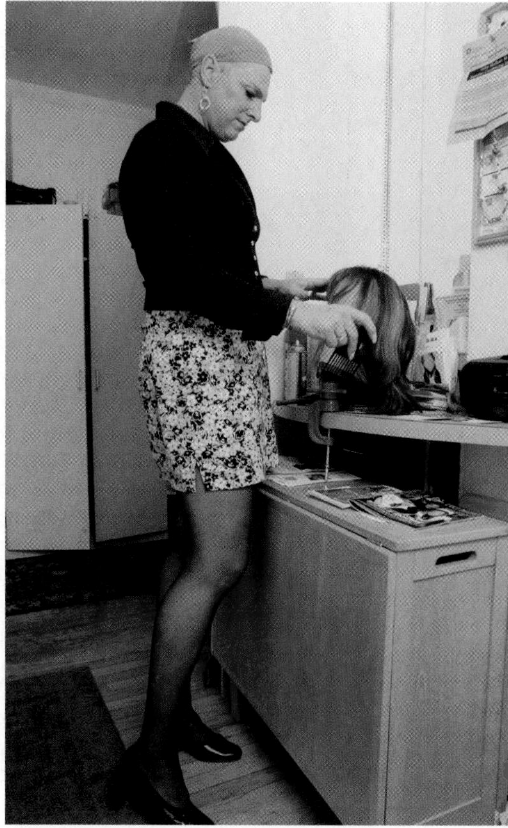

Transvestic fetishism involves wearing the clothes of the opposite sex, sometimes including wig and makeup for men, as a way to sexual arousal.

The sexual rituals in sadism and masochism are of four types: physical restriction, which involves the use of bondage, chains, or handcuffs as part of sex; the administration of pain, in which one partner inflicts pain or harm on the other with beatings, whippings, electrical shock, burning, cutting, stabbing, strangulation, torture, mutilation, or even death; hypermasculinity practices, including the aggressive use of enemas, fists, and dildos in the sexual act; and humiliation, in which one partner verbally and physically humiliates the other during sex (Sandnabba, Santtila, Alison, & Nordling, 2002). The partner who is the victim in such encounters may be either a masochist and a willing victim or a nonconsenting victim. A variety of props may be used in these encounters, including black leather garments, chains, shackles,

SHADES OF GRAY

Read the following case study.

Mr. A., a 65-year-old security guard, is distressed about his wife's objections to his wearing a nightgown at home in the evening, now that his youngest child has left home. His appearance and demeanor, except when he is dressing in women's clothes, are always masculine, and he is exclusively heterosexual. Occasionally, over the past 5 years, he has worn an inconspicuous item of female clothing even when dressed as a man—sometimes a pair of panties, sometimes an ambiguous pinkie ring. He always carries a photograph of himself dressed as a woman.

His first recollection of an interest in female clothing was putting on his sister's underwear at age 12, an act accompanied by sexual excitement. He continued periodically to put on women's underpants—an activity that invariably resulted in an erection, sometimes a spontaneous emission, and sometimes masturbation but never accompanied by fantasy. Although he occasionally wished to be a girl, this desire never figured into his sexual fantasies. During his single years he was always attracted to women but was shy about sex. Following his marriage at age 22, he had his first heterosexual intercourse.

His involvement with female clothes was of the same intensity even after his marriage. At age 45, after a chance exposure to a magazine called *Transvestia,* he began to increase his cross-dressing activity. He learned there were other men like himself, and he became more and more preoccupied with female clothing in fantasy and progressed to sometimes dressing completely as a woman. More recently he has become involved in a transvestite network, writing to other transvestites contacted through the magazine and occasionally attending transvestite parties. These parties have been the only times that he has cross-dressed outside his home.

Although still committed to his marriage, sex with his wife has dwindled over the past 20 years as his waking thoughts and activities have become increasingly centered on cross-dressing. Over time this activity has become less eroticized and more an end in itself, but it still is a source of some sexual excitement. He always has an increased urge to dress as a woman when under stress; it has a tranquilizing effect. If particular circumstances prevent him from cross-dressing, he feels extremely frustrated. (Reprinted from the *DSM-IV-TR Casebook: A Learning Companion to the Diagnostic and Statistical Manual of Mental Disorders,* Fourth Edition, Text Revision. Copyright © 2000 American Psychiatric Association.)

Should Mr. A. be diagnosed with transvestic fetishism? (Discussion appears at the end of this chapter.)

whips, harnesses, and ropes. Men are much more likely than women to enjoy sadomasochistic sex, in the roles of both sadist and masochist (Sandnabba et al., 2002). Some women find such activities exciting, but many consent to them only to please their partners or because they are paid to do so, and some are nonconsenting victims of sadistic men.

Although sadomasochistic sex between consenting adults typically does not result in physical injury, the activities can get out of control or go too far. A particularly dangerous activity is *hypoxyphilia,* which involves sexual arousal by means of oxygen deprivation, obtained by placing ropes around the neck, putting plastic bags or masks over the head, or exerting severe chest compression (Hucker, 2008). Accidents involving hypoxyphilia can result in permanent injury or death.

Rape is not defined as a disorder in the *DSM-IV-TR*, and only a minority of rapists meet the criteria for sexual sadism (Gannon & Ward, 2008). Rape is often part of a pattern of antisocial, aggressive behavior or an act motivated by anger and vindictiveness toward specific individuals or groups of individuals (McCabe & Wauchope, 2005). Some studies show that a subgroup of men convicted of rape show preferential arousal to coercive rape stimuli, indicating that rape functions as a means of sexual arousal for them (Lalumiere et al., 2003). Other researchers argue that these results suggest that these rapists should be diagnosed with sexual sadism, however, and not that a diagnosis specifically for rape behavior should be designated (Knight, 2009).

The authors of the *DSM-5* are proposing to add a diagnosis of *paraphilic coercive disorder*, which would be characterized by recurrent episodes of intense fantasies or desires involving sexual coercion. To qualify for the diagnosis, the individual will have had to initiate sexually coercive behavior with at least three nonconsenting others or be highly upset or impaired by the symptoms (American Psychiatric Association, 2010). This diagnosis has been proposed for previous versions of the *DSM* but has not been accepted (Knight, 2009). Whether it will be included in the *DSM-5* remains to be seen.

Voyeurism, Exhibitionism, and Frotteurism

Voyeurism, as a form of sexual arousal, involves watching another person undress, do things in the nude, or have sex. Voyeurism is probably the most common illegal paraphilia (Langstrom, 2009). A survey of 2,450 randomly selected adults from the general population of Sweden found that 12 percent of the men and 4 percent of the women reported at least one incident of being sexually aroused by spying on others having sex (Langstrom & Seto, 2006). A study of 60 male college students in the United States suggested that 42 percent had secretly watched others in sexual situations (Templeman & Stinnet, 1991).

For a diagnosis to be made, the voyeuristic behavior must be repeated over 6 months and must be compulsive. Further, for a diagnosis of voyeurism to be given, the urges must cause the person significant distress or impairment in functioning or the voyeur must have acted on these urges with a nonconsenting person (the *DSM-5* likely will specify that the behavior must have occurred on three or more separate occasions with different victims). Most people who engage in voyeurism are men who watch women (Lavin, 2008). They may masturbate during or immediately after the act of watching (American Psychiatric Association, 2000).

The person who engages in **exhibitionism** obtains sexual gratification by exposing his or her genitals to involuntary observers, who usually are strangers. The survey in Sweden mentioned above found that 4.1 percent of men and 2.1 percent of women reported having experienced sexual arousal from exposing their genitals to a stranger at least once in their life (Langstrom & Seto, 2006). In order to obtain the diagnosis of exhibitionism, individuals must have acted on their urges to engage in the behavior (the *DSM-5* may specify with three or more strangers on separate occasions; American Psychiatric Association, 2010), or the behavior must cause significant distress or impairment. Most exhibitionists are men, and their targets tend to be women, children, or adolescents (Murphy & Page, 2008). The exhibitionist typically confronts his victim in a public place, such as at a park or on a bus. His arousal comes from observing the victim's surprise, fear, or disgust or from a fantasy that his victim is becoming sexually aroused. His behavior often is compulsive and impulsive—he feels a sense of excitement, fear, restlessness, and sexual arousal and then feels compelled to find relief by exhibiting himself (Murphy & Page, 2008). Some people who engage in exhibitionism masturbate while exhibiting themselves. Others draw on memories or fantasies of exposing themselves to arouse themselves while masturbating, as in the following case study.

CASE STUDY

A 27-year-old engineer requested consultation at a psychiatric clinic because of irresistible urges to exhibit his penis to female strangers. At age 18, for reasons unknown to himself, he first experienced an overwhelming desire to engage in exhibitionism. He sought situations in which he was alone with a woman he did not know. As he approached her, he would become sexually excited. He would then walk up to her and display his erect penis. He found that her shock and fear further stimulated him, and usually he would then ejaculate. He also fantasized about past encounters while masturbating. He feels guilty and ashamed after exhibiting himself and vows never to repeat it. Nevertheless, the desire often overwhelms him, and the behavior recurs frequently, usually at periods of tension. (Reprinted from the *DSM-IV-TR Casebook: A Learning Companion to the Diagnostic and Statistical Manual of Mental Disorders,* Fourth Edition,Text Revision. Copyright © 2000 American Psychiatric Association.)

People who engage in exhibitionism are more likely than most sex offenders to get caught, in part because of the public nature of their behavior. In addition, some of them repeatedly return to places where they have already exhibited themselves. The danger of being caught heightens their arousal. People who engage in exhibitionism are also likely to continue their behavior after having been caught (Murphy & Page, 2008).

Frotteurism is a paraphilia that often co-occurs with voyeurism and exhibitionism. The person who engages in frotteurism gains sexual gratification from rubbing against and fondling parts of the body of a nonconsenting person. Often, this happens in crowded places, such as an elevator, and the target may not recognize the contact as sexual (Krueger & Kaplan, 2008). In order to receive this diagnosis, individuals must have acted on their urges to engage in the behavior (the *DSM-5* likely will specify on three or more occasions; American Psychiatric Association, 2010), or the urges must be causing significant distress or impairment. Most people who engage in frotteurism are males, and the onset of the disorder most often is in early adulthood (Lussier & Piché, 2008).

Defrocked priest Paul Shanley was convicted of pedophilia.

Pedophilia

People with **pedophilia** have sexual fantasies, urges, and behaviors focused on prepubescent children. To be diagnosed with pedophilia in the *DSM-IV-TR,* the individual must have acted on the urges, or the urges must have caused significant distress or impairment. Most people with pedophilia are heterosexual men attracted to young girls (Seto, 2008). Homosexual men with pedophilia typically are attracted to young boys. Women can have pedophilia, but this situation is rarer.

Not all individuals with pedophilia engage in sexual contact with children; instead, many use child pornography to become sexually aroused (Seto, 2009). Still, most of what we know about pedophilia is based on studies conducted with individuals who have committed sexual offenses with children. Sexual encounters between people with pedophilia and their child victims often are brief, although they may recur frequently. People with pedophilia may threaten children with harm, physically restrain them, or tell them that they will punish them or their loved ones if the children do not comply. Other people with pedophilia are loving, caring, and gentle to the child, using emotional closeness to gain sexual access to the child. This is especially true in incestuous relationships, in which people with pedophilia may see themselves as simply being good, loving parents. They believe that what they do to the child is not sexual but loving (Seto, 2009). Some predatory individuals with pedophilia develop elaborate plans for gaining access to children, such as winning the trust of the mother or marrying the mother, trading children with other people with pedophilia, or, in rare cases, abducting children or adopting children from foreign countries (McConaghy, 1998).

CASE STUDY

Dr. Crone, a 35-year-old, single child psychiatrist, has been arrested and convicted of fondling several neighborhood girls, ages 6 to 12. Friends and colleagues were shocked and dismayed, as he had been considered by all to be particularly caring and supportive of children.

Dr. Crone's first sexual experience was at age 6, when a 15-year-old female camp counselor performed fellatio on him several times over the course of the summer—an experience that he had always kept to himself. As he grew older, he was surprised to notice that the age range of girls who attracted him sexually did not change, and he continued to have recurrent erotic urges and fantasies about girls between ages 6 and 12. Whenever he masturbated, he would fantasize about a girl in that age range, and on a couple of occasions over the years, he had felt himself to be in love with such a youngster.

Intellectually, Dr. Crone knew that others would disapprove of his many sexual involvements with young girls. He never believed, however, that he had caused any of these youngsters harm, feeling instead that they were simply sharing pleasurable feelings together. He frequently prayed for help and that his actions would go undetected. He kept promising himself that he would stop, but the temptations were such that he could not. (Reprinted from the *DSM-IV-TR Casebook: A Learning Companion to the Diagnostic and Statistical Manual of Mental Disorders,* Fourth Edition, Text Revision. Copyright © 2000 American Psychiatric Association.)

The impact on the child victims of people with pedophilia can be great. The most frequent symptoms shown by sexually abused children are fearfulness, post-traumatic stress disorder, conduct disorder and hyperactivity, sexualized behaviors (promiscuity and sexual behavior inappropriate for their age), and poor self-esteem (Kendall-Tackett et al., 1993; McConaghy, 1998). More severe symptoms are experienced by children who endure frequent abuse over a long period, who are penetrated by the perpetrator, who are abused by a family member (typically, a father or stepfather), and whose mother does not provide support on learning of the abuse. About two-thirds of victimized children show significant recovery from their symptoms within 12 to 18 months following cessation of the abuse, but significant numbers of abused children continue to experience psychological problems even into adulthood (Burnam et al., 1988; Kendall-Tackett et al., 1993).

The *DSM-5* authors propose a number of changes in the diagnosis of pedophilia based on research done since publication of the *DSM-IV-TR* (Blanchard et al., 2009). First, whereas the *DSM-IV-TR* required that the child victims of the pedophile be prepubescent, the *DSM-5* will allow the diagnosis to be given to pedophiles whose victims are pubescent, reflecting research that shows little justification for distinguishing between attraction to prepubescent and pubescent children (Blanchard et al., 2009). As a result, the *DSM-5* authors are suggesting that the name of the disorder be changed to *pedohebephilic disorder* (hebephilia is the erotic preference for pubescent children, whereas pedophilia is the erotic preference for prepubescent children). In addition, *DSM-5* criteria will likely define the behaviors required for the diagnosis more precisely, specifying that the diagnosis not be given unless the individual has engaged in sexual behavior with at least two different prepubescent children or at least three different pubescent children, prefers child rather than adult pornography, or is distressed or impaired by the sexual attraction to children (American Psychiatric Association, 2010).

FIGURE 13.4 A Behavioral Account of the Development of Paraphilias

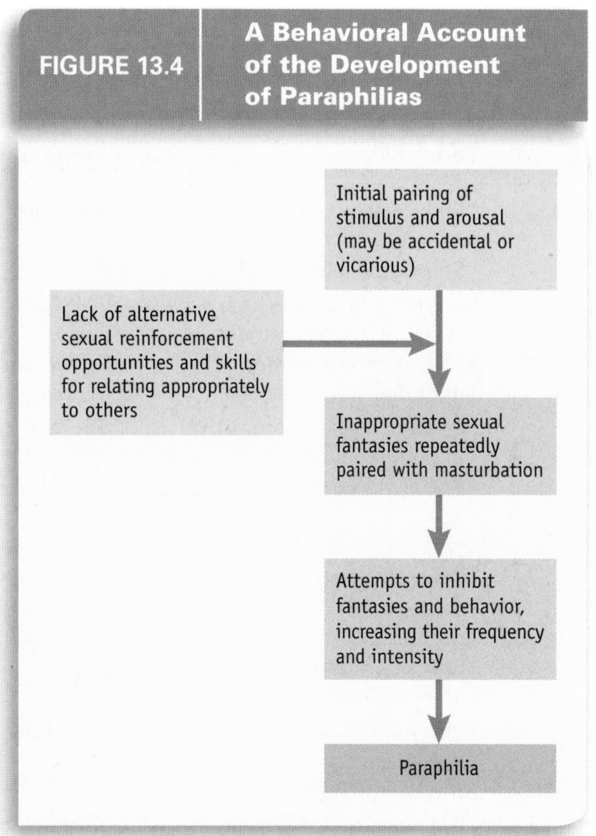
Initial pairing of stimulus and arousal (may be accidental or vicarious)
Lack of alternative sexual reinforcement opportunities and skills for relating appropriately to others
Inappropriate sexual fantasies repeatedly paired with masturbation
Attempts to inhibit fantasies and behavior, increasing their frequency and intensity
Paraphilia

Causes of Paraphilias

Several lines of evidence suggest that alterations in the development of the nervous system may contribute to pedophilia (Seto, 2008). Men with pedophilia are more likely to have had a head injury before age 13, to have cognitive and memory deficits, to have lower intelligence, and to have differences in brain structure volume (Cantor et al., 2008). How these factors contribute to pedophilia is not yet clear.

Behavioral theories of the paraphilias explain them as being due to an initial classical pairing of intense early sexual arousal with a particular stimulus (Gijs, 2008; Figure 13.4). For example, a child may become aroused when spying on the babysitter's lovemaking with her boyfriend or while being held down and tickled erotically. This may be followed by intensive operant conditioning in which the stimulus is present during masturbation. For example, the individual may repeatedly fantasize about a particular scenario, such as watching the babysitter have sex, while masturbating. This reinforces the association between the stimulus and sexual arousal. The individual may try to suppress the undesired arousal or behaviors, but these attempts at inhibition increase the frequency and intensity of the fantasies. Eventually, the sexual arousal may generalize to other stimuli similar to the initial fantasy, such as actually watching other people's lovemaking, leading to paraphilic behavior (e.g., voyeurism). Some people with paraphilia appear to have a strong sex drive and masturbate often, providing many opportunities for the pairing of their fantasies with sexual gratification (Kafka & Hennen, 2003). Often, the person with paraphilia also has few opportunities for other types of sexual reinforcement and has difficulty relating appropriately to other adults.

These classic behavioral theories have been supplemented with principles of social learning theory (see Chapter 2), which suggest that the larger environment of a child's home and culture influences his or her tendency to develop deviant sexual behavior. Children whose parents frequently use corporal punishment and engage in aggressive contact with each other are more likely to engage in impulsive, aggressive, and perhaps sexualized acts toward others as they grow older. Many people with pedophilia have poor interpersonal skills and feel intimidated when interacting sexually with adults (Seto, 2008).

TABLE 13.4 Distortions, Assumptions, and Justifications

People with paraphilia or who engage in rape may engage in cognitions that provide a rationale for their behaviors.

Category	Pedophilia	Exhibitionism	Rape
Misattributing blame	"She started it by being too cuddly." "She would always run around half dressed."	"She kept looking at me like she was expecting it." "The way she was dressed, she was asking for it."	"She was saying 'no' but her body said 'yes.'"
Minimizing or denying sexual intent	"I was teaching her about sex . . . better from her father than someone else."	"I was just looking for a place to pee." "My pants just slipped down."	"I was trying to teach her a lesson. . . . She deserved it."
Debasing the victim	"She'd had sex before with her boyfriend." "She always lies."	"She was just a slut anyway."	"The way she came on to me at the party, she deserved it." "She never fought back. . . . She must have liked it."
Minimizing consequences	"She's always been real friendly to me, even afterward." "She was messed up even before it happened."	"I never touched her, so I couldn't have hurt her." "She smiled, so she must have liked it."	"She'd had sex with hundreds of guys before. It was no big deal."
Deflecting censure	"This happened years ago. . . . Why can't everyone forget about it?"	"It's not like I raped anyone."	"I only did it once."
Justifying the cause	"If I wasn't molested as a kid, I'd never have done this."	"If I knew how to get dates, I wouldn't have to expose."	"If my girlfriend gave me what I want, I wouldn't be forced to rape."

Source: From *A Guide to Treatments That Work,* edited by Peter Nathan and Jack Gorman (1998): Table 24.5 (p. 448) from "The Paraphilias: Research and Treatment" by Barry M. Maletzky. By permission of Oxford University Press, Inc.

A study of 64 convicted sex offenders with various types of paraphilia found that they had higher rates of childhood abuse and family dysfunction than did offenders who had committed property crimes and did not have a paraphilia (Lee, Jackson, Pattison, & Ward, 2002). Childhood sexual abuse was a particularly strong predictor of pedophilia. Similarly, studies of juvenile sex offenders, most of whom assaulted a younger child, find that many likely suffered sexual abuse (Gerardin & Thibaut, 2004).

Cognitive theorists have also identified a number of distortions and assumptions that people with paraphilia have about their behaviors and the behaviors of their victims, as shown in Table 13.4 (Gerardin & Thibaut, 2004; Maletzky, 1998). These distortions may have been learned from parents' deviant messages about sexual behavior. They are used to justify the person's victimization of others.

Treatments for the Paraphilias

Most people with paraphilia do not seek treatment for their behaviors (Darcangelo et al., 2008). Treatment is often forced on those who are arrested after engaging in illegal acts including voyeurism, exhibitionism, frotteurism, or pedophilia. Simple incarceration does little to change these behaviors, and convicted sex offenders are likely to become repeat offenders (Seto, 2008).

Biological interventions generally are aimed at reducing the sex drive in order to reduce paraphilic behavior. Surgical castration, which almost completely eliminates the production of androgens, lowers repeat offense rates among sex offenders (Maletzky & Field, 2003; Seto, 2009). Castration has been performed on hundreds of convicted sex offenders in the Netherlands, Germany, and the United States, although it is rarely used today (Seto, 2009).

Sex offenders can be offered antiandrogen drugs that suppress the production of testosterone and thereby reduce the sex drive. These drugs typically are used in conjunction with psychotherapy and can be useful for hypersexual men who are motivated to change their behavior (Maletzky & Field, 2003). Follow-up studies have shown that people with paraphilia treated with antiandrogen drugs show reductions in their paraphilic behavior (Gerardin & Thibaut, 2004; Maletzky & Field, 2003). These drugs have a number of side effects, however, including fatigue, sleepiness, depression, weight gain, leg cramps, breast formation, hair loss, and osteoperosis (Gijs, 2008). Nine states have laws that require some sex offenders who want to be paroled to take antiandrogen drugs or undergo surgical castration (Seto, 2009).

The selective serotonin reuptake inhibitors (SSRIs) have been used to reduce sexual drive and paraphilic behavior. Some studies find that these drugs have positive effects on sexual drive and impulse control (e.g., Greenberg, Bradford, Curry & O'Rouch, 1996), although the effects are not totally consistent across studies (Gijs, 2008; Seto, 2009).

Behavior modification therapies commonly are used to treat paraphilia and can be successful if people with a paraphilia are willing to change their behavior (Seto, 2009). **Aversion therapy** is used to extinguish sexual responses to objects or situations a person with a paraphilia finds arousing. During such therapy, a person with a paraphilia might be exposed to painful but harmless electric shocks or loud bursts of noise while viewing photographs of what arouses them, such as children, or while actually touching objects that arouse them, such as women's panties. **Desensitization** procedures may be used to reduce the person's anxiety about engaging in normal sexual encounters with other adults. For example, people with a paraphilia might be taught relaxation exercises, which they then use to control their anxiety as they gradually build up fantasies of interacting sexually with other adults in ways that are fulfilling to them and to their partners (Maletzky, 1998). These behavioral treatments generally are effective in the treatment of nonpredatory paraphilias such as fetishism (Darcangelo et al., 2008).

Cognitive interventions may be combined with behavioral interventions designed to help people learn more socially acceptable ways to approach and interact with people they find attractive (Cole, 1992). Role playing might be used to give the person with a paraphilia practice in approaching another person and eventually negotiating a positive sexual encounter with him or her. Also, group therapy in which people with paraphilias support one another through changes in their behavior can be helpful. Multiple studies find that these combined cognitive-behavioral treatments can effectively treat nonpredatory paraphilias in individuals motivated to change (Darcangelo et al., 2008).

Cognitive-behavior therapy also has been used to help people with a predatory paraphilia (e.g., pedophilia, exhibitionism, voyeurism) identify and challenge thoughts and situations that trigger their behaviors and serve as justifications for their behaviors, such as those listed in Table 13.4 (Maletzky, 1998; McConaghy, 1998). Unfortunately, randomized clinical trials of cognitive-behavioral therapy for sex offenders have found no significant differences in the recidivism rate for men who received the therapy and those who did not (Camilleri & Quinsey, 2008; Marques et al., 2005).

Hypersexual Disorder: A Proposal for the *DSM-5*

Some people have an insatiable desire for sex that they feel is "out of control" (Bancroft & Vukadinovic, 2004; Kafka, 2009). These men and women describe themselves as addicted to sex and will seek to gratify their sexual fantasies and urges with consenting partners; through masturbation, pornography, cybersex, or telephone sex; and in strip clubs. They are at high risk for sexually transmitted diseases, unwanted pregnancies, social consequences such as the breakup of marriages, and work consequences such as being fired for downloading pornography at work (Bancroft et al., 2003; Cooper, Golden, & Kent-Ferraro, 2002; Kalichman et al., 2005; McBride, Reece, & Sanders, 2008). It is estimated that five times as many men as women exhibit this syndrome (Kafka, 2009).

The authors of the *DSM-5* are proposing to add the diagnosis *hypersexual disorder* to characterize these people. The diagnosis would require that individuals have a pattern lasting at least six months of repeated and powerful sexual desires, fantasies, and behaviors that consume much of their time, that arise in response to stress or dysphoria, that they unsuccessfully try to control or reduce, and that persist even when their behaviors cause them distress or social, occupational, or physical harm. (American Psychiatric Association, 2010).

Hypersexual disorder will not be classified as a paraphilia but will be a separate sexual disorder in the *DSM-5*. However, some people who are hypersexual also engage in paraphilic behavior, and many people who have a paraphilic disorder appear to have a very high sex drive (Kafka, 2009).

TEST YOURSELF

1. What is the definition of paraphilia?
2. What is fetishism? What is transvestic fetishism?
3. What are sexual sadism and sexual masochism?
4. What are voyeurism, exhibitionism, and frotteurism?
5. What is pedophilia?
6. What are some causes of the paraphilias?
7. What are effective treatments for the paraphilias?

APPLY IT George likes to become sexually aroused by watching his neighbor undress, while Fred likes to become aroused by rubbing against unsuspecting women on the subway. George could be diagnosed with __________, while Fred could be diagnosed with __________.

a. exhibitionism, frotteurism

b. fetishism, exhibitionism

c. voyeurism, frotteurism

d. sadism, fetishism

Answers appear online at www.mhhe.com/nolen5e.

GENDER IDENTITY DISORDER

Gender identity disorder (GID) is diagnosed when there is a discrepancy between individuals' gender identity and their biological sex (see the *DSM-IV-TR* criteria in Table 13.5). Stephanie, in the following case study, would be diagnosed with this disorder.

CASE STUDY

Stephanie was 30 when she first attended our clinic. She gave a history of conviction that she was, in fact, male and wished to rid herself of identifiably female attributes and acquire male traits and features. She said she had been cross-living and employed as a male for about 1 year, following the breakdown of a 10-year marriage. She was taking testosterone prescribed by her family physician. She presented at our clinic with a request for removal of her uterus and ovaries.

She did not give a childhood history of tomboy attitudes, thoughts, or behavior. She said social interaction with other children, boys or girls, was minimal. Desperate for a friend, she fantasized "an articulate and strong" boy, exactly her age, named Ronan. They were always together and they talked over everything: thoughts and feelings and the events of her life. Cross-dressing in her father's clothing also began during childhood. There was no history of sexual arousal associated with or erotic fantasy involving cross-dressing.

Puberty at age 12 and the accompanying bodily changes apparently did not overly distress Stephanie. Sexual and romantic feelings focused on "slender, feminine-appearing men." At 16, Stephanie met such a man and they were together for 2 years. Her next romantic involvement was with a "male bisexual transvestite." Sexual interaction, according to Stephanie, included experimentation with drugs and "role reversals." She and her partner cross-dressed, and Stephanie took the dominant and active role. During vaginal sex, she imagined herself as a male with another male.

At 19, she met a slender, good-looking man. They were compatible and married soon after. The marriage was a success. Stephanie's preferred position for intercourse was with both kneeling, she behind her husband, rubbing her pubic area against him while masturbating him. She would imagine she had a penis and was penetrating him. Stephanie's marriage broke down after the couple's business failed. She decided to live full-time in the male role as Jacob. While on the West Coast, she started treatment with male hormones. She moved back east and presented at our clinic for assessment. She saw herself as a male, primarily attracted to gay or gay-appearing males. She was uninterested in relationships with women, except perhaps as purely sexual encounters of short duration. (Adapted from Dickey & Stephens, 1995, pp. 442–443)

Gender identity disorder of childhood is a rare condition in which a child persistently rejects his or her anatomic sex and desires to be or insists he or she is a member of the opposite sex. Girls with this disorder seek masculine-type activities and male peer groups to a degree far beyond that of a tomboy. Sometimes, these girls express the belief that they will eventually grow a penis. Boys with the disorder seek feminine-type activities and female peer groups and tend to begin cross-dressing in girls' clothes at a very early age (Zucker, 2005). They express disgust with their penis and wish it would disappear. The

TABLE 13.5 *DSM-IV-TR* Criteria for a Diagnosis of Gender Identity Disorder

People with gender identity disorder believe they were born with the wrong sex's genitals and are truly members of the other sex.

A. Strong and persistent identification with the other sex. In children, this is manifested by four or more of the following:
   1. Repeatedly stated desire to be, or insistence that he or she is, the other sex
   2. In boys, preference for cross-dressing or simulating female attire; in girls, insistence on wearing only stereotypic masculine clothing
   3. Strong and persistent preferences for cross-sex roles in play and in fantasies
   4. Intense desire to participate in the stereotypic games and pastimes of the other sex
   5. Strong preference for playmates of the other sex

   In adolescents or adults, identification with the other sex may be manifested with symptoms such as the stated desire to be the other sex, frequently passing as the other sex, desire to live or be treated as the other sex, or the conviction that he or she has the typical feelings or reactions of the other sex.

B. Persistent discomfort with his or her sex and sense of inappropriateness in the gender role of that sex.

C. Disturbance is not concurrent with a physical intersex condition and causes significant distress or problems in functioning.

Source: Reprinted with permission from the *Diagnostic and Statistical Manual of Mental Disorders,* Fourth Edition, Text Revision.

onset of these behaviors typically is in the preschool years. Boys are referred more often than girls for concerns regarding gender identity. This may reflect a greater prevalence of gender identity disorder in males than females or it may reflect that parents are more concerned about violations of gender roles in boys than in girls (Zucker & Cohen-Kettenis, 2008).

Adults who might be diagnosed with gender identity disorder also are referred to as **transsexuals.** (The term *transgender* more broadly refers to individuals with varying degrees of cross-gender identity, including transsexuals but also individuals who cross-dress and those with transvestic fetishism; see Lawrence, 2008). People with gender identity disorder who cross-dress are not sexually aroused by this practice but simply believe they are putting on the clothes of the gender to which they really belong. The sexual preferences of individuals with gender identity disorder vary. Some are asexual, having little interest in either sex; some are heterosexual; and some are homosexual (Lawrence, 2008). People with gender identity disorder who can afford it may seek a sex-change operation. Gender identity disorder is rare, with an estimated prevalence of 1 per 12,900 for male to female transsexualism and 1 per 33,800 for female to male transsexualism (De Cuypere et al., 2007).

Some transsexual people are so disturbed by their misassignment of gender that they develop alcohol and other drug abuse problems and/or other psychological disorders (Lawrence, 2008). Low self-esteem and psychological distress also result from their rejection by others. High rates of HIV infection among transsexual people have been reported in some studies (Lawrence, 2008). HIV may be contracted through risky sexual behaviors or through the sharing of needles during drug use or hormone injections. Many transsexual people avoid seeking medical attention because of negative interactions with physicians. Indeed, some physicians refuse to treat transsexual people.

The *DSM-5* authors propose replacing the label *gender identity disorder* with *gender incongruence* because this label more accurately reflects the core of the problem: an incongruence between what identity these individuals experience and/or express and how they are expected to live based on their assigned gender at birth (Meyer-Bahlburg, 2009; Winters, 2005). A survey of transgendered people found that many rejected the term gender identity disorder because it contributes to the stigmatization of their condition (Vance et al., in press). Further, the *DSM-5* will likely specify that the gender incongruence be manifested in a subjective sense that one's feelings and identity are of the opposite gender, strong desires to be rid of one's genitals and to have the genitals of the other gender, and to the desire to be treated as the other gender (American Psychiatric Association, 2010).

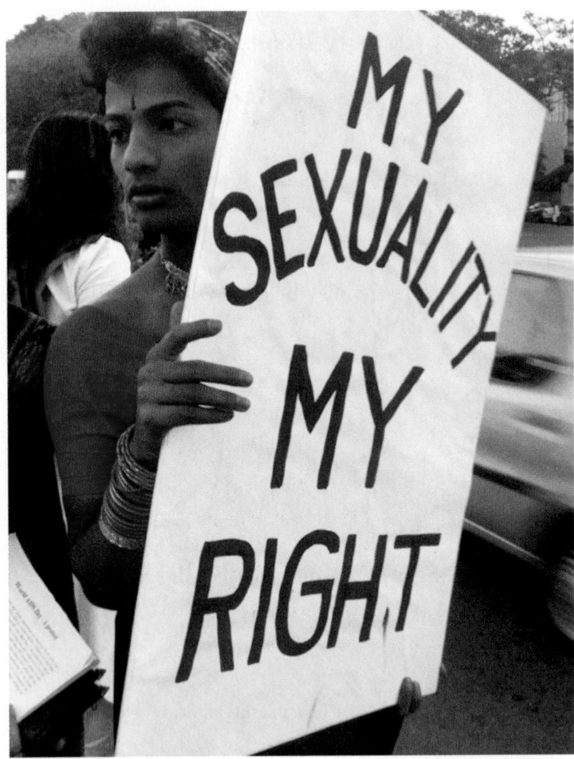

Some transsexual people argue that they do not have a disorder but do have a right to live their life as they wish.

Contributors to Gender Identity Disorder

Biological theories of gender identity disorder have focused on the effects of prenatal hormones on brain development (Bradley, 1995; Zucker, 2005). Although several specific mechanisms have been implicated, most theories suggest that people who develop gender identity disorder have been exposed to unusual levels of hormones, which influence later gender identity and sexual orientation by influencing the development of brain structures involved in sexuality. In genetic females, female-to-male transsexualism has been associated with hormonal disorders resulting in prenatal exposure to high levels of androgens (Baba et al., 2007), whereas in genetic males, male-to-female transsexualism has been associated with prenatal exposure to very low levels of androgens (Hines, Ahmed, & Hughes, 2003; Wisniewski & Migeon, 2002).

A cluster of cells in the hypothalamus called the bed nucleus of stria terminalis, which plays a role in sexual behavior, has been implicated in multiple studies (Chung, De Vries, & Swaab, 2002; Kruijver et al., 2000; Zhou, Hofman, & Swaab, 1995). Typically, this cluster of cells is smaller in women's brains than in men's. Studies have found that this cluster of cells is half as large in transsexual men as in nontranssexual men and is close to the size usually found in women's brains.

Hormonal disorders contributing to gender identity disorder may be tied to genetic abnormalities. Family and twin studies suggest that 62 percent of the variation in vulnerability to gender identity disorder is due to genetic causes (Coolidge, Thede, & Young, 2002; Green, 2000), although the specific genetic factors involved are not yet known (Ujike et al., 2009).

Most psychosocial theories of gender identity disorder focus on the role parents play in shaping their children's gender identity. Parents encourage children to identify with one sex or the other by reinforcing "gender-appropriate" behavior and punishing "gender-inappropriate" behavior. From early infancy, they buy male or female clothes for their children and sex-stereotyped toys (dolls or trucks). They encourage or discourage playing rough-and-tumble games or playing with dolls. A long-term study of a large sample of boys with gender identity disorder found that their parents were less likely than the parents of boys without gender identity disorder to discourage cross-gender behaviors (Green, 1986). That is, these boys were not punished, either subtly or overtly, for engaging in feminine behavior such as playing with dolls or wearing dresses as much as were boys who did not have gender identity disorder. Further, boys who were highly feminine (although not necessarily with gender identity disorder) tended to have mothers who had wanted a girl rather than a boy, saw their baby sons as girls, and dressed their baby sons as girls. When the boys were older, their mothers tended to prohibit rough-and-tumble play, and the boys had few opportunities to have male playmates. About one-third of these boys had no father in the home, and those who did have a father in the home tended to be very close to their mother. In general, however, the evidence in support of psychological contributors to gender identity disorder has been weak (Zucker, 2005).

Treatments for Gender Identity Disorder

Therapists who work with people with gender identity disorder help these individuals clarify their gender identity and their desire for treatment. In addition to psychotherapy, there are three principal means of treatment for gender identity disorder: (1) cross-sex hormone therapy, (2) full-time real-life experience in the desired gender role, and (3) sex reassignment surgery, which provides the genitalia and secondary sex characteristics (e.g., breasts) of the gender with which the individuals identify (Lawrence, 2008).

Cross-sex hormone therapy stimulates the development of secondary sex characteristics of the preferred sex and suppresses secondary sex characteristics of the birth sex. Estrogens are used in feminizing hormone therapy for male-to-female transsexuals. These cause fatty deposits to develop in the breasts and hips, soften the skin, and inhibit the growth of a beard. Testosterone is used to induce masculinization in female-to-male transsexuals. It causes the voice to deepen, hair to become distributed in a male pattern, fatty tissue in the breast to recede, and muscles to enlarge; the clitoris also may grow larger (Lawrence, 2008). Hormone therapy may be given to individuals whether or not they wish to undergo sex reassignment surgery.

Before undergoing sex reassignment surgery, individuals spend up to a year or more living full-time in the gender role they seek. Some choose to live full-time in their desired gender role even if they do not undertake sex reassignment surgery or hormone therapy (Lawrence, 2008).

Sex reassignment requires a series of surgeries and hormone treatments, often over a period of 2 years or longer. In male-to-female surgery, the penis and testicles are removed, and tissue from the penis is used to create an artificial vagina. The construction of male genitals for a female-to-male reassignment is technically more difficult (Lawrence, 2008). First, the internal sex organs (ovaries, fallopian tubes, uterus) and any fatty tissue remaining in the breasts are removed. Then the urethra is rerouted through the enlarged clitoris, or an artificial penis and scrotum are constructed from tissue taken from other parts of the body. This penis allows urination while standing but cannot achieve a natural erection. Other procedures, such as artificial implants, may be used to create an erection.

Sex reassignment surgery is controversial. Some follow-up studies suggest that the outcome tends to be positive when patients are carefully selected for gender reassignment procedures based on their motivation for change and their overall psychological health and are given psychological counseling to help them through the change (Bradley & Zucker, 1997; Lindemalm, Korlin, & Uddenberg, 1986; Smith, Van Goozen, & Cohen-Kettenis, 2001). A review of outcome studies found adequate levels of sexual functioning and high sexual satisfaction following sex reassignment surgery (Klein & Gorzalka, 2009).

Treatment of children and adolescents with gender identity disorder focuses primarily on psychotherapy to help them clarify their gender identity and deal with interpersonal and psychological issues created by that identity. Most clinicians consider hormone therapies and surgeries unacceptable for children and adolescents because they cannot give fully informed consent for such procedures (Zucker & Cohen-Kettenis, 2008).

TEST YOURSELF

1. What is gender identity disorder?
2. What biological factors may contribute to gender identity disorder?
3. What aspects of socialization may contribute to gender identity disorder?

APPLY IT Chris was born a genetic female but has had a lifelong desire to become a male both physically and in lifestyle. If Chris seeks treatment from an expert on gender identity disorder, which of the following treatments is *not* likely to be recommended?

a. cross-sex hormone therapy
b. full-time real-life experience living as a male
c. sex reassignment surgery
d. cognitive therapy to challenge distorted beliefs regarding gender

Answers appear online at www.mhhe.com/nolen5e.

CHAPTER INTEGRATION

Nowhere is the interplay of biological, psychological, and social forces more apparent than in matters of sexuality (Figure 13.5). Biological factors influence gender identity, sexual orientation, and

FIGURE 13.5 Interplay of Biological and Psychological Factors in Sexuality

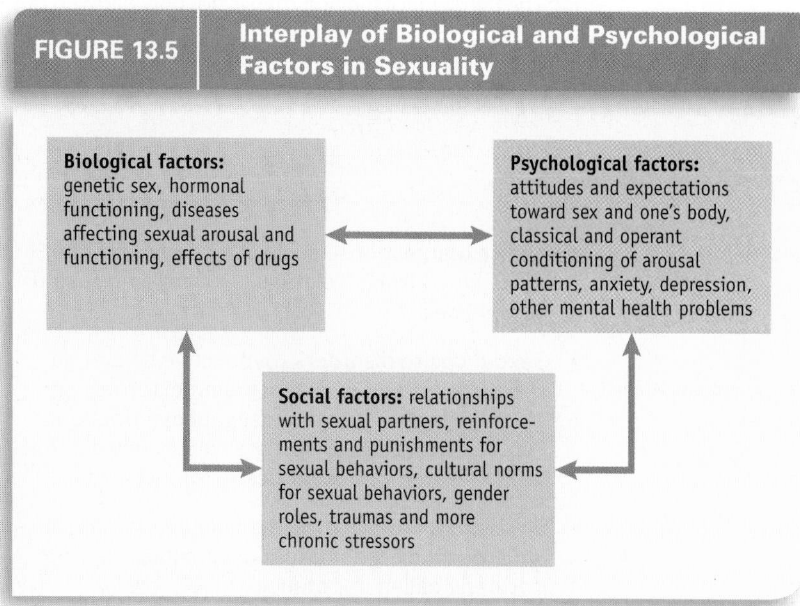
Biological factors: genetic sex, hormonal functioning, diseases affecting sexual arousal and functioning, effects of drugs
Psychological factors: attitudes and expectations toward sex and one's body, classical and operant conditioning of arousal patterns, anxiety, depression, other mental health problems
Social factors: relationships with sexual partners, reinforcements and punishments for sexual behaviors, cultural norms for sexual behaviors, gender roles, traumas and more chronic stressors

sexual functioning. These biological factors can be greatly moderated, however, by psychological and social factors. The meaning people assign to a sexual dysfunction, an unusual sexual practice, or an atypical gender identity is heavily influenced by their attitudes toward their sexuality and by the reactions of people around them. In addition, as we saw with sexual dysfunctions, purely psychological and social conditions can cause a person's body to stop functioning as it normally would.

SHADES OF GRAY DISCUSSION (review p. 410)

Although you may have thought the evidence of transvestic fetishism increased as his case grew from his wife's objection over a nightgown to his enjoyment of transvestite parties, Mr. A probably would not receive a diagnosis. In order to be diagnosed with transvestic fetishism, he would have to have shown that cross-dressing causes significant distress or impairment in his functioning. Currently there is no evidence that he is distressed over his behavior or over the consequences of his behavior, even though his wife objects to it. While Mr. A's case does not warrant a diagnosis now, he may receive one in the future if the decline in his marriage or difficulty at work due to cross-dressing causes him significant distress.

THINK CRITICALLY

One man goes to a public beach to watch women in skimpy bikinis. A second man pays to see a female topless dancer in a nightclub. A third man stands outside a woman's bedroom window at night, secretly watching her undress.

Our society—like all societies across cultures and throughout history—makes judgments about the types of sexual activities we allow and the types we do not. The actions of the three men described above are all motivated by the desire to be sexually aroused by the sight of women's naked, or almost naked, bodies. But consider how differently our society judges each behavior: The behavior of the first man is not only allowed but also promoted in many movies, television shows, and commercials. The behavior of the second man is a form of legal sexual commerce. Only the behavior of the third man is labeled a sexual disorder and is not allowed by cultural norms or by laws. Although we may like to think that, in our modern culture, we prohibit only those sexual behaviors that are truly "sick," our judgments are still subjective and culturally specific.

In your judgment, are there any sexual disorders in this chapter that you think should not be considered a disorder and instead should be considered simply a personal preference? (*Discussion appears on p. 520 at the back of this book.*)

CHAPTER SUMMARY

- The sexual response cycle can be divided into the desire, arousal, plateau, orgasm, and resolution phases.
- Sexual desire disorders (hypoactive sexual desire disorder and sexual aversion disorder) are among the most common sexual dysfunctions. Persons with these disorders experience a chronically lowered or absent desire for sex.
- The sexual arousal disorders include female sexual arousal disorder and male erectile disorder (formerly called impotence).
- Women with female orgasmic disorder experience a persistent or recurrent delay in or the complete absence of orgasm, after having reached the excitement phase of the sexual response cycle. Men with premature ejaculation persistently experience ejaculation (after minimal sexual stimulation) before, on, or shortly after penetration and before they wish it.
- Men with male orgasmic disorder experience a persistent or recurrent delay in or the absence of orgasm following the excitement phase of the sexual response cycle.

- The sexual pain disorders include dyspareunia, which is genital pain associated with intercourse, and vaginismus, in which a woman experiences involuntary contraction of the muscles surrounding the outer third of the vagina when the vagina is penetrated.
- The psychological factors leading to sexual dysfunction most commonly involve negative attitudes toward sex, traumatic or stressful experiences, or conflicts with sexual partners. A variety of biological factors, including medical illnesses, the side effects of drugs, nervous system injury, and hormonal deficiencies, can cause sexual dysfunction.
- Fortunately, most sexual dysfunctions can be treated successfully. Biological treatments include drugs that increase sexual functioning, such as Viagra, and the alleviation of medical conditions that might be contributing to sexual dysfunction.
- Psychological treatments combine (1) psychotherapy focused on the personal concerns of the individual with the dysfunction and on the conflicts between the individual and his or her partner and (2) sex therapy designed to decrease inhibitions about sex and teach new techniques for achieving optimal sexual enjoyment.
- One set of techniques in sex therapy is sensate focus exercises. The exercises lead partners through three stages, from gentle nongenital touching to direct genital stimulation and finally to intercourse focused on enhancing and sustaining pleasure, rather than on orgasm and performance.
- Men experiencing premature ejaculation can be helped with the stop-start technique or the squeeze technique.
- The paraphilias are a group of disorders in which the focus of the individual's sexual fantasies, urges, and behaviors is (1) nonliving objects, (2) nonconsenting adults, (3) suffering or humiliation of oneself or one's partner, or (4) children.
- Fetishism is a paraphilia that involves sexual fantasies, urges, or behaviors focused on nonliving objects. A particular form of fetish is transvestism, in which heterosexual men dress in women's clothes in order to become sexually aroused.
- Voyeurism involves sexual fantasies, urges, or behaviors focused on secretly watching another person undressing, doing things in the nude, or engaging in sex. Almost all people who engage in voyeurism are men who watch women.
- Exhibitionism involves sexual fantasies, urges, or behaviors focused on exposing the genitals to involuntary observers, usually strangers.
- Frotteurism often co-occurs with voyeurism and exhibitionism. The person who engages in frotteurism has sexual fantasies, urges, or behaviors focused on rubbing against and fondling parts of the body of a nonconsenting person. Usually this occurs in a crowded public space.
- Sexual sadism involves sexual fantasies, urges, or behaviors focused on inflicting pain and humiliation on a sex partner. Sexual masochism involves sexual fantasies, urges, or behaviors focused on experiencing pain or humiliation during sex.
- People with pedophilia have sexual fantasies, urges, or behaviors focused on prepubescent children.
- Some neurodevelopmental differences are found between people with pedophilia and people without the disorder.
- Behavioral theories suggest that the sexual behaviors of people with paraphilia result from classical and operant conditioning.
- Treatments for the paraphilias include biological interventions to reduce sexual drive, behavioral interventions to decondition arousal due to paraphilic objects, and cognitive-behavioral interventions to combat cognitions supporting paraphilic behavior and increase coping skills.
- Gender identity disorder (GID) is diagnosed when an individual believes that he or she was born with the wrong genitals and is fundamentally a person of the opposite sex. Gender identity disorder of childhood is a rare condition in which a child persistently rejects his or her anatomic sex and desires to be or insists he or she is a member of the opposite sex.
- Gender identity disorder in adulthood is often referred to as transsexualism. Transsexual persons experience a chronic discomfort and sense of inappropriateness with their gender and genitals, wish to be rid of them, and want to live as members of the opposite sex. Transsexual individuals often dress in the clothes of the opposite sex but, unlike transvestites, do not do so in order to gain sexual arousal.
- Biological theories suggest that gender identity disorder is due to prenatal exposure to hormones that affect development of the hypothalamus and other brain structures involved in sexuality. Socialization theories suggest that the parents of children (primarily boys) with gender identity disorder do not encourage gender-appropriate behaviors.
- Treatment for gender identity disorder includes cross-sex hormone therapy, real-life experience as a member of the desired sex, and sex reassignment surgery.

KEY TERMS

hypoactive sexual desire disorder 390
sexual desire 391
arousal phase 391
plateau phase 391
orgasm 391
resolution 392
sexual dysfunction 392
paraphilia 392
gender identity 392
gender identity disorder (GID) 392
sexual aversion disorder 393
female sexual arousal disorder 393
male erectile disorder 393
female orgasmic disorder 395
premature ejaculation 395
male orgasmic disorder 396
dyspareunia 396
vaginismus 396
substance-induced sexual dysfunction 397
performance anxiety 398
sensate focus therapy 404
stop-start technique 405
squeeze technique 405
fetishism 408
transvestic fetishism 409
sexual sadism 409
sexual masochism 409
sadomasochism 409
voyeurism 411
exhibitionism 411
frotteurism 411
pedophilia 412
aversion therapy 415
desensitization 415
transsexuals 417

Chapter 14

Substance-Related and Impulse-Control Disorders

CHAPTER OUTLINE

Extraordinary People

Celebrity Drug Abusers

Heath Ledger's portrayal of the Joker in *The Dark Knight* won an Oscar in 2009. However, the actor was not present to accept his award because on January 22, 2008, he had died of an overdose of prescription drugs, including oxycodone, hydrocodone, diazepam, temazepam, alprazolam, and doxylamine. Ledger was 28 and on the brink of a promising career. Many other celebrities have had public problems with drugs and alcohol, including Amy Winehouse, Kate Moss, Britney Spears, Lindsey Lohan, Robert Downey Jr., Whitney Houston, Drew Barrymore, and Courtney Love. Drug-related celebrity deaths include Michael Jackson, D.J. AM, Chris Farley, Anna Nicole Smith, John Belushi, Russell Jones (Ol' Dirty Bastard), and Rick James. As guitarist Keith Richards of the Rolling Stones said, "I used to know a few guys that did drugs all the time, but they're not alive anymore. . . . And you get the message after you've been to a few funerals."

But what message do fans get from celebrities who use, and die from, drugs? Some people may dismiss these deaths or recognize the tragic waste of human lives and talent. But others may look to celebrities as role models and see drug use as part of a glamorous lifestyle. Characters in popular movies and TV shows frequently use alcohol and illicit drugs to cope with stress, increase their sex appeal, and get through the day. However, some movies and television shows provide more realistic depictions of substance abuse and treatment. In 2009, the Partnership for a Drug-Free America recognized the performances of Anne Hathaway in *Rachel Getting Married* (a hit movie that shows the ruinous effect drugs have had on a young woman struggling through rehab) and Benjamin Bratt in *The Cleaner* (a TV series about a former addict helping others overcome drug dependence).

We all have our temptations, and some of us have more trouble resisting them than others. In this chapter, we consider disorders that involve chronic difficulties in resisting the desire to drink alcohol or take drugs, known in the *DSM-IV-TR* as **substance-related disorders.** We also consider a set of disorders involving the inability to resist other drives: to gamble, to shoplift, to set fires, to explode in rage, and even to pull out one's hair. These disorders are known collectively in the *DSM-IV-TR* as **impulse-control disorders.** The *DSM-5* authors have proposed combining the substance-related and impulse-control disorders into one new category, *addiction and related disorders*.

We begin with the substance-related disorders. A **substance** is any natural or synthesized product that has psychoactive effects—it changes perceptions, thoughts, emotions, and behaviors. Some of the substances we discuss in this chapter are popularly referred to as *drugs* (e.g., cocaine and heroin). People who abuse these drugs are often referred to as *drug addicts.* Yet a person need not be physically dependent on a substance, as the term *addict* implies, in order to have a problem with it. For example, some clubgoers who are not physically addicted to Ecstasy still may think they need the drug to have a good time.

Societies differ in their attitudes toward substances with psychoactive effects, with some seeing their use as a matter of individual choice and others seeing it as a grave public health and security concern. Within the United States, attitudes have varied greatly over time and across subgroups. U.S. ambivalence toward alcohol use is nicely illustrated in a letter from former Congressman Billy Mathews to one of his then-constituents, who wrote: "Dear Congressman, how do you stand on whiskey?" Because the congressman did not know how the constituent stood on alcohol, he fashioned the following safe response:

> My dear friend, I had not intended to discuss this controversial subject at this particular time. However, I want you to know that I do not shun a controversy. On the contrary, I will take a stand on any issue at any time, regardless of how fraught with controversy it may be. You have asked me how I feel about whiskey. Here is how I stand on the issue.
>
> If when you say whiskey, you mean the Devil's brew; the poison scourge; the bloody monster that defiles innocence, dethrones reason, destroys the home, creates

FIGURE 14.1 **Illicit Drug Use in the Past Year.** In the United States, ethnic and age groups have different rates of drug use.

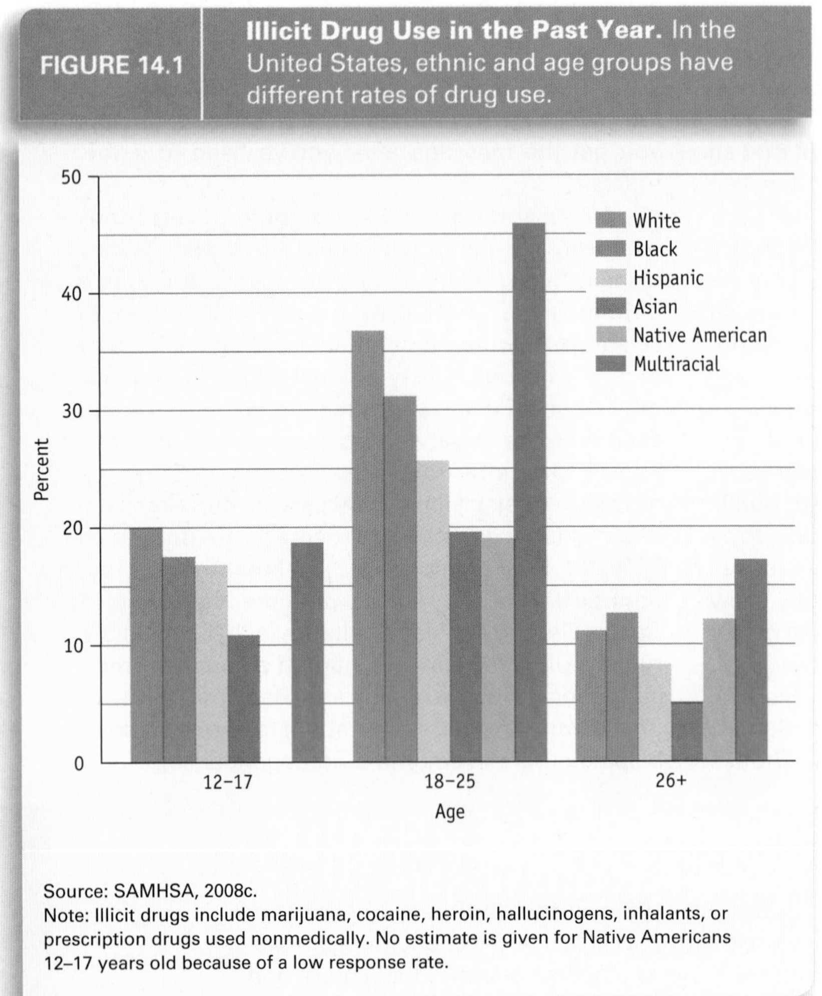

Source: SAMHSA, 2008c.
Note: Illicit drugs include marijuana, cocaine, heroin, hallucinogens, inhalants, or prescription drugs used nonmedically. No estimate is given for Native Americans 12–17 years old because of a low response rate.

Coca-Cola originally contained cocaine.

misery, poverty, fear; literally takes the bread from the mouths of little children; if you mean the evil drink that topples the Christian man and woman from the pinnacles of righteous, gracious living into the bottomless pit of degradation and despair, shame and helplessness and hopelessness; then certainly, I am against it with all of my power.

But, if when you say whiskey, you mean the oil of conversation, the philosophic wine, the ale that is assumed when great fellows get together, that puts a song in their hearts and laughter on their lips, and the warm glow of contentment in their eyes; if you mean Christmas cheer; if you mean that stimulating drink that puts the spring in the old gentleman's step on a frosty morning; if you mean the drink that enables the man to magnify his joy and his happiness and to forget, if only for a little while, life's great tragedies and heartbreaks and sorrows; if you mean that drink, the sale of which pours into our Treasury untold millions of dollars which are used to provide tender care for little crippled children, our blind, our deaf, our pitiful aged and infirm; to build highways, hospitals, and schools; then certainly, I am in favor of it. This is my stand, and I will not compromise. Your congressman. (Quoted in Marlatt, Larimer, Baer, & Quigley, 1993, p. 462)

Many substances have been used for medicinal purposes for centuries. As long ago as 1500 BCE., people in the Andes highlands chewed coca leaves to increase their endurance (Cocores, Pottash, & Gold, 1991). Coca leaves can be manufactured into cocaine, which was used legally throughout Europe and the United States into the twentieth century to relieve fatigue. It was an ingredient in the original Coca-Cola drink and in more than 50 other widely available beverages and elixirs.

Psychoactive substances also have traditionally appeared in religious ceremonies. When chewed, peyote causes visual hallucinations of colored lights or of geometric forms, animals, or people. Native groups in North America have used it in religious rituals for hundreds of years.

Substance Use Along the Continuum

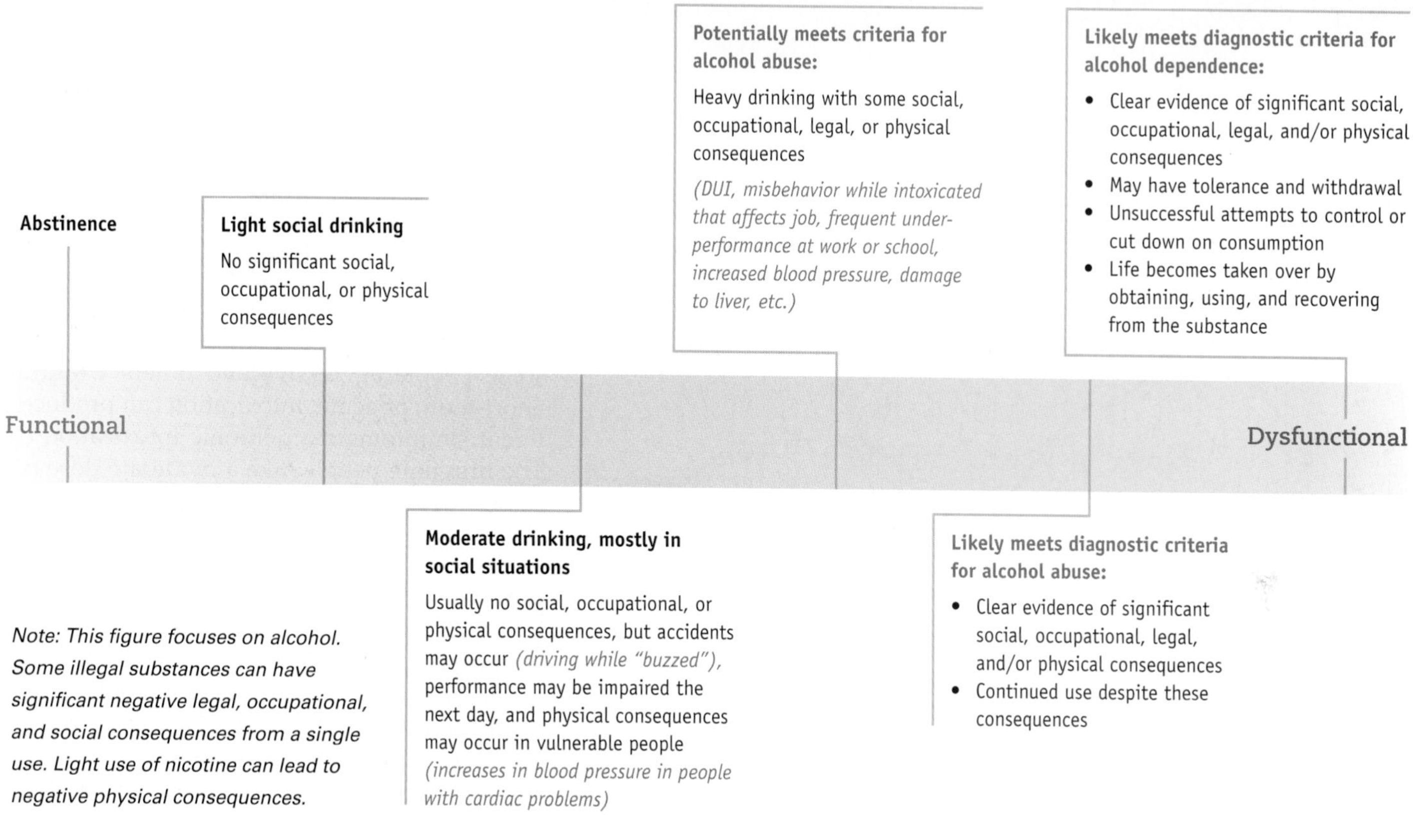

Abstinence

Light social drinking
No significant social, occupational, or physical consequences

Moderate drinking, mostly in social situations
Usually no social, occupational, or physical consequences, but accidents may occur *(driving while "buzzed")*, performance may be impaired the next day, and physical consequences may occur in vulnerable people *(increases in blood pressure in people with cardiac problems)*

Potentially meets criteria for alcohol abuse:
Heavy drinking with some social, occupational, legal, or physical consequences
(DUI, misbehavior while intoxicated that affects job, frequent underperformance at work or school, increased blood pressure, damage to liver, etc.)

Likely meets diagnostic criteria for alcohol abuse:
- Clear evidence of significant social, occupational, legal, and/or physical consequences
- Continued use despite these consequences

Likely meets diagnostic criteria for alcohol dependence:
- Clear evidence of significant social, occupational, legal, and/or physical consequences
- May have tolerance and withdrawal
- Unsuccessful attempts to control or cut down on consumption
- Life becomes taken over by obtaining, using, and recovering from the substance

Functional — Dysfunctional

Note: This figure focuses on alcohol. Some illegal substances can have significant negative legal, occupational, and social consequences from a single use. Light use of nicotine can lead to negative physical consequences.

As a student, you likely know more people along the continuum of substance use than along any other continuum in previous chapters. TV shows and movies often show substance use as a rite of passage into adulthood—think of the college drinking scenes in movies like *Animal House*—and statistics suggest there is some truth in this portrayal. Illegal drug use is highest among young adults (Figure 14.1; Substance Abuse and Mental Health Services Administration [SAMHSA], 2008b), with about 20 percent of college students reporting current use.

At one end of the continuum are people who abstain completely. Some do not enjoy the effects of substances; others hold to religious beliefs that prohibit the use of alcohol or drugs, as in the Mormon faith. Personal experiences—such as having a relative die from an accident caused by alcohol or drugs—also may impact people's decision to abstain.

Further along the continuum are people who use drugs and alcohol "recreationally." Nearly half the U.S. population admits to having tried an illegal substance at some time in their life, and approximately 14 percent have used one in the past year (SAMHSA, 2008b). Substance use varies across demographic groups as well. Figure 14.1 shows substantial differences among ethnic groups in the United States, and Figure 14.2 on page 428 outlines the use of illegal drugs among 12th-graders. Young adult usage peaked in the 1970s, saw another increase in the late 1990s, and has declined or held steady since then (Johnston, O'Malley, Bachman, & Schulenberg, 2008).

Although movies and TV often make substance use look cool, the consequences are staggeringly serious. There are more deaths from traffic accidents involving substance-impaired drivers than from all other types of accidents. In 2008, 15 percent of drivers in the United States reported driving under the influence of alcohol, and another 5 percent reported driving under the influence of an illicit drug (SAMHSA, 2008c). Over 10 percent of emergency room visits in the United States are related to the misuse of alcohol or of illegal or prescription drugs (SAMHSA, 2008a). Recreational drug use costs the United States over $181 billion a year in costs related to accidents, crime, health care, and lost productivity (Office of National Drug Control Policy, 2004). When you factor in alcohol, this amount rises to $500 billion (CDC, 2005).

Near the other end of the continuum are individuals who build their lives around substances. Their immoderate substance use impairs their everyday functioning—they may avoid job and family responsibilities, act impulsively or bizarrely, or endanger their own and others' lives. These people have a substance-related disorder.

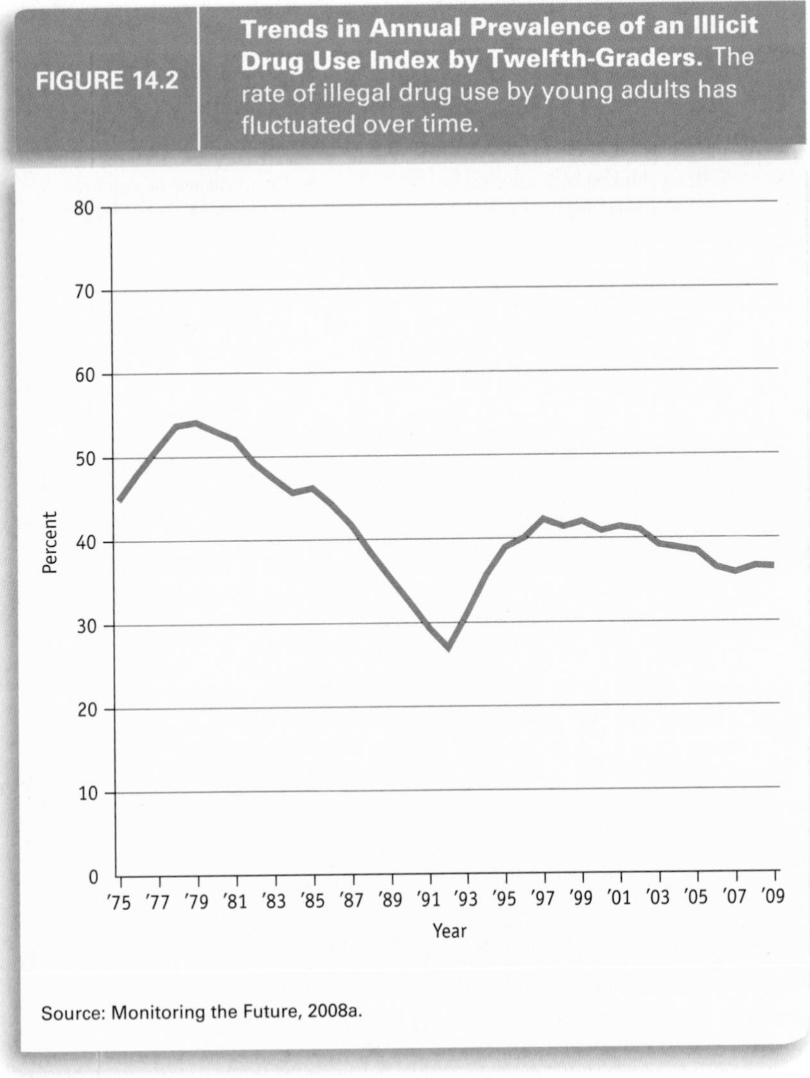

FIGURE 14.2 **Trends in Annual Prevalence of an Illicit Drug Use Index by Twelfth-Graders.** The rate of illegal drug use by young adults has fluctuated over time.

Source: Monitoring the Future, 2008a.

DEFINING SUBSTANCE-RELATED DISORDERS

Four substance-related conditions appear in the *DSM-IV-TR: substance intoxication, substance withdrawal, substance abuse,* and *substance dependence* (Table 14.1). This chapter first discusses the criteria for each condition. It then describes how the conditions are manifested in the context of those substances most commonly linked to them.

Abused substances fit into five categories: (1) central nervous system depressants, including alcohol, barbiturates, benzodiazepines, and inhalants; (2) central nervous system stimulants, including cocaine, amphetamines, nicotine, and caffeine; (3) opioids, including heroin and morphine; (4) hallucinogens and phencyclidine (PCP); and (5) cannabis. Intoxication, withdrawal, abuse, and dependence can occur with most, though not all, of these substances (Table 14.2).

Substance intoxication is a set of behavioral and psychological changes that occur as a result of the physiological effects of a substance on the central nervous system. People become intoxicated soon after they ingest a substance, and the more they ingest, the more intoxicated they become. Intoxication declines as the amount of substance in blood or tissue declines, but symptoms may last for hours or days after the substance no longer is detectable in the body (Virani, Bezchlybnik-Butler, & Jeffries, 2009).

The specific symptoms of intoxication depend on what substance is taken, how much of it and when, the user's tolerance, and the context. For example, you may have observed that alcohol makes some people aggressive and others withdrawn. Short-term, or acute, intoxication can produce different symptoms than chronic intoxication does. The first time people take a moderate dose of cocaine, they may be outgoing and upbeat. With chronic use over days or weeks, they may begin to withdraw socially (Virani et al., 2009). People's expectations about a substance's effects also can influence the types of symptoms shown. People who expect marijuana to make them relaxed may experience relaxation, whereas people who are frightened of disinhibition may experience anxiety (Ruiz, Strain, & Langrod, 2007).

The setting also can influence the types of symptoms people develop. People who consume a few alcoholic drinks at a party may become uninhibited and loud, but when they consume the same amount at home alone they may become tired and depressed (Brick, 2008). The environment can also influence how maladaptive the intoxication is. People who drink alcohol only at home may be less likely to cause harm to themselves or others than are people who drink at bars and drive home under the influence of alcohol. The diagnosis of substance intoxication is given only when the behavioral and psychological changes the person experiences are significantly maladaptive: They substantially disrupt the person's social and family relationships, cause occupational or financial problems, or place the individual at significant risk for adverse effects, such as a traffic accident, severe medical complications, or legal problems. For example, driving under the influence of a substance would merit a diagnosis of substance intoxication.

Substance withdrawal is a set of physiological and behavioral symptoms that result when people who have been using substances heavily for prolonged periods of time stop or greatly reduce their use. Symptoms typically are the opposite of those of intoxication. The diagnosis of substance withdrawal requires significant distress or impairment in a person's everyday functioning. Although the

TABLE 14.1 Definitions of Substance Intoxication, Withdrawal, Abuse, and Dependence

These definitions of substance intoxication, withdrawal, abuse, and dependence apply across a variety of substances, but the specific symptoms depend on the substance used.

Substance intoxication	Experience of significant maladaptive behavioral and psychological symptoms due to the effect of a substance on the central nervous system
Substance withdrawal	Experience of clinically significant distress in social, occupational, or other areas of functioning due to the cessation or reduction of substance use
Substance abuse	Diagnosis given when recurrent substance use leads to significant harmful consequences
Substance dependence	Diagnosis given when substance use leads to physiological dependence or significant impairment or distress

Source: Reprinted with permission from the *Diagnostic and Statistical Manual of Mental Disorders,* Fourth Edition, Text Revision.

TABLE 14.2 *DSM-IV-TR* Diagnosis for Each Class of Substances

The X's indicate which diagnoses are recognized for each substance in the *DSM-IV-TR.*

	Intoxication	Withdrawal	Abuse	Dependence
Alcohol	X	X	X	X
Barbiturates	X	X	X	X
Benzodiazepines	X	X	X	X
Inhalants	X		X	X
Cocaine	X	X	X	X
Amphetamines	X	X	X	X
Caffeine	X			
Opioids	X	X	X	X
Hallucinogens	X		X	X
Phencyclidine	X		X	X
Cannabis	X		X	X
Nicotine		X		X

Source: Reprinted with permission from the *Diagnostic and Statistical Manual of Mental Disorders,* Fourth Edition, Text Revision.

symptoms of caffeine withdrawal (nervousness, headaches) may be annoying, they typically do not cause significant impairment or distress. For this reason, caffeine withdrawal is not a diagnostic category in the *DSM-IV-TR* or the *DSM-5.*

The diagnosis of **substance abuse** is given in the *DSM-IV-TR* when a person's recurrent use of a substance results in significant harmful consequences. Four categories of harmful consequences suggest substance abuse (see the *DSM-IV-TR* criteria in Table 14.3). First, the individual *fails to fulfill important obligations* at work, school, or home. He or she may fail to show up at work or for classes, may be unable to concentrate and therefore performs poorly, or may even consume the substance at work or at school. Second, the individual *repeatedly uses the substance in situations in which it is physically hazardous to do so,* such as while driving. Third, the individual *repeatedly has legal problems as a result of substance use,* such as arrests for drunk driving or for the possession of illegal substances. Fourth, the individual *continues to use the substance* *despite repeated social or legal problems as a result of use.* A person must show repeated problems in at least one of these categories within a 12-month period to receive a diagnosis of substance abuse.

The diagnosis of **substance dependence** in the *DSM-IV-TR* is closest to what people often refer to as *drug addiction* (see the *DSM-IV-TR* criteria in Table 14.4). A person who is *physiologically dependent* on a substance shows either tolerance or withdrawal from the substance. **Tolerance** is present when a person experiences less effect from the same dose of a substance and needs more and more of it to achieve intoxication. People who have smoked cigarettes for years often smoke more than 20 cigarettes a day, an amount that would have made them violently ill when they first began smoking. A person highly tolerant of a substance may have a very high blood level of it without being aware of its effects. The risk for tolerance varies greatly among substances. Alcohol, opioids, stimulants, and nicotine have high risks for tolerance, whereas cannabis and PCP appear to have lower risks (Brick, 2008). Substance dependence and abuse are highly comorbid with all other psychological disorders, including depression, anxiety, and schizophrenia (Kessler et al., 2005).

People who are physiologically dependent on a substance often show severe withdrawal symptoms when they stop using it. Sometimes the substance must be withdrawn gradually to prevent the symptoms from becoming overwhelming or dangerous (Brick, 2008). Users may continue to take the substance to relieve or avoid withdrawal symptoms.

TABLE 14.3 *DSM-IV-TR* Criteria for Diagnosing Substance Abuse

The criteria for diagnosing substance abuse require repeated problems as a result of the use of a substance.

One or more of the following occurs during a 12-month period, leading to significant impairment or distress:

1. Failure to fulfill important obligations at work, home, or school as a result of substance use
2. Repeated use of the substance in situations in which it is physically hazardous to do so
3. Repeated legal problems as a result of substance use
4. Continued use of the substance despite repeated social or legal problems as a result of use

Source: Reprinted with permission from the *Diagnostic and Statistical Manual of Mental Disorders,* Fourth Edition, Text Revision. Copyright © 2000 American Psychiatric Association.

TABLE 14.4 *DSM-IV-TR* Criteria for Diagnosing Substance Dependence

Substance dependence often involves evidence of physiological dependence plus repeated problems due to the use of the substance.

A. Maladaptive pattern of substance use, leading to three or more of the following:
   1. Tolerance, as defined by either
      a. the need for markedly increased amounts of the substance to achieve intoxication or desired effect
      b. markedly diminished effect with continued use of the same amount of the substance
   2. Withdrawal, as manifested by either
      a. the characteristic withdrawal syndrome for the substance
      b. the same or a closely related substance is taken to relieve or avoid withdrawal symptoms
   3. The substance is often taken in larger amounts or over a longer period than was intended
   4. There is a persistent desire or unsuccessful effort to cut down or control substance use
   5. A great deal of time is spent in activities necessary to obtain the substance, use the substance, or recover from its effects
   6. Important social, occupational, or recreational activities are given up or reduced because of substance use
   7. The substance use is continued despite knowledge of having a persistent or recurrent physical or psychological problem caused by or exacerbated by the substance.

Source: Reprinted with permission from the *Diagnostic and Statistical Manual of Mental Disorders,* Fourth Edition, Text Revision. Copyright © 2000 American Psychiatric Association.

Physiological dependence (evidence of tolerance or withdrawal) is not required for a diagnosis of substance dependence in the *DSM-IV-TR*, however. A person need only compulsively use a substance despite experiencing significant social, occupational, psychological, or medical problems as a result. The diagnosis of substance dependence preempts the diagnosis of substance abuse. Some individuals abuse substances for years, severely disrupting their lives, without qualifying for a diagnosis of substance dependence.

Some people who are dependent on a substance will do almost anything to get it (steal, lie, prostitute themselves). Their lives may revolve around obtaining and ingesting the substance. They may have attempted repeatedly to reduce or stop its use, only to find themselves compulsively taking the substance again. In the following case study, Lucy is physically and psychologically dependent on both heroin and crack cocaine.

CASE STUDY

By age 18, Lucy was heavily addicted to heroin, and her mother took her to a detoxification program. After the 21-day regimen, Lucy was released but immediately relapsed. By age 24, she was mainlining heroin and turning tricks regularly to support her own and a boyfriend's drug habits. Lucy's boyfriend then admitted himself to a drug rehabilitation program, and when he completed treatment, they both stopped their heroin use. However, they began snorting cocaine. Lucy soon left her boyfriend and went to work in a massage parlor, where the other women introduced her to crack. By 1984 Lucy was 30 years old, a veteran drug addict and a prostitute.

Lucy left the massage parlor and began working on the streets. Her crack use increased continually until 1986, when she tried to stop. In her opinion, crack was worse than heroin, so she started injecting narcotics again. But she never stopped using crack.

Because of her crack use, Lucy began doing things she had never contemplated, even while on heroin. She had anal sex and sold herself for less than before. She even began trading sex for drugs rather than money and regularly worked in crack houses, which she described as "disgusting" and crowded. Lucy had five to seven customers a night, and most of the sex was oral. During this time, she either stayed with her sister or slept in cars. (Inciardi, James A., Lockwood, D., & Pottieger, A. E., *Women and Crack-Cocaine,* 1st edition, © 1993, pp. 160–161. Reprinted by permission of Pearson Education, Inc., Upper Saddle River, NJ.)

Smoking, snorting, or injecting a substance can lead to more intense intoxication and a greater chance of dependence than eating or drinking it.

The way a substance is administered can help determine how rapidly a person will become intoxicated and whether the substance will produce withdrawal symptoms or lead to abuse or dependence (Virani et al., 2009). Rapid and efficient absorption of the substance into the bloodstream, through injection, smoking, or snorting, leads to more intense intoxication and a greater likelihood of dependence. These routes of administration also are more likely to lead to overdose (Brick, 2008).

Some substances, such as cocaine and heroin, act more rapidly on the central nervous system and thus lead to faster intoxication. They also are more likely to lead to dependence or abuse. Substances whose effects wear off quickly also are more likely to lead to dependence or abuse than are substances with longer-lasting effects (Ruiz et al., 2007).

The *DSM-5* authors propose that substance abuse and dependence be combined into one diagnosis, *substance-use disorder*. This proposal reflects difficulties in distinguishing between abuse and dependence in clinical settings and research, as well as in the reliability of the diagnosis of abuse (Hasin & Beseler, 2009). The diagnostic criteria for substance-use disorder will include the continued use of substances despite negative social, occupational, and health consequences, as indicated in the *DSM-IV-TR* criteria for substance abuse, as well as evidence of tolerance or withdrawal. To these criteria the *DSM-5* authors have added "craving the substance," because craving is a common symptom of abuse and dependence. However, they have removed "legal problems" from the criteria because of its low prevalence. Users will have to show two or more of these symptoms over a year to receive the diagnosis. Clinicians will rate the severity of the disorder as moderate

(2 or 3 of the criteria are met) or severe (4 or more criteria are met). Clinicians will also specify if the individual shows physiological dependence, as indicated by tolerance or withdrawal (American Psychiatric Association, 2010).

TEST YOURSELF

1. What is substance intoxication?
2. What is substance withdrawal?
3. What are the criteria for substance abuse?
4. What are the criteria for substance dependence?

APPLY IT Jennifer lost her driver's license after her second drunk driving offense this year. Still, last weekend she went out with friends and got very drunk; she passed out and the next day couldn't remember anything about the evening before. For which *DSM-IV-TR* diagnosis would Jennifer most likely meet the criteria?

a. substance intoxication
b. substance withdrawal
c. substance abuse
d. substance dependence

Answers appear online at www.mhhe.com/nolen5e.

Drinking alcohol with food leads to slower absorption of the alcohol.

DEPRESSANTS

Depressants slow the central nervous system. In moderate doses, they make people relaxed and somewhat sleepy, reduce concentration, and impair thinking and motor skills. In heavy doses, they can induce stupor or even death.

Alcohol

Alcohol's effects on the brain occur in two distinct phases (Brick, 2008). In low doses, alcohol causes many people to feel more self-confident, more relaxed, and perhaps slightly euphoric. They may be less inhibited, and this disinhibitory effect may be what many people find attractive. At increasing doses, however, alcohol induces many of the symptoms of depression, including fatigue and lethargy, decreased motivation, sleep disturbances, depressed mood, and confusion. Also, although many people take alcohol to feel sexier (mainly by reducing their sexual inhibitions), even low doses can impair sexual functioning.

People intoxicated by alcohol slur their words, walk unsteadily, have trouble paying attention or remembering things, and are slow and awkward in their physical reactions. They may act inappropriately, becoming aggressive or saying rude things. Their moods may swing from exuberance to despair. With extreme intoxication, people may fall into a stupor or a coma. Often, they do not recognize that they are obviously intoxicated or may flatly deny it. Once sober, they may have amnesia, known as a *blackout,* for the events that occurred while they were intoxicated (Ruiz et al., 2007).

One critical determinant of how quickly people become intoxicated with alcohol is whether their stomach is full or empty. An empty stomach speedily delivers alcohol to the small intestine, where it is rapidly absorbed into the body. A person with a full stomach may ingest significantly more drinks before reaching a dangerous blood-alcohol level or showing clear signs of intoxication (Brick, 2008). People in countries where alcohol is usually consumed with meals, such as France, show lower rates of alcohol-related substance disorders than do people in countries where alcohol often is consumed on an empty stomach.

The legal definition of alcohol intoxication is much narrower than the criteria for a diagnosis of alcohol intoxication. Most U.S. states consider a person to be under the influence of alcohol if his or her blood-alcohol level is 0.08 or above. As Table 14.5 indicates, it does not take many drinks for most people to reach this level. Deficits in attention, reaction time, and coordination arise even with the first drink and can interfere with the ability to operate a car or machinery safely and to perform other tasks requiring a steady

TABLE 14.5 Relationships Among Sex, Weight, Oral Alcohol Consumption, and Blood-Alcohol Level

It doesn't take very many drinks for most people to reach a blood-alcohol level of 0.08, which is the legal definition of intoxication in most states.

		Blood-Alcohol Level (Percent)					
Total Alcohol Content (Ounces)	Beverage Intake*	Female (100 lb)	Male (100 lb)	Female (150 lb)	Male (150 lb)	Female (200 lb)	Male (200 lb)
1/2	1 oz spirits† 1 glass wine 1 can beer	0.045	0.037	0.03	0.025	0.022	0.019
1	2 oz spirits 2 glasses wine 2 cans beer	0.090	0.075	0.06	0.050	0.045	0.037
2	4 oz spirits 4 glasses wine 4 cans beer	0.180	0.150	0.12	0.100	0.090	0.070
3	6 oz spirits 6 glasses wine 6 cans beer	0.270	0.220	0.18	0.150	0.130	0.110
4	8 oz spirits 8 glasses wine 8 cans beer	0.360	0.300	0.24	0.200	0.180	0.150
5	10 oz spirits 10 glasses wine 10 cans beer	0.450	0.370	0.30	0.250	0.220	0.180

*In 1 hour
†100-proof spirits (50 percent alcohol)
Source: Data from Ray & Ksir, 1993, p. 194.

hand, coordination, clear thinking, and clear vision. These deficits are not always readily observable, even to trained eyes. People often leave parties or bars without appearing drunk but with a blood-alcohol level well above the legal limit and dangerous deficits in their ability to drive (Brick, 2008).

Drinking large quantities of alcohol can be fatal, even in people who are not chronic alcohol abusers. About one-third of these deaths result from respiratory paralysis, usually due to a final large dose of alcohol in people who are already intoxicated. Alcohol can also interact fatally with a number of substances, including some antidepressant drugs (Brick, 2008).

Unintentional alcohol-related injuries due to automobile accidents, drowning, burns, poisoning, and falls account for approximately 600,000 deaths per year internationally (WHO, 2005b). Nearly half of all fatal automobile accidents and deaths due to falls or fires and over one-third of all drownings are alcohol-related (Fleming & Manwell, 2000; Hunt, 1998). More than half of all murderers and their victims are believed to be intoxicated with alcohol at the time of the murders, and people who commit suicide often do so under the influence of alcohol.

Alcohol Abuse and Dependence

People given the diagnosis of **alcohol abuse** in the *DSM-IV-TR* use alcohol in dangerous situations (such as when driving), fail to meet important obligations at work or at home, and have recurrent legal or social problems as a result of their alcohol use. Almost 18 percent of U.S. adults meet the criteria for alcohol abuse at some time in their life (Hasin, Stinson, Ogburn, & Grant, 2007). People given the diagnosis of **alcohol dependence** in the

Heavy drinking can be part of the culture of a peer group, but it still can lead to alcohol abuse and dependence in some members.

DSM-IV-TR typically have all the problems of an alcohol abuser and may show physiological tolerance to alcohol. They spend a great deal of time intoxicated or withdrawing from alcohol, organize their lives around drinking, or continue to drink despite having significant social, occupational, medical, or legal problems as a result. The characteristics of alcohol dependence match what most people associate with the label *alcoholism* (although the *DSM* no longer uses this term). About 13 percent of U.S. adults meet the criteria for alcohol dependence at some time in their life (Hasin et al., 2007). In the *DSM-5,* alcohol abuse and alcohol dependence likely will be subsumed under the diagnosis *alcohol-use disorder,* which will be indicated by the presence of at least two symptoms from the combined list of symptoms for alcohol abuse and alcohol dependence (American Psychiatric Association, 2010).

Binge drinking is defined as consuming five or more drinks within a couple of hours (some researchers define a binge for women as consuming four or more drinks within a couple of hours). In a nationwide survey, 23 percent of respondents reported binge drinking in the previous month (SAMHSA, 2008c). Binge drinking on college campuses is common. Nationwide, 44 percent of college students report binge drinking in the past month, compared with 39 percent of 18- to 22-year-olds not in college (SAMHSA, 2005; Wechsler & Nelson, 2008). Binge drinking is especially common among members of fraternities and sororities, with 75 percent of members saying they binge drink (Wechsler et al., 2002).

Different subtypes of alcohol dependence have different causes and prognoses. One reliable distinction is between alcohol-dependent people who also have antisocial personalities (who are hostile and aggressive and violate social norms) and those who do not (Zucker et al., 1996). People in the antisocial group have more severe symptoms of alcohol dependency, tend to remain alcohol-dependent longer, and have poorer social functioning, more marital failures, and heavier drug involvement (Zucker et al., 1996). They are more likely to come from families with alcoholism, to have begun drinking earlier in life, and to have children with behavior problems (Puttler, Zucker, Fitzgerald, & Bingham, 1998).

Another distinction has been made between negative-affect alcohol disorders and other alcohol disorders (Sher, Grekin, & Williams, 2005). People with negative-affect alcohol disorders tend to have shown symptoms of depression and anxiety in childhood and adolescence and to have begun severe alcohol use and abuse only in adulthood. This pattern is more common in women than in men (Nolen-Hoeksema, 2004).

Alcohol Withdrawal

The symptoms of alcohol withdrawal manifest in three stages (Brick, 2008). The first, which usually begins within a few hours after drinking has been stopped or sharply curtailed, includes tremulousness (the "shakes"), weakness, and profuse perspiration. The person may complain of anxiety (the "jitters"), headache, nausea, and abdominal cramps and may retch and vomit. He or she is flushed, restless, and easily startled but alert. The EEG pattern may be mildly abnormal. The person may begin to see or hear things, at first only with eyes shut but later also with eyes open. Those whose dependence is moderate may experience only this first stage of withdrawal, and the symptoms may disappear within a few days.

The second stage includes convulsive seizures, which may begin as soon as 12 hours after drinking stops but more often appear during the second or third day. The third stage of withdrawal is characterized by **delirium tremens,** or **DTs.** Auditory, visual, and tactile hallucinations occur. The person also may develop bizarre, terrifying delusions, such as the belief that monsters are attacking. He or she may sleep little and may become agitated and disoriented. Fever, profuse perspiration, and an irregular heartbeat may develop. Delirium tremens is fatal in approximately 10 percent of cases. Death may occur from hyperthermia (extremely high body temperature) or the collapse of the peripheral vascular system. Fortunately, only about 11 percent of individuals with alcohol dependence ever experience seizures or DTs (Schuckit, Tip, Reich, Hesselbrock, 1995). These symptoms are more common among people who drink large amounts in a single sitting and have an existing medical illness.

Long-Term Effects of Alcohol Misuse

Heavy and prolonged use of alcohol can have toxic effects on several systems of the body, including the stomach, esophagus, pancreas, and liver (for a review, see Nolen-Hoeksema, 2004). One of the most common medical conditions associated with alcohol misuse is low-grade hypertension. This condition, combined with increases in the levels of triglycerides and low-density lipoprotein (or "bad") cholesterol, puts alcohol abusers at increased risk for heart disease. Alcohol abusers and alcohol dependents often are malnourished, in part because chronic alcohol ingestion decreases the absorption of critical nutrients from the gastrointestinal system and in part because they tend to "drink their meals." Some show a chronic thiamin deficiency, which can lead to several disorders of the central nervous system, including numbness and pain in the extremities, deterioration in the muscles, and the loss of visual acuity for both near and far objects (Martin & Bates, 1998).

Alcohol-induced persisting amnesic disorder, a permanent cognitive disorder caused by damage to the central nervous system, consists of two syndromes: *Wernicke's encephalopathy* brings mental confusion and disorientation and, in severe states, coma, while *Korsakoff's syndrome* includes memory loss for recent events and difficulty recalling distant ones. *Alcohol-induced dementia* is the loss of intellectual abilities, including memory, abstract thinking, judgment, and problem solving, often accompanied by personality changes such as increased paranoia. This syndrome occurs in approximately 9 percent of chronic alcohol abusers or dependents and is a common cause of adult dementia (Winger et al., 1992). Subtler deficits due to central nervous system damage are observed in many chronic abusers of alcohol, even after they quit drinking (Martin & Bates, 1998).

Some studies indicate that *moderate* alcohol consumption, particularly of red wine, carries health benefits. Red wine contains antioxidants that can increase good cholesterol, along with other chemicals that can help prevent damage to blood vessels and reduce bad cholesterol, producing positive cardiac effects (Fillmore et al., 2006). Several studies suggest that individuals who consume one or two drinks a day have better physical health and lower mortality rates than individuals who abstain from alcohol (Corrao, Bagnardi, Zambon, & La Vecchia, 2004; Rehm, Greenfield, & Rogers, 2001). However, abstainers and moderate drinkers differ on many other variables that can affect health: Abstainers are more likely than moderate drinkers to be older, less well educated, physically inactive, and overweight and to have diabetes, hypertension, and high cholesterol (Naimi et al., 2005). Some people classified as abstainers drank heavily earlier in life and have quit due to negative health effects (Fillmore et al., 2006). These factors make the health benefits of moderate drinking less clear.

FIGURE 14.3 **Consumption of Pure Alcohol in Various Regions of the World.** Cultures vary greatly in their consumption of alcohol. (Southeast Asia includes India and neighboring countries. Western Pacific includes Australia, China, Japan, and the Pacific Rim Countries.)

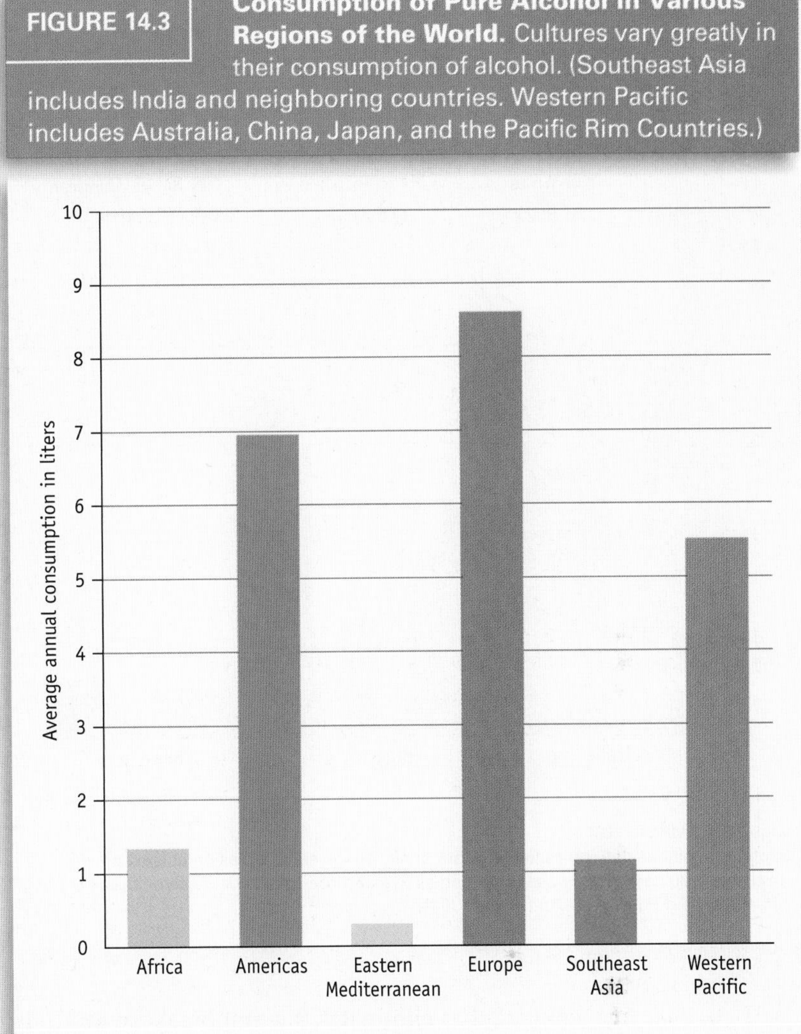

Source: World Health Organization, 2005b.

Cultural Differences in Alcohol Disorders

Cultures differ markedly in their use of alcohol and rates of alcohol-related problems (Figure 14.3). Low rates of consumption in Eastern Mediterranean and some African countries are tied to Islam's prohibitions against alcohol. Low consumption in Southeast Asia may be due in part to the absence in 50 percent of people of Asian descent of an

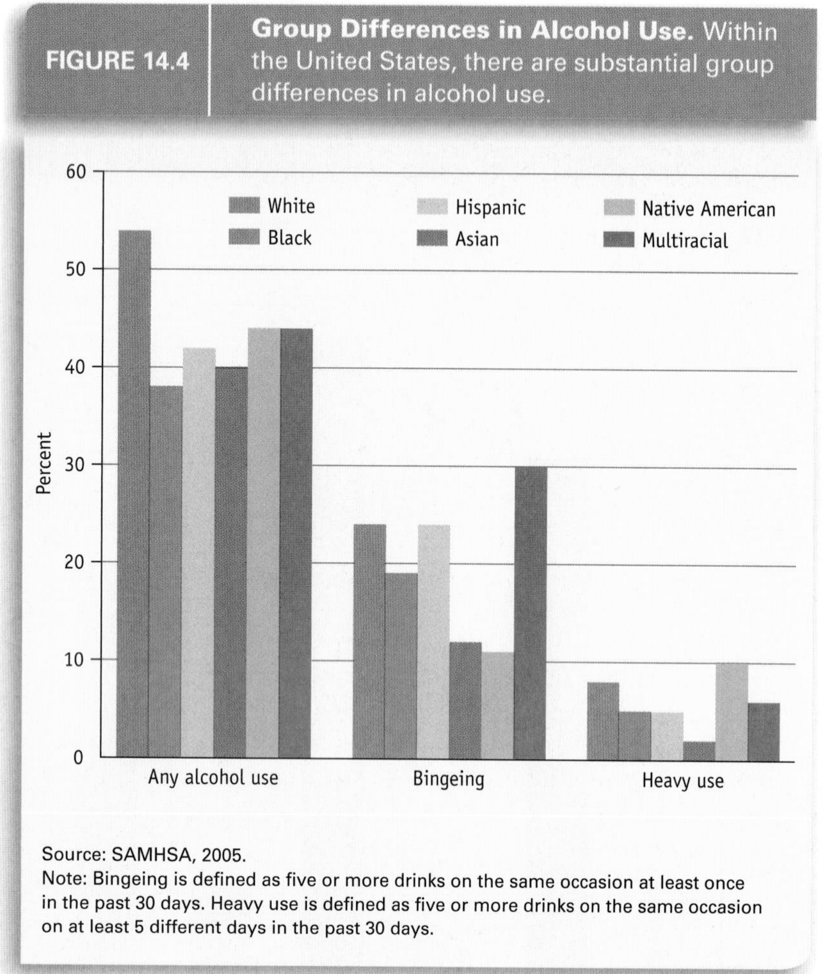

FIGURE 14.4 **Group Differences in Alcohol Use.** Within the United States, there are substantial group differences in alcohol use.

Source: SAMHSA, 2005.
Note: Bingeing is defined as five or more drinks on the same occasion at least once in the past 30 days. Heavy use is defined as five or more drinks on the same occasion on at least 5 different days in the past 30 days.

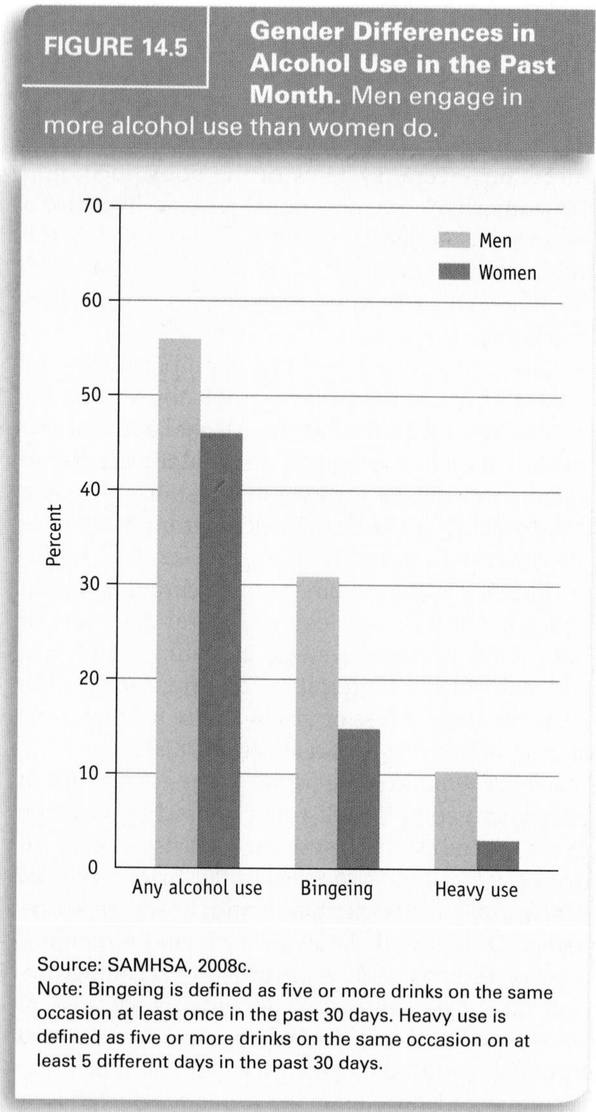

FIGURE 14.5 **Gender Differences in Alcohol Use in the Past Month.** Men engage in more alcohol use than women do.

Source: SAMHSA, 2008c.
Note: Bingeing is defined as five or more drinks on the same occasion at least once in the past 30 days. Heavy use is defined as five or more drinks on the same occasion on at least 5 different days in the past 30 days.

enzyme that eliminates the first breakdown product of alcohol, acetaldehyde. When these individuals consume alcohol, they experience a flushed face and heart palpitations, and the discomfort often leads them to avoid alcohol altogether.

Ethnic groups within the United States differ substantially in their alcohol use (Figure 14.4). One group at high risk for alcohol-related problems is Native Americans, 43 percent of whom meet the criteria for alcohol abuse or alcohol dependence at some time in their life (Hasin et al., 2007). Deaths related to alcohol are as much as five times more common among Native Americans than in the general U.S. population (Manson et al., 1992). This higher rate of alcohol-related problems has been tied to excessive rates of poverty and unemployment, lower levels of education, and a greater sense of helplessness and hopelessness (Manson et al., 1992).

Gender and Alcohol Use

In a community survey, about 56 percent of U.S. men over age 12 said they had consumed at least one alcoholic beverage in the past month, compared with 46 percent of women (Figure 14.5; SAMHSA, 2008c). Men are also more likely than women to binge drink, to drink heavily, and to have alcohol-use disorders. About 25 percent of U.S. men and 12 percent of U.S. women will meet the criteria for alcohol abuse at some time in their life, and about 17 percent of men and 8 percent of women will meet the criteria for alcohol dependence at some point (Keyes, Grant, & Hasin, 2008). The gender gap in alcohol use is much greater among men and women who subscribe to traditional gender roles, which condone drinking for men but not for women (Huselid & Cooper, 1992). Similarly, the gender gap is greater in U.S. ethnic minority groups that more widely accept traditional gender roles, such as Hispanics and recent Asian immigrants, than among European Americans, due largely to high percentages of minority women who completely abstain.

SHADES OF GRAY

As you may have observed, binge drinking on the weekends is fairly common on college campuses. Read about Nick and his friends, who may resemble people you know.

Nick began drinking in high school, but his drinking escalated when he moved away from home for college. After just a couple of weeks there, Nick became friends with a group that liked to party on the weekends. On Thursday nights, they would drink and get so loud and obnoxious that their neighbors in the dorm would sometimes complain. They would sleep off their hangovers on Friday, miss classes, and then begin drinking again from Friday afternoon through Saturday, finally stopping on Sunday to sleep and recover. Nick was able to keep decent grades through his first year, despite missing many classes. In sophomore year, classes in his major were harder, and he would abstain from drinking from Sunday afternoon until noon on Thursday. But Thursday afternoon he would get the keg of beer for his friends, and the old pattern would kick in.

One night during a drinking game, Nick accidentally punched a hole in the wall of his dorm room and was kicked off campus as a result. Between this incident and his declining grades, his parents threatened to stop paying his college tuition.

Would you diagnose Nick with either alcohol abuse or alcohol dependence? (Discussion appears at the end of this chapter.)

Trends Across the Life Span

Among adolescents and young adults, abuse of alcohol is widespread. One nationwide sample found that 16 percent, 33 percent, and 44 percent of eighth-, tenth-, and twelfth-graders, respectively, reported drinking an alcoholic beverage in the prior 30-day period (Monitoring the Future, 2008b). A study of more than 3,000 youths ages 14 to 24 found that 15 percent of males and about 5 percent of females could be diagnosed with alcohol abuse (Nelson & Wittchen, 1998). About 10 percent of males and 3 percent of females could be diagnosed with alcohol dependence.

Young and middle-aged adults diagnosed with alcohol dependence tend to show a chronic course. One study that followed 1,346 people found that two-thirds of those diagnosed with alcohol dependence still qualified for the diagnosis 5 years later (Schuckit et al., 2001). Of those initially diagnosed with alcohol abuse, 55 percent continued to show some signs of abuse or dependence 5 years later, but only 3.5 percent went on to develop the full dependence syndrome. Of participants with no alcohol diagnosis at baseline, only 2.5 percent met the criteria for alcohol dependence 5 years later, but 12.8 percent met the criteria for alcohol abuse at follow-up. Those more likely to receive a diagnosis at follow-up included men, people experiencing marital instability, and people who had also used illegal drugs.

As with illegal substances, abuse of and dependence on alcohol decline as people age (Sher et al., 2005). There are many reasons. First, with age the liver metabolizes alcohol at a slower rate, and the lower percentage of body water increases the absorption of alcohol. As a result, older people become intoxicated faster and experience the negative effects of alcohol more severely and quickly. Second, as people grow older, they may become more mature in their choices, including choices about drinking alcohol to excess. Third, older people have grown up under stronger prohibitions against alcohol use and abuse than have younger people. Fourth, people who have used alcohol excessively for many years may die from alcohol-related diseases before they reach old age (Sher et al., 2005).

Benzodiazepines, Barbiturates, and Inhalants

Three other groups of substances that, like alcohol, depress the central nervous system are benzodiazepines, barbiturates, and inhalants. Intoxication with and withdrawal from these substances are similar to alcohol intoxication and withdrawal. Users may initially feel euphoric and become disinhibited but then experience depressed moods, lethargy, perceptual distortions, loss of coordination, and other signs of central nervous system depression.

Benzodiazepines (such as Xanax, Valium, Halcion, Librium, and Klonopin) and **barbiturates** (such as Seconal) are legally manufactured and sold by prescription, usually as sedatives for the treatment of anxiety and insomnia. Benzodiazepines are also used as muscle relaxants and antiseizure medicines. In the United States, approximately 90 percent of people hospitalized for medical care or surgery are prescribed sedatives (Virani et al., 2009). Large quantities of these substances end up on the black market, however. They are especially likely to be abused in combination with other psychoactive substances to produce greater feelings of euphoria or to relieve the agitation created by other substances (Schuckit, 1995).

Barbiturates and benzodiazepines cause decreases in blood pressure, respiratory rate, and heart rate. In overdose, they can be extremely dangerous and even cause death from respiratory arrest or cardiovascular collapse. Overdose is especially likely when people take these substances (particularly benzodiazepines) with alcohol.

Inhalants are volatile substances that produce chemical vapors, which can be inhaled and which depress the central nervous system (Virani et al., 2009). One group of inhalants is solvents, including gasoline, glue, paint thinners, and spray paints. Users may inhale vapors directly from the can or bottle containing the substance, soak a rag with the substance and hold the rag to their mouth and nose, or place the substance in a paper or plastic bag and inhale the gases from the bag. The chemicals rapidly reach the lungs, bloodstream, and brain. Other inhalants are medical anesthetic gases, such as nitrous oxide ("laughing gas"), which also can be found in whipped cream dispensers and products that boost octane levels. Nitrites, another class of inhalants, dilate blood vessels and relax muscles and are used as sex enhancers. Illegally packaged nitrites are called "poppers" or "snappers" on the street (National Institute on Drug Abuse [NIDA], 2002d).

The greatest users of inhalants are young people. National surveys find that by fourth grade 6 percent of U.S. children have tried inhalants and that abuse peaks between seventh and ninth grades (NIDA, 2002d). Seventeen percent of eighth-graders report having used inhalants at sometime in their life (NIDA, 2002a). Some studies find that nearly all children on some Native American reservations have experimented with inhaling gasoline. Hispanic teenagers also appear to have higher rates of inhalant use than other groups of U.S. teenagers, and it is estimated that 500,000 children in Mexico City are addicted to inhalants (Hartman, 1998). Males are more likely than females to use inhalants.

Chronic users of inhalants may have a variety of respiratory irritations and rashes. Inhalants can cause permanent damage to the central nervous system, including degeneration and lesions of the brain; these can lead to cognitive deficits, including severe dementia. Recurrent use can also cause hepatitis and liver and kidney disease. Death can occur from depression of the respiratory or cardiovascular system. *Sudden sniffing death* is due to acute irregularities in heartbeat or loss of oxygen. Users sometimes suffocate when they fall unconscious with an inhalant-filled plastic bag over their nose and mouth. Users can also die or be seriously injured when the inhalants induce the delusion that they can do fantastic things, such as fly, and they then jump off a cliff or a tall building to test their ability (Virani et al., 2009).

TEST YOURSELF

1. What are the symptoms of alcohol intoxication and withdrawal?
2. What are the symptoms of benzodiazepine and barbiturate intoxication ?
3. What are the dangers of inhalant use?

APPLY IT Raul has been abusing alcohol much of his life. Now in his 50s, he has trouble remembering recent events or conversations and performing somewhat complex tasks, such as balancing his checkbook. His wife says he no longer has good judgment, for example, buying things the family can't afford just because a salesman is pressuring him. Which of the following might Raul's most recent symptoms be the result of?

a. alcohol withdrawal
b. alcohol-induced dementia
c. Korsakoff's syndrome
d. Wernicke's encephalopathy

Answers appear online at www.mhhe.com/nolen5e.

STIMULANTS

Stimulants activate the central nervous system, causing feelings of energy, happiness, and power; a decreased desire for sleep; and a diminished appetite (Table 14.6). Cocaine and the amphetamines (including the related methamphetamines) are the two types associated with severe substance-related disorders. Both impart a psychological lift or rush. They cause dangerous increases in blood pressure and heart rate, alter the rhythm and electrical activity of the heart, and constrict the blood vessels, which can lead to heart attacks, respiratory arrest, and seizures. In the United States, toxic reactions to cocaine and the amphetamines account for more than a third of drug-related emergency room visits (SAMHSA, 2008a).

Caffeine and nicotine also are stimulants and can result in diagnosable substance-related disorders.

TABLE 14.6 Intoxication with and Withdrawal from Stimulants

The stimulants activate the central nervous system.

Drug	Intoxication Symptoms	Withdrawal Symptoms
Cocaine and amphetamines	Behavioral changes (e.g., euphoria or affective blunting; changes in sociability; hypervigilance; interpersonal sensitivity; anxiety, tension, or anger; impaired judgment) Rapid heartbeat Dilation of pupils Elevated or lowered blood pressure Perspiration or chills Nausea or vomiting Weight loss Psychomotor agitation or retardation Muscular weakness Slowed breathing Chest pain Confusion, seizures, coma	Dysphoric mood Fatigue Vivid, unpleasant dreams Insomnia or hypersomnia Increased appetite Psychomotor retardation or agitation
Nicotine	Not a diagnosis in the *DSM-IV-TR*	Dysphoria or depressed mood Insomnia Irritability, frustration, or anger Anxiety Difficulty concentrating Restlessness Decreased heart rate Increased appetite or weight gain
Caffeine	Restlessness Nervousness Excitement Insomnia Flushed face Frequent urination Stomach upset Muscle twitching Rambling flow of thought or speech Rapid heartbeat Periods of inexhaustibility Psychomotor agitation	Marked fatigue or drowsiness Marked anxiety or depression Nausea or vomiting

Source: Reprinted with permission from the *Diagnostic and Statistical Manual of Mental Disorders,* Fourth Edition, Text Revision.

Although their psychological effects are not as severe as those of cocaine and amphetamines, these drugs—particularly nicotine—can have long-term negative effects.

Prescription stimulants, including Dexedrine and Ritalin, are used to treat asthma and other respiratory problems, obesity, neurological disorders, attention-deficit/hyperactivity disorder (ADHD, see Chapter 10), and a variety of other diseases. From 1990 to 2000, abuse of these drugs increased 165 percent; it has declined only slightly since 2000 (NIDA, 2002f; SAMHSA, 2008c). About 1 million people in the United States use stimulants for nonmedical reasons.

Cocaine

Cocaine, a white powder extracted from the coca plant, is one of the most addictive substances known. People snort the powder or inject it intravenously.

FIGURE 14.6 **Effects of Cocaine on Dopamine Systems.** Cocaine blocks transporters for the reuptake of dopamine, resulting in excess dopamine in the synapses.

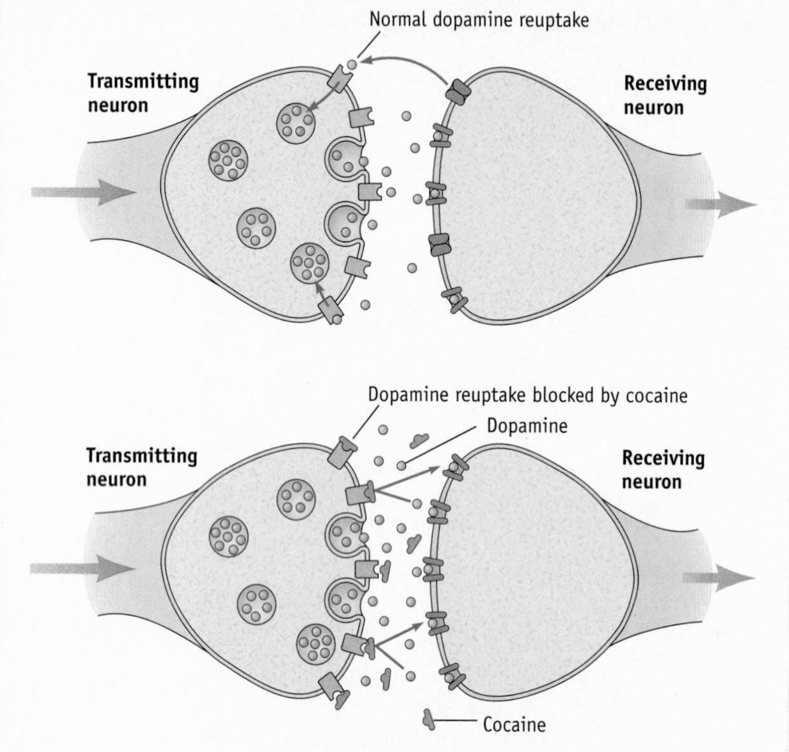

In the 1970s, even more powerful freebase cocaine appeared when users developed a method for separating the most potent chemicals in cocaine by heating it with ether. Freebase cocaine is usually smoked in a water pipe or mixed in a tobacco or marijuana cigarette. *Crack* is a form of freebase cocaine boiled down into tiny chunks, or rocks, and usually smoked.

Initially, cocaine produces a sudden rush of intense euphoria, followed by heightened self-esteem, alertness, energy, and feelings of competence and creativity. Users crave increasing amounts of the substance, for both its physiological and its psychological effects (Ruiz et al., 2007). When taken repeatedly or at high doses, however, it leads to grandiosity, impulsiveness, hypersexuality, compulsive behavior, agitation, and anxiety, reaching the point of panic and paranoia. Stopping use can induce exhaustion and depression.

Cocaine activates those areas of the brain that register reward and pleasure. Normally, a pleasurable event releases dopamine into the synapses in these areas. Dopamine then binds to receptors on neighboring synapses (Figure 14.6). Cocaine blocks the reuptake of dopamine into the transmitting neuron, causing it to accumulate in the synapse and maintaining the pleasurable feeling (Ruiz et al., 2007). The rapid, strong effects of cocaine on the brain's reward centers make this substance more likely than most to lead to abuse and dependence. The following case study illustrates this process.

CASE STUDY

Dr. Arnie Rosenthal is a 31-year-old white male dentist, married for 10 years with two children. His wife insisted he see a psychiatrist because of uncontrolled use of cocaine, which over the past year had made it increasingly difficult for him to function as a dentist. During the previous 5 years he used cocaine virtually every day, with only occasional 1- or 2-week periods of abstinence. For the past 4 years Rosenthal wanted to stop, but his desire was overridden by a "compulsion" to take the drug.

He began using marijuana after being married a year, smoking a joint each day after school and spending the evening staring at TV. When he graduated from dental school his wife was pregnant, and he was "scared to death" at the prospect of being a father. His deepening depression was characterized by social isolation, increased loss of interests, and frequent temper outbursts. He needed intoxication with marijuana, or occasionally sedatives, for sex, relaxation, and socialization. Following the birth of the child he "never felt so crazy," and his marijuana and sedative use escalated. Two years later, a second child was born. Dr. Rosenthal was financially successful, had moved to an expensive suburban home with a swimming pool, and had two cars and "everything my parents wanted for me." He was 27 years old, felt he had nothing to look forward to, and felt painfully isolated; drugs were no longer providing relief.

Rosenthal tried cocaine for the first time and immediately felt good. "I was no longer depressed. I used cocaine as often as possible because all my problems seemed to vanish, but I had to keep doing it. The effects were brief and it was very expensive, but I didn't care. When the immediate effects wore off, I'd feel even more miserable and depressed so that I did as much cocaine as I was able to obtain." He is now continuously nervous and irritable. (From Spitzer, R. L., Skodol, A. E., Gibbon, M., & Williams, J. B. W., 1983, *Psychopathology: A Case Book,* pp. 81–83. Copyright © 1983 The McGraw-Hill Companies, Inc. Reprinted with permission.)

Cocaine's effects wear off quickly, and the dependent person must take frequent doses to maintain a high. Tolerance also can develop, and the individual must obtain larger and larger amounts to experience a high (Ruiz et al., 2007). Cocaine dependents spend huge amounts of money on the substance and may engage in theft, prostitution, or drug dealing to obtain enough money to purchase it. Desperation can lead frequent users to participate in extremely dangerous behaviors. Many contract HIV, the virus that causes AIDS, by sharing needles with infected users or by having unprotected sex in exchange for money or cocaine (Ruiz et al., 2007).

Other frequent medical complications of cocaine use are disturbances in heart rhythm and heart attacks; respiratory failure; neurological effects, including strokes, seizures, and headaches; and gastrointestinal complications, including abdominal pain and nausea. Physical symptoms include chest pain, blurred vision, fever, muscle spasms, convulsions, and coma (Ruiz et al., 2007).

Fifteen percent of people in the United States have tried cocaine at least once (SAMHSA, 2008c). Its use has fallen since the mid-1980s. In 1986, 13 percent of adolescents said they had used cocaine in the past year; in 2007, a survey of twelfth-graders in U.S. high schools found that only 5 percent had used it in the past year (Monitoring the Future, 2008a). The decline has occurred primarily among casual users. There is some evidence that the use of crack has not fallen off in recent years (Monitoring the Future, 2008a).

Amphetamines

Amphetamines and the related *methamphetamines* are stimulants prescribed for the treatment of attention problems, narcolepsy, and chronic fatigue. They also are found in antihistamines (e.g., Sudafed) and diet drugs. Many stimulants are used appropriately under the supervision of physicians, but a great many doses are diverted to illegal use and abuse (Ruiz et al., 2007). Because of the potential for abuse, most states regulate over-the-counter sales of diet drugs and antihistamines. On the street, amphetamines are known as "speed," "meth," and "chalk." They are most often swallowed as pills but can be injected intravenously, and methamphetamine can be snorted ("crank") or smoked ("crystal meth" or "ice").

Amphetamines release the neurotransmitters dopamine and norepinephrine and block their reuptake. The symptoms of intoxication are similar to those of cocaine intoxication: euphoria, self-confidence, alertness, agitation, and paranoia (Ruiz et al., 2007).

Like cocaine, amphetamines can produce perceptual illusions. The movement of other people and objects may seem distorted or exaggerated. Users may hear frightening voices making derogatory statements about them, see sores all over their body, or feel snakes crawling on their arms. They may have delusions of being stalked that lead them to act out violently. Some users know that these experiences are not real, but others lose their grip on reality and develop *amphetamine-induced psychotic disorders* (Ruiz et al., 2007).

Legal problems typically arise for amphetamine abusers from aggressive or inappropriate behavior while intoxicated or as a result of buying the drug illegally. Tolerance develops quickly, as does physical dependence. Users may switch from swallowing pills to injecting amphetamines intravenously. Some go on a *speed run*, in which they inject amphetamines frequently over several days without eating or sleeping. Then they crash into a devastating depression. Acute withdrawal symptoms typically subside within a few days, but chronic users may experience mood instability, memory loss, confusion, paranoid thinking, and perceptual abnormalities for weeks, months, or even years. They often battle the withdrawal symptoms with another speed run (Ruiz et al., 2007).

Abuse of amphetamines and methamphetamines can lead to a number of medical issues, particularly cardiovascular problems—including rapid or irregular heartbeat, increased blood pressure, and irreversible, stroke-producing damage to the small blood vessels in the brain. Elevated body temperature and convulsions can occur during overdoses, leading to death. Sharing needles to inject amphetamines risks contracting HIV or hepatitis (Brick, 2008).

Abuse of these drugs has risen in recent years. In 2007, 7.5 percent of twelfth-graders reported using amphetamines in the past year, and 1.7 percent reported using methamphetamines (Monitoring the Future, 2008a). College students trying to stay up late to study may take them. Employers may even provide amphetamines to increase employee productivity. Use of methamphetamines is prevalent among gay and bisexual men, particularly among those who are HIV-positive (Halkitis, Green, & Mourgues, 2005).

With extended use, people become irritable and hostile and need more stimulants to avoid withdrawal effects. Their personal relationships and health decline. Between 1995 and 2002, emergency room visits involving amphetamines increased 54 percent in the United States (SAMHSA, 2005).

Nicotine

All the substances we have discussed thus far, except alcohol and the inhalants, are illegal for nonprescription use, and many laws regulate the use of alcohol. One of the most addictive substances known, however, is fully legal for use by adults and readily available to adolescents—nicotine.

Nicotine is an alkaloid found in tobacco. Cigarettes, the most popular nicotine delivery device, get this substance to the brain within seconds. In the United States, 70 percent of people over age 12 have smoked cigarettes at some time in their life, and 28 percent currently are smokers (SAMHSA, 2008c). Smoking usually begins in the early teens. A 2007 survey of twelfth-graders found that 46 percent had smoked a cigarette at some time in their life and that 9 percent were smoking regularly (Johnston et al., 2008). Among people who continue to smoke through age 20, 95 percent become daily smokers. Tobacco use has declined in the United States and other industrialized countries over the past few decades, thanks in part to significantly increased taxes on tobacco products, laws restricting their use in public places, and lawsuits limiting tobacco companies' ability to advertise. In contrast, tobacco use is increasing in developing countries.

In the United States, smoking rates have declined more for men than for women; men today are only slightly more likely than women to smoke (NIDA, 2002e; SAMHSA, 2008c). Female adolescents have been initiating smoking more frequently than males, and, once addicted to nicotine, women are less likely to quit smoking.

Nicotine operates on both the central and the peripheral nervous systems. It helps release several biochemicals in the brain, including dopamine, norepinephrine, serotonin, and the endogenous opioids. Although people often say they smoke to reduce stress, nicotine's physiological effects actually resemble the fight-or-flight response (see Chapter 5)—several systems in the body are aroused, including the cardiovascular and respiratory systems. The subjective sense that smoking reduces stress actually may reflect the reversal of tension and irritability that signal nicotine withdrawal. In other words, nicotine addicts need nicotine to feel normal because of its effects on the body and the brain (Ruiz et al., 2007).

In 1964, based on a review of 6,000 empirical studies, the surgeon general of the United States concluded that smoking, particularly cigarette smoking, causes lung cancer, bronchitis, and probably coronary heart disease. An estimated $80 billion in annual U.S. health care costs is attributable to smoking (NIDA, 2002e). Mortality rates for smokers are 70 percent greater than for nonsmokers, meaning that a person between ages 30 and 35 who smokes two packs a day will die 8 to 9 years earlier than a nonsmoker. Each year, an estimated 443,000 people in the United States die prematurely from smoking-related coronary heart disease, lung cancer, emphysema, or chronic bronchitis or from exposure to secondhand smoke. An additional 8.6 million people have a serious illness related to smoking (CDC, 2009). Women who smoke while pregnant give birth to smaller babies. The longer a person smokes and the more he or she smokes each day, the greater the health risks.

When chronic heavy smokers try to quit or are prohibited from smoking for an extended period, such as at work or on an airplane, they show severe withdrawal symptoms. They become depressed, irritable, angry, anxious, frustrated, restless, and hungry; they have trouble concentrating; and they desperately crave another cigarette. These symptoms are immediately relieved by smoking, another sign of physiological dependence (Ruiz et al., 2007).

Because nicotine is relatively cheap and available, dependents tend not to spend much time trying to obtain it. They may panic, however, if they run out of cigarettes and replacements are not available. They also may spend a large part of their day smoking or chewing tobacco, and they continue to use nicotine even though it is damaging their health (e.g., after they have been diagnosed with emphysema). They may skip social activities where smoking is not allowed or recreational activities such as sports because they have trouble breathing.

Over 70 percent of people who smoke say they want to quit (Goldstein, 1998). Quitting is difficult, however, in part because the withdrawal syndrome is difficult to withstand. Only about 7 percent of smokers who try to stop smoking are still abstinent after 1 year, and most relapse within a few days of quitting (NIDA, 2002e). The craving can remain after a smoker quits—50 percent of people who quit smoking report they have desired cigarettes in the past 24 hours (Goldstein, 1994). Nicotine patches and gum can help fight this urge.

Caffeine

Caffeine is by far the most heavily used stimulant; 75 percent of it is ingested through coffee (Chou, 1992). A cup of brewed coffee has about 100 milligrams of caffeine, and the average U.S. adult drinks about two cups per day. Other sources include tea (about 40 milligrams of caffeine per 6 ounces), caffeinated soda (45 milligrams per 12 ounces), over-the-counter analgesics and cold remedies (25–50 milligrams per tablet), weight-loss drugs (75–200 milligrams per tablet), and chocolate and cocoa (5 milligrams per bar).

Caffeine stimulates the central nervous system, increasing the levels of dopamine, norepinephrine, and serotonin. It also increases metabolism, body temperature, and blood pressure. The appetite wanes, and people feel more alert. But in doses equivalent to just two to three cups of coffee, caffeine can cause unpleasant symptoms, including restlessness, nervousness, and hand tremors. People may experience an upset stomach and feel their heart beating rapidly or irregularly. They may have trouble going to sleep later on and may need to urinate frequently. These are symptoms of *caffeine intoxication.* Extremely large doses of caffeine can cause extreme agitation, seizures, respiratory failure, and cardiac problems.

The *DSM-IV-TR* specifies that a diagnosis of caffeine intoxication should be given only if an individual experiences significant distress or impairment in functioning as a result of the symptoms. Someone who drinks too much coffee for several days in a row during exam week, for example, might be so agitated that she cannot sit through her exams and so shaky that she cannot drive a car; such a person could be given a diagnosis of caffeine intoxication.

Some heavy coffee drinkers who joke that they are "caffeine addicts" actually cannot be diagnosed with caffeine dependence disorder, according to the *DSM-IV-TR,* because dependence on the drug seems not to cause significant social and occupational problems. Still, caffeine users can develop tolerance and undergo withdrawal if they stop ingesting caffeine. They may require several cups of coffee in the morning to feel "normal" and may experience significant headaches, fatigue, and anxiety if they do not get their coffee.

TEST YOURSELF

1. What are the symptoms of intoxication from cocaine, amphetamines, and methamphetamines?
2. What are the symptoms of withdrawal from cocaine, amphetamines, and methamphetamines?
3. What are the dangers of using cocaine, amphetamines, and methamphetamines?
4. What effects does nicotine have on the body? What are the health effects of smoking?
5. What are the symptoms of caffeine intoxication?

APPLY IT Connie has been abusing amphetamines for 3 years. She was brought from a party to the emergency room, where she started thrashing around and attacking people, claiming they had turned into monsters and were trying to kill her. She did not seem to know where she was and claimed that the hospital personnel were part of a conspiracy to murder her. Connie may be suffering from which of the following?

a. Korsakoff's syndrome
b. amphetamine personality disorder
c. amphetamine-induced psychotic disorder
d. Wernicke's encephalopathy

Answers appear online at www.mhhe.com/nolen5e.

OPIOIDS

Morphine, heroin, codeine, and methadone are all **opioids.** They are derived from the sap of the opium poppy, which has been used for thousands of years to relieve pain. Our bodies produce natural opioids, including *endorphins* and *enkaphalins,* to cope with pain. For example, a sports injury induces the body to produce endorphins to reduce pain and avoid shock. Doctors also may prescribe synthetic opioids, such as hydrocodone (Lorcet, Lortab, Vicodin) or oxycodone (Percodan, Percocet, OxyContin) for pain.

Morphine was widely used as a pain reliever in the nineteenth century, until it was found to be highly addictive. Heroin was developed from morphine in the late nineteenth century and was used for a time for medicinal purposes. By 1917, however, it was clear that heroin and all the opioids have dangerous addictive properties, and Congress passed a law making heroin illegal and banning the other opioids except for specific medical needs. Heroin remained widely available on the street, however (Winger et al., 1992).

When used illegally, opioids often are injected into the veins (*mainlining*), snorted, or smoked. The initial symptom of opioid intoxication often is euphoria (Table 14.7). People describe a sensation in the abdomen like a sexual orgasm, referring to it as a *thrill, kick,* or *flash.* They may have a tingling sensation and a pervasive sense of warmth. They pass into a state of drowsiness, during which they are lethargic, their speech is slurred, and their mind may be clouded. They may experience periods of light sleep with vivid dreams. Pain is reduced (Ruiz et al., 2007). A person in this state is referred to as being *on the nod.* Severe intoxication can lead to unconsciousness, coma, and seizures.

TABLE 14.7 Intoxication with and Withdrawal from Opioids

The opioids include morphine, heroin, codeine, and methadone.

Drug	Intoxication Symptoms	Withdrawal Symptoms
Opioids	Behavioral changes (e.g., initial euphoria followed by apathy, dysphoria, psychomotor agitation or retardation, impaired judgment) Constriction of pupils Drowsiness or coma Slurred speech Attention and memory problems Hallucinations or illusions	Dysphoric mood Nausea or vomiting Muscle aches Tearing or nasal mucus discharge Dilation of pupils Goose bumps Sweating Diarrhea Yawning Fever Insomnia

Source: Reprinted with permission from the *Diagnostic and Statistical Manual of Mental Disorders,* Fourth Edition, Text Revision. Copyright © 2000 American Psychiatric Association.

Opioids can suppress the respiratory and cardiovascular systems to the point of death. The drugs are especially dangerous when combined with depressants, such as alcohol or sedatives. Withdrawal symptoms include dysphoria, an achy feeling in the back and legs, increased sensitivity to pain, and a craving for more opioids. The person may feel nausea, vomit, and experience profuse sweating and goose bumps, diarrhea, and fever (Ruiz et al., 2007). These symptoms usually appear within 8 to 16 hours of last use and peak within 36 to 72 hours. In chronic or heavy users, they may continue in strong form for 5 to 8 days and in a milder form for weeks to months.

Most street heroin is cut with other substances, so users do not know the actual strength of the drug or its true contents, leaving them at risk for overdose or death. Users also risk contracting HIV through contaminated needles or through unprotected sex, which many opioid abusers exchange for more heroin. In some areas of the United States, up to 60 percent of chronic heroin users have HIV. Intravenous users also can contract hepatitis, tuberculosis, serious skin abscesses, and deep infections. Women who use heroin during pregnancy risk miscarriage and premature delivery, and children born to addicted mothers are at increased risk for sudden infant death syndrome (Brady, Back, & Greenfield, 2009).

The abuse of and dependence on opioid pain relievers have increased significantly in the past decade, with 13 percent of the U.S. population admitting to nonmedical use of pain relievers at some time in their life (SAMHSA, 2008b). The most frequently abused drug is oxycodone (OxyContin); emergency room visits involving this drug increased 512 percent between 1995 and 2002 (SAMHSA, 2005). An estimated 11 million Americans age 12 and older have used oxycodone nonmedically at least once in their lifetime. About 5 percent of twelfth-graders report having used oxycodone in the past year, and nearly 10 percent report using hydrocodone (Vicodin) in the past year (Monitoring the Future, 2008a).

TEST YOURSELF

1. What drugs are considered opioids?
2. What are the symptoms of intoxication with opioids?
3. What are the symptoms of withdrawal from opioids?
4. What are the dangers of opioid use?

APPLY IT David is a college student who was prescribed oxycodone after painful knee surgery and who now is dependent on the drug. To his friends, he often appears how?

a. excessively happy or giddy
b. paranoid and hostile
c. hyper and agitated
d. drowsy and spacey

Answers appear online at www.mhhe.com/nolen5e.

HALLUCINOGENS AND PCP

Most of the substances we have discussed so far can produce perceptual illusions and distortions in large doses. The hallucinogens and phencyclidine (PCP) produce perceptual changes even in small doses (Table 14.8). A clear withdrawal syndrome has not been documented, so the *DSM-IV-TR* does not recognize withdrawal from these drugs as a diagnosis.

The **hallucinogens** are a mixed group of substances, including lysergic acid diethylamide (LSD) and peyote. The psychoactive effects of LSD were first discovered in 1943 when Dr. Albert Hoffman accidentally swallowed a minute amount and experienced visual hallucinations. He later purposefully swallowed a small amount of LSD and reported the effects.

VOICES

As far as I remember, the following were the most outstanding symptoms: vertigo, visual disturbances; the faces of those around me appeared as grotesque, colored masks; marked motor unrest, alternating with paresis; an intermittent heavy feeling in the head, limbs, and the entire body, as if they were filled with metal; cramps in the legs, coldness, and loss of feeling in the hands; a metallic taste on the tongue; dry constricted sensation in the throat; feeling of choking; confusion alternating between clear recognition of my condition, in which state I sometimes observed, in the manner of an independent, neutral observer, that I shouted half insanely or babbled incoherent words. Occasionally, I felt as if I were out of my body. The doctor found a rather weak pulse but an otherwise normal circulation. Six hours after ingestion of the LSD my condition had already improved considerably. Only the visual disturbances were still pronounced. Everything seemed to sway and the proportions were distorted like the reflections in the surface of moving water. Moreover, all objects appeared in unpleasant, constantly changing colors, the predominant shades being sickly green and blue. When I closed my eyes, an unending series of colorful, very realistic and fantastic images surged in upon me. A remarkable feature was the manner in which all acoustic perceptions (e.g., the noise of a passing car) were transformed into optical effects, every sound causing a corresponding colored hallucination constantly changing in shape and color like pictures in a kaleidoscope. (Hoffman, 1968, pp. 185–186)

TABLE 14.8 Intoxication with Hallucinogens and PCP

The hallucinogens and PCP cause a variety of perceptual and behavioral changes.

Drug	Intoxication Symptoms
Hallucinogens	Behavioral changes (e.g., marked anxiety or depression, the feeling that others are talking about you, fear of losing your mind, paranoia, impaired judgment)
	Perceptual changes while awake (e.g., intensification of senses, depersonalization, illusions, hallucinations)
	Dilation of pupils
	Rapid heartbeat
	Sweating
	Palpitations
	Blurring of vision
	Tremors
	Incoordination
PCP	Behavioral changes (e.g., belligerence, assaultiveness, impulsiveness, unpredictability, psychomotor agitation, impaired judgment)
	Involuntary rapid eyeball movement
	Hypertension
	Numbness
	Loss of muscle coordination
	Problems speaking due to poor muscle control
	Muscle rigidity
	Seizures or coma
	Exceptionally acute hearing
	Perceptual disturbances

Source: Reprinted with permission from the *Diagnostic and Statistical Manual of Mental Disorders,* Fourth Edition, Text Revision. Copyright © 2000 American Psychiatric Association.

As Hoffman describes, one symptom of intoxication from LSD and other hallucinogens is *synesthesia,* the overflow from one sensory modality to another. People say they hear colors and see sounds. They feel at one with their surroundings, and time seems to pass very slowly. Moods also may shift from depression to elation to fear. Some people become anxious. Others feel a sense of detachment and a great sensitivity for art, music, and feelings. These experiences lent the drugs the label *psychedelic,* from the Greek words for "soul" and "to make manifest." LSD was used in the 1960s as part of the consciousness-expanding movement (Winger et al., 1992).

The hallucinogens are dangerous drugs, however. Although LSD was legal for use in the early 1960s, by 1967 reports of "bad acid trips," or "bummers," had become common, particularly in the Haight-Ashbury district of San Francisco, where many LSD enthusiasts from around the United States congregated (Smith & Seymour, 1994). Symptoms included severe anxiety, paranoia, and loss of control. Some people on bad trips would walk off a roof or jump out a window, believing they could fly, or walk into the sea, believing they were "one with the universe." For some, the anxiety and hallucinations were severe enough to produce psychosis requiring hospitalization and long-term treatment. Some people experience flashbacks to their psychedelic experiences long after the drug has worn off.

Phencyclidine (PCP), also known as *angel dust, PeaCePill, Hog,* and *Tranq,* is manufactured as a powder to be snorted or smoked. Although PCP is not classified in the *DSM-IV-TR* as a hallucinogen, it has many of the same effects. At lower doses, it produces a sense of intoxication, euphoria or affective dulling, talkativeness, lack of concern, slowed reaction time, vertigo, eye twitching, mild hypertension, abnormal involuntary movements, and weakness. At intermediate doses, it leads to disorganized thinking, distortions of body image (e.g., feeling that one's arms are not part of one's body), depersonalization, and feelings of unreality. A user may become hostile, belligerent, and even violent (Morrison, 1998). At higher doses, PCP produces amnesia and coma, analgesia sufficient to allow surgery, seizures, severe respiratory problems, hypothermia, and hyperthermia. The effects begin immediately after injecting, snorting, or smoking and peak within minutes. Symptoms of severe intoxication can persist for several days; people with PCP intoxication often are misdiagnosed as having a psychotic disorder unrelated to substance use (Morrison, 1998).

Hallucinogen or PCP abuse is diagnosed when individuals repeatedly fail to fulfill major role obligations at school, work, or home due to intoxication with these drugs. They may use the drugs in dangerous situations, such as while driving a car, and they may have legal troubles due to their possession of the drugs. Because the drugs can cause paranoia or aggressive behavior, frequent users may find their work and social relationships affected. About 11 percent of the U.S. population reports having tried a hallucinogen or PCP, but only 0.4 percent report having used it in the past month (SAMHSA, 2002). Use is higher among teenagers, however, with 5 percent of twelfth-graders reporting use of a hallucinogen in the past year (Monitoring the Future, 2008a).

TEST YOURSELF

1. What are the symptoms of intoxication with hallucinogens?
2. What are the symptoms of intoxication with PCP?

APPLY IT Researchers in the 1950s thought that studying the effects of LSD would give them insights into another major psychiatric disorder. Which disorder do you think that was?

a. depression
b. schizophrenia
c. antisocial personality disorder
d. autism

Answers appear online at www.mhhe.com/nolen5e.

CANNABIS

The leaves of the **cannabis** (or hemp) plant can be cut, dried, and rolled into cigarettes or inserted into food and beverages. In North America, the result is known as *marijuana, weed, pot, grass, reefer,* and *Mary Jane*. Cannabis is the most commonly used illegal drug in the United States, with about 40 percent of the population reporting its use at some time in their life, and 6 percent in the past month (SAMHSA, 2008b). About 7 percent of the population would qualify for a diagnosis of cannabis abuse, and 2 to 3 percent for a diagnosis of cannabis dependence (Kendler & Prescott, 1998a; SAMHSA, 2008c).

Occasional use is widespread—30 percent of college students say they have used cannabis in the past year (Mohler-Kuo, Lee, & Wechsler, 2003). Use starts much earlier than college. About 50 percent of twelfth-graders say they have used it at some time in their life, and about 32 percent in the past year (Johnston et al., 2008). Some states have legalized the use of cannabis for medical purposes, such as reducing nausea among cancer patients.

The symptoms of cannabis intoxication may develop within minutes if the drug is smoked but may take a few hours to develop if it is taken orally (Table 14.9). The acute symptoms last 3 to 4 hours, but some may linger or recur for 12 to 24 hours. Intoxication usually begins with a "high" feeling of well-being, relaxation, and tranquillity. Users may feel dizzy, sleepy, or dreamy. They may become more aware of their environment, and everything may seem funny. They may become grandiose or lethargic. People who already are very anxious, depressed, or angry may become more so (Ruiz et al., 2007).

TABLE 14.9 Intoxication with Cannabis

Cannabis is the most commonly used illegal drug in the United States.

Drug	Intoxication Symptoms
Cannabis	Behavioral changes (e.g., impaired motor coordination, euphoria, anxiety, sensation of slowed time, impaired judgment)
	Red eyes
	Increased appetite
	Dry mouth
	Rapid heartbeat

Source: Reprinted with permission from the *Diagnostic and Statistical Manual of Mental Disorders,* Fourth Edition, Text Revision. Copyright © 2000 American Psychiatric Association.

Although many college students view cannabis as a benign or safe drug, it can significantly affect cognitive and motor functioning. People taking cannabis may believe they are thinking profound thoughts, but their short-term memories are impaired to the point that they cannot remember thoughts long enough to express them in sentences. Motor performance is also impaired. People's reaction times are slower and their concentration and judgment deficient, and as a result they are at risk for accidents. The cognitive impairments caused by cannabis can last up to a week after heavy use stops (Pope, Gruber, et al., 2001). These effects appear to be greater for women than for men (Pope et al., 1997).

At moderate to large doses, cannabis users experience perceptual distortions, feelings of depersonalization, and paranoid thinking. Some find these hallucinogenic effects pleasant, but others become frightened. Some users may have severe anxiety episodes resembling panic attacks (Phariss, Millman, & Beeder, 1998).

The physiological symptoms of cannabis intoxication include increased or irregular heartbeat, increased appetite, and dry mouth. Cannabis smoke is irritating and increases the risk of chronic cough, sinusitis, bronchitis, and emphysema. It contains even larger amounts of known carcinogens than does tobacco and thus creates a high risk of cancer. The chronic use of cannabis lowers sperm count in men and may cause irregular ovulation in women (Ruiz et al., 2007).

Physical tolerance to cannabis can develop, so users need greater amounts to avoid the symptoms of withdrawal, which include loss of appetite, hot flashes, runny nose, sweating, diarrhea, and hiccups (Kouri & Pope, 2000).

TEST YOURSELF

1. What are the symptoms of intoxication from cannabis?
2. What are the dangers of cannabis use?

APPLY IT Gail smoked a marijuana cigarette just before an exam in her abnormal psychology class to calm her nerves. What is the most likely consequence of Gail's action?

a. Gail develops hallucinations during the exam.
b. Gail passes out during the exam.
c. Gail performs very well on the exam because she is so calm.
d. Gail forgets her answer to an essay question before she can finish writing it.

Answers appear online at www.mhhe.com/nolen5e.

OTHER DRUGS OF ABUSE

Drug sellers are creative in coming up with new psychoactive substances. Often these start with legitimate medicinal purposes, then are hijacked or transformed into street drugs. We will discuss *ecstasy* (3,4-methylenedioxymethamphetamine, or MDMA), *GHB* (gamma-hydroxybutyrate), *ketamine,* and *rohypnol* (flunitrazepam). These drugs have been associated with nightclubs and all-night dance parties. Emergency room visits involving these drugs doubled from 1994 to 1999 but have decreased somewhat since 2000 (SAMHSA, 2008a).

Ecstasy has the stimulant effects of an amphetamine along with occasional hallucinogenic properties (NIDA, 2009). Users experience heightened energy and restlessness and claim that their social inhibitions decrease and their affection for others increases. Even short-term use can have long-term negative effects on cognition and health, however. People who use ecstasy score lower on tests related to attention, memory, learning, and general intelligence than do people who do not use the drug. The euphoric effects of ecstasy, and some of the brain damage, may be due to alterations in the functioning of serotonin in the brain—serotonin levels in ecstasy users are half those in people who do not use it (Gold, Tabrah, & Frost-Pineda, 2001). Long-term users risk

There has been an increase in recent years in the use of drugs as part of the club scene.

several cardiac problems and liver failure, and they show increased rates of anxiety, depression, psychotic symptoms, and paranoia (Gold, et al., 2001). Another effect of ecstasy is teeth-grinding; some users suck a baby's pacifier at parties to relieve this.

GHB is a central nervous system depressant approved for the treatment of the sleep disorder narcolepsy (NIDA, 2008a). At low doses, it can relieve anxiety and promote relaxation. At higher doses, it can result in sleep, coma, or death. In the 1980s, GHB was widely used by bodybuilders and athletes to lose fat and build muscle and was available over the counter in health food stores. In 1990, it was banned except under the supervision of a physician due to reports of severe side effects, including high blood pressure, wide mood swings, liver tumors, and violent behavior. Other side effects include sweating, headache, decreased heart rate, nausea, vomiting, impaired breathing, loss of reflexes, and tremors (NIDA, 2008a). GHB is also considered a *date-rape drug* because it has been associated with sexual assaults (NIDA, 2008a). It goes by the street names Grievous Bodily Harm, G., Liquid Ecstasy, and Georgia Home Boy.

Ketamine is a rapid-acting anesthetic that produces hallucinogenic effects ranging from rapture to paranoia to boredom (NIDA, 2008a). Ketamine can elicit an out-of-body or near-death experience. It also can render the user comatose. It has effects similar to those of PCP, including numbness, loss of coordination, a sense of invulnerability, muscle rigidity, aggressive or violent behavior, slurred or blocked speech, an exaggerated sense of strength, and a blank stare. Because ketamine is an anesthetic, users feel no pain, which can lead them to injure themselves (NIDA, 2008a).

A ketamine high usually lasts 1 hour but can last as long as 4 to 6 hours, and it takes 24 to 48 hours for users to feel normal again. Large doses can produce vomiting and convulsions and may lead to oxygen starvation in the brain and muscles. One gram can cause death. Ketamine is another date-rape drug used to anesthetize victims (NIDA, 2008a).

One widely known date-rape drug is rohypnol, which goes by the slang names Roofies, Rophies, Roche, and the Forget-Me-Not Pill. It is a benzodiazepine and has sedative and hypnotic effects (NIDA, 2008a). Users may experience a high, as well as muscle relaxation, drowsiness, impaired judgment, blackouts, hallucinations, dizziness, and confusion. Rohypnol tablets can easily be crushed and slipped into someone's drink. Rohypnol is odorless, colorless, and tasteless, so victims often don't notice their drink has been altered. Side effects can include headaches, muscle pain, and seizures. In combination with alcohol or other depressants, rohypnol can be fatal (NIDA, 2008a).

TEST YOURSELF

1. What are the symptoms of ecstasy intoxication? What are the dangers of its use?
2. What are the symptoms of GHB intoxication? What are the dangers of its use?
3. What are the symptoms of ketamine intoxication? What are the dangers of its use?
4. What are the symptoms of rohypnol intoxication? What are the dangers of its use?

APPLY IT Jerry has been using ecstasy almost every weekend for a few years. He loves the euphoric feeling it gives him, but he has noticed over the past year that he has had increasing problems maintaining his attention and concentration on the job. The mood and cognitive effects Jerry is experiencing may be due to changes in levels of ________ in his brain.

a. serotonin
b. GABA
c. steroids
d. hallucinogens

Answers appear online at www.mhhe.com/nolen5e.

THEORIES OF SUBSTANCE USE, ABUSE, AND DEPENDENCE

All the substances we have discussed affect several biochemicals that can have direct reinforcing effects on the brain. The brain appears to have its own "pleasure pathway" that affects our experience of reward. This pathway begins in the midbrain ventral tegmental area, then progresses through the nucleus accumbens and on to the anterior cingulate area of the frontal cortex. It is particularly rich in neurons sensitive to the neurotransmitter dopamine (Kalivas & Volkow, 2005).

Some drugs, such as amphetamines and cocaine, directly increase the availability of dopamine in this pathway, producing a strong sense of reward or a high. Other drugs increase the availability of dopamine more indirectly. For example, the neurons in the ventral tegmental area are inhibited from continuously firing by GABA neurons, so the firing of GABA neurons reduces the high caused by activity in the dopamine neurons. The opiate drugs inhibit GABA, which stops the GABA neurons from inhibiting dopamine, making dopamine available in the reward center (Kalivas & Volkow, 2005).

Other areas of the frontal cortex, including the orbitofrontal cortex, the dorsolateral frontal cortex, and the inferior frontal gyrus, play important roles in controlling the urge to drink alcohol or use drugs (Bechara, 2005; Goldstein & Volkow, 2002). Individuals whose reward network overpowers their control network may be more likely to use substances (Goldstein & Volkow, 2002; Hutchison, 2010).

The chronic use of psychoactive substances alters the reward centers, causing a craving for these substances (Robinson & Berridge, 1993). The repeated use of substances such as cocaine, heroin, and amphetamines causes the brain to reduce its production of dopamine, with the result that dopamine receptors in the brain become less sensitive. As the brain produces less dopamine, more of the drug is needed to produce the desired effects. If the individual stops taking the drug, the brain does not immediately compensate for the loss of dopamine, and withdrawal symptoms occur. Also, because the brain is not producing its typical amount of dopamine, the person may feel sad and unmotivated and may have difficulty experiencing pleasure from other sources, such as food or happy events. A powerful craving for the drug sets in because only the drug can produce pleasure (Robinson & Berridge, 1993).

Psychoactive drugs also affect a number of other biochemical and brain systems. Alcohol has sedative and antianxiety effects largely by enhancing the activity of the neurotransmitter GABA in the septal/hippocampal system. Alcohol also affects serotonin systems, which are associated with changes in mood (Brick, 2008).

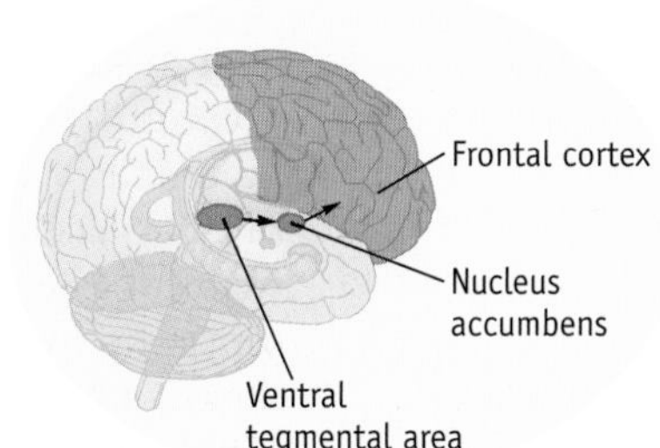

The brain's "pleasure pathway" begins in the ventral tegmental area, then goes through the nucleus accumbens and on to the frontal cortex. It is rich in neurons sensitive to dopamine.

Many people never try most of the substances discussed in this chapter, and most who do never abuse or become dependent on them. Why not? We turn now to theories of substance abuse and dependence that try to explain differences in vulnerability to substance-related disorders. Most theories focus on alcohol abuse and dependence, probably because these disorders are more widespread. However, several theories have been applied to explain abuse and dependence on substances other than alcohol, and we note these in our discussion.

Biological Theories

Many biological theories of substance-use disorders focus on genetics and neurotransmitters. Research suggests that people who become substance-dependent or -abusive may have different physiological reactions to substances than people who do not.

Genetic Factors

Family history, adoption, and twin studies all suggest that genetics may play a substantial role in determining who is at risk for substance-use disorders (see reviews by Agrawal & Lynskey, 2008; Gelernter & Kranzler, 2008; Kaufman, 2008). Family studies show that the relatives of people with substance-related disorders are eight times more likely to also have a substance disorder than are the relatives of people with no such disorder (Merikangas, Dierker, & Szatmari, 1998). There seems to be a common underlying genetic vulnerability to substance abuse and substance dependence in general (Tsuang et al., 1998), perhaps accounting for the fact that individuals who use one substance are likely to use several.

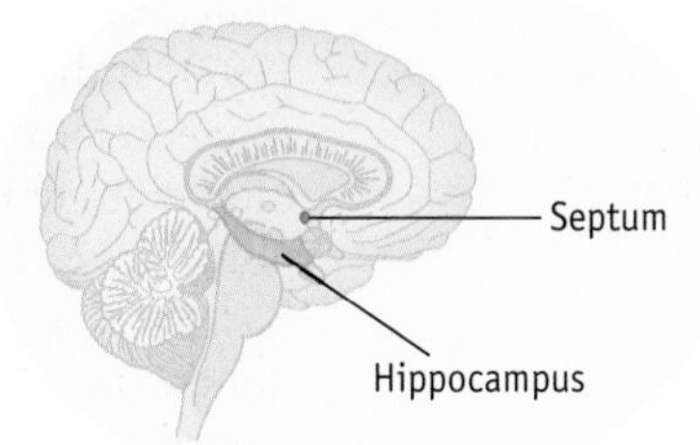

Alcohol has its sedative and antianxiety effects largely by enhancing the activity of the neurotransmitter GABA in the septal/hippocampal system. It also affects serotonin systems, which influence mood.

Twin studies also indicate a genetic component to substance abuse (Crabbe, 2002; Kendler & Prescott, 1998b; Lerman et al., 1999). A study of more than 3,000 male twins found a concordance rate for alcohol dependence among monozygotic twins of 0.48, compared with a rate of 0.32 among dizygotic twins (Prescott and Kendler, 1999). Evidence of heritability was strong for early-onset alcohol dependence (first symptoms before age 20), but not for late-onset alcohol dependence.

Much research has focused on the genes controlling the dopamine system, given its importance in the reinforcing properties of substances. Genetic variation in the dopamine receptor gene (labeled DRD2) and the dopamine transporter gene (labeled SLC6A3) may influence how the brain processes dopamine, thereby affecting how reinforcing a person finds substances such as nicotine (Hasin, Hatzenbuehler, & Waxman, 2006).

Reward Sensitivity

People clearly differ in their sensitivity to the rewarding properties of substances. Individuals dependent on various drugs score higher on self-report measures of reward sensitivity (Franken, Muris, & Georgieva, 2006). Higher reward sensitivity is also correlated with earlier onset of alcohol consumption in young adults (Pardo, Aguilar, Molinuevo, & Torrubia, 2007), alcohol use and abuse in nonclinical samples (Jorm et al., 1999; Loxton & Dawe, 2001), and craving and positive mood responses to alcohol cues in young-adult heavy drinkers (Zisserson & Palfai, 2007).

One physiological marker of reward sensitivity may be heart rate acceleration in response to rewarding stimuli (Fowles et al., 1982). Alcohol stimulates heart rate in humans, and an exaggerated heart rate response to an intoxicating dose of alcohol is found in people who are alcohol dependent or have a family history of alcohol dependence (Conrod, Peterson, Pihl, & Mankowski, 1997). Individuals who experience greater heart rate acceleration in response to alcohol also report more subjective feelings of elation, energy, and outgoingness as blood alcohol levels rise (Brunelle, Barrett, & Pihl, 2007). Children of alcohol dependents may experience these subjective stimulant effects more than do children of nondependents. These physiological and subjective responses to alcohol may make alcohol more rewarding and motivate its consumption (Newlin & Thomson, 1990). Individuals who show an exaggerated heart rate response to alcohol also show an increased quantity and frequency of consumption (Brunelle & Pihl, 2007).

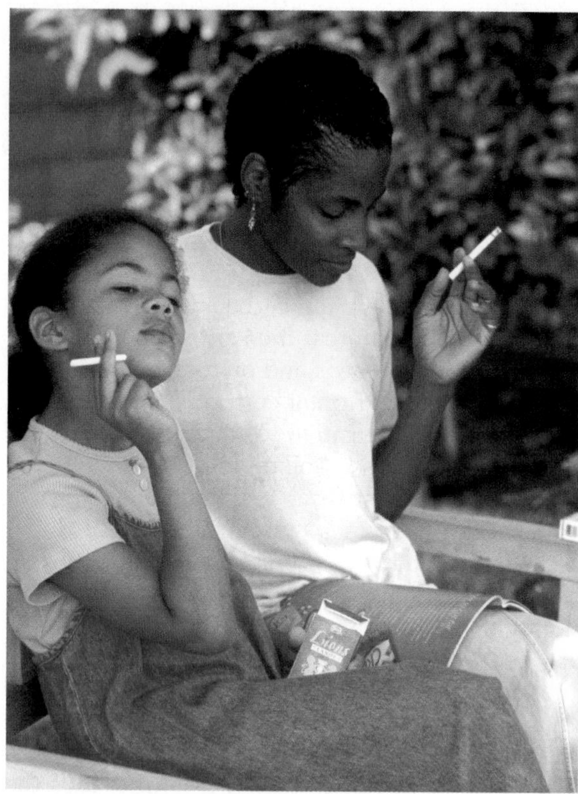

Children may learn substance-related behaviors from their parents.

Psychological Theories

Social learning theories (see Chapter 2) suggest that children and adolescents may learn substance-use behaviors from the modeling of their parents and important others in their culture. Even as preschoolers, the children of heavy drinkers are more likely than other children to be able to identify alcoholic drinks and view alcohol use as a part of daily life (Zucker, Kincaid, Fitzgerald, & Bingham, 1995). Children whose parents abuse alcohol by frequently getting drunk or by driving while intoxicated learn that these are acceptable behaviors, and thus they are more likely to engage in them (Chassin, Pitts, DeLucia, & Todd, 1999).

Because alcohol-related problems are more common among males than females, most of the adults modeling inappropriate use of alcohol are male. In turn, because children are more likely to learn from adults who are similar to themselves, male children and adolescents may be more likely to learn these behaviors than female children and adolescents. Thus, maladaptive patterns of alcohol use may be passed down through the males in a family through modeling (Chassin et al., 1999).

The cognitive theories of alcohol abuse have focused on people's expectations of alcohol's effects and their beliefs about the appropriateness of using it to cope with stress (Marlatt, Baer, Donovan, & Kivlahan, 1988). People who expect alcohol to reduce their distress and who do not have more adaptive means of coping (e.g., problem solving or supportive friends or family) are more likely than others to drink alcohol when they are upset and to have social problems related to drinking (Cooper et al., 1992). In long-term studies of the sons of alcohol dependents, men who used alcohol to cope and relax were more likely to develop alcohol abuse or dependence (Schuckit, 1998).

One personality characteristic consistently related to an increased risk of substance abuse and dependence is *behavioral undercontrol,* or the tendency to be impulsive, sensation-seeking, and prone to antisocial behaviors such as violating laws. People with high levels of behavioral undercontrol take psychoactive drugs at an earlier age, ingest more psychoactive drugs, and are more likely to be diagnosed with substance abuse or dependence (McGue et al., 2001; White, Xie, & Thompson, 2001). Behavioral undercontrol runs strongly in families, and twin studies suggest that this may be due in part to genes (Rutter et al., 1999). Thus, genetics may influence behavioral undercontrol, which in turn influences the risk that individuals will develop substance use disorders.

Sociocultural Perspectives

The reinforcing effects of substances—the highs stimulants produce, the calming and "zoning out" effects of the depressants and opioids—may be more attractive to people under chronic stress. Thus, rates of substance abuse and dependence are higher among people living in poverty, women in abusive relationships, and adolescents whose parents fight frequently and violently (Zucker, Chermack, & Curran, 1999). For these people, the effects of substances may be especially reinforcing. They also may think that they have little to lose. Many people dependent on substances were introduced to them by family members and grew up in horrible conditions that everyone around them sought to escape through substance use (Zucker et al., 1995), as did LaTisha.

VOICES

LaTisha, 35 years old when interviewed, was born and raised in Miami. Her mother was a barmaid and she never knew her father. She grew up with two brothers and four sisters, all of whom have different fathers. Her mother used pills during LaTisha's childhood, particularly Valium.

At 12 LaTisha took her first alcoholic drink, introduced to her by her mother. She didn't drink regularly until she was 17, although she started sniffing glue at 13. LaTisha's mother often brought men home from the bar to have sex with them for money. At 14, LaTisha's mother introduced her to prostitution by setting her up with "dates" from the bar. LaTisha was not aware until years later that the men had been paying her mother. LaTisha also recalls having been sexually abused by one of her mother's male friends when she was about 8.

When LaTisha was 16, her older brother returned home from the army. He and his friends smoked marijuana, and to "be with the crowd," LaTisha also began smoking it. At a party, her brother introduced her to "downers"—prescription sedatives and tranquilizers. LaTisha began taking pills regularly, eventually as many as 15 a day for about a year and a half. She most often used both Valium and Quaalude.

By the time she was 17, LaTisha's brother had introduced her to heroin. Almost immediately, she began speedballing—injecting as well as snorting heroin, cocaine, and various amphetamines. During all the phases of LaTisha's injection-substance use, sharing needles was common. By age 24, LaTisha was mainlining heroin and turning tricks every day. (Inciardi, James A., Lockwood, D., & Pottieger, A. E., *Women and Crack-Cocaine,* 1st edition, © 1993, pp. 160–161. Reprinted by permission of Pearson Education, Inc., Upper Saddle River, NJ.)

It does not take conditions as extreme as LaTisha's to create an atmosphere that promotes substance use and abuse. Subtler environmental reinforcements and punishments clearly influence people's substance-use habits. Some societies discourage any use of alcohol, often due to religious beliefs, and alcohol abuse and dependence are rare in these societies. Other societies, including many European cultures, allow the drinking of alcohol but strongly discourage excessive drinking and irresponsible behavior while intoxicated. Alcohol-related disorders are less common in these societies than in societies with few restrictions, either legal or cultural, on alcohol use (Sher et al., 2005).

Gender Differences

Substance use, particularly alcohol use, is more acceptable for men than for women in many societies.

Women suffer the effects of excessive alcohol use at lower doses than men do.

Heavy drinking is part of what "masculine" men do and is modeled by heroes and cultural icons. In contrast, until recently heavy drinking signified that a woman was "not a lady." Societal acceptance of heavy drinking by women has increased in recent generations, as has the rate of alcohol use among young women (Nolen-Hoeksema, 2004).

Women tend to be less likely than men to carry risk factors for drug and alcohol abuse and dependence (Nolen-Hoeksema, 2004). They appear less likely to have personality traits associated with substance-use disorder (behavioral undercontrol, sensation seeking). They also appear less motivated to use alcohol to reduce distress and less likely to expect drug consumption to have a positive outcome (Nolen-Hoeksema & Harrell, 2002).

Women suffer alcohol-related physical illnesses at lower levels of exposure to alcohol than men do (Fillmore et al., 1997). In addition, heavy alcohol use is associated with reproductive problems in women. Women may be more likely to experience greater cognitive and motor impairment due to alcohol than do men and to suffer physical harm and sexual assault following alcohol use (Abbey, Ross, McDuffie, & McAuslan, 1996).

When they do use alcohol, women may notice that they feel intoxicated much sooner than men, and they may be more likely to find these effects aversive or frightening, leading them to inhibit their consumption (Nolen-Hoeksema, 2004). This lower consumption, in turn, protects women from developing tolerance to high doses of alcohol, as well as from risking alcohol-related social and occupational problems.

When women become substance abusers, their patterns and reasons for use tend to differ from those of men. Men tend to begin using substances in the context of socializing with male friends, while women most often are initiated by family members, partners, or lovers (McCrady et al., 2009). One study found that 70 percent of female crack users were living with men who also were substance users, and many were living with multiple abusers (Inciardi et al., 1993). Perhaps because women's drug use is more closely tied to their intimate relationships, studies have found that treatments that include their partners tend to be more effective in reducing abuse and dependence in women (McCrady et al., 2009).

TEST YOURSELF

1. How do psychoactive substances affect reward systems in the brain?
2. What is the role of genetics in substance-use disorders?
3. What is the role of reward sensitivity in substance use?
4. What are the psychological theories of risk for substance-use disorders?
5. What role do sociocultural factors play in substance-use disorders?
6. What are some reasons for gender differences in substance-use disorders?

APPLY IT Thomas grew up in a home where both parents were dependent on alcohol; fought all the time, sometimes violently; and had trouble holding down jobs. The family was chronically impoverished. Thomas became dependent on alcohol at an early age. Which of the following theories explains why Thomas developed alcohol dependency?

a. genetic theory
b. behavioral theory
c. sociocultural theory
d. genetic, behavioral, and sociocultural theories

Answers appear online at www.mhhe.com/nolen5e.

TREATMENTS FOR SUBSTANCE-RELATED DISORDERS

The treatment of substance-related disorders is challenging, and media accounts of celebrity drug abusers who are in rehab one month, out the next, and back a short time later suggest that it seldom is effective. Meta-analyses and reviews of existing treatments suggest that, as a whole, they help only about 17 to 35 percent of substance-dependent individuals abstain for up to 1 year (Hutchison, 2010). We will review the most common and best-supported biological and psychosocial treatments.

Biological Treatments

Medications can help wean individuals off a substance, reduce their desire for it, and maintain their use at a controlled level (O'Malley & Kosten, 2006).

Antianxiety Drugs, Antidepressants, and Antagonists

Although many substance-dependent people can withstand withdrawal symptoms with emotional support, others may require medications. For alcohol dependents, a benzodiazepine, which has depressant effects similar to those of alcohol, can reduce tremors and anxiety, decrease pulse and respiration rates, and stabilize blood pressure (Ntais, Pakos, Kyzas, & Ioannidis, 2005). The dosage is decreased each day so that a patient withdraws from the alcohol slowly but does not become dependent on the benzodiazepine.

Antidepressant drugs sometimes are used to treat individuals with substance dependence who are depressed, but their efficacy in treating either alcohol or other drug problems or depression without psychotherapy has not been consistently supported (Nunes & Levine, 2004). People have widely different responses to the SSRIs, which currently are not well understood (Naranjo & Knoke, 2001).

Antagonist drugs block or change the effects of the addictive drug, reducing the desire for it. *Naltrexone* and *naloxone* are opioid antagonists—they block the effects of opioids such as heroin. Theoretically, this can reduce the desire for and therefore the use of the addictive drug. The opioid antagonists must be administered very carefully, however, because they can cause severe withdrawal reactions in people addicted to opioids (O'Malley & Kosten, 2006).

Naltrexone has also proven useful in treating alcohol dependents and abusers, possibly because it blocks the effects of endorphins during drinking. Alcohol dependents taking naltrexone report a diminished craving for alcohol and thus drink less (O'Malley & Kosten, 2006).

The drug acamprosate affects glutamate and GABA receptors in the brain, which are involved in the craving for alcohol. Meta-analyses of clinical trials show that acamprosate can maintain abstinence from alcohol better than a placebo (O'Malley & Kosten, 2006).

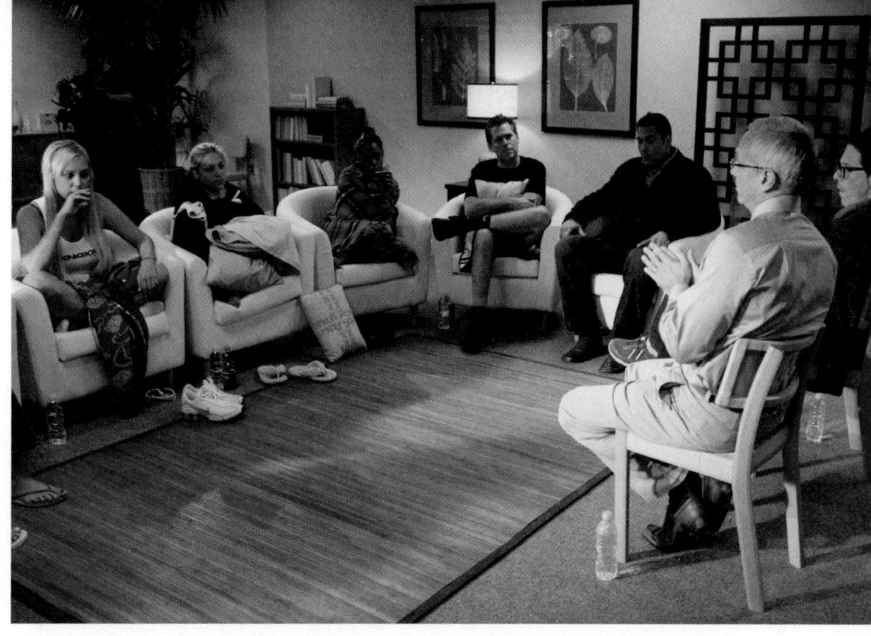

Dr. Drew Pinsky treats patients with various substance-related disorders on the VH1 TV show *Celebrity Rehab.*

A drug that can make alcohol actually punishing is *disulfiram,* commonly called *Antabuse* (Carroll, 2001). Just one alcoholic drink can make people taking disulfiram feel sick and dizzy and can make them vomit, blush, and even faint. People must be very motivated to remain on disulfiram, and it works to reduce alcohol consumption only as long as they take it.

The pharmacological treatment of nicotine dependence uses two general approaches (Mooney & Hatsukami, 2001). Most common is nicotine replacement therapy—the use of nicotine gum, patch, nasal spray, or inhaler to prevent withdrawal effects. It is hoped that the individual will gradually reduce use of the nicotine replacement, slowly being weaned off nicotine's physiological effects.

The other approach is using prescription medication that reduces the craving for nicotine. One drug approved for this use is the antidepressant bupropion (marketed for smoking cessation as Zyban). The ways bupropion helps people stop smoking are not currently clear but may involve changes in levels of the neurotransmitter dopamine (Mooney & Hatsukami, 2001). A drug called varenicline (Chantix), which binds to and partially stimulates nicotine receptors, also has been shown to reduce cravings for nicotine products and decrease their pleasure (Jorenby et al., 2006).

Methadone Maintenance Programs

Gradual withdrawal from heroin can be achieved with **methadone.** This drug is itself an opioid, but it has less potent and less long-lasting effects than heroin when taken orally. The person dependent on heroin takes methadone to reduce extreme negative withdrawal symptoms. Those who take heroin while on methadone do not experience heroin's intense psychological effects, because methadone blocks receptors for it (O'Malley & Kosten, 2006).

Although the goal of treatment is to eventually withdraw individuals from methadone, some patients use it for years under a physician's care. Such *methadone maintenance programs* are controversial. Some people believe they allow the heroin dependent to simply transfer dependency to another substance that is legal and provided by a physician. Others believe methadone maintenance is the only way to keep some heroin dependents from going back on the street and relapsing. Studies find that patients in such programs are much more likely to remain in psychological treatment than patients who try to withdraw from heroin without methadone and also are less likely to relapse into heroin use (Mattick et al., 2003).

Behavioral and Cognitive Treatments

Several behavioral and cognitive techniques have proven helpful in the treatment of substance-use disorders (Carroll & Rounsaville, 2006). They have certain goals in common. The first is to motivate the individual to stop using the addictive drug. People who enter treatment often are ambivalent about stopping use and may have been forced into treatment against their desire. The second goal is to teach new coping skills to replace the use of substances to cope with stress and negative feelings. The third goal is to change the reinforcements for using substances—for example, an individual may need to disengage from social circles that encourage drug use. The fourth is to enhance the individual's support from nonusing friends and family. The final goal often is to foster adherence to pharmacotherapies in conjunction with psychotherapy.

Behavioral Treatments

Behavioral treatments based on *aversive classical conditioning* are sometimes used to treat alcohol dependency and abuse, alone or in combination with biological or other psychosocial therapies (Finney & Moos, 1998; Schuckit, 1995). Drugs such as disulfiram (Antabuse) that make the ingestion of alcohol unpleasant or toxic are given to people who are alcohol dependent. Eventually, through classical conditioning, people develop conditioned responses to alcohol—namely, nausea and vomiting. They then learn to avoid alcohol, through operant conditioning, in order to avoid the aversive response. Aversive conditioning is effective in reducing alcohol consumption, at least in the short term (Schuckit, 1995). "Booster" sessions often are needed to reinforce this conditioning, because it tends to weaken with time.

Covert sensitization therapy uses imagery to create associations between thoughts of alcohol use and thoughts of highly unpleasant consequences. An example of a sensitization scene that a therapist might take a client through begins as follows.

VOICES

You finish the first sip of beer, and you . . . notice a funny feeling in your stomach. . . . Maybe another drink will help. . . . As you tip back . . . that funny feeling in your stomach is stronger, and you feel like you have to burp. . . . You swallow again, trying to force it down, but it doesn't work. You can feel the gas coming up. . . . You swallow more, but suddenly your mouth is filled with a sour liquid that burns the back of your throat and goes up your nose. . . . [You] spew the liquid all over the counter and sink. . . . (Rimmele, Miller, & Dougher, 1989, p. 135)

The imagery gets even more graphic. Covert sensitization techniques seem to be effective in creating conditioned aversive responses to the sight and smell of alcohol and in reducing alcohol consumption.

Contingency management programs provide reinforcements for individuals to curtail their use of substances, for example, employment, housing, or vouchers for purchases at local stores. Studies show that individuals dependent on heroin, cocaine, marijuana, or alcohol will remain in treatment longer and be much more likely to become abstinent when they are provided with incentives contingent on submitting drug-free urine specimens (Carroll & Rounsaville, 2006).

Cognitive Treatments

Interventions based on the cognitive models of alcohol abuse and dependency help clients identify situations in which they are most likely to drink and lose control over their drinking, as well as their expectations that alcohol will help them cope in those situations (Daley & Marlatt, 2006). Therapists work with clients to challenge these expectations by reviewing alcohol's negative effects on the clients' behavior. Perhaps a client was feeling anxious at a recent party and began to drink heavily.

The therapist might have the client recount his embarrassing behavior while intoxicated, challenging the notion that the alcohol helped him cope effectively. Therapists also help clients learn to handle stressful situations in adaptive ways, such as seeking the help of others or engaging in active problem solving. Finally, therapists help clients learn to say "No, thanks" when they are offered a drink and to deal with social pressure by using assertiveness skills.

The following is an excerpt from a discussion between a therapist and a client with alcohol-related problems in which the therapist is helping the client generate strategies for coping with the stress of a possible job promotion. The therapist encourages the client to brainstorm coping strategies and refrains from evaluating them for the moment so the client will feel free to generate as many strategies as possible.

VOICES

Client: I really want this job, and it'll mean a lot more money for me, not only now but also at retirement. Besides, if I refused the promotion, what would I tell my wife or my boss?

Therapist: Rather than worrying about that for the moment, why don't we explore what kinds of possible behavioral options you have regarding this job promotion? Remember, don't evaluate the options now. Alternatives, at this point, can include anything even remotely possible; what we want you to do is come up with a range of possible alternatives. You don't have to carry out an alternative just because you consider it.

Client: You know, I could do what I usually do in these kinds of situations. In fact, being as nervous as I've been these past couple of months, I've done that quite often.

Therapist: You mean drinking?

Client: Yeah, I've been drinking quite heavily some nights when I get home, and my wife is really complaining.

Therapist: Well, OK, drinking is one option. What other ways could you deal with this problem?

Client: Well, I could take the job, and on the side I could take some night courses in business at a local college. That way I could learn how to be a supervisor. But, gee, that would be a lot of work. I don't even know if I have the time. Besides, I don't know if they offer the kind of training I need.

Therapist: At this point, it's really not necessary to worry about how to carry out the options but simply to identify them. You're doing fine. What are some other ways you might handle the situation?

Client: Well, another thing I could do is to simply tell the boss that I'm not sure I'm qualified and either tell him that I don't want the job or ask him if he could give me some time to learn my new role.

Therapist: OK. Go on, you're doing fine.

Client: But what if the boss tells me that I have to take the job, I don't have any choice?

Therapist: Well, what general kinds of things might happen in that case?

Client: Oh, I could take the job and fail. That's one option. I could take the job and learn how to be a supervisor. I could refuse the job, risk being fired, and maybe end up having to look for another job. You know, I could just go and talk to my supervisor right now and explain the problem to him and see what comes of that.

Therapist: Well, you've delineated a lot of options. Let's take some time to evaluate them before you reach any decision.

(Adapted from Sobell & Sobell, 1978, pp. 97–98)

The therapist helps the client evaluate the effectiveness of each option and anticipate any negative consequences. In this case, the client decides to accept the promotion but to take some courses at the local college to increase his business background. The two discuss the stresses of managing a new job and classes, and they generate ways the client can manage these stresses other than by drinking.

In most cases, therapists using cognitive-behavioral approaches encourage their clients to abstain from alcohol, especially when they have a history of frequent relapses into abuse. When clients' goals are to learn to drink socially and therapists believe they can achieve these goals, therapy may focus on teaching the clients to engage in social, or controlled, drinking.

Studies have shown that cognitive-behavioral approaches are effective in treating abuse and dependence on alcohol, cannabis, nicotine, heroin, amphetamines, and cocaine (Dennis et al., 2000; McCrady, 2001; Mooney & Hatsukami, 2001; NIDA, 2002b, c, d; Waldron et al., 2001).

Motivational Interviewing

If individuals are not motivated to curtail their substance use, no treatment will be effective. William Miller (1983; Miller & Rose, 2009) developed **motivational interviewing** to elicit and solidify clients' motivation and commitment to changing their substance use. Rather than confronting the user, the motivational interviewer adopts an empathic interaction style, drawing out the user's statements of desire, ability, reasons, need, and, ultimately, commitment to change. The interviewer focuses on the client's ambivalence, helping the client voice his or her own arguments for change. Many controlled studies find that just four sessions of motivational interviewing lead to sustained reductions in substance use, particularly alcohol use (e.g., Ball et al., 2007; Carroll et al., 2006; see review by Miller & Rose, 2009).

Alcoholics Anonymous meetings seek to help individuals overcome alcohol dependence.

Relapse Prevention

Unfortunately, the relapse rate for people undergoing any kind of treatment for alcohol abuse and dependency is high. The **abstinence violation effect** contributes to relapse. It has two components. The first is a sense of conflict and guilt when an abstinent alcohol abuser or dependent violates abstinence and has a drink. He or she may continue to drink to try to suppress the conflict and guilt. The second component is a tendency to attribute a violation of abstinence to a lack of willpower and self-control rather than to situational factors. Thus, the person may think, "I'm an alcoholic and there's no way I can control my drinking. The fact that I had a drink proves this." This type of thinking may pave the way to continued, uncontrolled drinking.

Relapse prevention programs teach people who abuse alcohol to view slips as temporary and situationally caused. Therapists help clients identify high-risk situations, such as parties, and either avoid them or develop effective coping strategies for them. A client who decides to go to a party may first practice with the therapist some assertiveness skills for resisting friends' pressure to drink and write down other coping strategies to use if she feels tempted, such as starting a conversation with a supportive friend or practicing deep breathing exercises. She also may decide that, if the temptation becomes too great, she will ask a supportive friend to leave the party with her and go somewhere for coffee until the urge to drink passes.

Alcoholics Anonymous

Alcoholics Anonymous (AA) is an organization created by and for people with alcohol-related problems. Its philosophy is based on the *disease model* of alcoholism, which asserts that, because of biological, psychological, and spiritual deficits, some people will lose all control over their drinking once they have one drink. Therefore, the only way to control alcohol intake is to abstain completely. AA prescribes 12 steps that people dependent on alcohol must take toward recovery. The first is to admit their dependence on alcohol and their inability to control its effects. AA encourage its members to seek help from a higher power, to admit their weaknesses, and to ask forgiveness. The goal for all members is complete abstinence.

Group members provide moral and social support and make themselves available to one another in times of crisis. Once they are able, they are expected to devote themselves to helping others who are recovering from alcohol dependence. AA members believe that people are never completely cured of alcohol dependence—they are always "recovering alcoholics," with the potential for falling back into uncontrolled drinking with only one drink. To motivate others to abstain from alcohol, AA meetings include testimonials from members, such as the following.

VOICES

I am Duncan. I am an alcoholic. . . . I know that I will always be an alcoholic, that I can never again touch alcohol in any form. It'll kill me if I don't keep away from it. In fact, it almost did. . . . I must have been just past my 15th birthday when I had that first drink everybody talks about. And like so many of them—and you—it was like a miracle. With a little beer in my gut, the world was transformed. I wasn't a weakling anymore, I could lick almost anybody on the block. So, like for so many of you, my friends in the Fellowship, alcohol became the royal road to love, respect, and self-esteem. . . .

Though it's obvious to me now that my drinking even then, in high school, and after I got to college, was a problem, I didn't think so at the time. A couple of minor auto accidents, one conviction for drunken driving, a few fights—nothing out of the ordinary, it seemed to me at the time. True, I was drinking quite a lot, even then, but my friends seemed to be able to down as much beer as I did. I guess the fact that I hadn't really had any blackouts and that I could go for days without having to drink reassured me that things hadn't gotten out of control.

[Later] on, the drinking began to affect both my marriage and my career. With enough booze in me and under the pressures of guilt over my failure to carry out my responsibilities to my wife and children, I sometimes got kind of rough physically with them. I would break furniture, throw things around, then rush out and drive off in the car. I had a couple of wrecks, lost my license for two years because of one of them. Worst of all was when I tried to stop. By then I was totally hooked, so every time I tried to stop drinking, I'd experience withdrawal in all its horrors. I never had DTs, but I came awfully close many times, with the vomiting and the "shakes" and being unable to sit still or to lie down. And that would go on for days at a time. . . . Then, about four years ago, with my life in ruins, my wife given up on me and the kids with her, out of a job, and way down on my luck, the Fellowship and I found each other. Jim, over there, bless his heart, decided to sponsor me—we'd been friends for a long time, and I knew he'd found sobriety through this group. I've been dry now for a little over two years, and with luck and support, I may stay sober. (From Spitzer, R. L., Skodol, A. E., Gibbon, M., & Williams, J. B. W., 1983, *Psychopathology: A Case Book,* pp. 81–83. Copyright © 1983 The McGraw-Hill Companies, Inc. Reprinted with permission.)

The practices and philosophies of AA do not appeal to everyone. The emphases on one's powerlessness, need for a higher power, and complete abstinence turn away many. In addition, many people who subscribe to AA's philosophy still find it difficult to maintain complete abstinence, and they "fall off the wagon" throughout their lives. However, many believe that AA has been critical to their recovery from alcohol abuse and dependency, and it remains the most common source of treatment for people with alcohol-related problems. There are over 100,000 registered AA groups, and meetings take place all over the United States day and night, providing a supportive community as an alternative to drinking (Tonigan & Connors, 2008). Self-help groups modeled on AA—including Narcotics Anonymous, Cocaine Anonymous, and Marijuana Anonymous—assist people with dependencies on other drugs.

Evaluations of AA's effectiveness are complicated by differences between people who might attend and those who would not, the self-help nature of the intervention, and the fact that outcomes often are self-reported (Kelly, 2003). Perhaps as a result, meta-analyses and reviews of studies of AA's effectiveness have produced mixed results, with some suggesting that AA is effective and others suggesting that it is worse than no treatment (Emrick, Tonigan, Montgomery, & Little, 1993; Kaskutus, 2009; Kelly, 2003; Kownacki & Shadish, 1999; Tonigan, 1996).

Comparing Interventions

A large, multi-site clinical trial called Project MATCH compared three interventions designed to help people with alcohol dependency: cognitive-behavioral intervention, motivational interviewing and enhancement, and a 12-step program based on the AA model but led by professional counselors (Project MATCH Research Group, 1998). Surprisingly, the study showed that the three interventions were equally effective in reducing drinking behavior and preventing relapse over the following year (Project MATCH Research Group, 1998; Witkiewitz, Van der Maas, Hufford, & Marlatt, 2007).

Another multi-site study of over 1,300 alcohol-dependent individuals, Project COMBINE, indicated that combining psychosocial interventions with medications did not yield better outcomes than individual therapies (Anton et al., 2006). The psychosocial intervention was a combination of cognitive-behavioral therapy, motivational interviewing, a 12-step program facilitated by a professional, and community support. The medications were either naltrexone, acamprosate, or a combination. Both psychosocial intervention and naltrexone led to significant reductions in drinking, and the combination of the two was not superior to the individual therapies. Acamprosate did not perform better than a placebo either alone or combined with psychosocial treatment (Anton et al., 2006). A similar pattern was found in a 1-year follow-up of the same individuals, with indications that those who received psychosocial treatment were especially likely to have good outcomes whether or not they also received naltrexone (Donovan et al., 2008).

Prevention Programs

Only about 25 percent of alcohol dependents or abusers seek treatment (Dawson et al., 2005). About 25 percent may recover on their own, often due to maturation or positive changes in their environment (e.g., getting a good job or marrying a supportive person) that motivate them to control their drinking (Dawson et al., 2005). The remainder of people with significant alcohol problems carry these problems throughout their lives. Some become physically ill or unable to hold a job or maintain a relationship. Others hide or control their alcohol abuse and dependency and may be in relationships with people who facilitate it. Often they have periods of abstinence, sometimes long, but then—perhaps when facing stressful events—they begin drinking again. This is why preventing the development of substance abuse and dependency is so important.

In the United States, young adults between 18 and 24 have the highest rates of alcohol consumption and make up the largest proportion of problem drinkers of any age group. College students are even more likely to drink than their noncollege peers. Among students, 73 to 98 percent drink alcohol, in response to easy access to alcohol, social activities that focus on drinking, and peer pressure. About 25 percent of college students report having experienced alcohol-related problems, such as inability to complete schoolwork or an alcohol-related accident. Alcohol-related accidents are the leading cause of death among college students (Marlatt et al., 1993).

Many colleges have programs to reduce drinking and drinking-related problems. Programs that emphasize alcohol's health-related consequences tend not to impress young people, who are more likely to focus on the short-term gains of alcohol use. Some college counselors refer students with drinking problems to abstinence programs, such as Alcoholics Anonymous, but students often dislike admitting powerlessness and adopting lifelong abstinence. Finally, many colleges provide alternative activities that do not focus on alcohol. In general, however, prevention programs designed to stop drinking have had limited success.

Psychologist Alan Marlatt and his colleagues at the University of Washington (Marlatt, Blume, & Parks, 2001; Parks, Anderson, & Marlatt, 2001; Marlatt & Witkiewitz, 2010) have argued that a more credible approach to college drinking is to recognize it as normative behavior and focus education on the immediate risks of excess (alcohol-related accidents) and the payoffs of moderation (avoidance of hangovers). They view young drinkers as relatively inexperienced in regulating their use of alcohol and thus in need of skills training to prevent abuse. Learning to drink safely is compared to learning to drive safely in that people must learn to anticipate hazards and avoid "unnecessary accidents."

Based on this **harm reduction model,** the Alcohol Skills Training Program (ASTP) targets heavy-drinking college students for intervention. In eight weekly sessions of 90 minutes each, participants learn to be aware of their drinking habits—including when, where, and with whom they are most likely to overdrink—by keeping daily records of their alcohol consumption and the situations in which they drink. They also are taught to calculate their blood-alcohol level. It often comes as a surprise to them how few drinks it takes to become legally intoxicated.

Next, beliefs about the "magical" effects of drinking on social skills and sexual prowess are challenged. Participants discuss hangovers and alcohol's negative effects on social behaviors, ability to drive, and weight gain. They are encouraged to set personal goals for limiting consumption based on their blood-alcohol level and their desire to avoid drinking's negative effects. They learn skills for limiting consumption, such as alternating alcoholic and nonalcoholic beverages and selecting drinks for quality rather than quantity (buying two good beers rather than a six-pack of generic). Later, members are taught alternative ways to reduce negative emotional states, such as using relaxation exercises or reducing sources of stress. Finally, via role playing, participants learn skills for resisting peer pressure and avoiding high-risk situations in which they are likely to overdrink.

Evaluations of ASTP have shown that participants decrease their consumption and alcohol-related problems and increase their social skill at resisting alcohol abuse (Fromme, Marlatt, Baer, & Kivlahan, 1994; Marlatt, Baer, & Larimer, 1995). ASTP was designed for a group format, and the use of group pressure to encourage change and allow role playing has many advantages. Adaptations of this program, delivered in person or in written form as a self-help manual, also have shown positive effects (Baer et al., 1992, 2001).

TEST YOURSELF

1. What types of medications are used in the treatment of people with substance-related disorders?
2. How do behavioral and cognitive therapies treat substance-related disorders?
3. What is motivational interviewing?
4. Describe the abstinence violation effect and relapse prevention programs.
5. How do Alcoholics Anonymous and related programs treat substance-related disorders?
6. What are the goals of prevention programs based on the harm reduction model?

APPLY IT Renda sought treatment for alcohol dependence. Her therapist first asked Renda about her motivations for stopping drinking and encouraged her to set reasonable goals for change. They then talked about Renda's expectations that alcohol helped her cope with stress and identified alternative coping strategies she could use. Renda's therapist used a combination of ______ and ______ in treating Renda.

a. Alcoholics Anonymous, psychodynamic therapy
b. motivational interviewing, cognitive techniques
c. interpersonal therapy, cognitive therapy
d. harm reduction therapy, contingency management

Answers appear online at www.mhhe.com/nolen5e.

IMPULSE-CONTROL DISORDERS

People with substance-related disorders have difficulty controlling their impulses to drink or take drugs. People also can have trouble controlling many other types of impulses. In previous chapters, we have discussed people who act on the impulse to binge eat or to engage in socially unacceptable sexual acts.

The *DSM-IV-TR* recognizes another group of impulse-control disorders that includes pathological gambling, kleptomania, pyromania, intermittent explosive disorder, and trichotillomania. People with these disorders often feel a mounting sense of tension that is relieved only by engaging in their impulsive act. Some researchers consider these disorders to be similar to substance-related disorders and to be due to abnormalities in reward systems in the brain (Grant & Potenza, 2006). Others consider them part of the obsessive-compulsive disorder continuum, because people with these disorders seem to have obsessions (e.g., people with pyromania are preoccupied with fire-related images and objects) and seem compelled to engage in impulsive behaviors (e.g., stealing or gambling). As we describe in this section, the *DSM-5* authors have proposed moving these disorders to various categories based on the available research for each disorder.

Pathological Gambling

More than two-thirds of U.S. adults report having gambled in the past year, but most gamble only occasionally and recreationally (Potenza, Kosten, & Rounsaville, 2001). Approximately 5 percent of the population engages in chronic, compulsive gambling (Shaffer & Hall, 2001). The *DSM-IV-TR* criteria for **pathological gambling** are given in Table 14.10. This disorder frequently leads to serious financial, relationship, and employment problems. Pathological gamblers also tend to have problems with substance use, depression, and anxiety and family histories of substance abuse and gambling problems (Grant et al., 2008). Because of its connections to substance-use problems, pathological gambling is likely to be recategorized in the *DSM-5* with addictions and related disorders. The *DSM-5* authors also propose changing the name to *disordered gambling* (American Psychiatric Association, 2010).

Pathological gambling may be connected to decreased executive control over impulses in the frontal areas of the brain (Potenza et al., 2003). Pathological gamblers also may have a greater response of the brain's reward systems to gambling and related cues (van Holst, van den Brink, Veltman, & Goudriaan, 2010).

Cognitive-behavioral therapies concentrate on changing the individual's belief that he or she has more control than the average person over gambling outcomes and developing new activities and coping strategies to replace gambling. Controlled studies of CBT have shown that it can help reduce compulsive gambling (Ladouceur et al., 2001, 2003; Pallesen et al., 2005). Serotonin reuptake inhibitors have shown only mixed success in treating pathological

TABLE 14.10 *DSM-IV-TR* Criteria for Pathological Gambling

A. Persistent and recurrent maladaptive gambling behavior as indicated by five (or more) of the following:

1. Is preoccupied with gambling (e.g., preoccupied with reliving past gambling experiences, handicapping or planning the next venture, or thinking of ways to get money with which to gamble)
2. Needs to gamble with increasing amounts of money in order to achieve the desired excitement
3. Has repeated unsuccessful efforts to control, cut back, or stop gambling
4. Is restless or irritable when attempting to cut down or stop gambling
5. Gambles as a way of escaping from problems or of relieving a dysphoric mood (e.g., feelings of helplessness, guilt, anxiety, depression)
6. After losing money gambling, often returns another day to get even ("chasing" one's losses)
7. Lies to family members, therapist, or others to conceal the extent of involvement with gambling
8. Has committed illegal acts such as forgery, fraud, theft, or embezzlement to finance gambling
9. Has jeopardized or lost a significant relationship, job, or educational or career opportunity because of gambling
10. Relies on others to provide money to relieve a desperate financial situation caused by gambling

B. The gambling behavior is not better accounted for by a manic episode.

Source: Reprinted with permission from the *Diagnostic and Statistical Manual of Mental Disorders,* Fourth Edition, Text Revision.

gambling (Grant & Potenza, 2006; van Holst et al., 2010); naltrexone, which affects reward sensitivity, appears to be more effective than SSRIs in reducing symptoms (Grant & Kim, 2002b).

Kleptomania

Have you ever felt an urge to take an item from a store without paying for it? Over 11 percent of the U.S. public, and 28.6 percent of college students, admit to having shoplifted (Lejoyeux, Arbaretaz, McLoughlin, & Adès, 2002; National Association for Shoplifting Prevention, 2006; Odlaug & Grant, 2008). People with **kleptomania** are chronic shoplifters, taking items not needed for personal use or monetary value. Before the theft, they feel a mounting tension that turns to relief or gratification afterward.

Kleptomania is relatively rare, with one study estimating a lifetime prevalence of 0.4 percent (Odlaugh & Grant, 2008). People with kleptomania tend to have high rates of comorbid depression, anxiety, substance-use disorders, and family histories of substance-use disorders (Grant, 2008). The majority have been apprehended at least once, and 15 to 23 percent have been jailed for theft (Grant & Kim, 2002a). The *DSM-5* likely will continue to classify kleptomania as an impulse-control disorder.

People with kleptomania show deficits in the frontal areas of the brain that help control impulsive behavior (Grant, Correia, & Brendan-Krohn, 2006). People with more severe forms perform poorly on tests of impulse control and problem-solving skills (Grant, Odlaug, & Wozniak, 2007). Naltrexone, serotonin reuptake inhibitors, anticonvulsant medications, and lithium are used to treat kleptomania (Grant, Kim, & Odlaug, 2009).

Pyromania

Pyromania is a pattern of deliberate and purposeful fire setting triggered by tension or affective arousal and resulting in pleasure or relief (American Psychiatric Association, 2000). People with pyromania are fascinated with fire, its consequences, and associated paraphernalia. They set fires for gratification—not for monetary gain, to express anger or ideology, to conceal criminal activity, or in response to delusions or hallucinations. The *DSM-5* likely will continue to classify pyromania as an impulse-control disorder.

Little is known about the causes of pyromania, in part because it seems to be extremely rare both in the general population and among arsonists (Grant & Kim, 2007). One small study found that onset occurred most often in late adolescence and that rates of comorbid substance-related disorders and other impulse-control disorders were high (Grant & Kim, 2007). Many of the fires these individuals set did not constitute arson because they were not intended to cause harm to property.

Intermittent Explosive Disorder

The *DSM-IV-TR* criteria for **intermittent explosive disorder** are (a) failure on many occasions to resist aggressive impulses that result in serious assaultive acts or destruction of property, (b) a degree of aggressiveness grossly out of proportion to the situation, and (c) symptoms not better explained by another mental disorder (such as antisocial personality disorder), the effects of substances, or a medical condition (such as a head trauma) (American Psychiatric Association, 2000). Epidemiological studies suggest that as many as 7 percent of the population could be diagnosed with intermittent explosive disorder (Kessler, Coccaro, et al., 2006). This chronic disorder can lead to legal difficulties and to loss of relationships and employment. (McCloskey et al., 2008). The *DSM-5* likely will continue to classify intermittent explosive disorder as an impulse-control disorder.

Cognitive-behavioral treatments for intermittent explosive disorder help individuals identify and avoid triggers for explosive outbursts and appraise situations in ways that do not provoke their aggression. One study found that both individualized and group CBT were more effective than a wait-list control in reducing anger, aggression, hostile thinking, and depressive symptoms while improving anger control in individuals with intermittent explosive disorder (McCloskey et al., 2008). SSRIs also have been shown to reduce aggression in individuals with this disorder (Coccaro & Kavoussi, 1997).

Trichotillomania

People diagnosed with **trichotillomania** have a history of the recurrent pulling out of their hair, resulting in noticeable hair loss. They report tension immediately before or while attempting to resist the impulse, and pleasure or relief when pulling out their hair. The behavior must cause significant distress or impairment and must not be due to other mental or medical conditions (American Psychiatric Association, 2000). In the *DSM-5*, trichotillomania likely will be reclassified with the anxiety and obsessive-compulsive disorders.

The estimated prevalence of trichotillomania is 1 to 3 percent (Christenson, Pyle, & Mitchell, 1991), and the average age of onset is 13 (Christenson & Mansueto, 1999). Hair pulling is most likely when the individual is bored (Grant & Potenza, 2006). People with the disorder are at risk for comorbid depression, substance-use disorders, and anxiety disorders, particularly OCD (Grant & Potenza, 2006). Their family members have higher than typical rates of OCD, suggesting a relationship between the two disorders (Grant & Potenza, 2006).

Neuroimaging studies suggest that this disorder involves disruptions in brain areas responsible for habitual motor behavior and impulse control (Vythilingum et al., 2002). One antidepressant drug, clomipramine, has proven useful in the treatment of trichotillomania (Bloch et al., 2007). Effective cognitive-behavioral treatments help individuals recognize triggers for hair pulling, find alternate ways to relax or cope with stress, and resist the behavior (Tolin et al., 2007; Woods, Wetterneck, & Flessner, 2006).

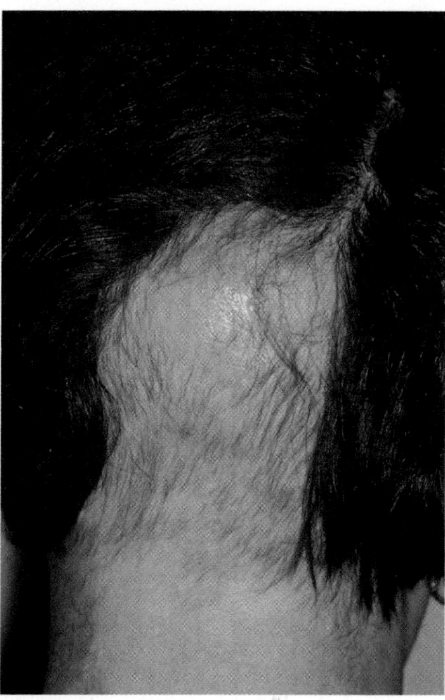

Trichotillomania is the compulsion to pull out one's own hair.

TEST YOURSELF

Briefly, what are the symptoms of and treatments for each of the impulse-control disorders?

APPLY IT Janet is diagnosed with an impulse-control disorder and OCD. Both her impulse-control disorder and her OCD symptoms are relieved when she takes clomipramine. Which impulse control disorder is Janet most likely diagnosed with?

a. pathological gambling
b. kleptomania
c. intermittent explosive disorder
d. trichotillomania

Answers appear online at www.mhhe.com/nolen5e.

CHAPTER INTEGRATION

The substances discussed in this chapter are powerful biological agents. They affect the brain directly, producing changes in mood, thoughts, and perceptions. Some people may be genetically or biochemically predisposed to find these changes

FIGURE 14.7 Integration of Biological and Psychological Pressures Toward the Development of Substance-Related Disorders

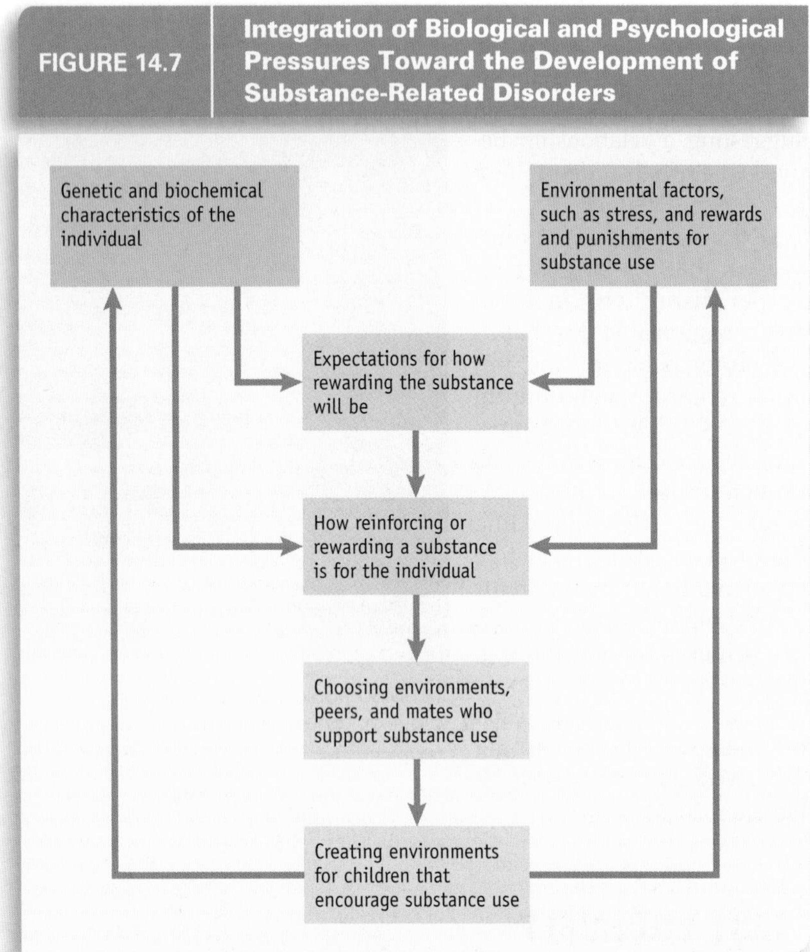

more positive or rewarding than other people do (Figure 14.7). Rewards and punishments in the environment clearly can affect an individual's choice to pursue the effects of substances, however. Even many long-term chronic substance abusers can abstain given strong environmental support for abstention.

People who find substances more rewarding, for either biological or environmental reasons, will develop expectations that the substances will be rewarding, which in turn will enhance how rewarding they actually are. Likewise, heavy substance users choose friends and environments that support their substance use. They tend to find partners who are also heavy substance users, creating a biological and psychosocial environment for their children that promotes substance abuse and dependence. Thus, the cycle of familial transmission of substance abuse and dependence has intersecting biological and psychosocial components.

Similar processes may play out for impulse-control behaviors that are connected to reward systems. For example, biological factors may influence how rewarding an individual finds gambling; the person will then associate with other gamblers, who reinforce the gambling behavior, and eventually the impulse to gamble may become pathological.

SHADES OF GRAY DISCUSSION (review p. 437)

Nick's behaviors definitely meet the criteria for alcohol abuse. He is failing to fulfill his obligations at school and continuing to use alcohol despite social problems (ejection from the campus and his parents' threat to withdraw their support). He also may meet the criteria for alcohol dependence: His hangovers are a sign of withdrawal, he spends much time drinking and recovering, and his drinking is hurting his grades. We don't know whether Nick has developed tolerance to alcohol, although the escalation of his drinking suggests that he needs more alcohol to get the desired effect. Nick doesn't seem to have any intention of cutting back on his drinking, so the criteria for attempting to control his substance use have not been met.

It may seem odd to think of a college student who drinks with his friends as having a psychiatric diagnosis. Some critics of the *DSM-IV-TR* argue that the criteria for alcohol abuse and dependence are too broad and that too many individuals meet them. Others argue that simply because a large percentage of the population meet the criteria for abuse or dependence doesn't mean we should ignore their behavior. What do you think?

THINK CRITICALLY

U.S. citizens can join the military, serve on a jury, and vote at age 18, but they can't drink alcohol legally until they are 21. In 1984, Congress passed the National Minimum Drinking Age Act in response to evidence that states with higher drinking ages had fewer traffic fatalities associated with alcohol. Some college administrators, however, believe that raising the drinking age has not reduced drinking among 18- to 21-year-olds but instead has driven it underground, where it is more difficult to regulate.

How do you think reducing the drinking age to 18 would change things? Would it increase drinking among 18- to 21-year-olds substantially? Would it increase alcohol-related negative consequences, such as drunk driving? If the drinking age were lowered to 18, are there programs that might counteract possible negative consequences? *(Discussion appears on pp. 520–521 at the back of this book.)*

CHAPTER SUMMARY

- A substance is any natural or synthesized product that has psychoactive effects. The five groups of substances most often leading to substance disorders are (1) central nervous system depressants, including alcohol, barbiturates, benzodiazepines, and inhalants; (2) central nervous system stimulants, including cocaine, amphetamines, nicotine, and caffeine; (3) opioids; (4) hallucinogens and phencyclidine; and (5) cannabis.
- Substance intoxication is indicated by a set of behavioral and psychological changes that occur as a direct result of the physiological effects of a substance on the central nervous system. Substance withdrawal is a set of physiological and behavioral symptoms that result from the cessation of or reduction in heavy and prolonged use of a substance. The specific symptoms of intoxication and withdrawal depend on the substance being used, the amount ingested, and the method of ingestion.
- Substance abuse is indicated when an individual shows persistent problems in one of four categories: (1) failure to fulfill major role obligations at work, school, or home; (2) substance use in situations in which such use is physically hazardous; (3) substance-related legal problems; and (4) continued substance use despite social or interpersonal problems.
- Substance dependence is characterized by a maladaptive pattern of substance use, leading to significant problems in a person's life and, usually, tolerance to the substance, withdrawal symptoms if it is discontinued, and compulsive substance-taking behavior.
- At low doses, alcohol produces relaxation and mild euphoria. At higher doses, it produces classic signs of depression and cognitive and motor impairment. A large proportion of deaths due to accidents, murders, and suicides are alcohol-related. Withdrawal symptoms can be mild or so severe as to be life-threatening. Alcohol abusers and alcohol dependents experience a wide range of social and interpersonal problems and are at risk for many serious health problems.
- Women drink less alcohol than men in most cultures and are less likely to have alcohol-related problems. Persons of Asian descent typically drink less and thus also are less prone to alcohol-related problems.
- Benzodiazepines and barbiturates can cause an initial rush plus a loss of inhibitions, followed by depressed mood, lethargy, and physical signs of central nervous system depression. These substances are dangerous in overdose and when mixed with other substances.
- The inhalants are volatile agents that people sniff to produce a sense of euphoria, disinhibition, and increased aggressiveness or sexual performance. They are extremely dangerous; even casual use may cause permanent brain damage or serious disease.
- Cocaine activates those parts of the brain that register reward and pleasure and produces a sudden rush of euphoria, followed by increased self-esteem, alertness, and energy and a greater sense of competence, creativity, and social acceptability. The user also may experience frightening perceptual changes. The symptoms of withdrawal from cocaine include exhaustion, a need for sleep, and depression. Cocaine's extraordinarily rapid and strong effects on the brain's reward centers seem to make it more likely than most illicit substances to lead to abuse and dependence.

- Amphetamines are readily available by prescription to treat certain disorders but often end up on the black market. They can make people feel euphoric, invigorated, self-confident, and gregarious, but they also can lead to restlessness, hypervigilance, anxiety, aggressiveness, and several dangerous physiological symptoms and changes.
- Nicotine is widely available. Smoking tobacco is legal, but it causes cancer, bronchitis, and coronary heart disease in users and a range of birth defects in the children of women who smoke when pregnant. People become physiologically dependent on nicotine and undergo withdrawal when they stop smoking.
- The opioids are developed from the juice of the poppy plant. The most commonly used illegal opioid is heroin. The initial symptom of opioid intoxication is euphoria, followed by drowsiness, lethargy, and periods of light sleep. Severe intoxication can lead to respiratory difficulties, unconsciousness, coma, and seizures. Withdrawal symptoms include dysphoria, anxiety, agitation, sensitivity to pain, and a craving for more substance.
- The hallucinogens, phencyclidine, and cannabis produce perceptual changes, including sensory distortions and hallucinations. These experiences are pleasant for some, frightening for others. Some people experience a sense of euphoria or relaxation from using these substances, and others become anxious and agitated.
- Some additional drugs of abuse are ecstasy (3,4-methylenedioxymethamphetamine, or MDMA), GHB (gamma-hydroxybutyrate), ketamine, and rohypnol (flunitrazepam). These drugs have several euphoric and sedative effects and are used at dance clubs and sometimes by perpetrators of date rape.
- Evidence indicates that genes play a role in vulnerability to substance-use disorders through their effects on the synthesis and metabolism of substances.
- Some people appear to be more sensitive than others to the rewarding effects of substances and are at increased risk for substance-related disorders.
- Behavioral theories of alcoholism note that people are reinforced or punished for their alcohol-related behaviors and also engage in behaviors modeled by important others. Cognitive theories argue that people who develop alcohol-related problems have expectations that alcohol will help them feel better and cope better with stressful events. One personality characteristic associated with substance-use disorders is behavioral undercontrol.
- Reasons for gender differences in substance-related disorders may be that men have more risk factors for substance use and that women are more sensitive to its negative consequences.
- Medications can ease withdrawal symptoms and reduce cravings for many substances. The symptoms of opioid withdrawal can be so severe that dependents are given methadone as they try to discontinue heroin use. Methadone also blocks the effects of subsequent doses of heroin, reducing the desire to obtain heroin. Methadone maintenance programs are controversial.
- People dependent on alcohol sometimes respond to behavior therapies based on aversive classical conditioning. They use a drug that makes them ill if they ingest alcohol or imagery that develops a conditioned aversive response to the sight and smell of alcohol. Contingency management programs provide incentives for reducing substance use.
- Cognitive therapies focus on training alcoholics in developing coping skills and in challenging positive expectations about alcohol's effects.
- Motivational interviewing attempts to empathetically draw out individuals' motivations and commitment to change their substance-use behavior.
- The abstinence violation effect comprises an individual's feeling of guilt over relapse and attribution of relapse to lack of self-control. Relapse prevention programs help identify triggers for relapse.
- The most common treatment for alcoholism is Alcoholics Anonymous, a self-help group that encourages alcoholics to admit their weaknesses and to call on a higher power and on other group members to help them abstain.
- Prevention programs based on harm reduction models seek to teach the responsible use of alcohol.
- The *DSM-IV-TR* impulse-control disorders include pathological gambling, kleptomania, pyromania, intermittent explosive disorder, and trichotillomania. People with these disorders often feel a mounting sense of tension that is relieved only by engaging in their impulsive act.

KEY TERMS

substance-related disorders 425
impulse-control disorders 425
substance 425
substance intoxication 428
substance withdrawal 428
substance abuse 429
substance dependence 430
tolerance 430
alcohol abuse 433
alcohol dependence 433
delirium tremens (DTs) 434
benzodiazepines 437
barbiturates 437
inhalants 438
cocaine 439
amphetamines 441
nicotine 442
caffeine 442
opioids 443
hallucinogens 445
phencyclidine (PCP) 446
cannabis 446
antagonist drugs 453
methadone 453
motivational interviewing 456
abstinence violation effect 456
relapse prevention programs 456
harm reduction model 458
pathological gambling 459
kleptomania 460
pyromania 460
intermittent explosive disorder 461
trichotillomania 461

Chapter 15

Health Psychology

CHAPTER OUTLINE

Extraordinary People

Norman Cousins, *Healing with Laughter*

In 1964, Norman Cousins, a successful writer at the *Saturday Review,* was diagnosed with ankylosing spondylitis, a painful collagen disease. After many medical tests and days in the hospital, doctors gave him a 1 in 500 chance of living. Cousins refused to believe that he would succumb to the disease and set out to find a course of action that might reverse its progression. His 1979 book *Anatomy of an Illness* describes his use of comedy and movies to raise his levels of positive emotions and thereby affect the functioning of his adrenal and endocrine systems:

> A good place to begin, I thought, was with amusing movies. Allen Funt, producer of the spoofing television program "Candid Camera," sent films of some of his "CC" classics, along with a motion-picture projector. The nurse was instructed in its use.
>
> It worked. I made the joyous discovery that ten minutes of genuine belly laughter had an anesthetic effect and would give me at least two hours of pain-free sleep. When the painkilling effect of the laughter wore off, we would switch on the motion-picture projector again, and not infrequently, it would lead to another pain-free sleep interval. Sometimes the nurse read to me out of a trove of humor books.
>
> How scientific was it to believe that laughter—as well as the positive emotions in general—was affecting my body chemistry for the better? If laughter did in fact have a salutary effect on the body's chemistry, it seemed at least theoretically likely that it would enhance the system's ability to fight the inflammation. So we took sedimentation-rate readings just before as well as several hours after the laughter episodes. Each time, there was a drop of at least five points. The drop by itself was not substantial, but it held and was cumulative.
>
> I was greatly elated by the discovery that there is a physiological basis for the ancient theory that laughter is good medicine. . . . (1985, p. 55–66)

Cousins eventually recovered from his illness. After returning to his career as a writer for several years, Cousins spent the last 12 years of his life at the UCLA Medical School, working with researchers to find scientific proof for his beliefs that positive emotions have healing properties. One of the leading institutes for the study of the impact of psychological factors on physical health is now named for him: The Cousins Center for Psychoneuroimmunology at UCLA.

In the years since Cousins's discovery that laughter was good medicine for him, considerable empirical evidence has emerged that positive emotions influence physiological functioning (Fredrickson & Joiner, 2002; Fredrickson, Tugade, Waugh, & Larkin, 2003). These findings evoke the ancient mind-body question: Does the mind affect the body, or does the body affect the mind? The answer now is clearly that the mind and the body affect each other.

In this chapter, we review the research in *health psychology* (also referred to as *behavioral medicine*), a field that explores how biological, psychological, and social/environmental factors interact to influence physical health. Figure 15.1 illustrates the components of a biopsychosocial approach to physical health (Baum, Perry, & Tarbell, 2004). First, biological factors, such as genetic makeup, age, and gender, clearly have a major influence on our susceptibility to disease. For example, genetics play a strong role in susceptibility to cancer, the risk of developing most cancers increases with age, and some forms of cancer, such as breast cancer, are much more common in women than in men. Second, social or environmental factors can directly impact health. The factor most often studied by health psychologists is stress, as we discuss in detail below. Another important social factor is culture, which influences our exposure to diseases and the treatments prescribed for these diseases. For example, the human immunodeficiency virus (HIV) is more widespread in Sub-Sarahan Africa than anywhere else in the world (UNAIDS, 2009), and cultural stigmas against condom use have played a role in the spread of HIV in this region (UNAIDS, 2004).

Third, a number of psychological factors can impact health. We can engage in behaviors that enhance our health, such as exercising regularly and brushing our teeth, or in behaviors that promote

FIGURE 15.1 Components in a Biopsychosocial Approach to Physical Health

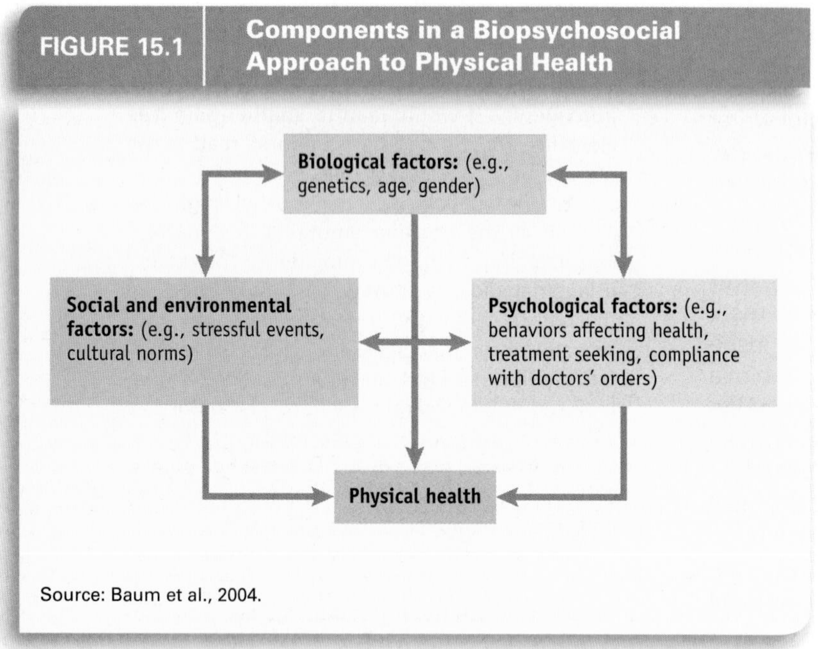

Source: Baum et al., 2004.

disease, such as smoking and eating fatty foods. When we are ill, we can seek treatment and follow our doctor's orders, or we can avoid treatment or not comply with the orders.

In addition to their direct effects on health, biological, psychological and social/environmental factors all interact to influence health. Consider a few examples: Genetics not only influences our vulnerability to a particular disease but also influences how much stress we are exposed to in our life and our perceptions of stress (Kendler, Karkowski, & Prescott, 1999; Kendler & Karkowski-Shuman, 1997). In turn, stress can make it more difficult to engage in healthy behaviors such as getting enough exercise. Our personalities influence how much stress we perceive in our lives, which in turn affects our health. Throughout this chapter, we discuss how interactions among biological, psychological, and social/environmental factors promote or damage health.

As a field, health psychology has grown rapidly in recent decades as psychological and social/environmental factors have become increasingly important determinants of both the length and the quality of our lives. At the beginning of the twentieth century, the leading causes of death, in addition to cardiovascular disease, were primarily infectious diseases, including influenza, pneumonia, and tuberculosis (Table 15.1). Over the past century, advances in medicine have greatly reduced the number of deaths due to these diseases. In the twenty-first century, the five leading causes of death are diseases significantly influenced by psychological and social factors such as smoking, diet, and stress. Thus, a critical part of maintaining people's physical health is understanding how psychological and social/environmental factors interact with each other and with biological vulnerabilities to create disease.

The concept of stress has been at the center of much research in health psychology. We begin this chapter by exploring the meaning of *stress* and describing how the body reacts to stress.

TABLE 15.1 Leading Causes of Death in the United States, 1900 and 2006

1900		2006	
Cause	**Rate (per 100,000)**	**Cause**	**Rate (per 100,000)**
1. Cardiovascular diseases (heart disease, stroke)	345	1. Heart disease	211
2. Influenza and pneumonia	202	2. Cancer	181
3. Tuberculosis	194	3. Cerebrovascular diseases (stroke)	44
4. Gastritis, duodenitis, enteritis, and colitis	143	4. Chronic lower respiratory diseases	42
5. Accidents	72	5. Accidents	41

Source: Data for 1900: U.S. Bureau of the Census, 1975, *Historical Statistics of the United States: Colonial Times to 1970,* I. Washington, DC: U.S. Government Printing Office. Data for 2006: Heron et al., 2009.

Stress Along the Continuum

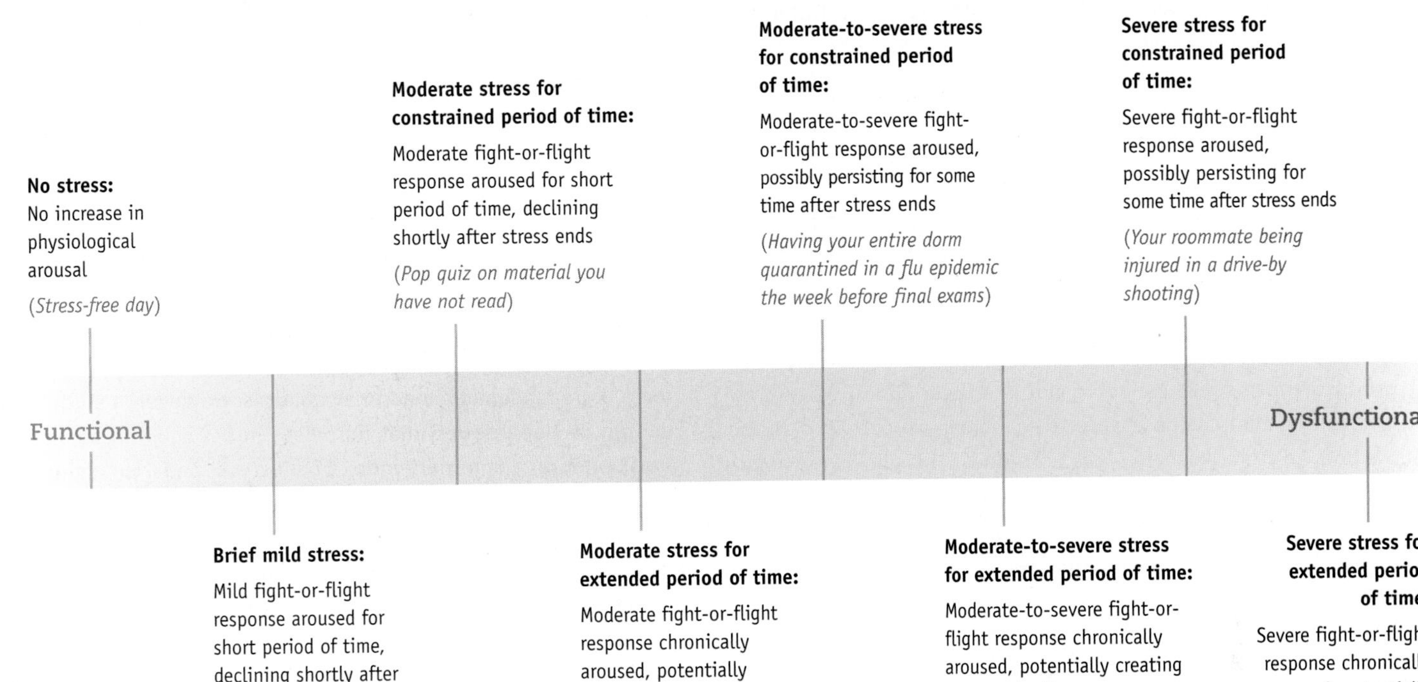

No stress:
No increase in physiological arousal
(Stress-free day)
Brief mild stress:
Mild fight-or-flight response aroused for short period of time, declining shortly after stress ends
(Pop quiz on material you have read)
Moderate stress for constrained period of time:
Moderate fight-or-flight response aroused for short period of time, declining shortly after stress ends
(Pop quiz on material you have not read)
Moderate stress for extended period of time:
Moderate fight-or-flight response chronically aroused, potentially creating harm to bodily systems
(Working on a difficult paper over several weeks for your final grade)
Moderate-to-severe stress for constrained period of time:
Moderate-to-severe fight-or-flight response aroused, possibly persisting for some time after stress ends
(Having your entire dorm quarantined in a flu epidemic the week before final exams)
Moderate-to-severe stress for extended period of time:
Moderate-to-severe fight-or-flight response chronically aroused, potentially creating harm to bodily systems
(Searching for a job and a place to live while you approach graduation saddled with student loans)
Severe stress for constrained period of time:
Severe fight-or-flight response aroused, possibly persisting for some time after stress ends
(Your roommate being injured in a drive-by shooting)
Severe stress for extended period of time:
Severe fight-or-flight response chronically aroused, potentially creating harm to bodily systems
(Your home being wiped out in a hurricane)
Functional
Dysfunctional

Stress is a familiar part of students' lives. Pop quizzes, papers that count for half the grade in a course, finding a job after graduation—all these can be stressful. In addition to academic stresses, many students face stresses in other parts of their lives: the break-up of close relationships, the death of loved ones, financial problems, and so on.

What makes some circumstances more stressful than others? Three factors seem key: uncontrollability, unpredictability, and duration. Uncontrollable events, such as the loss of a job, the sudden death of a loved one, or the loss of one's home to a natural disaster, are perceived by most people as stressful. In a classic experimental study, participants were shown vivid photographs of victims of violent deaths. The experimental group could stop their viewing by pressing a button. The other group could not stop their viewing of the photographs. Both groups of participants saw the same photographs for the same duration. The level of experienced stress in both groups was measured by their *galvanic skin response (GSR),* a drop in the electrical resistance of the skin that indicates sympathetic nervous system arousal. The experimental group showed much lower GSR response while viewing the photographs than did the other group, even though the only difference between the groups was their ability to control how much they saw (Geer & Maisel, 1972).

Unpredictability also makes events more stressful. Humans and other animals prefer negative events, such as painful electric shocks or loud bursts of noise, that are preceded by a warning tone (and therefore are predictable) to those that occur without warning (Abbott, Schoen, & Badia, 1984; Glass & Singer, 1972; Katz & Wykes, 1985). When you know a negative event is coming, you can prepare for it by finding ways to protect yourself from it; when you cannot predict when a negative event might strike, you can't prepare for it and thus its occurrence is more stressful. Also, if you can predict a negative event, then you can relax until the event is about to occur. With unpredictable events, you feel as if you can never relax because the event may occur at any time (Seligman & Binik, 1977).

Further, negative events are perceived as less stressful if they pass quickly, with no long-term consequences, but are perceived as more stressful if they last for a long time. For example, taking a pop quiz on material you have read may be less stressful than writing a long paper, because the pop quiz is over quickly while the paper writing can seem to go on forever.

(continued)

Anytime we face a stressor, whether mild or severe, a number of physiological responses kick in, as discussed in Chapter 5. Known collectively as the *fight-or-flight response* (refer to Figure 5.1, p. 114), bodily changes such as increased heart rate and elevated blood pressure prepare the body to either face the threat or flee from it. The sympathetic system also stimulates the release of a number of hormones—including epinephrine (adrenaline) and norepinephrine—that keep the body ready to react.

In more technical terms, the fight-or-flight response takes place when the hypothalamus releases corticotropin-release factor (CRF), which signals the pituitary gland to secrete adrenocorticotropic hormone (ACTH), the body's major stress hormone. ACTH stimulates the adrenal cortex, resulting in the release of a group of hormones, including cortisol. Eventually, when the threatening stimulus has passed, the increase in cortisol signals the body to stop releasing these hormones. This allows the body to adapt along a continuum of stress. Even mild stressors trigger the fight-or-flight response; when the stressor is immediate, the response is useful and then subsides. This adaptation is called *allostasis*—the body learns how to react more efficiently to stress when it comes and goes, is not severe, and does not persist for long periods of time (McEwen, 2000). But when a stressor is chronic—that is, when it lasts over a long period of time—and a person or animal cannot fight it or flee from it, then the chronic physiological arousal that results can be severely damaging to the body, a condition known as **allostatic load.**

Persistent uncontrollable and unpredictable stress can create allostatic load in humans and other animals. In studies of baboons living freely in a national reserve in Kenya, Robert Sapolsky (2007) showed that subordinate animals, who have less controllable and predictable access to food and sexual partners, show abnormal physiological responses to stress. Similarly, more dominant baboons whose dominance is threatened by other baboons also show an atypical response. The optimal stress responses are shown by dominant baboons whose dominance within the group is stable over time.

Many factors, including gender, minority status, socioeconomic status, and culture, may affect our exposure to uncontrollable and unpredictable events, our perceptions of these events, and our reactions to them. For example, many African Americans are exposed to excess stress due to racism, discrimination, and low socioeconomic status compared to many European Americans (Mays, Cochran, & Barnes, 2007). In turn, African Americans score higher on a number of indicators of allostatic load, such as persistent high blood pressure (Geronimus, Hicken, Keene, & Bound, 2006). This is particularly true of African American women, who bear extra responsibility in maintaining their families, often with few resources (Lewis et al., 2006). The higher allostatic load in African Americans may be due to all the factors seen in Figure 15.1: In addition to being exposed to racism and discrimination, they may have an increased biological vulnerability to risks such as hypertension and, on average, have less access to health care (Mays et al., 2007).

Culture can alter the very meaning of stress. Being homeless and living on the street might sound highly stressful and likely to create a great allostatic load in all cultures. However, a study of children in Nepal found that homeless street children actually fared better on a summary index of allostatic load than children living with their families in rural villages (Worthman & Panter-Brick, 2008). Although the homeless children were not with their families, they had formed family groups with other street children, protecting one another and collectively finding food and shelter. The rural village children had stable homes, but these homes had poor sanitation, and the children had only subsistence nutrition and faced heavy physical workloads. In more developed countries such as the United States, in contrast, being a homeless street child is associated with more stress and poorer health than is living with family in a rural small town (Worthman & Panter-Brick, 2008).

Finally, gender may influence typical responses to stress. Shelley Taylor and colleagues (2000) have suggested that females faced with threats engage in a pattern termed *tend and befriend.* Throughout evolutionary history, females have not been as physically capable as men of fighting off aggressors; also, because they have had primary responsibility for their offspring, they have not always been able to run from an aggressor. Instead of attempting to fight a threat or flee from it, females join social groups for protection and resources. Underlying this behavioral response to stress by females is a different neurobiological response to stress: The physiological changes associated with fight-or-flight are less prominent in females than in males, but stressed females experience the release of the hormone oxytocin, which is associated with increased affiliative behavior such as seeking out and caring for others.

PSYCHOLOGICAL FACTORS AND GENERAL HEALTH

We all know people who seem to be able to handle even severe stress extremely well—they bounce back from difficult times with renewed vigor, feeling as though they have grown psychologically from their stressful experiences. We call these people *resilient* (Masten & Powell, 2003). Other people, however, are more fragile—even mild stresses are overwhelming and seem to lead to psychological and physical decline.

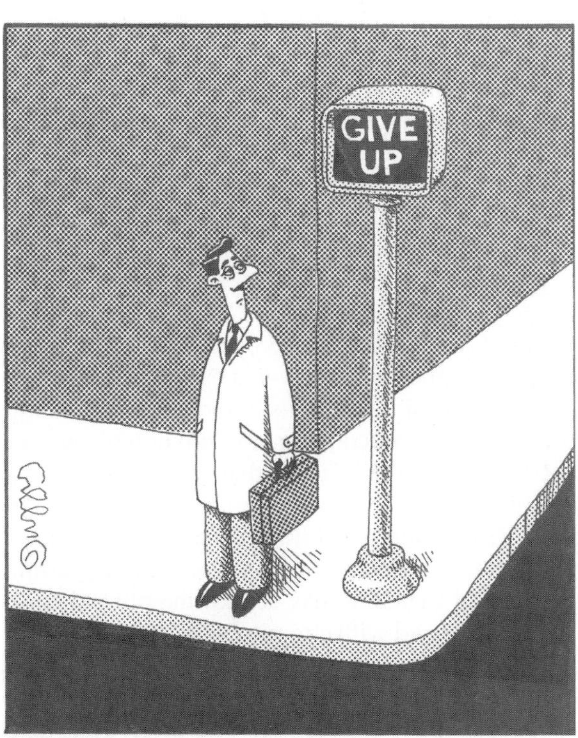

Cartoon by J. C. Duffy, www.cartoonstock.com. Used with permission.

Appraisals and Pessimism

One difference between resilient and fragile people is in how they appraise or interpret events. People who tend to have a pessimistic style of interpreting events—seeing negative events as their fault, likely to continue in the future, and subject to wide consequences—go through life seeing stress around every corner (Peterson et al., 1998). Pessimism may contribute to poor health by causing chronic arousal of the body's fight-or-flight response, resulting in physiological damage. Several studies have found evidence for this explanation. In one study, the blood pressure of pessimists and optimists was monitored daily for 3 days. The pessimists had chronically higher blood pressure levels than the optimists across the 3 days (Raikkonen et al., 1999). Another study found that older adults who were pessimistic showed poorer immune system functioning than those who were optimistic, even after the researchers statistically controlled for differences between the pessimists and optimists on measures of current health, depression, medication use, sleep, and alcohol use (Kamen-Siegel, Rodin, Seligman, & Dwyer, 1991).

A pessimistic outlook also may lead people to engage in unhealthy behaviors. In one study of people who were HIV-positive, researchers found that those who were more pessimistic were less likely to practice healthy behaviors, such as maintaining a proper diet, getting enough sleep, and exercising (Milam et al., 2004; Taylor, Kemeny, Aspinwall, & Schneider, 1992). These behaviors are particularly important for HIV-positive people because they can reduce the risk of developing AIDS.

The effects of pessimism may be lifelong. In a long-term study of men in the Harvard classes of 1939 and 1940, those who were pessimistic in college were more likely to develop physical illness over the subsequent 35 years than were those who were more optimistic in college (Peterson, Seligman, & Vaillant, 1988; see also Peterson et al., 1998).

In short, a pessimistic outlook may affect health directly by causing hyperarousal of the body's physiological response to stress or indirectly by reducing positive coping strategies and healthy behaviors. In contrast, an optimistic outlook, such as that Norman Cousins attempted to create in himself through laughter, may promote physical health by reducing physiological stress responses and promoting positive coping strategies.

« Extraordinary People: Norman Cousins

Coping Strategies

The ways people cope with illness and other stressful life circumstances can affect their health (Taylor & Stanton, 2007). One method of coping that can be bad for health is *avoidance coping,* denying that you are ill or are facing other obvious stresses. Avoidance coping has been linked to several health-related problems, such as greater pain after knee surgery (Rosenberger et al., 2004), compromised recovery of function following surgical procedures (Stephens, Druley, & Zautra, 2002), lower adherence to medical regimens and subsequently poorer health in HIV-positive individuals (Weaver et al., 2005), more risky behaviors in HIV-positive intravenous drug users (Avants, Warburton, & Margolin, 2001), and increased physical symptoms among AIDS caregivers (Billings, Folkman, Acree, & Moscowitz, 2000). Avoidance coping also predicts the chronic disease progression and/or mortality of people with cancer (Epping-Jordan, Compas, & Howell, 1994), HIV infection (Leserman et al., 2000), congestive heart failure (Murberg, Furze, & Bru, 2004), and rheumatoid arthritis (Evers et al., 2003).

In contrast, talking about negative emotions and important issues in one's life appears to have positive effects on health (e.g., Panagopoulou, Maes, Rime, & Montgomery, 2006). In a large series of studies, James Pennebaker (2007) found that encouraging people to reveal personal traumas in diaries or essays improves their health. In one study, 50 healthy college students were randomly assigned to write either about the most traumatic and upset-

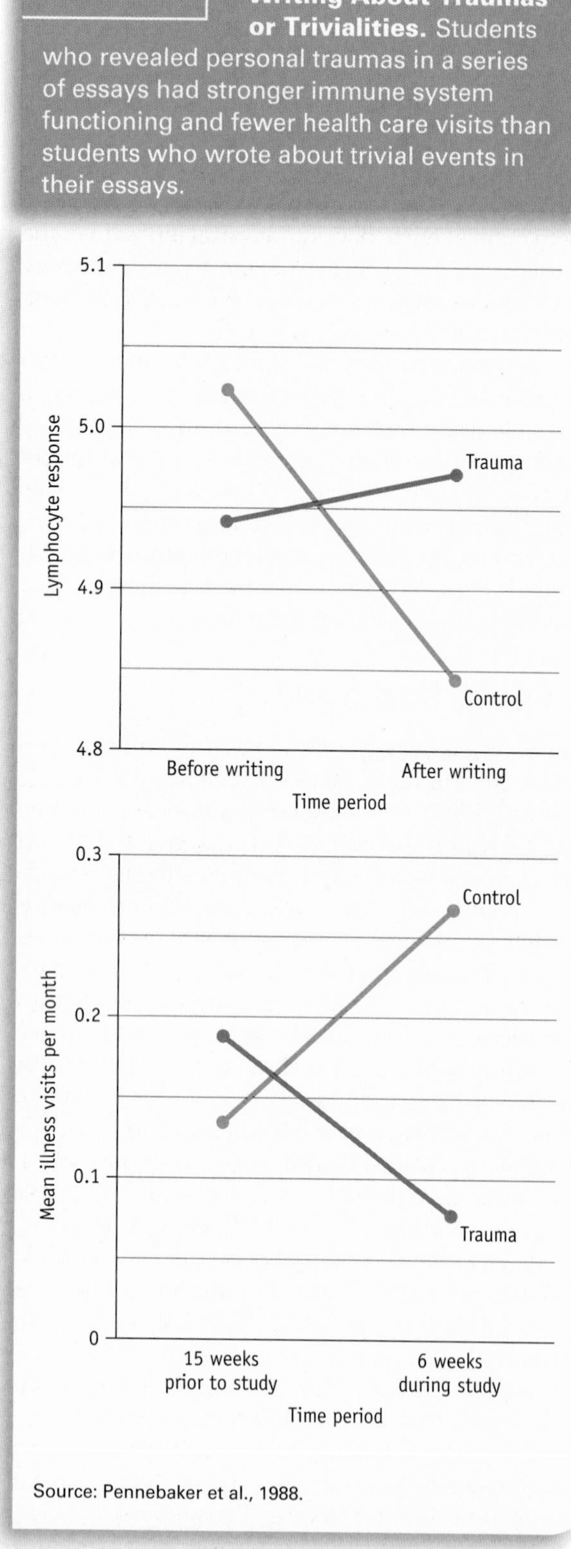

FIGURE 15.2 **Student's Health After Writing About Traumas or Trivialities.** Students who revealed personal traumas in a series of essays had stronger immune system functioning and fewer health care visits than students who wrote about trivial events in their essays.

Source: Pennebaker et al., 1988.

ting events in their lives or about trivial topics for 20 minutes on 4 consecutive days. Blood samples were taken from the students on the day before they began writing, on the last day of writing, and 6 weeks after their writing. The students' blood was tested for several markers of immune system functioning. The number of times the students visited the college health center over the 6 weeks following the writing task was also recorded and was compared with the number of health center visits the students had made before the study. As Figure 15.2 shows, students who revealed their personal traumas in their essays showed more positive immune system functioning and visited the health center less frequently than students in the control group (Pennebaker, Kiecolt-Glaser, & Glaser, 1988). In contrast, the group who wrote about trivial events experienced a slight increase in health center visits and a decrease in immune system functioning, for unknown reasons. Pennebaker (2007) believes that writing helps people understand and find meaning in the events of their lives. Understanding and finding meaning in turn reduce people's negative emotions regarding events and therefore may reduce the physiological strain associated with chronic negative emotions.

A related positive coping strategy is seeking social support. A wide variety of studies have found that people who seek and receive positive emotional support from others show more positive health outcomes, both on microlevel measures such as immune system activity and on macrolevel outcomes such as the progression of major diseases (Hallaraker, Arefjord, Havik, & Maeland, 2001; Pakenham, Chiu, Bursnall, & Cannon, 2007). Taylor and colleagues (2006) found that young adults who had grown up in supportive families showed less reactivity in certain areas of the brain to emotionally provocative photos. This reduced emotional reactivity could reduce physiological reactivity to stress in these individuals.

Gender Differences in Coping

Women are more likely than men to seek support from others in times of stress and to have larger social networks, including friends and extended family members (Kiecolt-Glaser & Newton, 2001). Men, in contrast, typically have a much smaller network of people they turn to for support and also are less likely than women to share personal issues and concerns with friends and family members. Thus, women may have more opportunity than men to benefit from the positive health effects of social support.

A major source of support is a partner or spouse. Married people have less physical illness and are less likely to die from a variety of conditions, including cancer, heart disease, and surgery, than nonmarried people (see Kiecolt-Glaser & Newton, 2001). A conflictual marriage, however, can be a major detriment to health. Experimental studies of married couples found that those who became hostile and negative toward each other while discussing marital problems showed greater decreases in four indicators of immune system functioning than did couples who remained calm and nonhostile in discussing marital problems. Those who became hostile also showed elevated blood pressure for longer periods of time (Kiecolt-Glaser, Malarkey, Chee, & Newton, 1993).

Women are more physiologically reactive than men to marital conflict (Kiecolt-Glaser & Newton, 2001). This may be because women's self-concepts, as well as their financial well-being, tend to be more closely tied to those of their spouse than are men's self-concepts (Cross & Madson, 1997). Also, women are more emotionally attuned to their partners and more conscious of conflict in their relationships. For these reasons, women may be more emotionally, cognitively, and physiologically sensitive to marital conflict, and this sensitivity may counteract any positive health effects they could derive from support from their partner (Kiecolt-Glaser & Newton, 2001). In general, women can benefit physiologically from being in a close relationship, but only if that relationship is a positive one.

Cultural Differences in Coping

Different cultures have different norms for coping with stressful events. People from Asian cultures tend to be more reluctant than European Americans to reach out to others for social support or to express their personal concerns, because they are more concerned about potential harm to their relationships if they do so (Kim, Sherman, & Taylor, 2008). People from Asian cultures instead may find ways to benefit from their social networks that don't involve revealing personal concerns or weaknesses or potentially burdening others. For example, they may remind themselves of their close relationships or simply enjoy the company of people they love. Studies of Asians and Asian Americans find that they derive more emotional and physiological benefit (in terms of lower cortisol levels) from this subtler, more implicit form of seeking social support than from explicitly asking others for support or revealing their needs (Kim et al., 2008). In contrast, European Americans benefit more from explicit forms of seeking social support than from implicit forms. Thus, while coping is important to health in all cultures, the specific forms of coping that are helpful may be influenced by cultural norms.

Psychological Disorders and Physical Health

People with psychological disorders have more physical health problems than people without psychological disorders. For example, a 20-year-long study of people who had been diagnosed with a *DSM* Axis I disorder or a personality disorder found that they had more physical health problems throughout this period than people without a psychological disorder (Chen et al., 2009). Serious health problems included severe allergies, chronic respiratory disease, chronic gastrointestinal disease, cardiovascular disease, cancer, and diabetes. In particular, several studies have found links between depression and a variety of diseases, including cancer, heart disease, diabetes, arthritis, and asthma (Everson-Rose & Lewis, 2005; Katon, 2003).

The mechanisms linking psychological disorders with physical health problems may be many. In some cases, psychopathology and medical illness may share a common genetic cause. For example, depression and cardiovascular disease are both related to genetic factors leading to dysfunction in serotonin systems (McCaffery et al., 2006). In other cases, medical disorders may create psychological disorders. Alzheimer's disease, a neurological disorder leading to dementia, also leads to depression, anxiety, personality changes, and psychotic symptoms such as hallucinations and delusions (see Chapter 11). Thyroid diseases can cause depressive symptoms. Further, the social and psychological stress of having a serious medical illness can cause depression or anxiety (Hammen, 2005).

In still other cases, psychological disorders may contribute to medical disorders. Self-starvation in anorexia nervosa can lead to osteroperosis and loss of bone density as well as to cardiovascular problems (Polivy & Herman, 2002). Substance abuse or dependence can cause many medical diseases, including hypertension and liver and kidney disease (see Chapter 14).

Living with a psychological disorder is stressful in many ways. An individual may have difficulty holding down a job, face discrimination and social rejection, and have trouble getting medical care (Everson-Rose & Lewis, 2005). People with many psychological disorders show signs of chronic arousal of the fight-or-flight response, including chronically elevated cortisol levels (McEwen, 2000). In turn, this excess allostatic load could contribute to physical illness.

Having a psychological disorder also may lead a person to be more pessimistic and to have poorer skills for coping with stress, which could then increase the allostatic load. For example, one study found that the greater rate of physical illness in people with depressive disorders compared to people with no psychological disorder was explained in part by higher levels of neuroticism in the depressed people (Rhebergen et al., 2010).

SHADES OF GRAY

As you read the following case study, ask yourself whether it presents a healthful way of coping with a stressful event.

John Park is a 62-year-old engineer, originally from South Korea and now living in Columbus, Ohio. John recently received news from his physician that he has prostate cancer. The urologist John consulted recommended that he undergo radiation therapy to treat it. John told his wife about the diagnosis and treatment, but he did not tell his children, all of whom are grown and living in other cities. John also did not tell any of his coworkers about the cancer. He took vacation time to receive treatment and recover from its aftereffects. John and his wife seldom spoke about the cancer. He preferred to go on with his life, living as normally as possible. He did enjoy talking with his wife about their children's lives, their grandchildren's escapades, and upcoming visits with friends and family.

Is John coping in a healthful way with his cancer? (Discussion appears at the end of this chapter.)

Neuroticism is a personality trait characterized by hyperreactivity to stress and poor coping skills.

People with psychological disorders also appear to be less likely to engage in positive health-related behaviors (Zvolensky & Smits, 2008). The rate of smoking is two to three times higher in people with psychological disorders than in people without a psychological disorder (Grant, Hasin, et al., 2004; Lasser et al., 2000). People with psychological disorders also appear to be less likely to exercise (Whooley et al., 2008) or to comply with medical regimens (Chen et al., 2009). These health-related behaviors put the individual at risk for the development or worsening of a medical illness.

TEST YOURSELF

1. What is the link between pessimism and health?
2. What is avoidance coping, and how is it linked to health?
3. How are expressive writing and social support linked to health?
4. How are psychological disorders linked to physical health?

APPLY IT Eeyore, the character in the *Winnie-the-Pooh* books who is always pointing out the negative aspects of situations to his friends, might be more susceptible to illness because of which of the following?

a. lack of social support
b. avoidance of difficult issues
c. stressful life
d. pessimism

Answers appear online at www.mhhe.com/nolen5e.

PSYCHOSOCIAL FACTORS IN SPECIFIC DISEASES

Health psychologists have intensively studied certain disease processes in which stress and psychological factors are expected to play a role. We consider two groups of diseases here: immune system diseases and cardiovascular diseases.

The Immune System

The **immune system** protects us from disease by identifying and killing pathogens and tumor cells. The immune system is divided into two branches, the *innate immune system* and the *specific immune system,* both of which have a number of cellular mechanisms for attacking invaders. The innate system reacts quickly and nonspecifically to any microorganism or toxin that enters the body, releasing cells that kill and ingest the invaders. The specific immune system is slower to respond, but its response is tailored to the particular type of pathogen present. The specific immune system remembers the pathogen so that if it attacks again the system is able to kill it more quickly and efficiently.

Stress may affect the immune system in several ways. Although short-term stress appears to increase the potency of immune responses, more chronic stress decreases immune functioning, in part because some of the biochemicals released as part of the fight-or-flight response, such as cortisol, suppress the immune system if a stressor persists for long periods (Segerstrom & Miller, 2004). The most controlled research linking stress and immune system functioning has been conducted with animals. The animals are experimentally exposed to stressors, and then the functioning of their immune system is measured directly. Studies have

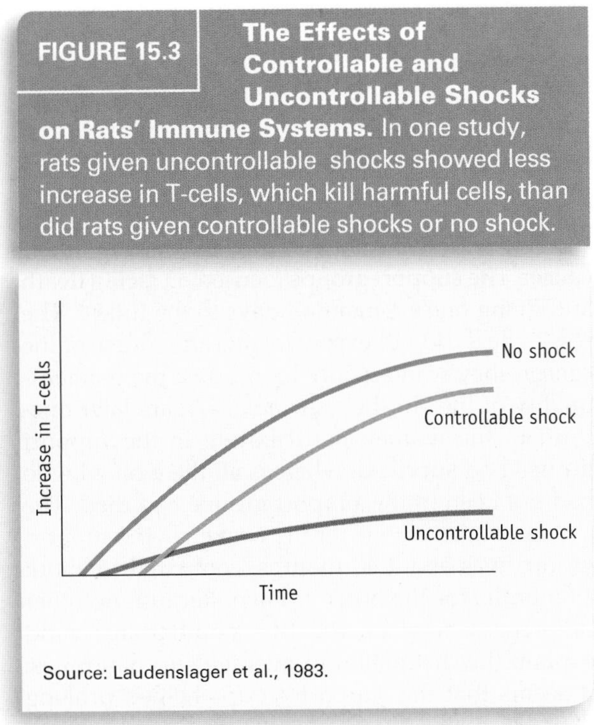

FIGURE 15.3 The Effects of Controllable and Uncontrollable Shocks on Rats' Immune Systems. In one study, rats given uncontrollable shocks showed less increase in T-cells, which kill harmful cells, than did rats given controllable shocks or no shock.

Source: Laudenslager et al., 1983.

shown that immune system cells are suppressed in animals exposed to loud noise, electric shock, separation from their mothers as infants, separation from their peers, and a variety of other stressors (Segerstrom & Miller, 2004).

Animals are most likely to show impairment of their immune system if they are exposed to stressors that are uncontrollable. In one experiment, one group of rats was subjected to an electric shock that the rats could turn off by pressing a lever (Laudenslager et al., 1983). Another group received an identical sequence of shocks but could not control the shock. A third group received no shock. The investigators examined how well the rats' *killer T-cells,* components of the specific immune system that secrete chemicals that kill harmful cells, multiplied when challenged by invaders. They found that the T-cells in the rats that could control the shock multiplied, as did those in the rats that were not shocked at all (Figure 15.3). The T-cells in the rats exposed to uncontrollable shock increased less, however. In another study following the same experimental design, investigators implanted tumor cells into rats, gave them controllable or uncontrollable shocks, and examined whether the rats' natural defenses rejected the tumors. Only 27 percent of the rats given uncontrollable shocks rejected the tumors, whereas 63 percent of the rats given controllable shocks rejected the tumors (Visintainer, Volpicelli, & Seligman, 1982).

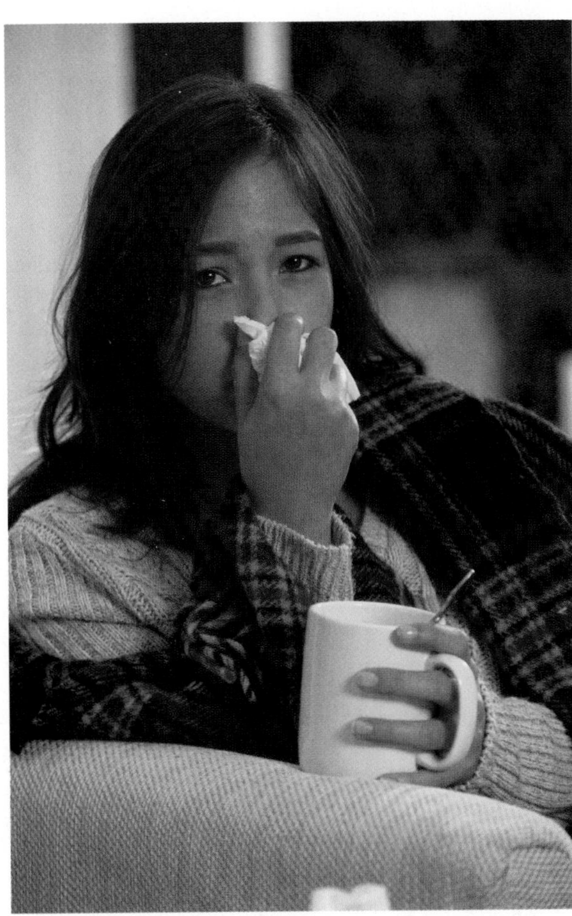

Studies suggest that immune-related diseases, such as colds, are more common among people who are under stress.

Uncontrollable stress also impairs immune system functioning in humans (Schneiderman, Ironson, & Siegel, 2005). The most common disease in which the immune system plays a role is the cold. You may have observed that you and your friends are more likely to get colds during times of stress. To test this common observation, investigators exposed about 400 healthy volunteers to a nasal wash containing either one of five cold viruses or an innocuous salt solution (Cohen, Tyrrell, & Smith, 1991). Participants received a stress score ranging from 3 (lowest stress) to 12 (highest stress) based on the number of stressful events they had experienced in the past year, the degree to which they felt able to cope with daily demands, and their frequency of negative emotions such as anger or depression. The participants were examined daily for cold symptoms and for the presence of cold viruses in their upper respiratory secretions. About 35 percent of the volunteers who reported the highest stress in their lives developed colds, compared to about 18 percent of those with the lowest stress scores.

Many other studies of humans have compared the functioning of the immune system in persons undergoing particular stressors with that of persons not undergoing these stressors. This research confirms that people show higher rates of infectious diseases, such as colds, herpes, and mononucleosis, during times of stress. For example, following the 1994 Northridge earthquake in the Los Angeles area, people whose lives had been more severely disrupted showed greater declines in immune system functioning than did those who had not experienced as much stress as a result of the earthquake (Solomon et al., 1997). People who worried more about the impact of the earthquake on their lives were especially likely to show detriments in immune system functioning (Segerstrom, Solomon, Kemony, & Fahey, 1998).

Negative interpersonal events seem particularly likely to affect immune system functioning. Married couples who argue more show poorer immunological functioning than married couples who have fewer arguments (Kiecolt-Glaser & Newton, 2001). Men and women who have recently been separated or divorced show poorer immune system functioning than married control subjects (Robles & Kiecolt-Glaser, 2003). However, the partner who has more control over the divorce or separation—that is, the partner who initiated it—shows better immune system functioning and better health than the other partner. This is another example of how perceptions of the controllability of a stressor can influence the impact of that stressor on health.

Cancer

Can psychosocial factors affect severe immune-related diseases such as cancer? One study of women with breast cancer found that those who felt they had little control over their cancer and other aspects of their lives were more likely to develop new tumors over a 5-year period than were women who felt more in control, even though the two groups of women did not differ in the type or initial seriousness of their cancers (Levy & Heiden, 1991; Watson et al., 1999). Another study found that pessimistic cancer patients are more likely to die during the first few years after their diagnosis than are optimistic cancer patients (Schulz et al., 1996). Coping also may affect cancer: Studies of women with breast cancer found that those who actively sought social support from others had greater immune system activity (Levy, Herberman, Whiteside, & Sanzo, 1990; Turner-Cobb et al., 2000).

If psychosocial factors such as social support and pessimism do influence the progression of cancer, this raises the possibility that the course of the disease can be affected by psychosocial interventions. Early studies gave hope. In a landmark study of women with advanced breast cancer who were expected to die within 2 years, one group of women participated in a series of weekly support groups and the other group did not (Spiegel, Bollm, Kraemer, & Gottheil, 1989). All the women received standard medical care for their cancer. The support groups focused on facing death and living one's remaining days to the fullest. The researchers did not expect to alter the course of the cancer; they wanted only to improve the women's quality of life. To their surprise, 4 years later one-third of the women participating in the support groups had survived, whereas all the women who had not been in the support groups had died. The average survival time for the women in the support groups was about 40 months, compared to about 19 months for the other women. Because no other differences between the two populations could explain the distinction in average survival times, it seems that the support groups helped prolong the participants' lives. The authors argued that the support groups reduced stress and distress for the women, reducing the release of corticosteroids, which can promote tumor growth (Spiegel, 2001). Having greater support might also help cancer patients engage in better health habits and adhere to difficult medical treatments such as chemotherapy.

Some subsequent studies also found that reducing stress can improve health in cancer patients (Fawzy, Kemeny, et al., 1990; Richardson, Shelton, Krailo, & Levine, 1990). In a study of patients with malignant melanoma (skin cancer), some patients were given six weekly treatment sessions in which they were taught stress-management procedures, relaxation, and methods for coping with their illness. Six months after treatment, the group that received the stress-reduction intervention showed better immune system functioning than the control group, whose members received only customary medical care (Fawzy, Cousins, et al., 1990; Fawzy, Kemeny, et al., 1990). At a 5-year follow-up, patients who had received the intervention were less likely to have had recurrences of the cancer and were significantly less likely to have died (Fawzy et al., 1993). At a 10-year follow-up, there were no differences between the intervention group and the control group in recurrences of the cancer, but the intervention group had a higher survival rate than the control group when other risk factors were taken into account (Fawzy, Canada, & Fawzy, 2003).

Other studies have failed to find effects of psychosocial interventions on the progression of cancer, however. For example, a large clinical trial attempting to replicate the effects in the study by David Spiegel and colleagues failed to find any effects of support groups on health in women with breast cancer (Goodwin et al., 2001; see also Kissane et al., 2007). Meta-analyses and reviews of the effects of psychosocial interventions on survival in cancer patients have not found overall positive effects (Chow, Tsao, & Harth, 2004; Coyne, Stefanek, & Palmer, 2007; Edwards, Hulbert-Williams, & Neal, 2008; Smedslund & Ringdal, 2004). Psychosocial interventions do improve cancer patients' quality of life, however (e.g., Antoni et al., 2001).

HIV/AIDS

The Centers for Disease Control estimates that well over a million people in the United States have been infected with the human immunodeficiency virus (HIV), which causes AIDS (CDC, 2008a). Worldwide, over 30 million people are infected with HIV (WHO, 2008). The progression of illness in people infected with HIV varies greatly. Individuals may live for years with no symptoms, then begin to develop relatively minor health problems such as weight loss, fever, and night sweats. Eventually, they may develop a number of serious and potentially fatal diseases, including pneumocystis pneumonia, cancer, dementia, and a wasting syndrome in which the body withers away. When these diseases emerge, a diagnosis of AIDS may be given. Fortunately, antiretroviral drugs appear to suppress the virus in those infected and to slow the development of AIDS. Unfortunately, these drugs do not eliminate the virus, and their side effects lead many people to discontinue their use. Moreover, millions of people around the world who are infected do not have access to these drugs.

Some studies suggest that psychological factors can affect the progression of illness in people infected with HIV (Leserman, 2008). Much of this research has been conducted with gay men, who have been affected disproportionately by the AIDS epidemic. Many men have lost their partners and many close friends to AIDS, particularly before antiretroviral drugs became available. One study that followed 85 HIV-infected gay men for 3 to 4 years found that those whose partner or close friend had died of AIDS showed a more rapid decline in immune system functioning (Kemeny & Dean, 1995). Another group of investigators followed 96 gay men for over 9 years and found that those who experienced more severe stressors, including the deaths of close friends and partners, showed a faster progression to AIDS (Leserman et al., 1999, 2000, 2002). For every increase of 1 on an index of stress experienced, their risk of developing an AIDS-related clinical condition (e.g., pneumocystis pneumonia) tripled. At the end of the study, 74 percent of the men above the median on the stress index progressed to AIDS, compared with 40 percent below the median.

Experiencing more chronic stressors also appears to affect the progression of HIV in gay men. Many gay men feel compelled to conceal their orientation from others in order to avoid discrimination and rejection. A study of HIV-positive gay men found that those who concealed their orientation showed a faster progression of disease than those who did not (Cole et al., 1995). The differences in health between the men who were "out" and those who were "closeted" did not reflect differences in health-related behaviors (e.g., smoking, exercise). It may be that the stress of chronic inhibition of one's identity can have direct effects on health. More generally, researchers found that HIV-positive men who experienced declines in social support and increases in loneliness showed poorer immune system control over the virus (Dixon et al., 2001).

Stress also affects the progression of the disease in children and adolescents who have been infected with HIV. In a year-long study of 618 HIV-positive young people, those who experienced two or more stressful life events, such as a parent becoming seriously ill, a death in the family, or the loss of their home, were three times more likely than other participants to show immune system declines (Howland et al., 2000).

Even stresses experienced long before an individual is infected with HIV seem to increase the risk for disease progression. The Coping with HIV/AIDS in the Southeast (CHASE) Study followed 490 HIV-positive adult men and women from five rural southern U.S. states for up to 41 months (Leserman et al., 2007). Those with a history of trauma, including childhood physical or sexual abuse or neglect or the murder of a family member, showed faster development of opportunistic infections and were more likely to die of AIDS-related causes than those without a history of trauma (Mugavero et al., 2007).

Interpretations of stress appear to be important moderators of their effects. In one study of 412 patients with HIV, those who scored high on questionnaires measuring pessimism at the beginning of the study had a greater load of the virus 18 months later than those who were less pessimistic (Milam et al., 2004). Similarly, a study of gay men who were HIV-positive found that those who blamed themselves for negative events and those who had more negative expectations showed a greater decline in immune system functioning and a greater development of HIV symptoms over time than did those who were more optimistic (Reed, Kemeny, Taylor, & Visscher, 1999; Segerstrom et al., 1996).

Coronary Heart Disease and Hypertension

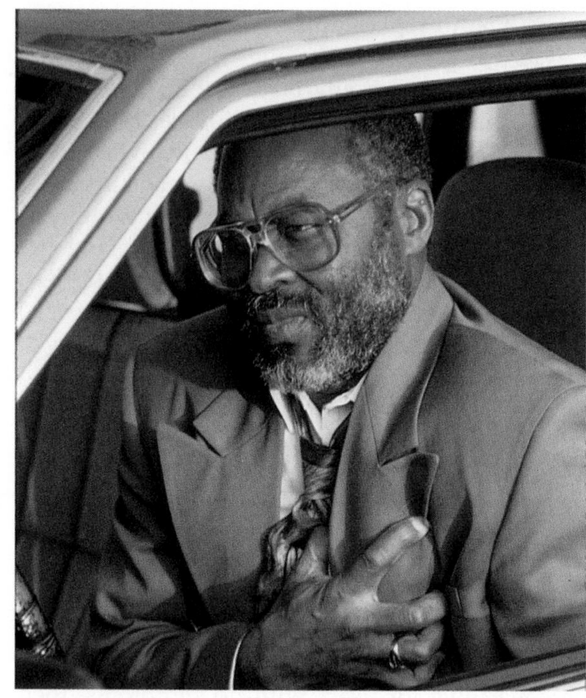

Coronary heart disease occurs when blood vessels supplying the heart are blocked by plaque; complete blockage causes a myocardial infarction—a heart attack.

CASE STUDY

Orrin was so mad he could scream. He had been told at 3:00 that afternoon to prepare a report on the financial status of his division of the company in time for a meeting of the board of directors the next morning. On the way home from work, someone rear-ended him at a stoplight and caused several hundred dollars in damage to his new car. When he got home from work, there was a message from his wife, saying she had been delayed at work and would not be home in time to cook dinner for the children, so Orrin would have to do it. Then, at dinner, Orrin's 12-year-old son revealed that he had flunked his math test that afternoon.

After finishing the dishes, Orrin went to his study to work on the report. The kids had the TV on so loud he couldn't concentrate. Orrin yelled to the kids to turn off the TV but they couldn't hear him. Furious, he stalked into the family room and began yelling at the children about the television and anything else that came to his mind.

Then, suddenly, Orrin began to feel a tremendous pressure on his chest, as if a truck were driving across it. Pain shot through his chest and down his left arm. Orrin felt dizzy and terrified. He collapsed onto the floor. His 7-year-old began screaming. Luckily, his 12-year-old called 911 for an ambulance.

Orrin was having a *myocardial infarction*—a heart attack. A myocardial infarction is one end point of **coronary heart disease,** or **CHD.** CHD occurs when the blood vessels that supply the heart muscles are narrowed or closed by the gradual buildup of a hard, fatty substance called *plaque* and inflammation of the vessel walls, blocking the flow of oxygen and nutrients to the heart. This process is known as *atherosclerosis.* The blockage of vessels can lead to pain, called *angina pectoris,* that radiates across the chest and arm. When oxygen to the heart is completely blocked a myocardial infarction can result.

Coronary heart disease is a leading cause of death and chronic illness around the world. Since 1990, more people have died from coronary heart disease than from any other cause (WHO, 2007). In the United States, CHD accounts for 35 percent of all deaths, or 1 in every 2.9 (American Heart Association, 2010). CHD is also a chronic disease, and more than 12 million Americans live daily with its symptoms. Men are more prone to CHD than are women, but CHD is the leading cause of death among women. African Americans and Hispanic Americans have higher rates of CHD than do European Americans. There seems to be a genetic contribution to coronary heart disease—people with family histories of CHD are at increased risk for the disease. However, 80 to 90 percent of people dying from coronary heart disease have one or more major risk factors that are affected by lifestyle choices, such as high blood pressure, high serum cholesterol, diabetes, smoking, and obesity (WHO, 2007).

People who live in a chronically stressful environment over which they have little control appear to be at increased risk for CHD. A study of 30,000 people in 52 countries found that about one-third of the risk for heart disease is connected to the stressfulness of people's environments (Rosengren et al., 2004; Yusuf et al., 2004). People in high-stress jobs are at increased risk for CHD, particularly if their jobs are highly demanding but provide them little control (Hintsanen et al., 2005; Schneiderman et al., 2005). For example, one study followed about 900 middle-aged men and women over 10 years and tracked the emergence of coronary heart disease (Karasek, Russell, & Theorell, 1982). The people in the study worked in a variety of jobs, and the researchers categorized these jobs in terms of how demanding they were and how much control they allowed a worker. Over the 10 years of this study, workers in jobs that were highly demanding but low in control, such as working on a factory production line, had a risk of coronary heart disease 1.5 times greater than that of workers in other occupations.

Experimental studies with animals have shown that disruption of the social environment can induce pathology that resembles coronary artery disease (Sapolsky, 2007). Some of these experiments have been conducted with a type of macaque monkey whose social organization involves the establishment of stable hierarchies of dominance—dominant and submissive animals can be identified within a given group on the basis of the animals' social behavior. Introduction of unfamiliar monkeys into an established social group is a stressor that leads to increased aggressive behavior as group members attempt to reestablish a social dominance hierarchy (Sapolsky, 2007).

In these studies, some monkey groups remained stable, with fixed memberships, and other groups were stressed by the repeated introduction of new members. After about 2 years under these conditions, the high-ranking or dominant males in the unstable social condition showed more extensive coronary heart disease than the subordinate males (Sapolsky, 2007).

Hypertension, or high blood pressure, is a condition in which blood flows through vessels with excessive force, putting pressure on vessel walls. Hypertension can be caused by blood being pushed with too much force by the heart through vessels or by constriction of the vessel walls. Chronic high blood pressure can cause hardening of the arterial walls and deterioration of the cell tissue, leading eventually to coronary heart disease, kidney failure, and stroke. Almost one-third of the population of the United States has hypertension (Hajjar, Kotchen, & Kotchen, 2006). Genetics appears to play a role in the predisposition to hypertension, but only about 10 percent of all cases of hypertension can be traced to genetics or to specific organic causes, such as kidney dysfunction. The other 90 percent of cases are known as *essential hypertension,* meaning that the causes are unknown (Klabunde, 2005).

Because part of the body's response to stress—the fight-or-flight response—is to increase blood pressure, it is not surprising that people who live in chronically stressful circumstances are more likely to develop hypertension (Schneiderman et al., 2005). As an example, people who move from quiet rural settings to crowded, noisy urban settings show increases in their rates of hypertension.

The chronic stress of poverty can contribute to diseases such as hypertension.

One group that lives in chronically stressful settings and has particularly high rates of hypertension is low-income African Americans (American Heart Association, 2002). They often do not have adequate financial resources for daily living, may be poorly educated and have trouble finding good employment, live in neighborhoods racked with violence, and frequently experience racism. All these conditions have been linked to higher blood pressure (Lehman, Taylor, Kiefe, & Seeman, 2009).

People with hypertension and the children of parents with hypertension tend to show a stronger blood pressure response to a wide variety of stressors. In experimental situations that have people solve arithmetic problems or immerse their hands in ice water, those with no personal or family history of hypertension show much less response than do those with a history of hypertension (Harrell, 1980). In addition, it takes longer for the blood pressure of persons with hypertension to return to normal following stressors than the blood pressure of those without hypertension.

Thus, people with hypertension and people with family or genetic histories of hypertension may have a heightened physiological reactivity to stress. If they are exposed to chronic stress, their chronically elevated blood pressure can lead to hardening and narrowing of the arteries, creating a physiologically based hypertension. Low-income African Americans may have both this physiological predisposition to heightened reactivity to stress *and* chronic exposure to stressful environments, making them doubly vulnerable to hypertension (Lehman et al., 2009).

Individuals with Type A personalities often put heightened stress on themselves, which may put them at risk for coronary heart disease.

Personality and CHD

The personality factor traditionally linked to coronary heart disease is the **Type A behavior pattern.** The three components of the Type A pattern, according to the physicians who identified it (Friedman & Rosenman, 1974), are a sense of time urgency, easily aroused hostility, and competitive striving for achievement. People who are Type A are always in a hurry, setting unnecessary deadlines for themselves and trying to do multiple things at once. They are competitive, even in situations in which being competitive is ridiculous. They also are chronically hostile and will fly into a rage with little provocation.

One of the most compelling studies to demonstrate the relationship between the Type A pattern and coronary heart disease followed more than 3,000 healthy middle-aged men for 8½ years (Rosenman et al., 1976). Over the 8½ years of the study, Type A men had twice as many heart attacks or other forms of coronary heart disease as non–Type A men. These results held up even after diet, age, smoking, and other variables associated with coronary heart disease were taken into account. Other studies have confirmed this twofold risk and have linked Type A behavior to heart disease in both men and women (Myrtek, 2007; Schneiderman et al., 2005). In addition, Type A behavior is correlated with the severity of coronary artery blockage as determined at autopsy or in X-ray studies (Friedman et al., 1968; Williams, Barefoot, Haney, & Harrell, 1988). Based on such evidence, in 1981 the American Heart Association classified Type A behavior as a risk factor for coronary heart disease.

Subsequent research suggests that the definition of Type A behavior as originally formulated is too diffuse. The crucial variable in predicting coronary heart disease may be hostility, particularly a cynical form of hostility characterized by suspiciousness, resentment, frequent anger, antagonism, and distrust of others (Barefoot et al., 1989; Miller, Smith, Turner, & Guijarro, 1996). Time urgency and competitiveness appear to be less predictive of heart disease.

For example, a 25-year study of 118 male lawyers found that those who scored high on hostility traits on a personality inventory taken in law school were five times more likely to die before age 50 than classmates who scored low (Barefoot et al., 1989). Similarly, in a study of physicians, hostility scores obtained in medical school predicted the incidence of coronary heart disease as well as mortality from all causes (Barefoot, Dahlstrom, & Williams, 1983). In both studies, the relationship between hostility and illness was independent of the effects of smoking, age, and high blood pressure.

How does hostility lead to coronary heart disease? Again, overarousal of the sympathetic nervous system may play a role. Hostile people show greater physiological arousal in the anticipation of stressors and in the early stages of dealing with stressors (Benotsch, Christensen, & McKelvey, 1997; Lepore, 1995). Their heart rates and blood pressures are higher, and they have greater secretion of the stress-related biochemicals known as *catecholamines.* They also return more slowly to baseline levels of sympathetic nervous system activity following stressors than do nonhostile people. This hyperreactivity may cause wear and tear on the coronary arteries, leading to coronary heart disease. Alternately, the excessive secretion of catecholamines in response to stress in hostile people may exert a direct chemical effect on blood vessels. The frequent rise and fall of catecholamine levels may cause frequent changes in blood pressure, reducing the resilience of the blood vessels. Hostile people also tend to engage in behaviors that increase their propensity for heart disease, including smoking, heavy drinking, and high-cholesterol diets (Schneiderman et al., 2005).

Some research has suggested that men are more likely than women to have the Type A personality pattern (Barefoot, Siegler, Nowlin, & Peterson, 1987; Haynes, Feinleib, & Kannel, 1980). Men also are more likely than women to carry three other risk factors for CHD: smoking, hypertension, and elevated cholesterol. Historically, far more men than women die of cardiovascular disease. In recent years, however, the number of women dying of cardiovascular disease has increased worldwide, while the number of men dying of cardiovascular disease has decreased (Espnes & Byrne, 2008).

Contrary to popular belief, women carry as much anger and hostility as men—they just don't express it as readily (Kring, 2000; Lavoie, Miller, Conway, & Flect, 2001; Nolen-Hoeksema & Rusting, 1999). Excessive hostility and anger, whether expressed or suppressed, are associated with risk factors for coronary heart disease in both women and men (Espnes & Byrne, 2008; Matthews et al., 1998).

Modifying Hostility to Improve Cardiovascular Functioning

A combination of cognitive and behavioral techniques has been shown to improve cardiovascular health by reducing Type A behavior, particularly hostility (Williams, 2008). One hallmark study included more than 1,000 individuals who had experienced at least one heart attack (Friedman et al., 1994). Treatment helped hostile participants learn to express themselves without exploding and to alter certain behaviors, such as interrupting others or talking or eating hurriedly. This treatment also targeted other aspects of Type A behavior, because the study was done before hostility was identified as the key factor. Participants were taught to overcome their sense of time urgency by practicing standing in line (which Type A individuals find irritating) and using the opportunity to reflect, to watch people, or to strike up a conversation with a stranger. Cognitive techniques helped participants reevaluate certain beliefs (such as the notion that success depends on the quantity of work produced) that might lead to urgent and hostile behavior. Also, participants found ways to make their home and work environments less stressful, such as by reducing unnecessary social engagements. By the end of the study 4½ years later, the intervention group had experienced half as many new heart attacks as the group whose participants were not taught to alter their lifestyles.

Depression and Coronary Heart Disease

Major depression occurs in 15 to 20 percent of hospitalized patients with coronary heart disease, and up to 50 percent have some depressive symptoms (Frasure-Smith & Lesperance, 2005). There are several third variables that could account for the link between depression and CHD. The blocked arteries that lead to CHD also lead to reduced oxygen in the brain and the marshaling of the immune system, both of which can contribute to mood changes, including depression (Alexopoulos et al., 1997; Dantzer, Wollman, & Yirmiya, 2002). Both CHD and depression may be caused by a relative deficiency in the polyunsaturated omega-3 fatty acids, found primarily in fatty fish (Ali et al., 2009). And, as noted earlier, both depression and CHD are linked to genes that alter the functioning of the serotonin system (Frasure-Smith & Lesperance, 2005).

Several studies suggest that depression doubles the risk of recurrent heart attacks and mortality in individuals with CHD (Frasure-Smith & Lesperance, 2005). For example, one study of patients with coronary heart disease found that those diagnosed with major depression were more than twice as likely to have a heart attack or some other major cardiac event (e.g., emergency heart surgery) over a 2-year follow-up period, even after taking into account a number of other risk factors for heart disease, such as age and high blood pressure (Frasure-Smith & Lesperance, 2008).

Depression could contribute to CHD through several pathways. Depression is associated with reduced heart rate variability (i.e., less variation from heart beat to heart beat), which is an indication of poorer functioning of the autonomic nervous system. In turn, low heart rate variability is a risk factor for CHD (Frasure-Smith & Lesperance, 2005).

Depressed people with CHD are less likely than nondepressed people with CHD to engage in behaviors that could reduce their risk of future cardiac events, such as eating a low-fat diet and increasing exercise (Gehi et al., 2005; Ziegelstein et al., 2000). In one longitudinal study of 1,017 adults with coronary heart disease, those who were depressed were more likely than those who were not depressed to smoke, to be less physically active, to not take prescribed medications, and to have a higher mean body mass index (Whooley et al., 2008). The depressed patients experienced 50 percent more cardiac events (e.g., heart attacks) over the 4-year follow-up than did nondepressed patients. The depressed patients' poor health behaviors accounted for their increased risk of cardiac events even after controlling for a number of physiological risk factors and possible third variables. In particular, the depressed patients' lower level of physical exercise accounted for 31 percent of the difference in cardiac events between the depressed and the nondepressed patients.

These results suggest that increasing physical exercise is an important target of intervention for depressed patients with coronary heart disease. Exercise is effective in reducing both CHD and depression (Blumenthal et al., 2005, 2007). In contrast, attempts to reduce depression in CHD patients through the use of antidepressants or cognitive-behavioral therapy have had limited effects on both the depression and the CHD (Berkman et al., 2003; Glassman et al., 2002; Rees et al., 2004; van Melle et al., 2007).

TEST YOURSELF

1. How does stress affect immune system functioning? What does research show about the links between stress, pessimism, and cancer?
2. How does stress affect HIV/AIDS?
3. What personality factors are linked to coronary heart disease?
4. What are the links between depression and coronary heart disease? What behaviors may account for this link?

APPLY IT Walter's wife describes him as a Type A personality: He fights to be first in line at the checkout stand and gets enraged if someone cuts in line before him. He's always in a hurry, driving his car too fast while simultaneously talking on the phone and eating his lunch. What aspect of Walter's behavior puts him most at risk for coronary heart disease?

a. his multitasking
b. his hostility
c. his being in a hurry
d. his competitiveness

Answers appear online at www.mhhe.com/nolen5e.

INTERVENTIONS TO IMPROVE HEALTH-RELATED BEHAVIORS

We know that our behaviors have a large influence on our health, yet most of us do not follow the recommendations of experts. Why? According to health psychologists, it takes more than information to change people's actions. People must have the motivation to change their behavior, believe they can change it, and have the skills to do so (Ajzen, 1991; Bandura, 2006; Leventhal, Weinman, Leventhal, & Phillips, 2008). Here we consider some attempts to give people the tools they need to change their health-related behaviors.

Guided Mastery Techniques

Guided mastery techniques provide people with explicit information about how to engage in positive health-related behaviors and with opportunities to do so in increasingly challenging situations. The goals are to increase people's skills as well as their beliefs that they can engage in the behaviors, known as *self-efficacy beliefs* (Bandura, 2006). The kinds of actions that might be targeted include using condoms during sex in order to prevent the spread of HIV and other sexually transmitted diseases, refusing alcohol when being pressured to drink, or starting an exercise program.

A guided mastery program for teaching women how to negotiate safe sexual practices might begin with information on condom use. A counselor then might model how a woman can ask a man to use a condom. The women would watch the counselor and then practice insisting on condom use in role-plays with the counselor or other group participants. In this role playing, the women would face increasingly difficult challenges to their insistence on condom use, learn strategies for meeting these challenges, and practice using those strategies. The women might also be taught to determine when it is useless to argue any longer and skills for removing themselves from unsafe sexual encounters.

Guided mastery techniques were used successfully in a program with African American women called Sister-to-Sister: The Black Women's Health Project Intervention (Jemmott, Jemmott III, & O'Leary, 2007). In five short interventions, nurses gave women information about the cause, transmission, and prevention of sexually transmitted diseases (STDs). The women then participated in guided mastery exercises to increase their skills and self-confidence for negotiating condom use by their male partners. The women also learned to eroticize condom use by incorporating putting on condoms into foreplay and intercourse in ways that increase positive attitudes toward their use. Compared to women who received only information, without guided mastery exercises, these women showed greater confidence in negotiating condom use and a stronger intention to use condoms (O'Leary, Jemmott, & Jemmott III, 2006). Most important, the program resulted in lower sexual risk behavior and lower incidence of STDs over the 12 months following it.

Cultural norms regarding health behaviors can affect people's willingness to engage in them (Azjen, 1991). Programs like the guided mastery program described above have been adapted to address cultural norms that might encourage or interfere with targeted health behaviors (Bandura, 2006). For example, a strong cultural value in many Hispanic groups is *familism*, or prioritizing the respect and care of one's family over one's individual needs. One study of Hispanic adolescents adapted a guided mastery program to include discussions of the impact of risky sexual behaviors on the loved ones of the adolescents (Koniak-Griffen et al., 2008). The adolescents in this program were all teen parents, so the program materials focused on cultural values of parental protectiveness, using traditional teachings of Chicano, Latino, and Native American ancestors. The adolescents who received this culturally adapted intervention showed greater increases in condom use than a comparison group of adolescents who received only general information about HIV prevention.

Internet-Based Health Interventions

Millions of people around the world get health information from the Internet every day. The Web can deliver high-quality health information and interventions to promote behaviors that improve health. Moreover, online interventions can be delivered to individuals who might not have access to in-person programs because none are available in their area or because they cannot afford them. Over half the population of most industrialized countries has access to the Internet, and the majority of Internet users say they get health information off the Web (Vandalenotte, Spathonis, Eakin, & Owan, 2007). Controlled studies of the effectiveness of these interventions offer hope that they can be effective in helping people change their behaviors and improve their health.

Many Internet-based behavioral interventions aim to increase people's exercise and improve their diet. Regular physical exercise significantly decreases the risk of cardiovascular disease, diabetes, and several forms of cancer (Ehrman, Gordon, Visich, & Keteyian, 2009). Yet most people do not exercise regularly. Similarly, while eating fresh fruits and vegetables every day reduces the risk of developing several major illnesses, the diets of people around the world increasingly are filled with high-fat, high-sugar, low-nutrition foods (Brownell & Horgen, 2004). As a result, obesity rates are skyrocketing, especially in developed countries. Intensive, in-person programs can spur people to increase their exercise and improve their diet. However, these programs are expensive, time-consuming, and unavailable to many people. The Internet provides the opportunity to deliver exercise and nutrition programs to large segments of the population for a relatively low cost.

One such program was designed by General Electric to improve the health of its workforce (Pratt et al., 2006). Employees were invited by e-mail to participate in the program, which involved increasing their daily exercise to 10,000 steps or 30 minutes of moderate-intensity physical exercise, eating five servings of fruits and vegetables

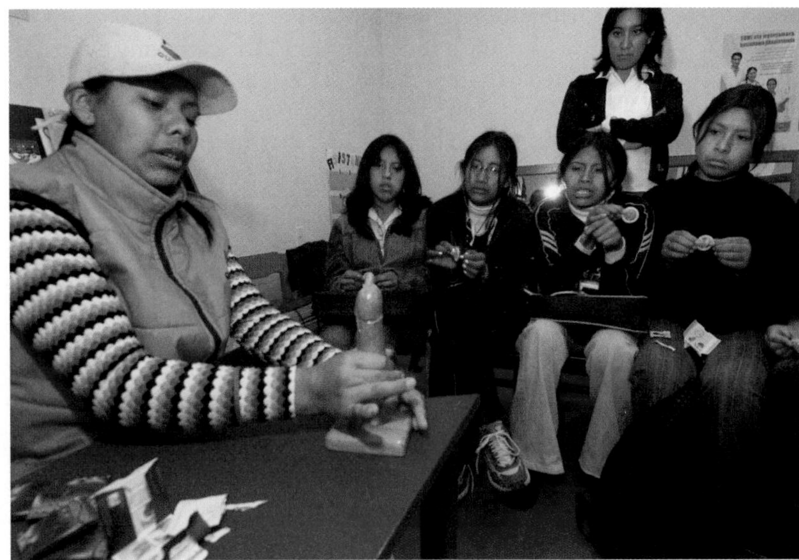

Programs to increase safe sexual behavior and promote the use of condoms may help prevent the spread of sexually transmitted diseases, especially if the programs are culturally sensitive.

Recent studies suggest that the Internet may be a good medium for delivering health-related interventions.

a day, and losing weight if significantly overweight. Participating employees completed an online assessment of their current behaviors and physical needs. Based on their profile, they received regular e-mails about their progress in the program, as well as e-newsletters with health tips and case studies of employees who had made major lifestyle changes. They were given phone and e-mail access to nutrition and fitness coaches who could answer their questions and provide personalized advice. Participants discussed exercise and diet in chat rooms. The Weight Watchers program was made available online. The company even created a "video reality series" that followed two employees who were participating in the program.

An evaluation of 2,498 employees across 53 nations who participated in the program for about 8 months showed that these employees significantly increased their physical activity and their consumption of fruits and vegetables (Pratt et al., 2006). They also lost an average of 4 to 5 pounds over the duration of the program.

A review of 15 Internet-based programs designed to improve both physical activity and diet found that the majority resulted in positive outcomes for participants compared to control groups (Vandelanotte et al., 2007). Gains tend to be relatively modest, and they are short-lived if the programs are not continued. Across thousands or even millions of people, however, the potential public health impact of these programs is great.

Busy students are often sleep deprived.

TEST YOURSELF

1. What are guided mastery techniques?
2. How can the Web be used to promote healthy behaviors?

APPLY IT Imagine that you want to design a program to discourage Hispanic college students from smoking. Which of the following components would be *least* likely to have a major impact on smoking in your target audience?

a. detailed information about the health risks of smoking
b. motivational messages focusing on the impact smoking has on their close relationships
c. skills messages showing how to use nicotine-gum and other strategies for lowering craving
d. self-efficacy messages enhancing their belief that they can stop smoking

Answers appear online at www.mhhe.com/nolen5e.

SLEEP AND HEALTH

Getting enough sleep is critically important to health. People who sleep fewer than 6 hours each night have a 70 percent higher mortality rate than those who sleep at least 7 or 8 hours each night (Ikehara et al., 2009; Kryger, Roth, & Dement, 1994). This is true for both men and women, for people of many ethnicities, and for people with many different health backgrounds. Lack of sleep weakens the immune system (Cruess et al., 2003; Irwin et al., 2008). Among middle-aged adults, those who sleep less show greater development of heart disease over time (King et al., 2008). People who work rotating shifts have higher rates of illness, including cardiovascular and gastrointestinal disease, than other people (Chatzitheochari & Arber, 2009).

Sleep deprivation also has many psychological effects: It impairs memory, learning, logical reasoning, arithmetic skills, complex verbal processing, and decision making. For example, reducing your amount of sleep to 5 hours each night for only 2 nights significantly reduces performance on math problems and creative-thinking tasks. This means that staying up to study for exams for only a couple of nights can significantly impair the ability to do well on those exams (Wolfson, 2010). Sleep deprivation also causes irritability, emotional ups and downs, and perceptual distortions, such as mild hallucinations (Harvey, 2008).

Sleep deprivation can literally kill. Each year in the United States, almost 20 percent of all serious car-crash injuries are due to driver sleepiness. Over half of automobile drivers admit to having driven when drowsy at least once in the past year, and 28 percent say they have fallen asleep at the wheel (National Sleep Foundation, 2009). Medical professionals work longer hours than members of almost any other profession, and as many as 98,000 deaths occur annually in the United States due to medical errors—many associated with sleep deprivation. Some of the most serious disasters in modern history have been the result of mistakes made by sleepy people (Mitler & Miller, 1995). In 1979, the worst nuclear plant accident in the United States

This train crash in Boston occurred when the driver fell asleep for only a few seconds.

occurred when fatigued workers at Three Mile Island failed to respond to a mechanical problem at the plant. In 1986, the world's worst nuclear disaster happened in Chernobyl in Ukraine (then part of the Soviet Union) during a test conducted by an exhausted team of engineers. In 2008, a Boston trolley car crashed into a stopped trolley after the driver of the first vehicle ran a red light; the National Transportation Safety Board concluded that the driver went into a "microsleep"—falling asleep for only a few seconds—resulting in the crash and her death (Ahlers, 2009).

It is frightening to realize that sleep deprivation is so widespread. Over half of Americans say they chronically feel sleep deprived (National Sleep Foundation, 2009). Young adults need, on average, 9.2 hours of sleep each day. Yet most young adults sleep 7.5 or fewer hours each day (National Sleep Foundation, 2009). Similarly, most middle-aged adults need at least 7 or 8 hours of sleep each day, but most get fewer than 7 hours. People who work rotating shifts or in jobs demanding long periods of activity, such as nurses, doctors, firefighters, police, and rescue personnel, often are chronically sleep deprived (Chatzitheochari & Arber, 2009). Even when they have time to sleep, they have trouble falling asleep because their body's natural rhythms have been disrupted by their irregular schedule. The effects of sleep deprivation are cumulative: A person builds up an increasing "sleep debt" for every 24-hour period in which he or she does not get adequate sleep (Wolfson, 2001).

Stress is a frequent contributor to sleep problems. A 2009 poll taken during a period of economic crisis found that one-third of Americans were losing sleep over the state of the U.S. economy and personal financial matters (National Sleep Foundation, 2009). In general, Americans are sleeping less while trying to cram more and more into the day, including multiple jobs, exercise, socializing, and school. Similar patterns are found in other developed countries, including Great Britain (Chatzitheochari & Arber, 2009). Over the past century, the average night's sleep time in these societies has declined more than 20 percent (National Sleep Foundation, 2009).

Assessing Sleep

What is sleep? Analysis of brain-wave activity suggests that there are five stages of sleep: four differing depths of sleep and a fifth stage, known as rapid eye movement (or REM) sleep (Figure 15.4). When a person closes his or her eyes and relaxes, the brain waves characteristically show a regular pattern of 8 to 12 hertz (cycles per second); these are known as *alpha waves.* As the individual drifts into Stage 1 sleep, the brain waves become less regular and have lower amplitude. Stage 2 includes *spindles*—short runs of rhythmical responses of 12 to 16 hertz—and an occasional sharp rise and fall in the amplitude of the entire EEG (referred to as a K-complex). The still deeper Stage 3 and Stage 4 are characterized by slow waves of 1 to 2 hertz, known as *delta waves.*

After an adult has been asleep for an hour or so, the EEG becomes very active. Electrodes near the person's eyes detect pronounced rapid eye movements. This stage is known as *REM sleep;* the other four stages are known as *non-REM* (or *NREM*) *sleep.* The stages alternate throughout the night, beginning with the NREM stages. Several sleep cycles occur, each containing some REM and some NREM sleep. There usually are four or five distinct REM periods over the course of an 8-hour night's sleep, with an occasional brief awakening as morning arrives. Dreaming occurs during REM sleep.

The pattern of the sleep cycles varies with a person's age. Newborn infants, for instance, spend about half their sleeping time in REM sleep. This drops to 20–25 percent of total sleep time by age 5 and remains fairly constant until old age, when it drops to 18 percent of total sleep time or less. Older

FIGURE 15.4 **EEG Recordings During Various Stages of Sleep.** The awake stage (relaxed with eyes closed) is characterized by alpha waves (8–12 hertz). Stage 1 is basically a transition from wakefulness to the deeper stages of sleep. Stage 2 is defined by the presence of sleep spindles (brief bursts of 12–16-hertz waves) and K-complexes (a sharp rise and fall in the brainwave pattern). Stages 3 and 4 are marked by the presence of delta waves (1–12 hertz), and the only difference between these two stages is the amount of delta waves found. Stage 3 is scored when 20–50 percent of the record contains delta waves, and Stage 4 when the percentage of delta waves is 50 percent or more.

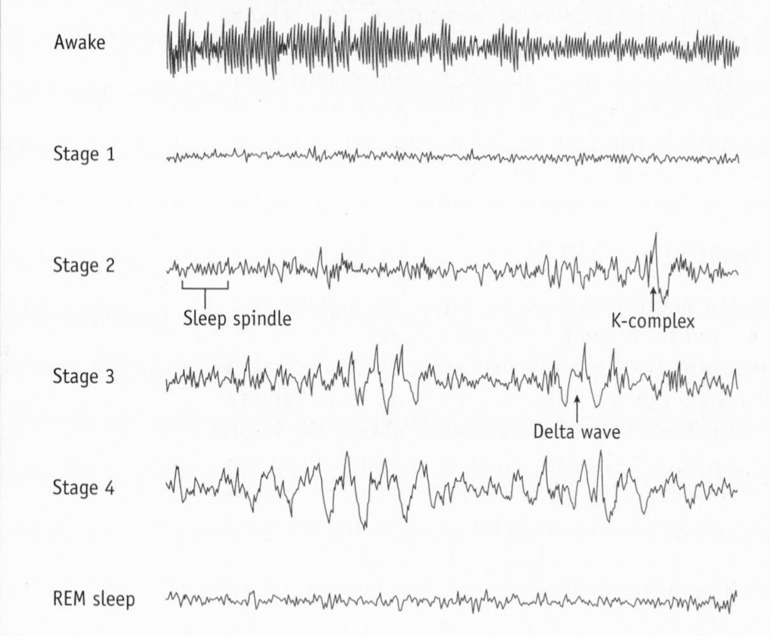

people tend to experience less Stage 3 and Stage 4 sleep (sometimes these stages disappear) and more frequent and longer nighttime awakenings (Liu & Ancoli-Israel, 2006).

A comprehensive assessment of how people sleep can be obtained by a *polysomnographic (PSG) evaluation.* This requires individuals to spend one or more nights in a lab, connected to instruments that measure respiration and oxygen desaturation (a measure of airflow), leg movements, eye movements, brain-wave activity, and heart activity (Buysse et al., 2006). An alternative is for individuals to wear a wristwatchlike device called an *actigraph,* which records movement (Morgenthaler et al., 2007). The data it gathers can be compared to known patterns of movement during sleep to determine when individuals are awake or asleep.

These methods of assessing sleep are objective and detailed, but they also are expensive and require special equipment. More frequently, people are asked to keep a detailed diary of their sleep patterns (what time they go to bed, when they awaken during the night, and when they get up in the morning). Questionnaires may be used to assess people's sleep patterns even more quickly.

Sleep Disorders

Some people experience so much difficulty sleeping that they may be diagnosed with a sleep disorder. The *DSM-IV-TR* recognizes four general types of sleep disorders. **Sleep disorders related to another mental disorder** are sleep disturbances that are directly attributable to psychological disorders. Sleep disturbances occur in many mental disorders. In particular, insomnia is a symptom of unipolar depression and co-occurs at high rates with other mental disorders, including bipolar disorder, schizophrenia, attention-deficit/hyperactivity disorder, the anxiety disorders, and substance use (Harvey, 2008). The symptoms of these disorders, such as anxiety, can make it difficult to sleep. In turn, insomnia can worsen the symptoms of these other disorders, perhaps in part because people who are sleep deprived are more emotionally reactive and have more difficulty regulating their emotions. They also have more difficulty functioning in their daily life due to decreased concentration and performance, which lead to the further accumulation of stressors (Harvey, 2008).

Sleep disorders due to a general medical condition are sleep disturbances that result from the physiological effects of a medical condition. Many medical conditions can disturb sleep, including degenerative neurological illnesses, such as Parkinson's disease; cerebrovascular disease, including strokes; endocrine conditions, such as hypo- or hyperthyroidism; viral and bacterial infections, such as viral encephalitis; pulmonary diseases, such as chronic bronchitis; and pain from musculoskeletal diseases, such as rheumatoid arthritis or fibromyalgia (Wolfson, 2001).

Substance-induced sleep disorders are sleep disturbances due to the use of substances, including prescription medications (e.g., medications that control hypertension or cardiac arrhythmias) and nonprescription substances (e.g., alcohol and caffeine).

The fourth type of sleep disorders is **primary sleep disorders.** These are further divided into *dyssomnias* (Table 15.2), and *parasomnias* (Table 15.3).

Dyssomnias

The **dyssomnias** are primary sleep disorders involving abnormalities in the amount, quality, or timing of sleep. These disorders are not due to a general medical condition, to a major mental disorder, or to substance use.

TABLE 15.2 Dyssomnias

These are the primary sleep disorders known as dyssomnias. Each condition must not be due to a general medical condition or substance use and must cause significant impairment in functioning to be diagnosed.

Type	Definition
Primary insomnia	Difficulty initiating or maintaining sleep, or nonrestorative sleep, for at least a month
Primary hypersomnia	Excessive sleepiness for at least 1 month, as evidenced by either prolonged sleep episodes or daytime sleep episodes that occur almost daily
Narcolepsy	Irresistible attacks of refreshing sleep that occur daily over at least 3 months plus either sudden loss of muscle tone or recurrent intrusions of elements of rapid eye movement (REM) sleep
Breathing-related sleep disorder	Sleep disruption leading to excessive sleepiness or insomnia that is due to a sleep-related breathing condition, such as apnea
Circadian rhythm sleep disorder	Sleep disruption leading to excessive sleepiness or insomnia that is due to a mismatch between the sleep-wake schedule required by a person's environment and his or her circadian sleep-wake pattern

Source: Reprinted with permission from the *Diagnostic and Statistical Manual of Mental Disorders,* Fourth Edition, Text Revision.

TABLE 15.3 Parasomnias

These are the primary sleep disorders known as parasomnias. Each condition must not be due to a general medical condition or substance use and must cause significant impairment in functioning to be diagnosed.

Type	Definition
Nightmare disorder	Repeated awakenings with detailed recall of extended and extremely frightening dreams, usually involving threats to survival, security, or self-esteem; on awakening, the person is alert and oriented.
Sleep terror disorder	Repeated, abrupt awakenings beginning with a panicky scream; intense fear and signs of autonomic arousal; relative unresponsiveness to the efforts of others to comfort the person; no detailed dream is recalled, and there is amnesia for the episode.
Sleepwalking disorder	Repeated episodes of rising from the bed during sleep and walking about; while sleepwalking, the person has a blank, staring face, is relatively unresponsive to others, and can be awakened only with great difficulty; on awakening, the person has amnesia for the episode; within several minutes after awakening, there is no impairment of mental activity or behavior, although there may initially be a short period of confusion and disorientation.

Source: Reprinted with permission from the *Diagnostic and Statistical Manual of Mental Disorders,* Fourth Edition, Text Revision.

Insomnia Probably the most familiar dyssomnia is **primary insomnia,** chronic difficulty initiating or maintaining sleep or sleep that does not restore energy and alertness. People with insomnia usually report a combination of difficulty falling asleep and intermittent wakefulness during the night.

Occasional problems with insomnia are extremely common, with up to 50 percent of adults

TABLE 15.4 *DSM-IV-TR* Criteria for Primary Insomnia

A. The predominant complaint is difficulty initiating or maintaining sleep, or nonrestorative sleep, for at least 1 month.

B. The sleep disturbance (or associated daytime fatigue) causes clinically significant distress or impairment in social, occupational, or other important areas of functioning.

C. The sleep disturbance does not occur exclusively during the course of narcolepsy, breathing-related sleep disorder, circadian rhythm sleep disorder, or a parasomnia.

D. The disturbance does not occur exclusively during the course of another mental disorder (e.g., major depressive disorder).

E. The disturbance is not due to the direct effects of a substance (e.g., a drug of abuse, a medication) or a general medical condition.

reporting they have had insomnia at some time in their life and one in three adults complaining they have had insomnia in the past year (National Sleep Foundation, 2009). Episodic insomnia is defined as difficulty falling asleep or staying asleep that lasts only a few days and is an isolated occurrence (Wolfson, 2001). This difficulty is often tied to a specific stressor, such as facing a major exam or being in an unfamiliar place, and it stops once the stressor has passed.

To receive the diagnosis of *primary insomnia,* the symptoms of insomnia must persist for at least 1 month, and the sleep disturbance must cause significant distress or impairment in functioning (Table 15.4). In addition, the insomnia must not be due to another mental disorder, to a medical condition, or to substance use. Chronic insomnia affects 10 to 15 percent of adults and is more frequent in women than in men and more common in older adults than in younger adults (Wolfson, 2001; Zhang & Wing, 2006).

As noted, insomnia very often is related to other mental disorders or general medical conditions (Harvey, 2008). The *DSM-5* is likely to classify these types of insomnias as primary insomnias instead of as sleep disorders due to another mental disorder or sleep disorders due to a general medical condition (American Psychiatric Association, 2010). This change is meant to acknowledge that insomnia is a condition of clinical importance whether it is due to other mental disorders, to general medical conditions, or to other biological or psychosocial factors.

When we fall asleep and when we awaken are strongly influenced by our biological rhythms, particularly body temperature rhythms (Lack et al., 2008). When we are on a schedule of sleeping at night and being awake and active during the day, our core body temperature typically reaches its minimum between 4 and 6 a.m.; falling asleep is easiest 5 to 6 hours before that minimum is reached (between about 11 p.m. and 1 a.m.). Wakening usually occurs 1 to 3 hours after the minimum core body temperature is reached. Some people have disruptions in this body temperature rhythm that interfere with their ability to fall asleep in the late evening or to stay asleep in the early morning (Lack et al., 2008).

Any major stressor can trigger an episode of insomnia, including relationship difficulties, job loss, the death of a loved one, and financial problems (Wolfson, 2001). In a vicious cycle, this episodic insomnia can become chronic insomnia. The longer the person lies in bed unable to go to sleep, the more distressed and restless he or she becomes. The person's wakefulness then becomes conditioned to the environment—to the bed and bedroom—leading to even more difficulty sleeping the next night.

Allison Harvey (2005) has proposed an empirically supported cognitive model of insomnia that suggests that cognitions maintain insomnia. First, during the day and when trying to sleep, individuals with insomnia worry about whether they will sleep. They may monitor the clock while trying to fall asleep, worrying more as time passes (Tang, Schmidt, & Harvey, 2007). This worry creates a cognitive and physiological arousal that keeps them awake. Second, they are hypervigilant for things that might keep them awake, such as noises in the environment or bodily aches and pains (Semler & Harvey, 2007). Third, they believe they get less sleep than they do and attribute daytime problems to their insomnia. This cognition feeds their anxiety about their insomnia. Fourth, they engage in counterproductive behaviors to try to help themselves sleep. They may drink alcohol, which can exacerbate insomnia, or avoid social engagements at night, which leaves them with more time alone to worry.

Cognitive-behavioral interventions for insomnia can be highly effective (e.g., Bastien et al., 2004; Harvey, McGlinchey, & Gruber, 2010). These interventions aim to reduce worries about sleep ("I wonder if I'm going to have a bad night again tonight!"), unhelpful beliefs about sleep ("Waking up during the night means I haven't slept well at all"), and misperceptions about the effects of sleep loss ("If I don't get 8 hours, I'll be a wreck tomorrow!"). The behavioral component of these interventions includes *stimulus control,* that is, controlling conditions that might interfere with sleep (Morin et al.,

2006). A person experiencing insomnia would be told to do the following:

1. Go to bed only when sleepy.
2. Use the bed and bedroom only for sleep and sex, not for reading, television watching, eating, or working.
3. Get out of bed and go to another room if you are unable to sleep for 15 to 20 minutes, and do not return to bed until you are sleepy.
4. Get out of bed at the same time each morning.
5. Don't nap during the day.

Sleep restriction therapy involves initially restricting the amount of time insomniacs can try to sleep in the night (Morin et al., 2006). Once they are able to sleep when they are in bed, they are gradually allowed to spend more time in bed. In addition, people often are taught relaxation exercises and are given information about the effects of diet, exercise, and substance use on sleep.

Various medications are used in the treatment of insomnia, including antidepressants, antihistamines, tryptophan, delta-sleep-inducing peptide (DSIP), melatonin, and benzodiazepines (Dündar et al., 2004). All these have proven effective in at least some studies, although the number of studies done on most of these agents is small. Those that have the least clear benefit are antihistamines and tryptophan (Lee, 2004; Nowell et al., 1998). Those that have proven most reliably effective are benzodiazepines and zolpidem (trade name Ambien). Individuals can become dependent on these sleep aids, however, and may experience withdrawal if they try to stop using them (Dündar et al., 2004). Rare cases of sleep-eating have been reported among users of Ambien—they get up during the night and consume large quantities of food, then don't remember doing so in the morning (Mahowald & Bornemann, 2006). Insomnia often returns after individuals stop taking the drugs. In contrast, the behavioral and cognitive interventions tend to have long-lasting positive effects (Nowell et al., 1998).

TABLE 15.5 *DSM-IV-TR* Criteria for Primary Hypersomnia

A. The predominant complaint is excessive sleepiness for at least 1 month (or less if recurrent) as evidenced by either prolonged sleep episodes or daytime sleep episodes that occur almost daily.

B. The excessive sleepiness causes clinically significant distress or impairment in social, occupational, or other important areas of functioning.

C. The excessive sleepiness is not better accounted for by insomnia and does not occur exclusively during the course of another sleep disorder (e.g., narcolepsy, breathing-related sleep disorder, circadian rhythm sleep disorder, or a parasomnia) and cannot be accounted for by an inadequate amount of sleep.

D. The disturbance does not occur exclusively during the course of another mental disorder (e.g., major depressive disorder).

E. The disturbance is not due to the direct effects of a substance (e.g., a drug of abuse, a medication) or a general medical condition.

TABLE 15.6 *DSM-IV-TR* Criteria for Narcolepsy

A. Irresistible attacks of refreshing sleep that occur daily over at least 3 months.

B. The presence of one or both of the following:
   1. Cataplexy
   2. Recurrent intrusions of elements of rapid eye movement (REM) sleep into the transition between sleep and wakefulness, as manifested by either hypnopompic or hypnagogic hallucinations or sleep paralysis at the beginning or end of sleep episodes

C. The disturbance is not due to the direct effects of a substance (e.g., a drug of abuse, a medication) or a general medical condition.

Hypersomnia and Narcolepsy **Primary hypersomnia** is the opposite of insomnia. People with hypersomnia are chronically sleepy and sleep for long periods. They may sleep 12 hours at a stretch and still wake up sleepy. A nap during the day may last an hour or more, and people may wake up unrefreshed. If their environment is not stimulating (e.g., during a boring lecture), they are sure to fall asleep. They may even fall asleep while driving. To qualify for a diagnosis, the hypersomnia must be present for at least 1 month and must cause significant distress or impairment in functioning (Table 15.5). The prevalence of hypersomnia in the general population is not known, but about 5 to 16 percent of people who go to sleep-disorder clinics are diagnosed with primary hypersomnia (American Psychiatric Association, 2000).

Narcolepsy involves irresistible attacks of sleep. Sleep episodes generally last 10 to 20 minutes but can last up to 1 hour. In addition to sleepiness, people diagnosed with narcolepsy must experience (1) cataplexy or (2) recurrent intrusions of elements of rapid eye movement (REM) sleep into the transition between sleep and wakefulness (Table 15.6). *Cataplexy* is episodes of sudden loss of muscle tone, lasting from a few seconds to minutes. People with cataplexy may suddenly drop objects, buckle at the knees, or even fall to the ground, but they are not asleep—their hearing and awareness may be normal. Cataplexy usually is triggered by a strong emotion, such as anger or surprise. When people with narcolepsy are asleep, they may experience *hypnagogic or hypnopompic hallucinations,* vivid dreamlike experiences involving all the senses. When they waken, they may experience brief periods when they can't move or speak, referred to as *sleep paralysis*. Narcolepsy most often starts in adolescence and is quite rare, affecting less than .05 percent of the general population (Longstreth et al., 2007).

Hypersomnia and narcolepsy are probably due to biological factors. Studies show that individuals with narcolepsy lack cells in the hypothalamus that secrete a neurotransmitter called hypocretin, which promotes wakefulness (Longstreth et al., 2007). Low levels of histamine, another neurotransmitter that promotes wakefulness, have also been found in people with narcolepsy and hypersomnia (Kanbayashi et al., 2009; Nishino et al., 2009). Hypersomnia and narcolepsy run in families, and specific genes have been implicated in narcolepsy (Longstreth et al., 2007).

Hypersomnia often is related to other mental disorders, particularly depression (Harvey, 2008). The *DSM-5* is likely to reclassify hypersomnia due to another mental disorder as *primary hypersomnia*. With this change, the *DSM-5* authors hope to call attention to hypersomnia in the context of another mental disorder as a clinical condition worthy of its own attention and to avoid its being neglected as simply a symptom of some other disorder (American Psychiatric Association, 2010).

The stimulant modafinil is consistently effective in the treatment of daytime sleepiness in individuals with narcolepsy or hypersomnia (Morgenthaler et al., 2007). Other stimulants, including amphetamines, methamphetamine, and methylphenidate, are also used as treatments for daytime sleepiness due to narcolepsy or hypersomnia. Sodium oxybate and selegiline can reduce cataplexy, hallucinations, and sleep paralysis in narcolepsy. In addition, some physicians prescribe antidepressants, but their effectiveness in treating narcolepsy or hypersomnia has not been shown in controlled studies (Morgenthaler et al., 2007).

Breathing-Related Sleep Disorder People with **breathing-related sleep disorder** have numerous brief sleep disturbances due to breathing problems (Table 15.7). People with **central sleep apnea** experience complete cessation of respiratory activity for brief periods of time (20 seconds or more) yet do not have frequent awakenings and do not tend to feel tired during the day. Central sleep apnea occurs when the brain does not send the signal to breathe to the respiratory system. It can be caused by central nervous system disorders, including cerebral vascular disease and head trauma, and by heart disease (Ramar & Guilleminault, 2008). It also occurs in premature infants. The first line of treatment is to treat the underlying disorder leading to central sleep apnea.

TABLE 15.7 *DSM-IV-TR* Criteria for Breathing-Related Sleep Disorder

A. Sleep disruption, leading to excessive sleepiness or insomnia, that is judged to be due to a sleep-related breathing condition (e.g., obstructive or central sleep apnea syndrome or central alveolar hypoventilation syndrome).

B. The disturbance is not better accounted for by another mental disorder and is not due to the direct effects of a substance (e.g., a drug of abuse, a medication) or another general medical condition (other than a breathing-related disorder).

Source: Reprinted with permission from the *Diagnostic and Statistical Manual of Mental Disorders,* Fourth Edition, Text Revision.

The more common breathing-related sleep disorder is **obstructive sleep apnea,** which involves repeated episodes of upper-airway obstruction during sleep. People with sleep apnea typically snore loudly, go silent and stop breathing for several seconds at a time, then gasp for air. Obstructive sleep apnea occurs when airflow is stopped due to a narrow airway or an obstruction (an abnormality or damage) in the airway. While associated with obesity, it also can occur in tonsillitis and other disorders that create inflammation in the airway (Ramar & Guilleminault, 2008). It occurs in up to 10 percent of the population and can begin throughout the life span.

Obstructive sleep apnea can be treated with a device called a continuous positive air pressure (CPAP) machine. The CPAP machine delivers a stream of compressed air via a hose to a nasal mask, keeping the airway open under air pressure so that unobstructed breathing is possible. CPAP is an effective treatment for obstructive sleep apnea, but 25 to 50 percent of people reject it because it makes them uncomfortable or does not give suf-

TABLE 15.8 *DSM-IV-TR* Criteria for Circadian Rhythm Sleep Disorder

A. A persistent or recurrent pattern of sleep disruption leading to excessive sleepiness or insomnia that is due to a mismatch between the sleep-wake schedule required by a person's environment and his or her circadian sleep-wake pattern.

B. The sleep disturbance causes clinically significant distress or impairment in social, occupational, or other important areas of functioning.

C. The sleep disturbance does not occur exclusively during the course of another sleep disorder or another mental disorder.

D. The disturbance is not due to the direct effects of a substance (e.g., a drug of abuse, a medication) or a general medical condition.

Source: Reprinted with permission from the *Diagnostic and Statistical Manual of Mental Disorders,* Fourth Edition, Text Revision. Copyright © 2000 American Psychiatric Association.

ficient relief from their breathing problems (Veasey et al., 2006). CPAP is also sometimes used to treat central sleep apnea.

Drugs that affect the serotonin system, including the serotonin reuptake inhibitors, have shown mixed effects in the treatment of obstructive sleep apnea; stimulants such as modafinil can reduce the daytime sleepiness associated with apnea (Veasey et al., 2006). Surgery to remove obstructive tissue blocking the airway or to increase the upper airway area can be used in extreme cases of obstructive sleep apnea, but meta-analyses of the small number of studies on the effectiveness of such surgeries do not show them to be consistently effective in treating the disorder (Franklin et al., 2009).

Circadian Rhythm Sleep Disorder As noted, insomnia can be caused by disruptions in biological rhythms, especially core body temperature. These biological rhythms, also known as *circadian rhythms,* are driven by mechanisms in the brain that keep people in sync with the regular patterns of light and dark over the course of the day. These mechanisms are located in a part of the hypothalamus called the superchiasmatic nucleus and modulate daily rhythms in many systems of the body, including sleep and alertness (Sack et al., 2007). Circadian rhythms are on a roughly 24-hour clock but can be affected by environmental time signals, especially the solar light/dark signal. Some people have more difficulty than others in adjusting their circadian rhythms after a disruption. Individual differences appear to have genetic roots (Sack et al., 2007). If sustained and distressing, this difficulty can be diagnosed as a **circadian rhythm sleep disorder** (Table 15.8).

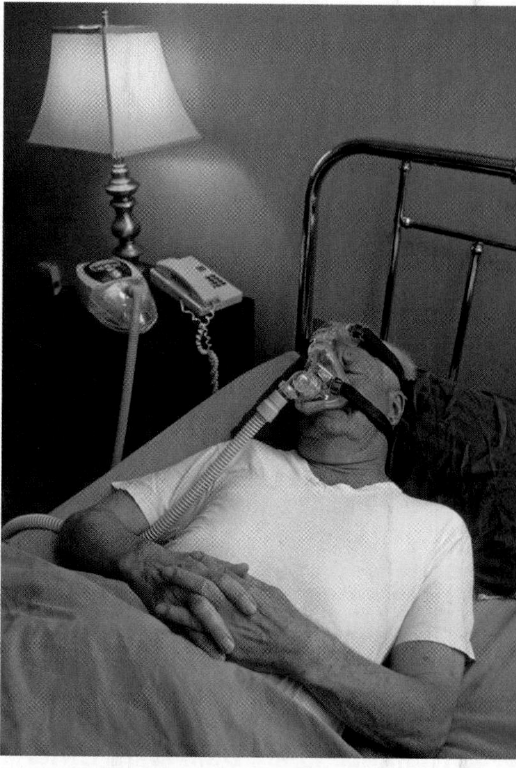

The CPAP machine helps people with breathing-related sleep problems.

The *DSM-IV-TR* recognizes three circadian rhythm sleep disorders. *Delayed sleep phase type* involves a persistent pattern of late sleep onset and late awakenings, and an inability to go to sleep or wake up earlier if desired. Adolescents typically experience a phase in their biological clock that makes them want to stay up late and sleep late (Wolfson, 2001). Delayed sleep phase type circadian rhythm disorder is diagnosed only when it seriously interfere with the person's functioning and causes distress. It is the most common circadian rhythm disorder diagnosed in clinical settings (Dagan & Eisenstein, 1999). *Jet lag type circadian rhythm disorder* is caused, as the name implies, by crossing several time zones in a short period of time. People feel sleepy when they want to be awake but have trouble going to sleep when they want to. No official prevalence data are available, but studies suggest that frequent jeg lag can negatively affect health and longevity (Davidson et al., 2006). *Shift work type circadian rhythm disorder* is caused by working rotating shifts or irregular hours. In one study, 31 percent of night workers and 26 percent of rotating shift workers met the criteria for this disorder (Drake et al., 2004).

Behavioral interventions can help treat circadian rhythm disorders. It is easier to stay up late than to go to sleep early, so rotating shift workers can more easily move their shifts clockwise than counterclockwise (Sack et al., 2007). Planned napping during night shifts also can help reduce worker sleepiness and associated accidents (Sallinen et al., 1998). Exposing shift workers to bright light during night shifts can help shift their circadian rhythms (Sack et al., 2007). Similarly, exposing individuals with delayed sleep phase type disorder to bright lights early in the morning can help shift their circadian rhythms.

TABLE 15.9 *DSM-IV-TR* Criteria for Nightmare Disorder

A. Repeated awakenings from the major sleep period or naps with detailed recall of extended and extremely frightening dreams, usually involving threats to survival, security, or physical integrity. The awakenings generally occur during the second half of the sleep period.

B. On awakening from the frightening dreams, the person rapidly becomes oriented and alert (in contrast to the confusion and disorientation seen in sleep terror disorder and some forms of epilepsy).

C. The dream experience, or the sleep disturbance resulting from the awakening, causes clinically significant distress or impairment in social, occupational, or other important areas of functioning.

D. The nightmares do not occur exclusively during the course of another mental disorder (e.g., a delirium, post-traumatic stress disorder) and are not due to the direct physiological effects of a substance (e.g., a drug of abuse, a medication) or a general medical condition.

Source: Reprinted with permission from the *Diagnostic and Statistical Manual of Mental Disorders*, Fourth Edition, Text Revision.

TABLE 15.10 *DSM-IV-TR* Criteria for Sleep Terror Disorder

A. Recurrent episodes of abrupt awakening from sleep, usually occurring during the first third of the major sleep episode and beginning with a panicky scream.

B. Intense fear and signs of autonomic arousal, such as tachycardia, rapid breathing, and sweating, during each episode.

C. Relative unresponsiveness to efforts of others to comfort the person during the episode.

D. No detailed dream is recalled, and there is amnesia for the episode.

E. The episodes cause clinically significant distress or impairment in social, occupational, or other important areas of functioning.

F. The disturbance is not due to the direct physiological effects of a substance (e.g., a drug of abuse, a medication) or a general medical condition.

Source: Reprinted with permission from the *Diagnostic and Statistical Manual of Mental Disorders*, Fourth Edition, Text Revision.

Administering melatonin at prescribed times during the day has been shown to enhance shifts of circadian rhythms in individuals with delayed sleep phase type, jet lag type, and shift work type circadian rhythm disorders (Sack et al., 2007). The dosage and timing of melatonin administration are tricky, however, and can vary from one individual to another (Arendt, 2009). Stimulants, such as modafinil, can improve alertness during night shifts and after crossing time zones, as can caffeine (Arendt, 2009; Sack et al., 2007).

Parasomnias

Unlike the dyssomnias, which involve difficulty sleeping, the **parasomnias** are unusual experiences that occur during sleep. They include *nightmare disorder, sleep terror disorder,* and *sleepwalking disorder.* Occasional problems with the symptoms of these disorders are common, but only a small proportion of the population ever develops a parasomnia.

About half of all adults have had nightmares, frightening dreams that wake them up (American Psychiatric Association, 2000). People often awaken from nightmares frightened, with a racing heart and sweating. They may have vivid memories of the dream, which often involves physical danger. Nightmares are more common in children than in adults, with 10 to 50 percent of children having a sufficient number of nightmares to disturb their parents (Neylan, Reynolds, & Kupfer, 2007). For a diagnosis of **nightmare disorder,** the nightmares must be frequent enough to cause significant distress or impairment in functioning (Table 15.9). Nightmares are common among people who have recently experienced a traumatic event (Krakow et al., 2007). Cognitive-behavioral interventions for nightmare disorder include desensitizing individuals to their nightmares. The person records the content of the nightmare in detail and then reads it repeatedly while doing relaxation exercises (Burgess, Gill, & Marks, 1998). Such interventions have been shown in small controlled trials to reduce the frequency of nightmares as well as the anxiety, depression, and sleeplessness associated with them. These gains persisted in a 4-year follow-up (Grandi et al., 2006).

Sleep terror disorder occurs most often in children (Neylan et al., 2007; Table 15.10). The sleeping child screams, sweating and with heart racing. Unlike nightmares, which occur during REM sleep, sleep terrors occur during NREM sleep. Children experiencing a sleep terror cannot be easily awakened. They usually do not remember their sleep terrors on awakening.

Like sleep terror disorder, **sleepwalking disorder** is relatively common in children, with 15 to 30 percent having at least one episode, but rare in adults (Neylan et al., 2007; Table 15.11). Sleepwalking occurs during NREM sleep, so the person sleepwalking is not acting out a dream. Sleepwalkers may respond to others' questions or commands but cannot hold a conversation. They may engage in nocturnal eating, going to the kitchen and eating food while asleep. They can injure themselves by running into furniture or thrashing about, especially if they are also experiencing a sleep terror (American Psychiatric Association, 2000). Sleepwalkers are difficult to waken (although doing so is not dangerous, as popularly believed). People typically do not remember their sleepwalking activity (Neylan et al., 2007).

Sleepwalking and sleep terrors tend to run in families (Szelenberger, Niemcewicz, & Dabrowska, 2005). Twin studies of sleep terrors show higher concordance rates in monozygotic twins than in dizygotic twins, suggesting a genetic influence on sleep terrors (Hublin et al., 1997). Stress, previous sleep deprivation, extreme fatigue, and the use of sedative or hypnotic drugs have been associated with both sleep terrors and sleepwalking (Neylan et al., 2007).

Antidepressants are sometimes used to treat sleep terrors, with mixed results (Neylan et al., 2007). A behavioral treatment involves waking a child 30 minutes before the time of night he or she typically would have a sleep terror or sleepwalking episode; after the child can go at least a week without a night terror, the scheduled wakenings are gradually ended. One study showed that such scheduled wakenings quickly reduced the frequency of children's night terrors; in a 1-year follow-up after the scheduled wakenings ended, the reductions in sleep terrors were maintained (Durand & Mindell, 1999).

In the *DSM-5*, sleepwalking and sleep terrors are likely to be subsumed under a new and more general category, *disorders of arousal,* that represents confusions of wakefulness with NREM sleep (American Psychiatric Association, 2010).

TEST YOURSELF

1. What are the four categories of sleep disorders?
2. What are the general characteristics of the dyssomnias and parasomnias?
3. What are insomnia, hypersomnia, narcolepsy, breathing-related sleep disorder, and circadian rhythm sleep disorder?
4. What are effective treatments for dyssomnias?
5. What three disorders are classified as parasomnias?

APPLY IT Janine was diagnosed with obstructive sleep apnea. Her doctor prescribed a machine she could use at night to prevent episodes of apnea. That machine was most likely which of the following?

a. a heart-lung machine
b. a machine that played soothing music
c. a continuous positive air pressure machine
d. a polysomnograph

Answers appear online at www.mhhe.com/nolen5e.

TABLE 15.11 *DSM-IV-TR* Criteria for Sleepwalking Disorder

A. Repeated episodes of rising from bed during sleep and walking about, usually occurring during the first third of the major sleep episode.

B. While sleepwalking, the person has a blank, staring face, is relatively unresponsive to the efforts of others to communicate with him or her, and can be awakened only with great difficulty.

C. On awakening (either from the sleepwalking episode or the next morning), the person has amnesia for the episode.

D. Within several minutes after awakening from the sleepwalking episode, there is no impairment of mental activity or behavior (although there may initially be a short period of confusion or disorientation).

E. The sleepwalking causes clinically significant distress or impairment in social, occupational, or other important areas of functioning.

F. The disturbance is not due to the direct physiological effects of a substance (e.g., a drug of abuse, a medication) or a general medical condition.

Source: Reprinted with permission from the *Diagnostic and Statistical Manual of Mental Disorders,* Fourth Edition, Text Revision. Copyright © 2000 American Psychiatric Association.

FIGURE 15.5 Reciprocal Effects of Psychological, Social, and Biological Factors in Stress-Related Disorders

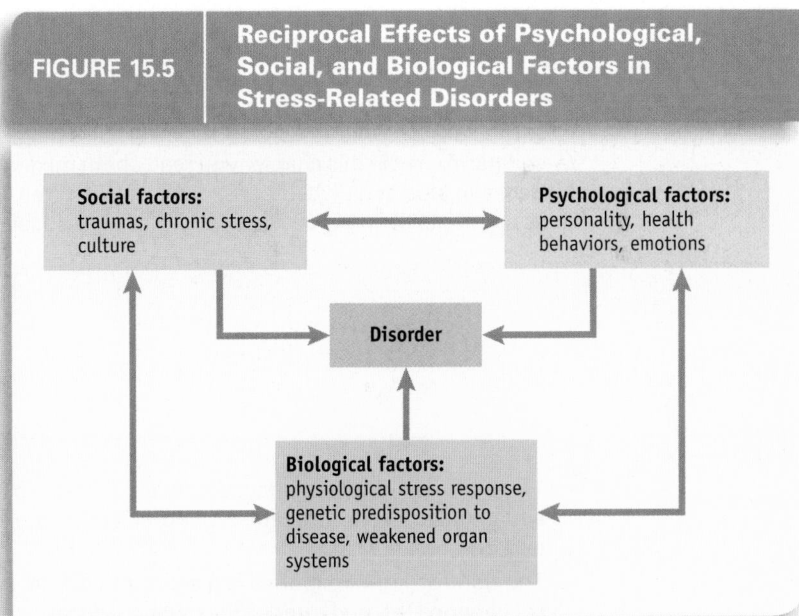

CHAPTER INTEGRATION

This chapter amply illustrates the reciprocal effects of the body, the mind, and the environment (Figure 15.5). Psychological and social factors can have direct effects on the physiology of the body and indirect effects on health by leading people to engage in behaviors that either promote or impair health. In turn, physical health affects people's emotional health and self-concept. People with life-threatening or debilitating physical illnesses are at a greatly increased risk for depression and other emotional problems. For these reasons, health psychologists begin with the assumption that biology, psychology, and the social environment have reciprocal influences on one another. Then they attempt to characterize these influences and determine their relative importance.

SHADES OF GRAY DISCUSSION (review p. 474)

At first glance you might think that John's avoidance of thinking or talking about his cancer is an unhealthy way of coping. He is not drawing on social support from his children or his co-workers. You might even wonder if he is living in denial of his serious illness. But look closer. John appears to be engaging in a subtler form of social support characteristic of Asian cultures. He enjoys talking with his wife about their children and grandchildren and about visiting friends and family. For John, this may be a more acceptable means of coping than overtly asking for support from people besides his wife.

THINK CRITICALLY

We would like to believe that we can improve our health by changing our attitudes and reducing stress in our lives. The self-help industry makes billions of dollars each year selling this hope to the public (see www.pbs.org/thisemotionallife/perspective/self-help-or-self-harm). Yet in this chapter you read about mixed evidence in studies of whether psychosocial interventions can affect the progression of diseases like cancer or heart disease. Although some studies have shown promise, many others show no effects of such interventions on the progression of disease. Given this mixed evidence, do you think psychologists should or should not offer psychosocial interventions to patients with cancer or cardiovascular disease? What should be the goals of these interventions? *(Discussion appears on p. 521 at the back of this book.)*

CHAPTER SUMMARY

- Three dimensions that affect the level of stress in situations are uncontrollability, unpredictability, and duration.
- The fight-or-flight response is a set of physiological changes the body undergoes when it faces a threat. In the short term it is adaptive, but if it persists for a long time it can cause damage to the body, a condition called allostatic load.
- Psychological factors associated with poorer health include pessimism and avoidance coping, while expressive writing and seeking social support are associated with better health. People with psychological disorders, especially depression, are at increased risk for a number of physical health problems.
- The immune system protects us from disease by identifying and killing pathogens and tumor cells. Chronic, uncontrollable stress; pessimism; and avoidance coping are associated with impaired immune system functioning, and with worse health in individuals with cancer or HIV/AIDS. Whether interventions to reduce stress or to improve cognitions about stress affect the progression of cancer is not clear, however.
- Chronic stress is also associated with coronary heart disease. The Type A behavior pattern, characterized by a sense of time urgency, easily aroused hostility, and competitive striving for achievement, predicts coronary heart disease. The component of Type A that is most predictive is hostility. Depression also is predictive of CHD.
- Guided mastery techniques help people increase their positive health-related behaviors. The Internet is being used to deliver guided mastery interventions worldwide.

- The *DSM-IV-TR* recognizes four general types of sleep disorders. Sleep disorders related to another mental disorder are directly attributable to psychological disorders. Sleep disorders due to a general medical condition result from the physiological effects of a medical condition. Substance-induced sleep disorders are due to the use of substances, including prescription medications (e.g., medications that control hypertension or cardiac arrhythmias) and nonprescription substances (e.g., alcohol and caffeine). Primary sleep disorders are dyssomnias (abnormalities in the amount, quality, or timing of sleep) and parasomnias (unusual behavior during sleep).
- Insomnia is difficulty initiating or maintaining sleep or sleep that chronically does not restore energy and alertness. It can be caused by disruptions in body temperature rhythms, stress, and faulty cognitions and habits concerning sleep. Cognitive-behavioral therapy is effective in treating insomnia. A variety of medications also are prescribed for insomnia, but CBT is the most effective treatment.
- Hypersomnia is chronic excessive sleepiness as evidenced by either prolonged sleep episodes or daytime sleep episodes that occur almost daily. Narcolepsy involves irresistible attacks of sleep; people with narcolepsy also have (1) cataplexy or (2) recurrent intrusions of elements of rapid eye movement (REM) sleep into the transition between sleep and wakefulness. Stimulants are prescribed for people with hypersomnia or narcolepsy.
- Breathing-related sleep disorder (central sleep apnea or obstructive sleep apnea) involves numerous brief sleep disturbances due to breathing problems. Continuous positive airway pressure (CPAP) machines are used to treat breathing-related sleep disorders. Obstructive sleep disorder is also sometimes treated with weight loss and surgery. Serotonin reuptake inhibitors and stimulants are sometimes prescribed.
- Circadian rhythm sleep disorder includes delayed sleep phase type, jet lag type, and shift work type. Melatonin, stimulants, light therapy, and behavioral techniques to change sleep habits are used to treat circadian rhythm sleep disorder.
- The parasomnias include nightmare disorder, sleep terror disorder, and sleepwalking disorder.

KEY TERMS

allostatic load 470
immune system 474
coronary heart disease (CHD) 478
hypertension 479
Type A behavior pattern 480
guided mastery techniques 482
sleep disorders related to another mental disorder 486
sleep disorders related to a general medical condition 486
substance-induced sleep disorders 486
primary sleep disorders 486
dyssomnias 486
primary insomnia 487
primary hypersomnia 489
narcolepsy 489
breathing-related sleep disorder 490
central sleep apnea 490
obstructive sleep apnea 490
circadian rhythm sleep disorder 491
parasomnias 492
nightmare disorder 492
sleep terror disorder 492
sleepwalking disorder 492

Chapter 16

Mental Health and The Law

CHAPTER OUTLINE

Extraordinary People

Greg Bottoms, *Angelhead*

Imagine a family member who is so violent that you and your parents must lock your bedroom doors at night. Now imagine that family member going after your youngest brother and your father with a baseball bat because he believes they deserve to die. These circumstances were a reality for Greg Bottoms, whose book *Angelhead* (2000) describes his brother Michael's schizophrenia and exposes mental health and judicial systems tragically inadequate to help Michael.

Michael's symptoms did not respond to antipsychotic drugs very well, at least when he actually took the medications. He came to believe that they were part of a conspiracy to control his mind and usually refused them. His violence toward his family became so severe that family members tried to have Michael institutionalized but were told they could not unless they proved he was an imminent danger to himself or others.

Eventually, the family found an institution that would take its insurance and placed Michael there. He hated the place, refused his medications, and attempted suicide. This landed him in a state psychiatric hospital for a while. Later he "confessed" to a murder he had not committed, having become convinced by the voices in his head that this was the sin he was paying such a high price for. He was jailed, but DNA evidence proved that Michael could not have committed the murder.

After he was exonerated for this murder, Michael was back home again, on high doses of antipsychotic medications but delusional, believing that God spoke directly to him and that his family was evil. Indeed, he decided that his father was the Antichrist and that, to save his family's souls, he had to kill them. One night, as his father lay dying of cancer and his family slept behind locked doors, Michael set the house on fire. He rode his bicycle to the end of the street and then sat watching, expecting his family's souls to float past him on the way to heaven. The family escaped. As they stood watching the firefighters try to extinguish the fire, Mr. Bottoms told the other family members this was the best thing that could happen, because now Michael could really be put away. In the next instant, however, he feared that Michael had been in the house and was dying in the fire. He tried to run into the house to look for Michael, but the firefighters held him back. Meanwhile, Michael rode up on his bicycle, completely nonchalant. A police officer asked Michael if he could ask him some questions, and Michael held out his hands for the handcuffs. Then he turned to his mother and casually asked her what she was going to make for breakfast. Michael confessed to setting the fire with the purpose of killing his family. He was convicted of attempted murder and arson and was sent to prison for 30 years.

Mental health professionals are asked regularly to help families such as the Bottoms family deal with the laws and social systems that guide the treatment of people with psychological disorders. Fundamental questions about society's values confront the personal wishes of people with mental disorders and their families: Does society have a right to impose treatment on an individual who doesn't want it? Under what conditions should people be absolved of responsibility for behaviors that harm others? Should the diagnosis of a psychological disorder entitle a person to special services and protection against discrimination?

This chapter explores cases that involve the law in the lives of people with mental health problems, focusing first on when a person can be committed against his or her will. Then we examine how the law regards a person charged with a crime who might have a mental disorder. Finally, we discuss how a person who has a mental disorder and is convicted of a crime is treated.

CIVIL COMMITMENT

In the best circumstances, people who need treatment for psychological disorders seek it themselves. They work with mental health professionals to find medication and/or psychotherapy to reduce their symptoms and keep their disorder under control. Many people who have serious psychological problems, however, do not recognize their need for treatment or may refuse treatment for a variety of reasons. For example, Michael Bottoms believed the doctors treating him were part of a conspiracy and refused to follow their prescriptions. A man experiencing a manic episode may enjoy many of the symptoms—the high energy, inflated self-esteem, and grandiose thoughts—and not want to take medication that would reduce these symptoms. A teenager who is abusing illegal drugs may believe that it is her right to do so and that there is nothing wrong with her abuse. Can these people be forced to enter mental institutions and to undergo treatment against their will? These are the questions we address in this section.

Criteria for Civil Commitment

Prior to the mid-twentieth century, in the United States the **need for treatment** was sufficient cause to hospitalize people against their will and force them to undergo treatment. Such involuntary hospitalization is called **civil commitment.** All that was needed for civil commitment was a certificate signed by two physicians stating that a person needed treatment and was not agreeing to it voluntarily. The person could then be confined, often indefinitely, without recourse to an attorney, a hearing, or an appeal (Meyer & Weaver, 2006).

The need for treatment alone is no longer sufficient legal cause for civil commitment in most states in the United States. This change came about as part of the patients' rights movement of the 1960s, which raised concerns about the personal freedom and civil liberties of mental patients. Opponents of the civil commitment process argued that it allowed people to be incarcerated simply for having alternative lifestyles or different political or moral values (Szasz, 1963, 1977). Certainly, there were many cases in the former Soviet Union and other countries of political dissidents being labeled mentally ill and in need of treatment and then being incarcerated in prisons for years. There also were disturbing cases of the misuse of civil commitment proceedings in the United States. In the 1860s, for example, Illinois law allowed husbands to have their wives involuntarily committed without evidence of insanity. Mrs. E. P. W. Packard was committed by her husband for holding "unacceptable" and "sick" political or moral views (Weiner & Wettstein, 1993). Mrs. Packard remained hospitalized for 3 years before winning her release; she then began crusading against civil commitment.

Procedurally, most states now mandate that persons being considered for involuntary commitment have the right to a public hearing, the right to counsel, the right to call and confront witnesses, the right to appeal decisions, and the right to be placed in the least restrictive treatment setting. In practice, however, judges typically defer to the judgment of mental health professionals about a person's mental illness and whether the criteria for commitment are met (Meyer & Weaver, 2006). Even attorneys who are supposed to be upholding an individual's rights tend to acquiesce to the judgment of mental health professionals, particularly if the attorney is court-appointed, as is often the case.

In the United States and many other countries, individuals musts be judged to meet one of the following criteria in order to be committed to a psychiatric facility against his or her will: (1) grave disability, (2) dangerousness to self, or (3) dangerousness to others. In addition, most states require that the danger people pose to themselves or to others be *imminent*—in other words, if they are not immediately incarcerated, they or someone else will likely be harmed in the very near future. Finally, all persons committed to psychiatric facilities must be diagnosed with a mental disorder, although the definition of mental disorders or mental illnesses varies from state to state (Meyer & Weaver, 2006). In particular, some states exclude substance abuse or dependence and mental retardation from their list of mental disorders or mental illnesses.

Grave Disability

The **grave disability** criterion requires that people be so incapacitated by mental disorders that they cannot provide for their basic needs of food, clothing, and shelter. This criterion is, in theory, much more severe than the need for treatment criterion because it requires that the person's survival be in immediate danger because of mental illness.

You might think that the grave disability criterion could be used to hospitalize homeless people living on the streets who appear to be psychotic and seem unable to take care of their basic needs. In the winter of 1988, New York City Mayor Ed Koch invoked the legal principle of *parens patriae* (sovereign as parent) to have mentally ill homeless people taken to mental health facilities. Mayor Koch argued that it was the city's duty to protect these mentally ill homeless people from the ravages of the winter weather because they were unable to protect themselves. One of the homeless people who was involuntarily hospitalized was 40-year-old Joyce Brown, who subsequently was diagnosed with paranoid schizophrenia. Brown had been living on the streets on and off for years, resisting efforts by her family to get her into psychiatric treatment. Brown and the American Civil Liberties Union contested her commitment and won her release on the grounds that the city had no right to incarcerate Brown if she had no intention of being treated (Kasindorf, 1988).

Mental Health Law Along the Continuum

A person with no mental health problems is suspected of having committed a crime

Legal decision does not need to take mental health into account

Mental health problems bring a person to the attention of the law, although the individual does not have a diagnosis and has not committed a crime

Legal decision may place the individual in a mental health facility involuntarily if he is a danger to himself or others

A person with mental health problems is suspected of having committed a crime

Legal decision must be informed by mental health experts

(mental health worker advises if the individual is fit to stand trial or should be considered not guilty by reason of insanity)

DSM-IV-TR **diagnosis of mental disorder**

A person with a diagnosed mental health disorder commits a crime

Legal decision must take the diagnosis into account, but the diagnosis does not guarantee that the person will receive specific treatment under the law

(The individual may or may not be found not guilty by reason of insanity)

Functional — Dysfunctional

Think back to before you took this course, before you had a sense of how fuzzy our definitions and understanding of mental disorders can be. Back then, if you had heard a news report about the violent behavior of Michael Bottoms, you might have thought that the authorities should simply determine whether he had a mental disorder that was leading him to be violent and then take appropriate action. If his violence was the result of a mental disorder, he should be given treatment to overcome the mental disorder; if his violence was not due to a mental disorder but was voluntary and intentional, he should be incarcerated.

Now you understand that the situation is not that clear-cut. The *DSM* provides criteria for diagnosing mental disorders, but whether a particular individual's behaviors meet those criteria is often a judgment call. Furthermore, we are limited in our ability to generalize from the research literature to individual cases. For example, we can know the likelihood that people with a particular mental disorder will commit violence in the future, but we cannot know for certain whether a given individual will be violent in the future.

When someone who appears to have mental health problems interacts with the judicial system, these judgment calls become even more complex. The fuzziness in our diagnostic criteria and in our understanding of mental disorders combines with the difficult ethical and social issues these cases create. A *DSM-IV-TR* diagnosis of a mental disorder does not ensure that an individual will be treated in a particular way by the law. For example, a diagnosed mental disorder is not enough to ensure that an individual receives needed treatment and may not exonerate an individual who has committed a crime. Mental health law is further complicated by the fact that the laws concerning people with mental health problems vary from region to region and have changed dramatically over the past 50 years.

One legal precedent relevant to Joyce Brown's release was *O'Connor v. Donaldson* (1975). Kenneth Donaldson had been committed to a Florida state hospital for 14 years. Donaldson's father originally had him committed, believing that Donaldson was delusional and therefore a danger to himself. At the time, Florida law allowed people to be committed if their mental disorder might impair their ability to manage their finances or to protect themselves against being cheated by others. Throughout his hospitalization, Donaldson refused medication because it violated his Christian Science beliefs. The superintendent, Dr. J. B. O'Connor, considered this refusal to be a symptom

One ethical question facing society is whether it has an obligation to provide mental health services to people who cannot take care of themselves.

of Donaldson's mental disorder. Even though Donaldson had been caring for himself adequately before his hospitalization and had friends who offered to help care for him if he was released from the hospital, O'Connor and the hospital continually refused Donaldson's requests for release. Donaldson sued on the grounds that he had received only custodial care during his hospitalization and was not a danger to himself. He requested to be released to the care of his friends and family. The Supreme Court agreed, ruling that "a State cannot constitutionally confine . . . a nondangerous individual, who is capable of surviving safely in freedom by himself or with the help of willing and responsible family and friends" (*O'Connor v. Donaldson*, 1975, p. 4).

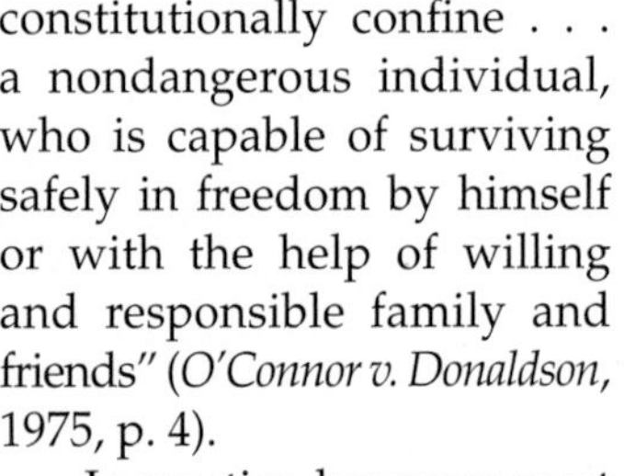

Serial killer Jeffrey Dahmer clearly had psychological problems, but mental health professionals did not foresee the terrible crimes he would commit.

In practice, however, most persons involuntarily committed because of grave disability do not have the ACLU championing their rights or the personal ability to file suit. Often, they are people with few financial resources or friends. Their families may have long histories of serious mental illness. The elderly mentally ill are especially likely to be committed because of grave disability (Turkheimer & Parry, 1992). Often, these people are committed to psychiatric facilities because not enough less restrictive treatment facilities are available in their communities and their families are unable to care for them.

Dangerousness to Self

The criterion **dangerousness to self** is most often invoked when it is believed that a person is imminently suicidal. In such cases, the person often is held in an inpatient psychiatric facility for a few days while undergoing further evaluation and possibly treatment. Most states allow short-term commitments without a court hearing in emergency situations such as this. All that is needed is a certification by the attending mental health professionals that the individual is in imminent danger to him- or herself. If the mental health professionals judge that the person needs further treatment but the person does not voluntarily agree to treatment, they can go to court to request that the person be committed for a longer period of time.

Dangerousness to Others

Dangerousness to others is the third criterion under which people can be committed involuntarily. If a person with a mental disorder is going to hurt another person if set free, then society has claimed the right to protect itself. While this action may seem justified, the appropriateness of this criterion rests on predictions of who will be dangerous and who will not. Some research has suggested that predictions of dangerousness tend to be wrong more often than they are right (McNiel & Binder, 1991; Monahan & Walker, 1990). As a tragic example, serial killer Jeffrey Dahmer was arrested and jailed in 1988 for sexually molesting a 13-year-old boy. He was released in 1990 with only limited follow-up by mental health professionals, despite concerns raised by his family about his mental health. Dahmer proceeded to drug, molest, kill, and dismember at least 17 additional victims over the next few years before being apprehended.

In 2009, Army psychiatrist Major Nidal Hasan shot and killed 13 people at Fort Hood, Texas. Students and faculty at Walter Reed Hospital, where Hasan trained, called Hasan's behavior "disconnected, aloof, paranoid, belligerent, and schizoid" (Zwerdling, 2009). Still, no one connected the dots to predict that Hasan could be a danger to others, and no action was taken to remove him from his post.

If clinicians believe that an individual may harm another person, they have a *duty to warn* that person, even if this violates a client's confidentiality. This duty to warn was established in a decision in the case of *Tarasoff v. Regents of the University of*

California (1974). Tatiana Tarasoff was a student at the University of California at Berkeley in the late 1960s. A graduate student named Prosenjit Poddar was infatuated with Tarasoff, who had rejected him. Poddar told his therapist in the student counseling service that he planned to kill Tarasoff when she returned to campus from vacation. The therapist informed the campus police, who picked up Poddar for questioning. Poddar agreed to leave Tarasoff alone, and the campus police released him. Two months later, Poddar killed Tarasoff. Tarasoff's parents sued the university, arguing that the therapist should have protected Tarasoff from Poddar. The California courts agreed and established the precedent that therapists have a duty to warn persons who are threatened by their clients during therapy sessions and to take actions to protect those persons (Meyer & Weaver, 2006).

Violence and People with Mental Disorders

Are people with psychological disorders more likely to be violent than people without them? Research suggests that disorders carry a moderately increased risk of violence (Arseneault et al., 2000; Banks et al., 2004; Monahan & Steadman, 2001).

In one major study, researchers followed 1,136 men and women with mental disorders for 1 year after their being discharged from a psychiatric hospital, monitoring their self-reports of violent behaviors, reports in police and hospital records, and reports by other informants, such as family members (Steadman et al., 1998). Serious violent acts were defined as battery that resulted in physical injury, sexual assaults, assaultive acts that involved the use of a weapon, and threats made with a weapon in hand. The former psychiatric patients' records of violent activity were compared to those of 519 people living in the same neighborhoods that the patients lived in after their hospital discharge. This community group was interviewed only once, at the end of the year-long study, and was asked about violent behavior in the past 10 weeks.

The likelihood that the former patients would commit a violent act was strongly related to their specific diagnosis and whether they had a substance abuse problem. About 18 percent of the former patients who had a diagnosis of a major mental disorder (e.g., schizophrenia, major depression, some other psychotic disorder) *without* a history of substance abuse committed a serious violent act in the year following discharge, compared to 31 percent of those with a major mental disorder *and* a history of substance abuse and 43 percent of those with a diagnosis of "other" mental disorder (i.e., a personality or adjustment disorder) *and* a co-occurring substance abuse problem. The researchers were somewhat surprised to find that the former patients were most likely to commit a violent act in the first couple of months following their discharge and less likely to do so as the year wore on (Figure 16.1). They suggested that patients might still be in crisis shortly after their hospitalization and that it may take some months for social support systems and treatment to begin to affect their behavior.

Nidal Hasan, who had previously exhibited behavior potentially indicative of a mental disorder, killed 13 people at Ft. Hood.

The rate of violence in the community sample was also strongly related to whether individuals had a history of substance abuse. Eleven percent of those with a substance abuse problem committed a violent act

FIGURE 16.1 **Likelihood of Violence.** The lines represent the percentage of patients with or without a substance abuse problem (SA), and the points represent community comparisons with or without a substance abuse problem, who committed a violent act in the previous 10 weeks in this study.

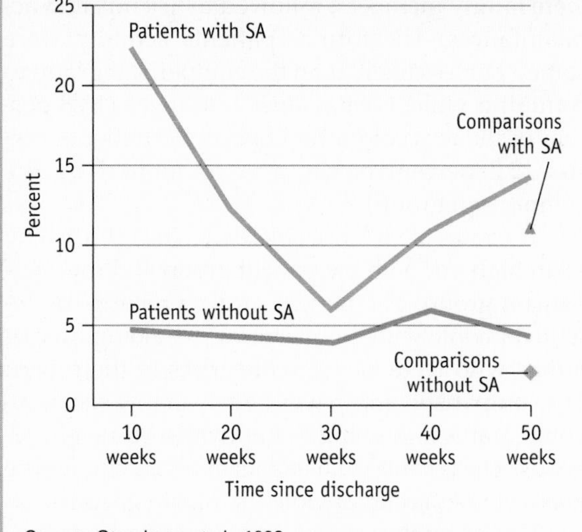

Source: Steadman et al., 1998.

Tragedies like the shootings by Seung-Hui Cho at Virginia Tech University have led the public to call for more intervention for troubled, potentially violent youth.

during the year of the study, compared to 3 percent of those with no substance abuse problem. Although the overall rate of violence in the community sample was lower than in the patient sample, this difference was statistically significant only when the researchers considered violence committed by the former patients shortly after their discharge. By the end of that year, the former patients were no more likely to commit a violent act than were people in the community comparison group.

The targets of violence by both the former patients and the community comparisons most often were family members, followed by friends and acquaintances. The former patients actually were somewhat less likely than the comparison group to commit a violent act against a stranger (13.8 percent of the acts committed by former patients versus 22.2 percent of the acts committed by the comparison group).

The rates of violence recorded in this study may seem high, for both the patient group and the comparison group. The patient group probably represented people with more serious psychological disorders who were facing acute crises in their lives. The comparison group was largely of low socioeconomic status and living in impoverished neighborhoods. These contextual factors may account for the relatively high rates of violence in both groups.

The researchers who conducted this study emphasized that their data show how inappropriate it is to consider "former mental patients" to be a homogeneous group of people all prone to violence. The presence of substance abuse problems was a strong predictor of violent behavior both in this group and in the group of people who had not been mental patients. Moreover, the majority of people with serious mental disorders did not commit any violent acts in the year after their discharge, especially against random strangers, as media depictions of former mental patients often suggest.

Other research has suggested that violence by mentally ill women tends to be *underestimated* by clinicians (Coontz, Lidz, & Mulvey, 1994; Robbins, Monahan, & Silver, 2003). Clinicians do not expect mentally ill women to be violent to the same degree that they expect mentally ill men to be violent. As a result, they do not probe mentally ill women for evidence of a tendency toward violence as much as they do mentally ill men. In reality, however, mentally ill women and mentally ill men are equally likely to commit violent acts toward others (Robbins et al., 2003). The victims of mentally ill women's violent acts are most likely to be family members; mentally ill men also are most often violent toward family members, but they commit violent acts against strangers more often than do mentally ill women (Newhill, Mulvey, & Lidz, 1995). Mentally ill men who commit violence are more likely to have been drinking before the violence and to be arrested following it than are mentally ill women who commit violence (Robbins et al., 2003).

Racial stereotypes lead people to expect mentally ill persons from ethnic minority groups to be more likely to commit acts of violence than White mentally ill people. However, there are no differences among the ethnic groups in rates of violence among mentally ill people (Mulvey, 1995). Thus, research is clarifying the true rates of violence among the mentally ill as well as some predictors of violence for this group.

Violence by children and teenagers with mental health problems has been in the news all too often in recent years. Depictions of youth going on shooting rampages lead to public demands for more intervention with troubled youth, regardless of whether they and their parents want it. One group of researchers examined the public's beliefs about the potential for harm to self or others by youth with mental health problems and the public's willingness to coerce these youth into treatment (Pescosolido et al., 2007). They asked over 1,100 adults to read vignettes depicting youth with attention-deficit/hyperactivity disorder (ADHD), major depression, asthma, or "daily troubles." Many more youth with ADHD or major depression were perceived as somewhat likely or very likely to be dangerous to themselves or others (33 percent for ADHD, 81 percent for major depression), compared to youth with asthma (15 percent) or "daily troubles" (13 percent). Over one-third of the adults in the study were willing to use legal means to force the youth with major depression to get mental health treatment. Adults who labeled the youth with ADHD or major depression "mentally ill" were twice as likely to see a potential for violence in these youth and five times more likely to support forced treatment, compared to adults who didn't apply the label "mentally ill" to the youth. These results suggest that the public associates diagnoses of mental disorders in youth with dangerousness and that a substantial portion of the public is ready to use the legal system to force children with mental disorders into treatment.

TABLE 16.1 Frequency of Involuntary Admissions to Psychiatric Facilities

These data reveal the percentage of all admissions to various types of psychiatric facilities that involve involuntary commitments. Data are from the United States in 1986.

Type of Facility	Percentage of All Admissions That Are Involuntary
State and county hospitals	61.6%
Multiservice mental health organizations (e.g., community mental health centers)	46.1
Private psychiatric hospitals	15.6
Nonfederal general hospitals	14.8
Veterans Administration hospitals	5.6

Source: Monahan et al., 2001.

Prevalence of Involuntary Commitment

How often are people involuntarily committed to a psychiatric facility? The data to answer this question are sparse, but the available studies suggest that about 25 percent of admissions to inpatient psychiatric facilities in the United States are involuntary and that about 15 to 20 percent of inpatient admissions in European countries are involuntary (Monahan et al., 2001). Admissions to state and county mental hospitals are much more likely to be involuntary than admissions to other types of hospitals (Table 16.1). In addition, 12 to 20 percent of patients of outpatient psychiatric facilities report having been ordered by civil courts to participate in outpatient treatment (Monahan et al., 2005). Court orders for outpatient care were more common among individuals who lived in residential psychiatric facilities and who had poor social support and poor psychosocial functioning, a recent history of violent behavior, recent police encounters, substance abuse problems, and higher rates of lifetime hospitalizations and involuntary hospitalizations (Swartz, Swanson, Kim, & Petrila, 2006).

These numbers probably underestimate the number of people coerced into mental health care treatment, because parents and legal guardians often "volunteer" a protesting child or incompetent adult for admission (Monahan et al., 2001). One study found that nearly 50 percent of the adults admitted voluntarily to inpatient psychiatric facilities said that someone other than themselves had initiated their going to the hospital, and 14 percent of the patients were under the custody of someone else at the time of admission (Hoge, Poythress, et al., 1997; Segal, Laurie, & Franskoviak, 2004). Nearly 40 percent of the voluntary patients believed they would have been involuntarily committed if they had not agreed to be hospitalized. Some of the patients felt they had been coerced by their therapists, who did not include them in the admissions process.

VOICES

I talked to him this morning. I said, "You . . . didn't even listen to me. You . . . call yourself a counselor. . . . Why did you decide to do this instead of . . . try to listen to me and understand . . . what I was going through." And he said, "Well, it doesn't matter, you know, you're going anyway." . . . He didn't listen to what I had to say. . . . He didn't listen to the situation. . . . He had decided before he ever got to the house . . . that I was coming up here. Either I come freely or the officers would have to subdue me and bring me in. (Bennett et al., 1993)

Patients involuntarily committed often may need treatment that they cannot acknowledge they need. About half of those patients who felt coerced into treatment eventually acknowledge that they needed treatment, but about half continue to believe treatment was unnecessary (Gardner et al., 1999).

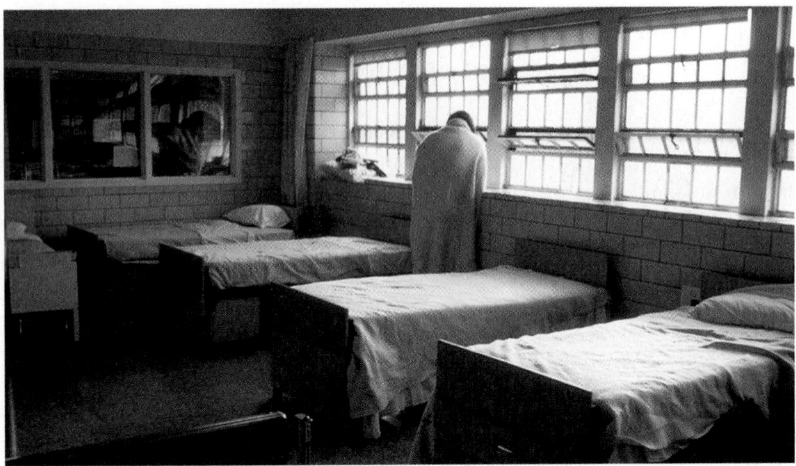

One fundamental right of people committed to a mental health facility is the right to be treated rather than simply warehoused.

TEST YOURSELF

1. What three criteria are used to determine whether an individual can be involuntarily committed?
2. What does research show about the risk of violence by people with mental disorders?

APPLY IT Which of the following individuals would most clearly meet the criteria for involuntary commitment?

a. George, a homeless person with schizophrenia who has lived for 5 years in a cardboard box under a bridge in Albany, New York
b. Jim, an unemployed stockbroker who wishes to die and just bought a handgun
c. Harry, who is diagnosed with heroin dependency and antisocial personality disorder and who believes people are out to get him
d. Phil, who refuses to take his medications for bipolar disorder because he does not like their side effects

Answers appear online at www.mhhe.com/nolen5e.

PATIENTS' RIGHTS

Numerous court cases over the years have established that people committed to mental health institutions retain most of their civil rights. They also have certain additional rights, which we discuss in this section.

Right to Treatment

One basic right of people who have been committed is the **right to treatment.** In the past, mental patients, including both those involuntarily committed and those seeking treatment voluntarily, were often warehoused. The conditions in which they lived were appalling, with little stimulation and few pleasantries let alone treatment for their disorders. In *Wyatt v. Stickney* (1971), patient Ricky Wyatt and others filed a class action suit against a custodial facility in Alabama, charging that they received no useful treatment and lived in minimally acceptable living conditions. After 33 years in the courts, the case finally was settled in 2003. From the court ruling came four standards, known as the "Wyatt Standards," for the evaluation of care of psychiatric patients: (1) They must be provided with a humane psychological and physical environment, (2) there must be qualified and sufficient staff for the administration of treatment, (3) there must be individualized treatment plans, and (4) restrictions of patient freedoms must be kept to a minimum (Sundram, 2009).

Right to Refuse Treatment

Another basic right is the **right to refuse treatment.** One of the greatest fears of people committed against their will is that they will be given drugs or other treatments that rob them of their consciousness and their free will. Many states now do not allow mental institutions or prisons to administer treatments without the informed consent of patients. **Informed consent** means that a patient accepts treatment after receiving a full and understandable explanation of the treatment being offered and making a decision based on his or her judgment of the risks and benefits of the treatment (Meyer & Weaver, 2006).

The right to refuse treatment is not recognized in some states, however, and in most states this right can be overruled in many circumstances (Monahan et al., 2001). Particularly if a patient is psychotic or manic, it may be judged that he or she cannot make a reasonable decision about treatment. In some jurisdictions, the simple fact that patients have a psychiatric diagnosis is enough to have them declared incompetent to make decisions about their treatment, particularly if it is a diagnosis of schizophrenia (Grisso & Appelbaum, 1998). Yet studies using reliable measures of patients' abilities to make rational decisions suggest that as many as 75 percent of those with schizophrenia and 90 percent of those with depression have adequate decision-making capacity (Grisso & Appelbaum, 1995).

Patients' psychiatrists and sometimes families may seek court rulings allowing them to administer treatment even if the patients refuse treatment. Judges most often agree with the psychiatrists' or families' requests to force treatment on patients. Most cases in which patients refuse treatment never go to court, however. Clinicians and family members pressure patients to accept treatment, and most eventually agree to treatment after initially refusing (Griffen, Steadman, & Petrila, 2002; Monahan et al., 2001).

TEST YOURSELF

What are the right to treatment, the right to refuse treatment, and informed consent?

APPLY IT Which of the following cases would be a clear violation of patients' rights?

a. Jane's psychiatrist goes to court to have Jane declared incompetent to make decisions about her treatment.

b. Joanne's psychiatrist enlists the help of Joanne's parents to pressure her into going into the hospital.

c. Vicki's psychiatrist gives her an antipsychotic medication but tells her it is an antidepressant to help her mood.

d. Maggie's psychiatrist tells her she is likely to lose her place in a halfway house if she doesn't start taking her medications.

Answers appear online at www.mhhe.com/nolen5e.

COMPETENCE TO STAND TRIAL

One fundamental principle of law is that, in order to stand trial, accused individuals must have a rational understanding of both the charges against them and the proceedings of the trial and must be able to participate in their defense. People who do not have an understanding of what is happening to them in a courtroom and who cannot participate in their defense are said to be **incompetent to stand trial.** Incompetence may involve impairment in several capacities, including the capacity to understand information, to think rationally about alternative courses of action, to make good choices, and to appreciate one's situation as a criminal defendant (Hoge, Bonnie, et al., 1997).

Impaired competence may be a common problem. Defense attorneys suspect impaired competence in their clients in up to 10 percent of cases. Although only a handful of these clients are referred for formal evaluation, between 24,000 and 60,000 evaluations of criminal defendants for competence to stand trial are performed every year in the United States (MacArthur Research Network on Mental Health and the Law, 1998). Thus, competence judgments are some of the most frequent

Competence to stand trial is one of the most common judgments psychologists are asked to help courts make.

types of judgments that mental health professionals are asked to make for courts. Judges appear to value the testimony of mental health experts concerning defendants' competence and rarely rule against these experts' recommendations.

The consequences of competence judgments for defendants are great. If defendants are judged incompetent, trials are postponed as long as there is reason to believe they will become competent in the foreseeable future, and defendants may be forced to receive treatment. On the other hand, incompetent defendants who are wrongly judged competent may not contribute adequately to their defense and may be wrongly convicted and incarcerated. Defendants who are suspected of being incompetent are described by their attorneys as much less helpful in establishing the facts of their case and much less actively involved in making decisions about their defense (MacArthur Research Network on Mental Health and the Law, 1998).

Not surprisingly, defendants with a long history of psychiatric problems, particularly schizophrenia or psychotic symptoms, are more likely to be referred for competence evaluations (Nicholson & Kugler, 1991). Defendants referred for competence evaluations also tend to have less education and to be poor, unemployed, and unmarried. Over half have been accused of violent offenses. Women are more likely than men to be judged incompetent, and members of ethnic minority groups are more likely than European Americans (Nicholson & Kugler, 1991). This may be because women and members of ethnic minorities who commit crimes are more likely to have severe psychological problems that make them incompetent to stand trial. Or perhaps evaluators have lower thresholds for judging women and ethnic minorities to be incompetent. In addition, when the evaluator does not speak the same language as the ethnic minority defendant, the defendant may not understand the evaluator's questions, and the evaluator may not understand the defendant's answers. In these instances, the evaluator may interpret the lack of communication as an indication of the defendant's incompetence to stand trial.

Psychologists have developed tests of those cognitive attributes important to the ability to follow legal proceedings, and people who perform poorly on these tests are more likely to be judged incompetent to stand trial. These tests have not been widely used, however. Instead, judgments of incompetence usually are made for people who have existing diagnoses of psychotic disorders or who have symptoms indicating severe psychopathology, such as gross disorientation, delusions, hallucinations, and thought disorders (Cochrane, Grisso, & Frederick, 2001).

TEST YOURSELF

What does it mean to be incompetent to stand trial?

APPLY IT Paul, who has a long history of paranoia and delusions, has been accused of shooting his wife. He has been judged incompetent to stand trial because he will not speak to his defense attorney, instead carrying on long, incoherent tirades about his wife having been unfaithful and the judicial system being corrupt. Which of the following describes how Paul's case will be handled?

a. Paul's trial will be postponed until he is judged competent.

b. Paul will not be forced to take treatments to reduce his psychiatric symptoms.

c. Paul will be sent to a psychiatric hospital and not be tried for shooting his wife.

d. Paul will be given a test that can definitively determine whether he is truly incompetent to stand trial.

Answers appear online at www.mhhe.com/nolen5e.

THE INSANITY DEFENSE

Insanity is a legal term rather than a psychological or medical term, and it has been defined in various ways. The **insanity defense** is based on the belief that people cannot be held fully responsible for illegal acts if they were so mentally incapacitated at the time of committing the acts that they could not conform to the rules of society (Meyer & Weaver, 2006). Note that people do not have to be chronically insane for the insanity defense to apply. They only have to be judged to have been insane at the time they committed the illegal acts. This judgment can be difficult to make.

John Hinckley was judged not guilty by reason of insanity in the shooting of President Ronald Reagan. This judgment inspired a reappraisal of the insanity defense.

The insanity defense has been one of the most controversial applications of psychology to the law. The lay public often thinks of the insanity defense as a means by which guilty people "get off." When the insanity defense has been used successfully in celebrated cases—as when John Hinckley successfully used this defense after shooting President Ronald Reagan and the president's press secretary, Jim Brady, in 1981—there have been calls to eliminate it altogether (Steadman et al., 1993). Indeed, these celebrated cases have often led to reappraisals of the insanity defense and redefinitions of the legal meaning of insanity.

The insanity defense actually is used much less often than the public tends to think. As shown in Table 16.2, fewer than 1 in 100 defendants in felony cases files an insanity plea, and only 26 percent of these result in acquittal (Silver, Cirincione, & Steadman, 1994). Thus, only about 1 in 400 people charged with a felony is judged not guilty by reason of insanity. About 265 of these people have diagnoses of schizophrenia, and most have a history of psychiatric hospitalizations and previous crimes (McGreevy, Steadman, & Callahan, 1991).

Almost 90 percent of the people who are acquitted after pleading the insanity defense are male, and 66 percent are White (McGreevy et al., 1991; Warren et al., 2004). The reasons men and Whites are more likely to successfully plead the insanity defense are unclear but may have to do with their greater access to competent attorneys

TABLE 16.2 Comparison of Public Perceptions of the Insanity Defense with Actual Use and Results

The public perceives that many more accused persons use the insanity defense successfully than is actually the case.

	Public Perception	Reality
Percentage of felony indictments for which an insanity plea is made	37%	1%
Percentage of insanity pleas resulting in "not guilty by reason of insanity"	44%	26%
Percentage of persons "not guilty by reason of insanity" sent to mental hospitals	51%	85%
Percentage of persons "not guilty by reason of insanity" set free	26%	15%
Conditional release		12%
Outpatient treatment		3%
Unconditional release		1%
Length of confinement of persons "not guilty by reason of insanity" (in months)		
All crimes	21.8	32.5
Murder		76.4

Source: Data from Silver et al., 1994.

who can effectively argue the insanity defense. In the past decade or two, as society has become more aware of the plight of abused and battered women, increasing numbers of women are pleading the insanity defense after injuring or killing a partner who had been abusing them.

One such case is that of Lorena Bobbitt. According to Bobbitt, her husband, John, had sexually and emotionally abused her for years. One night in 1994, John returned home drunk and raped Lorena. In what her attorneys described as a brief psychotic episode, Lorena cut off her husband's penis and threw it away. She was acquitted of charges of malicious injury by reason of temporary insanity. She was referred to a mental institution for further evaluation and was released a few months later.

Even when a defendant is judged not guilty by reason of insanity, he or she usually is not set free. Of those people acquitted because of insanity, about 85 percent are sent to mental hospitals, and all but 1 percent are put under some type of supervision and care. Of those who are sent to mental hospitals, the average length of stay (or incarceration) in the hospital is almost 3 years when all types of crimes are considered, and over 6 years for those who have been accused (and acquitted by reason of insanity) of murder (McGreevy et al., 1991; Silver et al., 1994). Some states stipulate that people judged not guilty by reason of insanity cannot be incarcerated in mental institutions for longer than they would have served in prison had they been judged guilty of their crimes, but not all states have this rule. In short, there is little evidence that the insanity defense is widely used to help people avoid incarceration for their crimes.

Insanity Defense Rules

Five rules have been used in modern history to evaluate defendants' pleas that they be judged not guilty by reason of insanity (Table 16.3).

M'Naghten Rule

The first insanity defense rule was the **M'Naghten rule** (Meyer & Weaver, 2006). Daniel M'Naghten lived in England in the mid-1800s and believed that the English Tory party was persecuting him. He set out to kill the Tory prime minister but mistakenly shot the prime minister's secretary. At his trial in 1843, the jury judged M'Naghten not guilty by reason of insanity. There was a public outcry at this verdict, leading the House of Lords to establish a rule formalizing when a person could be absolved from responsibility for his or her acts because of a mental disorder. This rule, known as the M'Naghten rule, still is used in many jurisdictions today:

> To establish a defense on the ground of insanity, it must be clearly proved that at the time of committing the act, the party accused was labouring under such a defect of reason, from disease of the mind, as not to know the nature and quality of the act he was doing, or if he did know it, that he did not know he was doing what was wrong.

TABLE 16.3 Insanity Defense Rules

Five rules have been used in determining whether an individual was insane at the time he or she committed a crime and therefore whether he or she should not be held responsible for the crime.

Rule	The Individual Is Not Held Responsible for a Crime If . . .
M'Naghten rule	At the time of the crime, the individual was so affected by a disease of the mind that he or she did not know the nature of the act he or she was committing or did not know it was wrong.
Irresistible impulse rule	At the time of the crime, the individual was driven by an irresistible impulse to perform the act or had a diminished capacity to resist performing the act.
Durham rule	The crime was a product of a mental disease or defect.
ALI rule	At the time of the crime, as a result of a mental disease or defect, the person lacked substantial capacity either to appreciate the criminality (wrongfulness) of the act or to conform his or her conduct to the law.
Insanity Defense Reform Act	At the time of the crime, as a result of mental disease or mental retardation, the person was unable to appreciate the wrongfulness of his or her conduct.

The M'Naghten rule reflects the doctrine that a person must have a "guilty mind"—in Latin, *mens rea*—or the intention to commit the illegal act in order to be held responsible for the act.

Applying the M'Naghten rule might seem to be a straightforward matter—one simply determines whether a person suffers from a disease of the mind and whether during the crime he or she understood that his or her actions were wrong. Unfortunately, it is not that simple. A major problem in applying the M'Naghten rule is determining what is meant by a "disease of the mind." The law has been unclear and inconsistent in what disorders it recognizes as diseases of the mind. The most consistently recognized diseases are psychoses. It has been relatively easy for the courts and the public to accept that someone experiencing severe delusions and hallucinations is suffering from a disease and, at times, may not know right from wrong. However, defendants have argued that several other disorders, including alcohol abuse, severe depression, and post-traumatic stress disorder, are diseases of the mind that impair judgments of right and wrong. It is much more difficult for courts, the lay public, and mental health professionals to agree on the validity of these claims (Meyer & Weaver, 2006).

Another major problem is that the M'Naghten rule requires that a person not know right from wrong at the time of the crime in order to be judged not guilty by reason of insanity (Meyer & Weaver, 2006). This is a difficult judgment to make because it is retrospective. Even when everyone agrees that a defendant suffers from a severe psychological disorder, this does not necessarily mean that at the time of the crime the person was incapable of knowing "right from wrong," as the M'Naghten rule requires. For example, serial killer Jeffrey Dahmer, who tortured, killed, dismembered, and ate his victims, clearly seemed to have a psychological disorder. Nevertheless, the jury denied his insanity defense in part because he took great care to hide his crimes from the local police, suggesting that he knew that what he was doing was wrong or against the law.

Irresistible Impulse Rule

The second rule used to judge the acceptability of the insanity defense is the **irresistible impulse rule.** First applied in Ohio in 1934, the irresistible impulse rule broadened the conditions under which a criminal act could be considered the product of insanity to include "acts of passion." Even if a person knew the act he or she was committing was wrong, the person could be absolved of responsibility for performing the act if he or she was driven by an irresistible impulse to perform the act or had a diminished capacity to resist performing it (Meyer & Weaver, 2006).

One of the most celebrated applications of the notion of diminished capacity was the "Twinkie Defense" of Dan White. As depicted in the movie *Milk* (2008), in 1979 Dan White assassinated San Francisco city council member Harvey Milk and Mayor George Moscone. White argued that he had had diminished capacity to resist the impulse to shoot Moscone and Milk due to the psychological effects of extreme stress and the consumption of large amounts of junk food. Using a particularly broad definition of diminished capacity in force in California law at the time, the jury convicted White of manslaughter instead of first-degree murder. Variations of the "Twinkie Defense" have rarely been attempted since White's trial.

Durham Rule

In 1954, Judge David Bazelon further broadened the criteria for the legal definition of insanity in his ruling on the case *Durham v. United States,* which produced the third rule for defining insanity—the **Durham rule.** According to the Durham rule, the insanity defense could be accepted for any crimes that were the "product of mental disease or mental defect." This rule allowed defendants to claim that the presence of any disorder recognized by mental health professionals could be the "cause" of their crimes. The Durham rule did not require that defendants show they were incapacitated by their disorders or did not understand that their acts were illegal. The rule eventually was dropped by almost all jurisdictions by the early 1970s (Meyer & Weaver, 2006).

ALI Rule

The fourth rule for deciding the acceptability of the insanity defense was proposed by the American Law Institute in 1962. Motivated by dissatisfaction with the existing legal definitions of insanity, a group of lawyers, judges, and scholars associated with the American Law Institute (ALI) worked to formulate a better definition, which eventually resulted in what is known as the **ALI rule:**

> A person is not responsible for criminal conduct if at the time of such conduct as the result of mental disease or defect he lacks substantial capacity either to appreciate the criminality (wrongfulness) of his conduct or to conform his conduct to the requirements of the law.

This rule is broader than the M'Naghten rule because it requires only that the defendant have a *lack* of appreciation of the criminality of his or her act, not an *absence* of understanding of the criminality of the act. The defendant's inability to conform his or her conduct to the requirements of the law can result from the emotional symptoms of a psychological disorder as well as from the cognitive deficits caused by the disorder. This expanded understanding incorporates some of the crimes recognized by the irresistible impulse rule. The ALI rule clearly is more restrictive than the Durham rule, however, because it requires some lack of appreciation of the criminality of an act, rather than the mere presence of a mental disorder (Meyer & Weaver, 2006). The ALI rule further restricts the types of mental disorders that can contribute to a successful insanity defense:

> As used in this Article, the term "mental disease or defect" does not include an abnormality manifested only by repeated criminal or otherwise antisocial conduct.

After Dan White killed Harvey Milk and Mayor George Moscone, he argued that he had diminished capacity due to the psychological effects of extreme stress and the consumption of large amounts of junk food.

This restriction prohibits defense attorneys from arguing that a defendant's long history of antisocial acts is itself evidence of the presence of a mental disease or defect. Further, in 1977, in *Barrett v. United States,* it was ruled that "temporary insanity created by voluntary use of alcohol or drugs" also does not qualify a defendant for acquittal by reason of insanity.

The ALI rule was widely adopted in the United States, including in the jurisdiction in which John Hinckley was tried for shooting Ronald Reagan. Hinckley had a long-standing diagnosis of schizophrenia and an obsession with the actress Jodi Foster. Letters he wrote to Foster before shooting Reagan indicated that he committed the act under the delusion that it would impress Foster and cause her to return his love. Hinckley's defense attorneys successfully argued that he had a diminished capacity to understand the wrongfulness of shooting Reagan or to conform his behaviors to the requirements of the law. The public outcry over the judgment that Hinckley was "not guilty by reason of insanity" initiated another reappraisal of the legal definition of insanity and the use of the insanity defense (Meyer & Weaver, 2006; Steadman et al., 1993).

Insanity Defense Reform Act

The reappraisal of the insanity defense led to the fifth rule for defining of insanity, codified in the **Insanity Defense Reform Act,** enacted by Congress in 1984. The Insanity Defense Reform Act adopted the **American Psychiatric Association**

definition of insanity in 1983. This definition dropped the provision in the ALI rule that absolved people of responsibility for criminal acts if they were unable to conform their behavior to the law and retained the wrongfulness criterion initially proposed in the M'Naghten rule (Meyer & Weaver, 2006). This definition reads as follows:

> A person charged with a criminal offense should be found not guilty by reason of insanity if it is shown that, as a result of mental disease or mental retardation, he was unable to appreciate the wrongfulness of his conduct at the time of his offense.

This definition now applies in all cases tried in federal courts and in the courts of about half the states. Also following the Hinckley verdict, most states now require that a defendant pleading not guilty by reason of insanity prove that he or she was insane at the time of the crime. Previously, the burden of proof had been on the prosecution to prove that the defendant was sane at the time the crime was committed (Steadman et al., 1993).

Problems with the Insanity Defense

Cases in which the insanity defense is pled often use mental health professionals to provide expert opinions. Despite their expertise, mental health professionals often disagree about the nature and causes of psychological disorders, the presence or absence of a psychological disorder, and the evaluation of defendants' states of mind at the time crimes were committed (Warren et al., 2004). Usually, lawyers on both sides of the case find mental health professionals who support their point of view, and the two professionals inevitably are in disagreement with each other. This disagreement leads to confusion on the part of judges, juries, and the public.

Mental health professionals also have raised concerns about the rules used to determine the acceptability of the insanity defense (Meyer & Weaver, 2006). Behind these rules is the assumption that most people, including most people with psychological disorders, have free will and usually can choose how they will act in any given situation. Many current models of both normal and abnormal behavior suggest that people do not have that much control over their behaviors. Biological predispositions, early life experiences, or disordered patterns of thinking can make people act in irrational and perhaps uncontrolled ways. This view makes it more difficult to determine when a person should or should not be held responsible for his or her behaviors.

Guilty but Mentally Ill

In a sixth and most recent reform of the insanity defense, some states have adopted as an alternative to the verdict "not guilty by reason of insanity" the verdict **guilty but mentally ill (GBMI).** Defendants convicted as guilty but mentally ill are incarcerated for the normal term designated for their crimes, with the expectation that they also will receive treatment for their mental illness. Proponents of the GBMI verdict argue that it recognizes the mental illness of defendants while still holding them responsible for their actions. Critics argue that the GBMI verdict is essentially a guilty verdict and a means of eliminating the insanity defense (Tanay, 1992). Juries may believe they are ensuring that a person gets treatment by judging him or her guilty but mentally ill, but there is no guarantee that a person convicted under GBMI will receive treatment. In most states, it is left to legal authorities to decide whether to incarcerate people judged guilty but mentally ill in mental institutions or prisons and, if they are sent to prisons, whether to provide them with treatment for their mental illness. As we discuss in the next section, people with mental disorders usually do not receive adequate—if any—treatment when they are incarcerated.

TEST YOURSELF

What rules have been used to determine whether an individual can be judged not guilty by reason of insanity?

APPLY IT Stan, who has a long history of paranoid schizophrenia, went into a local grocery store and began firing a semiautomatic weapon, acting under the delusion that he was commanded by Satan to "kill the unworthy." If Stan were judged "guilty but mentally ill," which of the following would be likely?

a. He would be sent to a mental hospital until his symptoms of paranoid schizophrenia were brought under control.
b. He would be sent to prison with the expectation that he would receive treatment for paranoid schizophrenia there.
c. He would be released into the custody of his family.
d. He would be given the death penalty.

Answers appear online at www.mhhe.com/nolen5e.

SHADES OF GRAY

Read the following case study.

On June 20, 2001, after her husband Rusty left for work, Andrea Yates methodically drowned all five of her young children in the bathtub. She then called 911 and asked that a police officer come to her house. She also called her husband at work and told him he needed to come home.

Andrea had a long history of psychotic depression. In the summer of 1999, she had tried to commit suicide and had been hospitalized twice. She had hallucinations and delusions that led her to believe she was evil and that her children were irreparably damaged and doomed to hell. Her psychiatrist diagnosed her with postpartum psychosis and successfully treated her, but urged the couple not to have any more children, saying future episodes of psychotic depression were inevitable. The Yates conceived their fifth child approximately 7 weeks after her discharge from the hospital.

Three months after the birth of her fifth child, Andrea's father died, and her condition worsened, leading her to be hospitalized. When she was discharged, her psychiatrist gave instructions that she be watched around the clock. On the day of the drowning, her husband left for work expecting his mother to arrive at the house soon to supervise Andrea and the children. It was then that Andrea drowned the children. She later told a psychiatrist, "My children weren't righteous. They stumbled because I was evil. The way I was raising them, they could never be saved. They were doomed to perish in the fires of hell." (*Houston Chronicle*, March 5, 2002)

Would you judge Andrea Yates "not guilty by reason of insanity"? Why or why not? (Discussion appears at the end of this chapter.)

MENTAL HEALTH CARE IN THE JUSTICE SYSTEM

Men with mental disorders are four times likelier to be incarcerated than men without a mental disorder, and women with a mental disorder are eight times likelier to be incarcerated than women without a mental disorder (Teplin, Abram, & McClelland, 1996). Although a subset of the crimes committed by people with mental disorders involve violence or theft, many of their crimes involve drug possession and use (Osher & Steadman, 2007). Many of these individuals are repeat offenders, going through a revolving door between prison and a freedom characterized by joblessness, homelessness, and poverty.

As a result, the prison system has become the *de facto* mental health system for millions of people with mental disorders (Osher & Steadman, 2007). Studies of male prison inmates find that over 50 percent can be diagnosed with a mental disorder, most often a substance use disorder or antisocial personality disorder (Collins & Schlenger, 1983; Hodgins & Cote, 1990; Neighbors et al., 1987). A study of women prison inmates found that 64 percent had a lifetime history of a major psychiatric disorder, including major depression, an anxiety disorder, a substance use disorder, or a personality disorder, and that 46 percent had suffered a major psychiatric disorder in the previous 6 months (Jordan, Schlenger, Fairbank, & Caddell, 1996). In addition, nearly 80 percent of these women had been exposed to an extreme trauma, such as sexual abuse, sometime in their lives. Another study of 1,272 women jail detainees awaiting trial in Chicago found that over 80 percent had a lifetime

Andrea Yates argued that severe psychosis and postpartum depression led her to drown her five young children in 2001.

history of a psychiatric disorder and that 70 percent were symptomatic within the previous 6 months (Teplin et al., 1996). In these studies, the most common diagnosis the women received was substance abuse or dependence, but substantial percentages of the women also had major depression and/or a borderline or antisocial personality disorder.

Numerous court decisions have mandated that prison inmates receive necessary mental health services, just as they should receive necessary medical services. Most inmates with mental disorders do not receive these services, however. A study of male inmates found that only 37 percent of those with schizophrenia or a major mood disorder received treatment while in jail (Teplin, 1990), and a study of female inmates found that only 23.5 percent of these with schizophrenia or a major mood disorder received treatment in jail (Teplin, Abram, & McClelland, 1997). Depression in inmates is particularly likely to go unnoticed and untreated, even though suicide is the second most frequent cause of death among jail detainees, accounting for 39 percent of all inmate deaths (Patterson, 1994).

The services inmates do receive often are minimal. Substance abuse treatments may involve only the provision of information about drugs and perhaps Alcoholics Anonymous or Narcotics Anonymous meetings held in the prison. Treatment for schizophrenia or depression may involve only occasional visits with a prison physician who prescribes a standard drug treatment but has neither the time nor the expertise to follow individuals closely.

Comprehensive treatment programs focusing on the special needs of prison inmates with mental disorders can successfully reduce their symptoms of mental disorder, their substance abuse, and their repeat offense rates. Many of these treatment programs focus on male inmates, because they greatly outnumber female inmates. The female inmate population has grown more rapidly than the male inmate population in the past decade, however, more than tripling in that time period (Teplin et al., 1997).

Female inmates may have different needs for services than male inmates (Teplin et al., 1997). Female inmates may be more likely than male inmates to have a history of sexual and physical abuse, which needs to be addressed in treatment. Also, female inmates are more likely than male inmates to be suffering from depression or anxiety, and to have children for whom they will become caregivers after they are released from prison.

Increasingly, communities are developing systems to divert criminal offenders with mental disorders into community-based treatment programs rather than incarceration (Redlich et al., 2006). The hope is that providing these individuals with comprehensive mental health treatment combined with occupational rehabilitation and social services will enable them to live in the community as healthy and productive citizens. Diversion from jail into community services is especially likely to be a goal when the offender is a youth (Steinberg, 2009).

Some states have developed *mental health courts,* in which the cases of offenders with mental disorders are reviewed by judges who specialize in working with mental health and social service professionals to divert offenders into treatment and rehabilitation. Courts that focus specifically on drug offenders often are called *drug courts*. Offenders diverted by mental health courts or drug courts into community treatment are still under the watchful eye of the court. If they do not cooperate with the plan developed by the mental health court for their treatment and rehabilitation, they can be diverted back into jail. This feature of these courts is controversial because it amounts to coercing offenders into treatment. Most courts attempt to avoid reincarceration and instead use milder sanctions, such as requiring offenders to reappear before the judge, to motivate them to cooperate with their treatment plan (Redlich et al., 2006).

The effectiveness of mental health courts and drug courts in reducing recidivism and rehabilitating offenders into the community relies heavily on the availability of high-quality community services, services sorely lacking in many communities.

TEST YOURSELF

What are mental health courts and drug courts?

APPLY IT Liz, who is cocaine-dependent, stole money from her employer to pay for cocaine. She was caught, and her case is being heard in a drug court. The judge in this court is more likely than a judge in a regular court to do which of the following?

a. rule that Liz is "not guilty by reason of mental defect"
b. require Liz to spend some time in jail before she goes into treatment for cocaine dependency
c. rule that Liz is "guilty but mentally ill"
d. require Liz to get treatment for her cocaine dependency as a condition of staying out of jail

Answers appear online at www.mhhe.com/nolen5e.

CHAPTER INTEGRATION

There has perhaps been less integration of biological, social, and psychological viewpoints in the law's approach to issues of mental health than in the mental health field itself. The rules governing the insanity defense suggest that the law takes a biological perspective on psychological disorders, conforming to the belief that a mental disease is like a medical disease (Figure 16.2). Similarly, civil commitment rules require certification that a person has a mental disorder or disease before he or she can be committed, further legitimating psychiatric diagnostic systems based on medical models.

In each area discussed in this chapter, however, there are mental health professionals advocating a more integrated and complex view of mental disorders than that traditionally held by the law. These professionals are trying to educate judges, juries, and laypeople to understand that some people have biological, psychological, or social predispositions to disorders and that other biological, psychological, or social factors can interact with these predispositions to trigger the onset of mental disorders or certain manifestations of mental disorders. What is most difficult to explain is the probabilistic nature of the predictions that can be made about mental disorders and the behavior of people with these disorders. While a predisposition or certain recent life experiences may make a person more likely to develop a disorder or to engage in a specific behavior (such as a violent behavior), they do not determine the disorder or the specific behavior.

FIGURE 16.2 Differences Between the Perspective of the Law and That of the Mental Health Profession

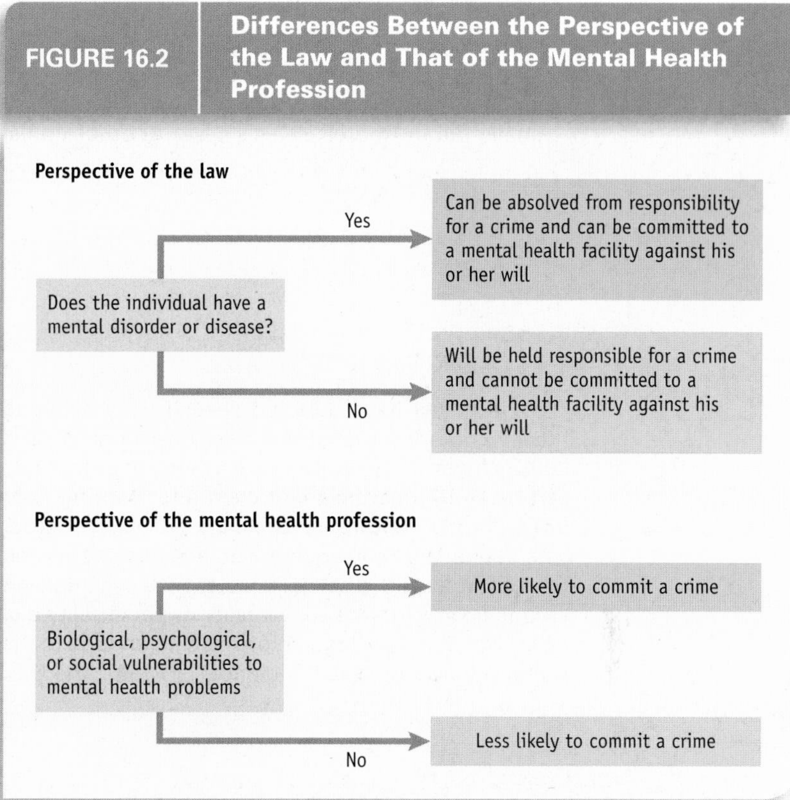

We all prefer to have predictions about the future that are definite, especially when we are making decisions that will determine a person's freedom or confinement. That kind of definitiveness is not possible, however, given our present knowledge of the ways biological, psychological, and social forces interact to influence people's behavior.

SHADES OF GRAY DISCUSSION (review p. 511)

The first point you might note in making your decision is that Andrea Yates had a well-documented history of psychotic depressions—in fact, the psychiatrist who treated her in 1999 warned that she could harm her children as a result of her psychosis. Yates testified that on the morning of the drownings, her delusions and hallucinations led her to believe that she had to kill her children to "save" them. But consider the fact that Yates called 911 and her husband after the drowning. Would this affect your decision? For the jury in Yates's 2002 murder trial it did. They rejected the insanity defense, accepting the assertion by the State of Texas that the fact that Yates called 911 proved she knew her actions were wrong despite her mental defect. Yates was convicted of murder and sentenced to life in prison. In 2005, Yates's conviction was overturned due to false testimony by one of the prosecution witnesses. In 2006 Yates was retried, and this time she was found not guilty by reason of insanity and committed to a Texas state mental hospital.

In making your judgment, you likely found yourself struggling with emotions related to accepting the killing of children by a parent. You are not alone. The public often cannot accept any excuse for such a crime, and therefore the plea of "not guilty by reason of insanity," supposedly as the result of psychotic postpartum depression, is highly controversial in such cases (Williamson, 1993). Severe postpartum depression with psychotic symptoms is very rare, and violence by these women against their newborns is even rarer (Nolen-Hoeksema, 1990). When such violence does occur, some courts have accepted that the

(continued)

mothers' behaviors are the result of the postpartum psychosis and have judged these women not guilty by reason of insanity, as the Texas courts finally did in Andrea Yates's case. At other times, however, even though the law is intended to be objective, its application can be influenced by people's emotional reactions to the behaviors of people with mental disorders.

THINK CRITICALLY

Several states have adopted special laws allowing the involuntary commitment of sex offenders (Winick, 2003). Under these laws, "sexually violent predators" can be kept in confinement even after serving their prison terms. In Kansas, "sexually violent predator" was defined as "any person who has been convicted of or charged with a sexually violent offense and who suffers from a mental abnormality or personality disorder which makes the person likely to engage in the predatory acts of sexual violence." In 1997, the U.S. Supreme Court upheld the Kansas sexual predator law, finding that the defendant in the case, who had committed sexual crimes against children, had a sufficient mental condition to authorize involuntary psychiatric hospitalization.

Do you support laws allowing the involuntary commitment of sexual offenders after they have served their sentence? Why or why not? *Discussion appears on p. 521 at the back of this book.*

CHAPTER SUMMARY

- Civil commitment is the procedure through which a person may be committed for treatment in a mental institution against his or her will. In most jurisdictions, three criteria are used to determine whether individuals may be committed: if they suffer from grave disability that impairs their ability to provide for their own basic needs, if they are an imminent danger to themselves, or if they are an imminent danger to others. Each of these criteria requires a subjective judgment on the part of clinicians and, often, predictions about the future that clinicians may not be competent to make. In particular, the prediction of who will pose a danger to others in the future is difficult to make and often is made incorrectly.
- When being considered for commitment, patients have the right to have an attorney, to have a public hearing, to call and confront witnesses, to appeal decisions, and to be placed in the least restrictive treatment setting. (The right to a hearing is often waived for short-term commitments in emergency settings.) Once committed, patients have the right to be treated and the right to refuse treatment.
- People with mental disorders, particularly those who also have a history of substance abuse, are somewhat more likely to commit violent acts, especially against family members and friends, than are people without a mental disorder. The prevalence of violence among people with mental disorders is not as great as is often assumed by the public and the media, however.
- One fundamental principle of law is that, in order to stand trial, an accused individual must have a reasonable degree of rational understanding both of the charges against him or her and the proceedings of the trial and must be able to participate in his or her defense. People who do not have an understanding of what is happening to them in a courtroom and who cannot participate in their defense are said to be incompetent to stand trial. Defendants who have a history of psychotic disorders, who have current symptoms of psychosis, or who perform poorly on tests of important cognitive skills may be judged incompetent to stand trial.
- Five rules for judging the acceptability of the insanity defense have been used in recent history: the M'Naghten rule, the irresistible impulse rule, the Durham rule, the ALI rule, and the Insanity Defense Reform Act. Each of these rules requires that the defendant be diagnosed with a mental disorder, and most of them require that it be shown that the defendant did not appreciate the criminality of his or her act or could not control his or her behaviors at the time of the crime.

- The verdict "guilty but mentally ill" was introduced following public uproar over uses of the insanity defense in high-profile cases. Persons judged guilty but mentally ill are confined for the duration of a regular prison term but with the assumption that they will receive psychiatric treatment while incarcerated.
- Mental health professionals have raised a number of concerns about the insanity defense. For one thing, it requires after-the-fact judgments of a defendant's state of mind at the time of the crime. In addition, the rules governing the insanity defense presume that people have free will and usually can control their actions. These presumptions contradict some models of normal and abnormal behavior that suggest that behavior is strongly influenced by biological, psychological, and social forces.
- Communities are increasingly attempting to divert persons with mental disorders who commit crimes away from jail and into community-based treatment programs. Mental health courts and drug courts have been established specifically for this purpose.

KEY TERMS

need for treatment 498
civil commitment 498
grave disability 498
dangerousness to self 500
dangerousness to others 500
right to treatment 504
right to refuse treatment 504
informed consent 504
incompetent to stand trial 505
insanity 506
insanity defense 506
M'Naghten rule 507
irresistible impulse rule 508
Durham rule 509
ALI rule 509
Insanity Defense Reform Act 509
American Psychiatric Association definition of insanity 509
guilty but mentally ill (GBMI) 510

DISCUSSIONS FOR THINK CRITICALLY

CHAPTER 1 (page 23)

Students often take a course in abnormal psychology because they want to understand the troubling behavior of someone in their life. Some students, while reading about the psychological problems covered in this book, recognize these problems in themselves. Recall that all the issues we discuss in this book fall along a continuum, such that only a small number of people are at the extreme and qualify for a disorder but many more people have moderate or mild versions. If you think you or someone you care about may have a disorder, refer to the four Ds to evaluate the degree of distress, dysfunction, deviance, and dangerousness in your behaviors and feelings or in another's behaviors and feelings. Most of the time you will find relatively little. If these behaviors and feelings are causing significant distress and difficulty in functioning, if you think they are highly deviant or possibly dangerous, consult a mental health professional. Most schools have counselors available and will also give referrals to mental health professionals in the area.

CHAPTER 2 (page 60)

Anika's difficult life puts her at high risk for psychological problems. If you were a biological theorist, you might look to Anika's mother. You might suggest that her use of alcohol and other drugs while pregnant affected Anika's brain development in ways that led to difficulties in controlling anger, problems in concentration, and self-destructive behaviors. You might also note that Anika may have inherited genes for impulsiveness and emotionality.

If you approached Anika's case from the perspective of a psychological theorist following a cognitive approach, you would focus on Anika's beliefs that she is no good and is defective. You might suggest that these beliefs have been shaped by her experiences of abuse and rejection by her mother and by her foster parents. If you were a behavioral theorist, you would search for reinforcements Anika may be getting for her aggressive and self-destructive behaviors—perhaps they bring her the attention she needs. You might note that behaviors such as skipping class and smoking are reinforced by her peers. If you were an interpersonal theorist, you would look for the roots of Anika's problems in her series of destructive families. You might examine whether the dynamics in Anika's current family contribute to her self-destructive behaviors.

Looking at Anika's case as a sociocultural theorist, you would view Anika's behaviors as a direct result of the stresses she has endured throughout her life. You would suggest that Anika's social environment—community, school, and family—feeds her negative behaviors and that she may need to be removed from this toxic environment.

Most forms of psychopathology are caused by multiple factors. All the explanations of Anika's behavior offered above could be at least partially true. Sometimes, intervening with just one factor improves a person's overall functioning. If an interpersonal therapist had Anika placed in a supportive and stable home situation, this alone might help her. Other times, interventions must happen on many different levels before the person's behaviors and feelings can improve. A biological theorist might offer medication for Anika's problems in addition to her receiving intervention from a behavioral theorist to help with peer pressure at school and intervention from an interpersonal theorist to help with problems at home. The combination of these approaches may be what Anika's complex case needs.

CHAPTER 3 (page 86)

A questionnaire or structured interview that systematically asks Brett about each of the criteria for the diagnosis of panic disorder, such as that in Table 3.1, would be extremely helpful in making a diagnosis. This questionnaire or structured interview would go point by point through the criteria in Table 3.4, determining whether a symptom was present, the frequency and duration of symptoms, and the circumstances that were present when the symptoms arose. Personality questionnaires might help determine whether Brett is chronically afraid of the symptoms or sees them as evidence of impending disaster. To establish whether his racing heart and shortness of breath might be due to a biological disorder (see Criterion E in Table 3.4), Brett should have a thorough physical exam focusing on factors such as drug use, cardiac functioning, and hormone functioning.

CHAPTER 4 (page 109)

Here are a few suggestions for how you could answer the questions.

1. The dependent variable is symptoms or diagnosis of eating disorders (see Chapter 12). The independent variable is some measure of "pressures to be thin."
2. Because adolescent girls and young women have high rates of eating disorders, you might want to recruit them for your sample.
3. You could measure pressures to be thin with a questionnaire that asks participants how much pressure they perceive in their lives. You could measure eating disorders with a questionnaire that asks participants if they have experienced each of the symptoms listed for eating disorders in the *DSM-IV-TR* (see Chapter 12).
4. A case study would allow you to explore in depth how pressures to be thin were related to the development of an eating disorder in one woman. The major disadvantage is that you cannot know whether what you discover is generalizable to other women.

5. A correlational study might examine the correlation between scores on a measure of pressures to be thin and scores on a measure of eating disorder symptoms.
6. An experimental study might include one group in which a confederate of the experimenter initiates a conversation with participants about how much men like women who are thin and another group in which the confederate initiates a conversation with participants about something unrelated to being thin. The dependent variable could be how much participants in each group say they are dissatisfied with their bodies (see Chapter 12 for a similar study).
7. A therapy outcome study might examine whether a therapy that helps young women with eating disorders reject pressures to be thin is more effective in reducing eating disorder symptoms than a therapy that does not specifically address pressures to be thin.
8. A meta-analysis could summarize all studies that have examined the relationship between pressures to be thin and symptoms of eating disorders to determine the average strength of the relationship across studies. The advantage of a meta-analysis is that it does not reflect the peculiarities of any one study (e.g., what sample or measures were used) but rather provides summary information across a range of studies.

CHAPTER 5 (page 149)

There is no clear right or wrong answer to this question—it depends on what you believe about how narrow or broad the definition of PTSD should be. Narrowing the definition will result in fewer people being diagnosed with the disorder. On one hand, this will focus resources for treatment and research on people who are most severely afflicted by the disorder. It also will prevent people from being labeled as having a psychiatric disorder, which can still carry a stigma in our society. On the other hand, narrowing the diagnosis may result in some people who are suffering significantly not getting help because they do not meet the diagnostic criteria.

CHAPTER 6 (page 178)

These are some of the facts from the actual trial of George Franklin, held in 1990, for the murder of Susan Nason, which occurred in 1969. In post-trial interviews, jurors reported that they had concluded the only way Eileen could have known the details to which she had testified was by being an eyewitness. They also had been impressed by the emotional recounting of the murder and by Eileen's confidence and firmness in asserting the truth of her memories. They deliberated for only one day before returning a verdict of "guilty of murder in the first degree."

This case was the first in America in which a conviction was based on a memory that apparently had been repressed and then recovered, but it was followed by a number of other cases in which individuals were charged with violence and sexual abuse based on repressed memories. As noted in the chapter, researchers have provided evidence for and against the claim that memories can be repressed, but this evidence can go only so far in helping us judge what is true in a given case. Often, this evidence is presented by competing expert witnesses in court cases. In the years since the Franklin case, jury verdicts and public opinion about repressed memories have shifted back and forth.

In 1996, George Franklin was set free after his conviction was overturned. It turned out that many of the details in Eileen Franklin's memory of the murder, such as the silver ring on Susan Nason's crushed finger, could have been known from newspaper accounts at the time. Indeed, some of the details Eileen recounted had factual inaccuracies that mirrored inaccuracies in the newspaper accounts of the murder. Other details, such as what Nason said during the incident, were unverifiable. The judge in the case ruled that George Franklin's rights had been violated, and the district attorney decided not to retry the case given the problems that had emerged with regard to Eileen Franklin's memories.

CHAPTER 7 (page 220)

Researchers have adapted CBT and IPT techniques to prevent depression in people at high risk (Munoz, Le, Clarke, & Jaycox, 2002). Working mostly in group settings, clinicians help individuals identify, and then dispute, negative patterns of thinking. The group setting allows the teaching and practicing of effective social skills, while the clinicians focus on individuals' concrete problems and help them devise solutions.

Adolescence is a notoriously difficult stage of life—you may remember painful experiences of your own. While for many people the difficulty lessens over time, evidence suggests that people with depression first developed it in adolescence. Based on this evidence, several researchers have focused on preventing depression in high-risk teens.

One study involved adolescents whose mild to moderate symptoms of depression put them at high risk for developing major depression. They were randomly assigned to a cognitive-behavioral intervention or to a no-intervention control group. The students receiving the cognitive-behavioral intervention met for 15 sessions in small groups, where they received therapy to help them overcome negative ways of thinking and learn more effective coping strategies. Over the course of the 15 sessions, the individuals in the intervention group benefited immediately and showed a decline in their depressive symptoms. Following the therapy, both the intervention group and the no-treatment control group were followed for up to 18 months. Relatively few members of the intervention group developed depression. In contrast, many members of the control group did develop depression. The intervention seemed to reduce the risk for future depression in its participants (Clarke et al., 1995).

Without therapy, these adolescents might have continued to struggle with low self-esteem, a negative outlook, and other symptoms that could adversely affect their lives and even lead to suicide attempts. Programs like this provide hope that vulnerable young people can be spared the debilitating effects of depression.

CHAPTER 8 (page 259)

In this chapter, you read about epigenetic processes, in which DNA can be changed chemically by different environmental conditions, leading to genes being turned on or off. These genetic changes alter the development of cells, tissues, and organs. What might have set these epigenetic processes in motion for these twins? An injury that Pamela suffered in the womb or in the birth process that Carolyn did not suffer—such as a birth complication that deprived her of oxygen—may be the reason. Or possibly Pamela, but not Carolyn, was exposed to an infectious disease early in life that affected her brain development.

CHAPTER 9 (pages 293–294)

"Ted" is Ted Bundy, one of the most infamous serial killers of the twentieth century. Researchers Douglas Samuel and Thomas Widiger (2006) asked 245 mental health professionals to engage in the same sort of evaluation of Ted as you did. Eighty percent of the clinicians diagnosed Ted with antisocial personality disorder because of his ruthless and violent criminal behavior. However, Ted actually lacks two key features of antisocial personality disorder: Criterion A3 for antisocial personality disorder requires "impulsivity or failure to plan ahead," but Bundy meticulously planned and carried out his murders; Criterion A6 for antisocial personality disorder is "consistent irresponsibility," but there is much evidence that Ted was considered quite responsible by his employers and close associates. In addition, 95 percent of the clinicians thought Ted met the criteria for narcissistic personality disorder, illustrating the problem of overlap between the diagnostic criteria for different disorders in the *DSM-IV-TR*.

When asked to rate Ted on the Big 5 personality factor facets, clinicians saw Ted as being low on most facets of negative emotionality, openness, and agreeableness but high on facets of extraversion, including assertiveness and excitement seeking. You might be surprised that they also rated him relatively high in conscientiousness, specifically in the facets of competence, orderliness, achievement, and deliberation. We often don't think of serial killers as having adaptive traits but these characteristics probably helped Ted avoid arrest for many years. They are not, however, captured by the diagnostic criteria for antisocial personality disorder. Samuel and Widiger (2006) argue that the Big 5 personality factor facets better describe Ted Bundy than do the *DSM-IV-TR* criteria and would have been a useful framework for clinicians and law enforcement officials as they were trying to capture and prosecute Bundy. It is this kind of empirical research that has led the *DSM-5* authors to reconceptualize personality disorders along dimensional traits like those represented in the Big 5.

CHAPTER 10 (page 331)

The decision of whether to give a child a particular medication is a highly personal one for parents. No one would want to deprive a child of a medication that could dramatically improve his or her functioning and quality of life. However, medications often are widely used to treat children when few controlled studies exist to show that the benefits clearly outweigh the possible risks of side effects and long-term effects on development. In their meta-analysis, Peter Jensen and colleagues (2007) argue that psychosocial treatments should be the first line of treatment for disruptive, aggressive, and self-injurious behaviors in children. When these treatments are not sufficiently effective, Jensen and colleagues affirm that existing studies show the potential benefits of the atypical antipsychotics to outweigh their apparent side effects. Still, they recommend that many more studies be done, particularly of the long-term effects of the atypical antipsychotics on growth and development in children.

CHAPTER 11 (page 356)

Different people have different strategies for responding to the challenges of being a caregiver to someone with dementia. Here are some tips from the Alzheimer's Association (www.alz.org):

1. Investigate the resources in your community. There may be support groups for you, financial resources for medical and custodial care for your family member, or groups that will provide respite care (for example, sitting with your family member when you need to be away from the house). You can find out about these resources through your family physician, your religious institution, or local chapters of the Alzheimer's Association or other groups focused on people with dementia.
2. Become educated about dementia and about caregiving techniques. It can be helpful to know what to expect from your family member and how to interpret and cope with his or her symptoms.

3. Engage in legal and financial planning. You may need to consult a financial adviser or attorney to plan for the day when you may need to place your family member in a care facility, or to ensure that his or her finances are appropriately managed. The Alzheimer's Association website has lots of good information about the legal and financial issues you may need to deal with.
4. Take care of yourself by watching your diet, exercising, and getting plenty of rest. Caregivers often neglect their own well-being, but this doesn't help their ill family member any more than it helps them. Consult your physician if you develop health problems, and consider getting help from a support group or a counselor to deal with the emotional issues you are facing.
5. Be realistic about what you can do. There may come a time when you cannot manage your family member physically because of his or her symptoms, or when the stress of caregiving becomes too much for you or your family. Give yourself credit for what you have done, and don't blame yourself if you can't do it all on your own. Ask for help from other family members, friends, and anyone else who may be able to relieve your stress.

CHAPTER 12 (page 386)

In designing an eating-disorder prevention program for your school, you would not be alone—a number of these programs have been developed and tested in school settings (see, for example, Stice et al., 2008). Most of these programs target known risk factors, including elevated pressure to be thin, internalization of the thin ideal, body dissatisfaction, and negative mood. Programs can consist of a single session or multiple sessions over time. They might involve a former sufferer of an eating disorder who tells others about her experience and how she overcame it. Or, over multiple sessions, a program might teach participants to manage a healthy weight, to reject social pressure to be thin, and to cope with stress. Finally, some programs target only individuals known to be at risk, while others target whole communities.

Meta-analyses of these programs find that 51 percent resulted in reduced eating-disorder risk factors (such as poor body image) and 29 percent in reduced current or future eating pathology (Stice, Shaw, & Marti, 2007). Although 29 percent may not sound like a high success rate, prevention programs for other public health problems, such as obesity and HIV, achieve about the same percentage. Larger positive effects were found for programs that (a) targeted participants who already had eating-disorder symptoms or risk factors, (b) focused solely on women over age 15, (c) were not lecture-based but instead encouraged participation, (d) were delivered by trained interventionists, and (e) focused on body acceptance and reducing thin-ideal internalization. Promising results come from prevention programs that teach women with risk factors to argue against the thin ideal and to recognize pressures from the media. Such programs have reduced participants' acceptance of the thin ideal and decreased their body dissatisfaction, dieting, and bulimic symptoms (Stice et al., 2008).

CHAPTER 13 (page 420)

Certain sexual disorders diagnosed in the *DSM-IV-TR*—including transvestism and other fetishes, sexual masochism, and consensual sexual sadism—are controversial because it can be argued that they represent variations in people's preferences for sexual activities rather than mental disorders (Moser, 2009). Many transsexual individuals argue that they do not have a mental disorder and have a right to live their life as they wish.

You might argue that any sexual behavior that negatively affects others—such as voyeurism, exhibitionism, frotteurism, and particularly pedophilia—should be considered a mental disorder. But many people with these sexual preferences do not act on them out of fear of being caught (Moser, 2009). Even in the case of pedophilia, studies find that the majority of individuals who are sexually attracted to prepubescent children have no history of sexual contact with a child according to self-reports, criminal records, or any other available information (Seto, 2009). On the other hand, 40 to 50 percent of individuals arrested for a sexual offense against a child would not be diagnosed as pedophiles based on their patterns of sexual arousal and their typical behavior (Seto, 2009). Other crimes that by definition victimize others, such as rape, are not considered mental disorders.

When the *DSM-IV-TR* was revised in 2000, attempts were made to narrow the definition of exhibitionism, voyeurism, frotteurism, and pedophilia so that only individuals who acted on these urges or who experienced clinically significant distress or impairment as a result of them would receive diagnoses. As we have discussed throughout this book, however, judgments as to what constitutes a mental disorder are subjective and are influenced by societal norms and historical trends. Nowhere is this truer than in the category of sexual disorders.

CHAPTER 14 (pages 462–463)

Both sides of this debate can marshal evidence for their positions. The presidents of about 100 U.S. colleges, including Duke, Ohio State, and Dartmouth, are calling on the U.S. government to lower the drinking age to 18, saying that the current law is routinely flouted and encourages dangerous binge drinking (see www.amethystinitiative.org). They suggest that legalizing drinking by 18- to 21-year-olds would bring their drinking out of hiding and afford colleges more opportunities to intervene in problem drinking. An analysis of federal records by the Associated Press found that 157 college-age people (ages 18 to 23) drank themselves to death between 1999 and 2005.

Other college presidents argue that lowering the drinking age will push illegal drinking even more into high schools. Statistics from the National Institute on Alcohol Abuse and Alcoholism show that the rate of accidents associated with alcohol among 16- to 20-year-olds has declined since the drinking age was raised to 21. Mothers Against Drunk Driving estimates that 25,000 lives have been saved (see www.madd.org). For further coverage of this debate, see www.cbsnews.com/stories/2009/02/19/60minutes/main4813571.shtml.

Prevention programs such as those described in this chapter could be used to reduce the harmful consequences of drinking by 18- to 21-year-olds. It is not known, however, how many colleges would institute such programs or whether the programs would counteract any negative consequences of lowering the drinking age.

CHAPTER 15 (page 494)

The scientific community is debating the ethical and practical issues raised by the failure to find significant effects of psychosocial interventions on the progression of cancer or cardiovascular disease. Some researchers argue that giving patients false hope that they can influence the course of their disease by changing their thoughts and by reducing stress is unethical and results in blaming the victim when health deteriorates (Coyne et al., 2007; see also Ehrenreich, 2009). Others argue that even if psychosocial interventions cannot influence patients' survival rates, they can improve their quality of life, which is itself a worthwhile goal (Frasure-Smith & Lesperence, 2005). The key, they say, is to give patients an honest and realistic expectation about what psychosocial interventions can and cannot do.

CHAPTER 16 (page 514)

On one hand, you may believe that justice requires freeing a sexual offender after he has served his sentence. On the other, you might fear future harm from the offender and therefore favor keeping him committed. In the 1997 case, the Supreme Court held that laws allowing involuntary commitment of sexual offenders were constitutional only if they were enacted with the intent to protect the public from further harm, not if they were enacted with the intent to further punish offenders. The public tends to support indefinitely incarcerating sex offenders, arguing that it protects the public against further harm (Carlsmith et al., 2007). However, predicting who is going to do harm to others in the future is difficult, and jurors' motives are not always purely for the public good. A study in which potential jurors were presented with a description based on the 1997 Kansas case found that they overwhelmingly favored confining the offender after he served his sentence, regardless of the probability that he would offend again (Carlsmith et al., 2007). This suggests that people's motives for supporting these laws have as much to do with exacting retribution against individuals who commit abhorrent crimes as with protecting the public.

GLOSSARY

A

ABAB (reversal) design type of experimental design in which an intervention is introduced, withdrawn, and then reinstated, and the behavior of a participant is examined on and off the treatment

abstinence violation effect what happens when a person attempting to abstain from alcohol use ingests alcohol and then endures conflict and guilt by making an internal attribution to explain why he or she drank, thereby making him or her more likely to continue drinking in order to cope with the self-blame and guilt

acute stress disorder disorder similar to post-traumatic stress disorder but occurs within 1 month of exposure to the stressor and does not last more than 4 weeks; often involves dissociative symptoms

adjustment disorder stress-related disorder that involves emotional and behavioral symptoms (depressive symptoms, anxiety symptoms, and/or antisocial behaviors) that arise within 3 months of the onset of a stressor

adoption study study of the heritability of a disorder by finding adopted people with a disorder and then determining the prevalence of the disorder among their biological and adoptive relatives, in order to separate out contributing genetic and environmental factors

affective flattening negative symptom of schizophrenia that consists of a severe reduction or the complete absence of affective responses to the environment

agnosia impaired ability to recognize objects or people

agoraphobia anxiety disorder characterized by fear of places and situations in which it would be difficult to escape, such as enclosed places, open spaces, and crowds

alcohol abuse diagnosis given to someone who uses alcohol in dangerous situations, fails to meet obligations at work or at home due to alcohol use, and has recurrent legal or social problems as a result of alcohol use

alcohol dependence diagnosis given to someone who has a physiological tolerance to alcohol, spends a lot of time intoxicated or in withdrawal, or continues to drink despite significant legal, social, medical, or occupational problems that result from alcohol (often referred to as alcoholism)

ALI rule legal principle stating that a person is not responsible for criminal conduct if he or she lacks the capacity to appreciate the criminality (wrongfulness) of the act or to conform his or her conduct to the requirements of the law as a result of mental disease

allostatic load physiological condition resulting from chronic arousal of the fight-or-flight response to stress

alogia deficit in both the quantity of speech and the quality of its expression

altruistic suicide suicide committed by people who believe that taking their own life will benefit society

Alzheimer's disease progressive neurological disease that is the most common cause of dementia

amenorrhea cessation of the menses

American Psychiatric Association definition of insanity definition of insanity stating that people cannot be held responsible for their conduct if, at the time they commit crimes, as the result of mental disease or mental retardation they are unable to appreciate the wrongfulness of their conduct

amnesia impairment in the ability to learn new information or to recall previously learned information or past events

amphetamines stimulant drugs that can produce symptoms of euphoria, self-confidence, alertness, agitation, paranoia, perceptual illusions, and depression

amygdala structure of the limbic system critical in emotions such as fear

animal studies studies that attempt to test theories of psychopathology using animals

animal type phobias extreme fears of specific animals that may induce immediate and intense panic attacks and cause the individual to go to great lengths to avoid the animals

anomic suicide suicide committed by people who experience a severe disorientation and role confusion because of a large change in their relationship to society

anorexia nervosa eating disorder in which people fail to maintain body weights that are normal for their age and height and have fears of becoming fat, distorted body images, and amenorrhea

antagonist drugs drugs that block or change the effects of an addictive drug, reducing desire for the drug

anterograde amnesia deficit in the ability to learn new information

antianxiety drugs drugs used to treat anxiety, insomnia, and other psychological symptoms

anticonvulsants drugs used to treat mania and depression

antidepressant drugs drugs used to treat the symptoms of depression, such as sad mood, negative thinking, and disturbances of sleep and appetite; common types are tricyclics, selective serotonin reuptake inhibitors, and serotonin-norepinephrine reuptake inhibitors

antipsychotic drugs drugs used to treat psychotic symptoms, such as delusions, hallucinations, and disorganized thinking

antisocial personality disorder (ASPD) pervasive pattern of criminal, impulsive, callous, and/or ruthless behavior, predicated on disregard for the rights of others and an absence of respect for social norms

anxiety state of apprehension, tension, and worry

anxiety sensitivity belief that bodily symptoms have harmful consequences

anxious-fearful personality disorders category including avoidant, dependent, and obsessive-compulsive personality disorders, which are characterized by a chronic sense of anxiety or fearfulness and behaviors intended to ward off feared situations

aphasia impaired ability to produce and comprehend language

applied tension technique technique used to treat blood-injection-injury type phobias in which the therapist teaches the client to increase his or her blood pressure and heart rate, thus preventing the client from fainting

apraxia impaired ability to initiate common voluntary behaviors

arousal phase in the sexual response cycle, psychological experience of arousal and pleasure as well as physiological changes, such as the tensing of muscles and enlargement of blood vessels and tissues (also called the excitement phase)

Asperger's disorder pervasive developmental disorder characterized by deficits in social skills and activities; similar to autism but does not include deficits in language or cognitive skills

assertive community treatment programs system of treatment that provides comprehensive services to people with schizophrenia, employing the expertise of medical professionals, social workers, and psychologists to meet the variety of patients' needs 24 hours a day

assessment process of gathering information about a person's symptoms and their possible causes

association studies genetic studies in which researchers identify physical disorders associated with a target psychological disorder for which genetic abnormalities or markers are known; the DNA of individuals with the psychological disorder and their first-degree relatives is then examined to determine if they also have this genetic marker (one form of molecular genetic studies)

attention-deficit/hyperactivity disorder (ADHD) syndrome marked by deficits in controlling attention, inhibiting impulses, and organizing behavior to accomplish long-term goals

atypical antipsychotics drugs that seem to be even more effective in treating schizophrenia than phenothiazines without the same neurological side effects; they bind to a different type of dopamine receptor than other neuroleptic drugs

auditory hallucination auditory perception of a phenomenon that is not real, such as hearing a voice when one is alone

autism childhood disorder marked by deficits in social interaction (such as a lack of interest in one's family or other children), communication (such as failing to modulate one's voice to signify emotional expression), and activities and interests (such as engaging in bizarre, repetitive behaviors)

aversion therapy treatment that involves the pairing of unpleasant stimuli with deviant or maladaptive sources of pleasure in order to induce an aversive reaction to the formerly pleasurable stimulus

avoidant personality disorder pervasive anxiety, sense of inadequacy, and fear of being criticized that lead to the avoidance of most social interactions with others and to restraint and nervousness in social interactions

avolition inability to persist at common goal-directed activities

B

barbiturates drugs used to treat anxiety and insomnia that work by suppressing the central nervous system and decreasing the activity level of certain neurons

behavioral approaches approaches to psychopathology that focus on the influence of reinforcements and punishments in producing behavior; the two core principles or processes of learning according to behaviorism are *classical conditioning* and *operant conditioning*

behavioral inhibition set of behavioral traits including shyness, fearfulness, irritability, cautiousness, and introversion; behaviorally inhibited children tend to avoid or withdraw from novel situations, are clingy with parents, and become excessively aroused when exposed to unfamiliar situations

behavioral observation method for assessing the frequency of a client's behaviors and the specific situations in which they occur

behavioral theories of depression theories that view depression as resulting from negative life events that represent a reduction in positive reinforcement; sympathetic responses to depressive behavior then serve as positive reinforcement for the depression itself

behavioral therapies psychotherapeutic approaches that focus on identifying the reinforcements and punishments contributing to a person's maladaptive behaviors and on changing specific behaviors

behavioral therapy therapy that focuses on changing a person's specific behaviors by replacing unwanted behaviors with desired behaviors

behavior genetics study of the processes by which genes affect behavior and the extent to which personality and abnormality are genetically inherited

behaviorism study of the impact of reinforcements and punishments on behavior

bell and pad method treatment for enuresis in which a pad placed under a sleeping child to detect traces of urine sets off a bell when urine is detected, awakening the child to condition him or her to wake up and use the bathroom before urinating

benzodiazepines drugs that reduce anxiety and insomnia

beta-amyloid class of proteins that accumulates in the spaces between neurons in the brain, contributing to Alzheimer's disease

binge-eating disorder eating disorder in which people compulsively overeat either continuously or on discrete binges but do not behave in ways to compensate for the overeating

bingeing eating a large amount of food in one sitting

binge/purge type of anorexia nervosa type of anorexia nervosa in which periodic bingeing or purging behaviors occur along with behaviors that meet the criteria for anorexia nervosa

biological approach view that biological factors cause and should be used to treat abnormality

biological theories theories of abnormality that focus on biological causes of abnormal behaviors

biopsychosocial approach approach to psychopathology that seeks to integrate biological, psychological, and social factors in understanding and treating psychopathology

bipolar disorder disorder marked by cycles between manic episodes and depressive episodes; also called manic-depression

bipolar I disorder form of bipolar disorder in which the full symptoms of mania are experienced; depressive aspects may be more infrequent or mild

bipolar II disorder form of bipolar disorder in which only hypomanic episodes are experienced and the depressive component is more pronounced

blood-injection-injury type phobias extreme fears of seeing blood or an injury or of receiving an injection or another invasive medical procedure, which cause a drop in heart rate and blood pressure and fainting

body dysmorphic disorder syndrome involving obsessive concern over a part of the body the individual believes is defective

borderline personality disorder syndrome characterized by rapidly shifting and unstable mood, self-concept, and interpersonal relationships, as well as impulsive behavior and transient dissociative states

breathing-related sleep disorder group of sleep disorders characterized by numerous brief sleep disturbances due to problems breathing

brief psychotic disorder disorder characterized by the sudden onset of delusions, hallucinations, disorganized speech, and/or disorganized behavior that lasts only between 1 day and 1 month, after which the symptoms vanish completely

bulimia nervosa eating disorder in which people engage in bingeing and behave in ways to prevent weight gain from the binges, such as self-induced vomiting, excessive exercise, and abuse of purging drugs (such as laxatives)

C

caffeine chemical compound with stimulant effects

calcium channel blockers drugs used to treat mania and depression

cannabis substance that causes feelings of well-being, perceptual distortions, and paranoid thinking

case studies in-depth analyses of individuals

catatonia group of disorganized behaviors that reflect an extreme lack of responsiveness to the outside world

catatonic schizophrenia type of schizophrenia in which people show a variety of motor behaviors and ways of speaking that suggest almost complete unresponsiveness to their environment

catharsis expression of emotions connected to memories and conflicts, which, according to Freud, leads to the release of energy used to keep these memories in the unconscious

causal attribution explanation for why an event occurred

central sleep apnea sleep disorder characterized by complete cessation of respiratory activity for brief periods of time (20 seconds or more); sufferers do not have frequent awakenings and do not tend to feel tired during the day; occurs when the brain does not send the signal to breathe to the respiratory system

cerebral cortex part of the brain that regulates complex activities, such as speech and analytical thinking

cerebrovascular disease disease that occurs when the blood supply to the brain is blocked, causing tissue damage to the brain

childhood disintegrative disorder pervasive developmental disorder in which children develop normally at first but later show permanent loss of basic skills in social interactions, language, and/or movement

chlorpromazine antipsychotic drug

circadian rhythm sleep disorder sleep disorder characterized by insomnia or excessive sleepiness during the day due to disruptions in circadian rhythms

civil commitment forcing of a person into a mental health facility against his or her will

classical conditioning form of learning in which a neutral stimulus becomes associated with a stimulus that naturally elicits a response, thereby making the neutral stimulus itself sufficient to elicit the same response

classification system set of syndromes and the rules for determining whether an individual's symptoms are part of one of these syndromes

client-centered therapy (CCT) Carl Rogers's form of psychotherapy, which consists of an equal relationship between therapist and client as the client searches for his or her inner self, receiving unconditional positive regard and an empathic understanding from the therapist

cocaine central nervous system stimulant that causes a rush of positive feelings initially but that can lead to impulsiveness, agitation, and anxiety and can cause withdrawal symptoms of exhaustion and depression

cognitions thoughts or beliefs

cognitive-behavioral therapy (CBT) treatment focused on changing negative patterns of thinking and solving concrete problems through brief sessions in which a therapist helps a client challenge negative thoughts, consider alternative perspectives, and take effective actions

cognitive disorders dementia, delirium, or amnesia characterized by impairments in cognition (such as deficits in memory, language, or planning) and caused by a medical condition or by substance intoxication or withdrawal

cognitive theories theories that focus on belief systems and ways of thinking as the causes of abnormal behavior

cognitive therapies therapeutic approaches that focus on changing people's maladaptive thought patterns

cohort effect effect that occurs when people born in one historical period are at different risk for a disorder than are people born in another historical period

collective unconscious according to Carl Jung, the wisdom accumulated by a society over hundreds of years of human existence and stored in the memories of individuals

community mental health centers institutions for the treatment of people with mental health problems in the community; may include teams of social workers, therapists, and physicians who coordinate care

community mental health movement movement launched in 1963 that attempted to provide coordinated mental health services to people in community-based treatment centers

compulsions repetitive behaviors or mental acts that an individual feels he or she must perform

computerized tomography (CT) method of analyzing brain structure by passing narrow X-ray beams through a person's head from several angles to produce measurements from which a computer can construct an image of the brain

concordance rate probability that both twins will develop a disorder if one twin has the disorder.

conditioned avoidance response behavior that is reinforced because it allows individuals to avoid situations that cause anxiety

conditioned response (CR) in classical conditioning, response that first followed a natural stimulus but that now follows a conditioned stimulus

conditioned stimulus (CS) in classical conditioning, previously neutral stimulus that, through pairing with a natural stimulus, becomes sufficient to elicit a response

conduct disorder syndrome marked by chronic disregard for the rights of others, including specific behaviors such as stealing, lying, and engaging in acts of violence

conscious refers to mental contents and processes of which we are actively aware

continuous variable factor that is measured along a continuum (such as 0–100) rather than falling into a discrete category (such as "diagnosed with depression")

continuum model model of abnormality that views mental disorders not as categorically different from "normal" experiences but as lying somewhere along a continuum from healthy, functional behaviors, thoughts, and feelings to unhealthy, dysfunctional behaviors, thoughts, and feelings

control group in an experimental study, group of subjects whose experience resembles that of the experimental group in all ways except that they do not receive the key manipulation

conversion disorder syndrome marked by a sudden loss of functioning in a part of the body, usually following an extreme psychological stressor

coronary heart disease (CHD) chronic illness that is a leading cause of death in the United States, occurring when the blood vessels that supply the heart with oxygen and nutrients are narrowed or closed by plaque, resulting in a myocardial infarction (heart attack) when closed completely

correlational studies method in which researchers assess only the relationship between two variables and do not manipulate one variable to determine its effects on another variable

correlation coefficient statistic used to indicate the degree of relationship between two variables

cortisol hormone that helps the body respond to stressors, inducing the fight-or-flight response

cross-sectional type of research examining people at one point in time but not following them over time

cultural relativism view that norms among cultures set the standard for what counts as normal behavior, which implies that abnormal behavior can only be defined relative to these norms and that no universal definition of abnormality is therefore possible; only definitions of abnormality relative to a specific culture are possible

cyclothymic disorder milder but more chronic form of bipolar disorder that consists of alternation between hypomanic episodes and mild depressive episodes over a period of at least 2 years

D

dangerousness to others legal criterion for involuntary commitment that is met when a person would pose a threat or danger to other people if not incarcerated

dangerousness to self legal criterion for involuntary commitment that is met when a person is imminently suicidal or a danger to him- or herself as judged by a mental health professional

day treatment centers mental health facilities that allow people to obtain treatment, along with occupational and rehabilitative therapies, during the day but to live at home at night

deep brain stimulation procedure to treat depression in which electrodes are surgically implanted in specific areas of the brain and connected to a pulse generator that is placed under the skin and stimulates these brain areas

defense mechanisms strategies the ego uses to disguise or transform unconscious wishes

degradation process in which a receiving neuron releases an enzyme into the synapse, breaking down neurotransmitters into other biochemicals

deinstitutionalization movement in which thousands of mental patients were released from mental institutions; a result of the patients' rights movement, which was aimed at stopping the dehumanization of mental patients and at restoring their basic legal rights

delirium cognitive disorder including disorientation and memory loss that is acute and usually transient

delirium tremens (DTs) symptoms that result during severe alcohol withdrawal, including hallucinations, delusions, agitation, and disorientation

delusional disorder disorder characterized by delusions lasting at least 1 month regarding situations that occur in real life, such as being followed, poisoned, or deceived by a spouse or having a disease; people with this disorder do not show any other symptoms of schizophrenia

delusion of reference false belief that external events, such as other people's actions or natural disasters, relate somehow to oneself

delusions fixed beliefs with no basis in reality

delusions of thought insertion beliefs that one's thoughts are being controlled by outside forces

demand characteristics factors in an experiment that suggest to participants how the experimenter would like them to behave

dementia cognitive disorder in which a gradual and usually permanent decline of intellectual functioning occurs; can be caused by a medical condition, substance intoxication, or withdrawal

dependent personality disorder pervasive selflessness, a need to be cared for, and fear of rejection, which lead to total dependence on and submission to others

dependent variable factor that an experimenter seeks to predict

depersonalization disorder syndrome marked by frequent episodes of feeling detached from one's own body and mental processes, as if one were an outside observer of oneself; symptoms must cause significant distress or interference with one's ability to function

depression state marked by either a sad mood or a loss of interest in one's usual activities, as well as feelings of hopelessness, suicidal ideation, psychomotor agitation or retardation, and trouble concentrating

desensitization treatment used to reduce anxiety by rendering a previously threatening stimulus innocuous by repeated and guided exposure to the stimulus under nonthreatening circumstances

developmental coordination disorder disorder involving deficits in the ability to walk, run, or hold on to objects

diagnosis label given to a set of symptoms that tend to occur together

***Diagnostic and Statistical Manual of Mental Disorders* (DSM)** official manual for diagnosing mental disorders in the United States, containing a list of specific criteria for each disorder, how long a person's symptoms must be present to qualify for a diagnosis, and requirements that the symptoms interfere with daily functioning in order to be called disorders

dialectical behavior therapy cognitive-behavioral intervention aimed at teaching problem-solving skills, interpersonal skills, and skill at managing negative emotions

diathesis-stress models models that assert that only when a diathesis or vulnerability interacts with a stress or trigger will a disorder emerge

disorder of written expression developmental disorder involving deficits in the ability to write

disorganized schizophrenia syndrome marked by incoherence in cognition, speech, and behavior as well as flat or inappropriate affect

dissociation process whereby different facets of an individual's sense of self, memories, or consciousness become split off from one another

dissociative amnesia loss of memory for important facts about a person's own life and personal identity, usually including the awareness of this memory loss

dissociative fugue disorder in which a person moves away and assumes a new identity, with amnesia for the previous identity

dissociative identity disorder (DID) syndrome in which a person develops more than one distinct identity or personality, each of which can have distinct facial and verbal expressions, gestures, interpersonal styles, attitudes, and even physiological responses

distress in defining abnormality, the view that behaviors should be considered abnormal only if the individual suffers distress and wishes to be rid of the behaviors

dizygotic (DZ) twins twins who average only 50 percent of their genes in common because they developed from two separate fertilized eggs

dopamine neurotransmitter in the brain, excess amounts of which have been thought to cause schizophrenia

double-blind experiment study in which both the researchers and the participants are unaware of which experimental condition the participants are in, in order to prevent demand effects

dramatic-emotional personality disorders category including antisocial, borderline, narcissistic, and histrionic personality disorders, which are characterized by dramatic and impulsive behaviors that are maladaptive and dangerous

Durham rule legal principle stating that the presence of a mental disorder is sufficient to absolve an individual of responsibility for a crime

dyspareunia genital pain associated with sexual intercourse

dyssomnias primary sleep disorders that involve abnormalities in the amount, quality, or timing of sleep

dysthymic disorder type of depression that is less acute than major depression but more chronic; diagnosis requires the presence of a sad mood or anhedonia, plus two other symptoms of depression, for at least 2 years, during which symptoms do not remit for 2 months or longer

E

eating disorder not otherwise specified diagnosis for individuals who have some symptoms of anorexia or bulimia nervosa but do not meet the full criteria

echolalia communication abnormality in which an individual simply repeats back what he or she hears rather than generating his or her own speech

effectiveness in therapy outcome research, how well a therapy works in real-world settings

efficacy in therapy outcome research, how well a therapy works in highly controlled settings with a narrowly defined group of people

ego part of the psyche that channels libido to be acceptable to the superego and within the constraints of reality

egoistic suicide suicide committed by people who feel alienated from others and who lack social support

ego psychology branch of psychodynamic theory emphasizing the importance of the individual's ability to regulate defenses in ways that allow healthy functioning within the realities of society

electroconvulsive therapy (ECT) treatment for depression that involves the induction of a brain seizure by passing electrical current through the patient's brain while he or she is anesthetized

electroencephalogram (EEG) procedure in which multiple electrodes are placed on the scalp to detect low-voltage electrical current produced by the firing of specific neurons in the brain

elimination disorders disorders in which a child shows frequent, uncontrolled urination or defecation far beyond the age at which children usually develop control over these functions

emotion-focused approaches theories of disorders that view poor regulation of emotions as being at the core of many types of psychopathology, including depression, anxiety, substance abuse, and most of the personality disorders

encopresis diagnosis given to children who are at least age 4 and who defecate inappropriately at least once a month for 3 months

endocrine system system of glands that produces many different hormones

enuresis diagnosis given to children at least age 5 who wet the bed or their clothes at least twice a week for 3 months

epidemiology study of the frequency and distribution of a disorder, or a group of disorders, in a population

epigenetics study of how environmental conditions can change the expression of genes without changing the gene sequence

excessive reassurance seeking constantly looking for assurances from others that one is accepted and loved

executive functions functions of the brain that involve the ability to sustain concentration; use abstract reasoning and concept formation; anticipate, plan, and program; initiate purposeful behavior; self-monitor; and shift from maladaptive patterns of behavior to more adaptive ones

exhibitionism obtainment of sexual gratification by exposing one's genitals to involuntary observers

experimental group in an experimental study, group of participants that receive the key manipulation

experimental studies studies in which the independent variables are directly manipulated and the effects on the dependent variable are examined

exposure and response prevention type of therapy in which individuals with anxiety symptoms are exposed repeatedly to the focus of their anxiety but prevented from avoiding it or engaging in compulsive responses to the anxiety

expressed emotion family interaction style in which families are overinvolved with each other, are overprotective of the disturbed family member, voice self-sacrificing attitudes to the disturbed family member, and simultaneously are critical, hostile, and resentful of this member

expressive language disorder disorder involving deficits in the ability to express oneself through language

external validity extent to which a study's results can be generalized to phenomena in real life

F

factitious disorder by proxy disorder in which the individual creates an illness in another individual in order to gain attention

factitious disorders disorders marked by deliberately faking physical or mental illness to gain medical attention

family-focused therapy treatment for people with bipolar disorder in which patients and their families are given education about bipolar disorder and training in communication and problem-solving skills

family history study study of the heritability of a disorder involving identifying people with the disorder and people without the disorder and then determining the disorder's frequency within each person's family

family systems theories theories that see the family as a complex system that works to maintain the status quo

family systems therapy psychotherapy that focuses on the family, rather than the individual, as the source of problems; family therapists challenge communication styles, disrupt pathological family dynamics, and challenge defensive conceptions in order to harmonize relationships among all members and within each member

female orgasmic disorder in women, recurrent delay in or absence of orgasm after having reached the excitement phase of the sexual response cycle (also called anorgasmia)

female sexual arousal disorder in women, recurrent inability to attain or maintain the swelling-lubrication response of sexual excitement

fetal alcohol syndrome (FAS) syndrome that occurs when a mother abuses alcohol during pregnancy, causing the baby to have lowered IQ, increased risk for mental retardation, distractibility, and difficulties with learning from experience

fetishism paraphilia in which a person uses inanimate objects as the preferred or exclusive source of sexual arousal

fight-or-flight response physiological changes in the human body that occur in response to a perceived threat, including the secretion of glucose, endorphins, and hormones as well as the elevation of heart rate, metabolism, blood pressure, breathing, and muscle tension

five-factor model personality theory that posits that any individual's personality is organized along five broad dimensions of personality: neuroticism, extraversion, openness to experience, agreeableness, and conscientiousness

flooding behavioral technique in which a client is intensively exposed to a feared object until the anxiety diminishes (also called implosive therapy)

formal thought disorder state of highly disorganized thinking (also known as loosening of associations)

free association method of uncovering unconscious conflicts in which the client is taught to talk about whatever comes to mind, without censoring any thoughts

frotteurism obtainment of sexual gratification by rubbing one's genitals against or fondling the body parts of a nonconsenting person

G

gender identity one's perception of oneself as male or female

gender identity disorder (GID) condition in which a person believes that he or she was born with the wrong sex's genitals and is fundamentally a person of the opposite sex

generalizability extent to which the results of a study generalize to, or inform us about, people other than those who were studied

generalized anxiety disorder (GAD) anxiety disorder characterized by chronic anxiety in daily life

general paresis disease that leads to paralysis, insanity, and eventually death; discovery of this disease helped establish a connection between biological diseases and mental disorders

global assumptions fundamental beliefs that encompass all types of situations

glove anesthesia state in which people lose all feeling in one hand, as if they were wearing a glove that wiped out all physical symptoms

grandiose delusions false, persistent beliefs that one has superior talents and traits

grave disability legal criterion for involuntary commitment that is met when a person is so incapacitated by a mental disorder that he or she cannot provide his or her own basic needs, such as food, clothing, or shelter, and his or her survival is threatened as a result

group comparison study study that compares two or more distinct groups on a variable of interest

guided mastery techniques interventions designed to increase health-promoting behaviors by providing explicit information about how to engage in these behaviors, as well as opportunities to engage in the behaviors in increasingly challenging situations

guilty but mentally ill (GBMI) verdict that requires a convicted criminal to serve the full sentence designated for his or her crime, with the expectation that he or she will also receive treatment for mental illness

H

halfway houses living facilities that offer people with long-term mental health problems the opportunity to live in a structured, supportive environment while they are trying to reestablish employment and ties to family and friends

hallucinations perceptual experiences that are not real

hallucinogens substances, including LSD and MDMA (ecstasy), that produce perceptual illusions and distortions even in small doses

harm-reduction model approach to treating substance use disorders that views alcohol use as normative behavior and focuses education on the immediate risks of the excessive use of alcohol (such as alcohol-related accidents) and on the payoffs of moderation (such as avoidance of hangovers)

hippocampus structure of the brain involved in memory and in the stress response

histrionic personality disorder syndrome marked by rapidly shifting moods, unstable relationships, and an intense need for attention and approval, which are sought by means of overly dramatic behavior, seductiveness, and dependence

hopelessness sense that the future is bleak and there is no way to make it more positive

hormone chemical that carries messages throughout the body, potentially affecting a person's mood, level of energy, and reaction to stress

humanistic theories views that people strive to develop their innate potential for goodness and self-actualization; abnormality arises as a result of societal pressures to conform to unchosen dictates that clash with a person's self-actualization needs and from an inability to satisfy more basic needs, such as hunger

humanistic therapy type of therapy in which the goal is to help the client discover his or her place in the world and to accomplish self-actualization through self-exploration; based on the assumption that the natural tendency for humans is toward growth (also called person-centered therapy)

human laboratory study experimental study involving human participants

hypertension condition in which the blood supply through the blood vessels is excessive and can lead to deterioration of the cell tissue and hardening of the arterial walls

hypoactive sexual desire disorder condition in which a person's desire for sex is diminished to the point that it causes him or her significant distress or interpersonal difficulties and is not due to transient life circumstances or another sexual dysfunction

hypochondriasis syndrome marked by chronic worry that one has a physical symptom or disease that one clearly does not have

hypomania state in which an individual shows mild symptoms of mania

hypothalamic-pituitary-adrenal axis (HPA axis) three key components of the neuroendocrine system that work together in a feedback system interconnected with the limbic system and the cerebral cortex

hypothalamus component of the brain that regulates eating, drinking, sex, and basic emotions; abnormal behaviors involving any of these activities may be the result of dysfunction in the hypothalamus

hypothesis testable statement about two or more variables and the relationship between them

I

id according to Freud, most primitive part of the unconscious; consists of drives and impulses seeking immediate gratification

immune system system that protects the body from disease-causing microorganisms and affects susceptibility to diseases

impulse-control disorders disorders characterized by difficulty controlling the desire to engage in certain impulsive acts; people with these disorders often feel a mounting sense of tension that is relieved only by engaging in their impulsive act

impulsivity difficulty controlling behaviors; acting without thinking first

incidence number of new cases of a specific disorder that develop during a specific period of time

incompetent to stand trial legal status of an individual who lacks a rational understanding of the charges against him or her, an understanding of the proceedings of his or her trial, or the ability to participate in his or her defense

independent variable factor that is manipulated by an experimenter or used to predict the dependent variable

informed consent procedure (often legally required prior to treatment administration) in which a patient receives a full and understandable explanation of the treatment being offered and makes a decision about whether to accept or refuse the treatment

inhalants solvents, such as gasoline, glue, or paint thinner, that one inhales to produce a high and that can cause permanent central nervous system damage as well as liver and kidney disease

insanity legal term denoting a state of mental incapacitation during the time a crime was committed

insanity defense defense used by people accused of a crime in which they state that they cannot be held responsible for their illegal acts because they were mentally incapacitated at the time of the act

Insanity Defense Reform Act 1984 law, affecting all federal courts and about half the state courts, that finds a person not guilty by reason of insanity if it is shown that, as a result of mental disease or mental retardation, the accused was unable to appreciate the wrongfulness of his or her conduct at the time of the offense

intelligence tests tests that assess a person's intellectual strengths and weaknesses

intermittent explosive disorder disorder characterized by (a) several episodes of failure to resist aggressive impulses that result in serious assaultive acts or destruction of property, (b) a degree of aggressiveness grossly out of proportion to the situation, and (c) symptoms not better explained by another mental disorder (such as antisocial personality disorder), the effects of substances, or a medical condition (e.g., a head trauma)

internal validity extent to which all factors that could extraneously affect a study's results are controlled within a laboratory study

interoceptive conditioning process by which symptoms of anxiety that have preceded panic attacks become the signals for new panic attacks

interpersonal and social rhythm therapy (ISRT) treatment for people with bipolar disorder that helps them manage their social relationships and daily rhythms to try to prevent relapse

interpersonal theories of depression theories that view the causes of depression as rooted in interpersonal relationships

interpersonal therapy (IPT) more structured, short-term version of psychodynamic therapies

irresistible impulse rule legal principle stating that even a person who knowingly performs a wrongful act can be absolved of responsibility if he or she was driven by an irresistible impulse to perform the act or had a diminished capacity to resist performing the act

K

kleptomania disorder characterized by chronic shoplifting, taking items not needed for personal use or monetary value; before the theft, these individuals feel a mounting tension that turns to relief or gratification after the theft

L

learned helplessness theory view that exposure to uncontrollable negative events leads to a belief in one's inability to control important outcomes and a subsequent loss of motivation, indecisiveness, and failure of action

libido according to Freud, psychical energy derived from physiological drives

light therapy treatment for seasonal affective disorder that involves exposure to bright lights during the winter months

limbic system part of the brain that relays information from the primitive brain stem about changes in bodily functions to the cortex, where the information is interpreted

linkage analysis genetic study that looks for associations between psychological disorders and physical disorders for which genetic causes are known

lithium drug used to treat manic and depressive symptoms

locus ceruleus area of the brain stem that plays a part in the emergency response and may be involved in panic attacks

longitudinal type of research evaluating the same group(s) of people for an extended period of time

M

magnetic resonance imaging (MRI) method of measuring both brain structure and brain function through the construction of a magnetic field that affects hydrogen atoms in the brain, emitting signals that a computer then records and uses to produce a three-dimensional image of the brain

major depression disorder involving a sad mood or anhedonia plus four or more of the following symptoms: weight loss or a decrease in appetite, insomnia or hypersomnia, psychomotor agitation or retardation, fatigue, feelings of worthlessness or severe guilt, trouble concentrating, and suicidal ideation; these symptoms must be present for at least 2 weeks and must produce marked impairments in normal functioning

male erectile disorder in men, recurrent inability to attain or maintain an erection until the completion of sexual activity

male orgasmic disorder in men, recurrent delay in or absence of orgasm following the excitement phase of the sexual response cycle

malingering feigning of a symptom or a disorder for the purpose of avoiding an unwanted situation, such as military service

managed care health care system in which all necessary services for an individual patient are supposed to be coordinated by a primary care provider; the goals are to coordinate services for an existing medical problem and to prevent future medical problems

mania state of persistently elevated mood, feelings of grandiosity, overenthusiasm, racing thoughts, rapid speech, and impulsive actions

mathematics disorder developmental disorder involving deficits in the ability to learn mathematics

mental hygiene movement movement to treat mental patients more humanely and to view mental disorders as medical diseases

mental illness phrase used to refer to a physical illness that causes severe abnormal thoughts, behaviors, and feelings

mental retardation developmental disorder marked by significantly subaverage intellectual functioning, as well as deficits (relative to others) in life skill areas, such as communication, self-care, work, and interpersonal relationships

mesmerism treatment for hysterical patients based on the idea that magnetic fluids in the patients' bodies are affected by the magnetic forces of other people and objects; the patients' magnetic forces are thought to be realigned by the practitioner through his or her own magnetic force

mesolimbic pathway subcortical part of the brain involved in cognition and emotion

meta-analysis statistical technique for summarizing results across several studies

methadone opioid that is less potent and longer-lasting than heroin; taken by heroin users to decrease their cravings and help them cope with negative withdrawal symptoms

mixed receptive-expressive language disorder disorder involving deficits in the ability to express oneself through language and to understand the language of others

M'Naghten rule legal principle stating that, in order to claim a defense of insanity, accused persons must have been burdened by such a defect of reason, from disease of the mind, as not to know the nature and quality of the act they were doing or, if they did know it, as not to know what they were doing was wrong

modeling process of learning behaviors by imitating others, especially authority figures or people like oneself

molecular genetic studies studies of the structure and function of genes that help in understanding how genetic mutations can lead to disease

monoamine oxidase inhibitors (MAOIs) class of antidepressant drugs

monoamines neurotransmitters, including catecholamines (epinephrine, norepinephrine, and dopamine) and serotonin, that have been implicated in the mood disorders

monozygotic (MZ) twins twins who share 100 percent of their genes because they developed from a single fertilized egg

moral treatment type of treatment delivered in mental hospitals in which patients were treated with respect and dignity and were encouraged to exercise self-control

motivational interviewing intervention for sufferers of substance use disorders to elicit and solidify individuals' motivation and commitment to changing their substance use; rather than confronting the user, the motivational interviewer adopts an empathic interaction style, drawing out the user's own statements of desire, ability, reasons, need, and, ultimately, commitment to change

multiple baseline design type of study in which an intervention is given to the same individual but begun in different settings or is given to different individuals but at different points in time and in which the effects of the intervention are systematically observed

N

narcissistic personality disorder syndrome marked by grandiose thoughts and feelings of one's own worth as well as an obliviousness to others' needs and an exploitive, arrogant demeanor

narcolepsy sleep disorder characterized by irresistible attacks of sleep plus (1) cataplexy or (2) recurrent intrusions of elements of rapid eye movement (REM) sleep into the transition between sleep and wakefulness

natural environment type phobias extreme fears of events or situations in the natural environment that cause impairment in one's ability to function normally

need for treatment legal criterion operationalized as a signed certificate by two physicians stating that a person requires treatment but will not agree to it voluntarily; formerly a sufficient cause to hospitalize the person involuntarily and force him or her to undergo treatment

negative cognitive triad perspective seen in depressed people in which they have negative views of themselves, of the world, and of the future

negative reinforcement process in which people avoid being exposed to feared objects and their avoidance is reinforced by the subsequent reduction of their anxiety

negative symptoms in schizophrenia, deficits in functioning that indicate the absence of a capacity present in people without schizophrenia, such as affective flattening (also called Type II symptoms)

neurofibrillary tangles twists or tangles of filaments within nerve cells, especially prominent in the cerebral cortex and hippocampus, common in the brains of Alzheimer's disease patients

neuroleptics drugs used to treat psychotic symptoms

neuropsychological tests tests of cognitive, sensory, and/or motor skills that attempt to differentiate people with deficits in these areas from normal subjects

neurotransmitters biochemicals, released from a sending neuron, that transmit messages to a receiving neuron in the brain and nervous system

nicotine alkaloid found in tobacco; operates on both the central and peripheral nervous systems, resulting in the release of biochemicals, including dopamine, norepinephrine, serotonin, and the endogenous opioids

nightmare disorder sleep disorder characterized by nightmares frequent enough to cause significant distress or impairment in functioning

nonpurging type of bulimia nervosa type of bulimia nervosa in which bingeing is followed by excessive exercise or fasting to control weight gain

nonsuicidal self-injury act of deliberately cutting, burning, puncturing, or otherwise significantly injuring one's skin with no intent to die

norepinephrine neurotransmitter that is involved in the regulation of mood

norepinephrine-dopamine reuptake inhibitor drug used to treat depression; inhibits the reuptake of both norepinephrine and dopamine

null hypothesis alternative to a primary hypothesis, stating that there is no relationship between the independent variable and the dependent variable

O

obesity condition of being significantly overweight, defined by the Centers for Disease Control as a body mass index (BMI) of 30 or over, where BMI is calculated as weight in pounds multiplied by 703, then divided by the square of height in inches

object relations view held by a group of modern psychodynamic theorists that one develops a self-concept and appraisals of others in a four-stage process during childhood and retains them throughout adulthood; psychopathology consists of an incomplete progression through these stages or an acquisition of poor self- and other concepts

observational learning learning that occurs when a person observes the rewards and punishments of another's behavior and then behaves in accordance with the same rewards and punishments

obsessions uncontrollable, persistent thoughts, images, ideas, or impulses that an individual feels intrude on his or her consciousness and that cause significant anxiety or distress

obsessive-compulsive disorder (OCD) anxiety disorder characterized by obsessions (persistent thoughts) and compulsions (rituals)

obsessive-compulsive personality disorder pervasive rigidity in one's activities and interpersonal relationships; includes qualities such as emotional constriction, extreme perfectionism, and anxiety resulting from even slight disruptions in one's routine

obstructive sleep apnea sleep disorder characterized by repeated episodes of upper-airway obstruction during sleep

odd-eccentric personality disorders disorders, including paranoid, schizotypal, and schizoid personality disorders, marked by chronic odd and/or inappropriate behavior with mild features of psychosis and/or paranoia

operant conditioning form of learning in which behaviors lead to consequences that either reinforce or punish the organism, leading to an increased or a decreased probability of a future response

operationalization specific manner in which variables in a study are measured or manipulated

opioids substances, including morphine and heroin, that produce euphoria followed by a tranquil state; in severe intoxication, can lead to unconsciousness, coma, and seizures; can cause withdrawal symptoms of emotional distress, severe nausea, sweating, diarrhea, and fever

oppositional defiant disorder syndrome of chronic misbehavior in childhood marked by belligerence, irritability, and defiance, although not to the extent found in a diagnosis of conduct disorder

organic amnesia loss of memory caused by brain injury resulting from disease, drugs, accidents (blows to head), or surgery

orgasm discharge of neuromuscular tension built up during sexual activity; in men, entails rhythmic contractions of the prostate, seminal vesicles, vas deferens, and penis and seminal discharge; in women, entails contractions of the orgasmic platform and uterus

P

pain disorder syndrome marked by the chronic experience of acute pain that appears to have no physical cause

palilalia continuous repetition of sounds and words

panic attacks short, intense periods during which an individual experiences physiological and cognitive symptoms of anxiety, characterized by intense fear and discomfort

panic disorder disorder characterized by recurrent, unexpected panic attacks

paranoid personality disorder chronic and pervasive mistrust and suspicion of other people that are unwarranted and maladaptive

paranoid schizophrenia syndrome marked by delusions and hallucinations that involve themes of persecution and grandiosity

paraphilia atypical sexual activity that involves one of the following: (1) nonhuman objects, (2) nonconsenting adults, (3)the suffering or humiliation of oneself or one's partner, or (4) children

parasomnias primary sleep disorders that involve abnormal behavioral and physiological events occurring during sleep

pathological gambling disorder characterized by chronic, compulsive gambling even when it leads to serious personal, financial, and legal problems

patients' rights movement movement to ensure that mental patients retain their basic rights and to remove them from institutions and care for them in the community

pedophilia adult obtainment of sexual gratification by engaging in sexual activities with young children

performance anxiety anxiety over sexual performance that interferes with sexual functioning

persecutory delusions false, persistent beliefs that one is being pursued by other people

personality disorder chronic pattern of maladaptive cognition, emotion, and behavior that begins by adolescence or early adulthood and continues into later adulthood

personality inventories questionnaires that assess people's typical ways of thinking, feeling, and behaving; used to obtain information about people's well-being, self-concept, attitudes, and beliefs

pervasive developmental disorders disorders characterized by severe and persisting impairment in several areas of development

phencyclidine (PCP) substance that produces euphoria, slowed reaction times, and involuntary movements at low doses; disorganized thinking, feelings of unreality, and hostility at intermediate doses; and amnesia, analgesia, respiratory problems, and changes in body temperature at high doses

phenothiazines drugs that reduce the functional level of dopamine in the brain and tend to reduce the symptoms of schizophrenia

phonological disorder disorder involving the use of speech sounds inappropriate for one's age or dialect

pituitary major endocrine gland that lies partly on the outgrowth of the brain and just below the hypothalamus; produces the largest number of different hormones and controls the secretions of other endocrine glands

placebo control group in a therapy outcome study, group of people whose treatment is an inactive substance (to compare with the effects of a drug) or a nontheory-based therapy providing social support (to compare with the effects of psychotherapy)

plaques deposits of amyloid protein that accumulate in the extracellular spaces of the cerebral cortex, hippocampus, and other forebrain structures in people with Alzheimer's disease

plateau phase in the sexual response cycle, period between arousal and orgasm, during which excitement remains high but stable

polygenic combination of many genes, each of which makes a small contribution to an inherited trait

positive symptoms in schizophrenia, hallucinations, delusions, and disorganization in thought and behavior (also called Type I symptoms)

positron-emission tomography (PET) method of localizing and measuring brain activity by detecting photons that result from the metabolization of an injected isotope

post-traumatic stress disorder (PTSD) anxiety disorder characterized by (1) repeated mental images of experiencing a traumatic event, (2) emotional numbing and detachment, and (3) hypervigilance and chronic arousal

preconscious according to Freud, area of the psyche that contains material from the unconscious before it reaches the conscious mind

premature ejaculation a man's inability to delay ejaculation after minimal sexual stimulation or until he wishes to ejaculate, causing significant distress or interpersonal problems

prepared classical conditioning theory that evolution has prepared people to be easily conditioned to fear objects or situations that were dangerous in ancient times

prevalence proportion of the population who have a specific disorder at a given point or period in time

primary hypersomnia sleep disorder in which people are chronically sleepy and sleep for long periods of time, leading to social and occupational impairment

primary insomnia difficulty in initiating or maintaining sleep, or sleep that chronically does not restore energy and alertness

primary prevention prevention of the development of psychological disorders before they start

primary sleep disorders category of sleep disorders including dyssomnias and parasomnias

prodromal symptoms in schizophrenia, milder symptoms prior to an acute phase of the disorder, during which behaviors are unusual and peculiar but not yet psychotic or completely disorganized

projective test presentation of an ambiguous stimulus, such as an inkblot, to a client, who then projects unconscious motives and issues onto the stimulus in his or her interpretation of its content

psychic epidemics phenomena in which large numbers of people begin to engage in unusual behaviors that appear to have a psychological origin

psychoanalysis form of treatment for psychopathology involving alleviating unconscious conflicts driving psychological symptoms by helping people gain insight into their conflicts and finding ways of resolving these conflicts

psychodynamic theories theories developed by Freud's followers but usually differing somewhat from Freud's original theories

psychodynamic therapies therapies focused on uncovering and resolving unconscious conflicts that drive psychological symptoms

psychogenic amnesia loss of memory in the absence of any brain injury or disease and thought to have psychological causes

psychological approaches approaches to abnormality that focus on personality, behavior, and ways of thinking as possible causes of abnormality

psychological theories theories that view mental disorders as caused by psychological processes, such as beliefs, thinking styles, and coping styles

psychopathology symptoms that cause mental, emotional, and/or physical pain

psychopathy set of broad personality traits including superficial charm, a grandiose sense of self-worth, a tendency toward boredom and need for stimulation, pathological lying, an ability to be cunning and manipulative, and a lack of remorse

psychophysiological tests tests in which instruments are attached to the periphery of the body to record changes due to activity in the nervous system

psychosexual stages according to Freud, stages in the developmental process children pass through; in each stage, sex drives are focused on the stimulation of certain areas of the body, and particular psychological issues can arouse anxiety

psychosis state involving a loss of contact with reality as well as an inability to differentiate between reality and one's subjective state

psychosomatic disorders syndromes marked by identifiable physical illness or defect caused at least partly by psychological factors

psychosurgery rare treatment for mental disorders in which a neurosurgeon attempts to destroy small areas of the brain thought to be involved in a patient's symptoms

purging type of bulimia nervosa type of bulimia nervosa in which bingeing is followed by the use of self-induced vomiting or purging medications to control weight gain

pyromania disorder characterized by repeated deliberate and purposeful fire setting triggered by tension or affective arousal and resulting in pleasure or relief

R

random assignment assignment of participants in an experiment to groups based on a random process

rapid cycling bipolar disorder diagnosis given when a person has four or more cycles of mania and depression within 1 year

reading disorder developmental disorder involving deficits in reading ability

receptors molecules on the membranes of neurons to which neurotransmitters bind

reflection method of responding in which a therapist expresses his or her attempt to understand what the client is experiencing and trying to communicate

reformulated learned helplessness theory view that people who attribute negative events to internal, stable, and global causes are more likely than other people to experience learned helplessness deficits following such events and thus are predisposed to depression

rejection sensitivity tendency to be hypervigilant and overreactive to signs of rejection from others

relapse prevention programs treatments that seek to offset continued alcohol use by identifying high-risk situations for those attempting to stop or cut down on drinking and teaching them either to avoid those situations or to use assertiveness skills when in them, while viewing setbacks as temporary

reliability degree of consistency in a measurement—that is, the extent to which it yields accurate measurements of a phenomenon across several trials, across different populations, and in different forms

repetitive transcranial magnetic stimulation (rTMS) biological treatment that exposes patients to repeated, high-intensity magnetic pulses that are focused on particular brain structures in order to stimulate those structures

repression defense mechanism in which the ego pushes anxiety-provoking material back into the unconscious

residual schizophrenia diagnosis made when a person has already experienced a single acute phase of schizophrenia but currently has milder and less debilitating symptoms

residual symptoms in schizophrenia, milder symptoms following an acute phase of the disorder, during which behaviors are unusual and peculiar but not psychotic or completely disorganized

resistance in psychodynamic therapy, when a client finds it difficult or impossible to address certain material, the client's resistance signals an unconscious conflict, which the therapist then tries to interpret

resolution in the sexual response cycle, state of deep relaxation following orgasm in which a man loses his erection and a woman's orgasmic platform subsides

restricting type of anorexia nervosa type of anorexia nervosa in which weight gain is prevented by refusal to eat

retrograde amnesia deficit in the ability to recall previously learned information or past events

Rett's disorder pervasive developmental disorder in which children develop normally at first but later show permanent loss of basic skills in social interactions, language, and/or movement

reuptake process in which a sending neuron reabsorbs some of the neurotransmitter in the synapse, decreasing the amount left in the synapse

right to refuse treatment right, not recognized by all states, of involuntarily committed people to refuse drugs or other treatment

right to treatment fundamental right of involuntarily committed people to receive active treatment for their disorders rather than shelter alone

risk factors conditions or variables associated with a higher risk of having a disorder

rumination focusing on one's personal concerns and feelings of distress repetitively and passively

S

sadomasochism pattern of sexual rituals between a sexually sadistic "giver" and a sexually masochistic "receiver"

sample group of people taken from a population of interest to participate in a study

schizoaffective disorder disorder in which individuals simultaneously experience schizophrenic symptoms (i.e., delusions, hallucinations, disorganized speech and behavior, and/or negative symptoms) and mood symptoms meeting the criteria for a major depressive episode, a manic episode, or an episode of mixed mania/depression

schizoid personality disorder syndrome marked by a chronic lack of interest in and avoidance of interpersonal relationships as well as emotional coldness in interactions with others

schizophrenia disorder consisting of unreal or disorganized thoughts and perceptions as well as verbal, cognitive, and behavioral deficits

schizophreniform disorder disorder in which individuals meet the primary criteria for schizophrenia but show symptoms lasting only 1 to 6 months.

schizotypal personality disorder chronic pattern of inhibited or inappropriate emotion and social behavior as well as aberrant cognitions and disorganized speech

scientific method systematic method of obtaining and evaluating information relevant to a problem

seasonal affective disorder (SAD) disorder identified by a 2-year period in which a person experiences major depression during winter months and then recovers fully during the summer; some people with this disorder also experience mild mania during summer months

secondary prevention detection of psychological disorders in their earliest stages and treatment designed to reduce their development

selective serotonin reuptake inhibitors (SSRIs) class of antidepressant drugs

self-actualization fulfillment of one's potential for love, creativity, and meaning

self-efficacy beliefs beliefs that one can engage in the behaviors necessary to overcome a situation

self-monitoring method of assessment in which a client records the number of times per day that he or she engages in a specific behavior and the conditions surrounding the behavior

sensate focus therapy treatment for sexual dysfunction in which partners alternate between giving and receiving stimulation in a relaxed, openly communicative atmosphere in order to reduce performance anxiety and concern over achieving orgasm by learning each partner's sexual fulfillment needs

separation anxiety disorder syndrome of childhood and adolescence marked by the presence of abnormal fear or worry over becoming separated from one's caregiver(s) as well as clinging behaviors in the presence of the caregiver(s)

serotonin neurotransmitter involved in the regulation of mood and impulsive responses

serotonin-norepinephrine reuptake inhibitors (SNRIs) drugs that affect both the serotonin system and the norepinephrine system and are used to treat anxiety and depression

sexual aversion disorder condition in which a person actively avoids sexual activities and experiences sex as unpleasant or anxiety-provoking

sexual desire in the sexual response cycle, an urge or inclination to engage in sexual activity

sexual dysfunction problems in experiencing sexual arousal or carrying through with sexual acts to the point of sexual arousal

sexual masochism sexual gratification obtained through experiencing pain and humiliation at the hands of one's partner

sexual sadism sexual gratification obtained through inflicting pain and humiliation on one's partner

shared psychotic disorder disorder in which individuals have a delusion that develops from a relationship with another person who already has delusions (also referred to as *folie à deux*)

single-case experimental design experimental design in which an individual or a small number of individuals are studied intensively; the individual is put through some sort of manipulation or intervention, and his or her behavior is examined before and after this manipulation to determine the effects

single photon emission computed tomography (SPECT) procedure to assess brain functioning in which a tracer substance is injected into the bloodstream and then travels to the brain, where it can indicate the activity level of specific areas of the brain when viewed through a SPECT scanner

situational type phobias extreme fears of situations such as public transportation, tunnels, bridges, elevators, flying, driving, or enclosed spaces

sleep disorders related to a general medical condition sleep disorders that result from the physiological effects of a medical condition, such as arthritis or pulmonary disease

sleep disorders related to another mental disorder sleep disorders caused by a mental disorder listed in the *DSM,* such as depression or substance abuse

sleep terror disorder sleep disorder in which the individual screams, sweats, and has a racing heart during NREM sleep; the person cannot be easily wakened and usually does not remember the episode on awakening

sleepwalking disorder sleep disorder characterized by repeated episodes of walking during NREM sleep

social drift explanation for the association between schizophrenia and low social status that says that because schizophrenia symptoms interfere with a person's ability to complete an education and hold a job, people with schizophrenia tend to drift downward in social class compared to their family of origin

social phobia extreme fear of being judged or embarrassed in front of people, causing the individual to avoid social situations

sociocultural approach approach to psychopathology focusing on the role of the environment, stress, and culture in producing psychopathology

somatic hallucinations unreal perceptions that something is happening inside one's body—for example, that worms are eating one's intestines

somatization disorder syndrome marked by the chronic experience of unpleasant or painful physical symptoms for which no organic cause can be found

somatoform disorders disorders marked by unpleasant or painful physical symptoms that have no apparent organic cause and that often are not physiologically possible, suggesting that psychological factors are involved

specific phobias extreme fears of specific objects or situations that cause an individual to routinely avoid those objects or situations

squeeze technique sex therapy technique used for premature ejaculation; the man's partner stimulates him to an erection, and then when he signals that ejaculation is imminent, the partner applies a firm but gentle squeeze to his penis, either at the glans or at the base, for 3 or 4 seconds; the goal of this technique is for the man to learn to identify the point of ejaculatory inevitability and to control his arousal level at that point

statistical significance likelihood that a study's results have occurred only by chance

stop-start technique sex therapy technique used for premature ejaculation; the man or his partner stimulates his penis until he is about to ejaculate; the man then relaxes and concentrates on the sensations in his body until his level of arousal declines; the goal of this technique is for the man to learn to identify the point of ejaculatory inevitability and to control his arousal level at that point

stress-management interventions strategies that teach clients to overcome the problems in their lives that are increasing their stress

stroke sudden damage to the brain due to blockage of blood flow or hemorrhaging

structured interview meeting between a clinician and a client or a client's associate(s) in which the clinician asks questions that are standardized and are usually designed to determine whether a diagnosis is warranted

stuttering significant problem in speech fluency, often including frequent repetitions of sounds or syllables

substance naturally occurring or synthetically produced product that alters perceptions, thoughts, emotions, and behaviors when ingested, smoked, or injected

substance abuse diagnosis given when a person's recurrent substance use leads to significant harmful consequences, as manifested by a failure to fulfill obligations at work, school, or home; the use of substances in physically hazardous situations; legal problems; and continued use despite social and legal problems

substance dependence diagnosis given when a person's substance use leads to physiological dependence or significant impairment or distress, as manifested by an inability to use the substance in moderation; a decline in social, occupational, or recreational activities; or the spending of large amounts of time obtaining substances or recovering from their effects

substance-induced sexual dysfunction problems in sexual functioning caused by substance use

substance-induced sleep disorders sleep disturbances due to the use of substances, including prescription medications (e.g., medications that control hypertension or cardiac arrhythmias) and nonprescription substances (e.g., alcohol and caffeine)

substance intoxication experience of significantly maladaptive behavioral and psychological symptoms due to the effect of a substance on the central nervous system that develops during or shortly after use of the substance

substance-related disorders disorders characterized by inability to use a substance in moderation and/or the intentional use of a substance to change one's thoughts, feelings, and/or behaviors, leading to impairment in work, academic, personal, or social endeavors

substance withdrawal experience of clinically significant distress in social, occupational, or other areas of functioning due to the cessation or reduction of substance use

suicide purposeful taking of one's own life

suicide attempts behaviors engaged in with some intent to kill oneself

suicide cluster when two or more suicides or attempted suicides nonrandomly occur closely together in space or time

suicide contagion phenomenon in which the suicide of a well-known person is linked to the acceptance of suicide by people who closely identify with that person

suicide ideation thoughts about killing oneself

superego part of the unconscious that consists of absolute moral standards internalized from one's parents during childhood and from one's culture

supernatural theories theories that see mental disorders as the result of supernatural forces, such as divine intervention, curses, demonic possession, and/or personal sins; mental disorders then can be cured through religious rituals, exorcisms, confessions, and/or death

symptom questionnaire questionnaire that assesses what symptoms a person is experiencing

synapse space between a sending neuron and a receiving neuron into which neurotransmitters are first released (also known as the synaptic gap)

syndrome set of symptoms that tend to occur together

systematic desensitization therapy type of behavior therapy that attempts to reduce client anxiety through relaxation techniques and progressive exposure to feared stimuli

T

tactile hallucinations unreal perceptions that something is happening to the outside of one's body—for example, that bugs are crawling up one's back

tardive dyskinesia neurological disorder marked by involuntary movements of the tongue, face, mouth, or jaw, resulting from taking neuroleptic drugs

tertiary prevention program focusing on people who already have a disease with the aim of preventing relapse and reducing the impact of the disease on the person's quality of life

thalamus structure of the brain that directs incoming information from sense receptors (such as vision and hearing) to the cerebrum

theory set of assumptions about the likely causes of abnormality and appropriate treatments

therapy outcome studies experimental studies that assess the effects of an intervention designed to reduce psychopathology in an experimental group, while performing no intervention or a different type of intervention on another group

third variable problem possibility that variables not measured in a study are the real cause of the relationship between the variables measured in the study

tolerance condition of experiencing less and less effect from the same dose of a substance

transference in psychodynamic therapies, the client's reaction to the therapist as if the therapist were an important person in his or her early development; the client's feelings and beliefs about this other person are transferred onto the therapist

transsexuals people who experience chronic discomfort with their gender and genitals as well as a desire to be rid of their genitals and to live as a member of the opposite sex

transvestic fetishism paraphilia in which a heterosexual man dresses in women's clothing as his primary means of becoming sexually aroused

trephination procedure in which holes were drilled in the skulls of people displaying abnormal behavior, presumably to allow evil spirits to depart their bodies; performed in the Stone Age

trichotillomania disorder characterized by recurrent pulling out of the hair resulting in noticeable hair loss; these individuals report tension immediately before or while attempting to resist the impulse, and pleasure or relief when they are pulling out their hair

tricyclic antidepressant drugs class of antidepressant drugs

twin studies studies of the heritability of a disorder by comparing concordance rates between monozygotic and dizygotic twins

Type A behavior pattern personality pattern characterized by time urgency, hostility, and competitiveness

U

unconditioned response (UR) in classical conditioning, response that naturally follows when a certain stimulus appears, such as a dog salivating when it smells food

unconditioned stimulus (US) in classical conditioning, stimulus that naturally elicits a reaction, as food elicits salivation in dogs

unconscious area of the psyche where memories, wishes, and needs are stored and where conflicts among the id, ego, and superego are played out

undifferentiated schizophrenia diagnosis made when a person experiences schizophrenic symptoms, such as delusions and hallucinations, but does not meet criteria for paranoid, disorganized, or catatonic schizophrenia

unipolar depression type of depression consisting of depressive symptoms but without manic episodes

unusualness criterion for abnormality that suggests that abnormal behaviors are rare or unexpected

V

vaginismus in women, involuntary contractions of the muscles surrounding the outer third of the vagina that interfere with penetration and sexual functioning

vagus nerve stimulation (VNS) treatment in which the vagus nerve—the part of the autonomic nervous system that carries information from the head, neck, thorax, and abdomen to several areas of the brain, including the hypothalamus and amygdala—is stimulated by a small electronic device much like a cardiac pacemaker, which is surgically implanted under a patient's skin in the left chest wall

validity degree of correspondence between a measurement and the phenomenon under study

variable measurable factor or characteristic that can vary within an individual, between individuals, or both

vascular dementia second most common type of dementia, associated with symptoms of cerebrovascular disease (tissue damage in the brain due to a blockage of blood flow)

visual hallucination visual perception of something that is not actually present

voyeurism obtainment of sexual arousal by compulsively and secretly watching another person undressing, bathing, engaging in sex, or being naked

W

wait list control group in a therapy outcome study, group of people that functions as a control group while an experimental group receives an intervention and then receives the intervention itself after a waiting period

working through method used in psychodynamic therapies in which the client repeatedly goes over and over painful memories and difficult issues as a way to understand and accept them

REFERENCES

A

Aarsland, D., & Kurz, M. W. (2009). The epidemiology of dementia associated with Parkinson disease. *Journal of the Neurological Sciences, 289,* 18–22.

Abbey, A., Ross, L. T., McDuffie, D., & McAuslan, P. (1996). Alcohol and dating risk factors for sexual assault among college women. *Psychology of Women Quarterly, 20,* 147–169.

Abbott, B. B., Schoen, L. S., & Badia, P. (1984). Predictable and unpredictable shock: Behavioral measures of aversion and physiological measures of stress. *Psychological Bulletin, 96,* 45–71.

Abi-Dargham, A., Kegeles, L. S., Zea-Ponce, Y., Mawlawi, O., Martinez, D., Mitropoulou, V., O'Flynn, K., Koenigsberg, H. W., van Heertum, R., Cooper, T., Laruelle, M., & Siever, L. J. (2004). Striatal amphetamine-induced dopamine release in patients with schizotypal personality disorder studied with single photon emission computed tomography and [123l]lodobenzamide. *Biological Psychiatry, 55,* 1001–1006.

Abramowitz, C. S., Kosson, D. S., & Seidenberg, M. (2004). The relationship between childhood attention deficit hyperactivity disorder and conduct problems and adult psychopathy in male inmates. *Personality and Individual Differences, 36,* 1031–1047.

Abramowitz, J. S. (1997). Effectiveness of psychological and pharmacological treatments for obsessive-compulsive disorder: A quantitative review. *Journal of Consulting & Clinical Psychology, 65,* 44–52.

Abramson, L. Y., Alloy, L. B., Hankin, B. L., Haeffel, G. J., MacCoon, D. G., & Gibb, B. E. (2002). Cognitive vulnerability-stress models of depression in a self-regulatory and psychobiological context. In I. H. Gotlib & C. L. Hammen (Eds.), *Handbook of depression* (pp. 268–294). New York: Guilford Press.

Abramson, L. Y., Metalsky, G. I., & Alloy, L. B. (1989). Hopelessness depression: A theory-based subtype of depression. *Psychological Review, 96,* 358–372.

Abramson, L. Y., Seligman, M. E. P., & Teasdale, J. (1978). Learned helplessness in humans: Critique and reformulation. *Journal of Abnormal Psychology, 87,* 49–74.

Adams, C. E., Awad, G., Rathbone, J., & Thornley, B. (2007). Chlorpromazine versus placebo for schizophrenia. *Cochrane Database of Systematic Reviews, 2,* CD000284.

Addis, M. E. (2008). Gender and depression in men. *Clinical Psychology: Science and Practice, 15,* 153–168.

Addis, M. E., Hatgis, C., Krasnow, A. D., Jacob, K., Bourne, L., & Mansfield, A. (2004). Effectiveness of cognitive-behavioral treatment for panic disorder versus treatment as usual in a managed care setting. *Journal of Consulting & Clinical Psychology, 72,* 625–635.

Aderibigbe, Y. A., Bloch, R. M., & Walker, W. R. (2001). Prevalence of depersonalization and derealization experiences in a rural population. *Social Psychiatry & Psychiatric Epidemiology, 36,* 63–69.

Adler, C. M., Adams, J., DelBello, M. P., Holland, S. K., Schmithorst, V., Levine, A., Jarvis, K., & Strakowski, S. M. (2006). Evidence of white matter pathology in bipolar disorder adolescents experiencing their first episode of mania: A diffusion tensor imaging study. *American Journal of Psychiatry, 163,* 322–324.

Agras, W. S., & Kirkley, B. G. (1986). Bulimia: Theories of etiology. In K. D. Brownell & J. P. Foreyt (Eds.), *Handbook of eating disorders: Physiology, psychology, and treatment of obesity, anorexia, and bulimia* (pp. 367–378). New York: Basic Books.

Agras, W. S., Walsh, B. T., Fairburn, C. C., Wilson, G. T., & Kraemer, H. C. (2000). A multicenter comparison of cognitive-behavioral therapy and interpersonal psychotherapy for bulimia nervosa. *Archives of General Psychiatry, 57,* 459–466.

Agrawal, A., & Lynskey, M. T. (2008). Are there genetic influences on addiction? Evidence from family, adoption and twin studies. *Addiction, 103,* 1069–1081.

Agronin, M. E. (2009). Sexual disorders in elderly patients. In R. Balon & R. T. Segraves (Eds.), *Clinical manual of sexual disorders* (pp. 403–422). Arlington, VA: American Psychiatric Publishing.

Aguero-Torres, H., Fratiglioni, L., & Winblad, B. (1998). Natural history of Alzheimer's disease and other dementias: Review of the literature in the light of the findings from the Kungholmen Project. *International Journal of Geriatric Psychiatry, 13,* 755–766.

Ahlers, M. M. (2009, July 14). NTSB: Sleep disorder may have contributed to Boston train crash. http://www.cnn.com/2009/US/07/14/ntsb.train.crash/index.html (accessed July 23, 2009)

Ajdacic-Gross, V., Killias, M., Hepp, U., Gadola, E., Bopp, M., Lauber, C., Schnyder, U., Gutzwiller, F., & Rossler, W. (2006). Changing times: A longitudinal analysis of international firearm suicide data. *American Journal of Public Health, 96,* 1752–1755.

Ajzen, I. (1991). The theory of planned behavior. *Organizational Behavior and Human Decision Processes, 50,* 179–211.

Akhtar, S., Wig, N. N., Varma, V. K., Pershad, D., & Verma, S. K. (1975). A phenomenological analysis of symptoms in obsessive-compulsive neurosis. *British Journal of Psychiatry, 127,* 342–348.

Alarcon, R. D., Becker, A. E., Lewis-Fernandez, R., Like, R. C., Desai, P., Foulks, E., Gonzales, J., Hansen, H., Kopelowicz, A., Lu, F. G., Oquendo, M. A., & Primm, A. (2009). Issues for *DSM-V:* The role of culture in psychiatric diagnosis. *Journal of Nervous and Mental Disease, 197,* 559–560.

Aleman, A., & Laroi, F. *Hallucinations: The science of idiosyncratic perception.* Washington, DC: American Psychological Association.

Alexander, K. L., Entwisle, D. R., & Thompson, M. S. (1987). School performance, status relations, and the structure of sentiment: Bringing the teacher back in. *American Sociological Review, 52,* 665–682.

Alexopoulos, G. S., Meyers, B. S., Young, R. C., Campbell, S., Silbersweig, D., & Charlson, M. (1997). "Vascular depression" hypothesis. *Archives of General Psychiatry, 54,* 915–922.

Ali, S., Garg, S., Cohen, B. E., Bhave, P., Harris, W. S., & Whooley, M. A. (2009). Association between omega-3 fatty acids and depressive symptoms among patients with established coronary artery disease: Data from the Heart and Soul Study. *Psychotherapy and Psychosomatics, 78,* 125–127.

Allderidge, P. (1979). Hospitals, madhouses and asylums: Cycles in the care of the insane. *British Journal of Psychiatry, 134,* 321–334.

Allen, J. B., & Iacono, W. G. (2001). Assessing the validity of amnesia in dissociative identity disorder: A dilemma for the DSM and the courts. *Psychology, Public Policy, & Law, 7,* 311–344.

Alloy, L. B., Abramson, L. Y., & Francis, E. L. (1999). Do negative cognitive styles confer vulnerability to depression? *Current Directions in Psychological Science, 8,* 128–132.

Alloy, L. B., Abramson, L. Y., Walshaw, P. D., Cogswell, A., Grandin, L. D., Hughes, M. E., Iacoviello, B. M., Whitehouse, W. G., Urosevic, S., Nusslock, R., & Hogan, M. E. (2008). Inhibition system sensitivities and bipolar spectrum disorders: Prospective prediction of bipolar mood episodes. *Bipolar Disorders, 10,* 310–322.

Alonso, J., Angermeyer, M. C., Bernert, S., Bruffaerts, R., Brugha, T. S., Bryson, H., de Girolamo, G., de Graaf, R., Demyttenaere, K., Gasquet, I., Haro, J. M., Katz, S. J., Kessler, R. C., Kovess, V., Lepine, J. P., Ormel, J., Polidori, G., Russo, L. J., & Vilagut, G. (2004). 12-month comorbidity patterns and associated factors in Europe: Results from the European Study of the Epidemiology of Mental Disorders (ESEMeD) project. *Acta Psychiatrica Scandinavica, 109,* 28–37.

Althof, S. E. (1995). Pharmacologic treatment of rapid ejaculation. *Psychiatric Clinics of North America, 18,* 85–94.

Althof, S. E. (2000). Erectile dysfunction: Psychotherapy with men and couples. In S. R. Leiblum & R. C. Rosen (Eds.), *Principles and practice of sex therapy* (3rd ed., pp. 242–275). New York: Guilford Press.

Altman, S., Haeri, S., Cohen, L. J., Ten, A., Harron, E., Galynker, I. I., et al. (2006). Predictors of relapse in bipolar disorder: A review. *Journal of Psychiatric Practice, 12,* 269–282.

American Heart Association. (2002). Diseases and conditions. Retrieved from www.americanheart.org

American Heart Association. (2010). Cardiovascular disease statistics. http://americanheart.org/presenter.jhtml?identifier=4478 (accessed April 27, 2010)

American Psychiatric Association (APA). (2000). *Diagnostic and statistical manual of mental disorders* (4th ed., Text Revision). Washington, DC: American Psychiatric Association.

American Psychiatric Association. (2010). *DSM-5* development. Retrieved May 10, 2010, from http://www.dsm5.org

American Psychological Association. (2000). Guidelines for psychotherapy with lesbian, gay, and bisexual clients. *American Psychologist, 55,* 1440–1451.

American Society for Aesthetic Plastic Surgery. (2005). Trends and demographic data. http://www.r4md.com/cosmetic_surgery/stats.html (accessed March 30, 2009)

Ananth, J., Burgoyne, K. S., Gadasalli, R., & Aquino, S. (2001). How do the atypical antipsychotics work? *Journal of Psychiatry & Neuroscience, 26,* 385–394.

Anders, S. L. (2003). Improving community-based care for the treatment of schizophrenia: Lessons from native Africa. *Psychiatric Rehabilitation Journal, 27,* 51–58.

Andersen, A. E. (Ed.). (1990). *Males with eating disorders.* New York: Brunner/Mazel.

Andersen, A. E., & DiDomenico, L. (1992). Diet vs. shape content of popular male and female magazines: A dose-response relationship to the incidence of eating disorders? *International Journal of Eating Disorders, 11,* 283–287.

Anderson, G., Yasenik, L., & Ross, C. A. (1993). Dissociative experiences and disorders among women who identify themselves as sexual abuse survivors. *Child Abuse & Neglect, 17,* 677–686.

Anderson, G. M., & Hoshino, Y. (1997). Neurochemical studies of autism. In D. J. Cohen & F. R. Volkmar (Eds.), *Handbook of autism and pervasive developmental disorders* (pp. 325–343). Toronto: Wiley.

Anderson, L., Shaw, J. M., & McCargar, L. (1997). Physiological effects of bulimia nervosa on the gastrointestinal tract. *Canadian Journal of Gastroenterology, 11,* 451–459.

Anderson, R. E., Bartlett, S. J., Morgan, G. D., & Brownell, K. D. (1995). Weight loss, psychological, and nutritional patterns in competitive male body builders. *International Journal of Eating Disorders, 18,* 49–57.

Andrade, L., Caraveo-Anduaga, J. J., Berglund, P., Bijl, R.V., DeGraaf, R., Volbergh, W., et al. (2003). The epidemiology of major depressive episodes: Results from the International Consortium of Psychiatric Epidemiology (ICPE) surveys. *International Journal of Methods in Psychiatric Research, 12,* 3–21.

Andreasen, N. (2001). Neuroimaging and neurobiology of schizophrenia. In K. Miyoshi, C. M. Shapiro, M. Gaviria, & Y. Morita (Eds.), *Contemporary neuropsychiatry* (pp. 265–271). Tokyo: Springer-Verlag.

Andreasen, N. C. (1998). Jeff: A difficult case of schizophrenia. In R. P. Halgin & S. K. Whitbourne (Eds.), *A casebook in abnormal psychology from the files of experts* (pp. 197–210). New York: Oxford University Press.

Andreasen, N. C., Flaum, M., Swayze, V. W., Tyrrell, G., & Arndt, S. (1990). Positive and negative symptoms in schizophrenia: A critical reappraisal. *Archives of General Psychiatry, 47,* 615–621.

Andrews, G., Hobbs, M. J., Borkovec, T. D., Beesdo, K., Craske, M. G., Heimberg, R. G., Rapee, R. M., Ruscio, A. M., & Stanley, M. A. (2010). Generalized worry disorder: A review of *DSM-IV* generalized anxiety disorder and options for *DSM-V. Depression and Anxiety, 0,* 1–14.

Angold, A., Costello, E. J., & Worthman, C. M. (1998). Puberty and depression: The roles of age, pubertal status, and pubertal timing. *Psychological Medicine, 28,* 51–61.

Angold, A., Erkanli, A., Egger, H. L., & Costello, J. (2000). Stimulant treatment for children: A community perspective. *Journal of the American Academy of Child & Adolescent Psychiatry, 39,* 975–994.

Angold, A., Erkanli, A., Farmer, E. M. Z., Fairbank, J. A., Burns, B. J., Keeler, G., & Costello, J. (2002). Psychiatric disorder, impairment, and service use in rural African American and white youth. *Archives of General Psychiatry, 59,* 893–901.

Angst, J., Gamma, A., Endrass, J., Goodwin, R., Ajdacic, V., Eich, D., & Rössler, W. (2004). Obsessive-compulsive severity spectrum in the community: Prevalence, comorbidity, and course. *European Archives of Psychiatry & Clinical Neuroscience, 254,* 156–164.

Angst, J., Gamma, A., Pezawas, L., Ajdacic-Gross, V., Eich, D., Rossler, W., & Altamura, C. (2007). Parsing the clinical phenotype of depression: The need to integrate brief depressive episodes. *Acta Psychiatrica Scandinavica, 115,* 221–228.

Anonymous. (1992). First-person account: Portrait of a schizophrenic. *Schizophrenia Bulletin, 18,* 333–334.

Anton, R. F., O'Malley, S. S., Ciraulo, D. A., Cisler, R. A., Couper, D., Donovan, D. M., Gastfriend, D. R., Hosking, J. D., Johnson, B. A., LoCastro, J. S., Longabaugh, R., Mason, B. J., Mattson, M. E., Miller, W. R., Pettinati, H. M., Randall, C. L., Swift, R., Weiss, R. D., Williams, L. D., & Zweben, A. (2006). Combined pharmacotherapies and behavioral interventions for alcohol dependence: The COMBINE study: A randomized controlled trial. *Journal of the American Medical Association, 295,* 2003–2017.

Antoni, M. H., Lehman, J. M., Kilbourn, K. M., Boyers, A. E., Culver, J. L., Alferi, S. M., Young, S. E., McGregor, B. A., Arena, P. L., Harris, S. D., Price, A. A., & Carver, C. S. (2001). Cognitive-behavioral stress management intervention decreases the prevalence of depression and enhances benefit finding among women under treatment for early-stage breast cancer. *Health Psychology, 20,* 20–32.

Arendt, J. (2009). Managing jet lag: Some of the problems and possible new solutions. *Sleep Medicine Reviews, 13,* 249–256.

Arseneault, L., Moffitt, T. E., Caspi, A., Taylor, A., Rijsdijk, F. V., Jaffee, S. R., Ablow, J. C., & Measelle, J. R. (2003). Strong genetic effects on cross-situational antisocial behaviour among 5-year-old children according to mothers, teachers, examiner-observers, and twins' self-reports. *Journal of Child Psychology & Psychiatry, 44,* 832–848.

Arseneault, L., Moffitt, T. E., Caspi, A., Taylor, P. J., & Silva, P. A. (2000). Mental disorders and violence in a total birth cohort. *Archives of General Psychiatry, 57,* 979–986.

Asberg, M., & Forslund, K. (2000). Neurobiological aspects of suicidal behavior. *International Review of Psychiatry, 12,* 62–74.

Atiya, M., Hyman, B. T., Albert, M. S., & Killiany, R. (2003). Structural magnetic resonance imaging in established and prodromal Alzheimer's disease: A review. *Alzheimer's Disease & Associated Disorders, 17,* 177–195.

Attia, E., & Roberto, C. A. (2009). Should amenorrhea be a diagnostic criterion for anorexia nervosa? *International Journal of Eating Disorders, 42,* 581–589.

Attia, E., & Walsh, B. T. (2007). Anorexia nervosa. *American Journal of Psychiatry, 164,* 1805–1810.

August, G. L., Realmutto, G. M., Hektner, J. M., & Bloomquist, M. L. (2001). An integrated components preventive intervention for aggressive elementary school children: The early risers' program. *Journal of Consulting & Clinical Psychology, 69,* 614–626.

Avants, S. K., Warburton, L. A., & Margolin, A. (2001). How injection drug users coped with testing HIV-seropositive: Implications for subsequent health-related behaviors. *AIDS Education and Prevention, 13,* 207–218.

B

Baba, T., Endo, T., Honnma, H., Kitajima, Y., Hayashi, T., Ikeda, H., et al. (2007). Association between polycystic ovary syndrome and female-to-male transsexuality. *Human Reproduction, 22,* 1011–1016.

Bach, A. K., Wincze, J. P., & Barlow, D. H. (2001). Sexual dysfunction. In D. H. Barlow (Ed.), *Clinical handbook of psychological disorders: A step-by-step treatment manual* (3rd ed., pp. 562–608). New York: Guilford Press.

Bachrach, H. M., Galatzer-Levy, R., Skolnikoff, A., & Waldron, S. (1991). On the efficacy of psychoanalysis. *Journal of the American Psychoanalytic Association, 39,* 871–916.

Baer, J. S., Kivlahan, D. R., Blume, A. W., McKnight, P., & Marlatt, G. A. (2001). Brief intervention for heavy-drinking college students: 4-year follow-up and natural history. *American Journal of Public Health, 91,* 1310–1316.

Baer, J. S., Marlatt, G. A., Kivlahan, D. R., & Fromme, K. (1992). An experimental test of three methods of alcohol risk reduction with young adults. *Journal of Consulting & Clinical Psychology, 60,* 974–979.

Bagge, C., Nickell, A., Stepp, S., Durrett, C., Jackson, K., & Trull, T. J. (2004). Borderline personality disorder features predict negative outcomes 2 years later. *Journal of Abnormal Psychology, 113,* 279–288.

Baghurst, T. (2006). Change in sociocultural ideal male physique: An examination of past and present action figures. *Body Image, 3,* 87–91.

Baker, D., Hunter, E., Lawrence, E., Medford, N., Patel, M., Senior, C., Sierra, M., Lambert, M. V., Phillips, M. L., & David, A. S. (2003). Depersonalisation disorder: Clinical features of 204 cases. *British Journal of Psychiatry, 182,* 428–433.

Baker, L. A., Jacobson, K. C., Raine, A., Lozano, D. I., & Bezdjian, S. (2007). Genetic and environmental bases of childhood antisocial behavior: A multi-informant twin study. *Journal of Abnormal Psychology, 116,* 219–235.

Baldessarini, R. J., Tondo, L., & Hennen, J. (2001). Treating the suicidal patient with bipolar disorder: Reducing suicide risk with lithium. *Annals of the New York Academy of Sciences, 932,* 24–38.

Ball, S. A., Martino, S., Nich, C., Frankforter, T. L., Van Horn, D., Crits-Christoph, P., Woody, G. E., Obert, J. L., Farentinos, C., & Carroll, K. M. (2007). Site matters: Multisite randomized trial of motivational enhancement therapy in community drug abuse clinics. *Journal of Consulting and Clinical Psychology, 75,* 556–567.

Ballenger, J. C., Davidson, J. R. T., Lecrubier, Y., Nutt, D. J., Marshall, R. D., Nemeroff, C. B., Shalev, A. Y., & Yehuda, R. (2004). Consensus statement update on posttraumatic stress disorder from the International Consensus Group on Depression and Anxiety. *Journal of Clinical Psychiatry, 65*(Suppl. 1), 55–62.

Balon, R., & Segraves, R. T. (Eds). (2008). *Clinical manual of sexual disorders.* Arlington, VA: American Psychiatric Publishing.

Bancroft, J., Janssen, E., Strong, D., Carnes, L., Vukadinovic, Z., & Long, J. S. (2003). Sexual risk-taking in gay men: The relevance of sexual arousability, mood and sensation seeking. *Archives of Sexual Behavior, 32,* 555–572.

Bancroft, J., & Vukadinovic, Z. (2004). Sexual addiction, sexual compulsivity, sexual impulsivity or what? Toward a theoretical model. *Journal of Sex Research, 41,* 225–234.

Bandura, A. (1969). *Principles of behavior modification.* New York: Holt, Rinehart & Winston.

Bandura, A. (2006). Going global with social cognitive theory: From prospect to paydirt. In S. I. Donaldson, D. E. Berger, & K. Pezdek (Eds.), *Applied psychology: New frontiers and rewarding careers* (pp. 53–79). Mahwah, NJ: Erlbaum.

Banks, S., Robbins, P. C., Silver, E., Vesselinov, R., Steadman, H. J., Monahan, J., Mulvey, E. P., Appelbaum, P. S., Grisso, T., & Roth, L. H. (2004). A multiple-models approach to violence risk assessment among people with mental disorder. *Criminal Justice & Behavior, 31,* 324–340.

Barch, D. M. (2003). Cognition in schizophrenia: Does working memory work? *Current Directions in Psychological Science, 12,* 146–150.

Barch, D. M. (2005). The cognitive neuroscience of schizophrenia. *Annual Review of Clinical Psychology, 1,* 321–353.

Barch, D. M., Csernansky, J. G., Conturo, T., & Snyder, A. Z. (2002). Working and long-term memory deficits in schizophrenia: Is there a common prefrontal mechanism? *Journal of Abnormal Psychology, 111,* 478–494.

Barefoot, J. C., Dahlstrom, W. G., & Williams, R. B. (1983). Hostility, CHD incidence, and total mortality: A 25-yr follow-up study of 255 physicians. *Psychosomatic Medicine, 45,* 59–63.

Barefoot, J. C., Dodge, K. A., Peterson, B. L., Dahlstrom, W. G., & Williams, R. B., Jr. (1989). The Cook-Medley Hostility Scale: Item content and ability to predict survival. *Psychosomatic Medicine, 51,* 46–57.

Barefoot, J. C., Siegler, I. C., Nowlin, J. B., & Peterson, B. L. (1987). Suspiciousness, health, and mortality: A follow-up study of 500 older adults. *Psychosomatic Medicine, 49,* 450–457.

Barkley, R. A. (1991). Attention deficit/hyperactivity disorder. *Psychiatric Annals, 21,* 725–733.

Barkley, R. A. (1996). Attention deficit/hyperactivity disorder. In E. J. Mash & R. A. Barkley (Eds.), *Child psychopathology* (pp. 63–112). New York: Guilford Press.

Barkley, R. A., Fischer, M., Edelbrock, C. S., & Smallish, L. (1990). The adolescent outcome of hyperactive children diagnosed by research criteria: I. An 8-year prospective follow-up study. *Journal of the American Academy of Child & Adolescent Psychiatry, 29,* 546–557.

Barlow, D. H. (1986). Causes of sexual dysfunction: The role of anxiety and cognitive interference. *Journal of Consulting & Clinical Psychology, 54,* 140–148.

Barlow, D. H. (2002). *Anxiety and its disorders: The nature and treatment of anxiety and panic* (2nd ed.). New York: Guilford Press.

Barlow, D. H., Gorman, J. M., Shear, M. K., & Woods, S. W. (2000). Cognitive-behavioral therapy, imipramine, or their combination for panic disorder: A randomized controlled trial. *Journal of the American Medical Association, 283,* 2529–2536.

Barlow, D. H., Sakheim, D. K., & Beck, J. G. (1983). Anxiety increases sexual arousal. *Journal of Abnormal Psychology, 92,* 49–54.

Baron-Cohen, S., & Swettenham, J. (1997). Theory of mind in autism: Its relationship to executive function and central coherence. In D. J. Cohen & F. R. Volkmar (Eds.), *Handbook of autism and pervasive developmental disorders* (pp. 880–893). Toronto: Wiley.

Barsky, A. J., & Ahern, D. K. (2005). Cognitive behavior therapy for hypochondriasis: A randomized controlled trial. *Journal of the American Medical Association, 291,* 1464–1470.

Barsky, A. J., Wyshak, G., & Klerman, G. L. (1992). Psychiatric comorbidity in *DSM-III-R* hypochondriasis. *Archives of General Psychiatry, 49,* 101–108.

Bartlik, B., & Goldstein, M. Z. (2001a). Practical geriatrics: Maintaining sexual health after menopause. *Psychiatric Services, 51,* 751–753.

Bartlik, B., & Goldstein, M. Z. (2001b). Practical geriatrics: Men's sexual health after midlife. *Psychiatric Services, 52,* 291–293.

Basson, R., Berman, J., Burnett, A., Derogatis, L., Ferguson, D., Fourcroy, J., Goldstein, I., Graziottin, A., Heiman, J., Laan, E., Leiblum, S., Padma-Nathan, H., Rosen, R., Segraves, K., Segraves, R. T., Shabsigh, R., Sipski, M., Wagner, G., & Whippie, B. (2001). Report of the international consensus development conference on female sexual dysfunction: Definitions and classifications. *Journal of Sex & Marital Therapy, 27,* 83–94.

Basson, R., McInnes, R., Smith, M. D., Hodgson, G., & Koppiker, N. (2002). Efficacy and safety of sildenafil citrate in women with sexual dysfunction associated with female sexual arousal disorder. *Journal of Women's Health & Gender-Based Medicine, 11,* 367–377.

Bastien, C. H., Morin, C. M., Ouellet, M.-C., Blais, F. C., & Bouchard, S. (2004). Cognitive-behavioral therapy for insomnia: Comparison of individual therapy, group therapy, and telephone consultations. *Journal of Consulting & Clinical Psychology, 72,* 653–659.

Bateman, A., & Fonagy, P. (2008). 8-year follow-up of patients treated for borderline personality disorder: Mentalization-based treatment versus treatment as usual. *American Journal of Psychiatry, 165,* 631–638.

Bateson, G., Jackson, D. D., Haley, J., & Weakland, J. (1956). Toward a theory of schizophrenia. *Behavioral Science, 1,* 251–264.

Bauermeister, J. J., Alegria, M., Bird, H. R., Rubio-Stipec, M., et al. (1992). Are attentional-hyperactivity deficits unidimensional or multidimensional syndromes? Empirical findings from a community survey. *Journal of the American Academy of Child & Adolescent Psychiatry, 31,* 423–431.

Baum, A., Perry, N. W., Jr., & Tarbell, S. (2004). The development of psychology as a health science. In T. J. Ball, R. G. Frank, A. Baum, & J. L. Wallander (Eds.), *Handbook of clinical health psychology: Volume 3. Models and perspectives in health psychology* (pp. 9–28). Washington, DC: American Psychological Association.

Baxter, L., Schwartz, J., Bergman, K., & Szuba, M. (1992). Caudate glucose metabolic rate changes with both drug and behavior therapy for obsessive-compulsive disorder. *Archives of General Psychiatry, 49,* 681–689.

Baxter, L. R., Jr., Clark, E. C., Iqbal, M., & Ackermann, R. F. (2001). Cortical-subcortical systems in the mediation of obsessive-compulsive disorder: Modeling the brain's mediation of a classic "neurosis." In D. G. Lichter & J. L. Cummings (Eds.), *Frontal-subcortical circuits in psychiatric and neurological disorders* (pp. 207–230). New York: Guilford Press.

Bayley, J. (1999). *Elegy for Iris.* New York: St. Martin's Press.

Bear, M. F., Dolen, G., Osterweil, E., & Nagarajan, N. (2008). Fragile X: Translation in action. *Neuropsychopharmacology Reviews, 33,* 84–87.

Beatty, J. (1995). *Principles of behavioral neuroscience.* Dubuque, IA: Wm. C. Brown.

Bechara, A. (2005). Decision making, impulse control and loss of willpower to resist drugs: A neurocognitive perspective. *Nature Neuroscience, 8,* 1458–1463.

Beck, A. T. (1967). *Depression: Clinical, experimental, and theoretical aspects.* New York: Harper & Row.

Beck, A. T. (1976). *Cognitive therapy and the emotional disorders.* New York: International Universities Press.

Beck, A. T. (1997). Cognitive therapy: Reflections. In J. K. Zeig (Ed.), *The evolution of psychotherapy:*

The third conference (pp. 55–69). New York: Brunner/Mazel.

Beck, A. T., & Beck, R. W. (1972). Screening depressed patients in family practice: A rapid technique. *Postgraduate Medicine, 52,* 81–85.

Beck, A. T., Butler, A. C., Brown, G. K., Dahlsgaard, K. K., Newman, C. F., & Beck, J. S. (2001). Dysfunctional beliefs discriminate personality disorders. *Behaviour Research & Therapy, 39,* 1213–1225.

Beck, A. T., & Emery, G. (1985). *Anxiety disorders and phobias: A cognitive perspective.* New York: Basic Books.

Beck, A. T., & Freeman, A. M. (1990). *Cognitive therapy of personality disorders.* New York: Guilford Press.

Beck, A. T., & Rector, N. A. (2005). Cognitive approaches to schizophrenia: Theory and therapy. *Annual Review of Clinical Psychology, 1,* 577–606.

Beck, A. T., Rush, A. J., Shaw, B. F., & Emery, G. (1979). *Cognitive therapy of depression.* New York: Guilford Press.

Beck, A. T., Steer, R. A., Kovacs, M., & Garrison, B. (1985). Hopelessness and eventual suicide: A 10-year prospective study of patients hospitalized with suicidal ideation. *American Journal of Psychiatry, 142,* 559–563.

Beck, A. T., Ward, C. H., Mendelson, M., Moch, J. E., & Erbaugh, J. (1962). Reliability of psychiatric diagnosis: II. A study of consistency of clinical judgments and ratings. *American Journal of Psychiatry, 119,* 351–357.

Beck, A. T., Weissman, A., Lester, D., & Trexler, L. (1974). The measurement of pessimism: The Hopelessness Scale. *Journal of Consulting & Clinical Psychology, 42,* 861–865.

Becker-Blease, K. A., Deater-Deckard, K., Eley, T., Freyd, J. J., Stevenson, J., & Plomin, R. (2004). A genetic analysis of individual differences in dissociative behaviors in childhood and adolescence. *Journal of Child Psychology & Psychiatry, 45,* 522–532.

Beekman, A. T., Bremmer, M. A., Deeg, D. J., van Balkom, A. J., Smit, J. H., deBeurs, E., van Dyck, R., & van Tilburg, W. (1998). Anxiety disorders in later life: A report from the Longitudinal Aging Study Amsterdam. *International Journal of Geriatric Psychiatry, 13,* 717–726.

Belle, D., & Doucet, J. (2003). Poverty, inequality, and discrimination as sources of depression among U.S. women. *Psychology of Women Quarterly, 27,* 101–113.

Belmaker, R. H. (2004). Medical progress: Bipolar disorder. *New England Journal of Medicine, 351,* 476–486.

Belmaker, R. H., & Agam, G. (2008). Major depressive disorder. *New England Journal of Medicine, 358,* 55–68.

Bender, D. S., Dolan, R. T., Skodol, A. E., Sanislow, C. A., Dyck, I. R., McGlasgan, T. H., Shea, M. T., Zanarini, M. C., Oldham, J. M., & Gunderson, J. G. (2001). Treatment utilization by patients with personality disorders. *American Journal of Psychiatry, 158,* 295–302.

Bender, D. S., Skodol, A. E., Dyck, I. R., Markowitz, J. C., Shea, M. T., Yen, S., Sanislow, C. A., Pinto, A., Zanarini, M. C., McGlashan, T. H., Gunderson, J. G., Daversa, M. T., & Grilo, C. M. (2007). Ethnicity and mental health treatment utilization by patients with personality disorders. *Journal of Consulting and Clinical Psychology, 75,* 992–999.

Bender, L. (1938). *A visual motor gestalt test and its clinical use.* New York: American Orthopsychiatric Association.

Benedetti, F., Sforzini, L., Colombo, C., Maffei, C., & Smeraldi, E. (1998). Low-dose clozapine in acute and continuation treatment of severe borderline personality disorder. *Journal of Clinical Psychology, 59,* 103–107.

Benet-Martinez, V., & John, O. P. (1998). Los Cinco Grandes across cultures and ethnic groups: Multitrait-multimethod analyses of the Big Five in Spanish and English. *Journal of Personality & Social Psychology, 75,* 729–750.

Benjamin, L. T., Jr. (2005). A history of clinical psychology as a profession in America (and a glimpse at its future). *Annual Review of Clinical Psychology, 1,* 1–30.

Bennett, N. S., Lidz, C. W., Monahan, J., Mulvey, E. P., Hoge, S. K., Roth, L. H., & Gardner, W. (1993). Inclusion, motivation, and good faith: The morality of coercion in mental hospital admission. *Behavioral Sciences and the Law, 11,* 295–306.

Benotsch, E. G., Christensen, A. J., & McKelvey, L. (1997). Hostility, social support, and ambulatory cardiovascular activity. *Journal of Behavioral Medicine, 20,* 163–176.

Bentall, R. P., Rouse, G., Kinderman, P., Blackwood, N., Howard, R., Moore, R., et al. (2008). Paranoid delusions in schizophrenia spectrum disorders and depression: The transdiagnostic role of expectations of negative events and negative self-esteem. *Journal of Nervous and Mental Disease, 196,* 375–383.

Berk, M., Dodd, S., Kauer-Sant'Anna, M., Malhi, G. S., Bourin, M., Kapczinski, F., Norman, T. (2007). Dopamine dysregulation syndrome: Implications for a dopamine hypothesis of bipolar disorder. *Acta Psychiatrica Scandinavica, 116,* 41–49.

Berkman, L. F., Blumenthal, J., Burg, M., et al. (2003). Effects of treating depression and low perceived social support on clinical events after myocardial infarction: The Enhancing Recovery in Coronary Heart Disease Patients (ENRICHD) randomized trial. *Journal of the American Medical Association, 289,* 3106–3116.

Berlin, L. J., Brooks-Gunn, J., McCartoon, C., & McCormick, M. C. (1998). The effectiveness of early intervention: Examining risk factors and pathways to enhanced development. *Preventive Medicine, 27,* 238–245.

Berman, A. L., & Jobes, D. A. (1995). Suicide prevention in adolescents (age 12–18). *Suicide & Life-Threatening Behavior, 25,* 143–154.

Bernstein, D. P., Useda, D., & Siever, L. J. (1995). Paranoid personality disorder. In W. J. Livesley (Ed.), *The* DSM-IV *personality disorders* (pp. 45–57). New York: Guilford Press.

Berthoud, H. R., & Morrison, C. (2008). The brain, appetite, and obesity. *Annual Review of Psychology, 59,* 55–92.

Bettelheim, B. (1967). *The empty fortress: Infantile autism and the birth of the self.* New York: Free Press.

Beutler, L. E., Daldrup, R., Engle, D., & Guest, P. D. (1988). Family dynamics and emotional expression among patients with chronic pain and depression. *Pain, 32,* 65–72.

Biederman, J., Faraone, S. V., Hirschfeld-Becker, D. R., Friedman, D., Robin, J. A., & Rosenbaum, J. F. (2001). Patterns of psychopathology and dysfunction in high-risk children of parents with panic disorder and major depression. *American Journal of Psychiatry, 158,* 49–57.

Biederman, J., Faraone, S. V., Monuteaux, M. C., Bober, M., & Cadogen, E. (2004). Gender effects on attention-deficit/hyperactivity disorder in adults, revisited. *Biological Psychiatry, 55,* 692–700.

Biederman, J., Hirshfeld-Becker, D. R., Rosenbaum, J. F., Hérot, C., Friedman, D., Snidman, N., Kagan, J., Faraone, S. V. (2001). Further evidence of association between behavioral inhibition and social anxiety in children. *American Journal of Psychiatry, 158,* 1673–1679.

Biederman, J., Mick, E., Faraone, S. V., Braaten, E., Doyle, A., Spencer, T., Wilens, T. E., Frazier, E., & Johnson, M. (2002). Influence of gender on attention deficit hyperactivity disorder in children referred to a psychiatric clinic. *American Journal of Psychiatry, 159,* 36–42.

Biederman, J., Rosenbaum, J. F., Bolduc-Murphy, E. A., Faraone, S. V., Chaloff, J., Hirshfeld, D. R., & Kagan, J. (1993). Behavioral inhibition as a temperamental risk factor for anxiety disorders. *Child & Adolescent Psychiatric Clinics of North America, 2,* 667–684.

Biederman, J., Rosenbaum, J. F., Hirshfeld, D. R., Faraone, V., Bolduc, E., Gersten, M., Meminger, S., & Reznick, S. (1990). Psychiatric correlates of behavioral inhibition in young children of parents with and without psychiatric disorders. *Archives of General Psychiatry, 47,* 21–26.

Billings, D. W., Folkman, S., Acree, M., & Moskowitz, J. T. (2000). Coping and physical health during caregiving: The roles of positive and negative affect. *Journal of Personality and Social Psychology, 79,* 131–142.

Bird, T. D., Lampe, T. H., Wijsman, E. M., & Schellenberg, G. D. (1998). Familial Alzheimer's: Genetic studies. In M. F. Folstein (Ed.), *Neurobiology of primary dementia* (pp. 27–42). Washington, DC: American Psychiatric Press.

Birmaher, B., Axelson, D., Strober, M., Gill, M. K., Valeri, S., Chiappetta, L., Ryan, N., Leonard, H., Junt, J., Iyengar, S., & Keller, M. (2006). Clinical course of children and adolescents with bipolar spectrum disorders. *Archive of General Psychiatry, 63,* 175–183.

Birmaher, B., Axelson, D. A., Monk, K., Kalas, C., Clark, D. B., Ehmann, M., Bridge, J., Heo, J., & Brent, D. A. (2003). Fluoxetine for the treatment of childhood anxiety disorders. *Journal of the American Academy of Child & Adolescent Psychiatry, 42,* 415–423.

Biron, M., Risch, N., Hamburger, R., Mandel, B., Kushner, S., Newman, M., Drumer, D., & Belmaker, R. H. (1987). Genetic linkage between X-chromosome markers and bipolar affective illness. *Nature, 326,* 289–292.

Blacher, J. B., Hanneman, R. A., & Rousey, A. B. (1992). Out-of-home placement of children with severe handicaps: A comparison of approaches. *American Journal on Mental Retardation, 96,* 607–616.

Blair, R. J. R., Peschardt, K. S., Budhani, S., Mitchell, D. G. V., & Pine, D. S. (2006). The development of psychopathy. *Journal of Child Psychology and Psychiatry, 47,* 262–275.

Blanchard, R., Lykins, A. D., Wherrett, D., Kuban, M. E., Cantor, J. M., Blak, T., Dickey, R., & Klassen, P. E. (2009). Pedophilia, hebephilia, and the *DSM-V. Archives of Sexual Behavior, 38,* 335–350.

Blaney, P. H. (1986). Affect and memory: A review. *Psychological Bulletin, 99,* 229–246.

Blazer, D. G., Kessler, R. C., McGonagle, K. A., & Swartz, M. S. (1994). The prevalence and distribution of major depression in a national community sample: The National Comorbidity Study. *American Journal of Psychiatry, 151,* 979–986.

Blazer, D. G., Kessler, R. C., & Swartz, M. (1998). Epidemiology of recurrent major and minor depression with a seasonal pattern: The National Comorbidity Study. *British Journal of Psychiatry, 172,* 164–167.

Bliss, E. L. (1980). Multiple personalities: A report of 14 cases with implications for schizophrenia and hysteria. *Archives of General Psychiatry, 37,* 1388–1397.

Bliss, E. L. (1986). *Multiple personality, allied disorders, and hypnosis.* New York: Oxford University Press.

Bloch, M. H., Landeros-Weisenberger, A., Dombrowski, P., Kelmendi, B., Wegner, R., Nudel, J., Pittenger, C., Leckman, J. F., & Coric, V. (2007). Systematic review: Pharmacological and behavioral treatment for trichotillomania. *Biological Psychiatry, 62,* 839–846.

Blond, A. (2008). Impacts of exposure to images of ideal bodies on male body dissatisfaction: A review. *Body Image, 5,* 244–250.

Blum, N., St. John, D., Pfohl, B., Stuart, S., McCormick, B., Allen, J., Arndt, S., & Black, D. W. (2008). Systems training for emotional predictability and problem solving (STEPPS) for outpatients with borderline personality disorder: A randomized controlled trial and 1-year follow-up. *American Journal of Psychiatry, 165,* 468–478.

Blumenthal, J. A., Babyak, M. A., Doraiswamy, P. M., Watkins, L., Hoffman, B. M., Barbour, K. A., Herman, S., Craighead, W. E., Brosse, A. L., Waugh, R., Hinderliter, A., & Sherwood, A. (2007). Exercise and pharmacotherapy in the treatment of major depressive disorder. *Psychosomatic Medicine, 69,* 587–596.

Blumenthal, J. A., Sherwood, A., Babyak, M. A., Watkins, L. L., Waugh, R., Georgiades, A., Bacon, S. L., Hayano, J., Coleman, R. E., & Hinderliter, A. (2005). Effects of exercise and stress management training on markers of cardiovascular risk in patients with ischemic heart disease: A randomized controlled trial. *Journal of the American Medical Association, 293,* 1626–1634.

Bohart, A. C. (1990). Psychotherapy integration from a client-centered perspective. In G. Lietaer (Ed.), *Client-centered and experiential psychotherapy in the nineties* (pp. 481–500). Leuven, Belgium: Leuven University Press.

Bohart, A. C. (1995). The person-centered psychotherapies. In A. S. Gurman (Ed.), *Essential psychotherapies: Theory and practice* (pp. 55–84). New York: Guilford Press.

Bohus, M., Haaf, B., Simms, T., Limberger, M. F., Schmahl, C., Unckel, C., Lieb, K., & Linehan, M. M. (2004). Effectiveness of inpatient dialectical behavioral therapy for borderline personality disorder: A controlled trial. *Behaviour Research & Therapy, 42,* 487–499.

Bölte, S., & Poustka, F. (2004). Comparing the intelligence profiles of savant and nonsavant individuals with autistic disorder. *Intelligence, 32,* 121–131.

Bonanno, G. A., Galea, S., Bucciarelli, A., & Vlahov, D. (2006). Psychological resilience after disaster: New York City in the aftermath of the September 11th terrorist attack. *Psychological Science, 17,* 181–186.

Bondolfi, G., Dufour, H., Patris, M., May, J. P., Billeter, U., Eap, C. B., & Bauman, P. (1998). Risperidone versus clozapine in treatment-resistant chronic schizophrenia: A randomized double-blind study. *American Journal of Psychiatry, 155,* 449–504.

Book, A. S., Starzyk, K. B., & Quinsey, V. L. (2001). The relationship between testosterone and aggression: A meta-analysis. *Aggression & Violent Behavior, 6,* 579–599.

Bookheimer, S.Y., Strojwas, M. H., Cohen, M. S., Saunders, A. M., Pericak-Vance, M. A., Mazziotta, J. C., & Small, G. W. (2000). Patterns of brain activation in people at risk for Alzheimer's disease. *New England Journal of Medicine, 343,* 450–456.

Borges, G., Angst, J., Nock, M. K., Ruscio, A. M., & Kessler, R. C. (2008). Risk factors for the incidence and persistence of suicide-related outcomes: A 10-year follow-up study using the national comorbidity surveys. *Journal of Affective Disorders, 105,* 25–33.

Borkovec, T. (2002). Life in the future versus life in the present. *Clinical Psychology: Science & Practice, 9,* 76–80.

Borkovec, T. D. (1994). The nature, functions, and origins of worry. In G. C. L. Davey & F. Tallis (Eds.), *Worrying: Perspectives on theory, assessment, and treatment* (pp. 5–34). Sussex, UK: Wiley.

Borkovec, T. D., Newman, M. G., & Castonguay, L. G. (2003). Cognitive-behavioral therapy for generalized anxiety disorder with integrations from interpersonal and experiential therapies. *CNS Spectrums, 8,* 382–389.

Borkovec, T. D., Newman, M. G., Pincus, A. L., & Lytle, R. (2002). A component analysis of cognitive-behavioral therapy for generalized anxiety disorder and the role of interpersonal problems. *Journal of Consulting & Clinical Psychology, 70,* 288–298.

Bottoms, G. (2000). *Angelhead.* New York: Three Rivers Press.

Bouchard, C. B. (1994). Genetics of obesity: Overview and research direction. In C. B. Bouchard (Ed.), *The genetics of obesity* (pp. 223–233). Boca Raton, FL: CRC Press.

Bouchard, T. J., & Loehlin, J. C. (2001). Genes, evolution, and personality. *Behavior Genetics, 31,* 243–273.

Bouton, M. E., Mineka, S., & Barlow, D. H. (2001). A modern learning theory perspective on the etiology of panic disorder. *Psychological Review, 108,* 4–32.

Bowen, R. C., Offord, D. R., & Boyle, M. H. (1990). The prevalence of overanxious disorder and separation anxiety disorder: Results from the Ontario Child Health Study. *Journal of the American Academy of Child & Adolescent Psychiatry, 29,* 753–758.

Bradley, J. D. D., & Golden, C. J. (2001). Biological contributions to the presentation and understanding of attention-deficit/hyperactivity disorder: A review. *Clinical Psychology Review, 21,* 907–929.

Bradley, S. J. (1995). Psychosexual disorders in adolescence. In J. M. Oldham & M. B. Riba (Eds.), *Review of psychiatry* (Vol. 14, pp. 735–754). Washington, DC: American Psychiatric Press.

Bradley, S. J., & Zucker, K. J. (1997). Gender identity disorder: A review of the past 10 years. *Journal of the American Academy of Child & Adolescent Psychiatry, 36,* 872–880.

Brady, K .T., Back, S. E., & Greenfield, S. F. (Eds.). (2009). *Women and addiction: A comprehensive handbook.* New York: Guilford Press.

Brain, P. F., & Susman, E. J. (1997). Hormonal aspects of aggression and violence. In D. M. Stoff, J. Breiling, & J. D. Maser (Eds.), *Handbook of antisocial personality disorder* (pp. 314–323). New York: Wiley.

Brambilla, F., Bellodi, L., Arancio, C., Ronchi, P., & Limonta, D. (2001). Central dopaminergic function in anorexia and bulimia nervosa: A psychoneuroendocrine approach. *Psychoneuroendocrinology, 26,* 393–409.

Braun, B. G. (Ed.). (1986). *Treatment of multiple personality disorder.* Washington, DC: American Psychiatric Press.

Brawman-Mintzer, O., & Yonkers, K. A. (2001). Psychopharmacology in women. In N. L. Stotland (Ed.), *Psychological aspects of women's health care: The interface between psychiatry and obstetrics and gynecology* (2nd ed., pp. 401–420). Washington, DC: American Psychiatric Press.

Bregman, J. D., & Gerdtz, J. (1997). Behavioral interventions. In D. J. Cohen & F. R. Volkmar (Eds.), *Handbook of autism and pervasive developmental disorders* (pp. 606–630). Toronto: Wiley.

Breier, A. (1995). Serotonin, schizophrenia and antipsychotic drug action. *Schizophrenia Research, 14,* 187–202.

Breier, A., Schreiber, J. L., Dyer, J., & Pickar, D. (1991). National Institute of Mental Health longitudinal study of chronic schizophrenia: Prognosis and predictors of outcome. *Archives of General Psychiatry, 48,* 239–246.

Bremner, J. D., Narayan, M., Anderson, E. R., Staib, L. H., Miller, H. L., & Charney, D. S. (2000). Hippocampal volume reduction in major depression. *American Journal of Psychiatry, 157,* 115–118.

Brent, D. A., & Bridge, J. (2003). Firearms availability and suicide. *American Behavioral Scientist, 46*(9), 1192–1210.

Brent, D. A., Kerr, M. M., Goldstein, C., Bozigar, J., Wartella, M., & Allan, M. J. (1989). An outbreak of suicide and suicidal behavior in a high school. *Journal of the American Academy of Child & Adolescent Psychiatry, 28,* 918–924.

Brent, D. A., Oquendo, M., Birmaher, B., Greenhill, L., Kolko, D., Stanley, B., Zelazny, J., Brodsky, B., Bridge, J., Ellis, S., Salazer, J. O., & Mann, J. J. (2002). Familial pathways to early-onset suicide attempt. *Archives of General Psychiatry, 59,* 801–807.

Brent, D. A., Oquendo, M., Birmaher, B., Greenhill, L., Kolko, D., Stanley, B., Zelazny, J., Brodsky, B., Firinciogullari, S., Ellis, S. P., & Mann, J. J. (2003). Peripubertal suicide attempts in offspring of suicide attempters with siblings concordant for suicidal behavior. *American Journal of Psychiatry, 160,* 1486–1493.

Brent, D. A., Perper, J. A., Allman, C. J., Moritz, G. M., Wartella, M. E., & Zelenak, J. P. (1991). The presence and accessibility of firearms in the homes of adolescent suicide: A case-control study. *Journal of the American Medical Association, 266,* 2989–2995.

Brent, D. A., Perper, J., Moritz, G., Baugher, M., & Allman, C. (1993). Suicide in adolescents with no apparent psychopathology. *Journal of the American Academy of Child and Adolescent Psychiatry, 32,* 494–500.

Brick, J. (Ed.). (2008). *Handbook of the medical consequences of alcohol and drug abuse* (2nd ed.). New York: Haworth Press/Taylor & Francis Group.

Bridges, F. S. (2004). Gun Control Law (Bill C-17), suicide, and homicide in Canada. *Psychological Reports, 94,* 819–826.

Briere, J., & Conte, J. R. (1993). Self-reported amnesia for abuse in adults molested as children. *Journal of Traumatic Stress, 6,* 21–31.

Broidy, L. M., Nagin, D. S., Tremblay, R. E., Bates, J. E., Brame, B., Dodge, K. A., Fergusson, D., Horwood, J. L., Loeber, R., Laird, R., Lynam, D. R., Moffitt, T. E., Pettit, G. S., & Vitaro, F. (2003). Developmental trajectories of childhood disruptive behaviors and adolescent delinquency: A six-site, cross-national study. *Developmental Psychology, 39,* 222–245.

Brookes, K., Xu, X., Chen, W., Zhou, K., Neale, B., Lowe, N., Aneey, R., Franke, B., Gill, M., Ebstein, R., Buitelaar, J., Sham, P., Campbell, D., Knight, J., Andreou, P., Altink, M., Arnold, R., Boer, F., Buschgens, C., Butler, L., Christiansen, H., et al. (2006). The analysis of 51 genes in *DSM-IV* combined type attention deficit hyperactivity disorder: Association signals in DRD4, DAT1 and 16 other genes. *Molecular Psychiatry, 11,* 934–953.

Brooks-Gunn, J., Klebanov, P. K., & Duncan, G. J. (1996). Ethnic differences in children's intelligence test scores: Role of economic deprivation, home environment, and maternal characteristics. *Child Development, 67,* 396–408.

Brotto, L. A., & Luria, M. (2008). Menopause, aging and sexual response in women. In D. L. Rowland & L. Incrocci (Eds.), *Handbook of sexual and gender identity disorders* (pp. 251–283). Hoboken, NJ: Wiley.

Brown, J. E., Ayowa, O. B., & Brown, R. C. (1993). Dry and tight: Sexual practices and potential risks in Zaire. *Social Science & Medicine, 37,* 989–994.

Brown, T. A., O'Leary, T. A., & Barlow, D. H. (2001). Generalized anxiety disorder. *Clinical handbook of psychological disorders: A step-by-step treatment manual* (3rd ed., pp. 154–208). New York: Guilford Press.

Brown, T. M., & Boyle, M. F. (2002). The ABC of psychological medicine: Delirium. *British Medical Journal, 325,* 644–647.

Browne, K. O. (2001). Cultural formulation of psychiatric diagnoses. *Culture, Medicine, & Psychiatry, 25,* 411–425.

Brownell, K., & Horgen, K. B. (2004). *Food fight: The inside story of the food industry, America's obesity crisis, and what we can do about it.* New York: McGraw-Hill.

Bruch, H. (1973). *Eating disorders: Obesity, anorexia nervosa, and the person within.* New York: Basic Books.

Bruch, H. (1982). Anorexia nervosa: Therapy and theory. *American Journal of Psychiatry, 139,* 1531–1538.

Brunelle, C., Barrett, S. P., & Pihl, R. O. (2007). Relationship between the cardiac response to acute intoxication and alcohol-induced subjective effects throughout the blood alcohol concentration curve. *Human Psychopharmacology, 22,* 437–443.

Brunelle, C., & Pihl, R. O. (2007). Effects of conditioned reward and nonreward cues on the heart rate response to alcohol intoxication in male social drinkers. *Alcoholism: Clinical and Experimental Research, 31,* 383–389.

Bryant, C., Jackson, H., & Ames, D. (2008). The prevalence of anxiety in older adults: Methodological issues and a review of the literature. *Journal of Affective Disorders, 109,* 233–250.

Buckwalter, J., Sobel, E., Dunn, M. E., & Diz, M. M. (1993). Gender differences on a brief measure of cognitive functioning in Alzheimer's disease. *Archives of Neurology, 50,* 757–760.

Buka, S. L., Cannon, T. D., Torrey, E. F., Yolken, R. H., and the Collaborative Study Group on the Perinatal Origins of Severe Psychotic Disorders. (2008). Maternal exposure to herpes simplex virus and risk of psychosis among adult offspring. *Biological Psychiatry, 63,* 809–815.

Bulik, C. M. (2005). Exploring the gene-environment nexus in eating disorders. *Journal of Psychiatry and Neuroscience, 30,* 335–339.

Bulik, C. M., Sullivan, P. F., & Kendler, K. S. (2003). Genetic and environmental contributions to obesity and binge eating. *International Journal of Eating Disorders, 33,* 293–298.

Bulik, C. M., Sullivan, P. F., Tozzi, F., Furberg, H., Lichtenstein, P., & Pedersen, N. L. (2006). Prevalence, heritability, and prospective risk factors for anorexia nervosa. *Archives of General Psychiatry, 63,* 305–312.

Burgess, M., Gill, M., & Marks, I. M. (1998). Postal self-exposure treatment of recurrent nightmares. *British Journal of Psychiatry, 172,* 257–267.

Burnam, M. A., Stein, J. A., Golding, J. M., & Siegel, J. M. (1988). Sexual assault and mental disorders in a community population. *Journal of Consulting & Clinical Psychology, 56,* 843–850.

Burr, J. A., Hartman, J. T., & Matteson, D. W. (1999). Black suicide in U.S. metropolitan areas: An examination of the racial inequality and social integration-regulation hypotheses. *Social Forces, 77,* 1049–1081.

Burton, E., Stice, E., Bearman, S. K., Rohde, P. (2007). Experimental test of the affect-regulation theory of bulimic symptoms and substance use: A randomized trial. *International Journal of Eating Disorders, 40,* 27–36.

Busfield, J. (1986). *Managing madness: Changing ideas and practice.* London: Hutchinson.

Bustillo, J. R., Lauriello, J., Horan, W. P., & Keith, S. J. (2001). The psychosocial treatment of schizophrenia: An update. *American Journal of Psychiatry, 158,* 163–175.

Butzel, J. S., Talbot, N. L., Duberstein, P. R., Houghtalen, R. P., Cox, C., & Giles, D. E. (2000). The relationship between traumatic events and dissociation among women with histories of childhood sexual abuse. *Journal of Nervous & Mental Disease, 188,* 547–549.

Butzlaff, R. L., & Hooley, J. M. (1998). Expressed emotion and psychiatric relapse. *Archives of General Psychiatry, 55,* 547–552.

Buysse, D. J., Ancoli-Israel, S., Edinger, J. D., Lichstein, K. L., & Morin, C. M. (2006). Recommendations for a standard research assessment of insomnia. *Sleep, 29,* 1155–1173.

Byrne, E. J. (1994). *Confusional states in older people.* Boston: E. Arnold.

Byrne, S., Cooper, Z., & Fairburn, C. (2003). Weight maintenance and relapse in obesity: A qualitative study. *International Journal of Obesity, 27,* 955–962.

Bystritsky, A., Ackerman, D. L., Rosen, R. M., Vapnik, T., Gorvis, E., Maidment, K. M., & Saxena, S. (2004). Augmentation of serotonin reuptake inhibitors in refractory obsessive-compulsive disorder using adjunctive olanzapine: A placebo-controlled trial. *Journal of Clinical Psychiatry, 65,* 565–568.

C

Caffey, J. (1972). On the theory and practice of shaking infants. *American Journal of Diseases of Children, 124,* 161–172.

Cale, E. M., & Lilienfeld, S. O. (2002). Sex differences in psychopathy and antisocial personality disorder: A review and integration. *Clinical Psychology Review, 22,* 1179–1207.

Caligiuri, M. P., Brown, G. G., Meloy, M. J., et al. (2003). An fMRI study of affective state and medication on cortical and subcortical brain regions during motor performance in bipolar disorder. *Psychiatry Research, 123,* 171–182.

Cameron, N., & Rychlak, J. F. (1985). *Personality development and psychopathology: A dynamic approach.* Boston: Houghton Mifflin.

Camilleri, J. A., & Quinsey, V. L. (2008). Pedophilia: Assessment and treatment. In D. R. Laws & W. T. O'Donohue (Eds.), *Sexual deviance: Theory, assessment, and treatment* (pp. 183–213). New York: Guilford Press.

Camp, B. W., Broman, S. H., Nichols, P. L., & Leff, M. (1998). Maternal and neonatal risk factors for mental retardation: Defining the "at-risk" child. *Early Human Development, 50,* 159–173.

Campbell-Sills, L., & Barlow, D. H. (2007). Incorporating emotion regulation into conceptualizations and treatments of anxiety and mood disorders. In J. J. Gross (Ed.), *Handbook of emotion regulation* (pp. 542–559). New York: Guilford Press.

Campo, J. V., & Fritz, G. (2001). A management model for pediatric somatization. *Psychosomatics, 42,* 467–476.

Cannon, T. D., & Keller, M. C. (2006). Endophenotypes in the genetic analysis of mental disorders. *Annual Review of Clinical Psychology, 2,* 267–290.

Cannon, T. D., Cadenhead, K., Cornblatt, B., Woods, S. W., Addington, J., Walker, E., Seidman, L. J., Perkins, D., Tsuang, M., McGalshan, T., & Heinssen, R. (2008). Prediction of psychosis in youth at high clinical risk: A multisite longitudinal study in North America. *Archives of General Psychiatry, 65,* 23–37.

Cannon, T. D., Kapiro, J., Lonnqvist, J., Huttunen, M., & Koskenvuo, M. (1998). The genetic epidemiology of schizophrenia in a Finnish twin cohort. *Archives of General Psychiatry, 55,* 67–74.

Cannon, T. D., Rosso, I. M., Bearden, C. E., Sanchez, L. E., & Hadley, T. (1999). A prospective cohort study of neurodevelopmental processes in the genesis and epigenesis of schizophrenia. *Development & Psychopathology, 11,* 467–485.

Cannon, T. D., van Erp, T. G. M., Bearden, C. E., Loewy, R., Thompson, P., Toga, A.W., Huttunen, M.O., Keshavan, M. S., Seidman, L. J., & Tsuang, M. T. (2003). Early and late neurodevelopmental influences in the prodrome to schizophrenia: Contributions of genes, environment, and their interactions. *Schizophrenia Bulletin, 29,* 653–669.

Cantor, J. M., Kabani, N., Christensen, B. K., Zipursky, R. B., Barbaree, H. E., Dickey, R., Klassen, P. E., Mikulis, D. J., Kuban, M. E., Blak, T., Richards, B. A., Hanratty, M. K., & Blanchard, R. (2008). Cerebral white matter deficiencies in pedophilic men. *Journal of Psychiatric Research, 42,* 167–183.

Cantor-Graae, E., & Selten, J. P. (2005). Schizophrenia and migration: A meta-analysis and review. *American Journal of Psychiatry, 162,* 12–24.

Cardozo, B. L., Bilukha, O. O., Gotway Crawford, C. A., et al. (2004). Mental health, social functioning, and disability in postwar Afghanistan. *Journal of the American Medical Association, 292,* 575–584.

Cardozo, B. L., Kaiser, R., Gotway, C. A., & Agani, F. (2003). Mental health, social functioning, and feelings of hatred and revenge in Kosovar Albanians one year after the war in Kosovo. *Journal of Traumatic Stress, 16,* 351–360.

Cardozo, B. L., Vergara, A., Agani, F., & Gotway, C. A. (2000). Mental health, social functioning, and attitudes of Kosovar Albanians following the war in Kosovo. *Journal of the American Medical Association, 284,* 569–577.

Carlsmith, K. M., Monahan, J., & Evans, A. (2007). The function of punishment in the civil commitment of sexually violent predators. *Behavioral Sciences and the Law, 25,* 437–448.

Carroll, J. K. (2004). *Murug, waali,* and *gini*: Expressions of distress in refugees from Somalia. *Primary Care Companion to the Journal of Clinical Psychiatry, 6,* 119–125.

Carroll, K. M. (2001). Combined treatments for substance dependence. In M. T. Sammons & N. B. Schmidt (Eds.), *Combined treatments for mental disorders.* Washington, DC: American Psychological Association.

Carroll, K. M., Ball, S. A., Nich, C., Martino, S., Frankforter, T. L., Farentinos, C., Kunkel, L. E., Mikulich-Gilbertson, S. K., Morgenstern, J., Obert, J. L., Polcin, D., Snead, N., & Woody, G. E. (2006). Motivational interviewing to improve treatment engagement and outcome in individuals seeking treatment for substance abuse: A multisite effectiveness study. *Drug and Alcohol Dependence, 81,* 301–312.

Carroll, K. M., & Rounsaville, B. J. (2006). Behavioral therapies: The glass would be half full if only we had a glass. In W. R. Miller & K. M. Carroll (Eds.), *Rethinking substance abuse: What the science shows and what we should do about it* (pp. 223–239). New York: Guilford Press.

Caspi, A., Harrington, H., Milne, B., Amell, J. W., Theodore, R. F., & Moffitt, T. E. (2003). Children's behavioral styles at age 3 are linked to their adult personality traits at age 26. *Journal of Personality, 71,* 495–513.

Caspi, A., McClay, J., Moffitt, T. E., Mill, J., Martin, J., Craig, I. W., et al. (2002). Role of genotype in the cycle of violence in maltreated children. *Science, 297,* 851–854.

Caspi, A., Sugden, K., Moffitt, T. E., Taylor, A., Craig, I. W., et al. (2003). Influence of life stress on depression: Moderation by a polymorphism in the 5-HTT gene. *Science, 301,* 386–389.

Castelli, F., Frith, C., Happe, F., & Frith, U. (2002). Autism, Asperger's syndrome and brain mechanisms for the attribution of mental states to animated shapes. *Brain, 125,* 1839–1849.

Castiglioni, A. (1946). *Adventures of the mind* (1st American ed.). New York: Knopf.

Castle, D. J., & Morgan, V. (2008). Epidemiology. In K. T. Mueser & Dilip V. Jeste (Eds.), *Clinical handbook of schizophrenia* (pp. 14–24). New York: Guilford Press.

Castro, F. G., Barrera, M., Jr., & Holleran Steiker, L. K. (2010). Issues and challenges in the design of culturally adapted evidence-based interventions. *Annual Review of Clinical Psychology, 6,* 213–239.

Ceci, S. J., & Bruck, M. (1995). *Jeopardy in the courtroom.* Washington, DC: American Psychological Association.

Centers for Disease Control (2005). Annual smoking-attributable mortality, years of potential life lost, and productivity losses—United States, 1997–2001. *Morbidity and Mortality Weekly Report, 54,* 625–628.

Centers for Disease Control (CDC). (2007). Suicide: Facts at a glance. www.cdc.gov/ncipc/dvp/suicide/SuicideDataSheet.pdf (accessed April 1, 2010)

Centers for Disease Control (CDC). (2008a). HIV/AIDS in the United States. http://www.cdc.gov (accessed March 13, 2009)

Centers for Disease Control (CDC). (2008b). Tracking fetal alcohol syndrome. http://www.cdc.gov/ncbddd/fas/fassurv.htm (accessed December 5, 2008)

Centers for Disease Control (CDC). (2009). The burden of tobacco use. http://www.cdc.gov/nccdphp/publications/aag/osh.htm (accessed March 26, 2009)

Centers for Disease Control (CDC). (2010). *Obesity.* Retrieved April 20, 2010, from http://www.cdc.gov/obesity

Centers for Disease Control (CDC), National Center for Injury Prevention and Control. (2004). Web-based injury statistics query and reporting system. Retrieved from http://www.cdc.gov/ncipc/wisqars/default.htm

Cervantes, R. C., Salgado de Snyder, V. N., & Padilla, A. M. (1989). Posttraumatic stress in immigrants from Central America and Mexico. *Hospital & Community Psychiatry, 40,* 615–619.

Chang, C.-J., Chen, W. J., Liu, S. K., Cheng, J. J., Yang, W.-C. O., Chang, H.-J., Lane, H.-Y., Lin, S.-K., Yang, T.-W., & Hwu, H.-G. (2002). Morbidity risk of psychiatric disorders among the first degree relatives of schizophrenia patients in Taiwan. *Schizophrenia Bulletin, 28,* 379–392.

Chang, K. D., & Simeonova, D. I. (2004). Mood stabilizers: Use in pediatric psychopharmacology. In H. Steiner (Ed.), *Handbook of mental health intervention in children and adolescents: An integrated developmental approach* (pp. 363–412). San Francisco: Jossey-Bass.

Chang, V. W., & Christakis, N. A. (2003). Self-perception of weight appropriateness in the United States. *American Journal of Preventative Medicine, 24,* 332–339.

Chapman, L. J., Edell, W. S., & Chapman, J. P. (1980). Physical anhedonia, perceptual aberration, and psychosis proneness. *Schizophrenia Bulletin, 6,* 639–653.

Chapman, T. F., Manuzza, S., & Fyer, A. J. (1995). Epidemiology and family studies of social phobia. In R. G. Heimberg, M. R. Liebowitz, D. A. Hope, & F. R. Schneier (Eds.), *Social phobia: Diagnosis, assessment, and treatment* (pp. 21–40). New York: Guilford Press.

Charney, D. S. (2004). Psychobiological mechanisms of resilience and vulnerability:

Implications for successful adaptation to extreme stress. *American Journal of Psychiatry, 161*, 195–216.

Charney, D. S., Nagy, L. M., Bremner, J. D., Goddard, A. W., Yehuda, R., & Southwick, S. M. (2000). Neurobiologic mechanisms of human anxiety. In B. S. Fogel (Ed.), *Synopsis of neuropsychiatry* (pp. 273–288). Philadelphia: Lippincott Williams & Wilkins.

Chassin, L., Pitts, S. C., DeLucia, C., & Todd, M. (1999). A longitudinal study of children of alcoholics: Predicting young adult substance use disorders, anxiety, and depression. *Journal of Abnormal Psychology, 108*, 106–119.

Chatzitheochari, S., & Arber, S. (2009). Lack of sleep, work and the long hours culture: Evidence from the UK time use survey. *Work, Employment and Society, 23*, 30–48.

Chavira, D. A., Grilo, C. M., Shea, M. T., Yen, S., Gunderson, J. G., Morey, L. C., et al. (2003). Ethnicity and four personality disorders. *Comprehensive Psychiatry, 44*, 483–491.

Chen, H., Cohen, P., Crawford, T. N., Kasen, S., Guan, B., & Gordon, K. (2009). Impact of early adolescent psychiatric and personality disorder on long-term physical health: A 20-year longitudinal follow-up study. *Psychological Medicine, 39*, 865–874.

Chevez, L. G. (2005). Latin American healers and healing: Healing as a redefinition process. In R. Moodley & W. West (Eds). *Integrating traditional healing practices into counseling and psychotherapy* (pp. 85–99). Thousand Oaks, CA: Sage.

Chilvers, R., Macdonald, G. M., & Hayes, A. A. (2006). Supported housing for people with severe mental disorders. *Cochrane Database of Systematic Reviews, 4*, CD000453.

Chou, T. (1992). Wake up and smell the coffee: Caffeine, coffee, and the medical consequences. *Western Journal of Medicine, 157*, 544–553.

Chow, E., Tsao, M. N., & Harth, T. (2004). Does psychosocial intervention improve survival in cancer? A meta-analysis. *Palliative Medicine, 18*, 25–31.

Christenson, G. A., & Mansueto, C. S. (1999). Trichotillomania: Descriptive characteristics and phenomenology. In D. J. Stein, G. A. Christenson, & E. Hollander (Eds.), *Trichotillomania* (pp. 1–42). Washington, DC: American Psychiatric Publishing.

Christenson, G. A., Pyle, R. L., & Mitchell, J. E. (1991). Estimated lifetime prevalence of trichotillomania in college students. *Journal of Clinical Psychiatry, 52*, 415–417.

Christophersen, E. R., & Mortweet, S. L. (2001). *Treatments that work with children: Empirically supported strategies for managing childhood problems.* Washington, DC: American Psychological Association.

Chui, H. C., & Gatz, M. (2005). Cultural diversity in Alzheimer disease: The interface between biology, belief, and behavior. *Alzheimer Disease and Associated Disorders, 19*, 250–255.

Chung, W. C., De Vries, G. J., & Swaab, D. F. (2002). Sexual differentiation of the bed nucleus of the striaterminalis in humans may extend into adulthood. *Journal of Neuroscience, 22*, 1027–1033.

Cicchetti, D., & Rogosch, F. A. (2001). Diverse patterns of neuroendocrine activity in maltreated children. *Development & Psychopathology, 13*, 677–694.

Cicchetti, D., & Toth, S. L. (2005). Child maltreatment. *Annual Review of Clinical Psychology, 1*, 409–438.

Clancy, S. A., McNally, R. J., Schacter, D. L., Lenzenweger, M. F., & Pitman, R. K. (2002). Memory distortion in people reporting abduction by aliens. *Journal of Abnormal Psychology, 111*, 455–461.

Clancy, S. A., Schacter, D. L., McNally, R. J., & Pitman, R. (2000). False recognition in women reporting recovered memories of sexual abuse. *Psychological Science, 11*, 26–31.

Clark, D. A., & Purdon, C. (1993). New perspectives for a cognitive theory of obsessions. *Australian Psychologist, 28*, 161–167.

Clark, D. M. (1988). A cognitive model of panic attacks. In S. Rachman & J. D. Maser (Eds.), *Panic: Psychological perspectives* (pp. 71–89). Hillsdale, NJ: Erlbaum.

Clark, D. M., Ehlers, A., McManus, F., Hackmann, A., Fennell, M., Campbell, H., Flower, T., Davenport, C., & Louis, B. (2003). Cognitive therapy versus fluoxetine in generalized social phobia: A randomized placebo-controlled trial. *Journal of Consulting & Clinical Psychology, 71*, 1058–1067.

Clark, D. M., Salkovskis, P. M. N., Hackman, A., Wells, A., Fennel, M., Ludgate, S., et al. (1998). Two psychological treatments for hypochondriasis. *British Journal of Psychiatry, 173*, 218–225.

Clark, D. M., & Wells, A. (1995). A cognitive model of social phobia. In R. G. Heimberg, M. R. Liebowitz, D. A. Hope, & F. R. Schneier (Eds.), *Social phobia: Diagnosis, assessment and treatment* (pp. 69–93). New York: Guilford Press.

Clarke, G. N., Hawkins, W., Murphy, M., Sheeber, L. B., Lewinsohn, P. M., & Seeley, J. R. (1995). Targeted prevention of unipolar depressive disorder in an at-risk sample of high school adolescents: A randomized trial of a group cognitive intervention. *Journal of the American Academy of Child & Adolescent Psychiatry, 34*, 312–321.

Clarkin, J. F., Levy, K. N., Lenzenweger, M. F., & Kernberg, O. F. (2007). Evaluating three treatments for borderline personality disorder: A multiwave study. *American Journal of Psychiatry, 164*, 922–928.

Clayton, A. H. (2007). Epidemiology and neurobiology of female sexual dysfunction. *Journal of Sexual Medicine, 4*, 260–268.

Cleckley, H. M. (1941/1982). *The mask of sanity: An attempt to reinterpret the so-called psychopathic personality.* St. Louis, MO: C. V. Mosby.

Cloninger, C. R. (2000). A practical way to diagnose personality disorder: A proposal. *Journal of Personality Disorders, 14*, 99–108.

Cloninger, C. R., & Gottesman, I. I. (1987). Genetic and environmental factors in antisocial behavior disorders. In S. A. Mednick, T. E. Moffitt, & S. A. Stack (Eds.), *The causes of crime: New biological approaches* (pp. 92–109). New York: Cambridge University Press.

Coccaro, E. F., & Kavoussi, R. J. (1997). Fluoxetine and impulsive aggressive behavior in personality-disordered subjects. *Archives of General Psychiatry, 54*, 1081–1088.

Cochrane, R. E., Grisso, T., & Frederick, R. I. (2001). The relationship between criminal charges, diagnoses, and psycholegal opinions among federal pretrial defendants. *Behavioral Sciences & the Law, 19*, 565–582.

Cocores, J., Pottash, A. C., & Gold, M. S. (1991). Cocaine. In N. S. Miller (Ed.), *Comprehensive handbook of drug and alcohol addiction* (pp. 341–352). New York: Marcel Dekker.

Cohen, J. A., Deblinger, E., Mannarino, A. P., & Steer, R. A. (2004). A multisite, randomized controlled trial for children with sexual abuse–related PTSD symptoms. *Journal of the American Academy of Child & Adolescent Psychiatry, 43*, 393–402.

Cohen, S., Tyrrell, D. A., & Smith, A. P. (1991). Psychological stress and susceptibility to the common cold. *New England Journal of Medicine, 325*, 606–612.

Cohen, S. A., Ohrig, K., Lott, R. S., & Kerrick, J. M. (1998). Risperidone for aggression and self-injurious behavior in adults with mental retardation. *Journal of Autism & Developmental Disorders, 28*, 229–233.

Coid, J. W., Kirkbride, J. B., Barker, D., Cowden, F., Stamps, R., Yang, M., et al. (2008). Raised incidence rates of all psychoses among migrant groups. *Archives of General Psychiatry, 65*, 1250–1258.

Colapinto, J. (2000). *As nature made him: The boy who was raised as a girl.* New York: HarperCollins.

Cole, M. G. (2004). Delirium in elderly patients. *American Journal of Geriatric Psychiatry, 12*, 7–21.

Cole, S. W., Kemeny, M. E., Taylor, S. E., Visscher, B. R., & Fahey, J. L. (1995). Accelerated course of human immunodeficiency virus infection in gay men who conceal their homosexual identity. *Psychosomatic Medicine, 58*, 219–238.

Cole, W. (1992). Incest perpetrators: Their assessment and treatment. *Psychiatric Clinics of North America, 15*, 689–701.

Coles, M. E., Hart, T. A., & Heimberg, R. G. (2005). Cognitive-behavioral group treatment for social phobia. In R. Crozier & L. E. Alden (Eds.), *International handbook of social anxiety.* London: Wiley.

Collins, J. J., & Schlenger, W. E. (1983, November 9–13). *The prevalence of psychiatric disorder among admissions to prison.* Paper presented at the American Society of Criminology 35th Annual Meeting, Denver.

Committee on Gulf War and Health. (2008). *Gulf War and health. Vol. 7: Long-term consequences of traumatic brain injury.* Washington, DC: National Academies Press.

Conklin, H. M., & Iacono, W. G. (2002). Schizophrenia: A neurodevelopmental perspective. *Current Directions in Psychological Science, 11*, 33–37.

Conner, K. R., & Zhong, Y. (2003). State firearm laws and rates of suicide in men and women.

American Journal of Preventive Medicine, 25, 320–324.

Conrod, P. J., Peterson, J. B., Pihl, R. O., & Mankowski, S. (1997). Biphasic effects of alcohol on heart rate are influenced by alcoholic family history and rate of alcohol ingestion. *Alcoholism: Clinical and Experimental Research, 21,* 140–149.

Conwell, Y., Duberstein, P. R., Cox, C., Hermann, J., Forbes, N., & Caine, E. D. (1998). Age differences in behaviors leading to completed suicide. *American Journal of Geriatric Psychiatry, 6,* 122–126.

Conwell, Y., & Thompson, C. (2008). Suicidal behavior in elders. *Psychiatric Clinics of North America, 31,* 333–356.

Cooley, E., & Toray, T. (2001). Body image and personality predictors of eating disorder symptoms during the college years. *International Journal of Eating Disorders, 30,* 28–36.

Coolidge, F. L., Thede, L., & Jang, K. L. (2004). Are personality disorders psychological manifestations of executive function deficits? Bivariate heritability evidence from a twin study. *Behavior Genetics, 34,* 75–84.

Coolidge, F. L., Thede, L. L., & Young, S. E. (2002). The heritability of gender identity disorder in a child and adolescent twin sample. *Behavior Genetics, 32,* 251–257.

Coons, P. M. (1980). Multiple personality: Diagnostic considerations. *Journal of Clinical Psychiatry, 41,* 330–336.

Coons, P. M. (1984). *Childhood antecedents of multiple personality.* Paper presented at the Meeting of the American Psychiatric Association, Los Angeles.

Coons, P. M. (1986). Treatment progress in 20 patients with multiple personality disorder. *Journal of Nervous & Mental Disease, 174,* 715–721.

Coons, P. M. (1994). Confirmation of childhood abuse in child and adolescent cases of multiple personality disorder and dissociative disorder not otherwise specified. *Journal of Nervous & Mental Disease, 182,* 461–464.

Coons, P. M., Cole, C., Pellow, T. A., & Milstein, V. (1990). Symptoms of posttraumatic stress disorder and dissociation in women victims of abuse. In R. P. Kluft (Ed.), *Incest-related syndromes of adult psychopathology* (pp. 205–226). Washington, DC: American Psychiatric Press.

Coons, P. M., & Milstein, V. (1986). Psychosexual disturbances in multiple personality: Characteristics, etiology, and treatment. *Journal of Clinical Psychiatry, 47,* 106–110.

Coons, P. M., & Milstein, V. (1990). Self-mutilation associated with dissociative disorders. *Dissociation: Progress in the Dissociative Disorders, 3,* 81–87.

Coontz, P. D., Lidz, C. W., & Mulvey, E. P. (1994). Gender and the assessment of dangerousness in the psychiatric emergency room. *International Journal of Law & Psychiatry, 17,* 369–376.

Cooper, A., Golden, G. H., & Kent-Ferraro, J. (2002). Online sexual behaviors in the workplace: How can human resource departments and employee assistance programs respond effectively? *Sexual Addiction & Compulsivity, 9,* 149–165.

Cooper, M. L., Russell, M., Skinner, J. B., Frone, M. R., & Mudar, P. (1992). Stress and alcohol use: Moderating effects of gender, coping, and alcohol expectancies. *Journal of Abnormal Psychology, 101,* 139–152.

Cope, M. B., Fernandez, J. R., & Allison, D. B. (2004). Genetic and biological risk factors. In K. J. Thompson (Ed.), *Handbook of eating disorders and obesity* (pp. 323–338). Hoboken, NJ: Wiley.

Cornelius, M. D., Goldschmidt, L., Day, N. L., & Larkby, C. (2002). Alcohol, tobacco and marijuana use among pregnant teenagers: 6-year follow-up of offspring growth effects. *Neurotoxicology & Teratology, 24,* 703–710.

Cororve, M. B., & Gleaves, D. H. (2001). Body dysmorphic disorder: A review of conceptualizations, assessments, and treatment strategies. *Clinical Psychology Review, 21,* 949–970.

Corrao, G., Bagnardi, V., Zambon, A., & La Vecchia, C. (2004). A meta-analysis of alcohol consumption and the risk of 15 diseases. *Prevention by Medicine, 38,* 613–619.

Costa, P. T., & Widiger, T. A. (Eds.). (2002). *Personality disorders and the five-factor model of personality* (2nd ed., pp. 215–221). Washington, DC: American Psychological Association.

Costello, E. J., Copeland, W., Cowell, A., & Keeler, G. (2007). Service costs of caring for adolescents with mental illness in a rural community, 1993–2000. *American Journal of Psychiatry, 164,* 36–42.

Costello, E. J., Keeler, G. P., & Angold, A. (2001). Poverty, race/ethnicity, and psychiatric disorder: A study of rural children. *American Journal of Public Health, 91,* 1494–1498.

Costello, E. J., Mustillo, S., Erkanli, A., Keeler, G., & Angold, A. (2003). Prevalence and development of psychiatric disorders in childhood and adolescence. *Archives of General Psychiatry, 60,* 837–844.

Courtet, P., Picot, M.-C., Bellivier, F., Torres, S., Jollant, F., Michelon, C., Castelnau, D., Astruc, B., Buresi, C., & Malafosse, A. (2004). Serotonin transporter gene may be involved in short-term risk of subsequent suicide attempts. *Biological Psychiatry, 55,* 46–51.

Cousins, N. (1985). Therapeutic value of laughter. *Integrative Psychiatry, 3,* 112.

Coyne, J. C. (1976). Toward an interactional description of depression. *Psychiatry, 39,* 28–40.

Coyne, J. C., & Gotlib, I. H. (1983). The role of cognition in depression: A critical appraisal. *Psychological Bulletin, 94,* 472–505.

Coyne, J. C., Stefanek, M., & Palmer, S. C. (2007). Psychotherapy and survival in cancer: The conflict between hope and evidence. *Psychological Bulletin, 133,* 367–394.

Crabbe, J. C. (2002). Genetic contributions to addiction. *Annual Review of Psychology, 53,* 435–462.

Craig, T. K., Boardman, A. P., Mills, K., & Daly-Jones, O. (1993). The South London Somatisation Study: I. Longitudinal course and the influence of early life experiences. *British Journal of Psychiatry, 163,* 579–588.

Cranston-Cuebas, M. A., & Barlow, D. H. (1990). Cognitive and affective contributions to sexual functioning. *Annual Review of Sex Research, 1,* 119–161.

Craske, M. G., & Barlow, D. H. (2001). Panic disorder and agoraphobia. In D. H. Barlow (Ed.), *Clinical handbook of psychological disorders: A step-by-step treatment manual* (3rd ed., pp. 1–59). New York: Guilford Press.

Craske, M. G., & Waters, A. M. (2005). Panic disorder, phobias, and generalized anxiety disorder. *Annual Review of Clinical Psychology, 1,* 197–226.

Crawford, T. N., Cohen, P., Johnson, J. G., et al. (2005). Self-reported personality disorder in the children in the community sample: Convergent and prospective validity in late adolescence and adulthood. *Journal of Personality Disorders, 19,* 30–52.

Crepault, C., & Couture, M. (1980). Men's erotic fantasies. *Archives of Sexual Behavior, 9,* 565–581.

Crick, N. R., & Dodge, K. A. (1994). A review and reformulation of social information-processing mechanisms in children's social adjustment. *Psychological Bulletin, 115,* 74–101.

Crick, N. R., & Grotpeter, J. K. (1995). Relational aggression, gender, and social-psychological adjustment. *Child Development, 66,* 710–722.

Crick, N. R., & Ladd, G. W. (1990). Children's perceptions of the outcomes of social strategies: Do the ends justify being mean? *Developmental Psychology, 26,* 612–620.

Crits-Christoph, P., & Barber, J. P. (2000). Long-term psychotherapy. In C. R. Snyder & R. E. Ingram (Eds.), *Handbook of psychological change: Psychotherapy processes and practices for the 21st century* (pp. 455–473). New York: Wiley.

Cronbach, L. J., & Meehl, P. E. (1955). Construct validity in psychological tests. *Psychological Bulletin, 52,* 281–302.

Crosby, A. E., Cheltenham, M. P., & Sacks, J. J. (1999). Incidence of suicidal ideation and behavior in the United States, 1994. *Suicide & Life-Threatening Behavior, 29,* 131–140.

Cross, S. E., & Madson, L. (1997). Models of the self: Self-construals and gender. *Psychological Bulletin, 122,* 5–37.

Cross-National Collaborative Group. (1992). The changing rate of major depression. *Journal of the American Medical Association, 268,* 3098–3105.

Crowther, J. H., Armey, M., Luce, K. H., Dalton, G. R., & Leahey, T. (2008). The point prevalence of bulimic disorders from 1990 to 2004. *International Journal of Eating Disorders, 41,* 491–497.

Cruess, D. G., Antoni, M. H., Gonzalez, J., Fletcher, M. A., Klimas, N., Duran, R., Ironson, G., & Schneiderman, N. (2003). Sleep disturbance mediates and association between psychological distress and immune status among HIV-positive men and women on combination antiretroviral therapy. *Journal of Psychosomatic Research, 54,* 185–189.

Csernansky, J. G., Mahmoud, R., & Brenner, R. (2002). A comparison of risperidone and haloperidol for the prevention of relapse in patients with schizophrenia. *New England Journal of Medicine, 346,* 16–22.

Cuijpers, P., Dekker, J., Hollon, S. D., & Andersson, G. (2009). Adding psychotherapy to pharmacotherapy in the treatment of depressive disorders in adults: A meta-analysis. *Journal of Clinical Psychiatry, 70,* 1219–1229.

Cuijpers, P., van Straten, A., van Oppen, P., & Andersson, G. (2008). Are psychological and pharmacological interventions equally effective in the treatment of adult depressive disorders? A meta-analysis of comparative studies. *Journal of Clinical Psychiatry, 69,* 1675–1685.

Cuijpers, P., van Straten, A., Warmerdam, L., & Andersson, G. (2009). Psychological treatment versus combined treatment of depression: A meta-analysis. *Depression & Anxiety, 26,* 279–288.

Culpepper, L. (2004). Identifying and treating panic disorder in primary care. *Journal of Clinical Psychiatry, 65*(Suppl. 5), 19–23.

D

Dagan, Y., & Eisenstein, M. (1999). Circadian rhythm sleep disorders: Toward a more precise definition and diagnosis. *Chronobiology International, 16,* 213–222.

Dahl, A. A. (1993). The personality disorders: A critical review of family, twin, and adoption studies. *Journal of Personality Disorders* (Spr. Suppl. 1), 86–99.

Daley, D. C., & Marlatt, G. A. (2006). *Overcoming your alcohol or drug problem: Effective recovery strategies* (2nd ed.): *Therapist guide.* New York: Oxford University Press.

Damasio, H., Grabowski, T., Frank, R., Galaburda, A. M., & Damasio, A. R. (1994). The return of Phineas Gage: Clues about the brain from the skull of a famous patient. *Science, 264,* 1102–1105.

Dana, R. H. (1998). *Understanding cultural identity in intervention and assessment.* Thousand Oaks, CA: Sage.

Dana, R. H. (2000). *Handbook on cross-cultural and multicultural personality assessment.* Mahwah, NJ: Erlbaum.

Dana, R. H. (2001). Clinical diagnosis of multicultural populations in the United States. In L. A. Suzuki & J. G. Ponterotto (Eds.), *Handbook of multicultural assessment: Clinical, psychological, and educational applications* (2nd ed., pp. 101–131). San Francisco: Jossey-Bass.

Dansinger, M. L., Gleason, J. A., Griffith, J. L., Selker, H. P., & Schaefer, E. J. (2005). Comparison of the Atkins, Ornish, Weight Watchers, and Zone diets for weight loss and heart disease risk reduction: A randomized trial. *Journal of the American Medical Association, 293,* 43–53.

Dantzer, R., Wollman, E. E., & Yirmiya, R. (2002). Cytokines and depression: An update. *Brain, Behavior and Immunity, 16,* 501–502.

Darcangelo, S. (2008). Fetishism: Psychopathology and treatment. In D. R. Laws & W. T. O'Donohue (Eds.), *Sexual deviance: Theory, assessment, and treatment* (pp. 108–119). New York: Guilford Press.

Darcangelo, S., Hollings, A., and Paladino, G. (2008). Fetishism: Assessment and treatment. In D. R. Laws & W. T. O'Donohue (Eds.), *Sexual deviance: Theory, assessment, and treatment* (pp. 119–131). New York: Guilford Press.

Davenport, D. S., & Yurich, J. M. (1991). Multicultural gender issues. *Journal of Counseling & Development, 70,* 64–71.

Davidson, J., Allgulander, C., Pollack, M. H., Hartford, J., Erickson, J. S., Russell, J. M., Perahia, D., Wohlreich, M. M., Carlson, J., & Raskin, J. (2008). Efficacy and tolerability of duloxetine in elderly patients with generalized anxiety disorder: A pooled analysis of four randomized, double-blind, placebo-controlled studies. *Human Psychopharmacology, 23,* 519–526.

Davidson, J. R. T. (2001). Pharmacotherapy of generalized anxiety disorder. *Journal of Clinical Psychiatry, 62*(Suppl. 11), 46–50.

Davidson, J. R. T. (2003). Pharmacotherapy of social phobia. *Acta Psychiatrica Scandinavica, 108*(Suppl. 417), 65–71.

Davidson, J. R. T. (2004). Long-term treatment and prevention of posttraumatic stress disorder. *Journal of Clinical Psychiatry, 65*(Suppl. 1), 44–48.

Davidson, J. R. T., Rothbaum, B. O., van der Kolk, B. A., Sikes, C. R., & Farfel, G. M. (2001). Multicenter, double-blind comparison of sertraline and placebo in the treatment of posttraumatic stress disorder. *Archives of General Psychiatry, 58,* 485–492.

Davidson, K., Norrie, J., Tyrer, P., Gumley, A., Tata, P., Murray, H., & Palmer, S. (2006). The effectiveness of cognitive behavior therapy for borderline personality disorder: Results from the borderline personality disorder of cognitive therapy (BOSCOT) trial. *Journal of Personality Disorders, 20,* 450–465.

Davidson, R. J., Pizzagalli, D. A., & Nitschke, J. B. (2009). Representation and regulation of emotion in depression: Perspectives from affective neuroscience. In I. H. Gotlib & C. L. Hammen (Eds.), *Handbook of depression* (2nd ed., pp. 218–248). New York: Guilford Press.

Davidson, R. J., Pizzagalli, D., Nitschke, J. B., & Putnam, K. (2002). Depression: Perspectives from affective neuroscience. *Annual Review of Psychology, 53,* 545–574.

Davis, K. L., Kahn, R. S., Ko, G., & Davidson, M. (1991). Dopamine in schizophrenia: A review and conceptualization. *American Journal of Psychiatry, 148,* 1474–1486.

Davis, O. S. P., Haworth, C. M. A., & Plomin, R. (2009). Learning abilities and disabilities: Generalist genes in early adolescence. *Cognitive Neuropsychiatry, 14,* 312–331.

Dawson, D. A., Grant, B. F., Stinson, F. S., Chou, P. S., Huang, B., & Ruan, W. J. (2005). Recovery from *DSM-IV* alcohol dependence: United States, 2001–2002. *Addiction, 100,* 281–292.

Deardorff, J., Hayward, C., Wilson, K. A., Bryson, S., Hammer, L. D., & Agras, S. (2007). Puberty and gender interact to predict social anxiety symptoms in early adolescence. *Journal of Adolescent Health, 41,* 102–104.

De Cuypere, G., van Hemelrijck, M., Michel, A., Carael, B., Heylens, G., Rubens, R., Hoebeke, P., & Mostrey, S. (2007). Prevalence and demography of transsexualism in Belgium. *European Psychiatry, 22,* 137–141.

Deeny, S. P., Poeppel, D., Zimmerman, J. B., Roth, S. M., Brandauer, J., Witkoswki, S., Hearn, J. W., Ludlow, A. T., Contreras-Vital, J. L., Brandt, J., & Hatfield, B. D. (2008). Exercise, APOE, and working memory: MEG and behavioral evidence for benefit of exercise in epsilon4 carriers. *Biological Psychology, 78,* 179–187.

Delizonna, L. L., Wincze, J. P., Litz, B. T., Brown, T. A., & Barlow, D. H. (2001). A comparison of subjective and physiological measures of mechanically produced and erotically produced erections (or, is an erection an erection?). *Journal of Sex & Marital Therapy, 27,* 21–31.

Dell, P. F. (1998). Axis II pathology in outpatients with dissociative identity disorder. *Journal of Nervous & Mental Disease, 186,* 352–356.

Dell, P. F., & Eisenhower, J. W. (1990). Adolescent multiple personality disorder: A preliminary study of eleven cases. *Journal of the American Academy of Child & Adolescent Psychiatry, 29,* 359–366.

Dennis, M. L., Babor, T. F., Diamond, G., Donaldson, J., Godley, S. H., Tims, F., Titus, J. C., Webb, C., Herrell, J., & the CYT Steering Committee. (2000). *The cannabis youth treatment (CYT) experiment: Preliminary findings.* Rockville, MD: Substance Abuse and Mental Health Services Administration, Center for Substance Abuse Treatment. http://samhsa.gov/centers/csat/content/recoverymonth/000907rptcover.html (accessed May 15, 2006)

Depression and Bipolar Support Alliance. (2008). Suicide prevention: Responding to an emergency situation. http://www.ndma.org (accessed May 15, 2008)

DePrince, A. P., & Freyd, J. J. (1999). Dissociation, attention, and memory. *Psychological Science, 10,* 449–452.

DePrince, A. P., & Freyd, J. J. (2001). Memory and dissociative tendencies: The roles of attentional context and word meaning in a directed forgetting task. *Journal of Trauma & Dissociation, 2,* 67–82.

Depue, R. Q., & Iacono, W. G. (1989). Neurobehavioral aspects of affective disorders. *Annual Review of Psychology, 40,* 457–492.

DeRose, L. M., Wright, A. J., & Brooks-Gunn, J. (2006). Does puberty account for the gender differential in depression? In C. L. M. Keyes & S. H. Goodman (Eds.), *Women and depression* (pp. 89–128). New York: Cambridge University Press.

DeRubeis, R. J., Gelfand, L. A., Tang, T. Z., & Simons, A. D. (1999). Medications versus cognitive behavior therapy for severely depressed outpatients: Mega-analysis of four randomized comparisons. *American Journal of Psychiatry, 156,* 1001–1013.

DeRubeis, R. J., Hollon, S. D., Amsterdam, J. D., Shelton, R. C., Young, P. R., Salomon, R. M., et al. (2005). Cognitive therapy vs. medications in the treatment of moderate to severe depression. *Archives of General Psychiatry, 62,* 409–416.

deSilva, P., Rachman, S., & Seligman, M. (1977). Prepared phobias and obsessions. *Behaviour Research & Therapy, 15,* 65–77.

Desmond, D. W., & Tatemichi, T. K. (1998). Vascular dementia. In M. F. Folstein (Ed.), *Neurobiology of primary dementia* (pp. 167–190). Washington, DC: American Psychiatric Press.

de Snyder, V. N. S ., Diaz-Perez, M. D., & Ojeda, V. D. (2000). The prevalence of nervios and associated symptomatology among inhabitants of Mexican rural communities. *Culture, Medicine & Psychiatry, 24,* 453–470.

Deutsch, A. (1937). *The mentally ill in America: A history of their care and treatment from colonial times.* Garden City, NY: Doubleday, Doran & Company.

Dewaraja, R., & Sasaki, Y. (1991). Semen-loss syndrome: A comparison between Sri Lanka and Japan. *American Journal of Psychotherapy, 45,* 14–20.

de Zwaan, M., Roerig, J. L., & Mitchell, J. E. (2004). Pharmacological treatment of anorexia nervosa, bulimia nervosa, and binge eating disorder. In J. K. Thompson (Ed.), *Handbook of eating disorders and obesity* (pp. 186–217). Hoboken, NJ: Wiley.

Dickey, R., & Stephens, J. (1995). Female-to-male transsexualism, heterosexual type: Two cases. *Archives of Sexual Behavior, 24,* 439–445.

Dimidjian, S., Hollon, S. D., Dobson, K. S., Schmaling, K. B., Kohlenberg, R. J., Addis, M. E., Gallop, R., McGlinchey, J. B., Markley, D. K., Gollan, J. K., Atkins, D. C., Dunner, D. L., & Jacobson, N. S. (2006). Randomized trial of behavioral activation, cognitive therapy, and antidepressant medication in the acute treatment of adults with major depression. *Journal of Consulting and Clinical Psychology, 74,* 658–670.

Dishion, T. J., & Patterson, G. R. (1997). The timing and severity of antisocial behavior: Three hypotheses within an ecological framework. In D. M. Stoff, J. Breiling, & J. D. Maser (Eds.), *Handbook of antisocial personality disorder* (pp. 205–217). New York: Wiley.

Distel, M. A., Trull, T. J., Derom, C. A., Thiery, E. W., Grimmer, M. A., Martin, N. G., Willemsen, G., & Boomsma, D. I. (2007). Heritability of borderline personality disorder features is similar across three countries. *Psychological Medicine, 38,* 1219–1229.

Dixon, D., Cruess, S., Kilbourn, K., Klimas, N., Fletcher, M. A., Ironson, G., Baum, A., Schneiderman, N., & Antoni, M. H. (2001). Social support mediates loneliness and human herpes virus Type 6 (HHV-6) antibody titers. *Journal of Applied Social Psychology, 31,* 1111–1132.

Docherty, N. M., Grosh, E. S., Wexler, B. E. (1996). Affective reactivity of cognitive functioning and family history in schizophrenia. *Psychiatry, 139,* 59–64.

Dodge, K., & Schwartz, D. (1997). Social information processing mechanisms in aggressive behavior. In D. M. Stoff, J. Breiling, & J. D. Maser (Eds.), *Handbook of antisocial personality disorder* (pp. 171–180). New York: Wiley.

Dodge, K. A., & Pettit, G. S. (2003). A biopsychosocial model of the development of chronic conduct problems in adolescence. *Developmental Psychology, 39,* 349–371.

Dohrenwend, B. P. (2000). The role of adversity and stress in psychopathology: Some evidence and its implications for theory and research. *Journal of Health and Social Behavior, 41,* 1–19.

Dohrenwend, B. P., Levav, I., Shrout, P. E., Link, B. G., Skodol, A. E., & Martin, J. L. (1987). Life stress and psychopathology: Progress on research begun with Barbara Snell Dohrenwend. *American Journal of Community Psychology, 15,* 677–715.

Dolan, A. (2006). The obsessive disorder that haunts my life. www.dailymail.co.uk (accessed February 26, 2009)

Dolder, C. R. (2008). Side effects of antipsychotics. In K. T. Mueser & Dilip V. Jeste (Eds.), *Clinical handbook of schizophrenia* (pp. 168–177). New York: Guilford Press.

Donegan, N. H., Sanislow, C. A., Blumberg, H. P., Fulbright, R. K., Lacadie, C., Skudlarski, P., Gore, J. C., Olson, I. R., McGlashan, T. H., & Wexler, B. E. (2003). Amygdala hyperreactivity in borderline personality disorder: Implications for emotional dysregulation. *Biological Psychiatry, 54,* 1284–1293.

Donovan, D. M., Anton, R. F., Miller, W. R., Longabaugh, R., Hosking, J. D., & Youngblood, M. (2008). Combined pharmacotherapies and behavioral interventions for alcohol dependence (the COMBINE study): Examination of posttreatment drinking outcomes. *Journal of Studies on Alcohol and Drugs, 69,* 5–13.

Dorfman, W. I., & Leonard, S. (2001). The Minnesota Multiphasic Personality Inventory-2 (MMPI-2). In W. I. Dorfman & S. M. Freshwater (Eds.), *Understanding psychological assessment* (pp. 145–171). Dordrecht, Netherlands: Kluwer Academic.

Dorris, M. (1989). *The unbroken cord.* New York: Harper & Row.

Dossenbach, M., Erol, A., el Mahfoud Kessaci, M., Shaheen, M. O., Sunbol, M. M., Boland, J., Hodge, A., O'Halloran, R. A., & Bitter, I. (2004). Effectiveness of antipsychotic treatments for schizophrenia: Interim 6-month analysis from a prospective observational study (IC-SOHO) comparing olanzapine, quetiapine, risperidone, and haloperidol. *Journal of Clinical Psychiatry, 65,* 312–321.

Dougherty, D. D., & Rauch, S. L. (2007a). Brain correlates of antidepressant treatment outcome from neuroimaging studies in depression. *Psychiatric Clinics of North America, 30,* 91–103.

Dougherty, D. D., & Rauch, S. L. (2007b). Somatic therapies for treatment-resistant depression: New neurotherapeutic interventions. *Psychiatric Clinics of North America, 30,* 31–37.

Downar, J., & Kapur, S. (2008). Biological theories. In K. T. Mueser & Dilip V. Jeste (Eds.), *Clinical handbook of schizophrenia* (pp. 25-34). New York: Guilford Press.

Downey, G., & Feldman, S. I. (1996). Implications of rejection sensitivity for intimate relationships. *Journal of Personality and Social Psychology, 70,* 1327–1343.

Drake, C. L., Roehrs, T., Richardson, G., Walsh, J. K., & Roth, T. (2004). Shift work sleep disorder: Prevalence and consequences beyond that of symptomatic day workers. *Sleep, 27,* 1453–1462.

Drevets, W. C. (2001). Neuroimaging and neuropathological studies of depression: Implications for the cognitive-emotional features of mood disorders. *Current Opinions in Neurobiology, 11,* 240–249.

Du, Y., Dodel, R., Hampel, H., Buerger, K., Lin, S., Eastwood, B., Bales, K., Gao, F., Moeller, H. J., Oertel, W., Farlow, M., & Paul, S. (2001). Reduced levels of amyloid B-peptide antibody in Alzheimer disease. *Neurology, 57,* 801–805.

Dudley-Grant, G. R. (2001). Eastern Caribbean family psychology with conduct disordered adolescents from the Virgin Islands. *American Psychologist, 56,* 47–57.

Duffy, J. D. (1995). General paralysis of the insane: Neuropsychiatry's first challenge. *Journal of Neuropsychiatry, 7,* 243–249.

Dündar, Y., Dodd, S., Strobl, J., Boland, A., Dickson, R., & Walley, T. (2004). Comparative efficacy of newer hypnotic drugs for the short-term management of insomnia: A systematic review and meta-analysis. *Human Psychopharmacology: Clinical & Experimental, 19,* 305–322.

DuPaul, G. J., & Barkley, R. A. (1993). Behavioral contributions to pharmacology: The utility of behavioral methodology in medication treatment of children with attention deficit hyperactivity disorder. *Behavior Therapy, 24,* 47–65.

Durand, V. M., & Mindell, J. A. (1999). Behavioral intervention for childhood sleep terrors. *Behavior Therapy, 30,* 705–715.

Durkheim, E. (1897). *Le suicide: Étude de sociologie.* Paris: F. Alcan.

E

Eaton, W. W., Moortensenk, P. B., Herrman, H., & Freeman, H. (1992). Long-term course of hospitalization for schizophrenia: I. Risk for rehospitalization. *Schizophrenia Bulletin, 18,* 217–228.

Eaton, W. W., Thara, R., Federman, E., & Tien, A. (1998). Remission and relapse in schizophrenia: The Madras longitudinal study. *Journal of Nervous & Mental Disease, 186,* 357–363.

Eaves, L. J., Silberg, J. L., Meyer, J. M., Maes, H. H., Simonoff, E., Pickles, A., Rutter, M., Neale, M. C., Reynolds, C. A., Erikson, M. T., Heath, A. C., Loeber, R., Truett, K. R., & Hewitt, J. K. (1997). Genetics and developmental psychopathology: 2. The main effects of genes and environment on behavior problems in the Virginia Twin Study of Adolescent Behavioral Development. *Journal of Child Psychology & Psychiatry, 38,* 965–980.

Edelmann, R. J. (1992). *Anxiety: Theory, research, and intervention in clinical and health psychology.* Chichester, NY: Wiley.

Edinger, D. (1963). *Bertha Pappenheim, Leben und Schriften.* Frankfurt, Germany: Ner-Tamid Verlag.

Edwards, A. G. K., Hulbert-Williams, S., & Neal, R. D. (2008). Psychological interventions for women with metastatic breast cancer. *Cochrane Database of Systematic Reviews, 3,* CD004253.

Egeland, J. A. (1986). Cultural factors and social stigma for manic-depression: The Amish Study. *American Journal of Social Psychiatry, 6,* 279–286.

Egeland, J. A. (1994). An epidemiologic and genetic study of affective disorders among the Old Order Amish. In D. F. Papolos & H. M. Lachman (Eds.), *Genetic studies in affective disorders: Overview of basic methods, current directions, and critical research issues* (pp. 70–90). Oxford, UK: Wiley.

Egeland, J. A., & Hostetter, A. M. (1983). Amish study: I. Affective disorders among the Amish, 1976–1980. *American Journal of Psychiatry, 140,* 56–61.

Ehlers, A., Clark, D. M., Dunmore, E., Jaycox, L., Meadows, E., & Foa, E. (1998). Predicating response to exposure treatment in PTSD: The role of mental defeat and alienation. *Journal of Traumatic Stress, 11,* 457–471.

Ehrenreich, B. (2009). *Bright-sided: How the relentless promotion of positive thinking has undermined America.* New York: Metropolitan Books.

Ehrman, J. K., Gordon, P. M., Visich, P. S., & Keteyian, S. J. (Eds.). (2009). *Clinical exercise physiology* (2nd ed.). Champaign, IL: Human Kinetics.

Eisler, I., Dare, C., Hodes, M., Russell, G., Dodge, E., & Le Grange, D. (2000). Family therapy for adolescent anorexia nervosa: The results of a controlled comparison of two family interventions. *Journal of Child Psychology and Psychiatry and Allied Disciplines, 41,* 727–736.

Ekselius, L., Tilfors, M., Furmark, T., & Fredrikson, M. (2001). Personality disorders in the general population: *DSM-IV* and ICD-10 defined prevalence as related to sociodemographic profile. *Personality & Individual Differences, 30,* 311–320.

Elder, G. H., & Clipp, E. C. (1989). Combat experience and emotional health: Impairment and resilience in later life. *Journal of Personality, 57,* 311–341.

Eley, T. C., Bolton, D., O'Connor, T. G., Perrin, S., Smith, P., & Plomin, R. (2003). A twin study of anxiety-related behaviours in preschool children. *Journal of Child Psychology & Psychiatry, 44,* 945–960.

Eley, T. C., Lichenstein, P., & Stevenson, J. (1999). Sex differences in the etiology of aggressive and nonaggressive antisocial behavior: Results from two twin studies. *Child Development, 70,* 155–168.

Ellason, J. W., & Ross, C. A. (1997). Two-year follow-up of inpatients with dissociative identity disorder. *American Journal of Psychiatry, 154,* 832–839.

Ellason, J. W., Ross, C. A., & Fuchs, D. L. (1996). Lifetime Axis I and II comorbidity and childhood trauma history in dissociative identity disorder. *Psychiatry, 59,* 255–266.

Ellis, A. (1997). The evolution of Albert Ellis and emotive behavior therapy. In J. K. Zeig (Ed.), *The rational evolution of psychotherapy: The third conference* (pp. 69–78). New York: Brunner/Mazel.

Ellis, A., & Harper, R. A. (1961). *A guide to rational living.* Englewood Cliffs, NJ: Prentice Hall.

Ellman, L. M., & Cannon, T. D. (2008). Environmental pre- and perinatal influences on etiology. In K. T. Mueser & D. V. Jeste (Eds.), *Clinical handbook of schizophrenia.* (pp. 65–73). New York: Guilford Press.

Emmelkamp, P. M. G. (1994). Behavior therapy with adults. In A. E. Bergin (Ed.), *Handbook of psychotherapy and behavior change* (4th ed., pp. 379–427). New York: Wiley.

Emmelkamp, P. M. G., Benner, A., Kuipers, A., Feiertag, G. A., Koster, H. C., & van Apeldoorn, F. J. (2006). Comparison of brief dynamic and cognitive-behavioural therapies in avoidant personality disorder. *British Journal of Psychiatry, 189,* 60–64.

Emrick, C. D., Tonigan, J. S., Montgomery, H. A., & Little, L. (1993). Alcoholics Anonymous: What is currently known? In B. S. McCrady & W. R. Miller (Ed.), *Research on Alcoholics Anonymous: Opportunities and alternatives* (pp. 41–78). New Brunswick, NJ: Rutgers Center of Alcohol Studies.

Emslie, G. J., Portteus, A. M., Kumar, E. C., & Hume, J. H. (2004). Antidepressants: SSRIs and novel atypical antidepressants—An update on psychopharmacology. In H. Steiner (Ed.), *Handbook of mental health intervention in children and adolescents: An integrated developmental approach* (pp. 318–362). San Francisco: Jossey-Bass.

Eng, W., Heimberg, R. G., Coles, M. E., Schneier, F. R., & Liebowitz, M. R. (2000). An empirical approach to subtype identification in individuals with social phobia. *Psychological Medicine, 30,* 1345–1357.

Ensminger, M. E., & Hee-Soon, J. (2001). The influence of patterns of welfare receipt during the child-rearing years on later physical and psychological health. *Women & Health, 32,* 25–46.

Epping-Jordan, J. E., Compas, B. E., & Howell, D. C. (1994). Predictors of cancer progression in young adult men and women: Avoidance, intrusive thoughts, and psychological symptoms. *Health Psychology, 13,* 539–547.

Epple, D. M. (2002). Senile dementia of the Alzheimer type. *Clinical Social Work Journal, 30,* 95–110.

Epstein, J., Saunders, B. E., & Kilpatrick, D. G. (1997). Predicting PTSD in women with a history of childhood rape. *Journal of Traumatic Stress, 10,* 573–588.

Erbes, C., Westermeyer, J., Engdahl, B., & Johnsen, E. (2007). Post-traumatic stress disorder and service utilization in a sample of service members from Iraq and Afghanistan. *Military Medicine, 172,* 359–363.

Erdelyi, M. H. (1992). Psychodynamics and the unconscious. *American Psychologist, 47,* 784–787.

Erickson, M. T. (1992). *Behavior disorders of children and adolescents.* Englewood Cliffs, NJ: Prentice Hall.

Erlenmeyer-Kimling, L., Rock, D., Squires-Wheeler, E., & Roberts, S. (1991). Early life precursors of psychiatric outcomes in adulthood in subjects at risk for schizophrenia or affective disorders. *Psychiatry Research, 39,* 239–256.

Escobar, J. I. (1993). Psychiatric epidemiology. In A. C. Gaw (Ed.), *Culture, ethnicity, and mental illness* (pp. 43–73). Washington, DC: American Psychiatric Press.

Escobar, J. I., Burnam, M. A., Karno, M., & Forsythe, A. (1987). Somatization in the community. *Archives of General Psychiatry, 44,* 713–718.

Escobar, J. I., Gara, M., Waitzkin, H., Cohen Silver, R., Holman, A., & Compton, W. (1998). *DSM-IV* hypochondriasis in primary care. *General Hospital Psychiatry, 20,* 155–159.

Espnes, G. A., & Byrne, D. (2008). Gender differences in psychological risk factors for the development of heart disease. *Stress and Health, 24,* 188–195.

Estrada, A. U., & Pinsof, W. M. (1995). The effectiveness of family therapies for selected behavioral disorders of childhood. *Journal of Marital & Family Therapy, 21,* 403–440.

Evers, A. W. M., Kraaimaat, F. W., Geenen, R., Jacobs, J. W. G., & Bijlsma, J. W. J. (2003). Stress-vulnerability factors as long-term predictors of disease activity in early rheumatoid arthritis. *Journal of Psychosomatic Research, 55,* 293–302.

Everson-Rose, S. A., and Lewis, T. T. (2005). Psychosocial factors and cardiovascular diseases. *Annual Review of Public Health, 26,* 469–500.

Exner, J. E. (1993). *The Rorschach: A comprehensive system: Vol. 1. Basic foundations* (3rd ed.). New York: Wiley.

Eysenck, H. J. (1994). The biology of morality. In B. Puka (Ed.), *Defining perspectives in moral development* (pp. 212–229). New York: Garland.

Eysenck, H. J. (Ed.). (1967). *The biological basis of personality.* Springfield, IL: Charles C Thomas.

F

Fabiano, G. A., Pelham, W. E., Jr., Coles, E. K., Gnagy, E. M., Chronis-Tuscano, A., & O'Connor, B. C. (2009). A meta-analysis of behavioral treatments for attention-deficit/hyperactivity disorder. *Clinical Psychology Review, 29,* 129–140.

Fabrega, H. (1993). Toward a social theory of psychiatric phenomena. *Behavioral Science, 38,* 75–100.

Fabrega, H., Ulrich, R., Pilkonis, P., & Mezzich, J. (1991). On the homogeneity of personality disorder clusters. *Comprehensive Psychiatry, 32,* 373–386.

Fahy, T. A. (1988). The diagnosis of multiple personality disorder: A critical review. *British Journal of Psychiatry, 153,* 597–606.

Fairbank, J. A., Hansen, D. J., & Fitterling, J. M. (1991). Patterns of appraisal and coping across different stressor conditions among former prisoners of war with and without posttraumatic stress disorder. *Journal of Consulting & Clinical Psychology, 59,* 274–281.

Fairburn, C. G. (1997). Eating disorders. In D. M. Clark & C. G. Fairburn (Eds.), *Science and practice of cognitive behaviour therapy* (pp. 209–241). London: Oxford University Press.

Fairburn, C. G. (2005). Evidence-based treatment of anorexia nervosa. *International Journal of Eating Disorders, 37,* 526–530.

Fairburn, C. G., & Cooper, Z. (2007). Thinking afresh about the classification of eating disorders. *International Journal of Eating Disorders, 40,* S107–S110.

Fairburn, C. G., Cooper, Z., Bohn, K., O'Connor, M. E., Doll, H. A., & Palmer, R. L. (2007). The severity and status of eating disorder NOS: Implications for *DSM-V*. *Behaviour Research and Therapy, 45,* 1705–1715.

Fairburn, C. G., Cooper, Z., Doll, H. A., Norman, P., & O'Connor, M. (2000). The natural course of bulimia nervosa and binge eating disorder in young women. *Archives of General Psychiatry, 57,* 659–665.

Fairburn, C. G., Jones, R., Peveler, R. C., & Carr, S. J. (1991). Three psychological treatments for bulimia nervosa: A comparative trial. *Archives of General Psychiatry, 48,* 463–469.

Fairburn, C. G., Norman, P. A., Welch, S. L., O'Connor, M. E., Doll, H. A., & Peveler, R. C. (1995). A prospective study of outcome in bulimia nervosa and the long-term effects of three psychological treatments. *Archives of General Psychiatry, 52,* 304–312.

Fairburn, C. G., Stice, E., Cooper, Z., Doll, H. A., Norman, P. A., & O'Connor, M. E. (2003). Understanding persistence in bulimia nervosa: A 5-year naturalistic study. *Journal of Consulting & Clinical Psychology, 71,* 103–109.

Fairburn, C. G., Welsh, S. L., Doll, H. A., Davies, B. A., & O'Connor, M. E. (1997). Risk factors for bulimia nervosa. *Archives of General Psychiatry, 54,* 509–517.

Fairweather, G. W., Sanders, D. H., Maynard, H., & Cressler, D. L. (1969). *Community life for the mentally ill: An alternative to institutional care.* Chicago: Aldine.

Fallon, A. E., & Rozin, P. (1985). Sex differences in perceptions of desirable body shape. *Journal of Abnormal Psychology, 94,* 102–105.

Falloon, I. R., Brooker, C., & Graham-Hole, V. (1992). Psychosocial interventions for schizophrenia. *Behavior Change, 9,* 238–245.

Fals-Stewart, W., Marks, A. P., & Schafer, J. (1993). A comparison of behavioral group therapy and individual behavior therapy in treating obsessive-compulsive disorder. *Journal of Nervous & Mental Disease, 181,* 189–193.

Fanous, A. H., Prescott, C. A., & Kendler, K. S. (2004). The prediction of thoughts of death or self-harm in a population-based sample of female twins. *Psychological Medicine, 34,* 301–312.

Faraone, S. V., Biederman, J., Keenan, K., & Tsuang, M. T. (1991). A family-genetic study of girls with *DSM-III* attention deficit disorder. *American Journal of Psychiatry, 148,* 112–117.

Faravelli, C., Giugni, A., Salvatori, S., & Ricca, V. (2004). Psychopathology after rape. *American Journal of Psychiatry, 161,* 1483–1485.

Farmer, A., Elkin, A., & McGuffin, P. (2007). The genetics of bipolar affective disorder. *Current Opinion in Psychiatry, 20,* 8–12.

Farmer, M. A., Kao, A., & Binik, Y. M. (2009). Dyspareunia and vaginismus. In R. Balon & E. R. Segraves (Eds.), *Clinical manual of sexual disorders* (pp. 305–334). Arlington, VA: American Psychiatric Publishing.

Farmer, M. A., Kukkonen, T., & Binik, Y. M. (2008). Female genital pain and its treatment. In D. L. Rowland & L. Incrocci (Eds.), *Handbook of sexual and gender identity disorders* (pp. 220–250). Hoboken, NJ: Wiley.

Farrer, L. A., Cupples, L. A., Haines, J. L., et al. (1997). Effects of age, sex, and ethnicity on the association between apolipoprotein E genotype and Alzheimer disease: A meta-analysis. *Journal of the American Medical Association, 278,* 1349–1356.

Fauerbach, J. A., Lawrence, J. W., Schmidt, C. W., Munster, A. M., & Costa, P. T. (2000). Personality predictors of injury-related posttraumatic stress disorder. *Journal of Nervous & Mental Disease, 188,* 510–517.

Fawzy, F. I., Canada, A. L., & Fawzy, N. W. (2003). Malignant melanoma: Effects of a brief, structured psychiatric intervention on survival and recurrence at 10-year follow-up. *Archives of General Psychiatry, 60,* 100–103.

Fawzy, F. I., Cousins, N., Fawzy, N. W., Kemeny, M. E., Elashoff, R., & Morton, D. (1990). A structured psychiatric intervention for cancer patients: I. Changes over time in methods of coping and affective disturbance. *Archives of General Psychiatry, 47,* 720–725.

Fawzy, F. I., Fawzy, N. W., Huyn, C. S., Elashoff, R., Morton, D., Cousins, N., & Fahey, J. L. (1993). Effects of an early structured psychiatric intervention, coping and affective state on recurrence and survival 6 years later. *Archives of General Psychiatry, 50,* 681–689.

Fawzy, F. I., Kemeny, M. E., Fawzy, N. W., Elashoff, R., et al. (1990). A structured psychiatric intervention for cancer patients: II. Changes over time in immunological measures. *Archives of General Psychiatry, 47,* 729–735.

Fazel, S., & Danesh, J. (2002). Serious mental disorder in 23,000 prisoners: A systematic review of 62 surveys. *Lancet, 359,* 545–550.

Feder, A., Olfson, M., Fuentes, M., Shea, S., Lantigua, R. A., & Weissman, M. M. (2001). Medically unexplained symptoms in an urban general medicine practice. *Psychosomatics, 42,* 261–268.

Feigon, S. A., Waldman, I. D., Levy, F., & Hay, D. A. (2001). Genetic and environmental influences on separation anxiety disorder symptoms and their moderation by age and sex. *Behavior Genetics, 31,* 403–411.

Feingold, A. (1994). Gender differences in personality: A meta-analysis. *Psychological Bulletin, 116,* 429–456.

Feldman, M. A. (Ed.). (2004). *Early intervention: The essential readings.* Malden, MA: Blackwell.

Feldman, R. P., and Goodrich, J. T. (2001). Psychosurgery: A historical overview. *Neurosurgery, 48,* 647–659.

Fennell, M. J. V., & Teasdale, J. D. (1987). Cognitive therapy for depression: Individual differences and the process of change. *Cognitive Therapy & Research, 11,* 253–271.

Fenton, W. S., & McGlashan, T. H. (1994). Antecedents, symptom progression, and long-term outcome of the deficit syndrome in schizophrenia. *American Journal of Psychiatry, 151,* 351–356.

Fergusson, D. M., Horwood, J. L., & Lynskey, M. T. (1993). Early dentine lead levels and subsequent cognitive and behavioural development. *Journal of Child Psychology & Psychiatry & Allied Disciplines, 34,* 215–227.

Ferri, C. P., Prince, M., Brayne, C., Brodaty, H., Fratiglioni, L., Ganguli, M., et al. (2005). Global prevalence of dementia: A Delphi consensus study. *Lancet, 366,* 2112–2117.

Fillmore, K. M., Golding, J. M., Leino, E. V., Motoyoshi, M., Shoemaker, C., Terry, H., et al. (1997). Patterns and trends in women's and men's drinking. In R. W. Wilsnack & S. C. Wilsnack (Eds.), *Gender and alcohol: Individual and social perspectives* (pp. 21–48). Piscataway, NJ: Rutgers Center of Alcohol Studies.

Fillmore, K. M., Kerr, W. C., Stockwell, T., Chikritzhs, T., & Bostrom, A. (2006). Moderate alcohol use and reduced mortality risk: Systematic error in prospective studies. *Addiction Research and Theory, 14,* 1–132.

Fink, M. (2001). Convulsive therapy: A review of the first 55 years. *Journal of Affective Disorders, 63,* 1–15.

Fink, P., Hansen, M. S., & Oxhøj, M.-L. (2004). The prevalence of somatoform disorders among internal medical inpatients. *Journal of Psychosomatic Research, 56,* 413–418.

Finney, J. W., & Moos, R. H. (1998). Psychosocial treatments for alcohol use disorders. In P. E. Nathan (Ed.), *A guide to treatments that work* (pp. 156–166). New York: Oxford University Press.

First, M. B., Spitzer, R. L., Gibbon, M., & Williams, J. B. W. (1997). *Structured Clinical Interview for* DSM-IV *Axis I Disorders—Non-patient edition* (version 2.0). New York: New York State Psychiatric Institute, Biometrics Research Department.

Fischer, M., & Barkley, R. (2006). Young adult outcomes of children with hyperactivity: Leisure, financial, and social activities. *International Journal of Disability, Development and Education, 53,* 229–245.

Fishbain, D. A., & Goldberg, M. (1991). The misdiagnosis of conversion disorder in a psychiatric emergency service. *General Hospital Psychiatry, 13,* 177–181.

Fiske, A., Wetherell, J. L., & Gatz, M. (2009). Depression in older adults. *Annual Review of Clinical Psychology, 9,* 363–391.

Fitzgerald, P. B., Brown, T. L., Daskalakis, Z. J., de Castella, A., Kulkarni, J., Marston, N. A. U., & Oxley, T. (2004). Reduced plastic brain responses in schizophrenia: A transcranial magnetic stimulation study. *Schizophrenia Research, 71,* 17–26.

Fitzsimmons, S., & Buettner, L. L. (2002). Therapeutic recreation interventions for need-driven dementia-compromised behaviors in community-dwelling elders. *American Journal of Alzheimer's Disorder and Other Dementias, 17,* 367–381.

Flakierska-Praquin, N., Lindstrom, M., & Gilberg, C. (1997). School phobia with separation anxiety disorder: A comparative 20- to 29-year follow up study of 35 school refusers. *Comprehensive Psychology, 38,* 17–22.

Flegal, K. M., Carroll, M. D., Ogden, C. L., & Johnson, C. L. (2002). Prevalence and trends in obesity among U.S. adults, 1999–2000. *Journal of the American Medical Association, 288,* 1723–1727.

Fleming, M., & Manwell, L. B. (2000). Epidemiology. In G. Zernig (Ed.), *Handbook of alcoholism* (pp. 271–286). Boca Raton, FL: CRC Press.

Fletcher, J. M., Lyon, G. R., Fuchs, L. S., & Barnes, M. A. (2007). *Learning disabilities: From identification to intervention.* New York: Guilford Press.

Fletchner-Mors, M., Ditschuneit, H. H., Johnson, T. D., Suchard, M. A., & Adler, G. (2000). Metabolic and weight-loss effects of a long-term dietary intervention in obese patients: A four-year follow-up. *Obesity Research, 8,* 399–402.

Foa, E., & Kozak, M. (1993). Obsessive-compulsive disorder: Long-term outcome of psychological treatment. In M. Mavissakalian & R. Prien (Eds.), *Long-term treatment of anxiety disorders.* Washington, DC: American Psychiatric Press.

Foa, E. B., Dancu, C. V., Hembree, E., Jaycox, L. H., Anonymous, & Street, G. P. (1999). A comparison of exposure therapy, stress inoculation training, and their combination for reducing posttraumatic stress disorder in female assault victims. *Journal of Consulting & Clinical Psychology, 67,* 194–200.

Foa, E. B., & Franklin, E. (2001). Obsessive-compulsive disorder. In D. H. Barlow (Ed.), *Clinical handbook of psychological disorders: A step-by-step treatment manual* (3rd ed., pp. 209–263). New York: Guilford Press.

Foa, E. B., & Jaycox, L. H. (1999). Cognitive-behavioral theory and treatment of posttraumatic stress disorder. In D. Spiegel (Ed.), *Efficacy and cost-effectiveness of psychotherapy* (pp. 23–61). Washington, DC: American Psychiatric Association.

Foa, E. D., & Riggs, D. S. (1995). Posttraumatic stress disorder following assault: Theoretical considerations and empirical findings. *Current Directions in Psychological Science, 4,* 61–65.

Follette, W. C., & Hayes, S. C. (2000). Contemporary behavior therapy. In C. R. Snyder & R. E. Ingram (Eds.), *Handbook of psychological change: Psychotherapy processes and practices for the 21st century* (pp. 381–408). New York: Wiley.

Folstein, S. E., & Rosen-Sheidley, B. (2001). Genetics of autism: Complex aetiology for a heterogeneous disorder. *Nature Review Genetics, 2,* 943–955.

Fombonne, E. (1999). The epidemiology of autism: A review. *Psychological Medicine, 29,* 769–786.

Fombonne, E. (2009). Epidemiology of pervasive developmental disorders. *Pediatric Research, 65,* 591–598.

Fonagy, P., & Bateman, A. (2008). The development of borderline personality disorder: A mentalizing model. *Journal of Personality Disorders, 22,* 4–21.

Fournier, J. C., DeRubeis, R. J., Hollon, S. D., et al. (2010). Antidepressant drug effect and depression severity: A patient-level meta-analysis. *Journal of the American Medical Association, 303,* 47–53.

Fowles, D. C., Fisher, A. E., & Tranel, D. T. (1982). The heart beats to reward: The effect of monetary incentive on heart rate. *Psychophysiology, 19,* 506–513.

Francati, V., Vermetten, E., & Bremner, J. D. (2007). Functional neuroimaging studies in posttraumatic stress disorder: Review of current methods and findings. *Depression and Anxiety, 24,* 202–218.

Francis, D. D., Diorio, J., Liu, D., & Meany, M. J. (1999). Nongenomic transmission across generations in maternal behavior and stress responses in the rat. *Science 286,* 1155–1158.

Frank, E., Kupfer, D. J., Thase, M. E., Mallinger, A. G., Swartz, H. A., Fagiolini, A. M., Grochocinski, V., Houck, P., Scott, J., Thompson, W., & Monk, T. (2005). Two-year outcomes for interpersonal and social rhythm therapy in individuals with bipolar I disorder. *Archives of General Psychiatry, 62,* 996–1004.

Frank, E., Swartz, H. A., & Kupfer, D. J. (2000). Interpersonal and social rhythm therapy: Managing the chaos of bipolar disorder. *Biological Psychiatry, 48,* 593–604.

Frank, G. K., Kaye, W. H., Weltzin, T. E., Perel, J., Moss, H., McConaha, C., & Pollice, C. (2001). Altered response to meta-chlorophenylpiperazine in anorexia nervosa: Support for a persistent alteration of serotonin activity after short-term weight restoration. *International Journal of Eating Disorders, 30,* 57–68.

Frank, J. D. (1978). *Effective ingredients of successful psychotherapy.* New York: Brunner/Mazel.

Franken, I. H. A., Muris, P., & Georgieva, I. (2006). Gray's model of personality and addiction. *Addictive Behaviors, 31,* 399–403.

Franklin, K. A., Anttila, H., Axelsson, S., Gislason, T., Maasita, P., Myhre, K.I., & Rehnqvist, N. (2009). Effects and side-effects of surgery for snoring and obstructive sleep apnea—a systematic review. *Sleep, 32,* 27–36.

Franko, D. L., Wonderlich, S. A., Little, D., & Herzog, D. B. (2004). Diagnosis and classification of eating disorders. In J. K. Thompson (Ed.), *Handbook of eating disorders and obesity* (pp. 58–80). Hoboken, NJ: Wiley.

Frasure-Smith, N., & Lesperance, F. (2005). Depression and coronary heart disease: Complex synergism of mind, body, and environment. *Current Directions in Psychological Science, 14,* 39–43.

Frasure-Smith, N., & Lesperance, F. (2008). Depression and anxiety as predictors of 2-year cardiac events in patients with stable coronary artery disease. *Archives of General Psychiatry, 65,* 62–71.

Frasure-Smith, N., Lesperance, F., & Talajic, M. (1995). Depression and 18-month prognosis after myocardial infarction. *Circulation, 91,* 999–1005.

Frazier, J. A., Breeze, J. L., Papadimitriou, G., Kennedy, D. M., Hodge, S. M., Moore, C. M., Howard, J. D., Rohan, M. P., Caviness, V. S., & Makris, N. (2007). White matter abnormalities in children with and at risk for bipolar disorder. *Bipolar Disorders, 9,* 799–809.

Fredrickson, B. L., & Joiner, T. (2002). Positive emotions trigger upward spirals toward emotional well-being. *Psychological Science, 13,* 172–175.

Fredrickson, B. L., Tugade, M. M., Waugh, C. E., & Larkin, G. R. (2003). What good are positive emotions in crisis? A prospective study of resilience and emotions following the terrorist attacks on the United States on September 11th, 2001. *Journal of Personality & Social Psychology, 84,* 365–376.

Freeman, A., & Reinecke, M. A. (1995). Cognitive therapy. In A. S. Gurman (Ed.), *Essential psychotherapies: Theory and practice* (pp. 182–225). New York: Guilford Press.

Freeston, M. H., Ladouceur, R., Thibodeau, N., & Gagnon, F. (1992). Cognitive intrusions in a non-clinical population: II. Associations with depressive, anxious, and compulsive symptoms. *Behaviour Research & Therapy, 30,* 263–271.

Freud, S. (1909). *Analysis of a phobia of a five-year-old boy* (Vol. III). New York: Basic Books.

Frewen, P. A., Dozois, D. J. A., & Lanius, R. A. (2008). Neuroimaging studies of psychological interventions for mood and anxiety disorders: Empirical and methodological review. *Clinical Psychology Review, 28,* 228–246.

Freyd, J. J. (1996). *Betrayal trauma: The logic of forgetting childhood abuse.* Cambridge, MA: Harvard University Press.

Freyd, J. J., DePrince, A. P., & Gleaves, D. H. (2007). The state of betrayal trauma theory: Reply to McNally—conceptual issues and future directions. *Memory, 15,* 295–311.

Freyd, J. J., Martorella, S. R., Alvarado, J. S., Hayes, A. E., & Christman, J. C. (1998). Cognitive environments and dissociative tendencies: Performance on the standard Stroop task for high versus low dissociators. *Applied Cognitive Psychology, 12,* S91–S103.

Friedman, M., & Rosenman, R. H. (1974). *Type A behavior and your heart.* New York: Knopf.

Friedman, M., Rosenman, R. H., Straus, R., Wurm, M., & Kositcheck, R. (1968). The relationship of behavior pattern A to the state of coronary vasculature. *American Journal of Medicine, 44,* 525–537.

Friedman, M., Thoresen, C. E., Gill, J. J., Ulmer, D., Powell, L. H., Price, V., Brown, B., Thompson, L., Rabin, D. D., et al. (1994). Alteration of Type A behavior and its effect on cardiac recurrences in post myocardial infarction patients: Summary results of the recurrent coronary prevention project. In A. Steptoe (Ed.), *Psychosocial processes and health: A reader.* Cambridge, England: Cambridge University Press.

Frith, M. (2006, April 3). Beckham reveals his battle with obsessive disorder. http://www.independent.co.uk/news/uk/this-britain/beckham-reveals-his-battle-with-obsessive-disorder-472573.html (accessed October 15, 2009)

Fritz, G. K., Fritsch, S., & Hagino, O. (1997). Somatoform disorders in children and adolescents: A review of the past 10 years. *Journal of the American Academy of Child & Adolescent Psychiatry, 36,* 1329–1338.

Fromme, K., Marlatt, G. A., Baer, J. S., & Kivlahan, D. R. (1994). The Alcohol Skills Training Program: A group intervention for young adult drinkers. *Journal of Substance Abuse Treatment, 11,* 143–154.

Fromm-Reichmann, F. (1948). Notes on the development of treatments of schizophrenia by psychoanalytic psychotherapy. *Psychiatry, 2,* 263–273.

Furr, S. R., Westefeld, J. S., McConnell, G. N., & Jenkins, J. M. (2001). Suicide and depression among college students: A decade later. *Professional Psychology: Research & Practice, 32,* 97–100.

Fyer, A. J., Mannuzza, S., Chapman, T. F., Martin, L. Y., et al. (1995). Specificity in familial aggregation of phobic disorders. *Archives of General Psychiatry, 52,* 564–573.

G

Gagnon, J. H. (1990). The explicit and implicit use of the scripting perspective in sex research. *Annual Review of Sex Research, 1,* 1–43.

Gajilian, A. C. (2008). Iraq vets and post-traumatic stress: No easy answers. Retrieved from cnnhealth.com, February 26, 2009.

Gajria, M., Jitendra, A. K., Sood, S., & Sacks, G. (2007). Improving comprehension of expository text in students with LD: A research synthesis. *Journal of Learning Disabilities, 40,* 210–225.

Galea, S., Ahern, J., Resnick, H., Kilpatrick, D., Bucuvalas, M., Gold, J., & Vlahov, D. (2002). Psychological sequelae of the September 11 terrorist attacks in New York City. *New England Journal of Medicine, 346,* 982–987.

Galea, S., Brewin, C. R., Gruber, M., Jones, R. T., King, D. W., King, L. A., McNally, R. J., Ursano, R. J., Petukhova, M., & Kessler, R. C. (2007). Exposure to hurricane-related stressors and mental illness after Hurricane Katrina. *Archives of General Psychiatry, 64,* 1427–1434.

Galea, S., Tracy, M., Norris, F., & Coffey, S. F. (2008). Financial and social circumstances and the incidence and course of PTSD in Mississippi during the first two years after Hurricane Katrina. *Journal of Traumatic Stress, 21,* 357–368.

Gannon, T. A., & Ward, T. (2008). Rape: Psychopathology and theory. In D. R. Laws & W. T. O'Donohue (Eds.), *Sexual deviance: Theory, assessment, and treatment* (pp. 336–356). New York: Guilford Press.

Garber, J., & Horowitz, J. L. (2002). Depression in children. In I. H. Gotlib & C. L. Hammen (Eds.), *Handbook of depression* (pp. 510–540). New York: Guilford Press.

Garber, J., Walker, L. S., & Zeman, J. (1991). Somatization symptoms in a community sample of children and adolescents: Further validation of the Children's Somatization Inventory. *Psychological Assessment, 3,* 588–595.

Gardner, C. D., Kiazand, A., Alhassan, S., Kim, S., Stafford, R. S., Balise, R. R., et al. (2007). Comparison of the Atkins, Zone, Ornish, and LEARN diets for change in weight and related risk factors among overweight premenopausal women, the A to Z weight loss story: A randomized trial. *Journal of the American Medical Association, 297,* 969–977.

Gardner, H. (2003). Three distinct meanings of intelligence. In R. J. Sternberg & J. Lautrey (Eds.), *Models of intelligence: International perspectives* (pp. 43–54). Washington, DC: American Psychological Association.

Gardner, W., Lidz, C. W., Hoge, S. K., Monahan, J., Eisenberg, M. M., Bennett, N. S., Mulvey, E. P., & Roth, L. H. (1999). Patients' revisions of their beliefs about the need for hospitalization. *American Journal of Psychiatry, 156,* 1385–1391.

Garfield, S. L. (1994). Research on client variables in psychotherapy. In A. E. Bergin (Ed.), *Handbook of psychotherapy and behavior change* (4th ed., pp. 190–228). New York: Wiley.

Garmezy, N. (1991). Resilience and vulnerability to adverse developmental outcomes associated with poverty. *American Behavioral Scientist, 34,* 416–430.

Garner, D., Cooke, A. K., & Marano, H. E. (1997, January/February). The 1997 body image survey results. *Psychology Today,* pp. 30–44.

Garner, D. M., & Garfinkel, P. E. (1980). Sociocultural factors in the development of anorexia nervosa. *Psychological Medicine, 10,* 647–656.

Garner, D. M., & Garfinkel, P. E. (Eds.). (1985). *Handbook of psychotherapy for anorexia nervosa and bulimia.* New York: Guilford Press.

Garner, D. M., Olmstead, M. P., & Polivy, J. (1984). *The EDI.* Odessa, FL: Psychological Assessment Resources.

Garner, D. M., Rockert, W., Davis, R., & Garner, M. V. (1993). Comparison of cognitive-behavioral and supportive-expressive therapy for bulimia nervosa. *American Journal of Psychiatry, 150,* 37–46.

Gatz, M. (2007). Genetics, dementia, and the elderly. *Current Directions in Psychological Science, 16,* 123–127.

Gatz, M., Kasl-Godley, J. E., & Karel, M. J. (1996). Aging and mental disorders. In J. E. Birren (Ed.), *Handbook of the psychology of aging* (4th ed., pp. 365–382). San Diego, CA: Academic Press.

Gatz, M., Prescott, C. A., & Pedersen, N. L. (2006). Lifestyle risk and delaying factors. *Alzheimer Disease and Associated Disorders, 20,* S84–S88.

Gatz, M., Reynolds, C. A., Fratiglioni, L., Johansson, B., Mortimer, J. A., Berg, S., Fiske, A., & Pedersen, N. L. (2006). Role of genes and environments for explaining Alzheimer disease. *Archives of General Psychiatry, 63,* 168–174.

Gauntlett-Gilbert, J., & Kuipers, E. (2003). Phenomenology of visual hallucinations in psychiatric conditions. *Journal of Nervous and Mental Disease, 191,* 203–205.

Ge, X., Conger, R. D., Cadoret, R. J., & Neiderhiser, J. M. (1996). The developmental interface between nature and nurture: A mutual influence model of child antisocial behavior and parent behaviors. *Developmental Psychology, 32,* 574–589.

Geddes, J. R., Burgess, S., Hawton, K., Jamison, K., & Goodwin, G. M. (2004). Long-term lithium therapy for bipolar disorder: Systematic review and meta-analysis of randomized controlled trials. *American Journal of Psychiatry, 161,* 217–222.

Geer, J. H., & Maisel, E. (1972). Evaluating the effects of the prediction-control confound. *Journal of Personality & Social Psychology, 23,* 314–319.

Geer, J. H., Morokoff, P., & Greenwood, P. (1974). Sexual arousal in women: The development of a measurement device for vaginal blood volume. *Archives of Sexual Behavior, 3,* 559–564.

Gehi, A., Haas, D., Pipkin, S., & Whooley, M. A. (2005). Depression and medication adherence in outpatients with coronary heart disease: Findings from the Heart and Soul Study. *Archives of Internal Medicine, 165,* 2508–2513.

Gelernter, J., & Kranzler, H. R. (2008). Genetics of addiction. In M. Galanter & H. D. Kleber (Eds.). *The American Psychiatric Publishing textbook of substance abuse treatment* (4th ed., pp. 17–27). Arlington, VA: American Psychiatric Publishing.

George, M., Sackeim, H. A., Marangell, L. B., Husain, M. M., Nahas, Z., Lisanby, S. H., Ballenger, J. C., & Rush, A. J. (2000). Vagus nerve stimulation: A potential therapy for resistant depression? *Psychiatric Clinics of North America, 23,* 757–783.

George, M. S. (2007). Stimulating the brain. In F. E. Bloom (Ed.), *Best of the brain from Scientific American* (pp. 20–34). Washington, DC: Dana Press.

Gerardin, P., & Thibaut, F. (2004). Epidemiology and treatment of juvenile sexual offending. *Pediatric Drugs, 6,* 79–91.

Geronimus, A. T., Hicken, M., Keene, D., & Bound, J. (2006). "Weathering" and age patterns of allostatic load scored among Blacks and Whites in the United States. *American Journal of Public Health, 96,* 826–833.

Ghaemi, S. N., Pardo, T. B., & Hsu, D. J. (2004). Strategies for preventing the recurrence of bipolar disorder. *Journal of Clinical Psychiatry, 65*(Suppl. 10), 16–23.

Gibbons, M. B. C., Crits-Christoph, P., & Hearon, B. (2008). The empirical status of psychodynamic therapies. *Annual Review of Clinical Psychology, 5,* 93–108.

Giesen-Bloo, J., van Dyck, R., Spinhoven, P., van Tilburg, W., Dirksen, C., van Asselt, T., Kremers, I., Nadort, M., & Arntz, A. (2006). Outpatient psychotherapy for borderline personality disorder: Randomized trial of schema-focused therapy vs. transference-focused psychotherapy. *Archives of General Psychiatry, 63,* 649–658.

Gijs, L. (2008). Paraphilia and paraphilia-related disorders: An introduction. In D. L. Rowland & L. Incrocci (Eds.), *Handbook of sexual and gender identity disorders* (pp. 491–528). Hoboken, NJ: Wiley.

Giles, J. (1994, April 18). The poet of alienation. *Newsweek,* pp. 46–47.

Gillespie, N. A., Zhu, G., Heath, A. C., Hickie, I. B., & Martin, N. G. (2000). The genetic aetiology of somatic distress. *Psychological Medicine, 30,* 1051–1061.

Gilman, S. E., Cochran, S. D., Mays, V. M., Hughes, M., Ostrow, D., & Kessler, R. C. (2001). Risk of psychiatric disorders among individuals reporting same-sex sexual partners in the National Comorbidity Survey. *American Journal of Public Health, 91,* 933–939.

Gilvarry, C. M., Russell, A., Hemsley, D., & Murray, R. M. (2001). Neuropsychological performance and spectrum personality traits in the relatives of patients with schizophrenia and affective psychosis. *Psychiatry Research, 101,* 89–100.

Gitlin, M., Nuechterlein, K., Subotnik, K. L., Ventura, J., Mintz, J., Fogelson, D. L., Bartzokis, G., & Aravagiri, M. (2001). Clinical outcome following neuroleptic discontinuation in patients with remitted recent-onset schizophrenia. *American Journal of Psychiatry, 158,* 1835–1842.

Glass, G. V., & Singer, J. E. (1972). *Urban stress: Experiments on noise and social stressors.* New York: Academic Press.

Glassman, A. (1969). Indoleamines and affective disorders. *Psychosomatic Medicine, 31,* 107–114.

Glassman, A. H., O'Connor, C. M., Califf, R. M., et al. (2002). Sertraline treatment of major depression in patients with acute MI or unstable angina. *Journal of the American Medical Association, 288,* 701–709.

Glazener, C. M. A., Evans, J. H. C., & Peto, R. (2003). Tricyclic and related drugs for nocturnal enuresis in children. *Cochrane Database of Systematic Reviews, 3,* CD002117.

Glazener, C. M. A., Evans, J. H. C., & Peto, R. E. (2005). Alarm interventions for nocturnal enuresis in children. *Cochrane Database of Systematic Reviews, 2,* CD002911.

Gleaves, D. H., & Freyd, J. J. (1997, September). Questioning additional claims about the false memory syndrome epidemic. *American Psychologist,* pp. 993–994.

Gleaves, D. H., Hernandez, E., & Warner, M. S. (2003). The etiology of dissociative identity disorder: Reply to Gee, Allen, and Powell (2003). *Professional Psychology: Research & Practice, 34,* 116–118.

Gleaves, D. H., Smith, S. M., Butler, L. D., & Spiegel, D. (2004). False and recovered memories in the laboratory and clinic: A review of experimental and clinical evidence. *Clinical Psychology: Science & Practice, 11,* 3–28.

Glowinski, A. L., Bucholz, K. K., Nelson, E. C., Fu, Q., Madden, P. A. F., Reich, W., & Heath, A. C. (2001). Suicide attempts in an adolescent female twin sample. *Journal of the American Academy of Child & Adolescent Psychiatry, 40,* 1300–1307.

Goate, A., Chartier-Harlin, M.-C., Mullan, M., Brown, J., Crawford, F., Fidani, L., Giuffa, L., Haynes, A., Irving, N., James, L., et al. (1991). Segregation of a missense mutation in the amyloid precursor protein gene with familial Alzheimer's disease. *Nature, 349,* 704–706.

Godfrey, J. R., & Brownell, K. (2008). Toward optimal health: The influence of the environment on obesity. *Journal of Women's Health, 17,* 325–330.

Gold, M. S., Tabrah, H., & Frost-Pineda, K. (2001). Psychopharmacology of MDMA (ecstasy). *Psychiatric Annals, 31,* 675–681.

Goldberg, E. M., & Morrison, S. L. (1963). Schizophrenia and social class. *British Journal of Psychiatry, 109,* 785–802.

Golden, C. J., & Freshwater, S. M. (2001). Luria-Nebraska Neuropsychological Battery. In W. I. Dorfman & S. M. Freshwater (Eds.), *Understanding psychological assessment* (pp. 59–75). Dordrecht, Netherlands: Kluwer Academic.

Goldstein, A. (1994). *Addiction: From biology to drug policy.* New York: W. H. Freeman.

Goldstein, J. M., & Lewine, R. R. J. (2000). Overview of sex differences in schizophrenia: Where have we been and where do we go from here? In D. J. Castle, J. McGrath, & J. Kulkarni (Eds.), *Women and schizophrenia* (pp. 111–141). Cambridge, UK: Cambridge University Press.

Goldstein, J. M., Seidman, L. J., Buka, S. L., Horton, N. J., Donatelli, J. L., Rieder, R. O., & Tsuang, M. T. (2000). Impact of genetic vulnerability and hypoxia on overall intelligence by age 7 in offspring at high risk for schizophrenia compared with affective psychoses. *Schizophrenia Bulletin, 26,* 323–334.

Goldstein, J. M., Seidman, L. J., O'Brien, L. M., Horton, N. J., Kennedy, D. N., Makris, N., Caviness, V. S., Faraone, S. V., & Tsuang, M. T. (2002). Impact of normal sexual dimorphisms on sex differences in structural brain abnormalities in schizophrenia assessed by magnetic resonance imaging. *Archives of General Psychiatry, 59,* 154–164.

Goldstein, M. G. (1998). Bupropion sustained release and smoking cessation. *Journal of Clinical Psychology, 59*(Suppl. 4), 66–72.

Goldstein, M. J., Talovic, S. A., Nuechterlein, K. H., & Fogelson, D. L. (1992). Family interaction versus individual psychopathology: Do they indicate the same processes in the families of schizophrenia? *British Journal of Psychiatry, 161,* 97–102.

Goldstein, R. Z., & Volkow, N. D. (2002). Drug addiction and its underlying neurobiological basis: Neuroimaging evidence for the involvement of the frontal cortex. *American Journal of Psychiatry,* 159, 1642–1652.

Goodwin, F. K., & Jamison, K. R. (1990). *Manic-depressive illness.* New York: Oxford University Press.

Goodwin, F. K., & Jamison, K. R. (Eds.). (2007). *Manic depressive illness: Bipolar disorders and recurrent depression* (2nd ed.). New York: Oxford University Press.

Goodwin, P. J., Leszcz, M., Ennis, M., et al. (2001). The effect of group psychosocial support on survival in metastatic breast cancer. *New England Journal of Medicine, 345,* 1719–1726.

Goodwin, R. D., & Roy-Byrne, P. (2006). Panic and suicidal ideation and suicide attempts: Results from the National Comorbidity Survey. *Depression and Anxiety, 23,* 124–132.

Gorman, J. M. (2003). Treating generalized anxiety disorder. *Journal of Clinical Psychiatry, 64*(Suppl. 2), 24–29.

Gorman, J. M., Papp, L. A., & Coplan, J. D. (1995). Neuroanatomy and neurotransmitter function in panic disorder. In S. P. Roose & R. A. Glick (Eds.), *Anxiety as symptom and signal* (pp. 39–56). Hillsdale, NJ: Analytic Press.

Gotlib, I. H., Krasnoperova, E., Yue, D. L., & Joormann, J. (2004). Attentional biases for negative interpersonal stimuli in clinical depression. *Journal of Abnormal Psychology, 113,* 127–135.

Gotlib, I. H., Lewinsohn, P. M., & Seeley, J. R. (1995). Symptoms versus a diagnosis of depression: Differences in psychosocial functioning. *Journal of Consulting and Clinical Psychology, 63,* 90–100.

Gottesman, I. I. (1991). *Schizophrenia genesis: The origins of madness.* New York: W. H. Freeman.

Gottesman, I. I., & Reilly, J. L. (2003). Strengthening the evidence for genetic factors in schizophrenia (without abetting genetic discrimination). In M. F. Lenzenweger & J. M. Hooley (Eds.), *Principles of experimental psychopathology: Essays in honor of Brendan A. Maher* (pp. 31–44). Washington, DC: American Psychological Association.

Gould, M., Jamieson, P., & Romer, D. (2003). Media contagion and suicide among the young. *American Behavioral Scientist, 46,* 1269–1284.

Gould, M., Marrocco, F., Kleinman, M., Thomas, J. G., Mostkoff, K., Cote, J., & Davies, M. (2005). Evaluating iatrogenic risk of youth suicide screening programs: A randomized controlled trial. *Journal of the American Medical Association, 293,* 1635–1643.

Gould, M. S., Greenberg, T., Velting, D. M., & Shaffer, D. (2003). Youth suicide risk and preventive interventions: A review of the past 10 years. *Journal of the American Academy of Child & Adolescent Psychiatry, 42,* 386–405.

Grabe, S., & Hyde, J. S. (2006). Ethnicity and body dissatisfaction among women in the United States: A meta-analysis. *Psychological Bulletin, 132,* 622–640.

Grandi, S., Fabbri, S., Panatoni, N., Gonnella, E., & Marks, I. (2006). Self-exposure treatment of recurrent nightmares: Waiting-list-controlled trial and 4-year follow-up. *Psychotherapy and Psychosomatics, 75,* 384–388.

Grandin, T. (1995). *Thinking in pictures and my other reports from my life with autism.* New York: Vintage Books.

Grant, B., Stinson, F., Dawson, D., Chou, P., Dufour, M., Compton, W., Pickering, R., & Kaplan, K. (2004). Prevalence and co-occurrence of substance use disorders and independent mood and anxiety disorders: Results from the National Epidemiologic Survey on Alcohol and Related Conditions. *Archives of General Psychiatry, 61,* 807–816.

Grant, B. F., Hasin, D. S., Chou, S. P., Stinson, F. S., & Dawson, D. A. (2004). Nicotine dependence and psychiatric disorders in the United States: Results from the National Epidemiologic Survey on Alcohol and Related Conditions. *Archives of General Psychiatry, 61,* 1107–1115.

Grant, J. E. (2008). *Impulse control disorders: A clinician's guide to understanding and treating behavioral addictions.* New York: W. W. Norton.

Grant, J. E., Correia, S., Brennan-Krohn, T. (2006). White matter integrity in kleptomania: A pilot study. *Psychiatric Research Neuroimaging, 147,* 233–237.

Grant, J. E., & Kim, S. W. (2002a). Clinical characteristics and associated psychopathology of 22 patients with kleptomania. *Comprehensive Psychiatry, 43,* 378–384.

Grant, J. E., & Kim, S. W. (2002b). Effectiveness of pharmacotherapy for pathological gambling: A chart review. *Annals of Clinical Psychiatry, 14,* 155–161.

Grant, J. E., & Kim, S. W. (2007). Clinical characteristics and psychiatric comorbidity of pyromania. *Journal of Clinical Psychiatry, 68,* 1717–1722.

Grant, J. E., Kim, S. W., & Odlaug, B. L. (2009). A double-blind, placebo-controlled study of the opiate antagonist, naltrexone, in the treatment of kleptomania. *Biological Psychiatry, 65,* 600–606.

Grant, J. E., Kim, S. W., Odlaug, B. L., Buchanan, S. N., & Potenza, M. N. (2008). Late-onset pathological gambling: Clinical correlates and gender differences. *Journal of Psychiatric Research, 43,* 380–387.

Grant, J. E., Odlaug, B. L., & Wozniak, J. R. (2007). Neuropsychological functioning in kleptomania. *Behaviour Research and Therapy, 45,* 1663–1670.

Grant, J. E., & Potenza, M. N. (2006). Compulsive aspects of impulse-control disorders. *Psychiatric Clinics of North America, 29,* 539–551.

Grattan-Smith, P., Fairly, M., & Procopis, P. (1988). Clinical features of conversion disorder. *Archives of Disease in Childhood, 63,* 408–414.

Gratz, K. L., Rosenthal, M. Z., Tull, M. T., Lejuez, C. W., & Gunderson, J. G. (2006). An experimental investigation of emotion dysregulation in borderline personality disorder. *Journal of Abnormal Psychology, 115,* 850–855.

Gray, J. A. (1987). *The psychology of fear and stress* (2nd ed.). Cambridge, UK: Cambridge University Press.

Greaves, G. B. (1980). Multiple personality: 165 years after Mary Reynolds. *Journal of Nervous & Mental Disease, 168,* 577–596.

Green, R. (1986). Gender identity in childhood and later sexual orientation: Follow-up of 78 males. *Annual Progress in Child Psychiatry & Child Development,* 214–220.

Green R. (2000). Family cooccurrence of "gender dysphoria": Ten sibling or parent-child pairs. *Archives of Sexual Behavior, 29,* 499–507.

Greenberg, D. M., Bradford, J. M., Curry, S., & O'Rouche, A. (1996, May). *A controlled study of the treatment of paraphilia disorders with selective serotonin inhibitors.* Paper presented at the annual meeting of the Canadian Academy of Psychiatry and the Law, Tremblay, Quebec.

Greenberg, L. S., Elliot, R., & Lietaer, G. (1994). Research on humanistic and experiential psychotherapies. In A. Bergin & S. Garfield (Eds.), *Handbook of psychotherapy and behavior change* (4th ed., pp. 509–542). New York: Wiley.

Griffin, P. A., Steadman, H. J., & Petrila, J. (2002). The use of criminal charges and sanctions in mental health courts. *Psychiatric Services, 53,* 1285–1289.

Grilo, C. M., Masheb, R., & Wilson, G. T. (2005). Efficacy of cognitive behavioral therapy and fluoxetine for the treatment of binge eating disorder: A randomized double-blind placebo-controlled comparison. *Biological Psychiatry, 57,* 301–309.

Grilo, C. M., Sanislow, C. A., & McGlashan, T. H. (2002). Co-occurrence of *DSM-IV* personality disorders with borderline personality disorder. *Journal of Nervous & Mental Disease, 190,* 552–554.

Grisso, T., & Appelbaum, P. S. (1995). The MacArthur Treatment Competence Study: III. Abilities of patients to consent to psychiatric and medical treatments. *Law & Human Behavior, 19,* 149–174.

Grob, G. N. (1994). *The mad among us: A history of the care of America's mentally ill.* Cambridge, MA: Harvard University Press.

Groesz, L. M., Levine, M. P., & Murnen, S. K. (2002). The effect of experimental presentation of thin media images on body satisfaction: A meta-analytic review. *International Journal of Eating Disorders, 31,* 1–16.

Gross, R. T., Brooks-Gunn, J., & Spiker, D. (1992). Efficacy of educational interventions for low birth weight infants: The Infant Health and Development Program. In S. L. Friedman & M. D. Sigman (Eds.), *The psychological development of low birth weight children: Advances in applied developmental psychology.* Norwood, NJ: Ablex.

Gross-Isseroff, R., Biegon, A., Voet, H., & Weizman, A. (1998). The suicide brain: A review of postmortem receptor/transporter binding studies. *Neuroscience & Biobehavioral Reviews, 22,* 653–661.

Grossman, H. (2008). The amnestic syndrome. In S. H. Fatemi & P. J. Clayton (Eds). *The medical basis of psychiatry* (3rd ed., pp. 39–45). Totowa, NJ: Humana Press.

Groth-Marnat, G. (2003). *Handbook of psychological assessment,* 4th ed. New York: Wiley.

Gruber, A. J., & Pope, H. G. (1998). Ephedrine abuse among 36 female weightlifters. *American Journal of Addiction, 7,* 256–261.

Guarnaccia, P. J., Guevara-Ramos, L. M., Gonzales, G., Canino, G. J., & Bird, H. (1992). Cross-cultural aspects of psychiatric symptoms in Puerto Rico. *Community & Mental Health, 7,* 99–110.

Guarnaccia, P. J., Rivera, M., Franco, F., Neighbors, C., & Allende-Ramos, C. (1996). The experiences of *ataques de nervios:* Toward an anthropology of emotions in Puerto Rico. *Culture, Medicine, & Psychiatry, 15,* 139–165.

Gumley, A., O'Grady, M., McNay, L., Reilly, J., Power, K., & Norrie, J. (2003). Early intervention for relapse in schizophrenia: Results of a 12-month randomized controlled trial of cognitive behavioural therapy. *Psychological Medicine, 33,* 419–431.

Gunderson, J. G. (2001). *Borderline personality disorder: A clinical guide.* Washington, DC: American Psychiatric Publishing.

Gunderson, J. G., Zanarini, M. C., & Kisiel, C. L. (1995). Borderline personality disorder. In W. J. Livesley (Ed.), *The* DSM-IV *personality disorders* (pp. 141–157). New York: Guilford Press.

Gur, R. E., Calkins, M. E., Gur, R. C., Horan, W. P., Nuechterlein, K. H., Seidman, L. J., & Stone, W. S. (2007). The Consortium on the Genetics of Schizophrenia: Neurocognitive endophenotypes. *Schizophrenia Bulletin, 33,* 49–68.

Gusella, J. F., MacDonald, M. E., Ambrose, C. M., & Duyao, M. P. (1993). Molecular genetics of Huntington's disease. *Archives of Neurology, 50,* 1157–1163.

Gustafsson, P. E., Larsson I., Nelson, N., & Gustafsson, P. A. (2009). Sociocultural disadvantage, traumatic life events, and psychiatric symptoms in preadolescent children. *American Journal of Orthopsychiatry, 79,* 387–397.

H

Haas, A. P., Hendin, H., & Mann, J. J. (2003). Suicide in college students. *American Behavioral Scientist, 46,* 1224–1240.

Hackett, G. I. (2008). Disorders of male sexual desire. In D. L. Rowland & L. Incrocci (Eds.), *Handbook of sexual and gender identity disorders* (pp. 5–31). Hoboken, NJ: Wiley.

Hafner, H., & van der Heiden, W. (2008). Course and outcome. In K. T. Mueser & D. V. Jeste (Eds.), *Clinical handbook of schizophrenia* (pp. 100–113). New York: Guilford Press.

Hajjar, I., Kotchen, J. M., & Kotchen, T. A. (2006). Hypertension: Trends in prevalence, incidence, and control. *Annual Review of Public Health, 27,* 465–490.

Halkitis, P. N., Green, K. A., & Mourgues, P. (2005). Longitudinal investigation of methamphetamine use among gay and bisexual men in New York City: Findings from project BUMPS. *Journal of Urban Health, 82,* 1099–3460.

Hall, G. C. N. (2001). Psychotherapy research with ethnic minorities: Empirical, ethical, and conceptual issues. *Journal of Consulting & Clinical Psychology, 69,* 502–510.

Hallaraker, E., Arefjord, K., Havik, O. E., & Maeland, J. G. (2001). Social support and emotional adjustment during and after a severe life event: A study of wives of myocardial infarction patients. *Psychology & Health, 16,* 343–355.

Halmi, K. A., Agras, W. S., Crow, S., Mitchell, J., Wilson, G. T., Bryson, S. W., & Kraemer, H. C. (2005). Predictors of treatment acceptance and completion in anorexia nervosa: Implications for future study designs. *Archives of General Psychiatry, 62*, 776–781.

Hammen, C. (2003). Social stress and women's risk for recurrent depression. *Archives of Women's Mental Health, 6*, 9–13.

Hammen, C. (2005). Stress and depression. *Annual Review of Clinical Psychology, 1*, 293–320.

Hanson, R. F., Borntrager, C., Self-Brown, S., et al. (2008). Relations among gender, violence exposure, and mental health: The National Survey of Adolescents. *American Journal of Orthopsychiatry, 78*, 313–321.

Hare, R. D., & Hart, S. D. (1993). Psychopathy, mental disorder, and crime. In S. Hodgins (Ed.), *Mental disorder and crime* (pp. 104–115). Thousand Oaks, CA: Sage.

Hare, R. D., & Neumann, C. S. (2008). Psychopathy as a clinical and empirical construct. *Annual Review of Clinical Psychology, 4*, 217–246.

Harrell, J. P. (1980). Psychological factors and hypertension: A status report. *Psychological Bulletin, 87*, 482–501.

Harris, M. J., Milich, R., Corbitt, E. M., & Hoover, D. W. (1992). Self-fulfilling effects of stigmatizing information on children's social interactions. *Journal of Personality & Social Psychology, 63*, 41–50.

Hart, S. D., & Hare, R. D. (1997). Psychopathy: Assessment and association with criminal conduct. In D. M. Stoff, J. Breiling, & J. D. Maser (Eds.), *Handbook of antisocial personality disorder* (pp. 22–35). New York: Wiley.

Harter, S. (1983). Developmental perspectives on the self-system. In P. H. Mussen (Ed.), *Handbook of child development* (pp. 275–385). New York: Wiley.

Hartman, D. E. (1998). Behavioral pharmacology of inhalants. In R. E. Tarter (Ed.), *Handbook of substance abuse: Neurobehavioral pharmacology* (pp. 263–268). New York: Plenum Press.

Hartung, C. M., & Widiger, T. A. (1998). Gender differences in the diagnosis of mental disorders: Conclusions and controversies of the *DSM-IV*. *Psychological Bulletin, 123*, 260–278.

Harvey, A., Watkins, E., Mansell, W., & Shafran, R. (2004). *Cognitive behavioural processes across psychological disorders: A transdiagnostic approach to research and treatment.* Oxford: Oxford University Press.

Harvey, A. G. (2005). A cognitive theory and therapy for chronic insomnia. *Journal of Cognitive Psychotherapy, 19*, 41–59.

Harvey, A. G. (2008). Insomnia, psychiatric disorders, and the transdiagnostic perspective. *Current Directions in Psychological Science, 17*, 299–303.

Harvey, A. G., McGlinchey, E., & Gruber, J. (2010). Toward an affective science of insomnia treatments. In A. M. Kring & D. M. Sloan (Eds.), *Emotion regulation and psychopathology: A transdiagnostic approach to etiology and treatment* (pp. 427–446). New York: Guilford Press.

Harwood, D. M. J., Hawton, K., Hope, T., & Jacoby, R. (2000). Suicide in older people: Mode of death, demographic factors, and medical contact before death. *International Journal of Geriatric Psychiatry, 15*, 736–743.

Hasin, D., Hatzenbuehler, M., & Waxman, R. (2006). Genetics of substance use disorders. In W. R. Miller & K. M. Carroll (Eds.), *Rethinking substance abuse: What the science shows and what we should do about it* (pp. 61–77). New York: Guilford Press.

Hasin, D. S., & Beseler, C. L. (2009). Dimensionality of lifetime alcohol abuse, dependence and binge drinking. *Drug and Alcohol Dependence, 101*, 53–61.

Hasin, D. S., Stinson, F. S., Ogburn, E., & Grant, B. F. (2007). Prevalence, correlates, disability and comorbidity of *DSM-IV* alcohol abuse and dependence in the United States: Results from the National Epidemiologic Survey on alcohol and related conditions. *Archives of General Psychiatry, 64*, 830–842.

Hatzenbuehler, M. L. (2009). How does sexual minority stigma "get under the skin"? A psychological mediation framework. *Pyschological Bulletin, 135*, 707–730.

Hatzenbuehler, M. L., Keyes, K. M., & Hasin, D. S. (2009). State-level policies and psychiatric morbidity in LGB populations. *American Journal of Public Health, 99*, 2275–2281.

Hatzenbuehler, M. L., McLaughlin, K. A., Keyes, K. M., & Hasin, D. S. (2010). The impact of institutional discrimination on psychopathology in LGB populations: A prospective study. *American Journal of Public Health, 100*, 452–459.

Hatzenbuehler, M. L., Nolen-Hoeksema, S., & Erickson, S. J. (2008). Minority stress predictors of HIV risk behavior, substance use, and depressive symptoms: Results from a prospective study of bereaved gay men. *Health Psychology, 27*, 455–462.

Hayes, S. C., Luoma, J. B., Bond. F. W., Masuda, A., & Lillis, J. (2006). Acceptance and commitment therapy: model, processes, and outcomes. *Behaviour Research and Therapy, 44*, 1–25.

Haynes, S. G., Feinleib, M., & Kannel, W. B. (1980). The relationship of psychosocial factors to coronary heart disease in the Framingham study: III. Eight-year incidence of coronary heart disease. *American Journal of Epidemiology, 111*, 37–58.

Hayward, C., Killen, J. D., Kraemer, H. C., & Taylor, C. B. (1998). Linking self-reported childhood behavioral inhibition to adolescent social phobia. *Journal of the American Academy of Child & Adolescent Psychiatry, 37*, 1308–1316.

Hayward, C., Killen, J. D., Kraemer, H. C., & Taylor, C. B. (2000). Predictors of panic attacks in adolescents. *Journal of the American Academy of Child & Adolescent Psychiatry, 39*, 207–214.

Hebert, L. E., Scherr, P. A., Bienias, J. L., Bennet, D. A., & Evans, D. A. (2003). Alzheimer disease in the US population: Prevalence estimates using the 2000 census. *Archives of Neurology, 60*, 1119–1122.

Hedley, A. A., Ogden, C. L., Johnson, C. L., Carroll, M. D., Curtin, L. R., & Flegal, K. M. (2004). Prevalence of overweight and obesity among U.S. children, adolescents, and adults, 1999–2002. *Journal of the American Medical Association, 291*, 2847–2850.

Heim, C., & Nemeroff, C. B. (2001). The role of childhood trauma in the neurobiology of mood and anxiety disorders: Preclinical and clinical studies. *Biological Psychiatry, 49*, 1023–1039.

Heim, C., Meinlschmidt, G., & Nemeroff, C. B. (2003). Neurobiology of early-life stress. *Psychiatric Annals, 33*, 18–26.

Heim, C., Plotsky, P. M., & Nemeroff, C. B. (2004). Importance of studying the contributions of early adverse experience to neurobiological findings in depression. *Neuropsychopharmacology, 29*, 641–648.

Heiman, J. R. (2000). Orgasmic disorders in women. In S. R. Leiblum & R. C. Rosen (Eds.), *Principles and practice of sex therapy* (3rd ed., pp. 118–153) New York: Guilford Press.

Heimberg, R. G. (2001). Current status of psychotherapeutic interventions for social phobia. *Journal of Clinical Psychiatry, 62*(Suppl. 1), 36–42.

Heimberg, R. G., Liebowitz, M., Hope, D. A., Schneier, F. R., Holt, C. S., Welkowitz, L. A., Juster, H. R., Campeas, R., Bruck, M. A., Cloitre, M., Fallon, B., & Klein, D. F. (1998). Cognitive behavioral group therapy vs. phenelzine therapy for social phobia: 12-week outcome. *Archives of General Psychiatry, 55*, 1113–1141.

Heinrichs, N., & Hofman, S. G. (2001). Information processing in social phobia: A critical review. *Clinical Psychology Review, 21*, 751–770.

Heiser, N. A., Turner, S. M., & Beidel, D. C. (2003). Shyness: Relationship to social phobia and other psychiatric disorders. *Behaviour Research & Therapy, 41*, 209–221.

Helgeland, M. I., & Torgersen, S. (2004). Developmental antecedents of borderline personality disorder. *Comprehensive Psychiatry, 45*, 138–147.

Helzer, J. E., Burnam, A., & McEvoy, L. T. (1991). Alcohol abuse and dependence. In L. Robins & D. Reiger (Eds.), *Psychiatric disorders in America: The Epidemiologic Catchment Area Study* (pp. 9–38). New York: Free Press.

Helzer, J. E., Kraemer, H. C., Krueger, R. F., Wittchen, H.-U., Sirovatka, P. J., & Regier, D. A. (2008). *Dimensional approaches in diagnostic classification: Refining the research agenda for* DSM-V. Arlington, VA: American Psychiatric Association.

Henry, B., & Moffitt, T. E. (1997). Neuropsychological and neuroimaging studies of juvenile delinquency and adult criminal behavior. In D. M. Stoff, J. Breiling, & J. D. Maser (Eds.), *Handbook of antisocial personality disorder* (pp. 280–288). New York: Wiley.

Henry, M. E., Schmidt, M. E., Matochik, J. A., Stoddard, E. P., & Potter, W. Z. (2001). The effects of ECT on brain glucose: A pilot FDG PET study. *Journal of ECT, 17*, 33–40.

Herman, J. L., & Harvey, M. R. (1997). Adult memories of childhood trauma: A naturalistic clinical study. *Journal of Traumatic Stress, 10*, 557–571.

Heron, M., Hoyert, D. L., Murphy, S. L., Xu, J., Kochanek, K. D., & Tejada-Vera, B. (2009).

Deaths: Final data for 2006. National Vital Statistics Reports (Vol. 57, No. 14).

Herpertz-Dahlmann, B., Muller, B., Herpertz, S., & Heussen, N. (2001). Prospective 10-year follow-up in adolescent anorexia nervosa—Course, outcome, psychiatric comorbidity, and psychosocial adaptation. *Journal of Child Psychology & Psychiatry, 42,* 603–612.

Hettema, J. M., Neale, M. C., & Kendler, K. S. (2001). A review and meta-analysis of the genetic epidemiology of anxiety disorders. *American Journal of Psychiatry, 158,* 1568–1578.

Hewlett, W. A. (2000). Benzodiazepines in the treatment of obsessive-compulsive disorder. In W. K. Goodman (Ed.), *Obsessive-compulsive disorder: Contemporary issues in treatment* (pp. 405–429). Mahwah, NJ: Erlbaum.

Hilgard, E. R. (1977/1986). *Divided consciousness: Multiple controls in human thought and action.* New York: Wiley.

Hilgard, E. R. (1992). Divided consciousness and dissociation. *Consciousness & Cognition: An International Journal, 1,* 16–31.

Hill, A. J., & Franklin, J. A. (1998). Mothers, daughters, and dieting: Investigating the transmission of weight control. *British Journal of Clinical Psychology, 37,* 3–13.

Hines, M., Ahmed, S. F., & Hughes, I. A. (2003). Psychological outcomes and gender-related development in complete androgen insensitivity syndrome. *Archives of Sexual Behavior, 32,* 93–101.

Hinshelwood, J. A. (1896). A case of dyslexia: A peculiar form of word-blindness. *Lancet, 2,* 1451–1454.

Hintsanen, M., Kivimaki, M., Elovainio, M., Pulkki-Raback, L., Keskivaara, P., Juonala, M., Raitakari, O. Y., & Keltikangas-Jarvinen, L. (2005). Job strain and early atherosclerosis: The Cardiovascular Risk in Young Finns Study. *Psychosomatic Medicine, 67,* 740–747.

Hite, S. (1976). *The Hite report: A nationwide study on female sexuality.* New York: Macmillan.

Hlastala, S. A., Frank, E., Kowalski, J., Sherrill, J. T., & Tu, X. M. (2000). Stressful life events, bipolar disorder, and the "kindling model." *Journal of Abnormal Psychology, 109,* 777–787.

Hodgins, S., & Cote, G. (1990). Prevalence of mental disorders among penitentiary inmates in Quebec. *Canadian Journal of Mental Health, 39,* 1–4.

Hoek, H. W., van Harten, P. N., Hermans, K. M. E., Katzman, M. A., Matroos, G. E., & Susser, E. S. (2005). The incidence of anorexia nervosa on Curaçao. *American Journal of Psychiatry, 162,* 748–752.

Hoek, H. W., & van Hoeken, D. (2003). Review of the prevalence and incidence of eating disorders. *International Journal of Eating Disorders, 34,* 383–396.

Hoffman, A. (1968). Psychotomimetic agents. In A. Burger (Ed.), *Drugs affecting the central nervous system* (Vol. 2). New York: Marcel Dekker.

Hofmann, S. G. (2004). Cognitive mediation of treatment change in social phobia. *Journal of Consulting & Clinical Psychology, 72,* 393–399.

Hogarty, G. E., Anderson, C. M., Reiss, D. J., Kornblith, S. J., Greenwald, D. P., Jaund, C. D., & Madonia, M. J. (1986). Family psychoeducation, social skills training, and maintenance chemotherapy in the aftercare treatment of schizophrenia: I. One-year effects of a controlled study on relapse and expressed emotion. *Archives of General Psychiatry, 43,* 633–642.

Hogarty, G. E., Anderson, C. M., Reiss, D. J., Kornblith, S. J., Greenwald, D. P., Ulrich, R. F., & Carter, M. (1991). Family psychoeducation, social skills training, and maintenance chemotherapy in the aftercare treatment of schizophrenia: II. Two-year effects of a controlled study on relapse and adjustment. *Archives of General Psychiatry, 48,* 340–347.

Hogarty, G. E., Greenwald, D., Ulrich, R. F., Kornblith, S. J., DiBarry, A. L., Cooley, S., Carter, M., & Flesher, S. (1997). Three-year trials of personal therapy among schizophrenic patients living with or independent of family: II. Effects of adjustment of patients. *American Journal of Psychiatry, 154,* 1514–1524.

Hogarty, G. E., Kornblith, S. J., Greenwald, D., DiBarry, A. L., Cooley, S., Ulrich, R. F., Carter, M., & Flesher, S. (1997). Three-year trials of personal therapy among schizophrenic patients living with or independent of family: I. Description of study and effects on relapse rates. *American Journal of Psychiatry, 154,* 1504–1513.

Hoge, C. W., Auchterlonie, J. L., Milliken, C. S. (2006). Mental health problems, use of mental health services, and attrition from military service after returning from deployment to Iraq or Afghanistan. *Journal of the American Medical Association, 295,* 1023–1032.

Hoge, C. W., Castro, C. A., Messer, S. C., McGurk, D., Cotting, D. I., & Koffman, R. L. (2004). Combat duty in Iraq and Afghanistan, mental health problems, and barriers to care. *New England Journal of Medicine, 351,* 13–22.

Hoge, S. K., Bonnie, R. J., Poythress, N., Monahan, J., Eisenberg, M., & Feucht-Haviar, T. (1997). The MacArthur Adjudicative Competence Study: Development and validation of a research instrument. *Law & Human Behavior, 21,* 141–179.

Hoge, S. K., Poythress, N., Bonnie, R. J., Monahan, J., Eisenberg, M., & Feucht-Haviar, T. (1997). The MacArthur Adjudicative Competence Study: Diagnosis, psychopathology, and competence-related abilities. *Behavioral Sciences & the Law, 15,* 329–345.

Holden, C. (1980). Identical twins reared apart. *Science, 207,* 1323–1328.

Hollander, E., Allen, A., Lopez, R. P., Bienstock, C. A., Grossman, R., Siever, L. J., Merkatz, L., & Stein, D. J. (2001). A preliminary double-blind, placebo-controlled trial of divalproex sodium in borderline personality disorder. *Journal of Clinical Psychiatry, 62,* 199–203.

Hollon, S. D., DeRubeis, R. J., Shelton, R. C., Amsterdam, J. D., Salomon, R. M., O'Reardon, J. P., et al. (2005). Prevention or relapse following cognitive therapy versus medications in moderate to severe depression. *Archives of General Psychiatry, 62,* 417–422.

Hollon, S. D., & Dimidjian, S. (2008). Cognitive and behavioral treatment of depression. In I. H. Gotlib & C. Hammen (Eds.), *Handbook of depression* (pp. 586–603). New York: Guilford Press.

Hollon, S. D., Haman, K. L., & Brown, L. L. (2002). Cognitive-behavioral treatment of depression. In I. H. Gotlib & C. L. Hammen (Eds.), *Handbook of depression* (pp. 383–403). New York: Guilford Press.

Holmans, P., Weissman, M. M., Zubenko, G. S., et al. (2007). Genetics of recurrent early-onset major depression (GenRED): Final genome scan report. *American Journal of Psychiatry, 164,* 248–258.

Holm-Denoma, J. M., Scaringi, V., Gordon, K. H., van Orden, K. A., & Joiner, T. E., Jr. (2009). Eating disorder symptoms among undergraduate varsity athletes, club athletes, independent exercisers, and nonexercisers. *International Journal of Eating Disorders, 42,* 47–53.

Hooley, J. M. (2007). Expressed emotion and relapse of psychopathology. *Annual Review of Clinical Psychology, 3,* 329–352.

Hooley, J. M., & Campbell, C. (2002). Control and controllability: Beliefs and behaviour in high and low expressed emotion relatives. *Psychological Medicine, 32,* 1091–1099.

Horesh, N., Ratner, S., Laor, N., & Toren, P. (2008). A comparison of life events in adolescents with major depression, borderline personality disorder and matched controls: A pilot study. *Psychopathology, 41,* 300–306.

Hornbacher, M. (1998). *Wasted.* New York: HarperPerennial.

Hornbacher, M. (2008). *Madness: A bipolar life.* New York: Houghton Miflin.

Hornstein, N. L., & Putnam, F. W. (1992). Clinical phenomenology of child and adolescent dissociative disorders. *Journal of the American Academy of Child & Adolescent Psychiatry, 31,* 1077–1085.

Horowitz, M. J. (1976). *Stress response syndromes.* New York: Aronson.

Hough, D. W. (2001). Low-dose olanzapine for self-mutilation behavior in patients with borderline personality disorder. *Journal of Clinical Psychiatry, 62,* 296–297.

Hough, R. L., Canino, G. J., Abueg, F. R., & Gusman, F. D. (1996). PTSD and related stress disorders among Hispanics. In A. J. Marsella, M. J. Friedman, E. T. Gerrity, & R. M. Scurfield (Eds.), *Ethnocultural aspects of post-traumatic stress disorder* (pp. 483–504). Washington, DC: American Psychological Association.

Houts, A. C. (2003). Behavioral treatment for enuresis. In A. E. Kazdin & J. R. Weisz (Eds.), *Evidence-based psychotherapies for children and adolescents* (pp. 389–406). New York: Guilford Press.

Howell, P. (2007). Signs of developmental stuttering up to age eight and at 12 plus. *Clinical Psychology Review, 27,* 287–306.

Howland, L. C., Gortmaker, S. L., Mofenson, L. M., Spino, C., Gardner, J. D., Gorski, H., Fowler, M. G., & Oleske, J. (2000). Effects of negative life events on immune suppression in children and youth infected with human immunodeficiency virus type 1. *Pediatrics, 106,* 540–546.

Howlin, P., Goode, S., Hutton, J., & Rutter, M. (2004). Adult outcome for children with autism. *Journal of Child Psychology & Psychiatry, 45,* 212–229.

Hoza, B., Mrug, S., Verdes, A. C., Hinshaw, S. P., Bukowski, W. M., Gold, J. A., Kraemer, H. C., Pelma, W. E., Jr., Wigal, T., & Arnold, L. E. (2005). What aspects of peer relationships are impaired in children with attention-deficit/hyperactivity disorder? *Journal of Consulting and Clinical Psychology, 73,* 411–423.

Hubbard, K., O'Neill, A.-M., Cheakalos, C., Baker, K., Berenstein, L., Breu, G., Duffy, T., Fowler, J., Greissinger, L. K., Matsumoto, N., Smith, P., Weinstein, F., & York, M. (1999, April 12). Out of control. *People,* pp. 52–69.

Hublin, C., Kaprio, J., Partinen, M., Heikkilä, K., & Koskenvuo, M. (1997). Prevalence and genetics of sleepwalking: A population-based twin study. *Neurology, 48,* 177–181.

Hucker, S. J. (2008). Sexual masochism: Psychopathology and theory. In D. R. Laws & W. T. O'Donohue (Eds.), *Sexual deviance: Theory, assessment, and treatment* (pp. 250–264). New York: Guilford Press.

Hudson, J. I., Hiripi, E., Pope, H. G., & Kessler, R. C. (2007). The prevalence and correlates of eating disorders in the National Comorbidity Survey Replication. *Biological Psychiatry, 61,* 348–358.

Hudziak, J. J., van Beijsterveldt, C. E. M., Althoff, R. R., Stanger, C., Rettew, D. C., Nelson, E. C., Todd, R. D., Bartels, M., & Boomsma, D. I. (2004). Genetic and environmental contributions to the Child Behavior Checklist Obsessive-Compulsive Scale: A cross-cultural twin study. *Archives of General Psychiatry, 61,* 608–616.

Hugdahl, K., & Ohman, A. (1977). Effects of instruction on acquisition and extinction of electrodermal response to fear-relevant stimuli. *Journal of Experimental Psychiatry: Human Learning & Memory, 3,* 608–618.

Hughes, A. A., Hedtke, K. A., & Kendall, P. C. (2008). Family functioning in families of children with anxiety disorders. *Journal of Family Psychology, 2,* 325–328.

Hunt, W. A. (1998). Pharmacology of alcohol. In R. E. Tarter, R. T. Ammerman, & P. J. Ott (Eds.), *Handbook of substance abuse: Neurobehavioral pharmacology* (pp. 7–21). New York: Plenum Press.

Huppert, J. D., Bufka, L. F., Barlow, D. H., Gorman, J. M., Shea, K. M., & Woods, S. W. (2001). Therapists, therapist variables, and cognitive-behavioral therapy outcome in a multicenter trial for panic disorder. *Journal of Consulting & Clinical Psychology, 69,* 747–755.

Huppert, J. D., Strunk, D. R., Ledley, D. R., Davidson, J. R. T., & Foa, E. B. (2008). Generalized social anxiety disorder and avoidant personality disorder: Structural analysis and treatment outcome. *Depression and Anxiety, 25,* 441–448.

Hurley, R. A., Saxena, S., Rauch, S. L., Hoehn-Saric, R., & Taber, K. H. (2008). Predicting treatment response in obsessive-compulsive disorder. In R. A. Hurley & K. H. Taber (Eds.). *Windows to the brain: Insights from neuroimaging* (pp. 213–219). Arlington, VA: American Psychiatric Publishing.

Huselid, R. F., & Cooper, M. L. (1992). Gender roles as mediators of sex differences in adolescent alcohol use and abuse. *Journal of Health & Social Behavior, 33,* 348–362.

Hutchison, K. E. (2010). Realizing the promise of pharmacogenomics and personalized medicine. *Annual Review of Clinical Psychology, 6,* 577–589.

Hwu, H.-G., Chen, C.-H., Hwang, T.-J., Liu, C.-M., Cheng, J. L., Lin, S.-K., Liu, S.-K., Chen, C.-H., Chi, Y.-Y., Ou-Young, C.-W., Lin, H.-N., & Chen, W. J. (2002). Symptom patterns and subgrouping of schizophrenic patients: Significance of negative symptoms assessed on admission. *Schizophrenic Research, 56,* 105–119.

Hyman, I. E., & Billings, F. J. (1998). Individual differences and the creation of false childhood memories. *Memory, 6,* 1–20.

I

Iervolino, A. C., Perroud, N., Rullana, M. A., Guipponi, M., Cherkas, L., Collier, D. A., & Mataix-Cols, D. (2009). Prevalence and heritability of compulsive hoarding: A twin study. *American Journal of Psychiatry,* 166, 1156–1161.

Ikehara, S., Iso, H., Date, C., Kikuchi, S., Watanabe, Y., Wada, Y., Inaba, Y., Tamakoshi, A., & JACC Study Group. (2009). Association of sleep duration with mortality from cardiovascular disease and other causes for Japanese men and women: The JACC Study. *Sleep, 32,* 259–301.

Inciardi, J. A., Lockwood, D., & Pottieger, A. E. (1993). *Women and crack cocaine.* New York: Macmillan.

Incrocci, L., & Gianotten, W. L. (2008). Disease and sexuality. In D. L. Rowland & L. Incrocci (Eds.), *Handbook of sexual and gender identity disorders* (pp. 284–324). Hoboken, NJ: Wiley.

Infant Health and Development Program. (1990). Enhancing the outcome of low-birth-weight, premature infants: A multisite randomized trial. *Journal of the American Medical Association, 263,* 3035–3042.

Ingram, R. E., Hayes, A., & Scott, W. (2000). Empirically supported treatments: A critical analysis. In C. R. Snyder & R. E. Ingram (Eds.), *Handbook of psychological change: Psychotherapy processes and practices for the 21st century* (pp. 40–60). New York: Wiley.

Insel, T. R. (Ed.). (1984). *New findings in obsessive-compulsive disorder.* Washington, DC: American Psychiatric Press.

Ironside, R. N., & Batchelor, I. R. C. (1945). *Aviation neuro-psychiatry.* Baltimore: Williams & Wilkins.

Irwin, M. R., Wang, M., Ribeiro, D., Cho, H. J., Olmstead, R., Breen, E. C., Martinez-Maza, O., & Cole, S. (2008). Sleep loss activates cellular inflammatory signaling. *Biological Psychiatry, 64,* 538–540.

Iversen, A. C., Fear, N. T., Ehlers, A., Hacker Hughes, J., Hull, L., Earnshaw, M., Greenberg, N., Rona, R., Wessely, S., & Hotopf, M. (2008). Risk factors for post-traumatic stress disorder among UK Armed Forces personnel. *Psychological Medicine, 38,* 511–522.

Iwamasa, G. Y., Larrabee, A. L., & Merritt, R. D. (2000). Are personality disorder criteria ethnically biased? A card-sort analysis. *Cultural Diversity and Ethnic Minority Psychology, 6,* 284–296.

J

Jablensky, A. (2000). Epidemiology of schizophrenia: The global burden of disease and disability. *European Archives of Psychiatry & Clinical Neuroscience, 250,* 274–285.

Jack, C. R., Jr., Petersen, R. C., Grundman, M., Jin, S., Gamst, A., Ward, C. P., Sencakova, D., Doody, R. S., & Thal, L. J. (2007). Longitudinal MRI findings from the vitamin E and donepezil treatment study for MCI. *Neurobiology of Aging, 29,* 1285–1295.

Jack, D. C. (1991). *Silencing the self: Women and depression.* New York: HarperPerennial.

Jack, R. (1992). *Women and attempted suicide.* Hillsdale, NJ: Erlbaum.

Jacobi, F., Wittchen, H.-U., Hölting, C., Höfler, M., Pfister, H., Muller, N., et al. (2004). Prevalence, co-morbidity and correlates of mental disorders in the general population: Results from the German Health Interview and Examination Survey (GHS). *Psychological Medicine, 34,* 597–611.

Jacobson, C. M., & Gould, M. (2009). Suicide and nonsuicidal self-injurious behaviors among youth: Risk and protective factors. In S. Nolen-Hoeksema & L. Hilt (Eds.), *Handbook of depression in adolescents* (pp. 207–236). New York: Routledge.

Jacobson, E. (1964). *The self and the object world.* New York: International Universities Press.

Jacobson, S. W., & Jacobson, J. L. (2000). Teratogenic insult and neurobehavioral function in infancy and childhood. In C. A. Nelson (Ed.), *The Minnesota symposia on child psychology, Vol. 31: The effects of early adversity on neurobehavioral development* (pp. 61–112). Mahwah, NJ: Erlbaum.

James, W. (1890). *The principles of psychology.* New York: Henry Holt.

Jamison, K. R. (1993). *Touched with fire: Manic-depressive illness and the artistic temperament.* New York: Free Press.

Jamison, K. R. (1995). *An unquiet mind: A memoir of moods and madness.* New York: Knopf.

Jang, K. L., McCrae, R. R., Angleitner, A., Riemann, R., & Livesley, W. J. (1998). Heritability of facet-level traits in a cross-cultural twin sample: Support for a hierarchical model of personality. *Journal of Personality & Social Psychology, 74,* 1556–1565.

Jang, K. L., Paris, J., Zweig-Frank, H., & Livesley, W. J. (1998). Twin study of dissociative experience. *Journal of Nervous & Mental Disease, 186,* 345–351.

Jefferson, J. W. (2001). Benzodiazepines and anticonvulsants for social phobia (social anxiety disorder). *Journal of Clinical Psychiatry, 62*(Suppl. 1), 50–53.

Jemmott, L. S., Jemmott, J. B., III, & O'Leary, A. (2007). A randomized controlled trial of brief HIV/STD prevention interventions for African American women in primary care settings: Effects on sexual risk behavior and STD incidence. *American Journal of Public Health, 97,* 1034–1040.

Jenkins, J. H., & Karno, M. (1992). The meaning of expressed emotion: Theoretical issues raised by cross-cultural research. *American Journal of Psychiatry, 149,* 9–21.

Jenkins, J. H., Kleinman, A., & Good, B. J. (1991). Cross-cultural studies of depression. In J. Becker (Ed.), *Psychosocial aspects of depression* (pp. 67–99). Hillsdale, NJ: Erlbaum.

Jenkins, R. L. (1973). *Behavior disorders of childhood and adolescence.* Springfield, IL: Charles C Thomas.

Jensen, P. S., Arnold, E., Swanson, J. M., Vitiello, B., Abikoff, H. B., Greenhill, L. L., Hechtman, L., Hinshaw, S. P., Pelma, W. E., Wells, K. C., Conners, C. K., Elliott, G. R., Epstein, J. N., Hoza, B., March, J. S., Molina, B. S. G., Newcorn, J. H., Severe, J. B., Wigal, T., Gibbons, R. D., & Hur, K. (2007). Three-year follow-up of the NIMH MTA study. *Journal of the American Academy of Child and Adolescent Psychiatry, 46,* 989–1002.

Jensen, P. S., Buitelaar, J., Pandina G. J., Binder, C., & Haas, M. (2007). Management of psychiatric disorders in children and adolescents with atypical antipsychotics: A systematic review of published clinical trials. *European Journal of Child and Adolescent Psychiatry, 16,* 104–120.

Jensen, P. S., Hinshaw, S. P., Swanson, J. M., Greenhill, L. L., Conners, C. K., Arnold, L. E., Abikoff, H. B., Elliott, G., Hechtman, L., Hoza, B., March, J. S., Newcorn, J. H., Severe, J. B., Vitiello, B., Wells, K., & Wigal, T. (2001). Findings from the NIMH Multimodal Treatment Study of ADHD (MTA): Implications and applications for primary care providers. *Journal of Developmental & Behavioral Pediatrics, 22,* 60–73.

Jesner, O. S., Aref-Adib, M., & Coren, E. (2007). Risperidone for autism spectrum disorder. *Cochrane Database of Systematic Reviews,* Issue 1.

Joe, S., & Kaplan, M. S. (2001). Suicide among African American men. *Suicide & Life-Threatening Behavior, 31*(Suppl.), 106–121.

Johns, L. C., Cannon, M., Singleton, N., Murray, R. M., Farrell, M., Brugha, T., et al. (2004). Prevalence and correlates of self-reported psychotic symptoms in the British population. *British Journal of Psychiatry, 185,* 298–305.

Johnson, S. L., Cuellar, A. K., & Miller, C. (2009). Bipolar and unipolar depression: A comparison of clinical phenomenology, biological vulnerability, and psychosocial factors. In I. H. Gotlib & C. L. Hammen (Eds.), *Handbook of depression* (2nd ed., pp. 142–162). New York: Guilford Press.

Johnson, W., McGue, M., Krueger, R. F., & Bouchard, T. J. (2004). Marriage and personality: A genetic analysis. *Journal of Personality & Social Psychology, 86,* 285–294.

Johnston, L. D., O'Malley, P. M., Bachman, J. G., & Schulenberg, J. E. (2008). *Monitoring the Future national survey results on drug use, 1975–2007: I. Secondary school students* (NIH Publication No. D6-6418A). Bethesda, MD: National Institute on Drug Abuse.

Joiner, T. (2005). *Why people die by suicide.* Cambridge, MA: Harvard University Press.

Joiner, T. E., Jr. (1999). The clustering and contagion of suicide. *Current Directions in Psychological Science, 8,* 89–92.

Joiner, T. E., Johnson, F., & Soderstrom, K. (2002). Association between serotonin transporter gene polymorphism and family history of completed and attempted suicide. *Suicide & Life-Threatening Behavior, 32,* 329–332.

Joiner, T. E., Jr., Brown, J. S., & Wingate, L. R. (2005). The psychology and neurobiology of suicidal behavior. *Annual Review of Psychology, 56,* 287–314.

Joiner, T. E., Jr., & Timmons, K. A. (2009). Depression in its interpersonal context. In I. H. Gotlib & C. L. Hammen (Eds.), *Handbook of depression* (2nd ed., pp. 322–339). New York: Guilford Press.

Joormann, J. (2004). Attentional bias in dysphoria: The role of inhibitory processes. *Cognition and Emotion, 18,* 125–147.

Joormann, J. (2008). Cognitive aspects of depression. In I. H. Gotlib & C. Hammen (Eds.), *Handbook of depression* (pp. 298–321). New York: Guilford Press.

Joormann, J. (2009). Cognitive aspects of depression. In I. H. Gotlib & C. L. Hammen (Eds.), *Handbook of depression* (2nd ed., pp. 298–321). New York: Guilford Press.

Jordan, B. K., Schlenger, W. E., Fairbank, J. A., & Caddell, J. M. (1996). Prevalence of psychiatric disorders among incarcerated women: II. Convicted felons entering prison. *Archives of General Psychiatry, 53,* 513–519.

Jorenby, D. E., Hays, J.,T., Rigotti, N. A., Azoulay, S., Watsky, E. J., Williams, K. E., Billing, C. B., Gong, J., & Reeves, K. R. (2006). Efficacy of varenicline, an alpha 4 beta 2 nicotinic acetylcholine receptor partial agonist, vs. placebo or sustained-release bupropion for smoking cessation: A randomized controlled trial. *Journal of the American Medical Association, 296,* 56–63.

Jorm, A. F., Christensen, H., Henderson, A. S., Jacomb, P. A., Korten, A. E., & Rodgers, B. (1999). Using the BIS/BAS scales to measure behavioural inhibition and behavioural activation: Factor structure, validity and norms in a large community sample. *Personality and Individual Differences, 26,* 49–58.

Joshi, S. V. (2004). Psychostimulants, atomoxetine, and alpha-agonists. In H. Steiner (Ed.), *Handbook of mental health intervention in children and adolescents: An integrated developmental approach* (pp. 258–287). San Francisco: Jossey-Bass.

Julien, D., O'Connor, K. P., & Aardema, F. (2007). Intrusive thoughts, obsessions, and appraisals in obsessive-compulsive disorder: A critical review. *Clinical Psychology Review, 27,* 366–383.

Kafka, M. P. (2009, November 24). Hypersexual disorder: A proposed diagnosis for *DSM-V*. *Archives of Sexual Behavior.* doi:10.1007/s10508-009-9574-7

Kafka, M. P., & Hennen, J. (2003). Hypersexual desire in males: Are males with paraphilias different from males with paraphilia-related disorders? *Sexual Abuse: A Journal of Research and Treatment, 15,* 307–321.

Kagan, J., Reznick, J. S., & Snidman, M. (1987). The physiology and psychology of behavioral inhibition in children. *Child Development, 58,* 1459–1473.

Kalat, J. W. (2007). *Biological psychiatry,* 9th ed. Belmont, CA: Thomson/Wadsworth.

Kalichman, S. C., Cherry, C., Cain, D., Pope, H., & Kalichman, M. (2005). Psychosocial and behavioral correlates of seeking sex partners on the Internet among HIV-positive men. *Annals of Behavioral Medicine, 30,* 243–250.

Kalivas, P. W., & Volkow, N. D. (2005). The neural basis of addiction: A pathology of motivation and choice. *American Journal of Psychiatry, 162,* 1403–1413.

Kamen-Siegel, L., Rodin, J., Seligman, M. E., & Dwyer, J. (1991). Explanatory style and cell-mediated immunity in elderly men and women. *Health Psychology, 10,* 229–235.

Kanbayashi, T., Kodama, T., Kondo, H., Satoh, S., Inoue, U., Chiba, S., Shimizu, T., & Nishino, S. (2009). CSF histamine contents in narcolepsy, idiopathic hypersomnia and obstructive sleep apnea syndrome. *Sleep, 32,* 181–187.

Kanner, L. (1943). Autistic disturbances of affective contact. *Nervous Child, 21,* 217–250.

Kaplan, H. S. (1974). *The new sex therapy: Active treatment of sexual dysfunction.* New York: Brunner/Mazel.

Kaplan, M. (1983). The issue of sex bias in *DSM-III*: Comments on the articles by Spitzer, Williams, and Kass. *American Psychologist, 38,* 802–803.

Karasek, R. A., Russell, R. S., & Theorell, T. (1982). Physiology of stress and regeneration in job related cardiovascular illness. *Journal of Human Stress, 8,* 29–42.

Karno, M., & Golding, J. M. (1991). Obsessive compulsive disorder. In L. R. Robins & D. A. Regier (Eds.), *Psychiatric disorders in America: The Epidemiologic Catchment Area study.* New York: Maxwell Macmillan International.

Karno, M., Hough, R., Burnam, A., Escobar, J. I., Timbers, D. M., Santana, F., & Boyd, J. H. (1987). Lifetime prevalence of specific psychiatric disorders among Mexican Americans and non-Hispanic whites in Los Angeles. *Archives of General Psychiatry, 44,* 695–701.

Karno, M., & Jenkins, J. H. (1993). Cross-cultural issues in the course and treatment of schizophrenia. *Psychiatric Clinics of North America, 16,* 339–350.

Karper, L. P., & Krystal, J. H. (1997). Pharmacotherapy of violent behavior. In D. M. Stoff, J. Breiling, & J. D. Maser (Eds.), *Handbook of antisocial personality disorder* (pp. 436–444). New York: Wiley.

Kartheiser, P. H., Ursano, A. M., & Barnhill, L. J. (2007). In R. Fletcher, E. Loschen, C. Stavrakaki, & M. First (Eds.), *Diagnostic manual of intellectual disability: A textbook of diagnosis of mental disorders in persons with intellectual disability* (pp. 97–106). Kingston, NY: National Association for the Dually Diagnosed.

Kasindorf, J. (1988, May 2). *The real story of Billie Boggs: Was Koch right—or the civil libertarians? New York*, pp. 35–44.

Kaskutas, L. A. (2009). Alcoholics Anonymous effectiveness: Faith meets science. *Journal of Addictive Diseases, 28*, 145–157.

Kaslow, N., Thompson, M., Meadows, L., Chance, S., Puett, R., Hollins, L., Jessee, S., & Kellermann, A. (2000). Risk factors for suicide attempts among African American women. *Depression & Anxiety, 12*, 13–20.

Katon, W., Sullivan, M., & Walker, E. (2001). Medical symptoms without identified pathology: Relationship to psychiatric disorders, childhood and adult trauma, and personality traits. *Annals of International Medicine, 134*, 917–925.

Katon, W. J. (2003). Clinical and health services relationships between major depression, depressive symptoms, and general medical illness. *Biological Psychiatry, 54*, 216–226.

Katon, W. J. (2006). Panic disorder. *New England Journal of Medicine, 35*, 2360–2367.

Katusic, S., Barbaresi, W., Colligan, R., Weaver, A., & Jacobsen, S. (2005). *Written language learning disorder: Incidence in a population-based birth cohort, 1976–1982, Rochester, Minnesota.* Rochester, MN: Mayo Clinic.

Katusic, S., Colligan, R., Barbaresi, W., Schaid, D., & Jacobsen, S. (2001). Incidence of reading disability in a population-based birth cohort, 1976–1982, Rochester, Minn. *Mayo Clinical Proceedings, 76*, 1081–1091.

Katz, R., & Wykes, T. (1985). The psychological difference between temporally predictable and unpredictable stressful events: Evidence for information control theories. *Journal of Personality & Social Psychology, 48*, 781–790.

Katzman, R. (1993). Education and the prevalence of dementia and Alzheimer's disease. *Neurology, 43*, 13–20.

Kaufman, J. (2008). Genetic and environmental modifiers of risk and resiliency in maltreated children. In J. J. Hudziak (Ed.). (2008). *Developmental psychopathology and wellness: Genetic and environmental influences* (pp. 141–160). Arlington, VA: American Psychiatric Publishing.

Kaufman, J., Yang, B. Z., Douglas-Palumberi, H., Grasso, D., Lipschitz, D., et al. (2006). Brain-derived neurotrophic factor-5-HTTLPR gene interactions and environmental modifiers of depression in children. *Biological Psychiatry, 59*, 673–680.

Kaufman, J., Yang, B.Z., Douglas-Palumberi, H., Houshyar, S., Lipschitz, D., et al. (2004). Social supports and serotonin transporter gene moderate depression in maltreated children. *Proceedings of the National Academy of Sciences, 101*, 17316–17321.

Kazdin, A. E. (2003a). Problem-solving skills training and parent management training for conduct disorder. In A. E. Kazdin & J. R. Weisz (Eds.), *Evidence-based psychotherapies for children and adolescents* (pp. 241–262). New York: Guilford Press.

Kazdin, A. E. (2003b). Psychotherapy for children and adolescents. *Annual Review of Psychology, 54*, 253–276.

Keane, T. M., Gerardi, R. J., Quinn, S. J., & Litz, B. T. (1992). Behavioral treatment of post-traumatic stress disorder. In S. M. Turner, K. S. Calhoun, & H. E. Adams (Eds.), *Handbook of clinical behavior therapy* (pp. 87–97). New York: Wiley.

Keck, P. E., McElroy, S. L., Strakowski, S., West, S., Sax, K., Hawkins, J., Bourne, M. L., & Haggard, P. (1998). 12-month outcome of patients with bipolar disorder following hospitalization for a manic or mixed episode. *American Journal of Psychiatry, 155*, 646–652.

Keel, P. K., Heatherton, T. F., Dorer, D. J., Joiner, T. E., & Zalta, A. K. (2006). Point prevalence of bulimia nervosa in 1982, 1992, and 2002. *Psychological Medicine, 36*, 119–127.

Keel, P. K., & Klump, K. L. (2003). Are eating disorders culture-bound syndromes? Implications for conceptualizing their etiology. *Psychological Bulletin, 129*, 747–769.

Kegel, M., Dam, H., Ali, F., & Bjerregaard, P. (2009). The prevalence of seasonal affective disorder (SAD) in Greenland is related to latitude. *Nordic Journal of Psychiatry, 63*, 331–335.

Keller, M. B., McCullough, J. P., Klein, D. N., Arnow, B., Dunner, D. L., Gelenberg, A. J., Markowitz, J. C., Nemeroff, C. B., Russell, J. M., Thase, M. E., Trivedi, M. H., & Zajecka, J. (2000). A comparison of nefazodone, the cognitive behavioral analysis system of psychotherapy, and their combination for the treatment of chronic depression. *New England Journal of Medicine, 342*, 1462–1470.

Kellermann, A. L., Rivara, F. P., Somes, G., & Reay, D. T. (1992). Suicide in the home in relation to gun ownership. *New England Journal of Medicine, 327*, 467–472.

Kelly, J. F. (2003). Self-help for substance-use disorders: History, effectiveness, knowledge gaps, and research opportunities. *Clinical Psychological Revue, 23*, 639–663.

Kelly, S. J., Day, N., & Streissguth, A. P. (2000). Effects of prenatal alcohol exposure on social behavior in humans and other species. *Neurotoxicology & Teratology, 22*, 143–149.

Kemeny, M. E., & Dean, L. (1995). Effects of AIDS-related bereavement on HIV progression among New York City gay men. *AIDS Education and Prevention, 7*, 36–47.

Kendall, P. C., Aschenbrand, S. G., & Hudson, J. L. (2003). Child-focused treatment of anxiety. In A. E. Kazdin & J. R. Weisz (Eds.), *Evidence-based psychotherapies for children and adolescents* (pp. 81–100). New York: Guilford Press.

Kendall, P. C., Hollon, S. D., Beck, A. T., Hammen, C. L., & Ingram, R. E. (1987). Issues and recommendations regarding use of the Beck Depression Inventory. *Cognitive Therapy & Research, 11*, 289–299.

Kendall, P. C., Hudson, J. L., Gosch, E., Flannery-Schroeder, E., & Suveg, C. (2008). Cognitive-behavioral therapy for anxiety disordered youth: A randomized clinical trial evaluating child and family modalities. *Journal of Consulting and Clinical Psychology, 76*, 282–297.

Kendall-Tackett, K. A., Williams, L. M., & Finkelhor, D. (1993). Impact of sexual abuse on children: A review and synthesis of recent empirical studies. *Psychological Bulletin, 113*, 164–180.

Kendler, K. S., Gallagher, T. J., Abelson, J. M., & Kessler, R. C. (1996). Lifetime prevalence, demographic risk factors, and diagnostic validity of nonaffective psychosis as assessed in a U.S. community sample. *Archives of General Psychiatry, 53*, 1022–1031.

Kendler, K. S., Karkowski, L. M., & Prescott, C. A. (1999). Causal relationship between stressful life events and the onset of major depression. *American Journal of Psychiatry, 156*, 837–848.

Kendler, K. S., & Karkowski-Shuman, L. (1997). Stressful life events and genetic liability to major depression: Genetic control of exposure to the environment? *Psychological Medicine, 27*, 539–547.

Kendler, K. S., McGuire, M., Gruenberg, A. M., & Walsh, D. (1994). Outcome and family study of the subtypes of schizophrenia in the west of Ireland. *American Journal of Psychiatry, 151*, 849–856.

Kendler, K. S., Myers, J., Prescott, C. A., & Neale, M. C. (2001). The genetic epidemiology of irrational fears and phobias in men. *Archives of General Psychiatry, 58*, 257–265.

Kendler, K. S., Neale, M. C., Kessler, R. C., & Heath, A. C. (1992). Major depression and generalized anxiety disorder: Same genes, (partly) different environments? *Archives of General Psychiatry, 49*, 716–722.

Kendler, K. S., Neale, M. C., Kessler, R. C., Heath, A. C., & Eaves, L. J. (1993). A test of the equal-environment assumption in twin studies of psychiatric illness. *Behavior Genetics, 23*, 21–28.

Kendler, K. S., & Prescott, C. A. (1998a). Cannabis use, abuse, and dependence in a population-based sample of female twins. *American Journal of Psychiatry, 155*, 1016–1022.

Kendler, K. S., & Prescott, C. A. (1998b). Cocaine use, abuse, and dependence in a population-based sample of female twins. *British Journal of Psychiatry, 173*, 345–350.

Kendler, K. S., & Prescott, C. A. (1999). A population based twin study of lifetime major depression in men and women. *Archives of General Psychiatry, 56*, 39–44.

Kennedy, S. H., Evans, K. R., Kruger, S., Mayberg, H. S., Meyer, J. H., et al. (2001). Changes in regional brain glucose metabolism measured with positron emission tomography after paroxetine treatment of major depression. *American Journal of Psychiatry, 158*, 899–905.

Kerbeshian, J., Burd, L., & Avery, K. (2001). Pharmacotherapy of autism: A review and clinical approach. *Journal of Developmental and Physical Disabilities, 13,* 199–228.

Kernberg, O. F. (1979). Psychoanalytic profile of the borderline adolescent. *Adolescent Psychiatry, 7,* 234–256.

Keshavan, M., Shad, M., Soloff, P., & Schooler, N. (2004). Efficacy and tolerability of olanzapine in the treatment of schizotypal personality disorder. *Schizophrenia Research, 71,* 97–101.

Kessing, L. V., Hansen, M. G., & Andersen, P. K. (2004). Course of illness in depressive and bipolar disorders: Naturalistic study, 1994–1999. *British Journal of Psychiatry, 185,* 372–377.

Kessler, R. C. (2003). The impairments caused by social phobia in the general population: Implications for intervention. *Acta Psychiatrica Scandinavica, 108*(Suppl. 417), 19–27.

Kessler, R. C., Adler, L., Barkley, R., Biederman, J., Conners, C. K., Demler, O., Faraone, S. V., Greenhill, L. L., Howes, M. J., Secnik, K., Spencer, T., Ustun, T. B., Walters, E. E., & Zaslavsky, A. M. (2006). The prevalence and correlates of adult ADHD in the United States: Results from the National Comorbidity Survey Replication. *American Journal of Psychiatry, 163,* 716–723.

Kessler, R. C., Andrade, L. H., Bijl, R. V., Offord, D. R., Demler, O. V., & Stein, D. J. (2002). The effects of co-morbidity on the onset and persistence of generalized anxiety disorder in the ICPE surveys. *Psychological Medicine, 32,* 1213–1225.

Kessler, R. C., Berglund, P. A., Bruce, M. L., Koch, J. R., et al. (2001). The prevalence and correlates of untreated serious mental illness. *Health Services Research, 36,* 987–1007.

Kessler, R. C., Berglund, P., Demler, O., Jin, R., Koretz, D., Merikangas, K. R., Rush, A. J., Walters, E. E., & Wang, P. S. (2003). The epidemiology of major depressive disorder: Results from the national comorbidity survey replication (NCS-R). *Journal of the American Medical Association, 289,* 3095–3105.

Kessler, R. C., Berglund, P., Demler, O., Jin, R., Merikangas, M. R., & Walters, E. E. (2005). Lifetime prevalence and age-of-onset distributions of *DSM-IV* disorders in the National Comorbidity Survey Replication. *Archives of General Psychiatry, 62,* 593–602.

Kessler, R. C., Chiu, W. T., Jin, R., Ruscio, A. M., Shear, K., & Walters, E. E. (2006). The epidemiology of panic attacks, panic disorder, and agoraphobia in the National Comorbidity Survey Replication. *Archives of General Psychiatry, 63,* 415–424.

Kessler, R. C., Coccaro, E. F., Fava, M., Jaeger, S., Jin, R., & Walters, E. (2006). The prevalence and correlates of *DSM–IV* intermittent explosive disorder in the National Comorbidity Survey Replication. *Archives of General Psychiatry, 63,* 669–678.

Kessler, R. C., Davis, C. G., & Kendler, K. S. (1997). Childhood adversity and adult psychiatric disorder in the U.S. National Comorbidity Survey. *Psychological Medicine, 27,* 1101–1119.

Kessler, R. C., McGonagle, K. A., Zhao, S., Nelson, C. B., Hughes, M., Eshleman, S., Wittchen, H., & Kendler, K. S. (1994). Lifetime and 12-month prevalence of *DSM-III-R* psychiatric disorders in the United States: Results from the National Comorbidity Study. *Archives of General Psychiatry, 51,* 8–19.

Kessler, R. C., Merikangas, K. R, & Wang, P. S. (2007). Prevalence, comorbidity, and service utilization for mood disorders in the United States at the beginning of the twenty-first century. *Annual Review of Clinical Psychology, 3,* 137–158.

Kessler, R. C., Sonnega, A., Bromet, E., Hughes, M., & Nelson, C. B. (1995). Posttraumatic stress disorder in the National Comorbidity Survey. *Archives of General Psychiatry, 52,* 1048–1060.

Kessler, R. C., Stein, M. B., & Berglund, P. (1998). Social phobia subtypes in the National Comorbidity Survey. *American Journal of Psychiatry, 155,* 613–619.

Kety, S. S., Wender, P. H., Jacobsen, B., Ingraham, L. J., Jansson, L., Faber, B., & Kinney, D. K. (1994). Mental illness in the biological and adoptive relative of schizophrenic adoptees: Replication of the Copenhagen study in the rest of Denmark. *Archives of General Psychiatry, 51,* 442–455.

Keyes, K. M., Grant, B. F., & Hasin, D. S. (2008). Evidence for a closing gender gap in alcohol use, abuse, and dependence in the United States population. *Drug and Alcohol Dependence, 93,* 21–29.

Khan, A., Leventhal, R. M., Khan, S. R., & Brown, W. A. (2002). Severity of depression and response to antidepressants and placebo: An analysis of the Food and Drug Administration database. *Journal of Clinical Psychopharmacology, 22,* 40–45.

Kiecolt-Glaser, J. K., Malarkey, W. B., Chee, M., & Newton, T. (1993). Negative behavior during marital conflict is associated with immunological down-regulation. *Psychosomatic Medicine, 55,* 395–409.

Kiecolt-Glaser, J. K., & Newton, T. L. (2001). Marriage and health: His and hers. *Psychological Bulletin, 127,* 472–503.

Kihlstrom, J. F. (2001). Dissociative disorders. In P. B. Sutker (Ed.), *Comprehensive handbook of psychopathology* (3rd ed., pp. 259–276). New York: Kluwer Academic/Plenum Publishers.

Kihlstrom, J. F. (2005). Dissociative disorders. *Annual Review of Clinical Psychology, 1,* 227–254.

Kihlstrom, J. F., & Couture, L. J. (1992). Awareness and information processing in general anesthesia. *Journal of Psychopharmacology, 6,* 410–417.

Kihlstrom, J. F., Glisky, M. L., & Angiulo, M. J. (1994). Dissociative tendencies and dissociative disorders. *Journal of Abnormal Psychology, 103,* 117–124.

Kim, H. S., Sherman, D. K., & Taylor, S. E. (2008). Culture and social support. *American Psychologist, 63,* 518–526.

Kim, L. I. C. (1993). Psychiatric care of Korean Americans. In A. C. Gaw (Ed.), *Culture, ethnicity, and mental illness* (pp. 347–375). Washington, DC: American Psychiatric Press.

Kim-Cohen, J., Caspi, A., Rutter, M., Polo Tomas, M., & Moffitt, T. E. (2006). The caregiving environments provided to children by depressed mothers with or without an antisocial history. *American Journal of Psychiatry, 163,* 1009–1018.

King, B. H., Hodapp, R. M., & Dykens, E. M. (2005). Mental retardation. In B. J. Sadock & V. A. Sadock (Eds.), *Kaplan & Sadock's comprehensive textbook of psychiatry* (pp. 3076–3206). Philadelphia: Lippincott Williams & Wilkins.

King, C. R., Knutson, K. L., Rathouz, P. J., Sidney, S., Liu, K., & Lauderdale, D. S. (2008). Short sleep duration and incident coronary artery calcification. *Journal of the American Medical Association, 300,* 2859–2866.

King, D. A., & Markus, H. E. (2000). Mood disorders in older adults. In S. K. Whitbourne (Ed.), *Psychopathology in later adulthood* (pp. 141–172). New York: Wiley.

King, D. W., King, L. A., Foy, D. W., Keane, T. M., & Fairbank, F. A. (1999). Posttraumatic stress disorder in a national sample of female and male Vietnam veterans: Risk factors, war-zone stressors, and resilience-recovery variables. *Journal of Abnormal Psychology, 108,* 164–170.

Kirk, S. A., & Kutchins, H. (1992). *The selling of* DSM: *The rhetoric of science in psychiatry.* New York: A. de Gruyter.

Kirkbride, J. B., Fearon, P., Morgan, C., Dazzan, P., Morgan, K., Tarrant, J., Lloyd, T., Holloway, J., Hutchinson, G., Leff, J. P., Mallett, R. M., Harrison, G. L., Murray, R. M., & Jones, P. B. (2006). Heterogeneity in incidence rates of schizophrenia and other psychotic syndromes: Findings from the 3-center ÆSOP study. *Archives of General Psychiatry, 63,* 250–258.

Kirmayer, L. J. (2001). Cultural variations in the clinical presentation of depression and anxiety: Implications for diagnosis and treatment. *Journal of Clinical Psychiatry, 62*(Suppl. 13), 22–28.

Kirmayer, L. J., & Taillefer, S. (1997). Somatoform disorders. In S. M. Turner & M. Hersen (Eds.), *Adult psychopathology and diagnosis* (3rd ed., pp. 333–383). New York: Wiley.

Kirsch, I., Deacon, B. J., Huedo-Medina, T. B., Scoboria, A., Moore, T. J., & Johnson, B. T. (2008). Initial severity and antidepressant benefits: A meta-analysis of data submitted to the Food and Drug Administration. *PLoS Medicine, 5,* e45.

Kirsch, I., & Lynn, S. J. (1998). Dissociation theories of hypnosis. *Psychological Bulletin, 123,* 100–115.

Kisiel, C. L., & Lyons, J. S. (2001). Dissociation as a mediator of psychopathology among sexually abused children and adolescents. *American Journal of Psychiatry, 158,* 1034–1039.

Kissane, D. W., Grabsch, B., Clarke, D. M., Smith, G. C., Love, A. W., Bloch, S., Snyder, R. D., & Li, Y. (2007). Supportive-expressive group therapy for women with metastatic breast cancer: Survival and psychosocial outcome from a randomized controlled trial. *Psycho-Oncology, 16,* 277–286.

Klabunde, R. (2005). *Cardiovascular physiology concepts.* Philadelphia: Lippincott Williams & Wilkins.

Klein, C., & Gorzalka, B. B. (2009). Sexual functioning in transsexuals following hormone therapy and genital surgery: A review. *Journal of Sexual Medicine, 6,* 2922–2939.

Klein, D. N., Lewinsohn, P. M., Seeley, J. R., & Rohde, P. (2001). A family study of major depressive disorder in a community sample of adolescents. *Archives of General Psychiatry, 58,* 13–20.

Klein, M. (1952). Notes on some schizoid mechanisms. In M. Klein, P. Heimann, S. Isaacs, & J. Riviere (Eds.), *Developments in psychoanalysis.* London: Hogarth Press.

Kleinman, A., & Kleinman, J. (1985). Somatization: The interconnections in Chinese society among culture, depressive experiences, and meanings of pain. In A. Kleinman & B. Good (Eds.), *Culture and depression* (pp. 429–490). Berkeley: University of California Press.

Klerman, G. L., & Weissman, M. M. (1989). Increasing rates of depression. *Journal of the American Medical Association, 261,* 2229–2235.

Klerman, G. L., Weissman, M. M., Rounsaville, B., & Chevron, E. (1984). *Interpersonal psychotherapy of depression.* New York: Basic Books.

Klorman, R., Cicchetti, D., Thatcher, J. E., & Ison, J. R. (2003). Acoustic startle in maltreated children. *Journal of Abnormal Child Psychology, 31,* 359–370.

Kluft, R. P. (1987). Unsuspected multiple personality disorder: An uncommon source of protracted resistance, interruption, and failure in psychoanalysis. *Hillside Journal of Clinical Psychiatry, 9,* 100–115.

Knable, M. B., Barci, B. M., Webster, M. J., Meador-Woodruff, J., & Torrey, E. F. (2004). Molecular abnormalities of the hippocampus in severe psychiatric illness: Postmortem findings from the Stanley Neuropathology Consortium. *Molecular Psychiatry, 9,* 609–620.

Knapp, M., Mangalore, R., & Simon, J. (2004). The global costs of schizophrenia. *Schizophrenia Bulletin, 30,* 279–293.

Knight, R. A. (2009, November 3). Is a diagnostic category for paraphilic coercive disorder defensible? *Archives of Sexual Behavior.* doi: 10.1007/s10508-009-9571-x

Knopman, D. (2003). Pharmacotherapy for Alzheimer's disease: 2002. *Clinical Neuropharmacology, 26,* 93–101.

Koegel, R. L., Koegel, L. K., & Brookman, L. I. (2003). Empirically supported pivotal response interventions for children with autism. In A. E. Kazdin & J. R. Weisz (Eds.), *Evidence-based psychotherapies for children and adolescents* (pp. 341–357). New York: Guilford Press.

Koenen, K. C., Harley, R., Lyons, M. J., Wolfe, J., Simpson, J. C., Goldberg, J., et al. (2002). A twin registry study of familial and individual risk factors for trauma exposure and posttraumatic stress disorder. *Journal of Nervous and Mental Disease, 190,* 209–218.

Koenen, K. C., Nugent, N. R., & Amstadter, A. B. (2008). Gene-environment interaction in posttraumatic stress disorder. *European Archives of Psychiatry and Clinical Neuroscience, 258,* 82–96.

Konarski, J. Z., McIntyre, R. S., Kennedy S. H., Rafi-Tari, S., Soczynska, J. K., & Ketter, T. A. (2008). Volumetric neuroimaging investigations in mood disorders: Bipolar disorder versus major depressive disorder. *Bipolar Disorder, 10,* 1–37.

Kong, L. L., Allen, J. J. B., & Glisky, E. L. (2008). Interidentity memory transfer in dissociative identity disorder. *Journal of Abnormal Psychology, 117,* 686–692.

Koniak-Griffin, D., Lesser, J., Henneman, T., Huang, R., Huang, X., Kappos, B., et al. (2008). HIV prevention for Latino adolescent mothers and their partners. *Western Journal of Nurse Research, 30,* 724.

Koopman, C., Classen, C., & Spiegel, D. A. (1994). Predictors of posttraumatic stress symptoms among survivors of the Oakland/Berkeley, California, firestorm. *American Journal of Psychiatry, 151,* 888–894.

Koopman, C., Drescher, K., Bowles, S., Gusman, F., Blake, D., Dondershine, H., Chang, V., Butler, L. D., & Spiegel, D. (2001). Acute, dissociative reactions in veterans with PTSD. *Journal of Trauma & Dissociation, 2,* 91–111.

Kopelman, M. D. (1987). Crime and amnesia: A review. *Behavioral Sciences & the Law, 5,* 323–342.

Kopelman, M. D. (2002). Disorders of memory. *Brain, 125,* 2152–2191.

Koss, J. D. (1990). Somatization and somatic complaint syndromes among Hispanics: Overview and ethnopsychological perspectives. *Transcultural Psychiatric Research Review, 27,* 5–29.

Koss, M. P., & Kilpatrick, D. G. (2001). Rape and sexual assault. In E. Gerrity (Ed.), *The mental health consequences of torture* (pp. 177–193). New York: Kluwer Academic/Plenum.

Koss-Chioino, J. D. (2000). Traditional and folk approaches among ethnic minorities. In J. F. Aponte & J. Wohl (Eds). *Psychological intervention and cultural diversity* (2nd ed., pp. 149–166). Needham Heights, MA: Allyn & Bacon.

Koukoui, S. D., & Chaudhuri, A. (2007). Neuroanatomical, molecular, genetic, and behavioral correlates of fragile X syndrome. *Brain Research Reviews, 53,* 27–38.

Kouri, E. M., & Pope, H. G. (2000). Abstinence symptoms during withdrawal from chronic marijuana use. *Experimental & Clinical Psychopharmacology, 8,* 483–492.

Kownacki, R. J., & Shadish, W. R. (1999). Does Alcoholics Anonymous work? The results from a meta-analysis of controlled experiments. *Substance Use and Misuse, 34,* 1897–1916.

Krakow, B., Haynes, P. L., Warner, T. D., Melendrez, D., Sisley, B.N., Johnston, L., Hollifield, M., & Lee, S. (2007). Clinical sleep disorder profiles in a large sample of trauma survivors: An interdisciplinary view of posttraumatic sleep disturbance. *Sleep and Hypnosis, 9,* 6–15.

Krakowski, M. (2003). Violence and serotonin: Influence of impulse control, affect regulation, and social functioning. *Journal of Neuropsychiatry & Clinical Neurosciences, 15,* 294–305.

Kratochvil, C. J., Michelson, D., Newcorn, J. H., Weiss, M. D., Busner, J., Moore, R. J., Ruff, D. D., Ramsey, J., Dickson, R., Turgay, A., Saylor, K. E., Luber, S., Vaughan, B., Allen, A. J., & the Atomoxetine High-Dose Study Group. (2007). High-dose atomoxetine treatment of ADHD in youths with limited response to standard doses. *Journal of the American Academy of Child and Adolescent Psychiatry, 46,* 1128–1137.

Kraus, G., & Reynolds, D. J. (2001). The "A-B-C's" of the Cluster B's: Identifying, understanding, and treating Cluster B personality disorders. *Clinical Psychology Review, 21,* 345–373.

Kring, A. M. (2000). Gender and anger. In A. H. Fischer (Ed.), *Gender and emotion: Social psychological perspectives* (pp. 211–231). New York: Cambridge University Press.

Kring, A. M., & Moran, E. K. (2008). Emotional response deficits in schizophrenia: Insights from affective science. *Schizophrenia Bulletin, 34,* 819–834.

Kring, A. M., & Neale, J. M. (1996). Do schizophrenic patients show a disjunctive relationship among expressive, experiential, and psychophysiological components of emotion? *Journal of Abnormal Psychology, 105,* 249–257.

Kroll, J. (1973). A reappraisal of psychiatry in the Middle Ages. *Archives of General Psychiatry, 29,* 276–283.

Krueger, R. B., and Kaplan, M. S. (2008). Frotteurism: Assessment and treatment. In D. R. Laws & W. T. O'Donohue (Eds.), *Sexual deviance: Theory, assessment, and treatment* (pp. 150–164). New York: Guilford Press.

Krueger, R. F., & Markon, K. E. (2006). Reinterpreting comorbidity: A model-based approach to understanding and classifying psychopathology. *Annual Review of Clinical Psychology, 2,* 111–134.

Krueger, R. F., Skodol, A. E., Livesley, W. J., Shrout, P. E., & Huang, Y. (2008). Synthesizing dimensional and categorical approaches to personality disorders. In J. Hezler, H. C. Kraemer, R. F. Krueger, H. U. Wittchen, P. J. Sirovatka, **et al.**, (Eds.), *Dimensional approaches in diagnostic classification. Refining the research agenda for* DSM-V (pp. 85–99). Washington, DC: American Psychiatric Association.

Kruijver, F. P., Zhou, J. N., Pool, C. W., Hofman, M. A., Gooren, L. J., & Swaab, D. F. (2000). Male-to-female transsexuals have female neuron numbers in a limbic nucleus. *Journal of Clinical Endocrinology and Metabolism, 85,* 2034–2041.

Kryger, M. H., Roth, T., & Dement, W. C. (Eds.). (1994). *Principles and practice of sleep medicine.* Philadelphia: Saunders.

Kumar, M. S., Murhekar, M. V., Hutin, Y., Subramanian, T., Ramachandran, V., & Gupte, M. D. (2007). Prevalence of posttraumatic stress disorder in a coastal fishing village in Tamil Nadu, India, after the December 2004 tsunami. *American Journal of Public Health, 97,* 99–101.

Kutscher, E. C. (2008). Antipsychotics. In K. T. Mueser & D. V. Jeste (Eds.), *Clinical handbook of schizophrenia* (pp. 159–167). New York: Guilford Press.

L

Lack, L. C., Gradisar, M., Van Someren, E. J. W., Wright, H. R., & Lushington, K. (2008). The relationship between insomnia and body temperatures. *Sleep Medicine Reviews, 12,* 307–317.

Ladouceur, R., Sylvain, C., Boutin, C., Lachance, S., Doucet, C., & Leblond, J. (2003). Group therapy for pathological gamblers: A cognitive approach. *Behavior Research and Therapy, 41,* 587–596.

Ladouceur, R., Sylvain, C., Boutin, C., Lachance, S., Doucet, C., Leblond, J., & Jacques, C. (2001). Cognitive treatment of pathological gambling. *Journal of Nervous and Mental Disorders, 189,* 774–780.

LaFromboise, T. D., Trimble, J. E., & Mohatt, G. V. (1998). Counseling intervention and American Indian tradition: An integrative approach. In D. R. Atkinson (Ed.), *Counseling American minorities* (5th ed., pp. 159–182). New York: McGraw-Hill.

Lagana, L., McGarvey, E. L., Classen, C., & Koopman, C. (2001). Psychosexual dysfunction among gynecological cancer survivors. *Journal of Clinical Psychology in Medical Settings, 8,* 73–84.

LaGreca, A. M., Silverman, W. K., Vernberg, E. M., & Prinstein, M. J. (1996). Symptoms of posttraumatic stress in children after Hurricane Andrew: A prospective study. *Journal of Consulting & Clinical Psychology, 64,* 712–723.

Lalonde, J. K., Hudson, J. I., Gigante, R. A., & Pope, H. G. (2001). Canadian and American psychiatrists' attitudes towards dissociative disorders diagnoses. *Canadian Journal of Psychiatry, 46,* 407–412.

Lalumière, M. L., Quinsey, V. L., Harris, G. T., Rice, M. E., & Trautrimas, C. (2003). Are rapists differentially aroused by coercive sex in phallometric assessments? In R. A. Prentky, E. Janus, & M. Seto (Eds.), *Sexual coercion: Understanding and management* (pp. 211–224). New York: New York Academy of Sciences.

Lamb, H. R. (2001). *Best of new directions for mental health services, 1979–2001.* San Francisco: Jossey-Bass.

Lambert, M. C., Knight, F., Overly, K., Weisz, J. R., Desrosiers, M., & Thesiger, C. (1992). Jamaican and American adult perspectives on child psychopathology: Further exploration of the threshold model. *Journal of Consulting & Clinical Psychology, 60,* 146–149.

Lambert, M. T., & Silva, P. S. (1998). An update on the impact of gun control legislation on suicide. *Psychiatric Quarterly, 69,* 127–134.

Lang, A. J., & Stein, M. B. (2001). Social phobia: Prevalence and diagnostic threshold. *Journal of Clinical Psychiatry, 62*(Suppl. 1), 5–10.

Langlois, J. A., Rutland-Brown, W., & Wald, M. M. (2006). The epidemiology and impact of traumatic brain injury: A brief overview. *Journal of Head Trauma Rehabilitation 21,* 375–378.

Langstrom, N. (2009, November 19). The *DSM* diagnostic criteria for exhibitionism, voyeurism, and frotteurism. *Archives of Sexual Behavior*. doi: 10.1007/s10508-009-9577-4

Langstrom, N., & Seto, M. C. (2006). Exhibitionistic and voyeuristic behavior in a Swedish national population survey. *Archives of Sexual Behavior, 35,* 427–435.

Langstrom, N., & Zucker, K. J. (2005). Transvestic fetishism in the general population: Prevalence and correlates. *Journal of Sex and Marital Therapy, 31,* 87–95.

Larsson, H., Tuvblad, C., Rijsdijk, F. V., Andershed, H., Grann, M., & Lichtenstein, P. (2007). A common genetic factor explains the association between psychopathic personality and antisocial behavior. *Psychological Medicine, 37,* 15–26.

Lasser, K., Boyd, J. W., Woolhandler, S., Himmelstein, D. U., McCormick, D., & Bor, D. H. (2000). Smoking and mental illness: A population-based prevalence study. *Journal of the American Medical Association, 284,* 2606–2610.

Laudenslager, M. L., Ryan, S. M., Drugan, R. C., Hyson, R. L., & Maier, S. F. (1983). Coping and immunosuppression: Inescapable but not escapable shock suppresses lymphocyte proliferation. *Science, 221,* 569–570.

Laumann, E. O., Das, A., & Waite, L. J. (2008). Sexual dysfunction among older adults: Prevalence and risk factors from a nationally representative U.S. probability sample of men and women 57–85 years of age. *Journal of Sexual Medicine, 5,* 2300–2311.

Laumann, E. O., Gagnon, J. H., Michael, R. T., & Michaels, S. (1994). *The social organization of sexuality: Sexual practices in the United States.* Chicago: University of Chicago Press.

Laumann, E. O., Paik, A., & Rosen, R. C. (1999). Sexual dysfunction in the United States. *Journal of the American Medical Association, 281,* 537–544.

Lavin, M. (2008). Voyeurism: Psychopathology and theory. In D. R. Laws & W. T. O'Donohue (Eds.), *Sexual deviance: Theory, assessment, and treatment* (pp. 305–320). New York: Guilford Press.

Lavoie, K. L., Miller, S. B., Conway, M., & Fleet, R. P. (2001). Anger, negative emotions, and cardiovascular reactivity during interpersonal conflict in women. *Journal of Psychosomatic Research, 51,* 503–512.

Lavretsky, H. (2008). History of schizophrenia as a psychiatric disorder. In K. T. Mueser & D. V. Jeste (Eds.), *Clinical handbook of schizophrenia* (pp. 3–13). New York: Guilford Press.

Lawrence, A. A. (2008). Gender identity disorders in adults: Diagnosis and treatment. In D. L. Rowland & L. Incrocci (Eds.), *Handbook of sexual and gender identity disorders* (pp. 423–456). Hoboken, NJ: Wiley.

Lawrie, S. M., McIntosh, A. M., Hall, J., Owens, D. G. C., & Johnstone, E. C. (2008). Brain structure and function changes during the development of schizophrenia: The evidence from studies of subjects at increased genetic risk. *Schizophrenia Bulletin, 34,* 330–340.

Laws, D. R., and O'Donohue, W. T. (2008). Introduction. In D. R. Laws & W. T. O'Donohue (Eds.) *Sexual deviance: Theory, assessment, and treatment* (pp. 1–21). New York: Guilford Press.

Leadbeater, B. J., Kuperminc, G. P., Blatt, S. J., & Herzog, C. (1999). A multivariate model of gender differences in adolescents' internalizing and externalizing problems. *Developmental Psychology, 35,* 1268–1282.

Le Doux, J. E. (1996). *The emotional brain: The mysterious underpinnings of emotional life.* New York: Simon & Schuster.

Le Doux, J. E., & Phelps, E. A. (2000). Emotional networks in the brain. In M. Lewis & J. M. Haviland-Jones (Eds.), *Handbook of emotions* (2nd ed., pp. 157–172). New York: Guilford Press.

Lee, J. K. P., Jackson, H. J., Pattison, P., & Ward, T. (2002). Developmental risk factors for sexual offending. *Child Abuse & Neglect, 26,* 73–92.

Lee, Y.-J. (2004). Overview of the therapeutic management of insomnia with zolpidem. *CNS Drugs, 18*(Suppl. 1), 17–23.

Leenaars, A. A. (2007). Gun-control legislation and the impact on suicide. *Crisis, 28,* 50–57.

Le Grange, D., Eisler, I., Dare, C., & Russell, G. F. M. (1992). Evaluation of family treatments in adolescent anorexia nervosa: A pilot study. *International Journal of Eating Disorders, 12,* 347–357.

Lehman, B. J., Taylor, S. E., Kiefe, C., & Seeman, T. E. (2009). Relationship of early life stress and psychological functioning to blood pressure in the CARDIA study. *Health Psychology, 28,* 338–346.

Leibenluft, E., & Rich, B. A. (2008). Pediatric bipolar disorder. *Annual Review of Clinical Psychology, 4,* 163–187.

Leiblum, S. R. (2000). Vaginismus: A most perplexing problem. In S. R. Leiblum & R. C. Rosen (Eds.), *Principles and practice of sex therapy* (3rd ed., pp. 181–202). New York: Guilford Press.

Leiblum, S. R., Koochaki, P. E., Rodenberg, C. A., Barton, I. P., & Rosen, R. C. (2006). Hypoactive sexual desire disorder in postmenopausal women: U.S. results from the Women's International Study of Health and Sexuality (WISHeS). *Menopause, 13,* 46–56.

Leiblum, S. R., & Rosen, R. C. (2000). *Principles and practice of sex therapy* (3rd ed.). New York: Guilford Press.

Lejoyeux, M., Arbaretaz, M., McLoughlin, M., & Adès, J. (2002). Impulse control disorders and depression. *Journal of Nervous and Mental Disorders, 190,* 310–314.

Lemke, W. (2007). Fostering internal cooperation through the use of imagery in the treatment of dissociative identity disorder. *Journal of Trauma & Dissociation, 8,* 53–68.

Lenzenweger, M. F. (2008). Epidemiology of personality disorders. *Psychiatric Clinics of North America, 31,* 395–403.

Lenzenweger, M. F., Lane, M. C., Loranger, A. W., & Kessler, R. C. (2007). *DSM-IV* personality disorders in the National Comorbidity Survey Replication. *Biological Psychiatry, 62,* 553–564.

Leon, G. R., Fulkerson, J. A., Perry, C. L., & Early-Zald, M. B. (1995). Prospective analysis of personality and behavioral vulnerabilities and gender influences in the later development of disordered eating. *Journal of Abnormal Psychology, 104,* 140–149.

Lepine, J.-P. (2001). Epidemiology, burden, and disability in depression and anxiety. *Journal of Clinical Psychiatry, 62*(Suppl. 13), 4–10.

Lepore, S. J. (1995). Cynicism, social support and cardiovascular reactivity. *Health Psychology, 14,* 210–216.

Lerman, C., Caporaso, N. E., Audrain, J., Main, D., Bowman, E. D., Lockshin, B., Boyd, N. R., & Shields, P. G. (1999). Evidence suggesting the role of specific genetic factors in cigarette smoking. *Health Psychology, 18,* 14–20.

Leserman J. (2008). Role of depression, stress, and trauma in HIV disease progression. *Psychosomatic Medicine, 70,* 539–545.

Leserman, J., Jackson, E. D., Petitto, J. M., Golden, R. N., Silva, S. G., Perkins, D. O., Cai, J., Folds, J. D., & Evans, D. L. (1999). Progression to AIDS: The effects of stress, depressive symptoms, and social support. *Psychosomatic Medicine, 61,* 397–406.

Leserman, J., Pence, B. W., Whetten, K., Mugavero, M. J., Thielman, N. M., Swartz, M. S., & Stangl, D. (2007). Relation of lifetime trauma and depressive symptoms to mortality in HIV. *American Journal of Psychiatry, 164,* 1707–1713.

Leserman, J., Petitto, J. M., Golden, R. N., Gaynes, B. N., Gu, H., et al. (2000). Impact of stressful life events, depression, social support, coping, and cortisol on progression to AIDS. *American Journal of Psychiatry, 157,* 1221–1228.

Leserman, J., Petitto, J. M., Gu, H., Gaynes, B. N., Barroso, J., Golden, R. N., Perkins, D. O., Folds, J. D., & Evans, D. L. (2002). Progression to AIDS, a clinical AIDS condition, and mortality: Psychosocial and physiological predictors. *Psychological Medicine, 32,* 1059–1073.

Leventhal, H., Weinman, J., Leventhal, E. A., & Phillips, L. A. (2008). Health psychology: The search for pathways between behavior and health. *Annual Review of Psychology, 59,* 477–506.

Levinson, D. F. (2006). The genetics of depression: A review. *Biological Psychiatry 60,* 84–92.

Levy, S. M., & Heiden, L. (1991). Depression, distress, and immunity: Risk factors for infectious disease. *Stress Medicine, 7,* 45–51.

Levy, S. M., Herberman, R. B., Whiteside, T., & Sanzo, K. (1990). Perceived social support and tumor estrogen/progesterone receptor status as predictors of natural killer cell activity in breast cancer patients. *Psychosomatic Medicine, 52,* 73–85.

Lewinsohn, P. M. (1974). A behavioral approach to depression. In R. J. Friedman & M. M. Katz (Eds.), *The psychology of depression: Contemporary theory and research.* Washington, DC: Winston-Wiley.

Lewinsohn, P. M., & Gotlib, I. H. (1995). Behavioral therapy and treatment of depression. In E. E. Beckham & W. R. Leber (Eds.), *Handbook of depression* (2nd ed., pp. 352–375). New York: Guilford Press.

Lewinsohn, P. M., Muñoz, R. F., Youngren, M. A., & Zeiss, A. M. (1986). *Control your depression.* Englewood Cliffs, NJ: Prentice Hall.

Lewinsohn, P. M., Striegel-Moore, R. H., & Seeley, J. R. (2000). Epidemiology and natural course of eating disorders in young women from adolescence to young adulthood. *Journal of the American Academy of Child & Adolescent Psychiatry, 39,* 1284–1292.

Lewinsohn, P. M., Zinbarg, R., Seeley, J. R., Lewinsohn, M., & Sack, W. H. (1997). Lifetime comorbidity among anxiety disorders and between anxiety disorders and other mental disorders in adolescents. *Journal of Anxiety Disorders, 11,* 377–394.

Lewis, G., David, A., Andreasson, S., & Allebeck, P. (1992). Schizophrenia and city life. *Lancet, 340,* 137–140.

Lewis, R. W., Fugl-Meyer, K. S., Bosch, R., Fugl-Meyer, A. R., Laumann, E. O., Lizza, E., & Martin-Morales, A. (2004). Epidemiology/risk factors of sexual dysfunction. *Journal of Sexual Medicine, 1,* 35–39.

Lewis, R. W., Yuan, J., & Wangt, R. (2008). Male sexual arousal disorder. In D. L. Rowland & L. Incrocci (Eds.), *Handbook of sexual and gender identity disorders* (pp. 32–67). Hoboken, NJ: Wiley.

Lewis, T. T., Everson-Rose, S. A., Powell, L. H., Matthews, K. A., Brown, C., & Karavolos, K. (2006). Chronic exposure to everyday discrimination and coronary artery calcification in African-American women: The SWAN heart study. *Psychosomatic Medicine, 68,* 362–368.

Liberman, R. P. (1994). Psychosocial treatments for schizophrenia. *Psychiatry, 57,* 104–114.

Liberman, R. P., Eckman, T. A., & Marder, S. R. (2001). Rehab rounds: Training in social problem solving among persons with schizophrenia. *Psychiatric Services, 52,* 31–33.

Liberman, R. P., Glynn, S., Blair, K. E., Ross, D., & Marder, S. R. (2002). In vivo amplified skills training: Promoting generalization of independent living skills for clients with schizophrenia. *Psychiatry: Interpersonal & Biological Processes, 65,* 137–155.

Liberto, J. G., Oslin, D. W., & Ruskin, P. E. (1996). Alcoholism in the older population. In L. L. Carstensen, B. A. Edelstein, & L. Dornbrand (Eds.), *The practical handbook of clinical gerontology* (pp. 324–348). Thousand Oaks, CA: Sage.

Lichtermann, D., Karbe, E., & Maier, W. (2000). The genetic epidemiology of schizophrenia and of schizophrenia spectrum disorders. *European Archives of Psychiatry & Clinical Neuroscience, 250,* 304–310.

Lieberman, J. A., Tollefson, G., Tohen, M., Green, A. I., Gur, R. E., Kahn, R., McEvoy, J., Perkins, D., Sharma, T., Zipursky, R., Wei, H., & Hamer, R. M. (2003). Comparative efficacy and safety of atypical and conventional antipsychotic drugs in first-episode psychosis: A randomized, double-blind trial of olanzapine versus haloperidol. *American Journal of Psychiatry, 160,* 1396–1404.

Lilienfeld, S. O., Lynn, S. J., Kirsch, I., Chaves, J. F., Sarvin, T. R., Ganaway, G. K., & Powell, R. A. (1999). Dissociative identity disorders and the sociocognitive model: Recalling the lessons of the past. *Psychological Bulletin, 125,* 507–523.

Lindemalm, G., Korlin, D., & Uddenberg, N. (1986). Long-term follow-up of "sex change" in 13 male-to-female transsexuals. *Archives of Sexual Behavior, 15,* 187–210.

Linehan, M. M. (1973). Suicide and attempted suicide: Study of perceived sex differences. *Perceptual & Motor Skills, 37,* 31–34.

Linehan, M. M. (1999). Standard protocol for assessing and treating suicidal behaviors for patients in treatment. In D. G. Jacobs (Ed.), *The Harvard Medical School guide to suicide assessment and intervention* (pp. 146–187). San Francisco: Jossey-Bass.

Linehan, M. M., Cochran, B. N., & Kehrer, C. A. (2001). Dialectical behavior therapy for borderline personality disorder. In D. H. Barlow (Ed.), *Clinical handbook of psychological disorders: A step-by-step treatment manual* (pp. 470–522). New York: Guilford Press.

Linehan, M. M., Heard, H. L., & Armstrong, H. E. (1993). Naturalistic follow-up of a behavioral treatment for chronically parasuicidal borderline patients. *Archives of General Psychiatry, 50,* 971–974.

Links, P. S., Heslegrave, R., & van Reekum, R. (1998). Prospective follow-up study of borderline personality disorder: Prognosis, prediction of outcome, and Axis II comorbidity. *Canadian Journal of Psychiatry, 43,* 265–270.

Linscott, R. J., Allardyce, J., & van Os, J. (2009). Seeking verisimilitude in a class: A systematic review of evidence that the criterial clinical symptoms of schizophrenia are taxonic. *Schizophrenia Bulletin.* doi:10.1093

Linscott, R. J., & van Os, J. (2010). Systematic reviews of categorical versus continuum models in psychosis: Evidence for discontinuous subpopulations underlying a psychometric continuum. Implications for *DSM-V, DSM-VI,* and *DSM-VII. Annual Review of Clinical Psychology,* 6. 391–419.

Lisansky-Gomberg, E. S. (2000). Substance abuse disorders. In S. K. Whitbourne (Ed.), *Psychopathology in later adulthood* (pp. 277–298). New York: Wiley.

Liu, L., & Ancoli-Israel, S. (2006). Insomnia in the older adult. *Sleep Medicine Clinics, 1,* 409–421.

Liu, X.-Q., Paterson, A. D., Szatmari, P., and the Autism Genome Project Consortium. (2008). Genome-wide linkage analyses of quantitative and categorical autism subphenotypes. *Biological Psychiatry, 64,* 561–570.

Livesley, W. J. (1998). Suggestions for a framework for an empirically based classification of personality disorder. *Canadian Journal of Psychiatry, 43,* 137–147.

Livesley, W. J. (2010). *Rationale for general diagnostic criteria for personality disorder.* http://www.dsm5.org/ProposedRevisions/pages/RationaleforDefinitionandGeneralDiagnosticCriteriaforPersonalityDisorder.aspx (accessed February 15, 2010)

Lloyd-Richardson, E. E., Perrine, N., Dierker, L., Kelley, M. L. (2007). Characteristics and functions of non-suicidal self-injury in a community sample of adolescents. *Psychological Medicine, 37,* 1183–1192.

Lochman, J. E., Barry, T. D., & Pardini, D. A. (2003). Anger control training for aggressive youth. In A. E. Kazdin & J. R. Weisz (Eds.), *Evidence-based psychotherapies for children and adolescents* (pp. 263–281). New York: Guilford Press.

Lochman, J. E., White, K. J., & Wayland, K. K. (1991). Cognitive-behavioral assessment and treatment with aggressive children. In P. Kendall (Ed.), *Therapy with children and adolescents: Cognitive behavioral procedures* (pp. 25–65). New York: Guilford Press.

Lock, J., Agras, W. S., Bryson, S., & Kraemer, H. C. (2005). A comparison of short- and long-term family therapy for adolescent anorexia nervosa. *Journal of the American Academy of Child and Adolescent Psychiatry, 44,* 632–639.

Lock, J., le Grange, D., Agras, W. S., & Dare, C. (2001). *Treatment manual for anorexia nervosa: A family-based approach.* New York: Guilford Press.

Loebel, J. P., Loebel, J. S., Dager, S. R., Centerwall, B. S., & Reay, D. T. (1991). Anticipation of nursing home placement may be a precipitant of suicide among the elderly. *Journal of the American Geriatric Society, 39,* 407–408.

Loeber, R. (1990). Development and risk factors of juvenile antisocial behavior and delinquency. *Clinical Psychology Review, 10,* 1–41.

Loeber, R., & Farrington, D. P. (1997). Strategies and yields of longitudinal studies on antisocial behavior. In D. M. Stoff, J. Breiling, & J. D. Maser (Eds.), *Handbook of antisocial personality disorder* (pp. 125–139). New York: Wiley.

Loehlin, J. C. (2009). History of behavior genetics. In Y.-K. Kim (Ed.), *Handbook of behavior genetics* (pp. 3–11). New York: Spring Science & Business Media.

Loftus, E. F. (1993). The reality of repressed memories. *American Psychologist, 48,* 518–537.

Loftus, E. F. (2003). Make-believe memories. *American Psychologist, 58,* 867–873.

Loftus, E. F., Garry, M., & Hayne, H. (2008). Repressed and recovered memory. In E. Borgida & S. T. Fiske (Eds.), *Beyond common sense: Psychological science in the courtroom* (pp. 177–194). Malden, MA: Blackwell.

Long, P. W. (1996). Internet mental health. http://www.mentalhealth.com/ (accessed June 1, 2006)

Longstreth, W. T., Koepsell, T. D., Ton, T. G., Hendrickson, A. F., & van Belle, G. (2007). The epidemiology of narcolepsy. *Sleep, 30,* 13–26.

Lopez, S. R., & Guarnaccia, P. J. J. (2000). Cultural psychopathology: Uncovering the social world of mental illness. *Annual Review of Psychology, 51,* 571–598.

Lopez, S. R., Kopelowicz, A., & Canive, J. M. (2002). Strategies in developing culturally congruent family interventions for schizophrenia: The case of Hispanics. In H. P. Lefley & D. L. Johnson (Eds.), *Family interventions in mental illness: International perspectives* (pp. 61–90). Westport, CT: Praeger.

LoPiccolo, J. (1992). Paraphilias. *Nordisk Sexologi, 10,* 1–14.

Lotspeich, L. J., Kwon, H., Schumann, C. M., Fryer, S. L., Goodlin-Jones, B. L., Buonocore, M. H., Lammers, C. R., Amaral, D. G., & Reiss, A. L. (2004). Investigation of neuroanatomical differences between autism and Asperger syndrome. *Archives of General Psychiatry, 61,* 291–298.

Lovaas, O. I. (1987). Behavioral treatment and normal educational and intellectual functioning in young autistic children. *Journal of Consulting & Clinical Psychology, 55,* 3–9.

Lovaas, O. I., & Smith, T. (2003). Early and intensive behavioral intervention in autism. In A. E. Kazdin & J. R. Weisz (Eds.), *Evidence-based psychotherapies for children and adolescents* (pp. 325–340). New York: Guilford Press.

Lowe, B., Zipfel, S., Buchholz, C., Dupont, Y., Reas, D. L., & Herzog, W. (2001). Long-term outcome of anorexia nervosa in a prospective 21-year follow-up study. *Psychological Medicine, 31,* 881–890.

Loxton, N. J., & Dawe, S. (2001). Alcohol abuse and dysfunctional eating in adolescent girls: The influence of individual differences in sensitivity to reward and punishment. *International Journal of Eating Disorders, 29,* 455–462.

Luborksy, L. (1984). *Principles of psychoanalytic psychotherapy: A manual for supportive-expressive treatment.* New York: Basic Books.

Luborsky, L., & Barrett, M. S. (2006). The historical and empirical status of key psychoanalytic concepts. *Annual Review of Clinical Psychology, 2,* 1–20.

Ludwig, A. M. (1992). Creative achievement and psychopathology: Comparison among professions. *American Journal of Psychotherapy, 46,* 330–356.

Ludwig, J., Cook, P. J. (2000). Homicide and suicide rates associated with implementation of the Brady Handgun Violence Prevention Act. *Journal of the American Medical Association, 284,* 585–591.

Luria, A. (1973). *The working brain.* New York: Basic Books.

Lussier, P., and Piché, L. (2008). Frotteurism: Psychopathology and Theory. In D. R. Laws & W. T. O'Donohue (Eds.), *Sexual deviance: Theory, assessment, and treatment* (pp. 131–150). New York: Guilford Press.

Luthar, S. S. (2003). *Resilience and vulnerability: Adaptation in the context of childhood adversities.* Cambridge, UK: Cambridge University Press.

Lyman, R. (1997, April 15). Michael Dorris dies at 52: Wrote of his son's suffering. *New York Times,* p. 24.

Lynam, D. R., Caspi, A., Moffitt, T. E., Wikstrom, P. H., Loeber, R., & Novak, S. (2000). The interaction between impulsivity and neighborhood context on offending: The effects of impulsivity are stronger in poorer neighborhoods. *Journal of Abnormal Psychology, 109,* 563–574.

Lynch, T. R., Trost, W. T., Salsman, N., & Linehan, M. M. (2007). Dialectical behavior therapy for borderline personality disorder. *Annual Review of Clinical Psychology, 3,* 181–206.

Lyness, J. M. (2004). Treatment of depressive conditions in later life: Real-world light for dark (or dim) tunnels. *Journal of the American Medical Association, 291,* 1626–1628.

Lyons-Ruth, K., Holmes, B. M., Sasvari-Szekely, M., Ronai, Z., Nemoda, Z., & Pauls, D. (2007). Serotonin transporter polymorphism and borderline or antisocial traits among low-income young adults. *Psychiatric Genetics, 17,* 339–343.

Lytton, H., & Romney, D. M. (1991). Parents' differential socialization of boys and girls: A meta-analysis. *Psychological Bulletin, 109,* 267–296.

M

MacArthur Research Network on Mental Health and the Law. (1998). Executive summary. http://ness.sys.Virginia.EDU/macarthur/violence.html (accessed June 1, 2006)

Maher, B. A. (1966). *Principles of psychotherapy: An experimental approach.* New York: McGraw-Hill.

Maher, W. B., & Maher, B. A. (1985). Psychopathology: I. From ancient times to eighteenth century. In G. A. Kimble & K. Schlesinger (Eds.), *Topics in the history of psychology* (Vol. 2). Hillsdale, NJ: Erlbaum.

Mahler, M. (1968). *On human symbiosis and the vicissitudes of individuation: Vol. I. Infantile psychosis.* New York: International Universities Press.

Mahowald, M. W., & Bornemann, M. A. C. (2006). Sleep disorders: Case studies. *Neurology Clinics, 24,* 267–289.

Maletzky, B. (1998). The paraphilias: Research and treatment. In P. E. Nathan (Ed.), *A guide to treatments that work* (pp. 472–500). New York: Oxford University Press.

Maletzky, B. M., & Field, G. (2003). The biological treatment of dangerous sexual offenders, a review and preliminary report of the Oregon pilot depo-Provera program. *Aggression and Violent Behavior, 8,* 391–412.

Mandel, H. (2005). *Hidden Howie: True stories from the private life of a public nuisance.* Available from Amazon Shorts, www.amazon.com

Mangweth, B., Pope, H. G., Kemmler, G., Ebenbichler, C., Hausmann, A., De Col, C., Kreutner, B., Kinzl, J., & Biebl, W. (2001). Body image and psychopathology in male bodybuilders. *Psychotherapy & Psychosomatics, 70,* 38–43.

Manicavasagar, V., Silove, D., Rapee, R., Waters, F., & Momartin, S. (2001). Parent-child concordance for separation anxiety: A clinical study. *Journal of Affective Disorders, 65,* 81–84.

Mann, J. J., Brent, D. A., & Arango, V. (2001). The neurobiology and genetics of suicide and attempted suicide: A focus on the serotonergic system. *Neuropsychopharmacology, 24,* 467–477.

Mannino, J. D. (1999). *Sexually speaking.* New York: McGraw-Hill.

Manson, J. E., Willett, W. C., Stampfer, M. J., Colditz, G. A., Hunter, D. J., Hankinson, S. E., et al. (1995). Body weight and mortality among women. *New England Journal of Medicine, 333,* 677–685.

Manson, S. M., Shore, J. H., Baron, A. E., Ackerson, L., & Neligh, G. (1992). Alcohol abuse and dependence among American Indians. In J. E. Helzer & G. J. Canino (Eds.), *Alcoholism in North America, Europe, and Asia* (pp. 113–127). New York: Oxford University Press.

Maramba, G. G., & Nagayama Hall, G. C. (2002). Meta-analyses of ethnic match as a predictor of dropout, utilization, and level of functioning. *Cultural Diversity & Ethnic Minority Psychology, 8,* 290–297.

Marangell, L. B. (2004). The importance of subsyndromal symptoms in bipolar disorder. *Journal of Clinical Psychiatry, 65*(Suppl. 10), 24–27.

Marazziti, D., Catena, M., & Pallanti, S. (2006). Pharmacologic treatment of obsessive-compulsive disorder. *Psychiatric Annals, 36,* 454–462.

Marcos, L. R. (1979). Effects of interpreters on the evaluation of psychopathology in non-English-speaking patients. *American Journal of Psychiatry, 136,* 171–174.

Marcus, D. K., & Church, S. E. (2003). Are dysfunctional beliefs about illness unique to hypochondriasis? *Journal of Psychosomatic Research, 54,* 543–547.

Markovitz, P. J. (2004). Recent trends in the pharmacotherapy of personality disorders. *Journal of Personality Disorders, 18,* 99–101.

Marks, I. M., & Swinson, R. (1992). Behavioral and/or drug therapy. In G. D. Burrows, S. M. Roth, & R. Noyes, Jr. (Eds.), *Handbook of anxiety* (Vol. 5). Oxford, UK: Elsevier.

Marlatt, G. A., Baer, J. S., Donovan, D. M., & Kivlahan, D. R. (1988). Addictive behaviors: Etiology and treatment. *Annual Review of Psychology, 39,* 223–252.

Marlatt, G. A., Baer, J. S., & Larimer, M. (1995). Preventing alcohol abuse in college students: A harm reduction approach. In G. M. Boyd, J. Howard, & R. A. Zucker (Eds.), *Alcohol problems among adolescents: Current directions in prevention research* (pp. 147–172). Hillsdale, NJ: Erlbaum.

Marlatt, G. A., Blume, A. W., & Parks, G. A. (2001). Integrating harm reduction therapy and traditional substance abuse treatment. *Journal of Psychoactive Drugs, 33,* 13–21.

Marlatt, G. A., Larimer, M. E., Baer, J. S., & Quigley, L. A. (1993). Harm reduction for alcohol problems: Moving beyond the controlled drinking economy. *Behavior Therapy, 24,* 461–503.

Marlatt, G. A., & Witkiewitz, K. (2010). Update on harm reduction policy and intervention research. *Annual Review of Clinical Psychology, 6,* 591–606.

Marques, J. K., Wiederanders, M., Day, M., Nelson, C., & van Ommeren, A. (2005). Effects of a relapse prevention program on sexual recidivism: Final results from California's Sex Offender Treatment Evaluation Project (SOTEP). *Sex Abuse, 17,* 79–107.

Marshall, G. N., & Orlando, M. (2002). Acculturation and peritraumatic dissociation in young adult Latino survivors of community violence. *Journal of Abnormal Psychology, 111,* 166–174.

Marshall, T., Jones, D. P. H., Ramchandrani, P. G., Stein, A., & Bass, C. (2007). Intergenerational transmission of health beliefs in somatoform disorders. *British Journal of Psychiatry, 191,* 449–450.

Martenyi, F., Brown, E. B., Zhang, H., Koke, S. C., & Prakash, A. (2002). Fluoxetine v. placebo in prevention of relapse in post-traumatic stress disorder. *British Journal of Psychiatry, 181,* 315–320.

Martin, C. S., & Bates, M. E. (1998). Psychological and psychiatric consequences of alcohol. In R. E. Tarter, R. T. Ammerman, & P. J. Ott (Eds.), *Handbook of substance abuse: Neurobehavioral pharmacology* (pp. 33–50). New York: Plenum Press.

Masten, A. S., & Powell, J. L. (2003). A resilience framework for research, policy, and practice. In S. E. Luthar (Ed.), *Resilience and vulnerability: Adaptation in the context of childhood adversities* (pp. 1–25). New York: Cambridge University Press.

Masters, W. H., & Johnson, V. E. (1970). *Human sexual inadequacy.* Boston: Little, Brown.

Masters, W. H., Johnson, V. E., & Kolodny, R. C. (1993). *Biological foundations of human sexuality.* New York: HarperCollins.

Matarazzo, J. D. (1985). Psychotherapy. In G. A. Kimble & K. Schlesinger (Eds.), *Topics in the history of psychology.* Hillsdale, NJ: Erlbaum.

Mathews, A., & MacLeod, C. (2005). Cognitive vulnerability to emotional disorders. *Annual Review of Clinical Psychology, 1,* 167–196.

Matt, G. E., Vasquez, C., & Campbell, W. K. (1992). Mood-congruent recall of affectively toned stimuli: A meta-analytic review. *Clinical Psychology Review, 12,* 227–255.

Matthews, K. A., Owens, J. F., Kuller, L. H., Sutton-Tyrrell, K., & Jansen-McWilliams, L. (1998). Are hostility and anxiety associated with carotid atherosclerosis in healthy post-menopausal women? *Psychosomatic Medicine, 5,* 633–638.

Mattick, R. P., Breen, C., Kimber, J., Davoli, M., & Breen, R. (2003). Methadone maintenance therapy versus no opioid replacement therapy for opioid dependence. *Cochrane Database of Systematic Reviews, 2,* CD002209.

Maughan, B., Pickles, A., Rowe, R., Costello, E. J., & Angold, A. (2000). Developmental trajectories of aggressive and non-aggressive conduct problems. *Journal of Quantitative Criminology, 16,* 199–221.

Maughan, B., Rowe, R., Messer, J., Goodman, R., & Meltzer, H. (2004). Conduct disorder and oppositional defiant disorder in a national sample: Developmental epidemiology. *Journal of Child Psychology & Psychiatry, 45,* 609–621.

Mausbach, B. T., Coon, D. W., Depp, C., Rabinowitz, Y. G., Wilson-Arias, E., Kraemer, H. C., Thompson, L. W., Lane, G., & Gallagher-Thompson, D. (2004). Ethnicity and time to institutionalization of dementia patients: A comparison of Latina and Caucasian female family caregivers. *Journal of the American Geriatrics Society, 52,* 1077–1084.

Maxmen, J. S., & Ward, N. G. (1995). *Essential psychopathology and its treatment.* New York: W. W. Norton.

Mayberg, H. S., Lozano, A. M., Voon, V., et al. (2005). Deep brain stimulation for treatment-resistant depression. *Neuron, 45,* 651–660.

Mayou, R., Bryant, B., & Ehlers, A. (2001). Prediction of psychological outcomes one year after a motor vehicle accident. *American Journal of Psychiatry, 158,* 1231–1238.

Mays, V. M., Cochran, S. D., & Barnes, N. W. (2007). Race, race-based discrimination, and health outcomes among African Americans. *Annual Review of Psychology, 58,* 201–225.

Mazure, C. M. (1998). Life stressors as risk factors in depression. *Clinical Psychology: Science & Practice, 5,* 291–313.

Mazzeo, S. E., Trace, S. E., Mitchell, K. S., & Gow, R. S. (2007). Effects of a reality TV cosmetic surgery makeover program on eating disordered attitudes and behaviors. *Eating Behaviors, 8,* 390–397.

Mazzoni, G., & Loftus, E. F. (1998). Dream interpretations can change beliefs about the past. *Psychotherapy, 35,* 177–187.

McBride, A. A., Joe, G. W., & Simpson, D. D. (1991). Prediction of long-term alcohol use, drug use, and criminality among inhalant users. *Hispanic Journal of Behavioral Sciences, 13,* 315–323.

McBride, K. R., Reece, M., & Sanders, S. (2008). Using the Sexual Compulsivity Scale to predict outcomes of sexual behavior in young adults. *Sexual Addiction & Compulsivity, 15,* 97–115.

McBurnett, K., Pfiffner, L. J., & Frick, P. J. (2001). Symptom properties as a function of ADHD type: An argument for continued study of sluggish cognitive tempo. *Journal of Abnormal Child Psychology, 29,* 207–213.

McCabe, M., & Wauchope, M. (2005). Behavioral characteristics of men accused of rape: Evidence for different types of rapists. *Archives of Sexual Behavior, 34,* 241–253.

McCabe, M. P., & Ricciardelli, L. A. (2004). Weight and shape concerns of boys and men. In J. K. Thompson (Ed.), *Handbook of eating disorders and obesity* (pp. 606–634). Hoboken, NJ: Wiley.

McCabe, R., Antony, M., Summerfeldt, L., Liss, A., & Swinson, R. (2003). Preliminary examination of the relationship between anxiety disorders in adults and self-reported history of teasing or bullying experiences. *Cognitive Behaviour Therapy, 32,* 187–193.

McCaffery, J. M., Frasure-Smith, N., Dubé, M. P., Théroux, P., Rouleau, G. A., Duan, Q., & Lesperance, F. (2006). Common genetic vulnerability to depressive symptoms and coronary artery disease: A review and development of candidate genes related to inflammation and serotonin. *Psychosomatic Medicine, 68,* 187–200.

McCarthy, B., & Thestrup, M. (2008). Integrating sex therapy interventions with couple therapy. *Journal of Contemporary Psychotherapy, 38,* 139–149.

McCarthy, B. W. (1989). Cognitive-behavioral strategies and techniques in the treatment of early ejaculation. In S. R. Leiblum & R. C. Rosen (Eds.), *Principles and practice of sex therapy: Update for the 1990s* (pp. 141–167). New York: Guilford Press.

McCarthy, B. W. (1997). Strategies and techniques for revitalizing a nonsexual marriage. *Journal of Sex & Marital Therapy, 23,* 231–240.

McCarthy, B. W. (2001). Relapse prevention strategies and techniques with erectile dysfunction. *Journal of Sex & Marital Therapy, 27,* 1–8.

McCarthy, M. (1990). The thin ideal, depression and eating disorders in women. *Behaviour Research & Therapy, 28,* 205–215.

McCloskey, M. S., Noblett, K. L., Deffenbacher, J. L., Gollan, J. K., & Coccaro, E. F. (2008). Cognitive-behavioral therapy for intermittent explosive disorder: A pilot randomized clinical trial. *Journal of Consulting and Clinical Psychology, 76,* 876–886.

McConaghy, N. (1998). Paedophilia: A review of the evidence. *Australian & New Zealand Journal of Psychiatry, 32,* 252–265.

McCormick, M. C., McCarton, C., Brooks-Gunn, J., Belt, P., & Gross, R. T. (1998). The Infant Health and Development Program: Interim summary. *Developmental & Behavioral Pediatrics, 19,* 359–370.

McCrady, B. S. (2001). Alcohol use disorders. In D. H. Barlow (Ed.), *Clinical handbook of psychological disorders: A step-by-step treatment manual* (3rd ed., pp. 376–433). New York: Guilford Press.

McCrady, B. S., Epstein, E. E., Cook, S., Jensen, N., & Hildebrandt, T. (2009). A randomized trial of individual and couple behavioral alcohol treatment for women. *Journal of Consulting and Clinical Psychology, 77,* 243–256.

McCrae, R. R., & Costa, P. T. (1999). A five-factor theory of personality. In L. A. Pervin (Ed.), *Handbook of personality: Theory and research* (2nd ed., pp. 139–153). New York: Guilford Press.

McCullough, J. P., Klein, D. N., Borian, F. E., Howland, R. H., Riso, L. P., Keller, M. B., Banks, P. L. C. (2008). Group comparisons of *DSM-IV* subtypes of chronic depression: Validity of the distinctions, Part II. *Journal of Abnormal Psychology 112,* 614–622.

McDaid, D., & Thornicroft, G. (2005). *Mental health II: Balancing institutional and community-based care.* Geneva: World Health Organization.

McEwen, B. S. (2000). Allostasis and allostatic load: Implications for neuropsychopharmacology. *Neuropsychopharmacology, 22,* 108–124.

McGhie, A., & Chapman, J. (1961). Disorders in attention and perception in early schizophrenia. *Schizophrenia Bulletin, 34,* 103–116.

McGlashan, T. H. (1988). A selective review of recent North American long-term follow-up studies of schizophrenia. *Schizophrenia Bulletin, 14,* 515–542.

McGovern, C. M. (1985). *Masters of madness.* Hanover, NH: University Press of New England.

McGreevy, M. A., Steadman, H. J., & Callahan, L. A. (1991). The negligible effects of California's 1982 reform of the insanity defense test. *American Journal of Psychiatry, 148,* 744–750.

McGue, M., Iacono, W. G., Legrand, L. N., Malone, S., & Elkins, I. (2001). Origins and consequences of age at first drink: I. Associations with substance-use disorders, disinhibitory behavior and psychopathology, and P3 amplitude. *Alcoholism: Clinical & Experimental Research, 25,* 1156–1165.

McGuffin, P., Rijsdijk, F., Andrew, M., Sham, P., Katz, R., & Cardno, A. (2003). The heritability of bipolar affective disorder and the genetic relationship to unipolar depression. *Archives of General Psychiatry, 60,* 497–502.

McIntosh, J. L. (1995). Suicide prevention in the elderly (age 65–99). *Suicide & Life-Threatening Behaviors, 25,* 180–192.

McKinnon, D. H., McLeod, S., & Reilly, S. (2008). The prevalence of stuttering, voice, and speech-sound disorders in primary school students in Australia. *Language, Speech, and Hearing Services in Schools, 38,* 5–15.

McLaughlin, K., Hilt, L., & Nolen-Hoeksema, S. (2007). Racial/ethnic differences in internalizing and externalizing symptoms in adolescents. *Journal of Abnormal Child Psychology, 35,* 801–806.

McLean, P. D., Whittal, M. L., Thordarson, D. S., Taylor, S., Soechting, I., Koch, W. J., Paterson, R., & Anderson, K. W. (2001). Cognitive versus behavior therapy in the group treatment of obsessive-compulsive disorder. *Journal of Consulting & Clinical Psychology, 69,* 205–214.

McMillan, T. M., & Rachman, S. J. (1987). Fearlessness and courage: A laboratory study of paratrooper veterans of the Falklands War. *British Journal of Psychology, 78,* 375–383.

McNally, R. J. (1999). Anxiety sensitivity and information-processing biases for threat. In S. Taylor (Ed.), *Anxiety sensitivity: Theory, research, and treatment of the fear of anxiety* (pp. 183–197). Mahwah, NJ: Erlbaum.

McNally, R. J. (2003). Recovering memories of trauma: A view from the laboratory. *Current Directions in Psychological Science, 12,* 32–35.

McNally, R. J., Clancy, S. A., & Schacter, D. L. (2001). Directed forgetting of trauma cues in adults reporting repressed or recovered memories of childhood sexual abuse. *Journal of Abnormal Psychology, 110,* 151–156.

McNally, R. J., Clancy, S. A., Schacter, D. L., & Pitman, R. K. (2000a). Cognitive processing of trauma cues in adults reporting repressed, recovered, or continuous memories of childhood sexual abuse. *Journal of Abnormal Psychology, 109,* 355–359.

McNally, R. J., Clancy, S. A, Schacter, D. L., & Pitman, R. K. (2000b). Personality profiles, dissociation, and absorption in women reporting repressed, recovered, or continuous memories of childhood sexual abuse. *Journal of Consulting Clinical Psychology, 68,* 1033–1037.

McNiel, D. E., & Binder, R. L. (1991). Clinical assessment of the risk of violence among psychiatric inpatients. *American Journal of Psychiatry, 148,* 1317–1321.

McWilliams, N., & Weinberger, J. (2003). Psychodynamic psychotherapy. In G. Stricker & T. A. Widiger (Eds.), *Handbook of psychology: Clinical psychology* (Vol. 8, pp. 253–277). New York: Wiley.

Meaney, M. J. (2001). Maternal care, gene expression, and the transmission of individual differences in stress reactivity across generations. *Annual Review of Neuroscience, 24,* 1161–1192.

Mechanic, D., & Bilder, S. (2004). Treatment of people with mental illness: A decade-long perspective. *Health Affairs, 23,* 84–95.

Mednick, B., Reznick, C., Hocevar, D., & Baker, R. (1987). Long-term effects of parental divorce on young adult male crime. *Journal of Youth & Adolescence, 16,* 31–45.

Mednick, S. A., Machon, R. A., Huttunen, M. O., & Bonett, D. (1988). Adult schizophrenia following prenatal exposure to an influenza epidemic. *Archives of General Psychiatry, 45,* 189–192.

Mednick, S. A., Watson, J. B., Huttunen, M., Cannon, T. D., Katila, H., Machon, R., Mednick, B., Hollister, M., Parnas, J., Schulsinger, F., Sajaniemi, N., Voldsgaard, P., Pyhala, R., Gutkind, D., & Wang, X. (1998). A two-hit working model of the etiology of schizophrenia. In M. F. Lenzenweger & R. H. Dworkin (Eds.), *Origins of the development of schizophrenia* (pp. 27–66). Washington, DC: American Psychological Association.

Mellon, M. W., & McGrath, M. L. (2000). Empirically supported treatments in pediatric psychology: Nocturnal enuresis. *Journal of Pediatric Psychology, 25,* 193–214.

Menezes, N. M., Arenovich, T., & Zipursky, R. B. (2006). A systematic review of longitudinal outcomes studies of first-episode psychosis. *Psychological Medicine, 36,* 1349–1362.

Menza, M., Lauritano, M., Allen, L., Warman, M., Ostella, F., Hamer, R. M., & Escobar, J. (2001). Treatment of somatization with nefazodone: A prospective, open-label study. *Annals of Clinical Psychiatry, 13,* 153–158.

Merckelbach, H., Devilly, G., & Rassin, R. (2002). Alters in dissociative identity disorder: Metaphors or genuine identities? *Clinical Psychology Review, 22,* 481–498.

Merikangas, K. R., Akiskal, H. S., Angst, J., Greenberg, P. E., Hirschfield, R. M. A., Petukhova, M., & Kessler, R. C. (2007). Lifetime and 12-month prevalence of bipolar spectrum disorder in the national comorbidity survey replication. *Archives of General Psychiatry, 64,* 543–552.

Merikangas, K. R., Dierker, L. C., & Szatmari, P. (1998). Psychopathology among offspring of parents with substance abuse and/or anxiety disorders: A high-risk study. *Journal of Child Psychology & Psychiatry, 5,* 711–720.

Merikangas, K. R., & Knight, E. (2009). Epidemiology of adolescent depression. In S. Nolen-Hoeksema & L. Hilt (Eds.), *Handbook of depression in adolescents* (pp. 53–74). New York: Routledge.

Merikangas, K. R., Lieb, R., Wittchen, H.-U., & Avenevoli, S. (2003). Family and high-risk studies of social anxiety disorder. *Acta Psychiatrica Scandinavica, 108*(Suppl. 417), 28–37.

Merrick, E. L., Horgan, C. M., Hodgkin, D., Garnick, D. W., Houghton, S. F., Panas, L., Saitz, R., & Blow, F. C. (2008). Unhealthy drinking patterns in older adults: Prevalence and associated characteristics. *Journal of the American Geriatric Society, 56,* 214–223.

Merrill, L. L., Thomsen, C. J., Sinclair, B. B., Gold, S. R., & Milner, J. S. (2001). Predicting the impact of child sexual abuse on women: The role of abuse severity, parental support, and coping strategies. *Journal of Consulting & Clinical Psychology, 69,* 992–1006.

Meston, C. M., & Bradford, A. (2007). Sexual dysfunctions in women. *Annual Review of Clinical Psychology, 3,* 233–256.

Meston, C. M., Seal, B. N., & Hamilton, L. D. (2008). Problems with arousal and orgasm in women. In D. L. Rowland & L. Incrocci (Eds.), *Handbook of sexual and gender identity disorders* (pp. 188–219). Hoboken, NJ: Wiley.

Meyer, I. H. (2003). Prejudice, social stress, and mental health in lesbian, gay, and bisexual populations: Conceptual issues and research evidence. *Psychological Bulletin, 129,* 674–697.

Meyer, R. G., & Weaver, C. M. (2006). *Law and mental health: A case-based approach.* New York: Guilford Press.

Meyer-Bahlburg, H. F. L. (2010). From mental disorder to iatrogenic hypogonadism: Dilemmas in conceptualizing gender identity variants as psychiatric conditions. *Archives of Sexual Behavior, 39,* 461–476.

Micallef, J., & Blin, O. (2001). Neurobiology and clinical pharmacology of obsessive-compulsive disorder. *Clinical Neuropharmacology, 24,* 191–207.

Michael, R. T., Gagnon, J. H., Laumann, E., & Kolata, G. (1994). *Sex in America: A definitive survey.* Boston: Little, Brown.

Michalak, E. E., & Lam, R. W. (2002). Seasonal affective disorder: The latitude hypothesis revisited. *Canadian Journal of Psychiatry / La Revue canadienne de psychiatrie, 47,* 787–788.

Michelson, D. (2004). *Results from a double-blind study of atomoxetine, OROS methylphenidate, and placebo.* Presented at the 51st Annual Meeting of the American Academy of Child and Adolescent Psychiatry, Washington, DC, October 19, 2004.

Mick, E., & Faraone, S.V. (2008). Genetics of attention deficit hyperactivity disorder. *Child and Adolescent Psychiatric Clinics of North America, 17,* 261–284.

Miklowitz, D. J., George, E. L., Richards, J. A., Simoneau, T. L., & Suddath, R. L. (2003). A randomized study of family-focused psychoeducation and pharmacotherapy in the outpatient management of bipolar disorder. *Archives of General Psychiatry, 60,* 904–912.

Miklowitz, D. J., Simoneau, T. L., George, E. L., Richards, J. A., Kalbag, A., Sachs-Ericsson, N., & Suddath, R. (2000). Family-focused treatment of bipolar disorder: 1-year effects of a psychoeducational program in conjunction with pharmacotherapy. *Biological Psychiatry, 48,* 582–592.

Milam, J. E., Richardson, J. L., Marks, G., Kemper, C. A., & McCutchan, A. J. (2004). The roles of dispositional optimism and pessimism in HIV disease progression. *Psychology & Health, 19,* 167–181.

Miller, T. Q., Smith, T. W., Turner, C. W., & Guijarro, M. L. (1996). Meta-analytic review of research on hostility and physical health. *Psychological Bulletin, 119,* 322–348.

Miller, W. R. (1983). Motivational interviewing with problem drinkers. *Behavioural Psychotherapy, 11,* 147–172.

Miller, W. R., & Rose, G. S. (2009). Toward a theory of motivational interviewing. *American Psychologist, 64,* 527–537.

Milliken, C. S., Auchterlonie, J. L., & Hoge, C. W. (2007). Longitudinal assessment of mental health problems among active and reserve component soldiers returning from the Iraq war. *Journal of the American Medical Association, 298,* 2141–2148.

Millon, T., Davis, R., Millon, C., Escovar, L., & Meagher, S. (2000). *Personality disorders in modern life.* New York: Wiley.

Milos, G., Spindler, A., Schnyder, U., & Fairburn, C. G. (2005). Instability of eating disorder diagnoses: A prospective study. *British Journal of Psychiatry, 187,* 573–578.

Mineka, S. (1985). Animal models of anxiety based disorders: Their usefulness and limitations. In A. H. Tuma & J. Maser (Eds.), *Anxiety and the anxiety disorders* (pp. 199–244). Hillsdale, NJ: Erlbaum.

Mineka, S., Davidson, M., Cook, M., & Keir, R. (1984). Observational conditioning of snake fear in rhesus monkeys. *Journal of Abnormal Psychology, 93,* 355–372.

Mineka, S., Gunnar, M., & Champoux, M. (1986). Control and early socioemotional development: Infant rhesus monkeys reared in controllable versus uncontrollable environments. *Child Development, 57,* 1241–1256.

Mineka, S., & Zinbarg, R. (2006). A contemporary learning theory perspective on the etiology of anxiety disorders: It's not what you thought it was. *American Psychologist, 61,* 10–26.

Minuchin, S. (1981). *Family therapy techniques.* Cambridge, MA: Harvard University Press.

Minuchin, S., Rosman, B. L., & Baker, L. (1978). *Psychosomatic families: Anorexia nervosa in context.* Cambridge, MA: Harvard University Press.

Miranda, J., Bernal, G., Lau, A., Kohn, L., Hwang, W. C., & La Fromboise, T. (2005). State of the science on psychosocial interventions for ethnic minorities. *Annual Review of Clinical Psychology, 1,* 113–142.

Mirsalimi, H., Perleberg, S. H., Stovall, E. L., & Kaslow, N. J. (2003). Family psychotherapy. In G. Stricker & T. A. Widiger (Eds.), *Handbook of psychology: Clinical psychology* (Vol. 8, pp. 367–387). New York: Wiley.

Mirsky, A. E., Bieliauskas, L. A., French, L. M., Van Kammen, D. P., Joensson, E., & Sedvall, S. (2000). A 39-year follow-up on the Genain quadruplets. *Schizophrenia Bulletin, 26,* 699–708.

Mitchell, J., Crow, S., Peterson, C. B., Wonderlich, S., & Crosby, R. D. (1998). Feeding laboratory studies in patients with eating disorders: A review. *International Journal of Eating Disorders, 24,* 115–124.

Mitler, M. M., & Miller, J. C. (1995). Some practical considerations and policy implications of studies and sleep patterns. *Behavioral Medicine, 21,* 184–185.

Mitropoulou, V., Barch, D., Harvey, P., Maldari, L., New, B., Cornblatt, B., & Siever, L. (2003). Two studies of attentional processing in schizotypal personality disorder. *Schizophrenia Research, 60,* S148.

Mitte, K. (2005). A meta-analysis of the efficacy of psycho- and pharmacotherapy in panic disorder with and without agoraphobia. *Journal of Affective Disorders, 88,* 27–45.

Moffitt, T. E. (1993). The neuropsychology of conduct disorder. *Development & Psychopathology, 5,* 135–151.

Moffitt, T. E. (2006). Life-course persistent versus adolescence-limited antisocial behavior. In D. Cicchetti & D. J. Cohen (Eds.), *Developmental psychopathology* (Vol. 3). *Risk, disorder, and adaptation* (2nd ed, pp. 570–598). New York: Wiley.

Moffitt, T. E., Arseneault, L., Jaffee, S. R., Kim-Cohen, J., Koenen, K. C., Odgers, C. L., Slutske, W. S., & Viding, E. (2008). Research review: *DSM-V* conduct disorder: Research needs for an evidence base. *Journal of Child Psychology and Psychiatry, 49,* 3–33.

Moffitt, T. E., Brammer, G. L., Caspi, A., Fawcet, J. P., Raleigh, M., Yuwiler, A., & Silva, P. A. (1998). Whole blood serotonin relates to violence in an epidemiological study. *Biological Psychiatry, 43,* 446–457.

Moffitt, T. E., & Caspi, A. (2001). Childhood predictors differentiate life-course persistent and adolescence-limited antisocial pathways among males and females. *Development & Psychopathology, 13,* 355–375.

Moffitt, T. E., Caspi, A., Rutter, M., & Silva, P. A. (2001). *Sex differences in antisocial behaviour: Conduct disorder, delinquency, and violence in the Dunedin Longitudinal Study.* Cambridge, UK: Cambridge University Press.

Mohler-Kuo, M., Lee, J. E., & Wechsler, H. (2003). Trends in marijuana and other illicit drug use among college students: Results. *Journal of American College Health, 52,* 17–24.

Molnar, B. E., Berkman, L. F., & Buka, S. L. (2001). Psychopathology, childhood sexual abuse and other childhood adversities: Relative links to subsequent suicidal behavior in the U.S. *Psychological Medicine, 31,* 965–977.

Monahan, J., Bonnie, R. J., Appelbaum, P. S., Hyde, P. S., Steadman, H. J., & Swartz, M. S.

(2001). Mandated community treatment: Beyond outpatient commitment. *Psychiatric Services, 52,* 1198–1205.

Monahan, J., Redlich, A., Swanson, J., Robbins, P., Appelbaum, P., Petrila, J., Steadman, H., Swartz, M., Angell, B., & McNiel, D. (2005). Use of leverage to improve psychiatric treatment in the community. *Psychiatric Services, 56,* 37–44.

Monahan, J., & Steadman, H. J. (2001). Violence risk assessment: A quarter century of research. In L. E. Frost (Ed.), *The evolution of mental health law* (pp. 195–211). Washington, DC: American Psychological Association.

Monahan, J., & Walker, L. (1990). *Social science in law: Cases and materials.* Westbury, NY: Foundation Press.

Monitoring the Future (2008a). Trends in 1-year Prevalence of use of various drugs for eighth, tenth, and twelfth graders. http://www.monitoringthefuture.org/data/07data/pr07t2.pdf (accessed December 6, 2008).

Monitoring the Future (2008b). *Trends in 30-day prevalence of use of various drugs for eighth, tenth, and twelfth Graders.* http://www.monitoringthefuture.org/data/07data/pr07t3.pdf (accessed December 6, 2008)

Mooney, M. E., & Hatsukami, D. K. (2001). Combined treatments for smoking cessation. In M. T. Sammons & N. B. Schmidt (Eds.), *Combined treatments for mental disorders* (pp. 191–213). Washington, DC: American Psychological Association.

Mora, G. (2008). Renaissance conceptions and treatments of madness. In E. Wallace, IV, & J. Gach (Eds.), *History of psychiatry and medical psychology: With an epilogue on psychiatry and the mind-body relation* (pp. 199–226). New York: Springer Science.

Morgan, A. B., & Lilienfeld, S. O. (2000). A meta-analytic review of the relation between antisocial behavior and neuropsychological measures of executive function. *Clinical Psychological Review, 20,* 113–136.

Morgan, C. A., Hazlett, G., Wang, S., Richardson, E. G., Jr., Schnurr, P., & Southwick, S. M. (2001). Symptoms of dissociation in humans experiencing acute, uncontrollable stress: A prospective investigation. *American Journal of Psychiatry, 158,* 1239–1247.

Morgenthaler, T., Alessi, C., Friedman, L., Owens, J., Kapur, V., Boehlecke, B., Brown, T., Chesson, A., Coleman, J., Lee-Chiong, T., Pancer, J., & Swick, T. J. (2007). Practice parameters for the use of actigraphy in the assessment of sleep and sleep disorders: An update for 2007. *Sleep, 30,* 519–529.

Morin, C. M., Bootzin, R., Buysse, D., Edinger, J. D., Espie, C. A., & Lichstein, K. L. (2006). Psychological and behavioral treatment of insomnia: Update of the recent evidence (1998–2004). *Sleep, 29,* 1398–1414.

Morokoff, P. J., & Gillilland, R. (1993). Stress, sexual functioning, and marital satisfaction. *Journal of Sex Research, 30,* 43–53.

Morrison, N. K. (1998). Behavioral pharmacology of hallucinogens. In R. E. Tarter (Ed.), *Handbook of substance abuse: Neurobehavioral pharmacology* (pp. 229–240). New York: Plenum Press.

Mortensen, P. B. (2003). Mortality and physical illness in schizophrenia. In R. M. Murray & P. B. Jones (Eds.), *The epidemiology of schizophrenia* (pp. 275–287). New York: Cambridge University Press.

Moser, C. (2009). When is an unusual sexual interest a mental disorder? *Archives of Sexual Behavior, 38,* 323–325.

Mowrer, O. H. (1939). A stimulus-response analysis of anxiety and its role as a reinforcing agent. *Psychological Review, 46,* 553–566.

Mueser, K. T., & Jeste, D. V. (Eds.). (2008). *Clinical handbook of schizophrenia.* New York: Guilford Press.

Mueser, K. T., Bellack, A. S., Morrison, R. L., & Wade, J. H. (1990). Gender, social competence, and symptomatology in schizophrenia: A longitudinal analysis. *Journal of Abnormal Psychology, 99,* 138–147.

Mueser, K. T., & McGurk, S. R. (2004). Schizophrenia. *Lancet, 363,* 2063–2072.

Mugavero, M. J,. Pence, B. W., Whetten, K., Leserman, J., Swartz, M., Stangl, D., & Thielman, N. M. (2007). Predictors of AIDS-related morbidity and mortality in a southern U.S. cohort. *AIDS Patient Care STDs, 21,* 681–690.

Mulvey, E. P. (1995). Personal communication.

Mundo, E., Zanoni, S., & Altamura, A. C. (2006). Genetic issues in obsessive-compulsive disorder and related disorders. *Psychiatric Annals, 36,* 495–512.

Munoz, R. F., Cuijpers, P., Smit, F., Barrera, A., & Leykin, Y. (2010). Prevention of onset and recurrence of major depression. *Annual Review of Clinical Psychology, 6,* 181–212.

Munoz, R. F., Le, H. N., Clarke, G., & Jaycox, L. (2002). Preventing the onset of major depression. In I. H. Gotlib & C. L. Hammen (Eds.), *Handbook of depression* (pp. 343–359). New York: Guilford Press.

Munro, A. (1999). *Delusional disorder: Paranoia and related illnesses.* New York: Cambridge University Press.

Murberg, T. A., Furze, G., & Bru, E. (2004). Avoidance coping styles predict mortality among patients with congestive heart failure: A 6-year follow-up study. *Personality and Individual Differences, 36,* 757–766.

Murphy, J. M. (1976). Psychiatric labeling in cross-cultural perspective. *Science, 191,* 1019–1028.

Murphy, W. D., and Page, I. J. (2008). Exhibitionism: Psychopathology and theory. In D. R. Laws & W. T. O'Donohue (Eds.), *Sexual deviance: Theory, assessment, and Treatment* (pp. 61–76). New York: Guilford Press.

Murray, H. A. (1943). *Thematic apperception test manual.* Cambridge, MA: Harvard University Press.

Myrtek, M. (2007). Type A behavior and hostility as independent risk factors for coronary heart disease. In J. Jordan, B. Barden, & A. M. Zeiher (Eds.), *Contributions toward evidence-based psychocardiology: A systematic review of the literature* (pp. 159–183). Washington, DC: American Psychological Association.

N

Naimi, T. S., Brown, D. W., Brewer, R. D, Giles, W. H., Mensah, G., Serdula, M. K., Mokdad, A. H., Hungerford, D. W., Lando, J., Naimi, S., & Stroup, D. F. (2005). Cardiovascular risk factors and confounders among nondrinking and moderate-drinking U.S. adults. *American Journal of Prevention Medicine, 28,* 369–373.

Naranjo, C. A., & Knoke, D. M. (2001). The role of selective serotonin reuptake inhibitors in reducing alcohol consumption. *Journal of Clinical Psychiatry, 62*(Suppl. 20), 18–25.

Narrow, W. E., Regier, D. A., Rae, D., Manderscheid, R. W., & Locke, B. Z. (1993). Use of services by persons with mental and addictive disorders. *Archives of General Psychiatry, 50,* 95–107.

Nasar, S. (1998). *A beautiful mind.* New York: Simon & Schuster.

Nath, A., Schless, N., Venkatesan, A., Rumbaugh, J., Sacktor, N., & McArthur, J. (2008). Evolution of HIV dementia with HIV infection. *International Review of Psychiatry, 20,* 25–31.

National Association for Shoplifting Prevention. (2006). Shoplifting statistics. http://www.shopliftingprevention.org/WhatNASPOffers/NRC/PublicEducStats.htm (accessed July 25, 2009)

National Institute of Mental Health (NIMH). (2002). Suicide facts. http://www.nimh.nih.gov/research/suifact.htm (accessed February 1, 2003)

National Insitute of Mental Health (NIMH). (2008). *Schizophrenia: Causes, symptoms, signs, diagnosis and treatments* (Kindle Edition). Washington, DC: Author.

National Institute on Drug Abuse (NIDA). (2002a). Cocaine abuse and addiction. http://www.drugabuse.gov/ResearchReports/Cocaine/cocaine2.html (accessed February 1, 2003)

National Institute on Drug Abuse (NIDA). (2002b). Heroin: Abuse and addiction. http://www.drugabuse.gov/ ResearchReports/heroin/heroin2.html (accessed February 1, 2003)

National Institute on Drug Abuse (NIDA). (2002c). Inhalant abuse. Retrieved from http://www.drugabuse.gov/ResearchReports/Inhalants/ inhalants2.html (accessed February 1, 2003)

National Institute on Drug Abuse (NIDA). (2002d). Methamphetamine: Abuse and addiction. http://www.drugabuse.gov/ Research Reports/Methamph/methamph2.html (accessed February 1, 2003)

National Institute on Drug Abuse (NIDA). (2002e). Nicotine addiction. http://www.drugabuse.gov/ResearchReports/Nicotine/nicotine2.html (accessed February 1, 2003)

National Institute on Drug Abuse (NIDA). (2002f). Prescription drugs: Abuse and addiction. http://www.drugabuse.gov/ResearchReports/Prescription/prescription2.html (accessed February 1, 2003)

National Institute on Drug Abuse (NIDA). (2008a). InfoFacts: Club drugs (GHB, ketamine, and rohypnol). http://www.drugabuse.gov/pdf/infofacts/ClubDrugs08.pdf (accessed March 5, 2009)

National Institute on Drug Abuse. (2008b). Trends in prescription drug abuse. http://www.drugabuse.gov/ResearchReports/Prescription/prescription5.html (accessed December 17, 2008).

National Institute on Drug Abuse (NIDA). (2009). Research report: MDMA (ecstasy). http://www.drugabuse.gov/PDF/RRmdma.pdf (accessed March 5, 2009)

National Sleep Foundation. (2009). 2009 Sleep in America poll. Washington, DC: Author.

Neal, J. A., & Edelmann, R. J. (2003). The etiology of social phobia: Toward a developmental profile. *Clinical Psychology Review, 23,* 761–786.

Neighbors, H. W. (1984). Professional help use among black Americans: Implications for unmet need. *American Journal of Community Psychology, 12,* 551–566.

Neighbors, H. W., Trierweiler, S. J., Ford, B. C., & Muroff, J. R. (2003). Racial differences in *DSM* diagnosis using a semi-structured instrument: The importance of clinical judgment in the diagnosis of African Americans. *Journal of Health & Social Behavior, 43,* 237–256.

Neighbors, H. W., Williams, D. H., Gunnings, T. S., Lipscomb, W. D., Broman, C., & Lepkowski, J. (1987). *The prevalence of mental disorder in Michigan prisons: Final report.* Ann Arbor: Michigan Department of Corrections, University of Michigan, School of Public Health, Department of Community Health Programs, Community Mental Health Program.

Nelson, B., & Yung, A. (2008). Treatment of the schizophrenia prodrome. In K. T. Mueser & D. V. Jeste (Eds.), *Clinical handbook of schizophrenia* (pp. 380–389). New York: Guilford Press.

Nelson, C. B., & Wittchen, H. (1998). *DSM-IV* alcohol disorders in a general population sample of adolescents and young adults. *Addiction, 93,* 1065–1077.

Nemeroff, C. B. (2000). An ever-increasing pharmacopoeia for the management of patients with bipolar disorder. *Journal of Clinical Psychiatry, 61*(Suppl. 13), 19–25.

Nemeroff, C. B. (2004). Neurobiological consequences of childhood trauma. *Journal of Clinical Psychiatry, 65*(Suppl. 1), 18–28.

Nemeroff, C. B., Kalali, A., Keller, M. B., Charney, D. S., Lendarts, S. E., Cascade, E. F., et al. (2007). Impact of publicity concerning pediatric suicidality data on physician practice patterns in the United States. *Archives of General Psychiatry, 64,* 466–472.

Nemeroff, C. J., Stein, R. I., Diehl, N. S., & Smilack, K. M. (1994). From the Cleavers to the Clintons: Role choices and body orientation as reflected in magazine article content. *International Journal of Eating Disorders, 16,* 167–176.

Nestadt, G., Romanoski, A. J., Chahal, R., & Merchant, A. (1990). An epidemiological study of histrionic personality disorder. *Psychological Medicine, 20,* 413–422.

Neugebauer, R. (1979). Medieval and early modern theories of mental illness. *Archives of General Psychiatry, 36,* 477–483.

Neumark-Sztainer, D., Story, M., Hannan, P. J., & Croll, J. (2002). Overweight status and eating patterns among adolescents: Where do youth stand in comparison to the Healthy People 2010 Objectives? *American Journal of Public Health, 82,* 844–851.

Newhill, C. E., Mulvey, E. P., & Lidz, C. W. (1995). Characteristics of violence in the community by female patients seen in a psychiatric emergency service. *Psychiatric Services, 46,* 785–789.

Newlin, D. B,. & Thomson, J. B. (1990). Alcohol challenge with sons of alcoholics: A critical review and analysis. *Psychological Bulletin, 108,* 383–402.

Newmann, J. P., Engel, R. J., & Jensen, J. E. (1991). Age differences in depressive symptom experiences. *Journal of Gerontology, 46,* P224–P235.

Newring, K. A. B., Wheeler, J., & Draper C. (2008). Transvestic fetishism: Assessment and treatment. In D. R. Laws & W. T. O'Donohue (Eds.), *Sexual deviance: Theory, assessment, and treatment* (pp. 285–304). New York: Guilford Press.

Neylan, T. C., Reynolds, C. F., III, & Kupfer, D. J. (2007). Sleep disorders. In J. A. Bourgeois, R. E. Hales, & S. C. Yudofsky (Eds.), *The American Psychiatric Publishing Board prep and review guide for psychiatry* (pp. 275–280). Arlington, VA: American Psychiatric Publishing.

Nicholson, R. A., & Kugler, K. E. (1991). Competent and incompetent criminal defendants: A quantitative review of comparative research. *Psychological Bulletin, 109,* 355–370.

Nigg, J. T., & Goldsmith, H. H. (1994). Genetics of personality disorders: Perspectives from personality and psychopathology research. *Psychological Bulletin, 115,* 346–380.

Nigg, J. T., & Huang-Pollock, C. L. (2003). An early onset model of the role of executive functions and intelligence in CD. In B. B. Lahey, T. E. Moffitt, & A. Caspi (Eds.), *Causes of conduct disorder and juvenile delinquency* (pp. 227–253). New York: Guilford Press.

Nishino, S., Sakurai, E., Nevsimalova, S., Yoshida, Y., Watanabe, T., Yanai, K., & Mignot, E. (2009). Decreased CSF histamine in narcolepsy with and without low CSF hypocretin-1 in comparison to healthy controls. *Sleep, 32,* 175–180.

Nobre, P. J., & Pinto-Gouveia, J. (2006). Dysfunctional sexual beliefs as vulnerability factors for sexual dysfunction. *Journal of Sex Research, 43,* 68–75.

Nock, M. (2010). Self-injury. *Annual Review of Clinical Psychology, 6,* 339–363.

Nock, M. K., Borges, G., Bromet, E. J., Alonso, J., Angermeyer, M., Beautrais, A., Bruffaerts, R., Chiu, W. T., de Girolamo, G., Gluzman, S., de Graaf, R., Gureje, O., Haro, J. M., Huang, Y., Karam, E., Kessler, R. C., Lepine, J. P., Levinson, D., Medina-Mora, M. E., Ono, Y., Posada-Villa, J., & Williams, D. (2008). Cross-national prevalence and risk factors for suicidal ideation, plans and attempts. *British Journal of Psychiatry, 192,* 98–105.

Nock, M. K., & Kazdin, A. E. (2001). Parent expectancies for child therapy: Assessment and relation to participant in treatment. *Journal of Child & Family Studies, 10,* 155–180.

Nock, M. K., & Kessler, R. C. (2006). Prevalence of and risk factors for suicide attempts versus suicide gestures: Analysis of the national comorbidity survey. *Journal of Abnormal Psychology, 115,* 616–623.

Nock, M. K., & Prinstein, M. J. (2004). A functional approach to the assessment of self-mutilative behavior. *Journal of Consulting and Clinical Psychology, 72,* 885–890.

Nolen-Hoeksema, S. (1990). *Sex differences in depression.* Stanford, CA: Stanford University Press.

Nolen-Hoeksema, S. (2004). Gender differences in risk factors and consequences for alcohol use and problems. *Clinical Psychology Review, 24,* 981–1010.

Nolen-Hoeksema, S., & Harrell, Z. A. T. (2002). Rumination, depression, and alcohol use: Tests of gender differences. *Journal of Cognitive Psychotherapy: An International Quarterly, 16,* 391–404.

Nolen-Hoeksema, S., & Hilt, L. (2009). Gender differences in depression. In I. H. Gotlib & C. L. Hammen (Eds.), *Handbook of Depression*, 2nd ed. (pp. 386-404). New York: Guilford Press.

Nolen-Hoeksema, S., & Rusting, C. (1999). Gender differences in well-being. In D. Kahneman, E. Diener, & N. Schwarz (Eds.), *Foundations of hedonic psychology: Scientific perspectives on enjoyment and suffering* (pp. 330–352). New York: Russell Sage Foundation.

Nolen-Hoeksema, S., Wisco, B. E., & Lyubomirsky, S. (2008). Rethinking rumination. *Perspectives on Psychological Science, 3,* 400–424.

Nopoulos, P., Flaum, M., & Andreasen, N. C. (1997). Sex differences in brain morphology in schizophrenia. *American Journal of Psychiatry, 154,* 1648–1654.

Norcross, J. C. (2002). Empirically supported therapy relationships. In J. C. Norcross (Ed.), *Psychotherapy relationships that work: Therapist contributions and responsiveness to patients* (pp. 3–16). London: Oxford University Press.

Nordin, V., & Gillberg, C. (1998). The long-term course of autistic disorders: Update on follow-up studies. *Acta Psychiatrica Scandinavica, 97,* 99–108.

Norman, R. M., & Malla, A. K. (1993). Stressful life events and schizophrenia: II. Conceptual and methodological issues. *British Journal of Psychiatry, 162,* 166–174.

Norris, F. H., Perilla, J. L., Ibanez, G. E., & Murphy, A. D. (2001). Sex differences in symptoms of posttraumatic stress: Does culture play a role? *Journal of Traumatic Stress, 14,* 7–28.

Nowell, P. D., Buysse, D. J., Morin, C. M., Reynolds, III, C. F., & Kuper, D. J. (1998). Effective treatments for selected sleep disorders. In P. E. Nathan (Ed.), *A guide to treatments* *that work* (pp. 531–543). New York: Oxford University Press.

Noyes, R., Langbehn, D. R., Happel, R. L., Stout, L. R., Muller, B. A., & Longley, S. L. (2001). Personality dysfunction among somatizing patients. *Psychosomatics, 42,* 320–329.

Ntais, C., Pakos, E., Kyzas, P., & Ioannidis, J. P. A. (2005). Benzodiazepines for alcohol withdrawal. *Cochrane Database of Systematic Reviews, 3,* CD005063.

Nunes, E. V., & Levin, F. R. (2004). Treatment of depression in patients with alcohol or other drug dependence: A meta-analysis. *Journal of the American Medical Association, 291,* 1887–1896.

Nurnberg, H. G., Hensley, P. L., Heiman, J. R., Croft, H. A., DeBattista, C., & Paine, S. (2008). Sildenafil treatment of women with antidepressant-associated sexual dysfunction: A randomized controlled trial. *Journal of the American Medical Association, 300,* 395–404.

Nusslock, R., Abramson, L. Y., Harmon-Jones, E., Alloy, L. B., & Hogan, M. E. (2007). A goal-striving life event and the onset of bipolar episodes: Perspective from the behavioral approach system (BAS) dysregulation theory. *Journal of Abnormal Psychology, 116,* 105–115.

O

O'Connor v. Donaldson. (1975). 422 U.S. 563.

O'Connor, B. P. (2005). A search for consensus on the dimensional structure of personality disorders. *Journal of Clinical Psychology, 61,* 323–345.

O'Connor, K., Hallam, R., & Rachman, S. (1985). Fearlessness and courage: A replication experiment. *British Journal of Psychology, 76,* 187–197.

Odgers, C. L., Milne, B., Caspi, A., Crump, R., Poulton, R., & Moffitt, T. E. (2007). Predicting prognosis for the conduct-problem boy: Can family history help? *Journal of the American Academy of Child and Adolescent Psychiatry, 46,* 1240–1249.

Odlaug, B. L., & Grant, J. E. (2008, May). *Prevalence of impulse control disorders in a college sample.* Poster presented at the Annual Meeting of the American Psychiatric Association, Washington, DC.

O'Donnell, L., O'Donnell, C., Wardlaw, D. M., & Stueve, A. (2004). Risk and resiliency factors influencing suicidality among urban African American and Latino youth. *American Journal of Community Psychology, 33,* 37–49.

O'Donohue (Eds.), *Sexual deviance: Theory, assessment, and treatment* (pp. 1–21). New York: Guilford Press.

Office of National Drug Control Policy. (2004). *The economic costs of drug abuse in the United States: 1992–2002* (Publication No. 207303). Washington, DC: Executive Office of the President.

Offord, D. R. (1997). Bridging development, prevention, and policy. In D. M. Stoff, J. Breiling, & J. D. Maser (Eds.), *Handbook of antisocial personality disorder* (pp. 357–364). New York: Wiley.

Ogden, C. L., Carroll, M. D., Curtin, L. R., McDowell, M. A., Tabak, C. J., & Flegal, K. M. (2006). Prevalence of overweight and obesity in the United States, 1999–2004. *Journal of the American Medical Association, 295,* 1549–1555.

Ogden, C. L., Flegal, K. M., Carroll, M. D., & Johnson, C. L. (2002). Prevalence and trends in overweight among US children and adolescents, 1999–2000. *Journal of the American Medical Association, 288,* 1728–1732.

Ohman, A., Fredrikson, M., Hugdahl, K., & Rimmo, P. (1976). The premise of equipotentiality in human classical conditioning: Conditioned electrodermal responses to potentially phobic stimuli. *Journal of Experimental Psychology: General, 105,* 313–337.

Okazaki, S., & Sue, S. (2003). Methodological issues in assessment research with ethnic minorities. In A. E. Kazdin (Ed.), *Methodological issues & strategies in clinical research* (3rd ed., pp. 349–367). Washington, DC: American Psychological Association.

O'Leary, A., Jemmott, L. S., & Jemmott, J. B., III. (2008). Mediation analysis of an effective sexual risk-reduction intervention for women: The importance of self-efficacy. *Health Psychology, 27,* S180–S184.

Olin, S. S., Raine, A., Cannon, T. D., Parnas, J., Schulsinger, F., & Mednick, S. A. (1999). Childhood behavior precursors of schizotypal personality disorder. *Schizophrenia Bulletin, 23,* 93–103.

Olivardia, R., Pope, H. G., Mangweth, B., & Hudson, J. I. (1995). Eating disorders in college men. *American Journal of Psychiatry, 152,* 1279–1285.

Olmos de Paz, T. (1990). Working-through and insight in child psychoanalysis. *Melanie Klein & Object Relations, 8,* 99–112.

Olson, H. C., Feldman, J. J., Streissguth, A. P., Sampson, P. D., & Boostein, F. L. (1998). Neuropsychological deficits in adolescents with fetal alcohol syndrome: Clinical findings. *Alcoholism: Clinical & Experimental Research, 22,* 1998–2012.

O'Malley, S. S., & Kosten, T. R. (2006). Pharmacotherapy of addictive disorders. In W. R. Miller & K. M. Carroll (Eds.), *Rethinking substance abuse: What the science shows and what we should do about it* (pp. 240–256). New York: Guilford Press.

Oquendo, M. A., Ellis, S. P., Greenwald, S., Malone, K. M., Weissman, M. M., & Mann, J. J. (2001). Ethnic and sex differences in suicide rates relative to major depression in the United States. *American Journal of Psychiatry, 158,* 1652–1658.

Ortiz, J., & Raine, A. (2004). Heart rate and antisocial behavior in children and adolescents: A meta-analysis. *Journal of the American Academy of Child and Adolescent Psychiatry, 43,* 154–162.

Osher, F. C., & Steadman, H. J. (2007). Adapting evidence-based practices for persons with mental illness involved with the criminal justice system. *Psychiatric Services, 58,* 1472–1478.

Öst, L. (1992). Blood and injection phobia: Background and cognitive, physiological, and behavioral variables. *Journal of Abnormal Psychology, 101,* 68–74.

Öst, L., Svensson, L., Hellström, K., & Lindwall, R. (2001). One-session treatment of phobias in youths: A randomized clinical trial. *Journal of Consulting & Clinical Psychology, 69,* 814–824.

Öst, L. S., & Sterner, U. (1987). Applied tension: A specific behavioral method for treatment of blood phobia. *Behaviour Research & Therapy, 25,* 25–29.

Overmier, J. B., & Seligman, M. E. (1967). Effects of inescapable shock upon subsequent escape and avoidance responding. *Journal of Comparative & Physiological Psychology, 63,* 28–33.

Ozonoff, S., & Cathcart, K. (1998). Effectiveness of a home program intervention for young children with autism. *Journal of Autism & Developmental Disorders, 28,* 25–32.

P

Pakenham, K. I., Chiu, J., Bursnall, S., & Cannon, T. (2007). Relations between social support, appraisal and coping and both positive and negative outcomes in young caregivers. *Journal of Health Psychology, 12,* 89–102.

Pallesen, S., Mitsem, M., Kvale, G., Johnsen, B.-H., & Molde, H. (2005). Outcome of psychological treatments of pathological gambling: A review and meta-analysis. *Addiction, 100,* 1412–1422.

Panagopoulou, E., Maes, S., Rime, B., & Montgomery, A. (2006). Social sharing of emotion in anticipation of cardiac surgery—effects on preoperative distress. *Journal of Health Psychology, 11,* 809–820.

Pappadopulos, E., Woolston, S., Chait, A., Perkins, M., Connor, D. F., & Jensen, P. S. (2006). Pharmacotherapy of aggression in children and adolescents: Efficacy and effect size. *Journal of the Canadian Academy of Child and Adolescent Psychiatry, 15,* 27–39.

Pardo, Y., Aguilar, R., Molinuevo, B., & Torrubia, R. (2007). Alcohol use as a behavioural sign of disinhibition: Evidence from J. A. Gray's model of personality. *Addictive Behaviors, 32,* 2398–2403.

Paris, J. (2008). *Treatment of borderline personality disorder: A guide to evidence-based practice.* New York: Guilford Press.

Park, D. C., & Reuter-Lorenz, P. (2009). The adaptive brain: Aging and neurocognitive scaffolding. *Annual Review of Psychology, 60,* 173–196.

Parker, G., Johnston, P., & Hayward, L. (1988). Parental "expressed emotion" as a predictor of schizophrenic relapse. *Archives of General Psychiatry, 45,* 806–813.

Parks, G. A., Anderson, B. K., & Marlatt, G. A. (2001). Relapse prevention therapy. In N. Heather, T. J. Peters, & T. Stockwell (Eds.), *International handbook of alcohol dependence and problems* (pp. 575–592). New York: Wiley.

Patrick, D. L., Althof, S. E., Pryor, J. L., Rosen, R., Rowland, D. L., Ho, K. F., McNulty, P., Rothman, M., & Jamieson, C. (2005). Premature ejaculation: An observational study of men and their partners. *Journal of Sexual Medicine, 2,* 358–367.

Patterson, R. (1994). *Opening remarks.* Paper presented at the National Forum on Creating Jail Mental Health Services for Tomorrow's Health Care Systems, San Francisco.

Pauls, D. A., Morton, L. A., & Egeland, J. A. (1992). Risks of affective illness among first-degree relatives of bipolar I old-order Amish probands. *Archives of General Psychiatry, 49,* 703–708.

Paunovic, N., & Öst, L. (2001). Cognitive-behavior therapy vs exposure therapy in the treatment of PTSD in refugees. *Behaviour Research & Therapy, 39,* 1183–1197.

Pennebaker, J. W. (2007). Current issues and new directions in psychology and health: Listening to what people say—the value of narrative and computational linguistics in health psychology. *Psychology & Health, 22,* 631–635.

Pennebaker, J. W., Kiecolt-Glaser, J. K., & Glaser, R. (1988). Disclosure of traumas and immune function: Health implications for psychotherapy. *Journal of Consulting and Clinical Psychology, 56,* 239–245.

Perelman, M. A., & Rowland, D. L. (2008). Retarded and inhibited ejaculation. In D. L. Rowland & L. Incrocci (Eds.), *Handbook of sexual and gender identity disorders* (pp. 100–121). Hoboken, NJ: Wiley.

Perry, J. C. (1993). Longitudinal studies of personality disorders. *Journal of Personality Disorders* (Suppl. 1), 63–85.

Perugi, G., Akiskal, H. S., Giannotti, D., Frare, F., Di Vaio, S., & Cassano, G. B. (1997). Gender-related differences in body dysmorphic disorder (dysmorphophobia). *Journal of Nervous & Mental Disease, 185,* 578–582.

Pescosolido, B. A., Fettes, D. L., Martin, J. K., Monahan, J., & McLeod, J. D. (2007). Perceived dangerousness of children with mental health problems and support for coerced treatment. *Psychiatric Services, 58,* 619–625.

Peterson, C., & Seligman, M. E. (1984). Causal explanations as a risk factor for depression: Theory and evidence. *Psychological Review, 91,* 347–374.

Peterson, C., Seligman, M. E., & Vaillant, G. E. (1988). Pessimistic explanatory style is a risk factor for physical illness: A thirty-five-year longitudinal study. *Journal of Personality & Social Psychology, 55,* 23–27.

Peterson, C., Seligman, M. E. P., Yurko, K. H., Martin, L. R., & Friedman, H. S. (1998). Catastrophizing and untimely death. *Psychological Science, 9,* 127–130.

Petronis, A., Gottesman, I. I., Kan, P., Kennedy, J. L., Basile, V. S., Paterson, A. D., & Popendikyte, V. (2003). Monozygotic twins exhibit numerous epigenetic differences: Clues to twin discordance? *Schizophrenia Bulletin, 29,* 168–178.

Pettit, G. S., Dodge, K. A., & Brown, M. M. (1988). Early family experience, social problem solving patterns, and children's social competence. *Child Development, 59,* 107–120.

Phariss, B., Millman, R. B., & Beeder, A. B. (1998). Psychological and psychiatric consequences of cannabis. In R. E. Tarter (Ed.), *Handbook of substance abuse: Neurobehavioral pharmacology* (pp. 147–158). New York: Plenum Press.

Pharoah, F., Mari, J., Rathbone, J., & Wong, W. (2006). Family intervention for schizophrenia. *Cochrane Database of Systematic Reviews, 4,* CD000088.

Phillips, K. A. (2001). *Somatoform and factitious disorders.* Washington, DC: American Psychiatric Association.

Phillips, K. A., & Diaz, S. F. (1997). Gender differences in body dysmorphic disorder. *Journal of Nervous & Mental Disease, 185,* 570–577.

Phillips, K. A., Didie, E. R., Feusner, J., & Wilhelm, S. (2008). Body dysmorphic disorder: Treating an underrecognized disorder. *American Journal of Psychiatry, 165,* 1111–1118.

Phillips, K. A., & Najjar, F. (2003). An open-label study of citalophram in body dysmorphic disorder. *Journal of Clinical Psychiatry, 64,* 715–720.

Phillips, K. A., Pagano, M. E., & Menard, W. (2006). Pharmacotherapy for body dysmorphic disorder: Treatment received and illness severity. *Annals of Clinical Psychiatry, 18,* 251–257.

Pike, K. M., Walsh, B. T., Vitousek, K., Wilson, G. T., & Bauer, J. (2003). Cognitive behavior therapy in the posthospitalization treatment of anorexia nervosa. *American Journal of Psychiatry, 160,* 2046–2049.

Pillai, J. J., Friedman, L., Stuve, T. A., Trinidad, S., Jesberger, J. A., Lewin, J. S., Findling, R. L., Swales, T. P., & Schultz, S. C. (2002). Increased presence of white matter hyperintensities in adolescent patients with bipolar disorder. *Psychiatry Research, 114,* 51–56.

Pipher, M. (1994). *Reviving Ophelia: Saving the selves of adolescent girls.* New York: Putnam.

Pitschel-Walz, G., Leucht, S., Baumi, J., Kissling, W., & Engel, R. (2001). The effect of family interventions on relapse and rehospitalization in schizophrenia—A meta-analysis. *Schizophrenia Bulletin, 27,* 73–92.

Pittenger, C., & Duman, R. S. (2008). Stress, depression, and neuroplasticity: A convergence of mechanisms. *Neuropsychopharmacology Reviews, 33,* 88–109.

Platt, S., & Hawton, K. (2000). Repetition of suicidal behavior. In K. Hawton (Ed.), *International book of suicide and attempted suicide.* New York: Wiley.

Plener, P. L., Libal, G., Keller, F., Fegert, J. M., & Muehlenkamp, J. J. (2009). An international comparison of adolescent non-suicidal self-injury (NSSI) and suicide attempts: Germany and the USA. *Psychological Medicine, 39,* 1549–1558.

Polanczyk, G., & Jensen, P. (2008). Epidemiological considerations in attention deficit hyperactivity disorder: A review and update. *Child and Adolescent Psychiatric Clinics of North America, 17,* 245–260.

Pole, N., Neylan, T. C., Otte, C., Metzler, T. J., Best, S. R., & Henn-Haase, C. (2007). Associations between childhood trauma and emotion-modulated psychophysiological responses to startling sounds: A study of police cadets. *Journal of Abnormal Psychology, 116,* 352–361.

Polivy, J., & Herman, C. P. (2002). Causes of eating disorders. *Annual Review of Psychology, 53,* 187–213.

Pope, H. G., Gruber, A. J, Hudson, J. I., Huestis, M. A., & Yurgelun-Todd, D. (2001). Neuropsychological performance in long-term cannabis users. *Archives of General Psychiatry, 58,* 909–915.

Pope, H. G., Gruber, A. J., Mangweth, B., Bureau, B., deCol, C., Jouvent, R., & Hudson, J. I. (2000). Body image perception among men in three countries. *American Journal of Psychiatry, 157,* 1297–1301.

Pope, H. G., Jacobs, A., Mialet, J., Yurgelun-Todd, D., & Gruber, S. (1997). Evidence for a sex-specific residual effect of cannabis on visuospatial memory. *Psychotherapy & Psychosomatics, 66,* 179–184.

Pope, H. G., Oliva, P. S., Hudson, J. I., Bodkin, J. A., & Grueber, A. J. (1999). Attitudes toward *DSM-IV* dissociative disorders diagnoses among board-certified American psychiatrists. *American Journal of Psychiatry, 156,* 321–323.

Pope, H. G., Jr., Lalonde, J. K., Pindyck, L. J., Walsh, B. T., Bulik, C. M., Crow, S., McElroy, L. L., Rosenthal, N., & Hudson, J. I. (2006). Binge eating disorder: A stable syndrome. *American Journal of Psychology, 163,* 2181–2183.

Potenza, M. N., Kosten, T. R., & Rounsaville, B. J. (2001). Pathological gambling. *Journal of the American Medical Association, 286,* 141–144.

Potenza, M. N., Steinberg, M. A., Skudlarski, P., Fulbright, R. K., Lacadie, C. M., Wilbur, M. K., Rounsaville, B. J., Gore, J. C., & Wexler, B. E. (2003). Gambling urges in pathological gambling: A functional magnetic resonance imaging study. *Archives of General Psychiatry, 60,* 828–836.

Pratt, D. S., Jandzio, M., Tomlinson, D., Kang, X., & Smith, E. (2006). The 5-10-25 challenge: An observational study of a Web-based wellness intervention for a global workforce. *Disease Management, 9,* 284–290.

Prescott, C. A., & Kendler, K. S. (1999). Genetic and environmental contributions to alcohol abuse and dependence in a population-based sample of male twins. *American Journal of Psychiatry, 156,* 34–40.

Pretzer, J. (2004). Cognitive therapy of personality disorders. In G. G. Magnavita (Ed.), *Handbook of personality disorders: Theory and practice* (pp. 169–193). New York: Wiley.

Pribor, E. F., Yutzy, S. H., Dean, J. T, & Wetzel, R. D. (1993). Briquet's syndrome, dissociation, and abuse. *American Journal of Psychiatry, 150,* 1507–1511.

Pridal, C. G., & LoPiccolo, J. (2000). Multi-element treatment of desire disorders: Integration of cognitive, behavioral, and systemic therapy. In S. R. Leiblum & R. C. Rosen

(Eds.), *Principles and practice of sex therapy* (3rd ed., pp. 57–81). New York: Guilford Press.

Prince, J. (2008). Catecholamine dysfunction in attention-deficit/hyperactivity disorder: An update. *Journal of Clinical Psychopharmacology, 28,* S39–S45.

Pritchard, J. C. (1837). *A treatise on insanity and other diseases affecting the mind.* Philadelphia: Harwell, Barrington, & Harwell.

Prochaska, J. O. (1995). Common problems: Common solutions. *Clinical Psychology: Science & Practice, 2,* 101–105.

Proctor, A., Yairi, E., Duff, M. C., & Zhang, J. (2008). Prevalence of stuttering in African American preschoolers. *Journal of Speech, Language and Hearing Research, 51,* 1465–1479.

Project MATCH Research Group. (1998). Matching alcoholism treatments to client heterogeneity: Treatment main effects and matching effects on drinking during treatment. *Journal of Studies on Alcohol, 59,* 631–639.

Puhl, R. M., & Heuer, C. A. (2009). The stigma of obesity: A review and update. *Obesity, 17,* 1–24.

Putnam, F., Zahn, T., & Post, R. (1990). Differential autonomic nervous system activity in multiple personality disorder. *Physical Review, 31,* 251–260.

Putnam, F. W. (1991). Recent research on multiple personality disorder. *Psychiatric Clinics of North America, 14,* 489–502.

Putnam, F. W., Guroff, J. J., Silberman, E. K., & Barban, L. (1986). The clinical phenomenology of multiple personality disorder: Review of 100 recent cases. *Journal of Clinical Psychiatry, 47,* 285–293.

Putnam, F. W., & Lowenstein, R. J. (1993). Treatment of multiple personality disorder: A survey of current practices. *American Journal of Psychiatry, 150,* 1048–1052.

Puttler, L. I., Zucker, R. A., Fitzgerald, H. E., & Bingham, C. R. (1998). Behavioral outcomes among children of alcoholics during the early and middle childhood years: Familial subtype variations. *Alcoholism: Clinical & Experimental Research, 22,* 1962–1972.

Q

Quality Assurance Project. (1990). Treatment outlines for paranoid, schizotypal, and schizoid personality disorders. *Australian & New Zealand Journal of Psychiatry, 24,* 339–350.

R

Rachman, S. (1993). Obsessions, responsibility and guilt. *Behaviour Research & Therapy, 31,* 149–154.

Rachman, S. (1997). A cognitive theory of obsessions. *Behaviour Research & Therapy, 35,* 667–682.

Rachman, S., & deSilva, P. (1978). Abnormal and normal obsessions. *Behaviour Research & Therapy, 16,* 233–248.

Rachman, S. J., & Hodgson, R. J. (1980). *Obsessions and compulsions.* Englewood Cliffs, NJ: Prentice Hall.

Ragin, D. F., Pilotti, M., Madry, L., Sage, R. E., Bingham, L. E., & Primm, B. J. (2002). Intergenerational substance abuse and domestic violence as familial risk factors for lifetime attempted suicide among battered women. *Journal of Interpersonal Violence, 17,* 1027–1045.

Raikkonen, K., Matthews, K. A., Flory, J. D., Owens, J. F., & Gump, B. B. (1999). Effects of optimism, pessimism, and trait anxiety on ambulatory blood pressure and mood during everyday life. *Journal of Personality & Social Psychology, 76,* 104–113.

Raine, A. (1997). Antisocial behavior and psychophysiology: A biological perspective. In D. M. Stoff, J. Breiling, & J. D. Maser (Eds.), *Handbook of antisocial personality disorder* (pp. 289–304). New York: Wiley.

Ramar, K., & Guilleminault, C. (2008). Sleep apnea (central and obstructive). In H. R. Smith, C. L. Comella, & B. Hogl (Eds.), *Sleep medicine* (pp. 129–156). New York: Cambridge University Press.

Rapee, R. M., & Barlow, D. H. (1993). Generalized anxiety disorder, panic disorder, and the phobias. In P. B. Sutker (Ed.), *Comprehensive handbook of psychopathology* (pp. 109–127). New York: Plenum Press.

Rapee, R. M., & Heimberg, R. G. (1997). A cognitive-behavioral model of anxiety in social phobia. *Behaviour Research & Therapy, 35,* 741–756.

Rapoport, J. L. (1989). The biology of obsessions and compulsions. *Scientific American,* 83–89.

Rapoport, J. L. (1990). *The boy who couldn't stop washing.* New York: Plume.

Rapoport, J. L. (1991). Recent advances in obsessive-compulsive disorder. *Neuropsychopharmacology, 5,* 1–10.

Rapoport, J. L., Jensen, P. S., Inoff-Germain, G., Weissman, M. M., Greenwald, S., Narrow, W. E., Lahey, B. B., & Canino, G. (2000). Childhood obsessive-compulsive disorder in the NIMH MECA study: Parent versus child identification of cases. *Journal of Anxiety Disorders, 14,* 535–548.

Rasekh, Z., Bauer, H. M., Manos, M. M., & Iacopino, V. (1998). Women's health and human rights in Afghanistan. *Journal of the American Medical Association, 280,* 449–455.

Rauch, S. L., Phillips, K. A., Segal, E., Makris, N., Shin, L. M., Whalen, P. J., Jenike, M. A., Caviness, V. S., Jr., & Kennedy, D. N. (2003). A preliminary morphometric magnetic resonance imaging study of regional brain volumes in body dysmorphic disorder. *Psychiatry Research: Neuroimaging, 122,* 13–19.

Ravussin, E., Valencia, M. E., Esparza, J., Bennett, P. H., & Schulz, L. O. (1994). Effects of a traditional lifestyle on obesity in Pima Indians. *Diabetes Care, 17,* 1067–1074.

Ray, O., & Ksir, C. (1993). *Drugs, society, and human behavior.* St. Louis: C. V. Mosby.

Razran, G. (1961). The observable unconscious and the inferable conscious in current Soviet psychophysiology: Interoceptive conditioning, semantic conditioning, and the orienting reflex. *Psychological Review, 68,* 81–150.

Read, J. D., & Lindsay, D. S. (Eds.). (1997). *Recollections of trauma: Scientific research and clinical practice.* New York: Plenum Press.

Reas, D. L., & Grilo, C. M. (2008). Review and meta-analysis of pharmacotherapy for binge-eating disorder. *Obesity, 16,* 2024–2038.

Redlick, A. D., Steadman, H. J., Monahan, J., Robbins, P. C., & Petrila, J. (2006). Patterns of practice in mental health courts: A national survey. *Law and Human Behavior, 30,* 347–362.

Reed, G. M., Kemeny, M. E., Taylor, S. E., & Visscher, B. R. (1999). Negative HIV-specific expectancies and AIDS-related bereavement as predictors of symptom onset in asymptomatic HIV-positive gay men. *Health Psychology, 18,* 354–363.

Rees, K., Bennett, P., West, R., Davey, S. G., & Ebrahim, S. (2004). Psychological interventions for coronary heart disease. *Cochrane Database Systematic Reviews, 2,* CD002902.

Regier, D. A., Boyd, J. H., Burke, J. D., Rae, D. S., Myers, J. K., Kramer, M., Robins, L. N., George, L. K., Karno, M., & Locke, B. Z. (1988). One-month prevalence of mental disorders in the United States: Based on five epidemiologic catchment area sites. *Archives of General Psychiatry, 45,* 977–986.

Regier, D. A., Narrow, W. E., Rae, D. S., Manderscheid, R. W., Locke, B. Z., & Goodwin, F. K. (1993). The de facto U.S. mental and addictive disorders service system. *Archives of General Psychiatry, 50,* 85–94.

Rehm, J., Greenfield, T. K., & Rogers, J. D. (2001). Average volume of alcohol consumption, patterns of drinking, and all-cause mortality: Results from the U.S. National Alcohol Survey. *American Journal of Epidemiology, 153,* 64–71.

Rehm, L. P. (1977). A self-control model of depression. *Behavior Therapy, 8,* 787–804.

Reichborn-Kuennerud, T., Czajkowski, N., Torgersen, S., Neale, M. C., Orstavik, R. E., Tambs, K., & Kendler, K. S. (2007). The relationship between avoidant personality disorder and social phobia. A population-based twin study. *American Journal of Psychiatry, 164,* 1722–1728.

Reid, J. B., & Eddy, J. M. (1997). The prevention of antisocial behavior: Some considerations in the search for effective interventions. In D. M. Stoff, J. Breiling, & J. D. Maser (Eds.), *Handbook of antisocial personality disorder* (pp. 343–356). New York: Wiley.

Reissing, E. D., Binik, Y. M., & Khalife, S. (1999). Does vaginismus exist? *Journal of Nervous & Mental Disease, 187,* 261–274.

Reitan, R. M., & Davidson, L. A. (1974). *Clinical neuropsychology: Current status and applications.* Washington, DC: V. H. Winston & Sons.

Resick, P. A. (1993). The psychological impact of rape. *Journal of Interpersonal Violence, 8,* 223–255.

Resick, P. A., & Calhoun, K. S. (2001). Posttraumatic stress disorder. In D. H. Barlow (Ed.), *Clinical handbook of psychological disorders: A step-by-step treatment manual* (3rd ed., pp. 60–113). New York: Guilford Press.

Resick, P. A., & Schnicke, M. K. (1992). Cognitive processing therapy for sexual assault victims. *Journal of Consulting & Clinical Psychology, 60,* 748–756.

Resnick, H. S., Kilpatrick, D. G., Dansky, B. S., & Saunders, B. E. (1993). Prevalence of civilian trauma and posttraumatic stress disorder in a representative national sample of women. *Journal of Consulting & Clinical Psychology, 61,* 984–991.

Rhebergen, D., Beekman, A. T. F., de Graaf, R., Nolen, W. A., Spijker, J., Hoogendijk, W. J., & Pennix, B.W.J.H. (2010). Trajectories of recovery of social and physical functioning in major depression, dysthymic disorder, and double depression: A 3-year follow-up. *Journal of Affective Disorders, 124,* 148–156.

Ricca, V., Mannucci, E., Mezzani, B., Moretti, S., Di Bernardo, M., Bertelli, M., Rotella, C. M., & Faravelli, C. (2001). Fluoxetine and fluvoxamine combined with individual cognitive-behaviour therapy in binge eating disorder: A one-year follow-up study. *Psychotherapy & Psychosomatics, 70,* 298–306.

Rich, B. A., Schmajuk, M., Perez-Edgar, K. E., Fox, N. A., Pine, D. S., & Leibenluft, E. (2007). Different psychophysiological and behavioral responses elicited by frustration in pediatric bipolar disorder and severe mood dysregulation. *American Journal of Psychiatry, 164,* 309–317.

Richards, T., Corina, D., Serafini, S., Steury, K., Echelard, D., Dager, S., et al. (2000). Effects of a phonologically driven treatment for dyslexia on lactate levels measured by proton MRI spectroscopic imaging. *American Journal of Neuroradiology, 21,* 916–922.

Richardson, J. L., Shelton, D. R., Krailo, M., & Levine, A. M. (1990). The effect of compliance with treatment in survival among patients with hematologic malignancies. *Journal of Clinical Oncology, 8,* 356.

Rief, W., Hiller, W., & Margraf, J. (1998). Cognitive aspects of hypochondriasis and the somatization syndrome. *Journal of Abnormal Psychology, 107,* 587–595.

Rifkin, A., Ghisalbert, D., Dimatou, S., Jin, C., & Sethi, M. (1998). Dissociative identity disorder in psychiatric inpatients. *American Journal of Psychiatry, 155,* 844–845.

Rimmele, C. T., Miller, W. R., & Dougher, M. J. (1989). Aversion therapies. In R. K. Hester & W. R. Miller (Eds.), *Handbook of alcoholism treatment approaches: Effective alternatives* (pp. 128–140). New York: Pergamon Press.

Risch, N., Herrell, R., Lehner, T., Liang, K. Y., Eaves, L., Hoh, J., Griem, A., Kovacs, M., Ott, J., & Merikangas, K. R. (2009). Interaction between the serotonin transporter gene (5-HTTLPR), stressful life events, and risk of depression: A meta-analysis. *Journal of the American Medical Association, 301,* 2462–2471.

Robbins, P. C., Monahan, J., & Silver, E. (2003). Mental disorder, violence, and gender. *Law and Human Behavior, 27,* 561–571.

Robin, A. L. (2003). Behavioral family systems therapy for adolescents with anorexia nervosa. In A. E. Kazdin & J. R. Weisz (Eds.), *Evidence-based psychotherapies for children and adolescents* (pp. 358–373). New York: Guilford Press.

Robinson, T. E., & Berridge, K. C. (1993). The neural basis of drug craving: An incentive-sensitization theory of addiction. *Brain Research Reviews, 18,* 247–291.

Robles, T. F., & Kiecolt-Glaser, J. K. (2003). The physiology of marriage: Pathways to health. *Physiology & Behavior, 79,* 409–416.

Rockney, R. M., & Lemke, T. (1992). Casualties from a junior-senior high school during the Persian Gulf War: Toxic poisoning or mass hysteria? *Journal of Developmental & Behavioral Pediatrics, 13,* 339–342.

Rockwood, K., Fay, S., Gorman, M., Carver, D., & Graham, J. E. (2007). The clinical meaningfulness of ADAS-Cog changes in Alzheimer's disease patients treated with donepezil in an open-label trial. *BMC Neurology, 7,* 26.

Roelofs, K., Hoogduin, K. A. L., Keijsers, G. P. J., Naring, G. W. B., Moene, F. C., & Sandijck, P. (2002). Hypnotic susceptibility in patients with conversion disorder. *Journal of Abnormal Psychology, 111,* 390–395.

Rogers, C. R. (1951). *Client-centered therapy, its current practice, implications, and theory.* Boston: Houghton Mifflin.

Rogler, L. H. (1989). The meaning of culturally sensitive research in mental health. *American Journal of Psychiatry, 146,* 296–303.

Rogler, L. H. (1999). Methodological sources of cultural insensitivity in mental health research. *American Psychologist, 54,* 424–433.

Rohan, K. J., Roecklein, K. A., Lindsey, K. T., Johnson, L. G., Lippy, R. D., Lacy, T. J., & Barton, F. B. (2007). A randomized controlled trial of cognitive-behavioral therapy, light therapy, and their combination for seasonal affective disorder. *Journal of Consulting and Clinical Psychology, 75,* 489–500.

Ron, M. (2001). Explaining the unexplained: Understanding hysteria. *Brain, 124,* 1065–1066.

Rosen, G. (1968). *Madness in society: Chapters in the historical sociology of mental illness.* Chicago: University of Chicago Press.

Rosen, G. M., Spitzer, R. L., & McHugh, P. R. (2008). Problems with the post-traumatic stress disorder diagnosis and its future in *DSM-V. British Journal of Psychiatry, 192,* 3–4.

Rosen, L. N., Targum, S. D., Terman, M., Bryant, M. J., Hoffman, H., Kasper, S. F., Hamovit, J. R., Docherty, J. P., Welch, B., & Rosenthal, N. E. (1990). Prevalence of seasonal affective disorder at four latitudes. *Psychiatry Research, 31,* 131–144.

Rosen, R. C., & Leiblum, S. R. (1995). Treatment of sexual disorders in the 1990s: An integrated approach. *Journal of Consulting & Clinical Psychology, 63,* 877–890.

Rosenbaum, M. (1980). The role of the term schizophrenia in the decline of the diagnoses of multiple personality. *Archives of General Psychiatry, 37,* 1383–1385.

Rosenberger, P. H., Ickovics, J. R., Epel, E. S., D'Entremont, D., & Jokl, P. (2004). Physical recovery in arthroscopic knee surgery: Unique contributions of coping behaviors to clinical outcomes and stress reactivity. *Psychology and Health, 19,* 307–320.

Rosengren, A., Hawken, S., Ounpuu, S., Sliwa, K., Zubaid, M., et al. (2004). Association of psychosocial risk factors with risk of acute myocardial infarction in 11,119 cases and 13,648 controls from 52 countries (the INTERHEART study): Case-control study. *Lancet, 364,* 953–962.

Rosenhan, D. L. (1973). On being sane in insane places. *Science, 179,* 250–258.

Rosenman, R. H., Brand, R. J., Jenkins, C. D., Friedman, M., Straus, R., & Wrum, M. (1976). Coronary heart disease in the Western Collaborative Group Study: Final follow-up experience of 8 years. *Journal of the American Medical Association, 233,* 877–878.

Rosenstein, M. J., Milazzo-Sayre, L. J., & Manderscheid, R. W. (1989). Care of persons with schizophrenia: A statistical profile. *Schizophrenia Bulletin, 15,* 45–58.

Rosenthal, M. Z., Gratz, K. L., Kosson, D. S., Cheavens, J. S., Lejuez, C. W., & Lynch, T. R. (2008). Borderline personality disorder and emotional responding: A review of the research literature. *Clinical Psychology Review, 28,* 75–91.

Ross, C. A. (1989). *Multiple personality disorder: Diagnosis, clinical features, and treatment.* New York: Wiley.

Ross, C. A. (1991). Epidemiology of multiple personality disorder and dissociation. *Psychiatric Clinics of North America, 14,* 503–517.

Ross, C. A. (1997). *Dissociative identity disorder: Diagnosis, clinical features, and treatment of multiple personality.* Toronto: Wiley.

Ross, C. A. (1999). Dissociative disorders. In T. Millon (Ed.), *Oxford textbook of psychopathology* (pp. 466–481). New York: Oxford University Press.

Ross, C. A., & Norton, G. R. (1989). Differences between men and women with multiple personality disorder. *Hospital & Community Psychiatry, 40,* 186–188.

Ross, C. A., Norton, G. R., & Wozney, K. (1989). Multiple personality disorder: An analysis of 236 cases. *Canadian Journal of Psychiatry, 34,* 413–418.

Ross, C. E., & Mirowsky, J. (1984). Socially-desirable response and acquiescence in a cross-cultural survey of mental health. *Journal of Health & Social Behavior, 25,* 189–197.

Ross, L., Lepper, M. R., & Hubbard, M. (1975). Perseverance in self-perception and social preparation: Biased attributional processes in the debriefing paradigm. *Journal of Personality & Social Psychology, 32,* 880–892.

Ross, S., & Heath, N. (2002). A study of the frequency of self-mutilation in a community sample of adolescents. *Journal of Youth and Adolescence, 31,* 67–77.

Rosselló, J., & Bernal, G. (2005). New developments in cognitive-behavioral and interpersonal treatments for depressed Puerto Rican adolescents. In E. D. Hibbs & P. S. Jensen (Eds.), *Psychosocial treatments for child and adolescent disorders: Empirically based strategies for clinical practice* (2nd ed., pp. 187–217). Washington, DC: American Psychological Association.

Rossiter, E., & Agras, W. S. (1990). An empirical test of the *DSM-III-R* definition of binge. *International Journal of Eating Disorders, 9,* 513–518.

Rothbaum, B. O., & Foa, E. B. (1991). Exposure treatment of PTSD concomitant with conversion mutism: A case study. *Behavior Therapy, 22,* 449–456.

Rothbaum, B. O., Foa, E. D., Riggs, D. S., & Murdock, T. (1992). A prospective examination of post-traumatic stress disorder in rape victims. *Journal of Traumatic Stress, 5,* 455–475.

Rovner, B. W. (1993). Depression and increased risk of mortality in the nursing home patient. *American Journal of Medicine, 94*(Suppl. 5A), 19S–22S.

Rowe, R., Maughan, B., Worthman, C. M., Costello, E. J., & Angold, A. (2004). Testosterone, antisocial behavior, and social dominance in boys: Pubertal development and biosocial interaction. *Biological Psychiatry, 55,* 546–552.

Rowland, D. L., & McMahon, C. G. (2008). Premature ejaculation. In D. L. Rowland & L. Incrocci (Eds.), *Handbook of sexual and gender identity disorders* (pp. 68–99). Hoboken, NJ: Wiley.

Roy, A. (1992). Genetics, biology, and suicide in the family. In R. W. Maris, A. L. Berman, J. T. Maltsberger, & R. I. Yufit (Eds.), *Assessment and prediction of suicide* (pp. 574–588). New York: Guilford Press.

Roy-Byrne, P. P., Craske, M. G., & Stein, M. B. (2006). Panic disorder. *Lancet, 368,* 1023–1032.

Rozin, P., Bauer, R., & Catanese, D. (2003). Food and life, pleasure and worry, among American college students: Gender differences and regional similarities. *Journal of Personality & Social Psychology, 85,* 132–141.

Rucker, D., Padwal, R., Li, S. K., Curloni, C., & Lau, D. C. W. (2007). Long term pharmacotherapy for obesity and overweight: Updated meta-analysis. *British Medical Journal, 335,* 1–10.

Rudnick, A., & Roe, D. (2008). Diagnostic interviewing. In K. T. Mueser & D. V. Jeste (Eds.), *Clinical handbook of schizophrenia* (pp. 117–124). New York: Guilford Press.

Rudolph, K. (2009). Interpersonal factors in adolescent depression. In S. Nolen-Hoeksema & L. Hilt (Eds.), *Handbook of depression in adolescents* (pp. 377–418). New York: Routledge.

Rudolph, K. D. (2008). The interpersonal context of adolescent depression. In S. Nolen-Hoeksema & L. M. Hilt (Eds.), *Handbook of depression in adolescents* (pp. 377–418). New York: Routledge.

Rudolph, K. D., & Conley, C. S. (2005). The socioeconomic costs and benefits of social-evaluative concerns: Do girls care too much? *Journal of Personality, 73,* 115–137.

Ruiz, P., Strain, E. C., & Langrod, J. G. (2007). *The substance abuse handbook.* Philadelphia: Lippincott Williams & Wilkins.

Rutter, M. (1987). Temperament, personality and personality disorder. *British Journal of Psychiatry, 150,* 443–458.

Rutter, M. (1997). Antisocial behavior: Developmental psychopathology perspectives. In D. M. Stoff, J. Breiling, & J. D. Maser (Eds.), *Handbook of antisocial personality disorder* (pp. 115–124). New York: Wiley.

Rutter, M., Caspi, A., Fergusson, D., Horwood, L. J., Goodman, R., Maughan, B., Moffitt, T. E., Meltzer, H., & Carroll, J. (2004). Sex differences in developmental reading disability: New findings from 4 epidemiological studies. *Journal of the American Medical Association, 291,* 2007–2012.

Rutter, M., MacDonald, H., Couteur, A. L., Harrington, R., Bolton, P., & Bailey, A. (1990). Genetic factors in child psychiatric disorders: II. Empirical findings. *Journal of Child Psychology & Psychiatry, 31,* 39–83.

Rutter, M., Silberg, J., O'Connor, T., & Simonoff, E. (1999). Genetics and child psychiatry: II. Empirical research findings. *Journal of Child Psychology & Psychiatry, 40,* 19–55.

Ryan, J. J., & Lopez, S. J. (2001). Wechsler Adult Intelligence Scale–III. In W. I. Dorfman & S. M. Freshwater (Eds.), *Understanding psychological assessment* (pp. 19–42). Dordrecht, Netherlands: Kluwer Academic.

S

Sack, R. L., Auckley, D., Auger, R. R., Carskadon, M. A., Wright, K. P., Jr., Vitiello, M. V., & Zhdanova, I. V. (2007). Circadian rhythm sleep disorders: Part I, Basic principles, shift work and jet lag disorders. *Sleep, 30,* 1460–1483.

Sackeim, H. A., Prudic, J., Fuller, R., Keilp, J., Lavori, P. W., & Olfson, M. (2007). The cognitive effects of electroconvulsive therapy in community settings. *Neuropsychopharmacology, 32,* 244–254.

Safer, D. L., Telch, C. F., & Chen, E. Y. (2009). *Dialectical behavior therapy for binge eating and bulimia.* New York: Guilford Press.

Saigal, C. S., Wessells, H., Pace, J., Schonlau, M., Wilt, T. J., The Urologic Diseases in America Project. (2006). Predictors and prevalence of erectile dysfunction in a racially diverse population. *Archives of Internal Medicine, 166,* 207–212.

Sajatovic, M., Madhusoodanan, S., & Fuller, M. A. (2008). Clozapine. In K. T. Mueser & D. V. Jeste (Eds.), *Clinical handbook of schizophrenia* (pp. 178–185). New York: Guilford Press.

Salkovskis, P. M. (1998). Psychological approaches to the understanding of obsessional problems. In R. Swinson (Ed.), *Obsessive-compulsive disorder: Theory, research, and treatment* (pp. 33–50). New York: Guilford Press.

Sallinen, M., Harma, M., Akerstedt, T., Rosa, R., & Lillqvist, O. (1998). Promoting alertness with a short nap during a night shift. *Journal of Sleep Research, 7,* 240–247.

Saluja, G., Iachan, R., Scheidt, P. C., Overpeck, M. D., Sun, W., & Giedd, J. N. (2004). Prevalence of and risk factors for depressive symptoms among young adolescents. *Archives of Pediatrics & Adolescent Medicine, 158,* 760–765.

Samii, A., Nutt, J. G., & Ransom, B. R. (2004). Parkinson's disease. *Lancet, 363,* 1783–1793.

Sampson, R. J., & Laub, J. H. (1992). Crime and deviance in the life course. *Annual Review of Sociology, 18,* 63–84.

Samuel, D. B., & Widiger, T. A. (2006). Clinicians' judgments of clinical utility: A comparison of the *DSM-IV* and five-factor models. *Journal of Abnormal Psychology, 115,* 298–308.

Sanderson, W. C., Rapee, R. M., & Barlow, D. H. (1989). The influence of illusion of control on panic attacks induced via inhalation of 5.5% carbon dioxide–enriched air. *Archives of General Psychology, 46,* 157–162.

Sandnabba, N. K., Santtila, P., Alison, L., & Nordling, N. (2002). Demographics, sexual behaviour, family background and abuse experiences of practitioners of sadomasochistic sex: A review of recent research. *Sexual & Relationship Therapy, 17,* 39–55.

Sapolsky, R. M. (2007). Why zebras don't get ulcers: Stress, metabolism, and liquidating your assets. In A. Monat, R. S. Lazarus, & G. Reevy (Eds.). *The Praeger handbook on stress and coping,* Vol. 1 (pp. 181–197). Westport, CT: Praeger.

Sarbin, T. R., & Juhasz, J. B. (1967). The historical background of the concept of hallucination. *Journal of the History of the Behavioral Sciences, 3,* 339–358.

Sarwer, D. B., Magee, L., & Crerand, C. E. (2004). Cosmetic surgery and cosmetic medical treatments. In J. K. Thompson (Ed.), *Handbook of eating disorders and obesity* (pp. 718–737). Hoboken, NJ: Wiley.

Satir, V. (1967). Family systems and approaches to family therapy. *Journal of the Fort Logan Mental Health Center, 4,* 81–93.

Saulsman, L. M., & Page, A. C. (2004). The five-factor model and personality disorder empirical literature: A meta-analytic review. *Clinical Psychology Review 23,* 1055–1085.

Saunders, B. E., Villeponteaux, L. A., Lipovsky, J. A., Kilpatrick, D. G., et al. (1992). Child sexual assault as a risk factor for mental disorders among women: A community survey. *Journal of Interpersonal Violence, 7,* 189–204.

Savla, G. N., Moore, D. J., & Palmer, B. W. Cognitive functioning. (2008). In K. T. Mueser & Dilip V. Jeste (Eds.), *Clinical handbook of schizophrenia* (pp. 91–99). New York: Guilford Press.

Saxena, S., Brody, A. L., Ho, M. L., Alborzian, S., Maidment, K. M., Zohrabi, N., Ho, M. K., Huang, S.-C., Wu, H.-M., & Baxter, L. R., Jr. (2002). Differential cerebral metabolic changes with paroxetine treatment of obsessivecompulsive disorder vs. major depression. *Archives of General Psychiatry, 59,* 250–261.

Saxena, S., Brody, A. L., Ho, M. L., Zohrabi, N., Maidment, K. M., & Baxter, L. R., Jr. (2003). Differential brain metabolic predictors of response to paroxetine in obsessive-compulsive disorder versus major depression. *American Journal of Psychiatry, 160,* 522–532.

Saxena, S., Brody, A. L., Maidment, K. M., Dunkin, J. J., Colgan, M., Alborzian, S., Phelps, M. E., & Baxter, L. R. (1999). Localized orbitofrontal and subcortical metabolic changes and predictors of response to paroxetine treatment in obsessive-compulsive disorder. *Neuropsychopharmacology, 21,* 683–693.

Saxena, S., & Prasad, K. V. (1989). *DSMIII* subclassification of dissociative disorders applied to psychiatric outpatients in India. *American Journal of Psychiatry, 146,* 261–262.

Scarr, S., Weinberg, R. A., & Waldman, I. D. (1993). IQ correlations in transracial adoptive families. *Intelligence, 17,* 541–555.

Schacter, D. L. (1999). The seven sins of memory. *American Psychologist, 54,* 182–203.

Schacter, D. L., Chiao, J. Y., & Mitchell, J. P. (2003). The seven sins of memory: Implications for the self. In J. LeDoux, J. Debiece, & H. Moss (Eds.), The self: From soul to brain. *Annals of the New York Academy of Sciences, 1001,* 226–239.

Scheeringa, M. S., Zeanah, C. H., Myers, L., & Putnam, F. W. (2003). New findings on alternative criteria for PTSD in preschool children. *Journal of the American Academy of Child and Adolescent Psychiatry, 42,* 561–570.

Schiavi, R. C., & Segraves, R. T. (1995). The biology of sexual dysfunction. *Psychiatric Clinics of North America, 18,* 7–23.

Schildkraut, J. J. (1965). The catecholamine hypothesis of affective disorder: A review of supporting evidence. *American Journal of Psychiatry, 122,* 509–522.

Schlenger, W. E., Kulka, R. A., Fairbank, J. A., & Hough, R. L. (1992). The prevalence of post-traumatic stress disorder in the Vietnam generation: A multimethod, multisource assessment of psychiatric disorder. *Journal of Traumatic Stress, 5,* 333–363.

Schmidt, N. B., & Keough, M. E. (2010). Treatment of panic. *Annual Review of Clinical Psychology, 6,* 241–256.

Schneider, J. A., O'Leary, A., & Jenkins, S. R. (1995). Gender, sexual orientation, and disordered eating. *Psychology & Health, 10,* 113–128.

Schneiderman, N., Ironson, G., & Siegel, S. D. (2005). Stress and health: Psychological, behavioral, and biological determinants. *Annual Review of Clinical Psychology, 1,* 607–628.

Scholte, W. F., Olff, M., Ventevogel, P., de Vries, G.-J., Jansveld, E., Cardozo, B. L., & Crawford, C. A. G. (2004). Mental health symptoms following war and repression in eastern Afghanistan. *Journal of the American Medical Association, 292,* 585–593.

Schonfeld, L., & Dupree, L. W. (2002). Age-specific cognitive-behavioral and self-management treatment approaches. In A. M. Gurnack, R. Atkinson, & N. J. Osgood (Eds.), *Treating alcohol and drug abuse in the elderly* (pp. 109–130). New York: Springer.

Schreibman, L., & Charlop-Christy, M. H. (1998). Autistic disorder. In T. H. Ollendick & M. Hersen (Eds.), *Handbook of child psychopathology* (pp. 157–180). New York: Plenum Press.

Schuckit, M. A. (1991). A longitudinal study of children of alcoholics. In M. Galanter (Ed.), *Recent developments in alcoholism* (Vol. 9, pp. 5–19). New York: Plenum Press.

Schuckit, M. A. (1995). *Drug and alcohol abuse: A clinical guide to diagnosis and treatment.* New York: Plenum Medical Book Company.

Schuckit, M. A. (1998). Biological, psychological, and environmental predictors of the alcoholism risk: A longitudinal study. *Journal of Studies on Alcohol, 59,* 485–494.

Schuckit, M. A., Smith, T. L., Danko, G. P., Bucholz, K. K., Reich, T., & Bierut, L. (2001). Five-year clinical course associated with *DSM-IV* alcohol abuse or dependence in a large group of men and women. *American Journal of Psychiatry, 158,* 1084–1090.

Schuckit, M. A., Tip, J. E., Reich, T., & Hesselbrock, V. M. (1995). The histories of withdrawal convulsions and delirium tremens in 1648 alcohol dependent subjects. *Addiction, 90,* 1335–1347.

Schultz, R. T. (2005). Developmental deficits in social perception in autism: The role of the amygdala and fusiform face area. *International Journal of Developmental Neuroscience, 23,* 125–141.

Schulz, R., Bookwala, J., Knapp, J. E., Scheier, M., & Williamson, G. M. (1996). Pessimism, age, and cancer mortality. *Psychology & Aging, 11,* 304–309.

Schuster, M. A., Stein, B. D., Jaycox, L. H., Collins, R. L., Marshall, G. N., Elliott, M. N., Zhou, A. J., Kanouse, D. E., Morrison, J. L., & Berry, S. H. (2001). A national survey of stress reactions after the September 11, 2001, terrorist attacks. *New England Journal of Medicine, 345,* 1507–1512.

Schwartz, J., Stoessel, P. W., Baxter, L. R., Martin, K. M., & Phelps, M. C. (1996). Systemic changes in cerebral glucose metabolic rate after successful behavior modification treatment of obsessive-compulsive disorder. *Archives of General Psychiatry, 53,* 109–113.

Scogin, F., Floyd, M., & Forde, J. (2000). Anxiety in older adults. In S. K. Whitbourne (Ed.), *Psychopathology in later adulthood* (pp. 117–140). New York: Wiley.

Scogin, F., Welsh, D., Hanson, A., Stump, J., & Coates, A. (2005). Evidence-based psychotherapies for depression in older adults. *Psychological Science and Practice, 12,* 222–237.

Scull, A. (1993). *The most solitary of afflictions.* New Haven: Yale University Press.

Seedat, S., Stein, M. B., & Forde, D. R. (2003). Prevalence of dissociative experiences in a community sample. *Journal of Nervous & Mental Disorders, 191,* 115–120.

Seeman, M. V. (2008) Gender. In K. T. Mueser & Dilip V. Jeste (Eds.), *Clinical handbook of schizophrenia* (pp. 575–580). New York: Guilford Press.

Segal, S. P., Laurie, T. A., & Franskoviak, P. (2004). Ambivalence of PES patients toward hospitalization and factors in their disposition. *International Journal of Law & Psychiatry, 27,* 87–99.

Segerstrom, S. C., & Miller, G. E. (2004). Psychological stress and the human immune system: A meta-analytic study of 30 years of inquiry. *Psychological Bulletin, 130,* 601–630.

Segerstrom, S. C., Solomon, G. F., Kemeny, M. E., & Fahey, J. L. (1998). Relationship of worry to immune sequelae of the Northridge earthquake. *Journal of Behavioral Medicine, 21,* 433–450.

Segerstrom, S. C., Taylor, S. E., Kemeny, M. E., Reed, G. M., & Visscher, B. R. (1996). Causal attributions predict rate of immune decline in HIV seropositive gay men. *Health Psychology, 15,* 485–493.

Segraves, R. T. (2003). Pharmacologic management of sexual dysfunction: Benefits and limitations. *CNS Spectrums, 8,* 225–229.

Segraves, R. T., Clayton, A., Croft, H., Wolf, A., & Warnock, J. (2004). Bupropion sustained release for the treatment of hypoactive sexual desire disorder in premenopausal women. *Journal of Clinical Psychopharmacology, 24,* 339–342.

Seidman, L. J., Faraone, S. V., Goldstein, J. M., Kremen, W. S., Horton, N. J., Makris, N., Toomey, R., Kennedy, D., Caviness, V. S., & Tsuang, M. T. (2002). Left hippocampal volume as a vulnerability indicator for schizophrenia. *Archives of General Psychiatry, 59,* 839–849.

Seligman, M. (1970). On the generality of the laws of learning. *Psychological Review, 77,* 406–418.

Seligman, M. E. (1993). *What you can change and what you can't: The complete guide to self-improvement.* New York: Knopf.

Seligman, M. E., & Maier, S. F. (1967). Failure to escape traumatic shock. *Journal of Experimental Psychology, 74,* 1–9.

Seligman, M. E. P. (1975). *Helplessness: On depression, development, and death.* San Francisco: Freeman, Cooper.

Seligman, M. E. P., & Binik, Y. M. (1977). The safety signal hypothesis. In H. Davis & H. Hurwitz (Eds.), *Pavlovian operant interactions.* Hillsdale, NJ: Erlbaum.

Selling, L. H. (1940). *Men against madness.* New York: Greenberg.

Semans, J. H. (1956). Premature ejaculation: A new approach. *Southern Medical Journal, 49,* 353–357.

Semler, C. N., & Harvey, A. G. (2007). An experimental investigation of daytime monitoring for sleep-related threat in primary insomnia. *Cognition and Emotion, 21,* 146–161.

Serfaty, M. A., Turkington, D., Heap, M., Ledsham, L., & Jolley, E. (1999). Cognitive-therapy versus dietary counseling in the outpatient treatment of anorexia nervosa: Effects of the treatment phase. *European Eating Disorders Review, 7,* 334–350.

Seto, M. C. (2008). Pedophilia: Psychopathology and theory. In D. R. Laws & W. T. O'Donohue (Eds.) *Sexual deviance: Theory, assessment, and treatment* (pp. 164–183). New York: Guilford Press.

Seto, M. C. (2009). Pedophilia. *Annual Review of Clinical Psychology, 5,* 391–407.

Shaffer, D., & Gould, M. (2000). Suicide prevention in the schools. In K. Hawton (Ed.), *The international handbook of suicide and attempted suicide* (pp. 585–724). New York: Wiley.

Shaffer, D., Gould, M. S., Fisher, P., Trautman, P., Moreau, D., Kleinman, M., & Flory, M. (1996). Psychiatric diagnosis in child and adolescent suicide. *Archives of General Psychiatry, 53,* 339–348.

Shaffer, D., & Jacobson, C. (2010). *Proposal to the* DSM-V *childhood disorder and mood disorder* *work groups to include non-suicidal self-injury (NSSI) as a* DSM-V *disorder*. http://www.dsm5.org/Proposed%20Revision%20Attachments/APA%20DSM-5%20NSSI%20Proposal.pdf (accessed February 15, 2010).

Shaffer, H. J., & Hall, M. N. (2001). Updating and refining prevalence estimates of disordered gambling behaviour in the United States and Canada. *Canadian Journal of Public Health, 92,* 168–172.

Shalev, A. Y., Peri, T., Canetti, L., & Schreiber, S. (1996). Predictors of PTSD in injured trauma survivors: A prospective study. *American Journal of Psychiatry, 153,* 219–225.

Shaw, D. S., Keenan, K., & Vondra, J. I. (1994). Developmental precursors of externalizing behavior: Ages 1 to 3. *Developmental Psychology, 30,* 355–364.

Shaw, D. S., & Winslow, E. B. (1997). Precursors and correlates of antisocial behavior from infancy to preschool. In D. M. Stoff, J. Breiling, & J. D. Maser (Eds.), *Handbook of antisocial personality disorder* (pp. 148–158). New York: Wiley.

Shaw, P., Lerch, J. P., Pruessner, J. C., Taylor, K. N., Rose, A. B., et al. (2007). Cortical morphology in children and adolescents with different apolipoprotein E gene polymorphisms: An observational study. *Lancet Neurology, 6,* 494–500.

Shaywitz, B., Shaywitz, S., Blachman, B., Pugh, K., Fulbright, R., Skudlarski, P., et al. (2004). Development of left occipito-temporal systems for skilled reading in children after a phonologically-based intervention. *Biological Psychiatry, 55,* 926–933.

Shaywitz, S. (2003). *Overcoming dyslexia: A new and complete science-based program for reading problems at any level.* New York: Knopf.

Shaywitz, S. E., & Shaywitz, B. A. (2008). Paying attention to reading: The neurobiology of reading and dyslexia. *Development and Psychopathology, 20,* 1329–1349.

Shea, M. T. (1993). Psychosocial treatment of personality disorders. *Journal of Personality Disorders* (Suppl. 1), 167–180.

Shea, M. T., Stout, R., Gunderson, J., Morey, L. C., Grilo, C. M., McGlashan, T., Skodol, A. E., Dolan-Sewell, R., Dyck, I., Zanarini, M. C., & Keller, M. B. (2002). Short-term diagnostic stability of schizotypal, borderline, avoidant, and obsessive-compulsive personality disorders. *American Journal of Psychiatry, 159,* 2036–2041.

Shenton, M. E., Frumin, M., McCarley, R. W., Maier, S. E., Westin, C.-F., Fischer, I. A., Dickey, C., & Kikinis, R. (2001). Morphometric magnetic resonance imaging studies: Findings in schizophrenia. In D. D. Dougherty & S. L. Rauch (Eds.), *Psychiatric neuroimaging research: Contemporary strategies* (pp. 1–60). Washington, DC: American Psychiatric Association.

Sher, K. J., Grekin, E. R., & Williams, N. A. (2005). The development of alcohol use disorders. In S. Nolen-Hoeksema, T. D. Cannon, & T. A. Widiger (Eds.), *Annual Review of Clinical Psychology* (Vol. 1, pp. 493–523). Palo Alto, CA: Annual Reviews.

Sher, K. J., & Trull, T. J. (1994). Personality and disinhibitory psychopathology: Alcoholism and antisocial personality disorder. *Journal of Abnormal Psychology, 103,* 92–102.

Sheridan, M. A., Hinshaw, S., & D'Esposito, M. (2007). Efficiency of the prefrontal cortex during working memory in attention-deficit/hyperactivity disorder. *Journal of the American Academy of Child and Adolescent Psychiatry, 46,* 1357–1366.

Sherman, J. C. (2008). Normal and learning disabled (LD) development of academic skills. In L. E. Wolf, H. E. Schreiber, & J. Wasserstein (Eds). *Adult learning disorders: Contemporary issues* (pp. 3–24). New York: Psychology Press.

Shifren, J., Braunstein, G., Simon, J., Casson, P., Buster, J., Redmond, G., Burki, R., Ginsburg, E., Rosen, R., Leiblum, S., Caramelli, K., Mazer, N., Jones, K., & Daugherty, C. (2000). Transdermal testosterone treatment in women with impaired sexual function after oophorectomy. *New England Journal of Medicine, 343,* 682–688.

Shin, L. M., Wright, C. I., Cannistraro, P. A., Wedig, M. M., McMullin, K., Martis, B., Macklin, M. L., Lasko, N. B., Cavanaugh, S. R., Krangel, T. S., Orr, S. P., Pitman, R. K., Whalen, P. J., & Rauch, S. L. (2005). A functional magnetic resonance imaging study of amygdala and medial prefrontal cortex responses to overtly presented fearful faces in posttraumatic stress disorder. *Archives of General Psychiatry, 62,* 273–281.

Shortt, A. L., Barrett, P. M., & Fox, T. L. (2001). Evaluating the FRIENDS program: A cognitive-behavioral group treatment for anxious children and their parents. *Journal of Clinical Child Psychology, 30,* 525–535.

Siev, J., & Chambless, D. L. (2007). Specificity of treatment effects: Cognitive therapy and relaxation for generalized anxiety and panic disorders. *Journal of Consulting and Clinical Psychology, 75,* 513–522.

Siever, L. J., Bernstein, D. P., & Silverman, J. M. (1995). Schizotypal personality disorder. In W. J. Livesley (Ed.), *The* DSM-IV *personality disorders* (pp. 71–90). New York: Guilford Press.

Siever, L. J., & Davis, K. L. (1991). A psychobiological perspective on the personality disorders. *American Journal of Psychiatry, 148,* 1647–1658.

Siever, L. J., & Davis, K. L. (2004). The pathophysiology of schizophrenia disorders: Perspectives from the spectrum. *American Journal of Psychiatry, 161,* 398–413.

Siever, L. J., & Kendler, K. S. (1985). Paranoid personality disorder. In R. Michels, J. Cavenar, & H. Bradley (Eds.), *Psychiatry* (Vol. 1, pp. 1–11). New York: Basic Books.

Siever, L. J., New, A. S., Kirrane, R., Novotny, S., Koenigsberg, H., & Grossman, R. (1998). New biological research strategies for personality disorders. In K. R. Silk (Ed.), *Biology of personality disorders* (pp. 27–61). Washington, DC: American Psychiatric Press.

Sigman, M., Spence, S. J., & Wang, A. T. (2006). Autism from developmental and neuropsychological perspectives. *Annual Review of Clinical Psychology, 2,* 327–355.

Silberg, J. L., Parr, T., Neale, M. C., Rutter, M., Angold, A., & Eaves, L. J. (2003). Maternal smoking during pregnancy and risk to boys' conduct disturbance: An examination of the causal hypothesis. *Biological Psychiatry, 53,* 130–135.

Silver, E., Cirincione, C., & Steadman, H. J. (1994). Demythologizing inaccurate perceptions of the insanity defense. *Law & Human Behavior, 18,* 63–70.

Simeon, D., Guralnik, O., Schmeidler, J., Sirof, B., & Knutelska, M. (2001). The role of childhood interpersonal trauma in depersonalization disorder. *American Journal of Psychiatry, 158,* 1027–1033.

Simons, J. A., & Helms, J. E. (1976). Influence of counselors' marital status, sex, and age on college and noncollege women's counselor preferences. *Journal of Counseling Psychology, 23,* 380–386.

Simpson, E. B., Yen, S., Costello, E., Rosen, K., Begin, A., Pistorello, J., & Pearlstein, T. (2004). Combined dialectical behavior therapy and fluoxetine in the treatment of borderline personality disorder. *Journal of Clinical Psychiatry, 65,* 379–385.

Sing, L. (1995). Self-starvation in context: Towards a culturally sensitive understanding of anorexia nervosa. *Social Science & Medicine, 41,* 25–36.

Singh, N. N., Oswald, D. P., & Ellis, C. R. (1998). Mental retardation. In T. H. Ollendick & M. Hersen (Eds.), *Handbook of child psychopathology* (pp. 91–116). New York: Plenum Press.

Skodol, A. E. (2010). Rationale for proposing five specific personality disorder types. http://www.dsm5.org/ProposedRevisions/Pages/RationaleforProposingFiveSpecificPersonalityDisorderTypes.aspx (accessed April 3, 2010)

Slate. (2004, June 3). Gender gap: What were the real reasons behind David Reimer's suicide? http://slate.msn.com/id/2101678/ (accessed February 11, 2005)

Small, G. W. (1998). The pathogenesis of Alzheimer's disease. *Journal of Clinical Psychiatry, 59,* 7–14.

Smedslund, G., & Ringdal, G. I. (2004). Meta-analysis of the effects of psychosocial interventions on survival time in cancer patients. *Journal of Psychosomatic Research, 57,* 123–131.

Smith, C. A., & Farrington, D. P. (2004). Continuities in antisocial behavior and parenting across three generations. *Journal of Child Psychology & Psychiatry, 45,* 230–247.

Smith, D. E., & Seymour, R. B. (1994). LSD: History and toxicity. *Psychiatric Annals, 24,* 145–147.

Smith, Y. L. S., van Goozen, S. H. M., & Cohen-Kettenis, P. T. (2001). Adolescents with gender identity disorder who were accepted or rejected for sex reassignment surgery: A prospective follow-up study. *Journal of the American Academy of Child & Adolescent Psychiatry, 40,* 472–481.

Smolak, L., Murnen, S. K., & Ruble, A. E. (2000). Female athletes and eating problems: A meta-analysis. *International Journal of Eating Disorders, 27,* 371–380.

Smolak, L., & Striegel-Moore, R. H. (2001). Challenging the myth of the golden girl: Ethnicity and eating disorders. In R. H. Striegel-Moore & L. Smolak (Eds.), *Eating disorders: Innovative directions in research and practice* (pp. 111–132). Washington, DC: American Psychological Association.

Smoller, J. W., Rosenbaum, J. F., Biederman, J., Kennedy, J., Dai, D., Racette, S. R., Laird, N. M., Kagan, J., Snidman, N., Hirshfeld-Becker, D., Tsuang, M. T., Sklar, P. B., & Slaugenhaupt, S. A. (2003). Association of a genetic marker at the corticotrophin-releasing hormone locus with behavioral inhibition. *Biological Psychiatry, 54,* 1376–1381.

Snitz, B. E., MacDonald, A. W., III, & Carter, C. S. (2006). Cognitive deficits in unaffected first-degree relatives of schizophrenia patients: A meta-analytic review of putative endophenotypes. *Schizophrenia Bulletin, 32,* 179–194.

Snowden, L. R., & Cheung, F. K. (1990). Use of inpatient mental health services by members of ethnic minority groups. *American Psychologist, 45,* 347–355.

Snowden, L. R., & Yamada, A. M. (2005). Cultural differences in access to care. *Annual Review of Clinical Psychology, 1,* 143–166.

Snowdon, D. A. (1997). Aging and Alzheimer's disease: Lessons from the Nun Study. *Gerontologist, 37,* 150–156.

Snowdon, D. A., Greiner, L. H., Mortimer, J. A., Riley, K. P., et al. (1997). Brain infarction and the clinical expression of Alzheimer's disease: The Nun Study. *Journal of the American Medical Association, 277,* 813–817.

Snowdon, D. A., Kemper, S. J., Mortimer, J. A., Greiner, L. H., Wekstein, D. R., & Markesbery, W. R. (1996). Linguistic ability in early life and cognitive function and Alzheimer's disease in late life: Findings from the Nun Study. *Journal of the American Medical Association, 275,* 528–532.

Snyder, C. R., Ilardi, S., Michael, S. T., & Cheavens, J. (2000). Hope theory: Updating a common process for psychological change. In C. R. Snyder & R. E. Ingram (Eds.), *Handbook of psychological change: Psychotherapy processes and practices for the 21st century* (pp. 128–153). New York: Wiley.

Sobal, J., & Stunkard, A. J. (1989). Socioeconomic status and obesity: A review of the literature. *Psychological Bulletin, 105,* 260–275.

Sobell, M. B., & Sobell, L. C. (1978). *Behavioral treatment of alcohol problems.* New York: Plenum Press.

Soloff, P. H., Cornelius, J., George, A., Nathan, S., Perel, J. M., & Ulrich, R. F. (1993). Efficacy of phenelzine and haloperidol in borderline personality disorder. *Archives of General Psychiatry, 50,* 377–385.

Soloff, P. H., Meltzer, C. C., Greer, P. J., Constantine, D., & Kelly, T. M. (2000). A fenfluramine-activated FDG-PET study of borderline personality disorder. *Biological Psychiatry, 47,* 540–547.

Solomon, G. F., Segerstrom, S. C., Grohr, P., Kemeny, M., & Fahey, J. (1997). Shaking up immunity: Psychological and immunologic changes following a natural disaster. *Psychosomatic Medicine, 59,* 114–127.

Somerset, W., Newport, D. J., Ragan, K., & Stowe, Z. N. (2006). Depressive disorders in women: From menarche to beyond the menopause. In C. L. M. Keyes & S. H. Goodman (Eds.), *Women and depression* (pp. 62–88). New York: Cambridge University Press.

Southwick, S. M., Vythilingam, M., & Charney, D. S. (2005). The psychobiology of depression and resilience to stress: Implications for prevention and treatment. *Annual Review of Clinical Psychology, 1,* 255–292.

Spanos, N. (1994). Multiple identity enactments and multiple personality disorder: A sociocognitive perspective. *Psychological Bulletin, 120,* 42–59.

Spanos, N. P. (1978). Witchcraft in histories of psychiatry: A critical analysis and an alternative conceptualization. *Psychological Bulletin, 85,* 417–439.

Spiegel, D. (2001). Mind matters—group therapy and survival in breast cancer. *New England Journal of Medicine, 345,* 1767–1768.

Spiegel, D., Bollm, J. R., Kraemer, H. C., & Gottheil, E. (1989). Psychological support for cancer patients. *Lancet, 2,* 1447.

Spierings, C., Poels, P. J., Sijben, N., Gabreels, F. J., & Renier, W. O. (1990). Conversion disorders in childhood: A retrospective follow-up study of 84 inpatients. *Developmental Medicine & Child Neurology, 32,* 865–871.

Spitzer, R. L. (1981). The diagnostic status of homosexuality in *DSM-III*: A reformulation of the issues. *American Journal of Psychiatry, 138,* 210–215.

Spitzer, R. L., First, M. B., & Wakefield, J. C. (2007). Saving PTSD from itself in *DSM-V. Journal of Anxiety Disorders, 21,* 233–241.

Spitzer, R. L., Gibbon, M., Skodol, A. E., Williams, J. B. W., & First, M. B. (Eds.). (1994). DSM-IV *case book: A learning companion to the* Diagnostic and Statistical Manual of Mental Disorders (4th ed.). Washington, DC: American Psychiatric Association.

Spitzer, R. L., Gibbon, M., Skodol, A. E., Williams, J. B. W., & First, M. B. (Eds.). (2002). DSM-IV-TR *Case Book: A learning companion to the* Diagnostic and Statistical Manual of Mental Disorders, *Fourth Edition, Text Revision.* Washington, DC: American Psychiatric Publishing.

Spitzer, R. L., Skodol, A. E., Gibbon, M., & Williams, J. B. W. (1981). DSM-III *case book: A learning companion to the* Diagnostic and Statistical Manual of Mental Disorders (3rd ed.). Washington, DC: American Psychiatric Association.

Spitzer, R. L., Skodol, A. E., Gibbon, M., & Williams, J. B. W. (1983). *Psychopathology, a case book.* New York: McGraw-Hill.

Sprock, J. (2000). Gender-typed behavioral examples of histrionic personality disorder. *Journal of Psychopathology and Behavioral Assessment, 22,* 107–122.

Sprock, J., Blashfield, R. K., & Smith, B. (1990). Gender weighting of *DSM-III-R* personality disorder criteria. *American Journal of Psychiatry, 147,* 586–590.

Stack, S. (1991). Social correlates of suicide by age: Media impacts. In A. A. Leenaars (Ed.), *Life span perspectives of suicide* (pp. 187–213). New York: Plenum Press.

Stadler, C., Sterzer, P., Schmeck, K., Krebs, A., Kleinschmidt, A., & Poustka, F. (2006, Mar. 2). Reduced anterior cingulate activation in aggressive children and adolescents during affective stimulation: Association with temperament *Journal of Psychiatric Research.*

Stahl, S. M. (2001). Dopamine system stabilizers, aripiprazole, and the next generation of antipsychotics, Part II: Illustrating their mechanisms of action. *Journal of Clinical Psychiatry, 62,* 923–924.

Stahl, S. M. (2006). *Essential psychopharmacology: The prescriber's guide.* New York: Cambridge University Press.

Stark, L. J., Opipari, L. C., Donaldson, D. L., Danovsky, M. B., Rasile, D. A., & DelSanto, A. F. (1997). Evaluation of a standard protocol for retentive encopresis: A replication. *Journal of Pediatric Psychology, 22,* 619–633.

Statham, D. J., Heath, A. C., Madden, P., Bucholz, K., Bierut, L., Dinwiddie, S. H., Slutske, W. S., Dunne, M. P., & Martin, N. G. (1998). Suicidal behavior: An epidemiological study. *Psychological Medicine, 28,* 839–855.

Steadman, H. J., McGreevy, M. A., Morrissey, J. P., Callahan, L. A., Robbins, P. C., & Cirincione, C. (1993). *Before and after Hinckley: Evaluating insanity defense reform.* New York: Guilford Press.

Steadman, H. J., Mulvey, E. P., Monahan, J., Robbins, P. C., Appelbaum, P. S., Grisso, T., Roth, L. H., & Silver, E. (1998). Violence by people discharged from acute psychiatric inpatient facilities and by others in the same neighborhoods. *Archives of General Psychiatry, 55,* 393–401.

Stein, A., Woolley, H., Cooper, S., Winterbottom, J., Fairburn, C. G., & Cortina-Borja, M. (2006). Eating habits and attitudes among 10-year-old children of mothers with eating disorders. *British Journal of Psychiatry, 189,* 324–329.

Stein, B. D., Elliott, M. N., Jaycox, L. H., Collins, R. L., Berry, S. H., Klein, D. J., & Schuster, M. A. (2004). A national longitudinal study of the psychological consequences of the September 11, 2001 terrorist attacks: Reactions, impairments, and help-seeking. *Psychiatry, 67,* 105–117.

Stein, M. B., Jang, K. J., Taylor, S., Vernon, P. A., & Livesley, W. J. (2002). Genetic and environmental influences on trauma exposure and posttraumatic stress disorder: A twin study. *American Journal of Psychiatry 159,* 1675–1681.

Steinberg, L. (2009). Adolescent development and juvenile justice. *Annual Review of Clinical Psychology, 5,* 459–486.

Steinberg, L., Dahl, R., Keating, D., Kupfer, D. J., Masten, A. S., & Pine, D. (2006). The study of developmental psychopathology in adolescence: Integrating affective neuroscience with the study of context. In D. Cicchetti & D. Cohen (Eds.), *Developmental psychopathology, Vol. 2: Developmental neuroscience* (pp. 710–741). New York: Wiley.

Steiner, M., Dunn, E., & Born, L. (2003). Hormones and mood: From menarche to menopause and beyond. *Journal of Affective Disorders, 74,* 67–83.

Steketee, G., & Frost, R. (2003). Compulsive hoarding: Current status of the research. *Clinical Psychology Review, 23,* 905–927.

Stephens, M. A. P., Druley, J. A., & Zautra, A. J. (2002). Older adults' recovery from surgery for osteoarthritis of the knee: Psychosocial resources and constraints as predictors of outcomes. *Health Psycholology, 21,* 377–383.

Stephens, S., Kenny, R. A., Rowan, E., Allan, L., Kalaria, R. N., Bradbury, M., & Ballard, C. G. (2004). Neuropsychological characteristics of mild vascular cognitive impairment and dementia after stroke. *International Journal of Geriatric Psychiatry, 19,* 1053–1057.

Stern, Y., Gurland, B., Tatemichi, T. K., & Tang, M. X. (1994). Influence of education and occupation on the incidence of Alzheimer's disease. *Journal of the American Medical Association, 271,* 1004–1010.

Sternberg, R. J. (2004). Culture and intelligence. *American Psychologist, 59,* 325–338.

Sterzer, P., Stadler, C., Krebs, A., Kleinschmidt, A., & Poustka F. (2005). Abnormal neural responses to emotional visual stimuli in adolescents with conduct disorder. *Biological Psychiatry, 57,* 7–15.

Stewart, S. E., Stack, D. E., & Wilhelm, S. (2008). Severe obsessive-compulsive disorder with and without body dysmorphic disorder: Clinical correlates and implications. *Annals of Clinical Psychiatry, 20,* 33–38.

St. George-Hyslop, P. H., Tanzi, R. E., Polinsky, R. J., Haines, J. L., Nee, L., Watkins, P. C., & Meyers, R. H. (1987). The genetic defect causing familial Alzheimer's disease maps on chromosome 21. *Science, 235,* 885–890.

Stice, E. (2002). Risk and maintenance factors for eating pathology: A meta-analytic review. *Psychological Bulletin, 128,* 825–848.

Stice, E. (2003). Puberty and body image. In C. Hayward (Ed.), *Gender differences at puberty* (pp. 61–76). New York: Cambridge University Press.

Stice, E., & Agras, W. S. (1998). Predicting the onset and remission of bulimic behaviors in adolescence: A longitudinal grouping analysis. *Behavior Therapy, 29,* 257–276.

Stice, E., Bohon, C., Marti, C. N., & Fischer, K. (2008). Subtyping women with bulimia nervosa along dietary and negative affect dimensions: Further evidence of reliability and validity. *Journal of Counseling and Clinical Psychology, 76,* 1022–1033.

Stice, E., Burton, E. M., & Shaw, H. (2004). Prospective relations between bulimic pathology, depression, and substance abuse: Unpacking comorbidity in adolescent girls. *Journal of Consulting & Clinical Psychology, 72,* 62–71.

Stice, E., Chase, A., Stormer, S., & Appel, A. (2001). A randomized trial of a dissonance-based eating disorder prevention program. *International Journal of Eating Disorders, 29,* 247–262.

Stice, E., & Fairburn, C. G. (2003). Dietary and dietary-depressive subtypes of bulimia nervosa show differential symptom presentation, social impairment, comorbidity, and course of illness. *Journal of Consulting & Clinical Psychology, 71,* 1090–1094.

Stice, E., Maxfield, J., & Wells, T. (2003). Adverse effects of social pressure to be thin on young women: An experimental investigation of the effects of "fat talk." *International Journal of Eating Disorders, 34,* 108–117.

Stice, E., Mazotti, L., Weibel, D., & Agras, W. S. (2000). Dissonance prevention program decreases thin-ideal internalization, body dissatisfaction, dieting, negative affect, and bulimic symptoms: A preliminary experiment. *International Journal of Eating Disorders, 27,* 206–217.

Stice, E., Presnell, K., & Spangler, D. (2002). Risk factors for binge eating onset in adolescent girls: A 2-year prospective investigation. *Health Psychology, 21,* 131–138.

Stice, E., Shaw, H., & Marti, C. N. (2007). A meta-analytic review of eating disorder prevention programs: Encouraging findings. *Annual Review of Clinical Psychology, 3,* 233–257.

Stice, E., & Shaw, H. E. (1994). Adverse effects of the media-portrayed thin-ideal on women and linkages to bulimic symptomatology. *Journal of Social & Clinical Psychology, 13,* 288–308.

Stice, E., Spangler, D., & Agras, W. S. (2001). Exposure to media-portrayed thin-ideal images adversely affects vulnerable girls: A longitudinal experiment. *Journal of Social & Clinical Psychology, 20,* 270–288.

Stice, E., & Spoor, S. T. P. (2007). Stability of eating disorder diagnoses. *International Journal of Eating Disorders, 40,* S79–S82.

Stoney, C. M. (2003). Gender and cardiovascular disease: A psychobiological and integrative approach. *Current Directions in Psychological Science, 12,* 129–133.

Stormer, S. M., & Thompson, J. K. (1998, November). *Challenging media messages regarding appearance: A psychoeducational program for males and females.* Paper presented at the annual meeting of the Association for the Advancement of Behavior Therapy, Washington, DC.

Stouthamer-Loeber, M., Loeber, R., Homish, D. L., & Wei, E. (2001). Maltreatment of boys and the development of disruptive and delinquent behavior. *Development & Psychopathology, 13,* 941–955.

Strauss, J. S. (1969). Hallucinations and delusions as points on continua function: Rating scale evidence. *Archives of General Psychiatry, 21,* 581–586.

Striegel-Moore, R. (1995). Psychological factors in the etiology of binge eating. *Addictive Behaviors, 20,* 713–723.

Striegel-Moore, R., Wilson, G. T., Wilfley, D. E., Elder, K. A., & Brownell, K. D. (1998). Binge eating in an obese community sample. *International Journal of Eating Disorders, 23,* 27–37.

Striegel-Moore, R. H. (1993). Etiology of binge eating: A developmental perspective. In C. G. Fairburn & G. T. Wilson (Eds.), *Binge eating: Nature, assessment, and treatment* (pp. 144–172). New York: Guilford Press.

Striegel-Moore, R. H., & Bulik, C. M. (2007). Risk factors for eating disorders. *American Psychologist, 62,* 181–198.

Striegel-Moore, R. H., Dohm, F. A., Kraemer, H. C., Taylor, C. B., Daniels, S., Crawford, P. B., & Schreiber, G. B. (2003). Eating disorders in white and black women. *American Journal of Psychiatry, 160,* 1326–1331.

Striegel-Moore, R. H., Fairburn, C. G., Wilfley, D. E., Pike, K. M., Dohm, F.-A., & Kraemer, H. C. (2005). Toward an understanding of risk factors for binge-eating disorder in black and white women: A community-based case-control study. *Psychological Medicine, 35,* 907–917.

Striegel-Moore, R. H., & Franko, D. L. (2008). Should binge eating disorder be included in the *DSM-V?* A critical review of the state of the evidence. *Annual Review of Clinical Psychology, 4,* 305–324.

Striegel-Moore, R. H., Seeley, J. R., & Lewinsohn, P. M. (2003). Psychosocial adjustment in young adulthood of women who experienced an eating disorder during adolescence. *Journal of the American Academy of Child & Adolescent Psychiatry, 42,* 587–593.

Striegel-Moore, R. H., Silberstein, L. R., & Rodin, J. (1993). The social self in bulimia nervosa: Public self-consciousness, social anxiety, and perceived fraudulence. *Journal of Abnormal Psychology, 102,* 297–303.

Stringaris, A., Cohen, P., Pine, D. S., & Leibenluft, E. (2009). Adult outcomes of adolescent irritability: A 20-year community follow-up. *American Journal of Psychiatry, 166,* 1048–1054.

Stroebe, M., Gergen, M., Gergen, K., & Stroebe, W. (1992). Broken hearts or broken bonds: Love and death in historical perspective. *American Psychologist, 47,* 1205–1212.

Stroebe, M.S., Hansson, R. O., Schut, H., & Stroebe, W. (2008). Bereavement research: Contemporary perspectives. In M. S. Stroebe, R. O. Hansson, H. Schut, W. Stroebe, & E. Van den Blink (Eds). *Handbook of bereavement research and practice: Advances in theory and intervention* (pp. 3–25). Washington, DC: American Psychological Association.

Stunkard, A. (1997). Eating disorders: The last 25 years. *Appetite, 29,* 181–190.

Stunkard, A. J. (1993). A history of binge eating. In C. G. Fairburn & G. T. Wilson (Eds.), *Binge eating: Nature, assessment, and treatment* (pp. 15–34). New York: Guilford Press.

Substance Abuse and Mental Health Services Administration (SAMHSA). (2002). National household survey on drug abuse. http://dawninfo.samhsa.gov/ (accessed November 1, 2004)

Substance Abuse and Mental Health Services Administration (SAMHSA). (2005). Overview of findings from the 2003 National Survey on Drug Use and Health. http://www.oas.samhsa.gov/nhsda/2k3nsduh/2k3Overview.htm (accessed November 1, 2004)

Substance Abuse and Mental Health Services Administration (SAMHSA). (2008a). *Drug Abuse Warning Network, 2006: National estimates of drug-related emergency department visits* (DAWN Series D-30, DHHS Publication No. SMA 08-4339). Rockville, MD: author.

Substance Abuse and Mental Health Services Administration (SAMHSA). (2008b). National Survey on Drug Use and Health, 2006 and 2007. http://www.oas.samhsa.gov (accessed March 26, 2009)

Substance Abuse and Mental Health Services Administration (SAMHSA). (2008c). *Results from the 2007 National Survey on Drug Use and Health: National findings* (Office of Applied Studies, NSDUH Series H-34, DHHS Publication No. SMA 08-4343). Rockville, MD: author.

Suddath, R. L., Christison, G. W., Torrey, E. F., & Casanova, M. F. (1990). Anatomical abnormalities in the brains of monozygotic twins discordant for schizophrenia. *New England Journal of Medicine, 322,* 789–794.

Sue, D. W., & Sue, D. (2003). *Counseling the culturally diverse: Theory and practice* (4th ed.). New York: Wiley.

Sue, S., & Lam, A. G. (2002). Cultural and demographic diversity. In J. C. Norcross (Ed.), *Psychotherapy relationships that work: Therapist contributions and responsiveness to patients* (pp. 401–421). London: Oxford University Press.

Sue, S., & Zane, N. (1987). The role of culture and cultural techniques in psychotherapy: A critique and reformulation. *American Psychologist, 42,* 37–51.

Suhail, K., & Cochrane, R. (2002). Effect of culture and environment on the phenomenology of delusions and hallucinations. *International Journal of Social Psychiatry, 48,* 126–138.

Suhara, T., Okubo, Y., Yasuno, F., Sudo, Y., Inoue, M., Ichimiya, T., Nakashima, Y., Nakayama, K., Tanada, S., Suzuki, K., Halldin, C., & Farde, L. (2002). Decreased dopamine D2 receptor binding in the anterior cingulated cortex in schizophrenia. *Archives of General Psychiatry, 59,* 25–30.

Sultzer, D. L., Davis, S. M., Tariot, P. N., Dagerman, K. S., Lebowitz, B. D., Lyketsos, C. G., Rosenheck, R. A., Hsiao, J. K., Lieberman, J. A., & Schneider, L. S. (2008). Clinical symptom responses to atypical antipsychotic medications in Alzheimer's disease: Phase 1 outcomes from the CATIE-AD effectiveness trial. *American Journal of Psychiatry, 165,* 844–854.

Sundgot-Borgen, J. (1994). Risk and trigger factors for the development of eating disorders in female elite athletes. *Medicine & Science in Sports & Exercise, 26,* 414–419.

Sundram, C. J. (2009). *Wyatt v. Stickney—a long odyssey reaches an end.* http://www.cqcapd.state.ny.us/pressreleases/wyattclarence.htm (accessed September 29, 2009)

Suomi, S. J. (1999). Developmental trajectories, early experiences, and community consequences: Lessons from studies with rhesus monkeys. In D. P. Keating (Ed.), *Developmental health and the wealth of nations: Social, biological, and educational dynamics* (pp. 185–200). New York: Guilford Press.

Sutker, P. B., Allain, A. N., & Winstead, D. K. (1993). Psychopathology and psychiatric diagnoses of World War II Pacific theater prisoners of war and combat veterans. *American Journal of Psychiatry, 150,* 240–245.

Sutker, P. B., Davis, J. M., Uddo, M., & Ditta, S. R. (1995). Assessment of psychological distress in Persian Gulf troops: Ethnicity and gender comparisons. *Journal of Personality Assessment, 64,* 415–427.

Svenningsson, P., Chergui, K., Rachleff, I., Flajolet, M., Zhang, X., El Yacoubi, M., Vaugeois, J.-M., Nomikos, G. G., & Greengard, P. (2006). Alterations in 5-HT1B receptor function by p11 in depression-like states. *Science, 311,* 77–80.

Swanson, J., Arnold, L. E., Kraemer, H., Hechtman, L., Molina, B., Hinshaw, S., Vitiello, B., Jensen, P., Steinhoff, K., Lerner, M., Greenhill, L., Abikoff, H., Wells, K., Epstein, J., Elliot, G., Newcorn, J., Hoza, B., & Wigal, T. (2008). Evidence, interpretation, and qualification from multiple reports of long-term outcomes in the multimodal treatment study of children with ADHD (MTA): I. Executive Summary. *Journal of Attention Disorders, 12,* 4–14.

Swanson, J. M., Elliott, G. R., Greenhill, L. L., Wigal, T., Arnold, L. E., Vitiello, B., Hechtman, L., Epstein, J. N., Pelham, W. E., Abikoff, H. B., Newcorn, J. H., Molina, B. S. G., Hinshaw, S. P., Wells, K. C., Hoza, B., Jensen, P. S., Gibbons, R. D., Hur, K., Stehli, A., Davies, M., March, J. S., Conners, C. K., Caron, M., & Volkow, N. D. (2007). Effects of stimulant medication on growth rates across 3 years in the MTA follow-up. *Journal of the American Academy of Child and Adolescent Psychiatry, 46,* 1015–1027.

Swartz, H. A., & Frank, E. (2001). Psychotherapy for bipolar depression: A phase-specific treatment strategy? *Bipolar Disorders, 3,* 11–12.

Swartz, M., Blazer, D., George, L., & Winfield, I. (1990). Estimating the prevalence of borderline personality disorder in the community. *Journal of Personality Disorders, 4,* 257–272.

Swartz, M., Swanson, J., Kim, M., & Petrila, J. (2006). Use of outpatient commitment or related civil court treatment orders in five U.S. communities. *Psychiatric Services, 57,* 343–349.

Sylvers, P., Brubaker, N., Alden, S. A., Brennan, P. A., & Lilienfeld, S. O. (2008). Differential endophenotypic markers of narcissistic and antisocial personality features: A psychophysiological investigation. *Journal of Research in Personality, 42,* 1260–1270.

Szasz, T. (1961). *The myth of mental illness.* New York: Hoeber-Harper.

Szasz, T. S. (1963). *Law, liberty, and psychiatry: An inquiry into the social uses of mental health practice.* New York: Collier Books.

Szasz, T. S. (1971). The sane slave: An historical note on the use of medical diagnosis as justificatory rhetoric. *American Journal of Psychotherapy, 25,* 228–239.

Szasz, T. S. (1977). *Psychiatric slavery.* New York: Free Press.

Szelenberger, W., Niemcewicz, S., & Dabrowska, A. J. (2005). Sleepwalking and night terrors: Psychopathological and psychophysiological correlates. *International Review of Psychiatry, 17,* 263–270.

T

Tager-Flusberg, H., Joseph, R., & Folstein, S. (2001). Current directions in research on autism. *Mental Retardation & Developmental Disabilities Research Review, 7,* 21–29.

Takahashi, Y. (1990). Is multiple personality disorder really rare in Japan? *Dissociation: Progress in the Dissociative Disorders, 3,* 57–59.

Takei, N., Sham, P. C., O'Callaghan, E., & Murray, R. M. (1992). Cities, winter birth, and schizophrenia. *Lancet, 340,* 558–559.

Takei, N., Sham, P. C., O'Callaghan, R., Glover, G., et al. (1995). Early risk factors in schizophrenia: Place and season of birth. *European Psychiatry, 10,* 165–170.

Talkowski, M. E., Bamne, M., Mansour, H., & Nimgaonkar, V. L. (2007). Dopamine genes and schizophrenia: Case closed or evidence pending? *Schizophrenia Bulletin, 33,* 1071–1081.

Tanay, E. (1992). The verdict with two names. *Psychiatric Annals, 22,* 571–573.

Tang, N. K. Y., Schmidt, D. A., & Harvey, A. G. (2007). Sleeping with the enemy: Clock monitoring in the maintenance of insomnia. *Journal of Behavior Therapy and Experimental Psychiatry, 38,* 40–55.

Tannock, R. (2005). Mathematics disorder. In B. J. Sadock & V. A. Sadock (Eds.), *Kaplan & Sadock's comprehensive textbook of psychiatry* (pp. 3116–3123). Philadelphia: Lippincott Williams & Wilkins.

Tariot, P. N. (2003). Alzheimer disease: Current challenges, emerging treatments. *Alzheimer Disease & Associated Disorders, 17*(Suppl. 4), 98.

Tateyama, M., Asai, M., Hashimoto, M., Bartels, M., & Kasper, S. (1998). Transcultural study of schizophrenic delusions: Tokyo versus Vienna versus Tuebingen (Germany). *Psychopathology, 31,* 59–68.

Tateyama, M., Asai, M., Kamisada, M., Hashimoto, M., Bartels, M., & Heimann, H. (1993). Comparison of schizophrenia delusions between Japan and Germany. *Psychopathology, 26,* 151–158.

Taylor, D. O., & Miklowitz, D. J. (2009). Bipolar disorder in childhood and adolescence. In S. Nolen-Hoeksema & L. Hilt (Eds.), *Handbook of depression in adolescents* (pp. 179–208). New York: Routledge.

Taylor, J., Iacono, W. G., & McGue, M. (2000). Evidence for a genetic etiology of early-onset delinquency. *Journal of Abnormal Psychology, 109,* 634–643.

Taylor, S., Fedoroff, I., Koch, W. J., Thordarson, D. S., Fecteau, G., & Nicki, R. M. (2001). Posttraumatic stress disorder arising after road traffic collisions: Patterns of response to cognitive-behavior therapy. *Journal of Consulting & Clinical Psychology, 69,* 541–551.

Taylor, S. E., Eisenberger, N. I., Saxbe, D., Lehman, B. J., & Lieberman M. D. (2006). Neural responses to emotional stimuli are associated with childhood family stress. *Biological Psychiatry, 60,* 296–301.

Taylor, S. E., Kemeny, M. E., Aspinwall, L. G., & Schneider, S. G. (1992). Optimism, coping, psychological distress, and high-risk sexual behavior among men at risk for acquired immunodeficiency syndrome (AIDS). *Journal of Personality & Social Psychology, 63,* 460–473.

Taylor, S. E., Klein, L. C., Lewis, B. P., Gruenwald, T. L., Gurung, R. A. R., & Updegraff, J. A. (2000). Biobehavioral responses to stress in females: Tend-and-befriend, not fight-or-flight. *Psychological Review, 3,* 411–429.

Taylor, S. E., & Stanton, A. L. (2007). Coping resources, coping processes and mental health. *Annual Review of Clinical Psychology, 3,* 377–401.

Telles, C., Karno, M., Mintz, J., Paz, G., Arias, M., Tucker, D., & Lopez, S. (1995). Immigrant families coping with schizophrenia. *British Journal of Psychiatry, 167,* 473–479.

Temple, E., Deutsch, G., Poldrack, R., Miller, S., Tallal, P., Merzenich, M., et al. (2003). Neural deficits in children with dyslexia ameliorated by behavioral remediation: Evidence from fMRI. *Proceedings of the National Academy of Science of the United States of America, 100,* 2860–2865.

Temple, N. (2001). Psychodynamic psychotherapy in the treatment of conversion hysteria. In P. W. Halligan, C. Bass, & J. Marshall (Eds.), *Contemporary approaches to the study of hysteria: Clinical and theoretical perspectives* (pp. 283–297). Oxford, UK: Oxford University Press.

Templeman, T. N., & Stinnet, R. D. (1991). Patterns of sexual arousal and history in a "normal" sample of young men. *Archives of Sexual Behavior, 20,* 137–150.

Teplin, L. A. (1990). The prevalence of severe mental disorder among male urban jail detainers: Comparison with the Epidemiologic Catchment Area program. *American Journal of Public Health, 80,* 663–669.

Teplin, L. A., Abram, K. M., & McClelland, G. M. (1996). Prevalence of psychiatric disorders among incarcerated women. I. Pretrial jail detainees. *Archives of General Psychiatry, 53,* 505–512.

Teplin, L. A., Abram, K. M., & McClelland, G. M. (1997). Mentally disordered women in jail: Who receives services? *American Journal of Public Health, 87,* 604–609.

Teri, L., Gibbons, L. E., McCurry, S. M., Logsdon, R. G., Buchner, D. M., Barlow, W. E., Kukull, W. A., LaCroix, A. Z., McCormick, W., & Larson, E. B. (2003). Exercise plus behavioral management in patients with Alzheimer disease: A randomized controlled trial. *Journal of the American Medical Association, 290,* 2015–2022.

Test, M. A., & Stein, L. I. (1980). Alternative to mental hospital treatment: III. Social cost. *Archives of General Psychiatry, 37,* 409–412.

Teyber, E., & McClure, F. (2000). Therapist variables. In C. R. Snyder & R. E. Ingram (Eds.), *Handbook of psychological change: Psychotherapy processes and practices for the 21st century* (pp. 62–87). New York: Wiley.

Thase, M. E., & Denko, T. (2008). Pharmacotherapy of mood disorders. *Annual Review of Clinical Psychology, 4,* 53–92.

Thermenos, H. W., Seidman, L. J., Breiter, H., Goldstein, J. M., Goodman, J. M., Poldrack, R., Faraone, S. V., & Tsuang, M. T. (2004). Functional magnetic resonance imaging during auditory verbal working memory in nonpsychotic relatives of persons with schizophrenia: A pilot study. *Biological Psychiatry, 55,* 490–500.

Thienemann, M. (2004). Medications for pediatric anxiety. In H. Steiner (Ed.), *Handbook of mental health intervention in children and adolescents: An integrated developmental approach* (pp. 288–317). San Francisco: Jossey-Bass.

Thompson, J. K., Heinberg, L. J., Altabe, M. N., & Tantleff-Dunn, S. (1999). *Exacting beauty: Theory, assessment and treatment of body image disturbance.* Washington, DC: American Psychological Association.

Thompson, J. K., & Stice, E. (2001). Thin ideal internalization: Mounting evidence for a new risk factor for body image disturbance and eating pathology. *Current Directions in Psychological Science, 10,* 181–183.

Thompson, L. W., Coon, D. W., Gallagher-Thompson, D., Sommer, B., & Koin, D. (2001). Comparison of desipramine and cognitive/behavioral therapy in the treatment of late-life depression. *American Journal of Geriatric Psychiatry, 9,* 225–240.

Thompson, P. M., Hayashi, K. M., De Zubicaray, G. I., Janke, A. L., Rose, S. E., et al. (2004). Mapping hippocampal and ventricular change in Alzheimer disease. *Neuroimage, 22,* 1754–1766.

Thompson, P. M., Vidal, C., Giedd, J. N., Gochman, P., Blumenthal, J., Nicolson, R., Toga, A. W., & Rapoport, J. L. (2001). Mapping adolescent brain change reveals dynamic wave of accelerated gray matter loss in very early-onset schizophrenia. *Proceedings of the National Academy of Sciences of the United States of America, 98,* 11650–11655.

Thompson, R. F., & Krupa, D. J. (1994). Organization of memory traces in the mammalian brain. *Annual Review of Neuroscience, 17,* 519–549.

Thorpe, G. L., & Olson, S. L. (1997). *Behavior therapy: Concepts, procedures, and applications* (2nd ed.). Boston: Allyn & Bacon.

Tienari, P. (1991). Interaction between genetic vulnerability and family environment: The Finnish adoptive family study of schizophrenia. *Acta Psychiatrica Scandinavica, 84,* 460–465.

Tiet, Q. Q., Wasserman, G. A., Loeber, R., McReynolds, L. S., & Miller, L. S. (2001). Developmental and sex differences in types of conduct problems. *Journal of Child & Family Studies, 10,* 181–197.

Tiggemann, M., Martins, Y., & Kirkbride, A. (2007). Oh to be lean and muscular: Body image ideals in gay and heterosexual men. *Psychology of Men and Masculinity, 8,* 15–24.

Tiihonen, J., & Wahlbeck, K. (2006). Glutamertergic drugs for schizophrenia. *Cochrane Database of Systematic Reviews, 2,* CD003730.

Todd, R. D., Lobos, E. A., Sun, L. W., & Neuman, R. J. (2003). Mutational analysis of the nicotinic acetylcholine receptor alpha 4 subunit gene in attention deficit/hyperactivity disorder: Evidence for association of an intronic polymorphism with attention problems. *Molecular Psychiatry, 8,* 103–108.

Tolin, D. F., Franklin, M. E., Diefenbach, G. J., Anderson, E., & Meunier, S. A. (2007). Pediatric trichotillomania: Descriptive psychopathology and an open trial of cognitive behavioral therapy. *Cognitive Behaviour Therapy, 36,* 129–144.

Tonigan, J. S., & Connors, G. J. (2008). Psychological mechanisms in Alcoholics Anonymous. In M. Galanter & H. D. Kleber (Eds), *The American Psychiatric Publishing textbook of substance abuse treatment* (4th ed., pp. 491–498). Arlington, VA: American Psychiatric Publishing.

Torrey, E. F. (1995). *Surviving schizophrenia: A manual for families, consumers, and providers* (3rd ed.). New York: HarperPerennial.

Torrey, E. F. (1997). *Out of the shadows: Confronting America's mental illness crisis.* New York: Wiley.

Torrey, E. F. (2006). *Surviving Schizophrenia: A manual for families, patients, and providers.* New York: HarperPaperbacks.

Torrey, E. F., Bowler, A. E., & Clark, K. (1997). Urban birth and residence as risk factors for psychosis: An analysis of 1880 data. *Schizophrenia Research, 25,* 169–176.

Torrey, E. F., & Yolken, R. H. (1998). At issue: Is household crowding a risk factor for schizophrenia and bipolar disorder? *Schizophrenia Bulletin, 24,* 321–324.

Torti, F. M., Jr., Gwyther, L. P., Reed, S. D., Friedman, J. Y., & Schulman, K. A. (2004). A multinational review of recent trends and reports in dementia caregiver burden. *Alzheimer Disease & Associated Disorders, 18,* 99–109.

Toufexis, A., Blackman, A., & Drummond, T. (1996, April 29). Why Jennifer got sick. http://www.time.com/time/magazine/article/0,9171,984465,00.html (accessed October 29, 2009)

Trestman, R. L., Ford, J., Zhang, W., & Wiesbrock, V. (2007). Current and lifetime psychiatric illness among inmates not identified as acutely mentally ill at intake in Connecticut's jails. *Journal of the American Academy of Psychiatry and Law, 35,* 490–500.

True, W. R., Rice, J., Eisen, S. A., Heath, A. C., Goldberg, J., Lyons, M. J., & Nowak, J. (1993).

A twin study of genetic and environmental contributions to liability for posttraumatic stress symptoms. *Archives of General Psychiatry, 50,* 257–264.

Trull, T. J., & Durrett, C. A. (2005). Categorical and dimensional models of personality disorder. *Annual review of clinical psychology 1,* 355–380.

Trull, T. J., Solhan, M. B., Tragesser, S. L., Jahng, S., Wood, P. K., Paisecki, T. M., & Watson, D., (2008). Affective instability: Measuring a core feature of borderline personality disorder with ecological momentary assessment. *Journal of Abnormal Psychology, 117,* 647–661.

Trull, T. J., Waudby, C. J., & Sher, K. J. (2004). Alcohol, tobacco, and drug use disorders and personality disorder symptoms. *Experimental & Clinical Psychopharmacology, 12,* 65–75.

Tsai, J. L., Butcher, J. N., Muñoz, R. F., & Vitousek, K. (2001). Culture, ethnicity, and psychopathology. In P. B. Sutker (Ed.), *Comprehensive handbook of psychopathology* (3rd ed., pp. 105–127). New York: Kluwer Academic/Plenum.

Tsai, J. L., & Chentsova-Dutton, Y. (2002). Understanding depression across cultures. In I. H. Gotlib & C. L. Hammen (Eds.), *Handbook of depression* (pp. 467–491). New York: Guilford Press.

Tseng, W. (1973). The development of psychiatric concepts in traditional Chinese medicine. *Archives of General Psychiatry, 29,* 569–575.

Tseng, W.-S. (2001). *Culture and psychotherapy: A guide to clinical practice.* Washington, DC: American Psychiatric Press.

Tsuang, M. T., Lyons, M. J., Meyer, J. M., Doyle, T., Eisen, S. A., Goldberg, J., True, W., Lin, N., Toomey, R., & Eaves, L. (1998). Co-occurrence of abuse of different drugs in men: The role of drug-specific and shared vulnerabilities. *Archives of General Psychiatry, 55,* 967–972.

Tugrul, C., & Kabakci, E. (1997). Vaginismus and its correlates. *Sexual & Marital Therapy, 12,* 23–34.

Turk, C. L., Heimberg, R. G., & Hope, D. A. (2001). Social anxiety disorder. *Clinical handbook of psychological disorders: A step-by-step treatment manual* (3rd ed., pp. 114–153). New York: Guilford Press.

Turk, D. C., & Ruby, T. E. (1992). Cognitive factors and persistent pain: A glimpse into Pandora's box. *Cognitive Therapy & Research, 16,* 99–122.

Turkheimer, E., & Parry, C. D. (1992). Why the gap? Practice and policy in civil commitment hearings. *American Psychologist, 47,* 646–655.

Turner-Cobb, J. M., Sephton, S. E., Koopman, C., Blake-Mortimer, J., & Spiegel, D. (2000). Social support and salivary cortisol in women with metastatic breast cancer. *Psychosomatic Medicine, 62,* 337–345.

Twenge, J. M., & Nolen-Hoeksema, S. (2002) Age, gender, race, SES, and birth cohort differences on the Children's Depression Inventory: A meta-analysis. *Journal of Abnormal Psychology, 111,* 578–588.

U

Ujike, H., Otani, K., Nakatsuka, M., Ishii, K., Sasaki, A., Oishi, T., Sato, T., Okahisa, Y., Matsumoto, Y., Namba, Y., Kimata, Y., & Kuroda, S. (2009). Association study of gender identity disorder and sex hormone–related genes. *Progress in Neuro-Psychopharmacology & Biological Psychiatry, 3,* 1241–1244.

Ulbricht, J. A., & Neiderhiser, J. M. (2009). Genotype-environment correlation and family relationships. In Y.-K. Kim (Ed.), *Handbook of behavior genetics* (pp. 209–221). New York: Spring Science & Business Media.

Ullman, L. P., & Krasner, L. (1975). *A psychological approach to abnormal behavior* (2nd ed.). Oxford, UK: Prentice Hall.

UNAIDS. (2004). *Making condoms work for HIV prevention.* Geneva, Switzerland: Joint United Nations Programme on HIV/AIDS.

UNAIDS. (2009). *AIDS epidemic update 2009.* http://www.unaids.org/en/Knowledge-Centre/HIVData/EpiUpdate/EpiUpd Archive/2009/default.asp (accessed February 5, 2010)

Ungvari, G. S., Leung, S. K., Ng, F. S., Cheung, H. -K., & Leung, T. (2005). Schizophrenia with prominent catatonic features ("catatonic schizophrenia"): I. Demographic and clinical correlates in the chronic phase. *Progress in Neuro-Psychopharmacology & Biological Psychiatry, 29,* 27–38.

Unützer, J., Patrick, D. L., Diehr, P., Simon, G., Grembowski, D., & Katon, W. (2000). Quality adjusted life years in older adults with depressive symptoms and chronic medical disorders. *International Psychogeriatrics, 12,* 15–33.

U.S. Department of Health and Human Services (USDHHS). (2001a). *Mental health: Culture, race, and ethnicity. A supplement to mental health: A report of the surgeon general.* Rockville, MD: U.S. Department of Health and Human Services, Public Health Services, Office of the Surgeon General.

U.S. Department of Health and Human Services (USDHHS). (2001b). *The Surgeon General's call to action to prevent and decrease obesity.* Rockville, MD: U.S. Department of Health and Human Services, U.S. Public Health Service, Office of the Surgeon General. http://www.surgeongeneral.gov/topics/obesity/calltoaction/CalltoAction.pdf. (accessed February 1, 2009)

U.S. Department of Health and Human Services: Centers for Disease Control and Prevention. (2009). Japanese encephalitis among three U.S. travelers returning from Asia, 2003–2008. *Morbidity and Mortality Weekly Report, 58,* 737–768.

V

Vakoch, D. A., & Strupp, H. H. (2000). Psychodynamic approaches to psychotherapy: Philosophical and theoretical foundations of effective practice. In C. R. Snyder & R. E. Ingram (Eds.), *Handbook of psychological change: Psychotherapy processes and practices for the 21st century* (pp. 200–216). New York: Wiley.

Valenstein, E. S. (1986). *Great and desperate cures: The rise and decline of psychosurgery and other radical treatments for mental illness.* New York: Basic Books.

Valenstein, R. S. (1998). *Blaming the brain: The truth about drugs and mental health.* New York: Free Press.

Valenzuela, M. J. (2008). Brain reserve and the prevention of dementia. *Current Opinion in Psychiatry 21,* 296–302.

Valera, E., Faraone, S., Murray, K., & Seidman, L. (2007). Meta-analysis of structural imaging findings in attention-deficit/hyperactivity disorder. *Biological Psychiatry, 61,* 1361–1369.

Vance, S., Cohen-Kettenis, P. T., Drescher, J., Meyer-Bahlburg, H. F. L., Pfäfflin, F., & Zucker, K. J. (in press). Transgender advocacy groups' opinions on the current *DSM* gender identity disorder diagnosis: Results from an international survey. *International Journal of Transgenderism.*

Vandelanotte, C., Spathonis, K. M., Eakin, E. G., & Owen, N. (2007). Website-delivered physical activity interventions: A review of the literature. *American Journal of Preventative Medicine, 33,* 54–64.

van Goozen, S., Fairchild, G., Snoek, H., & Harold, G. T. (2007). The evidence for a neurobiological model of childhood antisocial behavior. *Psychological Bulletin,133,* 149–182.

Van Hemert, A. M., Hengeveld, M. W., Bolk, J. H., & Rooijmans, H. G. (1993). Psychiatric disorders in relation to medical illness among patients of a general medical outpatient clinic. *Psychological Medicine, 23,* 167–173.

van Holst, R. J., van den Brink, W., Veltman, D. J., & Goudriaan, A. E. (2010). Why gamblers fail to win: A review of cognitive and neuroimaging findings in pathological gambling. *Neuroscience and Biobehavioral Reviews, 34,* 87–107.

van Lankveld, J. (2008). Problems with sexual interest and desire in women. In D. L. Rowland & L. Incrocci (Eds.), *Handbook of sexual and gender identity disorders* (pp. 154–187). Hoboken, NJ: Wiley.

van Melle, J. P., de Jonge, P., Honig, A., Schene, A. H., Kuyper, A. M. G., Crijns, H.J.G.M., Schins, A., Tulner, D., van den Berg, M. P., & Ormel, J. (2007). Effects of antidepressant treatment following myocardial infarction. *British Journal of Psychiatry, 190,* 460–466.

van Ommeren, M., De Jong, J. T. V. M., Bhogendra, S., Komproe, I., Thapa, S. B., & Cardena, E. (2001). Psychiatric disorders among tortured Bhutanese refugees in Nepal. *Archives of General Psychiatry, 58,* 475–482.

van Os, J., Hanssen, M., Bijl, R. V., & Vollebergh, W. (2001). Prevalence of psychotic disorder and community level of psychotic symptoms. *Archives of General Psychiatry, 58,* 663–668.

Vazquez-Nuttall, E., Romero-Garcia, I., & DeLeon, R. (1987). Sex roles and perceptions of femininity and masculinity of Hispanic women: A review of the literature. *Psychology of Women Quarterly, 11*, 409–425.

Veasey, S. C., Guilleminault, C., Strohl, K. P., Sanders, M. H., Ballard, R. D., & Magalang, U. J. (2006). Medical therapy for obstructive sleep apnea: A review by the Medical Therapy for Obstructive Sleep Apnea Task Force of the Standards of Practice Committee of the American Academy of Sleep Medicine. *Sleep, 29*, 1036–1044.

Veith, I. (1965). *Hysteria: The history of a disease.* Chicago: University of Chicago Press.

Velting, O. N., Setzer, N. J., & Albano, A. M. (2004). Update on and advances in assessment and cognitive-behavioral treatment of anxiety disorders in children and adolescents. *Professional Psychology: Research & Practice, 35*, 42–54.

Ventura, J., Neuchterlein, K. H., Lukoff, D., & Hardesty, J. P. (1989). A prospective study of stressful life events and schizophrenic relapse. *Journal of Abnormal Psychology, 98*, 407–411.

Verhulst, J., & Heiman, J. (1988). A systems perspective on sexual desire. In S. R. Leiblum & R. C. Rosen (Eds.), *Sexual desire disorders* (pp. 243–270). New York: Guilford Press.

Verma, K. K., Khaitan, B. K., & Singh, O. P. (1998). The frequency of sexual dysfunctions in patients attending a sex therapy clinic in north India. *Archives of Sexual Behavior, 27*, 309–314.

Vermetten, E., Schmahl, C., Lindner, S., Loewenstein, R., & Bremner, J. (2006). Hippocampal and amygdalar volumes in dissociative identity disorder. *American Journal of Psychiatry, 163*, 630–636.

Viken, R. J., Treat, T. A., Nosofsky, R. M., McFall, R. M., & Palmeri, T. J. (2002). Modeling individual differences in perceptual and attentional processes. *Journal of Abnormal Psychology, 111*, 598–609.

Villarreal, G., Hamilton, D. A., Petropoulos, H., Driscoll, I., Rowland, L. M., Griego, J. A., Kodituwakku, P. W., Hart, B. L., Escalona, R., & Brooks, W. M. (2002). Reduced hippocampal volume and total white matter volume in posttraumatic stress disorder. *Biological Psychiatry, 52*, 119–125.

Virani, A. S., Bezchlybnik-Butler, K. Z., & Jeffries, J. J. (Eds.). (2009). *Clinical handbook of psychotropic drugs* (18th rev. ed.). Ashland, OH: Hogrefe & Huber.

Visintainer, M. A., Volpicelli, J. R., & Seligman, M. E. (1982). Tumor rejection in rats after inescapable or escapable shock. *Science, 216*, 437–439.

Vismara, L. A., & Rogers, S. J. (2010). Behavioral treatments in autism spectrum disorder: What do we know? *Annual Review of Clinical Psychology, 6*, 447–468.

Visser, F. E., Aldenkamp, A. P., van Huffelen, A. C., Kuilman, M., Overweg, J., & van Wijk, J. (1997). Prospective study of the prevalence of Alzheimer-type dementia in institutionalized individuals with Down syndrome. *American Journal on Mental Retardation, 101*, 400–412.

Vitkus, J. (2004). *Casebook in abnormal psychology.* New York: McGraw-Hill.

Vohs, K. D., Bardone, A. M., Joiner, T. E., Jr., & Abramson, L. Y. (1999). Perfectionism, perceived weight status, and self-esteem interact to predict bulimic symptoms: A model of bulimic symptom development. *Journal of Abnormal Psychology, 108*, 695–700.

Vohs, K. D., Voelz, Z. R., Pettit, J. W., Bardone, A. M., Katz, J., Abramson, L. Y., Heatherton, T. F., & Joiner, T. E. (2001). Perfectionism, body dissatisfaction, and self-esteem: An interactive model of bulimic symptom development. *Journal of Social & Clinical Psychology, 20*, 476–497.

Volkmar, F. G. (2001). Pharmacological intervention in autism: Theoretical and practical issues. *Journal of Clinical Child Psychology, 30*, 80–87.

Volkmar, F. R., Lord, C., Bailey, A., Schultz, R. T., & Klin, A. (2004). Autism and pervasive developmental disorders. *Journal of Child Psychology and Psychiatry, 45*, 135–170.

Volkmar, F. R., State, M., & Klin, A. (2009). Autism and autism spectrum disorders: Diagnostic issues for the coming decade. *Journal of Child Psychology and Psychiatry, 50*, 108–115.

Vuilleumier, P., Chicherio, C., Assal, F., Schwartz, S., Slosmen, D., & Landis, T. (2001). Functional neuroanatomical correlates of hysterical sensorimotor loss. *Brain, 124*, 1077–1090.

Vythilingam, M., Heim, C., Newport, J., Miller, A. H., Anderson, E., Bronen, R., Brummer, M., Staib, L., Vermetten, E., Charney, D. S., Nemeroff, C. B., & Bremner, J. D. (2002). Childhood trauma associated with smaller hippocampal volume in women with major depression. *American Journal of Psychiatry, 159*, 2072–2080.

Vythilingum, B., Warwick, J., van Kradenburg, J., Hugo, C., van Heerden, B., & Stein, D. J. (2002). SPECT scans in identical twins with trichotillomania. *Journal of Neuropsychiatry and Clinical Neuroscience, 14*, 340–342.

W

Wadden, T. A., Brownell, K. D., & Foster, G. D. (2002). Obesity: Responding to the global epidemic. *Journal of Consulting & Clinical Psychology, 70*, 510–525.

Wade, T. D., Bergin, J. L., Tiggemann, M., Bulik, C. M., & Fairburn, C. G. (2006). Prevalence and long-term course of lifetime eating disorders in an adult Australian twin cohort. *Australian and New Zealand Journal of Psychiatry, 40*, 121–128.

Wade, T. D., Tiggemann, M., Bulik, C. M., Fairburn, C. G., Wray, N. R., & Martin, N. G. (2008). Shared temperament risk factors for anorexia nervosa: A twin study. *Psychosomatic Medicine, 70*, 239–244.

Wagner, P. S., & Spiro, C. (2005). *Divided minds: Twin sisters and their journey through schizophrenia.* New York: St. Martin's Press.

Wakschlag, L. S., Pickett, K. E., Kasza, K. E., & Loeber, R. (2006). Is prenatal smoking associated with a developmental pattern of conduct problems in young boys? *Journal of the American Academy of Child and Adolescent Psychiatry, 45*, 461–467.

Waldron, H. B., Slesnick, N., Brody, J. L., Turner, C. W., & Peterson, T. R. (2001). Treatment outcomes for adolescent substance abuse at 4- and 7-month assessments. *Journal of Consulting & Clinical Psychology, 69*, 802–813.

Walker, E., Kestler, L., Bollini, A., & Hochman, K. M. (2004). Schizophrenia: Etiology and course. *Annual Review of Psychology, 55*, 401–430.

Walker, L. E. A. (1994). Are personality disorders gender biased? In S. A. Kirk & S. D. Einbinder (Eds.), *Controversial issues in mental health* (pp. 22–29). Boston: Allyn & Bacon.

Wallace, E. R., IV., & Gach, J. (Eds.). (2008). *History of psychiatry and medical psychology: With an epilogue on psychiatry and the mind-body relation.* New York: Springer Science.

Wang, P. S., Aguilar-Gaxiola, S., Alonso, J., Angermeyer, M. C., Borges, G., & Bromet E. J. (2007). Use of mental health services for anxiety, mood, and substance disorders in 17 countries in the WHO World Mental Health surveys. *Lancet, 370*, 841–850.

Warga, C. (1988, September). You are what you think. *Psychology Today*, pp. 54–58.

Warren, J. I., Burnette, M., South, S. C., Chauhan, P., Bale, R., & Friend, R. (2002). Personality disorders and violence among female prison inmates. *Journal of the American Academy of Psychiatry and the Law*, 502–509.

Warren, J. I., Murrie, D. C., Chauhan, P., Dietz, P. E., & Morris, J. (2004). Opinion formation in evaluating sanity at the time of the offense: An examination of 5175 pre-trial evaluations. *Behavioral Sciences and the Law, 22*, 171–186.

Waschbusch, D. A. (2002). A meta-analytic examination of comorbid hyperactive-impulsive-attention problems and conduct problems. *Psychological Bulletin, 128*, 118–150.

Watson, C. G., & Buranen, C. (1979). The frequencies of conversion reaction symptoms. *Journal of Abnormal Psychology, 88*, 209–211.

Watson, D. (2009). Differentiating the mood and anxiety disorders: A quadripartite model. *Annual Review of Clinical Psychology, 5*, 221–247.

Watson, J. B. (1930). *Behaviorism.* Chicago: University of Chicago Press.

Watson, J. B., & Raynor, R. (1920). Conditioned emotional reactions. *Journal of Experimental Psychology, 3*, 1–14.

Watson, M., Haviland, J. S., Greer, S., Davidson, J., & Bliss, J. M. (1999). Influence of psychological response on survival in breast cancer: A population-based cohort study. *Lancet, 354*, 1331–1336.

Weaver, I. C. G., Cervoni, N., Champagne, F. A., D'Alessio, A. C. D., Sharma, S., Seckl, J. R., Dymov, S., Szyf, M., & Meaney, M. J. (2004). Epigenetic programming by maternal behavior. *Nature Neuroscience, 7*, 847–854.

Weaver, K. E., Llabre, M. M., Duran, R. E., Antoni, M. H., Ironson, G. I., Penedo, F. J., & Schneiderman, N. (2005). A stress and coping model of medication adherence and viral load in HIV-positive men and women on highly active antiretroviral therapy (HAART). *Health Psychology, 24,* 385–392.

Webster-Stratton, C., & Reid, M. J. (2003). The incredible years parents, teachers, and children training series: A multifaceted treatment approach for young children with conduct problems. In A. E. Kazdin & J. R. Weisz (Eds.), *Evidence-based psychotherapies for children and adolescents* (pp. 224–240). New York: Guilford Press.

Wechsler, H., Lee, J. E., Kuo, M., Seibring, M., Nelson, T. F., & Lee, H. (2002). Trends in alcohol use, related problems and experience of prevention efforts among U.S. college students 1993 to 2001: Results from the 2001 Harvard School of Public Health College Alcohol Study. *Journal of American College Health, 50,* 203–217.

Wechsler, H., & Nelson, T. E. (2008). What we have learned from the Harvard School of Public Health College Alcohol Study: Focusing attention on college student alcohol consumption and the environmental conditions that promote it. *Journal of Studies on Alcohol and Drugs, 69,* 481–490.

Weeks, D., & James, J. (1995). *Eccentrics.* New York: Villard.

Weems, C. F., Pina, A. A., Costa, N. M., Watts, S. E., Taylor, L. K., & Cannon, M. F. (2007). Predisaster trait anxiety and negative affect predict posttraumatic stress in youths after Hurricane Katrina. *Journal of Counseling and Clinical Psychology, 75,* 154–159.

Weiner, B. A., & Wettstein, R. M. (1993). *Legal issues in mental health care.* New York: Plenum Press.

Weissman, M. M., & Markowitz, J. C. (2002). Interpersonal psychotherapy for depression. In I. H. Gotlib & C. L. Hammen (Eds.), *Handbook of depression* (pp. 404–421). New York: Guilford Press.

Weisz, J. R., Donenberg, G., Han, S., & Kauneckis, D. (1995). Child and adolescent psychotherapy outcomes in experiments versus clinics: Why the disparity? *Journal of Abnormal Child Psychology, 23,* 83–106.

Wentz, E., Gillberg, C., Gillberg, I. C., & Ratsam, M. (2001). Ten-year follow-up of adolescent-onset anorexia nervosa: Psychiatric disorders and overall functioning scales. *Journal of Child Psychology & Psychiatry, 42,* 613–622.

Westen, D. (1998). The scientific legacy of Sigmund Freud: Toward a psychodynamically informed psychological science. *Psychological Bulletin, 124,* 333–371.

Westen, D., & Morrison, K. (2001). A multidimensional meta-analysis of treatments for depression, panic, and generalized anxiety disorder: An empirical examination of the status of empirically supported therapies. *Journal of Consulting & Clinical Psychology, 69,* 875–899.

Westermeyer, J. (1993). Cross-cultural psychiatric assessment. In A. C. Gaw (Ed.), *Culture, ethnicity, and mental illness* (pp. 125–144). Washington, DC: American Psychiatric Press.

Westermeyer, J., Bouafuely, M., Neider, J., & Callies, A. (1989). Somatization among refugees: An epidemiologic study. *Psychosomatics, 30,* 34–43.

Weston, S. C., & Siever, L. J. (1993). Biologic correlates of personality disorders. NIMH Conference: Personality disorders (1990, Williamsburg, Virginia). *Journal of Personality Disorders* (Suppl. 1), 129–148.

Westrin, A., & Lam, R. W. (2007). Seasonal affective disorder: A clinical update. *Annals of Clinical Psychiatry, 19,* 239–246.

Wetherell, J. L., Lenze, E. J., & Stanley, M. A. (2005). Evidence-based treatment of geriatric anxiety disorders. *Psychiatric Clinics of North America, 28,* 871-896.

Whalen, C. K., & Henker, B. (1998). Attention-deficit/hyperactivity disorder. In T. H. Ollendick & M. Hersen (Eds.), *Handbook of child psychopathology* (pp. 181–212). New York: Plenum Press.

Wheeler, J., Newring, K. A. B., and Draper, C. (2008). Transvestic fetishism: Psychopathology and theory. In D. R. Laws & W. T. O'Donohue (Eds.), *Sexual deviance: Theory, assessment, and treatment* (pp. 272–284). New York: Guilford Press.

Whitbourne, S. K. (2000). The normal aging process. In S. K. Whitbourne (Ed.), *Psychopathology in later adulthood* (pp. 27–59). New York: Wiley.

White, H. R., Xie, M., & Thompson, W. (2001). Psychopathology as a predictor of adolescent drug use trajectories. *Psychology of Addictive Behaviors, 15,* 210–218.

White, S. (2002). The neuropathogenesis of delirium. *Review of Clinical Gerontology, 12,* 62–67.

Whittal, M. L., Agras, W. S., & Gould, R. A. (1999). Bulimia nervosa: A meta-analysis of psychosocial and pharmacological treatments. *Behavior Therapy, 30,* 117–135.

WHO World Mental Health Survey Consortium. (2004). Prevalence, severity, and unmet need for treatment of mental disorders in the World Health Organization World Mental Health Surveys. *Journal of the American Medical Association, 291,* 2581–2590.

Whooley, M. A., de Jonge, P., Vittinghoff, E., Otte, C., Moos, R., Carney, R. M., Ali, S., Dowray, S., Na, B., Feldman, M. D., Schiller, N., & Browner, W. S. (2008). Depressive symptoms, health behaviors, and risk of cardiovascular events in patients with coronary heart disease. *Journal of the American Medical Association, 300,* 2379–2388.

Widiger, T. A. (1998). Invited essay: Sex biases in the diagnosis of personality disorders. *Journal of Personality Disorders, 12,* 95–118.

Widiger, T. A. (2002). Values, politics, and science in the construction of the *DSM*s. In J. Z. Sadler (Ed.), *Descriptions and prescriptions: Values, mental disorders, and the* DSMs (pp. 25–41). Baltimore: Johns Hopkins University Press.

Widiger, T. A., Mangine, S., Corbitt, E. M., Ellis, C. G., & Thomas, G. V. (1995). *Personality disorder interview-IV: A semistructured interview for the assessment of personality disorders.* Odessa, FL: Psychological Assessment Resources.

Widiger, T. A., & Mullins-Sweatt, S. N. (2009). Five-factor model of personality disorder: A proposal for *DSM-V. Annual Review of Clinical Psychology, 5,* 197–220.

Widiger, T. A., Simonsen, E. (2005). Alternative dimensional models of personality disorder: Finding a common ground. *Journal of Personality Disorders 19,* 110–130.

Widom, C. S., DuMont, K., & Czaja, S. J. (2007). A prospective investigation of major depressive disorder and comorbidity in abused and neglected children grown up. *Archives of General Psychiatry, 64,* 49–56.

Wikan, U. (1991). *Managing turbulent hearts.* Chicago: University of Chicago Press.

Wilens, T. E., Biederman, J., & Spencer, T. J. (2002). Attention deficit/hyperactivity disorder across the lifespan. *Annual Review of Medicine, 53,* 113–131.

Wilfley, D. E., Agras, W. S., Telch, C. F., Rossiter, E. M., Schneider, J. A., Cole, A. G., Sifford, L., & Raeburn, S. D. (1993). Group cognitive-behavioral therapy and group interpersonal psychotherapy for the nonpurging bulimic individual: A controlled comparison. *Journal of Consulting & Clinical Psychology, 61,* 296–305.

Wilfley, D. E., Pike, K. M., & Striegel-Moore, R. H. (1997). Toward an integrated model of risk for binge-eating disorder. *Journal of Gender, Culture, & Health, 2,* 1–32.

Wilfley, D. E., Welch, R. R., Stein, R. I., Spurrell, E. B., Cohen, L. R., Saelens, B. E., Dounchis, J. Z., Frank, M. A., Wiseman, C. V., & Matt, G. E. (2002). A randomized comparison of group cognitive-behavioral therapy and group interpersonal psychotherapy for the treatment of overweight individuals with binge-eating disorder. *Archives of General Psychiatry, 59,* 713–721.

Williams, D. L. (2010). *Developmental language disorders: Learning, language, and the brain. San Diego,* CA: Plural Publishing.

Williams, D. R., Gonzalez, H. M., Neighbors, H., Nesse, R., Abelson, J. M., Sweetman, J., & Jackson, J. S. (2007). Prevalence and distribution of major depressive disorder in African Americans, Caribbean Blacks, and non-Hispanic Whites. Results from the National Survey of American Life. *Archives of General Psychiatry, 64,* 305–315.

Williams, L. M. (1995). Recovered memories of abuse in women with documented child sexual victimization histories. *Journal of Traumatic Stress, 8,* 649–673.

Williams, R. B. (2008). Psychosocial and biobehavioral factors and their interplay in coronary heart disease. *Annual Review of Clinical Psychology, 4,* 349–365.

Williams, R. B., Barefoot, J. C., Haney, T. L., & Harrell, F. E. (1988). Type A behavior and angiographically documented coronary atherosclerosis in a sample of 2,289 patients. *Psychosomatic Medicine, 50,* 139–152.

Williamson, G. L. (1993). Postpartum depression syndrome as a defense to criminal behavior. *Journal of Family Violence, 8,* 151–165.

Wilps, R. F., Jr. (1990). Male bulimia nervosa: An autobiographical case study. In A. E.

Andersen (Ed.), *Males with eating disorders* (pp. 9–29). New York: Brunner/Mazel.

Wilson, G. R., Loeb, K. L., Walsh, B. T., Labouvie, R., Petkova, E., Xinhua, L., & Waternaux, C. (1999). Psychological versus pharmacological treatments of bulimia nervosa: Predictors and processes of change. *Journal of Consulting & Clinical Psychology, 67,* 451–459.

Wilson, G. T., Fairburn, C. G., & Agras, W. S. (1997). Cognitive-behavioral treatment for anorexia nervosa. In D. M. Garner & P. E. Garfinkel (Eds.), *Handbook of treatment for eating disorders* (pp. 67–93). New York: Guilford Press.

Wilson, G. T, Fairburn, C. C., Agras, W. S., Walsh, B. T., & Kraemer, H. (2002). Cognitive-behavioral therapy for bulimia nervosa: Time course and mechanisms of change. *Journal of Consulting & Clinical Psychology, 70,* 267–274.

Wilson, G. T., Grilo, C. M., & Vitousek, K. M. (2007). Psychological treatment of eating disorders. *American Psychologist, 62,* 199–216.

Wilson, K. A., & Hayward, C. (2005). A prospective evaluation of agoraphobia and depression symptoms following panic attacks in a community sample of adolescents. *Journal of Anxiety Disorders, 19,* 87–103.

Winger, G., Hofmann, F. G., & Woods, J. H. (1992). *Handbook on drug and alcohol abuse.* New York: Oxford University Press.

Winick, B. J. (2003). A therapeutic jurisprudence assessment of sexually violent predator laws. In B. J. Winick & J. Q. LaFond (Eds.), *Protecting society from sexually dangerous offenders: Law, justice, and therapy* (pp. 317–331). Washington, DC: American Psychological Association.

Winstanley, C. A., Theobald, D. E., Dalley, J. W., Robbins, T. W. (2005). Interactions between serotonin and dopamine in the control of impulsive choice in rats: Therapeutic implications for impulse control disorders. *Neuropsychopharmacology, 30,* 669–682.

Wintemute, G. J., Parham, C. A., Beaumont, J. J., Wright, M., & Drake, C. (1999). Mortality among recent purchasers of handguns. *New England Journal of Medicine, 341,* 1583–1589.

Winters, K. (2005). Gender dissonance: Diagnostic reform of gender identity disorder for adults. *Journal of Psychology and Human Sexuality, 17,* 71–89.

Wiseman, C. V., Gray, J. J., Mosimann, J. E., & Ahrens, A. H. (1992). Cultural expectations of thinness in women: An update. *International Journal of Eating Disorders, 11,* 85–89.

Wisniewski, A. B. & Migeon, C. J. (2002). Long-term perspectives for 46,XY patients affected by complete androgen insensitivity syndrome or congenital micropenis. *Seminars in Reproductive Medicine, 20,* 297–304.

Witkiewitz, K., Van der Maas, H. L. J., Hufford, M. R., & Marlatt, G. A. (2007). Nonnormality and divergence in posttreatment alcohol use: Reexamining the project MATCH data "another way." *Journal of Abnormal Psychology, 116,* 378–394.

Wittchen, H.-U., & Fehm, L. (2003). Epidemiology and natural course of social fears and social phobia. *Acta Psychiatrica Scandinavica, 108*(Suppl. 417), 4–18.

Wittke-Thompson, J. K., Ambrose, N., Yairi, E., Roe, C., Cook, E. H., Ober, C., & Cox, N. J. (2007). Genetic studies of stuttering in a founder population. *Journal of Fluency Disorders, 32,* 33–50.

Wolfsdorf, B. A., & Zlotnick, C. (2001). Affect management in group therapy for women with posttraumatic stress disorder and histories of childhood sexual abuse. *Journal of Clinical Psychology, 57,* 169–181.

Wolfson, A. R. (2001). *The woman's book of sleep: A complete resource guide.* Oakland, CA: New Harbinger.

Wolfson, A. R. (2010). Adolescents and emerging adults' sleep patterns: New developments. *Journal of Adolescent Health, 46,* 97–99.

Wolpe, J. (1997). Thirty years of behavior therapy. *Behavior Therapy, 28,* 633–635.

Woods, D. W., Wetterneck, C. T., & Flessner, C. A. (2006). A controlled evaluation of acceptance and commitment therapy plus habit reversal for trichotillomania. *Behaviour Research and Therapy, 44,* 639–656.

World Health Organization (WHO). (2004). Distribution of suicide rates (per 100,000) by gender and age, 2000. http://www.who.int/mental_health/prevention/suicide/suicidecharts/en/ (accessed February 18, 2008)

World Health Organization (WHO). (2005a, January 12–15). Alcohol and mental health. Briefing from the WHO European Ministerial Conference on Mental Health, Helsinki, Finland. http://www.who.int/substance_abuse/facts/psychoactives/en/ (accessed February 18, 2008)

World Health Organization (WHO). (2005b). *Global alcohol database.* http://www.who.int/whosis (accessed February 6, 2006)

World Health Organization (WHO). (2005c). WHO SUPRE suicide prevention: Live your life. http://www.who.int/mental_health/management/en/SUPRE_flyer1.pdf (accessed February 20, 2006)

World Health Organization (WHO). (2007). Deaths from coronary heart disease. http://www.who.int/cardiovascular_disease/en/cvd_atlas_14_deathHD.pdf (accessed October 31, 2007)

World Health Organization (WHO). (2008). Global summary of the AIDS epidemic, December 2007. http://www.who.int/2008_global_summary_AIDS_ep (accessed March 13, 2009)

Worthman, C. M., & Panter-Brick, C. (2008). Homeless street children in Nepal: Use of allostatic load to assess the burden of childhood adversity. *Development and Psychopathology, 20,* 233–255.

Wurtzel, E. (1995). *Prozac nation.* New York: Berkley.

Wyatt, E. (2009, November 24). On "The Biggest Loser," health can take a back seat. http://www.nytimes.com/2009/11/25/ business/media/25loser.html?_r=1 (accessed January 6, 2010)

Y

Yairi, E., & Ambrose, N. G. (2005). *Early childhood stuttering.* Austin, TX: PRO-ED.

Yang, J., Dai, X., Yao, S., Cai, T., Gao, B., McCrae, R. R., & Costa, P. T. (2002). Personality disorders and the five-factor model of personality in Chinese psychiatric patients. In P. T. Costa & T. A. Widiger (Eds.), *Personality Disorders and the Five-factor Model of Personality* (2nd ed., pp. 215–221). Washington, DC: American Psychological Association.

Yapko, M. D. (1997). *Breaking the patterns of depression.* New York: Golden Books.

Yeh, M., & Weisz, J. R. (2001). Why are we here at the clinic? Parent-child (dis)agreement on referral problems at outpatient treatment entry. *Journal of Consulting & Clinical Psychology, 69,* 1019–1025.

Yehuda, R. (2004). Risk and resilience in posttraumatic stress disorder. *Journal of Clinical Psychiatry, 65*(Suppl. 1), 29–36.

Yehuda, R., Blair, W., Labinsky, E., & Bierer, L. M. (2007). Effects of parental PTSD on the cortisol response to dexamethasone administration in their adult offspring. *American Journal of Psychiatry, 164,* 163–166.

Yehuda, R., McFarlane, A. C., & Shalev, A. Y. (1998). Predicting the development of posttraumatic stress disorder from the acute response to a traumatic event. *Biological Psychiatry, 44,* 1305–1313.

Yirmiya, N., Erel, O., Shaked, M., & Solomonica-Levi, D. (1998). Meta-analysis comparing theory of mind abilities of individuals with autism, individuals with mental retardation, and normally developed individuals. *Psychological Bulletin, 124,* 283–307.

Young, E., & Korzun, A. (1999). Psychoneuroendocrinology of depression: Hypothalamic-pituitary-gonadal axis. *Psychiatric Clinics of North America, 21,* 309–323.

Yusuf, S., Hawken, S., Ounpuu, S., Dans, T., Avezum, A., Lanas, F., Budaj, A., Pais, P., Varigos, J., & Lisheng, L. (2004). Effect of potentially modifiable risk factors associated with myocardial infarction in 52 countries (the INTERHEART study): Case-control study. *Lancet, 364,* 937–952.

Z

Zaider, T. I., & Heimberg, R. G. (2003). Nonpharmacologic treatments for social anxiety disorder. *Acta Psychiatrica Scandinavica, 108*(Suppl. 417), 72–84.

Zalsman, G., Shoval, G., & Rotstein, L. (2009). Pharmactherapy for adolescent depression. In S. Nolen-Hoeksema & L. Hilt (Eds.), *Handbook of depression in adolescents* (pp. 571–588). New York: Routledge.

Zanarini, M. C. (Ed.). (1997). *Role of sexual abuse in the etiology of borderline personality disorder.* Washington, DC: American Psychiatric Press.

Zanarini, M. C., Skodol, A.-E., Bender, D., Dolan, R., Sanislow, C., Schaefer, E., Morey, L., Grilo, C. M., Shea, M. T., McGlashan, T. H., & Gunderson, G. (2000). The Collaborative Longitudinal Personality Disorders Study: Reliability of Axis I and II diagnoses. *Journal of Personality Disorder, 14,* 291–299.

Zarit, S. H., & Haynie, D. A. (2000). Introduction to clinical issues. In S. K. Whitbourne (Ed.), *Psychopathology in later adulthood* (pp. 1–25). New York: Wiley.

Zayas, L. H., Lester, R. J., Cabassa., L. J., & Fortuna, L. R. (2005). Why do so many Latina teens attempt suicide? A conceptual model for research. *American Journal of Orthopsychiatry, 75,* 275–287.

Zelt, D. (1981). First person account: The Messiah quest. *Schizophrenia Bulletin, 7,* 527–531.

Zhang, B., & Wing, Y.-K. (2006). Sex differences in insomnia: A meta-analysis. *Sleep, 29,* 85–93.

Zhang, X., Beaulieu, J. M., Sotnikova, T. D., Gainetdinov, R. R., & Caron, M. G. (2004). Tryptophan hydroxylase-2 controls brain serotonin. *Science, 305,* 217.

Zhou, J.-N., Hofman, M. A., & Swaab, D. F. (1995). No changes in the number of vasoactive intestinal polypeptide (VIP)-expressing neurons in the suprachiasmatic nucleus of homosexual men; comparison with vasopressin-expressing neurons. *Brain Research, 672,* 285–288.

Ziegelstein, R. C., Fauerbach, J. A., Stevens, S. S., Romanelli, J., Richter, D. P., & Bush, D. E. (2000). Patients with depression are less likely to follow recommendations to reduce cardiac risk during recovery from a myocardial infarction. *Archives of Internal Medicine, 160,* 1818–1823.

Zigler, E., Gilliam, W. S., & Jones, S. M. (2006). *A vision for universal preschool education.* New York: Cambridge University Press.

Zigler, E., & Hodapp, R. M. (1991). Behavioral functioning in individuals with mental retardation. *Annual Review of Psychology, 42,* 29–50.

Zigler, E., & Styfco, S. J. (2004). Applying the findings of developmental psychology to improve early childhood intervention. In M. A. Feldman (Ed.), *Early intervention: The essential readings* (pp. 54–72). Malden, England: Blackwell.

Zigler, E., & Styfco, S. J. (2008). America's Head Start program: An effort for social justice. In C. Wainryb, J. Smetana, & E. Turiel (Eds.), *Social development, social inequalities, and social justice* (pp. 53–80). New York: Taylor & Francis Group/Lawrence Erlbaum.

Zilboorg, G., & Henry, G. W. (1941). *A history of medical psychology.* New York: W. W. Norton.

Zimmerman, M., Rothschild, L., & Chelminski, I. (2005). The prevalence of *DSM-IV* personality disorders in psychiatric outpatients. *American Journal of Psychiatry, 162,* 1911–1918.

Zisserson, R. N., & Palfai, T. P. (2007). Behavioral activation system (BAS) sensitivity and reactivity to alcohol cues among hazardous drinkers. *Addictive Behaviors, 32,* 2178–2186.

Zoccolillo, M. (1993). Gender and the development of conduct disorder. *Development & Psychopathology, 5,* 65–78.

Zubenko, G. S., Hughes, H. B., III, Stiffler, J. S., Zubenko, W. N., & Kaplan, B. B. (2002). D2S2944 identifies a likely susceptibility locus for recurrent, early-onset, major depression in women. *Molecular Psychiatry, 7,* 460–467.

Zucker, K. J. (2005). Gender identity disorder in children and adolescents. *Annual Review of Clinical Psychology 1,* pp. 467–492.

Zucker K. J., & Cohen-Kettenis, P. T. (2008). Gender identity disorder in children and adolescents. In D. L. Rowland & L. Incrocci (Eds.), *Handbook of sexual and gender identity disorders* (pp. 376–422). Hoboken, NJ: Wiley.

Zucker, R. A., Chermack, S. T., & Curran, G. M. (1999). Alcoholism: A lifespan perspective on etiology and course. In M. Lewis & A. J. Sameroff (Eds.), *Handbook of developmental psychopatholgy* (2nd ed.). New York: Plenum Press.

Zucker, R. A., Ellis, D. A., Fitzgerald, H. E., Bingham, C. R., & Sanford, K. (1996). Other evidence for at least two alcoholisms: II. Life course variation in antisociality and heterogeneity of alcoholic outcome. *Development & Psychopathology, 8,* 831–848.

Zucker, R. A., Kincaid, S. B., Fitzgerald, H. E., & Bingham, C. R. (1995). Alcohol schema acquisition in preschoolers: Differences between children of alcoholics and children of nonalcoholics. *Alcoholism: Clinical & Experimental Research, 19,* 1011–1017.

Zvolensky, M. J., & Smits, J. A. J. (Eds.). (2008). *Anxiety in health behaviors and physical illness.* New York: Springer Science & Business Media.

Zwerdling, D. (2009, November 11). Walter Reed officials asked: Was Hasan psychotic? http://www.npr.org/templates/story/story.php?storyId=120313570 (accessed January 19, 2009)

CREDITS

TEXT & ILLUSTRATIONS

CHAPTER 1

p. 3: Anonymous, 1992. "First-person account: Portrait of a schizophrenic." *Schizophrenia Bulletin*, 18, 333–334; **p. 3:** From *An Unquiet Mind* by Kay Redfield Jamison. Copyright © 1995 by Kay Redfield Jamison. Used by permission of Alfred A. Knopf, a division of Random House, Inc.; **Fig. 1.1:** Graph of Trends in the numbers of psychiatric beds in western Europe 1978–2002, from European health for all database, WHO Regional Office for Europe, 2004. Data from The WHO World Mental Health Survey Consortium (2004). Prevalence, severity, and unmet need for treatment of mental disorders in the World Health Organization World Mental Health Surveys. *Journal of the American Medical Association*, 291, 2581–2590. As found in David McDaid and Graham Thornicroft, Policy Brief: Mental health II: Balancing institutional and community-based care, p. 3. *European Observatory on Health Systems and Policies*, © World Health Organization 2005. Used with permission from the World Health Organization; **p. 21:** Excerpt from pp. 105–106 from E. Fuller Torrey, *Surviving Schizophrenia*. Copyright © 2006, 2001, 1995, 1988, 1983 by E. Fuller Torrey. Reprinted by permission of HarperCollins Publishers.

CHAPTER 2

p. 27: Excerpts by Ellis from Wargh (1988). "You are what you think," *Psychology Today*, pp. 54–58. Reprinted with permission from *Psychology Today* magazine. Copyright © 1988 Sussex Publishers, LLC; **Fig. 2.2 and p. 30:** From H. Damasio, T. Grabowski, Frank R. Galaburda, and A. R. Damasio (1994), "The Return of Phineas Gage: Clues About the Brain from the Skull of a Famous Patient," *Science*, Vol. 264, pp. 1102–1105. Dornslife Neuroscience Imaging Center and Brain and Creativity Institute, University of Southern California. Copyright © 1994 American Association for the Advancement of Science. Reprinted with permission from AAAS and Dr. Hanna M. Damasio; **Fig. 2.6:** Adapted from Robert S. Feldman, *Understanding Psychology*, 7e, Fig. 4, p. 85. Copyright © 2005 The McGraw-Hill Companies, Inc. Reprinted with permission; **pp. 54–55:** Sue, S. & Zane, N., 1987, "The Role of Culture and Cultural Techniques in Psychotherapy: A Critique and Reformulation," *American Psychologist*, 42, pp. 42–43. Copyright © 1987 by the American Psychological Association. Reproduced with permission. The use of this information does not imply endorsement by the publisher.

CHAPTER 3

Fig. 3.3: From J. M. Sattler, *Assessment of Children*, 3rd edition. Reprinted with permission.

CHAPTER 5

pp. 140, 142: From Brown, T. A., O'Leary, T. A. & Barlow, D. H. 2001. Generalized Anxiety Disorder, *Clinical Handbook of Psychological Disorders: A Step-By-Step Treatment Manual*, 3rd ed., pp. 187, 193–194. New York: Guilford Press. Reprinted with permission; **pp. 143–145:** From Dr. Judith Rapoport, *The Boy Who Couldn't Stop Washing*. Copyright © 1989 by Judith L. Rapoport, M.D. Used by permission of Dutton, a division of Penguin Group (USA) Inc.

CHAPTER 6

Table 6.1: From Colin A. Ross, *Dissociative Identity Disorder*. Copyright © 1997 John Wiley & Sons, Inc. Reprinted with permission of John Wiley & Sons, Inc.; **p. 158:** Reprinted from *Behavior Therapy*, Vol 22, Barbara Olasov Rothbaum and Edna B. Foa, Exposure Treatment of PTSD Concomitant with Conversion Mutism: A Case Study, Pages 449–456, Copyright 1991, with permission from Elsevier; **Fig. 6.2:** From p. 353 of "Somatoform Disorders," by L. J. Kirmayer and S. Taillefer, in *Adult Psychopathology and Diagnosis*, 3rd ed., eds. S. M. Turner and M. Hersen, 1997, pp. 333–383. Copyright © 1997 John Wiley & Sons, Inc. Reproduced with permission of John Wiley & Sons, Inc.; **p. 163:** Reproduced with permission from Koss J. D. (1990). Somatization and Somatic Complaint Syndromes Among Hispanics: Overview and Ethnopsychological Perspectives. *Transcultural Psychiatric Research Review*, 27, p. 5–29. Copyright © 1990 McGill University; **p. 164:** Norman Cameron, *Personality Development and Psychopathology: A Dynamic Approach*, Second Edition. Copyright © 1985 by Wadsworth, a part of Cengage Learning, Inc. Reproduced with permission. www.cengage.com/permissions; **pp. 165–166:** Phillips, K. A., Didie, E. R., Feusner, J., & Wilhelm, S. (2008). Body dysmorphic disorder: Treating an underrecognized disorder. Reprinted with permission from the *American Journal of Psychiatry*. Copyright © 2008 American Psychiatric Association; **p. 168:** From C. H. Thigpen and H. M. Cleckley, *The Three Faces of Eve*, Copyright © 1957 McGraw-Hill. Reprinted with permission; **p. 170:** From Hornstein, N. L. & Putnam, F. W., 1992, "Clinical Phenomenology of Child and Adolescent Dissociative Disorders," *Journal of the American Academy of Child & Adolescent Psychiatry*, 31, 1077–1085; **p. 174:** From Hilgard, E. R. (1986). *Divided consciousness: Multiple controls in human thought and action*, p. 68. New York: Wiley. Reprinted with permission of the estate of Ernest R. Hilgard; **p. 176:** Loftus, E. F., 1993, "The Reality of Repressed Memories," *American Psychologist*, 48, 518–537. Copyright © 1993 by the American Psychological Association. Reproduced with permission. The use of this information does not imply endorsement by the publisher.

CHAPTER 7

p. 181: From *An Unquiet Mind* by Kay Redfield Jamison. Copyright © 1995 by Kay Redfield Jamison. Used by permission of Alfred A. Knopf, a division of Random House, Inc.; **p. 197:** Byron Good, *Culture and Depression*. Copyright © 1985 by University of California Press–Books. Reproduced with permission of University of California–Books in the format Textbook via Copyright Clearance Center; **p. 206:** From *Breaking the Patterns of Depression* by Michael D. Yapko. Copyright © 1997 by Michael D. Yapko. Used by permission of Doubleday, a division of Random House, Inc.; **p. 207–208:** Thorpe/Olson, *Behavior Therapy: Concepts, Procedures & Applications*, "Case Study: Susan." Copyright © 1997 Allyn & Bacon. Reproduced by permission of Pearson Education, Inc.;

Fig. 7.8: Adapted from World Health Organization (WHO). (2004). Distribution of suicide rates (per 100,000) by gender and age, 2000. Retrieved from: http://www.who.int/mental_health/prevention/suicide/suicidecharts/en/. Reprinted with permission from the World Health Organization; **Fig. 7.9:** From World Health Organization (WHO). (2005). *WHO SUPRE suicide prevention: Live your life*. Retrieved from: http://www.who.int/mental_health/management/en/SUPRE_flyer1.pdf. Reprinted with permission from the World Health Organization.

CHAPTER 8

Fig. 8.1: From E. Fuller Torrey, *Surviving Schizophrenia*. Copyright © 2006, 2001, 1995, 1988, 1983 by E. Fuller Torrey. Reprinted by permission of HarperCollins Publishers; **pp. 241, 258:** *Casebook in Abnormal Psychology* edited by Halgin & Whitbourne, "A Difficult Case of Schizophrenia," pp. 197–210. Copyright © 1998 by Oxford University Press, Inc. By permission of Oxford University Press, Inc.; **p. 247:** From McGhie, A. & Chapman, J., 1961, "Disorders in Attention and Perception in Early Schizophrenia," *British Journal of Medical Psychology*, 34, p. 104. Reproduced with permission from Psychology and Psychotherapy: Theory Research and Practice (formerly the British Journal of Medical Psychology) © The British Psychological Society; **Fig. 8.3:** From *Schizophrenia Genesis: The Origins of Madness* by Irving I. Gottesman. © 1991 by Irving I. Gottesman. Used with permission of Worth Publishers; **Fig. 8.5:** Barch, D. M. (April 2005). The cognitive neuroscience of schizophrenia. *Annual Review of Clinical Psychology* by D. M. Barch. Copyright © 2005 by Annual Reviews, Inc. Reproduced with permission of Annual Reviews, Inc. in the format Textbook via Copyright Clearance Center, and with permission of the author; **Fig. 8.8:** Barch, D. M. (April 2005). The cognitive neuroscience of schizophrenia. *Annual Review of Clinical Psychology* by D. M. Barch. Copyright © 2005 by Annual Reviews, Inc. Reproduced with permission of Annual Reviews, Inc. in the format Textbook via Copyright Clearance Center, and with permission of the author; **p. 251:** From Brown, T. A., O'Leary, T. A. & Barlow, D. H., 2001, in Barlow, D. H. (Ed.) "Generalized Anxiety Disorder," *Clinical Handbook of Psychological Disorders: A Step-by-Step Treatment Manual*, Third Edition, New York: Guilford Press, p. 502. Reprinted with permission.

CHAPTER 9

p. 263: From *Girl, Interrupted* by Susanna Kaysen. Copyright © 1993 by Susanna Kaysen. Used by permission of Turtle Bay Books, a division of Random House, Inc., and of the UK publisher, Little, Brown; **pp. 268–269:** From Beck, A. T. & Freeman, A. M., 1990, *Cognitive Therapy of Personality Disorders*, pp. 111–112. New York: Guilford Press. Reprinted with permission; **p. 277:** From Linehan, M. M., Cochran, B. N. & Kehrer, K. C., "Dialectical Behavior Therapy for Borderline Personality Disorder," in D. H. Barlow (Ed.), *Clinical Handbook of Psychological Disorders: A Step-by-Step Treatment Manual*, Third Edition, pp. 502–504. NY: Guilford Press. Reprinted with permission; **pp. 282, 283:** From Beck, A. T. & Freeman, A. M., 1990, *Cognitive Therapy of Personality Disorders*, pp. 111–112, 245–247. New York: Guilford Press. Reprinted with permission.

CHAPTER 10

p. 297: Excerpts from *THINKING IN PICTURES and Other Reports from My Life with Autism* by Temple Grandin. Copyright © 1995, 2006 by Temple Grandin, published in the US by Vintage and in the UK by Bloomsbury. Used by permission of Doubleday, a division of Random House, Inc., and by permission of the author; **p. 304:** From Jenkins, R. L., *Behavior Disorders of Childhood and Adolescence*, 1973. Courtesy of Charles C. Thomas Publisher, Ltd., Springfield, Illinois; **Fig. 10.1:** From "The Prevention of Antisocial Behavior: Some Considerations in the Search for Effective Interventions," by J. B. Reid and J. M. Eddy, in *Handbook of Antisocial Personality Disorder*, eds. David M. Stoff, James Breiling, and Jack D. Maser. Copyright © 1997 John Wiley & Sons, Inc. Reproduced with permission of John Wiley & Sons, Inc.; **p. 318:** Adapted from John Vitkus, *The McGraw-Hill Casebook for Abnormal Psychology*, 5th ed., p. 193–199. Copyright © 2004 The McGraw-Hill Companies, Inc. Reprinted with permission.

CHAPTER 11

p. 335: From *Elegy for Iris* by John Bayley. Copyright © 1998 by the author and reprinted by permission of St. Martin's Press, LLC. In the UK from *Iris: A Memoir* by John Bayley, reprinted by permission of Gerald Duckworth & Co. Ltd.; **Fig. 11.1:** *Annual Review of Psychology* by Park, D. C. & Reuter-Lorenz, P. Copyright 2009 by Annual Reviews, Inc. Reproduced with permission of Annual Reviews, Inc. in the format Textbook via Copyright Clearance Center; **p. 351:** Adapted from Anxiety in Older Adults, by F. Scogin, M. Floyd, and J. Forde, in *Psychopathology in Later Adulthood*, ed. S. K. Whitbourne. Copyright © 2000 John Wiley & Sons, Inc. Reproduced with permission of John Wiley & Sons, Inc.; **p. 352:** Adapted from Mood Disorders in Older Adults, by D. A. King and H. E. Markus, in *Psychopathology in Later Adulthood*, ed. S. K. Whitbourne. Copyright © 2000 John Wiley & Sons, Inc. Reproduced with permission of John Wiley & Sons, Inc.; **p. 355:** Substance Abuse Disorders, by E. Lisansky-Gomberg, in *Psychopathology in Later Adulthood*, ed. S. K. Whitbourne. Copyright © 2000 John Wiley & Sons, Inc. Reproduced with permission of John Wiley & Sons, Inc.

CHAPTER 12

p. 362: Excerpt from pp. 254–255 from *Wasted: A Memoir of Anorexia and Bulimia* by Marya Hornbacher. Copyright © 1998 by Marya Hornbacher-Beard. Reprinted by permission of HarperCollins Publishers; **Fig. 12.2:** From D. Garner, A. K. Cooke, and H. E. Marano, "The 1997 Body Image Survey," in *Psychology Today*, pp. 30–44. Reprinted with permission from Psychology Today magazine. Copyright © 1997 Sussex Publishers, LLC; **pp. 367–368:** From Stunkard, A. J., 1993, "A History of Binge Eating," in C. G. Fairburn and G. T. Wilson (Eds.), *Binge Eating: Nature, Assessment, and Treatment*, pp. 20–21. New York: Guilford Press. Reprinted with permission; **pp. 370–371:** Reprinted from *Social Science & Medicine*, Vol. 41, Issue 1, L. Sing, "Self-starvation in context: Towards a culturally sensitive understanding of anorexia nervosa," pp. 27–29. Copyright © 1995. With permission from Elsevier; **Fig. 12.4:** From C. V. Wiseman, et al., "Cultural Expectations of Thinness in Women: An Update," in *International Journal of Eating Disorders*, Vol. 11. Copyright © 1992 John Wiley & Sons, Inc. Reprinted with permission; **p. 378:** "Worshipping The

Gods of Thinness," from *Reviving Ophelia* by Mary Pipher, Ph.D. Copyright © 1994 by Mary Pipher, Ph.D. Used by permission of G.P. Putnam's Sons, a division of Penguin Group (USA) Inc., and the author.

CHAPTER 13

p. 389: Excerpt from pp. 57, 180 from *As Nature Made Him* by John Colapinto. Copyright © 1999 by John Colapinto. Reprinted by permission of HarperCollins Publishers; **pp. 395–396:** From McCarthy, B. W., 1989, "Cognitive Behavioral Strategies and Techniques in the Treatment of Early Ejaculation," in S. R. Leiblum & R. C. Rosen (Eds.), *Principles and Practice of Sex Therapy: Update for the 1990s*, pp. 151–152. New York: Guilford Press. Reprinted with permission; **p. 405:** From Althof, S. E. (2000). Erectile dysfunction: Psychotherapy with men and couples. In S. R. Leiblum & R. C. Rosen (Eds.), *Principles and Practice of Sex Therapy* (3rd ed.), p. 270. New York, NY: Guilford Press. Reprinted with permission; **p. 416:** Adapted from Springer and the International Academy of Sex Research, *Archives of Sexual Behavior*, vol. 24, 1995, pp. 439–445, "Female-to-Male Transsexualism, Heterosexual Type: Two Cases," R. Dickey and J. Stephens. Copyright © 1995 Plenum Publishing Corporation, with kind permission from Springer Science and Business Media and the author.

CHAPTER 14

Fig. 14.2: Monitoring the Future Study, University of Michigan. Reprinted with permission; **Fig. 14.3:** From *Global Status Report on Alcohol*, World Health Organization, 2001, www.who.int/substance_abuse. Reprinted with permission from the World Health Organization; **p. 445:** From Psychotomimetic Agents by A. Hoffman, as found in *Drugs Affecting the Central Nervous System*, Vol. 2 by A. Burger (Ed). Copyright © 1968. Reproduced by permission; **p. 454:** Reprinted from Hester, R. K. and W. R. Miller (eds). *Handbook of Alcoholism Treatment Approaches: Effective Alternatives*, C. T. Rimmele, W. R. Miller, M. J. Dougher, "Aversion Therapies," p. 135. Copyright © 1989. With permission; **p. 455:** Adapted from Springer and Plenum Publishing Corporation, *Behavioral Treatment of Alcohol Problems*, 1978, pp. 97–98, M. B. Sobell and L. C. Sobell. Copyright © 1978. With kind permission from Springer Science and Business Media and the author.

CHAPTER 15

p. 467: From *Anatomy of an Illness as Perceived by the Patient: Reflections on Healing and Regeneration* by Norman Cousins. Copyright © 1979 by W. W. Norton & Company, Inc. Used by permission of W. W. Norton & Company, Inc.

CHAPTER 16

p. 503: Bennett N. S., Lidz C. W., Monahan J., Mulvey E. P., Hoge S. K., Roth L. H., Gardner W., "Inclusion, motivation, and good faith: The morality of coercion in mental hospital admission," *Behavioral Sciences and the Law*. 1993; 11(3): 298. Used with permission of the publisher, Wiley-Blackwell.

PHOTOS

PREFACE

© PhotoAlto/PunchStock

CHAPTER 1

p. 2: © Will Crocker/Getty Images; **p. 3:** © Corbis; **p. 4:** © AP Images/Aaron Favila; **p. 6:** © The Granger Collection, New York; **p. 7:** © Courtesy of Gary Holloway. Photo by Josef Astor; **p. 10**(left): © Sandved B. Kjell/Visuals Unlimited; **p. 10**(right): © The Granger Collection; **p. 12:** © Bettmann/Corbis; **p. 14**(left): © US National Library of Medicine/Science Photo Library/Photo Researchers; **p. 14**(right): © Jean-Loup Charmet/Photo Researchers; **p. 15**(top): © Robert Fleeury/Photo Researchers; **p. 15**(bottom): © Library of Congress Prints and Photographs Division [LC-USZ62-9797]; **p. 16:** © The Granger Collection; **p. 17:** © Jean-Loup Charmet/Photo Researchers; **p. 21:** © Sonda Dawes/The The Image Works

CHAPTER 2

p. 26: © Daly and Newton/Getty Images; **p. 27:** Courtesy, Albert Ellis, Albert Ellis Institute; **p. 36:** © Enrico Ferorelli; **p. 38:** © 1994 Newsweek, Inc. All rights reserved. Reprinted by permission. Photo by Myko Photography; **p. 41:** © Syracuse Newspapers/Dennis Nett /The Image Works; **p. 43:** © Michael Newman/PhotoEdit; **p. 44**(top): Courtesy Aaron Beck; **p. 44**(bottom): © David Young-Wolff/PhotoEdit; **p. 45:** © Library of Congress Prints and Photographs Division [LC-USZ62-72266]; **p. 49:** National Library of Medicine; **p. 51:** © Michael Newman/PhotoEdit; **p. 56**(left): © Jose Luis Pelaėz Inc./Getty Images; **p. 56**(right): © David R. Frazier/Photo Researchers; **p. 58:** © Geoff Manasse/Getty Images

CHAPTER 3

p. 64: © Dona Monroe/Getty Images; **p. 65:** Courtesy, Marya Hornbacher; **p. 71:** © Michael Newman/PhotoEdit; **p. 73:** © Living Art Enterprises, LLC/Photo Researchers; **p. 76:** © Michael Newman/PhotoEdit; **p. 84:** © Royalty-Free/Corbis

CHAPTER 4

p. 88: © Zephyr/SPL/Getty Images; **p. 89:** © Royalty-Free/Corbis; **p. 93:** © Charles Peterson/Retna Ltd./Corbis; **p. 97:** © Peter Hvizdak/The Image Works; **p. 99:** © Liquidlibrary/PictureQuest; **p. 101:** © Getty Images

CHAPTER 5

p. 112: © Asia Images/Getty Images; **p. 113:** © AP Images/Antonio Calann; **p. 117:** © Library of Congress Prints and Photographs Division [LC-DIG-ppmsca-01814]; **p. 119:** © AP Images/Andrea Booher; **p. 120:** © AP Images/Marco Di Lauro; **p. 126:** © Ryan McVay/Getty Images; **p. 132:** © AP Images/G. Paul Burnett; **p. 134:** Courtesy Prof. Ben Harris, University of New Hampshire; **p. 136:** © Digital Vision/Superstock; **p. 137**(all): Courtesy, Albert Bandura; **p. 144**(top): © Royalty-Free/Corbis; **p. 144**(bottom): © Trae Patton/NBCU Photo Bank via AP Images; **p. 146:** © Lewis Baxter/Peter Arnold/Photolibrary

CHAPTER 6

p. 152: © Adam Gault/Getty Images; **p. 153:** © The Granger Collection; **p. 156:** © AP Images/Alan Diaz; **p. 161:** © Comstock Images/Jupiter Images/Alamy; **p. 165:** © David Young-Wolff/PhotoEdit; **p. 169:** © The Kobal Collection/20th Century Fox; **p. 170:** © Cindy Charles/Photo Edit; **p. 175:** © Consolidated News/Getty Images

CHAPTER 7

p. 80: © Rubberball/Getty Images; **p. 181:** © Johns Hopkins Medicine; **p. 188:** © Chris Knapton/Alamy; **p. 189**(top): Library of Congress Prints and Photographs Division [LC-DIG-npcc-17934]; **p. 189**(bottom): © Royalty-Free/Corbis; **p. 190:** © Art Streiber/CBS via Getty Images; **p. 194:** © AP Image/Eric Gay; **p. 195:** © Digital Vision/Getty Images; **p. 199**(both): Rich, B. A., Vinton, D., Roberson-Nay, R., Hommer, R., Berghorst, L., McClure, E., Fromm, S., Pine, D., Leibenluft, E. (2006). Limbic hyperactivation during processing of neutral facial expressions in children with bipolar disorder. Proceedings of the National Academy of Science, 103(23), 8900–8905. Reproduced with permission; **p. 202:** © Robin Nelson/PhotoEdit; **p. 203:** © Will McIntyre/Photo Researchers; **p. 204:** © John Ulan/Canadian Press/Phototake; **p. 205:** © John Griffin/The Image Works; **p. 206:** © Shuji Kobayashi/Getty Images; **p. 213:** © Jack Spratt/The Image Works; **p. 216:** © Reuters/Corbis; **p. 218:** © Gary D. Landsman/Corbis

CHAPTER 8

p. 224: © Joe Madeira/Getty Images; **p. 225:** © Reuters/Corbis; **p. 232:** © AP Images/CP, Kevin Frayer; **p. 233:** © Justin Sullivan/Getty Images; **p. 242:** Courtesy, The Genain Quadrulplets; **p. 243:** © Science Source/Photo Researchers; **p. 245:** © Paul Thompson, Arthur Toga, Judith Rapoport/UCLA Lab of Neuro Imaging and NIMH; **p. 253:** Courtesy, Skyland Trail, Atlanta, GA

CHAPTER 9

p. 262: © Siri Stafford/Getty Images; **p. 263:** © Ed Quinn/Corbis; **p. 270:** © David Harry Stewart/Getty Images; **p. 274:** © The Kobal Collection/Ken Regan/Orion; **p. 280:** Donegan Nelson, H., et al. (2003) "Amygdala hyperreactivity in borderline personality disorder: implications for emotional dysregulation." Biological Psychiatry, *54(11)*, 1284–1293. © 2003 with permission from Elsevier; **p. 281:** © Esbin-Anderson/The Image Works; **p. 282:** © Plush Studios/Getty Images; **p. 285:** © Walter Hodges/Getty Images; **p. 287:** © Christian Hoehn/Getty Images; **p. 290**(left): © DK1961/Alamy; **p. 290**(right): © Royalty-Free/Corbis

CHAPTER 10

p. 296: © Adam Gault/Getty Images; **p. 297:** Courtesy, Temple Grandin; **p. 302:** © Dan McCoy/Rainbow; **p. 306:** © Paramount/The Kobal Collection; **p. 308:** © Patrick Olear/PhotoEdit; **p. 312:** © Geri Engberg/The Image Works; **p. 315:** © Eric A. Wessman/Stock Boston; **p. 317:** © Geoff Franklin; **p. 320:** © John Birdsall/The Image Works; **p. 326:** United Artists/The Kobal Collection/Stephen Vaughan; **p. 329**(top): Schultz, Robert, T. (2005). Developmental deficits in social perception in autism: The role of the amygdala and fusiform face area. International Journal of Developmental Neuroscience, 23(2–3), 125–141. © 2005 with permission from Elsevier; **p. 329**(bottom): © Ellen Senisi/The Image Works

CHAPTER 11

p. 334: © Peter Skinner/Photo Researchers; **p. 335:** © Sophie Bassouls/Sygma/Corbis; **p. 339:** © Corbis/Bettmann; **p. 340**(right): © Alfred Pasieka/Photo Researchers; **p. 345:** © J.M. Loubat/Vandystadt/Photo Researchers; **p. 346:** © Judy Griesedieck; **p. 348:** © David Grossman/Photo Researchers; **p. 353:** © Fritz Hoffmann/The Image Works; **p. 354:** © Macduff Everton/Getty Images

CHAPTER 12

p. 358: © Daniel Grill/Getty Images; **p. 359:** © KMazur/WireImage/Getty Images; **p. 360:** © N.M.S.B./Custom Medical Stock Photo; **p. 365:** © Hulton Archive/Getty Images; **p. 366:** © Jim West; **p. 370**(left): © Petre Buzoianu/ZUMA; **p. 370**(right): © Charles O'Rear/Corbis; **p. 372:** © Altrendo Images/Getty Images; **p. 373**(left): © Steve Freeman/WireImage/Getty Images; **p. 373**(right): © Jason LaVeris/FilmMagic/Getty Images; **p. 375:** © David J. Green/Lifestyle/Alamy; **p. 377:** © AP Images/Trae Patton/NBCU Photo Bank; **p. 378:** © Ryan McVay/Getty Images; **p. 380:** © Peter Widmann/Alamy; **p. 382:** © A. Chederros/Onoky/Corbis

CHAPTER 13

p. 388: © Jeffrey Coolidge/Getty Images; **p. 389:** © Reuters/Corbis; **p. 393:** © AP Images/Elaine Thompson; **p. 397:** © A. Collins/The Image Works; **p. 401:** © Bill Bachmann/PhotoEdit; **p. 404:** © Grace/Zefa/Corbis; **p. 406:** © Digital Vision/PunchStock; **p. 409:** © Bartomeu Amengual/Age Fotostock; **p. 412:** © AP Images; **p. 418:** © AP Images/Gautam Singh

CHAPTER 14

p. 424: © Phil Ashley/Getty Images; **p. 425:** © Jim Spellman/WireImage/Getty Images; **p. 426:** © Bettmann/Corbis; **p. 431:** © Bob Daemmrich/The Image Works; **p. 432:** © Philip Lee Harvey/Getty Images; **p. 434:** © Jim Arbogast/Getty Images; **p. 448:** © G. Baden/Zefa/Corbis; **p. 450:** © David Young-Wolff/PhotoEdit; **p. 452:** © M.C. Photograph/Alamy; **p. 453:** © VH1/PhotoFest; **p. 456:** © Larry Mulvehill/Photo Researchers; **p. 461:** © Dr. Ken Greer/Visuals Unlimited

CHAPTER 15

p. 466: © Brigitte Sporrer/Getty Images; **p. 467:** © AP Images/Ron Frehm; **p. 475:** © Bill Losh/Getty Images; **p. 478:** © W. Hill, Jr./The Image Works; **p. 479:** © Stephen D. Cannerelli/Syracuse Newspapers/The Image Works; **p. 480:** © Rachel Epstein/The Image Works; **p. 483**(top): © Anja Kessler/Photolibrary; **p. 483**(bottom): © Michael Newman/PhotoEdit; **p. 484:** © Ellen Senisi/The Image Works; **p. 485:** © Dina Rudick/Boston Globe/Landov; **p. 491:** © Don Garbera/PhotoTake

CHAPTER 16

p. 496: © Christine Balderas/Getty Images; **p. 497:** © William DiLillo; **p. 500**(top): © AP Images; **p. 500**(bottom): © AP Images/Eugene Garcia; **p. 501:** © AP Images/USUHS; **p. 502:** © Reuters/NBC News Handout; **p. 504:** © Eric Roth/Index Stock Imagery/Photolibrary; **p. 505:** © Bob Daemmrich/Stock Boston; **p. 506:** © AP Images/Barry Thumma; **p. 509:** © AP Images; **p. 511:** © Mike Stewart/Sygma/Corbis

NAME INDEX

C

D

E

F

G

H

M

T

U

V

W

X

Y

Z

SUBJECT INDEX

Page numbers in *italics* indicate figures, photo, or tables.

A

SUBJECT INDEX

Page numbers in *italics* indicate figures, photo, or tables.

A

D

N

O

P

T

U

V

W

Z

DSM-IV-TR Classification

Multiaxial System (Abbreviated)

Axis I — Clinical Disorders
Other Conditions That May Be a Focus of Clinical Attention (Conditions that do not meet precise diagnostic criteria are designated "NOS" ["Not Otherwise Specified"])

Axis II — Personality Disorders
Mental Retardation

Axis III — General Medical Conditions

Axis IV — Psychosocial and Environmental Problems

Axis V — Global Assessment of Functioning

Disorders Usually First Diagnosed in Infancy, Childhood, or Adolescence

Mental Retardation (Axis II)
- Mild Mental Retardation
- Moderate Mental Retardation
- Severe Mental Retardation
- Profound Mental Retardation
- Mental Retardation, Severity Unspecified

Learning Disorders
- Reading Disorder
- Mathematics Disorder
- Disorder of Written Expression

Motor Skills Disorder
- Developmental Coordination Disorder

Communication Disorders
- Expressive Language Disorder
- Mixed Receptive-Expressive Language Disorder
- Phonological Disorder
- Stuttering

Pervasive Developmental Disorders
- Autistic Disorder
- Rett's Disorder
- Childhood Disintegrative Disorder
- Asperger's Disorder

Attention-Deficit and Disruptive Behavior Disorders
- Attention-Deficit/Hyperactivity Disorder
- Conduct Disorder
- Oppositional Defiant Disorder

Feeding and Eating Disorders of Infancy or Early Childhood
- Pica
- Rumination Disorder
- Feeding Disorder of Infancy or Early Childhood

Tic Disorders
- Tourette's Disorder
- Chronic Motor or Vocal Tic Disorder
- Transient Tic Disorder

Elimination Disorders
- Encopresis
- Enuresis

Other Disorders of Infancy, Childhood, or Adolescence
- Separation Anxiety Disorder
- Selective Mutism
- Reactive Attachment Disorder of Infancy or Early Childhood
- Stereotypic Movement Disorder

Delirium, Dementia, and Amnestic and Other Cognitive Disorders

- Delirium Due to a General Medical Condition
- Substance Intoxication Delirium
- Substance Withdrawal Delirium
- Delirium Due to Multiple Etiologies

Dementia
- Dementia of the Alzheimer's Type, with Early Onset
- Dementia of the Alzheimer's Type, with Late Onset
- Vascular Dementia
- Dementia Due to HIV Disease
- Dementia Due to Head Trauma
- Dementia Due to Parkinson's Disease
- Dementia Due to Huntington's Disease
- Dementia Due to Pick's Disease
- Dementia Due to Creutzfeldt-Jakob Disease
- Dementia Due to a General Medical Condition
- Substance-Induced Persisting Dementia
- Dementia Due to Multiple Etiologies

Amnestic Disorders
- Amnestic Disorder Due to a General Medical Condition
- Substance-Induced Persisting Amnestic Disorder

Mental Disorders Due to a General Medical Condition Not Elsewhere Specified

- Catatonic Disorder Due to a General Medical Condition
- Personality Change Due to a General Medical Condition
- Mental Disorder NOS Due to a General Medical Condition

Substance-Related Disorders

Alcohol-Related Disorders
- Alcohol Use Disorders
- Alcohol-Induced Disorders

Amphetamine-Related Disorders
- Amphetamine Use Disorders
- Amphetamine-Induced Disorders

Caffeine-Related Disorders
- Caffeine-Induced Disorders

Cannabis-Related Disorders
- Cannabis Use Disorders
- Cannabis-Induced Disorders

Cocaine-Related Disorders
- Cocaine Use Disorders
- Cocaine-Induced Disorders

Hallucinogen-Related Disorders
- Hallucinogen Use Disorders
- Hallucinogen-Induced Disorders

Inhalant-Related Disorders
- Inhalant Use Disorders
- Inhalant-Induced Disorders

Nicotine-Related Disorders
- Nicotine Use Disorders
- Nicotine-Induced Disorders

Opioid-Related Disorders
- Opioid Use Disorders
- Opioid-Induced Disorders

Phencyclidine-Related Disorders
- Phencyclidine Use Disorders
- Phencyclidine-Induced Disorders

Sedative-, Hypnotic-, or Anxiolytic-Related Disorders
- Sedative, Hypnotic, or Anxiolytic Use Disorders
- Sedative-, Hypnotic-, or Anxiolytic-Induced Disorders

Polysubstance-Related Disorder
- Polysubstance Use Disorders
- Polysubstance-Induced Disorders

Other (or Unknown) Substance-Related Disorders
- Other (or Unknown) Substance Use Disorders
- Other (or Unknown) Substance-Induced Disorders

Schizophrenia and Other Psychotic Disorders

- Schizophrenia
  - Paranoid Type
  - Disorganized Type
  - Catatonic Type
  - Undifferentiated Type
  - Residual Type
- Schizophreniform Disorder
- Schizoaffective Disorder
- Delusional Disorder
- Brief Psychotic Disorder
- Shared Psychotic Disorder